Statistical Handbook of Working America

ISSN 1083-1398

Statistical Handbook of Working America

Statistics on Occupations, Careers, Employment, & the Work Environment

Charity Anne Dorgan, Editor

Gale Research

An ITP Information/Reference Group Company

Changing the Way the World Learns

NEW YORK • LONDON • BONN • BOSTON • DETROIT
MADRID • MELBOURNE • MEXICO CITY • PARIS
SINGAPORE • TOKYO • TORONTO • WASHINGTON
ALBANY NY • BELMONT CA • CINCINNATI OH

Charity Anne Dorgan, *Editor*

Editorial Code & Data, Inc., Staff

Robert S. Lazich and Susan M. Turner, *Contributing Editors*
Marlita A. Reddy, *Research Director*
Gary Alampi, *Programmer/Analyst*

Gale Research Inc. Staff

Kathleen E. Maki, *Coordinating Editor*
Mary Beth Trimper, *Production Director*
Cynthia Baldwin, *Product Design Manager*
Shanna P. Heilveil, *Production Assistant*
Pamela A. E. Galbreath, *Art Director*

Copyright c 1995
Gale Research Inc.
835 Penobscot Building
Detroit, MI 48226-4094

ISBN 0-7876-0087-3
ISSN 1083-1398

Printed in the United States of America

I⟨T⟩P™   Gale Research Inc., an International Thomson Publishing Company.
         ITP logo is a trademark under license.

10 9 8 7 6 5 4 3 2 1

TABLE OF CONTENTS

CHAPTER 2 - STATISTICS BY OCCUPATION continued:

CHAPTER 3 - STATISTICS BY INDUSTRY continued:

CHAPTER 5 - EARNINGS AND COSTS OF EMPLOYMENT continued:

Introduction

Statistical Handbook of Working America (SHWA) is a comprehensive compilation of statistics on occupations, careers, employment, and the work environment. Data in *SHWA* are drawn from more than 190 government, academic, association, trade, technical, and media sources, thus providing broad subject coverage of the American workplace. *SHWA* features:

- More than 900 statistical tables.

- More than 675 occupations.

- More than 190 sources.

- More than 50 original graphic presentations of statistical data.

- National, state, and local coverage.

- Comparative international statistics.

- Coverage of all industry sectors.

This edition also features 10 summary indicator tables, comprehensive occupation and keyword indexes, annotated source listings, explanations of acronyms and abbreviations, and a glossary of statistical and labor-related terms.

Scope and Coverage

Subjects Covered. *SHWA* provides a comprehensive overview of the U.S. workplace. Data include general statistics such as complete profiles of employment status and labor participation in each state; or, thorough summaries of employee benefits at establishments of all sizes in the private and public sectors; or, the educational attainment of the U.S. workforce by state.

In addition, data are included for topics related to recent news stories and national issues of particular interest to human resources and legal professionals, top executives and union leaders, workers at all levels, researchers, and students. Some examples might be:

- Affirmative Action

- AIDS

- Americans With Disabilities Act

- Broadbanding and other pay programs

- Casual business attire

- Downsizing

- Family and Medical Leave Act

- Health promotion initiatives

- Information Superhighway

- Pay disparities based on gender, race, or sexual preference

- Reengineering

- Repetitive motion injuries

- Telecommuting

- Work and family benefits

- Workforce diversity

- Workplace stress and violence

SHWA presents data in tabular format within 11 topical chapters. Coverage is as follows:

Summary Indicators. Provides an overview of the data contained throughout *SHWA*. The 10 summary indicator tables offer snapshots of the American workplace for convenient, easy reference to data used most frequently.

Statistics by Occupation. Topics include compensation; earnings; employee benefits; employment and unemployment, including employment for college graduates; industrial relations; jobs; leading occupations; occupational outlook; projected job openings; work hours and schedules; and workers.

Statistics by Industry. Covers compensation; employee benefits; employees and earnings; employment and unemployment; health and safety; industrial relations; industry summaries; occupational outlook; production and technology; work hours and schedules; and workers.

Employment and Unemployment. Presents statistics on employers; employment status; job growth; labor force participation; recruiting and placement; unemployment; work hours and schedules; workers, particularly special groups such as minorities and women.

Earnings and Costs of Employment. Covers compensation; compensation methods; cost control; business travel costs; health and safety costs; health care costs; relocation costs; Social Security; taxes; earnings; pay and pay increases; and wage rates, such as the hourly minumum wage.

Employee Benefits. Topics include benefit programs and packages; health care; incentives; insurance plans; pension and retirement plans; benefits for retirees; time off; and work and family benefits.

Skills, Training, and Education. Offers data on academic awards and degrees; basic skills; educational attainment; job training and retraining; school enrollment; and schools.

Health and Safety. Covered topics include AIDS; ergonomics; fatalities; lost work time; occupational illness and injuries; Occupational Safety and Health Administration; stress; substance abuse; wellness; workers' compensation; and workplace violence.

Legal and Ethical Issues. Topics include Affirmative Action; Americans With Disabilities Act; discrimination; ethics; Family and Medical Leave Act; lawsuits; sexual harassment; social issues such as domestic violence and workplace attire; and worker satisfaction.

Production and Technology. Covers productivity measures; quality and reengineering; technologies; and telecommuting.

Industrial Relations. Presents data on collective bargaining; labor disputes; unions; and worker displacement, including downsizing.

Occupations Covered. *SHWA* features a variety of statistics for more than 600 occupations–from chief executive officers to nude movie body doubles. Specifically, data will show:

- Most dangerous occupations
- Fastest growing occupations
- Projected job openings by occupation
- Occupational outlook in each industry
- Leading occupations by major metropolitan area
- Racial/ethnic backgrounds of workers by occupation
- Earnings by occupation
- Earnings for occupations by industry
- Employment by occupation
- Employment of college graduates by occupation
- Union membership and earnings by occupation
- Occupational tenures
- Work schedules by occupation

The amount of data provided depends in large part on the occupations themselves. Long-established professions with well-rooted networks–for example, nursing–frequently collect and maintain statistics through trade associations and other agencies. Hence, data are available in greater detail. Migrant farmworkers, on the other hand, are not easily surveyed due to the nature of their work and lifestyle. Every effort has been made to offer as much information as possible for as many occupations as possible within space limitations of this edition. When decisions needed to be made regarding coverage, occupations were ranked according to employment figures so that the most respresentative data could be provided. This is the rationale for selecting leading occupations and for choosing employment projections by occupation in each industry.

Geographic Area Covered. *SHWA* covers employment in the United States. For the most part, data exclude Americans living and working abroad for foreign establishments or at overseas branches and affiliates of U.S.-headquartered firms. Depending on the table, data presented may reflect the national, state, or local level. Some tables offer comparisons of the United States and foreign countries on topics such as labor productivity. Nations selected for these tables usually are similar to the United States in economic development.

Period Covered. Material in *SHWA* dates from 1990 or later. Some of the tables also present earlier data for historical purposes; for example, to illustrate changes—growth or decline—over time. Whenever possible, projections have been provided to indicate trends and forecasts. In any case, the most recent data available at the time of compilation have been included in this edition.

Sources

Thousands of work-related statistics are produced by a variety of reliable sources each year. Data were selected for inclusion in *SHWA* on the basis of their timeliness, interest or value to researchers and the general public, and their ability to contribute to the comprehensive coverage of the field.

Much of the statistical material included in *SHWA* comes from the U.S. federal government or from state and other government levels under federal mandate. Many of the tables were drawn from statistical services or special reports of major federal departments; for example, the Department of Labor's Bureau of Labor Statistics, the body that administers programs and collects statistics on employment-related matters in the United States. Statistics from the departments of Commerce and Education frequently are cited as well.

SHWA also features data from media sources, including newspapers, business periodicals, trade magazines, professional journals, and association publications. These media often rely on the government or other sources for the information they provide. Nevertheless, presentation of material in current literature is indicative of issues, anxieties, and aspirations occupying the American consciousness. In addition, *SHWA* offers statistics collected by consultants and consulting organizations, associations, special surveys and studies, and opinion polls.

Special Features

Abbreviations and Acronyms. This list shows all the abbreviations, acronyms, and initialisms that appear in tables throughout *SHWA*. While explanations and translations of abbreviations will be found within the text of tables, a general listing is provided here for the convenience of *SHWA* users. Abbreviations and acronyms are listed in alphabetic order, with explanations following.

Summary Indicators. A brief introductory chapter provides quick access to some of the more conventional material included in the body of *SHWA*. These graphic summaries contain data extracted from one or more tables located elsewhere in the text to offer a convenient overview of work issues.

Glossary of Terms. Statistical terms such as "median" and "average" and work-related jargon (for example, "reentrants") are explained to assist users in understanding tabular data and the context in which the data were gathered or compiled.

Sources. An appendix lists all the sources cited in tables included in *SHWA*. Sources are arranged alphabetically by author name or title as appropriate. In the case of periodicals, dates of issues consulted are shown. The list provides table references, showing all data citing a particular source.

Occupation Index. This index presents all occupations covered in *SHWA* by their official Bureau of Labor Statistics job titles, alternate career names, occupation names contained within job titles, popular names, and synonymous or related names. Each citation is followed by table and page reference numbers. Page references do not necessarily identify the page on which a table begins. In the cases where tables span two or more pages, references point to the page on which the index term appears—which may be the second or subsequent page of a table. Many cross-references have been added to index citations to facilitate the location of related topics and tables.

Keyword Index. This index allows users to access all subjects, issues, government agencies, companies, unions, programs, associations, schools, educational institutions, personal names, and locations cited in the tables of *SHWA*. Each citation is followed by table and page reference numbers. Page references do not necessarily identify the page on which a table begins. In the cases where tables span two or more pages, references point to the page on which the index term appears—which may be the second or subsequent page of a table. Many cross-references have been added to index citations to facilitate the location of related topics and tables.

Acknowledgments

Many people and organizations contributed data, suggestions, permission, and advice in the compilation of *SHWA*. The editorial staff thanks them all for their help and guidance.

Comments and Suggestions

Although every effort has been made to ensure the accuracy and timeliness of the data in *SHWA*, errors and omissions may occur. Notification of changes or additions deemed appropriate by users of this edition are appreciated. Comments and suggestions for the improvement of *SHWA* are welcome. Please contact:

Statistical Handbook of Working America
Gale Research Inc.
835 Penobscot Building
Detroit, MI 48226-4094
Phone: (313)961-2242
Toll-free: 800-347-GALE
Fax: (313)961-6815

How to Use This Book

Statistical Handbook of Working America (SHWA) is organized into 11 chapters, the first of which contains summary indicators. (See the Table of Contents or the Introduction on the preceding pages for a list of chapters.) Each chapter begins with notes that explain its contents and reference related material elsewhere in *SHWA*. To facilitate browsing through *SHWA* tables, the chapter titles also appear in the upper right- or upper left-hand corners of pages.

Arrangement

SHWA chapters are subdivided by alphabetically arranged topics. Topics are alphabetized in a word-by-word, letter-by-letter arrangement. Topic notations are placed above the first table in subject groupings for easy identification. The topic is shown again in italic type below each subsequent table's reference number.

Organization of Tables

Tables are arranged alphabetically by title within each topic grouping. Table titles are alphabetized in a word-by-word, letter-by-letter arrangement. In addition, each table is numbered sequentially, beginning with the first table in the first chapter. Hence, data may be accessed through table reference numbers or alphabetically by topic and table title.

Tables appear in the Sources list by table number. Tables can be accessed by reference number or by page number using the Table of Contents, the Occupation Index, or the Keyword Index.

Special Presentations

Some tables display graphic presentations such as bar graphs and pie charts to facilitate analysis of provided data. If the table has more than one column of data, the number of the column represented by the graphic is identified. Complete tabular data follow each graphic.

A selection of material in *SHWA* is of a textual nature. Nevertheless, these entries contain predominantly statistical data. Occasionally, such entries offer explanatory material.

Sample Table

The following sample table shows elements commonly included in *SHWA* tables. Each numbered paragraph corresponds to the numbered item in the sample.

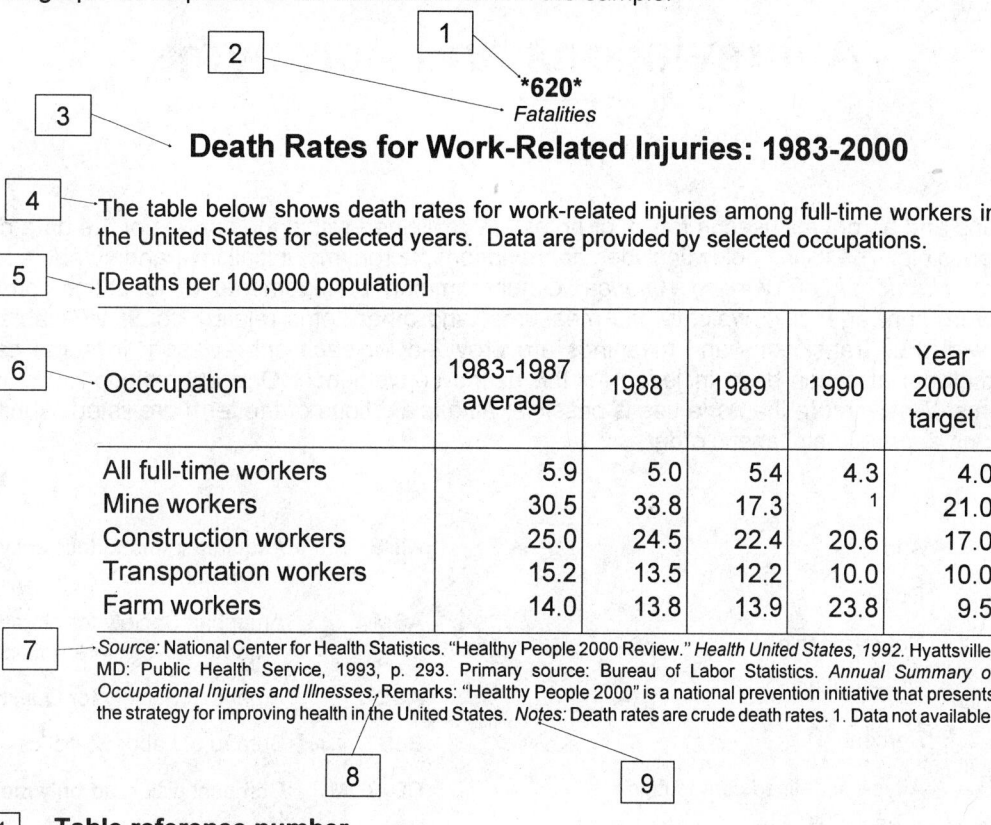

| 1 |
| 2 |
620
Fatalities

| 3 |
Death Rates for Work-Related Injuries: 1983-2000

| 4 | The table below shows death rates for work-related injuries among full-time workers in the United States for selected years. Data are provided by selected occupations.

| 5 | [Deaths per 100,000 population]

| 6 |

Occcupation	1983-1987 average	1988	1989	1990	Year 2000 target
All full-time workers	5.9	5.0	5.4	4.3	4.0
Mine workers	30.5	33.8	17.3	[1]	21.0
Construction workers	25.0	24.5	22.4	20.6	17.0
Transportation workers	15.2	13.5	12.2	10.0	10.0
Farm workers	14.0	13.8	13.9	23.8	9.5

| 7 | *Source:* National Center for Health Statistics. "Healthy People 2000 Review." *Health United States, 1992.* Hyattsville, MD: Public Health Service, 1993, p. 293. Primary source: Bureau of Labor Statistics. *Annual Summary of Occupational Injuries and Illnesses.* Remarks: "Healthy People 2000" is a national prevention initiative that presents the strategy for improving health in the United States. *Notes:* Death rates are crude death rates. 1. Data not available.

| 8 | | 9 |

| 1 | **Table reference number.**

| 2 | **Topic within chapter.**

| 3 | **Table title.**

| 4 | **Headnote.** Provides a brief explanation of the table, or explains unusual terminology. Note that this material, unless enclosed within quotes, has been prepared by the editors and is not taken from the original source unless otherwise stated.

| 5 | **Quantifying information.** Indicates measurement or units used within the table.

| 6 | **Table.**

| 7 | **Source.** Identifies the material from which table originated. If data for the table were not compiled by the source cited, a **primary source** notation will follow.

| 8 | **Remarks.** In some instances, additional remarks appear for clarification of source notations or other reasons.

| 9 | **Footnotes.** Footnotes or other explanations help to clarify data in the table (for example, missing information or special criteria for reported information) or to explain and clarify as in the case of translating acronyms and abbreviations.

Abbreviations and Acronyms

Abbreviations and acronyms used in tables or notes are explained within the context of the data presented whenever possible. The listing below includes abbreviations, acronyms, initialisms, and symbols appearing in *Statistical Handbook of Working America.* Other common abridgements of locations, organization names, government agencies, weights and measures, and other items related to *SHWA* tables are included as well. Full translations and meanings are provided for each abbreviation. In some cases, explanatory material also has been included for the user's convenience. One abbreviation may represent multiple items. Where more than one use is possible, all explanations of the term are listed. Abbreviations and acronyms appear in alphabetic order.

&	And
$	Dollars
-	Not applicable
-	Not available
%	Percent
401(k)	A type of defined contribution pension plan
a.m.	*Ante meridiem* [before noon]
AARP	American Association of Retired Persons
ABA	American Bar Association
ACTWU	Amalgamated Clothing and Textile Workers Union
ADA	Americans With Disabilities Act
admin.	Administrative
AFGE	American Federation of Government Employees
AFL	American Federation of Labor
AFSCME	American Federation of State, County, and Municipal Employees
AFT	American Federation of Teachers

AIDS	Acquired immunodeficiency syndrome
ASM	American Society for Metals (former name of ASM International)
ASQC	American Society for Quality Control
BLS	Bureau of Labor Statistics
CD-ROM	Compact disk read-only memory
CEO	Chief executive officer
CFOI	Census of Fatal Occupational Injuries
CIO	Chief information officer
CIO	Congress of Industrial Organizations
CIP	Classification of Instructional Programs
CMSA	Consolidated Metropolitan Statistical Area
CNN	Cable News Network
Co.	Company
COBRA	Consolidated Omnibus Budget Reconciliation Act (1985)
COLA	Cost-of-living adjustment
Corp.	Corporation

CPDF	Central Personnel Data File (U.S. Office of Personnel Management)
CPI	Consumer Price Index
CPS	Current Population Survey
CWA	Communications Workers of America
DC	District of Columbia
e.g.	*Exempli gratia* [for example]
E-mail	Electronic mail
EAP	Employee Assistance Program
EBRI	Employee Benefit Research Institute
ECI	Employment Cost Index
ed.	Edition
EDI	Electronic data interchange
EDP	Electronic data processing
EEG	Electroencephalogram
EEG	Electroencephalography
EEO	Equal Employment Opportunity
EEOC	Equal Employment Opportunity Commission
EKG	Electrocardiogram
EKG	Electrocardiograph
EPA	Environmental Protection Agency
ERISA	Employee Retirement Income Security Act
ESOP	Employee Stock Ownership Plans
exc.	Except
exc.	Excluding
exec.	Executive
FAS 106	Financial accounting standard 106 (1993)
FMLA	Family and Medical Leave Act
FSA	Flexible spending account
GDP	Gross domestic product
GED	General educational development
GIC	Guaranteed income contract
GIC	Guaranteed investment contract

H	High
HI	Health Insurance
HIV	Human immunodeficiency virus
HMO	Health maintenance organization
HR	Human resources
IAM	International Association of Machinists and Aerospace Workers
IBEW	International Brotherhood of Electrical Workers
ICC	Interstate Commerce Commission
ILGWU	International Ladies' Garment Workers' Union
Inc.	Incorporated
IT	Information technology
L	Low
LAN	Local-area network
Ltd.	Limited
MBA	Master's of Business Administration
MD	Maryland
mgrl.	Managerial
misc.	Miscellaneous
MS	Microsoft Corporation
MSA	Metropolitan Statistical Area
MSHA	Mine Safety and Health Administration
N/A	Not available
N/A	Not applicable
n.e.c.	Not elsewhere classified
NA	Not available
NA	Not applicable
NALC	National Association of Letter Carriers
NCES	National Center for Education Statistics
NECMA	New England County Metropolitan Area
NETS	Network of Employers for Traffic Safety
NIOSH	National Institute of Occupational Safety and Health

no.	Number	R&D	Research and development
NYBGH	New York Business Group on Health	SEIU	Service Employees International Union
OASDHI	Old-Age, Survivors, Disability, and Health Insurance	SES	Senior Executive Services
OASDI	Old-Age, Survivors, and Disability Insurance	SIC	Standard Industrial Classification
		SMI	Supplementary Medical Insurance
OCAW	Oil, Chemical, and Atomic Workers International Union	St.	Saint
OECD	Organization for Economic Cooperation and Development	T&D	Training and development
		TEC	The Executive Committee
OPM	U.S. Office of Personnel Management	TV	Television
		U.S.	United States
OSHA	Occupational Safety and Health Administration	USA	United States of America
OTA	Office of Technology Assessment, U.S. Congress	UAW	International Union, United Automobile, Aerospace, and Agricultural Implement Workers of America [also known as United Auto Workers]
p.	Page		
PAC	Political action committee	UFCW	United Food and Commercial Workers International Union
PBX	Private branch exchange		
PC	Personal computer	USDL	U.S. Department of Labor
Ph.D.	Doctor of Philosophy	VA	Virginia
PIN	Personal identification number	VCR	Videocassette recorder
PIN	Personal information network	VH	Very high
PIN	Progam integrated network	VIP	Very important passenger
PMSA	Primary Metropolitan Statistical Area	VIP	Very important person
POS	Point-of-service plan	VL	Very low
pp.	Pages		
PPO	Preferred provider organization		

Chapter 1
SUMMARY INDICATORS

The 10 tables in this chapter profile the material included in *Statistical Handbook of Working America.* Each table features data included elsewhere in *SHWA,* highlighting major aspects of the American workplace. Locations of full data are indicated in the Table column. Numbers listed in this column reference table (not page) numbers.

★1★

Chapter 2: Occupations

Occupation	Data	Denomination	Date	Table
Highest employment: Managers and administrators (salaried)	4,941,606	Number	1990	159
Most highly compensated: Managers	30.25	Dollars per hour	1993	11
Longest occupational tenure: Barbers	27.2	Years	1991	88
Longest employer tenure: Firefighting and fire prevention supervisors	20.3	Years	1991	88
Highest growth occupation: Home health aides	+138.1	Percent	1992	206
Most projected job openings: Service occupations	6,441,000	Number	1992-2005	207
Riskiest job: Cab driver/chauffeur	15.1	Murders per 100,000 workers	1992	87
Fastest declining: Central office frame wirers	-75.3	Percent	1992	204

Source: Data are drawn from tables elsewhere in *Statistical Handbook of Working America.*

★2★

Chapter 3: Industries

Industry	Data	Denomination	Date	Table
Highest employment: Services	41,817,000	Number	1993	319
Most self-employed workers: Services	4,062,000	Number	1993	475
Highest unemployment rate: Construction	14.3	Percent	1993	328
Highest wages and salaries: Electric, gas, and sanitary services	42,998	Dollars	1992	279

[Continued]

★ 2 ★

Chapter 3: Industries
[Continued]

Industry	Data	Denomination	Date	Table
Highest injury/illness rate: Meat packing plants	44.4	Percent	1992	330
Most work-related deaths: Government	1,700	Number	1992	334

Source: Data are drawn from tables elsewhere in *Statistical Handbook of Working America.*

★ 3 ★

Chapter 4: Employment and Unemployment

	Total employment	Date	Total unemployment	Date	Demonination	Tables
United States	119,306	1993	9,384	1992	Thousands	539, 549
Alabama	1,840	1993	143	1992	Thousands	539, 549
Alaska	276	1993	26	1992	Thousands	539, 549
Arizona	1,723	1993	135	1992	Thousands	539, 549
Arkansas	1,091	1993	83	1992	Thousands	539, 549
California	13,853	1993	1,393	1992	Thousands	539, 549
Colorado	1,805	1993	108	1992	Thousands	539, 549
Connecticut	1,678	1993	137	1992	Thousands	539, 549
Delaware	354	1993	19	1992	Thousands	539, 549
District of Columbia	280	1993	26	1992	Thousands	539, 549
Florida	6,166	1993	533	1992	Thousands	539, 549
Georgia	3,267	1993	232	1992	Thousands	539, 549
Hawaii	558	1993	26	1992	Thousands	539, 549
Idaho	512	1993	34	1992	Thousands	539, 549
Illinois	5,538	1993	451	1992	Thousands	539, 549
Indiana	2,780	1993	185	1992	Thousands	539, 549
Iowa	1,488	1993	70	1992	Thousands	539, 549
Kansas	1,253	1993	55	1992	Thousands	539, 549
Kentucky	1,684	1993	122	1992	Thousands	539, 549
Louisiana	1,740	1993	156	1992	Thousands	539, 549
Maine	581	1993	46	1992	Thousands	539, 549
Maryland	2,507	1993	176	1992	Thousands	539, 549
Massachusetts	2,953	1993	267	1992	Thousands	539, 549
Michigan	4,374	1993	408	1992	Thousands	539, 549
Minnesota	2,341	1993	124	1992	Thousands	539, 549
Mississippi	1,135	1993	97	1992	Thousands	539, 549
Missouri	2,481	1993	151	1992	Thousands	539, 549
Montana	401	1993	28	1992	Thousands	539, 549
Nebraska	830	1993	25	1992	Thousands	539, 549
Nevada	692	1993	47	1992	Thousands	539, 549
New Hampshire	579	1993	46	1992	Thousands	539, 549
New Jersey	3,706	1993	337	1992	Thousands	539, 549
New Mexico	700	1993	51	1992	Thousands	539, 549
New York	7,985	1993	734	1992	Thousands	539, 549

[Continued]

★ 3 ★

Chapter 4: Employment and Unemployment
[Continued]

	Total employment	Date	Total unemployment	Date	Demonination	Tables
North Carolina	3,383	1993	210	1992	Thousands	539, 549
North Dakota	305	1993	15	1992	Thousands	539, 549
Ohio	5,132	1993	397	1992	Thousands	539, 549
Oklahoma	1,432	1993	86	1992	Thousands	539, 549
Oregon	1,473	1993	116	1992	Thousands	539, 549
Pennsylvania	5,479	1993	442	1992	Thousands	539, 549
Rhode Island	472	1993	46	1992	Thousands	539, 549
South Carolina	1,685	1993	112	1992	Thousands	539, 549
South Dakota	347	1993	11	1992	Thousands	539, 549
Tennessee	2,358	1993	156	1992	Thousands	539, 549
Texas	8,508	1993	675	1992	Thousands	539, 549
Utah	875	1993	42	1992	Thousands	539, 549
Vermont	299	1993	21	1992	Thousands	539, 549
Virginia	3,208	1993	216	1992	Thousands	539, 549
Washington	2,490	1993	198	1992	Thousands	539, 549
West Virginia	702	1993	87	1992	Thousands	539, 549
Wisconsin	2,589	1993	135	1992	Thousands	539, 549
Wyoming	226	1993	13	1992	Thousands	539, 549

Source: Data are drawn from tables elsewhere in *Statistical Handbook of Working America.*

★ 4 ★

Chapter 5: Compensation

Component	Data	Denomination	Date	Table
Total employer compensation costs	16.70	Dollars per hour worked	1993	595
Wages and salaries	11.90	Dollars per hour worked	1993	595
Benefits	4.80	Dollars per hour worked	1993	595
Average annual pay	25,903	Dollars	1992	643
Median earnings of all men	26,472	Dollars	1992	633
Earnings of white men	31,012	Dollars	1992	641
Earnings of black men	22,369	Dollars	1992	641
Earnings of Hispanic men	20,049	Dollars	1992	641
Average income of heterosexual men	28,312	Dollars	1991	642
Average income of gay men	26,321	Dollars	1991	642
Median earnings of all women	16,227	Dollars	1992	636
Earnings of white women	21,659	Dollars	1992	641
Earnings of black women	19,819	Dollars	1992	641
Earnings of Hispanic women	17,138	Dollars	1992	641
Average income of heterosexual women	18,341	Dollars	1991	642
Average income of lesbians	15,068	Dollars	1991	642

[Continued]

★ 4 ★

Chapter 5: Compensation
[Continued]

Component	Data	Denomination	Date	Table
Median annual earnings of high school graduates	21,241	Dollars	1992	638
Median annual earnings of bachelor's degree holders	34,385	Dollars	1992	638
Average total salary increases	4.5-4.6	Percent	1994	647

Source: Data are drawn from tables elsewhere in *Statistical Handbook of Working America.*

★ 5 ★

Chapter 6: Employee Benefits
[In percentages]

Benefit	Employees at small private establishments 1992	Employees at medium and large private establishments, 1991	Employees in state and local government, 1992	Tables
Paid time off				
Vacations	88	96	67	703, 705, 706
Holidays	82	92	75	703, 705, 706
Jury duty leave	58	86	97	703, 705, 706
Funeral leave	50	80	65	703, 705, 706
Rest time	49	67	53	703, 705, 706
Military leave	21	54	83	703, 705, 706
Sick leave	53	67	95	703, 705, 706
Personal leave	12	21	38	703, 705, 706
Lunch time	9	8	10	703, 705, 706
Maternity leave	2	2	-	703, 705, 706
Paternity leave	1	1	-	703, 705, 706
Unpaid time off				
Maternity leave	18	37	59	703, 705, 706
Paternity leave	8	26	44	703, 705, 706
Insurance plans				
Medical care	71	83	90	669, 671, 672
Life	64	94	89	669, 671, 672
Accident/sickness	26	45	22	669, 671, 672
Long-term disability	23	40	28	669, 671, 672
Retirement and savings plans				
Defined benefit pension	22	59	87	685, 687, 688
Defined contribution	33	48	9	685, 687, 688
Miscellaneous benefits				
Parking	86	88	-	655, 657, 659
Educational assistance	36	72	66	655, 657, 659
Travel accident insurance	16	42	15	655, 657, 659
Severance pay	15	41	32	655, 657, 659

[Continued]

★5★

Chapter 6: Employee Benefits
[Continued]

Benefit	Employees at small private establishments 1992	Employees at medium and large private establishments, 1991	Employees in state and local government, 1992	Tables
Relocation allowance	12	31	-	655, 657, 659
Recreation facilities	7	26	15	655, 657, 659
Nonproduction bonuses, cash	47	35	38	655, 657, 659
Child care	2	8	8	655, 657, 659
Flexible benefits plans	2	10	5	655, 657, 659
Reimbursement accounts[1]	14	36	50	655, 657, 659
Eldercare	3	9	13	655, 657, 659
Long-term care insurance	1	4	5	655, 657, 659
Wellness programs	17	35	30	655, 657, 659
Employee assistance programs	17	56	63	655, 657, 659
Inhouse infirmary	-	-	17	655, 657, 659
Prepaid legal services	-	-	7	655, 657, 659

Source: Data are drawn from tables elsewhere in *Statistical Handbook of Working America*. *Note:* "-" indicates "not available."

★6★

Chapter 7: Education and Training

Persons receiving--	Data	Denomination	Date	Table
Associate's degrees	529,392	Number	1991-1992	715
Bachelor's degrees	1,158,895	Number	1991-1992	715
Master's degrees	356,414	Number	1991-1992	715
Doctoral degrees	41,545	Number	1991-1992	715
First professional degrees	75,688	Number	1991-1992	715
Work-related training	152,815,000	Number	1990	776

Source: Data are drawn from tables elsewhere in *Statistical Handbook of Working America*.

★7★

Chapter 8: Occupational Health and Safety

Health and Safety	Data	Denomination	Date	Table
Americans With Disabilities Act complaints	12,962	Number	1992-1993	794
Disabling work injuries	3,200,000	Number	1993	801
Work fatalities	6,083	Number	1992	789
People experiencing workplace violence	30,000	Number	-	824
Workers' compensation payments	42,169	Million $	1991	819

Source: Data are drawn from tables elsewhere in *Statistical Handbook of Working America*. *Note:* "-" indicates "not available."

★8★

Chapter 9: Discrimination

Discrimination	Data	Denomination	Date	Table
Total discrimination claims	85,000	Number	1993	832
Civil rights complaints	50,000	Number	1993	831
Racial discrimination	3,700	Number	-	834
Sexual harassment	11,908	Number	1993	845
Family and Medical Leave Act violations	564	Number	1993-1994	839

Source: Data are drawn from tables elsewhere in *Statistical Handbook of Working America*. *Note:* "-" indicates "not available."

★9★

Chapter 10: Technology

Use of technology	Data	Denomination	Table
800 numbers	75.0	Percent	871
Beepers and pagers	12.1	Percent	872
Cellular phones	8.7	Percent	872
E-mail	49.0	Percent	871
Fax machines	97.0	Percent	871
Online services	5.9	Percent	872
Personal digital assistants	0.8	Percent	872
Portable computers	7.3	Percent	872

[Continued]

★9★

Chapter 10: Technology
[Continued]

Use of technology	Data	Denomination	Table
Video conferencing	20.0	Percent	871
Voice mail	57.0	Percent	871

Source: Data are drawn from tables elsewhere in *Statistical Handbook of Working America.*

★10★

Chapter 11: Unions

Item	Data	Denomination	Date	Table
AFL-CIO affiliated-union membership	13,299,000	Number	1993	899
Union mergers	5	Number	1994	905
Workers covered by collective bargaining agreements	8,141,000	Number	1995	893
Strikes	601	Number	1993-1994	895
Work stoppages	3,981,000	Days	1993	897
Workers on strike	321,395	Number	1993-1994	895
Displaced workers	5,584,000	Number	1992	904

Source: Data are drawn from tables elsewhere in *tatistical Handbook of Working America.*

Chapter 2
STATISTICS BY OCCUPATION

"What do you want to be when you grow up?" is probably one of the most frequently asked questions posed to young people. One Gallup poll indicates that boys want to be sports stars or doctors, while girls aspire to be teachers or performing artists. In the long run, though, most people opt for less glamorous careers as indicated by the nearly 270 tables in this chapter. Data in these tables show the state of more than 600 occupations in the American workplace. Coverage includes compensation, earnings, employee benefits, employment and unemployment, industrial relations, jobs, job openings, work hours and schedules, and workers. In addition, the leading 115 occupations are profiled in detail by race and ethnicity for the largest metropolitan areas. See chapter 3 for employment projections for occupations by industry.

Compensation

★ 11 ★

Private Industry Employee Compensation Costs, by Occupational Group: 1993

Table shows the average employer costs for employee compensation for each occupational group. Data are for private industry from March 1993.

[Dollars per hour]

Occupational group	Benefits	Wages and salaries
Service	2.06	6.48
Handlers, equipment cleaners, helpers, and laborers	3.64	8.14
Sales	3.17	10.15
Administrative support	4.12	10.02
Machine operators, assemblers, and inspectors	5.47	10.03
Transportation and material moving	5.43	10.96
Precision production	6.84	14.21

[Continued]

★ 11 ★

Private Industry Employee Compensation Costs, by Occupational Group: 1993

[Continued]

Occupational group	Benefits	Wages and salaries
Professional and technical	7.37	19.76
Managerial	8.31	22.14

Source: Levine, Chester. "Employee Benefits: Growing in Diversity and Cost." *Occupational Outlook Quarterly* (winter 1993-1994), p. 40. Primary source: Bureau of Labor Statistics. Employment Cost Index.

★ 12 ★

Compensation

State and Local Government Employee Compensation, by Occupational Group: 1993

Table shows the employer costs per hour worked for state and local government employee compensation as of March.

[In dollars]

Occupational group	Total compen-sation	Wages and salaries	Benefits						
			Total	Paid leave	Supple-mental pay	Insur-ance	Retire-ment and savings	Legally required benefits	Other[1]
All state and local government workers	24.44	17.00	7.44	1.86	0.21	2.02	1.87	1.44	0.03
White-collar occupations	27.67	19.72	7.95	1.98	0.14	2.17	2.08	1.55	0.03
Professional specialty and technical	32.91	24.07	8.83	1.95	0.16	2.37	2.54	1.77	0.04
Teachers	36.02	26.87	9.15	1.72	0.09	2.55	2.91	1.84	0.04
Executive, administrative, and managerial	30.66	21.26	9.39	3.07	0.15	2.02	2.35	1.80	0.02
Administrative support, including clerical	15.59	10.18	5.41	1.44	0.09	1.85	1.01	0.99	0.02
Blue-collar occupations	18.78	12.13	6.65	1.71	0.35	1.84	1.32	1.42	(Z)
Service occupations	17.04	10.83	6.21	1.58	0.37	1.65	1.50	1.09	0.02

Source: U.S. Bureau of the Census. *Statistical Abstract of the United States, 1994.* 114th ed. Washington, DC: U.S. Government Printing Office, 1994, p. 320. Primary source: U.S. Bureau of Labor Statistics. *News: Employer Costs for Employee Compensation.* USDL 93-220. *Notes:* Data based on a sample. "Z" indicates cost per hour less than one cent. 1. Includes severance pay and supplemental unemployment benefits.

Earnings

★ 13 ★

Average Earnings for Selected Occupations: 1993

The table below shows the average earnings of selected occupations in Los Angeles, California, in 1993.

[In dollars]

Job	Average earnings
Michael Eisner, Walt Disney	203,950,000
Bruce Willis[1]	20,000,000
John McGrain, Conversion Industries	11,429,990
Whoopi Goldberg[1]	8,500,000
Ray Irani, Occidental Petroleum	5,707,857
Harry Gluck, Caesars World	4,170,422
Lodwrick Cook, ARCO	2,000,000
Jill Barad, Mattel	1,029,727
Chief executive officer[2]	770,000
Senior law partner	300,000
Drug dealer	200,000
Chief of police	160,000
Mayor[3]	123,778
Waiter at Spago's[4]	62,400
Aerospace engineer	60,200
Taxi driver	42,170
Police officer	40,080
Computer programmer	36,800
Bartender	35,000
Nanny	19,000
Hotel maids	14,000
Actor	12,500
Nude movie double[5]	3,700
Bank robber[6]	3,250
Porn actress[1]	350
Car thief[7]	200
Prostitute[8]	45

Source: "To Have and to Have Not." *The Economist,* 12 March 1994, p. 35. Primary source: *Los Angeles* magazine. *Notes:* 1. Per film. 2. Average. 3. Mayor Richard Riordan donated salary to charity. 4. Tips only. 5. Per day. 6. Per heist. 7. Per vehicle. 8. Per trick.

★ 14 ★
Earnings

Earnings and Number of Full-Time Wage and Salary Workers, by Occupation: 1983-1993

Table shows the number of workers and median salary earnings for selected occupations. Data represent annual averages of quarterly data. Based on Current Population Survey.

[In current dollars of usual weekly earnings]

Characteristic	Number of workers (1,000)				Median weekly earnings ($)			
	1983	1985	1990	1993	1983	1985	1990	1993
All workers	70,976	77,002	85,082	85,211	313	343	415	463
Male:								
Managerial and professional	10,312	11,078	12,263	12,454	516	583	731	791
Executive, administrative, managerial	5,344	5,835	6,401	6,611	530	593	742	791
Professional specialty	4,967	5,243	5,863	5,843	506	571	720	791
Technical, sales, and administrative support	8,125	8,803	9,596	9,774	385	420	496	534
Technical and related support	1,428	1,563	1,747	1,773	424	472	570	615
Sales	3,853	4,227	4,666	4,664	389	431	505	544
Administrative support[1]	2,844	3,013	3,183	3,337	362	391	440	492
Service	3,723	3,947	4,476	4,680	255	272	320	350
Private household	11	13	12	25	(B)	(B)	(B)	(B)
Protective	1,314	1,327	1,523	1,646	355	391	477	524
Other service	2,398	2,607	2,942	3,009	217	230	273	290
Precision production[2]	9,180	10,026	10,169	9,609	387	408	488	511
Mechanics and repairers	3,418	3,752	3,669	3,578	377	400	477	509
Construction trades	2,966	3,308	3,603	3,275	375	394	480	495
Other	2,796	2,966	2,897	2,756	408	433	510	539
Operators, fabricators and laborers	9,833	10,585	11,257	10,685	308	325	378	399
Machine operators, assemblers, and inspectors	4,138	4,403	4,510	4,242	319	341	391	407
Transportation and material moving	3,199	3,459	3,721	3,681	335	369	418	456
Handlers, equipment cleaners, helpers, and laborers	2,496	2,724	3,027	2,762	251	261	308	319
Farming, forestry, fishing	1,137	1,150	1,253	1,182	200	216	263	274
Female:								
Managerial and professional	7,139	8,302	10,595	11,636	357	399	511	580
Executive, administrative, managerial	2,772	3,492	4,764	5,131	339	383	485	528
Professional specialty	4,367	4,810	5,831	6,505	367	408	534	605
Technical, sales, and administrative support	13,517	14,622	16,202	16,120	247	269	332	376
Technical and related support	1,146	1,200	1,470	1,587	299	331	417	468
Sales	2,460	2,929	3,531	3,398	204	226	292	329
Administrative support[1]	9,911	10,494	11,202	11,135	248	270	332	375
Service	3,598	3,963	4,531	4,699	173	185	230	259
Private household	267	330	298	313	116	130	171	183
Protective	139	156	216	286	250	278	405	417
Other service	3,193	3,477	4,017	4,099	176	188	231	259
Precision production[2]	784	906	893	880	256	268	316	344
Mechanics and repairers	120	144	139	140	337	392	459	543
Construction trades	45	53	50	38	(B)	265	394	(B)
Other	619	709	704	702	244	253	300	319
Operators, fabricators, and laborers	3,486	3,482	3,675	3,335	204	216	262	288

[Continued]

★ 14 ★

Earnings and Number of Full-Time Wage and Salary Workers, by Occupation: 1983-1993
[Continued]

Characteristic	Number of workers (1,000)				Median weekly earnings ($)			
	1983	1985	1990	1993	1983	1985	1990	1993
Machine operators, assemblers, and inspectors	2,853	2,778	2,840	2,539	202	216	260	284
Transportation and material moving	159	189	227	244	253	252	314	358
Handlers, equipment cleaners, helpers and laborers	474	514	608	551	211	209	250	286
Farming, forestry, fishing	143	138	171	158	169	185	216	242

Source: U.S. Bureau of the Census. Statistical Abstract of the United States, 1994. 114th ed. Washington, DC: U.S. Government Printing Office, 1994, p. 429. Primary sources: U.S. Bureau of Labor Statistics. Bulletin 2307; and Employment and Earnings (monthly, January issues). Notes: "B" represents base is less than 50,000; data not shown. The median of a group of numbers is the middle number or value when each item in the group is arranged according to size, either from lowest to highest or highest to lowest. The median generally has the same number of items above it and below it. If there is an even number of items in the group, the median is taken to be the average of the two middle numbers. 1. Includes clerical occupations. 2. Includes craft and repair.

★ 15 ★

Earnings

Earnings and Number of Workers, by Occupation and Sex: 1992

Data show the number of male and female workers with earnings and median earnings by occupation of longest job held. Covers persons 15 years old and over as of March 1993. Based on Current Population Survey.

Major occupation of longest job held	All workers				Year-round, full-time workers			
	Women		Men		Women		Men	
	Number (1,000)	Median earnings ($)	Number (1,000)	Median earnings ($)	Number (1,000)	Median earnings ($)	Number (1,000)	Median earnings ($)
Total[1]	62,050	13,677	72,318	22,173	33,180	21,440	48,308	30,358
Executive, administrators, and managerial	7,097	24,338	9,400	40,100	5,334	27,495	7,826	42,509
Professional specialty	9,579	25,759	8,214	40,059	5,749	31,261	6,347	44,015
Technical and related support	2,235	20,601	2,095	29,711	1,396	24,797	1,614	32,720
Sales	8,258	8,565	8,012	23,485	3,408	17,924	5,675	31,346
Administrative support[2]	15,906	15,746	4,367	20,708	9,589	20,321	2,949	27,186
Precision production, craft and repair	1,202	14,794	12,980	23,219	728	19,045	8,786	28,923
Machine operators, assemblers, and inspectors	3,391	11,834	5,004	19,498	1,952	15,714	3,412	23,884
Transportation and material moving	559	10,874	4,893	21,167	204	20,131	3,136	25,787
Handlers, equipment cleaners, helpers, and laborers	1,107	7,461	4,755	10,043	397	14,522	2,004	18,793
Service workers	11,972	6,506	8,110	10,739	4,174	12,931	4,060	20,606
Private household	1,090	2,350	73	(B)	202	9,668	25	(B)

[Continued]

★ 15 ★

Earnings and Number of Workers, by Occupation and Sex: 1992
[Continued]

Major occupation of longest job held	All workers				Year-round, full-time workers			
	Women		Men		Women		Men	
	Number (1,000)	Median earnings ($)	Number (1,000)	Median earnings ($)	Number (1,000)	Median earnings ($)	Number (1,000)	Median earnings ($)
Service, except private household	10,882	6,917	8,037	10,785	3,972	13,195	4,035	20,656
Farming, forestry, and fishing	678	3,686	3,630	7,858	208	10,079	1,769	14,897

Source: U.S. Bureau of the Census. *Statistical Abstract of the United States, 1994.* 114th ed. Washington, DC: U.S. Government Printing Office, 1994, p. 431. Primary source: U.S. Bureau of the Census. *Current Population Reports.* P60-184. *Notes:* "B" represents base less than 75,000. The median of a group of numbers is the middle number or value when each item in the group is arranged according to size, either from lowest to highest or highest to lowest. The median generally has the same number of items above it and below it. If there is an even number of items in the group, the median is taken to be the average of the two middle numbers. 1. Includes persons whose longest job was in the Armed Forces. 2. Includes clerical.

★ 16 ★
Earnings

Earnings for Selected Administrative Support Occupations: 1993

```
Mail carrier - 32,900
Secretary - 20,100
Telephone operator - 20,100
Bookkeeper - 19,500
Receptionist - 16,400
Bank teller - 15,200
```

Table shows the median annual earnings in 1993 for selected administrative support occupations.

[In dollars]

Occupation	Average earnings
Mail carrier	32,900
Secretary	20,100
Telephone operator	20,100
Bookkeeper	19,500
Receptionist	16,400
Bank teller	15,200

Source: "The Best Jobs in America? How *Money* Ranks Today's Occupations." *Career Opportunities News* 12, no. 4 (January-February 1995), pp. 1-3. Primary source: *Money* magazine.

★ 17 ★
Earnings

Earnings for Selected Art and Entertainment Occupations: 1993

Technical writers - 37,400	
Public relations worker - 31,900	
Actor - 31,300	
Journalist - 29,900	
Fashion designer - 29,600	
Musician - 28,900	
Graphic artist - 25,800	
Photographer - 23,400	
Television news reporter - 21,400	
Dancer - 14,800	

Table shows the median annual earnings in 1993 for selected art and entertainment occupations.

[In dollars]

Occupation	Average earnings
Technical writers	37,400
Public relations worker	31,900
Actor	31,300
Journalist	29,900
Fashion designer	29,600
Musician	28,900
Graphic artist	25,800
Photographer	23,400
Television news reporter	21,400
Dancer	14,800

Source: "The Best Jobs in America? How *Money* Ranks Today's Occupations." *Career Opportunities News* 12, no. 4 (January-February 1995), pp. 1-3. Primary source: *Money* magazine.

★ 18 ★

Earnings

Earnings for Selected Education-Related Occupations: 1993

| High school teacher - 32,500 |
| Grade school teacher - 31,000 |
| Librarian - 29,500 |
| Preschool teacher - 18,400 |

Table shows the median annual earnings in 1993 for selected education-related occupations.

[In dollars]

Occupation	Average earnings
High school teacher	32,500
Grade school teacher	31,000
Librarian	29,500
Preschool teacher	18,400

Source: "The Best Jobs in America? How *Money* Ranks Today's Occupations." *Career Opportunities News* 12, no. 4 (January-February 1995), pp. 1-3. Primary source: *Money* magazine.

★ 19 ★
Earnings

Earnings for Selected Engineering and Architectural Occupations: 1993

```
┌─────────────────────────────────────────────────┐
│  ┌─────────────────────────────────────────────┐ │
│  │ Electrical engineer - 59,100                │ │
│  └─────────────────────────────────────────────┘ │
│  ┌─────────────────────────────────────────────┐ │
│  │ Aeronautical engineer - 56,700             │ │
│  └─────────────────────────────────────────────┘ │
│  ┌─────────────────────────────────────────────┐ │
│  │ Civil engineer - 55,800                     │ │
│  └─────────────────────────────────────────────┘ │
│  ┌──────────────────────────┐                    │
│  │ Architect - 36,100       │                    │
│  └──────────────────────────┘                    │
│  ┌────────────────────┐                          │
│  │ Surveyor - 28,700  │                          │
│  └────────────────────┘                          │
└─────────────────────────────────────────────────┘
```

Table shows the median annual earnings in 1993 for selected engineering and architectural occupations.

[In dollars]

Occupation	Average earnings
Electrical engineer	59,100
Aeronautical engineer	56,700
Civil engineer	55,800
Architect	36,100
Surveyor	28,700

Source: "The Best Jobs in America? How *Money* Ranks Today's Occupations." *Career Opportunities News* 12, no. 4 (January-February 1995), pp. 1-3. Primary source: *Money* magazine.

★ 20 ★

Earnings

Earnings for Selected Health Occupations: 1993

```
Physician - 148,000
Dentist - 93,000
Pharmacist - 47,500
            Veterinarian - 46,900
              Physical therapist - 37,200
              Registered nurse - 35,700
            Dental hygienist - 28,600
            Paramedic - 28,100
            Medical lab technician - 27,700
          Nutritionist - 25,700
          Licensed practical nurse - 22,600
```

Table shows the median annual earnings in 1993 for selected health occupations.

[In dollars]

Occupation	Average earnings
Physician	148,000
Dentist	93,000
Pharmacist	47,500
Veterinarian	46,900
Physical therapist	37,200
Registered nurse	35,700
Dental hygienist	28,600
Paramedic	28,100
Medical lab technician	27,700
Nutritionist	25,700
Licensed practical nurse	22,600

Source: "The Best Jobs in America? How *Money* Ranks Today's Occupations." *Career Opportunities News* 12, no. 4 (January-February 1995), pp. 1-3. Primary source: *Money* magazine.

★ 21 ★
Earnings

Earnings for Selected Managerial Occupations: 1993

```
Lobbyist - 91,300
Management consultant - 61,900
School principal - 57,300
Financial planner - 55,100
Hotel manager - 54,000
Bank officer - 43,000
            Purchasing manager - 40,200
Funeral director - 36,500
            Hospital administrator - 36,000
Accountant - 31,800
            Personnel manager - 31,100
            Property manager - 26,600
            Retail buyer - 25,700
            Fast food manager - 21,100
```

Table shows the median annual earnings in 1993 for selected managerial occupations.

[In dollars]

Occupation	Average earnings
Lobbyist	91,300
Management consultant	61,900
School principal	57,300
Financial planner	55,100
Hotel manager	54,000
Bank officer	43,000
Purchasing manager	40,200
Funeral director	36,500
Hospital administrator	36,000
Accountant	31,800
Personnel manager	31,100
Property manager	26,600
Retail buyer	25,700
Fast food manager	21,100

Source: "The Best Jobs in America? How *Money* Ranks Today's Occupations." *Career Opportunities News* 12, no. 4 (January-February 1995), pp. 1-3. Primary source: *Money* magazine.

★ 22 ★
Earnings

Earnings for Selected Operator, Fabricator, and Laborer Occupations: 1993

Welder - 23,600

Truck driver - 23,100

Heavy equipment operator - 22,000

Garbage collector - 18,800

Taxi driver - 16,200

Table shows the median annual earnings in 1993 for selected operator, fabricator, and laborer occupations.

[In dollars]

Occupation	Average earnings
Welder	23,600
Truck driver	23,100
Heavy equipment operator	22,000
Garbage collector	18,800
Taxi driver	16,200

Source: "The Best Jobs in America? How *Money* Ranks Today's Occupations." *Career Opportunities News* 12, no. 4 (January-February 1995), pp. 1-3. Primary source: *Money* magazine.

★ 23 ★
Earnings

Earnings for Selected Precision Production, Craft, and Repair Occupations: 1993

```
Construction superintendent - 44,900
Computer repairer - 30,500
Plumber - 27,000
Machinist - 26,600
Carpenter - 22,800
Auto mechanic - 21,900
                          Construction worker - 19,700
Butcher - 18,400
Tailor - 16,600
```

Table shows the median annual earnings in 1993 for selected precision production, craft, and repair occupations.

[In dollars]

Occupation	Average earnings
Construction superintendent	44,900
Computer repairer	30,500
Plumber	27,000
Machinist	26,600
Carpenter	22,800
Auto mechanic	21,900
Construction worker	19,700
Butcher	18,400
Tailor	16,600

Source: "The Best Jobs in America? How *Money* Ranks Today's Occupations." *Career Opportunities News* 12, no. 4 (January-February 1995), pp. 1-3. Primary source: *Money* magazine.

★ 24 ★

Earnings

Earnings for Selected Sales Occupations: 1993

Advertising executive - 44,300	
Stockbroker - 40,700	
Real estate agent - 31,700	
Advertising salesperson - 30,700	
Insurance agent - 29,400	
Auto salesperson - 25,800	
Travel agent - 23,800	
Appliance salesperson - 23,300	
	Apparel salesperson - 13,600
Cashier - 11,700	

Table shows the median annual earnings in 1993 for selected sales occupations.

[In dollars]

Occupation	Average earnings
Advertising executive	44,300
Stockbroker	40,700
Real estate agent	31,700
Advertising salesperson	30,700
Insurance agent	29,400
Auto salesperson	25,800
Travel agent	23,800
Appliance salesperson	23,300
Apparel salesperson	13,600
Cashier	11,700

Source: "The Best Jobs in America? How *Money* Ranks Today's Occupations." *Career Opportunities News* 12, no. 4 (January-February 1995), pp. 1-3. Primary source: *Money* magazine.

★ 25 ★
Earnings

Earnings for Selected Scientific Occupations: 1993

Geologist - 50,800	
Biologist - 46,000	
Chemist - 43,500	
Computer systems anaylst - 42,700	
Mathematician - 42,700	
Forest ranger - 29,400	

Table shows the median annual earnings in 1993 for selected scientific occupations.

[In dollars]

Occupation	Average earnings
Geologist	50,800
Biologist	46,000
Chemist	43,500
Computer systems anaylst	42,700
Mathematician	42,700
Forest ranger	29,400

Source: "The Best Jobs in America? How *Money* Ranks Today's Occupations." *Career Opportunities News* 12, no. 4 (January-February 1995), pp. 1-3. Primary source: *Money* magazine.

★ 26 ★
Earnings

Earnings for Selected Service Occupations: 1993

| Police officer - 32,900 |
| Firefighter - 32,200 |
| Flight attendant - 26,300 |
| Hairstylist - 14,200 |
| Restaurant cook - 13,100 |
| Waiter or waitress - 12,000 |

Table shows the median annual earnings in 1993 for selected service occupations.

[In dollars]

Occupation	Average earnings
Police officer	32,900
Firefighter	32,200
Flight attendant	26,300
Hairstylist	14,200
Restaurant cook	13,100
Waiter or waitress	12,000

Source: "The Best Jobs in America? How *Money* Ranks Today's Occupations." *Career Opportunities News* 12, no. 4 (January-February 1995), pp. 1-3. Primary source: *Money* magazine.

★ 27 ★
Earnings

Earnings for Selected Social Science Occupations: 1993

Lawyer - 60,500	
Psychologist - 53,000	
Sociologist - 46,600	
Urban planner - 42,800	
Economist - 41,200	
Social worker - 26,600	
Clergy member - 26,000	

Table shows the median annual earnings in 1993 for selected social science occupations.

[In dollars]

Occupation	Average earnings
Lawyer	60,500
Psychologist	53,000
Sociologist	46,600
Urban planner	42,800
Economist	41,200
Social worker	26,600
Clergy member	26,000

Source: "The Best Jobs in America? How *Money* Ranks Today's Occupations." *Career Opportunities News* 12, no. 4 (January-February 1995), pp. 1-3. Primary source: *Money* magazine.

★ 28 ★

Earnings

Earnings for Selected Technical Occupations: 1993

| Airline pilot - 56,500 |
| Air traffic controller - 43,300 |
| Computer programmer - 38,800 |
| Paralegal - 27,900 |

Table shows the median annual earnings in 1993 for selected technical occupations.

[In dollars]

Occupation	Average earnings
Airline pilot	56,500
Air traffic controller	43,300
Computer programmer	38,800
Paralegal	27,900

Source: "The Best Jobs in America? How *Money* Ranks Today's Occupations." *Career Opportunities News* 12, no. 4 (January-February 1995), pp. 1-3. Primary source: *Money* magazine.

★ 29 ★

Earnings

State and Local Government Full-Time Employee Salaries, by Sex and Race/Ethnicity: 1991

As of June 30. Excludes school systems and educational institutions. Based on reports from state governments (44 in 1973; 48 in 1975, 1976, and 1979; 47 in 1977 and 1983; 45 in 1978; 42 in 1980; 49 in 1981 and 1984 through 1987; and 50 in 1989 through 1991) and a sample of county, municipal, township, and special district jurisdictions employing 15 or more nonelected, nonappointed full-time employees. Data for 1982 and 1988 are not available.

Occupation	Median annual salary ($1,000)					
	Male	Female	White[1]	Minority		
				Total[2]	Black[1]	Hispanic[3]
Total	28.4	22.7	26.4	23.8	22.7	24.5
Officials/administrators	43.7	37.0	41.9	41.2	41.6	41.8
Professionals	35.9	30.8	33.1	30.9	30.4	32.5
Technicians	28.9	23.0	26.6	23.6	23.3	25.8
Protective service	29.5	24.9	29.1	28.3	27.1	31.9
Paraprofessionals	21.3	19.3	20.0	19.6	19.1	20.0
Administrative support	21.2	19.6	19.6	19.8	19.9	20.1

[Continued]

★ 29 ★

State and Local Government Full-Time Employee Salaries, by Sex and Race/Ethnicity: 1991
[Continued]

Occupation	Median annual salary ($1,000)					
	Male	Female	White[1]	Minority		
				Total[2]	Black[1]	Hispanic[3]
Skilled craft	26.0	20.7	25.7	25.6	25.0	26.5
Service/maintenance	21.1	16.6	20.4	20.5	18.9	20.7

Source: U.S. Bureau of the Census. *Statistical Abstract of the United States, 1994.* 114th ed. Washington, DC: U.S. Government Printing Office, 1994, p. 320. Primary source: U.S. Equal Employment Opportunity Commission. *State and Local Government Information Report* (annual). *Notes:* 1. Non-Hispanic. 2. Includes other minority groups not shown separately. 3. Persons of Hispanic origin may be of any race.

Employee Benefits

★ 30 ★

Employee Benefit Plan Financing, by Occupation: 1991

Table shows full-time participants in selected employee benefit programs by financing source. Data are for medium and large private establishments in 1991.

[In percentages]

Occupational group	Sickness and accident insurance	Long-term disability insurance	Medical care for employee	Medical care for family	Dental care for employee	Dental care for family	Life insurance	Defined benefit pension
All participants								
Total	100	100	100	100	100	100	100	100
Wholly employer financed	74	78	49	31	58	43	85	95
Partly employer financed	26	22	51	69	42	57	15	5
Professional, technical, and related								
Total	100	100	100	100	100	100	100	100
Wholly employer financed	59	76	45	25	54	37	85	95
Partly employer financed	41	24	55	75	46	63	15	5
Clerical and sales								
Total	100	100	100	100	100	100	100	100
Wholly employer financed	67	77	43	27	51	38	86	97
Partly employer financed	33	23	57	73	49	62	14	3
Production and service								
Total	100	100	100	100	100	100	100	100
Wholly employer financed	82	83	55	37	66	50	84	95
Partly employer financed	18	17	45	63	34	50	16	5

Source: U.S. Department of Labor. Bureau of Labor Statistics. *Employee Benefits in Medium and Large Private Establishments, 1991.* Bulletin 2422. Washington, DC: U.S. Government Printing Office, May 1993, p. 124.

★ 31 ★

Employee Benefits

Group Health Plans Provided by Employers or Unions, by Occupation: 1992

Table shows the number of employees and percentages with employer- or union-provided group health plans. Data are for wage and salary workers 15 years old and over as of March 1993. Based on Current Population Survey.

[In thousands, except percentages]

Occupation	Total	Percent with group health plan
Total	134,516	50.8
Executive, administrative, managerial	16,501	65.9
Professional specialty	17,793	66.0
Technical/related support	4,330	68.4
Sales workers	16,286	41.1
Administrative support, including clerical	20,341	56.5
Precision production, craft/repair	14,185	55.1
Machine operators, assemblers[1]	8,395	59.2
Transportation and material moving	5,457	55.3
Handlers, equipment cleaners[2]	5,868	36.8
Service workers	20,091	28.7
Private households	1,163	3.2
Other	18,928	30.3
Farming, forestry and fishing	4,344	16.8
Armed Forces	924	6.5

Source: U.S. Bureau of the Census. *Statistical Abstract of the United States, 1994.* 114th ed. Washington, DC: U.S. Government Printing Office, 1994, p. 433. Primary source: U.S. Bureau of the Census. Unpublished data. *Notes:* 1. Includes inspectors. 2. Includes helpers and laborers.

★ 32 ★

Employee Benefits

Health-Related Benefit Programs, by Occupation: 1991

The table below presents the percentages of full-time employees participating in selected employee benefit programs in medium and large private establishments during 1991. Participants are workers covered by a paid time off, insurance, retirement, or capital accumulation plan. Employees subject to a minimum service requirement before they are eligible for benefit coverage are counted as participants even if they have not met the requirement at the time of the survey. If employees are required to pay part of the cost of a benefit, only those who elect the coverage and pay their shares are counted as participants. Benefits for which the employee must pay the full premium are outside the scope of the survey. Only current employees are counted as participants; retirees are excluded.

Benefit programs	All employees	Professional, technical, and related employees	Clerical and sales employees	Production and service employees
Paid:				
Sick leave	67	87	82	48
Maternity leave	2	3	2	1
Paternity leave	1	1	1	1
Unpaid:				
Maternity leave	37	43	38	33
Paternity leave	26	31	26	23
Sickness and accident insurance	45	32	35	57
Wholly employer financed	33	19	23	46
Partly employer financed	11	13	12	10
Long-term disability insurance	40	61	49	24
Wholly employer financed	31	46	38	20
Partly employer financed	9	15	11	4
Medical care	83	85	81	84
Employee coverage:				
Wholly employer financed	41	38	35	46
Partly employer financed	42	47	46	38
Family coverage:				
Wholly employer financed	26	21	22	31
Partly employer financed	57	64	59	53
Dental care	60	67	60	57
Employee coverage:				
Wholly employer financed	35	36	31	37
Partly employer financed	25	31	29	20
Family coverage:				
Wholly employer financed	26	25	23	29
Partly employer financed	34	42	37	28

Source: U.S. Department of Labor. Bureau of Labor Statistics. *Employee Benefits in Medium and Large Private Establishments, 1991.* Bulletin 2422. Washington, DC: U.S. Government Printing Office, May 1993, p. 5. *Notes:* Because of rounding, sums of individual items may not equal totals. 1. Less than 0.5 percent.

★ 33 ★

Employee Benefits

Pension Plans Provided by Employers or Unions, by Occupation: 1992

Table shows the number of employees and percentages with employer- or union-provided pension plans. Data are for wage and salary workers 15 years old and over as of March 1993. Based on Current Population Survey.

[In thousands, except percentages]

Occupation	Total	Percent with pension plan
Total	134,516	40.1
Executive, administrative, managerial	16,501	52.6
Professional specialty	17,793	59.1
Technical/related support	4,330	55.7
Sales workers	16,286	27.6
Administrative support, including clerical	20,341	46.9
Precision production, craft/repair	14,185	41.6
Machine operators, assemblers[1]	8,395	42.1
Transportation and material moving	5,457	39.4
Handlers, equipment cleaners[2]	5,868	24.4
Service workers	20,091	20.8
Private households	1,163	2.2
Other	18,928	22.0
Farming, forestry and fishing	4,344	8.5
Armed Forces	924	72.3

Source: U.S. Bureau of the Census. *Statistical Abstract of the United States, 1994.* 114th ed. Washington, DC: U.S. Government Printing Office, 1994, p. 433. Primary source: U.S. Bureau of the Census. Unpublished data. *Notes:* 1. Includes inspectors. 2. Includes helpers and laborers.

Employment and Unemployment

★ 34 ★

Adjuster and Investigator Employment, by Sex, Race, and Hispanic Origin: 1983 and 1993

For employed civilian noninstitutional population 16 years old and over. Annual average of monthly figures. Based on Current Population Survey.

Occupation	1983				1993			
	Total employed (1,000)	Percent of total			Total employed (1,000)	Percent of total		
		Female	Black	Hispanic		Female	Black	Hispanic
Total	100,834	43.7	9.3	5.3	119,306	45.8	10.2	7.8
Adjusters and investigators	675	69.9	11.1	5.1	1,372	74.0	12.2	6.1
Insurance adjusters, examiners, and investigators	199	65.0	11.5	3.3	372	71.5	12.1	4.0
Investigators and adjusters, except insurance	301	70.1	11.3	4.8	748	76.2	11.2	6.3
Eligibility clerks, social welfare	69	88.7	12.9	9.4	86	84.7	16.2	6.0
Bill and account collectors	106	66.4	8.5	6.5	166	64.3	14.8	9.5

Source: U.S. Bureau of the Census. *Statistical Abstract of the United States, 1994.* 114th ed. Washington, DC: U.S. Government Printing Office, 1994, p. 408. Primary source: U.S. Bureau of Labor Statistics. *Employment and Earnings* (monthly; January issues).

★ 35 ★

Employment and Unemployment

Administrative Support Employment, by Sex, Race, and Hispanic Origin: 1983 and 1993

For employed civilian noninstitutional population 16 years old and over. Annual average of monthly figures. Based on Current Population Survey.

Occupation	1983				1993			
	Total employed (1,000)	Percent of total			Total employed (1,000)	Percent of total		
		Female	Black	Hispanic		Female	Black	Hispanic
Total	100,834	43.7	9.3	5.3	119,306	45.8	10.2	7.8
Administrative support, including clerical	16,395	79.9	9.6	5.0	18,555	78.8	11.2	6.8
Supervisors	676	53.4	9.3	5.0	778	58.4	11.9	6.8
Miscellaneous administrative support[1]	2,397	85.2	12.5	5.9	3,694	82.3	12.4	7.8
General office clerks	648	80.6	12.7	5.2	731	82.0	11.4	9.6
Bank tellers	480	91.0	7.5	4.3	446	88.4	6.9	6.2
Data entry keyers	311	93.6	18.6	5.6	623	82.4	16.4	8.3
Statistical clerks	96	75.7	7.5	3.4	50	78.4	15.4	3.3
Teachers' aides	348	93.7	17.8	12.6	508	92.2	15.7	12.3

Source: U.S. Bureau of the Census. *Statistical Abstract of the United States, 1994.* 114th ed. Washington, DC: U.S. Government Printing Office, 1994, p. 408. Primary source: U.S. Bureau of Labor Statistics. *Employment and Earnings* (monthly; January issues). *Note:* 1. Includes other occupations, not shown separately.

★ 36 ★

Employment and Unemployment

Architectural and Engineering Employment, by Sex, Race, and Hispanic Origin: 1983 and 1993

For employed civilian noninstitutional population 16 years old and over. Annual average of monthly figures. Based on Current Population Survey.

Occupation	1983				1993			
	Total employed (1,000)	Percent of total			Total employed (1,000)	Percent of total		
		Female	Black	Hispanic		Female	Black	Hispanic
Total	100,834	43.7	9.3	5.3	119,306	45.8	10.2	7.8
Architects	103	12.7	1.6	1.5	123	18.6	3.1	2.3
Engineers[1]	1,572	5.8	2.7	2.2	1,716	8.6	3.7	3.6
Aerospace	80	6.9	1.5	2.1	83	7.5	2.1	3.9
Chemical	67	6.1	3.0	1.4	58	10.0	2.5	4.9
Civil	211	4.0	1.9	3.2	221	9.4	4.7	3.8
Electrical and electronic	450	6.1	3.4	3.1	533	7.6	4.5	3.4
Industrial	210	11.0	3.3	2.4	201	16.4	3.4	4.4
Mechanical	259	2.8	3.2	1.1	296	5.2	4.4	3.3

Source: U.S. Bureau of the Census. *Statistical Abstract of the United States, 1994.* 114th ed. Washington, DC: U.S. Government Printing Office, 1994, p. 407. Primary source: U.S. Bureau of Labor Statistics. *Employment and Earnings* (monthly; January issues). *Note:* 1. Includes other occupations, not shown separately.

★ 37 ★

Employment and Unemployment

Art-Related Employment, by Sex, Race, and Hispanic Origin: 1983 and 1993

For employed civilian noninstitutional population 16 years old and over. Annual average of monthly figures. Based on Current Population Survey.

Occupation	1983				1993			
	Total employed (1,000)	Percent of total			Total employed (1,000)	Percent of total		
		Female	Black	Hispanic		Female	Black	Hispanic
Total	100,834	43.7	9.3	5.3	119,306	45.8	10.2	7.8
Writers, artists, entertainers, and athletes[1]	1,544	42.7	4.8	2.9	2,026	46.6	5.3	4.7
Designers	393	52.7	3.1	2.7	541	52.6	3.7	4.4
Painters, sculptors, craft-artists, and artist printmakers	186	47.4	2.1	2.3	222	48.0	3.5	4.1
Photographers	113	20.7	4.0	3.4	135	26.2	6.5	7.1

Source: U.S. Bureau of the Census. *Statistical Abstract of the United States, 1994.* 114th ed. Washington, DC: U.S. Government Printing Office, 1994, p. 407. Primary source: U.S. Bureau of Labor Statistics. *Employment and Earnings* (monthly; January issues). *Note:* 1. Includes other occupations, not shown separately.

★ 38 ★

Employment and Unemployment

Cleaning and Building Service Employment, by Sex, Race, and Hispanic Origin: 1983 and 1993

For employed civilian noninstitutional population 16 years old and over. Annual average of monthly figures. Based on Current Population Survey.

Occupation	1983				1993			
	Total employed (1,000)	Percent of total			Total employed (1,000)	Percent of total		
		Female	Black	Hispanic		Female	Black	Hispanic
Total	100,834	43.7	9.3	5.3	119,306	45.8	10.2	7.8
Cleaning and building service occupations[1]	2,736	38.8	24.4	9.2	2,959	42.2	22.4	16.2
Maids and housemen	531	81.2	32.3	10.1	661	81.7	27.3	18.6
Janitors and cleaners	2,031	28.6	22.6	8.9	2,086	30.7	21.5	16.1

Source: U.S. Bureau of the Census. *Statistical Abstract of the United States, 1994.* 114th ed. Washington, DC: U.S. Government Printing Office, 1994, p. 409. Primary source: U.S. Bureau of Labor Statistics. *Employment and Earnings* (monthly; January issues). *Note:* 1. Includes other occupations, not shown separately.

★ 39 ★

Employment and Unemployment

Communications Equipment Operator Employment, by Sex, Race, and Hispanic Origin: 1983 and 1993

For employed civilian noninstitutional population 16 years old and over. Annual average of monthly figures. Based on Current Population Survey.

Occupation	1983				1993			
	Total employed (1,000)	Percent of total			Total employed (1,000)	Percent of total		
		Female	Black	Hispanic		Female	Black	Hispanic
Total	100,834	43.7	9.3	5.3	119,306	45.8	10.2	7.8
Communications equipment operators	256	89.1	17.0	4.4	208	86.1	20.9	8.0
Telephone operators	244	90.4	17.0	4.3	197	86.9	21.0	7.9

Source: U.S. Bureau of the Census. *Statistical Abstract of the United States, 1994.* 114th ed. Washington, DC: U.S. Government Printing Office, 1994, p. 408. Primary source: U.S. Bureau of Labor Statistics. *Employment and Earnings* (monthly; January issues).

★ 40 ★

Employment and Unemployment

Computer Equipment Operator Employment, by Sex, Race, and Hispanic Origin: 1983 and 1993

For employed civilian noninstitutional population 16 years old and over. Annual average of monthly figures. Based on Current Population Survey.

Occupation	1983				1993			
	Total employed (1,000)	Percent of total			Total employed (1,000)	Percent of total		
		Female	Black	Hispanic		Female	Black	Hispanic
Total	100,834	43.7	9.3	5.3	119,306	45.8	10.2	7.8
Computer equipment operators	605	63.9	12.5	6.0	603	61.9	13.8	6.2
Computer operators	597	63.7	12.1	6.0	597	61.9	13.7	6.1

Source: U.S. Bureau of the Census. *Statistical Abstract of the United States, 1994.* 114th ed. Washington, DC: U.S. Government Printing Office, 1994, p. 408. Primary source: U.S. Bureau of Labor Statistics. *Employment and Earnings* (monthly; January issues).

★ 41 ★

Employment and Unemployment

Construction Employment, by Sex, Race, and Hispanic Origin: 1983 and 1993

For employed civilian noninstitutional population 16 years old and over. Annual average of monthly figures. Based on Current Population Survey.

Occupation	1983				1993			
	Total employed (1,000)	Percent of total			Total employed (1,000)	Percent of total		
		Female	Black	Hispanic		Female	Black	Hispanic
Total	100,834	43.7	9.3	5.3	119,306	45.8	10.2	7.8
Construction trades	4,289	1.8	6.6	6.0	5,004	1.9	6.5	9.5
Construction trades, except supervisors	3,784	1.9	7.1	6.1	4,269	1.9	7.0	10.2
Carpenters	1,160	1.4	5.0	5.0	1,276	0.9	4.5	7.7

Source: U.S. Bureau of the Census. *Statistical Abstract of the United States, 1994.* 114th ed. Washington, DC: U.S. Government Printing Office, 1994, p. 409. Primary source: U.S. Bureau of Labor Statistics. *Employment and Earnings* (monthly; January issues).

★ 42 ★

Employment and Unemployment

Education-Related Employment, by Sex, Race, and Hispanic Origin: 1983 and 1993

For employed civilian noninstitutional population 16 years old and over. Annual average of monthly figures. Based on Current Population Survey.

Occupation	1983				1993			
	Total employed (1,000)	Percent of total			Total employed (1,000)	Percent of total		
		Female	Black	Hispanic		Female	Black	Hispanic
Total	100,834	43.7	9.3	5.3	119,306	45.8	10.2	7.8
Teachers, college and university	606	36.3	4.4	1.8	772	42.5	4.8	3.1
Teachers, except college and university[1]	3,365	70.9	9.1	2.7	4,397	75.1	8.6	3.6
Prekindergarten and kindergarten	299	98.2	11.8	3.4	501	97.7	11.7	5.0
Elementary school	1,350	83.3	11.1	3.1	1,668	85.9	9.3	3.9
Secondary school	1,209	51.8	7.2	2.3	1,237	57.5	6.9	3.1
Special education	81	82.2	10.2	2.3	286	84.0	10.1	2.3
Counselors, educational and vocational	184	53.1	13.9	3.2	224	67.6	14.3	6.9
Librarians, archivists, and curators	213	84.4	7.8	1.6	223	83.5	6.2	3.8
Librarians	193	87.3	7.9	1.8	195	88.3	7.0	3.5

Source: U.S. Bureau of the Census. *Statistical Abstract of the United States, 1994.* 114th ed. Washington, DC: U.S. Government Printing Office, 1994, p. 407. Primary source: U.S. Bureau of Labor Statistics. *Employment and Earnings* (monthly; January issues). *Note:* 1. Includes other occupations, not shown separately.

★ 43 ★

Employment and Unemployment

Electrical and Electronic Equipment Repair Employment, by Sex, Race, and Hispanic Origin: 1983 and 1993

For employed civilian noninstitutional population 16 years old and over. Annual average of monthly figures. Based on Current Population Survey.

Occupation	1983				1993			
	Total employed (1,000)	Percent of total			Total employed (1,000)	Percent of total		
		Female	Black	Hispanic		Female	Black	Hispanic
Total	100,834	43.7	9.3	5.3	119,306	45.8	10.2	7.8
Electrical and electronic equipment repairers[1]	674	7.4	7.3	4.5	655	9.5	9.0	5.8
Data processing equipment repairers	98	9.3	6.1	4.5	152	10.7	10.2	5.0
Telephone installers and repairers	247	9.9	7.8	3.7	188	12.5	9.9	3.4

Source: U.S. Bureau of the Census. *Statistical Abstract of the United States, 1994.* 114th ed. Washington, DC: U.S. Government Printing Office, 1994, p. 409. Primary source: U.S. Bureau of Labor Statistics. *Employment and Earnings* (monthly; January issues). *Note:* 1. Includes other occupations, not shown separately.

★ 44 ★

Employment and Unemployment

Engineering Technology-Related Employment, by Sex, Race, and Hispanic Origin: 1983 and 1993

For employed civilian noninstitutional population 16 years old and over. Annual average of monthly figures. Based on Current Population Survey.

Occupation	1983				1993			
	Total employed (1,000)	Percent of total			Total employed (1,000)	Percent of total		
		Female	Black	Hispanic		Female	Black	Hispanic
Total	100,834	43.7	9.3	5.3	119,306	45.8	10.2	7.8
Engineering and related technologists and technicians[1]	822	18.4	6.1	3.5	870	17.8	7.4	4.9
Electrical and electronic technicians	260	12.5	8.2	4.6	297	15.5	7.4	5.6
Drafting occupations	273	17.5	5.5	2.3	244	18.1	6.9	5.9
Surveying and mapping technicians	(2)	(2)	(2)	(2)	73	5.0	4.8	2.8

Source: U.S. Bureau of the Census. *Statistical Abstract of the United States, 1994.* 114th ed. Washington, DC: U.S. Government Printing Office, 1994, p. 408. Primary source: U.S. Bureau of Labor Statistics. *Employment and Earnings* (monthly; January issues). *Notes:* 1. Includes other occupations, not shown separately. 2. Level of total employment below 50,000.

★ 45 ★

Employment and Unemployment

Entertainment-Related Employment, by Sex, Race, and Hispanic Origin: 1983 and 1993

For employed civilian noninstitutional population 16 years old and over. Annual average of monthly figures. Based on Current Population Survey.

Occupation	1983				1993			
	Total employed (1,000)	Percent of total			Total employed (1,000)	Percent of total		
		Female	Black	Hispanic		Female	Black	Hispanic
Total	100,834	43.7	9.3	5.3	119,306	45.8	10.2	7.8
Writers, artists, entertainers, and athletes[1]	1,544	42.7	4.8	2.9	2,026	46.6	5.3	4.7
Musicians and composers	155	28.0	7.9	4.4	174	32.8	8.8	5.8
Actors and directors	60	30.8	6.6	3.4	96	38.3	10.4	4.7
Athletes	58	17.6	9.4	1.7	80	23.9	10.1	3.9

Source: U.S. Bureau of the Census. *Statistical Abstract of the United States, 1994.* 114th ed. Washington, DC: U.S. Government Printing Office, 1994, p. 407. Primary source: U.S. Bureau of Labor Statistics. *Employment and Earnings* (monthly; January issues). *Note:* 1. Includes other occupations, not shown separately.

★ 46 ★

Employment and Unemployment

Executive, Administrative, and Managerial Employment, by Sex, Race, and Hispanic Origin: 1983 and 1993

For employed civilian noninstitutional population 16 years old and over. Annual average of monthly figures. Based on Current Population Survey.

Occupation	1983				1993			
	Total employed (1,000)	Percent of total			Total employed (1,000)	Percent of total		
		Female	Black	Hispanic		Female	Black	Hispanic
Total	100,834	43.7	9.3	5.3	119,306	45.8	10.2	7.8
Executive, administrative, and managerial[1]	10,772	32.4	4.7	2.8	15,376	42.0	6.2	4.5
Officials and administrators, public	417	38.5	8.3	3.8	581	45.2	11.3	4.5
Financial managers	357	38.6	3.5	3.1	529	46.2	4.4	4.2
Personnel and labor relations managers	106	43.9	4.9	2.6	96	60.7	7.9	4.6
Purchasing managers	82	23.6	5.1	1.4	109	34.9	8.0	5.3
Managers, marketing, advertising and public relations	396	21.8	2.7	1.7	496	31.2	3.1	3.5
Administrators, education and related fields	415	41.4	11.3	2.4	635	59.9	13.0	3.8
Managers, medicine and health	91	57.0	5.0	2.0	450	70.5	6.5	4.2
Managers, properties and real estate	305	42.8	5.5	5.2	4٤ ،	45.7	6.6	6.3

Source: U.S. Bureau of the Census. *Statistical Abstract of the United States, 1994.* 114th ed. Washington, DC: U.S. Government Printing Office, 1994, p. 407. Primary source: U.S. Bureau of Labor Statistics. *Employment and Earnings* (monthly; January issues). *Note:* 1. Includes other occupations, not shown separately.

★ 47 ★

Employment and Unemployment

Farming, Forestry, and Fishing Employment, by Sex, Race, and Hispanic Origin: 1983 and 1993

For employed civilian noninstitutional population 16 years old and over. Annual average of monthly figures. Based on Current Population Survey.

Occupation	1983				1993			
	Total employed (1,000)	Percent of total			Total employed (1,000)	Percent of total		
		Female	Black	Hispanic		Female	Black	Hispanic
Total	100,834	43.7	9.3	5.3	119,306	45.8	10.2	7.8
Farming, forestry, and fishing	3,700	16.0	7.5	8.2	3,326	15.4	6.3	16.0
Farm operators and managers	1,450	12.1	1.3	0.7	1,170	14.3	0.9	2.4
Other agricultural and related occupations	2,072	19.9	11.7	14.0	1,963	17.0	9.5	24.8
Farm workers	1,149	24.8	11.6	15.9	801	20.0	7.0	28.5
Forestry and logging occupations	126	1.4	12.8	2.1	132	5.9	10.4	11.8
Fishers, hunters, and trappers	53	4.5	1.8	2.5	61	4.4	1.7	4.8

Source: U.S. Bureau of the Census. *Statistical Abstract of the United States, 1994.* 114th ed. Washington, DC: U.S. Government Printing Office, 1994, p. 409. Primary source: U.S. Bureau of Labor Statistics. *Employment and Earnings* (monthly; January issues).

★ 48 ★

Employment and Unemployment

Finance and Business Services Sales Employment, by Sex, Race, and Hispanic Origin: 1983 and 1993

For employed civilian noninstitutional population 16 years old and over. Annual average of monthly figures. Based on Current Population Survey.

Occupation	1983				1993			
	Total employed (1,000)	Percent of total			Total employed (1,000)	Percent of total		
		Female	Black	Hispanic		Female	Black	Hispanic
Total	100,834	43.7	9.3	5.3	119,306	45.8	10.2	7.8
Sales representatives, finance and business services[1]	1,853	37.2	2.7	2.2	2,317	40.5	4.7	3.7
Insurance sales	551	25.1	3.8	2.5	583	33.3	5.1	3.8
Real estate sales	570	48.9	1.3	1.5	710	51.4	2.5	4.1
Securities and financial services sales	212	23.6	3.1	1.1	355	28.1	4.1	2.2
Advertising and related sales	124	47.9	4.5	3.3	161	50.8	4.5	3.1

Source: U.S. Bureau of the Census. *Statistical Abstract of the United States, 1994.* 114th ed. Washington, DC: U.S. Government Printing Office, 1994, p. 408. Primary source: U.S. Bureau of Labor Statistics. *Employment and Earnings* (monthly; January issues). *Note:* 1. Includes other occupations, not shown separately.

★ 49 ★

Employment and Unemployment

Financial Records Processing Employment, by Sex, Race, and Hispanic Origin: 1983 and 1993

For employed civilian noninstitutional population 16 years old and over. Annual average of monthly figures. Based on Current Population Survey.

Occupation	1983				1993			
	Total employed (1,000)	Percent of total			Total employed (1,000)	Percent of total		
		Female	Black	Hispanic		Female	Black	Hispanic
Total	100,834	43.7	9.3	5.3	119,306	45.8	10.2	7.8
Financial records processing[1]	2,457	89.4	4.6	3.7	2,272	89.9	5.4	5.3
Bookkeepers, accounting, and auditing clerks	1,970	91.0	4.3	3.3	1,806	90.9	4.5	4.9
Payroll and time keeping clerks	192	82.2	5.9	5.0	173	88.3	6.6	5.2
Billing clerks	146	88.4	6.2	3.9	160	88.5	8.4	6.6
Cost and rate clerks	96	75.6	5.9	5.3	60	72.9	10.9	9.7
Billing, posting, and calculating machine operators	(2)	(2)	(2)	(2)	72	86.1	12.0	8.2

Source: U.S. Bureau of the Census. *Statistical Abstract of the United States, 1994.* 114th ed. Washington, DC: U.S. Government Printing Office, 1994, p. 408. Primary source: U.S. Bureau of Labor Statistics. *Employment and Earnings* (monthly; January issues). *Notes:* 1. Includes other occupations, not shown separately. 2. Level of total employment below 50,000.

★ 50 ★

Employment and Unemployment

Firefighting and Fire Prevention Employment, by Sex, Race, and Hispanic Origin: 1983 and 1993

For employed civilian noninstitutional population 16 years old and over. Annual average of monthly figures. Based on Current Population Survey.

Occupation	1983				1993			
	Total employed (1,000)	Percent of total			Total employed (1,000)	Percent of total		
		Female	Black	Hispanic		Female	Black	Hispanic
Total	100,834	43.7	9.3	5.3	119,306	45.8	10.2	7.8
Firefighting and fire prevention	189	1.0	6.7	4.1	208	3.7	7.6	4.5
Firefighting occupations	170	1.0	7.3	3.8	188	3.3	7.5	5.0

Source: U.S. Bureau of the Census. *Statistical Abstract of the United States, 1994.* 114th ed. Washington, DC: U.S. Government Printing Office, 1994, p. 409. Primary source: U.S. Bureau of Labor Statistics. *Employment and Earnings* (monthly; January issues).

★ 51 ★

Employment and Unemployment

Food Preparation and Service Employment, by Sex, Race, and Hispanic Origin: 1983 and 1993

For employed civilian noninstitutional population 16 years old and over. Annual average of monthly figures. Based on Current Population Survey.

Occupation	1983				1993			
	Total employed (1,000)	Percent of total			Total employed (1,000)	Percent of total		
		Female	Black	Hispanic		Female	Black	Hispanic
Total	100,834	43.7	9.3	5.3	119,306	45.8	10.2	7.8
Food preparation and service occupations[1]	4,860	63.3	10.5	6.8	5,691	58.4	12.8	11.7
Bartenders	338	48.4	2.7	4.4	321	53.3	3.8	3.1
Waiters and waitresses	1,357	87.8	4.1	3.6	1,414	80.0	4.6	7.5
Cooks	1,452	50.0	15.8	6.5	1,992	44.2	19.0	13.9
Food counter, fountain, and related occupations	326	76.0	9.1	6.7	367	69.2	12.6	8.1
Kitchen workers, food preparation	138	77.0	13.7	8.1	260	75.3	15.0	10.8
Waiters' and waitresses' assistants	364	38.8	12.6	14.2	368	43.7	11.4	18.1

Source: U.S. Bureau of the Census. *Statistical Abstract of the United States, 1994.* 114th ed. Washington, DC: U.S. Government Printing Office, 1994, p. 409. Primary source: U.S. Bureau of Labor Statistics. *Employment and Earnings* (monthly; January issues). *Note:* 1. Includes other occupations, not shown separately.

★ 52 ★

Employment and Unemployment

Handler, Helper, and Laborer Employment, by Sex, Race, and Hispanic Origin: 1983 and 1993

For employed civilian noninstitutional population 16 years old and over. Annual average of monthly figures. Based on Current Population Survey.

Occupation	1983				1993			
	Total employed (1,000)	Percent of total			Total employed (1,000)	Percent of total		
		Female	Black	Hispanic		Female	Black	Hispanic
Total	100,834	43.7	9.3	5.3	119,306	45.8	10.2	7.8
Handlers, equipment cleaners, helpers, and laborers[1]	4,147	16.8	15.1	8.6	4,619	18.3	16.1	12.9
Freight, stock, and material handlers	1,488	15.4	15.3	7.1	1,850	20.7	16.7	9.9
Laborers, except construction	1,024	19.4	16.0	8.6	1,127	17.0	16.7	13.7

Source: U.S. Bureau of the Census. *Statistical Abstract of the United States, 1994.* 114th ed. Washington, DC: U.S. Government Printing Office, 1994, p. 409. Primary source: U.S. Bureau of Labor Statistics. *Employment and Earnings* (monthly; January issues). *Note:* 1. Includes other occupations, not shown separately.

★ 53 ★

Employment and Unemployment

Health Assessment and Treating Employment, by Sex, Race, and Hispanic Origin: 1983 and 1993

For employed civilian noninstitutional population 16 years old and over. Annual average of monthly figures. Based on Current Population Survey.

Occupation	1983				1993			
	Total employed (1,000)	Percent of total			Total employed (1,000)	Percent of total		
		Female	Black	Hispanic		Female	Black	Hispanic
Total	100,834	43.7	9.3	5.3	119,306	45.8	10.2	7.8
Health assessment and treating occupations	1,900	85.8	7.1	2.2	2,602	86.4	8.3	3.5
Registered nurses	1,372	95.8	6.7	1.8	1,859	94.4	8.4	3.2
Pharmacists	158	26.7	3.8	2.6	187	38.1	6.1	2.7
Dietitians	71	90.8	21.0	3.7	94	92.8	17.5	6.0
Physicians' assistants	51	36.3	7.7	4.4	([1])	([1])	([1])	([1])

Source: U.S. Bureau of the Census. *Statistical Abstract of the United States, 1994.* 114th ed. Washington, DC: U.S. Government Printing Office, 1994, p. 407. Primary source: U.S. Bureau of Labor Statistics. *Employment and Earnings* (monthly; January issues). *Note:* 1. Level of total employment below 50,000.

★ 54 ★

Employment and Unemployment

Health Diagnosing Employment, by Sex, Race, and Hispanic Origin: 1983 and 1993

For employed civilian noninstitutional population 16 years old and over. Annual average of monthly figures. Based on Current Population Survey.

Occupation	1983				1993			
	Total employed (1,000)	Percent of total			Total employed (1,000)	Percent of total		
		Female	Black	Hispanic		Female	Black	Hispanic
Total	100,834	43.7	9.3	5.3	119,306	45.8	10.2	7.8
Health diagnosing occupations[1]	735	13.3	2.7	3.3	909	20.5	3.0	3.9
Physicians	519	15.8	3.2	4.5	605	21.8	3.7	4.6
Dentists	126	6.7	2.4	1.0	152	10.5	1.9	3.0

Source: U.S. Bureau of the Census. *Statistical Abstract of the United States, 1994.* 114th ed. Washington, DC: U.S. Government Printing Office, 1994, p. 407. Primary source: U.S. Bureau of Labor Statistics. *Employment and Earnings* (monthly; January issues). *Note:* 1. Includes other occupations, not shown separately.

★ 55 ★

Employment and Unemployment

Health Service Employment, by Sex, Race, and Hispanic Origin: 1983 and 1993

For employed civilian noninstitutional population 16 years old and over. Annual average of monthly figures. Based on Current Population Survey.

Occupation	1983				1993			
	Total employed (1,000)	Percent of total			Total employed (1,000)	Percent of total		
		Female	Black	Hispanic		Female	Black	Hispanic
Total	100,834	43.7	9.3	5.3	119,306	45.8	10.2	7.8
Health service occupations	1,739	89.2	23.5	4.8	2,213	87.4	27.3	7.7
Dental assistants	154	98.1	6.1	5.7	181	97.8	3.4	10.4
Health aides, except nursing	316	86.8	16.5	4.8	312	78.9	22.2	4.7
Nursing aides, orderlies, and attendants	1,269	88.7	27.3	4.7	1,719	87.9	30.7	7.9

Source: U.S. Bureau of the Census. *Statistical Abstract of the United States, 1994.* 114th ed. Washington, DC: U.S. Government Printing Office, 1994, p. 409. Primary source: U.S. Bureau of Labor Statistics. *Employment and Earnings* (monthly; January issues).

★ 56 ★

Employment and Unemployment

Health Technology-Related Employment, by Sex, Race, and Hispanic Origin: 1983 and 1993

For employed civilian noninstitutional population 16 years old and over. Annual average of monthly figures. Based on Current Population Survey.

Occupation	1983				1993			
	Total employed (1,000)	Percent of total			Total employed (1,000)	Percent of total		
		Female	Black	Hispanic		Female	Black	Hispanic
Total	100,834	43.7	9.3	5.3	119,306	45.8	10.2	7.8
Health technologists and technicians[1]	1,111	84.3	12.7	3.1	1,522	81.0	12.4	5.8
Clinical laboratory technologists and technicians	255	76.2	10.5	2.9	315	76.1	12.1	6.1
Dental hygienists	66	98.6	1.6	-	76	99.3	0.4	2.0
Health record technologists and technicians	(2)	(2)	(2)	(2)	63	88.8	20.4	5.7
Radiologic technicians	101	71.7	8.6	4.5	146	70.2	8.3	7.0
Licensed practical nurses	443	97.0	17.7	3.1	425	94.6	17.2	3.4

Source: U.S. Bureau of the Census. *Statistical Abstract of the United States, 1994.* 114th ed. Washington, DC: U.S. Government Printing Office, 1994, p. 408. Primary source: U.S. Bureau of Labor Statistics. *Employment and Earnings* (monthly; January issues). *Notes:* "-" represents or rounds to zero. 1. Includes other occupations, not shown separately. 2. Level of total employment below 50,000.

★ 57 ★

Employment and Unemployment

Law-Related Employment, by Sex, Race, and Hispanic Origin: 1983 and 1993

For employed civilian noninstitutional population 16 years old and over. Annual average of monthly figures. Based on Current Population Survey.

Occupation	1983				1993			
	Total employed (1,000)	Percent of total			Total employed (1,000)	Percent of total		
		Female	Black	Hispanic		Female	Black	Hispanic
Total	100,834	43.7	9.3	5.3	119,306	45.8	10.2	7.8
Lawyers and judges	651	15.8	2.7	1.0	815	22.8	2.8	2.1
Lawyers	612	15.3	2.6	0.9	777	22.9	2.7	2.1

Source: U.S. Bureau of the Census. *Statistical Abstract of the United States, 1994.* 114th ed. Washington, DC: U.S. Government Printing Office, 1994, p. 407. Primary source: U.S. Bureau of Labor Statistics. *Employment and Earnings* (monthly; January issues).

★ 58 ★

Employment and Unemployment

Machine Operator and Related Employment, by Sex, Race, and Hispanic Origin: 1983 and 1993

For employed civilian noninstitutional population 16 years old and over. Annual average of monthly figures. Based on Current Population Survey.

Occupation	1983				1993			
	Total employed (1,000)	Percent of total			Total employed (1,000)	Percent of total		
		Female	Black	Hispanic		Female	Black	Hispanic
Total	100,834	43.7	9.3	5.3	119,306	45.8	10.2	7.8
Operators, fabricators, and laborers	16,091	26.6	14.0	8.3	17,038	24.5	14.9	12.1
Machine operators, assemblers, and inspectors[1]	7,744	42.1	14.0	9.4	7,415	38.7	14.7	13.8
Textile, apparel, and furnishings machine operators[1]	1,414	82.1	18.7	12.5	1,159	74.4	20.8	19.9
Textile sewing machine operators	806	94.0	15.5	14.5	616	85.8	18.5	24.1
Pressing machine operators	141	66.4	27.1	14.2	147	62.7	24.0	20.4
Fabricators, assemblers, and hand working occupations	1,715	33.7	11.3	8.7	1,882	32.7	12.7	12.0
Production inspectors, testers, samplers, and weighers	794	53.8	13.0	7.7	777	52.4	15.0	13.7

Source: U.S. Bureau of the Census. *Statistical Abstract of the United States, 1994.* 114th ed. Washington, DC: U.S. Government Printing Office, 1994, p. 409. Primary source: U.S. Bureau of Labor Statistics. *Employment and Earnings* (monthly; January issues). *Note:* 1. Includes other occupations, not shown separately.

★ 59 ★

Employment and Unemployment

Mail-Related Employment, by Sex, Race, and Hispanic Origin: 1983 and 1993

For employed civilian noninstitutional population 16 years old and over. Annual average of monthly figures. Based on Current Population Survey.

Occupation	1983				1993			
	Total employed (1,000)	Percent of total			Total employed (1,000)	Percent of total		
		Female	Black	Hispanic		Female	Black	Hispanic
Total	100,834	43.7	9.3	5.3	119,306	45.8	10.2	7.8
Duplicating, mail and other office machine operators	68	62.6	16.0	6.1	63	47.8	19.2	9.2
Mail and message distributing occupations	799	31.6	18.1	4.5	953	37.6	19.0	7.4
Postal clerks, except mail carriers	248	36.7	26.2	5.2	297	44.8	26.8	6.8
Mail carriers, postal service	259	17.1	12.5	2.7	333	28.4	12.6	7.0
Mail clerks, except postal service	170	50.0	15.8	5.9	166	51.5	22.5	8.8
Messengers	122	26.2	16.7	5.2	157	29.1	14.2	7.9

Source: U.S. Bureau of the Census. *Statistical Abstract of the United States, 1994.* 114th ed. Washington, DC: U.S. Government Printing Office, 1994, p. 408. Primary source: U.S. Bureau of Labor Statistics. *Employment and Earnings* (monthly; January issues).

★ 60 ★

Employment and Unemployment

Managerial and Professional Specialty Employment, by Sex, Race, and Hispanic Origin: 1983 and 1993

For employed civilian noninstitutional population 16 years old and over. Annual average of monthly figures. Based on Current Population Survey. See also related tables for specific occupations.

Occupation	1983				1993			
	Total employed (1,000)	Percent of total			Total employed (1,000)	Percent of total		
		Female	Black	Hispanic		Female	Black	Hispanic
Total	100,834	43.7	9.3	5.3	119,306	45.8	10.2	7.8
Managerial and professional specialty	23,592	40.9	5.6	2.6	32,280	47.8	6.6	4.0
Management-related occupations[1]	2,966	40.3	5.8	3.5	4,155	52.7	7.5	4.6
Accountants and auditors	1,105	38.7	5.5	3.3	1,387	49.2	7.0	4.2
Professional specialty[1]	12,820	48.1	6.4	2.5	16,904	53.2	7.0	3.6

Source: U.S. Bureau of the Census. *Statistical Abstract of the United States, 1994.* 114th ed. Washington, DC: U.S. Government Printing Office, 1994, p. 407. Primary source: U.S. Bureau of Labor Statistics. *Employment and Earnings* (monthly; January issues). *Note:* 1. Includes other occupations, not shown separately.

★ 61 ★

Employment and Unemployment

Material Recording, Scheduling, and Distributing Employment, by Sex, Race, and Hispanic Origin: 1983 and 1993

For employed civilian noninstitutional population 16 years old and over. Annual average of monthly figures. Based on Current Population Survey.

Occupation	1983				1993			
	Total employed (1,000)	Percent of total			Total employed (1,000)	Percent of total		
		Female	Black	Hispanic		Female	Black	Hispanic
Total	100,834	43.7	9.3	5.3	119,306	45.8	10.2	7.8
Material recording, scheduling, and distributing[1]	1,562	37.5	10.9	6.6	1,852	44.0	14.0	8.3
Dispatchers	157	45.7	11.4	4.3	221	52.7	11.8	5.7
Production coordinators	182	44.0	6.1	2.2	196	50.2	7.8	4.7
Traffic, shipping, and receiving clerks	421	22.6	9.1	11.1	570	30.9	15.1	11.9
Stock and inventory clerks	532	38.7	13.3	5.5	489	43.4	14.5	6.8
Weighers, measurers, and checkers	79	47.2	16.9	5.8	67	45.6	15.9	10.4
Expediters	112	57.5	8.4	4.3	227	67.0	13.9	7.1

Source: U.S. Bureau of the Census. *Statistical Abstract of the United States, 1994.* 114th ed. Washington, DC: U.S. Government Printing Office, 1994, p. 408. Primary source: U.S. Bureau of Labor Statistics. *Employment and Earnings* (monthly; January issues). *Note:* 1. Includes other occupations, not shown separately. Includes clerks.

★ 62 ★

Employment and Unemployment

Mathematical and Computer Science Employment, by Sex, Race, and Hispanic Origin: 1983 and 1993

For employed civilian noninstitutional population 16 years old and over. Annual average of monthly figures. Based on Current Population Survey.

Occupation	1983				1993			
	Total employed (1,000)	Percent of total			Total employed (1,000)	Percent of total		
		Female	Black	Hispanic		Female	Black	Hispanic
Total	100,834	43.7	9.3	5.3	119,306	45.8	10.2	7.8
Mathematical and computer scientists[1]	463	29.6	5.4	2.6	1,051	32.4	6.0	2.5
Computer systems analysts, scientists	276	27.8	6.2	2.7	769	29.9	5.8	2.4
Operations and systems researchers and analysts	142	31.3	4.9	2.2	236	39.7	6.3	3.0

Source: U.S. Bureau of the Census. *Statistical Abstract of the United States, 1994.* 114th ed. Washington, DC: U.S. Government Printing Office, 1994, p. 407. Primary source: U.S. Bureau of Labor Statistics. *Employment and Earnings* (monthly; January issues). *Note:* 1. Includes other occupations, not shown separately.

★ 63 ★

Employment and Unemployment

Mechanic- and Repair-Related Employment, by Sex, Race, and Hispanic Origin: 1983 and 1993

For employed civilian noninstitutional population 16 years old and over. Annual average of monthly figures. Based on Current Population Survey.

Occupation	1983				1993			
	Total employed (1,000)	Percent of total			Total employed (1,000)	Percent of total		
		Female	Black	Hispanic		Female	Black	Hispanic
Total	100,834	43.7	9.3	5.3	119,306	45.8	10.2	7.8
Mechanics and repairers	4,158	3.0	6.8	5.3	4,416	3.5	7.3	7.9
Mechanics and repairers, except supervisors[1]	3,906	2.8	7.0	5.5	4,196	3.3	7.3	8.1
Vehicle and mobile equipment mechanics/repairers[1]	1,683	0.8	6.9	6.0	1,800	1.0	6.1	9.9
Automobile mechanics	800	0.5	7.8	6.0	854	0.6	6.4	10.8
Aircraft engine mechanics	95	2.5	4.0	7.6	139	4.1	5.1	11.5

Source: U.S. Bureau of the Census. *Statistical Abstract of the United States, 1994.* 114th ed. Washington, DC: U.S. Government Printing Office, 1994, p. 409. Primary source: U.S. Bureau of Labor Statistics. *Employment and Earnings* (monthly; January issues). *Note:* 1. Includes other occupations, not shown separately.

★ 64 ★

Employment and Unemployment

Natural Science Employment, by Sex, Race, and Hispanic Origin: 1983 and 1993

For employed civilian noninstitutional population 16 years old and over. Annual average of monthly figures. Based on Current Population Survey.

Occupation	1983				1993			
	Total employed (1,000)	Percent of total			Total employed (1,000)	Percent of total		
		Female	Black	Hispanic		Female	Black	Hispanic
Total	100,834	43.7	9.3	5.3	119,306	45.8	10.2	7.8
Natural scientists[1]	357	20.5	2.6	2.1	531	30.1	3.6	1.9
Chemists, except biochemists	98	23.3	4.3	1.2	133	28.8	4.3	3.0
Geologists and geodesists	65	18.0	1.1	2.6	54	14.0	1.0	2.1
Biological and life scientists	55	40.8	2.4	1.8	114	40.4	3.9	1.4

Source: U.S. Bureau of the Census. *Statistical Abstract of the United States, 1994.* 114th ed. Washington, DC: U.S. Government Printing Office, 1994, p. 407. Primary source: U.S. Bureau of Labor Statistics. *Employment and Earnings* (monthly; January issues). *Note:* 1. Includes other occupations, not shown separately.

★ 65 ★

Employment and Unemployment

Personal Service Employment, by Sex, Race, and Hispanic Origin: 1983 and 1993

For employed civilian noninstitutional population 16 years old and over. Annual average of monthly figures. Based on Current Population Survey.

Occupation	1983				1993			
	Total employed (1,000)	Percent of total			Total employed (1,000)	Percent of total		
		Female	Black	Hispanic		Female	Black	Hispanic
Total	100,834	43.7	9.3	5.3	119,306	45.8	10.2	7.8
Personal service occupations[1]	1,870	79.2	11.1	6.0	2,594	80.7	12.9	7.6
Barbers	92	12.9	8.4	12.1	86	22.3	27.5	8.5
Hairdressers and cosmetologists	622	88.7	7.0	5.7	758	90.1	9.4	6.3
Attendants, amusement and recreation facilities	131	40.2	7.1	4.3	161	39.4	7.4	5.8
Public transportation attendants	63	74.3	11.3	5.9	104	80.4	8.8	7.4
Welfare service aides	77	92.5	24.2	10.5	73	82.1	21.2	16.6
Family child care providers	(NA)	(NA)	(NA)	(NA)	302	99.0	9.4	10.2
Early childhood teachers' assistants	(NA)	(NA)	(NA)	(NA)	418	96.6	15.7	6.4

Source: U.S. Bureau of the Census. *Statistical Abstract of the United States, 1994.* 114th ed. Washington, DC: U.S. Government Printing Office, 1994, p. 409. Primary source: U.S. Bureau of Labor Statistics. *Employment and Earnings* (monthly; January issues). *Notes:* "NA" stands for "not available." 1. Includes other occupations, not shown separately.

★ 66 ★

Employment and Unemployment

Precision Production, Craft, and Repair Employment, by Sex, Race, and Hispanic Origin: 1983 and 1993

For employed civilian noninstitutional population 16 years old and over. Annual average of monthly figures. Based on Current Population Survey.

Occupation	1983				1993			
	Total employed (1,000)	Percent of total			Total employed (1,000)	Percent of total		
		Female	Black	Hispanic		Female	Black	Hispanic
Total	100,834	43.7	9.3	5.3	119,306	45.8	10.2	7.8
Precision production, craft, and repair occupations	12,328	8.1	6.8	6.2	13,326	8.6	7.4	9.2
Extractive occupations	196	2.3	3.3	6.0	148	1.8	4.6	7.9
Precision production occupations	3,685	21.5	7.3	7.4	3,758	23.6	8.8	10.5

Source: U.S. Bureau of the Census. *Statistical Abstract of the United States, 1994.* 114th ed. Washington, DC: U.S. Government Printing Office, 1994, p. 409. Primary source: U.S. Bureau of Labor Statistics. *Employment and Earnings* (monthly; January issues).

★ 67 ★

Employment and Unemployment

Private Household Employment, by Sex, Race, and Hispanic Origin: 1983 and 1993

For employed civilian noninstitutional population 16 years old and over. Annual average of monthly figures. Based on Current Population Survey.

Occupation	1983				1993			
	Total employed (1,000)	Percent of total			Total employed (1,000)	Percent of total		
		Female	Black	Hispanic		Female	Black	Hispanic
Total	100,834	43.7	9.3	5.3	119,306	45.8	10.2	7.8
Private household workers[1]	980	96.1	27.8	8.5	912	95.1	17.1	21.6
Child care workers	408	96.9	7.9	3.6	345	97.2	9.0	15.0
Cleaners and servants	512	95.8	42.4	11.8	534	94.0	21.6	25.7

Source: U.S. Bureau of the Census. *Statistical Abstract of the United States, 1994.* 114th ed. Washington, DC: U.S. Government Printing Office, 1994, p. 409. Primary source: U.S. Bureau of Labor Statistics. *Employment and Earnings* (monthly; January issues). *Note:* 1. Includes other occupations, not shown separately.

★ 68 ★

Employment and Unemployment

Protective Service Employment, by Sex, Race, and Hispanic Origin: 1983 and 1993

For employed civilian noninstitutional population 16 years old and over. Annual average of monthly figures. Based on Current Population Survey.

Occupation	1983				1993			
	Total employed (1,000)	Percent of total			Total employed (1,000)	Percent of total		
		Female	Black	Hispanic		Female	Black	Hispanic
Total	100,834	43.7	9.3	5.3	119,306	45.8	10.2	7.8
Protective service occupations	1,672	12.8	13.6	4.6	2,152	17.2	17.4	6.6
Supervisors, protective service	127	4.7	7.7	3.1	185	7.8	12.2	4.8
Supervisors, police and detectives	58	4.2	9.3	1.2	96	10.3	6.6	6.1
Police and detectives	645	9.4	13.1	4.0	923	16.0	18.0	5.4
Police and detectives, public service	412	5.7	9.5	4.4	511	12.0	14.5	5.9
Sheriffs, bailiffs, and other law enforcement officers	87	13.2	11.5	4.0	117	19.5	13.4	4.6
Correctional institution officers	146	17.8	24.0	2.8	295	21.6	25.8	5.0
Guards	711	20.6	17.0	5.6	836	23.9	20.4	8.8
Guards and police, except public service	602	13.0	18.9	6.2	711	17.2	22.6	9.5

Source: U.S. Bureau of the Census. *Statistical Abstract of the United States, 1994.* 114th ed. Washington, DC: U.S. Government Printing Office, 1994, p. 409. Primary source: U.S. Bureau of Labor Statistics. *Employment and Earnings* (monthly; January issues).

★ 69 ★

Employment and Unemployment

Records Processing Employment, by Sex, Race, and Hispanic Origin: 1983 and 1993

For employed civilian noninstitutional population 16 years old and over. Annual average of monthly figures. Based on Current Population Survey.

Occupation	1983				1993			
	Total employed (1,000)	Percent of total			Total employed (1,000)	Percent of total		
		Female	Black	Hispanic		Female	Black	Hispanic
Total	100,834	43.7	9.3	5.3	119,306	45.8	10.2	7.8
Records processing occupations, except financial[1]	866	82.4	13.9	4.8	908	79.1	14.9	6.6
Order clerks	188	78.1	10.6	4.4	212	78.1	17.1	6.5
Personnel clerks, except payroll and time keeping	64	91.1	14.9	4.6	63	89.2	15.2	3.9
Library clerks	147	81.9	15.4	2.5	146	75.9	11.6	3.4
File clerks	287	83.5	16.7	6.1	288	79.6	15.0	10.4
Records clerks	157	82.8	11.6	5.6	184	77.9	14.3	4.8

Source: U.S. Bureau of the Census. *Statistical Abstract of the United States, 1994.* 114th ed. Washington, DC: U.S. Government Printing Office, 1994, p. 408. Primary source: U.S. Bureau of Labor Statistics. *Employment and Earnings* (monthly; January issues). *Note:* 1. Includes other occupations, not shown separately.

★ 70 ★

Employment and Unemployment

Sales Employment, by Sex, Race, and Hispanic Origin: 1983 and 1993

For employed civilian noninstitutional population 16 years old and over. Annual average of monthly figures. Based on Current Population Survey.

Occupation	1983				1993			
	Total employed (1,000)	Percent of total			Total employed (1,000)	Percent of total		
		Female	Black	Hispanic		Female	Black	Hispanic
Total	100,834	43.7	9.3	5.3	119,306	45.8	10.2	7.8
Sales occupations	11,818	47.5	4.7	3.7	14,245	48.1	6.7	5.9
Supervisors and proprietors	2,958	28.4	3.6	3.4	4,016	36.4	4.4	5.3
Sales representatives, commodities, except retail	1,442	15.1	2.1	2.2	1,538	21.0	2.9	3.9
Sales workers, retail and personal services	5,511	69.7	6.7	4.8	6,281	64.9	9.7	7.5
Cashiers	2,009	84.4	10.1	5.4	2,581	78.4	13.2	8.7
Sales-related occupations	54	58.7	2.8	1.3	93	60.5	5.3	6.1

Source: U.S. Bureau of the Census. *Statistical Abstract of the United States, 1994.* 114th ed. Washington, DC: U.S. Government Printing Office, 1994, p. 408. Primary source: U.S. Bureau of Labor Statistics. *Employment and Earnings* (monthly; January issues).

★ 71 ★

Employment and Unemployment

Science Technician Employment, by Sex, Race, and Hispanic Origin: 1983 and 1993

For employed civilian noninstitutional population 16 years old and over. Annual average of monthly figures. Based on Current Population Survey.

Occupation	1983				1993			
	Total employed (1,000)	Percent of total			Total employed (1,000)	Percent of total		
		Female	Black	Hispanic		Female	Black	Hispanic
Total	100,834	43.7	9.3	5.3	119,306	45.8	10.2	7.8
Science technicians[1]	202	29.1	6.6	2.8	261	37.5	7.2	5.2
Biological technicians	52	37.7	2.9	2.0	85	59.7	6.1	3.8
Chemical technicians	82	26.9	9.5	3.5	74	26.0	7.1	3.9

Source: U.S. Bureau of the Census. *Statistical Abstract of the United States, 1994.* 114th ed. Washington, DC: U.S. Government Printing Office, 1994, p. 408. Primary source: U.S. Bureau of Labor Statistics. *Employment and Earnings* (monthly; January issues). *Note:* 1. Includes other occupations, not shown separately.

★ 72 ★

Employment and Unemployment

Secretarial Employment, by Sex, Race, and Hispanic Origin: 1983 and 1993

For employed civilian noninstitutional population 16 years old and over. Annual average of monthly figures. Based on Current Population Survey.

Occupation	1983				1993			
	Total employed (1,000)	Percent of total			Total employed (1,000)	Percent of total		
		Female	Black	Hispanic		Female	Black	Hispanic
Total	100,834	43.7	9.3	5.3	119,306	45.8	10.2	7.8
Secretaries, stenographers, and typists[1]	4,861	98.2	7.3	4.5	4,174	96.2	8.9	5.9
Secretaries	3,891	99.0	5.8	4.0	3,586	98.9	7.7	5.8
Typists	906	95.6	13.8	6.4	494	94.3	18.8	7.4
Information clerks	1,174	88.9	8.5	5.5	1,678	88.8	9.3	7.9
Receptionists	602	96.8	7.5	6.6	899	97.2	8.6	7.6

Source: U.S. Bureau of the Census. *Statistical Abstract of the United States, 1994.* 114th ed. Washington, DC: U.S. Government Printing Office, 1994, p. 408. Primary source: U.S. Bureau of Labor Statistics. *Employment and Earnings* (monthly; January issues). *Note:* 1. Includes other occupations, not shown separately.

★ 73 ★

Employment and Unemployment

Service Employment, by Sex, Race, and Hispanic Origin: 1983 and 1993

For employed civilian noninstitutional population 16 years old and over. Annual average of monthly figures. Based on Current Population Survey. See also tables for various services; for example, personal service occupations.

Occupation	1983				1993			
	Total employed (1,000)	Percent of total			Total employed (1,000)	Percent of total		
		Female	Black	Hispanic		Female	Black	Hispanic
Total	100,834	43.7	9.3	5.3	119,306	45.8	10.2	7.8
Service occupations	13,857	60.1	16.6	6.8	16,522	59.5	17.3	11.2
Services, except private household and protective	11,205	64.0	16.0	6.9	13,457	63.9	17.3	11.2

Source: U.S. Bureau of the Census. *Statistical Abstract of the United States, 1994.* 114th ed. Washington, DC: U.S. Government Printing Office, 1994, p. 409. Primary source: U.S. Bureau of Labor Statistics. *Employment and Earnings* (monthly; January issues).

★ 74 ★

Employment and Unemployment

Social Science-Related Employment, by Sex, Race, and Hispanic Origin: 1983 and 1993

For employed civilian noninstitutional population 16 years old and over. Annual average of monthly figures. Based on Current Population Survey.

Occupation	1983				1993			
	Total employed (1,000)	Percent of total			Total employed (1,000)	Percent of total		
		Female	Black	Hispanic		Female	Black	Hispanic
Total	100,834	43.7	9.3	5.3	119,306	45.8	10.2	7.8
Social scientists and urban planners[1]	261	46.8	7.1	2.1	399	57.0	5.9	3.0
Economists	98	37.9	6.3	2.7	117	47.6	4.8	3.5
Psychologists	135	57.1	8.6	1.1	241	64.1	7.1	3.1
Social, recreation, and religious workers[1]	831	43.1	12.1	3.8	1,096	50.5	15.6	5.0
Social workers	407	64.3	18.2	6.3	586	68.9	21.4	6.0
Recreation workers	65	71.9	15.7	2.0	89	75.1	14.8	4.7
Clergy	293	5.6	4.9	1.4	350	11.4	8.7	3.1

Source: U.S. Bureau of the Census. *Statistical Abstract of the United States, 1994.* 114th ed. Washington, DC: U.S. Government Printing Office, 1994, p. 407. Primary source: U.S. Bureau of Labor Statistics. *Employment and Earnings* (monthly; January issues). *Note:* 1. Includes other occupations, not shown separately.

★ 75 ★

Employment and Unemployment

State and Local Government Full-Time Employment, by Sex and Race/Ethnicity: 1991

As of June 30. Excludes school systems and educational institutions. Based on reports from state governments (44 in 1973; 48 in 1975, 1976, and 1979; 47 in 1977 and 1983; 45 in 1978; 42 in 1980; 49 in 1981 and 1984 through 1987; and 50 in 1989 through 1991) and a sample of county, municipal, township, and special district jurisdictions employing 15 or more nonelected, nonappointed full-time employees. Data for 1982 and 1988 are not available.

Occupation	Employment (1,000)						
	Total	Male	Female	White[1]	Minority		
					Total[2]	Black[1]	Hispanic[3]
Total	5,459	3,110	2,349	3,965	1,494	1,011	340
Officials/administrators	304	212	93	262	43	28	10
Professionals	1,227	609	619	957	270	164	53
Technicians	501	294	207	381	120	74	30
Protective service	913	792	121	697	216	148	56
Paraprofessionals	403	110	292	245	158	126	23
Administrative support	976	121	856	683	293	190	75
Skilled craft	455	436	19	349	106	67	30
Service/maintenance	679	537	141	390	288	213	62

Source: U.S. Bureau of the Census. *Statistical Abstract of the United States, 1994.* 114th ed. Washington, DC: U.S. Government Printing Office, 1994, p. 320. Primary source: U.S. Equal Employment Opportunity Commission. *State and Local Government Information Report* (annual). *Notes:* 1. Non-Hispanic. 2. Includes other minority groups not shown separately. 3. Persons of Hispanic origin may be of any race.

★ 76 ★

Employment and Unemployment

Technical, Sales, and Administrative Support Employment, by Sex, Race, and Hispanic Origin: 1983 and 1993

For employed civilian noninstitutional population 16 years old and over. Annual average of monthly figures. Based on Current Population Survey.

Occupation	1983				1993			
	Total employed (1,000)	Percent of total			Total employed (1,000)	Percent of total		
		Female	Black	Hispanic		Female	Black	Hispanic
Total	100,834	43.7	9.3	5.3	119,306	45.8	10.2	7.8
Technical, sales, and administrative support	31,265	64.6	7.6	4.3	36,814	63.8	9.3	6.3
Technicians and related support	3,053	48.2	8.2	3.1	4,014	50.5	9.6	5.0
Technicians, except health, engineering, and science[1]	917	35.3	5.0	2.7	1,361	39.9	8.4	4.0
Airplane pilots and navigators	69	2.1	-	1.6	101	3.9	5.5	2.4
Computer programmers	443	32.5	4.4	2.1	578	31.5	6.7	3.5
Legal assistants	128	74.0	4.3	3.6	254	79.6	8.6	4.9

Source: U.S. Bureau of the Census. *Statistical Abstract of the United States, 1994.* 114th ed. Washington, DC: U.S. Government Printing Office, 1994, p. 408. Primary source: U.S. Bureau of Labor Statistics. *Employment and Earnings* (monthly; January issues). *Notes:* "-" represents or rounds to zero. 1. Includes other occupations, not shown separately.

★ 77 ★

Employment and Unemployment

Therapist Employment, by Sex, Race, and Hispanic Origin: 1983 and 1993

For employed civilian noninstitutional population 16 years old and over. Annual average of monthly figures. Based on Current Population Survey.

Occupation	1983				1993			
	Total employed (1,000)	Percent of total			Total employed (1,000)	Percent of total		
		Female	Black	Hispanic		Female	Black	Hispanic
Total	100,834	43.7	9.3	5.3	119,306	45.8	10.2	7.8
Therapists[1]	247	76.3	7.6	2.7	416	74.9	6.9	4.1
Inhalation therapists	69	69.4	6.5	3.7	92	58.4	10.0	6.9
Physical therapists	55	77.0	9.7	1.5	115	72.5	3.0	5.0
Speech therapists	51	90.5	1.5	-	83	91.8	6.7	1.2

Source: U.S. Bureau of the Census. *Statistical Abstract of the United States, 1994.* 114th ed. Washington, DC: U.S. Government Printing Office, 1994, p. 407. Primary source: U.S. Bureau of Labor Statistics. *Employment and Earnings* (monthly; January issues). *Notes:* "-" represents or rounds to zero. 1. Includes other occupations, not shown separately.

★ 78 ★

Employment and Unemployment

Transportation Employment, by Sex, Race, and Hispanic Origin: 1983 and 1993

For employed civilian noninstitutional population 16 years old and over. Annual average of monthly figures. Based on Current Population Survey.

Occupation	1983				1993			
	Total employed (1,000)	Percent of total			Total employed (1,000)	Percent of total		
		Female	Black	Hispanic		Female	Black	Hispanic
Total	100,834	43.7	9.3	5.3	119,306	45.8	10.2	7.8
Transportation and material moving occupations	4,201	7.8	13.0	5.9	5,004	9.3	14.0	8.6
Motor vehicle operators	2,978	9.2	13.5	6.0	3,825	10.8	14.2	8.9
Trucks, heavy and light	2,195	3.1	12.3	5.7	2,786	4.5	12.3	8.8
Transportation occupations, except motor vehicles	212	2.4	6.7	3.0	170	4.1	10.2	3.1
Material moving equipment operators	1,011	4.8	12.9	6.3	1.009	4.5	13.9	8.5
Industrial truck and tractor operators	369	5.6	19.6	8.2	432	7.3	20.9	12.0

Source: U.S. Bureau of the Census. *Statistical Abstract of the United States, 1994.* 114th ed. Washington, DC: U.S. Government Printing Office, 1994, p. 409. Primary source: U.S. Bureau of Labor Statistics. *Employment and Earnings* (monthly; January issues).

★ 79 ★

Employment and Unemployment

Unemployment and Unemployment Rates, by Occupation and Sex: 1983-1993

For civilian noninstitutional population 16 years old and over. Beginning 1985, annual averages of monthly data; 1983 data are estimated. Rate represents unemployment as a percent of the labor force for each specified group. Data for 1992 are not fully comparable with data for prior years because of the introduction of the occupational and industrial classification used in the 1990 Census. Based on the Current Population Survey.

Occupation	Number (1,000)			Unemployment rate				
				1983	1985	1993		
	1983	1985	1993			Total	Male	Female
Total[1]	10,717	8,312	8,734	9.6	7.2	6.8	7.1	6.5
Managerial and professional specialty	795	645	983	3.3	2.4	3.0	2.8	3.1
Executive, administrative, and managerial	396	329	527	3.5	2.6	3.3	2.9	3.8
Professional specialty	399	316	456	3.0	2.3	2.6	2.7	2.5
Technical, sales, and administrative support	2,116	1,694	2,075	6.3	4.9	5.3	4.8	5.6
Technicians and related support	152	110	163	4.7	3.3	3.9	3.9	3.9
Sales occupations	850	702	908	6.7	5.3	6.0	4.8	7.3
Administrative support, including clerical	1,114	882	1,003	6.4	4.9	5.1	5.5	5.0
Service occupations	1,697	1,386	1,359	10.9	8.8	7.6	7.9	7.4
Private household	79	69	63	7.4	6.4	6.5	9.6	6.3
Protective service	120	85	105	6.7	4.7	4.7	4.3	6.5
Service, except private household and protective	1,498	1,233	1,190	11.8	9.5	8.1	9.2	7.5
Precision production, craft, and repair	1,466	1,038	1,141	10.6	7.2	7.9	7.9	7.7
Mechanics and repairers	344	225	256	7.6	4.8	5.5	5.5	5.3

[Continued]

★ 79 ★

Unemployment and Unemployment Rates, by Occupation and Sex: 1983-1993
[Continued]

Occupation	Number (1,000)			Unemployment rate				
				1983	1985	1993		
	1983	1985	1993			Total	Male	Female
Construction trades	709	531	624	14.2	10.1	11.1	11.1	10.1
Other precision production, craft, and repair	412	281	262	9.6	6.4	6.3	5.8	7.9
Operators, fabricators, and laborers	2,955	2,140	1,877	15.5	11.3	9.9	9.7	10.6
Machine operators, assemblers, inspectors	1,411	980	795	15.4	11.1	9.7	8.9	10.9
Transportation and material moving occupations	596	422	399	12.4	8.5	7.4	7.4	7.0
Handlers, equipment cleaners, helpers, laborers	948	739	682	18.6	14.3	12.9	13.2	11.5
Construction laborers	207	186	167	25.8	21.3	20.2	20.2	(B)
Farming, forestry, and fishing	407	315	296	9.9	8.3	8.2	7.8	10.1

Source: U.S. Bureau of the Census. *Statistical Abstract of the United States, 1994.* 114th ed. Washington, DC: U.S. Government Printing Office, 1994, p. 417. Primary source: U.S. Bureau of Labor Statistics. *Employment and Earnings* (monthly; January issues). *Notes:* "B" notes base less than 35,000. 1. Includes persons with no previous work experience and those whose last job was in the Armed Forces.

★ 80 ★

Employment and Unemployment

Writing-Related Employment, by Sex, Race, and Hispanic Origin: 1983 and 1993

For employed civilian noninstitutional population 16 years old and over. Annual average of monthly figures. Based on Current Population Survey.

Occupation	1983				1993			
	Total employed (1,000)	Percent of total			Total employed (1,000)	Percent of total		
		Female	Black	Hispanic		Female	Black	Hispanic
Total	100,834	43.7	9.3	5.3	119,306	45.8	10.2	7.8
Writers, artists, entertainers, and athletes[1]	1,544	42.7	4.8	2.9	2,026	46.6	5.3	4.7
Authors	62	46.7	2.1	0.9	139	57.2	2.4	1.9
Technical writers	(2)	(2)	(2)	(2)	63	52.8	2.7	2.3
Editors and reporters	204	48.4	2.9	2.1	266	48.5	5.0	3.4
Public relations specialists	157	50.1	6.2	1.9	155	59.6	7.0	3.5

Source: U.S. Bureau of the Census. *Statistical Abstract of the United States, 1994.* 114th ed. Washington, DC: U.S. Government Printing Office, 1994, p. 407. Primary source: U.S. Bureau of Labor Statistics. *Employment and Earnings* (monthly; January issues). *Notes:* 1. Includes other occupations, not shown separately. 2. Level of total employment below 50,000.

Employment and Unemployment: College Graduates

★ 81 ★

College Graduate Employment, by Occupation: 1992

Professional specialty - 12,115

Exec., admin., and mgrl. - 6,905

Marketing and sales workers - 3,381

Administrative support - 2,516

Craft, operatives, and laborers - 1,449

Technologists and technicians - 1,169

Service - 1,062

Unemployed - 996

Agricultural - 273

According to the source: "Bureau of Labor Statistics (BLS) projections indicate that about three-fourths of the college graduates who enter the labor force between 1992 and 2005 can expect to find college-level jobs" (p. 5). The table below shows colleges graduates in the labor force during 1992.

[In thousands]

Occupation	College graduates in the labor force
Professional specialty	12,115
Exec., admin., and mgrl.	6,905
Marketing and sales workers	3,381
Administrative support	2,516
Craft, operatives, and laborers	1,449
Technologists and technicians	1,169
Service	1,062
Unemployed	996
Agricultural	273

Source: Shelley, Kristina J. "More Job Openings—Even More New Entrants: The Outlook for College Graduates, 1992-2005." Occupational Outlook Quarterly 38, no. 2 (summer 1994), p. 5. Notes: "Exec." represents "executive"; "admin." represents "administrative." "mgrl." represents "managerial."

★ 82 ★

Employment and Unemployment: College Graduates

College Graduates Hired by the Federal Government, by Occupation: 1992

Table shows the 20 occupations for which the largest number of college graduates were hired by the federal government during the 1992 fiscal year.

Occupation	Number of new hires
Computer specialists	1,140
General attorneys	917
Nurses	901
Miscellaneous administrators and analysts	805
Financial institution examiners	797
Medical officers	674
Auditors	603
Electronics engineers	566
Civil engineers	558
Criminal investigators	538
General engineers	486
Accountants	443
General educators and trainers	438
Management and program analysts	382
Contracting specialists	369
Social scientists	344
Medical technologists	291
Social workers	290
General biological scientists	290
Chemists	282

Source: U.S. Department of Labor. Bureau of Labor Statistics. *Working for US in the 1990's.* Washington, DC: U.S. Department of Labor. Bureau of Labor Statistics, 1993, p. 17. Reprinted from *Occupational Outlook Quarterly* (summer 1993). Primary source: Office of Personnel Management (OPM). Central Personnel Data File. *Note:* 1. Full-time permanent positions.

★ 83 ★

Employment and Unemployment: College Graduates

Employment Status of Bachelor's Degree Recipients, by Occupation: 1991

Table shows the employment status of those who received bachelor's degrees during the 1989-1990 school year. Figures show the graduates' employment status one year after earning their degrees. Data are provided by field of study for selected occupations.

[Percent distribution]

Occupational area in April 1991	All fields of study	Business and manage-ment	Educa-tion	Engi-neering	Health profes-sions	Public affairs and/or social services	Bio-logical sciences	Mathematics, computer, and physical sciences	Social sciences	Human-ities	Psy-chology	Other fields[1]
Total	100	100	100	100	100	100	100	100	100	100	100	100
Employed	84	89	91	87	97	84	65	79	80	78	73	85
Business	21	45	4	7	3	3	10	7	22	13	15	28
Educators	13	1	73	1	1	3	7	9	6	18	10	3
Engineers	5	1	(2)	61	(2)	(2)	1	5	1	(2)	(2)	4
Health professionals	5	(2)	1	(2)	91	(2)	8	1	1	(2)	5	1
Public affairs/social service	3	(2)	1	(2)	(2)	57	1	(2)	6	2	15	1
Biological scientists	1	1	(2)	(2)	(2)	(2)	4	(2)	1	1	(2)	(2)
Computer scientists, physical scientists, mathematicians	1	1	(2)	1	(2)	(2)	(2)	7	(2)	(2)	(2)	(2)
Communications	2	1	(2)	1	(2)	1	1	(2)	2	9	1	14
Technicians	6	3	(2)	8	(2)	(2)	13	29	5	4	3	8
Other	3	3	1	2	(2)	(2)	5	7	4	2	1	(2)
Nonprofessional, nonmanagerial, nontechnical	23	33	11	6	3	21	16	14	33	30	24	27
Unemployed[3]	4	5	2	3	(2)	3	2	4	4	4	5	6
Not in labor force[4]	12	6	6	9	2	13	33	16	15	18	21	9
Enrolled in school[5]	8	2	2	6	(2)	4	29	13	11	12	16	5

Source: U.S. Department of Education. Office of Educational Research and Improvement. National Center for Education Statistics. *Digest of Education Statistics, 1994.* NCES 94-115. Lanham, MD: Bernan, November 1994, p. 405. Primary source: U.S. Department of Education. National Center for Education Statistics. "Recent College Graduates, 1991" (survey). Table was prepared in July 1993. *Notes:* Details may not add to totals due to rounding. 1. Includes agriculture and natural resources, architecture and environmental design, area and ethnic studies, communications, consumer/personal/miscellaneous services, home economics, industrial arts, law, liberal/general studies, library and archival sciences, military sciences, multi/interdisciplinary studies, personal and social development, and trade and industrial. 2. Less than 0.5 percent. 3. Percent looking for work. 4. Percent not looking for work. 5. Enrolled full-time or part-time.

Industrial Relations

★ 84 ★

Layoffs, by Job Category

Sixty-six percent of the businesses surveyed by the American Management Association in 1993 reported laying off workers as a method of business turnaround. The table below shows selected job categories affected by layoffs.

[In percentages]

Job category	Jobs cut
Professional and technical	20.3
Middle management	19.3
Supervisory	15.0

Source: Balagopal, Sudha Sethu. "Life From Square One." *India Today,* 31 March 1994, p. 6C. Primary source: American Management Association.

★ 85 ★
Industrial Relations

Union Members' Weekly Earnings, by Occupation: 1983 and 1993

Annual averages of monthly data. Covers employed wage and salary workers 16 years old and over. Excludes self-employed workers whose businesses are incorporated, although they technically qualify as wage and salary workers. Based on Current Population Survey.

Occupation	Median usual weekly earnings[1] ($)						Not represented by unions	
	Total		Union members[2]		Represented by unions[3]			
	1983	1993	1983	1993	1983	1993	1983	1993
Total	313	463	388	575	383	569	288	426
Managerial and professional specialty	437	675	423	696	421	688	446	670
Technical, sales, and administrative support	281	419	350	509	341	501	270	408
Service occupations	205	293	305	478	299	467	182	265
Precision, production, craft, and repair	377	501	456	642	450	637	322	453
Operators, fabricators, and laborers	275	365	366	501	361	497	226	321
Farming, forestry, and fishing	196	269	292	436	287	413	189	264

Source: U.S. Bureau of the Census. *Statistical Abstract of the United States, 1994.* 114th ed. Washington, DC: U.S. Government Printing Office, 1994, p. 439. Primary source: U.S. Bureau of Labor Statistics. *Employment and Earnings* (January issues). *Notes:* 1. For full-time employed wage and salary workers; 1983 data revised. 2. Members of a labor union or an employee association similar to a labor union. 3. Members of a labor union or an employee association similar to a union as well as workers who report no union affiliation but whose jobs are covered by a union or an employee association contract.

★ 86 ★

Industrial Relations

Union Membership, by Occupation: 1983 and 1993

Annual averages of monthly data. Covers employed wage and salary workers 16 years old and over. Excludes self-employed workers whose businesses are incorporated, although they technically qualify as wage and salary workers. Based on Current Population Survey.

Occupation	Employed wage and salary workers					
	Total (1,000)		Union members[1] (%)		Represented by unions[2] (%)	
	1983	1993	1983	1993	1983	1993
Total	88,290	105,067	20.1	15.8	23.3	17.7
Managerial and professional specialty	19,657	27,168	17.1	14.9	21.9	18.0
Technical, sales, and administrative support	28,024	33,429	12.1	10.4	15.0	12.1
Service occupations	12,875	15,371	15.3	13.8	17.9	15.3
Precision, production, craft, and repair	10,542	11,024	32.9	25.6	35.7	27.2
Operators, fabricators, and laborers	15,416	16,316	35.4	24.7	37.9	26.0
Farming, forestry, and fishing	1,775	1,759	5.5	5.1	6.9	5.7

Source: U.S. Bureau of the Census. *Statistical Abstract of the United States, 1994.* 114th ed. Washington, DC: U.S. Government Printing Office, 1994, p. 439. Primary source: U.S. Bureau of Labor Statistics. *Employment and Earnings* (January issues). *Notes:* 1. Members of a labor union or an employee association similar to a labor union. 2. Members of a labor union or an employee association similar to a union as well as workers who report no union affiliation but whose jobs are covered by a union or an employee association contract.

Jobs

★ 87 ★

High Risk Jobs

Cab driver/chauffeur - 15.1	
Police officer - 9.3	
Hotel clerk - 5.1	
Gas station worker - 4.5	
Security guard - 3.6	
Stock handler/bagger - 3.1	
Store owner/manager - 2.8	
Bartender - 2.1	

According to the source, 2 million workers were victims of workplace violence in 1992. The table below shows the riskiest occupations for on-the-job murders.

[In percentages]

Occupation	Murders per 100,000 workers
Cab driver/chauffeur	15.1
Police officer	9.3
Hotel clerk	5.1
Gas station worker	4.5
Security guard	3.6
Stock handler/bagger	3.1
Store owner/manager	2.8
Bartender	2.1

Source: Castelli, Jim. "A Digest of Developments in Occupational Safety and Health." *Safety + Health* (February 1994), p. 88. Primary source: National Institute of Occupational Safety and Health (NIOSH).

★ 88 ★
Jobs

Occupational and Employer Tenure, by Occupation: 1991

As of January. For the 35 occupations with the longest occupational tenure. Covers occupations with 50,000 or more workers. Based on Current Population Survey.

Current occupation	Number (1,000)	Occupational tenure[1] Total (years)	Rank	Employer tenure[2] Total (years)	Rank	Median age[3]
Total employed, 16 years old and over[4]	114,979	6.5	(X)	4.5	(X)	37.2
Airplane pilots and navigators	116	12.2	30	4.5	32	36.2
Automobile body and related repairers	202	12.1	31	3.1	34	34.1
Barbers	111	27.2	1	11.0	12	51.7
Brickmasons and stonemasons	160	12.6	21	5.1	30	38.2
Chemical engineers	72	12.6	21	6.4	22	38.0
Civil engineers	284	13.2	15	7.4	18	42.0
Crane and tower operators	77	13.7	13	6.1	24	41.9
Dental laboratory & medical appliance technicians	59	12.9	17	5.5	27	39.9
Dentists	136	15.1	7	13.7	7	40.5
Electrical power installers and repairers	128	12.6	21	12.5	9	39.2
Electricians	718	12.3	27	4.9	31	38.3
Farmers, except horticultural	1,037	21.8	2	20.2	2	48.0
Geologists and geodesists	60	12.3	27	7.3	19	40.8
Health specialties teachers	50	15.1	7	11.4	11	45.7
Heavy equipment mechanics	158	13.7	13	6.7	20	38.1
Locomotive operators	58	19.8	3	19.7	3	46.5
Machinists	526	12.3	27	6.6	21	39.3
Managers, farms, except horticultural	145	11.6	34	8.9	15	36.9
Millwrights	79	12.5	24	6.2	23	43.1
Musicians and composers	143	15.2	5	5.4	29	36.8
Operating engineers	247	12.0	32	5.7	26	37.8
Pharmacists	182	12.7	20	5.8	25	39.1
Plumbers, pipefitters, and steamfitters	427	13.1	16	5.5	27	38.4
Public transportation attendants	60	12.5	24	8.2	17	39.2
Railroad conductors and yardmasters	56	15.2	5	18.8	4	43.1
Stationary engineers	120	15.4	4	11.8	10	42.2
Structural metal workers	52	12.4	26	1.1	35	36.5
Supervisors, firefighting and fire prevention	65	15.0	10	20.3	1	44.5
Supervisors, police and detectives	69	12.9	17	15.1	6	41.5
Teachers, elementary school	1,592	12.0	32	8.4	16	41.3
Teachers, secondary school	1,392	14.1	11	9.5	14	42.0
Telephone installers and repairers	193	12.9	17	16.5	5	40.3
Timber cutting and logging	68	11.5	35	3.5	33	33.3
Tool and die makers	125	15.1	7	12.6	8	39.5
Veterinarians	66	14.0	12	10.2	13	39.5

Source: U.S. Bureau of the Census. *Statistical Abstract of the United States, 1994.* 114th ed. Washington, DC: U.S. Government Printing Office, 1994, p. 415. Primary sources: U.S. Bureau of Labor Statistics. *News.* USDL 92-386; and unpublished data. *Notes:* "X" represents "not applicable." 1. Cumulative tenure in current occupation. 2. Continuous tenure with current employer. 3. The median of a group of numbers is the middle number or value when each item in the group is arranged according to size, either from lowest to highest or highest to lowest. The median generally has the same number of items above it and below it. If there is an even number of items in the group, the median is taken to be the average of the two middle numbers. 4. Includes other occupations, not shown separately.

★ 89 ★
Jobs

Occupational Employment, by Sex: 1993

Figures show the number employed, participation rate, and distribution for all employees in each occupational grouping. Table shows 1993 data for men and women in U.S. private industry, excluding Hawaii. Data cover all industries, 163,039 units.

Group	Total employment	Officials and managers	Professionals	Technicians	Sales workers	Office and clerical workers	Craft workers	Operatives	Laborers	Service workers
Number employed										
All employees	36,321,236	3,976,608	5,251,884	2,224,637	3,849,873	5,578,787	3,360,333	5,534,879	2,652,578	3,891,657
Male	19,425,287	2,789,118	2,613,254	1,182,134	1,675,551	959,091	2,975,681	3,750,207	1,740,266	1,739,985
Female	16,895,949	1,187,490	2,638,630	1,042,503	2,174,322	4,619,696	384,652	1,784,672	912,312	2,151,672
Participation rate										
All employees	100.0	100.0	100.0	100.0	100.0	100.0	100.0	100.0	100.0	100.0
Male	53.5	70.1	49.8	53.1	43.5	17.2	88.6	67.8	65.6	44.7
Female	46.5	29.9	50.2	46.9	56.5	82.8	11.4	32.2	34.4	55.3
Occupational distribution										
All employees	100.0	10.9	14.5	6.1	10.6	15.4	9.3	15.2	7.3	10.7
Male	100.0	14.4	13.5	6.1	8.6	4.9	15.3	19.3	9.0	9.0
Female	100.0	7.0	15.6	6.2	12.9	27.3	2.3	10.6	5.4	12.7

Source: U.S. Equal Employment Opportunity Commission. *Job Patterns for Minorities and Women in Private Industry, 1993.* Washington, DC: U.S. Government Printing Office, 1994, p. 1.

★ 90 ★
Jobs

Occupations of the Employed, by Sex, Race, and Educational Attainment: 1993

Annual averages of monthly figures. For civilian noninstitutional population 25 years and over. Based on Current Population Survey.

[In thousands]

Sex, race, and years of school completed	Total employed	Managerial/ professional	Technical/ sales/ adminis-trative	Service[1]	Precision production[2]	Operators/ fabricators[3]	Farming forestry, fishing
Male, total[4]	55,508	16,020	11,250	4,720	10,943	10,297	2,278
Less than a high school diploma	6,851	352	518	903	1,870	2,460	749
High school graduates, no college	18,596	2,001	3,153	1,853	5,324	5,352	912
Less than a bachelor's degree	13,894	3,145	3,877	1,429	3,024	2,009	409
College graduates	16,167	10,522	3,702	534	725	476	208
White	48,449	14,541	9,947	3,582	9,885	8,430	2,063
Less than a high school diploma	5,709	314	449	658	1,666	1,978	643
High school graduates, no college	16,115	1,828	2,808	1,357	4,858	4,429	835
Less than a bachelor's degree	12,174	2,860	3,422	1,146	2,723	1,641	382
College graduates	14,451	9,540	3,268	421	638	382	203
Black	5,052	816	869	888	766	1,553	160
Less than a high school diploma	884	27	52	181	149	396	80
High school graduates, no college	1,983	118	259	398	349	799	60
Less than a bachelor's degree	1,324	207	346	229	222	301	19
College graduates	860	464	212	79	46	58	2

[Continued]

★ 90 ★

Occupations of the Employed, by Sex, Race, and Educational Attainment: 1993
[Continued]

Sex, race, and years of school completed	Total employed	Managerial/ professional	Technical/ sales/ adminis- trative	Service[1]	Precision production[2]	Operators/ fabricators[3]	Farming forestry, fishing
Female, total[4]	46,132	14,349	19,198	7,486	1,040	3,626	433
Less than a high school diploma	4,181	210	896	1,734	198	1,030	114
High school graduates, no college	16,871	2,233	8,351	3,626	535	1,943	183
Less than a bachelor's degree	13,040	3,555	6,962	1,681	219	536	89
College graduates	12,040	8,352	2,990	445	90	116	48
White	39,107	12,624	16,689	5,733	837	2,814	410
Less than a high school diploma	3,276	181	779	1,241	159	815	102
High school graduates, no college	14,367	2,020	7,458	2,788	427	1,497	176
Less than a bachelor's degree	11,035	3,104	5,930	1,329	177	408	86
College graduates	10,428	7,319	2,522	373	73	94	47
Black	5,301	1,181	1,875	1,453	142	635	16
Less than a high school diploma	703	22	81	420	25	146	9
High school graduates, no college	2,024	162	706	702	80	371	3
Less than a bachelor's degree	1,611	344	834	291	30	111	-
College graduates	963	652	255	40	7	8	-

Source: U.S. Bureau of the Census. Statistical Abstract of the United States, 1994. 114th ed. Washington, DC: U.S. Government Printing Office, 1994, p. 412. Primary source: U.S. Bureau of Labor Statistics. Unpublished data. Notes: "-" represents or rounds to zero. 1. Includes private household workers. 2. Includes craft and repair. 3. Includes laborers. 4. Includes other races, not shown separately.

Leading Occupations

★ 91 ★

Accountants and Auditors, by Metropolitan Area

According to the 1990 Census of Population and Housing, accountants and auditors ranked 13 among occupations employing the most people in the United States. Table presents the number of civilians 16 years old or older who reported working as accountants and auditors during the 1990 Census. Data show the total employment figures, employment per 100,000 population, and employment data for men and women of various races and ethnicities in the 25 metropolitan statistical areas with the largest concentrations of accountants and auditors.

[Total for all of the U.S. was 1,590,178; 639.4 per 100,000 persons]

Metropolitan area	Total employees	Employees per 100,000 population	Men American Indian, Eskimo & Aleut	Asian, Pacific Islander	Black	Hispanic	White	Women American Indian, Eskimo & Aleut	Asian, Pacific Islander	Black	Hispanic	White
New York, New York New Jersey (northern) Long Island, New York CMSA	175,318	969.3	80	7,161	8,740	5,180	83,298	41	7,241	10,406	5,883	54,712
Los Angeles, California Anaheim, California Riverside, California CMSA	106,103	730.2	149	9,515	2,362	4,469	34,376	275	12,000	4,103	5,806	39,167
Chicago, Illinois Gary, Indiana Lake County, Illinois CMSA	68,686	851.6	21	2,120	2,252	1,063	29,507	74	2,224	4,063	1,553	27,499
San Francisco, California Oakland, California San Jose, California CMSA	62,542	1,000	59	5,939	1,376	1,619	19,489	200	9,552	2,101	2,601	22,346
Washington, District of Columbia MSA	49,586	1,264	30	1,552	3,754	705	18,213	29	2,092	6,750	849	16,871

[Continued]

★ 91 ★

Accountants and Auditors, by Metropolitan Area
[Continued]

Metropolitan area	Total employees	Employees per 100,000 population	Men American Indian, Eskimo & Aleut	Men Asian, Pacific Islander	Men Black	Men Hispanic	Men White	Women American Indian, Eskimo & Aleut	Women Asian, Pacific Islander	Women Black	Women Hispanic	Women White
Philadelphia, Pennsylvania												
Wilmington, Delaware												
Trenton, New Jersey CMSA	47,058	797.7	12	410	1,507	221	23,164	37	651	3,428	319	17,675
Boston, Massachusetts												
Lawrence, Massachusetts												
Salem, Massachusetts CMSA	44,542	1,068	9	623	641	246	20,866	38	980	799	319	20,419
Dallas, Texas												
Fort Worth, Texas CMSA	40,872	1,052	43	579	933	728	17,158	74	716	2,049	982	18,571
Houston, Texas												
Galveston, Texas												
Brazoria, Texas CMSA	36,151	974.2	5	836	1,122	978	14,410	53	1,177	2,508	1,302	15,228
Detroit, Michigan												
Ann Arbor, Michigan CMSA	29,892	640.7	7	276	1,101	109	12,554	56	201	2,164	206	13,400
Atlanta, Georgia MSA	29,662	1,047	7	224	1,561	119	10,704	24	335	4,121	293	12,605
Minneapolis, Minnesota												
St. Paul, Minnesota MSA	24,379	989.4	2	157	155	103	11,510	33	174	307	74	11,983
Miami, Florida												
Fort Lauderdale, Florida CMSA	22,664	709.9	18	189	753	3,427	10,375	11	277	1,043	4,134	9,458
Seattle, Washington												
Tacoma, Washington CMSA	21,002	820.7	50	826	127	93	7,754	80	1,242	315	275	10,431
Denver, Colorado												
Boulder, Colorado CMSA	19,216	1,040	64	151	284	330	8,049	16	181	362	627	9,722
Cleveland, Ohio												
Akron, Ohio												
Lorain, Ohio CMSA	18,815	681.8	0	159	490	31	9,229	7	115	1,005	73	7,765
St. Louis, Missouri MSA	18,225	745.7	6	64	376	82	8,249	36	95	769	70	8,609
Baltimore, Maryland MSA	17,989	755.2	0	250	693	73	7,896	10	232	1,381	65	7,500
San Diego, California MSA	16,376	655.6	20	589	180	444	5,803	56	1,279	387	824	7,569
Phoenix, Arizona MSA	14,954	704.7	46	238	70	291	5,984	106	153	111	521	7,872
Pittsburgh, Pennsylvania												
Beaver Valley, Pennsylvania CMSA	13,780	614.4	9	20	170	19	7,157	0	45	371	29	6,008
Cincinnati, Ohio												
Hamilton, Ohio CMSA	13,389	767.7	0	48	238	47	6,145	0	62	458	46	6,410
Kansas City, Missouri												
Kansas City, Kansas MSA	13,232	844.8	13	36	257	87	5,363	26	94	562	128	6,807
Tampa, Florida												
St. Petersburg, Florida												
Clearwater, Florida MSA	12,795	618.7	0	68	179	487	5,655	33	76	316	421	6,359
Columbus, Ohio MSA	11,402	827.8	10	80	336	15	5,316	15	34	382	15	5,211

Source: Census of Population and Housing, 1990: Equal Employment Opportunity (EEO) File on CD-ROM [machine-readable datafiles]. Prepared by the Bureau of the Census. Washington, DC: The Bureau, 1992. *Notes:* "MSA" represents "metropolitan statistical area"; "CMSA" stands for "consolidated metropolitan statistical area."

★ 92 ★

Leading Occupations

Administrative Support Occupations, by Metropolitan Area

According to the 1990 Census of Population and Housing, administrative support occupations ranked 37 among occupations employing the most people in the United States. Table presents the number of civilians 16 years old or older who reported working in administrative support occupations during the 1990 Census. Data show the total employment figures, employment per 100,000 population, and employment data for men and women of various races and ethnicities in the 25 metropolitan statistical areas with the largest concentrations of administrative support occupations. Figures are for miscellaneous administrative support occupations. See also tables for specific occupations such as secretaries and typists.

[Total for all of the U.S. was 688,288; 276.7 per 100,000 persons]

Metropolitan area	Total employees	Employees per 100,000 population	Men					Women				
			American Indian, Eskimo & Aleut	Asian, Pacific Islander	Black	Hispanic	White	American Indian, Eskimo & Aleut	Asian, Pacific Islander	Black	Hispanic	White
New York, New York New Jersey (northern) Long Island, New York CMSA	60,942	336.9	47	1,062	3,970	2,248	14,468	62	1,369	8,774	3,939	28,773
Los Angeles, California Anaheim, California Riverside, California CMSA	43,003	295.9	98	1,728	1,590	2,644	9,004	143	3,186	3,353	5,708	20,061
Chicago, Illinois Gary, Indiana Lake County, Illinois CMSA	26,133	324.0	6	193	1,045	388	5,908	25	382	3,518	1,010	14,383
San Francisco, California Oakland, California San Jose, California CMSA	22,294	356.5	30	1,043	665	747	4,540	83	2,471	1,464	1,612	10,982
Philadelphia, Pennsylvania Wilmington, Delaware Trenton, New Jersey CMSA	20,610	349.4	0	75	818	108	4,931	22	160	3,098	271	11,370
Washington, District of Columbia MSA	16,697	425.6	41	295	1,546	273	3,481	40	309	3,413	424	7,312
Boston, Massachusetts Lawrence, Massachusetts Salem, Massachusetts CMSA	15,526	372.2	11	90	206	65	3,759	27	270	793	286	10,237
Detroit, Michigan Ann Arbor, Michigan CMSA	14,920	319.8	14	73	646	55	3,461	56	63	2,395	110	8,146
Dallas, Texas Fort Worth, Texas CMSA	13,117	337.6	41	81	421	300	3,314	58	79	1,558	655	7,125
Houston, Texas Galveston, Texas Brazoria, Texas CMSA	11,207	302.0	15	66	337	274	2,651	18	112	1,646	1,192	5,614
Atlanta, Georgia MSA	10,691	377.3	0	25	512	33	2,447	21	39	2,316	98	5,295
Minneapolis, Minnesota St. Paul, Minnesota MSA	10,515	426.7	5	64	90	24	2,517	56	41	199	60	7,519
Miami, Florida Fort Lauderdale, Florida CMSA	9,222	288.9	5	11	296	720	2,023	11	93	1,159	2,125	5,436
Seattle, Washington Tacoma, Washington CMSA	8,964	350.3	24	181	140	44	2,259	99	264	180	194	5,753
Baltimore, Maryland MSA	7,973	334.7	8	0	477	48	1,746	9	77	1,390	38	4,239
Phoenix, Arizona MSA	7,238	341.1	67	14	100	233	2,024	99	49	237	580	4,314
St. Louis, Missouri MSA	7,191	294.2	0	35	166	3	1,415	16	34	1,041	56	4,463
Cleveland, Ohio Akron, Ohio Lorain, Ohio CMSA	7,014	254.2	9	20	180	29	1,652	14	44	842	58	4,221
San Diego, California MSA	6,728	269.3	35	153	89	207	1,641	19	386	185	669	3,926
Denver, Colorado Boulder, Colorado CMSA	6,669	360.8	5	24	101	151	1,535	40	51	287	500	4,328
Pittsburgh, Pennsylvania Beaver Valley, Pennsylvania CMSA	5,813	259.2	5	0	155	11	1,423	0	50	513	26	3,667
Tampa, Florida St. Petersburg, Florida Clearwater, Florida MSA	5,688	275.1	7	0	145	105	1,304	37	30	410	271	3,661
Kansas City, Missouri Kansas City, Kansas MSA	5,520	352.4	7	10	154	45	1,156	10	9	657	82	3,485
Columbus, Ohio MSA	5,475	397.5	0	10	82	22	1,431	5	4	474	17	3,464
Sacramento, California MSA	5,278	356.4	5	75	117	143	1,252	31	214	261	480	3,118

Source: Census of Population and Housing, 1990: Equal Employment Opportunity (EEO) File on CD-ROM [machine-readable datafiles]. Prepared by the Bureau of the Census. Washington, DC: The Bureau, 1992. *Notes:* "MSA" represents "metropolitan statistical area"; "CMSA" stands for "consolidated metropolitan statistical area."

★ 93 ★

Leading Occupations

Apparel Sales Workers, by Metropolitan Area

According to the 1990 Census of Population and Housing, apparel sales workers ranked 74 among occupations employing the most people in the United States. Table presents the number of civilians 16 years old or older who reported working as apparel sales workers during the 1990 Census. Data show the total employment figures, employment per 100,000 population, and employment data for men and women of various races and ethnicities in the 25 metropolitan statistical areas with the largest concentrations of apparel sales workers.

[Total for all of the U.S. was 444,577; 178.8 per 100,000 persons]

Metropolitan area	Total employees	Employees per 100,000 population	Men					Women				
			American Indian, Eskimo & Aleut	Asian, Pacific Islander	Black	Hispanic	White	American Indian, Eskimo & Aleut	Asian, Pacific Islander	Black	Hispanic	White
New York, New York New Jersey (northern) Long Island, New York CMSA	42,874	237.0	33	998	1,256	1,869	7,269	78	1,213	4,064	4,711	25,086
Los Angeles, California Anaheim, California Riverside, California CMSA	28,400	195.4	23	1,141	518	1,595	4,226	115	2,407	1,510	5,541	14,835
Chicago, Illinois Gary, Indiana Lake County, Illinois CMSA	16,886	209.4	0	294	505	374	2,466	4	295	1,935	983	10,647
San Francisco, California Oakland, California San Jose, California CMSA	12,996	207.8	30	374	261	367	1,830	74	1,309	687	1,323	7,823
Philadelphia, Pennsylvania Wilmington, Delaware Trenton, New Jersey CMSA	10,809	183.2	0	56	359	91	1,870	12	177	1,220	235	6,950
Detroit, Michigan Ann Arbor, Michigan CMSA	9,387	201.2	22	54	473	19	1,043	13	115	1,238	122	6,386
Boston, Massachusetts Lawrence, Massachusetts Salem, Massachusetts CMSA	9,048	216.9	5	51	183	59	1,336	23	229	284	173	6,815
Dallas, Texas Fort Worth, Texas CMSA	7,810	201.0	7	73	166	181	1,532	34	177	551	588	4,967
Miami, Florida Fort Lauderdale, Florida CMSA	7,510	235.2	0	51	271	683	1,488	0	21	555	2,307	4,853
Houston, Texas Galveston, Texas Brazoria, Texas CMSA	7,296	196.6	0	75	179	229	918	21	249	1,042	1,040	4,251
Washington, District of Columbia MSA	7,055	179.8	0	164	477	123	1,002	10	310	1,025	315	3,935
Seattle, Washington Tacoma, Washington CMSA	5,759	225.0	5	154	31	20	717	41	314	139	106	4,343
San Diego, California MSA	4,918	196.9	0	142	77	191	667	43	350	156	725	3,135
Atlanta, Georgia MSA	4,841	170.9	0	19	233	23	799	0	47	755	125	2,959
Minneapolis, Minnesota St. Paul, Minnesota MSA	4,714	191.3	6	10	61	0	799	47	59	105	36	3,613
Cleveland, Ohio Akron, Ohio Lorain, Ohio CMSA	4,555	165.1	1	23	120	7	596	0	53	564	87	3,165
Baltimore, Maryland MSA	4,536	190.4	0	12	361	71	778	0	126	660	23	2,535
St. Louis, Missouri MSA	4,119	168.5	0	2	142	14	694	4	17	387	33	2,856
Pittsburgh, Pennsylvania Beaver Valley, Pennsylvania CMSA	3,803	169.6	0	0	54	0	686	0	16	169	9	2,867
Phoenix, Arizona MSA	3,249	153.1	6	32	0	69	516	32	46	88	290	2,418
Tampa, Florida St. Petersburg, Florida Clearwater, Florida MSA	3,174	153.5	0	18	31	65	509	0	8	125	115	2,451
Denver, Colorado Boulder, Colorado CMSA	3,145	170.2	0	32	38	81	696	28	47	125	212	2,058
Portland, Oregon Vancouver, Washington CMSA	2,882	195.0	0	47	29	45	452	16	39	51	64	2,210
Cincinnati, Ohio Hamilton, Ohio CMSA	2,715	155.7	0	13	60	12	372	0	23	231	14	2,016
Norfolk, Virginia Virginia Beach, Virginia Newport News, Virginia MSA	2,704	193.7	0	14	118	14	270	6	45	578	43	1,651

Source: Census of Population and Housing, 1990: Equal Employment Opportunity (EEO) File on CD-ROM [machine-readable datafiles]. Prepared by the Bureau of the Census. Washington, DC: The Bureau, 1992. *Notes:* "MSA" represents "metropolitan statistical area"; "CMSA" stands for "consolidated metropolitan statistical area."

★94★

Leading Occupations

Assemblers, by Metropolitan Area

According to the 1990 Census of Population and Housing, assemblers ranked 14 among occupations employing the most people in the United States. Table presents the number of civilians 16 years old or older who reported working as assemblers during the 1990 Census. Data show the total employment figures, employment per 100,000 population, and employment data for men and women of various races and ethnicities in the 25 metropolitan statistical areas with the largest concentrations of assemblers.

[Total for all of the U.S. was 1,573,979; 632.9 per 100,000 persons]

Metropolitan area	Total employees	Employees per 100,000 population	Men					Women				
			American Indian, Eskimo & Aleut	Asian, Pacific Islander	Black	Hispanic	White	American Indian, Eskimo & Aleut	Asian, Pacific Islander	Black	Hispanic	White
Los Angeles, California Anaheim, California Riverside, California CMSA	109,389	752.8	287	5,551	3,649	42,451	30,610	160	6,005	2,711	29,011	20,342
New York, New York New Jersey (northern) Long Island, New York CMSA	75,975	420.1	169	1,829	9,173	12,875	23,273	110	2,155	8,286	14,554	19,225
Detroit, Michigan Ann Arbor, Michigan CMSA	65,463	1,403	183	287	14,573	1,078	28,701	86	311	7,130	547	13,272
Chicago, Illinois Gary, Indiana Lake County, Illinois CMSA	53,484	663.1	79	933	5,856	8,498	15,231	80	1,741	4,880	9,299	13,831
Philadelphia, Pennsylvania Wilmington, Delaware Trenton, New Jersey CMSA	30,858	523.1	78	547	4,184	1,357	12,537	28	535	2,942	862	8,516
Dallas, Texas Fort Worth, Texas CMSA	28,730	739.4	100	1,000	2,909	4,972	9,621	75	772	3,420	3,657	5,434
San Francisco, California Oakland, California San Jose, California CMSA	27,625	441.8	165	4,102	1,174	4,458	8,275	100	4,157	748	3,353	5,108
Minneapolis, Minnesota St. Paul, Minnesota MSA	23,369	948.4	204	727	850	280	10,251	147	1,035	479	198	9,428
Cleveland, Ohio Akron, Ohio Lorain, Ohio CMSA	23,232	841.8	32	135	3,186	655	10,466	20	141	2,305	317	6,450
Boston, Massachusetts Lawrence, Massachusetts Salem, Massachusetts CMSA	22,217	532.6	46	624	917	1,240	8,665	17	951	879	1,157	8,665
St. Louis, Missouri MSA	19,622	802.8	45	123	3,329	349	9,866	37	45	1,980	56	4,086
Milwaukee, Wisconsin Racine, Wisconsin CMSA	17,608	1,096	42	64	1,764	514	7,122	61	146	1,877	459	6,042
Atlanta, Georgia MSA	16,271	574.2	17	301	4,113	271	5,872	16	280	2,748	106	2,735
Flint, Michigan MSA	14,661	3,406	30	16	2,309	279	7,002	29	0	2,323	100	2,746
Seattle, Washington Tacoma, Washington CMSA	13,313	520.2	121	749	410	295	7,554	58	716	152	126	3,395
Rochester, New York MSA	12,448	1,242	11	163	1,055	315	5,064	59	255	1,178	266	4,352
Miami, Florida Fort Lauderdale, Florida CMSA	12,296	385.1	8	54	1,529	4,494	5,233	0	99	1,109	2,943	3,251
Dayton, Ohio Springfield, Ohio MSA	12,195	1,282	0	24	1,266	47	6,569	11	40	1,083	27	3,182
Cincinnati, Ohio Hamilton, Ohio CMSA	12,091	693.2	22	54	1,070	34	6,419	13	40	769	44	3,686
Kansas City, Missouri Kansas City, Kansas MSA	12,050	769.3	61	118	1,563	456	6,025	21	80	1,181	213	2,646
Houston, Texas Galveston, Texas Brazoria, Texas CMSA	11,771	317.2	36	513	1,531	2,956	4,318	7	452	770	1,159	1,809
San Diego, California MSA	11,629	465.5	63	935	442	2,227	3,467	32	1,996	170	1,984	2,279
Phoenix, Arizona MSA	11,240	529.7	252	271	304	2,058	4,163	111	344	487	1,892	3,041
Baltimore, Maryland MSA	10,519	441.6	29	87	2,827	76	3,631	6	60	1,792	61	2,049
Buffalo, New York Niagara Falls, New York CMSA	10,494	882.4	18	6	882	145	5,498	33	58	759	99	3,110

Source: Census of Population and Housing, 1990: Equal Employment Opportunity (EEO) File on CD-ROM [machine-readable datafiles]. Prepared by the Bureau of the Census. Washington, DC: The Bureau, 1992. *Notes:* "MSA" represents "metropolitan statistical area"; "CMSA" stands for "consolidated metropolitan statistical area."

★ 95 ★

Leading Occupations

Automobile Mechanics, by Metropolitan Area

According to the 1990 Census of Population and Housing, automobile mechanics ranked 24 among occupations employing the most people in the United States. Table presents the number of civilians 16 years old or older who reported working as automobile mechanics during the 1990 Census. Data show the total employment figures, employment per 100,000 population, and employment data for men and women of various races and ethnicities in the 25 metropolitan statistical areas with the largest concentrations of automobile mechanics, excluding apprentices.

[Total for all of the U.S. was 954,623; 383.8 per 100,000 persons]

Metropolitan area	Total employees	Employees per 100,000 population	Men					Women				
			American Indian, Eskimo & Aleut	Asian, Pacific Islander	Black	Hispanic	White	American Indian, Eskimo & Aleut	Asian, Pacific Islander	Black	Hispanic	White
Los Angeles, California Anaheim, California Riverside, California CMSA	58,669	403.7	356	4,714	2,806	24,315	36,206	0	36	57	352	718
New York, New York New Jersey (northern) Long Island, New York CMSA	56,949	314.9	133	1,646	9,089	9,861	41,254	0	9	173	228	550
Detroit, Michigan Ann Arbor, Michigan CMSA	27,360	586.5	116	190	3,796	423	21,849	0	0	279	26	946
Chicago, Illinois Gary, Indiana Lake County, Illinois CMSA	25,214	312.6	36	552	3,135	2,709	19,584	0	10	110	70	263
San Francisco, California Oakland, California San Jose, California CMSA	22,316	356.9	142	3,061	1,275	3,638	15,863	6	31	13	65	280
Philadelphia, Pennsylvania Wilmington, Delaware Trenton, New Jersey CMSA	22,071	374.1	29	216	2,636	567	18,488	0	6	14	23	353
Houston, Texas Galveston, Texas Brazoria, Texas CMSA	16,551	446.0	53	621	2,802	4,561	10,376	0	23	28	78	184
Dallas, Texas Fort Worth, Texas CMSA	16,102	414.4	117	240	1,795	2,478	12,033	0	0	34	27	200
Miami, Florida Fort Lauderdale, Florida CMSA	14,395	450.9	38	209	2,497	6,648	10,725	0	0	21	70	137
Boston, Massachusetts Lawrence, Massachusetts Salem, Massachusetts CMSA	13,887	332.9	18	220	601	687	12,466	12	0	51	25	207
Washington, District of Columbia MSA	12,908	329.0	85	941	2,713	890	8,619	0	4	65	13	64
Atlanta, Georgia MSA	10,842	382.6	26	51	2,081	216	8,421	0	0	45	6	135
Cleveland, Ohio Akron, Ohio Lorain, Ohio CMSA	10,402	376.9	29	19	987	226	9,121	0	0	27	0	125
St. Louis, Missouri MSA	9,486	388.1	22	19	860	44	8,450	0	0	26	0	95
San Diego, California MSA	9,349	374.3	67	563	267	2,290	7,196	0	7	0	29	98
Baltimore, Maryland MSA	8,875	372.6	34	65	1,764	53	6,869	0	0	27	0	105
Phoenix, Arizona MSA	8,490	400.1	130	39	205	1,329	7,345	0	0	7	0	76
Seattle, Washington Tacoma, Washington CMSA	8,097	316.4	80	350	212	206	7,297	4	0	0	0	82
Pittsburgh, Pennsylvania Beaver Valley, Pennsylvania CMSA	7,872	351.0	9	46	201	26	7,533	0	0	5	3	78
Tampa, Florida St. Petersburg, Florida Clearwater, Florida MSA	7,558	365.5	52	84	374	634	6,778	0	0	22	8	123
Minneapolis, Minnesota St. Paul, Minnesota MSA	7,534	305.8	32	64	163	46	7,188	0	4	0	0	69
Denver, Colorado Boulder, Colorado CMSA	7,113	384.8	36	85	237	607	6,393	6	0	0	12	70
Cincinnati, Ohio Hamilton, Ohio CMSA	6,000	344.0	19	6	365	18	5,539	0	7	10	0	44
Kansas City, Missouri Kansas City, Kansas MSA	5,717	365.0	83	52	421	130	4,987	0	0	8	0	86
Sacramento, California MSA	5,671	382.9	53	245	196	505	4,793	0	8	13	5	95

Source: Census of Population and Housing, 1990: Equal Employment Opportunity (EEO) File on CD-ROM [machine-readable datafiles]. Prepared by the Bureau of the Census. Washington, DC: The Bureau, 1992. *Notes:* "MSA" represents "metropolitan statistical area"; "CMSA" stands for "consolidated metropolitan statistical area."

★ 96 ★

Leading Occupations

Bank Tellers, by Metropolitan Area

According to the 1990 Census of Population and Housing, bank tellers ranked 67 among occupations employing the most people in the United States. Table presents the number of civilians 16 years old or older who reported working as bank tellers during the 1990 Census. Data show the total employment figures, employment per 100,000 population, and employment data for men and women of various races and ethnicities in the 25 metropolitan statistical areas with the largest concentrations of bank tellers.

[Total for all of the U.S. was 509,023; 204.7 per 100,000 persons]

Metropolitan area	Total employees	Employees per 100,000 population	Men					Women				
			American Indian, Eskimo & Aleut	Asian, Pacific Islander	Black	Hispanic	White	American Indian, Eskimo & Aleut	Asian, Pacific Islander	Black	Hispanic	White
New York, New York New Jersey (northern) Long Island, New York CMSA	40,782	225.5	0	727	1,718	1,225	4,394	9	1,970	7,371	3,500	22,525
Los Angeles, California Anaheim, California Riverside, California CMSA	29,594	203.7	18	1,182	650	1,619	3,599	70	3,767	2,225	5,626	14,218
Chicago, Illinois Gary, Indiana Lake County, Illinois CMSA	18,946	234.9	9	340	305	327	2,122	6	580	2,727	1,594	11,773
San Francisco, California Oakland, California San Jose, California CMSA	13,306	212.8	7	968	143	394	1,275	37	2,469	573	1,467	7,093
Philadelphia, Pennsylvania Wilmington, Delaware Trenton, New Jersey CMSA	11,341	192.2	5	5	220	69	1,025	19	209	1,540	250	8,142
Detroit, Michigan Ann Arbor, Michigan CMSA	10,086	216.2	4	8	219	0	416	6	92	1,690	163	7,592
Boston, Massachusetts Lawrence, Massachusetts Salem, Massachusetts CMSA	9,843	236.0	12	62	156	143	1,156	9	280	508	263	7,495
Washington, District of Columbia MSA	8,677	221.2	4	226	451	163	1,083	16	797	2,204	444	3,729
Miami, Florida Fort Lauderdale, Florida CMSA	6,933	217.2	0	17	92	735	1,049	0	109	1,061	2,006	4,349
Dallas, Texas Fort Worth, Texas CMSA	6,131	157.8	13	9	60	77	604	22	79	473	554	4,520
Cleveland, Ohio Akron, Ohio Lorain, Ohio CMSA	5,793	209.9	0	0	107	6	377	0	30	866	143	4,348
St. Louis, Missouri MSA	5,429	222.1	0	20	52	5	388	0	48	597	41	4,311
Houston, Texas Galveston, Texas Brazoria, Texas CMSA	5,329	143.6	0	46	120	141	470	14	99	685	811	3,294
Atlanta, Georgia MSA	5,149	181.7	0	9	50	13	332	0	54	987	87	3,681
San Diego, California MSA	4,957	198.4	0	85	46	96	764	28	429	230	828	2,885
Baltimore, Maryland MSA	4,782	200.7	0	13	86	0	240	13	51	937	41	3,429
Pittsburgh, Pennsylvania Beaver Valley, Pennsylvania CMSA	4,777	213.0	0	11	26	0	239	0	20	309	37	4,166
Seattle, Washington Tacoma, Washington CMSA	4,412	172.4	9	56	47	45	452	30	290	124	101	3,321
Phoenix, Arizona MSA	4,265	201.0	0	8	19	66	444	45	64	213	515	3,133
Tampa, Florida St. Petersburg, Florida Clearwater, Florida MSA	4,230	204.6	0	0	30	18	417	11	51	303	197	3,364
Minneapolis, Minnesota St. Paul, Minnesota MSA	4,088	165.9	0	26	10	0	433	20	72	47	41	3,452
Cincinnati, Ohio Hamilton, Ohio CMSA	3,458	198.3	0	0	0	0	179	0	0	242	6	3,037
Denver, Colorado Boulder, Colorado CMSA	3,241	175.4	0	6	18	43	417	2	40	70	316	2,555
Kansas City, Missouri Kansas City, Kansas MSA	3,150	201.1	6	0	9	11	246	9	20	300	62	2,525
Milwaukee, Wisconsin Racine, Wisconsin CMSA	3,140	195.4	0	0	83	11	152	0	22	226	102	2,591

Source: Census of Population and Housing, 1990: Equal Employment Opportunity (EEO) File on CD-ROM [machine-readable datafiles]. Prepared by the Bureau of the Census. Washington, DC: The Bureau, 1992. *Notes:* "MSA" represents "metropolitan statistical area"; "CMSA" stands for "consolidated metropolitan statistical area."

★ 97 ★

Leading Occupations

Bartenders, by Metropolitan Area

According to the 1990 Census of Population and Housing, bartenders ranked 97 among occupations employing the most people in the United States. Table presents the number of civilians 16 years old or older who reported working as bartenders during the 1990 Census. Data show the total employment figures, employment per 100,000 population, and employment data for men and women of various races and ethnicities in the 25 metropolitan statistical areas with the largest concentrations of bartenders.

[Total for all of the U.S. was 330,710; 133.0 per 100,000 persons]

Metropolitan area	Total employees	Employees per 100,000 population	Men					Women				
			American Indian, Eskimo & Aleut	Asian, Pacific Islander	Black	Hispanic	White	American Indian, Eskimo & Aleut	Asian, Pacific Islander	Black	Hispanic	White
New York, New York New Jersey (northern) Long Island, New York CMSA	19,133	105.8	28	592	824	1,365	11,541	3	85	247	388	5,227
Los Angeles, California Anaheim, California Riverside, California CMSA	15,369	105.8	91	403	299	2,755	7,161	49	251	209	645	5,131
Chicago, Illinois Gary, Indiana Lake County, Illinois CMSA	11,595	143.8	30	178	563	945	4,879	60	39	317	268	4,929
San Francisco, California Oakland, California San Jose, California CMSA	8,464	135.4	18	547	246	964	4,373	22	293	89	286	2,421
Philadelphia, Pennsylvania Wilmington, Delaware Trenton, New Jersey CMSA	7,159	121.4	0	23	598	163	3,685	25	37	166	21	2,474
Boston, Massachusetts Lawrence, Massachusetts Salem, Massachusetts CMSA	6,536	156.7	0	237	48	142	3,810	0	22	80	28	2,288
Detroit, Michigan Ann Arbor, Michigan CMSA	5,272	113.0	8	27	178	100	1,932	23	15	142	18	2,911
Miami, Florida Fort Lauderdale, Florida CMSA	4,952	155.1	0	0	52	615	2,721	3	0	66	122	2,066
Dallas, Texas Fort Worth, Texas CMSA	4,621	118.9	3	84	167	387	2,062	10	9	47	106	1,943
Seattle, Washington Tacoma, Washington CMSA	4,568	178.5	11	65	83	90	1,515	103	97	62	61	2,571
Pittsburgh, Pennsylvania Beaver Valley, Pennsylvania CMSA	4,465	199.1	4	0	53	6	2,667	4	8	71	0	1,658
Milwaukee, Wisconsin Racine, Wisconsin CMSA	4,296	267.3	6	11	148	95	2,152	18	4	39	35	1,834
Las Vegas, Nevada MSA	4,012	541.1	31	129	157	253	2,435	42	26	18	71	1,048
Houston, Texas Galveston, Texas Brazoria, Texas CMSA	3,975	107.1	11	35	175	646	1,587	8	63	158	137	1,514
San Diego, California MSA	3,932	157.4	0	85	47	415	2,095	60	195	4	96	1,244
Washington, District of Columbia MSA	3,845	98.00	4	156	208	292	1,785	6	85	104	81	1,348
Minneapolis, Minnesota St. Paul, Minnesota MSA	3,789	153.8	13	44	56	33	2,245	20	24	17	2	1,370
Tampa, Florida St. Petersburg, Florida Clearwater, Florida MSA	3,501	169.3	7	6	58	24	1,407	20	19	37	31	1,945
Cleveland, Ohio Akron, Ohio Lorain, Ohio CMSA	3,373	122.2	0	6	97	18	1,461	28	0	80	21	1,688
Phoenix, Arizona MSA	3,354	158.1	10	38	42	203	1,420	0	21	14	108	1,666
St. Louis, Missouri MSA	3,294	134.8	19	5	179	8	1,314	15	7	53	0	1,700
Denver, Colorado Boulder, Colorado CMSA	2,962	160.3	12	12	68	145	1,119	10	12	41	156	1,611
Atlanta, Georgia MSA	2,911	102.7	18	18	284	83	1,335	0	2	85	9	1,145
Portland, Oregon Vancouver, Washington CMSA	2,726	184.5	5	9	31	24	966	66	24	13	39	1,603
Baltimore, Maryland MSA	2,671	112.1	6	36	116	22	1,209	23	57	15	12	1,209

Source: Census of Population and Housing, 1990: Equal Employment Opportunity (EEO) File on CD-ROM [machine-readable datafiles]. Prepared by the Bureau of the Census. Washington, DC: The Bureau, 1992. *Notes:* "MSA" represents "metropolitan statistical area"; "CMSA" stands for "consolidated metropolitan statistical area."

★ 98 ★
Leading Occupations

Bookkeepers, Accounting, and Auditing Clerks, by Metropolitan Area

According to the 1990 Census of Population and Housing, bookkeepers, accounting, and auditing clerks ranked 9 among occupations employing the most people in the United States. Table presents the number of civilians 16 years old or older who reported working as bookkeepers, accounting, and auditing clerks during the 1990 Census. Data show the total employment figures, employment per 100,000 population, and employment data for men and women of various races and ethnicities in the 25 metropolitan statistical areas with the largest concentrations of bookkeepers, accounting, and auditing clerks.

[Total for all of the U.S. was 1,921,952; 772.8 per 100,000 persons]

Metropolitan area	Total employees	Employees per 100,000 population	Men					Women				
			American Indian, Eskimo & Aleut	Asian, Pacific Islander	Black	Hispanic	White	American Indian, Eskimo & Aleut	Asian, Pacific Islander	Black	Hispanic	White
New York, New York New Jersey (northern) Long Island, New York CMSA	158,909	878.6	19	2,394	4,686	3,198	15,503	175	5,737	15,930	11,650	108,728
Los Angeles, California Anaheim, California Riverside, California CMSA	113,997	784.5	90	2,986	1,421	3,505	10,093	606	11,224	5,535	14,591	73,961
Chicago, Illinois Gary, Indiana Lake County, Illinois CMSA	60,926	755.4	4	686	1,087	443	5,593	84	1,426	5,711	2,939	44,910
San Francisco, California Oakland, California San Jose, California CMSA	57,225	915.1	18	1,736	599	621	4,680	317	7,033	2,503	4,595	38,314
Philadelphia, Pennsylvania Wilmington, Delaware Trenton, New Jersey CMSA	45,952	778.9	8	146	769	73	4,186	73	497	4,260	550	35,724
Boston, Massachusetts Lawrence, Massachusetts Salem, Massachusetts CMSA	36,891	884.3	6	231	320	262	4,087	43	673	886	415	30,371
Dallas, Texas Fort Worth, Texas CMSA	33,984	874.7	17	143	378	196	3,026	137	319	2,362	1,878	26,582
Detroit, Michigan Ann Arbor, Michigan CMSA	31,461	674.4	0	19	487	31	2,496	118	217	3,051	303	25,009
Houston, Texas Galveston, Texas Brazoria, Texas CMSA	29,935	806.7	3	178	473	359	2,416	86	699	2,934	2,690	21,860
Miami, Florida Fort Lauderdale, Florida CMSA	28,090	879.9	3	99	360	1,823	3,196	43	190	1,858	7,911	21,599
Washington, District of Columbia MSA	27,886	710.7	12	426	1,265	244	2,773	91	1,032	4,970	988	16,910
Atlanta, Georgia MSA	25,159	887.9	0	74	778	52	1,865	13	133	3,686	304	18,508
Seattle, Washington Tacoma, Washington CMSA	24,067	940.4	0	231	105	19	1,729	205	949	424	396	20,239
Minneapolis, Minnesota St. Paul, Minnesota MSA	23,638	959.3	5	46	86	70	2,726	97	205	247	115	20,168
Cleveland, Ohio Akron, Ohio Lorain, Ohio CMSA	20,415	739.7	0	53	192	17	1,659	46	140	1,516	178	16,689
San Diego, California MSA	19,001	760.6	6	289	157	362	1,643	91	1,307	582	1,434	14,164
St. Louis, Missouri MSA	18,732	766.4	0	12	199	15	1,654	43	62	1,183	154	15,538
Denver, Colorado Boulder, Colorado CMSA	17,810	963.6	8	51	87	123	1,749	107	220	401	1,214	14,689
Baltimore, Maryland MSA	17,221	722.9	16	11	420	46	1,461	6	151	1,923	115	13,213
Phoenix, Arizona MSA	16,588	781.7	12	10	76	262	1,736	216	162	235	1,210	13,527
Tampa, Florida St. Petersburg, Florida Clearwater, Florida MSA	14,874	719.3	0	24	91	185	1,433	26	87	420	673	12,674
Portland, Oregon Vancouver, Washington CMSA	14,638	990.5	12	83	74	37	1,433	87	253	123	209	12,468
Pittsburgh, Pennsylvania Beaver Valley, Pennsylvania CMSA	14,397	641.9	0	0	135	8	1,422	6	41	639	40	12,147
Kansas City, Missouri Kansas City, Kansas MSA	13,897	887.3	17	37	107	9	1,183	53	47	685	235	11,695
Sacramento, California MSA	13,404	905.0	4	107	44	106	1,055	105	616	366	845	10,797

Source: Census of Population and Housing, 1990: Equal Employment Opportunity (EEO) File on CD-ROM [machine-readable datafiles]. Prepared by the Bureau of the Census. Washington, DC: The Bureau, 1992. *Notes:* "MSA" represents "metropolitan statistical area"; "CMSA" stands for "consolidated metropolitan statistical area."

★ 99 ★
Leading Occupations

Bus Drivers, by Metropolitan Area

According to the 1990 Census of Population and Housing, bus drivers ranked 73 among occupations employing the most people in the United States. Table presents the number of civilians 16 years old or older who reported working as bus drivers during the 1990 Census. Data show the total employment figures, employment per 100,000 population, and employment data for men and women of various races and ethnicities in the 25 metropolitan statistical areas with the largest concentrations of bus drivers.

[Total for all of the U.S. was 447,570; 180.0 per 100,000 persons]

Metropolitan area	Total employees	Employees per 100,000 population	Men					Women				
			American Indian, Eskimo & Aleut	Asian, Pacific Islander	Black	Hispanic	White	American Indian, Eskimo & Aleut	Asian, Pacific Islander	Black	Hispanic	White
New York, New York New Jersey (northern) Long Island, New York CMSA	43,783	242.1	85	395	11,675	4,670	15,528	81	69	2,713	906	10,916
Los Angeles, California Anaheim, California Riverside, California CMSA	17,880	123.0	129	588	3,761	3,023	5,137	108	30	2,333	1,458	3,576
Chicago, Illinois Gary, Indiana Lake County, Illinois CMSA	15,709	194.8	17	59	5,444	1,090	3,626	19	30	2,170	209	3,605
Philadelphia, Pennsylvania Wilmington, Delaware Trenton, New Jersey CMSA	12,875	218.2	7	25	3,273	157	3,764	19	18	968	74	4,668
Washington, District of Columbia MSA	9,470	241.4	21	59	3,594	62	1,210	71	32	1,678	41	2,752
San Francisco, California Oakland, California San Jose, California CMSA	8,398	134.3	56	503	1,903	732	2,096	76	50	953	496	2,191
Boston, Massachusetts Lawrence, Massachusetts Salem, Massachusetts CMSA	7,184	172.2	6	65	858	304	2,785	24	15	351	98	2,877
Detroit, Michigan Ann Arbor, Michigan CMSA	7,000	150.1	29	6	1,511	43	1,103	26	0	707	36	3,589
Houston, Texas Galveston, Texas Brazoria, Texas CMSA	6,308	170.0	6	72	1,469	284	822	0	6	1,099	359	2,493
Seattle, Washington Tacoma, Washington CMSA	5,527	216.0	28	100	444	28	2,403	11	13	159	31	2,344
Minneapolis, Minnesota St. Paul, Minnesota MSA	5,481	222.4	64	33	318	55	3,356	14	0	98	0	1,563
Atlanta, Georgia MSA	5,426	191.5	0	10	1,355	8	823	38	16	963	14	2,213
Cleveland, Ohio Akron, Ohio Lorain, Ohio CMSA	5,282	191.4	10	10	1,163	38	1,165	2	0	646	14	2,269
Pittsburgh, Pennsylvania Beaver Valley, Pennsylvania CMSA	5,052	225.3	10	0	559	36	2,649	2	0	231	2	1,570
St. Louis, Missouri MSA	4,936	202.0	13	10	1,079	7	1,225	4	0	859	49	1,746
Dallas, Texas Fort Worth, Texas CMSA	4,713	121.3	7	8	1,332	149	1,289	12	0	888	67	1,051
Baltimore, Maryland MSA	4,498	188.8	8	12	1,459	0	892	30	7	585	0	1,505
Miami, Florida Fort Lauderdale, Florida CMSA	4,237	132.7	0	0	1,014	783	1,149	3	0	1,379	424	591
Milwaukee, Wisconsin Racine, Wisconsin CMSA	3,264	203.1	6	4	938	40	1,154	17	3	338	25	793
San Diego, California MSA	3,178	127.2	39	114	391	272	1,323	33	37	168	184	857
Norfolk, Virginia Virginia Beach, Virginia Newport News, Virginia MSA	3,132	224.3	14	0	466	0	325	7	0	833	18	1,476
Portland, Oregon Vancouver, Washington CMSA	3,099	209.7	17	25	103	36	1,417	12	16	32	31	1,457
Cincinnati, Ohio Hamilton, Ohio CMSA	3,076	176.4	0	18	350	0	995	5	0	194	0	1,514
Buffalo, New York Niagara Falls, New York CMSA	3,046	256.1	16	0	326	30	1,213	0	0	78	0	1,407
Phoenix, Arizona MSA	3,035	143.0	11	19	160	219	1,581	4	15	15	177	1,034

Source: Census of Population and Housing, 1990: Equal Employment Opportunity (EEO) File on CD-ROM [machine-readable datafiles]. Prepared by the Bureau of the Census. Washington, DC: The Bureau, 1992. *Notes:* "MSA" represents "metropolitan statistical area"; "CMSA" stands for "consolidated metropolitan statistical area."

★ 100 ★

Leading Occupations

Business Services Sales Occupations, by Metropolitan Area

According to the 1990 Census of Population and Housing, business service sales occupations ranked 63 among occupations employing the most people in the United States. Table presents the number of civilians 16 years old or older who reported working in business service sales occupations during the 1990 Census. Data show the total employment figures, employment per 100,000 population, and employment data for men and women of various races and ethnicities in the 25 metropolitan statistical areas with the largest concentrations of miscellaneous business services sales occupations. See also tables for related business services sales occupations such as securities and financial services sales occupations.

[Total for all of the U.S. was 549,247; 220.8 per 100,000 persons]

Metropolitan area	Total employees	Employees per 100,000 population	Men					Women				
			American Indian, Eskimo & Aleut	Asian, Pacific Islander	Black	Hispanic	White	American Indian, Eskimo & Aleut	Asian, Pacific Islander	Black	Hispanic	White
New York, New York New Jersey (northern) Long Island, New York CMSA	48,825	269.9	9	508	1,809	1,174	27,558	50	410	2,056	1,048	15,672
Los Angeles, California Anaheim, California Riverside, California CMSA	37,966	261.3	56	896	1,296	2,844	20,515	47	739	938	1,731	11,545
Chicago, Illinois Gary, Indiana Lake County, Illinois CMSA	26,238	325.3	36	122	838	460	15,662	8	132	869	360	8,226
San Francisco, California Oakland, California San Jose, California CMSA	18,339	293.3	31	709	508	605	9,212	29	652	593	529	6,260
Philadelphia, Pennsylvania Wilmington, Delaware Trenton, New Jersey CMSA	15,964	270.6	0	60	639	144	10,224	0	19	485	58	4,501
Dallas, Texas Fort Worth, Texas CMSA	15,430	397.1	63	60	557	409	9,392	40	28	559	219	4,516
Boston, Massachusetts Lawrence, Massachusetts Salem, Massachusetts CMSA	12,816	307.2	0	84	182	47	7,609	27	45	119	29	4,727
Atlanta, Georgia MSA	12,736	449.5	16	42	718	106	7,337	0	10	796	30	3,796
Washington, District of Columbia MSA	11,965	305.0	26	197	906	216	6,008	0	92	785	139	3,903
Houston, Texas Galveston, Texas Brazoria, Texas CMSA	11,231	302.6	12	82	531	518	6,741	0	25	461	307	3,073
Detroit, Michigan Ann Arbor, Michigan CMSA	10,179	218.2	0	6	397	53	5,925	0	26	505	47	3,299
Miami, Florida Fort Lauderdale, Florida CMSA	9,537	298.7	6	0	311	1,427	5,436	18	15	266	913	3,375
Minneapolis, Minnesota St. Paul, Minnesota MSA	9,337	378.9	16	29	134	32	5,869	9	24	67	5	3,184
Seattle, Washington Tacoma, Washington CMSA	7,752	302.9	10	49	75	60	4,314	53	100	26	37	3,092
Cleveland, Ohio Akron, Ohio Lorain, Ohio CMSA	7,548	273.5	16	6	212	40	4,766	7	0	179	30	2,348
Phoenix, Arizona MSA	7,142	336.6	17	0	84	169	4,332	48	29	56	202	2,483
Denver, Colorado Boulder, Colorado CMSA	6,981	377.7	0	22	116	232	4,284	0	26	55	150	2,332
St. Louis, Missouri MSA	6,951	284.4	0	8	201	19	4,144	0	9	218	25	2,371
San Diego, California MSA	6,942	277.9	49	46	138	249	3,748	14	103	102	140	2,602
Baltimore, Maryland MSA	6,918	290.4	21	11	437	8	3,915	6	0	521	72	2,001
Tampa, Florida St. Petersburg, Florida Clearwater, Florida MSA	6,654	321.8	12	13	122	188	4,173	0	5	161	123	2,156
Kansas City, Missouri Kansas City, Kansas MSA	5,312	339.2	0	15	193	50	3,021	40	22	243	14	1,764
Cincinnati, Ohio Hamilton, Ohio CMSA	5,074	290.9	0	19	98	12	3,120	0	14	102	0	1,718
Pittsburgh, Pennsylvania Beaver Valley, Pennsylvania CMSA	4,929	219.8	0	0	83	18	3,208	0	5	68	2	1,565
Milwaukee, Wisconsin Racine, Wisconsin CMSA	4,920	306.1	12	0	146	73	3,035	0	18	82	14	1,596

Source: Census of Population and Housing, 1990: Equal Employment Opportunity (EEO) File on CD-ROM [machine-readable datafiles]. Prepared by the Bureau of the Census. Washington, DC: The Bureau, 1992. *Notes:* "MSA" represents "metropolitan statistical area"; "CMSA" stands for "consolidated metropolitan statistical area."

★ 101 ★

Leading Occupations

Butchers and Meat Cutters, by Metropolitan Area

According to the 1990 Census of Population and Housing, butchers and meat cutters ranked 108 among occupations employing the most people in the United States. Table presents the number of civilians 16 years old or older who reported working as butchers and meat cutters during the 1990 Census. Data show the total employment figures, employment per 100,000 population, and employment data for men and women of various races and ethnicities in the 25 metropolitan statistical areas with the largest concentrations of butchers and meat cutters.

[Total for all of the U.S. was 278,902; 112.1 per 100,000 persons]

Metropolitan area	Total employees	Employees per 100,000 population	Men					Women				
			American Indian, Eskimo & Aleut	Asian, Pacific Islander	Black	Hispanic	White	American Indian, Eskimo & Aleut	Asian, Pacific Islander	Black	Hispanic	White
New York, New York New Jersey (northern) Long Island, New York CMSA	14,393	79.58	8	250	1,368	2,387	10,843	0	0	138	171	647
Los Angeles, California Anaheim, California Riverside, California CMSA	11,615	79.93	73	728	554	6,016	5,925	0	40	54	566	463
Chicago, Illinois Gary, Indiana Lake County, Illinois CMSA	8,370	103.8	24	13	961	1,847	5,041	4	20	193	216	771
Philadelphia, Pennsylvania Wilmington, Delaware Trenton, New Jersey CMSA	5,697	96.57	5	52	719	231	3,574	11	31	210	70	900
San Francisco, California Oakland, California San Jose, California CMSA	5,066	81.01	74	800	188	1,031	3,159	13	80	0	83	268
Detroit, Michigan Ann Arbor, Michigan CMSA	4,092	87.71	19	5	774	158	2,635	4	0	203	9	383
Miami, Florida Fort Lauderdale, Florida CMSA	3,231	101.2	0	0	329	1,643	2,455	0	12	34	93	229
Houston, Texas Galveston, Texas Brazoria, Texas CMSA	3,073	82.81	2	128	337	1,094	1,689	11	8	88	188	170
Boston, Massachusetts Lawrence, Massachusetts Salem, Massachusetts CMSA	2,983	71.51	0	41	119	69	2,519	0	23	18	39	225
Dallas, Texas Fort Worth, Texas CMSA	2,651	68.23	27	18	270	643	1,662	0	0	54	125	172
Washington, District of Columbia MSA	2,187	55.74	0	30	585	57	1,314	3	32	70	19	119
Cleveland, Ohio Akron, Ohio Lorain, Ohio CMSA	2,164	78.41	0	0	176	19	1,630	0	0	67	0	281
Baltimore, Maryland MSA	2,161	90.72	7	10	391	9	1,391	0	17	138	0	202
Pittsburgh, Pennsylvania Beaver Valley, Pennsylvania CMSA	2,152	95.95	0	0	47	0	1,705	0	8	16	1	376
Atlanta, Georgia MSA	2,149	75.84	4	61	307	79	1,182	0	76	230	46	199
St. Louis, Missouri MSA	2,141	87.60	0	5	264	34	1,585	0	0	84	0	202
Sioux City, Iowa MSA	2,102	1,828	38	235	82	514	759	26	152	17	143	364
Minneapolis, Minnesota St. Paul, Minnesota MSA	2,006	81.41	2	33	37	103	1,800	7	8	7	3	83
Seattle, Washington Tacoma, Washington CMSA	1,968	76.90	16	94	84	49	1,352	9	123	13	49	217
Cincinnati, Ohio Hamilton, Ohio CMSA	1,800	103.2	0	7	138	8	1,388	0	20	14	13	226
Tampa, Florida St. Petersburg, Florida Clearwater, Florida MSA	1,788	86.46	0	0	103	141	1,466	0	0	14	18	161
Omaha, Nebraska MSA	1,735	280.6	9	10	207	433	1,111	0	28	36	48	148
Denver, Colorado Boulder, Colorado CMSA	1,726	93.38	21	50	20	463	1,163	0	24	0	39	162
Phoenix, Arizona MSA	1,699	80.06	15	18	25	581	1,105	15	0	9	117	77
San Antonio, Texas MSA	1,682	129.2	0	15	53	1,177	957	0	3	0	173	104

Source: Census of Population and Housing, 1990: Equal Employment Opportunity (EEO) File on CD-ROM [machine-readable datafiles]. Prepared by the Bureau of the Census. Washington, DC: The Bureau, 1992. *Notes:* "MSA" represents "metropolitan statistical area"; "CMSA" stands for "consolidated metropolitan statistical area."

★ 102 ★

Leading Occupations

Carpenters, by Metropolitan Area

According to the 1990 Census of Population and Housing, carpenters ranked 18 among occupations employing the most people in the United States. Table presents the number of civilians 16 years old or older who reported working as carpenters during the 1990 Census. Data show the total employment figures, employment per 100,000 population, and employment data for men and women of various races and ethnicities in the 25 metropolitan statistical areas with the largest concentrations of carpenters, excluding apprentices.

[Total for all of the U.S. was 1,360,707; 547.1 per 100,000 persons]

Metropolitan area	Total employees	Employees per 100,000 population	Men					Women				
			American Indian, Eskimo & Aleut	Asian, Pacific Islander	Black	Hispanic	White	American Indian, Eskimo & Aleut	Asian, Pacific Islander	Black	Hispanic	White
New York, New York New Jersey (northern) Long Island, New York CMSA	90,148	498.4	144	1,518	9,025	10,128	74,409	0	0	258	223	920
Los Angeles, California Anaheim, California Riverside, California CMSA	77,194	531.2	600	2,042	2,562	31,568	53,111	14	56	67	504	826
Chicago, Illinois Gary, Indiana Lake County, Illinois CMSA	40,694	504.5	120	140	1,987	3,464	36,139	10	41	40	65	336
San Francisco, California Oakland, California San Jose, California CMSA	37,874	605.7	359	1,703	1,512	5,858	30,912	33	12	22	169	693
Philadelphia, Pennsylvania Wilmington, Delaware Trenton, New Jersey CMSA	32,035	543.0	106	209	2,181	886	28,688	0	0	41	12	369
Boston, Massachusetts Lawrence, Massachusetts Salem, Massachusetts CMSA	27,293	654.3	27	159	788	485	25,768	0	0	24	16	353
Washington, District of Columbia MSA	22,637	577.0	91	1,237	2,757	3,380	16,480	0	12	79	34	241
Miami, Florida Fort Lauderdale, Florida CMSA	19,841	621.5	59	119	2,262	8,933	16,086	0	0	5	73	204
Houston, Texas Galveston, Texas Brazoria, Texas CMSA	19,050	513.3	99	120	1,295	7,311	13,336	0	0	0	48	196
Detroit, Michigan Ann Arbor, Michigan CMSA	17,699	379.4	105	19	907	171	16,385	6	0	39	0	180
Seattle, Washington Tacoma, Washington CMSA	17,243	673.8	262	276	341	363	15,740	6	0	0	4	447
Dallas, Texas Fort Worth, Texas CMSA	15,753	405.4	83	114	753	3,486	12,309	16	2	15	16	239
Baltimore, Maryland MSA	14,475	607.6	44	38	1,515	202	12,517	0	0	28	12	275
Atlanta, Georgia MSA	14,448	509.9	82	86	1,591	659	12,212	12	0	49	7	186
San Diego, California MSA	14,158	566.8	168	322	384	3,385	11,169	0	0	18	49	210
St. Louis, Missouri MSA	12,763	522.2	31	51	493	71	12,029	0	0	11	5	138
Minneapolis, Minnesota St. Paul, Minnesota MSA	12,058	489.3	112	7	115	90	11,646	20	0	12	2	110
Cleveland, Ohio Akron, Ohio Lorain, Ohio CMSA	10,915	395.5	43	6	486	87	10,187	0	0	23	8	145
Pittsburgh, Pennsylvania Beaver Valley, Pennsylvania CMSA	10,024	446.9	0	5	286	34	9,603	0	0	7	0	121
Tampa, Florida St. Petersburg, Florida Clearwater, Florida MSA	9,982	482.7	123	71	496	627	8,920	0	0	27	2	213
Sacramento, California MSA	9,557	645.3	131	186	232	770	8,588	0	7	0	0	132
Portland, Oregon Vancouver, Washington CMSA	9,016	610.1	86	95	126	217	8,390	0	4	0	25	197
Providence, Rhode Island Pawtucket, Rhode Island Fall River, Massachusetts CMSA	8,482	743.1	34	7	195	239	7,992	0	16	0	0	111
Phoenix, Arizona MSA	8,098	381.6	205	29	147	1,172	6,929	0	0	7	28	111
Cincinnati, Ohio Hamilton, Ohio CMSA	7,972	457.1	13	0	220	37	7,641	3	0	9	0	68

Source: Census of Population and Housing, 1990: Equal Employment Opportunity (EEO) File on CD-ROM [machine-readable datafiles]. Prepared by the Bureau of the Census. Washington, DC: The Bureau, 1992. *Notes:* "MSA" represents "metropolitan statistical area"; "CMSA" stands for "consolidated metropolitan statistical area."

★ 103 ★
Leading Occupations

Cashiers, by Metropolitan Area

According to the 1990 Census of Population and Housing, cashiers ranked 6 among occupations employing the most people in the United States. Table presents the number of civilians 16 years old or older who reported working as cashiers during the 1990 Census. Data show the total employment figures, employment per 100,000 population, and employment data for men and women of various races and ethnicities in the 25 metropolitan statistical areas with the largest concentrations of cashiers.

[Total for all of the U.S. was 2,855,680; 1,148 per 100,000 persons]

Metropolitan area	Total employees	Employees per 100,000 population	Men					Women				
			American Indian, Eskimo & Aleut	Asian, Pacific Islander	Black	Hispanic	White	American Indian, Eskimo & Aleut	Asian, Pacific Islander	Black	Hispanic	White
New York, New York New Jersey (northern) Long Island, New York CMSA	172,671	954.7	113	4,412	7,982	10,012	28,799	385	8,840	27,818	20,736	80,572
Los Angeles, California Anaheim, California Riverside, California CMSA	155,403	1,069	261	8,259	3,757	17,105	26,263	802	12,424	9,444	38,148	63,234
Chicago, Illinois Gary, Indiana Lake County, Illinois CMSA	92,708	1,149	43	1,160	4,109	2,059	12,815	281	2,707	18,339	7,572	48,084
San Francisco, California Oakland, California San Jose, California CMSA	65,221	1,043	206	5,106	2,006	3,774	12,992	343	8,719	4,759	7,513	25,843
Philadelphia, Pennsylvania Wilmington, Delaware Trenton, New Jersey CMSA	63,409	1,075	41	636	2,721	526	10,835	187	1,426	10,056	1,875	36,179
Detroit, Michigan Ann Arbor, Michigan CMSA	57,147	1,225	57	194	2,142	196	8,357	221	478	11,579	1,004	33,641
Dallas, Texas Fort Worth, Texas CMSA	48,951	1,260	78	460	1,866	1,548	8,946	218	1,079	7,973	5,016	24,589
Houston, Texas Galveston, Texas Brazoria, Texas CMSA	47,855	1,290	40	1,455	2,096	1,825	5,602	133	1,888	10,886	7,796	20,319
Boston, Massachusetts Lawrence, Massachusetts Salem, Massachusetts CMSA	46,354	1,111	24	573	864	487	9,447	75	1,228	1,967	1,528	31,131
Washington, District of Columbia MSA	42,662	1,087	51	1,774	3,955	1,003	6,737	132	3,635	9,956	1,988	15,001
Miami, Florida Fort Lauderdale, Florida CMSA	41,350	1,295	30	261	1,600	3,916	6,971	72	712	8,726	11,162	20,825
Atlanta, Georgia MSA	36,692	1,295	10	372	2,447	224	5,376	55	790	10,959	367	16,503
Cleveland, Ohio Akron, Ohio Lorain, Ohio CMSA	31,889	1,155	28	80	879	78	4,036	40	313	4,595	401	21,664
St. Louis, Missouri MSA	29,004	1,187	8	34	1,136	78	4,444	60	230	5,489	299	17,447
Baltimore, Maryland MSA	28,905	1,213	39	365	1,532	66	3,896	87	623	7,309	331	14,965
San Diego, California MSA	27,971	1,120	85	827	605	1,464	5,520	175	1,823	1,728	4,678	14,090
Seattle, Washington Tacoma, Washington CMSA	27,541	1,076	85	824	402	181	5,600	342	1,777	1,351	743	16,853
Minneapolis, Minnesota St. Paul, Minnesota MSA	27,498	1,116	10	190	345	92	5,801	232	386	750	328	19,633
Tampa, Florida St. Petersburg, Florida Clearwater, Florida MSA	25,293	1,223	7	168	363	395	4,860	111	288	1,954	1,149	17,268
Pittsburgh, Pennsylvania Beaver Valley, Pennsylvania CMSA	24,134	1,076	30	31	291	28	3,693	2	105	1,413	127	18,543
Phoenix, Arizona MSA	23,566	1,111	77	188	215	926	5,442	388	329	766	2,835	14,136
Denver, Colorado Boulder, Colorado CMSA	20,354	1,101	35	123	325	861	5,426	152	398	742	2,391	11,846
Cincinnati, Ohio Hamilton, Ohio CMSA	20,174	1,157	27	57	480	13	3,432	41	200	1,957	76	13,956
Norfolk, Virginia Virginia Beach, Virginia Newport News, Virginia MSA	19,190	1,375	13	87	936	56	1,630	90	770	6,968	449	8,521
Milwaukee, Wisconsin Racine, Wisconsin CMSA	17,967	1,118	8	51	365	87	2,205	71	100	2,549	537	12,319

Source: Census of Population and Housing, 1990: Equal Employment Opportunity (EEO) File on CD-ROM [machine-readable datafiles]. Prepared by the Bureau of the Census. Washington, DC: The Bureau, 1992. *Notes:* "MSA" represents "metropolitan statistical area"; "CMSA" stands for "consolidated metropolitan statistical area."

★ 104 ★

Leading Occupations

Clergy, by Metropolitan Area

According to the 1990 Census of Population and Housing, clergy ranked 100 among occupations employing the most people in the United States. Table presents the number of civilians 16 years old or older who reported working as clergy during the 1990 Census. Data show the total employment figures, employment per 100,000 population, and employment data for men and women of various races and ethnicities in the 25 metropolitan statistical areas with the largest concentrations of clergy.

[Total for all of the U.S. was 324,889; 130.6 per 100,000 persons]

Metropolitan area	Total employees	Employees per 100,000 population	Men					Women				
			American Indian, Eskimo & Aleut	Asian, Pacific Islander	Black	Hispanic	White	American Indian, Eskimo & Aleut	Asian, Pacific Islander	Black	Hispanic	White
New York, New York New Jersey (northern) Long Island, New York CMSA	15,448	85.41	7	944	2,023	736	10,182	0	116	260	114	1,735
Los Angeles, California Anaheim, California Riverside, California CMSA	13,623	93.75	71	1,690	829	1,518	8,393	20	182	98	261	1,605
Chicago, Illinois Gary, Indiana Lake County, Illinois CMSA	8,345	103.5	7	273	845	319	5,813	0	28	137	85	1,078
Philadelphia, Pennsylvania Wilmington, Delaware Trenton, New Jersey CMSA	6,287	106.6	10	177	709	174	4,441	0	30	143	36	657
Dallas, Texas Fort Worth, Texas CMSA	6,068	156.2	20	158	550	368	4,507	4	7	40	26	622
San Francisco, California Oakland, California San Jose, California CMSA	5,896	94.29	0	693	333	312	3,853	13	33	49	15	782
Detroit, Michigan Ann Arbor, Michigan CMSA	4,284	91.83	8	46	469	31	3,201	0	0	73	15	480
Boston, Massachusetts Lawrence, Massachusetts Salem, Massachusetts CMSA	4,263	102.2	6	145	254	95	3,270	0	0	23	0	530
Washington, District of Columbia MSA	4,169	106.3	3	280	728	89	2,621	0	19	79	0	415
Atlanta, Georgia MSA	3,862	136.3	0	125	462	42	2,896	0	0	55	0	305
Houston, Texas Galveston, Texas Brazoria, Texas CMSA	3,670	98.89	0	124	453	408	2,609	0	7	34	4	282
Minneapolis, Minnesota St. Paul, Minnesota MSA	3,276	133.0	0	35	46	9	2,600	0	0	34	0	561
Seattle, Washington Tacoma, Washington CMSA	3,260	127.4	15	203	84	18	2,489	0	38	27	0	389
St. Louis, Missouri MSA	3,203	131.1	6	35	209	15	2,645	21	0	15	2	270
Cleveland, Ohio Akron, Ohio Lorain, Ohio CMSA	3,081	111.6	9	0	248	10	2,430	0	0	50	0	334
Pittsburgh, Pennsylvania Beaver Valley, Pennsylvania CMSA	2,894	129.0	0	18	196	13	2,343	0	2	2	0	333
Tampa, Florida St. Petersburg, Florida Clearwater, Florida MSA	2,463	119.1	31	21	128	49	2,062	0	12	0	6	198
Baltimore, Maryland MSA	2,390	100.3	7	82	312	7	1,724	0	0	42	0	223
San Diego, California MSA	2,360	94.47	0	117	149	203	1,726	0	16	10	26	269
Cincinnati, Ohio Hamilton, Ohio CMSA	2,336	133.9	7	16	174	0	1,881	0	0	23	0	235
Kansas City, Missouri Kansas City, Kansas MSA	2,256	144.0	6	32	75	16	1,723	0	0	97	18	301
Charlotte, North Carolina Gastonia, North Carolina Rock Hill, South Carolina MSA	2,251	193.7	0	0	222	27	1,793	0	0	31	0	200
Miami, Florida Fort Lauderdale, Florida CMSA	2,235	70.01	0	18	317	390	1,607	0	0	87	54	193
Phoenix, Arizona MSA	2,204	103.9	5	48	37	103	1,858	0	0	24	22	194
Denver, Colorado Boulder, Colorado CMSA	2,115	114.4	14	43	52	88	1,677	0	3	4	6	297

Source: Census of Population and Housing, 1990: Equal Employment Opportunity (EEO) File on CD-ROM [machine-readable datafiles]. Prepared by the Bureau of the Census. Washington, DC: The Bureau, 1992. *Notes:* "MSA" represents "metropolitan statistical area"; "CMSA" stands for "consolidated metropolitan statistical area."

★ 105 ★

Leading Occupations

Clinical Laboratory Technologists and Technicians, by Metropolitan Area

According to the 1990 Census of Population and Housing, clinical laboratory technologists and technicians ranked 98 among occupations employing the most people in the United States. Table presents the number of civilians 16 years old or older who reported working as clinical laboratory technologists and technicians during the 1990 Census. Data show the total employment figures, employment per 100,000 population, and employment data for men and women of various races and ethnicities in the 25 metropolitan statistical areas with the largest concentrations of clinical laboratory technologists and technicians.

[Total for all of the U.S. was 329,892; 132.6 per 100,000 persons]

Metropolitan area	Total employees	Employees per 100,000 population	Men					Women				
			American Indian, Eskimo & Aleut	Asian, Pacific Islander	Black	Hispanic	White	American Indian, Eskimo & Aleut	Asian, Pacific Islander	Black	Hispanic	White
New York, New York New Jersey (northern) Long Island, New York CMSA	24,130	133.4	22	1,399	2,127	1,207	3,628	33	2,058	4,105	2,192	9,507
Los Angeles, California Anaheim, California Riverside, California CMSA	15,629	107.6	35	1,837	385	788	3,155	6	3,053	953	1,045	5,402
Chicago, Illinois Gary, Indiana Lake County, Illinois CMSA	12,380	153.5	0	738	652	226	1,481	0	1,154	2,081	506	5,957
Philadelphia, Pennsylvania Wilmington, Delaware Trenton, New Jersey CMSA	10,435	176.9	22	157	363	98	1,211	10	433	1,389	133	6,734
San Francisco, California Oakland, California San Jose, California CMSA	8,104	129.6	11	696	223	193	1,417	37	1,773	350	350	3,391
Boston, Massachusetts Lawrence, Massachusetts Salem, Massachusetts CMSA	7,687	184.3	7	212	183	128	1,210	12	241	508	167	5,231
Detroit, Michigan Ann Arbor, Michigan CMSA	7,183	154.0	5	58	229	32	1,377	10	282	1,117	69	4,073
Washington, District of Columbia MSA	5,937	151.3	7	315	727	80	707	0	517	1,371	126	2,244
Houston, Texas Galveston, Texas Brazoria, Texas CMSA	5,550	149.6	0	274	431	170	610	13	308	1,215	532	2,393
Miami, Florida Fort Lauderdale, Florida CMSA	5,010	156.9	0	101	240	787	1,272	2	93	666	1,131	2,469
Baltimore, Maryland MSA	4,898	205.6	0	139	389	39	786	0	211	1,073	54	2,276
Dallas, Texas Fort Worth, Texas CMSA	4,542	116.9	0	106	220	130	768	31	277	598	218	2,375
Cleveland, Ohio Akron, Ohio Lorain, Ohio CMSA	4,509	163.4	0	46	153	33	670	0	178	623	37	2,786
St. Louis, Missouri MSA	4,449	182.0	0	13	160	35	715	10	135	781	48	2,621
Seattle, Washington Tacoma, Washington CMSA	3,977	155.4	0	114	61	37	758	30	355	196	86	2,424
Atlanta, Georgia MSA	3,863	136.3	0	20	341	14	514	7	88	887	77	1,962
Pittsburgh, Pennsylvania Beaver Valley, Pennsylvania CMSA	3,838	171.1	0	7	35	0	677	9	30	205	22	2,875
Minneapolis, Minnesota St. Paul, Minnesota MSA	3,816	154.9	19	28	51	0	676	11	50	33	40	2,920
San Diego, California MSA	3,483	139.4	5	239	105	174	874	7	469	101	167	1,568
Tampa, Florida St. Petersburg, Florida Clearwater, Florida MSA	2,980	144.1	8	24	62	93	784	0	45	145	134	1,848
Cincinnati, Ohio Hamilton, Ohio CMSA	2,774	159.1	0	32	76	0	515	0	64	260	23	1,822
Milwaukee, Wisconsin Racine, Wisconsin CMSA	2,739	170.4	0	11	45	10	413	0	24	186	16	2,050
Denver, Colorado Boulder, Colorado CMSA	2,686	145.3	6	28	53	89	502	6	74	153	81	1,810
Phoenix, Arizona MSA	2,685	126.5	0	10	49	93	684	44	46	52	115	1,732
Kansas City, Missouri Kansas City, Kansas MSA	2,612	166.8	0	26	43	30	373	0	61	324	48	1,748

Source: Census of Population and Housing, 1990: Equal Employment Opportunity (EEO) File on CD-ROM [machine-readable datafiles]. Prepared by the Bureau of the Census. Washington, DC: The Bureau, 1992. *Notes:* "MSA" represents "metropolitan statistical area"; "CMSA" stands for "consolidated metropolitan statistical area."

★ 106 ★

Leading Occupations

Commodity Sales Workers, by Metropolitan Area

According to the 1990 Census of Population and Housing, commodity sales workers ranked 12 among occupations employing the most people in the United States. Table presents the number of civilians 16 years old or older who reported working as commodity sales workers during the 1990 Census. Data show the total employment figures, employment per 100,000 population, and employment data for men and women of various races and ethnicities in the 25 metropolitan statistical areas with the largest concentrations of sales workers for miscellaneous commodities. See also tables for specific types of commodities such as apparel sales workers.

[Total for all of the U.S. was 1,857,857; 747.0 per 100,000 persons]

Metropolitan area	Total employees	Employees per 100,000 population	Men					Women				
			American Indian, Eskimo & Aleut	Asian, Pacific Islander	Black	Hispanic	White	American Indian, Eskimo & Aleut	Asian, Pacific Islander	Black	Hispanic	White
New York, New York New Jersey (northern) Long Island, New York CMSA	135,936	751.6	165	4,722	7,006	7,036	39,160	84	3,917	9,796	8,047	65,444
Los Angeles, California Anaheim, California Riverside, California CMSA	113,001	777.6	195	5,788	2,707	10,573	32,051	381	6,708	4,289	14,899	48,461
Chicago, Illinois Gary, Indiana Lake County, Illinois CMSA	58,326	723.1	56	744	2,408	1,178	15,698	16	1,011	4,762	2,266	32,041
San Francisco, California Oakland, California San Jose, California CMSA	56,097	897.1	68	2,748	1,250	2,329	15,500	282	4,560	2,225	3,856	27,224
Philadelphia, Pennsylvania Wilmington, Delaware Trenton, New Jersey CMSA	44,741	758.4	25	385	1,371	355	13,135	88	612	3,182	600	25,495
Boston, Massachusetts Lawrence, Massachusetts Salem, Massachusetts CMSA	33,683	807.4	26	221	348	255	11,267	32	313	447	498	20,706
Detroit, Michigan Ann Arbor, Michigan CMSA	33,279	713.3	30	85	1,078	133	8,993	84	268	3,000	362	19,621
Dallas, Texas Fort Worth, Texas CMSA	32,111	826.5	44	293	978	790	10,388	83	482	1,908	1,492	16,707
Miami, Florida Fort Lauderdale, Florida CMSA	30,572	957.6	11	266	1,053	4,484	10,831	36	290	1,878	6,019	15,173
Houston, Texas Galveston, Texas Brazoria, Texas CMSA	28,275	761.9	26	483	1,250	1,359	7,560	57	856	3,099	2,415	13,208
Washington, District of Columbia MSA	26,744	681.6	18	476	1,699	382	7,110	70	1,323	3,282	850	12,344
Atlanta, Georgia MSA	22,711	801.5	10	124	1,396	149	7,224	29	147	2,778	242	10,844
San Diego, California MSA	21,603	864.8	87	520	373	1,273	6,775	87	1,065	399	2,217	10,680
Cleveland, Ohio Akron, Ohio Lorain, Ohio CMSA	21,338	773.2	16	37	487	47	5,714	18	93	1,644	281	13,234
Seattle, Washington Tacoma, Washington CMSA	20,784	812.1	34	337	164	127	6,257	129	561	431	418	12,721
Minneapolis, Minnesota St. Paul, Minnesota MSA	20,600	836.0	21	69	121	56	7,199	85	151	230	203	12,644
Pittsburgh, Pennsylvania Beaver Valley, Pennsylvania CMSA	20,546	916.1	22	23	310	47	5,618	7	77	594	48	13,862
St. Louis, Missouri MSA	19,956	816.5	9	20	565	48	6,007	17	112	1,357	144	11,826
Tampa, Florida St. Petersburg, Florida Clearwater, Florida MSA	18,525	895.8	22	86	166	285	6,764	49	242	466	670	10,607
Phoenix, Arizona MSA	17,428	821.3	41	87	145	513	6,063	194	85	173	949	9,974
Baltimore, Maryland MSA	17,075	716.8	0	57	706	65	4,553	18	232	2,018	101	9,409
Denver, Colorado Boulder, Colorado CMSA	16,478	891.5	21	84	169	443	6,061	119	168	293	618	9,171
Cincinnati, Ohio Hamilton, Ohio CMSA	14,921	855.5	0	21	321	27	4,524	25	41	720	15	9,269
Kansas City, Missouri Kansas City, Kansas MSA	12,420	793.0	31	22	239	94	3,976	27	52	542	186	7,421
Milwaukee, Wisconsin Racine, Wisconsin CMSA	12,219	760.3	13	30	195	52	3,539	36	38	417	143	7,881

Source: Census of Population and Housing, 1990: Equal Employment Opportunity (EEO) File on CD-ROM [machine-readable datafiles]. Prepared by the Bureau of the Census. Washington, DC: The Bureau, 1992. *Notes:* "MSA" represents "metropolitan statistical area"; "CMSA" stands for "consolidated metropolitan statistical area."

★ 107 ★
Leading Occupations

Computer Operators, by Metropolitan Area

According to the 1990 Census of Population and Housing, computer operators ranked 42 among occupations employing the most people in the United States. Table presents the number of civilians 16 years old or older who reported working as computer operators during the 1990 Census. Data show the total employment figures, employment per 100,000 population, and employment data for men and women of various races and ethnicities in the 25 metropolitan statistical areas with the largest concentrations of computer operators.

[Total for all of the U.S. was 660,318; 265.5 per 100,000 persons]

Metropolitan area	Total employees	Employees per 100,000 population	Men					Women				
			American Indian, Eskimo & Aleut	Asian, Pacific Islander	Black	Hispanic	White	American Indian, Eskimo & Aleut	Asian, Pacific Islander	Black	Hispanic	White
New York, New York New Jersey (northern) Long Island, New York CMSA	63,658	352.0	70	2,072	6,118	3,827	17,519	99	1,371	9,712	4,351	23,556
Los Angeles, California Anaheim, California Riverside, California CMSA	36,942	254.2	104	2,833	2,033	3,271	9,628	123	2,459	3,126	4,208	12,943
Chicago, Illinois Gary, Indiana Lake County, Illinois CMSA	27,050	335.4	60	565	2,333	860	7,783	38	507	3,597	1,081	11,289
Philadelphia, Pennsylvania Wilmington, Delaware Trenton, New Jersey CMSA	20,025	339.4	7	240	1,584	199	6,880	29	162	2,388	188	8,529
San Francisco, California Oakland, California San Jose, California CMSA	17,506	280.0	70	1,889	767	1,027	4,865	94	1,936	1,399	1,265	5,523
Dallas, Texas Fort Worth, Texas CMSA	15,613	401.8	58	166	1,234	554	5,214	30	167	1,594	617	6,493
Washington, District of Columbia MSA	14,374	366.4	21	483	2,514	290	3,684	39	385	3,204	303	3,870
Boston, Massachusetts Lawrence, Massachusetts Salem, Massachusetts CMSA	13,528	324.3	20	197	551	254	5,229	23	130	571	154	6,540
Detroit, Michigan Ann Arbor, Michigan CMSA	13,050	279.7	6	93	715	74	4,073	24	119	1,818	141	6,122
Houston, Texas Galveston, Texas Brazoria, Texas CMSA	11,488	309.6	16	337	1,055	551	3,576	30	207	1,430	777	4,294
Atlanta, Georgia MSA	10,846	382.8	0	78	1,202	9	2,921	7	95	2,026	82	4,487
St. Louis, Missouri MSA	8,281	338.8	16	31	461	42	2,870	13	20	899	58	3,971
Miami, Florida Fort Lauderdale, Florida CMSA	8,171	255.9	0	132	306	1,074	2,209	0	113	1,014	1,883	4,098
Baltimore, Maryland MSA	8,119	340.8	0	56	671	55	2,311	25	81	1,568	19	3,388
Minneapolis, Minnesota St. Paul, Minnesota MSA	8,009	325.0	0	99	178	25	3,002	2	56	152	57	4,485
Cleveland, Ohio Akron, Ohio Lorain, Ohio CMSA	8,002	290.0	8	34	369	24	2,604	8	22	915	32	4,031
Seattle, Washington Tacoma, Washington CMSA	7,327	286.3	0	226	108	105	2,435	56	308	323	43	3,806
Denver, Colorado Boulder, Colorado CMSA	6,784	367.0	0	95	225	268	2,690	27	61	228	357	3,167
Kansas City, Missouri Kansas City, Kansas MSA	6,178	394.4	3	33	377	66	1,971	14	41	676	96	3,032
Phoenix, Arizona MSA	5,689	268.1	31	76	62	166	1,921	58	47	154	498	3,007
Columbus, Ohio MSA	5,610	407.3	7	46	300	15	1,943	6	20	485	42	2,783
San Diego, California MSA	5,548	222.1	46	199	283	208	1,781	29	301	299	461	2,271
Cincinnati, Ohio Hamilton, Ohio CMSA	5,388	308.9	0	37	136	8	1,571	0	15	387	34	3,236
Pittsburgh, Pennsylvania Beaver Valley, Pennsylvania CMSA	5,350	238.5	7	14	197	6	2,096	8	17	325	14	2,686
Tampa, Florida St. Petersburg, Florida Clearwater, Florida MSA	5,245	253.6	5	0	111	103	1,614	4	60	263	138	3,167

Source: Census of Population and Housing, 1990: Equal Employment Opportunity (EEO) File on CD-ROM [machine-readable datafiles]. Prepared by the Bureau of the Census. Washington, DC: The Bureau, 1992. *Notes:* "MSA" represents "metropolitan statistical area"; "CMSA" stands for "consolidated metropolitan statistical area."

★ 108 ★

Leading Occupations

Computer Programmers, by Metropolitan Area

According to the 1990 Census of Population and Housing, computer programmers ranked 41 among occupations employing the most people in the United States. Table presents the number of civilians 16 years old or older who reported working as computer programmers during the 1990 Census. Data show the total employment figures, employment per 100,000 population, and employment data for men and women of various races and ethnicities in the 25 metropolitan statistical areas with the largest concentrations of computer programmers.

[Total for all of the U.S. was 662,759; 266.5 per 100,000 persons]

Metropolitan area	Total employees	Employees per 100,000 population	Men					Women				
			American Indian, Eskimo & Aleut	Asian, Pacific Islander	Black	Hispanic	White	American Indian, Eskimo & Aleut	Asian, Pacific Islander	Black	Hispanic	White
New York, New York New Jersey (northern) Long Island, New York CMSA	67,683	374.2	60	5,129	3,479	2,529	35,693	14	2,948	2,514	1,185	16,686
Los Angeles, California Anaheim, California Riverside, California CMSA	39,932	274.8	75	5,536	1,254	2,051	20,740	0	3,224	798	984	6,838
San Francisco, California Oakland, California San Jose, California CMSA	33,874	541.7	24	4,089	629	991	18,744	23	2,881	531	339	6,559
Washington, District of Columbia MSA	29,181	743.7	42	1,517	2,394	502	14,183	4	1,288	2,489	249	7,020
Chicago, Illinois Gary, Indiana Lake County, Illinois CMSA	27,517	341.2	9	1,371	1,183	734	15,806	7	692	1,201	238	6,890
Philadelphia, Pennsylvania Wilmington, Delaware Trenton, New Jersey CMSA	20,851	353.5	20	578	938	134	12,097	0	517	869	77	5,789
Boston, Massachusetts Lawrence, Massachusetts Salem, Massachusetts CMSA	20,012	479.7	17	759	400	172	11,793	16	536	215	123	6,209
Dallas, Texas Fort Worth, Texas CMSA	19,810	509.9	52	775	503	615	12,207	19	478	541	292	4,879
Minneapolis, Minnesota St. Paul, Minnesota MSA	13,530	549.1	22	336	96	34	9,022	14	155	83	24	3,802
Detroit, Michigan Ann Arbor, Michigan CMSA	13,054	279.8	5	266	690	71	8,037	8	218	517	39	3,256
Atlanta, Georgia MSA	13,006	459.0	11	366	885	122	7,437	8	235	800	27	3,220
Houston, Texas Galveston, Texas Brazoria, Texas CMSA	12,687	341.9	31	623	608	582	6,817	14	540	497	268	3,136
Denver, Colorado Boulder, Colorado CMSA	11,303	611.5	42	301	155	329	7,344	28	117	141	134	3,002
Seattle, Washington Tacoma, Washington CMSA	9,696	378.9	55	381	118	67	6,283	9	399	73	34	2,346
Baltimore, Maryland MSA	9,501	398.8	6	185	441	89	5,416	7	151	540	28	2,713
St. Louis, Missouri MSA	8,167	334.2	26	89	373	43	4,723	12	96	363	44	2,474
San Diego, California MSA	7,953	318.4	31	494	180	259	5,046	8	451	74	66	1,583
Cleveland, Ohio Akron, Ohio Lorain, Ohio CMSA	6,959	252.2	0	96	191	14	4,391	0	82	241	25	1,928
Raleigh, North Carolina Durham, North Carolina MSA	6,892	937.1	12	202	352	94	4,243	0	146	298	0	1,599
Phoenix, Arizona MSA	6,664	314.0	0	110	80	132	4,375	18	64	69	117	1,816
Miami, Florida Fort Lauderdale, Florida CMSA	6,587	206.3	0	156	209	1,242	4,029	0	69	220	637	1,776
Hartford, Connecticut New Britain, Connecticut Middletown, Connecticut CMSA	6,431	592.3	33	149	199	89	3,533	0	107	144	81	2,196
Kansas City, Missouri Kansas City, Kansas MSA	5,928	378.5	25	37	119	47	3,829	0	66	145	65	1,696
Austin, Texas MSA	5,893	754.0	19	313	211	273	3,573	5	112	78	154	1,337
Columbus, Ohio MSA	5,725	415.6	0	129	219	9	3,652	8	97	103	0	1,516

Source: Census of Population and Housing, 1990: Equal Employment Opportunity (EEO) File on CD-ROM [machine-readable datafiles]. Prepared by the Bureau of the Census. Washington, DC: The Bureau, 1992. *Notes:* "MSA" represents "metropolitan statistical area"; "CMSA" stands for "consolidated metropolitan statistical area."

★ 109 ★

Leading Occupations

Computer Systems Analysts and Scientists, by Metropolitan Area

According to the 1990 Census of Population and Housing, computer systems analysts and scientists ranked 71 among occupations employing the most people in the United States. Table presents the number of civilians 16 years old or older who reported working as computer systems analysts and scientists during the 1990 Census. Data show the total employment figures, employment per 100,000 population, and employment data for men and women of various races and ethnicities in the 25 metropolitan statistical areas with the largest concentrations of computer systems analysts and scientists.

[Total for all of the U.S. was 471,290; 189.5 per 100,000 persons]

Metropolitan area	Total employees	Employees per 100,000 population	Men					Women				
			American Indian, Eskimo & Aleut	Asian, Pacific Islander	Black	Hispanic	White	American Indian, Eskimo & Aleut	Asian, Pacific Islander	Black	Hispanic	White
New York, New York New Jersey (northern) Long Island, New York CMSA	43,156	238.6	23	3,252	2,010	1,301	23,913	53	1,135	1,711	655	10,517
San Francisco, California Oakland, California San Jose, California CMSA	31,697	506.9	18	5,016	548	792	17,585	8	2,121	394	374	5,666
Washington, District of Columbia MSA	29,690	756.7	55	1,351	2,321	551	15,504	22	606	2,034	271	7,519
Los Angeles, California Anaheim, California Riverside, California CMSA	28,172	193.9	129	3,266	883	1,107	14,609	29	1,608	734	521	6,193
Boston, Massachusetts Lawrence, Massachusetts Salem, Massachusetts CMSA	23,092	553.6	25	1,241	424	239	14,724	6	544	168	96	5,898
Chicago, Illinois Gary, Indiana Lake County, Illinois CMSA	19,819	245.7	4	1,185	772	305	11,712	0	454	687	168	4,911
Philadelphia, Pennsylvania Wilmington, Delaware Trenton, New Jersey CMSA	15,009	254.4	4	405	507	64	9,066	0	217	548	79	4,193
Dallas, Texas Fort Worth, Texas CMSA	13,968	359.5	28	651	466	328	8,748	14	181	334	75	3,389
Seattle, Washington Tacoma, Washington CMSA	11,659	455.6	23	699	109	119	7,457	13	270	108	81	2,895
Baltimore, Maryland MSA	9,496	398.6	31	230	513	121	5,393	15	73	303	50	2,893
Atlanta, Georgia MSA	9,295	328.0	15	314	510	68	5,443	0	135	473	16	2,405
Detroit, Michigan Ann Arbor, Michigan CMSA	9,044	193.9	12	349	309	47	5,344	5	94	298	26	2,601
Minneapolis, Minnesota St. Paul, Minnesota MSA	8,951	363.3	34	259	168	46	5,748	2	58	49	0	2,594
Houston, Texas Galveston, Texas Brazoria, Texas CMSA	8,918	240.3	28	507	312	300	5,423	5	317	195	70	1,980
Denver, Colorado Boulder, Colorado CMSA	7,887	426.7	14	172	83	234	5,048	4	78	98	86	2,259
San Diego, California MSA	7,053	282.3	32	305	76	283	4,631	10	256	26	159	1,632
Phoenix, Arizona MSA	5,751	271.0	9	162	66	148	3,896	4	122	41	39	1,429
St. Louis, Missouri MSA	5,529	226.2	7	175	137	44	3,364	0	19	220	29	1,607
Cleveland, Ohio Akron, Ohio Lorain, Ohio CMSA	4,845	175.6	0	105	120	22	3,122	13	30	164	26	1,291
Hartford, Connecticut New Britain, Connecticut Middletown, Connecticut CMSA	4,413	406.4	0	77	137	53	2,493	5	67	92	7	1,534
Portland, Oregon Vancouver, Washington CMSA	4,073	275.6	11	234	15	45	2,807	0	70	5	7	924
Columbus, Ohio MSA	3,882	281.8	7	156	195	18	2,475	0	25	71	7	953
Pittsburgh, Pennsylvania Beaver Valley, Pennsylvania CMSA	3,854	171.8	0	83	79	51	2,546	0	14	48	8	1,047
Raleigh, North Carolina Durham, North Carolina MSA	3,753	510.3	0	133	140	45	2,310	0	48	126	0	988
Cincinnati, Ohio Hamilton, Ohio CMSA	3,614	207.2	0	41	110	28	2,287	0	27	94	0	1,048

Source: Census of Population and Housing, 1990: Equal Employment Opportunity (EEO) File on CD-ROM [machine-readable datafiles]. Prepared by the Bureau of the Census. Washington, DC: The Bureau, 1992. *Notes:* "MSA" represents "metropolitan statistical area"; "CMSA" stands for "consolidated metropolitan statistical area."

★110★

Leading Occupations

Construction and Maintenance Painters, by Metropolitan Area

According to the 1990 Census of Population and Housing, construction and maintenance painters ranked 62 among occupations employing the most people in the United States. Table presents the number of civilians 16 years old or older who reported working as construction and maintenance painters during the 1990 Census. Data show the total employment figures, employment per 100,000 population, and employment data for men and women of various races and ethnicities in the 25 metropolitan statistical areas with the largest concentrations of construction and maintenance painters.

[Total for all of the U.S. was 559,026; 224.8 per 100,000 persons]

Metropolitan area	Total employees	Employees per 100,000 population	Men					Women				
			American Indian, Eskimo & Aleut	Asian, Pacific Islander	Black	Hispanic	White	American Indian, Eskimo & Aleut	Asian, Pacific Islander	Black	Hispanic	White
Los Angeles, California Anaheim, California Riverside, California CMSA	46,910	322.8	348	2,814	2,067	22,920	25,914	46	240	122	962	1,594
New York, New York New Jersey (northern) Long Island, New York CMSA	34,956	193.3	44	1,225	4,394	9,017	24,081	0	89	150	310	1,315
San Francisco, California Oakland, California San Jose, California CMSA	17,840	285.3	96	1,057	1,206	4,890	12,270	15	25	69	105	873
Chicago, Illinois Gary, Indiana Lake County, Illinois CMSA	16,867	209.1	61	146	1,843	2,172	12,489	0	31	65	172	658
Houston, Texas Galveston, Texas Brazoria, Texas CMSA	12,858	346.5	52	64	1,038	7,096	7,126	0	42	33	124	443
Dallas, Texas Fort Worth, Texas CMSA	11,679	300.6	72	66	869	3,709	7,628	2	26	23	118	547
Philadelphia, Pennsylvania Wilmington, Delaware Trenton, New Jersey CMSA	10,942	185.5	42	89	1,182	385	8,882	0	0	66	17	475
Washington, District of Columbia MSA	10,716	273.1	33	320	1,989	3,261	6,265	0	30	45	58	438
Boston, Massachusetts Lawrence, Massachusetts Salem, Massachusetts CMSA	9,465	226.9	12	87	483	508	8,048	13	27	41	21	573
Miami, Florida Fort Lauderdale, Florida CMSA	9,171	287.3	0	29	1,174	4,152	6,936	0	7	62	235	357
Atlanta, Georgia MSA	8,896	314.0	62	60	1,661	759	5,944	0	0	73	32	611
Detroit, Michigan Ann Arbor, Michigan CMSA	8,769	188.0	52	23	1,413	239	6,697	6	0	75	8	440
San Diego, California MSA	6,608	264.5	44	275	290	1,746	4,617	11	14	0	110	320
Seattle, Washington Tacoma, Washington CMSA	5,836	228.0	51	121	202	94	4,777	22	15	30	9	575
Tampa, Florida St. Petersburg, Florida Clearwater, Florida MSA	5,358	259.1	39	22	204	377	4,614	0	0	23	66	405
Cleveland, Ohio Akron, Ohio Lorain, Ohio CMSA	5,165	187.2	37	0	696	127	4,024	0	0	39	7	308
St. Louis, Missouri MSA	4,851	198.5	15	7	631	28	3,884	0	1	35	0	277
Baltimore, Maryland MSA	4,763	199.9	22	13	818	147	3,576	0	0	79	7	207
Minneapolis, Minnesota St. Paul, Minnesota MSA	4,702	190.8	40	6	156	67	4,072	6	5	0	18	371
Phoenix, Arizona MSA	4,676	220.4	142	21	63	822	3,684	21	0	9	13	274
Denver, Colorado Boulder, Colorado CMSA	4,132	223.6	42	27	206	616	3,215	0	0	0	3	384
Cincinnati, Ohio Hamilton, Ohio CMSA	3,887	222.9	0	0	264	7	3,360	0	0	7	0	256
Norfolk, Virginia Virginia Beach, Virginia Newport News, Virginia MSA	3,870	277.2	24	18	1,037	32	2,383	6	7	87	0	295
San Antonio, Texas MSA	3,817	293.1	6	0	105	2,686	2,407	11	0	0	44	120
Portland, Oregon Vancouver, Washington CMSA	3,665	248.0	35	103	111	164	3,047	0	26	6	6	262

Source: Census of Population and Housing, 1990: Equal Employment Opportunity (EEO) File on CD-ROM [machine-readable datafiles]. Prepared by the Bureau of the Census. Washington, DC: The Bureau, 1992. *Notes:* "MSA" represents "metropolitan statistical area"; "CMSA" stands for "consolidated metropolitan statistical area."

★ 111 ★
Leading Occupations

Construction Laborers, by Metropolitan Area

According to the 1990 Census of Population and Housing, construction laborers ranked 20 among occupations employing the most people in the United States. Table presents the number of civilians 16 years old or older who reported working as construction laborers during the 1990 Census. Data show the total employment figures, employment per 100,000 population, and employment data for men and women of various races and ethnicities in the 25 metropolitan statistical areas with the largest concentrations of construction laborers.

[Total for all of the U.S. was 1,149,780; 462.3 per 100,000 persons]

Metropolitan area	Total employees	Employees per 100,000 population	Men					Women				
			American Indian, Eskimo & Aleut	Asian, Pacific Islander	Black	Hispanic	White	American Indian, Eskimo & Aleut	Asian, Pacific Islander	Black	Hispanic	White
Los Angeles, California Anaheim, California Riverside, California CMSA	89,898	618.6	602	1,635	4,104	53,999	50,872	33	63	117	1,346	1,695
New York, New York New Jersey (northern) Long Island, New York CMSA	71,323	394.3	255	2,251	13,353	13,449	47,898	7	68	618	462	1,097
Chicago, Illinois Gary, Indiana Lake County, Illinois CMSA	32,222	399.5	213	128	4,654	6,592	22,414	7	6	249	127	611
San Francisco, California Oakland, California San Jose, California CMSA	29,853	477.4	247	1,755	2,486	10,534	19,059	0	68	150	266	670
Philadelphia, Pennsylvania Wilmington, Delaware Trenton, New Jersey CMSA	24,151	409.4	34	199	5,567	1,174	17,017	0	0	211	64	490
Houston, Texas Galveston, Texas Brazoria, Texas CMSA	22,862	616.1	146	177	3,751	11,203	11,272	11	16	177	373	588
Dallas, Texas Fort Worth, Texas CMSA	18,151	467.2	86	40	2,169	7,937	9,910	21	6	64	143	465
Washington, District of Columbia MSA	18,031	459.6	118	160	5,510	5,092	8,514	0	20	234	152	510
Miami, Florida Fort Lauderdale, Florida CMSA	16,763	525.1	47	26	4,978	6,894	10,088	0	0	116	258	406
San Diego, California MSA	15,290	612.1	205	213	499	6,110	10,500	0	59	33	184	427
Detroit, Michigan Ann Arbor, Michigan CMSA	14,776	316.7	142	15	2,439	600	11,135	5	0	183	22	519
Atlanta, Georgia MSA	14,520	512.4	49	74	5,353	1,159	7,738	23	23	104	7	418
Boston, Massachusetts Lawrence, Massachusetts Salem, Massachusetts CMSA	14,321	343.3	31	53	944	594	12,621	0	19	53	23	363
Seattle, Washington Tacoma, Washington CMSA	10,862	424.4	225	195	504	417	8,935	6	21	64	60	628
Baltimore, Maryland MSA	10,701	449.2	14	41	3,805	78	6,323	0	0	141	0	323
St. Louis, Missouri MSA	10,449	427.5	12	10	1,515	139	8,534	0	0	61	0	287
Cleveland, Ohio Akron, Ohio Lorain, Ohio CMSA	9,802	355.2	21	0	1,404	246	7,928	0	0	80	0	271
Pittsburgh, Pennsylvania Beaver Valley, Pennsylvania CMSA	9,768	435.5	13	23	758	40	8,656	0	4	34	0	280
Sacramento, California MSA	9,591	647.6	137	160	532	1,792	7,292	19	8	40	126	338
Phoenix, Arizona MSA	9,182	432.7	301	66	417	3,582	6,079	30	6	16	42	298
Tampa, Florida St. Petersburg, Florida Clearwater, Florida MSA	8,365	404.5	44	13	1,217	692	6,490	0	0	85	20	349
Minneapolis, Minnesota St. Paul, Minnesota MSA	7,761	315.0	68	41	161	103	7,148	0	8	15	0	247
Cincinnati, Ohio Hamilton, Ohio CMSA	7,377	423.0	14	4	1,067	22	5,978	0	12	40	0	246
Kansas City, Missouri Kansas City, Kansas MSA	7,142	456.0	47	22	888	205	5,818	3	0	42	0	223
Denver, Colorado Boulder, Colorado CMSA	6,841	370.1	80	34	261	1,976	5,027	16	0	0	124	268

Source: Census of Population and Housing, 1990: Equal Employment Opportunity (EEO) File on CD-ROM [machine-readable datafiles]. Prepared by the Bureau of the Census. Washington, DC: The Bureau, 1992. *Notes:* "MSA" represents "metropolitan statistical area"; "CMSA" stands for "consolidated metropolitan statistical area."

★ 112 ★

Leading Occupations

Construction Supervisors, by Metropolitan Area

According to the 1990 Census of Population and Housing, construction supervisors ranked 44 among occupations employing the most people in the United States. Table presents the number of civilians 16 years old or older who reported working as construction supervisors during the 1990 Census. Data show the total employment figures, employment per 100,000 population, and employment data for men and women of various races and ethnicities in the 25 metropolitan statistical areas with the largest concentrations of construction supervisors.

[Total for all of the U.S. was 652,964; 262.5 per 100,000 persons]

Metropolitan area	Total employees	Employees per 100,000 population	Men					Women				
			American Indian, Eskimo & Aleut	Asian, Pacific Islander	Black	Hispanic	White	American Indian, Eskimo & Aleut	Asian, Pacific Islander	Black	Hispanic	White
New York, New York New Jersey (northern) Long Island, New York CMSA	43,426	240.1	40	851	3,030	3,643	36,930	9	13	323	118	923
Los Angeles, California Anaheim, California Riverside, California CMSA	40,511	278.8	375	1,142	1,318	9,262	31,070	7	23	74	271	1,248
San Francisco, California Oakland, California San Jose, California CMSA	16,217	259.3	173	666	492	1,906	13,439	22	41	44	42	448
Philadelphia, Pennsylvania Wilmington, Delaware Trenton, New Jersey CMSA	15,147	256.8	38	41	1,317	177	13,358	0	0	43	27	257
Chicago, Illinois Gary, Indiana Lake County, Illinois CMSA	14,041	174.1	36	77	776	829	12,164	0	0	107	21	337
Houston, Texas Galveston, Texas Brazoria, Texas CMSA	12,039	324.4	53	110	748	2,462	8,420	0	0	48	33	304
Washington, District of Columbia MSA	12,038	306.8	51	138	1,778	795	9,162	0	40	113	34	398
Atlanta, Georgia MSA	10,612	374.5	49	28	1,152	228	8,852	0	0	88	0	342
Dallas, Texas Fort Worth, Texas CMSA	10,412	268.0	88	27	426	1,275	8,794	4	0	13	28	305
Boston, Massachusetts Lawrence, Massachusetts Salem, Massachusetts CMSA	10,359	248.3	31	66	266	62	9,679	0	13	35	0	252
Miami, Florida Fort Lauderdale, Florida CMSA	10,087	316.0	40	41	1,143	2,908	8,214	0	0	65	70	315
Detroit, Michigan Ann Arbor, Michigan CMSA	9,034	193.7	44	8	560	118	8,171	5	0	25	0	202
Baltimore, Maryland MSA	8,910	374.0	37	41	1,182	66	7,382	0	0	46	0	209
San Diego, California MSA	8,211	328.7	90	93	143	1,470	6,963	0	0	38	70	217
Seattle, Washington Tacoma, Washington CMSA	7,450	291.1	64	99	112	152	6,841	1	31	0	0	218
Phoenix, Arizona MSA	6,398	301.5	82	34	106	774	5,592	0	0	6	36	189
Tampa, Florida St. Petersburg, Florida Clearwater, Florida MSA	5,955	288.0	16	20	257	153	5,403	0	0	0	0	246
Sacramento, California MSA	5,076	342.7	58	61	84	363	4,492	0	7	10	14	172
Cleveland, Ohio Akron, Ohio Lorain, Ohio CMSA	4,951	179.4	12	11	307	64	4,414	0	6	40	0	128
Norfolk, Virginia Virginia Beach, Virginia Newport News, Virginia MSA	4,832	346.1	35	0	464	41	4,170	0	0	43	0	105
Pittsburgh, Pennsylvania Beaver Valley, Pennsylvania CMSA	4,811	214.5	2	7	127	40	4,617	0	0	0	0	53
Minneapolis, Minnesota St. Paul, Minnesota MSA	4,700	190.7	0	9	0	18	4,587	0	0	0	0	86
Denver, Colorado Boulder, Colorado CMSA	4,520	244.6	42	18	154	586	3,991	0	0	15	5	82
Orlando, Florida MSA	4,097	381.9	39	0	329	173	3,496	0	0	7	37	192
Cincinnati, Ohio Hamilton, Ohio CMSA	4,056	232.6	0	0	277	10	3,700	0	0	0	0	79

Source: Census of Population and Housing, 1990: Equal Employment Opportunity (EEO) File on CD-ROM [machine-readable datafiles]. Prepared by the Bureau of the Census. Washington, DC: The Bureau, 1992. *Notes:* "MSA" represents "metropolitan statistical area"; "CMSA" stands for "consolidated metropolitan statistical area."

★ 113 ★

Leading Occupations

Cooks, by Metropolitan Area

According to the 1990 Census of Population and Housing, cooks ranked 8 among occupations employing the most people in the United States. Table presents the number of civilians 16 years old or older who reported working as cooks during the 1990 Census. Data show the total employment figures, employment per 100,000 population, and employment data for men and women of various races and ethnicities in the 25 metropolitan statistical areas with the largest concentrations of cooks.

[Total for all of the U.S. was 2,073,260; 833.6 per 100,000 persons]

Metropolitan area	Total employees	Employees per 100,000 population	Men					Women				
			American Indian, Eskimo & Aleut	Asian, Pacific Islander	Black	Hispanic	White	American Indian, Eskimo & Aleut	Asian, Pacific Islander	Black	Hispanic	White
Los Angeles, California Anaheim, California Riverside, California CMSA	108,843	749.0	413	8,490	4,017	51,011	35,617	165	3,471	2,722	17,270	15,991
New York, New York New Jersey (northern) Long Island, New York CMSA	106,458	588.6	192	15,620	13,067	20,159	40,650	94	1,932	6,312	4,314	17,848
Chicago, Illinois Gary, Indiana Lake County, Illinois CMSA	58,721	728.0	127	2,615	9,428	13,057	18,708	47	880	5,780	2,560	12,625
San Francisco, California Oakland, California San Jose, California CMSA	48,001	767.6	203	8,807	2,359	10,553	14,946	184	3,450	1,405	4,471	9,459
Detroit, Michigan Ann Arbor, Michigan CMSA	38,066	816.0	137	962	6,519	576	13,963	93	208	4,063	277	11,719
Philadelphia, Pennsylvania Wilmington, Delaware Trenton, New Jersey CMSA	37,831	641.3	133	1,489	7,773	1,699	13,564	43	474	3,290	444	9,739
Dallas, Texas Fort Worth, Texas CMSA	32,915	847.1	116	876	5,171	7,279	9,626	58	455	4,175	2,598	6,366
Houston, Texas Galveston, Texas Brazoria, Texas CMSA	30,503	822.0	62	1,105	4,571	6,633	7,209	53	689	4,996	4,147	5,698
Boston, Massachusetts Lawrence, Massachusetts Salem, Massachusetts CMSA	29,330	703.1	45	2,919	1,635	1,927	14,337	13	353	419	720	8,414
Washington, District of Columbia MSA	27,769	707.8	54	2,360	5,247	3,911	7,185	35	1,613	3,784	1,983	4,414
Miami, Florida Fort Lauderdale, Florida CMSA	23,883	748.1	51	1,167	5,577	4,598	8,942	27	297	2,984	2,448	3,811
Atlanta, Georgia MSA	23,663	835.1	20	760	5,828	666	5,850	54	338	5,346	268	4,962
St. Louis, Missouri MSA	22,301	912.4	52	516	3,981	162	7,724	28	131	2,634	148	7,132
Cleveland, Ohio Akron, Ohio Lorain, Ohio CMSA	21,368	774.3	30	441	2,685	207	7,735	8	145	2,140	182	7,998
Minneapolis, Minnesota St. Paul, Minnesota MSA	20,603	836.1	177	551	839	411	10,042	81	330	302	116	8,048
San Diego, California MSA	20,196	808.5	74	1,622	901	6,829	7,706	34	724	424	1,889	3,391
Seattle, Washington Tacoma, Washington CMSA	20,017	782.2	221	2,133	902	851	8,286	198	944	442	263	6,407
Pittsburgh, Pennsylvania Beaver Valley, Pennsylvania CMSA	17,958	800.7	28	210	1,269	172	7,587	14	48	805	46	7,958
Baltimore, Maryland MSA	16,792	704.9	35	730	4,287	191	4,633	40	385	2,905	100	3,711
Phoenix, Arizona MSA	15,696	739.6	235	520	562	2,801	7,855	161	143	210	1,501	3,823
Tampa, Florida St. Petersburg, Florida Clearwater, Florida MSA	15,348	742.2	45	399	1,295	807	7,566	38	177	1,027	433	4,616
Denver, Colorado Boulder, Colorado CMSA	15,061	814.9	108	397	1,133	1,943	7,103	78	332	509	1,005	4,052
Cincinnati, Ohio Hamilton, Ohio CMSA	14,551	834.3	35	226	1,768	43	5,861	2	70	1,090	38	5,495
Kansas City, Missouri Kansas City, Kansas MSA	13,190	842.1	71	245	2,099	492	5,085	77	59	1,078	219	4,068
Milwaukee, Wisconsin Racine, Wisconsin CMSA	12,462	775.4	19	205	1,432	401	4,626	67	80	1,001	167	4,727

Source: Census of Population and Housing, 1990: Equal Employment Opportunity (EEO) File on CD-ROM [machine-readable datafiles]. Prepared by the Bureau of the Census. Washington, DC: The Bureau, 1992. *Notes:* "MSA" represents "metropolitan statistical area"; "CMSA" stands for "consolidated metropolitan statistical area."

★114★

Leading Occupations

Data Entry Keyers, by Metropolitan Area

According to the 1990 Census of Population and Housing, data entry keyers ranked 47 among occupations employing the most people in the United States. Table presents the number of civilians 16 years old or older who reported working as data entry keyers during the 1990 Census. Data show the total employment figures, employment per 100,000 population, and employment data for men and women of various races and ethnicities in the 25 metropolitan statistical areas with the largest concentrations of data entry keyers.

[Total for all of the U.S. was 639,265; 257.0 per 100,000 persons]

Metropolitan area	Total employees	Employees per 100,000 population	Men					Women				
			American Indian, Eskimo & Aleut	Asian, Pacific Islander	Black	Hispanic	White	American Indian, Eskimo & Aleut	Asian, Pacific Islander	Black	Hispanic	White
New York, New York New Jersey (northern) Long Island, New York CMSA	59,859	331.0	48	1,255	2,989	1,874	5,403	158	2,533	15,691	7,308	28,408
Los Angeles, California Anaheim, California Riverside, California CMSA	43,068	296.4	66	1,500	905	2,056	4,215	353	5,174	5,678	7,857	20,073
Chicago, Illinois Gary, Indiana Lake County, Illinois CMSA	29,015	359.7	0	229	813	469	2,194	63	1,187	7,030	2,219	16,180
Philadelphia, Pennsylvania Wilmington, Delaware Trenton, New Jersey CMSA	20,379	345.5	6	96	558	78	1,596	31	328	5,493	509	11,955
San Francisco, California Oakland, California San Jose, California CMSA	19,619	313.7	73	980	587	387	2,010	118	3,928	2,177	2,151	8,528
Dallas, Texas Fort Worth, Texas CMSA	15,532	399.8	0	153	375	89	1,444	142	207	3,164	1,292	9,330
Boston, Massachusetts Lawrence, Massachusetts Salem, Massachusetts CMSA	14,570	349.3	31	95	221	56	1,448	25	428	1,252	325	10,845
Washington, District of Columbia MSA	13,820	352.2	12	195	938	91	1,235	68	802	5,343	416	5,069
Minneapolis, Minnesota St. Paul, Minnesota MSA	11,778	478.0	17	18	56	26	1,427	62	249	378	142	9,523
Atlanta, Georgia MSA	11,276	398.0	0	38	532	43	869	10	106	4,388	102	5,298
Detroit, Michigan Ann Arbor, Michigan CMSA	11,015	236.1	6	40	280	17	920	50	116	2,704	73	6,863
Houston, Texas Galveston, Texas Brazoria, Texas CMSA	10,204	275.0	0	92	269	198	688	21	289	2,563	1,254	5,477
Miami, Florida Fort Lauderdale, Florida CMSA	8,873	277.9	9	16	203	506	866	10	81	1,848	2,953	5,520
Baltimore, Maryland MSA	8,405	352.8	0	21	449	0	572	8	146	3,025	106	4,179
Seattle, Washington Tacoma, Washington CMSA	8,141	318.1	0	118	66	48	986	39	871	475	157	5,508
Cleveland, Ohio Akron, Ohio Lorain, Ohio CMSA	7,560	273.9	8	21	185	6	421	6	22	1,562	127	5,318
Phoenix, Arizona MSA	7,427	350.0	37	42	81	133	827	279	49	315	1,094	5,127
St. Louis, Missouri MSA	7,403	302.9	3	0	207	3	580	4	67	1,567	31	4,969
Kansas City, Missouri Kansas City, Kansas MSA	7,356	469.7	0	11	168	6	620	38	56	1,316	218	5,037
Denver, Colorado Boulder, Colorado CMSA	6,997	378.6	2	35	86	46	941	39	123	583	784	4,807
Columbus, Ohio MSA	6,896	500.7	0	0	128	14	519	6	40	1,558	32	4,620
San Diego, California MSA	6,447	258.1	20	183	121	130	870	24	801	491	760	3,470
Cincinnati, Ohio Hamilton, Ohio CMSA	6,064	347.7	0	7	78	8	605	18	24	980	22	4,346
Tampa, Florida St. Petersburg, Florida Clearwater, Florida MSA	5,844	282.6	0	22	64	54	495	16	81	726	455	4,298
Milwaukee, Wisconsin Racine, Wisconsin CMSA	5,641	351.0	0	5	69	25	560	8	67	739	116	4,136

Source: Census of Population and Housing, 1990: Equal Employment Opportunity (EEO) File on CD-ROM [machine-readable datafiles]. Prepared by the Bureau of the Census. Washington, DC: The Bureau, 1992. *Notes:* "MSA" represents "metropolitan statistical area"; "CMSA" stands for "consolidated metropolitan statistical area."

★ 115 ★

Leading Occupations

Designers, by Metropolitan Area

According to the 1990 Census of Population and Housing, designers ranked 55 among occupations employing the most people in the United States. Table presents the number of civilians 16 years old or older who reported working as designers during the 1990 Census. Data show the total employment figures, employment per 100,000 population, and employment data for men and women of various races and ethnicities in the 25 metropolitan statistical areas with the largest concentrations of designers.

[Total for all of the U.S. was 596,802; 240.0 per 100,000 persons]

Metropolitan area	Total employees	Employees per 100,000 population	Men					Women				
			American Indian, Eskimo & Aleut	Asian, Pacific Islander	Black	Hispanic	White	American Indian, Eskimo & Aleut	Asian, Pacific Islander	Black	Hispanic	White
New York, New York New Jersey (northern) Long Island, New York CMSA	68,941	381.2	70	2,177	2,396	2,972	27,223	101	2,318	1,927	2,535	30,870
Los Angeles, California Anaheim, California Riverside, California CMSA	49,419	340.1	122	3,087	838	4,367	18,861	124	2,449	542	3,961	19,426
San Francisco, California Oakland, California San Jose, California CMSA	24,443	390.9	40	2,005	371	763	8,613	54	1,433	262	964	11,105
Chicago, Illinois Gary, Indiana Lake County, Illinois CMSA	23,094	286.3	12	458	550	485	9,462	13	399	511	387	11,320
Detroit, Michigan Ann Arbor, Michigan CMSA	16,470	353.0	9	220	457	111	9,877	26	103	325	81	5,412
Philadelphia, Pennsylvania Wilmington, Delaware Trenton, New Jersey CMSA	15,298	259.3	2	195	452	98	6,419	20	115	437	132	7,589
Boston, Massachusetts Lawrence, Massachusetts Salem, Massachusetts CMSA	14,107	338.2	11	163	95	124	6,178	8	215	154	156	7,189
Washington, District of Columbia MSA	12,578	320.6	7	352	656	266	3,962	6	291	484	311	6,623
Dallas, Texas Fort Worth, Texas CMSA	11,516	296.4	17	183	174	370	4,517	7	177	149	327	5,958
Houston, Texas Galveston, Texas Brazoria, Texas CMSA	10,170	274.1	11	372	451	515	4,386	13	220	197	541	4,122
Atlanta, Georgia MSA	9,732	343.5	0	51	450	81	3,921	0	48	376	29	4,872
Miami, Florida Fort Lauderdale, Florida CMSA	8,690	272.2	0	38	178	1,274	3,561	0	51	287	1,679	4,199
Seattle, Washington Tacoma, Washington CMSA	8,678	339.1	34	186	58	54	3,182	44	307	38	77	4,798
Minneapolis, Minnesota St. Paul, Minnesota MSA	8,601	349.1	2	80	31	20	3,994	6	39	11	29	4,434
San Diego, California MSA	7,376	295.3	62	318	95	309	2,771	41	216	45	428	3,519
Cleveland, Ohio Akron, Ohio Lorain, Ohio CMSA	6,508	235.8	7	19	132	45	2,982	0	12	63	20	3,273
Denver, Colorado Boulder, Colorado CMSA	5,930	320.8	22	24	30	110	2,430	10	33	38	143	3,236
St. Louis, Missouri MSA	5,871	240.2	7	41	113	2	2,444	6	9	73	43	3,168
Baltimore, Maryland MSA	5,815	244.1	0	82	150	23	2,319	0	65	242	46	2,953
Phoenix, Arizona MSA	5,612	264.5	20	72	66	197	2,590	21	22	63	158	2,622
Pittsburgh, Pennsylvania Beaver Valley, Pennsylvania CMSA	5,108	227.8	15	0	62	5	2,449	0	19	35	11	2,522
Tampa, Florida St. Petersburg, Florida Clearwater, Florida MSA	5,028	243.1	0	38	83	119	2,100	0	49	13	118	2,710
Portland, Oregon Vancouver, Washington CMSA	4,826	326.6	14	115	32	79	2,069	5	45	14	11	2,496
Cincinnati, Ohio Hamilton, Ohio CMSA	4,746	272.1	9	16	41	31	2,349	0	12	88	42	2,220
Milwaukee, Wisconsin Racine, Wisconsin CMSA	4,454	277.1	3	34	42	33	2,142	12	0	35	26	2,167

Source: Census of Population and Housing, 1990: Equal Employment Opportunity (EEO) File on CD-ROM [machine-readable datafiles]. Prepared by the Bureau of the Census. Washington, DC: The Bureau, 1992. *Notes:* "MSA" represents "metropolitan statistical area"; "CMSA" stands for "consolidated metropolitan statistical area."

★116★
Leading Occupations

Drafting Occupations, by Metropolitan Area

According to the 1990 Census of Population and Housing, drafting occupations ranked 101 among occupations employing the most people in the United States. Table presents the number of civilians 16 years old or older who reported working in drafting occupations during the 1990 Census. Data show the total employment figures, employment per 100,000 population, and employment data for men and women of various races and ethnicities in the 25 metropolitan statistical areas with the largest concentrations of drafting occupations.

[Total for all of the U.S. was 324,764; 130.6 per 100,000 persons]

Metropolitan area	Total employees	Employees per 100,000 population	Men American Indian, Eskimo & Aleut	Men Asian, Pacific Islander	Men Black	Men Hispanic	Men White	Women American Indian, Eskimo & Aleut	Women Asian, Pacific Islander	Women Black	Women Hispanic	Women White
Los Angeles, California Anaheim, California Riverside, California CMSA	20,628	142.0	65	3,020	647	3,316	11,375	30	693	158	395	2,958
New York, New York New Jersey (northern) Long Island, New York CMSA	18,823	104.1	0	1,089	1,273	1,622	12,054	18	266	340	416	3,143
Detroit, Michigan Ann Arbor, Michigan CMSA	12,091	259.2	12	145	441	109	9,986	20	31	90	16	1,341
San Francisco, California Oakland, California San Jose, California CMSA	11,378	182.0	51	1,754	384	893	5,917	19	627	90	166	2,104
Chicago, Illinois Gary, Indiana Lake County, Illinois CMSA	9,817	121.7	3	506	631	458	6,666	13	192	113	108	1,484
Houston, Texas Galveston, Texas Brazoria, Texas CMSA	9,338	251.6	28	371	585	1,164	6,152	15	112	152	224	1,378
Philadelphia, Pennsylvania Wilmington, Delaware Trenton, New Jersey CMSA	8,295	140.6	2	174	581	74	6,143	0	43	107	37	1,211
Boston, Massachusetts Lawrence, Massachusetts Salem, Massachusetts CMSA	6,987	167.5	7	124	188	95	5,282	0	77	60	12	1,210
Seattle, Washington Tacoma, Washington CMSA	6,538	255.5	29	399	146	137	4,275	12	157	29	25	1,433
Washington, District of Columbia MSA	6,266	159.7	12	323	726	342	3,738	6	93	217	116	1,023
Dallas, Texas Fort Worth, Texas CMSA	6,077	156.4	44	141	217	421	4,246	3	69	109	82	967
Pittsburgh, Pennsylvania Beaver Valley, Pennsylvania CMSA	5,115	228.1	0	26	91	8	4,425	5	12	34	18	514
Minneapolis, Minnesota St. Paul, Minnesota MSA	4,689	190.3	25	56	27	33	3,981	0	5	10	0	574
Cleveland, Ohio Akron, Ohio Lorain, Ohio CMSA	4,108	148.9	4	63	159	27	3,339	0	3	84	9	420
St. Louis, Missouri MSA	3,958	161.9	0	7	213	24	3,050	0	0	39	4	649
Baltimore, Maryland MSA	3,859	162.0	0	77	383	33	2,743	0	13	61	18	564
Atlanta, Georgia MSA	3,745	132.2	13	65	472	57	2,324	0	6	152	25	684
San Diego, California MSA	3,743	149.8	21	252	177	469	2,189	3	40	6	128	757
Denver, Colorado Boulder, Colorado CMSA	3,695	199.9	21	56	68	226	2,459	0	10	13	60	926
Milwaukee, Wisconsin Racine, Wisconsin CMSA	3,154	196.2	14	57	96	35	2,539	0	10	44	12	386
Phoenix, Arizona MSA	3,063	144.3	60	94	48	191	2,077	6	6	9	39	639
Miami, Florida Fort Lauderdale, Florida CMSA	2,830	88.64	7	41	168	889	1,924	0	0	32	325	549
Tampa, Florida St. Petersburg, Florida Clearwater, Florida MSA	2,711	131.1	15	28	62	185	1,970	0	13	22	31	594
Cincinnati, Ohio Hamilton, Ohio CMSA	2,500	143.3	8	32	124	55	2,081	0	0	18	0	237
Kansas City, Missouri Kansas City, Kansas MSA	2,291	146.3	10	9	90	23	1,730	0	10	57	15	355

Source: Census of Population and Housing, 1990: Equal Employment Opportunity (EEO) File on CD-ROM [machine-readable datafiles]. Prepared by the Bureau of the Census. Washington, DC: The Bureau, 1992. *Notes:* "MSA" represents "metropolitan statistical area"; "CMSA" stands for "consolidated metropolitan statistical area."

★ 117 ★

Leading Occupations

Early Childhood Teachers' Assistants, by Metropolitan Area

According to the 1990 Census of Population and Housing, early childhood teachers' assistants ranked 95 among occupations employing the most people in the United States. Table presents the number of civilians 16 years old or older who reported working as early childhood teachers' assistants during the 1990 Census. Data show the total employment figures, employment per 100,000 population, and employment data for men and women of various races and ethnicities in the 25 metropolitan statistical areas with the largest concentrations of early childhood teachers' assistants.

[Total for all of the U.S. was 338,928; 136.3 per 100,000 persons]

Metropolitan area	Total employees	Employees per 100,000 population	Men					Women				
			American Indian, Eskimo & Aleut	Asian, Pacific Islander	Black	Hispanic	White	American Indian, Eskimo & Aleut	Asian, Pacific Islander	Black	Hispanic	White
New York, New York New Jersey (northern) Long Island, New York CMSA	19,395	107.2	11	35	564	201	506	45	360	5,835	2,770	10,811
Los Angeles, California Anaheim, California Riverside, California CMSA	13,633	93.82	11	61	132	254	653	86	677	1,284	3,873	8,858
Philadelphia, Pennsylvania Wilmington, Delaware Trenton, New Jersey CMSA	9,234	156.5	0	0	83	24	182	18	70	2,219	287	6,484
San Francisco, California Oakland, California San Jose, California CMSA	8,337	133.3	4	51	71	114	349	42	718	975	1,293	5,562
Chicago, Illinois Gary, Indiana Lake County, Illinois CMSA	7,433	92.16	0	5	328	75	208	9	64	1,346	467	5,148
Dallas, Texas Fort Worth, Texas CMSA	7,148	184.0	0	7	37	23	109	61	82	1,107	680	5,355
Washington, District of Columbia MSA	7,046	179.6	7	17	123	8	162	16	213	1,787	616	4,463
Boston, Massachusetts Lawrence, Massachusetts Salem, Massachusetts CMSA	6,027	144.5	0	0	49	17	233	6	53	407	331	5,119
Detroit, Michigan Ann Arbor, Michigan CMSA	6,003	128.7	0	0	88	0	169	7	20	1,152	89	4,561
Houston, Texas Galveston, Texas Brazoria, Texas CMSA	5,833	157.2	0	0	31	55	130	21	55	1,297	889	3,874
Atlanta, Georgia MSA	5,422	191.4	0	0	71	10	102	29	14	1,438	49	3,717
Minneapolis, Minnesota St. Paul, Minnesota MSA	4,988	202.4	0	3	19	0	198	13	54	176	44	4,513
Seattle, Washington Tacoma, Washington CMSA	4,548	177.7	0	14	22	2	126	44	228	316	148	3,747
Miami, Florida Fort Lauderdale, Florida CMSA	4,243	132.9	0	0	78	43	211	15	0	1,200	1,038	2,602
Denver, Colorado Boulder, Colorado CMSA	3,711	200.8	0	0	18	25	86	0	54	240	431	3,150
St. Louis, Missouri MSA	3,402	139.2	0	0	58	6	97	2	35	696	36	2,497
San Diego, California MSA	3,312	132.6	0	16	17	29	63	20	117	260	733	2,388
Baltimore, Maryland MSA	3,215	135.0	0	8	74	0	49	0	44	933	57	2,092
Cleveland, Ohio Akron, Ohio Lorain, Ohio CMSA	2,762	100.1	0	8	33	16	93	0	8	557	41	2,049
Tampa, Florida St. Petersburg, Florida Clearwater, Florida MSA	2,692	130.2	0	0	3	18	95	6	7	445	320	2,071
San Antonio, Texas MSA	2,687	206.4	0	0	16	70	88	5	0	223	1,296	1,821
Phoenix, Arizona MSA	2,650	124.9	0	0	0	19	24	59	47	47	392	2,307
Charlotte, North Carolina Gastonia, North Carolina Rock Hill, South Carolina MSA	2,533	218.0	0	0	16	0	45	0	0	564	13	1,902
Kansas City, Missouri Kansas City, Kansas MSA	2,404	153.5	6	0	0	0	84	10	0	330	36	1,952
Pittsburgh, Pennsylvania Beaver Valley, Pennsylvania CMSA	2,371	105.7	0	0	32	0	43	0	9	345	6	1,942

Source: Census of Population and Housing, 1990: Equal Employment Opportunity (EEO) File on CD-ROM [machine-readable datafiles]. Prepared by the Bureau of the Census. Washington, DC: The Bureau, 1992. *Notes:* "MSA" represents "metropolitan statistical area"; "CMSA" stands for "consolidated metropolitan statistical area."

★118★

Leading Occupations

Education Administrators, by Metropolitan Area

According to the 1990 Census of Population and Housing, education administrators ranked 52 among occupations employing the most people in the United States. Table presents the number of civilians 16 years old or older who reported working as education administrators during the 1990 Census. Data show the total employment figures, employment per 100,000 population, and employment data for men and women of various races and ethnicities in the 25 metropolitan statistical areas with the largest concentrations of education and related administrators.

[Total for all of the U.S. was 623,612; 250.7 per 100,000 persons]

Metropolitan area	Total employees	Employees per 100,000 population	Men					Women				
			American Indian, Eskimo & Aleut	Asian, Pacific Islander	Black	Hispanic	White	American Indian, Eskimo & Aleut	Asian, Pacific Islander	Black	Hispanic	White
New York, New York New Jersey (northern) Long Island, New York CMSA	46,982	259.8	24	683	2,319	1,257	18,260	65	593	4,757	1,411	19,364
Los Angeles, California Anaheim, California Riverside, California CMSA	32,632	224.6	55	794	1,260	1,552	10,730	140	1,045	2,545	2,903	14,341
Chicago, Illinois Gary, Indiana Lake County, Illinois CMSA	18,257	226.4	0	126	1,153	351	6,570	16	183	2,222	541	7,591
San Francisco, California Oakland, California San Jose, California CMSA	17,975	287.5	16	472	448	601	5,681	61	687	1,032	881	9,006
Philadelphia, Pennsylvania Wilmington, Delaware Trenton, New Jersey CMSA	16,356	277.3	0	96	1,086	152	6,493	27	110	1,592	150	6,874
Boston, Massachusetts Lawrence, Massachusetts Salem, Massachusetts CMSA	16,344	391.8	4	196	397	110	6,272	12	150	643	242	8,537
Washington, District of Columbia MSA	13,491	343.8	21	206	1,494	166	3,691	23	165	2,046	164	5,769
Detroit, Michigan Ann Arbor, Michigan CMSA	10,346	221.8	13	59	844	28	3,876	30	97	1,156	124	4,232
Dallas, Texas Fort Worth, Texas CMSA	9,619	247.6	6	54	393	192	3,565	11	30	708	383	4,558
Houston, Texas Galveston, Texas Brazoria, Texas CMSA	8,615	232.1	4	140	604	227	2,678	16	119	1,052	400	3,704
Baltimore, Maryland MSA	7,736	324.8	0	31	641	43	2,616	8	18	1,150	22	3,272
Atlanta, Georgia MSA	7,343	259.2	0	45	561	13	2,468	9	33	1,096	31	3,106
Minneapolis, Minnesota St. Paul, Minnesota MSA	7,020	284.9	11	41	125	51	2,881	43	29	134	40	3,722
Miami, Florida Fort Lauderdale, Florida CMSA	6,974	218.4	0	28	639	506	2,354	6	12	821	842	3,043
Seattle, Washington Tacoma, Washington CMSA	6,756	264.0	12	110	138	67	2,444	58	152	162	105	3,619
San Diego, California MSA	6,159	246.6	20	85	225	165	2,175	21	119	159	329	3,158
St. Louis, Missouri MSA	6,082	248.8	0	48	431	37	2,375	5	70	495	31	2,628
Cleveland, Ohio Akron, Ohio Lorain, Ohio CMSA	5,872	212.8	21	57	315	14	2,422	0	22	572	13	2,455
Denver, Colorado Boulder, Colorado CMSA	5,339	288.9	8	13	49	174	2,126	21	16	153	188	2,832
Pittsburgh, Pennsylvania Beaver Valley, Pennsylvania CMSA	5,206	232.1	0	49	135	34	2,428	0	30	159	12	2,385
Phoenix, Arizona MSA	4,402	207.4	60	33	112	188	1,475	11	19	142	125	2,402
Columbus, Ohio MSA	4,249	308.5	3	61	138	8	1,844	19	38	292	5	1,854
Cincinnati, Ohio Hamilton, Ohio CMSA	3,818	218.9	0	16	154	0	1,638	0	6	164	8	1,840
Tampa, Florida St. Petersburg, Florida Clearwater, Florida MSA	3,785	183.0	0	0	123	91	1,470	6	11	243	152	1,881
Sacramento, California MSA	3,752	253.3	24	89	88	120	1,388	18	78	141	227	1,808

Source: Census of Population and Housing, 1990: Equal Employment Opportunity (EEO) File on CD-ROM [machine-readable datafiles]. Prepared by the Bureau of the Census. Washington, DC: The Bureau, 1992. *Notes:* "MSA" represents "metropolitan statistical area"; "CMSA" stands for "consolidated metropolitan statistical area."

★ 119 ★

Leading Occupations

Electrical and Electronic Engineers, by Metropolitan Area

According to the 1990 Census of Population and Housing, electrical and electronic engineers ranked 72 among occupations employing the most people in the United States. Table presents the number of civilians 16 years old or older who reported working as electrical and electronic engineers during the 1990 Census. Data show the total employment figures, employment per 100,000 population, and employment data for men and women of various races and ethnicities in the 25 metropolitan statistical areas with the largest concentrations of electrical and electronic engineers.

[Total for all of the U.S. was 467,023; 187.8 per 100,000 persons]

Metropolitan area	Total employees	Employees per 100,000 population	Men					Women				
			American Indian, Eskimo & Aleut	Asian, Pacific Islander	Black	Hispanic	White	American Indian, Eskimo & Aleut	Asian, Pacific Islander	Black	Hispanic	White
New York, New York New Jersey (northern) Long Island, New York CMSA	35,976	198.9	58	3,430	2,212	1,480	25,770	9	499	479	256	3,065
Los Angeles, California Anaheim, California Riverside, California CMSA	35,413	243.7	87	6,047	1,097	2,083	23,806	51	746	292	276	2,493
San Francisco, California Oakland, California San Jose, California CMSA	33,432	534.6	109	7,381	656	1,180	21,018	0	1,171	204	248	2,408
Boston, Massachusetts Lawrence, Massachusetts Salem, Massachusetts CMSA	19,831	475.4	18	998	441	347	16,461	6	104	27	17	1,698
Washington, District of Columbia MSA	18,509	471.7	40	1,358	1,303	554	13,262	8	242	442	57	1,698
Chicago, Illinois Gary, Indiana Lake County, Illinois CMSA	17,213	213.4	13	1,522	1,088	371	12,647	0	113	347	52	1,315
Dallas, Texas Fort Worth, Texas CMSA	15,990	411.5	37	816	504	576	12,701	4	70	198	37	1,448
Philadelphia, Pennsylvania Wilmington, Delaware Trenton, New Jersey CMSA	11,539	195.6	20	610	480	104	9,384	0	94	167	0	762
Detroit, Michigan Ann Arbor, Michigan CMSA	9,557	204.9	5	524	399	102	7,380	0	59	135	7	1,033
Baltimore, Maryland MSA	8,823	370.4	21	189	453	189	7,247	0	35	156	38	656
Phoenix, Arizona MSA	8,253	388.9	54	572	169	307	6,645	0	72	7	24	610
Houston, Texas Galveston, Texas Brazoria, Texas CMSA	7,378	198.8	12	626	319	380	5,513	0	101	153	26	521
San Diego, California MSA	7,220	289.0	24	750	195	224	5,431	0	131	23	51	560
Atlanta, Georgia MSA	6,636	234.2	15	279	431	153	4,781	0	26	233	16	825
Seattle, Washington Tacoma, Washington CMSA	6,474	253.0	40	420	58	50	5,315	6	102	8	0	514
Minneapolis, Minnesota St. Paul, Minnesota MSA	6,297	255.6	2	167	155	15	5,417	0	24	29	0	496
Denver, Colorado Boulder, Colorado CMSA	6,286	340.1	15	181	84	183	5,208	0	38	27	39	673
St. Louis, Missouri MSA	5,098	208.6	0	111	203	46	4,293	0	22	72	0	379
Cleveland, Ohio Akron, Ohio Lorain, Ohio CMSA	4,435	160.7	0	150	182	37	3,742	0	0	64	8	287
Portland, Oregon Vancouver, Washington CMSA	4,086	276.5	13	305	53	54	3,366	0	28	17	0	289
Pittsburgh, Pennsylvania Beaver Valley, Pennsylvania CMSA	3,961	176.6	0	88	62	19	3,462	0	0	7	2	322
Miami, Florida Fort Lauderdale, Florida CMSA	3,779	118.4	7	199	218	820	2,882	0	20	16	174	390
Melbourne, Florida Titusville, Florida Palm Bay, Florida MSA	3,743	938.2	16	73	80	120	3,340	0	0	17	14	210
Austin, Texas MSA	3,652	467.3	9	262	54	127	2,941	0	38	14	9	281
Raleigh, North Carolina Durham, North Carolina MSA	3,647	495.9	7	168	242	39	2,864	0	10	23	7	320

Source: Census of Population and Housing, 1990: Equal Employment Opportunity (EEO) File on CD-ROM [machine-readable datafiles]. Prepared by the Bureau of the Census. Washington, DC: The Bureau, 1992. *Notes:* "MSA" represents "metropolitan statistical area"; "CMSA" stands for "consolidated metropolitan statistical area."

★ 120 ★

Leading Occupations

Electrical and Electronic Equipment Assemblers, by Metropolitan Area

According to the 1990 Census of Population and Housing, electrical and electronic equipment assemblers ranked 102 among occupations employing the most people in the United States. Table presents the number of civilians 16 years old or older who reported working as electrical and electronic equipment assemblers during the 1990 Census. Data show the total employment figures, employment per 100,000 population, and employment data for men and women of various races and ethnicities in the 25 metropolitan statistical areas with the largest concentrations of electrical and electronic equipment assemblers.

[Total for all of the U.S. was 309,406; 124.4 per 100,000 persons]

Metropolitan area	Total employees	Employees per 100,000 population	Men					Women				
			American Indian, Eskimo & Aleut	Asian, Pacific Islander	Black	Hispanic	White	American Indian, Eskimo & Aleut	Asian, Pacific Islander	Black	Hispanic	White
Los Angeles, California Anaheim, California Riverside, California CMSA	29,587	203.6	39	2,490	511	5,863	4,289	163	4,858	1,002	9,863	7,819
San Francisco, California Oakland, California San Jose, California CMSA	19,166	306.5	19	3,790	287	1,603	2,044	82	6,415	416	2,984	3,922
New York, New York New Jersey (northern) Long Island, New York CMSA	15,248	84.30	8	457	1,005	1,633	3,622	8	879	1,648	3,109	5,640
Chicago, Illinois Gary, Indiana Lake County, Illinois CMSA	11,883	147.3	24	386	789	1,417	1,839	19	865	1,061	2,506	4,702
Boston, Massachusetts Lawrence, Massachusetts Salem, Massachusetts CMSA	10,635	254.9	0	446	178	390	2,285	25	873	310	712	5,958
Dallas, Texas Fort Worth, Texas CMSA	8,275	213.0	9	474	357	393	1,190	77	679	1,953	889	2,807
Philadelphia, Pennsylvania Wilmington, Delaware Trenton, New Jersey CMSA	5,504	93.30	7	188	306	46	1,338	0	365	737	181	2,442
Phoenix, Arizona MSA	5,337	251.5	24	127	149	386	965	85	383	198	1,030	2,673
San Diego, California MSA	5,130	205.4	2	663	76	474	607	23	2,080	290	582	829
Milwaukee, Wisconsin Racine, Wisconsin CMSA	4,161	258.9	9	22	158	48	1,352	26	89	528	141	1,908
Cleveland, Ohio Akron, Ohio Lorain, Ohio CMSA	3,602	130.5	0	27	150	31	1,102	0	45	462	39	1,768
Minneapolis, Minnesota St. Paul, Minnesota MSA	3,592	145.8	0	229	78	14	1,099	44	278	56	2	1,797
Portland, Oregon Vancouver, Washington CMSA	3,097	209.6	26	221	16	89	839	45	354	35	60	1,475
Atlanta, Georgia MSA	2,862	101.0	0	68	262	38	536	6	186	689	60	1,051
Louisville, Kentucky MSA	2,775	291.3	0	0	219	6	1,344	8	6	311	2	887
Seattle, Washington Tacoma, Washington CMSA	2,749	107.4	18	248	52	20	604	10	502	34	98	1,238
Tampa, Florida St. Petersburg, Florida Clearwater, Florida MSA	2,634	127.4	4	61	96	37	602	9	116	367	153	1,305
Detroit, Michigan Ann Arbor, Michigan CMSA	2,274	48.74	9	18	231	27	762	12	74	199	60	933
Miami, Florida Fort Lauderdale, Florida CMSA	2,142	67.09	0	35	52	302	434	0	35	312	961	1,089
Houston, Texas Galveston, Texas Brazoria, Texas CMSA	2,134	57.50	16	137	152	229	432	0	246	345	313	575
Washington, District of Columbia MSA	2,090	53.27	0	184	69	28	220	0	703	228	70	654
Kansas City, Missouri Kansas City, Kansas MSA	2,052	131.0	0	33	87	56	526	0	66	290	24	1,005
Baltimore, Maryland MSA	1,961	82.32	0	35	237	20	480	10	10	475	10	714
Denver, Colorado Boulder, Colorado CMSA	1,852	100.2	6	136	44	57	418	0	202	65	326	818
Raleigh, North Carolina Durham, North Carolina MSA	1,783	242.4	0	31	256	7	248	6	48	644	11	550

Source: Census of Population and Housing, 1990: Equal Employment Opportunity (EEO) File on CD-ROM [machine-readable datafiles]. Prepared by the Bureau of the Census. Washington, DC: The Bureau, 1992. *Notes:* "MSA" represents "metropolitan statistical area"; "CMSA" stands for "consolidated metropolitan statistical area."

★ 121 ★

Leading Occupations

Electrical and Electronic Technicians, by Metropolitan Area

According to the 1990 Census of Population and Housing, electrical and electronic technicians ranked 84 among occupations employing the most people in the United States. Table presents the number of civilians 16 years old or older who reported working as electrical and electronic technicians during the 1990 Census. Data show the total employment figures, employment per 100,000 population, and employment data for men and women of various races and ethnicities in the 25 metropolitan statistical areas with the largest concentrations of electrical and electronic technicians.

[Total for all of the U.S. was 401,463; 161.4 per 100,000 persons]

Metropolitan area	Total employees	Employees per 100,000 population	Men					Women				
			American Indian, Eskimo & Aleut	Asian, Pacific Islander	Black	Hispanic	White	American Indian, Eskimo & Aleut	Asian, Pacific Islander	Black	Hispanic	White
New York, New York New Jersey (northern) Long Island, New York CMSA	26,512	146.6	61	1,635	2,962	2,332	17,703	0	150	753	510	2,205
Los Angeles, California Anaheim, California Riverside, California CMSA	25,766	177.3	137	4,318	1,552	3,441	14,155	26	813	414	754	2,415
San Francisco, California Oakland, California San Jose, California CMSA	20,635	330.0	120	4,868	969	1,432	10,308	23	1,271	318	519	1,997
Chicago, Illinois Gary, Indiana Lake County, Illinois CMSA	11,890	147.4	29	437	1,173	682	8,040	0	184	419	119	1,251
Boston, Massachusetts Lawrence, Massachusetts Salem, Massachusetts CMSA	11,428	273.9	18	360	434	214	8,477	16	103	89	100	1,721
Dallas, Texas Fort Worth, Texas CMSA	10,546	271.4	87	470	824	627	7,324	7	67	296	65	1,087
Philadelphia, Pennsylvania Wilmington, Delaware Trenton, New Jersey CMSA	9,140	154.9	13	315	747	134	6,664	5	17	246	54	1,036
Washington, District of Columbia MSA	8,941	227.9	34	569	1,444	292	5,105	0	120	687	29	910
San Diego, California MSA	7,441	297.9	34	870	457	842	4,867	2	169	17	76	567
Houston, Texas Galveston, Texas Brazoria, Texas CMSA	7,299	196.7	10	379	696	835	4,838	11	71	177	92	681
Minneapolis, Minnesota St. Paul, Minnesota MSA	6,987	283.6	8	245	86	36	5,653	0	29	30	3	923
Detroit, Michigan Ann Arbor, Michigan CMSA	6,356	136.2	6	118	480	62	4,905	0	14	129	0	685
Phoenix, Arizona MSA	6,191	291.7	42	139	152	389	4,531	21	61	28	183	893
Seattle, Washington Tacoma, Washington CMSA	5,822	227.5	37	355	213	126	4,415	4	53	21	14	665
Atlanta, Georgia MSA	5,751	203.0	9	43	967	81	3,784	0	25	258	20	596
Baltimore, Maryland MSA	4,966	208.5	5	58	630	88	3,528	0	22	196	14	501
Miami, Florida Fort Lauderdale, Florida CMSA	4,627	144.9	0	74	471	1,139	3,185	10	7	150	150	580
Cleveland, Ohio Akron, Ohio Lorain, Ohio CMSA	4,235	153.5	0	42	225	23	3,402	0	0	161	0	393
Tampa, Florida St. Petersburg, Florida Clearwater, Florida MSA	4,055	196.1	8	67	145	261	3,271	16	6	85	19	418
Denver, Colorado Boulder, Colorado CMSA	4,001	216.5	4	113	75	275	3,050	0	24	38	54	607
Norfolk, Virginia Virginia Beach, Virginia Newport News, Virginia MSA	3,581	256.5	6	82	303	91	2,758	0	18	98	24	290
Sacramento, California MSA	3,388	228.8	6	232	83	265	2,414	7	47	33	70	409
Portland, Oregon Vancouver, Washington CMSA	3,344	226.3	12	208	35	71	2,382	2	52	4	23	637
St. Louis, Missouri MSA	3,036	124.2	0	44	80	51	2,511	0	5	107	0	276
Pittsburgh, Pennsylvania Beaver Valley, Pennsylvania CMSA	2,844	126.8	0	19	79	0	2,523	0	0	8	7	208

Source: Census of Population and Housing, 1990: Equal Employment Opportunity (EEO) File on CD-ROM [machine-readable datafiles]. Prepared by the Bureau of the Census. Washington, DC: The Bureau, 1992. *Notes:* "MSA" represents "metropolitan statistical area"; "CMSA" stands for "consolidated metropolitan statistical area."

★ 122 ★

Leading Occupations

Electricians, by Metropolitan Area

According to the 1990 Census of Population and Housing, electricians ranked 49 among occupations employing the most people in the United States. Table presents the number of civilians 16 years old or older who reported working as electricians during the 1990 Census. Data show the total employment figures, employment per 100,000 population, and employment data for men and women of various races and ethnicities in the 25 metropolitan statistical areas with the largest concentrations of electricians, excluding apprentices.

[Total for all of the U.S. was 635,017; 255.3 per 100,000 persons]

Metropolitan area	Total employees	Employees per 100,000 population	Men					Women				
			American Indian, Eskimo & Aleut	Asian, Pacific Islander	Black	Hispanic	White	American Indian, Eskimo & Aleut	Asian, Pacific Islander	Black	Hispanic	White
New York, New York New Jersey (northern) Long Island, New York CMSA	45,758	253.0	56	754	5,371	4,415	36,499	0	31	360	237	831
Los Angeles, California Anaheim, California Riverside, California CMSA	34,732	239.0	229	1,908	2,167	8,300	24,855	13	94	158	369	741
Chicago, Illinois Gary, Indiana Lake County, Illinois CMSA	21,030	260.7	59	233	2,102	1,308	17,563	0	0	58	58	334
Philadelphia, Pennsylvania Wilmington, Delaware Trenton, New Jersey CMSA	15,915	269.8	35	156	1,088	245	14,019	0	0	196	10	295
San Francisco, California Oakland, California San Jose, California CMSA	13,281	212.4	106	1,271	683	1,337	10,106	19	76	45	84	416
Boston, Massachusetts Lawrence, Massachusetts Salem, Massachusetts CMSA	11,676	279.9	15	109	233	133	11,033	0	4	0	7	203
Houston, Texas Galveston, Texas Brazoria, Texas CMSA	11,011	296.7	2	211	841	1,679	8,731	0	22	51	13	248
Detroit, Michigan Ann Arbor, Michigan CMSA	10,676	228.8	45	33	888	167	9,369	0	0	96	11	185
Washington, District of Columbia MSA	8,997	229.3	36	134	2,075	385	6,340	0	8	101	0	88
Miami, Florida Fort Lauderdale, Florida CMSA	8,882	278.2	18	94	1,118	3,308	7,188	0	14	44	52	113
Dallas, Texas Fort Worth, Texas CMSA	8,560	220.3	84	134	523	822	7,184	12	6	49	17	107
Seattle, Washington Tacoma, Washington CMSA	7,604	297.1	85	446	282	188	6,401	15	4	15	16	294
Atlanta, Georgia MSA	7,018	247.7	17	126	927	77	5,715	0	0	54	0	133
Baltimore, Maryland MSA	6,764	283.9	17	23	846	67	5,635	0	0	74	0	149
Cleveland, Ohio Akron, Ohio Lorain, Ohio CMSA	6,699	242.7	12	0	522	88	5,996	0	0	24	0	138
San Diego, California MSA	5,885	235.6	67	479	318	638	4,503	0	49	16	29	95
St. Louis, Missouri MSA	5,684	232.6	0	19	425	79	5,070	2	0	11	0	140
Pittsburgh, Pennsylvania Beaver Valley, Pennsylvania CMSA	5,309	236.7	11	0	244	19	4,931	0	0	7	0	99
Minneapolis, Minnesota St. Paul, Minnesota MSA	5,248	213.0	33	31	63	27	4,974	0	9	6	0	114
Norfolk, Virginia Virginia Beach, Virginia Newport News, Virginia MSA	5,003	358.4	30	110	869	135	3,729	0	14	47	14	158
Phoenix, Arizona MSA	4,923	232.0	96	46	68	519	4,417	9	0	0	4	89
Cincinnati, Ohio Hamilton, Ohio CMSA	4,740	271.8	6	3	246	13	4,330	0	0	43	0	108
Tampa, Florida St. Petersburg, Florida Clearwater, Florida MSA	4,487	217.0	22	24	147	245	4,164	0	0	8	0	91
Charlotte, North Carolina Gastonia, North Carolina Rock Hill, South Carolina MSA	4,080	351.1	9	0	235	7	3,773	0	0	0	0	63
Denver, Colorado Boulder, Colorado CMSA	3,805	205.9	22	28	104	359	3,372	0	17	0	5	63

Source: Census of Population and Housing, 1990: Equal Employment Opportunity (EEO) File on CD-ROM [machine-readable datafiles]. Prepared by the Bureau of the Census. Washington, DC: The Bureau, 1992. *Notes:* "MSA" represents "metropolitan statistical area"; "CMSA" stands for "consolidated metropolitan statistical area."

★ 123 ★

Leading Occupations

Elementary School Teachers, by Metropolitan Area

According to the 1990 Census of Population and Housing, elementary school teachers ranked 3 among occupations employing the most people in the United States. Table presents the number of civilians 16 years old or older who reported working as elementary school teachers during the 1990 Census. Data show the total employment figures, employment per 100,000 population, and employment data for men and women of various races and ethnicities in the 25 metropolitan statistical areas with the largest concentrations of elementary school teachers.

[Total for all of the U.S. was 3,024,189; 1,216 per 100,000 persons]

Metropolitan area	Total employees	Employees per 100,000 population	Men American Indian, Eskimo & Aleut	Men Asian, Pacific Islander	Men Black	Men Hispanic	Men White	Women American Indian, Eskimo & Aleut	Women Asian, Pacific Islander	Women Black	Women Hispanic	Women White
New York, New York New Jersey (northern) Long Island, New York CMSA	242,325	1,340	87	927	6,818	3,065	50,997	230	2,666	25,208	12,490	150,266
Los Angeles, California Anaheim, California Riverside, California CMSA	149,863	1,031	190	1,614	3,056	4,745	26,861	427	6,712	11,390	16,702	90,695
Chicago, Illinois Gary, Indiana Lake County, Illinois CMSA	90,162	1,118	35	242	3,674	682	14,110	104	701	15,540	2,764	54,268
Philadelphia, Pennsylvania Wilmington, Delaware Trenton, New Jersey CMSA	73,091	1,239	12	105	2,384	158	14,369	81	237	10,650	1,003	44,800
San Francisco, California Oakland, California San Jose, California CMSA	64,685	1,034	69	900	950	1,166	12,039	192	3,725	3,417	3,696	41,823
Detroit, Michigan Ann Arbor, Michigan CMSA	53,906	1,155	8	106	1,688	94	10,722	115	198	7,649	309	33,289
Boston, Massachusetts Lawrence, Massachusetts Salem, Massachusetts CMSA	49,694	1,191	7	172	508	166	10,926	21	345	1,506	791	35,789
Houston, Texas Galveston, Texas Brazoria, Texas CMSA	49,320	1,329	38	85	1,480	445	6,483	77	275	7,197	3,030	32,454
Dallas, Texas Fort Worth, Texas CMSA	47,425	1,221	13	82	1,057	301	6,235	114	144	4,909	2,002	33,920
Washington, District of Columbia MSA	46,609	1,188	11	93	2,206	125	5,450	72	704	9,198	640	28,710
Atlanta, Georgia MSA	36,348	1,283	0	23	1,437	21	3,504	28	94	6,985	197	24,246
Miami, Florida Fort Lauderdale, Florida CMSA	34,666	1,086	13	29	1,454	1,113	5,420	48	153	6,076	5,863	20,962
Cleveland, Ohio Akron, Ohio Lorain, Ohio CMSA	30,732	1,114	5	11	642	68	6,176	25	89	2,870	158	20,829
St. Louis, Missouri MSA	29,945	1,225	9	16	934	42	4,824	14	66	4,379	167	19,681
Minneapolis, Minnesota St. Paul, Minnesota MSA	29,641	1,203	66	78	146	83	7,505	113	109	380	183	21,177
Baltimore, Maryland MSA	28,903	1,213	5	55	1,120	51	4,899	46	109	5,800	170	16,844
Seattle, Washington Tacoma, Washington CMSA	27,900	1,090	71	231	297	91	6,500	98	693	637	261	19,285
San Diego, California MSA	26,490	1,060	50	200	328	558	4,667	139	384	1,053	2,369	18,475
Pittsburgh, Pennsylvania Beaver Valley, Pennsylvania CMSA	23,716	1,057	0	4	240	11	6,983	12	36	961	47	15,475
Denver, Colorado Boulder, Colorado CMSA	23,651	1,280	7	82	259	356	4,811	40	149	610	1,364	17,010
Phoenix, Arizona MSA	22,881	1,078	31	35	80	500	4,588	115	180	418	1,521	16,522
Tampa, Florida St. Petersburg, Florida Clearwater, Florida MSA	21,287	1,029	18	16	341	152	3,862	31	31	2,117	941	14,763
Kansas City, Missouri Kansas City, Kansas MSA	20,746	1,325	12	17	360	35	3,295	13	61	2,030	204	14,854
Milwaukee, Wisconsin Racine, Wisconsin CMSA	20,473	1,274	2	20	367	55	4,388	5	111	1,277	229	14,186
Cincinnati, Ohio Hamilton, Ohio CMSA	19,067	1,093	0	12	300	15	3,395	11	70	1,449	106	13,809

Source: Census of Population and Housing, 1990: Equal Employment Opportunity (EEO) File on CD-ROM [machine-readable datafiles]. Prepared by the Bureau of the Census. Washington, DC: The Bureau, 1992. *Notes:* "MSA" represents "metropolitan statistical area"; "CMSA" stands for "consolidated metropolitan statistical area."

★ 124 ★

Leading Occupations

Engineers, by Metropolitan Area

According to the 1990 Census of Population and Housing, engineers ranked 94 among occupations employing the most people in the United States. Table presents the number of civilians 16 years old or older who reported working as engineers during the 1990 Census. Data show the total employment figures, employment per 100,000 population, and employment data for men and women of various races and ethnicities in the 25 metropolitan statistical areas with the largest concentrations of miscellaneous engineers. See also tables for specific types of engineers such as electrical and electronic engineers.

[Total for all of the U.S. was 341,963; 137.5 per 100,000 persons]

Metropolitan area	Total employees	Employees per 100,000 population	Men					Women				
			American Indian, Eskimo & Aleut	Asian, Pacific Islander	Black	Hispanic	White	American Indian, Eskimo & Aleut	Asian, Pacific Islander	Black	Hispanic	White
New York, New York New Jersey (northern) Long Island, New York CMSA	25,659	141.9	6	2,517	1,070	954	18,446	0	317	308	160	2,698
Los Angeles, California Anaheim, California Riverside, California CMSA	21,978	151.2	66	4,165	652	1,257	14,461	18	441	137	128	1,378
San Francisco, California Oakland, California San Jose, California CMSA	17,705	283.1	34	3,556	306	774	11,352	6	469	92	170	1,600
Washington, District of Columbia MSA	13,332	339.8	21	1,109	899	305	9,851	0	82	241	28	1,080
Boston, Massachusetts Lawrence, Massachusetts Salem, Massachusetts CMSA	13,271	318.1	0	660	165	176	10,919	9	198	54	39	1,245
Chicago, Illinois Gary, Indiana Lake County, Illinois CMSA	12,970	160.8	21	1,035	531	278	9,917	0	74	110	59	1,136
Philadelphia, Pennsylvania Wilmington, Delaware Trenton, New Jersey CMSA	11,626	197.1	8	805	495	217	9,106	0	58	55	50	1,024
Detroit, Michigan Ann Arbor, Michigan CMSA	8,454	181.2	19	535	308	73	6,920	0	26	70	0	570
Houston, Texas Galveston, Texas Brazoria, Texas CMSA	7,181	193.5	7	693	291	235	5,473	0	19	43	47	548
Baltimore, Maryland MSA	6,396	268.5	23	246	272	83	5,076	0	52	80	30	593
Dallas, Texas Fort Worth, Texas CMSA	6,295	162.0	0	312	250	217	5,078	8	40	12	7	519
Minneapolis, Minnesota St. Paul, Minnesota MSA	4,837	196.3	21	158	38	10	4,320	8	19	12	10	249
Atlanta, Georgia MSA	4,678	165.1	9	236	252	65	3,617	0	43	34	40	457
Denver, Colorado Boulder, Colorado CMSA	4,476	242.2	14	81	32	116	3,803	0	0	23	47	465
Cleveland, Ohio Akron, Ohio Lorain, Ohio CMSA	4,426	160.4	0	213	97	48	3,727	0	0	46	12	327
Rochester, New York MSA	4,400	438.9	6	150	104	35	3,527	0	7	39	5	557
San Diego, California MSA	4,329	173.3	6	386	103	244	3,280	5	56	0	18	399
Seattle, Washington Tacoma, Washington CMSA	4,308	168.3	6	275	83	58	3,345	0	95	25	0	468
Pittsburgh, Pennsylvania Beaver Valley, Pennsylvania CMSA	4,182	186.5	0	182	72	31	3,486	0	12	18	0	400
Cincinnati, Ohio Hamilton, Ohio CMSA	3,215	184.3	0	99	64	9	2,676	0	6	49	6	321
St. Louis, Missouri MSA	3,155	129.1	16	105	137	50	2,605	0	8	32	18	213
Norfolk, Virginia Virginia Beach, Virginia Newport News, Virginia MSA	3,147	225.4	0	94	232	28	2,606	0	10	8	7	185
Phoenix, Arizona MSA	2,802	132.0	16	165	43	165	2,313	0	6	0	29	235
Dayton, Ohio Springfield, Ohio MSA	2,517	264.6	5	129	111	30	2,094	0	6	45	0	114
Columbus, Ohio MSA	2,514	182.5	16	144	81	16	2,043	0	0	33	10	197

Source: Census of Population and Housing, 1990: Equal Employment Opportunity (EEO) File on CD-ROM [machine-readable datafiles]. Prepared by the Bureau of the Census. Washington, DC: The Bureau, 1992. *Notes:* "MSA" represents "metropolitan statistical area"; "CMSA" stands for "consolidated metropolitan statistical area."

★ 125 ★

Leading Occupations

Family Child Care Providers, by Metropolitan Area

According to the 1990 Census of Population and Housing, family child care providers ranked 78 among occupations employing the most people in the United States. Table presents the number of civilians 16 years old or older who reported working as family child care providers during the 1990 Census. Data show the total employment figures, employment per 100,000 population, and employment data for men and women of various races and ethnicities in the 25 metropolitan statistical areas with the largest concentrations of family child care providers.

[Total for all of the U.S. was 434,643; 174.8 per 100,000 persons]

Metropolitan area	Total employees	Employees per 100,000 population	Men					Women				
			American Indian, Eskimo & Aleut	Asian, Pacific Islander	Black	Hispanic	White	American Indian, Eskimo & Aleut	Asian, Pacific Islander	Black	Hispanic	White
Los Angeles, California Anaheim, California Riverside, California CMSA	22,627	155.7	0	18	90	165	196	161	1,218	1,001	9,680	14,702
New York, New York New Jersey (northern) Long Island, New York CMSA	15,080	83.37	0	29	109	46	232	78	832	3,764	3,173	8,785
San Francisco, California Oakland, California San Jose, California CMSA	13,384	214.0	0	31	75	78	236	106	1,077	933	2,795	9,799
Washington, District of Columbia MSA	10,430	265.8	0	0	56	0	38	74	642	1,674	1,319	7,285
Minneapolis, Minnesota St. Paul, Minnesota MSA	9,655	391.8	0	0	0	0	92	73	64	99	113	9,266
Chicago, Illinois Gary, Indiana Lake County, Illinois CMSA	8,656	107.3	0	0	49	6	103	2	191	1,199	864	6,672
Dallas, Texas Fort Worth, Texas CMSA	7,164	184.4	5	0	9	5	82	43	62	426	696	6,127
Boston, Massachusetts Lawrence, Massachusetts Salem, Massachusetts CMSA	6,051	145.1	0	0	18	11	53	8	127	458	343	5,264
Denver, Colorado Boulder, Colorado CMSA	5,931	320.9	0	0	14	6	70	42	89	187	555	5,325
Seattle, Washington Tacoma, Washington CMSA	5,931	231.8	0	0	5	0	104	28	179	183	187	5,378
Houston, Texas Galveston, Texas Brazoria, Texas CMSA	5,898	158.9	0	0	17	15	75	51	129	860	1,389	4,150
San Diego, California MSA	5,232	209.5	0	0	0	15	92	41	312	354	1,187	3,928
Detroit, Michigan Ann Arbor, Michigan CMSA	5,112	109.6	0	0	8	0	36	31	24	644	63	4,355
Philadelphia, Pennsylvania Wilmington, Delaware Trenton, New Jersey CMSA	4,978	84.38	0	0	21	7	66	23	30	860	194	3,876
Portland, Oregon Vancouver, Washington CMSA	4,814	325.7	0	0	0	0	100	53	26	110	105	4,481
Baltimore, Maryland MSA	4,782	200.7	0	0	17	0	6	0	61	1,120	42	3,558
Kansas City, Missouri Kansas City, Kansas MSA	4,780	305.2	0	0	0	0	48	56	62	172	94	4,398
Phoenix, Arizona MSA	4,628	218.1	0	0	6	0	67	55	46	52	508	4,159
St. Louis, Missouri MSA	4,466	182.7	0	7	0	0	40	19	24	397	23	3,979
Atlanta, Georgia MSA	3,953	139.5	0	0	10	0	42	0	19	744	86	3,116
Sacramento, California MSA	3,691	249.2	0	0	9	9	59	45	188	177	349	3,104
Norfolk, Virginia Virginia Beach, Virginia Newport News, Virginia MSA	3,404	243.8	0	0	6	0	0	14	51	704	76	2,588
Columbus, Ohio MSA	3,030	220.0	0	0	0	0	6	11	23	198	15	2,792
Salt Lake City, Utah Ogden, Utah MSA	2,930	273.3	0	0	0	0	17	11	24	4	143	2,810
Indianapolis, Indiana MSA	2,867	229.4	0	0	0	0	5	5	6	182	32	2,658

Source: Census of Population and Housing, 1990: Equal Employment Opportunity (EEO) File on CD-ROM [machine-readable datafiles]. Prepared by the Bureau of the Census. Washington, DC: The Bureau, 1992. *Notes:* "MSA" represents "metropolitan statistical area"; "CMSA" stands for "consolidated metropolitan statistical area."

★ 126 ★
Leading Occupations

Farm Workers, by Metropolitan Area

According to the 1990 Census of Population and Housing, farm workers ranked 30 among occupations employing the most people in the United States. Table presents the number of civilians 16 years old or older who reported working as farm workers during the 1990 Census. Data show the total employment figures, employment per 100,000 population, and employment data for men and women of various races and ethnicities in the 25 metropolitan statistical areas with the largest concentrations of farm workers.

[Total for all of the U.S. was 759,669; 305.4 per 100,000 persons]

Metropolitan area	Total employees	Employees per 100,000 population	Men					Women				
			American Indian, Eskimo & Aleut	Asian, Pacific Islander	Black	Hispanic	White	American Indian, Eskimo & Aleut	Asian, Pacific Islander	Black	Hispanic	White
Los Angeles, California Anaheim, California Riverside, California CMSA	29,318	201.8	99	347	404	19,561	11,155	25	90	108	6,238	3,825
Fresno, California MSA	19,555	2,930	66	251	86	15,223	6,100	10	107	0	2,598	816
Visalia, California Tulare, California Porterville, California MSA	15,609	5,004	30	371	11	10,568	4,655	0	189	0	2,535	706
Bakersfield, California MSA	14,961	2,753	64	766	94	9,270	2,285	33	561	0	3,272	686
Salinas, California Seaside, California Monterey, California MSA	13,437	3,778	34	276	10	9,401	2,511	15	51	17	3,333	1,023
San Francisco, California Oakland, California San Jose, California CMSA	12,859	205.6	35	272	160	8,348	5,547	30	112	28	2,084	1,687
McAllen, Texas Edinburg, Texas Mission, Texas MSA	7,893	2,058	13	7	18	5,456	3,776	4	20	0	2,295	1,537
Stockton, California MSA	7,599	1,581	14	540	45	5,228	4,311	9	88	0	847	746
Yakima, Washington MSA	6,980	3,697	88	39	0	4,689	1,650	14	0	0	996	328
Merced, California MSA	6,368	3,569	24	89	30	4,182	2,593	7	42	5	743	390
Tampa, Florida St. Petersburg, Florida Clearwater, Florida MSA	5,791	280.0	28	46	259	2,827	2,677	18	39	108	1,212	1,297
Modesto, California MSA	5,592	1,509	18	90	0	3,208	2,311	9	41	0	726	455
Santa Barbara, California Santa Maria, California Lompoc, California MSA	5,564	1,505	0	89	15	3,958	1,257	8	6	0	1,133	440
New York, New York New Jersey (northern) Long Island, New York CMSA	4,889	27.03	8	180	519	982	2,345	0	87	66	128	1,259
Miami, Florida Fort Lauderdale, Florida CMSA	4,657	145.9	2	16	847	2,066	1,754	0	22	583	647	656
Phoenix, Arizona MSA	4,603	216.9	160	24	102	3,102	2,010	8	0	0	317	281
San Diego, California MSA	4,548	182.1	92	164	57	3,173	2,428	0	75	6	380	445
Philadelphia, Pennsylvania Wilmington, Delaware Trenton, New Jersey CMSA	4,399	74.57	17	9	387	1,063	2,486	6	4	80	42	914
West Palm Beach, Florida Boca Raton, Florida Delray Beach, Florida MSA	4,010	464.4	36	20	1,052	1,894	1,711	0	0	492	281	289
Portland, Oregon Vancouver, Washington CMSA	3,666	248.1	75	19	56	1,733	1,918	10	4	6	223	522
Sacramento, California MSA	3,536	238.7	16	91	48	1,959	1,379	6	67	28	400	415
Richland, Washington Kennewick, Washington Pasco, Washington MSA	3,355	2236	15	9	0	2,130	1,174	0	0	0	608	261
Dallas, Texas Fort Worth, Texas CMSA	3,094	79.63	42	41	129	1,032	1,586	5	0	49	124	405
Chicago, Illinois Gary, Indiana Lake County, Illinois CMSA	3,075	38.12	0	24	131	917	1,739	0	16	0	110	584
Lexington-Fayette, Kentucky MSA	2,964	850.7	8	0	125	111	2,184	7	5	28	0	525

Source: Census of Population and Housing, 1990: Equal Employment Opportunity (EEO) File on CD-ROM [machine-readable datafiles]. Prepared by the Bureau of the Census. Washington, DC: The Bureau, 1992. *Notes:* "MSA" represents "metropolitan statistical area"; "CMSA" stands for "consolidated metropolitan statistical area."

★ 127 ★

Leading Occupations

Farmers, by Metropolitan Area

According to the 1990 Census of Population and Housing, farmers ranked 27 among occupations employing the most people in the United States. Table presents the number of civilians 16 years old or older who reported working as farmers during the 1990 Census. Data show the total employment figures, employment per 100,000 population, and employment data for men and women of various races and ethnicities in the 25 metropolitan statistical areas with the largest concentrations of farmers, excluding horticultural farmers.

[Total for all of the U.S. was 795,187; 319.7 per 100,000 persons]

Metropolitan area	Total employees	Employees per 100,000 population	Men					Women				
			American Indian, Eskimo & Aleut	Asian, Pacific Islander	Black	Hispanic	White	American Indian, Eskimo & Aleut	Asian, Pacific Islander	Black	Hispanic	White
Los Angeles, California Anaheim, California Riverside, California CMSA	4,651	32.01	21	252	43	953	2,441	17	121	0	214	1,047
Minneapolis, Minnesota St. Paul, Minnesota MSA	4,527	183.7	0	0	9	10	3,698	0	0	0	0	818
San Francisco, California Oakland, California San Jose, California CMSA	3,487	55.76	10	165	17	430	2,300	8	31	0	86	738
Lancaster, Pennsylvania MSA	3,314	783.8	0	0	0	9	2,836	0	0	0	0	471
Chicago, Illinois Gary, Indiana Lake County, Illinois CMSA	3,139	38.92	0	4	18	5	2,595	0	0	0	0	521
Philadelphia, Pennsylvania Wilmington, Delaware Trenton, New Jersey CMSA	3,109	52.70	0	11	36	26	2,423	6	12	28	0	582
St. Cloud, Minnesota MSA	3,069	1,607	0	0	0	0	2,477	0	0	0	0	592
Dallas, Texas Fort Worth, Texas CMSA	2,928	75.36	11	10	45	91	2,287	8	0	0	13	486
New York, New York New Jersey (northern) Long Island, New York CMSA	2,861	15.82	6	57	18	72	2,057	0	0	0	22	704
Kansas City, Missouri Kansas City, Kansas MSA	2,843	181.5	0	0	8	4	2,481	6	0	5	0	343
St. Louis, Missouri MSA	2,752	112.6	0	0	3	10	2,415	0	0	7	0	327
Fresno, California MSA	2,718	407.2	7	283	7	343	1,911	0	24	0	75	253
Portland, Oregon Vancouver, Washington CMSA	2,597	175.7	35	18	7	56	1,934	0	7	0	0	566
Detroit, Michigan Ann Arbor, Michigan CMSA	2,483	53.22	1	0	0	3	1,974	0	2	7	4	499
Columbus, Ohio MSA	2,431	176.5	0	5	12	0	2,203	0	0	0	0	211
Appleton, Wisconsin Oshkosh, Wisconsin Neenah, Wisconsin MSA	2,362	749.6	0	0	0	4	1,793	0	0	0	0	567
Washington, District of Columbia MSA	2,310	58.87	7	17	50	0	1,645	0	7	10	5	574
Wausau, Wisconsin MSA	2,257	1,956	0	2	0	0	1,696	0	0	0	0	559
Nashville, Tennessee MSA	2,120	215.2	0	0	81	7	1,812	0	0	0	0	227
Eau Claire, Wisconsin MSA	2,085	1,516	0	0	2	0	1,602	0	0	0	0	481
Indianapolis, Indiana MSA	2,075	166.0	0	0	10	6	1,861	6	0	0	0	198
Houston, Texas Galveston, Texas Brazoria, Texas CMSA	1,995	53.76	8	17	73	44	1,533	0	0	13	0	347
Rochester, New York MSA	1,994	198.9	12	0	2	5	1,736	0	2	0	0	237
Visalia, California Tulare, California Porterville, California MSA	1,963	629.3	9	125	0	267	1,447	4	14	0	41	118
Madison, Wisconsin MSA	1,947	530.4	0	0	0	0	1,557	0	0	0	3	387

Source: Census of Population and Housing, 1990: Equal Employment Opportunity (EEO) File on CD-ROM [machine-readable datafiles]. Prepared by the Bureau of the Census. Washington, DC: The Bureau, 1992. *Notes:* "MSA" represents "metropolitan statistical area"; "CMSA" stands for "consolidated metropolitan statistical area."

★ 128 ★
Leading Occupations

Financial Managers, by Metropolitan Area

According to the 1990 Census of Population and Housing, financial managers ranked 48 among occupations employing the most people in the United States. Table presents the number of civilians 16 years old or older who reported working as financial managers during the 1990 Census. Data show the total employment figures, employment per 100,000 population, and employment data for men and women of various races and ethnicities in the 25 metropolitan statistical areas with the largest concentrations of financial managers.

[Total for all of the U.S. was 635,911; 255.7 per 100,000 persons]

Metropolitan area	Total employees	Employees per 100,000 population	Men					Women				
			American Indian, Eskimo & Aleut	Asian, Pacific Islander	Black	Hispanic	White	American Indian, Eskimo & Aleut	Asian, Pacific Islander	Black	Hispanic	White
New York, New York New Jersey (northern) Long Island, New York CMSA	87,557	484.1	44	3,442	3,101	2,387	43,925	91	1,590	4,307	2,304	29,814
Los Angeles, California Anaheim, California Riverside, California CMSA	42,758	294.2	96	2,747	920	1,996	17,508	101	2,071	1,326	2,317	16,243
Chicago, Illinois Gary, Indiana Lake County, Illinois CMSA	26,311	326.2	19	544	633	339	13,808	15	262	1,196	430	9,583
San Francisco, California Oakland, California San Jose, California CMSA	24,801	396.6	16	1,538	364	753	10,163	63	1,844	576	758	9,744
Philadelphia, Pennsylvania Wilmington, Delaware Trenton, New Jersey CMSA	20,713	351.1	0	179	497	120	10,847	6	107	776	110	8,210
Boston, Massachusetts Lawrence, Massachusetts Salem, Massachusetts CMSA	19,786	474.3	0	177	238	121	10,079	19	145	376	156	8,645
Washington, District of Columbia MSA	16,500	420.5	8	423	933	272	7,239	3	386	1,154	245	6,227
Dallas, Texas Fort Worth, Texas CMSA	13,552	348.8	19	132	260	283	7,297	12	49	386	268	5,198
Detroit, Michigan Ann Arbor, Michigan CMSA	11,683	250.4	11	64	259	22	5,860	0	35	668	29	4,786
Atlanta, Georgia MSA	11,457	404.3	6	130	492	101	5,408	7	48	651	9	4,708
Miami, Florida Fort Lauderdale, Florida CMSA	11,009	344.8	15	117	148	1,846	5,252	16	80	378	1,663	4,773
Houston, Texas Galveston, Texas Brazoria, Texas CMSA	10,046	270.7	6	229	200	250	5,221	17	77	395	321	3,715
Minneapolis, Minnesota St. Paul, Minnesota MSA	8,492	344.6	23	61	79	39	4,858	20	14	39	23	3,396
Seattle, Washington Tacoma, Washington CMSA	8,089	316.1	7	214	71	82	3,691	15	193	62	102	3,793
Baltimore, Maryland MSA	7,965	334.4	10	44	235	27	3,649	6	66	451	50	3,483
San Diego, California MSA	7,116	284.9	0	119	83	155	2,916	19	194	158	224	3,497
Cleveland, Ohio Akron, Ohio Lorain, Ohio CMSA	7,002	253.7	0	24	107	41	3,949	14	25	197	11	2,661
Phoenix, Arizona MSA	6,811	321.0	12	50	39	174	3,293	13	52	42	253	3,165
Denver, Colorado Boulder, Colorado CMSA	6,359	344.0	8	99	39	96	3,386	11	64	40	131	2,649
Pittsburgh, Pennsylvania Beaver Valley, Pennsylvania CMSA	6,118	272.8	5	12	81	1	3,418	0	0	110	2	2,492
St. Louis, Missouri MSA	6,104	249.7	0	1	35	19	3,531	0	17	225	10	2,295
Tampa, Florida St. Petersburg, Florida Clearwater, Florida MSA	5,644	272.9	0	22	83	154	2,600	7	4	46	173	2,868
Columbus, Ohio MSA	4,677	339.6	0	22	94	17	2,495	0	16	87	24	1,963
Hartford, Connecticut New Britain, Connecticut Middletown, Connecticut CMSA	4,657	428.9	0	37	173	39	2,261	0	35	87	50	2,021
Cincinnati, Ohio Hamilton, Ohio CMSA	4,611	264.4	9	14	66	0	2,499	2	0	86	13	1,935

Source: Census of Population and Housing, 1990: Equal Employment Opportunity (EEO) File on CD-ROM [machine-readable datafiles]. Prepared by the Bureau of the Census. Washington, DC: The Bureau, 1992. *Notes:* "MSA" represents "metropolitan statistical area"; "CMSA" stands for "consolidated metropolitan statistical area."

★ 129 ★

Leading Occupations

Financial Officers, by Metropolitan Area

According to the 1990 Census of Population and Housing, financial officers ranked 38 among occupations employing the most people in the United States. Table presents the number of civilians 16 years old or older who reported working as financial officers during the 1990 Census. Data show the total employment figures, employment per 100,000 population, and employment data for men and women of various races and ethnicities in the 25 metropolitan statistical areas with the largest concentrations of financial officers.

[Total for all of the U.S. was 679,275; 273.1 per 100,000 persons]

Metropolitan area	Total employees	Employees per 100,000 population	Men					Women				
			American Indian, Eskimo & Aleut	Asian, Pacific Islander	Black	Hispanic	White	American Indian, Eskimo & Aleut	Asian, Pacific Islander	Black	Hispanic	White
New York, New York New Jersey (northern) Long Island, New York CMSA	64,410	356.1	48	1,960	2,282	1,772	31,157	60	1,164	3,736	2,149	22,867
Los Angeles, California Anaheim, California Riverside, California CMSA	49,834	342.9	36	2,746	1,299	2,713	18,845	117	2,658	2,324	3,942	19,114
Chicago, Illinois Gary, Indiana Lake County, Illinois CMSA	26,795	332.2	13	369	725	343	12,060	32	316	1,511	775	11,382
San Francisco, California Oakland, California San Jose, California CMSA	24,675	394.6	34	1,161	586	614	9,579	75	2,098	1,029	1,045	9,603
Washington, District of Columbia MSA	19,368	493.6	20	321	1,023	309	7,621	94	371	2,290	309	7,514
Boston, Massachusetts Lawrence, Massachusetts Salem, Massachusetts CMSA	16,842	403.7	9	157	233	120	7,946	0	185	368	156	7,883
Philadelphia, Pennsylvania Wilmington, Delaware Trenton, New Jersey CMSA	16,826	285.2	0	110	525	68	8,221	0	144	1,067	102	6,663
Dallas, Texas Fort Worth, Texas CMSA	14,343	369.2	20	60	233	287	7,146	31	110	606	349	5,924
Atlanta, Georgia MSA	11,197	395.2	12	45	531	54	5,088	0	19	1,093	47	4,403
Detroit, Michigan Ann Arbor, Michigan CMSA	10,880	233.2	0	41	348	56	4,827	10	48	798	60	4,761
Houston, Texas Galveston, Texas Brazoria, Texas CMSA	10,805	291.2	4	141	211	254	4,985	30	123	625	477	4,349
San Diego, California MSA	9,791	392.0	26	197	211	162	3,878	41	310	313	462	4,588
Miami, Florida Fort Lauderdale, Florida CMSA	8,968	280.9	11	38	268	1,107	4,095	0	48	325	1,579	4,008
Seattle, Washington Tacoma, Washington CMSA	8,795	343.7	14	241	100	99	3,668	49	220	213	52	4,259
Minneapolis, Minnesota St. Paul, Minnesota MSA	8,657	351.3	6	14	51	3	4,548	11	32	117	25	3,867
Baltimore, Maryland MSA	7,852	329.6	0	65	284	25	3,084	5	25	756	58	3,626
Phoenix, Arizona MSA	7,755	365.4	16	18	58	203	3,475	43	77	91	341	3,775
Denver, Colorado Boulder, Colorado CMSA	7,296	394.7	14	35	100	89	3,167	2	44	149	356	3,655
St. Louis, Missouri MSA	7,070	289.3	22	0	173	21	3,012	0	11	314	29	3,536
Cleveland, Ohio Akron, Ohio Lorain, Ohio CMSA	6,541	237.0	0	16	158	34	3,099	0	9	350	0	2,901
Tampa, Florida St. Petersburg, Florida Clearwater, Florida MSA	5,870	283.9	0	31	82	108	2,620	16	17	102	166	2,956
Portland, Oregon Vancouver, Washington CMSA	5,464	369.7	0	6	0	9	2,211	7	49	49	19	3,132
Pittsburgh, Pennsylvania Beaver Valley, Pennsylvania CMSA	5,198	231.8	15	4	46	17	2,501	0	0	141	8	2,491
Kansas City, Missouri Kansas City, Kansas MSA	5,059	323.0	0	10	108	26	2,313	8	22	145	42	2,415
Sacramento, California MSA	4,947	334.0	9	50	128	62	1,947	13	197	199	281	2,260

Source: Census of Population and Housing, 1990: Equal Employment Opportunity (EEO) File on CD-ROM [machine-readable datafiles]. Prepared by the Bureau of the Census. Washington, DC: The Bureau, 1992. *Notes:* "MSA" represents "metropolitan statistical area"; "CMSA" stands for "consolidated metropolitan statistical area."

★ 130 ★

Leading Occupations

Food Preparation and Service Occupation Supervisors, by Metropolitan Area

According to the 1990 Census of Population and Housing, food preparation and service occupation supervisors ranked 110 among occupations employing the most people in the United States. Table presents the number of civilians 16 years old or older who reported working as food preparation and service occupation supervisors during the 1990 Census. Data show the total employment figures, employment per 100,000 population, and employment data for men and women of various races and ethnicities in the 25 metropolitan statistical areas with the largest concentrations of food preparation and service occupation supervisors.

[Total for all of the U.S. was 276,420; 111.1 per 100,000 persons]

Metropolitan area	Total employees	Employees per 100,000 population	Men					Women				
			American Indian, Eskimo & Aleut	Asian, Pacific Islander	Black	Hispanic	White	American Indian, Eskimo & Aleut	Asian, Pacific Islander	Black	Hispanic	White
New York, New York New Jersey (northern) Long Island, New York CMSA	17,508	96.80	52	1,442	1,531	2,023	6,780	0	315	1,321	615	4,972
Los Angeles, California Anaheim, California Riverside, California CMSA	14,175	97.55	79	959	503	2,777	4,224	36	547	477	1,759	4,962
Chicago, Illinois Gary, Indiana Lake County, Illinois CMSA	8,123	100.7	11	221	647	744	2,242	19	171	716	317	3,564
San Francisco, California Oakland, California San Jose, California CMSA	7,206	115.2	38	874	248	765	2,131	42	473	247	456	2,564
Philadelphia, Pennsylvania Wilmington, Delaware Trenton, New Jersey CMSA	6,225	105.5	21	130	736	181	2,107	4	84	593	64	2,431
Detroit, Michigan Ann Arbor, Michigan CMSA	5,549	118.9	3	67	532	22	1,586	13	34	465	91	2,837
Boston, Massachusetts Lawrence, Massachusetts Salem, Massachusetts CMSA	4,779	114.6	19	167	119	136	2,090	0	68	91	36	2,103
Washington, District of Columbia MSA	4,607	117.4	8	413	597	274	1,344	0	161	550	171	1,345
Atlanta, Georgia MSA	4,416	155.9	0	124	645	76	1,274	0	73	626	63	1,674
Dallas, Texas Fort Worth, Texas CMSA	4,362	112.3	27	160	304	448	1,313	27	91	391	313	1,603
Seattle, Washington Tacoma, Washington CMSA	4,173	163.1	21	173	112	51	1,343	53	166	133	67	2,143
Houston, Texas Galveston, Texas Brazoria, Texas CMSA	3,953	106.5	0	68	243	427	1,122	6	76	403	319	1,759
Miami, Florida Fort Lauderdale, Florida CMSA	3,623	113.5	12	140	468	622	1,466	0	62	270	321	1,067
Cleveland, Ohio Akron, Ohio Lorain, Ohio CMSA	3,451	125.0	0	25	230	26	936	10	70	277	25	1,898
Minneapolis, Minnesota St. Paul, Minnesota MSA	3,260	132.3	5	37	85	9	1,177	10	40	23	32	1,870
Phoenix, Arizona MSA	3,204	151.0	2	38	44	239	1,129	12	86	10	133	1,694
St. Louis, Missouri MSA	2,961	121.2	0	37	306	1	802	8	22	354	7	1,432
Baltimore, Maryland MSA	2,842	119.3	0	88	345	16	702	22	134	434	5	1,098
Denver, Colorado Boulder, Colorado CMSA	2,778	150.3	23	79	137	201	1,005	14	72	27	71	1,322
San Diego, California MSA	2,738	109.6	0	190	75	418	896	14	114	58	233	1,088
Tampa, Florida St. Petersburg, Florida Clearwater, Florida MSA	2,653	128.3	5	37	138	123	1,122	12	42	174	62	1,104
Pittsburgh, Pennsylvania Beaver Valley, Pennsylvania CMSA	2,495	111.2	0	16	107	16	799	0	30	61	18	1,475
Orlando, Florida MSA	2,333	217.5	0	69	97	205	995	0	19	63	130	1,023
Cincinnati, Ohio Hamilton, Ohio CMSA	2,109	120.9	9	25	107	11	632	11	20	107	19	1,190
Kansas City, Missouri Kansas City, Kansas MSA	1,975	126.1	0	18	144	36	694	0	35	117	6	930

Source: Census of Population and Housing, 1990: Equal Employment Opportunity (EEO) File on CD-ROM [machine-readable datafiles]. Prepared by the Bureau of the Census. Washington, DC: The Bureau, 1992. *Notes:* "MSA" represents "metropolitan statistical area"; "CMSA" stands for "consolidated metropolitan statistical area."

★ 131 ★

Leading Occupations

Food Preparation Occupations, by Metropolitan Area

According to the 1990 Census of Population and Housing, food preparation occupations ranked 32 among occupations employing the most people in the United States. Table presents the number of civilians 16 years old or older who reported working in food preparation occupations during the 1990 Census. Data show the total employment figures, employment per 100,000 population, and employment data for men and women of various races and ethnicities in the 25 metropolitan statistical areas with the largest concentrations of miscellaneous food preparation occupations. See also tables for specific types of food preparation occupations such as cooks.

[Total for all of the U.S. was 743,777; 299.1 per 100,000 persons]

Metropolitan area	Total employees	Employees per 100,000 population	Men					Women				
			American Indian, Eskimo & Aleut	Asian, Pacific Islander	Black	Hispanic	White	American Indian, Eskimo & Aleut	Asian, Pacific Islander	Black	Hispanic	White
New York, New York New Jersey (northern) Long Island, New York CMSA	43,526	240.6	162	1,931	5,754	11,551	11,852	9	684	4,594	2,994	12,341
Los Angeles, California Anaheim, California Riverside, California CMSA	36,900	253.9	156	1,587	1,040	16,819	10,667	104	1,262	1,682	6,660	8,054
Chicago, Illinois Gary, Indiana Lake County, Illinois CMSA	20,451	253.6	35	385	2,669	5,182	5,495	11	479	1,869	1,432	5,735
San Francisco, California Oakland, California San Jose, California CMSA	18,604	297.5	27	2,836	711	5,749	5,097	22	1,817	737	1,463	3,710
Philadelphia, Pennsylvania Wilmington, Delaware Trenton, New Jersey CMSA	16,736	283.7	11	327	3,292	738	4,764	26	280	1,780	293	5,611
Detroit, Michigan Ann Arbor, Michigan CMSA	14,187	304.1	75	188	2,422	240	4,574	42	113	1,430	147	5,170
Boston, Massachusetts Lawrence, Massachusetts Salem, Massachusetts CMSA	13,033	312.4	38	405	646	1,467	5,014	12	307	401	337	5,370
Dallas, Texas Fort Worth, Texas CMSA	11,343	291.9	23	262	1,046	3,182	2,841	35	173	1,084	1,246	3,122
Washington, District of Columbia MSA	10,228	260.7	36	487	1,610	1,986	2,276	18	521	1,625	842	2,105
Cleveland, Ohio Akron, Ohio Lorain, Ohio CMSA	8,753	317.2	0	34	1,354	126	2,899	0	88	897	87	3,379
Miami, Florida Fort Lauderdale, Florida CMSA	8,723	273.2	16	41	2,039	2,013	2,339	0	182	1,703	1,511	1,963
Minneapolis, Minnesota St. Paul, Minnesota MSA	8,699	353.0	135	149	413	219	3,729	14	184	179	115	3,743
Houston, Texas Galveston, Texas Brazoria, Texas CMSA	8,291	223.4	29	154	911	2,210	1,570	13	178	1,233	1,512	2,169
Seattle, Washington Tacoma, Washington CMSA	8,237	321.9	112	769	371	202	3,189	83	637	202	126	2,707
San Diego, California MSA	7,873	315.2	13	434	243	2,560	2,496	23	459	286	969	2,104
St. Louis, Missouri MSA	7,216	295.2	11	54	1,326	53	2,286	13	53	1,001	61	2,422
Pittsburgh, Pennsylvania Beaver Valley, Pennsylvania CMSA	7,207	321.3	0	66	595	56	2,839	8	83	315	8	3,274
Phoenix, Arizona MSA	7,179	338.3	105	89	205	2,104	2,549	106	114	99	880	2,435
Tampa, Florida St. Petersburg, Florida Clearwater, Florida MSA	6,144	297.1	21	56	889	394	2,410	19	112	525	217	1,907
Atlanta, Georgia MSA	6,124	216.1	9	68	1,455	445	1,274	0	126	1,261	175	1,691
Denver, Colorado Boulder, Colorado CMSA	6,027	326.1	67	155	200	1,345	2,535	36	149	235	533	1,601
Las Vegas, Nevada MSA	5,979	806.4	18	121	793	1,982	1,619	21	188	458	584	1,164
Cincinnati, Ohio Hamilton, Ohio CMSA	5,926	339.8	10	28	754	0	2,054	0	61	554	33	2,465
Milwaukee, Wisconsin Racine, Wisconsin CMSA	5,764	358.6	3	70	536	304	1,810	13	71	676	59	2,391
Baltimore, Maryland MSA	5,588	234.6	26	93	1,321	84	1,481	7	123	981	66	1,511

Source: Census of Population and Housing, 1990: Equal Employment Opportunity (EEO) File on CD-ROM [machine-readable datafiles]. Prepared by the Bureau of the Census. Washington, DC: The Bureau, 1992. *Notes:* "MSA" represents "metropolitan statistical area"; "CMSA" stands for "consolidated metropolitan statistical area."

★ 132 ★

Leading Occupations

Food Serving and Lodging Establishment Managers, by Metropolitan Area

According to the 1990 Census of Population and Housing, food serving and lodging establishment managers ranked 21 among occupations employing the most people in the United States. Table presents the number of civilians 16 years old or older who reported working as food serving and lodging establishment managers during the 1990 Census. Data show the total employment figures, employment per 100,000 population, and employment data for men and women of various races and ethnicities in the 25 metropolitan statistical areas with the largest concentrations of food serving and lodging establishment managers.

[Total for all of the U.S. was 1,030,651; 414.4 per 100,000 persons]

Metropolitan area	Total employees	Employees per 100,000 population	Men					Women				
			American Indian, Eskimo & Aleut	Asian, Pacific Islander	Black	Hispanic	White	American Indian, Eskimo & Aleut	Asian, Pacific Islander	Black	Hispanic	White
New York, New York New Jersey (northern) Long Island, New York CMSA	59,988	331.7	74	4,706	3,222	4,658	31,783	22	1,383	2,373	1,442	14,234
Los Angeles, California Anaheim, California Riverside, California CMSA	58,328	401.4	214	6,229	1,683	8,977	23,606	104	3,355	1,292	4,723	15,089
Chicago, Illinois Gary, Indiana Lake County, Illinois CMSA	32,401	401.7	37	1,125	1,915	1,592	14,808	15	644	1,950	798	10,763
San Francisco, California Oakland, California San Jose, California CMSA	28,465	455.2	83	3,530	723	1,942	11,778	72	2,034	610	1,188	8,356
Washington, District of Columbia MSA	20,205	515.0	19	1,550	2,069	812	8,037	19	1,000	1,555	433	5,576
Philadelphia, Pennsylvania Wilmington, Delaware Trenton, New Jersey CMSA	19,414	029.1	53	775	1,274	246	9,401	20	331	1,050	190	6,325
Detroit, Michigan Ann Arbor, Michigan CMSA	18,564	397.9	22	298	1,212	131	7,949	51	249	1,331	166	7,335
Dallas, Texas Fort Worth, Texas CMSA	17,978	462.7	70	649	1,156	1,272	8,455	48	196	912	714	5,323
Miami, Florida Fort Lauderdale, Florida CMSA	16,942	530.7	34	458	816	3,260	9,269	12	187	839	1,546	4,686
Boston, Massachusetts Lawrence, Massachusetts Salem, Massachusetts CMSA	16,849	403.9	8	825	285	407	9,187	44	296	102	57	5,865
Houston, Texas Galveston, Texas Brazoria, Texas CMSA	15,659	422.0	0	920	1,343	1,448	5,984	16	483	1,527	934	4,134
Atlanta, Georgia MSA	15,639	551.9	38	606	2,057	292	6,684	38	267	1,695	56	4,089
San Diego, California MSA	12,174	487.4	88	581	322	1,211	5,728	33	425	210	745	3,882
Seattle, Washington Tacoma, Washington CMSA	11,074	432.7	46	897	190	228	5,154	64	471	176	61	3,955
Cleveland, Ohio Akron, Ohio Lorain, Ohio CMSA	10,881	394.3	5	202	604	100	4,923	7	86	611	90	4,396
Minneapolis, Minnesota St. Paul, Minnesota MSA	10,656	432.5	21	221	152	98	5,619	9	154	105	51	4,335
Tampa, Florida St. Petersburg, Florida Clearwater, Florida MSA	10,475	506.5	23	221	237	395	5,693	5	141	307	145	3,792
St. Louis, Missouri MSA	10,393	425.2	7	181	804	102	4,614	17	115	721	36	3,876
Phoenix, Arizona MSA	10,390	489.6	20	291	172	585	5,378	54	105	70	416	3,966
Baltimore, Maryland MSA	9,872	414.4	10	422	799	79	4,133	10	190	828	33	3,458
Denver, Colorado Boulder, Colorado CMSA	9,455	511.6	34	282	270	506	4,579	44	168	170	434	3,546
Orlando, Florida MSA	8,310	774.7	7	296	291	459	4,318	8	150	306	212	2,813
Cincinnati, Ohio Hamilton, Ohio CMSA	8,247	472.8	0	88	331	28	4,170	12	32	199	12	3,407
Pittsburgh, Pennsylvania Beaver Valley, Pennsylvania CMSA	8,204	365.8	8	128	203	15	4,447	0	37	113	11	3,264
Las Vegas, Nevada MSA	6,924	933.8	14	224	247	434	3,704	29	110	120	189	2,268

Source: Census of Population and Housing, 1990: Equal Employment Opportunity (EEO) File on CD-ROM [machine-readable datafiles]. Prepared by the Bureau of the Census. Washington, DC: The Bureau, 1992. *Notes:* "MSA" represents "metropolitan statistical area"; "CMSA" stands for "consolidated metropolitan statistical area."

★ 133 ★

Leading Occupations

Freight, Stock, and Material Handlers, by Metropolitan Area

According to the 1990 Census of Population and Housing, freight, stock, and material handlers ranked 60 among occupations employing the most people in the United States. Table presents the number of civilians 16 years old or older who reported working as freight, stock, and material handlers during the 1990 Census. Data show the total employment figures, employment per 100,000 population, and employment data for men and women of various races and ethnicities in the 25 metropolitan statistical areas with the largest concentrations of miscellaneous freight, stock, and material handlers. See also tables for specific types of freight, stock, and material handlers such as stock handlers and baggers.

[Total for all of the U.S. was 572,957; 230.4 per 100,000 persons]

Metropolitan area	Total employees	Employees per 100,000 population	Men					Women				
			American Indian, Eskimo & Aleut	Asian, Pacific Islander	Black	Hispanic	White	American Indian, Eskimo & Aleut	Asian, Pacific Islander	Black	Hispanic	White
New York, New York New Jersey (northern) Long Island, New York CMSA	34,360	190.0	69	820	9,038	6,331	19,094	14	102	627	622	1,690
Los Angeles, California Anaheim, California Riverside, California CMSA	29,859	205.5	197	1,268	3,760	12,318	15,304	25	138	458	1,042	1,297
Chicago, Illinois Gary, Indiana Lake County, Illinois CMSA	24,440	303.0	98	308	5,440	3,515	14,609	0	3	702	384	1,153
Philadelphia, Pennsylvania Wilmington, Delaware Trenton, New Jersey CMSA	12,198	206.8	20	120	3,007	449	7,475	0	6	308	49	926
San Francisco, California Oakland, California San Jose, California CMSA	12,023	192.3	91	1,066	1,728	2,675	6,441	6	228	250	276	713
Dallas, Texas Fort Worth, Texas CMSA	11,145	286.8	99	56	2,978	1,505	5,818	2	6	403	181	663
Detroit, Michigan Ann Arbor, Michigan CMSA	9,001	192.9	38	49	1,595	239	6,215	18	6	256	15	721
Atlanta, Georgia MSA	8,773	309.6	15	82	3,574	81	4,344	0	3	369	7	335
Houston, Texas Galveston, Texas Brazoria, Texas CMSA	7,954	214.3	21	73	2,456	2,151	3,525	0	17	197	108	261
Boston, Massachusetts Lawrence, Massachusetts Salem, Massachusetts CMSA	6,653	159.5	0	51	506	347	5,100	14	23	23	34	688
St. Louis, Missouri MSA	6,480	265.1	12	5	1,241	62	4,739	0	0	75	12	400
Cleveland, Ohio Akron, Ohio Lorain, Ohio CMSA	6,404	232.0	0	5	1,011	83	4,722	0	24	142	8	441
Minneapolis, Minnesota St. Paul, Minnesota MSA	6,023	244.4	144	27	278	84	4,850	19	0	19	19	614
Charlotte, North Carolina Gastonia, North Carolina Rock Hill, South Carolina MSA	5,394	464.2	19	30	1,690	42	2,850	0	7	273	10	508
Memphis, Tennessee MSA	5,330	542.9	0	28	2,470	48	2,052	0	0	534	7	226
Washington, District of Columbia MSA	5,294	134.9	38	88	2,502	269	2,186	0	7	154	4	243
Seattle, Washington Tacoma, Washington CMSA	5,243	204.9	73	156	468	118	3,966	11	34	29	28	449
Columbus, Ohio MSA	5,172	375.5	4	22	388	48	4,013	6	24	85	0	585
Kansas City, Missouri Kansas City, Kansas MSA	5,112	326.4	84	10	584	128	3,918	6	0	57	35	381
Miami, Florida Fort Lauderdale, Florida CMSA	5,061	158.5	18	43	1,612	1,552	2,685	0	0	171	166	283
Pittsburgh, Pennsylvania Beaver Valley, Pennsylvania CMSA	4,554	203.1	8	9	231	14	4,030	0	0	35	0	241
Cincinnati, Ohio Hamilton, Ohio CMSA	4,529	259.7	0	4	509	6	3,536	0	0	126	0	354
Denver, Colorado Boulder, Colorado CMSA	4,384	237.2	33	53	353	739	3,115	19	8	22	58	359
Indianapolis, Indiana MSA	4,233	338.7	33	25	613	31	3,012	0	0	169	0	356
Baltimore, Maryland MSA	4,226	177.4	33	16	1,634	33	2,151	0	7	158	0	210

Source: Census of Population and Housing, 1990: Equal Employment Opportunity (EEO) File on CD-ROM [machine-readable datafiles]. Prepared by the Bureau of the Census. Washington, DC: The Bureau, 1992. *Notes:* "MSA" represents "metropolitan statistical area"; "CMSA" stands for "consolidated metropolitan statistical area."

★ 134 ★

Leading Occupations

Garage and Service Station Occupations, by Metropolitan Area

According to the 1990 Census of Population and Housing, garage and service station occupations ranked 115 among occupations employing the most people in the United States. Table presents the number of civilians 16 years old or older who reported working in garage and service station occupations during the 1990 Census. Data show the total employment figures, employment per 100,000 population, and employment data for men and women of various races and ethnicities in the 25 metropolitan statistical areas with the largest concentrations of garage and service station-related occupations.

[Total for all of the U.S. was 270,227; 108.7 per 100,000 persons]

Metropolitan area	Total employees	Employees per 100,000 population	Men American Indian, Eskimo & Aleut	Men Asian, Pacific Islander	Men Black	Men Hispanic	Men White	Women American Indian, Eskimo & Aleut	Women Asian, Pacific Islander	Women Black	Women Hispanic	Women White
New York, New York New Jersey (northern) Long Island, New York CMSA	16,972	93.83	32	922	2,364	2,567	11,607	0	39	253	180	718
Los Angeles, California Anaheim, California Riverside, California CMSA	12,669	87.18	137	740	887	4,688	7,381	33	57	46	319	671
Philadelphia, Pennsylvania Wilmington, Delaware Trenton, New Jersey CMSA	6,997	118.6	18	63	931	281	5,332	9	14	128	31	353
Chicago, Illinois Gary, Indiana Lake County, Illinois CMSA	6,521	80.85	20	80	1,188	741	3,925	0	0	165	52	661
San Francisco, California Oakland, California San Jose, California CMSA	5,961	95.33	39	635	556	1,137	3,848	15	37	58	51	270
Boston, Massachusetts Lawrence, Massachusetts Salem, Massachusetts CMSA	4,752	113.9	14	32	166	164	4,273	0	0	0	24	189
Detroit, Michigan Ann Arbor, Michigan CMSA	4,565	97.85	0	7	930	92	3,063	0	5	54	7	479
Houston, Texas Galveston, Texas Brazoria, Texas CMSA	3,653	98.44	20	99	727	938	1,992	9	10	128	61	205
Dallas, Texas Fort Worth, Texas CMSA	3,428	88.23	13	88	571	278	2,067	0	0	120	38	349
Washington, District of Columbia MSA	3,422	87.22	30	143	769	126	2,133	0	26	44	43	205
Pittsburgh, Pennsylvania Beaver Valley, Pennsylvania CMSA	3,158	140.8	12	0	129	2	2,864	0	0	21	0	132
Miami, Florida Fort Lauderdale, Florida CMSA	3,038	95.16	0	36	412	1,275	2,117	0	8	67	162	252
Cleveland, Ohio Akron, Ohio Lorain, Ohio CMSA	2,990	108.3	36	0	366	53	2,217	0	4	53	0	280
Portland, Oregon Vancouver, Washington CMSA	2,760	186.8	27	33	100	56	2,323	12	0	0	0	224
San Diego, California MSA	2,617	104.8	33	120	115	507	1,744	0	17	0	60	278
St. Louis, Missouri MSA	2,556	104.6	21	8	255	13	1,965	0	0	32	0	275
Baltimore, Maryland MSA	2,525	106.0	0	16	645	12	1,635	0	0	47	0	171
Minneapolis, Minnesota St. Paul, Minnesota MSA	2,464	99.99	10	12	60	16	2,107	0	3	13	0	254
Atlanta, Georgia MSA	2,429	85.72	5	41	710	56	1,361	0	16	83	18	154
Phoenix, Arizona MSA	2,114	99.62	69	16	115	268	1,605	9	0	0	4	183
Seattle, Washington Tacoma, Washington CMSA	1,961	76.63	8	93	81	25	1,570	0	11	21	6	169
Cincinnati, Ohio Hamilton, Ohio CMSA	1,686	96.67	0	0	167	0	1,276	0	0	29	6	214
Milwaukee, Wisconsin Racine, Wisconsin CMSA	1,593	99.12	8	10	195	31	1,167	0	0	18	0	190
Columbus, Ohio MSA	1,508	109.5	0	7	52	15	1,238	0	0	32	0	179
Tampa, Florida St. Petersburg, Florida Clearwater, Florida MSA	1,470	71.08	7	0	229	72	1,028	0	0	7	20	181

Source: Census of Population and Housing, 1990: Equal Employment Opportunity (EEO) File on CD-ROM [machine-readable datafiles]. Prepared by the Bureau of the Census. Washington, DC: The Bureau, 1992. *Notes:* "MSA" represents "metropolitan statistical area"; "CMSA" stands for "consolidated metropolitan statistical area."

★ 135 ★
Leading Occupations

General Maintenance Mechanics and Repairers, by Metropolitan Area

According to the 1990 Census of Population and Housing, general maintenance mechanics and repairers ranked 69 among occupations employing the most people in the United States. Table presents the number of civilians 16 years old or older who reported working as general maintenance mechanics and repairers during the 1990 Census. Data show the total employment figures, employment per 100,000 population, and employment data for men and women of various races and ethnicities in the 25 metropolitan statistical areas with the largest concentrations of general maintenance mechanics and repairers.

[Total for all of the U.S. was 492,093; 197.9 per 100,000 persons]

Metropolitan area	Total employees	Employees per 100,000 population	Men American Indian, Eskimo & Aleut	Men Asian, Pacific Islander	Men Black	Men Hispanic	Men White	Women American Indian, Eskimo & Aleut	Women Asian, Pacific Islander	Women Black	Women Hispanic	Women White
New York, New York New Jersey (northern) Long Island, New York CMSA	31,162	172.3	34	1,030	4,381	6,098	22,026	0	47	251	214	758
Los Angeles, California Anaheim, California Riverside, California CMSA	25,664	176.6	149	1,473	1,426	9,967	16,297	6	72	49	257	656
Chicago, Illinois Gary, Indiana Lake County, Illinois CMSA	16,761	207.8	80	356	2,050	2,099	12,330	0	21	201	87	466
Philadelphia, Pennsylvania Wilmington, Delaware Trenton, New Jersey CMSA	11,501	195.0	3	39	1,321	442	9,467	0	0	63	0	368
San Francisco, California Oakland, California San Jose, California CMSA	10,623	169.9	71	1,248	734	1,574	7,322	15	85	72	88	304
Detroit, Michigan Ann Arbor, Michigan CMSA	7,700	165.1	39	46	1,070	123	6,206	0	8	91	10	208
Houston, Texas Galveston, Texas Brazoria, Texas CMSA	7,381	198.9	26	182	1,062	1,582	4,950	0	15	47	16	187
Boston, Massachusetts Lawrence, Massachusetts Salem, Massachusetts CMSA	6,790	162.8	0	88	323	335	5,859	0	14	19	6	275
Dallas, Texas Fort Worth, Texas CMSA	6,691	172.2	39	98	556	1,015	5,067	6	24	37	40	237
Miami, Florida Fort Lauderdale, Florida CMSA	6,600	206.7	0	67	1,088	2,812	4,906	0	0	58	86	114
Atlanta, Georgia MSA	5,440	192.0	26	74	969	58	4,001	0	6	120	0	228
Baltimore, Maryland MSA	4,929	206.9	27	47	733	83	3,984	0	0	25	0	74
Cleveland, Ohio Akron, Ohio Lorain, Ohio CMSA	4,791	173.6	16	43	326	89	4,191	0	0	33	0	144
Washington, District of Columbia MSA	4,479	114.2	32	174	1,147	203	2,726	7	13	76	18	181
Seattle, Washington Tacoma, Washington CMSA	4,394	171.7	48	122	176	104	3,753	0	0	0	5	235
Tampa, Florida St. Petersburg, Florida Clearwater, Florida CMSA	4,239	205.0	11	37	301	278	3,558	0	0	8	18	225
Phoenix, Arizona MSA	4,216	198.7	40	16	90	745	3,423	13	0	4	33	117
Minneapolis, Minnesota St. Paul, Minnesota MSA	4,205	170.7	77	60	114	42	3,745	0	13	0	7	172
St. Louis, Missouri MSA	4,176	170.9	0	18	373	30	3,608	0	0	33	0	140
San Diego, California MSA	3,908	156.4	28	349	190	830	2,780	0	6	31	23	139
Pittsburgh, Pennsylvania Beaver Valley, Pennsylvania CMSA	3,838	171.1	0	0	121	12	3,622	0	0	16	1	74
Denver, Colorado Boulder, Colorado CMSA	3,246	175.6	48	55	103	296	2,824	0	0	2	8	39
Norfolk, Virginia Virginia Beach, Virginia Newport News, Virginia MSA	3,094	221.6	0	25	665	41	2,247	0	0	17	0	110
Cincinnati, Ohio Hamilton, Ohio CMSA	3,083	176.8	2	0	218	6	2,742	0	0	16	0	105
Milwaukee, Wisconsin Racine, Wisconsin CMSA	2,945	183.2	19	0	189	43	2,580	0	0	25	0	120

Source: Census of Population and Housing, 1990: Equal Employment Opportunity (EEO) File on CD-ROM [machine-readable datafiles]. Prepared by the Bureau of the Census. Washington, DC: The Bureau, 1992. *Notes:* "MSA" represents "metropolitan statistical area"; "CMSA" stands for "consolidated metropolitan statistical area."

★ 136 ★

Leading Occupations

General Office Clerks, by Metropolitan Area

According to the 1990 Census of Population and Housing, general office clerks ranked 16 among occupations employing the most people in the United States. Table presents the number of civilians 16 years old or older who reported working as general office clerks during the 1990 Census. Data show the total employment figures, employment per 100,000 population, and employment data for men and women of various races and ethnicities in the 25 metropolitan statistical areas with the largest concentrations of general office clerks.

[Total for all of the U.S. was 1,491,116; 599.5 per 100,000 persons]

Metropolitan area	Total employees	Employees per 100,000 population	Men					Women				
			American Indian, Eskimo & Aleut	Asian, Pacific Islander	Black	Hispanic	White	American Indian, Eskimo & Aleut	Asian, Pacific Islander	Black	Hispanic	White
New York, New York New Jersey (northern) Long Island, New York CMSA	158,362	875.5	106	3,084	9,587	6,389	23,335	291	4,847	32,485	14,377	76,339
Los Angeles, California Anaheim, California Riverside, California CMSA	95,171	654.9	101	3,305	2,251	5,175	10,484	568	7,909	9,480	19,168	49,241
Chicago, Illinois Gary, Indiana Lake County, Illinois CMSA	56,070	695.2	24	507	2,379	1,022	7,182	92	1,360	10,224	3,344	32,093
San Francisco, California Oakland, California San Jose, California CMSA	46,643	745.9	52	2,385	1,126	1,139	5,374	237	6,954	3,902	5,129	23,935
Philadelphia, Pennsylvania Wilmington, Delaware Trenton, New Jersey CMSA	40,273	682.7	0	149	1,696	271	5,872	47	397	6,649	703	25,022
Boston, Massachusetts Lawrence, Massachusetts Salem, Massachusetts CMSA	31,003	743.2	3	165	521	274	5,319	24	540	1,775	868	22,095
Detroit, Michigan Ann Arbor, Michigan CMSA	29,870	640.3	6	76	1,015	163	3,614	86	207	5,902	383	18,761
Washington, District of Columbia MSA	28,660	730.5	5	516	2,948	437	4,195	73	848	8,061	946	11,527
Dallas, Texas Fort Worth, Texas CMSA	24,838	639.3	23	130	614	468	2,812	96	238	3,745	1,810	15,932
Miami, Florida Fort Lauderdale, Florida CMSA	22,715	711.5	20	106	593	2,164	3,605	43	148	2,902	7,369	14,546
Houston, Texas Galveston, Texas Brazoria, Texas CMSA	21,378	576.1	5	165	636	649	2,163	38	324	4,213	2,489	12,364
Atlanta, Georgia MSA	20,216	713.5	0	48	854	38	2,105	26	177	5,541	247	11,367
Baltimore, Maryland MSA	19,318	810.9	0	31	1,120	52	2,230	25	225	5,723	129	9,918
Seattle, Washington Tacoma, Washington CMSA	16,864	659.0	45	308	166	118	2,308	221	869	1,060	426	11,639
Minneapolis, Minnesota St. Paul, Minnesota MSA	16,523	670.5	16	77	66	32	2,658	103	158	382	155	12,978
St. Louis, Missouri MSA	15,877	649.6	0	22	363	17	2,061	30	5	2,593	118	10,762
Cleveland, Ohio Akron, Ohio Lorain, Ohio CMSA	15,247	552.5	0	0	398	28	1,764	31	75	2,353	178	10,565
Sacramento, California MSA	13,907	939.0	0	295	270	279	1,665	125	861	1,061	1,599	8,791
San Diego, California MSA	13,396	536.3	42	327	180	361	1,399	112	1,108	773	2,102	8,362
Denver, Colorado Boulder, Colorado CMSA	12,504	676.5	18	61	269	197	1,848	53	219	778	1,202	8,598
Phoenix, Arizona MSA	12,215	575.6	24	36	50	309	1,860	177	196	436	1,384	8,459
Tampa, Florida St. Petersburg, Florida Clearwater, Florida MSA	11,704	566.0	0	15	88	176	1,755	28	141	668	717	8,872
Pittsburgh, Pennsylvania Beaver Valley, Pennsylvania CMSA	11,323	504.9	2	14	272	29	2,085	16	25	924	74	7,943
Kansas City, Missouri Kansas City, Kansas MSA	11,007	702.8	3	3	140	31	1,432	48	75	1,380	345	7,723
Cincinnati, Ohio Hamilton, Ohio CMSA	10,858	622.6	0	13	228	7	1,586	7	53	1,200	39	7,753

Source: Census of Population and Housing, 1990: Equal Employment Opportunity (EEO) File on CD-ROM [machine-readable datafiles]. Prepared by the Bureau of the Census. Washington, DC: The Bureau, 1992. *Notes:* "MSA" represents "metropolitan statistical area"; "CMSA" stands for "consolidated metropolitan statistical area."

★ 137 ★

Leading Occupations

General Office Supervisors, by Metropolitan Area

According to the 1990 Census of Population and Housing, general office supervisors ranked 58 among occupations employing the most people in the United States. Table presents the number of civilians 16 years old or older who reported working as general office supervisors during the 1990 Census. Data show the total employment figures, employment per 100,000 population, and employment data for men and women of various races and ethnicities in the 25 metropolitan statistical areas with the largest concentrations of general office supervisors.

[Total for all of the U.S. was 579,625; 233.1 per 100,000 persons]

Metropolitan area	Total employees	Employees per 100,000 population	Men					Women				
			American Indian, Eskimo & Aleut	Asian, Pacific Islander	Black	Hispanic	White	American Indian, Eskimo & Aleut	Asian, Pacific Islander	Black	Hispanic	White
New York, New York New Jersey (northern) Long Island, New York CMSA	59,248	327.6	15	1,057	4,704	3,448	16,680	80	992	9,979	3,616	23,289
Los Angeles, California Anaheim, California Riverside, California CMSA	35,465	244.1	105	1,437	1,772	3,002	8,429	160	1,745	2,964	4,485	15,553
Chicago, Illinois Gary, Indiana Lake County, Illinois CMSA	20,507	254.3	20	198	1,045	443	5,180	32	237	2,698	732	10,523
Philadelphia, Pennsylvania Wilmington, Delaware Trenton, New Jersey CMSA	17,819	302.1	8	121	1,122	223	4,794	0	72	2,509	198	8,987
Washington, District of Columbia MSA	16,191	412.7	46	184	2,005	225	4,924	25	279	3,190	263	5,396
San Francisco, California Oakland, California San Jose, California CMSA	15,605	249.6	19	783	653	768	3,561	80	1,268	1,340	1,125	7,168
Boston, Massachusetts Lawrence, Massachusetts Salem, Massachusetts CMSA	11,330	271.6	4	26	287	118	3,609	12	31	346	211	6,913
Atlanta, Georgia MSA	9,976	352.1	0	36	1,064	61	2,585	10	65	1,759	86	4,432
Detroit, Michigan Ann Arbor, Michigan CMSA	9,802	210.1	0	32	614	62	2,481	14	80	1,651	31	4,901
Miami, Florida Fort Lauderdale, Florida CMSA	9,761	305.7	0	76	537	1,299	2,816	0	119	953	2,214	4,949
Dallas, Texas Fort Worth, Texas CMSA	9,364	241.0	12	22	608	267	3,023	46	38	709	326	4,615
Baltimore, Maryland MSA	8,713	365.8	0	40	655	24	2,821	0	62	1,543	50	3,559
Houston, Texas Galveston, Texas Brazoria, Texas CMSA	7,866	212.0	9	48	474	519	1,991	11	21	1,144	508	3,603
Minneapolis, Minnesota St. Paul, Minnesota MSA	6,333	257.0	18	28	23	26	1,768	5	15	62	33	4,384
Sacramento, California MSA	5,993	404.6	19	143	224	180	1,660	39	180	238	380	3,275
Seattle, Washington Tacoma, Washington CMSA	5,947	232.4	21	80	70	40	1,693	27	155	163	99	3,713
Cleveland, Ohio Akron, Ohio Lorain, Ohio CMSA	5,685	206.0	0	27	242	22	1,621	3	17	728	15	3,033
St. Louis, Missouri MSA	5,674	232.2	28	26	290	19	1,670	8	30	592	36	3,008
San Diego, California MSA	5,624	225.1	10	175	126	292	1,570	18	192	309	459	2,860
Phoenix, Arizona MSA	5,275	248.6	26	43	90	159	1,523	59	7	201	410	3,092
Denver, Colorado Boulder, Colorado CMSA	5,217	282.3	23	33	188	187	1,522	23	22	165	335	3,068
Kansas City, Missouri Kansas City, Kansas MSA	4,792	306.0	23	0	240	34	1,388	27	32	407	36	2,652
Tampa, Florida St. Petersburg, Florida Clearwater, Florida MSA	4,744	229.4	0	0	150	132	1,148	7	71	334	306	2,907
Pittsburgh, Pennsylvania Beaver Valley, Pennsylvania CMSA	4,560	203.3	0	0	162	0	1,263	0	13	296	22	2,826
Columbus, Ohio MSA	4,354	316.1	8	0	211	7	1,473	3	12	357	26	2,290

Source: Census of Population and Housing, 1990: Equal Employment Opportunity (EEO) File on CD-ROM [machine-readable datafiles]. Prepared by the Bureau of the Census. Washington, DC: The Bureau, 1992. *Notes:* "MSA" represents "metropolitan statistical area"; "CMSA" stands for "consolidated metropolitan statistical area."

★ 138 ★

Leading Occupations

Groundskeepers and Gardeners, by Metropolitan Area

According to the 1990 Census of Population and Housing, groundskeepers and gardeners ranked 33 among occupations employing the most people in the United States. Table presents the number of civilians 16 years old or older who reported working as groundskeepers and gardeners during the 1990 Census. Data show the total employment figures, employment per 100,000 population, and employment data for men and women of various races and ethnicities in the 25 metropolitan statistical areas with the largest concentrations of groundskeepers and gardeners, excluding farm groundskeepers and gardeners.

[Total for all of the U.S. was 735,556; 295.8 per 100,000 persons]

Metropolitan area	Total employees	Employees per 100,000 population	Men					Women				
			American Indian, Eskimo & Aleut	Asian, Pacific Islander	Black	Hispanic	White	American Indian, Eskimo & Aleut	Asian, Pacific Islander	Black	Hispanic	White
Los Angeles, California Anaheim, California Riverside, California CMSA	69,669	479.4	317	4,474	2,631	47,937	33,284	35	244	184	1,483	1,975
New York, New York New Jersey (northern) Long Island, New York CMSA	36,276	200.6	60	193	4,091	7,109	27,288	24	25	234	393	1,367
San Francisco, California Oakland, California San Jose, California CMSA	25,044	400.5	194	2,094	993	10,888	14,526	12	191	94	546	1,647
Chicago, Illinois Gary, Indiana Lake County, Illinois CMSA	14,974	185.7	116	57	1,414	6,335	8,469	0	0	210	135	591
Philadelphia, Pennsylvania Wilmington, Delaware Trenton, New Jersey CMSA	14,190	240.5	68	52	1,423	1,140	10,952	3	6	94	57	796
Dallas, Texas Fort Worth, Texas CMSA	13,513	347.8	41	124	1,584	5,800	7,326	3	8	68	126	531
Miami, Florida Fort Lauderdale, Florida CMSA	13,243	414.8	16	29	4,814	3,911	7,224	6	0	149	184	476
San Diego, California MSA	13,157	526.7	107	638	433	7,511	6,996	9	74	34	435	696
Houston, Texas Galveston, Texas Brazoria, Texas CMSA	11,953	322.1	24	121	1,697	6,492	6,029	0	0	61	164	397
Phoenix, Arizona MSA	10,402	490.2	390	75	268	4,852	6,718	20	0	17	76	319
Tampa, Florida St. Petersburg, Florida Clearwater, Florida MSA	10,273	496.8	34	49	1,069	665	7,962	16	8	86	57	891
Washington, District of Columbia MSA	9,951	253.6	37	244	2,334	1,673	5,604	0	5	201	40	595
Detroit, Michigan Ann Arbor, Michigan CMSA	9,796	210.0	102	47	1,432	246	7,300	11	0	185	22	580
Atlanta, Georgia MSA	9,313	328.7	22	56	2,317	503	6,118	0	0	65	11	451
Boston, Massachusetts Lawrence, Massachusetts Salem, Massachusetts CMSA	8,254	197.9	11	56	290	414	7,261	8	4	8	26	471
Seattle, Washington Tacoma, Washington CMSA	7,504	293.2	135	459	335	238	5,536	12	93	37	17	765
Cleveland, Ohio Akron, Ohio Lorain, Ohio CMSA	6,947	251.7	12	11	775	161	5,523	6	0	81	0	484
West Palm Beach, Florida Boca Raton, Florida Delray Beach, Florida MSA	6,430	744.6	30	28	1,908	1,446	3,805	0	23	108	109	262
Sacramento, California CMSA	6,140	414.6	134	393	230	1,810	3,855	11	29	7	58	398
Baltimore, Maryland MSA	6,018	252.6	35	14	1,511	114	4,030	0	0	68	0	311
Orlando, Florida MSA	5,932	553.0	43	18	1,020	431	4,076	6	0	71	31	554
St. Louis, Missouri MSA	5,364	219.5	29	9	961	45	4,020	8	16	32	0	277
Pittsburgh, Pennsylvania Beaver Valley, Pennsylvania CMSA	5,072	226.2	9	0	243	0	4,540	0	0	25	0	255
Denver, Colorado Boulder, Colorado CMSA	4,813	260.4	53	113	263	1,264	3,423	7	0	32	76	339
Portland, Oregon Vancouver, Washington CMSA	4,734	320.3	35	36	149	694	3,650	20	0	7	118	496

Source: Census of Population and Housing, 1990: Equal Employment Opportunity (EEO) File on CD-ROM [machine-readable datafiles]. Prepared by the Bureau of the Census. Washington, DC: The Bureau, 1992. *Notes:* "MSA" represents "metropolitan statistical area"; "CMSA" stands for "consolidated metropolitan statistical area."

★ 139 ★

Leading Occupations

Guards and Police, by Metropolitan Area

According to the 1990 Census of Population and Housing, guards and police ranked 28 among occupations employing the most people in the United States. Table presents the number of civilians 16 years old or older who reported working as guards and police during the 1990 Census. Data show the total employment figures, employment per 100,000 population, and employment data for men and women of various races and ethnicities in the 25 metropolitan statistical areas with the largest concentrations of guards and police, excluding public service police.

[Total for all of the U.S. was 785,511; 315.8 per 100,000 persons]

Metropolitan area	Total employees	Employees per 100,000 population	Men					Women				
			American Indian, Eskimo & Aleut	Asian, Pacific Islander	Black	Hispanic	White	American Indian, Eskimo & Aleut	Asian, Pacific Islander	Black	Hispanic	White
New York, New York New Jersey (northern) Long Island, New York CMSA	87,892	485.9	171	2,016	28,701	13,449	37,721	56	247	6,307	1,937	5,349
Los Angeles, California Anaheim, California Riverside, California CMSA	56,644	389.8	538	3,614	10,717	10,873	27,288	123	434	1,951	1,765	5,426
Chicago, Illinois Gary, Indiana Lake County, Illinois CMSA	30,064	372.7	86	391	9,140	2,270	13,924	40	76	2,624	336	2,431
Philadelphia, Pennsylvania Wilmington, Delaware Trenton, New Jersey CMSA	23,073	391.1	66	123	6,756	629	11,693	40	61	1,740	104	2,198
San Francisco, California Oakland, California San Jose, California CMSA	22,280	356.3	183	2,581	3,987	2,087	10,792	31	382	904	511	2,378
Washington, District of Columbia MSA	18,272	465.7	41	391	7,342	491	6,667	60	40	1,999	158	1,431
Detroit, Michigan Ann Arbor, Michigan CMSA	17,207	368.8	70	22	5,634	237	8,127	7	12	1,382	73	1,904
Miami, Florida Fort Lauderdale, Florida CMSA	16,469	515.9	82	80	2,960	4,867	10,264	16	28	925	680	1,512
Boston, Massachusetts Lawrence, Massachusetts Salem, Massachusetts CMSA	16,268	390.0	52	272	1,747	470	11,468	5	45	306	135	2,041
Houston, Texas Galveston, Texas Brazoria, Texas CMSA	15,549	419.0	73	133	4,206	1,735	7,469	25	39	966	355	1,646
Dallas, Texas Fort Worth, Texas CMSA	13,396	344.8	79	83	2,532	893	8,142	15	31	444	188	1,462
Baltimore, Maryland MSA	10,483	440.1	48	66	3,545	47	4,517	7	17	1,248	18	1,026
Atlanta, Georgia MSA	9,178	323.9	15	68	3,361	97	3,812	3	7	1,041	0	830
Pittsburgh, Pennsylvania Beaver Valley, Pennsylvania CMSA	8,492	378.6	14	28	1,138	29	6,120	0	4	296	28	849
San Diego, California MSA	8,448	338.2	131	357	1,132	973	5,023	3	79	170	175	1,084
Cleveland, Ohio Akron, Ohio Lorain, Ohio CMSA	8,295	300.6	34	60	1,758	89	4,953	5	8	412	33	999
Phoenix, Arizona MSA	7,984	376.2	65	46	381	647	6,042	27	9	76	80	1,069
St. Louis, Missouri MSA	7,705	315.3	18	23	1,744	53	4,528	12	0	403	22	934
Tampa, Florida St. Petersburg, Florida Clearwater, Florida MSA	7,255	350.8	58	17	572	378	5,704	0	0	112	60	723
Las Vegas, Nevada MSA	6,963	939.1	99	90	581	323	5,235	5	15	156	60	635
Seattle, Washington Tacoma, Washington CMSA	6,530	255.2	89	180	505	135	4,331	36	48	121	59	1,120
Minneapolis, Minnesota St. Paul, Minnesota MSA	6,504	264.0	64	70	491	116	4,832	34	11	8	34	940
Denver, Colorado Boulder, Colorado CMSA	5,439	294.3	56	17	469	410	3,454	14	17	161	169	1,043
New Orleans, Louisiana MSA	5,395	435.5	40	18	2,206	68	2,114	0	0	663	0	341
Kansas City, Missouri Kansas City, Kansas MSA	4,820	307.7	33	33	880	109	3,005	0	0	218	20	598

Source: Census of Population and Housing, 1990: Equal Employment Opportunity (EEO) File on CD-ROM [machine-readable datafiles]. Prepared by the Bureau of the Census. Washington, DC: The Bureau, 1992. *Notes:* "MSA" represents "metropolitan statistical area"; "CMSA" stands for "consolidated metropolitan statistical area."

★ 140 ★

Leading Occupations

Hairdressers and Cosmetologists, by Metropolitan Area

According to the 1990 Census of Population and Housing, hairdressers and cosmetologists ranked 34 among occupations employing the most people in the United States. Table presents the number of civilians 16 years old or older who reported working as hairdressers and cosmetologists during the 1990 Census. Data show the total employment figures, employment per 100,000 population, and employment data for men and women of various races and ethnicities in the 25 metropolitan statistical areas with the largest concentrations of hairdressers and cosmetologists.

[Total for all of the U.S. was 733,576; 295.0 per 100,000 persons]

Metropolitan area	Total employees	Employees per 100,000 population	Men					Women				
			American Indian, Eskimo & Aleut	Asian, Pacific Islander	Black	Hispanic	White	American Indian, Eskimo & Aleut	Asian, Pacific Islander	Black	Hispanic	White
New York, New York New Jersey (northern) Long Island, New York CMSA	47,476	262.5	11	404	802	1,348	7,100	85	2,457	4,488	5,683	29,756
Los Angeles, California Anaheim, California Riverside, California CMSA	46,334	318.9	62	1,047	592	1,600	4,619	270	5,317	2,863	9,265	26,623
Chicago, Illinois Gary, Indiana Lake County, Illinois CMSA	22,727	281.8	6	37	604	300	1,889	34	384	2,598	1,647	16,270
San Francisco, California Oakland, California San Jose, California CMSA	19,055	304.7	32	566	213	423	1,833	164	3,017	1,139	2,325	11,097
Philadelphia, Pennsylvania Wilmington, Delaware Trenton, New Jersey CMSA	15,548	263.6	26	25	117	127	1,758	14	231	1,716	399	11,450
Detroit, Michigan Ann Arbor, Michigan CMSA	13,730	294.3	4	5	369	32	1,038	66	93	1,567	203	10,502
Dallas, Texas Fort Worth, Texas CMSA	12,186	313.6	11	37	235	177	1,207	19	214	1,693	1,087	8,175
Boston, Massachusetts Lawrence, Massachusetts Salem, Massachusetts CMSA	12,120	290.5	16	45	93	72	2,077	6	232	421	338	9,044
Miami, Florida Fort Lauderdale, Florida CMSA	12,054	377.6	0	0	140	899	2,200	8	178	1,297	4,260	7,736
Washington, District of Columbia MSA	11,333	288.8	0	61	476	116	825	45	931	2,481	1,019	6,114
Houston, Texas Galveston, Texas Brazoria, Texas CMSA	10,152	273.6	10	26	179	275	762	60	649	2,000	1,641	5,641
Atlanta, Georgia MSA	8,680	306.3	9	11	371	57	818	25	125	1,753	241	5,450
San Diego, California MSA	7,702	308.3	3	12	50	190	847	57	738	216	1,145	5,214
Seattle, Washington Tacoma, Washington CMSA	7,670	299.7	13	57	34	65	634	122	443	194	268	6,109
St. Louis, Missouri MSA	7,655	313.2	0	0	106	0	631	32	0	716	107	6,143
Cleveland, Ohio Akron, Ohio Lorain, Ohio CMSA	7,488	271.3	0	0	93	8	563	14	62	961	84	5,771
Minneapolis, Minnesota St. Paul, Minnesota MSA	7,342	298.0	6	0	50	71	571	35	54	101	72	6,458
Pittsburgh, Pennsylvania Beaver Valley, Pennsylvania CMSA	7,305	325.7	0	0	73	18	792	8	14	246	39	6,172
Phoenix, Arizona MSA	7,154	337.1	32	15	52	139	789	43	35	138	846	5,598
Baltimore, Maryland MSA	6,918	290.4	0	0	169	7	508	8	170	1,293	134	4,715
Tampa, Florida St. Petersburg, Florida Clearwater, Florida MSA	6,815	329.6	8	17	88	70	718	23	113	207	440	5,605
Denver, Colorado Boulder, Colorado CMSA	5,778	312.6	0	20	63	149	400	57	114	188	813	4,577
Portland, Oregon Vancouver, Washington CMSA	4,932	333.7	8	31	5	65	407	32	145	45	115	4,167
Kansas City, Missouri Kansas City, Kansas MSA	4,747	303.1	0	0	64	14	381	9	47	412	114	3,779
Cincinnati, Ohio Hamilton, Ohio CMSA	4,667	267.6	0	0	50	0	382	0	5	411	20	3,819

Source: Census of Population and Housing, 1990: Equal Employment Opportunity (EEO) File on CD-ROM [machine-readable datafiles]. Prepared by the Bureau of the Census. Washington, DC: The Bureau, 1992. *Notes:* "MSA" represents "metropolitan statistical area"; "CMSA" stands for "consolidated metropolitan statistical area."

★ 141 ★

Leading Occupations

Hand Packers and Packagers, by Metropolitan Area

According to the 1990 Census of Population and Housing, hand packers and packagers ranked 86 among occupations employing the most people in the United States. Table presents the number of civilians 16 years old or older who reported working as hand packers and packagers during the 1990 Census. Data show the total employment figures, employment per 100,000 population, and employment data for men and women of various races and ethnicities in the 25 metropolitan statistical areas with the largest concentrations of hand packers and packagers.

[Total for all of the U.S. was 368,341; 148.1 per 100,000 persons]

Metropolitan area	Total employees	Employees per 100,000 population	Men					Women				
			American Indian, Eskimo & Aleut	Asian, Pacific Islander	Black	Hispanic	White	American Indian, Eskimo & Aleut	Asian, Pacific Islander	Black	Hispanic	White
New York, New York New Jersey (northern) Long Island, New York CMSA	26,451	146.2	3	502	2,347	4,556	5,040	127	897	3,354	6,514	9,008
Los Angeles, California Anaheim, California Riverside, California CMSA	26,130	179.8	31	494	645	8,397	4,606	39	1,009	644	11,667	6,557
Chicago, Illinois Gary, Indiana Lake County, Illinois CMSA	17,932	222.3	30	313	1,276	2,864	3,235	18	378	2,356	4,513	5,840
Philadelphia, Pennsylvania Wilmington, Delaware Trenton, New Jersey CMSA	9,550	161.9	45	113	838	439	1,922	0	224	1,528	618	4,254
San Francisco, California Oakland, California San Jose, California CMSA	6,638	106.2	5	402	238	1,011	1,306	0	989	194	1,686	2,113
Dallas, Texas Fort Worth, Texas CMSA	5,894	151.7	7	82	478	903	1,206	22	92	722	1,335	1,854
Detroit, Michigan Ann Arbor, Michigan CMSA	5,102	109.4	13	16	800	95	1,052	17	16	825	52	2,268
Boston, Massachusetts Lawrence, Massachusetts Salem, Massachusetts CMSA	4,874	116.8	8	82	146	324	1,487	6	171	155	390	2,384
Atlanta, Georgia MSA	3,870	136.6	0	29	527	26	572	14	78	1,323	61	1,299
Minneapolis, Minnesota St. Paul, Minnesota MSA	3,780	153.4	35	82	194	39	1,278	47	113	133	45	1,859
Cleveland, Ohio Akron, Ohio Lorain, Ohio CMSA	3,571	129.4	0	6	270	82	883	11	22	376	47	1,891
Miami, Florida Fort Lauderdale, Florida CMSA	3,417	107.0	0	14	288	711	843	10	36	384	1,355	1,573
Milwaukee, Wisconsin Racine, Wisconsin CMSA	3,214	200.0	15	7	412	119	751	9	22	344	147	1,491
Baltimore, Maryland MSA	2,909	122.1	0	32	479	10	377	0	35	886	12	1,085
Seattle, Washington Tacoma, Washington CMSA	2,777	108.5	13	115	94	28	604	54	265	72	146	1,483
Charlotte, North Carolina Gastonia, North Carolina Rock Hill, South Carolina MSA	2,742	236.0	9	12	236	10	472	16	40	893	19	1,050
Houston, Texas Galveston, Texas Brazoria, Texas CMSA	2,741	73.86	20	67	163	484	447	15	84	231	749	992
St. Louis, Missouri MSA	2,717	111.2	0	14	310	17	784	0	21	415	3	1,173
Cincinnati, Ohio Hamilton, Ohio CMSA	2,651	152.0	5	6	208	0	691	0	33	378	0	1,330
Pittsburgh, Pennsylvania Beaver Valley, Pennsylvania CMSA	2,312	103.1	7	18	89	2	734	0	0	107	0	1,357
Providence, Rhode Island Pawtucket, Rhode Island Fall River, Massachusetts CMSA	2,251	197.2	0	6	40	204	534	6	20	172	185	1,222
Fresno, California MSA	2,216	332.0	0	33	11	427	191	1	38	3	1,343	773
Scranton, Pennsylvania Wilkes-Barre, Pennsylvania MSA	2,188	298.0	0	0	11	6	720	0	14	0	3	1,437

[Continued]

★ 141 ★

Hand Packers and Packagers, by Metropolitan Area

[Continued]

Metropolitan area	Total employees	Employees per 100,000 population	Men					Women				
			American Indian, Eskimo & Aleut	Asian, Pacific Islander	Black	Hispanic	White	American Indian, Eskimo & Aleut	Asian, Pacific Islander	Black	Hispanic	White
Greensboro, North Carolina Winston-Salem, North Carolina High Point, North Carolina MSA	2,130	226.1	0	23	297	0	401	12	5	485	6	901
Columbus, Ohio MSA	2,072	150.4	3	0	101	6	746	10	35	101	16	1,070

Source: Census of Population and Housing, 1990: Equal Employment Opportunity (EEO) File on CD-ROM [machine-readable datafiles]. Prepared by the Bureau of the Census. Washington, DC: The Bureau, 1992. Notes: "MSA" represents "metropolitan statistical area"; "CMSA" stands for "consolidated metropolitan statistical area."

★ 142 ★

Leading Occupations

Health Technologists and Technicians, by Metropolitan Area

According to the 1990 Census of Population and Housing, health technologists and technicians ranked 81 among occupations employing the most people in the United States. Table presents the number of civilians 16 years old or older who reported working as health technologists and technicians during the 1990 Census. Data show the total employment figures, employment per 100,000 population, and employment data for men and women of various races and ethnicities in the 25 metropolitan statistical areas with the largest concentrations of miscellaneous health technologists and technicians. See also tables for specific types of health technologists and technicians such as clinical laboratory technologists and technicians.

[Total for all of the U.S. was 411,191; 165.3 per 100,000 persons]

Metropolitan area	Total employees	Employees per 100,000 population	Men					Women				
			American Indian, Eskimo & Aleut	Asian, Pacific Islander	Black	Hispanic	White	American Indian, Eskimo & Aleut	Asian, Pacific Islander	Black	Hispanic	White
New York, New York New Jersey (northern) Long Island, New York CMSA	26,587	147.0	43	710	1,567	1,055	5,524	45	852	3,508	2,543	12,786
Los Angeles, California Anaheim, California Riverside, California CMSA	23,606	162.5	53	859	704	1,701	4,244	116	1,618	1,547	4,630	11,371
Chicago, Illinois Gary, Indiana Lake County, Illinois CMSA	13,602	168.6	5	314	686	419	2,978	26	452	1,922	583	6,744
Philadelphia, Pennsylvania Wilmington, Delaware Trenton, New Jersey CMSA	11,388	193.0	6	116	702	19	2,096	19	166	1,387	175	6,750
Detroit, Michigan Ann Arbor, Michigan CMSA	10,872	233.0	19	57	318	18	1,792	25	179	1,355	56	7,085
San Francisco, California Oakland, California San Jose, California CMSA	10,838	173.3	11	570	270	451	2,412	41	993	533	1,001	5,261
Boston, Massachusetts Lawrence, Massachusetts Salem, Massachusetts CMSA	7,652	183.4	0	148	139	92	2,331	31	126	342	199	4,419
Miami, Florida Fort Lauderdale, Florida CMSA	7,391	231.5	0	25	366	694	1,683	6	62	902	1,636	4,143
Washington, District of Columbia MSA	7,174	182.8	8	231	927	146	1,581	27	223	1,459	130	2,615
Houston, Texas Galveston, Texas Brazoria, Texas CMSA	6,580	177.3	17	158	446	358	1,365	22	229	1,204	771	2,610
Pittsburgh, Pennsylvania Beaver Valley, Pennsylvania CMSA	5,541	247.1	0	20	94	12	1,591	0	29	229	17	3,574
St. Louis, Missouri MSA	5,458	223.3	12	26	203	57	1,189	17	43	696	85	3,253
Cleveland, Ohio Akron, Ohio Lorain, Ohio CMSA	5,410	196.0	0	28	189	11	1,001	2	50	722	39	3,391
Dallas, Texas Fort Worth, Texas CMSA	5,281	135.9	5	52	222	127	1,361	31	45	651	326	2,696
Baltimore, Maryland MSA	5,219	219.1	0	86	486	19	1,201	9	53	888	34	2,480
Atlanta, Georgia MSA	4,847	171.1	19	38	444	19	1,047	15	24	1,096	74	2,134

[Continued]

★ 142 ★

Health Technologists and Technicians, by Metropolitan Area
[Continued]

Metropolitan area	Total employees	Employees per 100,000 population	Men					Women				
			American Indian, Eskimo & Aleut	Asian, Pacific Islander	Black	Hispanic	White	American Indian, Eskimo & Aleut	Asian, Pacific Islander	Black	Hispanic	White
San Diego, California MSA	4,714	188.7	0	153	89	162	1,096	14	390	131	488	2,484
Seattle, Washington Tacoma, Washington CMSA	4,354	170.1	12	73	49	63	1,110	28	165	137	55	2,730
Tampa, Florida St. Petersburg, Florida Clearwater, Florida MSA	4,274	206.7	19	25	75	101	1,194	28	12	206	226	2,636
Minneapolis, Minnesota St. Paul, Minnesota MSA	4,176	169.5	20	19	43	12	958	24	46	53	46	3,003
Phoenix, Arizona MSA	3,912	184.4	28	29	24	73	857	27	67	52	318	2,615
Cincinnati, Ohio Hamilton, Ohio CMSA	3,415	195.8	0	39	124	3	796	0	16	233	0	2,207
Denver, Colorado Boulder, Colorado CMSA	3,383	183.0	0	0	67	121	911	24	15	103	219	2,116
Milwaukee, Wisconsin Racine, Wisconsin CMSA	3,255	202.5	0	5	38	27	539	18	23	175	35	2,444
Kansas City, Missouri Kansas City, Kansas MSA	3,002	191.7	0	8	122	21	757	7	7	256	70	1,794

Source: Census of Population and Housing, 1990: Equal Employment Opportunity (EEO) File on CD-ROM [machine-readable datafiles]. Prepared by the Bureau of the Census. Washington, DC: The Bureau, 1992. *Notes:* "MSA" represents "metropolitan statistical area"; "CMSA" stands for "consolidated metropolitan statistical area."

★ 143 ★

Leading Occupations

Industrial Machinery Repairers, by Metropolitan Area

According to the 1990 Census of Population and Housing, industrial machinery repairers ranked 96 among occupations employing the most people in the United States. Table presents the number of civilians 16 years old or older who reported working as industrial machinery repairers during the 1990 Census. Data show the total employment figures, employment per 100,000 population, and employment data for men and women of various races and ethnicities in the 25 metropolitan statistical areas with the largest concentrations of industrial machinery repairers.

[Total for all of the U.S. was 332,779; 133.8 per 100,000 persons]

Metropolitan area	Total employees	Employees per 100,000 population	Men					Women				
			American Indian, Eskimo & Aleut	Asian, Pacific Islander	Black	Hispanic	White	American Indian, Eskimo & Aleut	Asian, Pacific Islander	Black	Hispanic	White
Los Angeles, California Anaheim, California Riverside, California CMSA	13,758	94.68	100	720	572	5,178	8,933	0	40	63	379	389
New York, New York New Jersey (northern) Long Island, New York CMSA	13,006	71.91	10	362	1,569	2,286	9,574	0	7	101	114	241
Chicago, Illinois Gary, Indiana Lake County, Illinois CMSA	11,294	140.0	18	253	950	1,908	8,630	0	14	49	125	271
Detroit, Michigan Ann Arbor, Michigan CMSA	7,444	159.6	26	14	588	93	6,579	0	7	40	17	157
Philadelphia, Pennsylvania Wilmington, Delaware Trenton, New Jersey CMSA	6,142	104.1	17	19	416	194	5,457	0	0	40	16	109
San Francisco, California Oakland, California San Jose, California CMSA	5,356	85.65	25	620	272	837	3,830	9	93	16	38	112
Charlotte, North Carolina Gastonia, North Carolina Rock Hill, South Carolina MSA	4,389	377.7	33	18	430	26	3,546	0	0	76	0	271

[Continued]

★ 143 ★

Industrial Machinery Repairers, by Metropolitan Area
[Continued]

Metropolitan area	Total employees	Employees per 100,000 population	Men					Women				
			American Indian, Eskimo & Aleut	Asian, Pacific Islander	Black	Hispanic	White	American Indian, Eskimo & Aleut	Asian, Pacific Islander	Black	Hispanic	White
Greensboro, North Carolina Winston-Salem, North Carolina High Point, North Carolina MSA	4,325	459.1	8	7	518	8	3,473	0	0	51	0	268
Cleveland, Ohio Akron, Ohio Lorain, Ohio CMSA	4,249	154.0	9	5	325	29	3,702	0	0	38	0	150
Dallas, Texas Fort Worth, Texas CMSA	3,857	99.27	43	66	283	568	2,989	6	11	54	35	84
Boston, Massachusetts Lawrence, Massachusetts Salem, Massachusetts CMSA	3,401	81.53	17	32	98	81	3,061	0	8	36	7	119
Greenville, South Carolina Spartanburg, South Carolina MSA	3,214	501.5	5	0	251	26	2,783	0	0	24	0	132
Houston, Texas Galveston, Texas Brazoria, Texas CMSA	3,091	83.29	0	76	358	644	2,202	0	0	46	15	41
Milwaukee, Wisconsin Racine, Wisconsin CMSA	2,964	184.4	26	15	126	105	2,647	0	0	7	0	114
Minneapolis, Minnesota St. Paul, Minnesota MSA	2,803	113.8	22	29	31	41	2,531	0	12	0	0	137
Atlanta, Georgia MSA	2,669	94.19	0	52	336	13	2,167	0	0	68	0	40
Cincinnati, Ohio Hamilton, Ohio CMSA	2,661	152.6	10	6	96	19	2,461	0	0	12	0	76
St. Louis, Missouri MSA	2,484	101.6	0	0	159	21	2,170	0	0	12	0	143
Baltimore, Maryland MSA	2,447	102.7	9	14	421	16	1,912	0	0	5	0	86
Norfolk, Virginia Virginia Beach, Virginia Newport News, Virginia MSA	2,162	154.9	8	66	493	49	1,501	0	0	22	0	64
Providence, Rhode Island Pawtucket, Rhode Island Fall River, Massachusetts CMSA	2,110	184.8	7	0	24	224	1,674	0	7	0	42	186
Pittsburgh, Pennsylvania Beaver Valley, Pennsylvania CMSA	2,032	90.60	0	0	56	3	1,934	0	0	0	0	42
Indianapolis, Indiana MSA	2,019	161.5	8	22	140	30	1,742	0	0	0	0	85
Miami, Florida Fort Lauderdale, Florida CMSA	1,980	62.02	0	14	130	904	1,655	0	0	22	20	56
Rochester, New York MSA	1,979	197.4	0	7	100	29	1,736	0	0	15	0	103

Source: Census of Population and Housing, 1990: Equal Employment Opportunity (EEO) File on CD-ROM [machine-readable datafiles]. Prepared by the Bureau of the Census. Washington, DC: The Bureau, 1992. *Notes:* "MSA" represents "metropolitan statistical area"; "CMSA" stands for "consolidated metropolitan statistical area."

★ 144 ★

Leading Occupations

Industrial Truck and Tractor Equipment Operators, by Metropolitan Area

According to the 1990 Census of Population and Housing, industrial truck and tractor equipment operators ranked 75 among occupations employing the most people in the United States. Table presents the number of civilians 16 years old or older who reported working as industrial truck and tractor equipment operators during the 1990 Census. Data show the total employment figures, employment per 100,000 population, and employment data for men and women of various races and ethnicities in the 25 metropolitan statistical areas with the largest concentrations of industrial truck and tractor equipment operators.

[Total for all of the U.S. was 441,859; 177.7 per 100,000 persons]

Metropolitan area	Total employees	Employees per 100,000 population	Men					Women				
			American Indian, Eskimo & Aleut	Asian, Pacific Islander	Black	Hispanic	White	American Indian, Eskimo & Aleut	Asian, Pacific Islander	Black	Hispanic	White
Los Angeles, California Anaheim, California Riverside, California CMSA	23,277	160.2	200	527	2,125	13,200	12,003	34	37	118	519	607
Chicago, Illinois Gary, Indiana Lake County, Illinois CMSA	14,433	178.9	42	141	3,699	2,938	7,871	7	12	260	103	613
New York, New York New Jersey (northern) Long Island, New York CMSA	14,321	79.18	21	245	3,289	3,380	8,697	8	0	201	60	312
Detroit, Michigan Ann Arbor, Michigan CMSA	10,875	233.1	123	13	2,376	235	7,682	22	0	165	27	382
Philadelphia, Pennsylvania Wilmington, Delaware Trenton, New Jersey CMSA	9,709	164.6	56	70	2,578	623	6,193	40	0	123	30	253
San Francisco, California Oakland, California San Jose, California CMSA	8,479	135.6	81	581	1,030	2,903	4,839	0	29	83	189	324
Dallas, Texas Fort Worth, Texas CMSA	6,643	171.0	61	71	1,547	1,660	3,551	3	3	81	57	207
Atlanta, Georgia MSA	6,241	220.3	12	63	2,711	60	2,925	0	0	253	0	250
Houston, Texas Galveston, Texas Brazoria, Texas CMSA	4,860	131.0	24	22	1,699	1,808	1,947	0	8	51	27	87
Cleveland, Ohio Akron, Ohio Lorain, Ohio CMSA	4,467	161.9	12	24	912	117	3,227	0	0	64	0	185
St. Louis, Missouri MSA	3,952	161.7	0	7	803	41	2,781	0	0	127	0	202
Baltimore, Maryland MSA	3,817	160.2	19	23	1,364	30	2,112	0	0	113	0	164
Seattle, Washington Tacoma, Washington CMSA	3,667	143.3	46	119	259	158	2,983	0	12	9	24	153
Columbus, Ohio MSA	3,610	262.1	18	0	415	22	2,963	0	0	37	0	177
Minneapolis, Minnesota St. Paul, Minnesota MSA	3,534	143.4	18	24	98	41	3,225	13	0	0	0	146
Milwaukee, Wisconsin Racine, Wisconsin CMSA	3,511	218.5	17	0	683	269	2,399	10	0	44	0	232
Portland, Oregon Vancouver, Washington CMSA	3,210	217.2	35	37	76	233	2,731	0	0	0	0	207
Boston, Massachusetts Lawrence, Massachusetts Salem, Massachusetts CMSA	3,122	74.84	0	15	245	135	2,672	0	7	0	0	93
Greensboro, North Carolina Winston-Salem, North Carolina High Point, North Carolina MSA	3,107	329.8	5	14	841	37	1,943	0	0	87	0	188
Memphis, Tennessee MSA	3,064	312.1	0	4	1,775	10	1,063	0	0	154	0	58
Cincinnati, Ohio Hamilton, Ohio CMSA	3,012	172.7	0	0	222	13	2,574	0	0	23	0	182
Miami, Florida Fort Lauderdale, Florida CMSA	3,000	93.97	12	69	839	1,396	1,798	0	0	23	48	71
Kansas City, Missouri Kansas City, Kansas MSA	2,859	182.5	30	12	367	100	2,191	0	0	34	0	188
Grand Rapids, Michigan MSA	2,849	413.9	34	7	190	137	2,294	0	0	15	21	208
Sacramento, California MSA	2,777	187.5	14	86	293	694	1,832	0	4	15	8	136

Source: Census of Population and Housing, 1990: Equal Employment Opportunity (EEO) File on CD-ROM [machine-readable datafiles]. Prepared by the Bureau of the Census. Washington, DC: The Bureau, 1992. *Notes:* "MSA" represents "metropolitan statistical area"; "CMSA" stands for "consolidated metropolitan statistical area."

★ 145 ★

Leading Occupations

Insurance Adjusters, Examiners, and Investigators, by Metropolitan Area

According to the 1990 Census of Population and Housing, insurance adjusters, examiners, and investigators ranked 93 among occupations employing the most people in the United States. Table presents the number of civilians 16 years old or older who reported working as insurance adjusters, examiners, and investigators during the 1990 Census. Data show the total employment figures, employment per 100,000 population, and employment data for men and women of various races and ethnicities in the 25 metropolitan statistical areas with the largest concentrations of insurance adjusters, examiners, and investigators.

[Total for all of the U.S. was 344,639; 138.6 per 100,000 persons]

Metropolitan area	Total employees	Employees per 100,000 population	Men					Women				
			American Indian, Eskimo & Aleut	Asian, Pacific Islander	Black	Hispanic	White	American Indian, Eskimo & Aleut	Asian, Pacific Islander	Black	Hispanic	White
New York, New York New Jersey (northern) Long Island, New York CMSA	28,457	157.3	6	312	1,056	654	7,811	50	563	3,975	1,171	14,080
Los Angeles, California Anaheim, California Riverside, California CMSA	21,072	145.0	50	678	590	895	5,167	100	1,465	2,102	2,037	9,485
Chicago, Illinois Gary, Indiana Lake County, Illinois CMSA	13,645	169.2	6	65	543	73	3,350	27	168	1,829	441	7,452
Philadelphia, Pennsylvania Wilmington, Delaware Trenton, New Jersey CMSA	13,568	230.0	25	50	445	63	3,456	11	71	1,946	141	7,490
Dallas, Texas Fort Worth, Texas CMSA	9,574	246.4	6	2	260	122	2,335	32	114	1,195	474	5,332
San Francisco, California Oakland, California San Jose, California CMSA	8,801	140.7	11	322	260	233	2,173	75	747	840	593	4,087
Boston, Massachusetts Lawrence, Massachusetts Salem, Massachusetts CMSA	8,394	201.2	23	19	184	14	2,270	6	57	424	66	5,375
Detroit, Michigan Ann Arbor, Michigan CMSA	7,110	152.4	0	10	275	28	1,304	40	45	1,649	66	3,738
Hartford, Connecticut New Britain, Connecticut Middletown, Connecticut CMSA	6,863	632.1	0	63	116	49	1,485	18	66	611	140	4,451
Minneapolis, Minnesota St. Paul, Minnesota MSA	6,236	253.1	0	28	99	0	1,506	1	39	112	72	4,426
Atlanta, Georgia MSA	6,146	216.9	6	0	250	5	1,400	10	48	1,404	55	3,019
Washington, District of Columbia MSA	5,976	152.3	15	65	580	63	1,225	26	154	1,555	133	2,301
Seattle, Washington Tacoma, Washington CMSA	5,052	197.4	23	66	45	24	1,205	22	238	140	132	3,268
Tampa, Florida St. Petersburg, Florida Clearwater, Florida MSA	4,641	224.4	0	14	65	81	1,052	9	35	348	290	3,069
Columbus, Ohio MSA	4,584	332.8	0	17	128	0	856	8	64	717	22	2,779
Baltimore, Maryland MSA	4,462	187.3	0	7	167	9	1,064	22	29	968	48	2,186
Houston, Texas Galveston, Texas Brazoria, Texas CMSA	4,372	117.8	0	21	171	94	1,248	9	71	681	233	2,016
St. Louis, Missouri MSA	4,280	175.1	0	2	128	9	1,002	7	19	661	21	2,455
Kansas City, Missouri Kansas City, Kansas MSA	3,918	250.2	6	0	47	23	1,004	27	19	469	63	2,304
Milwaukee, Wisconsin Racine, Wisconsin CMSA	3,865	240.5	0	0	26	7	740	24	42	377	52	2,623
Jacksonville, Florida MSA	3,741	412.6	0	0	110	16	476	0	51	1,030	78	2,049
Pittsburgh, Pennsylvania Beaver Valley, Pennsylvania CMSA	3,722	166.0	0	0	18	6	916	0	0	386	0	2,393
Phoenix, Arizona MSA	3,695	174.1	42	0	75	54	917	30	71	86	158	2,436
Cleveland, Ohio Akron, Ohio Lorain, Ohio CMSA	3,509	127.2	0	0	144	0	766	0	9	457	55	2,120
Indianapolis, Indiana MSA	3,427	274.2	0	0	33	0	700	5	0	518	0	2,171

Source: Census of Population and Housing, 1990: Equal Employment Opportunity (EEO) File on CD-ROM [machine-readable datafiles]. Prepared by the Bureau of the Census. Washington, DC: The Bureau, 1992. *Notes:* "MSA" represents "metropolitan statistical area"; "CMSA" stands for "consolidated metropolitan statistical area."

★ 146 ★

Leading Occupations

Insurance Sales Occupations, by Metropolitan Area

According to the 1990 Census of Population and Housing, insurance sales occupations ranked 39 among occupations employing the most people in the United States. Table presents the number of civilians 16 years old or older who reported working in insurance sales occupations during the 1990 Census. Data show the total employment figures, employment per 100,000 population, and employment data for men and women of various races and ethnicities in the 25 metropolitan statistical areas with the largest concentrations of insurance sales occupations.

[Total for all of the U.S. was 666,542; 268.0 per 100,000 persons]

Metropolitan area	Total employees	Employees per 100,000 population	Men					Women				
			American Indian, Eskimo & Aleut	Asian, Pacific Islander	Black	Hispanic	White	American Indian, Eskimo & Aleut	Asian, Pacific Islander	Black	Hispanic	White
New York, New York New Jersey (northern) Long Island, New York CMSA	47,136	260.6	56	972	2,017	1,394	26,639	5	495	2,661	1,293	13,432
Los Angeles, California Anaheim, California Riverside, California CMSA	36,619	252.0	75	2,045	1,329	2,763	18,339	97	1,041	1,334	1,966	10,229
Chicago, Illinois Gary, Indiana Lake County, Illinois CMSA	25,446	315.5	29	448	1,376	398	13,872	34	213	1,593	449	7,501
Philadelphia, Pennsylvania Wilmington, Delaware Trenton, New Jersey CMSA	17,385	294.7	6	163	825	168	9,496	0	65	1,154	110	5,587
San Francisco, California Oakland, California San Jose, California CMSA	16,121	257.8	15	935	456	532	8,242	24	783	406	544	4,875
Dallas, Texas Fort Worth, Texas CMSA	14,332	368.9	70	113	572	385	7,779	0	96	866	219	4,499
Boston, Massachusetts Lawrence, Massachusetts Salem, Massachusetts CMSA	12,121	290.6	0	30	210	50	6,872	9	80	251	104	4,620
Atlanta, Georgia MSA	10,861	383.3	25	27	838	60	5,973	0	60	700	16	3,222
Houston, Texas Galveston, Texas Brazoria, Texas CMSA	10,806	291.2	23	251	660	480	5,864	20	119	482	309	3,122
Detroit, Michigan Ann Arbor, Michigan CMSA	10,317	221.2	11	32	736	53	5,408	7	12	695	20	3,400
Miami, Florida Fort Lauderdale, Florida CMSA	9,559	299.4	0	44	545	1,636	5,203	0	8	309	1,197	3,210
Minneapolis, Minnesota St. Paul, Minnesota MSA	8,687	352.5	21	41	55	10	5,272	12	52	75	15	3,148
Washington, District of Columbia MSA	8,601	219.2	7	200	680	62	4,134	15	165	735	91	2,610
St. Louis, Missouri MSA	7,909	323.6	8	39	303	0	4,977	9	30	387	9	2,142
Seattle, Washington Tacoma, Washington CMSA	7,114	278.0	16	185	163	51	4,153	5	123	69	18	2,400
Phoenix, Arizona MSA	7,027	331.1	8	15	95	196	4,089	19	17	42	142	2,625
Hartford, Connecticut New Britain, Connecticut Middletown, Connecticut CMSA	6,990	643.7	0	27	215	60	3,307	10	27	382	96	2,993
Tampa, Florida St. Petersburg, Florida Clearwater, Florida MSA	6,977	337.4	8	23	155	228	3,791	0	27	164	228	2,765
Cleveland, Ohio Akron, Ohio Lorain, Ohio CMSA	6,891	249.7	0	35	335	15	4,438	0	24	216	0	1,843
Baltimore, Maryland MSA	6,560	275.4	15	20	441	42	3,619	0	0	478	16	1,970
Denver, Colorado Boulder, Colorado CMSA	6,471	350.1	0	74	100	128	3,779	12	29	152	147	2,225
San Diego, California MSA	6,412	256.7	7	130	55	258	3,708	8	155	134	178	2,060
Kansas City, Missouri Kansas City, Kansas MSA	6,219	397.1	0	17	181	49	3,702	4	0	168	47	2,130
Pittsburgh, Pennsylvania Beaver Valley, Pennsylvania CMSA	5,944	265.0	0	6	147	21	4,095	0	5	75	6	1,608
San Antonio, Texas MSA	5,330	409.3	18	39	97	817	2,417	16	7	183	936	2,022

Source: Census of Population and Housing, 1990: Equal Employment Opportunity (EEO) File on CD-ROM [machine-readable datafiles]. Prepared by the Bureau of the Census. Washington, DC: The Bureau, 1992. *Notes:* "MSA" represents "metropolitan statistical area"; "CMSA" stands for "consolidated metropolitan statistical area."

★147★

Leading Occupations

Investigators and Adjusters, by Metropolitan Area

According to the 1990 Census of Population and Housing, investigators and adjusters ranked 57 among occupations employing the most people in the United States. Table presents the number of civilians 16 years old or older who reported working as investigators and adjusters during the 1990 Census. Data show the total employment figures, employment per 100,000 population, and employment data for men and women of various races and ethnicities in the 25 metropolitan statistical areas with the largest concentrations of investigators and adjusters, excluding insurance investigators and adjusters.

[Total for all of the U.S. was 581,830; 233.9 per 100,000 persons]

Metropolitan area	Total employees	Employees per 100,000 population	Men					Women				
			American Indian, Eskimo & Aleut	Asian, Pacific Islander	Black	Hispanic	White	American Indian, Eskimo & Aleut	Asian, Pacific Islander	Black	Hispanic	White
New York, New York New Jersey (northern) Long Island, New York CMSA	49,517	273.8	31	609	2,116	1,260	10,576	99	778	7,813	3,640	25,707
Los Angeles, California Anaheim, California Riverside, California CMSA	44,127	303.7	70	1,203	1,480	2,414	9,179	162	2,832	3,908	6,802	20,682
Chicago, Illinois Gary, Indiana Lake County, Illinois CMSA	26,114	323.8	5	176	1,030	400	5,630	35	293	3,742	1,197	14,462
San Francisco, California Oakland, California San Jose, California CMSA	22,587	361.2	54	958	629	606	4,672	87	2,218	1,935	1,909	10,992
Philadelphia, Pennsylvania Wilmington, Delaware Trenton, New Jersey CMSA	18,703	317.0	0	56	807	129	3,620	10	132	2,619	183	11,276
Dallas, Texas Fort Worth, Texas CMSA	13,297	342.2	30	32	347	203	3,057	51	66	1,561	828	7,725
Boston, Massachusetts Lawrence, Massachusetts Salem, Massachusetts CMSA	13,021	312.1	0	81	244	108	3,078	10	163	573	202	8,740
Atlanta, Georgia MSA	11,948	421.7	0	16	654	136	2,275	15	40	2,503	178	6,313
Washington, District of Columbia MSA	11,724	298.8	37	208	851	177	2,437	43	347	2,499	414	5,127
Detroit, Michigan Ann Arbor, Michigan CMSA	10,312	221.0	0	29	414	53	2,347	43	38	1,714	120	5,694
Minneapolis, Minnesota St. Paul, Minnesota MSA	10,108	410.2	27	12	82	24	2,719	26	57	217	39	6,937
Miami, Florida Fort Lauderdale, Florida CMSA	9,435	295.5	12	21	252	827	2,036	6	130	1,035	2,474	5,665
Seattle, Washington Tacoma, Washington CMSA	8,040	314.2	0	103	90	64	1,946	132	245	345	145	5,065
Phoenix, Arizona MSA	7,480	352.5	7	32	57	168	1,946	39	128	171	483	4,799
Houston, Texas Galveston, Texas Brazoria, Texas CMSA	7,438	200.4	0	67	338	187	1,601	16	79	1,288	735	3,619
St. Louis, Missouri MSA	7,389	302.3	0	0	164	26	1,813	13	28	777	82	4,568
Baltimore, Maryland MSA	7,283	305.7	6	20	488	7	1,297	11	60	1,870	54	3,519
San Diego, California MSA	6,962	278.7	27	72	125	262	1,508	19	458	412	785	3,790
Denver, Colorado Boulder, Colorado CMSA	6,863	371.3	7	28	102	159	1,673	51	68	332	544	4,372
Cleveland, Ohio Akron, Ohio Lorain, Ohio CMSA	6,859	248.5	0	0	192	37	1,587	11	16	770	64	4,221
Tampa, Florida St. Petersburg, Florida Clearwater, Florida MSA	6,501	314.4	12	0	85	146	1,302	0	48	439	388	4,474
Kansas City, Missouri Kansas City, Kansas MSA	5,394	344.4	0	10	130	62	1,153	2	39	530	99	3,454
Columbus, Ohio MSA	4,892	355.2	26	7	159	7	1,098	6	20	500	27	3,071
Milwaukee, Wisconsin Racine, Wisconsin CMSA	4,890	304.3	0	0	152	10	1,123	0	16	338	71	3,225
Cincinnati, Ohio Hamilton, Ohio CMSA	4,877	279.6	0	10	140	12	1,125	0	13	359	16	3,218

Source: Census of Population and Housing, 1990: Equal Employment Opportunity (EEO) File on CD-ROM [machine-readable datafiles]. Prepared by the Bureau of the Census. Washington, DC: The Bureau, 1992. *Notes:* "MSA" represents "metropolitan statistical area"; "CMSA" stands for "consolidated metropolitan statistical area."

★ 148 ★

Leading Occupations

Janitors and Cleaners, by Metropolitan Area

According to the 1990 Census of Population and Housing, janitors and cleaners ranked 7 among occupations employing the most people in the United States. Table presents the number of civilians 16 years old or older who reported working as janitors and cleaners during the 1990 Census. Data show the total employment figures, employment per 100,000 population, and employment data for men and women of various races and ethnicities in the 25 metropolitan statistical areas with the largest concentrations of janitors and cleaners.

[Total for all of the U.S. was 2,481,545; 997.8 per 100,000 persons]

Metropolitan area	Total employees	Employees per 100,000 population	Men					Women				
			American Indian, Eskimo & Aleut	Asian, Pacific Islander	Black	Hispanic	White	American Indian, Eskimo & Aleut	Asian, Pacific Islander	Black	Hispanic	White
New York, New York New Jersey (northern) Long Island, New York CMSA	175,664	971.2	464	2,873	36,037	41,918	73,551	222	955	11,207	17,215	24,355
Los Angeles, California Anaheim, California Riverside, California CMSA	131,746	906.6	710	5,412	12,280	53,132	48,611	190	1,776	4,090	22,954	16,940
Chicago, Illinois Gary, Indiana Lake County, Illinois CMSA	85,715	1,063	179	1,059	17,489	11,136	38,212	83	384	4,795	3,507	15,291
San Francisco, California Oakland, California San Jose, California CMSA	57,319	916.6	295	5,922	5,925	15,839	23,264	150	1,541	1,497	6,220	7,917
Philadelphia, Pennsylvania Wilmington, Delaware Trenton, New Jersey CMSA	55,230	936.2	188	432	13,791	1,907	23,057	53	174	6,999	858	8,864
Detroit, Michigan Ann Arbor, Michigan CMSA	49,752	1,066	145	169	10,556	765	22,935	97	79	4,783	250	10,581
Houston, Texas Galveston, Texas Brazoria, Texas CMSA	41,956	1,131	107	678	6,044	10,787	11,565	62	319	4,364	9,687	6,935
Dallas, Texas Fort Worth, Texas CMSA	39,573	1,019	166	1,033	7,448	6,179	14,818	50	371	3,615	3,534	5,704
Boston, Massachusetts Lawrence, Massachusetts Salem, Massachusetts CMSA	36,891	884.3	101	376	2,610	3,823	24,048	21	174	741	1,562	6,095
Washington, District of Columbia MSA	36,297	925.1	52	1,003	12,213	3,871	6,948	96	617	7,271	3,701	4,134
Miami, Florida Fort Lauderdale, Florida CMSA	31,626	990.6	69	141	6,887	9,048	12,770	13	114	3,443	5,859	6,234
Cleveland, Ohio Akron, Ohio Lorain, Ohio CMSA	31,090	1,127	72	80	5,021	361	15,531	37	39	2,833	348	7,169
Minneapolis, Minnesota St. Paul, Minnesota MSA	27,456	1,114	301	605	1,408	556	18,119	67	119	500	166	6,012
St. Louis, Missouri MSA	27,366	1,120	108	60	6,370	179	12,871	0	96	2,946	68	4,850
Atlanta, Georgia MSA	24,413	861.6	0	503	7,775	701	7,424	0	241	4,723	303	3,370
Pittsburgh, Pennsylvania Beaver Valley, Pennsylvania CMSA	24,294	1,083	0	26	2,495	87	14,271	38	0	1,022	42	6,386
Baltimore, Maryland MSA	22,519	945.3	61	66	8,119	122	6,290	79	52	4,467	67	3,336
San Diego, California MSA	21,989	880.3	154	1,691	1,646	5,718	9,118	63	620	339	3,252	3,243
Seattle, Washington Tacoma, Washington CMSA	21,623	844.9	359	1,422	1,497	813	11,331	201	700	594	320	5,058
Phoenix, Arizona MSA	21,098	994.2	431	220	814	4,203	10,837	189	69	315	2,416	4,424
Denver, Colorado Boulder, Colorado CMSA	20,140	1,090	111	412	1,333	3,570	10,229	123	214	534	2,092	4,599
Cincinnati, Ohio Hamilton, Ohio CMSA	18,434	1,057	43	46	3,242	71	9,175	35	13	1,516	18	4,327
Tampa, Florida St. Petersburg, Florida Clearwater, Florida MSA	17,922	866.7	39	80	1,984	1,334	9,711	0	120	1,243	829	4,260
Milwaukee, Wisconsin Racine, Wisconsin CMSA	17,554	1,092	101	153	2,141	606	8,946	75	19	1,389	385	4,214
Kansas City, Missouri Kansas City, Kansas MSA	16,251	1,038	101	64	3,282	387	8,107	31	87	1,319	118	3,062

Source: Census of Population and Housing, 1990: Equal Employment Opportunity (EEO) File on CD-ROM [machine-readable datafiles]. Prepared by the Bureau of the Census. Washington, DC: The Bureau, 1992. *Notes:* "MSA" represents "metropolitan statistical area"; "CMSA" stands for "consolidated metropolitan statistical area."

★ 149 ★

Leading Occupations

Laborers, by Metropolitan Area

According to the 1990 Census of Population and Housing, laborers in wholesale and retail trades ranked 92; those in durable manufacturing ranked 104; those in miscellaneous industries ranked 114; those in nondurable manufacturing ranked 137; and those in transportation, communications, and utilities ranked 205 among occupations employing the most people in the United States. Table presents the number of civilians 16 years old or older who reported working as laborers in any industry except construction during the 1990 Census. (See separate table for data on construction laborers.) Data show the total employment figures, employment per 100,000 population, and employment data for men and women of various races and ethnicities in the 25 metropolitan statistical areas with the largest concentrations of laborers.

[Total for all of the U.S. was 1,291,166; 519.2 per 100,000 persons]

Metropolitan area	Total employees	Employees per 100,000 population	Men					Women				
			American Indian, Eskimo & Aleut	Asian, Pacific Islander	Black	Hispanic	White	American Indian, Eskimo & Aleut	Asian, Pacific Islander	Black	Hispanic	White
New York, New York New Jersey (northern) Long Island, New York CMSA	71,675	396.3	183	2,029	13,316	14,251	32,274	68	1,253	4,262	6,619	9,368
Los Angeles, California Anaheim, California Riverside, California CMSA	66,468	457.4	458	2,569	4,656	30,735	28,332	91	1,075	891	8,441	6,722
Chicago, Illinois Gary, Indiana Lake County, Illinois CMSA	45,629	565.7	134	641	7,556	9,193	21,388	29	347	2,034	3,345	5,938
Philadelphia, Pennsylvania Wilmington, Delaware Trenton, New Jersey CMSA	25,843	438.1	50	201	5,722	1,114	14,101	8	92	1,367	357	3,004
San Francisco, California Oakland, California San Jose, California CMSA	25,319	404.9	222	2,235	2,601	6,648	12,375	85	764	555	1,531	2,442
Detroit, Michigan Ann Arbor, Michigan CMSA	21,318	457.0	97	69	4,291	562	11,853	7	89	1,512	69	3,054
Dallas, Texas Fort Worth, Texas CMSA	18,685	480.9	67	179	3,210	3,867	8,427	46	161	1,035	1,172	2,153
Houston, Texas Galveston, Texas Brazoria, Texas CMSA	17,163	462.5	36	388	3,662	6,055	7,148	0	129	605	978	1,121
Cleveland, Ohio Akron, Ohio Lorain, Ohio CMSA	15,776	571.6	32	59	2,828	449	9,583	12	11	745	101	2,190
Boston, Massachusetts Lawrence, Massachusetts Salem, Massachusetts CMSA	15,719	376.8	20	105	835	907	11,222	4	92	147	341	2,529
Atlanta, Georgia MSA	14,022	494.9	20	174	4,163	426	5,691	20	110	1,844	111	1,677
Pittsburgh, Pennsylvania Beaver Valley, Pennsylvania CMSA	13,724	611.9	17	28	763	37	11,188	9	5	126	17	1,566
Miami, Florida Fort Lauderdale, Florida CMSA	13,285	416.1	15	58	2,879	4,707	6,300	6	8	878	1,993	2,201
Seattle, Washington Tacoma, Washington CMSA	13,058	510.2	201	567	819	406	9,019	22	194	111	67	1,964
St. Louis, Missouri MSA	12,584	514.9	40	42	2,188	186	7,891	4	0	619	20	1,743
Minneapolis, Minnesota St. Paul, Minnesota MSA	11,104	450.6	200	61	445	202	8,123	36	18	82	36	2,034
Baltimore, Maryland MSA	10,944	459.4	41	81	3,853	76	4,741	6	44	767	44	1,370
Washington, District of Columbia MSA	10,186	259.6	115	172	4,155	564	3,589	14	81	769	283	835
Milwaukee, Wisconsin Racine, Wisconsin CMSA	9,641	599.9	73	58	1,341	749	5,504	25	23	515	117	1,639
Cincinnati, Ohio Hamilton, Ohio CMSA	9,298	533.1	15	21	1,154	0	6,074	0	9	290	9	1,720
Portland, Oregon Vancouver, Washington CMSA	8,971	607.0	93	149	288	695	6,487	18	76	63	111	1,315
Phoenix, Arizona MSA	8,590	404.8	191	82	426	2,200	5,127	93	90	123	412	1,070
Kansas City, Missouri Kansas City, Kansas MSA	8,322	531.3	43	56	1,194	477	5,107	11	17	324	75	1,273
Columbus, Ohio MSA	8,291	601.9	14	17	844	34	5,360	0	24	244	36	1,759
Denver, Colorado Boulder, Colorado CMSA	8,273	447.6	89	107	567	1,635	5,164	43	72	92	520	1,135

Source: Census of Population and Housing, 1990: Equal Employment Opportunity (EEO) File on CD-ROM [machine-readable datafiles]. Prepared by the Bureau of the Census. Washington, DC: The Bureau, 1992. *Notes:* "MSA" represents "metropolitan statistical area"; "CMSA" stands for "consolidated metropolitan statistical area."

★ 150 ★

Leading Occupations

Lawyers, by Metropolitan Area

According to the 1990 Census of Population and Housing, lawyers ranked 31 among occupations employing the most people in the United States. Table presents the number of civilians 16 years old or older who reported working as lawyers during the 1990 Census. Data show the total employment figures, employment per 100,000 population, and employment data for men and women of various races and ethnicities in the 25 metropolitan statistical areas with the largest concentrations of lawyers.

[Total for all of the U.S. was 747,077; 300.4 per 100,000 persons]

Metropolitan area	Total employees	Employees per 100,000 population	Men					Women				
			American Indian, Eskimo & Aleut	Asian, Pacific Islander	Black	Hispanic	White	American Indian, Eskimo & Aleut	Asian, Pacific Islander	Black	Hispanic	White
New York, New York 　New Jersey (northern) 　Long Island, New York CMSA	103,809	573.9	40	898	2,045	1,481	72,298	32	749	2,296	1,121	24,977
Los Angeles, California 　Anaheim, California 　Riverside, California CMSA	51,201	352.3	84	1,350	1,111	1,720	34,537	49	803	813	861	11,774
Washington, District of Columbia MSA	43,580	1111	31	521	1,803	600	27,724	6	311	1,558	303	11,393
Chicago, Illinois 　Gary, Indiana 　Lake County, Illinois CMSA	35,792	443.8	7	231	745	460	26,041	13	126	514	284	7,854
San Francisco, California 　Oakland, California 　San Jose, California CMSA	30,280	484.2	36	843	538	630	19,503	29	649	347	461	8,089
Philadelphia, Pennsylvania 　Wilmington, Delaware 　Trenton, New Jersey CMSA	23,077	391.2	12	61	594	207	16,205	0	41	495	83	5,635
Boston, Massachusetts 　Lawrence, Massachusetts 　Salem, Massachusetts CMSA	21,504	515.5	10	80	169	136	14,404	7	118	312	140	6,276
Houston, Texas 　Galveston, Texas 　Brazoria, Texas CMSA	14,928	402.3	16	57	346	429	10,433	6	63	327	254	3,528
Miami, Florida 　Fort Lauderdale, Florida CMSA	13,950	437.0	0	16	177	1,259	10,396	0	13	192	716	3,053
Detroit, Michigan 　Ann Arbor, Michigan CMSA	13,676	293.2	5	43	609	55	10,063	0	0	428	24	2,520
Dallas, Texas 　Fort Worth, Texas CMSA	12,750	328.2	8	26	210	265	9,468	8	42	179	154	2,687
Atlanta, Georgia MSA	11,615	409.9	0	19	519	84	8,240	7	22	347	32	2,425
Minneapolis, Minnesota 　St. Paul, Minnesota MSA	10,121	410.7	3	39	84	41	7,308	22	23	37	36	2,564
Denver, Colorado 　Boulder, Colorado CMSA	9,844	532.6	48	13	88	182	6,954	35	21	44	81	2,583
San Diego, California MSA	9,336	373.7	31	166	45	295	6,528	0	71	10	161	2,302
Seattle, Washington 　Tacoma, Washington CMSA	9,150	357.5	47	237	114	29	6,291	0	86	41	7	2,334
Cleveland, Ohio 　Akron, Ohio 　Lorain, Ohio CMSA	9,143	331.3	0	13	324	20	6,819	9	9	110	28	1,841
Baltimore, Maryland MSA	9,046	379.7	5	18	350	25	6,036	0	27	337	25	2,273
St. Louis, Missouri MSA	7,009	286.8	0	5	93	20	5,434	0	0	99	27	1,365
Pittsburgh, Pennsylvania 　Beaver Valley, Pennsylvania CMSA	6,657	296.8	0	24	97	14	5,006	0	36	52	0	1,442
Phoenix, Arizona MSA	6,608	311.4	0	64	53	157	4,847	11	22	19	74	1,504
New Orleans, Louisiana MSA	6,505	525.1	0	7	289	95	4,567	0	0	172	42	1,458
Kansas City, Missouri 　Kansas City, Kansas MSA	5,767	368.2	8	0	92	34	4,464	0	7	54	20	1,127
Sacramento, California MSA	5,562	375.5	25	58	89	66	3,910	0	71	52	46	1,315
Tampa, Florida 　St. Petersburg, Florida 　Clearwater, Florida MSA	5,420	262.1	0	0	70	300	4,129	10	0	39	42	1,159

Source: Census of Population and Housing, 1990: Equal Employment Opportunity (EEO) File on CD-ROM [machine-readable datafiles]. Prepared by the Bureau of the Census. Washington, DC: The Bureau, 1992. *Notes:* "MSA" represents "metropolitan statistical area"; "CMSA" stands for "consolidated metropolitan statistical area."

★ 151 ★

Leading Occupations

Licensed Practical Nurses, by Metropolitan Area

According to the 1990 Census of Population and Housing, licensed practical nurses ranked 79 among occupations employing the most people in the United States. Table presents the number of civilians 16 years old or older who reported working as licensed practical nurses during the 1990 Census. Data show the total employment figures, employment per 100,000 population, and employment data for men and women of various races and ethnicities in the 25 metropolitan statistical areas with the largest concentrations of licensed practical nurses.

[Total for all of the U.S. was 429,473; 172.7 per 100,000 persons]

Metropolitan area	Total employees	Employees per 100,000 population	Men American Indian, Eskimo & Aleut	Men Asian, Pacific Islander	Men Black	Men Hispanic	Men White	Women American Indian, Eskimo & Aleut	Women Asian, Pacific Islander	Women Black	Women Hispanic	Women White
New York, New York New Jersey (northern) Long Island, New York CMSA	22,459	124.2	8	298	842	224	887	53	1,262	8,391	1,691	10,095
Los Angeles, California Anaheim, California Riverside, California CMSA	15,872	109.2	0	283	376	430	876	135	2,288	2,979	2,964	7,166
Philadelphia, Pennsylvania Wilmington, Delaware Trenton, New Jersey CMSA	9,616	163.0	0	5	235	29	359	18	84	2,700	153	6,160
Chicago, Illinois Gary, Indiana Lake County, Illinois CMSA	8,506	105.5	0	19	243	106	357	10	278	3,335	357	4,031
Detroit, Michigan Ann Arbor, Michigan CMSA	7,226	154.9	4	25	156	31	273	21	121	2,416	68	4,199
Cleveland, Ohio Akron, Ohio Lorain, Ohio CMSA	6,488	235.1	0	0	143	33	194	30	11	1,277	122	4,799
San Francisco, California Oakland, California San Jose, California CMSA	6,431	102.8	0	177	97	120	419	48	1,127	1,034	698	3,117
Boston, Massachusetts Lawrence, Massachusetts Salem, Massachusetts CMSA	6,288	150.7	6	14	60	10	353	17	45	496	118	5,250
Houston, Texas Galveston, Texas Brazoria, Texas CMSA	5,481	147.7	0	22	110	40	168	62	244	2,171	495	2,493
Dallas, Texas Fort Worth, Texas CMSA	4,800	123.5	0	3	41	49	301	41	120	1,251	286	2,863
Tampa, Florida St. Petersburg, Florida Clearwater, Florida MSA	4,702	227.4	0	12	25	42	317	24	15	592	130	3,684
Miami, Florida Fort Lauderdale, Florida CMSA	4,532	142.0	0	7	132	116	259	2	57	1,738	552	2,249
St. Louis, Missouri MSA	4,464	182.6	0	14	9	0	209	7	24	1,471	11	2,726
Minneapolis, Minnesota St. Paul, Minnesota MSA	4,402	178.6	0	0	27	0	206	34	19	153	51	3,958
Baltimore, Maryland MSA	3,970	166.7	0	0	233	0	173	0	25	1,811	31	1,723
Pittsburgh, Pennsylvania Beaver Valley, Pennsylvania CMSA	3,893	173.6	0	4	53	0	112	0	9	551	22	3,151
Cincinnati, Ohio Hamilton, Ohio CMSA	3,827	219.4	0	0	24	6	229	6	0	723	24	2,845
Washington, District of Columbia MSA	3,682	93.84	0	19	253	7	150	16	118	1,685	119	1,413
Atlanta, Georgia MSA	3,444	121.6	0	0	116	0	92	0	24	1,613	21	1,599
San Antonio, Texas MSA	3,277	251.7	8	0	89	214	421	0	42	547	1,168	1,639
Seattle, Washington Tacoma, Washington CMSA	3,086	120.6	0	27	48	12	263	41	131	232	56	2,320
San Diego, California MSA	2,999	120.1	6	47	55	62	283	33	488	235	326	1,721
Milwaukee, Wisconsin Racine, Wisconsin CMSA	2,998	186.5	0	0	19	8	112	0	9	455	29	2,389
Buffalo, New York Niagara Falls, New York CMSA	2,836	238.5	0	0	45	0	118	45	6	366	36	2,249
Kansas City, Missouri Kansas City, Kansas MSA	2,639	168.5	0	6	51	28	206	16	12	538	47	1,763

Source: Census of Population and Housing, 1990: Equal Employment Opportunity (EEO) File on CD-ROM [machine-readable datafiles]. Prepared by the Bureau of the Census. Washington, DC: The Bureau, 1992. *Notes:* "MSA" represents "metropolitan statistical area"; "CMSA" stands for "consolidated metropolitan statistical area."

★ 152 ★

Leading Occupations

Machine Operators in Durable Manufacturing, by Metropolitan Area

According to the 1990 Census of Population and Housing, machine operators in durable manufacturing ranked 76 among occupations employing the most people in the United States. Table presents the number of civilians 16 years old or older who reported working as machine operators in durable manufacturing during the 1990 Census. Data show the total employment figures, employment per 100,000 population, and employment data for men and women of various races and ethnicities in the 25 metropolitan statistical areas with the largest concentrations of operators of unspecified machinery in durable manufacturing. See also tables for other types of machine operators.

[Total for all of the U.S. was 439,484; 176.7 per 100,000 persons]

Metropolitan area	Total employees	Employees per 100,000 population	Men					Women				
			American Indian, Eskimo & Aleut	Asian, Pacific Islander	Black	Hispanic	White	American Indian, Eskimo & Aleut	Asian, Pacific Islander	Black	Hispanic	White
Los Angeles, California Anaheim, California Riverside, California CMSA	29,259	201.4	68	1,292	1,038	16,355	10,144	34	468	362	5,684	3,198
New York, New York New Jersey (northern) Long Island, New York CMSA	22,483	124.3	66	428	2,658	6,249	7,150	67	386	1,799	5,160	4,711
Chicago, Illinois Gary, Indiana Lake County, Illinois CMSA	19,811	245.6	54	591	2,302	5,840	7,891	16	187	926	2,178	2,916
Detroit, Michigan Ann Arbor, Michigan CMSA	12,679	271.8	62	94	1,557	276	8,434	11	20	480	86	1,927
Philadelphia, Pennsylvania Wilmington, Delaware Trenton, New Jersey CMSA	8,636	146.4	18	192	1,239	546	4,608	0	129	514	209	1,379
Cleveland, Ohio Akron, Ohio Lorain, Ohio CMSA	7,798	282.6	4	73	1,070	183	4,596	6	35	342	43	1,510
San Francisco, California Oakland, California San Jose, California CMSA	6,238	99.76	23	1,291	398	1,199	2,017	0	910	152	526	624
Dallas, Texas Fort Worth, Texas CMSA	5,786	148.9	23	235	728	1,595	2,058	9	100	385	546	777
Providence, Rhode Island Pawtucket, Rhode Island Fall River, Massachusetts CMSA	4,805	420.9	6	201	148	493	2,062	10	42	80	395	1,718
Boston, Massachusetts Lawrence, Massachusetts Salem, Massachusetts CMSA	4,541	108.9	21	138	325	536	2,377	0	111	166	228	1,101
Milwaukee, Wisconsin Racine, Wisconsin CMSA	4,209	261.9	0	15	393	199	2,318	2	13	293	35	1,034
St. Louis, Missouri MSA	4,141	169.4	0	52	600	54	2,399	5	0	310	5	735
Pittsburgh, Pennsylvania Beaver Valley, Pennsylvania CMSA	3,725	166.1	0	10	162	5	3,204	0	2	36	0	311
Hartford, Connecticut New Britain, Connecticut Middletown, Connecticut CMSA	3,588	330.4	11	97	263	384	1,914	11	47	95	132	846
Miami, Florida Fort Lauderdale, Florida CMSA	3,392	106.3	0	18	458	1,204	1,330	0	11	144	1,187	1,100
Minneapolis, Minnesota St. Paul, Minnesota MSA	3,368	136.7	62	181	53	36	2,134	55	43	21	16	787
Atlanta, Georgia MSA	3,178	112.2	9	115	695	36	1,249	3	53	469	41	547
Seattle, Washington Tacoma, Washington CMSA	3,133	122.4	0	162	134	131	2,144	0	67	39	6	517
Grand Rapids, Michigan MSA	3,119	453.1	30	74	182	209	1,927	0	4	97	106	629
Greensboro, North Carolina Winston-Salem, North Carolina High Point, North Carolina MSA	3,115	330.7	11	33	476	27	1,383	5	10	334	12	847
Houston, Texas Galveston, Texas Brazoria, Texas CMSA	3,040	81.92	11	106	369	1,282	1,365	0	14	87	192	206
Baltimore, Maryland MSA	2,844	119.4	0	13	917	0	1,419	0	0	154	5	336
Rochester, New York MSA	2,730	272.3	13	13	279	119	1,602	0	34	93	12	600
Buffalo, New York Niagara Falls, New York CMSA	2,637	221.7	11	12	219	59	1,551	0	0	182	14	633
Portland, Oregon Vancouver, Washington CMSA	2,544	172.1	7	212	54	107	1,533	10	71	9	17	553

Source: Census of Population and Housing, 1990: Equal Employment Opportunity (EEO) File on CD-ROM [machine-readable datafiles]. Prepared by the Bureau of the Census. Washington, DC: The Bureau, 1992. *Notes:* "MSA" represents "metropolitan statistical area"; "CMSA" stands for "consolidated metropolitan statistical area."

★ 153 ★

Leading Occupations

Machine Operators in Nondurable Manufacturing, by Metropolitan Area

According to the 1990 Census of Population and Housing, machine operators in nondurable manufacturing ranked 103 among occupations employing the most people in the United States. Table presents the number of civilians 16 years old or older who reported working as machine operators in nondurable manufacturing during the 1990 Census. Data show the total employment figures, employment per 100,000 population, and employment data for men and women of various races and ethnicities in the 25 metropolitan statistical areas with the largest concentrations of operators of unspecified machinery in nondurable manufacturing. See also tables for other types of machine operators.

[Total for all of the U.S. was 309,226; 124.3 per 100,000 persons]

Metropolitan area	Total employees	Employees per 100,000 population	Men					Women				
			American Indian, Eskimo & Aleut	Asian, Pacific Islander	Black	Hispanic	White	American Indian, Eskimo & Aleut	Asian, Pacific Islander	Black	Hispanic	White
New York, New York New Jersey (northern) Long Island, New York CMSA	19,782	109.4	8	493	2,094	4,709	6,172	9	618	1,629	4,067	4,893
Los Angeles, California Anaheim, California Riverside, California CMSA	16,756	115.3	24	529	446	7,981	5,059	12	210	278	5,164	2,902
Chicago, Illinois Gary, Indiana Lake County, Illinois CMSA	13,361	165.7	37	318	1,190	3,495	3,779	17	211	1,230	2,416	3,005
Philadelphia, Pennsylvania Wilmington, Delaware Trenton, New Jersey CMSA	7,589	128.6	6	53	994	412	3,219	9	125	903	261	1,831
San Francisco, California Oakland, California San Jose, California CMSA	4,331	69.26	20	576	197	1,041	1,471	7	451	102	487	657
Detroit, Michigan Ann Arbor, Michigan CMSA	4,080	87.46	12	53	343	82	1,623	0	44	474	68	1,472
Atlanta, Georgia MSA	4,012	141.6	20	72	1,099	62	1,171	0	23	828	31	769
Dallas, Texas Fort Worth, Texas CMSA	3,963	102.0	28	134	535	898	1,295	6	38	446	545	586
Houston, Texas Galveston, Texas Brazoria, Texas CMSA	3,645	98.22	11	52	582	971	1,756	0	61	203	270	254
Cleveland, Ohio Akron, Ohio Lorain, Ohio CMSA	3,598	130.4	13	25	328	59	1,522	7	30	379	34	1,222
Richmond, Virginia Petersburg, Virginia MSA	3,482	402.3	30	46	1,275	20	1,147	7	13	581	0	383
Boston, Massachusetts Lawrence, Massachusetts Salem, Massachusetts CMSA	3,259	78.12	4	41	187	470	1,725	0	79	129	269	686
Minneapolis, Minnesota St. Paul, Minnesota MSA	2,837	115.1	15	65	100	97	1,672	4	35	55	37	823
Appleton, Wisconsin Oshkosh, Wisconsin Neenah, Wisconsin MSA	2,818	894.3	3	0	0	14	1,814	11	6	0	12	968
Greensboro, North Carolina Winston-Salem, North Carolina High Point, North Carolina MSA	2,751	292.0	0	0	433	27	1,159	3	4	293	0	856
Baltimore, Maryland MSA	2,687	112.8	6	15	503	10	763	5	37	598	0	755
St. Louis, Missouri MSA	2,533	103.6	16	16	325	46	1,126	0	8	319	0	701
Greenville, South Carolina Spartanburg, South Carolina MSA	2,449	382.1	8	0	348	0	925	0	10	284	9	874
Kansas City, Missouri Kansas City, Kansas MSA	2,351	150.1	9	19	231	159	1,171	4	32	131	46	631
Miami, Florida Fort Lauderdale, Florida CMSA	2,294	71.85	0	6	126	780	739	0	19	160	1,066	988
Cincinnati, Ohio Hamilton, Ohio CMSA	2,253	129.2	0	9	143	7	1,249	0	0	193	6	653
Milwaukee, Wisconsin Racine, Wisconsin CMSA	2,217	137.9	4	15	200	156	1,090	5	22	145	38	616
Providence, Rhode Island Pawtucket, Rhode Island Fall River, Massachusetts CMSA	2,185	191.4	0	27	110	167	1,014	20	5	45	92	756

[Continued]

★ 153 ★

Machine Operators in Nondurable Manufacturing, by Metropolitan Area

[Continued]

Metropolitan area	Total employees	Employees per 100,000 population	Men					Women				
			American Indian, Eskimo & Aleut	Asian, Pacific Islander	Black	Hispanic	White	American Indian, Eskimo & Aleut	Asian, Pacific Islander	Black	Hispanic	White
Charlotte, North Carolina Gastonia, North Carolina Rock Hill, South Carolina MSA	2,144	184.5	6	29	335	0	837	6	25	328	4	574
Buffalo, New York Niagara Falls, New York CMSA	1,890	158.9	10	22	99	27	1,001	0	5	166	0	580

Source: Census of Population and Housing, 1990: Equal Employment Opportunity (EEO) File on CD-ROM [machine-readable datafiles]. Prepared by the Bureau of the Census. Washington, DC: The Bureau, 1992. *Notes:* "MSA" represents "metropolitan statistical area"; "CMSA" stands for "consolidated metropolitan statistical area."

★ 154 ★

Leading Occupations

Machine Operators (Miscellaneous) in Durable Manufacturing, by Metropolitan Area

According to the 1990 Census of Population and Housing, miscellaneous machine operators in durable manufacturing ranked 109 among occupations employing the most people in the United States. Table presents the number of civilians 16 years old or older who reported working as miscellaneous machine operators in durable manufacturing during the 1990 Census. Data show the total employment figures, employment per 100,000 population, and employment data for men and women of various races and ethnicities in the 25 metropolitan statistical areas with the largest concentrations of miscellaneous machine operators in durable manufacturing.

[Total for all of the U.S. was 277,112; 111.4 per 100,000 persons]

Metropolitan area	Total employees	Employees per 100,000 population	Men					Women				
			American Indian, Eskimo & Aleut	Asian, Pacific Islander	Black	Hispanic	White	American Indian, Eskimo & Aleut	Asian, Pacific Islander	Black	Hispanic	White
Los Angeles, California Anaheim, California Riverside, California CMSA	22,127	152.3	38	883	511	12,783	7,081	53	317	233	5,095	2,770
New York, New York New Jersey (northern) Long Island, New York CMSA	15,547	85.96	30	514	1,690	4,527	4,661	15	209	1,274	3,736	3,282
Chicago, Illinois Gary, Indiana Lake County, Illinois CMSA	13,834	171.5	42	346	1,366	4,313	5,140	14	126	870	1,762	2,120
Detroit, Michigan Ann Arbor, Michigan CMSA	5,851	125.4	19	49	882	131	3,433	6	6	501	44	864
San Francisco, California Oakland, California San Jose, California CMSA	5,441	87.01	0	1,174	157	1,150	1,619	25	817	108	553	786
Philadelphia, Pennsylvania Wilmington, Delaware Trenton, New Jersey CMSA	4,445	75.35	0	80	868	397	1,961	8	15	295	141	967
Cleveland, Ohio Akron, Ohio Lorain, Ohio CMSA	4,269	154.7	6	31	548	138	2,563	0	32	232	32	759
Dallas, Texas Fort Worth, Texas CMSA	3,551	91.39	7	169	418	868	1,220	0	70	311	350	527
Boston, Massachusetts Lawrence, Massachusetts Salem, Massachusetts CMSA	3,356	80.45	14	135	169	442	1,739	0	59	213	117	701
Milwaukee, Wisconsin Racine, Wisconsin CMSA	3,085	192.0	6	15	311	141	1,690	27	4	196	58	722
Providence, Rhode Island Pawtucket, Rhode Island Fall River, Massachusetts CMSA	2,595	227.3	59	64	59	351	1,262	6	34	59	157	874

[Continued]

★ 154 ★

Machine Operators (Miscellaneous) in Durable Manufacturing, by Metropolitan Area

[Continued]

Metropolitan area	Total employees	Employees per 100,000 population	Men					Women				
			American Indian, Eskimo & Aleut	Asian, Pacific Islander	Black	Hispanic	White	American Indian, Eskimo & Aleut	Asian, Pacific Islander	Black	Hispanic	White
Houston, Texas Galveston, Texas Brazoria, Texas CMSA	2,531	68.20	15	93	275	1,151	1,105	0	39	76	155	152
Hartford, Connecticut New Britain, Connecticut Middletown, Connecticut CMSA	2,482	228.6	0	67	238	333	1,034	5	53	140	177	682
Minneapolis, Minnesota St. Paul, Minnesota MSA	2,459	99.79	2	185	95	37	1,486	9	33	16	12	596
Indianapolis, Indiana MSA	2,238	179.1	0	6	259	8	1,446	8	0	88	0	431
St. Louis, Missouri MSA	1,991	81.46	0	5	204	21	1,094	0	16	139	0	522
Greensboro, North Carolina Winston-Salem, North Carolina High Point, North Carolina MSA	1,989	211.1	18	12	366	1	699	0	0	317	0	576
Cincinnati, Ohio Hamilton, Ohio CMSA	1,970	113.0	9	17	109	10	1,336	0	8	76	0	415
Rochester, New York MSA	1,865	186.1	5	7	161	46	1,132	7	14	92	30	422
Miami, Florida Fort Lauderdale, Florida CMSA	1,856	58.13	0	25	262	765	857	0	14	93	451	480
Pittsburgh, Pennsylvania Beaver Valley, Pennsylvania CMSA	1,717	76.56	0	0	41	3	1,436	0	2	11	3	224
Greenville, South Carolina Spartanburg, South Carolina MSA	1,666	260.0	0	26	181	15	558	2	15	339	10	523
York, Pennsylvania MSA	1,662	397.8	0	20	45	31	1,152	0	5	0	15	432
Atlanta, Georgia MSA	1,642	57.95	5	124	344	49	536	0	35	287	13	265
Seattle, Washington Tacoma, Washington CMSA	1,571	61.39	17	115	67	31	954	3	49	29	0	317

Source: Census of Population and Housing, 1990: Equal Employment Opportunity (EEO) File on CD-ROM [machine-readable datafiles]. Prepared by the Bureau of the Census. Washington, DC: The Bureau, 1992. *Notes:* "MSA" represents "metropolitan statistical area"; "CMSA" stands for "consolidated metropolitan statistical area."

★ 155 ★

Leading Occupations

Machinists, by Metropolitan Area

According to the 1990 Census of Population and Housing, machinists ranked 61 among occupations employing the most people in the United States. Table presents the number of civilians 16 years old or older who reported working as machinists during the 1990 Census. Data show the total employment figures, employment per 100,000 population, and employment data for men and women of various races and ethnicities in the 25 metropolitan statistical areas with the largest concentrations of machinists, excluding apprentices.

[Total for all of the U.S. was 569,081; 228.8 per 100,000 persons]

Metropolitan area	Total employees	Employees per 100,000 population	Men					Women				
			American Indian, Eskimo & Aleut	Asian, Pacific Islander	Black	Hispanic	White	American Indian, Eskimo & Aleut	Asian, Pacific Islander	Black	Hispanic	White
Los Angeles, California Anaheim, California Riverside, California CMSA	40,045	275.6	369	4,186	1,992	13,440	24,669	23	111	119	998	1,063
New York, New York New Jersey (northern) Long Island, New York CMSA	24,415	135.0	50	1,017	3,046	3,327	17,470	2	21	312	458	809
Chicago, Illinois Gary, Indiana Lake County, Illinois CMSA	22,476	278.7	43	595	2,303	2,149	17,084	0	17	425	277	575
Cleveland, Ohio Akron, Ohio Lorain, Ohio CMSA	13,794	499.8	16	136	983	180	11,777	7	16	69	17	662

[Continued]

★ 155 ★

Machinists, by Metropolitan Area
[Continued]

Metropolitan area	Total employees	Employees per 100,000 population	Men					Women				
			American Indian, Eskimo & Aleut	Asian, Pacific Islander	Black	Hispanic	White	American Indian, Eskimo & Aleut	Asian, Pacific Islander	Black	Hispanic	White
San Francisco, California Oakland, California San Jose, California CMSA	13,102	209.5	163	1,981	462	2,012	9,152	0	53	35	82	268
Philadelphia, Pennsylvania Wilmington, Delaware Trenton, New Jersey CMSA	12,954	219.6	14	236	1,400	298	10,830	0	15	71	6	266
Houston, Texas Galveston, Texas Brazoria, Texas CMSA	12,554	338.3	27	698	1,406	3,294	8,449	0	0	123	57	151
Detroit, Michigan Ann Arbor, Michigan CMSA	12,123	259.9	40	68	739	120	10,838	9	7	92	6	299
Boston, Massachusetts Lawrence, Massachusetts Salem, Massachusetts CMSA	11,469	274.9	13	201	319	306	10,234	6	17	48	56	404
Dallas, Texas Fort Worth, Texas CMSA	9,437	242.9	90	340	957	1,115	6,903	5	18	135	90	273
Milwaukee, Wisconsin Racine, Wisconsin CMSA	9,385	583.9	37	55	443	395	8,247	0	3	55	2	381
Seattle, Washington Tacoma, Washington CMSA	9,195	359.3	101	344	446	222	7,912	0	40	31	13	248
Minneapolis, Minnesota St. Paul, Minnesota MSA	8,453	343.0	59	219	221	72	7,529	19	0	18	15	363
St. Louis, Missouri MSA	6,752	276.3	22	0	477	53	6,037	0	0	81	0	118
Pittsburgh, Pennsylvania Beaver Valley, Pennsylvania CMSA	6,055	270.0	0	7	97	17	5,842	0	0	4	0	95
Hartford, Connecticut New Britain, Connecticut Middletown, Connecticut CMSA	6,053	557.5	15	149	330	309	4,958	8	6	75	57	297
San Diego, California MSA	5,308	212.5	9	738	232	781	3,653	0	41	19	50	145
Cincinnati, Ohio Hamilton, Ohio CMSA	5,302	304.0	12	13	329	8	4,611	0	22	60	0	255
Portland, Oregon Vancouver, Washington CMSA	4,925	333.2	45	218	56	137	4,436	2	0	8	14	98
Phoenix, Arizona MSA	4,781	225.3	63	97	100	570	4,024	0	13	6	26	110
Baltimore, Maryland MSA	4,732	198.6	9	22	551	18	3,938	0	0	99	0	113
Dayton, Ohio Springfield, Ohio MSA	4,404	463.0	9	11	279	9	3,809	0	0	56	0	240
Buffalo, New York Niagara Falls, New York CMSA	4,175	351.1	7	22	143	11	3,907	0	0	16	0	80
Providence, Rhode Island Pawtucket, Rhode Island Fall River, Massachusetts CMSA	4,054	355.1	16	29	108	111	3,617	0	0	17	24	186
Charlotte, North Carolina Gastonia, North Carolina Rock Hill, South Carolina MSA	4,008	344.9	18	29	503	29	3,142	12	13	90	10	193

Source: Census of Population and Housing, 1990: Equal Employment Opportunity (EEO) File on CD-ROM [machine-readable datafiles]. Prepared by the Bureau of the Census. Washington, DC: The Bureau, 1992. *Notes:* "MSA" represents "metropolitan statistical area"; "CMSA" stands for "consolidated metropolitan statistical area."

★ 156 ★

Leading Occupations

Maids and Housemen, by Metropolitan Area

According to the 1990 Census of Population and Housing, maids and housemen ranked 35 among occupations employing the most people in the United States. Table presents the number of civilians 16 years old or older who reported working as maids and housemen during the 1990 Census. Data show the total employment figures, employment per 100,000 population, and employment data for men and women of various races and ethnicities in the 25 metropolitan statistical areas with the largest concentrations of maids and housemen.

[Total for all of the U.S. was 712,789; 286.6 per 100,000 persons]

Metropolitan area	Total employees	Employees per 100,000 population	Men					Women				
			American Indian, Eskimo & Aleut	Asian, Pacific Islander	Black	Hispanic	White	American Indian, Eskimo & Aleut	Asian, Pacific Islander	Black	Hispanic	White
New York, New York New Jersey (northern) Long Island, New York CMSA	43,122	238.4	82	475	6,293	6,303	5,186	112	925	11,659	9,060	11,576
Los Angeles, California Anaheim, California Riverside, California CMSA	36,384	250.4	69	556	787	5,872	3,739	205	1,022	1,843	21,535	13,081
Chicago, Illinois Gary, Indiana Lake County, Illinois CMSA	18,872	234.0	7	193	2,387	1,209	1,497	54	329	5,171	3,665	6,436
San Francisco, California Oakland, California San Jose, California CMSA	17,651	282.3	15	1,446	485	1,215	1,498	103	3,334	1,401	6,104	5,837
Miami, Florida Fort Lauderdale, Florida CMSA	13,462	421.7	11	7	1,230	1,612	1,486	48	59	5,856	3,982	4,007
Philadelphia, Pennsylvania Wilmington, Delaware Trenton, New Jersey CMSA	12,223	207.2	0	68	1,931	343	1,179	52	178	4,313	541	3,946
Washington, District of Columbia MSA	11,906	303.5	5	262	1,552	731	600	12	869	3,858	2,896	2,908
Dallas, Texas Fort Worth, Texas CMSA	10,941	281.6	6	113	784	831	726	37	217	3,089	3,347	3,326
Las Vegas, Nevada MSA	10,765	1,452	4	350	820	710	1,346	77	676	2,298	2,557	3,428
Detroit, Michigan Ann Arbor, Michigan CMSA	10,649	228.3	12	52	937	65	1,042	47	62	3,413	185	4,981
Boston, Massachusetts Lawrence, Massachusetts Salem, Massachusetts CMSA	10,306	247.1	12	115	973	782	1,922	50	264	1,288	1,024	4,751
Houston, Texas Galveston, Texas Brazoria, Texas CMSA	10,302	277.6	0	41	739	840	591	62	141	3,022	4,203	2,801
Atlanta, Georgia MSA	7,521	265.4	0	33	890	79	329	0	146	4,567	140	1,451
San Diego, California MSA	7,252	290.3	2	254	130	598	586	16	633	341	3,584	2,889
St. Louis, Missouri MSA	7,153	292.7	0	16	982	6	738	15	22	2,468	68	2,894
Phoenix, Arizona MSA	6,856	323.1	70	0	109	594	824	233	82	293	2,571	3,564
Tampa, Florida St. Petersburg, Florida Clearwater, Florida MSA	6,408	309.9	12	11	406	180	791	50	65	1,828	430	3,052
Baltimore, Maryland MSA	6,213	260.8	18	17	1,058	36	314	13	37	3,294	76	1,416
Cleveland, Ohio Akron, Ohio Lorain, Ohio CMSA	6,139	222.4	0	0	802	23	713	2	41	1,710	85	2,810
Orlando, Florida MSA	6,101	568.7	0	35	521	543	659	10	128	1,766	1,331	2,437
Seattle, Washington Tacoma, Washington CMSA	5,936	232.0	10	193	172	84	647	112	939	483	201	3,243
Honolulu, Hawaii MSA	5,755	688.2	0	1,458	16	62	143	7	3,737	34	241	311
Minneapolis, Minnesota St. Paul, Minnesota MSA	5,637	228.8	22	67	195	57	847	86	199	261	84	3,905
Pittsburgh, Pennsylvania Beaver Valley, Pennsylvania CMSA	5,289	235.8	2	6	384	8	940	11	53	670	25	3,210
New Orleans, Louisiana MSA	5,146	415.4	0	0	794	119	195	19	38	3,420	289	531

Source: Census of Population and Housing, 1990: Equal Employment Opportunity (EEO) File on CD-ROM [machine-readable datafiles]. Prepared by the Bureau of the Census. Washington, DC: The Bureau, 1992. *Notes:* "MSA" represents "metropolitan statistical area"; "CMSA" stands for "consolidated metropolitan statistical area."

★ 157 ★

Leading Occupations

Management Analysts, by Metropolitan Area

According to the 1990 Census of Population and Housing, management analysts ranked 106 among occupations employing the most people in the United States. Table presents the number of civilians 16 years old or older who reported working as management analysts during the 1990 Census. Data show the total employment figures, employment per 100,000 population, and employment data for men and women of various races and ethnicities in the 25 metropolitan statistical areas with the largest concentrations of management analysts.

[Total for all of the U.S. was 281,789; 113.3 per 100,000 persons]

Metropolitan area	Total employees	Employees per 100,000 population	Men					Women				
			American Indian, Eskimo & Aleut	Asian, Pacific Islander	Black	Hispanic	White	American Indian, Eskimo & Aleut	Asian, Pacific Islander	Black	Hispanic	White
New York, New York New Jersey (northern) Long Island, New York CMSA	30,375	167.9	27	848	744	449	18,547	9	364	1,028	335	8,642
Los Angeles, California Anaheim, California Riverside, California CMSA	19,575	134.7	83	757	519	735	11,671	0	496	437	511	5,134
Washington, District of Columbia MSA	18,758	478.1	15	224	1,016	274	10,132	53	166	1,154	159	5,937
San Francisco, California Oakland, California San Jose, California CMSA	14,579	233.1	51	627	246	390	8,268	14	363	302	163	4,551
Chicago, Illinois Gary, Indiana Lake County, Illinois CMSA	13,944	172.9	7	294	446	147	8,400	9	63	427	172	4,210
Boston, Massachusetts Lawrence, Massachusetts Salem, Massachusetts CMSA	11,905	285.4	0	164	114	99	7,822	19	124	59	28	3,577
Philadelphia, Pennsylvania Wilmington, Delaware Trenton, New Jersey CMSA	9,632	163.3	18	95	233	99	6,219	0	92	219	57	2,730
Dallas, Texas Fort Worth, Texas CMSA	6,096	156.9	9	48	83	129	3,955	10	12	177	48	1,779
Atlanta, Georgia MSA	5,841	206.1	6	87	317	48	3,440	6	7	326	81	1,617
Minneapolis, Minnesota St. Paul, Minnesota MSA	5,827	236.5	14	56	69	14	3,224	7	50	31	50	2,361
Detroit, Michigan Ann Arbor, Michigan CMSA	5,651	121.1	1	69	248	27	3,137	24	30	385	20	1,756
Houston, Texas Galveston, Texas Brazoria, Texas CMSA	4,632	124.8	18	41	172	136	3,126	0	39	191	59	989
Seattle, Washington Tacoma, Washington CMSA	4,045	158.1	0	66	54	45	2,669	20	68	8	18	1,146
Denver, Colorado Boulder, Colorado CMSA	3,939	213.1	9	24	77	84	2,483	13	0	19	87	1,248
Baltimore, Maryland MSA	3,839	161.2	10	36	205	29	1,920	0	37	234	10	1,391
San Diego, California MSA	3,627	145.2	18	58	93	157	2,282	0	65	35	81	975
Phoenix, Arizona MSA	3,192	150.4	6	18	39	58	2,136	0	6	13	71	933
Miami, Florida Fort Lauderdale, Florida CMSA	3,086	96.66	8	7	88	356	1,911	0	0	60	176	978
Cleveland, Ohio Akron, Ohio Lorain, Ohio CMSA	2,940	106.5	10	6	74	12	2,029	0	16	85	18	714
St. Louis, Missouri MSA	2,817	115.3	9	7	69	9	1,838	8	0	56	14	823
Sacramento, California MSA	2,588	174.7	42	119	36	60	1,353	7	13	89	48	867
Pittsburgh, Pennsylvania Beaver Valley, Pennsylvania CMSA	2,389	106.5	0	31	56	3	1,693	0	0	47	0	562
Tampa, Florida St. Petersburg, Florida Clearwater, Florida MSA	2,202	106.5	0	0	45	30	1,492	0	8	29	23	615
Portland, Oregon Vancouver, Washington CMSA	2,199	148.8	0	5	24	33	1,355	0	12	25	13	773
Columbus, Ohio MSA	2,145	155.7	0	3	124	9	1,115	8	11	106	10	772

Source: Census of Population and Housing, 1990: Equal Employment Opportunity (EEO) File on CD-ROM [machine-readable datafiles]. Prepared by the Bureau of the Census. Washington, DC: The Bureau, 1992. *Notes:* "MSA" represents "metropolitan statistical area"; "CMSA" stands for "consolidated metropolitan statistical area."

★ 158 ★

Leading Occupations

Management-Related Occupations, by Metropolitan Area

According to the 1990 Census of Population and Housing, management-related occupations ranked 87 among occupations employing the most people in the United States. Table presents the number of civilians 16 years old or older who reported working in management-related occupations during the 1990 Census. Data show the total employment figures, employment per 100,000 population, and employment data for men and women of various races and ethnicities in the 25 metropolitan statistical areas with the largest concentrations of miscellaneous management-related occupations. See also tables for specific management-related occupations such as personnel, training, and labor relations specialists.

[Total for all of the U.S. was 368,073; 148.0 per 100,000 persons]

Metropolitan area	Total employees	Employees per 100,000 population	Men					Women				
			American Indian, Eskimo & Aleut	Asian, Pacific Islander	Black	Hispanic	White	American Indian, Eskimo & Aleut	Asian, Pacific Islander	Black	Hispanic	White
New York, New York New Jersey (northern) Long Island, New York CMSA	42,891	237.1	18	531	1,546	1,075	6,333	60	1,032	5,330	3,632	26,367
Los Angeles, California Anaheim, California Riverside, California CMSA	24,384	167.8	51	640	547	1,588	4,289	142	1,600	1,672	2,514	13,418
Washington, District of Columbia MSA	18,501	471.5	0	97	769	155	2,357	82	564	4,422	489	10,001
San Francisco, California Oakland, California San Jose, California CMSA	15,429	246.7	34	396	166	298	1,999	69	1,385	780	1,141	9,976
Chicago, Illinois Gary, Indiana Lake County, Illinois CMSA	15,193	188.4	0	64	454	212	2,443	7	288	2,029	608	9,576
Philadelphia, Pennsylvania Wilmington, Delaware Trenton, New Jersey CMSA	11,727	198.8	0	11	347	52	2,266	29	101	1,228	163	7,673
Boston, Massachusetts Lawrence, Massachusetts Salem, Massachusetts CMSA	11,054	265.0	0	3	77	30	1,668	27	164	489	227	8,505
Dallas, Texas Fort Worth, Texas CMSA	7,863	202.4	33	13	105	125	1,199	34	123	502	389	5,642
Atlanta, Georgia MSA	7,291	257.3	0	25	311	0	887	38	23	1,125	90	4,836
Detroit, Michigan Ann Arbor, Michigan CMSA	6,144	131.7	12	19	185	17	1,669	15	42	697	71	3,481
Houston, Texas Galveston, Texas Brazoria, Texas CMSA	6,029	162.5	0	42	224	212	1,008	24	75	536	441	3,849
Seattle, Washington Tacoma, Washington CMSA	5,449	212.9	7	47	40	16	1,324	38	141	78	74	3,731
Baltimore, Maryland MSA	5,169	217.0	0	10	208	0	700	24	24	722	62	3,470
Minneapolis, Minnesota St. Paul, Minnesota MSA	4,865	197.4	10	39	12	8	1,099	17	22	18	49	3,635
San Diego, California MSA	4,729	189.3	10	38	18	133	800	57	308	203	330	3,128
Miami, Florida Fort Lauderdale, Florida CMSA	4,658	145.9	0	18	80	319	757	0	23	428	1,022	3,255
Cleveland, Ohio Akron, Ohio Lorain, Ohio CMSA	4,076	147.7	0	6	139	6	930	28	11	369	9	2,578
Phoenix, Arizona MSA	3,855	181.7	11	7	23	89	719	70	83	49	306	2,707
St. Louis, Missouri MSA	3,684	150.7	6	5	41	10	938	9	26	342	11	2,308
Denver, Colorado Boulder, Colorado CMSA	3,573	193.3	0	17	27	58	538	3	25	132	269	2,726
Pittsburgh, Pennsylvania Beaver Valley, Pennsylvania CMSA	2,887	128.7	0	0	26	0	601	0	6	156	17	2,098
Milwaukee, Wisconsin Racine, Wisconsin CMSA	2,860	178.0	0	0	28	5	647	11	15	91	41	2,056
Portland, Oregon Vancouver, Washington CMSA	2,650	179.3	0	23	16	22	477	10	23	14	40	2,075
Kansas City, Missouri Kansas City, Kansas MSA	2,533	161.7	0	0	39	16	565	0	7	175	45	1,741
Columbus, Ohio MSA	2,493	181.0	0	7	72	0	548	7	23	230	11	1,606

Source: Census of Population and Housing, 1990: Equal Employment Opportunity (EEO) File on CD-ROM [machine-readable datafiles]. Prepared by the Bureau of the Census. Washington, DC: The Bureau, 1992. *Notes:* "MSA" represents "metropolitan statistical area"; "CMSA" stands for "consolidated metropolitan statistical area."

★ 159 ★

Leading Occupations

Managers and Administrators (Salaried), by Metropolitan Area

According to the 1990 Census of Population and Housing, salaried managers and administrators ranked 1 among occupations employing the most people in the United States. Table presents the number of civilians 16 years old or older who reported working as salaried managers and administrators during the 1990 Census. Data show the total employment figures, employment per 100,000 population, and employment data for men and women of various races and ethnicities in the 25 metropolitan statistical areas with the largest concentrations of miscellaneous managers and administrators. See also tables for specific types of managers and administrators such as personnel and labor relations managers.

[Total for all of the U.S. was 4,941,606; 1,987 per 100,000 persons]

Metropolitan area	Total employees	Employees per 100,000 population	Men					Women				
			American Indian, Eskimo & Aleut	Asian, Pacific Islander	Black	Hispanic	White	American Indian, Eskimo & Aleut	Asian, Pacific Islander	Black	Hispanic	White
New York, New York New Jersey (northern) Long Island, New York CMSA	476,771	2,636	336	15,350	16,606	17,922	273,706	261	5,462	16,634	10,765	139,826
Los Angeles, California Anaheim, California Riverside, California CMSA	344,209	2,369	812	19,909	7,892	25,919	189,923	713	8,473	6,262	14,035	93,001
Chicago, Illinois Gary, Indiana Lake County, Illinois CMSA	196,666	2,438	185	3,453	6,435	4,269	122,624	107	1,183	5,580	2,121	54,433
San Francisco, California Oakland, California San Jose, California CMSA	183,549	2,935	462	11,498	3,700	6,414	99,984	344	6,180	3,059	4,591	54,537
Philadelphia, Pennsylvania Wilmington, Delaware Trenton, New Jersey CMSA	136,725	2,318	132	1,244	4,353	1,117	87,949	80	651	3,704	624	37,954
Washington, District of Columbia MSA	127,724	3,255	144	2,715	7,889	2,027	67,701	130	1,290	8,774	1,411	37,970
Boston, Massachusetts Lawrence, Massachusetts Salem, Massachusetts CMSA	127,190	3,049	64	1,525	1,600	1,089	80,816	50	524	1,146	611	40,909
Dallas, Texas Fort Worth, Texas CMSA	104,573	2,691	201	1,238	2,659	2,561	67,027	147	398	1,792	1,368	29,535
Detroit, Michigan Ann Arbor, Michigan CMSA	97,058	2,080	227	1,057	3,270	648	62,202	172	282	2,578	319	26,983
Houston, Texas Galveston, Texas Brazoria, Texas CMSA	89,123	2,402	156	1,449	2,812	4,004	57,519	75	438	2,066	2,018	22,159
Atlanta, Georgia MSA	82,100	2,897	125	890	3,543	818	50,882	56	222	3,333	369	22,796
Miami, Florida Fort Lauderdale, Florida CMSA	72,080	2,258	67	575	1,907	14,359	43,878	31	291	1,350	7,112	22,479
Minneapolis, Minnesota St. Paul, Minnesota MSA	65,825	2,671	72	380	539	375	44,091	47	97	165	98	20,288
Seattle, Washington Tacoma, Washington CMSA	63,685	2,489	174	1,306	532	654	40,166	156	735	497	344	19,777
Cleveland, Ohio Akron, Ohio Lorain, Ohio CMSA	59,357	2,151	68	380	1,645	298	39,961	0	114	1,093	148	15,953
Baltimore, Maryland MSA	58,962	2,475	88	421	3,000	357	36,088	68	288	2,383	196	16,522
San Diego, California MSA	57,117	2,286	184	1,846	773	3,008	33,286	208	838	630	1,816	17,585
Denver, Colorado Boulder, Colorado CMSA	54,380	2,942	66	425	649	1,591	33,984	82	294	593	1,016	17,447
St. Louis, Missouri MSA	52,693	2,156	51	237	1,353	289	34,577	47	110	962	196	15,292
Phoenix, Arizona MSA	47,814	2,253	107	359	428	1,634	30,687	73	135	189	870	14,783
Tampa, Florida St. Petersburg, Florida Clearwater, Florida MSA	42,240	2,043	57	207	738	1,198	26,762	17	121	414	613	13,742
Pittsburgh, Pennsylvania Beaver Valley, Pennsylvania CMSA	40,579	1,809	30	252	563	185	27,569	8	40	415	55	11,671
Cincinnati, Ohio Hamilton, Ohio CMSA	39,380	2,258	15	261	617	92	26,613	0	71	593	49	11,156
Kansas City, Missouri Kansas City, Kansas MSA	35,704	2,280	112	153	801	398	23,203	53	10	509	242	10,542
Portland, Oregon Vancouver, Washington CMSA	34,519	2,336	150	514	116	320	22,228	106	227	86	220	10,953

Source: Census of Population and Housing, 1990: Equal Employment Opportunity (EEO) File on CD-ROM [machine-readable datafiles]. Prepared by the Bureau of the Census. Washington, DC: The Bureau, 1992. *Notes:* "MSA" represents "metropolitan statistical area"; "CMSA" stands for "consolidated metropolitan statistical area."

★ 160 ★
Leading Occupations

Managers and Administrators (Self-Employed), by Metropolitan Area

According to the 1990 Census of Population and Housing, self-employed managers and administrators ranked 82 among occupations employing the most people in the United States. Table presents the number of civilians 16 years old or older who reported working as self-employed managers and administrators during the 1990 Census. Data show the total employment figures, employment per 100,000 population, and employment data for men and women of various races and ethnicities in the 25 metropolitan statistical areas with the largest concentrations of miscellaneous managers and administrators. See also tables for specific types of managers and administrators such as personnel and labor relations managers.

[Total for all of the U.S. was 404,387; 162.6 per 100,000 persons]

Metropolitan area	Total employees	Employees per 100,000 population	Men					Women				
			American Indian, Eskimo & Aleut	Asian, Pacific Islander	Black	Hispanic	White	American Indian, Eskimo & Aleut	Asian, Pacific Islander	Black	Hispanic	White
Los Angeles, California Anaheim, California Riverside, California CMSA	38,202	262.9	153	3,210	704	3,706	23,945	74	1,229	309	841	6,614
New York, New York New Jersey (northern) Long Island, New York CMSA	21,780	120.4	32	989	1,048	1,300	14,400	7	286	176	305	4,253
San Francisco, California Oakland, California San Jose, California CMSA	19,237	307.6	55	1,271	379	825	12,131	47	640	84	319	4,220
Chicago, Illinois Gary, Indiana Lake County, Illinois CMSA	9,496	117.7	17	259	460	181	6,422	0	125	89	79	2,012
Dallas, Texas Fort Worth, Texas CMSA	8,498	218.7	49	142	156	308	5,971	0	49	64	80	1,924
Philadelphia, Pennsylvania Wilmington, Delaware Trenton, New Jersey CMSA	8,079	137.0	0	135	462	82	5,666	0	114	89	31	1,542
San Diego, California MSA	7,334	293.6	62	204	82	460	5,065	5	99	35	87	1,522
Houston, Texas Galveston, Texas Brazoria, Texas CMSA	7,248	195.3	17	275	322	595	4,422	0	72	85	145	1,706
Washington, District of Columbia MSA	5,839	148.8	10	299	555	136	3,363	0	122	122	105	1,295
Seattle, Washington Tacoma, Washington CMSA	5,766	225.3	26	176	36	29	4,017	8	63	6	8	1,425
Boston, Massachusetts Lawrence, Massachusetts Salem, Massachusetts CMSA	5,387	129.1	0	35	37	33	3,962	0	21	22	29	1,287
Atlanta, Georgia MSA	5,203	183.6	21	73	396	47	3,460	4	61	115	12	1,050
Detroit, Michigan Ann Arbor, Michigan CMSA	4,884	104.7	28	71	296	14	3,313	0	29	75	30	1,061
Sacramento, California MSA	4,551	307.3	19	144	24	111	3,219	15	110	0	26	954
Phoenix, Arizona MSA	4,261	200.8	23	39	30	163	3,153	0	0	10	81	908
Miami, Florida Fort Lauderdale, Florida CMSA	3,892	121.9	0	17	224	1,161	2,632	0	18	47	288	901
Denver, Colorado Boulder, Colorado CMSA	3,615	195.6	13	38	31	122	2,709	0	28	9	30	726
Minneapolis, Minnesota St. Paul, Minnesota MSA	3,584	145.5	5	16	38	24	2,728	0	23	9	5	765
Pittsburgh, Pennsylvania Beaver Valley, Pennsylvania CMSA	3,555	158.5	4	4	40	18	2,781	0	8	4	15	714
Cleveland, Ohio Akron, Ohio Lorain, Ohio CMSA	3,492	126.5	0	25	155	20	2,580	0	4	23	6	701
Tampa, Florida St. Petersburg, Florida Clearwater, Florida MSA	3,264	157.8	11	24	75	131	2,391	11	8	0	23	735
Portland, Oregon Vancouver, Washington CMSA	3,011	203.7	13	66	15	8	2,149	0	20	0	8	737
St. Louis, Missouri MSA	2,921	119.5	3	0	145	23	2,066	0	11	61	6	623
Baltimore, Maryland MSA	2,782	116.8	4	37	165	33	1,850	0	38	53	9	635
Cincinnati, Ohio Hamilton, Ohio CMSA	2,421	138.8	0	11	72	3	1,772	0	0	22	0	544

Source: Census of Population and Housing, 1990: Equal Employment Opportunity (EEO) File on CD-ROM [machine-readable datafiles]. Prepared by the Bureau of the Census. Washington, DC: The Bureau, 1992. *Notes:* "MSA" represents "metropolitan statistical area"; "CMSA" stands for "consolidated metropolitan statistical area."

★ 161 ★
Leading Occupations

Marketing, Advertising, and Public Relations Managers, by Metropolitan Area

According to the 1990 Census of Population and Housing, marketing, advertising, and public relations managers ranked 54 among occupations employing the most people in the United States. Table presents the number of civilians 16 years old or older who reported working as marketing, advertising, and public relations managers during the 1990 Census. Data show the total employment figures, employment per 100,000 population, and employment data for men and women of various races and ethnicities in the 25 metropolitan statistical areas with the largest concentrations of marketing, advertising, and public relations managers.

[Total for all of the U.S. was 609,109; 244.9 per 100,000 persons]

Metropolitan area	Total employees	Employees per 100,000 population	Men					Women				
			American Indian, Eskimo & Aleut	Asian, Pacific Islander	Black	Hispanic	White	American Indian, Eskimo & Aleut	Asian, Pacific Islander	Black	Hispanic	White
New York, New York New Jersey (northern) Long Island, New York CMSA	65,842	364.0	43	1,408	1,300	1,260	38,471	31	780	1,200	1,071	22,259
Los Angeles, California Anaheim, California Riverside, California CMSA	44,277	304.7	65	2,042	819	1,928	26,151	46	928	583	1,287	12,573
Chicago, Illinois Gary, Indiana Lake County, Illinois CMSA	32,491	402.8	16	418	797	359	21,205	7	59	579	339	9,207
San Francisco, California Oakland, California San Jose, California CMSA	29,172	466.5	61	1,272	493	774	16,636	64	762	322	533	9,253
Philadelphia, Pennsylvania Wilmington, Delaware Trenton, New Jersey CMSA	18,656	316.2	26	115	315	145	12,627	6	64	274	27	5,206
Boston, Massachusetts Lawrence, Massachusetts Salem, Massachusetts CMSA	17,138	410.8	12	136	221	135	10,829	5	58	111	48	5,718
Dallas, Texas Fort Worth, Texas CMSA	16,315	419.9	29	185	293	289	11,083	0	38	234	182	4,300
Atlanta, Georgia MSA	15,719	554.8	29	141	526	165	10,621	9	18	452	82	3,868
Washington, District of Columbia MSA	12,941	329.8	39	184	607	122	7,066	13	110	602	164	4,273
Minneapolis, Minnesota St. Paul, Minnesota MSA	12,297	499.0	6	28	106	50	8,075	12	8	58	47	3,973
Detroit, Michigan Ann Arbor, Michigan CMSA	11,927	255.7	21	138	458	43	7,975	10	14	265	19	3,027
Houston, Texas Galveston, Texas Brazoria, Texas CMSA	10,598	285.6	11	149	335	407	7,069	9	50	109	204	2,682
Miami, Florida Fort Lauderdale, Florida CMSA	9,175	287.4	0	28	158	1,674	5,603	10	21	180	744	3,073
Cleveland, Ohio Akron, Ohio Lorain, Ohio CMSA	8,906	322.7	0	47	194	56	6,345	0	27	88	10	2,194
St. Louis, Missouri MSA	7,692	314.7	0	23	117	50	5,167	0	6	111	31	2,265
Seattle, Washington Tacoma, Washington CMSA	7,560	295.4	34	209	76	48	4,918	5	51	38	37	2,209
Denver, Colorado Boulder, Colorado CMSA	7,172	388.0	8	25	96	126	4,716	10	34	42	115	2,184
San Diego, California MSA	6,916	276.9	17	160	58	303	4,129	0	48	95	147	2,236
Baltimore, Maryland MSA	6,304	264.6	11	20	237	28	4,161	0	18	138	38	1,690
Cincinnati, Ohio Hamilton, Ohio CMSA	6,018	345.0	0	35	102	13	4,196	4	19	37	16	1,620
Phoenix, Arizona MSA	5,907	278.4	35	33	30	134	4,006	10	4	19	55	1,688
Milwaukee, Wisconsin Racine, Wisconsin CMSA	5,851	364.1	0	41	53	31	4,096	12	2	61	30	1,571
Pittsburgh, Pennsylvania Beaver Valley, Pennsylvania CMSA	5,626	250.9	0	60	33	17	4,006	0	0	40	12	1,487
Tampa, Florida St. Petersburg, Florida Clearwater, Florida MSA	5,456	263.8	9	42	69	155	3,691	19	14	28	42	1,572
Kansas City, Missouri Kansas City, Kansas MSA	5,447	347.8	4	13	45	48	3,635	0	18	53	26	1,659

Source: Census of Population and Housing, 1990: Equal Employment Opportunity (EEO) File on CD-ROM [machine-readable datafiles]. Prepared by the Bureau of the Census. Washington, DC: The Bureau, 1992. *Notes:* "MSA" represents "metropolitan statistical area"; "CMSA" stands for "consolidated metropolitan statistical area."

★ 162 ★

Leading Occupations

Mechanic and Repairer Supervisors, by Metropolitan Area

According to the 1990 Census of Population and Housing, mechanic and repairer supervisors ranked 113 among occupations employing the most people in the United States. Table presents the number of civilians 16 years old or older who reported working as mechanic and repairer supervisors during the 1990 Census. Data show the total employment figures, employment per 100,000 population, and employment data for men and women of various races and ethnicities in the 25 metropolitan statistical areas with the largest concentrations of mechanic and repairer supervisors.

[Total for all of the U.S. was 270,582; 108.8 per 100,000 persons]

Metropolitan area	Total employees	Employees per 100,000 population	Men					Women				
			American Indian, Eskimo & Aleut	Asian, Pacific Islander	Black	Hispanic	White	American Indian, Eskimo & Aleut	Asian, Pacific Islander	Black	Hispanic	White
New York, New York New Jersey (northern) Long Island, New York CMSA	18,776	103.8	16	270	1,337	1,524	14,246	0	61	767	104	1,541
Los Angeles, California Anaheim, California Riverside, California CMSA	13,537	93.16	55	662	773	2,198	9,597	32	89	241	241	1,010
Chicago, Illinois Gary, Indiana Lake County, Illinois CMSA	8,363	103.7	21	141	591	390	6,587	0	20	268	22	563
Philadelphia, Pennsylvania Wilmington, Delaware Trenton, New Jersey CMSA	6,421	108.8	14	27	537	62	5,312	0	0	48	0	458
San Francisco, California Oakland, California San Jose, California CMSA	6,136	98.12	34	514	326	517	4,143	16	102	215	106	479
Detroit, Michigan Ann Arbor, Michigan CMSA	5,072	108.7	0	22	389	52	3,900	0	5	245	0	483
Houston, Texas Galveston, Texas Brazoria, Texas CMSA	4,852	130.7	37	19	275	540	3,960	0	0	77	32	261
Dallas, Texas Fort Worth, Texas CMSA	4,712	121.3	20	48	330	315	3,671	0	0	124	26	409
Washington, District of Columbia MSA	3,996	101.9	13	45	637	61	2,604	11	17	310	16	348
Atlanta, Georgia MSA	3,935	138.9	0	24	392	70	2,987	0	0	130	0	383
Boston, Massachusetts Lawrence, Massachusetts Salem, Massachusetts CMSA	3,592	86.11	11	0	80	31	3,085	0	0	22	23	379
Miami, Florida Fort Lauderdale, Florida CMSA	3,499	109.6	7	18	338	1,020	2,785	0	0	64	61	221
Baltimore, Maryland MSA	3,002	126.0	19	0	292	5	2,440	0	0	55	0	196
St. Louis, Missouri MSA	2,914	119.2	21	0	127	18	2,434	7	0	50	6	270
Cleveland, Ohio Akron, Ohio Lorain, Ohio CMSA	2,799	101.4	12	0	110	8	2,421	2	0	43	0	211
Seattle, Washington Tacoma, Washington CMSA	2,611	102.0	15	23	41	26	2,295	0	0	19	0	209
Pittsburgh, Pennsylvania Beaver Valley, Pennsylvania CMSA	2,448	109.2	0	9	17	0	2,292	0	0	7	9	123
Tampa, Florida St. Petersburg, Florida Clearwater, Florida MSA	2,389	115.5	0	0	102	128	2,020	0	0	7	33	256
Minneapolis, Minnesota St. Paul, Minnesota MSA	2,324	94.31	0	0	27	6	2,045	0	10	0	0	242
Denver, Colorado Boulder, Colorado CMSA	2,238	121.1	6	11	105	148	1,745	0	14	28	48	249
Kansas City, Missouri Kansas City, Kansas MSA	2,226	142.1	3	13	112	40	1,795	0	0	13	34	263
Phoenix, Arizona MSA	2,147	101.2	8	12	23	207	1,783	0	0	0	19	183
San Diego, California MSA	2,078	83.19	11	104	78	235	1,599	8	8	26	9	159
Cincinnati, Ohio Hamilton, Ohio CMSA	2,035	116.7	0	0	52	0	1,762	0	0	56	0	159
Norfolk, Virginia Virginia Beach, Virginia Newport News, Virginia MSA	1,905	136.5	8	42	190	15	1,515	0	12	59	0	72

Source: Census of Population and Housing, 1990: Equal Employment Opportunity (EEO) File on CD-ROM [machine-readable datafiles]. Prepared by the Bureau of the Census. Washington, DC: The Bureau, 1992. *Notes:* "MSA" represents "metropolitan statistical area"; "CMSA" stands for "consolidated metropolitan statistical area."

★ 163 ★

Leading Occupations

Mining, Manufacturing, and Wholesale Sales Representatives, by Metropolitan Area

According to the 1990 Census of Population and Housing, mining, manufacturing, and wholesale sales representatives ranked 15 among occupations employing the most people in the United States. Table presents the number of civilians 16 years old or older who reported working as mining, manufacturing, and wholesale sales representatives during the 1990 Census. Data show the total employment figures, employment per 100,000 population, and employment data for men and women of various races and ethnicities in the 25 metropolitan statistical areas with the largest concentrations of mining, manufacturing, and wholesale sales representatives.

[Total for all of the U.S. was 1,527,816; 614.3 per 100,000 persons]

Metropolitan area	Total employees	Employees per 100,000 population	Men					Women				
			American Indian, Eskimo & Aleut	Asian, Pacific Islander	Black	Hispanic	White	American Indian, Eskimo & Aleut	Asian, Pacific Islander	Black	Hispanic	White
New York, New York New Jersey (northern) Long Island, New York CMSA	126,576	699.8	97	3,477	4,272	6,309	82,601	9	1,132	2,568	3,075	28,838
Los Angeles, California Anaheim, California Riverside, California CMSA	103,865	714.8	270	5,244	2,527	10,306	61,673	114	2,459	1,156	5,097	22,967
Chicago, Illinois Gary, Indiana Lake County, Illinois CMSA	67,462	836.4	59	685	2,530	1,243	46,870	14	286	1,065	858	15,049
San Francisco, California Oakland, California San Jose, California CMSA	45,909	734.2	62	2,159	786	1,901	27,505	73	1,175	633	1,128	12,295
Philadelphia, Pennsylvania Wilmington, Delaware Trenton, New Jersey CMSA	42,108	713.8	55	231	1,277	388	31,192	41	126	687	220	8,289
Dallas, Texas Fort Worth, Texas CMSA	38,358	987.2	89	233	895	1,025	26,815	32	117	483	441	8,911
Boston, Massachusetts Lawrence, Massachusetts Salem, Massachusetts CMSA	32,991	790.8	31	182	382	295	23,589	0	132	110	94	8,440
Houston, Texas Galveston, Texas Brazoria, Texas CMSA	32,069	864.2	53	407	1,026	1,774	23,036	10	168	423	760	5,861
Detroit, Michigan Ann Arbor, Michigan CMSA	31,866	683.1	70	212	1,019	223	23,180	16	61	574	50	6,686
Atlanta, Georgia MSA	31,459	1,110	23	159	1,211	191	22,705	17	58	589	91	6,643
Minneapolis, Minnesota St. Paul, Minnesota MSA	25,950	1,053	9	109	200	116	19,735	15	74	82	37	5,674
Miami, Florida Fort Lauderdale, Florida CMSA	25,866	810.2	36	196	787	6,978	17,293	0	49	302	2,757	6,305
Cleveland, Ohio Akron, Ohio Lorain, Ohio CMSA	21,876	792.7	0	53	485	117	16,326	13	43	271	55	4,648
Seattle, Washington Tacoma, Washington CMSA	21,177	827.5	57	421	256	210	14,935	38	187	59	125	5,128
St. Louis, Missouri MSA	17,998	736.4	24	24	524	79	13,445	3	12	251	10	3,700
Denver, Colorado Boulder, Colorado CMSA	15,998	865.5	33	57	136	532	11,566	0	85	86	246	3,725
Washington, District of Columbia MSA	15,815	403.1	18	249	1,183	267	9,994	9	122	490	88	3,668
Phoenix, Arizona MSA	15,750	742.2	28	31	102	741	11,683	26	41	27	252	3,424
Tampa, Florida St. Petersburg, Florida Clearwater, Florida MSA	15,733	760.8	59	28	204	553	11,528	0	23	124	219	3,646
Pittsburgh, Pennsylvania Beaver Valley, Pennsylvania CMSA	14,916	665.1	0	33	239	14	11,419	3	5	77	10	3,122
Baltimore, Maryland MSA	14,900	625.5	11	116	721	103	10,528	12	53	354	25	3,076
San Diego, California MSA	14,497	580.3	69	235	211	1,153	9,086	45	167	48	529	3,867
Kansas City, Missouri Kansas City, Kansas MSA	13,744	877.5	35	47	193	97	10,535	0	17	176	50	2,664
Portland, Oregon Vancouver, Washington CMSA	13,696	926.7	20	131	37	102	10,744	19	73	16	63	2,629
Cincinnati, Ohio Hamilton, Ohio CMSA	13,674	784.0	0	35	274	33	10,342	0	28	173	0	2,822

Source: Census of Population and Housing, 1990: Equal Employment Opportunity (EEO) File on CD-ROM [machine-readable datafiles]. Prepared by the Bureau of the Census. Washington, DC: The Bureau, 1992. *Notes:* "MSA" represents "metropolitan statistical area"; "CMSA" stands for "consolidated metropolitan statistical area."

★ 164 ★

Leading Occupations

Motor Vehicle and Boat Sales Workers, by Metropolitan Area

According to the 1990 Census of Population and Housing, motor vehicle and boat sales workers ranked 90 among occupations employing the most people in the United States. Table presents the number of civilians 16 years old or older who reported working as motor vehicle and boat sales workers during the 1990 Census. Data show the total employment figures, employment per 100,000 population, and employment data for men and women of various races and ethnicities in the 25 metropolitan statistical areas with the largest concentrations of motor vehicle and boat sales workers.

[Total for all of the U.S. was 352,279; 141.6 per 100,000 persons]

Metropolitan area	Total employees	Employees per 100,000 population	Men						Women				
			American Indian, Eskimo & Aleut	Asian, Pacific Islander	Black	Hispanic	White		American Indian, Eskimo & Aleut	Asian, Pacific Islander	Black	Hispanic	White
Los Angeles, California Anaheim, California Riverside, California CMSA	19,216	132.2	99	1,208	1,060	3,385	12,675		22	178	176	350	2,100
New York, New York New Jersey (northern) Long Island, New York CMSA	15,366	84.95	25	263	1,116	1,015	11,645		9	32	218	67	1,639
Chicago, Illinois Gary, Indiana Lake County, Illinois CMSA	9,116	113.0	2	142	662	560	6,966		0	14	152	17	932
San Francisco, California Oakland, California San Jose, California CMSA	7,066	113.0	22	587	498	775	4,811		0	117	91	122	666
Philadelphia, Pennsylvania Wilmington, Delaware Trenton, New Jersey CMSA	7,041	119.4	8	26	523	165	5,644		0	13	38	7	714
Dallas, Texas Fort Worth, Texas CMSA	6,731	173.2	40	47	399	419	5,344		0	0	94	21	591
Detroit, Michigan Ann Arbor, Michigan CMSA	5,983	128.3	6	9	343	55	4,751		0	0	80	12	772
Houston, Texas Galveston, Texas Brazoria, Texas CMSA	5,877	158.4	19	125	659	850	4,188		8	0	56	90	453
Miami, Florida Fort Lauderdale, Florida CMSA	5,272	165.1	19	13	391	1,637	4,190		4	0	32	167	517
Washington, District of Columbia MSA	4,734	120.7	27	83	915	190	3,168		0	4	81	11	380
Boston, Massachusetts Lawrence, Massachusetts Salem, Massachusetts CMSA	4,356	104.4	0	49	116	74	3,751		0	0	28	0	378
Atlanta, Georgia MSA	4,350	153.5	0	39	483	48	3,398		0	12	40	8	378
Seattle, Washington Tacoma, Washington CMSA	4,181	163.4	47	84	151	103	3,460		5	14	7	13	381
Cleveland, Ohio Akron, Ohio Lorain, Ohio CMSA	4,104	148.7	8	13	204	57	3,481		0	0	31	6	342
San Diego, California MSA	3,858	154.4	34	88	63	506	2,887		0	9	5	91	460
Minneapolis, Minnesota St. Paul, Minnesota MSA	3,639	147.7	19	53	63	4	3,117		0	0	0	0	383
Phoenix, Arizona MSA	3,529	166.3	0	9	43	339	2,994		8	0	0	21	268
Tampa, Florida St. Petersburg, Florida Clearwater, Florida MSA	3,472	167.9	0	14	78	147	2,923		0	0	12	5	411
St. Louis, Missouri MSA	3,354	137.2	5	22	138	22	2,908		0	5	19	0	257
Baltimore, Maryland MSA	3,220	135.2	0	38	418	15	2,373		0	0	29	0	362
Pittsburgh, Pennsylvania Beaver Valley, Pennsylvania CMSA	3,167	141.2	2	0	86	13	2,719		0	6	0	0	354
Denver, Colorado Boulder, Colorado CMSA	2,975	161.0	24	37	123	212	2,414		0	19	5	12	262
Portland, Oregon Vancouver, Washington CMSA	2,586	175.0	15	25	47	30	2,223		0	0	8	12	256
Kansas City, Missouri Kansas City, Kansas MSA	2,480	158.3	0	19	133	47	2,052		0	0	27	6	228
Cincinnati, Ohio Hamilton, Ohio CMSA	2,279	130.7	0	4	113	10	1,965		0	0	7	0	190

Source: Census of Population and Housing, 1990: Equal Employment Opportunity (EEO) File on CD-ROM [machine-readable datafiles]. Prepared by the Bureau of the Census. Washington, DC: The Bureau, 1992. *Notes:* "MSA" represents "metropolitan statistical area"; "CMSA" stands for "consolidated metropolitan statistical area."

★ 165 ★

Leading Occupations

Nursing Aides, Orderlies, and Attendants, by Metropolitan Area

According to the 1990 Census of Population and Housing, nursing aides, orderlies, and attendants ranked 11 among occupations employing the most people in the United States. Table presents the number of civilians 16 years old or older who reported working as nursing aides, orderlies, and attendants during the 1990 Census. Data show the total employment figures, employment per 100,000 population, and employment data for men and women of various races and ethnicities in the 25 metropolitan statistical areas with the largest concentrations of nursing aides, orderlies, and attendants.

[Total for all of the U.S. was 1,859,694; 747.7 per 100,000 persons]

Metropolitan area	Total employees	Employees per 100,000 population	Men					Women				
			American Indian, Eskimo & Aleut	Asian, Pacific Islander	Black	Hispanic	White	American Indian, Eskimo & Aleut	Asian, Pacific Islander	Black	Hispanic	White
New York, New York New Jersey (northern) Long Island, New York CMSA	181,173	1,002	118	1,080	10,281	4,173	8,175	745	5,628	93,642	25,248	49,327
Los Angeles, California Anaheim, California Riverside, California CMSA	73,157	503.4	127	1,817	2,543	4,649	6,920	424	6,681	12,675	20,412	29,059
Chicago, Illinois Gary, Indiana Lake County, Illinois CMSA	43,965	545.1	46	631	2,470	589	2,447	92	2,201	17,744	2,402	16,981
Philadelphia, Pennsylvania Wilmington, Delaware Trenton, New Jersey CMSA	43,855	743.4	11	171	3,154	375	2,889	190	724	18,706	1,278	17,131
Boston, Massachusetts Lawrence, Massachusetts Salem, Massachusetts CMSA	34,968	838.2	22	249	1,363	402	3,316	60	480	6,291	1,833	22,106
San Francisco, California Oakland, California San Jose, California CMSA	34,278	548.2	36	1,003	1,110	825	3,281	361	5,803	6,249	5,170	13,852
Detroit, Michigan Ann Arbor, Michigan CMSA	31,681	679.1	8	99	1,776	45	2,577	103	417	11,468	358	15,073
Miami, Florida Fort Lauderdale, Florida CMSA	23,608	739.5	4	36	1,051	774	1,311	99	319	13,228	4,254	6,795
Houston, Texas Galveston, Texas Brazoria, Texas CMSA	20,983	565.4	39	97	1,083	391	1,072	65	533	10,728	1,968	6,159
Dallas, Texas Fort Worth, Texas CMSA	20,764	534.4	3	91	971	238	1,415	185	274	7,956	1,425	9,050
Cleveland, Ohio Akron, Ohio Lorain, Ohio CMSA	20,180	731.2	7	36	965	45	1,243	76	155	6,339	358	11,249
Washington, District of Columbia MSA	19,945	508.3	0	222	1,935	276	1,135	59	603	10,513	861	4,996
St. Louis, Missouri MSA	18,788	768.7	2	49	867	37	1,207	68	113	7,142	99	9,299
Pittsburgh, Pennsylvania Beaver Valley, Pennsylvania CMSA	18,505	825.1	3	29	467	17	1,933	41	66	3,095	96	12,853
Minneapolis, Minnesota St. Paul, Minnesota MSA	17,794	722.1	46	84	439	53	2,324	167	293	1,266	207	13,060
Baltimore, Maryland MSA	17,239	723.7	8	43	1,189	40	687	16	150	9,597	175	5,492
Seattle, Washington Tacoma, Washington CMSA	15,546	607.5	24	255	426	133	2,059	237	1,030	1,285	655	9,919
Tampa, Florida St. Petersburg, Florida Clearwater, Florida MSA	14,117	682.7	33	37	409	135	1,455	57	136	2,839	660	8,981
San Diego, California MSA	13,287	531.9	20	331	450	466	1,849	130	1,506	1,600	2,385	6,031
Milwaukee, Wisconsin Racine, Wisconsin CMSA	13,118	816.2	10	19	631	17	759	109	90	4,147	279	7,215
Atlanta, Georgia MSA	12,920	456.0	0	11	886	0	785	29	62	6,514	97	4,624
Buffalo, New York Niagara Falls, New York CMSA	12,773	1,074	22	38	525	40	982	117	61	3,718	234	7,149
Cincinnati, Ohio Hamilton, Ohio CMSA	11,595	664.8	0	2	460	6	845	0	83	3,048	65	7,141
Providence, Rhode Island Pawtucket, Rhode Island Fall River, Massachusetts CMSA	11,574	1,014	17	22	225	26	1,223	52	111	941	462	8,731
Phoenix, Arizona MSA	11,016	519.1	58	39	159	260	1,390	510	125	842	1,365	7,016

Source: Census of Population and Housing, 1990: Equal Employment Opportunity (EEO) File on CD-ROM [machine-readable datafiles]. Prepared by the Bureau of the Census. Washington, DC: The Bureau, 1992. *Notes:* "MSA" represents "metropolitan statistical area"; "CMSA" stands for "consolidated metropolitan statistical area."

★ 166 ★

Leading Occupations

Packaging and Filling Machine Operators, by Metropolitan Area

According to the 1990 Census of Population and Housing, packaging and filling machine operators ranked 107 among occupations employing the most people in the United States. Table presents the number of civilians 16 years old or older who reported working as packaging and filling machine operators during the 1990 Census. Data show the total employment figures, employment per 100,000 population, and employment data for men and women of various races and ethnicities in the 25 metropolitan statistical areas with the largest concentrations of packaging and filling machine operators.

[Total for all of the U.S. was 281,245; 113.1 per 100,000 persons]

Metropolitan area	Total employees	Employees per 100,000 population	Men					Women				
			American Indian, Eskimo & Aleut	Asian, Pacific Islander	Black	Hispanic	White	American Indian, Eskimo & Aleut	Asian, Pacific Islander	Black	Hispanic	White
New York, New York New Jersey (northern) Long Island, New York CMSA	20,548	113.6	31	352	2,075	3,355	4,156	19	786	2,693	5,504	6,470
Los Angeles, California Anaheim, California Riverside, California CMSA	19,828	136.5	12	411	581	6,243	3,661	13	502	599	9,380	4,948
Chicago, Illinois Gary, Indiana Lake County, Illinois CMSA	13,155	163.1	28	136	1,137	2,375	2,610	0	276	1,953	3,292	3,627
Philadelphia, Pennsylvania Wilmington, Delaware Trenton, New Jersey CMSA	7,674	130.1	0	128	728	337	1,660	5	172	1,256	516	3,103
San Francisco, California Oakland, California San Jose, California CMSA	6,736	107.7	25	521	349	1,182	1,506	42	527	322	2,037	1,733
Dallas, Texas Fort Worth, Texas CMSA	4,060	104.5	33	42	317	923	868	7	83	554	1,005	999
Detroit, Michigan Ann Arbor, Michigan CMSA	3,665	78.56	7	21	710	85	945	6	22	781	72	1,126
Atlanta, Georgia MSA	3,049	107.6	0	18	656	72	402	2	104	1,137	28	653
St. Louis, Missouri MSA	3,038	124.3	0	6	234	44	1,209	27	0	476	9	1,083
Boston, Massachusetts Lawrence, Massachusetts Salem, Massachusetts CMSA	3,022	72.44	10	49	152	239	950	10	115	132	218	1,375
Cleveland, Ohio Akron, Ohio Lorain, Ohio CMSA	2,739	99.25	0	11	274	112	759	0	28	371	55	1,174
Modesto, California MSA	2,588	698.5	9	85	0	380	408	0	151	25	981	946
Baltimore, Maryland MSA	2,557	107.3	0	13	377	12	491	0	56	769	19	851
Columbus, Ohio MSA	2,365	171.7	14	29	261	12	930	0	2	174	2	949
Providence, Rhode Island Pawtucket, Rhode Island Fall River, Massachusetts CMSA	2,356	206.4	0	33	29	113	481	9	35	77	281	1,494
Minneapolis, Minnesota St. Paul, Minnesota MSA	2,333	94.68	20	36	133	73	1,018	23	74	44	10	955
Houston, Texas Galveston, Texas Brazoria, Texas CMSA	2,280	61.44	0	39	279	435	531	8	19	227	760	486
Kansas City, Missouri Kansas City, Kansas MSA	2,258	144.2	4	18	248	44	638	23	7	329	109	916
Cincinnati, Ohio Hamilton, Ohio CMSA	2,252	129.1	0	0	100	0	770	0	0	384	4	998
Milwaukee, Wisconsin Racine, Wisconsin CMSA	2,143	133.3	0	2	138	81	740	30	34	291	40	822
Charlotte, North Carolina Gastonia, North Carolina Rock Hill, South Carolina MSA	2,138	184.0	8	6	195	0	347	0	52	694	0	836
Miami, Florida Fort Lauderdale, Florida CMSA	2,045	64.05	0	7	249	463	454	0	14	282	822	845
Greensboro, North Carolina Winston-Salem, North Carolina High Point, North Carolina MSA	1,888	200.4	10	9	250	6	461	0	0	417	16	735
Memphis, Tennessee MSA	1,831	186.5	0	0	428	7	200	0	0	939	9	264

[Continued]

★ 166 ★

Packaging and Filling Machine Operators, by Metropolitan Area
[Continued]

Metropolitan area	Total employees	Employees per 100,000 population	Men					Women				
			American Indian, Eskimo & Aleut	Asian, Pacific Islander	Black	Hispanic	White	American Indian, Eskimo & Aleut	Asian, Pacific Islander	Black	Hispanic	White
Seattle, Washington Tacoma, Washington CMSA	1,635	63.89	0	113	110	41	456	58	117	70	45	685

Source: Census of Population and Housing, 1990: Equal Employment Opportunity (EEO) File on CD-ROM [machine-readable datafiles]. Prepared by the Bureau of the Census. Washington, DC: The Bureau, 1992. *Notes:* "MSA" represents "metropolitan statistical area"; "CMSA" stands for "consolidated metropolitan statistical area."

★ 167 ★

Leading Occupations

Personnel and Labor Relations Managers, by Metropolitan Area

According to the 1990 Census of Population and Housing, personnel and labor relations managers ranked 112 among occupations employing the most people in the United States. Table presents the number of civilians 16 years old or older who reported working as personnel and labor relations managers during the 1990 Census. Data show the total employment figures, employment per 100,000 population, and employment data for men and women of various races and ethnicities in the 25 metropolitan statistical areas with the largest concentrations of personnel and labor relations managers.

[Total for all of the U.S. was 275,495; 110.8 per 100,000 persons]

Metropolitan area	Total employees	Employees per 100,000 population	Men					Women				
			American Indian, Eskimo & Aleut	Asian, Pacific Islander	Black	Hispanic	White	American Indian, Eskimo & Aleut	Asian, Pacific Islander	Black	Hispanic	White
New York, New York New Jersey (northern) Long Island, New York CMSA	26,613	147.1	11	975	1,433	1,813	10,003	33	448	2,139	1,129	10,509
Los Angeles, California Anaheim, California Riverside, California CMSA	19,344	133.1	46	1,352	697	2,572	6,580	102	719	771	1,803	6,862
Washington, District of Columbia MSA	9,750	248.5	14	152	881	271	3,301	20	122	1,746	258	3,355
Chicago, Illinois Gary, Indiana Lake County, Illinois CMSA	9,610	119.2	9	269	454	325	3,736	0	98	862	315	3,878
San Francisco, California Oakland, California San Jose, California CMSA	8,578	137.2	8	552	338	364	2,906	30	262	483	399	3,650
Philadelphia, Pennsylvania Wilmington, Delaware Trenton, New Jersey CMSA	7,122	120.7	8	73	423	79	2,930	23	60	596	50	2,925
Boston, Massachusetts Lawrence, Massachusetts Salem, Massachusetts CMSA	6,438	154.3	0	48	132	53	2,783	0	25	162	31	3,238
Dallas, Texas Fort Worth, Texas CMSA	5,387	138.7	22	43	236	220	2,392	36	38	230	176	2,191
Detroit, Michigan Ann Arbor, Michigan CMSA	5,133	110.0	10	55	280	17	2,408	8	36	453	29	1,870
Houston, Texas Galveston, Texas Brazoria, Texas CMSA	4,500	121.3	0	89	168	403	1,909	30	65	273	258	1,670
Miami, Florida Fort Lauderdale, Florida CMSA	4,121	129.1	3	33	220	933	1,984	0	45	142	678	1,560
Atlanta, Georgia MSA	4,093	144.5	0	31	249	20	1,589	9	36	508	53	1,647
Baltimore, Maryland MSA	3,436	144.2	0	46	205	22	1,413	20	41	280	26	1,416
Seattle, Washington Tacoma, Washington CMSA	3,416	133.5	0	68	38	38	1,577	8	77	70	48	1,527
Minneapolis, Minnesota St. Paul, Minnesota MSA	3,193	129.6	9	0	24	6	1,289	9	10	19	0	1,827
San Diego, California MSA	3,143	125.8	18	85	71	189	1,098	0	103	74	266	1,503
Denver, Colorado Boulder, Colorado CMSA	2,922	158.1	0	24	41	110	1,300	7	14	120	83	1,350

[Continued]

★ 167 ★

Personnel and Labor Relations Managers, by Metropolitan Area

[Continued]

Metropolitan area	Total employees	Employees per 100,000 population	Men					Women				
			American Indian, Eskimo & Aleut	Asian, Pacific Islander	Black	Hispanic	White	American Indian, Eskimo & Aleut	Asian, Pacific Islander	Black	Hispanic	White
Cleveland, Ohio Akron, Ohio Lorain, Ohio CMSA	2,743	99.39	5	11	152	8	1,413	0	0	120	2	1,034
St. Louis, Missouri MSA	2,496	102.1	0	22	85	15	1,140	11	0	87	27	1,131
Phoenix, Arizona MSA	2,468	116.3	28	6	58	163	945	38	0	57	91	1,155
Cincinnati, Ohio Hamilton, Ohio CMSA	2,114	121.2	0	8	65	0	981	0	0	54	1	1,006
Pittsburgh, Pennsylvania Beaver Valley, Pennsylvania CMSA	2,052	91.49	0	0	62	8	1,127	0	0	57	0	806
Tampa, Florida St. Petersburg, Florida Clearwater, Florida MSA	1,993	96.38	0	14	35	36	772	0	8	74	91	1,076
Kansas City, Missouri Kansas City, Kansas MSA	1,870	119.4	0	0	118	12	850	0	0	58	23	837
Milwaukee, Wisconsin Racine, Wisconsin CMSA	1,848	115.0	0	23	60	10	831	0	8	95	42	803

Source: Census of Population and Housing, 1990: Equal Employment Opportunity (EEO) File on CD-ROM [machine-readable datafiles]. Prepared by the Bureau of the Census. Washington, DC: The Bureau, 1992. *Notes:* "MSA" represents "metropolitan statistical area"; "CMSA" stands for "consolidated metropolitan statistical area."

★ 168 ★

Leading Occupations

Personnel, Training, and Labor Relations Specialists, by Metropolitan Area

According to the 1990 Census of Population and Housing, personnel, training, and labor relations specialists ranked 66 among occupations employing the most people in the United States. Table presents the number of civilians 16 years old or older who reported working as personnel, training, and labor relations specialists during the 1990 Census. Data show the total employment figures, employment per 100,000 population, and employment data for men and women of various races and ethnicities in the 25 metropolitan statistical areas with the largest concentrations of personnel, training, and labor relations specialists.

[Total for all of the U.S. was 513,625; 206.5 per 100,000 persons]

Metropolitan area	Total employees	Employees per 100,000 population	Men					Women				
			American Indian, Eskimo & Aleut	Asian, Pacific Islander	Black	Hispanic	White	American Indian, Eskimo & Aleut	Asian, Pacific Islander	Black	Hispanic	White
New York, New York New Jersey (northern) Long Island, New York CMSA	46,731	258.4	33	391	2,812	1,544	15,019	20	652	4,380	2,201	22,000
Los Angeles, California Anaheim, California Riverside, California CMSA	30,962	213.1	69	622	1,308	2,626	8,834	90	1,139	2,332	3,226	14,005
Chicago, Illinois Gary, Indiana Lake County, Illinois CMSA	20,572	255.1	40	155	1,289	742	7,486	13	156	2,261	609	8,644
Washington, District of Columbia MSA	19,424	495.1	40	84	1,392	150	4,992	49	226	3,949	352	8,591
San Francisco, California Oakland, California San Jose, California CMSA	19,012	304.0	70	540	732	796	5,224	78	1,073	1,133	1,015	9,553
Philadelphia, Pennsylvania Wilmington, Delaware Trenton, New Jersey CMSA	15,440	261.7	11	26	693	202	5,534	12	71	1,720	166	7,200
Boston, Massachusetts Lawrence, Massachusetts Salem, Massachusetts CMSA	12,639	303.0	0	71	224	100	4,350	7	71	487	225	7,239
Detroit, Michigan Ann Arbor, Michigan CMSA	10,998	235.7	7	26	590	101	4,228	28	44	1,322	125	4,682
Dallas, Texas Fort Worth, Texas CMSA	10,064	259.0	19	67	439	300	3,333	57	51	892	253	4,989
Atlanta, Georgia MSA	8,966	316.4	0	21	552	109	2,752	5	7	1,510	84	3,997

[Continued]

★ 168 ★

Personnel, Training, and Labor Relations Specialists, by Metropolitan Area
[Continued]

Metropolitan area	Total employees	Employees per 100,000 population	Men					Women				
			American Indian, Eskimo & Aleut	Asian, Pacific Islander	Black	Hispanic	White	American Indian, Eskimo & Aleut	Asian, Pacific Islander	Black	Hispanic	White
Houston, Texas Galveston, Texas Brazoria, Texas CMSA	8,706	234.6	32	67	408	298	3,384	16	82	695	510	3,737
Minneapolis, Minnesota St. Paul, Minnesota MSA	7,472	303.2	39	27	205	52	2,867	32	45	156	68	4,057
Baltimore, Maryland MSA	7,471	313.6	18	21	623	19	2,338	15	52	1,208	20	3,188
Seattle, Washington Tacoma, Washington CMSA	6,892	269.3	38	149	233	130	2,042	87	211	284	98	3,787
Cleveland, Ohio Akron, Ohio Lorain, Ohio CMSA	5,712	207.0	3	23	300	41	2,229	14	51	497	18	2,570
St. Louis, Missouri MSA	5,709	233.6	19	20	283	34	2,262	0	12	420	23	2,675
San Diego, California MSA	5,395	216.0	0	115	185	278	1,824	21	151	294	408	2,522
Miami, Florida Fort Lauderdale, Florida CMSA	5,337	167.2	11	10	255	545	1,633	3	38	656	812	2,557
Phoenix, Arizona MSA	5,306	250.0	0	38	89	181	2,158	23	9	177	192	2,667
Denver, Colorado Boulder, Colorado CMSA	4,602	249.0	9	18	78	149	1,669	22	74	192	240	2,355
Columbus, Ohio MSA	4,153	301.5	10	0	184	9	1,607	3	26	301	0	2,022
Sacramento, California MSA	3,916	264.4	26	58	168	166	990	19	91	221	260	2,103
Kansas City, Missouri Kansas City, Kansas MSA	3,900	249.0	0	10	158	26	1,408	35	0	305	64	1,944
Pittsburgh, Pennsylvania Beaver Valley, Pennsylvania CMSA	3,899	173.9	0	0	154	4	1,700	0	12	223	14	1,806
Tampa, Florida St. Petersburg, Florida Clearwater, Florida MSA	3,800	183.8	10	17	72	113	1,481	6	32	200	91	1,923

Source: Census of Population and Housing, 1990: Equal Employment Opportunity (EEO) File on CD-ROM [machine-readable datafiles]. Prepared by the Bureau of the Census. Washington, DC: The Bureau, 1992. *Notes:* "MSA" represents "metropolitan statistical area"; "CMSA" stands for "consolidated metropolitan statistical area."

★ 169 ★

Leading Occupations

Physicians, by Metropolitan Area

According to the 1990 Census of Population and Housing, physicians ranked 56 among occupations employing the most people in the United States. Table presents the number of civilians 16 years old or older who reported working as physicians during the 1990 Census. Data show the total employment figures, employment per 100,000 population, and employment data for men and women of various races and ethnicities in the 25 metropolitan statistical areas with the largest concentrations of physicians.

[Total for all of the U.S. was 586,715; 235.9 per 100,000 persons]

Metropolitan area	Total employees	Employees per 100,000 population	Men					Women				
			American Indian, Eskimo & Aleut	Asian, Pacific Islander	Black	Hispanic	White	American Indian, Eskimo & Aleut	Asian, Pacific Islander	Black	Hispanic	White
New York, New York New Jersey (northern) Long Island, New York CMSA	68,056	376.3	43	7,169	2,584	3,223	40,489	18	3,894	1,444	1,053	11,564
Los Angeles, California Anaheim, California Riverside, California CMSA	36,656	252.3	69	4,920	1,051	1,933	22,173	17	2,024	654	552	4,987
Chicago, Illinois Gary, Indiana Lake County, Illinois CMSA	22,529	279.3	17	3,101	660	973	12,807	0	1,361	466	259	3,818
Philadelphia, Pennsylvania Wilmington, Delaware Trenton, New Jersey CMSA	20,639	349.9	5	1,196	619	375	13,876	6	815	268	108	3,746
San Francisco, California Oakland, California San Jose, California CMSA	19,971	319.4	10	1,686	501	461	12,838	10	873	171	243	3,721

[Continued]

★ 169 ★

Physicians, by Metropolitan Area
[Continued]

Metropolitan area	Total employees	Employees per 100,000 population	Men					Women				
			American Indian, Eskimo & Aleut	Asian, Pacific Islander	Black	Hispanic	White	American Indian, Eskimo & Aleut	Asian, Pacific Islander	Black	Hispanic	White
Boston, Massachusetts Lawrence, Massachusetts Salem, Massachusetts CMSA	15,667	375.6	6	690	141	308	10,460	0	482	133	110	3,652
Washington, District of Columbia MSA	14,043	357.9	7	1,151	908	592	8,011	10	571	574	180	2,651
Detroit, Michigan Ann Arbor, Michigan CMSA	13,849	296.9	9	1,614	615	501	8,192	17	675	320	100	2,237
Miami, Florida Fort Lauderdale, Florida CMSA	9,695	303.7	0	360	296	2,933	7,285	10	146	74	614	1,321
Houston, Texas Galveston, Texas Brazoria, Texas CMSA	9,477	255.4	16	694	326	918	6,057	6	286	122	248	1,718
Baltimore, Maryland MSA	9,216	386.9	15	974	355	324	5,547	0	464	265	92	1,568
Dallas, Texas Fort Worth, Texas CMSA	8,758	225.4	13	346	191	267	6,388	6	163	95	65	1,475
Cleveland, Ohio Akron, Ohio Lorain, Ohio CMSA	8,707	315.5	0	952	347	251	5,316	0	434	157	64	1,441
Seattle, Washington Tacoma, Washington CMSA	7,360	287.6	21	344	83	113	5,180	0	165	28	30	1,518
Atlanta, Georgia MSA	6,540	230.8	17	261	489	256	4,327	0	120	243	19	1,061
San Diego, California MSA	6,526	261.3	7	307	64	348	4,926	7	121	20	79	945
Pittsburgh, Pennsylvania Beaver Valley, Pennsylvania CMSA	6,522	290.8	5	470	109	176	4,370	0	159	17	25	1,372
St. Louis, Missouri MSA	6,506	266.2	0	678	172	179	4,278	0	255	92	41	966
Minneapolis, Minnesota St. Paul, Minnesota MSA	6,204	251.8	0	276	47	79	4,428	10	56	8	24	1,333
Denver, Colorado Boulder, Colorado CMSA	5,540	299.7	0	63	53	122	4,141	9	90	41	55	1,126
Tampa, Florida St. Petersburg, Florida Clearwater, Florida MSA	5,203	251.6	4	407	57	575	3,858	9	123	0	85	697
Phoenix, Arizona MSA	4,860	229.0	4	198	30	163	3,845	0	66	26	36	655
Kansas City, Missouri Kansas City, Kansas MSA	4,481	286.1	21	239	80	136	3,129	7	145	39	29	795
Milwaukee, Wisconsin Racine, Wisconsin CMSA	4,178	260.0	0	334	60	59	3,003	0	116	38	14	591
Portland, Oregon Vancouver, Washington CMSA	4,114	278.4	13	129	49	38	3,027	0	72	13	12	793

Source: Census of Population and Housing, 1990: Equal Employment Opportunity (EEO) File on CD-ROM [machine-readable datafiles]. Prepared by the Bureau of the Census. Washington, DC: The Bureau, 1992. *Notes:* "MSA" represents "metropolitan statistical area"; "CMSA" stands for "consolidated metropolitan statistical area."

★ 170 ★

Leading Occupations

Plumbers, Pipefitters, and Steamfitters, by Metropolitan Area

According to the 1990 Census of Population and Housing, plumbers, pipefitters, and steamfitters ranked 70 among occupations employing the most people in the United States. Table presents the number of civilians 16 years old or older who reported working as plumbers, pipefitters, and steamfitters during the 1990 Census. Data show the total employment figures, employment per 100,000 population, and employment data for men and women of various races and ethnicities in the 25 metropolitan statistical areas with the largest concentrations of plumbers, pipefitters, and steamfitters, excluding apprentices.

[Total for all of the U.S. was 488,858; 196.6 per 100,000 persons]

Metropolitan area	Total employees	Employees per 100,000 population	Men					Women				
			American Indian, Eskimo & Aleut	Asian, Pacific Islander	Black	Hispanic	White	American Indian, Eskimo & Aleut	Asian, Pacific Islander	Black	Hispanic	White
New York, New York New Jersey (northern) Long Island, New York CMSA	34,892	192.9	49	352	4,207	2,836	28,683	0	0	65	123	272
Los Angeles, California Anaheim, California Riverside, California CMSA	30,831	212.2	298	956	1,785	9,917	22,071	0	22	53	97	431
Chicago, Illinois Gary, Indiana Lake County, Illinois CMSA	14,428	178.9	48	46	1,085	737	12,749	0	0	16	8	95
Philadelphia, Pennsylvania Wilmington, Delaware Trenton, New Jersey CMSA	13,811	234.1	2	26	1,032	231	12,508	0	0	8	0	66
San Francisco, California Oakland, California San Jose, California CMSA	11,761	188.1	138	824	856	1,959	8,734	0	32	15	29	197
Houston, Texas Galveston, Texas Brazoria, Texas CMSA	11,444	308.4	58	94	1,100	2,478	8,810	0	0	0	24	74
Detroit, Michigan Ann Arbor, Michigan CMSA	9,464	202.9	29	0	952	121	8,324	0	0	44	0	53
Boston, Massachusetts Lawrence, Massachusetts Salem, Massachusetts CMSA	8,932	214.1	21	46	302	84	8,405	0	0	17	0	112
Washington, District of Columbia MSA	7,058	179.9	40	65	1,633	305	5,067	0	0	25	0	75
Dallas, Texas Fort Worth, Texas CMSA	6,574	169.2	37	33	590	927	5,244	0	0	17	0	72
Baltimore, Maryland MSA	6,006	252.1	28	28	734	54	5,105	0	0	19	0	76
San Diego, California MSA	5,629	225.3	79	146	399	1,193	4,337	2	0	13	6	94
Miami, Florida Fort Lauderdale, Florida CMSA	5,318	166.6	18	0	889	1,573	4,223	0	0	31	0	20
Seattle, Washington Tacoma, Washington CMSA	5,031	196.6	119	137	169	141	4,440	0	0	5	0	137
Cleveland, Ohio Akron, Ohio Lorain, Ohio CMSA	5,001	181.2	14	0	515	108	4,303	0	0	36	0	72
Atlanta, Georgia MSA	4,769	168.3	12	51	608	2	4,025	0	0	16	0	57
Norfolk, Virginia Virginia Beach, Virginia Newport News, Virginia MSA	4,609	330.1	44	38	1,235	87	3,008	0	0	46	0	205
St. Louis, Missouri MSA	4,510	184.5	6	0	403	27	4,066	0	0	0	0	24
Pittsburgh, Pennsylvania Beaver Valley, Pennsylvania CMSA	4,447	198.3	0	0	148	9	4,232	0	0	0	10	57
Phoenix, Arizona MSA	4,086	192.6	119	0	110	596	3,551	0	0	0	0	44
Minneapolis, Minnesota St. Paul, Minnesota MSA	3,913	158.8	8	11	46	26	3,776	0	0	5	0	60
Tampa, Florida St. Petersburg, Florida Clearwater, Florida MSA	3,796	183.6	36	0	281	207	3,420	0	0	0	0	53
Cincinnati, Ohio Hamilton, Ohio CMSA	3,415	195.8	15	14	165	0	3,184	0	0	6	0	31
Denver, Colorado Boulder, Colorado CMSA	3,231	174.8	34	0	182	378	2,821	0	0	0	0	46
Sacramento, California MSA	2,956	199.6	37	63	83	368	2,595	0	0	0	11	38

Source: Census of Population and Housing, 1990: Equal Employment Opportunity (EEO) File on CD-ROM [machine-readable datafiles]. Prepared by the Bureau of the Census. Washington, DC: The Bureau, 1992. *Notes:* "MSA" represents "metropolitan statistical area"; "CMSA" stands for "consolidated metropolitan statistical area."

★ 171 ★

Leading Occupations

Postal Clerks, by Metropolitan Area

According to the 1990 Census of Population and Housing, postal clerks ranked 91 among occupations employing the most people in the United States. Table presents the number of civilians 16 years old or older who reported working as postal clerks during the 1990 Census. Data show the total employment figures, employment per 100,000 population, and employment data for men and women of various races and ethnicities in the 25 metropolitan statistical areas with the largest concentrations of postal clerks, excluding mail carriers.

[Total for all of the U.S. was 350,565; 141.0 per 100,000 persons]

Metropolitan area	Total employees	Employees per 100,000 population	Men					Women				
			American Indian, Eskimo & Aleut	Asian, Pacific Islander	Black	Hispanic	White	American Indian, Eskimo & Aleut	Asian, Pacific Islander	Black	Hispanic	White
New York, New York New Jersey (northern) Long Island, New York CMSA	40,670	224.9	45	1,426	6,900	2,935	14,545	57	1,347	8,394	1,980	5,995
Los Angeles, California Anaheim, California Riverside, California CMSA	20,844	143.4	49	2,427	3,008	2,116	4,648	37	2,022	3,835	1,457	3,190
Chicago, Illinois Gary, Indiana Lake County, Illinois CMSA	17,419	216.0	17	403	4,766	444	2,859	23	332	6,740	241	1,951
San Francisco, California Oakland, California San Jose, California CMSA	12,204	195.2	35	2,809	1,103	1,258	2,242	35	2,110	1,131	909	1,610
Philadelphia, Pennsylvania Wilmington, Delaware Trenton, New Jersey CMSA	11,094	188.1	7	88	2,544	287	3,942	21	120	2,473	104	1,751
Washington, District of Columbia MSA	9,741	248.3	20	250	3,101	107	1,732	16	463	3,162	53	913
Boston, Massachusetts Lawrence, Massachusetts Salem, Massachusetts CMSA	8,444	202.4	0	83	301	27	5,425	0	110	157	0	2,362
Dallas, Texas Fort Worth, Texas CMSA	7,424	191.1	11	211	1,485	570	2,061	7	190	1,689	255	1,308
Detroit, Michigan Ann Arbor, Michigan CMSA	6,844	146.7	6	63	1,239	32	1,396	30	39	2,336	46	1,712
Atlanta, Georgia MSA	5,299	187.0	0	27	1,715	9	815	0	26	2,136	0	571
Miami, Florida Fort Lauderdale, Florida CMSA	4,770	149.4	13	26	812	441	1,402	6	60	1,183	473	1,113
Houston, Texas Galveston, Texas Brazoria, Texas CMSA	4,662	125.6	0	122	1,022	377	761	0	157	1,533	276	770
Minneapolis, Minnesota St. Paul, Minnesota MSA	4,472	181.5	17	75	149	57	2,469	30	88	58	26	1,552
Cleveland, Ohio Akron, Ohio Lorain, Ohio CMSA	4,385	158.9	8	6	1,060	19	1,282	0	7	1,252	10	741
St. Louis, Missouri MSA	4,320	176.8	2	14	1,079	25	1,117	0	7	1,351	0	742
Baltimore, Maryland MSA	4,099	172.1	0	30	1,034	22	926	4	23	1,304	8	770
Denver, Colorado Boulder, Colorado CMSA	3,902	211.1	9	155	439	523	1,778	8	114	171	297	892
Pittsburgh, Pennsylvania Beaver Valley, Pennsylvania CMSA	3,823	170.5	7	0	321	0	2,141	0	0	269	3	1,085
Seattle, Washington Tacoma, Washington CMSA	3,269	127.7	27	361	155	73	1,259	20	487	100	47	821
Tampa, Florida St. Petersburg, Florida Clearwater, Florida MSA	3,183	153.9	2	55	167	156	1,614	10	25	210	98	1,048
Cincinnati, Ohio Hamilton, Ohio CMSA	2,996	171.8	2	0	456	8	1,434	0	12	369	13	715
Phoenix, Arizona MSA	2,973	140.1	43	17	148	342	1,244	79	26	113	253	977
Milwaukee, Wisconsin Racine, Wisconsin CMSA	2,855	177.6	0	29	306	60	1,143	0	39	491	31	775
Kansas City, Missouri Kansas City, Kansas MSA	2,842	181.5	6	20	303	65	1,159	17	15	600	50	659
San Diego, California MSA	2,765	110.7	0	487	175	119	828	25	458	150	176	543

Source: Census of Population and Housing, 1990: Equal Employment Opportunity (EEO) File on CD-ROM [machine-readable datafiles]. Prepared by the Bureau of the Census. Washington, DC: The Bureau, 1992. *Notes:* "MSA" represents "metropolitan statistical area"; "CMSA" stands for "consolidated metropolitan statistical area."

★ 172 ★
Leading Occupations

Postal Service Mail Carriers, by Metropolitan Area

According to the 1990 Census of Population and Housing, postal service mail carriers ranked 99 among occupations employing the most people in the United States. Table presents the number of civilians 16 years old or older who reported working as postal service mail carriers during the 1990 Census. Data show the total employment figures, employment per 100,000 population, and employment data for men and women of various races and ethnicities in the 25 metropolitan statistical areas with the largest concentrations of postal service mail carriers.

[Total for all of the U.S. was 328,241; 132.0 per 100,000 persons]

Metropolitan area	Total employees	Employees per 100,000 population	Men American Indian, Eskimo & Aleut	Asian, Pacific Islander	Black	Hispanic	White	Women American Indian, Eskimo & Aleut	Asian, Pacific Islander	Black	Hispanic	White
New York, New York New Jersey (northern) Long Island, New York CMSA	29,662	164.0	53	892	4,522	2,925	18,061	12	86	1,587	756	3,014
Los Angeles, California Anaheim, California Riverside, California CMSA	18,393	126.6	102	2,011	2,346	2,981	7,391	18	235	1,208	1,061	3,000
Chicago, Illinois Gary, Indiana Lake County, Illinois CMSA	11,365	140.9	17	202	2,947	356	4,875	2	33	1,563	179	1,526
San Francisco, California Oakland, California San Jose, California CMSA	9,994	159.8	49	2,466	903	1,318	3,406	25	368	310	720	1,504
Philadelphia, Pennsylvania Wilmington, Delaware Trenton, New Jersey CMSA	8,886	150.6	31	57	1,131	165	5,766	0	7	383	25	1,411
Detroit, Michigan Ann Arbor, Michigan CMSA	6,780	145.3	15	12	915	41	2,792	7	10	951	46	2,047
Boston, Massachusetts Lawrence, Massachusetts Salem, Massachusetts CMSA	6,687	160.3	13	36	166	40	5,236	0	27	27	18	1,159
Washington, District of Columbia MSA	6,574	167.6	15	251	2,354	77	2,565	8	19	753	17	574
Dallas, Texas Fort Worth, Texas CMSA	5,630	144.9	42	30	1,045	510	2,921	11	11	247	58	1,113
Miami, Florida Fort Lauderdale, Florida CMSA	4,793	150.1	0	36	732	843	2,403	0	0	636	228	906
Houston, Texas Galveston, Texas Brazoria, Texas CMSA	4,532	122.1	20	111	1,173	512	1,438	0	28	588	102	887
Atlanta, Georgia MSA	4,185	147.7	0	13	1,109	12	1,578	0	0	498	0	987
St. Louis, Missouri MSA	4,141	169.4	6	3	684	33	2,376	0	0	250	8	813
Cleveland, Ohio Akron, Ohio Lorain, Ohio CMSA	4,023	145.8	9	6	756	37	2,322	5	5	269	0	631
Baltimore, Maryland MSA	3,441	144.5	7	28	807	16	1,548	0	0	289	30	754
Minneapolis, Minnesota St. Paul, Minnesota MSA	3,439	139.6	18	8	35	11	2,522	0	7	0	6	849
San Diego, California MSA	3,227	129.2	18	339	224	219	1,686	21	86	60	127	683
Pittsburgh, Pennsylvania Beaver Valley, Pennsylvania CMSA	3,226	143.8	14	7	132	0	2,448	0	0	74	5	551
Seattle, Washington Tacoma, Washington CMSA	3,080	120.4	4	199	198	72	1,690	0	21	20	0	897
Denver, Colorado Boulder, Colorado CMSA	3,011	162.9	9	38	169	412	1,895	5	37	32	72	624
Tampa, Florida St. Petersburg, Florida Clearwater, Florida MSA	2,966	143.4	0	16	147	115	2,085	0	0	43	14	670
Phoenix, Arizona MSA	2,913	137.3	16	48	46	384	1,810	0	8	23	78	680
Kansas City, Missouri Kansas City, Kansas MSA	2,263	144.5	0	0	194	51	1,578	0	0	82	9	381
Cincinnati, Ohio Hamilton, Ohio CMSA	2,222	127.4	0	28	218	4	1,430	0	0	90	0	456
Sacramento, California MSA	2,136	144.2	9	100	107	158	1,274	0	22	70	31	460

Source: Census of Population and Housing, 1990: Equal Employment Opportunity (EEO) File on CD-ROM [machine-readable datafiles]. Prepared by the Bureau of the Census. Washington, DC: The Bureau, 1992. *Notes:* "MSA" represents "metropolitan statistical area"; "CMSA" stands for "consolidated metropolitan statistical area."

★ 173 ★
Leading Occupations

Postsecondary Teachers, by Metropolitan Area

According to the 1990 Census of Population and Housing, postsecondary teachers ranked 53 among occupations employing the most people in the United States. Table presents the number of civilians 16 years old or older who reported working as postsecondary teachers (subjects not specified) during the 1990 Census. Data show the total employment figures, employment per 100,000 population, and employment data for men and women of various races and ethnicities in the 25 metropolitan statistical areas with the largest concentrations of postsecondary teachers, subjects taught not specified.

[Total for all of the U.S. was 615,068; 247.3 per 100,000 persons]

Metropolitan area	Total employees	Employees per 100,000 population	Men					Women				
			American Indian, Eskimo & Aleut	Asian, Pacific Islander	Black	Hispanic	White	American Indian, Eskimo & Aleut	Asian, Pacific Islander	Black	Hispanic	White
New York, New York New Jersey (northern) Long Island, New York CMSA	37,071	205.0	61	2,398	1,316	948	17,600	27	886	1,409	883	12,832
Los Angeles, California Anaheim, California Riverside, California CMSA	29,338	201.9	101	2,122	638	1,025	14,223	62	1,088	714	1,089	9,559
San Francisco, California Oakland, California San Jose, California CMSA	20,555	328.7	27	1,796	390	678	9,531	29	995	446	507	6,995
Chicago, Illinois Gary, Indiana Lake County, Illinois CMSA	16,983	210.6	0	968	705	342	7,858	27	425	824	236	5,997
Boston, Massachusetts Lawrence, Massachusetts Salem, Massachusetts CMSA	16,784	402.3	31	942	326	324	8,480	17	505	177	260	6,182
Philadelphia, Pennsylvania Wilmington, Delaware Trenton, New Jersey CMSA	15,955	270.5	17	1,088	428	260	8,260	17	283	547	167	5,158
Washington, District of Columbia MSA	10,544	268.7	37	532	917	296	4,562	20	296	583	130	3,501
Detroit, Michigan Ann Arbor, Michigan CMSA	9,715	208.2	17	655	395	67	4,959	0	204	421	89	3,052
Minneapolis, Minnesota St. Paul, Minnesota MSA	8,243	334.5	5	697	101	111	4,130	22	215	86	55	2,956
Houston, Texas Galveston, Texas Brazoria, Texas CMSA	7,252	195.4	0	552	493	154	3,005	0	247	510	202	2,358
San Diego, California MSA	6,761	270.7	47	381	112	180	3,360	19	150	112	189	2,477
Dallas, Texas Fort Worth, Texas CMSA	6,739	173.4	6	454	124	186	3,350	19	135	175	159	2,333
Seattle, Washington Tacoma, Washington CMSA	6,625	258.9	11	385	65	66	3,525	13	138	96	83	2,353
Baltimore, Maryland MSA	6,342	266.2	25	345	357	56	3,102	0	184	241	48	2,076
Cleveland, Ohio Akron, Ohio Lorain, Ohio CMSA	6,276	227.4	0	349	140	62	3,252	0	182	187	20	2,132
Raleigh, North Carolina Durham, North Carolina MSA	5,938	807.4	6	357	278	44	3,476	0	88	210	27	1,498
Columbus, Ohio MSA	5,699	413.7	5	421	167	72	3,135	6	213	115	50	1,633
Austin, Texas MSA	5,698	729.0	6	619	72	297	3,141	0	127	45	123	1,557
Pittsburgh, Pennsylvania Beaver Valley, Pennsylvania CMSA	5,591	249.3	5	352	112	69	2,921	0	68	79	50	2,041
Champaign, Illinois Urbana, Illinois Rantoul, Illinois MSA	5,301	3064	0	635	105	123	2,898	8	306	31	32	1,274
Atlanta, Georgia MSA	5,184	183.0	15	271	456	59	2,264	11	60	457	59	1,597
Denver, Colorado Boulder, Colorado CMSA	5,040	272.7	0	216	71	179	2,973	4	55	49	69	1,630
Miami, Florida Fort Lauderdale, Florida CMSA	4,954	155.2	0	253	193	372	2,304	0	74	179	420	1,862
Phoenix, Arizona MSA	4,658	219.5	54	215	47	242	2,552	13	68	44	187	1,530
St. Louis, Missouri MSA	4,629	189.4	0	190	92	84	2,420	0	31	255	77	1,587

Source: Census of Population and Housing, 1990: Equal Employment Opportunity (EEO) File on CD-ROM [machine-readable datafiles]. Prepared by the Bureau of the Census. Washington, DC: The Bureau, 1992. *Notes:* "MSA" represents "metropolitan statistical area"; "CMSA" stands for "consolidated metropolitan statistical area."

★ 174 ★

Leading Occupations

Printing Press Operators, by Metropolitan Area

According to the 1990 Census of Population and Housing, printing press operators ranked 88 among occupations employing the most people in the United States. Table presents the number of civilians 16 years old or older who reported working as printing press operators during the 1990 Census. Data show the total employment figures, employment per 100,000 population, and employment data for men and women of various races and ethnicities in the 25 metropolitan statistical areas with the largest concentrations of printing press operators.

[Total for all of the U.S. was 359,781; 144.7 per 100,000 persons]

Metropolitan area	Total employees	Employees per 100,000 population	Men					Women				
			American Indian, Eskimo & Aleut	Asian, Pacific Islander	Black	Hispanic	White	American Indian, Eskimo & Aleut	Asian, Pacific Islander	Black	Hispanic	White
New York, New York New Jersey (northern) Long Island, New York CMSA	28,014	154.9	43	867	3,832	4,743	17,541	21	86	666	1,061	2,231
Los Angeles, California Anaheim, California Riverside, California CMSA	22,378	154.0	70	1,724	1,258	8,022	11,877	35	302	154	1,678	2,098
Chicago, Illinois Gary, Indiana Lake County, Illinois CMSA	17,193	213.2	18	395	1,473	1,854	11,885	26	41	352	391	1,706
Philadelphia, Pennsylvania Wilmington, Delaware Trenton, New Jersey CMSA	10,316	174.9	30	135	764	201	7,889	7	29	272	35	1,037
San Francisco, California Oakland, California San Jose, California CMSA	9,210	147.3	41	1,267	434	1,314	5,602	12	211	105	182	922
Dallas, Texas Fort Worth, Texas CMSA	7,162	184.3	46	158	620	1,135	4,375	11	11	193	168	979
Washington, District of Columbia MSA	7,145	182.1	6	234	2,205	266	3,630	0	31	390	46	483
Boston, Massachusetts Lawrence, Massachusetts Salem, Massachusetts CMSA	6,952	166.7	0	90	351	166	5,479	0	0	50	63	855
Minneapolis, Minnesota St. Paul, Minnesota MSA	6,577	266.9	75	39	60	50	5,247	6	12	26	9	1,063
Atlanta, Georgia MSA	5,617	198.2	7	84	904	42	3,623	5	22	402	9	544
Detroit, Michigan Ann Arbor, Michigan CMSA	5,327	114.2	6	6	219	96	4,176	4	12	129	21	727
Miami, Florida Fort Lauderdale, Florida CMSA	4,394	137.6	9	44	581	1,555	2,810	0	0	129	404	529
St. Louis, Missouri MSA	4,168	170.5	17	19	299	11	3,088	0	5	124	0	616
Houston, Texas Galveston, Texas Brazoria, Texas CMSA	4,160	112.1	7	126	416	915	2,410	6	13	146	221	488
Cleveland, Ohio Akron, Ohio Lorain, Ohio CMSA	4,107	148.8	0	8	281	14	3,121	0	7	163	0	523
Milwaukee, Wisconsin Racine, Wisconsin CMSA	4,045	251.7	6	13	119	71	3,252	5	6	46	8	555
Baltimore, Maryland MSA	4,024	168.9	25	18	746	10	2,521	0	7	185	0	522
Kansas City, Missouri Kansas City, Kansas MSA	3,872	247.2	11	21	287	181	2,802	16	9	111	14	514
Seattle, Washington Tacoma, Washington CMSA	3,610	141.1	28	235	84	135	2,522	0	53	13	41	630
Cincinnati, Ohio Hamilton, Ohio CMSA	3,540	203.0	0	3	158	7	2,882	0	2	67	0	421
Denver, Colorado Boulder, Colorado CMSA	3,017	163.2	39	43	79	379	2,151	0	6	28	103	460
San Diego, California MSA	3,012	120.6	36	218	98	346	1,933	10	97	46	119	347
Portland, Oregon Vancouver, Washington CMSA	3,010	203.7	13	92	53	44	2,272	0	17	4	9	550
Tampa, Florida St. Petersburg, Florida Clearwater, Florida MSA	2,992	144.7	0	45	254	179	2,191	13	12	33	38	415
Phoenix, Arizona MSA	2,975	140.2	16	28	63	360	2,098	0	35	0	72	518

Source: Census of Population and Housing, 1990: Equal Employment Opportunity (EEO) File on CD-ROM [machine-readable datafiles]. Prepared by the Bureau of the Census. Washington, DC: The Bureau, 1992. *Notes:* "MSA" represents "metropolitan statistical area"; "CMSA" stands for "consolidated metropolitan statistical area."

★ 175 ★

Leading Occupations

Private Household Cleaners and Servants, by Metropolitan Area

According to the 1990 Census of Population and Housing, private household cleaners and servants ranked 89 among occupations employing the most people in the United States. Table presents the number of civilians 16 years old or older who reported working as private household cleaners and servants during the 1990 Census. Data show the total employment figures, employment per 100,000 population, and employment data for men and women of various races and ethnicities in the 25 metropolitan statistical areas with the largest concentrations of private household cleaners and servants.

[Total for all of the U.S. was 354,351; 142.5 per 100,000 persons]

Metropolitan area	Total employees	Employees per 100,000 population	Men					Women				
			American Indian, Eskimo & Aleut	Asian, Pacific Islander	Black	Hispanic	White	American Indian, Eskimo & Aleut	Asian, Pacific Islander	Black	Hispanic	White
Los Angeles, California Anaheim, California Riverside, California CMSA	44,791	308.2	13	226	185	1,774	1,389	193	1,762	2,267	33,479	19,608
New York, New York New Jersey (northern) Long Island, New York CMSA	31,476	174.0	20	190	705	791	1,112	85	1,717	11,469	10,209	12,146
San Francisco, California Oakland, California San Jose, California CMSA	10,504	168.0	0	237	66	332	689	73	1,181	997	3,957	5,485
Miami, Florida Fort Lauderdale, Florida CMSA	10,375	325.0	0	8	185	241	354	30	82	3,915	5,207	4,950
Houston, Texas Galveston, Texas Brazoria, Texas CMSA	9,819	264.6	0	35	87	244	246	37	98	3,701	4,542	3,021
Washington, District of Columbia MSA	9,244	235.6	0	63	164	153	162	63	811	3,165	3,826	3,229
Dallas, Texas Fort Worth, Texas CMSA	7,522	193.6	0	24	145	117	123	33	52	3,124	2,321	2,638
Chicago, Illinois Gary, Indiana Lake County, Illinois CMSA	6,859	85.04	0	37	165	136	253	24	118	2,122	973	3,588
Philadelphia, Pennsylvania Wilmington, Delaware Trenton, New Jersey CMSA	5,270	89.33	5	0	161	21	230	17	35	2,397	281	2,320
San Diego, California MSA	5,227	209.3	2	0	14	231	312	26	221	328	3,224	2,589
Atlanta, Georgia MSA	4,472	157.8	0	0	165	7	108	0	49	3,090	107	1,004
Detroit, Michigan Ann Arbor, Michigan CMSA	3,780	81.02	15	0	176	3	102	22	23	1,503	113	1,899
Boston, Massachusetts Lawrence, Massachusetts Salem, Massachusetts CMSA	3,086	73.98	0	30	43	100	302	5	38	279	600	2,158
San Antonio, Texas MSA	2,716	208.6	0	0	6	104	61	0	34	467	1,816	1,506
New Orleans, Louisiana MSA	2,715	219.2	0	0	79	15	60	11	0	1,948	355	465
Baltimore, Maryland MSA	2,690	112.9	0	0	197	25	58	10	41	1,525	115	805
Memphis, Tennessee MSA	2,663	271.3	0	0	96	0	19	0	7	2,320	8	221
Tampa, Florida St. Petersburg, Florida Clearwater, Florida MSA	2,619	126.7	0	0	37	5	133	26	11	936	137	1,432
St. Louis, Missouri MSA	2,583	105.7	0	8	55	8	96	12	0	1,353	43	1,045
West Palm Beach, Florida Boca Raton, Florida Delray Beach, Florida MSA	2,580	298.8	0	24	27	29	103	0	2	982	538	1,308
Cleveland, Ohio Akron, Ohio Lorain, Ohio CMSA	2,188	79.28	0	0	30	0	105	7	19	825	45	1,181
Phoenix, Arizona MSA	2,166	102.1	18	0	0	26	139	65	33	62	655	1,502
Seattle, Washington Tacoma, Washington CMSA	2,143	83.74	10	4	0	11	195	7	71	136	84	1,699
Denver, Colorado Boulder, Colorado CMSA	2,004	108.4	0	0	10	8	130	15	44	152	365	1,511
Sacramento, California MSA	1,877	126.7	0	0	30	20	106	46	209	157	333	1,170

Source: Census of Population and Housing, 1990: Equal Employment Opportunity (EEO) File on CD-ROM [machine-readable datafiles]. Prepared by the Bureau of the Census. Washington, DC: The Bureau, 1992. *Notes:* "MSA" represents "metropolitan statistical area"; "CMSA" stands for "consolidated metropolitan statistical area."

★ 176 ★

Leading Occupations

Production Inspectors, Checkers, and Examiners, by Metropolitan Area

According to the 1990 Census of Population and Housing, production inspectors, checkers, and examiners ranked 50 among occupations employing the most people in the United States. Table presents the number of civilians 16 years old or older who reported working as production inspectors, checkers, and examiners during the 1990 Census. Data show the total employment figures, employment per 100,000 population, and employment data for men and women of various races and ethnicities in the 25 metropolitan statistical areas with the largest concentrations of production inspectors, checkers, and examiners.

[Total for all of the U.S. was 625,008; 251.3 per 100,000 persons]

Metropolitan area	Total employees	Employees per 100,000 population	Men					Women				
			American Indian, Eskimo & Aleut	Asian, Pacific Islander	Black	Hispanic	White	American Indian, Eskimo & Aleut	Asian, Pacific Islander	Black	Hispanic	White
Los Angeles, California Anaheim, California Riverside, California CMSA	37,013	254.7	208	2,221	1,369	6,747	11,220	73	2,000	1,225	10,746	9,618
New York, New York New Jersey (northern) Long Island, New York CMSA	27,672	153.0	43	1,121	2,261	2,224	9,425	44	1,034	2,956	3,532	8,611
Chicago, Illinois Gary, Indiana Lake County, Illinois CMSA	22,043	273.3	27	592	1,618	1,540	8,192	36	773	2,430	2,348	6,249
San Francisco, California Oakland, California San Jose, California CMSA	13,613	217.7	87	1,346	438	995	3,925	87	2,279	492	2,183	3,559
Detroit, Michigan Ann Arbor, Michigan CMSA	12,924	277.0	36	81	1,372	121	6,797	18	35	1,218	67	3,263
Philadelphia, Pennsylvania Wilmington, Delaware Trenton, New Jersey CMSA	12,397	210.1	23	179	1,038	188	4,993	29	246	1,433	303	4,174
Boston, Massachusetts Lawrence, Massachusetts Salem, Massachusetts CMSA	11,522	276.2	13	156	230	315	4,772	27	203	449	461	5,209
Dallas, Texas Fort Worth, Texas CMSA	9,578	246.5	31	245	581	631	3,690	52	292	1,274	875	2,491
Cleveland, Ohio Akron, Ohio Lorain, Ohio CMSA	8,550	309.8	29	74	646	95	4,354	13	9	626	92	2,707
Minneapolis, Minnesota St. Paul, Minnesota MSA	6,593	267.6	9	93	75	30	2,991	40	63	109	41	3,204
Houston, Texas Galveston, Texas Brazoria, Texas CMSA	6,249	168.4	0	130	580	888	3,461	0	91	355	557	784
Seattle, Washington Tacoma, Washington CMSA	6,029	235.6	46	200	126	60	3,488	16	282	128	60	1,701
Greensboro, North Carolina Winston-Salem, North Carolina High Point, North Carolina MSA	6,021	639.1	5	13	389	0	1,085	22	16	1,294	27	3,179
Charlotte, North Carolina Gastonia, North Carolina Rock Hill, South Carolina MSA	5,583	480.4	8	21	281	7	1,340	18	58	1,085	22	2,772
Milwaukee, Wisconsin Racine, Wisconsin CMSA	5,526	343.8	27	6	294	132	2,588	4	30	408	115	2,031
Atlanta, Georgia MSA	5,394	190.4	7	49	642	24	1,473	0	56	1,241	48	1,906
Providence, Rhode Island Pawtucket, Rhode Island Fall River, Massachusetts CMSA	5,047	442.1	6	13	33	59	1,562	26	83	69	265	3,062
St. Louis, Missouri MSA	4,745	194.1	14	26	475	49	2,408	0	5	367	9	1,425
Cincinnati, Ohio Hamilton, Ohio CMSA	4,730	271.2	0	0	271	5	2,283	12	0	289	14	1,875
San Diego, California MSA	4,289	171.7	15	268	163	361	1,585	12	834	92	559	853
Greenville, South Carolina Spartanburg, South Carolina MSA	4,252	663.5	11	0	220	0	1,049	5	12	885	0	2,070
Phoenix, Arizona MSA	4,241	199.9	9	72	73	306	1,623	49	204	185	640	1,490
Baltimore, Maryland MSA	4,029	169.1	6	38	580	68	1,738	12	12	471	7	1,135
Miami, Florida Fort Lauderdale, Florida CMSA	3,948	123.7	3	21	280	700	1,357	0	29	465	1,381	1,521
Pittsburgh, Pennsylvania Beaver Valley, Pennsylvania CMSA	3,900	173.9	0	0	210	0	2,391	0	0	99	10	1,200

Source: Census of Population and Housing, 1990: Equal Employment Opportunity (EEO) File on CD-ROM [machine-readable datafiles]. Prepared by the Bureau of the Census. Washington, DC: The Bureau, 1992. *Notes:* "MSA" represents "metropolitan statistical area"; "CMSA" stands for "consolidated metropolitan statistical area."

★ 177 ★

Leading Occupations

Production Occupation Supervisors, by Metropolitan Area

According to the 1990 Census of Population and Housing, production occupation supervisors ranked 19 among occupations employing the most people in the United States. Table presents the number of civilians 16 years old or older who reported working as production occupation supervisors during the 1990 Census. Data show the total employment figures, employment per 100,000 population, and employment data for men and women of various races and ethnicities in the 25 metropolitan statistical areas with the largest concentrations of production occupation supervisors.

[Total for all of the U.S. was 1,299,637; 522.6 per 100,000 persons]

Metropolitan area	Total employees	Employees per 100,000 population	Men					Women				
			American Indian, Eskimo & Aleut	Asian, Pacific Islander	Black	Hispanic	White	American Indian, Eskimo & Aleut	Asian, Pacific Islander	Black	Hispanic	White
Los Angeles, California Anaheim, California Riverside, California CMSA	81,422	560.3	434	4,032	3,494	24,350	43,954	105	1,373	1,052	7,741	10,508
New York, New York New Jersey (northern) Long Island, New York CMSA	75,481	417.3	103	2,491	8,133	10,283	44,881	55	754	2,538	3,587	11,043
Chicago, Illinois Gary, Indiana Lake County, Illinois CMSA	48,498	601.3	55	1,023	4,416	5,359	32,475	26	162	1,241	1,248	5,628
Detroit, Michigan Ann Arbor, Michigan CMSA	30,596	655.8	139	174	2,563	425	23,859	39	23	774	64	2,840
San Francisco, California Oakland, California San Jose, California CMSA	28,924	462.5	196	2,395	1,449	3,782	16,030	44	1,271	477	1,403	4,919
Philadelphia, Pennsylvania Wilmington, Delaware Trenton, New Jersey CMSA	28,749	487.3	48	305	2,416	767	20,596	26	118	767	195	3,991
Dallas, Texas Fort Worth, Texas CMSA	21,904	563.8	73	289	1,664	2,457	14,443	44	62	692	674	2,912
Boston, Massachusetts Lawrence, Massachusetts Salem, Massachusetts CMSA	20,369	488.3	33	123	579	595	14,937	19	52	194	199	4,054
Houston, Texas Galveston, Texas Brazoria, Texas CMSA	18,165	489.5	36	391	1,964	2,328	12,294	0	44	380	466	1,593
Cleveland, Ohio Akron, Ohio Lorain, Ohio CMSA	16,200	587.0	43	43	845	242	13,083	0	9	231	27	1,805
Minneapolis, Minnesota St. Paul, Minnesota MSA	14,442	586.1	56	124	258	120	11,067	4	29	69	20	2,805
Seattle, Washington Tacoma, Washington CMSA	13,540	529.1	158	308	375	329	9,956	15	227	106	81	2,228
Atlanta, Georgia MSA	13,285	468.9	19	108	2,030	121	8,522	21	13	755	8	1,767
St. Louis, Missouri MSA	12,422	508.2	38	45	851	24	9,523	0	10	297	7	1,658
Milwaukee, Wisconsin Racine, Wisconsin CMSA	11,655	725.2	33	31	404	292	9,085	10	6	191	49	1,744
Miami, Florida Fort Lauderdale, Florida CMSA	11,262	352.8	7	106	999	3,688	7,018	0	30	312	1,754	2,269
Charlotte, North Carolina Gastonia, North Carolina Rock Hill, South Carolina MSA	10,311	887.3	23	91	1,159	77	7,198	0	13	279	0	1,504
Baltimore, Maryland MSA	10,230	429.4	6	75	1,564	70	7,000	24	14	437	0	1,105
Providence, Rhode Island Pawtucket, Rhode Island Fall River, Massachusetts CMSA	9,639	844.4	31	44	105	206	7,123	4	7	35	132	2,070
Greensboro, North Carolina Winston-Salem, North Carolina High Point, North Carolina MSA	9,638	1,023	46	31	934	14	6,785	5	10	363	0	1,451
Cincinnati, Ohio Hamilton, Ohio CMSA	9,537	546.8	0	47	491	32	7,555	2	4	87	5	1,351
San Diego, California MSA	9,494	380.1	49	350	262	1,283	6,249	16	293	106	483	1,357
Phoenix, Arizona MSA	9,372	441.6	36	68	229	1,119	6,329	11	13	115	422	1,751
Portland, Oregon Vancouver, Washington CMSA	8,753	592.3	106	161	183	246	6,649	6	66	21	33	1,417
Pittsburgh, Pennsylvania Beaver Valley, Pennsylvania CMSA	8,330	371.4	2	13	229	5	7,249	0	8	48	0	781

Source: Census of Population and Housing, 1990: Equal Employment Opportunity (EEO) File on CD-ROM [machine-readable datafiles]. Prepared by the Bureau of the Census. Washington, DC: The Bureau, 1992. *Notes:* "MSA" represents "metropolitan statistical area"; "CMSA" stands for "consolidated metropolitan statistical area."

★ 178 ★

Leading Occupations

Property and Real Estate Managers, by Metropolitan Area

According to the 1990 Census of Population and Housing, property and real estate managers ranked 80 among occupations employing the most people in the United States. Table presents the number of civilians 16 years old or older who reported working as property and real estate managers during the 1990 Census. Data show the total employment figures, employment per 100,000 population, and employment data for men and women of various races and ethnicities in the 25 metropolitan statistical areas with the largest concentrations of property and real estate managers.

[Total for all of the U.S. was 411,466; 165.4 per 100,000 persons]

Metropolitan area	Total employees	Employees per 100,000 population	Men					Women				
			American Indian, Eskimo & Aleut	Asian, Pacific Islander	Black	Hispanic	White	American Indian, Eskimo & Aleut	Asian, Pacific Islander	Black	Hispanic	White
Los Angeles, California Anaheim, California Riverside, California CMSA	38,108	262.2	76	1,463	655	2,299	16,921	121	908	615	2,365	15,322
New York, New York New Jersey (northern) Long Island, New York CMSA	33,184	183.5	61	572	2,859	4,889	18,365	0	184	1,258	866	7,716
San Francisco, California Oakland, California San Jose, California CMSA	17,074	273.0	17	690	418	514	7,938	72	501	340	683	6,694
Dallas, Texas Fort Worth, Texas CMSA	11,703	301.2	34	60	207	223	4,555	27	58	418	396	6,037
Chicago, Illinois Gary, Indiana Lake County, Illinois CMSA	11,132	138.0	10	92	661	224	5,156	12	43	924	161	4,045
Washington, District of Columbia MSA	10,508	267.8	9	76	922	193	4,252	6	84	937	124	4,102
Houston, Texas Galveston, Texas Brazoria, Texas CMSA	9,926	267.5	0	134	356	271	3,693	9	63	348	647	4,857
San Diego, California MSA	9,275	371.3	39	132	136	245	3,952	16	98	138	423	4,466
Boston, Massachusetts Lawrence, Massachusetts Salem, Massachusetts CMSA	8,031	192.5	6	92	212	149	4,929	7	4	227	53	2,447
Seattle, Washington Tacoma, Washington CMSA	7,455	291.3	24	137	135	30	3,457	91	75	117	60	3,390
Miami, Florida Fort Lauderdale, Florida CMSA	7,403	231.9	12	0	223	874	4,060	10	0	124	696	2,872
Philadelphia, Pennsylvania Wilmington, Delaware Trenton, New Jersey CMSA	7,340	124.4	0	55	424	133	3,812	7	62	355	51	2,532
Atlanta, Georgia MSA	7,281	257.0	17	45	358	39	3,388	13	7	483	54	2,925
Denver, Colorado Boulder, Colorado CMSA	6,329	342.4	22	12	84	121	3,261	6	19	28	187	2,783
Phoenix, Arizona MSA	5,994	282.5	8	23	71	60	2,675	25	10	25	129	3,102
Detroit, Michigan Ann Arbor, Michigan CMSA	5,768	123.6	6	23	340	37	2,795	28	12	400	38	2,141
Tampa, Florida St. Petersburg, Florida Clearwater, Florida MSA	5,077	245.5	21	16	42	83	2,462	14	22	44	54	2,442
Minneapolis, Minnesota St. Paul, Minnesota MSA	4,591	186.3	7	6	52	20	2,506	0	15	7	12	1,992
Baltimore, Maryland MSA	4,404	184.9	10	35	385	36	2,077	18	23	364	11	1,460
Sacramento, California MSA	4,317	291.5	9	32	55	48	1,979	38	19	63	134	2,049
Portland, Oregon Vancouver, Washington CMSA	3,951	267.3	9	35	50	31	1,849	2	14	5	34	1,964
Cleveland, Ohio Akron, Ohio Lorain, Ohio CMSA	3,212	116.4	0	0	181	0	1,781	0	0	153	30	1,097
St. Louis, Missouri MSA	3,126	127.9	0	0	157	0	1,255	0	19	190	8	1,493
San Antonio, Texas MSA	2,914	223.8	0	0	42	216	1,085	6	8	29	335	1,595
Kansas City, Missouri Kansas City, Kansas MSA	2,795	178.5	0	16	89	12	1,350	7	0	118	0	1,215

Source: Census of Population and Housing, 1990: Equal Employment Opportunity (EEO) File on CD-ROM [machine-readable datafiles]. Prepared by the Bureau of the Census. Washington, DC: The Bureau, 1992. *Notes:* "MSA" represents "metropolitan statistical area"; "CMSA" stands for "consolidated metropolitan statistical area."

★ 179 ★
Leading Occupations

Public Administration Administrators and Officials, by Metropolitan Area

According to the 1990 Census of Population and Housing, public administration administrators and officials ranked 68 among occupations employing the most people in the United States. Table presents the number of civilians 16 years old or older who reported working as public administration administrators and officials during the 1990 Census. Data show the total employment figures, employment per 100,000 population, and employment data for men and women of various races and ethnicities in the 25 metropolitan statistical areas with the largest concentrations of public administration administrators and officials.

[Total for all of the U.S. was 506,683; 203.7 per 100,000 persons]

Metropolitan area	Total employees	Employees per 100,000 population	Men					Women				
			American Indian, Eskimo & Aleut	Asian, Pacific Islander	Black	Hispanic	White	American Indian, Eskimo & Aleut	Asian, Pacific Islander	Black	Hispanic	White
Washington, District of Columbia MSA	57,096	1,455	119	918	3,937	936	26,614	122	443	7,314	623	17,362
New York, New York New Jersey (northern) Long Island, New York CMSA	28,283	156.4	46	709	2,268	938	11,743	55	319	3,491	1,087	8,992
Los Angeles, California Anaheim, California Riverside, California CMSA	17,461	120.2	46	630	1,025	1,333	7,151	92	560	1,440	1,470	5,494
Baltimore, Maryland MSA	16,854	707.5	8	21	1,112	108	8,012	15	39	2,133	138	5,483
Philadelphia, Pennsylvania Wilmington, Delaware Trenton, New Jersey CMSA	12,685	215.0	13	71	1,133	80	5,727	34	22	1,782	116	3,794
San Francisco, California Oakland, California San Jose, California CMSA	10,917	174.6	32	579	764	444	4,260	38	530	833	426	3,556
Chicago, Illinois Gary, Indiana Lake County, Illinois CMSA	10,389	128.8	15	109	1,043	336	4,436	0	56	1,651	227	2,781
Sacramento, California MSA	10,286	694.5	65	399	319	385	4,117	58	358	479	447	4,230
Boston, Massachusetts Lawrence, Massachusetts Salem, Massachusetts CMSA	9,475	227.1	22	134	307	89	4,083	0	48	433	109	4,360
Atlanta, Georgia MSA	6,442	227.4	12	9	701	22	2,671	9	14	981	40	2,040
Detroit, Michigan Ann Arbor, Michigan CMSA	5,851	125.4	0	6	611	98	2,210	15	15	1,046	54	1,865
Dallas, Texas Fort Worth, Texas CMSA	5,032	129.5	23	8	279	196	2,269	13	8	500	118	1,770
Seattle, Washington Tacoma, Washington CMSA	5,026	196.4	22	199	176	63	2,353	42	205	207	73	1,794
Albany, New York Schenectady, New York Troy, New York MSA	4,820	551.3	22	32	117	24	2,701	0	5	152	38	1,791
Denver, Colorado Boulder, Colorado CMSA	4,590	248.3	0	35	149	235	2,189	5	22	140	187	1,868
San Diego, California MSA	4,216	168.8	7	153	289	244	1,902	27	97	162	214	1,446
Norfolk, Virginia Virginia Beach, Virginia Newport News, Virginia MSA	4,181	299.5	0	19	376	32	1,907	0	24	448	37	1,379
Columbus, Ohio MSA	4,105	298.0	2	6	334	21	1,895	10	8	469	17	1,374
Miami, Florida Fort Lauderdale, Florida CMSA	4,077	127.7	3	12	298	459	1,936	12	0	438	392	1,300
Minneapolis, Minnesota St. Paul, Minnesota MSA	4,065	165.0	15	13	94	39	2,345	40	0	46	30	1,496
Oklahoma City, Oklahoma MSA	3,903	407.1	59	28	222	76	1,749	125	5	174	16	1,506
St. Louis, Missouri MSA	3,857	157.8	2	12	289	23	1,825	12	8	399	22	1,310
Houston, Texas Galveston, Texas Brazoria, Texas CMSA	3,824	103.0	0	27	336	151	1,637	17	51	429	234	1,207
Phoenix, Arizona MSA	3,749	176.7	63	4	108	157	1,799	40	26	159	170	1,400
Austin, Texas MSA	3,556	455.0	18	0	100	224	1,513	0	9	193	262	1,500

Source: Census of Population and Housing, 1990: Equal Employment Opportunity (EEO) File on CD-ROM [machine-readable datafiles]. Prepared by the Bureau of the Census. Washington, DC: The Bureau, 1992. *Notes:* "MSA" represents "metropolitan statistical area"; "CMSA" stands for "consolidated metropolitan statistical area."

★ 180 ★

Leading Occupations

Public Service Police and Detectives, by Metropolitan Area

According to the 1990 Census of Population and Housing, public service police and detectives ranked 65 among occupations employing the most people in the United States. Table presents the number of civilians 16 years old or older who reported working as public service police and detectives during the 1990 Census. Data show the total employment figures, employment per 100,000 population, and employment data for men and women of various races and ethnicities in the 25 metropolitan statistical areas with the largest concentrations of public service police and detectives.

[Total for all of the U.S. was 519,184; 208.8 per 100,000 persons]

Metropolitan area	Total employees	Employees per 100,000 population	Men					Women				
			American Indian, Eskimo & Aleut	Asian, Pacific Islander	Black	Hispanic	White	American Indian, Eskimo & Aleut	Asian, Pacific Islander	Black	Hispanic	White
New York, New York New Jersey (northern) Long Island, New York CMSA	66,923	370.0	44	501	6,698	5,274	49,522	21	79	3,034	913	4,424
Los Angeles, California Anaheim, California Riverside, California CMSA	25,723	177.0	214	857	2,219	3,880	16,693	41	151	745	718	2,757
Chicago, Illinois Gary, Indiana Lake County, Illinois CMSA	22,801	282.7	51	54	3,385	1,274	16,168	0	9	874	119	1,812
Philadelphia, Pennsylvania Wilmington, Delaware Trenton, New Jersey CMSA	16,765	284.2	29	28	2,335	492	12,240	0	7	755	44	1,065
Washington, District of Columbia MSA	14,004	356.9	23	99	3,663	259	7,467	6	0	1,183	94	1,409
San Francisco, California Oakland, California San Jose, California CMSA	11,045	176.6	111	595	619	1,010	7,406	40	86	236	148	1,389
Detroit, Michigan Ann Arbor, Michigan CMSA	10,738	230.2	49	42	2,166	80	6,800	4	24	805	32	804
Boston, Massachusetts Lawrence, Massachusetts Salem, Massachusetts CMSA	10,425	249.9	16	17	517	216	8,863	0	8	181	27	726
Miami, Florida Fort Lauderdale, Florida CMSA	9,860	308.8	18	0	896	1,832	6,917	7	8	443	328	1,366
Baltimore, Maryland MSA	7,927	332.8	5	9	1,378	53	5,285	15	0	454	0	753
Dallas, Texas Fort Worth, Texas CMSA	7,824	201.4	37	54	611	531	5,893	0	0	185	56	850
Houston, Texas Galveston, Texas Brazoria, Texas CMSA	7,776	209.5	30	44	758	941	5,622	4	4	241	104	677
Atlanta, Georgia MSA	5,778	203.9	0	0	1,230	74	3,750	0	0	237	36	536
Cleveland, Ohio Akron, Ohio Lorain, Ohio CMSA	5,367	194.5	36	5	541	171	4,055	12	0	176	25	453
San Diego, California MSA	5,355	214.4	79	97	211	947	3,719	3	28	130	82	667
St. Louis, Missouri MSA	5,248	214.7	10	0	757	60	4,061	0	0	68	8	327
Seattle, Washington Tacoma, Washington CMSA	4,609	180.1	39	160	176	92	3,629	27	30	44	0	480
Phoenix, Arizona MSA	4,338	204.4	76	34	159	364	3,278	12	0	57	113	448
Tampa, Florida St. Petersburg, Florida Clearwater, Florida MSA	3,840	185.7	18	35	197	277	3,017	0	0	121	18	415
Denver, Colorado Boulder, Colorado CMSA	3,653	197.6	31	61	86	279	2,741	0	4	25	83	552
Pittsburgh, Pennsylvania Beaver Valley, Pennsylvania CMSA	3,634	162.0	7	5	276	4	2,974	0	0	101	0	271
Buffalo, New York Niagara Falls, New York CMSA	3,464	291.3	15	0	287	54	2,808	0	0	112	0	225
Minneapolis, Minnesota St. Paul, Minnesota MSA	3,388	137.5	11	5	90	21	2,869	10	0	20	13	360
Kansas City, Missouri Kansas City, Kansas MSA	3,370	215.2	6	5	287	81	2,550	0	0	118	13	354
Milwaukee, Wisconsin Racine, Wisconsin CMSA	3,317	206.4	10	0	231	69	2,683	0	7	70	5	286

Source: Census of Population and Housing, 1990: Equal Employment Opportunity (EEO) File on CD-ROM [machine-readable datafiles]. Prepared by the Bureau of the Census. Washington, DC: The Bureau, 1992. *Notes:* "MSA" represents "metropolitan statistical area"; "CMSA" stands for "consolidated metropolitan statistical area."

★ 181 ★

Leading Occupations

Real Estate Sales Occupations, by Metropolitan Area

According to the 1990 Census of Population and Housing, real estate sales occupations ranked 26 among occupations employing the most people in the United States. Table presents the number of civilians 16 years old or older who reported working in real estate sales occupations during the 1990 Census. Data show the total employment figures, employment per 100,000 population, and employment data for men and women of various races and ethnicities in the 25 metropolitan statistical areas with the largest concentrations of real estate sales occupations.

[Total for all of the U.S. was 801,238; 322.2 per 100,000 persons]

Metropolitan area	Total employees	Employees per 100,000 population	Men					Women				
			American Indian, Eskimo & Aleut	Asian, Pacific Islander	Black	Hispanic	White	American Indian, Eskimo & Aleut	Asian, Pacific Islander	Black	Hispanic	White
Los Angeles, California Anaheim, California Riverside, California CMSA	78,057	537.2	103	4,068	1,624	4,536	33,071	120	3,366	1,326	3,392	31,399
New York, New York New Jersey (northern) Long Island, New York CMSA	60,207	332.9	33	1,334	2,282	1,841	23,549	21	1,191	1,331	1,431	29,298
San Francisco, California Oakland, California San Jose, California CMSA	32,806	524.6	47	1,814	584	671	14,361	99	1,733	433	907	13,251
Chicago, Illinois Gary, Indiana Lake County, Illinois CMSA	26,844	332.8	8	309	679	386	10,773	11	248	805	463	13,694
Washington, District of Columbia MSA	20,989	535.0	16	297	1,171	249	8,040	22	327	1,019	315	9,958
Philadelphia, Pennsylvania Wilmington, Delaware Trenton, New Jersey CMSA	17,751	300.9	9	78	357	47	7,715	0	104	449	116	8,997
Miami, Florida Fort Lauderdale, Florida CMSA	16,952	531.0	23	36	292	1,801	7,595	0	63	347	1,771	8,383
Dallas, Texas Fort Worth, Texas CMSA	15,117	389.1	46	84	272	171	7,168	51	101	343	302	6,935
San Diego, California MSA	14,920	597.3	24	332	90	330	7,408	19	246	101	491	6,427
Atlanta, Georgia MSA	13,893	490.3	0	45	490	57	5,906	8	48	569	92	6,803
Boston, Massachusetts Lawrence, Massachusetts Salem, Massachusetts CMSA	13,772	330.1	10	85	223	109	6,080	0	132	38	69	7,142
Houston, Texas Galveston, Texas Brazoria, Texas CMSA	13,380	360.6	4	237	378	359	5,708	11	231	289	342	6,288
Seattle, Washington Tacoma, Washington CMSA	12,790	499.8	36	259	128	85	6,690	14	246	39	104	5,341
Detroit, Michigan Ann Arbor, Michigan CMSA	12,430	266.4	7	42	286	50	5,326	12	59	341	92	6,329
Phoenix, Arizona MSA	11,379	536.2	0	32	7	123	6,475	21	40	67	157	4,658
Tampa, Florida St. Petersburg, Florida Clearwater, Florida MSA	10,088	487.8	0	22	58	172	4,832	8	31	51	180	5,030
Minneapolis, Minnesota St. Paul, Minnesota MSA	9,712	394.1	2	12	56	69	5,172	7	42	54	49	4,338
Baltimore, Maryland MSA	8,363	351.1	0	6	243	13	2,994	7	31	263	34	4,790
Denver, Colorado Boulder, Colorado CMSA	8,304	449.3	11	104	93	111	4,610	27	37	65	146	3,291
Sacramento, California MSA	7,616	514.2	25	168	155	128	3,651	10	82	36	112	3,408
Cleveland, Ohio Akron, Ohio Lorain, Ohio CMSA	7,423	269.0	0	8	204	26	2,955	19	53	127	34	4,057
St. Louis, Missouri MSA	7,149	292.5	9	6	88	0	2,791	26	25	127	23	4,077
West Palm Beach, Florida Boca Raton, Florida Delray Beach, Florida MSA	6,819	789.7	15	19	92	90	3,134	12	15	13	124	3,519
Orlando, Florida MSA	6,564	611.9	0	81	57	120	3,065	0	11	137	173	3,133
Portland, Oregon Vancouver, Washington CMSA	5,845	395.5	14	51	28	37	2,885	8	56	26	29	2,767

Source: Census of Population and Housing, 1990: Equal Employment Opportunity (EEO) File on CD-ROM [machine-readable datafiles]. Prepared by the Bureau of the Census. Washington, DC: The Bureau, 1992. *Notes:* "MSA" represents "metropolitan statistical area"; "CMSA" stands for "consolidated metropolitan statistical area."

★ 182 ★

Leading Occupations

Receptionists, by Metropolitan Area

According to the 1990 Census of Population and Housing, receptionists ranked 25 among occupations employing the most people in the United States. Table presents the number of civilians 16 years old or older who reported working as receptionists during the 1990 Census. Data show the total employment figures, employment per 100,000 population, and employment data for men and women of various races and ethnicities in the 25 metropolitan statistical areas with the largest concentrations of receptionists.

[Total for all of the U.S. was 822,093; 330.5 per 100,000 persons]

Metropolitan area	Total employees	Employees per 100,000 population	Men					Women				
			American Indian, Eskimo & Aleut	Asian, Pacific Islander	Black	Hispanic	White	American Indian, Eskimo & Aleut	Asian, Pacific Islander	Black	Hispanic	White
New York, New York New Jersey (northern) Long Island, New York CMSA	70,842	391.7	7	239	1,130	665	2,353	208	1,356	10,675	8,836	50,517
Los Angeles, California Anaheim, California Riverside, California CMSA	57,860	398.2	11	331	304	1,042	1,790	474	3,496	5,119	15,224	37,985
Chicago, Illinois Gary, Indiana Lake County, Illinois CMSA	32,015	396.9	0	146	313	63	1,020	31	375	4,657	2,577	24,252
San Francisco, California Oakland, California San Jose, California CMSA	28,224	451.3	19	346	214	229	1,121	263	2,290	2,474	3,908	19,768
Philadelphia, Pennsylvania Wilmington, Delaware Trenton, New Jersey CMSA	21,634	366.7	7	19	158	5	484	24	198	3,155	593	17,255
Washington, District of Columbia MSA	18,351	467.7	0	50	434	53	621	40	483	4,762	686	11,691
Detroit, Michigan Ann Arbor, Michigan CMSA	16,506	353.8	8	13	132	21	365	62	89	2,603	226	13,166
Boston, Massachusetts Lawrence, Massachusetts Salem, Massachusetts CMSA	16,081	385.5	0	3	81	13	861	43	181	873	359	13,809
Dallas, Texas Fort Worth, Texas CMSA	14,502	373.2	0	47	44	54	322	70	175	1,205	1,203	11,868
Houston, Texas Galveston, Texas Brazoria, Texas CMSA	13,795	371.7	0	14	83	93	226	12	169	1,474	2,461	10,555
Minneapolis, Minnesota St. Paul, Minnesota MSA	13,080	530.8	0	28	18	21	559	56	87	375	109	11,874
Seattle, Washington Tacoma, Washington CMSA	12,509	488.8	0	32	51	0	364	112	419	536	220	10,947
Miami, Florida Fort Lauderdale, Florida CMSA	12,255	383.9	10	12	50	219	573	15	45	1,180	4,270	9,952
Atlanta, Georgia MSA	11,566	408.2	0	0	108	7	230	35	38	2,060	152	9,031
San Diego, California MSA	11,237	449.8	6	24	58	61	287	96	629	642	1,894	8,494
Baltimore, Maryland MSA	9,159	384.5	0	16	136	12	309	46	60	1,971	52	6,599
Cleveland, Ohio Akron, Ohio Lorain, Ohio CMSA	9,036	327.4	0	7	49	0	236	33	18	1,211	155	7,397
Phoenix, Arizona MSA	8,696	409.8	11	0	0	31	269	121	69	195	997	7,596
Denver, Colorado Boulder, Colorado CMSA	8,511	460.5	13	4	73	64	280	71	66	415	849	7,158
St. Louis, Missouri MSA	8,308	339.9	0	16	20	23	264	10	51	942	104	6,988
Portland, Oregon Vancouver, Washington CMSA	6,959	470.9	0	13	12	6	169	56	126	194	132	6,351
Tampa, Florida St. Petersburg, Florida Clearwater, Florida MSA	6,898	333.6	4	0	21	17	273	11	24	367	310	6,156
Cincinnati, Ohio Hamilton, Ohio CMSA	6,784	389.0	0	4	16	10	183	13	2	646	19	5,910
Pittsburgh, Pennsylvania Beaver Valley, Pennsylvania CMSA	6,531	291.2	0	0	18	0	134	7	7	458	12	5,892
Milwaukee, Wisconsin Racine, Wisconsin CMSA	6,292	391.5	0	0	11	0	175	23	27	339	211	5,588

Source: Census of Population and Housing, 1990: Equal Employment Opportunity (EEO) File on CD-ROM [machine-readable datafiles]. Prepared by the Bureau of the Census. Washington, DC: The Bureau, 1992. *Notes:* "MSA" represents "metropolitan statistical area"; "CMSA" stands for "consolidated metropolitan statistical area."

★ 183 ★

Leading Occupations

Registered Nurses, by Metropolitan Area

According to the 1990 Census of Population and Housing, registered nurses ranked 10 among occupations employing the most people in the United States. Table presents the number of civilians 16 years old or older who reported working as registered nurses during the 1990 Census. Data show the total employment figures, employment per 100,000 population, and employment data for men and women of various races and ethnicities in the 25 metropolitan statistical areas with the largest concentrations of registered nurses.

[Total for all of the U.S. was 1,885,129; 758.0 per 100,000 persons]

Metropolitan area	Total employees	Employees per 100,000 population	Men American Indian, Eskimo & Aleut	Men Asian, Pacific Islander	Men Black	Men Hispanic	Men White	Women American Indian, Eskimo & Aleut	Women Asian, Pacific Islander	Women Black	Women Hispanic	Women White
New York, New York New Jersey (northern) Long Island, New York CMSA	154,588	854.7	19	1,105	1,941	802	4,242	227	16,769	31,555	6,936	96,479
Los Angeles, California Anaheim, California Riverside, California CMSA	90,853	625.2	94	1,045	630	1,042	3,807	413	17,073	8,687	7,855	55,597
Chicago, Illinois Gary, Indiana Lake County, Illinois CMSA	67,351	835.0	0	432	479	139	2,036	64	7,276	7,972	1,513	48,424
Philadelphia, Pennsylvania Wilmington, Delaware Trenton, New Jersey CMSA	57,777	979.4	0	175	468	131	2,513	72	2,089	6,081	589	46,114
San Francisco, California Oakland, California San Jose, California CMSA	49,907	798.1	0	420	274	297	2,835	302	7,775	3,210	2,363	34,209
Boston, Massachusetts Lawrence, Massachusetts Salem, Massachusetts CMSA	45,789	1,098	0	65	172	30	2,023	60	764	1,293	486	41,226
Detroit, Michigan Ann Arbor, Michigan CMSA	36,224	776.5	0	79	279	5	1,293	69	1,549	4,281	338	28,612
Washington, District of Columbia MSA	31,739	808.9	0	104	500	54	891	75	1,655	7,052	605	21,280
Cleveland, Ohio Akron, Ohio Lorain, Ohio CMSA	25,497	923.9	7	27	101	27	1,189	38	283	2,029	289	21,741
Houston, Texas Galveston, Texas Brazoria, Texas CMSA	25,328	682.5	0	119	302	149	950	88	2,698	4,982	1,441	15,532
Dallas, Texas Fort Worth, Texas CMSA	24,762	637.3	13	67	180	71	1,093	91	1,343	2,593	834	19,009
Pittsburgh, Pennsylvania Beaver Valley, Pennsylvania CMSA	24,455	1,090	0	0	53	12	1,036	0	104	940	74	22,313
Minneapolis, Minnesota St. Paul, Minnesota MSA	24,305	986.4	0	18	48	9	1,168	70	175	170	148	22,583
Miami, Florida Fort Lauderdale, Florida CMSA	23,615	739.7	23	99	266	586	1,332	54	1,193	5,630	2,558	14,771
Baltimore, Maryland MSA	22,864	959.8	7	33	295	0	890	50	452	3,604	204	17,492
St. Louis, Missouri MSA	21,966	898.7	0	11	110	8	1,300	50	232	2,602	176	17,641
Seattle, Washington Tacoma, Washington CMSA	20,805	813.0	12	118	61	45	1,188	79	1,098	536	287	17,595
Atlanta, Georgia MSA	20,779	733.3	2	16	209	12	737	22	362	3,833	115	15,570
Phoenix, Arizona MSA	17,061	804.0	19	69	9	19	1,222	237	268	347	717	14,583
San Diego, California MSA	16,984	679.9	13	154	148	97	802	49	2,380	789	796	12,392
Tampa, Florida St. Petersburg, Florida Clearwater, Florida MSA	16,745	809.7	0	54	72	78	1,001	36	298	759	714	14,396
Cincinnati, Ohio Hamilton, Ohio CMSA	16,080	922.0	0	8	73	6	708	17	69	1,099	47	14,098
Denver, Colorado Boulder, Colorado CMSA	15,362	831.1	0	0	56	71	846	51	248	469	415	13,569
Milwaukee, Wisconsin Racine, Wisconsin CMSA	15,128	941.3	6	3	75	6	625	31	75	812	91	13,458
Portland, Oregon Vancouver, Washington CMSA	13,352	903.5	0	7	18	21	953	69	319	158	156	11,761

Source: Census of Population and Housing, 1990: Equal Employment Opportunity (EEO) File on CD-ROM [machine-readable datafiles]. Prepared by the Bureau of the Census. Washington, DC: The Bureau, 1992. *Notes:* "MSA" represents "metropolitan statistical area"; "CMSA" stands for "consolidated metropolitan statistical area."

★ 184 ★

Leading Occupations

Sales Occupation Supervisors and Proprietors (Salaried), by Metropolitan Area

According to the 1990 Census of Population and Housing, salaried sales occupation supervisors and proprietors ranked 4 among occupations employing the most people in the United States. Table presents the number of civilians 16 years old or older who reported working as salaried sales occupation supervisors and proprietors during the 1990 Census. Data show the total employment figures, employment per 100,000 population, and employment data for men and women of various races and ethnicities in the 25 metropolitan statistical areas with the largest concentrations of salaried sales occupation supervisors and proprietors.

[Total for all of the U.S. was 3,015,374; 1,212 per 100,000 persons]

Metropolitan area	Total employees	Employees per 100,000 population	Men					Women				
			American Indian, Eskimo & Aleut	Asian, Pacific Islander	Black	Hispanic	White	American Indian, Eskimo & Aleut	Asian, Pacific Islander	Black	Hispanic	White
New York, New York New Jersey (northern) Long Island, New York CMSA	241,720	1,336	214	11,677	12,309	15,378	134,304	171	3,143	8,206	6,940	63,383
Los Angeles, California Anaheim, California Riverside, California CMSA	169,154	1,164	619	12,677	5,197	18,623	85,733	395	5,278	2,994	9,954	42,077
Chicago, Illinois Gary, Indiana Lake County, Illinois CMSA	104,331	1,294	102	2,077	4,822	3,570	59,688	112	704	4,125	1,791	30,174
San Francisco, California Oakland, California San Jose, California CMSA	77,861	1,245	265	5,512	1,967	4,668	40,801	223	2,840	1,526	2,252	22,146
Philadelphia, Pennsylvania Wilmington, Delaware Trenton, New Jersey CMSA	75,342	1,277	79	1,102	3,188	856	44,316	41	437	2,883	375	22,701
Dallas, Texas Fort Worth, Texas CMSA	60,243	1,550	229	940	2,226	2,443	34,658	67	320	1,801	1,063	18,286
Boston, Massachusetts Lawrence, Massachusetts Salem, Massachusetts CMSA	58,383	1,400	48	619	944	688	36,386	51	252	470	296	19,226
Detroit, Michigan Ann Arbor, Michigan CMSA	54,893	1,177	84	281	2,223	261	32,015	45	184	2,410	216	17,529
Houston, Texas Galveston, Texas Brazoria, Texas CMSA	49,440	1,332	151	1,776	2,180	3,653	27,276	28	763	2,109	1,946	12,558
Atlanta, Georgia MSA	49,117	1,733	51	763	3,124	383	28,675	48	238	3,027	205	13,079
Miami, Florida Fort Lauderdale, Florida CMSA	49,100	1,538	38	863	2,219	12,234	29,913	12	302	1,282	4,501	13,018
Washington, District of Columbia MSA	48,551	1,237	71	2,008	4,353	951	24,325	21	1,118	3,134	657	13,045
Minneapolis, Minnesota St. Paul, Minnesota MSA	36,978	1,501	67	197	348	91	23,754	85	65	200	105	12,193
Seattle, Washington Tacoma, Washington CMSA	34,430	1,345	119	890	337	386	20,697	107	403	257	225	11,467
Baltimore, Maryland MSA	33,890	1,423	38	524	1,926	210	18,955	31	214	2,060	104	10,122
Cleveland, Ohio Akron, Ohio Lorain, Ohio CMSA	31,902	1,156	19	135	889	174	19,505	31	78	870	128	10,263
Tampa, Florida St. Petersburg, Florida Clearwater, Florida MSA	31,867	1,541	26	160	504	1,161	19,791	48	73	342	493	10,720
St. Louis, Missouri MSA	29,355	1,201	25	114	826	55	17,591	54	105	786	94	9,835
San Diego, California MSA	29,208	1,169	115	922	476	2,416	16,273	50	554	415	1,331	8,897
Denver, Colorado Boulder, Colorado CMSA	27,573	1,492	42	181	505	1,130	16,717	31	116	274	724	8,955
Phoenix, Arizona MSA	27,566	1,299	38	240	254	1,418	17,085	60	89	136	621	8,737
Pittsburgh, Pennsylvania Beaver Valley, Pennsylvania CMSA	23,885	1,065	35	86	329	20	14,986	10	81	344	66	8,007
Kansas City, Missouri Kansas City, Kansas MSA	22,380	1,429	88	36	609	208	14,226	48	39	363	147	6,830
Cincinnati, Ohio Hamilton, Ohio CMSA	21,645	1,241	31	95	461	79	13,520	23	39	534	48	6,924
Portland, Oregon Vancouver, Washington CMSA	20,784	1,406	54	361	222	173	13,305	49	184	87	133	6,455

Source: Census of Population and Housing, 1990: Equal Employment Opportunity (EEO) File on CD-ROM [machine-readable datafiles]. Prepared by the Bureau of the Census. Washington, DC: The Bureau, 1992. *Notes:* "MSA" represents "metropolitan statistical area"; "CMSA" stands for "consolidated metropolitan statistical area."

★ 185 ★

Leading Occupations

Sales Occupation Supervisors and Proprietors (Self-Employed), by Metropolitan Area

According to the 1990 Census of Population and Housing, self-employed sales occupation supervisors and proprietors ranked 77 among occupations employing the most people in the United States. Table presents the number of civilians 16 years old or older who reported working as self-employed sales occupation supervisors and proprietors during the 1990 Census. Data show the total employment figures, employment per 100,000 population, and employment data for men and women of various races and ethnicities in the 25 metropolitan statistical areas with the largest concentrations of self-employed sales occupation supervisors and proprietors.

[Total for all of the U.S. was 436,087; 175.3 per 100,000 persons]

Metropolitan area	Total employees	Employees per 100,000 population	Men					Women				
			American Indian, Eskimo & Aleut	Asian, Pacific Islander	Black	Hispanic	White	American Indian, Eskimo & Aleut	Asian, Pacific Islander	Black	Hispanic	White
Los Angeles, California Anaheim, California Riverside, California CMSA	33,733	232.1	30	6,226	478	2,688	15,018	40	3,319	296	1,159	6,727
New York, New York New Jersey (northern) Long Island, New York CMSA	24,595	136.0	14	3,111	841	2,395	12,181	37	1,358	368	635	5,405
San Francisco, California Oakland, California San Jose, California CMSA	14,780	236.4	12	2,069	184	617	7,140	14	1,169	138	228	3,718
Chicago, Illinois Gary, Indiana Lake County, Illinois CMSA	9,110	113.0	9	817	366	441	4,670	10	426	218	248	2,248
Philadelphia, Pennsylvania Wilmington, Delaware Trenton, New Jersey CMSA	8,156	138.3	0	679	337	266	4,371	10	286	111	66	2,203
Dallas, Texas Fort Worth, Texas CMSA	6,857	176.5	12	361	75	242	4,158	9	162	78	87	1,906
Houston, Texas Galveston, Texas Brazoria, Texas CMSA	6,351	171.1	0	743	287	335	3,136	15	241	101	194	1,632
Detroit, Michigan Ann Arbor, Michigan CMSA	5,491	117.7	13	87	209	62	3,284	8	98	153	39	1,610
San Diego, California MSA	5,486	219.6	13	297	50	428	3,211	10	148	9	162	1,477
Boston, Massachusetts Lawrence, Massachusetts Salem, Massachusetts CMSA	5,418	129.9	0	93	43	101	3,490	0	28	21	64	1,628
Seattle, Washington Tacoma, Washington CMSA	4,614	180.3	0	374	30	35	2,365	4	222	54	53	1,535
Washington, District of Columbia MSA	4,373	111.5	0	636	220	66	1,953	0	307	88	52	1,147
Atlanta, Georgia MSA	3,987	140.7	6	247	255	21	2,227	8	142	76	8	1,013
Miami, Florida Fort Lauderdale, Florida CMSA	3,782	118.5	10	107	157	1,071	2,426	6	34	51	287	894
Pittsburgh, Pennsylvania Beaver Valley, Pennsylvania CMSA	3,697	164.8	0	49	43	12	2,458	0	46	21	7	1,080
Phoenix, Arizona MSA	3,606	169.9	20	119	13	79	2,276	0	93	5	54	1,034
Cleveland, Ohio Akron, Ohio Lorain, Ohio CMSA	3,099	112.3	0	18	134	16	1,908	0	12	28	21	994
Sacramento, California MSA	3,024	204.2	22	233	43	122	1,724	0	102	6	21	849
Tampa, Florida St. Petersburg, Florida Clearwater, Florida MSA	3,022	146.1	0	69	28	111	1,785	0	37	0	43	1,059
Portland, Oregon Vancouver, Washington CMSA	2,973	201.2	5	201	22	27	1,902	0	65	15	5	754
Denver, Colorado Boulder, Colorado CMSA	2,773	150.0	6	76	7	40	1,634	0	31	39	28	943
Minneapolis, Minnesota St. Paul, Minnesota MSA	2,739	111.2	0	31	0	0	1,695	0	29	0	0	984
Baltimore, Maryland MSA	2,462	103.4	0	294	146	10	1,118	5	202	64	0	633
St. Louis, Missouri MSA	2,454	100.4	9	39	97	15	1,464	0	38	22	14	785
Kansas City, Missouri Kansas City, Kansas MSA	2,255	144.0	2	59	41	5	1,289	8	21	30	0	805

Source: Census of Population and Housing, 1990: Equal Employment Opportunity (EEO) File on CD-ROM [machine-readable datafiles]. Prepared by the Bureau of the Census. Washington, DC: The Bureau, 1992. *Notes:* "MSA" represents "metropolitan statistical area"; "CMSA" stands for "consolidated metropolitan statistical area."

★ 186 ★

Leading Occupations

Secondary School Teachers, by Metropolitan Area

According to the 1990 Census of Population and Housing, secondary school teachers ranked 51 among occupations employing the most people in the United States. Table presents the number of civilians 16 years old or older who reported working as secondary school teachers during the 1990 Census. Data show the total employment figures, employment per 100,000 population, and employment data for men and women of various races and ethnicities in the 25 metropolitan statistical areas with the largest concentrations of secondary school teachers.

[Total for all of the U.S. was 624,400; 251.1 per 100,000 persons]

Metropolitan area	Total employees	Employees per 100,000 population	Men					Women				
			American Indian, Eskimo & Aleut	Asian, Pacific Islander	Black	Hispanic	White	American Indian, Eskimo & Aleut	Asian, Pacific Islander	Black	Hispanic	White
New York, New York New Jersey (northern) Long Island, New York CMSA	50,028	276.6	18	366	1,532	880	18,724	47	432	2,757	1,414	25,541
Los Angeles, California Anaheim, California Riverside, California CMSA	25,952	178.6	102	513	504	1,321	10,099	83	614	1,072	1,849	11,778
Chicago, Illinois Gary, Indiana Lake County, Illinois CMSA	22,960	284.7	11	110	709	277	9,468	15	108	1,374	275	10,962
Philadelphia, Pennsylvania Wilmington, Delaware Trenton, New Jersey CMSA	15,304	259.4	9	25	582	83	6,305	0	88	1,002	126	7,212
San Francisco, California Oakland, California San Jose, California CMSA	13,370	213.8	42	277	192	570	5,594	24	414	335	476	6,270
Boston, Massachusetts Lawrence, Massachusetts Salem, Massachusetts CMSA	12,055	289.0	0	50	138	103	4,981	0	35	121	100	6,677
Detroit, Michigan Ann Arbor, Michigan CMSA	8,550	183.3	0	8	313	21	3,508	7	42	579	45	4,068
Dallas, Texas Fort Worth, Texas CMSA	8,308	213.8	16	14	255	142	2,313	0	39	446	277	5,037
Houston, Texas Galveston, Texas Brazoria, Texas CMSA	7,963	214.6	3	2	397	143	2,230	0	0	637	327	4,468
Washington, District of Columbia MSA	7,778	198.2	40	31	541	62	2,073	35	87	783	216	4,139
Rochester, New York MSA	6,643	662.7	8	15	72	19	2,165	0	12	51	24	4,304
St. Louis, Missouri MSA	6,531	267.2	0	20	189	34	2,676	6	18	540	38	3,052
Cleveland, Ohio Akron, Ohio Lorain, Ohio CMSA	6,050	219.2	0	15	124	33	2,575	7	10	222	37	3,054
Minneapolis, Minnesota St. Paul, Minnesota MSA	5,565	225.8	6	8	76	39	2,701	0	25	49	37	2,666
Atlanta, Georgia MSA	5,493	193.9	8	0	194	0	1,593	0	7	690	104	2,984
Buffalo, New York Niagara Falls, New York CMSA	5,395	453.6	3	0	45	20	2,000	0	5	64	46	3,259
San Diego, California MSA	5,207	208.5	5	39	5	305	2,286	16	90	145	251	2,397
Miami, Florida Fort Lauderdale, Florida CMSA	5,160	161.6	7	12	337	386	1,819	0	0	420	584	2,444
Pittsburgh, Pennsylvania Beaver Valley, Pennsylvania CMSA	5,106	227.7	0	9	94	10	2,207	0	13	80	25	2,696
Baltimore, Maryland MSA	4,764	200.0	0	9	226	24	1,623	6	46	322	17	2,526
Albany, New York Schenectady, New York Troy, New York MSA	4,723	540.2	0	0	0	13	1,690	0	23	7	11	3,003
Seattle, Washington Tacoma, Washington CMSA	4,723	184.6	13	51	90	46	2,355	3	58	100	42	2,019
Phoenix, Arizona MSA	4,446	209.5	8	0	42	134	1,953	20	19	21	175	2,244
Cincinnati, Ohio Hamilton, Ohio CMSA	4,264	244.5	0	14	92	0	1,830	8	0	160	20	2,160
Syracuse, New York MSA	3,896	590.4	2	0	0	12	1,279	0	18	29	17	2,562

Source: Census of Population and Housing, 1990: Equal Employment Opportunity (EEO) File on CD-ROM [machine-readable datafiles]. Prepared by the Bureau of the Census. Washington, DC: The Bureau, 1992. *Notes:* "MSA" represents "metropolitan statistical area"; "CMSA" stands for "consolidated metropolitan statistical area."

★ 187 ★

Leading Occupations

Secretaries, by Metropolitan Area

According to the 1990 Census of Population and Housing, secretaries ranked 2 among occupations employing the most people in the United States. Table presents the number of civilians 16 years old or older who reported working as secretaries during the 1990 Census. Data show the total employment figures, employment per 100,000 population, and employment data for men and women of various races and ethnicities in the 25 metropolitan statistical areas with the largest concentrations of secretaries.

[Total for all of the U.S. was 4,018,671; 1,616 per 100,000 persons]

Metropolitan area	Total employees	Employees per 100,000 population	Men					Women				
			American Indian, Eskimo & Aleut	Asian, Pacific Islander	Black	Hispanic	White	American Indian, Eskimo & Aleut	Asian, Pacific Islander	Black	Hispanic	White
New York, New York New Jersey (northern) Long Island, New York CMSA	363,767	2,011	18	366	1,479	624	4,236	469	7,017	48,485	35,695	286,921
Los Angeles, California Anaheim, California Riverside, California CMSA	210,326	1,447	30	486	409	929	2,955	1,180	14,948	15,854	38,341	156,326
Chicago, Illinois Gary, Indiana Lake County, Illinois CMSA	150,390	1,865	6	131	329	167	1,385	272	1,887	18,715	8,814	123,322
Philadelphia, Pennsylvania Wilmington, Delaware Trenton, New Jersey CMSA	122,028	2,069	11	4	282	46	1,145	237	453	14,820	2,241	104,029
Washington, District of Columbia MSA	100,631	2,565	0	131	648	97	1,117	397	2,826	29,355	3,728	65,080
San Francisco, California Oakland, California San Jose, California CMSA	94,086	1,505	0	241	209	210	2,012	503	8,998	5,980	10,289	72,149
Boston, Massachusetts Lawrence, Massachusetts Salem, Massachusetts CMSA	84,713	2,031	8	47	78	42	1,214	49	545	3,256	1,578	78,745
Detroit, Michigan Ann Arbor, Michigan CMSA	77,581	1,663	11	0	237	22	481	309	243	9,557	948	66,384
Dallas, Texas Fort Worth, Texas CMSA	74,416	1,915	5	31	95	95	649	345	437	4,799	4,568	65,820
Houston, Texas Galveston, Texas Brazoria, Texas CMSA	70,578	1,902	0	28	174	141	484	222	906	6,692	7,346	58,708
Miami, Florida Fort Lauderdale, Florida CMSA	57,457	1,800	0	21	86	263	716	118	541	6,369	19,876	47,772
Atlanta, Georgia MSA	54,119	1,910	0	0	116	15	450	129	301	8,264	629	44,731
Cleveland, Ohio Akron, Ohio Lorain, Ohio CMSA	52,053	1,886	0	6	103	2	437	79	270	5,438	560	45,523
Baltimore, Maryland MSA	47,722	2,003	0	26	136	0	463	128	376	7,774	360	38,719
St. Louis, Missouri MSA	46,169	1,889	0	18	61	8	356	75	135	3,941	290	41,524
Minneapolis, Minnesota St. Paul, Minnesota MSA	45,785	1,858	6	23	75	1	538	182	236	779	300	43,813
Pittsburgh, Pennsylvania Beaver Valley, Pennsylvania CMSA	43,414	1,936	0	22	71	13	364	42	62	2,047	160	40,794
Seattle, Washington Tacoma, Washington CMSA	35,701	1,395	17	6	37	16	572	532	1,439	1,008	691	31,847
Denver, Colorado Boulder, Colorado CMSA	33,931	1,836	0	16	19	29	227	219	331	1,072	2,546	31,170
San Diego, California MSA	32,820	1,314	8	53	46	93	613	282	1,513	1,237	3,945	27,199
Phoenix, Arizona MSA	32,744	1,543	15	14	27	56	296	340	248	754	3,013	29,622
Tampa, Florida St. Petersburg, Florida Clearwater, Florida MSA	31,150	1,506	0	7	44	49	237	55	152	1,146	1,763	29,201
Cincinnati, Ohio Hamilton, Ohio CMSA	28,412	1,629	0	0	14	0	178	4	65	1,623	58	26,506
Kansas City, Missouri Kansas City, Kansas MSA	27,151	1,733	7	13	12	0	283	83	80	1,685	483	24,790
Milwaukee, Wisconsin Racine, Wisconsin CMSA	26,305	1,637	0	6	33	11	193	59	84	1,351	516	24,331

Source: Census of Population and Housing, 1990: Equal Employment Opportunity (EEO) File on CD-ROM [machine-readable datafiles]. Prepared by the Bureau of the Census. Washington, DC: The Bureau, 1992. *Notes:* "MSA" represents "metropolitan statistical area"; "CMSA" stands for "consolidated metropolitan statistical area."

Leading Occupations

Securities and Financial Services Sales Occupations, by Metropolitan Area

According to the 1990 Census of Population and Housing, securities and financial services sales occupations ranked 105 among occupations employing the most people in the United States. Table presents the number of civilians 16 years old or older who reported working in securities and financial services sales occupations during the 1990 Census. Data show the total employment figures, employment per 100,000 population, and employment data for men and women of various races and ethnicities in the 25 metropolitan statistical areas with the largest concentrations of securities and financial services sales occupations.

[Total for all of the U.S. was 297,548; 119.6 per 100,000 persons]

Metropolitan area	Total employees	Employees per 100,000 population	Men					Women				
			American Indian, Eskimo & Aleut	Asian, Pacific Islander	Black	Hispanic	White	American Indian, Eskimo & Aleut	Asian, Pacific Islander	Black	Hispanic	White
New York, New York New Jersey (northern) Long Island, New York CMSA	65,457	361.9	12	1,756	1,731	1,643	44,639	8	872	1,646	948	14,135
Chicago, Illinois Gary, Indiana Lake County, Illinois CMSA	21,421	265.6	0	309	576	256	15,917	6	80	416	150	4,024
Los Angeles, California Anaheim, California Riverside, California CMSA	18,555	127.7	47	1,011	578	824	11,458	24	569	385	575	3,908
San Francisco, California Oakland, California San Jose, California CMSA	12,149	194.3	26	737	324	334	7,445	18	450	145	297	2,809
Philadelphia, Pennsylvania Wilmington, Delaware Trenton, New Jersey CMSA	8,989	152.4	0	30	166	80	5,842	11	73	266	79	2,559
Boston, Massachusetts Lawrence, Massachusetts Salem, Massachusetts CMSA	8,327	199.6	11	86	63	36	5,410	0	70	134	69	2,539
Dallas, Texas Fort Worth, Texas CMSA	5,966	153.6	5	34	123	152	4,000	6	13	132	62	1,556
Miami, Florida Fort Lauderdale, Florida CMSA	5,392	168.9	0	36	168	490	3,473	0	0	48	463	1,586
Atlanta, Georgia MSA	5,151	181.8	18	7	255	18	3,241	16	0	242	76	1,365
Minneapolis, Minnesota St. Paul, Minnesota MSA	5,043	204.7	9	15	9	1	3,437	6	8	20	0	1,539
Washington, District of Columbia MSA	4,948	126.1	0	91	311	105	2,975	0	53	220	108	1,222
Houston, Texas Galveston, Texas Brazoria, Texas CMSA	4,840	130.4	0	150	127	158	3,134	0	74	150	144	1,112
Denver, Colorado Boulder, Colorado CMSA	4,544	245.9	11	19	36	123	3,358	34	23	17	48	1,014
Seattle, Washington Tacoma, Washington CMSA	4,377	171.0	0	97	73	28	2,723	10	87	12	47	1,370
Detroit, Michigan Ann Arbor, Michigan CMSA	4,240	90.89	0	47	164	47	2,911	0	8	82	13	1,021
San Diego, California MSA	3,674	147.1	18	76	69	105	2,377	0	37	25	100	982
Tampa, Florida St. Petersburg, Florida Clearwater, Florida MSA	3,435	166.1	0	11	40	91	2,403	0	7	5	48	958
St. Louis, Missouri MSA	3,275	134.0	0	3	70	0	2,166	0	0	56	5	980
Phoenix, Arizona MSA	3,163	149.1	0	47	24	61	2,307	4	0	32	57	714
Baltimore, Maryland MSA	2,853	119.8	0	7	151	7	1,616	5	33	201	14	840
Cleveland, Ohio Akron, Ohio Lorain, Ohio CMSA	2,791	101.1	0	45	30	8	1,907	0	2	36	2	771
West Palm Beach, Florida Boca Raton, Florida Delray Beach, Florida MSA	2,623	303.8	0	10	18	15	2,007	0	0	17	14	561
Pittsburgh, Pennsylvania Beaver Valley, Pennsylvania CMSA	2,179	97.16	0	0	46	0	1,518	0	6	42	8	559
Kansas City, Missouri Kansas City, Kansas MSA	2,141	136.7	0	0	54	15	1,536	0	0	35	4	512
Portland, Oregon Vancouver, Washington CMSA	2,085	141.1	5	44	7	19	1,377	0	34	0	0	610

Source: Census of Population and Housing, 1990: Equal Employment Opportunity (EEO) File on CD-ROM [machine-readable datafiles]. Prepared by the Bureau of the Census. Washington, DC: The Bureau, 1992. *Notes:* "MSA" represents "metropolitan statistical area"; "CMSA" stands for "consolidated metropolitan statistical area."

★ 189 ★

Leading Occupations

Service Organization Managers, by Metropolitan Area

According to the 1990 Census of Population and Housing, service organization managers ranked 83 among occupations employing the most people in the United States. Table presents the number of civilians 16 years old or older who reported working as service organization managers during the 1990 Census. Data show the total employment figures, employment per 100,000 population, and employment data for men and women of various races and ethnicities in the 25 metropolitan statistical areas with the largest concentrations of miscellaneous service organization managers. See also tables for specific types of service organization managers such as marketing, advertising, and public relations managers.

[Total for all of the U.S. was 404,073; 162.5 per 100,000 persons]

Metropolitan area	Total employees	Employees per 100,000 population	Men					Women				
			American Indian, Eskimo & Aleut	Asian, Pacific Islander	Black	Hispanic	White	American Indian, Eskimo & Aleut	Asian, Pacific Islander	Black	Hispanic	White
New York, New York New Jersey (northern) Long Island, New York CMSA	35,547	196.5	40	402	2,000	1,304	14,255	90	359	3,074	1,211	14,421
Los Angeles, California Anaheim, California Riverside, California CMSA	22,868	157.4	95	700	742	1,732	9,879	128	461	1,142	1,232	8,372
Washington, District of Columbia MSA	16,726	426.3	6	154	888	352	6,519	29	174	1,668	256	7,124
Chicago, Illinois Gary, Indiana Lake County, Illinois CMSA	15,928	197.5	0	125	1,024	431	6,395	19	117	1,211	348	6,637
San Francisco, California Oakland, California San Jose, California CMSA	12,714	203.3	18	583	378	471	5,075	75	340	568	511	5,311
Philadelphia, Pennsylvania Wilmington, Delaware Trenton, New Jersey CMSA	10,022	169.9	15	00	667	77	4,438	9	47	912	121	3,779
Boston, Massachusetts Lawrence, Massachusetts Salem, Massachusetts CMSA	9,209	220.8	0	8	179	107	4,201	0	40	282	130	4,404
Detroit, Michigan Ann Arbor, Michigan CMSA	6,575	140.9	18	32	590	34	2,671	16	21	553	54	2,606
Dallas, Texas Fort Worth, Texas CMSA	5,541	142.6	0	20	232	136	2,588	17	6	176	81	2,386
Minneapolis, Minnesota St. Paul, Minnesota MSA	5,160	209.4	5	24	92	35	2,282	26	40	151	20	2,523
Seattle, Washington Tacoma, Washington CMSA	4,877	190.6	27	70	132	51	2,117	47	54	91	35	2,314
Miami, Florida Fort Lauderdale, Florida CMSA	4,690	146.9	8	0	235	535	2,221	9	21	309	390	1,776
Atlanta, Georgia MSA	4,612	162.8	14	15	350	28	2,084	0	0	451	57	1,664
Cleveland, Ohio Akron, Ohio Lorain, Ohio CMSA	4,556	165.1	18	6	192	30	2,242	13	20	320	9	1,730
Baltimore, Maryland MSA	4,484	188.2	0	0	392	2	1,670	34	23	564	21	1,801
Houston, Texas Galveston, Texas Brazoria, Texas CMSA	4,377	118.0	0	65	160	254	2,012	0	15	304	162	1,706
San Diego, California MSA	4,109	164.5	29	73	75	185	1,704	12	80	137	193	1,854
St. Louis, Missouri MSA	3,760	153.8	8	0	219	6	1,720	0	5	210	3	1,595
Denver, Colorado Boulder, Colorado CMSA	3,736	202.1	8	15	90	168	1,649	5	0	74	76	1,772
Pittsburgh, Pennsylvania Beaver Valley, Pennsylvania CMSA	3,580	159.6	0	0	144	5	1,581	0	18	258	13	1,574
Portland, Oregon Vancouver, Washington CMSA	3,182	215.3	8	36	68	26	1,445	18	0	73	24	1,510
Tampa, Florida St. Petersburg, Florida Clearwater, Florida MSA	3,173	153.4	6	7	137	13	1,434	8	14	138	60	1,429
Phoenix, Arizona MSA	3,134	147.7	13	24	82	90	1,530	4	0	16	92	1,424
Milwaukee, Wisconsin Racine, Wisconsin CMSA	2,962	184.3	0	28	98	20	1,447	0	0	113	10	1,266
Kansas City, Missouri Kansas City, Kansas MSA	2,903	185.3	0	0	90	30	1,450	0	0	128	47	1,201

Source: Census of Population and Housing, 1990: Equal Employment Opportunity (EEO) File on CD-ROM [machine-readable datafiles]. Prepared by the Bureau of the Census. Washington, DC: The Bureau, 1992. *Notes:* "MSA" represents "metropolitan statistical area"; "CMSA" stands for "consolidated metropolitan statistical area."

★ 190 ★

Leading Occupations

Social Workers, by Metropolitan Area

According to the 1990 Census of Population and Housing, social workers ranked 43 among occupations employing the most people in the United States. Table presents the number of civilians 16 years old or older who reported working as social workers during the 1990 Census. Data show the total employment figures, employment per 100,000 population, and employment data for men and women of various races and ethnicities in the 25 metropolitan statistical areas with the largest concentrations of social workers.

[Total for all of the U.S. was 658,919; 264.9 per 100,000 persons]

Metropolitan area	Total employees	Employees per 100,000 population	Men					Women				
			American Indian, Eskimo & Aleut	Asian, Pacific Islander	Black	Hispanic	White	American Indian, Eskimo & Aleut	Asian, Pacific Islander	Black	Hispanic	White
New York, New York New Jersey (northern) Long Island, New York CMSA	73,591	406.9	96	488	7,896	2,724	13,045	225	942	17,684	6,363	29,123
Los Angeles, California Anaheim, California Riverside, California CMSA	30,561	210.3	87	808	2,430	2,365	6,411	160	1,283	4,319	3,811	12,103
Chicago, Illinois Gary, Indiana Lake County, Illinois CMSA	22,599	280.2	6	286	2,227	492	3,798	51	144	6,408	1,187	8,850
Philadelphia, Pennsylvania Wilmington, Delaware Trenton, New Jersey CMSA	20,438	346.5	23	51	2,154	298	3,716	16	98	5,560	673	8,344
San Francisco, California Oakland, California San Jose, California CMSA	16,620	265.8	43	610	951	825	4,144	94	811	1,417	1,144	7,687
Boston, Massachusetts Lawrence, Massachusetts Salem, Massachusetts CMSA	15,726	377.0	21	104	502	147	3,718	22	187	1,216	487	9,722
Detroit, Michigan Ann Arbor, Michigan CMSA	14,193	304.2	31	27	1,432	38	2,397	28	44	4,073	128	6,063
Washington, District of Columbia MSA	11,296	287.9	16	77	1,213	108	1,813	30	189	3,039	249	4,824
Minneapolis, Minnesota St. Paul, Minnesota MSA	8,985	364.6	71	44	235	28	2,442	124	63	348	44	5,611
Baltimore, Maryland MSA	8,678	364.3	0	21	772	25	1,307	0	84	3,129	49	3,341
Cleveland, Ohio Akron, Ohio Lorain, Ohio CMSA	7,524	272.6	6	18	625	97	1,447	4	18	1,682	102	3,638
Seattle, Washington Tacoma, Washington CMSA	7,091	277.1	66	205	273	76	1,846	103	139	354	131	4,020
Dallas, Texas Fort Worth, Texas CMSA	6,811	175.3	10	47	539	200	1,697	7	29	1,033	269	3,223
Pittsburgh, Pennsylvania Beaver Valley, Pennsylvania CMSA	6,735	300.3	0	0	337	6	1,891	30	6	808	22	3,655
St. Louis, Missouri MSA	6,727	275.2	13	21	684	18	1,200	17	41	1,786	17	2,956
Miami, Florida Fort Lauderdale, Florida CMSA	6,483	203.1	0	36	686	676	1,460	0	32	1,402	1,081	2,701
San Diego, California MSA	6,323	253.1	3	89	275	342	1,553	34	241	473	491	3,317
Houston, Texas Galveston, Texas Brazoria, Texas CMSA	6,171	166.3	0	46	688	306	1,065	36	69	1,588	485	2,391
Atlanta, Georgia MSA	5,980	211.1	14	14	637	32	1,058	17	13	1,883	52	2,329
Denver, Colorado Boulder, Colorado CMSA	5,023	271.8	22	13	188	212	1,158	28	44	208	424	3,064
Phoenix, Arizona MSA	4,802	226.3	37	34	174	273	1,311	79	20	257	338	2,573
Tampa, Florida St. Petersburg, Florida Clearwater, Florida MSA	4,768	230.6	9	30	299	94	1,320	16	7	641	185	2,354
Cincinnati, Ohio Hamilton, Ohio CMSA	4,702	269.6	5	0	309	21	915	2	6	824	38	2,607
Buffalo, New York Niagara Falls, New York CMSA	4,589	385.9	12	0	224	43	1,258	17	26	551	90	2,441
Milwaukee, Wisconsin Racine, Wisconsin CMSA	4,394	273.4	32	44	295	68	1,125	62	21	505	62	2,244

Source: Census of Population and Housing, 1990: Equal Employment Opportunity (EEO) File on CD-ROM [machine-readable datafiles]. Prepared by the Bureau of the Census. Washington, DC: The Bureau, 1992. *Notes:* "MSA" represents "metropolitan statistical area"; "CMSA" stands for "consolidated metropolitan statistical area."

★ 191 ★

Leading Occupations

Stock and Inventory Clerks, by Metropolitan Area

According to the 1990 Census of Population and Housing, stock and inventory clerks ranked 36 among occupations employing the most people in the United States. Table presents the number of civilians 16 years old or older who reported working as stock and inventory clerks during the 1990 Census. Data show the total employment figures, employment per 100,000 population, and employment data for men and women of various races and ethnicities in the 25 metropolitan statistical areas with the largest concentrations of stock and inventory clerks.

[Total for all of the U.S. was 711,772; 286.2 per 100,000 persons]

Metropolitan area	Total employees	Employees per 100,000 population	Men					Women				
			American Indian, Eskimo & Aleut	Asian, Pacific Islander	Black	Hispanic	White	American Indian, Eskimo & Aleut	Asian, Pacific Islander	Black	Hispanic	White
Los Angeles, California Anaheim, California Riverside, California CMSA	44,015	302.9	214	3,170	3,327	10,366	16,819	139	1,233	1,404	4,575	9,769
New York, New York New Jersey (northern) Long Island, New York CMSA	42,334	234.1	64	1,333	7,296	6,596	17,607	25	545	2,840	1,876	8,755
Chicago, Illinois Gary, Indiana Lake County, Illinois CMSA	23,910	296.4	6	605	2,999	2,201	10,922	42	197	1,572	591	6,022
San Francisco, California Oakland, California San Jose, California CMSA	19,901	318.3	173	2,624	1,370	2,634	7,454	67	1,154	753	1,185	4,596
Detroit, Michigan Ann Arbor, Michigan CMSA	16,351	350.5	50	116	2,337	181	8,171	30	29	974	71	4,557
Philadelphia, Pennsylvania Wilmington, Delaware Trenton, New Jersey CMSA	15,507	262.9	41	138	1,642	357	7,181	3	93	1,356	167	4,771
Dallas, Texas Fort Worth, Texas CMSA	15,259	392.7	61	220	2,170	1,651	7,108	5	91	927	418	3,425
Houston, Texas Galveston, Texas Brazoria, Texas CMSA	12,519	337.3	19	199	2,238	1,960	5,290	48	71	944	607	2,315
Boston, Massachusetts Lawrence, Massachusetts Salem, Massachusetts CMSA	11,350	272.1	0	112	645	306	6,294	9	107	327	180	3,693
Washington, District of Columbia MSA	10,285	262.1	22	377	2,854	282	3,230	9	140	1,435	148	2,021
Atlanta, Georgia MSA	9,749	344.1	15	93	1,960	150	3,976	0	41	1,147	69	2,416
Miami, Florida Fort Lauderdale, Florida CMSA	9,056	283.7	27	123	1,313	2,572	4,636	4	20	569	827	1,954
Seattle, Washington Tacoma, Washington CMSA	8,643	337.7	22	449	336	173	4,343	32	167	213	124	2,936
San Diego, California MSA	8,189	327.8	16	776	562	1,094	3,050	36	477	232	742	2,181
Cleveland, Ohio Akron, Ohio Lorain, Ohio CMSA	7,991	289.6	0	3 .	847	55	3,988	ҁ 9	22	484	66	2,574
Minneapolis, Minnesota St. Paul, Minnesota MSA	7,572	307.3	34	92	251	47	4,599	0	12	40	26	2,520
St. Louis, Missouri MSA	7,080	289.7	0	31	755	32	3,355	7	8	633	14	2,279
Phoenix, Arizona MSA	6,603	311.2	77	63	202	692	3,684	48	47	24	347	2,050
Baltimore, Maryland MSA	6,582	276.3	0	96	1,568	53	2,633	18	19	497	11	1,732
Denver, Colorado Boulder, Colorado CMSA	6,313	341.6	62	58	258	593	3,287	46	53	201	304	1,978
Pittsburgh, Pennsylvania Beaver Valley, Pennsylvania CMSA	5,648	251.8	5	0	274	12	3,527	0	9	125	48	1,701
Tampa, Florida St. Petersburg, Florida Clearwater, Florida MSA	5,643	272.9	0	33	359	194	2,880	0	29	306	179	1,978
Milwaukee, Wisconsin Racine, Wisconsin CMSA	5,558	345.8	18	19	566	91	3,018	12	3	242	32	1,596
Kansas City, Missouri Kansas City, Kansas MSA	5,509	351.7	33	30	445	158	2,978	9	0	301	39	1,652
Columbus, Ohio MSA	5,404	392.3	16	12	633	20	2,691	13	32	273	11	1,718

Source: Census of Population and Housing, 1990: Equal Employment Opportunity (EEO) File on CD-ROM [machine-readable datafiles]. Prepared by the Bureau of the Census. Washington, DC: The Bureau, 1992. *Notes:* "MSA" represents "metropolitan statistical area"; "CMSA" stands for "consolidated metropolitan statistical area."

★ 192 ★

Leading Occupations

Stock Handlers and Baggers, by Metropolitan Area

According to the 1990 Census of Population and Housing, stock handlers and baggers ranked 22 among occupations employing the most people in the United States. Table presents the number of civilians 16 years old or older who reported working as stock handlers and baggers during the 1990 Census. Data show the total employment figures, employment per 100,000 population, and employment data for men and women of various races and ethnicities in the 25 metropolitan statistical areas with the largest concentrations of stock handlers and baggers.

[Total for all of the U.S. was 1,030,362; 414.3 per 100,000 persons]

Metropolitan area	Total employees	Employees per 100,000 population	Men					Women				
			American Indian, Eskimo & Aleut	Asian, Pacific Islander	Black	Hispanic	White	American Indian, Eskimo & Aleut	Asian, Pacific Islander	Black	Hispanic	White
New York, New York New Jersey (northern) Long Island, New York CMSA	56,570	312.8	148	1,812	9,578	9,381	29,720	42	449	1,523	1,504	8,412
Los Angeles, California Anaheim, California Riverside, California CMSA	48,130	331.2	248	3,076	3,053	12,642	20,982	145	980	1,084	4,558	9,753
Chicago, Illinois Gary, Indiana Lake County, Illinois CMSA	40,496	502.1	81	855	6,130	3,810	19,487	8	294	2,182	1,390	8,491
Detroit, Michigan Ann Arbor, Michigan CMSA	23,670	507.4	91	116	3,384	365	13,419	50	76	1,174	169	5,157
San Francisco, California Oakland, California San Jose, California CMSA	23,318	372.9	160	2,077	1,235	2,834	11,437	42	758	472	1,219	5,421
Philadelphia, Pennsylvania Wilmington, Delaware Trenton, New Jersey CMSA	22,936	388.8	58	207	2,976	475	12,627	55	123	1,209	157	5,412
Boston, Massachusetts Lawrence, Massachusetts Salem, Massachusetts CMSA	17,422	417.6	6	62	542	524	11,670	0	120	189	181	4,511
Houston, Texas Galveston, Texas Brazoria, Texas CMSA	16,018	431.6	45	545	2,908	3,049	7,466	0	190	722	956	2,022
Dallas, Texas Fort Worth, Texas CMSA	14,707	378.5	39	360	2,236	1,535	7,636	22	203	789	511	2,380
Cleveland, Ohio Akron, Ohio Lorain, Ohio CMSA	12,047	436.5	20	73	1,422	173	7,332	10	6	441	38	2,635
Miami, Florida Fort Lauderdale, Florida CMSA	11,865	371.6	7	116	2,159	3,881	6,944	0	67	502	625	1,331
St. Louis, Missouri MSA	11,780	482.0	5	20	1,474	53	6,774	15	25	556	63	2,875
Atlanta, Georgia MSA	11,512	406.3	8	101	2,591	81	5,956	0	77	977	46	1,765
Minneapolis, Minnesota St. Paul, Minnesota MSA	11,169	453.3	96	157	254	150	7,955	55	5	69	66	2,492
Washington, District of Columbia MSA	11,066	282.0	66	352	2,573	448	4,892	0	228	862	125	1,830
Pittsburgh, Pennsylvania Beaver Valley, Pennsylvania CMSA	10,050	448.1	5	2	799	49	6,578	0	0	118	18	2,548
Phoenix, Arizona MSA	9,739	458.9	130	89	273	1,138	5,592	68	80	95	506	2,539
Tampa, Florida St. Petersburg, Florida Clearwater, Florida MSA	9,572	462.9	15	98	635	447	6,840	20	21	180	84	1,659
Cincinnati, Ohio Hamilton, Ohio CMSA	9,420	540.1	0	13	630	16	5,370	11	18	334	14	3,031
Seattle, Washington Tacoma, Washington CMSA	9,075	354.6	77	388	301	131	4,950	44	184	110	89	2,945
Denver, Colorado Boulder, Colorado CMSA	8,378	453.3	50	74	475	908	4,505	39	36	118	471	2,449
San Diego, California MSA	8,160	326.7	41	517	375	1,146	4,113	48	77	92	587	2,102
Baltimore, Maryland MSA	8,156	342.4	17	85	1,818	52	3,890	4	51	607	9	1,658
Kansas City, Missouri Kansas City, Kansas MSA	7,984	509.7	36	50	563	243	4,850	29	19	333	90	1,918
Columbus, Ohio MSA	6,846	497.0	6	19	517	86	3,901	6	3	203	25	2,158

Source: Census of Population and Housing, 1990: Equal Employment Opportunity (EEO) File on CD-ROM [machine-readable datafiles]. Prepared by the Bureau of the Census. Washington, DC: The Bureau, 1992. *Notes:* "MSA" represents "metropolitan statistical area"; "CMSA" stands for "consolidated metropolitan statistical area."

★ 193 ★

Leading Occupations

Teachers, by Metropolitan Area

According to the 1990 Census of Population and Housing, teachers ranked 59 among occupations employing the most people in the United States. Table presents the number of civilians 16 years old or older who reported working as teachers during the 1990 Census. Data show the total employment figures, employment per 100,000 population, and employment data for men and women of various races and ethnicities in the 25 metropolitan statistical areas with the largest concentrations of miscellaneous teachers. See also tables for specific types of teachers such as elementary school teachers.

[Total for all of the U.S. was 579,391; 233.0 per 100,000 persons]

Metropolitan area	Total employees	Employees per 100,000 population	Men					Women				
			American Indian, Eskimo & Aleut	Asian, Pacific Islander	Black	Hispanic	White	American Indian, Eskimo & Aleut	Asian, Pacific Islander	Black	Hispanic	White
New York, New York New Jersey (northern) Long Island, New York CMSA	43,368	239.8	50	918	1,837	1,224	12,902	49	944	3,086	1,741	22,610
Los Angeles, California Anaheim, California Riverside, California CMSA	33,284	229.1	53	1,284	909	1,518	10,575	65	1,501	1,415	2,208	15,877
San Francisco, California Oakland, California San Jose, California CMSA	19,727	315.5	78	928	452	612	6,138	25	788	595	787	10,255
Chicago, Illinois Gary, Indiana Lake County, Illinois CMSA	17,719	219.7	0	251	888	423	5,140	48	218	1,357	415	9,477
Philadelphia, Pennsylvania Wilmington, Delaware Trenton, New Jersey CMSA	14,330	242.9	3	146	664	66	4,491	19	96	911	148	7,962
Washington, District of Columbia MSA	12,732	324.5	0	216	913	186	3,775	5	220	1,021	239	6,472
Boston, Massachusetts Lawrence, Massachusetts Salem, Massachusetts CMSA	12,679	303.9	0	154	312	132	3,739	19	132	224	158	7,990
Dallas, Texas Fort Worth, Texas CMSA	10,850	279.3	20	73	397	260	4,022	32	126	417	276	5,544
Houston, Texas Galveston, Texas Brazoria, Texas CMSA	9,412	253.6	34	119	322	276	2,431	3	179	935	467	5,069
Detroit, Michigan Ann Arbor, Michigan CMSA	8,744	187.4	3	86	477	45	2,566	17	55	767	78	4,733
Atlanta, Georgia MSA	8,426	297.4	23	96	651	113	2,843	17	50	809	83	3,891
San Diego, California MSA	7,793	312.0	44	179	211	364	2,820	23	199	170	437	3,830
Minneapolis, Minnesota St. Paul, Minnesota MSA	7,145	290.0	11	13	90	14	2,520	29	68	98	35	4,299
Seattle, Washington Tacoma, Washington CMSA	7,004	273.7	20	167	81	56	2,529	31	143	56	75	3,924
Miami, Florida Fort Lauderdale, Florida CMSA	6,978	218.6	20	22	367	641	2,571	3	41	557	932	3,305
Denver, Colorado Boulder, Colorado CMSA	6,119	331.1	39	46	102	158	2,384	14	59	112	117	3,304
Phoenix, Arizona MSA	5,922	279.1	3	40	68	125	2,516	24	68	88	229	3,017
Cleveland, Ohio Akron, Ohio Lorain, Ohio CMSA	5,334	193.3	0	66	188	13	1,476	5	49	306	31	3,227
St. Louis, Missouri MSA	5,004	204.7	0	20	157	0	1,703	3	25	295	62	2,778
Baltimore, Maryland MSA	4,846	203.4	0	52	289	47	1,440	6	59	542	44	2,443
Pittsburgh, Pennsylvania Beaver Valley, Pennsylvania CMSA	4,732	211.0	0	18	138	0	1,430	5	9	148	7	2,984
Tampa, Florida St. Petersburg, Florida Clearwater, Florida MSA	4,206	203.4	6	13	80	129	1,601	6	34	193	165	2,258
Sacramento, California MSA	4,050	273.5	47	80	108	63	1,421	0	60	175	99	2,114
Milwaukee, Wisconsin Racine, Wisconsin CMSA	4,022	250.3	6	32	109	43	1,292	1	40	135	61	2,368
Salt Lake City, Utah Ogden, Utah MSA	4,013	374.3	0	34	0	38	1,219	0	58	5	50	2,665

Source: Census of Population and Housing, 1990: Equal Employment Opportunity (EEO) File on CD-ROM [machine-readable datafiles]. Prepared by the Bureau of the Census. Washington, DC: The Bureau, 1992. *Notes:* "MSA" represents "metropolitan statistical area"; "CMSA" stands for "consolidated metropolitan statistical area."

★ 194 ★
Leading Occupations

Teachers' Aides, by Metropolitan Area

According to the 1990 Census of Population and Housing, teachers' aides ranked 111 among occupations employing the most people in the United States. Table presents the number of civilians 16 years old or older who reported working as teachers' aides during the 1990 Census. Data show the total employment figures, employment per 100,000 population, and employment data for men and women of various races and ethnicities in the 25 metropolitan statistical areas with the largest concentrations of teachers' aides.

[Total for all of the U.S. was 275,543; 110.8 per 100,000 persons]

Metropolitan area	Total employees	Employees per 100,000 population	Men					Women				
			American Indian, Eskimo & Aleut	Asian, Pacific Islander	Black	Hispanic	White	American Indian, Eskimo & Aleut	Asian, Pacific Islander	Black	Hispanic	White
New York, New York New Jersey (northern) Long Island, New York CMSA	25,723	142.2	0	222	504	337	1,240	58	321	4,993	3,429	16,687
Los Angeles, California Anaheim, California Riverside, California CMSA	24,756	170.4	0	477	340	1,116	1,522	113	1,106	2,136	8,761	13,732
San Francisco, California Oakland, California San Jose, California CMSA	8,281	132.4	0	235	75	134	729	41	549	594	1,403	5,454
Chicago, Illinois Gary, Indiana Lake County, Illinois CMSA	6,871	85.19	0	96	228	154	445	6	109	1,419	646	4,131
Philadelphia, Pennsylvania Wilmington, Delaware Trenton, New Jersey CMSA	6,621	112.2	0	44	193	54	375	23	90	1,567	241	4,201
Detroit, Michigan Ann Arbor, Michigan CMSA	5,216	111.8	0	52	84	7	422	14	84	848	65	3,683
Boston, Massachusetts Lawrence, Massachusetts Salem, Massachusetts CMSA	4,787	114.8	8	138	31	73	488	12	91	228	232	3,674
Washington, District of Columbia MSA	4,048	103.2	0	62	293	101	249	14	149	1,081	240	2,056
San Diego, California MSA	3,542	141.8	7	94	48	104	322	64	192	159	668	2,349
Houston, Texas Galveston, Texas Brazoria, Texas CMSA	3,162	85.21	0	32	74	107	190	0	59	656	715	1,719
Minneapolis, Minnesota St. Paul, Minnesota MSA	2,886	117.1	5	62	35	0	319	3	21	98	19	2,339
Miami, Florida Fort Lauderdale, Florida CMSA	2,882	90.27	0	0	71	43	108	0	20	886	702	1,736
Dallas, Texas Fort Worth, Texas CMSA	2,645	68.08	0	50	74	46	149	15	6	493	268	1,711
Atlanta, Georgia MSA	2,407	84.95	0	55	74	5	114	0	44	492	9	1,623
Denver, Colorado Boulder, Colorado CMSA	2,347	127.0	0	29	19	49	269	21	23	73	340	1,723
Seattle, Washington Tacoma, Washington CMSA	2,187	85.46	5	75	42	0	234	30	95	63	40	1,633
Baltimore, Maryland MSA	1,949	81.82	0	28	46	0	150	0	10	679	20	1,026
Buffalo, New York Niagara Falls, New York CMSA	1,941	163.2	0	13	150	18	98	17	22	154	28	1,465
Sacramento, California MSA	1,873	126.5	23	91	27	35	163	10	80	87	209	1,264
Cleveland, Ohio Akron, Ohio Lorain, Ohio CMSA	1,848	66.96	0	11	53	15	184	0	25	313	22	1,253
Milwaukee, Wisconsin Racine, Wisconsin CMSA	1,745	108.6	0	30	76	26	76	17	25	298	66	1,176
Albany, New York Schenectady, New York Troy, New York MSA	1,631	186.6	0	18	13	0	132	0	24	60	34	1,378
Phoenix, Arizona MSA	1,598	75.30	0	8	9	13	136	17	34	40	400	1,139
Fresno, California MSA	1,569	235.1	0	20	6	50	84	31	54	115	519	940
Pittsburgh, Pennsylvania Beaver Valley, Pennsylvania CMSA	1,510	67.33	0	31	15	9	169	0	21	116	27	1,149

Source: Census of Population and Housing, 1990: Equal Employment Opportunity (EEO) File on CD-ROM [machine-readable datafiles]. Prepared by the Bureau of the Census. Washington, DC: The Bureau, 1992. *Notes:* "MSA" represents "metropolitan statistical area"; "CMSA" stands for "consolidated metropolitan statistical area."

★ 195 ★

Leading Occupations

Technicians, by Metropolitan Area

According to the 1990 Census of Population and Housing, technicians ranked 64 among occupations employing the most people in the United States. Table presents the number of civilians 16 years old or older who reported working as technicians during the 1990 Census. Data show the total employment figures, employment per 100,000 population, and employment data for men and women of various races and ethnicities in the 25 metropolitan statistical areas with the largest concentrations of technicians.

[Total for all of the U.S. was 527,799; 212.2 per 100,000 persons]

Metropolitan area	Total employees	Employees per 100,000 population	Men					Women				
			American Indian, Eskimo & Aleut	Asian, Pacific Islander	Black	Hispanic	White	American Indian, Eskimo & Aleut	Asian, Pacific Islander	Black	Hispanic	White
New York, New York New Jersey (northern) Long Island, New York CMSA	38,773	214.4	57	3,080	3,202	2,339	19,235	12	1,114	1,988	821	8,910
Los Angeles, California Anaheim, California Riverside, California CMSA	31,850	219.2	115	4,023	1,450	3,753	16,207	74	1,262	879	1,218	5,365
San Francisco, California Oakland, California San Jose, California CMSA	23,017	368.1	57	4,001	888	1,564	10,972	23	1,386	503	591	4,382
Washington, District of Columbia MSA	18,860	480.7	29	1,254	1,910	413	8,015	13	568	1,961	285	4,992
Boston, Massachusetts Lawrence, Massachusetts Salem, Massachusetts CMSA	16,440	394.1	37	1,091	453	329	9,276	0	538	204	169	4,644
Chicago, Illinois Gary, Indiana Lake County, Illinois CMSA	15,033	186.4	8	987	939	631	8,096	19	374	760	247	3,417
Philadelphia, Pennsylvania Wilmington, Delaware Trenton, New Jersey CMSA	13,786	233.7	15	564	907	254	7,829	11	256	606	79	3,415
Detroit, Michigan Ann Arbor, Michigan CMSA	10,120	216.9	35	529	649	166	5,982	0	151	503	53	2,221
Dallas, Texas Fort Worth, Texas CMSA	9,884	254.4	41	379	562	566	5,946	23	128	506	148	1,965
Houston, Texas Galveston, Texas Brazoria, Texas CMSA	9,853	265.5	34	725	957	679	5,418	0	293	539	263	1,487
Minneapolis, Minnesota St. Paul, Minnesota MSA	7,222	293.1	23	337	139	51	4,580	30	122	59	28	1,916
Atlanta, Georgia MSA	7,191	253.8	16	224	902	86	4,141	0	62	456	23	1,355
Baltimore, Maryland MSA	7,095	297.8	0	155	569	67	3,861	0	223	524	39	1,750
Seattle, Washington Tacoma, Washington CMSA	6,975	272.6	6	317	110	83	3,901	30	227	80	70	2,281
San Diego, California MSA	6,968	278.9	42	533	214	477	3,946	8	230	140	204	1,588
Denver, Colorado Boulder, Colorado CMSA	6,182	334.5	40	202	200	279	3,712	17	73	138	189	1,615
Cleveland, Ohio Akron, Ohio Lorain, Ohio CMSA	5,818	210.8	12	287	359	96	3,701	0	96	273	8	1,020
Phoenix, Arizona MSA	5,437	256.2	13	199	136	412	3,303	0	69	64	201	1,321
St. Louis, Missouri MSA	5,054	206.8	0	191	253	101	2,924	0	64	320	49	1,269
Miami, Florida Fort Lauderdale, Florida CMSA	5,015	157.1	4	74	403	1,177	2,893	0	48	312	325	1,006
Sacramento, California MSA	5,011	338.3	15	413	155	147	2,355	23	227	154	198	1,534
Raleigh, North Carolina Durham, North Carolina MSA	4,740	644.5	0	328	256	62	2,209	0	171	340	35	1,414
Columbus, Ohio MSA	4,398	319.3	9	371	190	53	2,458	5	90	142	9	1,109
Pittsburgh, Pennsylvania Beaver Valley, Pennsylvania CMSA	4,182	186.5	7	178	172	29	2,580	0	80	68	33	1,075
Tampa, Florida St. Petersburg, Florida Clearwater, Florida MSA	3,999	193.4	4	56	189	147	2,509	14	12	107	71	1,090

Source: Census of Population and Housing, 1990: Equal Employment Opportunity (EEO) File on CD-ROM [machine-readable datafiles]. Prepared by the Bureau of the Census. Washington, DC: The Bureau, 1992. *Notes:* "MSA" represents "metropolitan statistical area"; "CMSA" stands for "consolidated metropolitan statistical area."

★ 196 ★
Leading Occupations

Textile Sewing Machine Operators, by Metropolitan Area

According to the 1990 Census of Population and Housing, textile sewing machine operators ranked 29 among occupations employing the most people in the United States. Table presents the number of civilians 16 years old or older who reported working as textile sewing machine operators during the 1990 Census. Data show the total employment figures, employment per 100,000 population, and employment data for men and women of various races and ethnicities in the 25 metropolitan statistical areas with the largest concentrations of textile sewing machine operators.

[Total for all of the U.S. was 783,799; 315.2 per 100,000 persons]

Metropolitan area	Total employees	Employees per 100,000 population	Men					Women				
			American Indian, Eskimo & Aleut	Asian, Pacific Islander	Black	Hispanic	White	American Indian, Eskimo & Aleut	Asian, Pacific Islander	Black	Hispanic	White
New York, New York New Jersey (northern) Long Island, New York CMSA	76,283	421.8	37	1,714	1,196	5,143	4,302	150	18,980	6,090	29,218	28,435
Los Angeles, California Anaheim, California Riverside, California CMSA	74,545	513.0	45	1,421	261	19,136	6,883	182	8,369	1,076	42,622	17,906
Miami, Florida Fort Lauderdale, Florida CMSA	14,195	444.6	0	6	217	819	789	10	88	1,651	11,248	10,014
Philadelphia, Pennsylvania Wilmington, Delaware Trenton, New Jersey CMSA	11,356	192.5	7	104	291	229	726	64	1,100	2,644	1,546	5,379
San Francisco, California Oakland, California San Jose, California CMSA	10,602	169.5	11	463	17	238	354	12	7,848	126	946	1,147
Greensboro, North Carolina Winston-Salem, North Carolina High Point, North Carolina MSA	9,081	963.9	4	87	363	10	819	26	148	1,468	42	6,145
Chicago, Illinois Gary, Indiana Lake County, Illinois CMSA	8,160	101.2	0	63	240	612	625	35	1,166	880	2,552	3,212
Charlotte, North Carolina Gastonia, North Carolina Rock Hill, South Carolina MSA	8,098	696.9	0	68	408	46	750	44	215	2,002	85	4,588
Scranton, Pennsylvania Wilkes-Barre, Pennsylvania MSA	7,544	1,028	0	13	0	0	519	0	123	29	56	6,836
Allentown, Pennsylvania Bethlehem, Pennsylvania Easton, Pennsylvania MSA	7,058	1,028	0	28	1	75	325	0	192	18	528	6,187
Providence, Rhode Island Pawtucket, Rhode Island Fall River, Massachusetts CMSA	6,485	568.1	7	16	49	174	1,269	7	93	42	384	4,672
Atlanta, Georgia MSA	6,220	219.5	0	25	186	39	324	0	333	2,156	139	3,119
El Paso, Texas MSA	6,065	1,025	0	0	0	1,131	860	14	51	32	4,789	3,375
Dallas, Texas Fort Worth, Texas CMSA	5,986	154.1	5	332	64	499	363	70	841	581	1,952	2,289
Greenville, South Carolina Spartanburg, South Carolina MSA	5,885	918.3	0	9	543	8	860	7	69	1,126	34	3,257
Boston, Massachusetts Lawrence, Massachusetts Salem, Massachusetts CMSA	5,537	132.7	0	19	163	685	659	0	556	315	739	3,039
Knoxville, Tennessee MSA	5,527	913.8	0	0	14	0	214	9	108	364	43	4,818
Hickory, North Carolina Morganton, North Carolina MSA	5,454	2,460	0	1	32	0	471	18	52	327	23	4,553
Detroit, Michigan Ann Arbor, Michigan CMSA	3,784	81.11	0	3	113	20	317	4	169	853	277	2,183
Johnson City, Tennessee Kingsport, Tennessee Bristol, Tennessee Bristol, Virginia MSA	3,704	849.5	0	0	0	0	300	5	27	76	14	3,296
Seattle, Washington Tacoma, Washington CMSA	3,340	130.5	8	97	25	9	126	24	1,679	112	60	1,224
San Antonio, Texas MSA	3,263	250.6	0	18	10	213	129	7	115	42	2,670	1,866
Chattanooga, Tennessee MSA	3,198	738.2	0	0	24	0	414	0	45	292	19	2,411
San Diego, California MSA	2,934	117.5	12	42	0	397	302	24	682	31	1,300	990
New Bedford, Massachusetts MSA	2,912	1,658	0	0	0	33	328	0	11	8	73	2,475

Source: Census of Population and Housing, 1990: Equal Employment Opportunity (EEO) File on CD-ROM [machine-readable datafiles]. Prepared by the Bureau of the Census. Washington, DC: The Bureau, 1992. *Notes:* "MSA" represents "metropolitan statistical area"; "CMSA" stands for "consolidated metropolitan statistical area."

★ 197 ★

Leading Occupations

Traffic, Shipping, and Receiving Clerks, by Metropolitan Area

According to the 1990 Census of Population and Housing, traffic, shipping, and receiving clerks ranked 45 among occupations employing the most people in the United States. Table presents the number of civilians 16 years old or older who reported working as traffic, shipping, and receiving clerks during the 1990 Census. Data show the total employment figures, employment per 100,000 population, and employment data for men and women of various races and ethnicities in the 25 metropolitan statistical areas with the largest concentrations of traffic, shipping, and receiving clerks.

[Total for all of the U.S. was 648,602; 260.8 per 100,000 persons]

Metropolitan area	Total employees	Employees per 100,000 population	Men					Women				
			American Indian, Eskimo & Aleut	Asian, Pacific Islander	Black	Hispanic	White	American Indian, Eskimo & Aleut	Asian, Pacific Islander	Black	Hispanic	White
Los Angeles, California Anaheim, California Riverside, California CMSA	52,309	360.0	265	2,856	3,444	20,305	20,606	86	879	848	5,850	8,004
New York, New York New Jersey (northern) Long Island, New York CMSA	47,459	262.4	109	1,565	9,894	10,245	21,363	49	263	2,003	2,196	6,676
Chicago, Illinois Gary, Indiana Lake County, Illinois CMSA	28,771	356.7	64	717	4,466	4,520	14,550	42	179	1,143	599	4,910
San Francisco, California Oakland, California San Jose, California CMSA	18,735	299.6	157	2,382	1,493	2,755	8,359	29	690	602	802	3,417
Philadelphia, Pennsylvania Wilmington, Delaware Trenton, New Jersey CMSA	16,328	276.8	19	88	2,772	473	9,406	14	27	615	125	2,979
Dallas, Texas Fort Worth, Texas CMSA	14,998	386.0	100	272	2,695	1,847	6,757	35	121	642	486	3,094
Boston, Massachusetts Lawrence, Massachusetts Salem, Massachusetts CMSA	14,775	354.2	32	93	717	745	10,624	4	38	136	83	2,726
Atlanta, Georgia MSA	12,146	428.7	44	112	3,131	176	5,232	0	34	1,156	58	2,405
Detroit, Michigan Ann Arbor, Michigan CMSA	12,113	259.6	46	61	1,264	193	6,925	29	4	566	45	3,123
Houston, Texas Galveston, Texas Brazoria, Texas CMSA	9,750	262.7	27	194	1,931	1,721	3,868	25	39	626	492	1,773
Cleveland, Ohio Akron, Ohio Lorain, Ohio CMSA	9,189	333.0	9	34	976	190	5,647	5	17	387	30	2,023
Minneapolis, Minnesota St. Paul, Minnesota MSA	8,822	358.0	83	44	188	80	5,966	18	20	42	47	2,418
Miami, Florida Fort Lauderdale, Florida CMSA	8,746	274.0	14	62	1,388	3,057	4,249	0	21	462	1,219	1,997
Seattle, Washington Tacoma, Washington CMSA	7,725	301.9	43	302	354	182	4,402	30	129	120	41	2,239
St. Louis, Missouri MSA	6,176	252.7	6	20	816	39	3,632	1	0	225	21	1,467
Charlotte, North Carolina Gastonia, North Carolina Rock Hill, South Carolina MSA	5,800	499.1	11	24	1,322	20	2,599	11	0	298	0	1,507
Cincinnati, Ohio Hamilton, Ohio CMSA	5,770	330.8	34	17	455	49	3,515	0	0	179	0	1,558
Milwaukee, Wisconsin Racine, Wisconsin CMSA	5,556	345.7	22	12	460	186	3,457	18	0	68	20	1,408
Phoenix, Arizona MSA	5,452	256.9	56	21	207	677	2,728	18	21	76	320	1,677
Denver, Colorado Boulder, Colorado CMSA	5,445	294.6	30	90	230	723	3,232	36	28	67	152	1,402
San Diego, California MSA	5,062	202.6	43	296	296	976	2,374	6	217	105	377	1,123
Portland, Oregon Vancouver, Washington CMSA	4,971	336.4	3	112	58	108	3,158	23	37	22	50	1,486
Providence, Rhode Island Pawtucket, Rhode Island Fall River, Massachusetts CMSA	4,901	429.3	0	25	170	277	3,495	0	12	13	36	1,046
Washington, District of Columbia MSA	4,818	122.8	0	127	1,521	148	1,722	5	36	341	33	1,013
Tampa, Florida St. Petersburg, Florida Clearwater, Florida MSA	4,675	226.1	0	23	461	245	2,862	0	7	147	59	1,086

Source: Census of Population and Housing, 1990: Equal Employment Opportunity (EEO) File on CD-ROM [machine-readable datafiles]. Prepared by the Bureau of the Census. Washington, DC: The Bureau, 1992. *Notes:* "MSA" represents "metropolitan statistical area"; "CMSA" stands for "consolidated metropolitan statistical area."

★ 198 ★
Leading Occupations

Truck Drivers, by Metropolitan Area

According to the 1990 Census of Population and Housing, truck drivers ranked 5 among occupations employing the most people in the United States. Table presents the number of civilians 16 years old or older who reported working as truck drivers during the 1990 Census. Data show the total employment figures, employment per 100,000 population, and employment data for men and women of various races and ethnicities in the 25 metropolitan statistical areas with the largest concentrations of truck drivers.

[Total for all of the U.S. was 2,908,952; 1,170 per 100,000 persons]

Metropolitan area	Total employees	Employees per 100,000 population	Men					Women				
			American Indian, Eskimo & Aleut	Asian, Pacific Islander	Black	Hispanic	White	American Indian, Eskimo & Aleut	Asian, Pacific Islander	Black	Hispanic	White
New York, New York New Jersey (northern) Long Island, New York CMSA	166,130	918.5	390	4,221	35,352	29,107	106,651	46	120	1,657	928	4,543
Los Angeles, California Anaheim, California Riverside, California CMSA	158,358	1,090	1,285	5,551	13,963	61,738	93,211	83	329	1,076	2,762	6,789
Chicago, Illinois Gary, Indiana Lake County, Illinois CMSA	85,226	1,057	247	681	14,049	7,970	62,325	0	22	872	135	2,662
Philadelphia, Pennsylvania Wilmington, Delaware Trenton, New Jersey CMSA	60,501	1,026	244	240	11,160	1,822	44,988	23	33	501	51	2,193
San Francisco, California Oakland, California San Jose, California CMSA	54,910	878.1	433	3,936	5,411	10,119	36,645	70	250	517	586	3,192
Detroit, Michigan Ann Arbor, Michigan CMSA	46,884	1,005	279	156	6,935	571	36,166	34	13	510	89	2,585
Dallas, Texas Fort Worth, Texas CMSA	45,953	1,183	393	201	9,445	4,928	30,775	18	12	407	145	1,904
Houston, Texas Galveston, Texas Brazoria, Texas CMSA	44,705	1,205	175	392	12,947	8,775	22,923	7	11	771	418	2,495
Boston, Massachusetts Lawrence, Massachusetts Salem, Massachusetts CMSA	36,749	880.9	32	149	1,633	1,145	32,001	5	32	164	58	2,099
Atlanta, Georgia MSA	35,579	1,256	116	144	11,843	436	20,972	13	2	782	8	1,554
Miami, Florida Fort Lauderdale, Florida CMSA	35,382	1,108	82	223	8,175	16,013	23,042	3	0	479	698	1,561
Washington, District of Columbia MSA	31,248	796.4	142	513	14,026	1,408	13,880	12	37	661	85	1,332
Cleveland, Ohio Akron, Ohio Lorain, Ohio CMSA	29,540	1,070	88	57	3,896	461	23,569	6	7	268	6	1,456
St. Louis, Missouri MSA	27,742	1,135	125	38	3,247	183	22,630	10	2	277	12	1,353
Baltimore, Maryland MSA	27,187	1,141	103	82	8,387	190	17,118	14	0	457	11	959
Seattle, Washington Tacoma, Washington CMSA	26,420	1,032	321	535	893	575	22,101	48	8	42	22	2,281
Minneapolis, Minnesota St. Paul, Minnesota MSA	26,223	1,064	220	123	466	213	23,942	19	13	26	18	1,317
Pittsburgh, Pennsylvania Beaver Valley, Pennsylvania CMSA	22,902	1,021	17	15	1,430	124	20,450	0	0	68	8	895
Phoenix, Arizona MSA	22,799	1,074	224	59	973	3,351	17,877	57	14	69	149	1,616
Tampa, Florida St. Petersburg, Florida Clearwater, Florida MSA	22,297	1,078	76	80	2,325	1,743	17,571	29	0	133	76	1,622
Denver, Colorado Boulder, Colorado CMSA	21,160	1,145	176	175	1,083	2,583	16,709	5	5	80	128	1,580
Cincinnati, Ohio Hamilton, Ohio CMSA	20,259	1,162	44	34	1,511	29	17,534	0	0	149	0	980
San Diego, California MSA	19,458	778.9	172	683	1,085	4,005	13,625	8	35	138	200	1,495
Portland, Oregon Vancouver, Washington CMSA	19,088	1,292	209	206	383	311	16,853	18	13	44	61	1,228
Kansas City, Missouri Kansas City, Kansas MSA	18,477	1,180	223	30	1,793	347	15,028	24	0	146	0	1,031

Source: Census of Population and Housing, 1990: Equal Employment Opportunity (EEO) File on CD-ROM [machine-readable datafiles]. Prepared by the Bureau of the Census. Washington, DC: The Bureau, 1992. *Notes:* "MSA" represents "metropolitan statistical area"; "CMSA" stands for "consolidated metropolitan statistical area."

★ 199 ★

Leading Occupations

Typists, by Metropolitan Area

According to the 1990 Census of Population and Housing, typists ranked 40 among occupations employing the most people in the United States. Table presents the number of civilians 16 years old or older who reported working as typists during the 1990 Census. Data show the total employment figures, employment per 100,000 population, and employment data for men and women of various races and ethnicities in the 25 metropolitan statistical areas with the largest concentrations of typists.

[Total for all of the U.S. was 662,775; 266.5 per 100,000 persons]

Metropolitan area	Total employees	Employees per 100,000 population	Men					Women				
			American Indian, Eskimo & Aleut	Asian, Pacific Islander	Black	Hispanic	White	American Indian, Eskimo & Aleut	Asian, Pacific Islander	Black	Hispanic	White
New York, New York New Jersey (northern) Long Island, New York CMSA	75,304	416.3	15	375	1,633	974	4,376	220	1,711	18,960	7,467	44,345
Los Angeles, California Anaheim, California Riverside, California CMSA	44,213	304.3	34	738	604	849	2,494	273	3,939	6,674	9,006	24,348
Chicago, Illinois Gary, Indiana Lake County, Illinois CMSA	25,877	320.8	0	75	376	106	700	37	440	7,212	1,864	16,014
Philadelphia, Pennsylvania Wilmington, Delaware Trenton, New Jersey CMSA	22,763	385.9	0	18	212	28	539	13	181	5,634	491	15,948
Washington, District of Columbia MSA	21,612	550.8	0	130	1,029	147	997	65	679	9,627	736	8,798
San Francisco, California Oakland, California San Jose, California CMSA	20,048	320.6	15	474	220	260	1,665	109	3,155	2,535	2,167	10,892
Detroit, Michigan Ann Arbor, Michigan CMSA	14,000	306.7	0	7	294	7	347	30	60	4,027	118	9,497
Boston, Massachusetts Lawrence, Massachusetts Salem, Massachusetts CMSA	12,545	300.7	0	54	140	48	765	11	129	1,023	342	10,252
Dallas, Texas Fort Worth, Texas CMSA	10,276	264.5	4	35	99	40	377	60	47	1,711	532	7,645
Houston, Texas Galveston, Texas Brazoria, Texas CMSA	9,217	248.4	0	0	36	72	162	0	94	2,700	1,144	5,677
Minneapolis, Minnesota St. Paul, Minnesota MSA	9,212	373.8	24	37	25	0	376	78	73	340	107	8,166
Atlanta, Georgia MSA	9,185	324.2	0	0	85	12	296	29	41	3,200	123	5,484
Baltimore, Maryland MSA	8,479	355.9	0	0	206	0	181	6	65	2,896	82	5,117
St. Louis, Missouri MSA	7,795	318.9	0	7	115	0	250	19	62	1,944	38	5,394
Miami, Florida Fort Lauderdale, Florida CMSA	7,615	238.5	0	8	50	151	284	8	20	1,943	2,062	5,109
Cleveland, Ohio Akron, Ohio Lorain, Ohio CMSA	7,533	273.0	0	0	66	0	232	10	36	1,685	107	5,446
Seattle, Washington Tacoma, Washington CMSA	7,275	284.3	16	26	71	16	490	51	352	486	184	5,689
San Diego, California MSA	6,629	265.4	6	71	56	65	394	74	480	554	873	4,489
Pittsburgh, Pennsylvania Beaver Valley, Pennsylvania CMSA	6,443	287.3	0	0	59	9	178	12	0	626	24	5,560
Phoenix, Arizona MSA	5,872	276.7	26	0	21	0	143	181	28	409	897	4,583
Denver, Colorado Boulder, Colorado CMSA	5,848	316.4	0	8	30	48	288	65	91	397	639	4,628
Sacramento, California MSA	5,636	380.5	11	82	52	6	248	40	370	622	707	3,837
Milwaukee, Wisconsin Racine, Wisconsin CMSA	5,466	340.1	0	8	7	0	180	26	27	653	196	4,448
Tampa, Florida St. Petersburg, Florida Clearwater, Florida MSA	5,270	254.8	16	8	62	10	157	25	36	683	373	4,215
Cincinnati, Ohio Hamilton, Ohio CMSA	5,152	295.4	0	0	23	6	134	0	38	713	44	4,223

Source: Census of Population and Housing, 1990: Equal Employment Opportunity (EEO) File on CD-ROM [machine-readable datafiles]. Prepared by the Bureau of the Census. Washington, DC: The Bureau, 1992. *Notes:* "MSA" represents "metropolitan statistical area"; "CMSA" stands for "consolidated metropolitan statistical area."

★ 200 ★

Leading Occupations

Unemployed (Experienced), by Metropolitan Area

According to the 1990 Census of Population and Housing, the experienced unemployed ranked 23 among occupations of the most people in the United States. Table presents the number of civilians 16 years old or older who reported being unemployed during the 1990 Census. Data show the total employment figures, employment per 100,000 population, and employment data for men and women of various races and ethnicities in the 25 metropolitan statistical areas with the largest concentrations of experienced unemployed people with no recent civilian work experience.

[Total for all of the U.S. was 999,951; 402.1 per 100,000 persons]

Metropolitan area	Total employees	Employees per 100,000 population	Men					Women				
			American Indian, Eskimo & Aleut	Asian, Pacific Islander	Black	Hispanic	White	American Indian, Eskimo & Aleut	Asian, Pacific Islander	Black	Hispanic	White
New York, New York New Jersey (northern) Long Island, New York CMSA	94,533	522.7	147	2,124	17,285	14,124	16,601	230	2,923	18,637	16,882	21,911
Los Angeles, California Anaheim, California Riverside, California CMSA	88,609	609.8	266	3,881	6,088	23,788	18,867	278	4,220	6,210	26,499	20,060
Chicago, Illinois Gary, Indiana Lake County, Illinois CMSA	51,025	632.6	23	609	14,225	4,131	6,479	147	803	14,838	5,041	8,259
Detroit, Michigan Ann Arbor, Michigan CMSA	31,690	679.3	62	166	10,122	363	4,568	101	172	10,421	316	5,731
Philadelphia, Pennsylvania Wilmington, Delaware Trenton, New Jersey CMSA	23,729	402.2	7	270	5,797	1,086	4,391	49	406	5,939	1,193	5,295
San Francisco, California Oakland, California San Jose, California CMSA	21,741	347.7	84	2,214	2,350	2,889	4,086	96	2,619	2,435	3,348	4,630
Houston, Texas Galveston, Texas Brazoria, Texas CMSA	19,179	516.8	37	406	3,570	2,401	3,079	11	612	4,154	3,408	4,039
Miami, Florida Fort Lauderdale, Florida CMSA	16,984	532.0	8	72	2,776	2,831	3,562	6	195	3,289	5,446	6,186
Cleveland, Ohio Akron, Ohio Lorain, Ohio CMSA	13,800	500.0	45	33	3,706	231	2,791	0	74	3,446	298	3,433
Dallas, Texas Fort Worth, Texas CMSA	13,013	334.9	25	174	2,352	1,492	2,674	19	314	2,286	1,673	3,243
Pittsburgh, Pennsylvania Beaver Valley, Pennsylvania CMSA	12,513	557.9	40	6	1,591	67	4,611	0	57	1,386	19	4,801
Boston, Massachusetts Lawrence, Massachusetts Salem, Massachusetts CMSA	12,236	293.3	2	360	924	1,070	3,602	60	374	1,102	1,357	4,468
New Orleans, Louisiana MSA	10,619	857.2	8	59	3,058	189	1,128	18	94	4,472	226	1,678
St. Louis, Missouri MSA	10,466	428.2	47	21	2,786	62	2,093	0	52	3,019	52	2,410
San Diego, California MSA	9,642	386.0	113	669	362	2,096	2,500	50	621	506	2,181	2,683
Washington, District of Columbia MSA	9,516	242.5	12	292	2,195	620	1,391	0	434	2,514	820	1,801
San Antonio, Texas MSA	7,852	603.0	6	64	326	2,535	2,214	28	77	303	3,023	2,663
Atlanta, Georgia MSA	7,507	264.9	6	97	1,824	105	1,091	0	179	2,450	151	1,725
Baltimore, Maryland MSA	7,010	294.3	0	29	1,894	8	1,058	9	92	2,466	50	1,426
Milwaukee, Wisconsin Racine, Wisconsin CMSA	6,272	390.3	14	56	1,443	212	1,077	69	91	1,729	377	1,454
Memphis, Tennessee MSA	6,131	624.5	8	11	2,353	10	382	7	23	2,765	18	572
Phoenix, Arizona MSA	5,913	278.6	107	115	197	987	1,610	160	62	221	1,300	2,094
Buffalo, New York Niagara Falls, New York CMSA	5,406	454.6	31	5	1,104	155	1,431	49	123	915	128	1,598
Cincinnati, Ohio Hamilton, Ohio CMSA	5,277	302.6	6	11	861	0	1,432	18	60	1,055	13	1,825
El Paso, Texas MSA	5,181	875.8	8	22	151	1,835	1,602	8	41	95	2,611	

Source: Census of Population and Housing, 1990: Equal Employment Opportunity (EEO) File on CD-ROM [machine-readable datafiles]. Prepared by the Bureau of the Census. Washington, DC: The Bureau, 1992. *Notes:* "MSA" represents "metropolitan statistical area"; "CMSA" stands for "consolidated metropolitan statistical area."

★ 201 ★

Leading Occupations

Waiters and Waitresses, by Metropolitan Area

According to the 1990 Census of Population and Housing, waiters and waitresses ranked 17 among occupations employing the most people in the United States. Table presents the number of civilians 16 years old or older who reported working as waiters and waitresses during the 1990 Census. Data show the total employment figures, employment per 100,000 population, and employment data for men and women of various races and ethnicities in the 25 metropolitan statistical areas with the largest concentrations of waiters and waitresses.

[Total for all of the U.S. was 1,488,253; 598.4 per 100,000 persons]

Metropolitan area	Total employees	Employees per 100,000 population	Men					Women				
			American Indian, Eskimo & Aleut	Asian, Pacific Islander	Black	Hispanic	White	American Indian, Eskimo & Aleut	Asian, Pacific Islander	Black	Hispanic	White
New York, New York New Jersey (northern) Long Island, New York CMSA	88,274	488.1	43	6,731	2,904	8,030	20,419	93	2,683	3,692	5,358	46,431
Los Angeles, California Anaheim, California Riverside, California CMSA	79,531	547.3	81	3,053	761	10,159	16,625	365	5,275	1,497	11,438	41,143
Chicago, Illinois Gary, Indiana Lake County, Illinois CMSA	42,976	532.8	29	949	917	2,119	5,571	88	1,006	2,606	2,180	29,550
San Francisco, California Oakland, California San Jose, California CMSA	35,354	565.4	53	2,648	553	2,450	7,312	213	3,328	516	2,905	18,529
Detroit, Michigan Ann Arbor, Michigan CMSA	32,877	704.7	32	107	943	143	3,464	216	555	1,803	453	25,543
Philadelphia, Pennsylvania Wilmington, Delaware Trenton, New Jersey CMSA	32,323	547.9	16	559	966	372	4,665	52	579	1,906	448	23,284
Boston, Massachusetts Lawrence, Massachusetts Salem, Massachusetts CMSA	28,273	677.7	19	886	238	534	4,151	67	555	379	394	21,595
Miami, Florida Fort Lauderdale, Florida CMSA	23,130	724.5	17	273	592	2,570	5,407	47	585	1,121	3,757	14,172
Dallas, Texas Fort Worth, Texas CMSA	22,292	573.7	9	472	623	2,205	5,359	116	592	1,019	1,910	11,555
Houston, Texas Galveston, Texas Brazoria, Texas CMSA	21,221	571.8	9	540	842	2,965	4,951	126	719	1,237	2,797	9,948
Washington, District of Columbia MSA	21,194	540.2	28	1,133	1,181	1,553	4,854	16	1,237	2,025	943	9,624
Minneapolis, Minnesota St. Paul, Minnesota MSA	17,756	720.6	26	122	79	60	2,455	128	365	142	230	14,365
Cleveland, Ohio Akron, Ohio Lorain, Ohio CMSA	16,831	609.9	0	28	326	39	1,738	10	200	900	160	13,546
Atlanta, Georgia MSA	16,761	591.5	13	357	1,130	391	3,291	42	526	1,478	278	9,588
Pittsburgh, Pennsylvania Beaver Valley, Pennsylvania CMSA	15,656	698.1	0	75	102	34	1,627	32	108	233	32	13,448
Seattle, Washington Tacoma, Washington CMSA	15,536	607.1	14	485	216	244	2,459	138	1,138	162	310	10,662
San Diego, California MSA	15,403	616.6	15	465	107	1,137	3,196	84	858	137	1,375	9,324
Tampa, Florida St. Petersburg, Florida Clearwater, Florida MSA	15,259	737.9	49	73	208	398	2,995	52	364	226	452	11,157
St. Louis, Missouri MSA	14,026	573.9	25	81	622	133	2,524	39	142	878	99	9,641
Phoenix, Arizona MSA	12,826	604.4	39	182	27	645	3,193	129	234	75	908	8,239
Baltimore, Maryland MSA	11,939	501.2	11	167	518	90	1,845	23	367	991	89	7,990
Denver, Colorado Boulder, Colorado CMSA	11,851	641.2	8	92	192	373	2,499	81	275	148	985	8,031
Orlando, Florida MSA	11,738	1,094	15	120	207	514	2,961	38	334	295	439	7,533
Las Vegas, Nevada MSA	10,488	1,415	0	232	164	540	1,899	79	469	326	674	6,902
Cincinnati, Ohio Hamilton, Ohio CMSA	10,341	592.9	6	52	110	41	1,393	5	121	290	90	8,329

Source: Census of Population and Housing, 1990: Equal Employment Opportunity (EEO) File on CD-ROM [machine-readable datafiles]. Prepared by the Bureau of the Census. Washington, DC: The Bureau, 1992. *Notes:* "MSA" represents "metropolitan statistical area"; "CMSA" stands for "consolidated metropolitan statistical area."

★ 202 ★

Leading Occupations

Waiters' and Waitresses' Assistants, by Metropolitan Area

According to the 1990 Census of Population and Housing, waiters' and waitresses' assistants ranked 85 among occupations employing the most people in the United States. Table presents the number of civilians 16 years old or older who reported working as waiters' and waitresses' assistants during the 1990 Census. Data show the total employment figures, employment per 100,000 population, and employment data for men and women of various races and ethnicities in the 25 metropolitan statistical areas with the largest concentrations of waiters' and waitresses' assistants.

[Total for all of the U.S. was 378,558; 152.2 per 100,000 persons]

Metropolitan area	Total employees	Employees per 100,000 population	Men					Women				
			American Indian, Eskimo & Aleut	Asian, Pacific Islander	Black	Hispanic	White	American Indian, Eskimo & Aleut	Asian, Pacific Islander	Black	Hispanic	White
Los Angeles, California Anaheim, California Riverside, California CMSA	29,003	199.6	57	915	518	15,163	11,093	32	599	539	2,292	6,016
New York, New York New Jersey (northern) Long Island, New York CMSA	17,443	96.44	33	833	1,649	4,442	6,888	30	226	1,280	609	4,393
Chicago, Illinois Gary, Indiana Lake County, Illinois CMSA	14,602	181.0	32	196	1,412	5,127	5,442	19	87	956	498	3,186
San Francisco, California Oakland, California San Jose, California CMSA	13,667	218.6	77	1,910	502	3,690	4,930	7	662	330	724	3,198
Philadelphia, Pennsylvania Wilmington, Delaware Trenton, New Jersey CMSA	8,588	145.6	7	148	1,284	222	3,310	8	103	737	92	2,845
Detroit, Michigan Ann Arbor, Michigan CMSA	7,964	170.7	22	72	1,191	156	3,625	13	48	495	60	2,432
Las Vegas, Nevada MSA	6,742	909.3	41	349	341	1,462	2,101	10	475	414	579	2,070
Dallas, Texas Fort Worth, Texas CMSA	6,412	165.0	19	68	444	2,249	2,034	13	61	700	472	1,433
Phoenix, Arizona MSA	6,330	298.3	84	123	107	1,251	3,156	47	77	56	356	1,928
San Diego, California MSA	5,926	237.2	7	344	132	1,790	2,600	13	199	64	388	1,419
Houston, Texas Galveston, Texas Brazoria, Texas CMSA	5,901	159.0	17	96	461	2,298	1,601	17	61	604	854	1,188
Washington, District of Columbia MSA	5,757	146.7	32	328	985	1,646	1,818	0	273	532	251	922
Seattle, Washington Tacoma, Washington CMSA	5,654	220.9	54	313	185	149	2,131	55	180	130	57	2,491
Miami, Florida Fort Lauderdale, Florida CMSA	5,389	168.8	46	76	969	1,464	2,471	12	49	519	415	1,024
Boston, Massachusetts Lawrence, Massachusetts Salem, Massachusetts CMSA	5,207	124.8	8	156	421	352	2,055	0	46	149	101	2,176
Cleveland, Ohio Akron, Ohio Lorain, Ohio CMSA	4,914	178.1	3	34	643	55	2,154	18	21	289	31	1,714
St. Louis, Missouri MSA	4,894	200.2	7	51	686	108	2,178	7	37	414	35	1,484
Cincinnati, Ohio Hamilton, Ohio CMSA	4,571	262.1	0	31	358	19	2,000	0	21	182	26	1,973
Denver, Colorado Boulder, Colorado CMSA	4,296	232.4	5	97	106	447	2,209	32	92	110	174	1,333
Minneapolis, Minnesota St. Paul, Minnesota MSA	4,200	170.5	15	131	160	66	1,904	13	32	52	36	1,847
Tampa, Florida St. Petersburg, Florida Clearwater, Florida MSA	4,055	196.1	0	35	294	279	1,830	12	37	231	121	1,531
Baltimore, Maryland MSA	3,670	154.1	22	72	642	76	1,442	0	22	467	39	980
Orlando, Florida MSA	3,664	341.6	0	53	298	635	1,742	22	43	175	131	1,123
Pittsburgh, Pennsylvania Beaver Valley, Pennsylvania CMSA	3,653	162.9	0	17	331	30	1,877	7	10	107	6	1,292
Atlanta, Georgia MSA	3,596	126.9	0	77	784	190	1,051	0	32	678	60	870

Source: Census of Population and Housing, 1990: Equal Employment Opportunity (EEO) File on CD-ROM [machine-readable datafiles]. Prepared by the Bureau of the Census. Washington, DC: The Bureau, 1992. *Notes:* "MSA" represents "metropolitan statistical area"; "CMSA" stands for "consolidated metropolitan statistical area."

★ 203 ★

Leading Occupations

Welders and Cutters, by Metropolitan Area

According to the 1990 Census of Population and Housing, welders and cutters ranked 46 among occupations employing the most people in the United States. Table presents the number of civilians 16 years old or older who reported working as welders and cutters during the 1990 Census. Data show the total employment figures, employment per 100,000 population, and employment data for men and women of various races and ethnicities in the 25 metropolitan statistical areas with the largest concentrations of welders and cutters.

[Total for all of the U.S. was 643,978; 258.9 per 100,000 persons]

Metropolitan area	Total employees	Employees per 100,000 population	Men American Indian, Eskimo & Aleut	Men Asian, Pacific Islander	Men Black	Men Hispanic	Men White	Women American Indian, Eskimo & Aleut	Women Asian, Pacific Islander	Women Black	Women Hispanic	Women White
Los Angeles, California Anaheim, California Riverside, California CMSA	29,062	200.0	270	1,300	1,406	16,493	14,969	10	49	100	1,135	800
New York, New York New Jersey (northern) Long Island, New York CMSA	17,724	97.99	50	435	4,144	3,657	10,268	0	22	297	407	521
Chicago, Illinois Gary, Indiana Lake County, Illinois CMSA	16,965	210.3	27	258	2,281	4,312	10,837	0	0	181	327	615
Houston, Texas Galveston, Texas Brazoria, Texas CMSA	15,269	411.5	151	287	1,785	6,021	9,443	0	15	9	61	120
Detroit, Michigan Ann Arbor, Michigan CMSA	14,483	310.5	128	100	2,813	312	10,286	3	15	359	37	593
Philadelphia, Pennsylvania Wilmington, Delaware Trenton, New Jersey CMSA	9,802	166.2	9	71	1,439	474	7,476	0	0	209	31	295
Dallas, Texas Fort Worth, Texas CMSA	9,082	233.8	80	236	799	2,906	5,733	9	13	12	203	243
Cleveland, Ohio Akron, Ohio Lorain, Ohio CMSA	8,352	302.6	28	24	1,041	310	6,387	7	9	219	15	445
San Francisco, California Oakland, California San Jose, California CMSA	8,171	130.7	176	674	490	2,270	5,266	19	33	18	140	147
Pittsburgh, Pennsylvania Beaver Valley, Pennsylvania CMSA	6,110	272.4	3	0	173	8	5,690	0	0	37	0	207
St. Louis, Missouri MSA	5,752	235.3	8	37	730	53	4,733	0	0	63	2	179
Milwaukee, Wisconsin Racine, Wisconsin CMSA	5,658	352.0	66	37	748	338	4,346	0	0	36	0	204
Seattle, Washington Tacoma, Washington CMSA	5,415	211.6	67	293	234	270	4,509	3	29	0	16	168
Boston, Massachusetts Lawrence, Massachusetts Salem, Massachusetts CMSA	5,140	123.2	17	117	256	241	4,266	0	6	12	38	276
Minneapolis, Minnesota St. Paul, Minnesota MSA	5,126	208.0	42	64	84	46	4,673	5	20	0	2	214
Norfolk, Virginia Virginia Beach, Virginia Newport News, Virginia MSA	4,924	352.7	55	72	1,797	72	2,691	0	0	179	7	130
New Orleans, Louisiana MSA	4,630	373.7	18	120	1,147	212	3,254	0	4	29	0	21
Cincinnati, Ohio Hamilton, Ohio CMSA	4,612	264.4	0	8	287	16	4,143	0	0	0	2	166
Atlanta, Georgia MSA	4,529	159.8	6	134	973	225	3,152	0	0	39	0	92
Portland, Oregon Vancouver, Washington CMSA	4,507	305.0	42	74	80	185	4,106	0	6	8	13	91
Miami, Florida Fort Lauderdale, Florida CMSA	4,482	140.4	32	34	740	1,960	3,077	0	0	85	187	223
San Diego, California MSA	4,394	175.9	22	252	305	1,321	2,819	0	24	13	80	132
Baltimore, Maryland MSA	4,110	172.5	23	15	985	43	2,863	0	0	93	0	107
Birmingham, Alabama MSA	4,052	446.4	38	7	949	15	2,878	0	0	76	0	95
Tulsa, Oklahoma MSA	3,983	561.8	424	15	127	110	3,313	15	0	0	0	45

Source: Census of Population and Housing, 1990: Equal Employment Opportunity (EEO) File on CD-ROM [machine-readable datafiles]. Prepared by the Bureau of the Census. Washington, DC: The Bureau, 1992. *Notes:* "MSA" represents "metropolitan statistical area"; "CMSA" stands for "consolidated metropolitan statistical area."

Occupational Outlook

★ 204 ★

Fastest Declining Occupations: 1992-2005

Data show civilian employment for 35 fastest declining occupations. Occupations are in descending order of absolute employment percent change for 1992 through 2005 (moderate growth). Includes wage and salary jobs, self-employed and unpaid family members. Estimates based on the Current Employment Statistics estimates and the Occupational Employment Statistics estimates. Minus sign (-) indicates decrease.

| Occupation | Employment (1,000) | | | | Percentage change 1992-2005 | | |
| | 1992 | 2005[1] | | | | | |
		Low	Moderate	High	Low	Moderate	High
Total, all occupations[2]	121,099	139,007	147,482	154,430	14.8	21.8	27.5
Frame wirers, central office	11	2	3	3	-77.4	-75.3	-74.7
Signal or track switch maintainers	3	1	1	1	-76.6	-74.6	-72.9
Peripheral EDP equipment operators	30	11	12	12	-62.6	-60.2	-59.0
Directory assistance operators	27	12	13	14	-54.9	-50.6	-49.4
Central office operators	48	22	24	24	-54.7	-50.3	-49.1
Station installers and repairers, telephone	40	18	20	20	-54.7	-50.3	-49.1
Portable machine cutters	11	5	6	6	-48.3	-40.1	-39.4
Computer operators, except peripheral equipment	266	151	161	168	-43.2	-39.3	-36.6
Shoe sewing machine operators and tenders	16	9	10	10	-46.3	-38.4	-35.8
Central office and PBX installers and repairers	70	41	45	46	-41.3	-35.6	-34.1
Child care workers, private household	350	220	227	242	-37.1	-35.1	-31.0
Job printers	15	9	10	10	-39.4	-35.0	-33.2
Roustabouts	33	20	22	32	-38.4	-33.2	-2.0
Separating and still machine operators and tenders	21	13	14	15	-37.0	-32.8	-29.8
Cleaners and servants, private household	483	316	326	347	-34.6	-32.5	-28.2
Coil winders, tapers, and finishers	20	12	14	16	-41.2	-32.4	-22.1
Billing, posting, and calculating machine operators	93	62	66	68	-33.6	-29.5	-27.0
Sewing machine operators, garment	556	338	393	396	-39.1	-29.2	-28.7
Compositors and typesetters, precision	11	7	8	8	-30.7	-26.5	-23.3
Data entry keyers, composing	16	11	12	12	-31.7	-26.4	-23.8
Motion picture projectionists	9	7	7	7	-29.3	-25.8	-24.0
Telephone and cable TV line intallers	165	117	125	134	-29.4	-24.4	-18.7
Cutting and slicing machine setters [3]	94	68	73	76	-28.1	-22.6	-19.5
Watchmakers	9	7	7	8	-26.5	-22.6	-18.4
Tire building machine operators	14	10	11	12	-29.4	-22.3	-19.0
Packaging and filling machine operators and tenders	319	232	248	257	-27.1	-22.3	-19.4
Head sawyers and sawing machine operators and tenders[4]	59	44	46	53	-25.7	-22.3	-10.3
Switchboard operators	239	177	188	194	-25.9	-21.3	-18.8
Farmers	1,088	831	857	914	-23.7	-21.2	-16.0
Machine forming operators and tenders, metal and plastic	155	112	123	133	-27.8	-20.8	-14.3
Cement and gluing machine operators and tenders	35	26	28	30	-25.7	-20.2	-12.7

Source: U.S. Bureau of the Census. *Statistical Abstract of the United States, 1994.* 114th ed. Washington, DC: U.S. Government Printing Office, 1994, p. 411. Primary source: U.S. Bureau of Labor Statistics. *Monthly Labor Review* (November 1993). *Notes:* 1. Based on low, moderate, or high trend assumptions. 2. Includes other occupations, not shown separately. 3. Includes operators and tenders. 4. Includes set-up operators.

★ 205 ★
Occupational Outlook
Fastest Growing Occupations: 1992-2005

Data show civilian employment for 35 fastest growing occupations. Occupations are in descending order of absolute employment percent change for 1992 through 2005 (moderate growth). Includes wage and salary jobs, self-employed and unpaid family members. Estimates based on the Current Employment Statistics estimates and the Occupational Employment Statistics estimates.

Occupation	Employment (1,000)				Percentage change 1992-2005		
	1992	Low	Moderate	High	Low	Moderate	High
Total, all occupations[2]	121,099	139,007	147,482	154,430	14.8	21.8	27.5
Home health aides	347	794	827	835	128.7	138.1	140.6
Human services workers	189	429	445	451	127.6	135.9	139.2
Personal and home care aides	127	283	293	296	122.0	129.8	132.0
Computer engineers and scientists	211	409	447	484	93.9	111.9	129.2
Systems analysts	455	891	956	1,001	95.7	110.1	120.0
Physical and corrective therapy assistants and aides	61	113	118	119	84.6	92.7	95.1
Physical therapists	90	163	170	173	80.2	88.0	91.4
Paralegals	95	166	176	180	75.8	86.1	89.8
Occupational therapy assistants and aides	12	20	21	21	70.5	78.1	80.1
Electronic pagination systems workers	18	29	32	33	65.1	77.9	84.0
Teachers, special education	358	594	625	648	65.9	74.4	81.0
Medical assistants	181	296	308	313	63.5	70.5	73.0
Detectives, except public	59	94	100	104	60.1	70.2	76.8
Correction officers	282	452	479	503	60.0	69.9	78.1
Child care workers	684	1,100	1,135	1,183	60.6	65.8	72.8
Travel agents	115	167	191	196	45.2	65.7	69.9
Radiologic technologists and technicians	162	252	264	267	55.4	62.7	64.6
Nursery (farm) workers	72	110	116	123	53.1	62.0	71.3
Medical records technicians	76	118	123	125	54.4	61.5	63.6
Operations research analysts	45	67	72	75	50.1	61.4	68.0
Occupational therapists	40	61	64	65	52.9	59.6	62.5
Subway and streetcar operators	22	33	35	37	48.1	57.2	64.9
Legal secretaries	280	415	439	447	48.3	57.1	59.9
Teachers, preschool and kindergarten	434	646	669	682	48.9	54.3	57.2
Manicurists	35	54	55	56	51.2	54.1	58.3
EEG technologists	6	9	10	10	46.6	53.8	55.4
Producers, directors, actors, and entertainers	129	190	198	205	47.0	53.5	58.7
Speech-language pathologists and audiologists	73	105	110	113	44.6	51.3	55.7
Flight attendants	93	121	140	144	30.3	51.0	55.5
Guards	803	1,138	1,211	1,255	41.7	50.8	56.2
Nuclear medicine technologists	12	17	18	18	43.1	50.1	51.6
Insurance adjusters, examiners, and investigators	147	205	220	220	39.3	49.1	49.5
Respiratory therapists	74	104	109	110	41.4	48.3	49.9
Psychologists	143	204	212	222	42.1	48.0	54.7

Source: U.S. Bureau of the Census. *Statistical Abstract of the United States, 1994.* 114th ed. Washington, DC: U.S. Government Printing Office, 1994, p. 411. Primary source: U.S. Bureau of Labor Statistics. *Monthly Labor Review* (November 1993). *Notes:* 1. Based on low, moderate, or high trend assumptions. 2. Includes other occupations, not shown separately.

★ 206 ★

Occupational Outlook

High Growth Occupations: 1992-2005

Data show civilian employment for 35 occupations with the largest job growth. Occupations are in descending order of absolute employment change for 1992 through 2005 (moderate growth). Includes wage and salary jobs, self-employed and unpaid family members. Estimates based on the Current Employment Statistics estimates and the Occupational Employment Statistics estimates.

Occupation	Employment (1,000)				Percentage change 1992-2005		
	1992	2005[1]			Low	Moderate	High
		Low	Moderate	High			
Total, all occupations[2]	121,099	139,007	147,482	154,430	14.8	21.8	27.5
Salespersons, retail	3,660	4,137	4,446	4,611	13.1	21.5	26.0
Registered nurses	1,835	2,479	2,601	2,637	35.1	41.7	43.7
Cashiers	2,747	3,201	3,417	3,520	16.5	24.4	28.1
General office clerks	2,688	3,143	3,342	3,489	16.9	24.3	29.8
Truck drivers, light and heavy	2,391	2,836	3,039	3,235	18.6	27.1	35.3
Waiters and waitresses	1,756	2,280	2,394	2,415	29.8	36.3	37.5
Nursing aides, orderlies, and attendants	1,308	1,824	1,903	1,937	39.4	45.4	48.0
Janitors and cleaners[3]	2,862	3,246	3,410	3,519	13.4	19.1	23.0
Food preparation workers	1,223	1,661	1,748	1,775	35.8	42.9	45.1
Systems analysts	455	891	956	1,001	95.7	110.1	120.0
Home health aides	347	794	827	835	128.7	138.1	140.6
Teachers, secondary school	1,263	1,640	1,724	1,789	29.9	36.6	41.7
Child care workers	684	1,100	1,135	1,183	60.6	65.8	72.8
Guards	803	1,138	1,211	1,255	41.7	50.8	56.2
Marketing and sales worker supervisors	2,036	2,303	2,443	2,565	13.1	20.0	26.0
Teacher aides and educational assistants	885	1,209	1,266	1,308	36.6	43.1	47.8
General managers and top executives	2,871	3,050	3,251	3,418	6.2	13.2	19.0
Maintenance repairers, general utility	1,145	1,388	1,464	1,542	21.2	27.8	34.7
Gardeners and groundskeepers, except farm	884	1,152	1,195	1,261	30.3	35.2	42.7
Teachers, elementary	1,456	1,683	1,767	1,830	15.6	21.3	25.6
Food counter, fountain, and related workers	1,564	1,776	1,872	1,895	13.6	19.7	21.2
Receptionists and information clerks	904	1,149	1,210	1,245	27.1	33.8	37.7
Accountants and auditors	939	1,167	1,243	1,301	24.3	32.3	38.6
Clerical supervisors and managers	1,267	1,473	1,568	1,622	16.3	23.8	28.0
Cooks, restaurant	602	837	879	889	39.0	45.8	47.5
Teachers, special education	358	594	625	648	65.9	74.4	81.0
Licensed practical nurses	659	879	920	933	33.4	39.7	41.6
Cooks, short order and fast food	714	921	971	978	29.0	36.0	37.0
Human services workers	189	429	445	451	127.6	135.9	139.2
Computer engineers and scientists	211	409	447	484	93.9	111.9	129.2
Teachers, preschool and kindergarten	434	646	669	682	48.9	54.3	57.2
Food service and lodging managers	532	732	764	787	37.6	43.5	48.0
Hairdressers, hair stylists, and cosmetologists	628	824	846	876	31.2	34.7	39.4
Blue-collar worker supervisors	1,757	1,844	1,974	2,131	5.0	12.4	21.3
College and university faculty	812	976	1,026	1,064	20.2	26.4	31.1

Source: U.S. Bureau of the Census. *Statistical Abstract of the United States, 1994.* 114th ed. Washington, DC: U.S. Government Printing Office, 1994, p. 410. Primary source: U.S. Bureau of Labor Statistics. *Monthly Labor Review* (November 1993). *Notes:* 1. Based on low, moderate, or high trend assumptions. 2. Includes other occupations, not shown separately. 3. Includes maids and housekeepers.

Occupational Outlook: Job Openings

★ 207 ★

Job Openings, by Occupational Group: 1992-2005

Table shows the average annual job openings due to growth, total replacement, and net replacement needs for 1992 through 2005.

[In thousands]

Occupation	Number of annual average job openings due to growth and total replacement needs	Number of annual average job openings due to growth and net replacement needs
Total, all occupations	24,423	4,667
Executive, administrative, and managerial occupations	1,376	440
Professional specialty occupations	2,290	753
Miscellaneous professional specialty occupations	166	45
Technicians and related support occupations	562	182
Marketing and sales occupations	3,473	536
Administrative support occupations[1]	4,632	694
Service occupations	6,441	973
Miscellaneous service workers	296	41
Agriculture, forestry, fishing, and related occupations	768	94
Precision production, craft, and repair occupations	1,747	470
Operators, fabricators, and laborers	3,133	525

Source: U.S. Department of Labor. Bureau of Labor Statistics. *Occupational Projections and Training Data.* 1994 ed. Bulletin 2451. Washington, DC: U.S. Government Printing Office, May 1994, pp. 4-35. A statistical and research supplement to the 1994-1995 *Occupational Outlook Handbook. Note:* 1. Including clerical.

★ 208 ★

Occupational Outlook: Job Openings

Job Openings for Adjusters, Investigators, and Collectors: 1992-2005

Table shows the average annual job openings due to growth, total replacement, and net replacement needs for 1992 through 2005. Jobs also are ranked by growth expected.

[In thousands]

Occupation	Annual average job openings due to growth and total replacement needs		Annual average job openings due to growth and net replacement needs	
	Number	Rank	Number	Rank
Adjusters, investigators, and collectors	244	-	40	-
Adjustment clerks	67	L	10	L
Bill and account collectors	64	L	9	L
Insurance claims and policy processing occupations	89	-	17	-
Insurance adjusters, examiners, and investigators	25	VL	7	VL
Insurance claims clerks	18	VL	4	VL
Insurance policy processing clerks	46	L	7	VL
Welfare eligibility workers and interviewers	16	VL	3	VL
All other adjusters and investigators	7	VL	1	VL

Source: U.S. Department of Labor. Bureau of Labor Statistics. *Occupational Projections and Training Data.* 1994 ed. Bulletin 2451. Washington, DC: U.S. Government Printing Office, May 1994, pp. 12-13. A statistical and research supplement to the 1994-1995 *Occupational Outlook Handbook. Notes:* Rankings are based on all detailed occupations in the National Industry-Occupation Matrix. Codes for describing the ranked variables are: VH - very high; H - high; L - low; or VL - very low. A dash (-) indicates data are not applicable.

★ 209 ★

Occupational Outlook: Job Openings

Job Openings for Agriculture, Forestry, and Fishing Occupations: 1992-2005

Table shows the average annual job openings due to growth, total replacement, and net replacement needs for 1992 through 2005. Jobs also are ranked by growth expected.

[In thousands]

Occupation	Annual average job openings due to growth and total replacement needs		Annual average job openings due to growth and net replacement needs	
	Number	Rank	Number	Rank
Animal caretakers[1]	28	VL	5	VL
Farm occupations	218	-	28	-
Farm workers	192	H	23	L
Nursery workers	26	VL	5	VL
Farm operators and managers	96	-	14	-
Farmers	82	L	10	L
Farm managers	15	VL	4	VL
Fishers, hunters, and trappers	3	-	1	-
Captains and other officers, fishing vessels	0	VL	0	VL

[Continued]

★ 209 ★

Job Openings for Agriculture, Forestry, and Fishing Occupations: 1992-2005

[Continued]

Occupation	Annual average job openings due to growth and total replacement needs		Annual average job openings due to growth and net replacement needs	
	Number	Rank	Number	Rank
Fishers, hunters, and trappers	3	VL	1	VL
Foresty and logging occupations	27	-	4	-
Forest and conservation workers	9	VL	2	VL
Timber cutting and logging occupations	18	-	2	-
Fallers and buckers	6	VL	1	VL
Log handling equipment operators	3	VL	0	VL
Logging tractor operators	4	VL	1	VL
All other timber cutting and related logging workers	4	VL	1	VL
Gardeners and groundskeepers[1]	343	VH	33	H
Supervisors, farming, forestry, and agricultural-related occupations	8	VL	2	VL
All other agricultural, forestry, fishing, and related workers	44	L	7	VL

Source: U.S. Department of Labor. Bureau of Labor Statistics. *Occupational Projections and Training Data.* 1994 ed. Bulletin 2451. Washington, DC: U.S. Government Printing Office, May 1994, pp. 18-21. A statistical and research supplement to the 1994-1995 *Occupational Outlook Handbook. Notes:* Rankings are based on all detailed occupations in the National Industry-Occupation Matrix. Codes for describing the ranked variables are: VH - very high; - H - high; L - low; or VL - very low. A dash (-) indicates data are not applicable. 1. Except farm.

★ 210 ★

Occupational Outlook: Job Openings

Job Openings for Architects and Surveyors: 1992-2005

Table shows the average annual job openings due to growth, total replacement, and net replacement needs for 1992 through 2005. Jobs also are ranked by growth expected.

[In thousands]

Occupation	Annual average job openings due to growth and total replacement needs		Annual average job openings due to growth and net replacement needs	
	Number	Rank	Number	Rank
Architects and surveyors	27	-	7	-
Architects[1]	12	VL	3	VL
Landscape architects	2	VL	1	VL
Surveyors	12	VL	3	VL

Source: U.S. Department of Labor. Bureau of Labor Statistics. *Occupational Projections and Training Data.* 1994 ed. Bulletin 2451. Washington, DC: U.S. Government Printing Office, May 1994, pp. 6-7. A statistical and research supplement to the 1994-1995 *Occupational Outlook Handbook. Notes:* Rankings are based on all detailed occupations in the National Industry-Occupation Matrix. Codes for describing the ranked variables are: VH - very high; H - high; L - low; or VL - very low. A dash (-) indicates data are not applicable. 1. Except landscape and marine architects.

★ 211 ★

Occupational Outlook: Job Openings

Job Openings for Cleaning and Building Service Occupations: 1992-2005

Table shows the average annual job openings due to growth, total replacement, and net replacement needs for 1992 through 2005. Jobs also are ranked by growth expected. See also table for private household occupations.

[In thousands]

Occupation	Annual average job openings due to growth and total replacement needs		Annual average job openings due to growth and net replacement needs	
	Number	Rank	Number	Rank
Cleaning and building service occupations[1]	856	-	107	-
Institutional cleaning supervisors	21	VL	8	VL
Janitors and cleaners[2]	768	VH	92	VH
Pest controllers and assistants	12	VL	6	VL
All other cleaning and building service workers	55	L	6	VL

Source: U.S. Department of Labor. Bureau of Labor Statistics. *Occupational Projections and Training Data.* 1994 ed. Bulletin 2451. Washington, DC: U.S. Government Printing Office, May 1994, pp. 16-17. A statistical and research supplement to the 1994-1995 *Occupational Outlook Handbook. Notes:* Rankings are based on all detailed occupations in the National Industry-Occupation Matrix. Codes for describing the ranked variables are: VH - very high; H - high; L - low; or VL - very low. A dash (-) indicates data are not applicable. 1. Except private household. 2. Includes maids and housekeeping cleaners.

★ 212 ★

Occupational Outlook: Job Openings

Job Openings for Clerical and Administrative Support Workers: 1992-2005

Table shows the average annual job openings due to growth, total replacement, and net replacement needs for 1992 through 2005. Jobs also are ranked by growth expected. See also tables for specific clerical and administrative support workers; for example, secretaries, stenographers, and typists.

[In thousands]

Occupation	Annual average job openings due to growth and total replacement needs		Annual average job openings due to growth and net replacement needs	
	Number	Rank	Number	Rank
Clerical and administrative support workers, other[1]	1,675	-	246	-
Bank tellers	116	L	21	L
Clerical supervisors and managers	139	L	53	H
Court clerks	9	VL	1	VL
Credit authorizers, credit checkers, and loan and credit clerks	45	-	7	-
Credit authorizers	4	VL	0	VL
Credit checkers	7	VL	1	VL
Loan and credit clerks	31	VL	5	VL
Loan interviewers	4	VL	1	VL
Customer service representatives, utilities	25	VL	4	VL
Data entry keyers[2]	126	L	10	L

[Continued]

★ 212 ★

Job Openings for Clerical and Administrative Support Workers: 1992-2005
[Continued]

Occupation	Annual average job openings due to growth and total replacement needs		Annual average job openings due to growth and net replacement needs	
	Number	Rank	Number	Rank
Data entry keyers, composing	4	VL	0	VL
Duplicating, mail, and other office machine operators	49	L	8	L
General office clerks	702	VH	95	VH
Municipal clerks	4	VL	0	VL
Proofreaders and copy markers	6	VL	1	VL
Real estate clerks	7	VL	1	VL
Statistical clerks	5	VL	1	VL
Teacher aides and educational assistants	338	H	39	H
All other clerical and administrative support workers	100	L	6	VL

Source: U.S. Department of Labor. Bureau of Labor Statistics. *Occupational Projections and Training Data.* 1994 ed. Bulletin 2451. Washington, DC: U.S. Government Printing Office, May 1994, pp. 14-17. A statistical and research supplement to the 1994-1995 *Occupational Outlook Handbook. Notes:* Rankings are based on all detailed occupations in the National Industry-Occupation Matrix. Codes for describing the ranked variables are: VH - very high; H - high; L - low; or VL - very low. A dash (-) indicates data are not applicable. 1. Includes miscellaneous clerical occupations not found in other administrative occupational groupings. 2. Except composing.

★ 213 ★

Occupational Outlook: Job Openings

Job Openings for Communications Equipment Mechanics, Installers, and Repairers: 1992-2005

Table shows the average annual job openings due to growth, total replacement, and net replacement needs for 1992 through 2005. Jobs also are ranked by growth expected.

[In thousands]

Occupation	Annual average job openings due to growth and total replacement needs		Annual average job openings due to growth and net replacement needs	
	Number	Rank	Number	Rank
Communications equipment mechanics, installers, and repairers	3	-	2	-
Central office and PBX installers and repairers	1	VL	1	VL
Frame wirers, central office	0	VL	0	VL
Radio mechanics	1	VL	0	VL
Signal or track switch maintainers	0	VL	0	VL
All other communications equipment mechanics, installers, and repairers	2	VL	0	VL

Source: U.S. Department of Labor. Bureau of Labor Statistics. *Occupational Projections and Training Data.* 1994 ed. Bulletin 2451. Washington, DC: U.S. Government Printing Office, May 1994, pp. 22-23. A statistical and research supplement to the 1994-1995 *Occupational Outlook Handbook. Notes:* Rankings are based on all detailed occupations in the National Industry-Occupation Matrix. Codes for describing the ranked variables are: VH - very high; H - high; L - low; or VL - very low. A dash (-) indicates data are not applicable.

★ 214 ★
Occupational Outlook: Job Openings

Job Openings for Communications Equipment Operators: 1992-2005

Table shows the average annual job openings due to growth, total replacement, and net replacement needs for 1992 through 2005. Jobs also are ranked by growth expected.

[In thousands]

Occupation	Annual average job openings due to growth and total replacement needs		Annual average job openings due to growth and net replacement needs	
	Number	Rank	Number	Rank
Commmunications equipment operators	39	-	8	-
Telephone operators	37	-	8	-
Central office operators	5	VL	1	VL
Directory assistance operators	3	VL	1	VL
Switchboard operators	29	VL	6	VL
All other communications equipment operators	2	VL	0	VL

Source: U.S. Department of Labor. Bureau of Labor Statistics. *Occupational Projections and Training Data.* 1994 ed. Bulletin 2451. Washington, DC: U.S. Government Printing Office, May 1994, pp. 12-13. A statistical and research supplement to the 1994-1995 *Occupational Outlook Handbook. Notes:* Rankings are based on all detailed occupations in the National Industry-Occupation Matrix. Codes for describing the ranked variables are: VH - very high; H - high; L - low; or VL - very low. A dash (-) indicates data are not applicable.

★ 215 ★
Occupational Outlook: Job Openings

Job Openings for Computer and Peripheral Equipment Operators: 1992-2005

Table shows the average annual job openings due to growth, total replacement, and net replacement needs for 1992 through 2005. Jobs also are ranked by growth expected.

[In thousands]

Occupation	Annual average job openings due to growth and total replacement needs		Annual average job openings due to growth and net replacement needs	
	Number	Rank	Number	Rank
Computer operators and peripheral equipment operators	36	-	7	-
Computer operators[1]	33	VL	7	VL
Peripheral EDP equipment operators	3	VL	1	VL

Source: U.S. Department of Labor. Bureau of Labor Statistics. *Occupational Projections and Training Data.* 1994 ed. Bulletin 2451. Washington, DC: U.S. Government Printing Office, May 1994, pp. 12-13. A statistical and research supplement to the 1994-1995 *Occupational Outlook Handbook. Notes:* Rankings are based on all detailed occupations in the National Industry-Occupation Matrix. Codes for describing the ranked variables are: VH - very high; H - high; L - low; or VL - very low. A dash (-) indicates data are not applicable. 1. Except peripheral equipment.

★ 216 ★

Occupational Outlook: Job Openings

Job Openings for Computer, Mathematical, and Operations Research Occupations: 1992-2005

Table shows the average annual job openings due to growth, total replacement, and net replacement needs for 1992 through 2005. Jobs also are ranked by growth expected.

[In thousands]

Occupation	Annual average job openings due to growth and total replacement needs		Annual average job openings due to growth and net replacement needs	
	Number	Rank	Number	Rank
Computer, mathematical, and operations research occupations	135	-	65	-
Actuaries	1	VL	1	VL
Computer systems analysts, engineers, and scientists	125	-	61	-
Computer engineers and scientists	40	L	20	L
Systems analysts	85	L	42	H
Mathematicians and other mathematical scientists	1	VL	0	VL
Operations research analysts	6	VL	3	VL
Statisticians	1	VL	0	VL

Source: U.S. Department of Labor. Bureau of Labor Statistics. *Occupational Projections and Training Data.* 1994 ed. Bulletin 2451. Washington, DC: U.S. Government Printing Office, May 1994, pp. 6-7. A statistical and research supplement to the 1994-1995 *Occupational Outlook Handbook. Notes:* Rankings are based on all detailed occupations in the National Industry-Occupation Matrix. Codes for describing the ranked variables are: VH - very high; H - high; L - low; or VL - very low. A dash (-) indicates data are not applicable.

★ 217 ★

Occupational Outlook: Job Openings

Job Openings for Construction Trades: 1992-2005

Table shows the average annual job openings due to growth, total replacement, and net replacement needs for 1992 through 2005. Jobs also are ranked by growth expected.

[In thousands]

Occupation	Annual average job openings due to growth and total replacement needs		Annual average job openings due to growth and net replacement needs	
	Number	Rank	Number	Rank
Construction trades	579	-	135	-
Bricklayers and stonemasons	29	VL	6	VL
Carpenters	182	H	36	H
Carpet installers	7	VL	3	VL
Ceiling and tile installers	2	VL	0	VL
Concrete and terrazzo finishers	3	VL	4	VL
Drywall installers and finishers	33	VL	7	VL

[Continued]

★ 217 ★

Job Openings for Construction Trades: 1992-2005

[Continued]

Occupation	Annual average job openings due to growth and total replacement needs		Annual average job openings due to growth and net replacement needs	
	Number	Rank	Number	Rank
Electricians	42	L	18	L
Glaziers	7	VL	2	VL
Hard tile setters	5	VL	1	VL
Highway maintenance workers	22	VL	6	VL
Insulation workers	22	VL	4	VL
Painters and paperhangers, construction and maintenance	79	L	20	L
Paving, surfacing, and tamping equipment operators	15	VL	4	VL
Pipelayers and pipelaying pipefitters	6	VL	2	VL
Plasterers	5	VL	1	VL
Plumbers, pipefitters, and steamfitters	46	L	10	L
Roofers	41	L	4	VL
Structural and reinforcing metal workers	13	VL	3	VL
All other construction trades workers	20	VL	5	VL

Source: U.S. Department of Labor. Bureau of Labor Statistics. *Occupational Projections and Training Data.* 1994 ed. Bulletin 2451. Washington, DC: U.S. Government Printing Office, May 1994, pp. 20-21. A statistical and research supplement to the 1994-1995 *Occupational Outlook Handbook. Notes:* Rankings are based on all detailed occupations in the National Industry-Occupation Matrix. Codes for describing the ranked variables are: VH - very high; H - high; L - low; or VL - very low. A dash (-) indicates data are not applicable.

★ 218 ★

Occupational Outlook: Job Openings

Job Openings for Electrical and Electronic Equipment Mechanics, Installers, and Repairers: 1992-2005

Table shows the average annual job openings due to growth, total replacement, and net replacement needs for 1992 through 2005. Jobs also are ranked by growth expected.

[In thousands]

Occupation	Annual average job openings due to growth and total replacement needs		Annual average job openings due to growth and net replacement needs	
	Number	Rank	Number	Rank
Electrical and electronic equipment mechanics, installers, and repairers	36	-	16	-
Data processing equipment repairers	10	VL	4	VL
Electrical powerline installers and repairers	7	VL	4	VL
Electronic home entertainment equipment repairers	5	VL	1	VL
Electronics repairers, commercial and industrial equipment	10	VL	2	VL

[Continued]

★ 218 ★

Job Openings for Electrical and Electronic Equipment Mechanics, Installers, and Repairers: 1992-2005
[Continued]

Occupation	Annual average job openings due to growth and total replacement needs		Annual average job openings due to growth and net replacement needs	
	Number	Rank	Number	Rank
Station installers and repairers, telephone	1	VL	1	VL
Telephone and cable TV line installers and repairers	4	VL	4	VL
All other electrical and electronic equipment mechanics, installers, and repairers	4	VL	1	VL

Source: U.S. Department of Labor. Bureau of Labor Statistics. *Occupational Projections and Training Data.* 1994 ed. Bulletin 2451. Washington, DC: U.S. Government Printing Office, May 1994, pp. 22-23. A statistical and research supplement to the 1994-1995 *Occupational Outlook Handbook. Notes:* Rankings are based on all detailed occupations in the National Industry-Occupation Matrix. Codes for describing the ranked variables are: VH - very high; H - high; L - low; or VL - very low. A dash (-) indicates data are not applicable.

★ 219 ★

Occupational Outlook: Job Openings

Job Openings for Engineering and Science Technicians and Technologists: 1992-2005

Table shows the average annual job openings due to growth, total replacement, and net replacement needs for 1992 through 2005. Jobs also are ranked by growth expected.

[In thousands]

Occupation	Annual average job openings due to growth and total replacement needs		Annual average job openings due to growth and net replacement needs	
	Number	Rank	Number	Rank
Engineering and science technicians and technologists	165	-	43	-
Drafters	52	L	11	L
Engineering technicians	85	-	22	-
Electrical and electronic technicians and technologists	36	VL	10	L
All other engineering technicians and technologists	49	L	12	L
Science and mathematics technicians	28	VL	10	L

Source: U.S. Department of Labor. Bureau of Labor Statistics. *Occupational Projections and Training Data.* 1994 ed. Bulletin 2451. Washington, DC: U.S. Government Printing Office, May 1994, pp. 10-11. A statistical and research supplement to the 1994-1995 *Occupational Outlook Handbook. Notes:* Rankings are based on all detailed occupations in the National Industry-Occupation Matrix. Codes for describing the ranked variables are: VH - very high; H - high; L - low; or VL - very low. A dash (-) indicates data are not applicable.

★ 220 ★

Occupational Outlook: Job Openings

Job Openings for Engineers: 1992-2005

Table shows the average annual job openings due to growth, total replacement, and net replacement needs for 1992 through 2005. Jobs also are ranked by growth expected.

[In thousands]

Occupation	Annual average job openings due to growth and total replacement needs		Annual average job openings due to growth and net replacement needs	
	Number	Rank	Number	Rank
Engineers	83	-	52	-
Aeronautical and astronautical engineers	5	VL	2	VL
Chemical engineers	2	VL	2	VL
Civil enginers[1]	15	VL	7	VL
Electrical and electronics engineers	21	VL	15	L
Industrial engineers[2]	5	VL	5	VL
Mechanical engineers	14	VL	8	VL
Metallurgists and metallurgical, ceramic, and materials engineers	1	VL	1	VL
Mining engineers[3]	0	VL	0	VL
Nuclear engineers	1	VL	0	VL
Petroleum engineers	1	VL	0	VL
All other engineers	20	VL	11	L

Source: U.S. Department of Labor. Bureau of Labor Statistics. *Occupational Projections and Training Data.* 1994 ed. Bulletin 2451. Washington, DC: U.S. Government Printing Office, May 1994, pp. 4-7. A statistical and research supplement to the 1994-1995 *Occupational Outlook Handbook. Notes:* Rankings are based on all detailed occupations in the National Industry-Occupation Matrix. Codes for describing the ranked variables are: VH - very high; H - high; L - low; or VL - very low. A dash (-) indicates data are not applicable. 1. Including traffic engineers. 2. Excluding safety engineers. 3. Including mine safety engineers.

★ 221 ★

Occupational Outlook: Job Openings

Job Openings for Extractive Occupations: 1992-2005

Table shows the average annual job openings due to growth, total replacement, and net replacement needs for 1992 through 2005. Jobs also are ranked by growth expected.

[In thousands]

Occupation	Annual average job openings due to growth and total replacement needs		Annual average job openings due to growth and net replacement needs	
	Number	Rank	Number	Rank
Extractive and related workers[1]	43	-	4	-
Oil and gas extractive occupations	11	-	1	-
Roustabouts	5	VL	0	VL
All other oil and gas extraction occupations	6	VL	0	VL

[Continued]

★ 221 ★

Job Openings for Extractive Occupations: 1992-2005
[Continued]

Occupation	Annual average job openings due to growth and total replacement needs		Annual average job openings due to growth and net replacement needs	
	Number	Rank	Number	Rank
Mining, quarrying, and tunneling occupations	4	VL	0	VL
All other extraction and related workers	28	VL	3	VL

Source: U.S. Department of Labor. Bureau of Labor Statistics. *Occupational Projections and Training Data.* 1994 ed. Bulletin 2451. Washington, DC: U.S. Government Printing Office, May 1994, pp. 20-23. A statistical and research supplement to the 1994-1995 *Occupational Outlook Handbook. Notes:* Rankings are based on all detailed occupations in the National Industry-Occupation Matrix. Codes for describing the ranked variables are: VH - very high; H - high; L - low; or VL - very low. A dash (-) indicates data are not applicable. 1. Including blasters.

★ 222 ★

Occupational Outlook: Job Openings

Job Openings for Food Preparation and Service Occupations: 1992-2005

Table shows the average annual job openings due to growth, total replacement, and net replacement needs for 1992 through 2005. Jobs also are ranked by growth expected.

[In thousands]

Occupation	Annual average job openings due to growth and total replacement needs		Annual average job openings due to growth and net replacement needs	
	Number	Rank	Number	Rank
Food preparation and service occupations	3,276	-	427	-
Chefs, cooks, and kitchen workers	1,349	-	164	-
Cooks[1]	411	-	57	-
Bakers, bread and pastry	56	L	9	VL
Cooks, institution or cafeteria	127	L	14	L
Cooks, restaurant	228	H	35	H
Cooks, short order and fast food	225	H	35	H
Food preparation workers	684	VH	72	VH
Food and beverage service occupations	1,840	-	251	-
Bartenders	105	L	12	L
Dining room and cafeteria attendants and bar helpers	172	H	28	L
Food counter, fountain, and related workers	778	VH	79	VH
Hosts and hostesses, restaurant, lounge, or coffee shop	69	L	9	L
Waiters and waitresses	716	VH	122	VH
All other food preparation and service workers	87	L	12	L

Source: U.S. Department of Labor. Bureau of Labor Statistics. *Occupational Projections and Training Data.* 1994 ed. Bulletin 2451. Washington, DC: U.S. Government Printing Office, May 1994, pp. 16-17. A statistical and research supplement to the 1994-1995 *Occupational Outlook Handbook. Notes:* Rankings are based on all detailed occupations in the National Industry-Occupation Matrix. Codes for describing the ranked variables are: VH - very high; H - high; L - low; or VL - very low. A dash (-) indicates data are not applicable. 1. Except short order.

★ 223 ★

Occupational Outlook: Job Openings

Job Openings for Hand Helpers, Laborers, and Material Movers: 1992-2005

Table shows the average annual job openings due to growth, total replacement, and net replacement needs for 1992 through 2005. Jobs also are ranked by growth expected.

[In thousands]

Occupation	Annual average job openings due to growth and total replacement needs		Annual average job openings due to growth and net replacement needs	
	Number	Rank	Number	Rank
Helpers, laborers, and material movers, hand	1,309	-	176	-
Freight, stock, and material movers, hand	288	H	35	H
Hand packers and packagers	189	H	21	L
Helpers, construction trades	124	L	21	L
Machine feeders and offbearers	30	VL	8	VL
Parking lot attendants	13	VL	3	VL
Refuse collectors	18	VL	3	VL
Service station attendants	71	L	7	VL
Vehicle washers and equipment cleaners	93	L	7	VL
All other helpers, laborers, and material movers, hand	482	VH	70	H

Source: U.S. Department of Labor. Bureau of Labor Statistics. *Occupational Projections and Training Data.* 1994 ed. Bulletin 2451. Washington, DC: U.S. Government Printing Office, May 1994, pp. 34-35. A statistical and research supplement to the 1994-1995 *Occupational Outlook Handbook. Notes:* Rankings are based on all detailed occupations in the National Industry-Occupation Matrix. Codes for describing the ranked variables are: VH - very high; H - high; L - low; or VL - very low. A dash (-) indicates data are not applicable.

★ 224 ★

Occupational Outlook: Job Openings

Job Openings for Hand Workers: 1992-2005

Table shows the average annual job openings due to growth, total replacement, and net replacement needs for 1992 through 2005. Jobs also are ranked by growth expected. Data include assemblers and fabricators.

[In thousands]

Occupation	Annual average job openings due to growth and total replacement needs		Annual average job openings due to growth and net replacement needs	
	Number	Rank	Number	Rank
Hand workers[1]	424	-	68	-
Cannery workers	17	VL	2	VL
Coil winders, tapers, and finishers	3	VL	0	VL
Cutters and trimmers, hand	7	VL	1	VL
Electrical and electronic assemblers	33	VL	4	VL
Grinders and polishers, hand	11	VL	2	VL
Machine assemblers	8	VL	1	VL

[Continued]

★ 224 ★

Job Openings for Hand Workers: 1992-2005
[Continued]

Occupation	Annual average job openings due to growth and total replacement needs		Annual average job openings due to growth and net replacement needs	
	Number	Rank	Number	Rank
Meat, poultry, and fish cutters and trimmers, hand	26	VL	6	VL
Metal pourers and casters, basic shapes	1	VL	0	VL
Painting, coating, and decorating workers, hand	6	VL	1	VL
Portable machine cutters	1	VL	0	VL
Pressers, hand	2	VL	0	VL
Sewers, hand	2	VL	0	VL
Solderers and brazers	4	VL	1	VL
Welders and cutters	41	L	12	L
All other assemblers and fabricators	177	H	19	L
All other hand workers	83	L	19	L

Source: U.S. Department of Labor. Bureau of Labor Statistics. *Occupational Projections and Training Data.* 1994 ed. Bulletin 2451. Washington, DC: U.S. Government Printing Office, May 1994, pp. 32-33. A statistical and research supplement to the 1994-1995 *Occupational Outlook Handbook.*
Notes: Rankings are based on all detailed occupations in the National Industry-Occupation Matrix. Codes for describing the ranked variables are: VH - very high; H - high; L - low; or VL - very low. A dash (-) indicates data are not applicable. 1. Including assemblers and fabricators.

★ 225 ★
Occupational Outlook: Job Openings

Job Openings for Health Assessment and Treating Occupations: 1992-2005

Table shows the average annual job openings due to growth, total replacement, and net replacement needs for 1992 through 2005. Jobs also are ranked by growth expected.

[In thousands]

Occupation	Annual average job openings due to growth and total replacement needs		Annual average job openings due to growth and net replacement needs	
	Number	Rank	Number	Rank
Health assessment and treating occupations	261	-	118	-
Dietitians and nutritionists	4	VL	2	VL
Pharmacists	15	VL	6	VL
Physician assistants	6	VL	2	VL
Registered nurses	186	H	86	VH
Therapists	51	-	21	-
Occupational therapists	6	VL	2	VL
Physical therapists	17	VL	8	VL
Recreational therapists	4	VL	1	VL
Respiratory therapists	10	VL	4	VL

[Continued]

★ 225 ★

Job Openings for Health Assessment and Treating Occupations: 1992-2005
[Continued]

Occupation	Annual average job openings due to growth and total replacement needs		Annual average job openings due to growth and net replacement needs	
	Number	Rank	Number	Rank
Speech-language pathologists and audiologists	10	VL	4	VL
All other therapists	3	VL	1	VL

Source: U.S. Department of Labor. Bureau of Labor Statistics. *Occupational Projections and Training Data.* 1994 ed. Bulletin 2451. Washington, DC: U.S. Government Printing Office, May 1994, pp. 8-9. A statistical and research supplement to the 1994-1995 *Occupational Outlook Handbook. Notes:* Rankings are based on all detailed occupations in the National Industry-Occupation Matrix. Codes for describing the ranked variables are: VH - very high; H - high; L - low; or VL - very low. A dash (-) indicates data are not applicable.

★ 226 ★

Occupational Outlook: Job Openings

Job Openings for Health Diagnosing Occupations: 1992-2005

Table shows the average annual job openings due to growth, total replacement, and net replacement needs for 1992 through 2005. Jobs also are ranked by growth expected.

[In thousands]

Occupation	Annual average job openings due to growth and total replacement needs		Annual average job openings due to growth and net replacement needs	
	Number	Rank	Number	Rank
Health diagnosing occupations	49	-	35	-
Chiropractors	3	VL	2	VL
Dentists	6	VL	5	VL
Optometrists	1	VL	1	VL
Physicians	35	VL	25	L
Podiatrists	1	VL	1	VL
Veterinarians and veterinary inspectors	3	VL	2	VL

Source: U.S. Department of Labor. Bureau of Labor Statistics. *Occupational Projections and Training Data.* 1994 ed. Bulletin 2451. Washington, DC: U.S. Government Printing Office, May 1994, pp. 8-9. A statistical and research supplement to the 1994-1995 *Occupational Outlook Handbook. Notes:* Rankings are based on all detailed occupations in the National Industry-Occupation Matrix. Codes for describing the ranked variables are: VH - very high; H - high; L - low; or VL - very low. A dash (-) indicates data are not applicable.

★ 227 ★

Occupational Outlook: Job Openings

Job Openings for Health Service Occupations: 1992-2005

Table shows the average annual job openings due to growth, total replacement, and net replacement needs for 1992 through 2005. Jobs also are ranked by growth expected.

[In thousands]

Occupation	Annual average job openings due to growth and total replacement needs		Annual average job openings due to growth and net replacement needs	
	Number	Rank	Number	Rank
Health service occupations	520	-	106	-
Ambulance drivers and attendants[1]	3	VL	0	VL
Dental assistants	42	L	10	L
Medical assistants	31	VL	12	L
Nursing aides and psychiatric aides	361	-	64	-
Nursing aides, orderlies, and attendants	343	H	62	H
Psychiatric aides	19	VL	3	VL
Occupational therapy assistants and aides	3	VL	1	VL
Pharmacy assistants	9	VL	2	VL
Physical and corrective therapy assistants and aides	21	VL	5	VL
All other health service workers	49	L	11	L

Source: U.S. Department of Labor. Bureau of Labor Statistics. *Occupational Projections and Training Data.* 1994 ed. Bulletin 2451. Washington, DC: U.S. Government Printing Office, May 1994, pp. 16-19. A statistical and research supplement to the 1994-1995 *Occupational Outlook Handbook. Notes:* Rankings are based on all detailed occupations in the National Industry-Occupation Matrix. Codes for describing the ranked variables are: VH - very high; H - high; L - low; or VL - very low. A dash (-) indicates data are not applicable. 1. Except emergency medical technicians.

★ 228 ★

Occupational Outlook: Job Openings

Job Openings for Health Technicians and Technologists: 1992-2005

Table shows the average annual job openings due to growth, total replacement, and net replacement needs for 1992 through 2005. Jobs also are ranked by growth expected.

[In thousands]

Occupation	Annual average job openings due to growth and total replacement needs		Annual average job openings due to growth and net replacement needs	
	Number	Rank	Number	Rank
Health technicians and technologists	261	-	94	-
Cardiology technologists	2	VL	1	VL
Clinical lab technologists and technicians	27	VL	10	L
Dental hygienists	15	VL	5	VL
EEG technologists	1	VL	0	VL
EKG technicians	1	VL	0	VL
Emergency medical technicians	15	VL	5	VL

[Continued]

★ 228 ★

Job Openings for Health Technicians and Technologists: 1992-2005
[Continued]

Occupation	Annual average job openings due to growth and total replacement needs		Annual average job openings due to growth and net replacement needs	
	Number	Rank	Number	Rank
Licensed practical nurses	83	L	30	L
Medical records technicians	12	VL	5	VL
Nuclear medicine technologists	1	VL	1	VL
Opticians, dispensing and measuring	9	VL	3	VL
Psychiatric technicians	16	VL	2	VL
Radiologic technologists and technicians	16	VL	10	L
Surgical technologists	6	VL	2	VL
All other health professionals and paraprofessionals	56	L	20	L

Source: U.S. Department of Labor. Bureau of Labor Statistics. Occupational Projections and Training Data. 1994 ed. Bulletin 2451. Washington, DC: U.S. Government Printing Office, May 1994, pp. 10-11. A statistical and research supplement to the 1994-1995 Occupational Outlook Handbook. Notes: Rankings are based on all detailed occupations in the National Industry-Occupation Matrix. Codes for describing the ranked variables are: VH - very high; H - high; L - low; or VL - very low. A dash (-) indicates data are not applicable.

★ 229 ★

Occupational Outlook: Job Openings

Job Openings for Information Clerks: 1992-2005

Table shows the average annual job openings due to growth, total replacement, and net replacement needs for 1992 through 2005. Jobs also are ranked by growth expected.

[In thousands]

Occupation	Annual average job openings due to growth and total replacement needs		Annual average job openings due to growth and net replacement needs	
	Number	Rank	Number	Rank
Information clerks	443	-	57	-
Hotel desk clerks	52	L	8	VL
Interviewing clerks[1]	22	VL	4	VL
New accounts clerks, banking	27	VL	4	VL
Receptionists and information clerks	300	H	37	H
Reservation and transportation ticket agents and travel clerks	43	L	5	VL

Source: U.S. Department of Labor. Bureau of Labor Statistics. Occupational Projections and Training Data. 1994 ed. Bulletin 2451. Washington, DC: U.S. Government Printing Office, May 1994, pp. 12-13. A statistical and research supplement to the 1994-1995 Occupational Outlook Handbook. Notes: Rankings are based on all detailed occupations in the National Industry-Occupation Matrix. Codes for describing the ranked variables are: VH - very high; H - high; L - low; or VL - very low. A dash (-) indicates data are not applicable. 1. Except personnel and social welfare.

★ 230 ★

Occupational Outlook: Job Openings

Job Openings for Lawyers and Judicial Workers: 1992-2005

Table shows the average annual job openings due to growth, total replacement, and net replacement needs for 1992 through 2005. Jobs also are ranked by growth expected.

[In thousands]

Occupation	Annual average job openings due to growth and total replacement needs		Annual average job openings due to growth and net replacement needs	
	Number	Rank	Number	Rank
Lawyers and judicial workers	48	-	25	-
Judges, magistrates, and other judicial workers	4	VL	2	VL
Lawyers	43	L	24	L

Source: U.S. Department of Labor. Bureau of Labor Statistics. *Occupational Projections and Training Data.* 1994 ed. Bulletin 2451. Washington, DC: U.S. Government Printing Office, May 1994, pp. 8-9. A statistical and research supplement to the 1994-1995 *Occupational Outlook Handbook. Notes:* Rankings are based on all detailed occupations in the National Industry-Occupation Matrix. Codes for describing the ranked variables are: VH - very high; H - high; L - low; or VL - very low. A dash (-) indicates data are not applicable.

★ 231 ★

Occupational Outlook: Job Openings

Job Openings for Life Scientists: 1992-2005

Table shows the average annual job openings due to growth, total replacement, and net replacement needs for 1992 through 2005. Jobs also are ranked by growth expected.

[In thousands]

Occupation	Annual average job openings due to growth and total replacement needs		Annual average job openings due to growth and net replacement needs	
	Number	Rank	Number	Rank
Life scientists	14	-	8	-
Agricultural and food scientists	2	VL	1	VL
Biological scientists	6	VL	4	VL
Foresters and conservation scientists	2	VL	1	VL
Medical scientists	3	VL	2	VL
All other life scientists	0	VL	0	VL

Source: U.S. Department of Labor. Bureau of Labor Statistics. *Occupational Projections and Training Data.* 1994 ed. Bulletin 2451. Washington, DC: U.S. Government Printing Office, May 1994, pp. 6-7. A statistical and research supplement to the 1994-1995 *Occupational Outlook Handbook. Notes:* Rankings are based on all detailed occupations in the National Industry-Occupation Matrix. Codes for describing the ranked variables are: VH - very high; H - high; L - low; or VL - very low. A dash (-) indicates data are not applicable.

Occupational Outlook: Job Openings

Job Openings for Machine Setters, Set-up Operators, Operators, and Tenders: 1992-2005

Table shows the average annual job openings due to growth, total replacement, and net replacement needs for 1992 through 2005. Jobs also are ranked by growth expected. See also tables for specific machine workers; for example, printing, binding, and related workers.

[In thousands]

Occupation	Annual average job openings due to growth and total replacement needs		Annual average job openings due to growth and net replacement needs	
	Number	Rank	Number	Rank
Machine setters, set-up operators, operators and tenders	677	-	123	-
Combination machine tool setters, set-up operators, operators, and tenders	17	VL	4	VL
Machine forming operators and tenders, metal and plastic	11	VL	4	VL
Machine tool cut and form setters, operators, and tenders, metal and plastic	73	-	14	-
Drilling and boring machine tool setters and set-up operators, metal and plastic	5	VL	1	VL
Grinding machine setters and set-up operators, metal and plastic	9	VL	1	VL
Lathe and turning machine tool setters and set-up operators, metal and plastic	8	VL	1	VL
Machine tool cutting operators and tenders, metal and plastic	13	VL	2	VL
Numerical control machine tool operators and tenders, metal and plastic	12	VL	2	VL
Punching and machine setters and set-up operators, metal and plastic	5	VL	1	VL
All other machine tool cutting and forming operators	21	VL	4	VL
Other machine setters, set-up operators, and tenders	267	-	48	-
Boiler operators and tenders, low pressure	1	VL	1	VL
Cement and gluing machine operators and tenders	5	VL	1	VL
Chemical equipment controllers, operators, and tenders	10	VL	2	VL
Cooking and roasting machine operators and tenders, food and tobacco	4	VL	1	VL
Crushing and mixing machine operators and tenders	20	VL	3	VL
Cutting and slicing machine setters, operators, and tenders	10	VL	2	VL
Dairy processing equipment operators[1]	2	VL	1	VL
Electronic semiconductor processors	4	VL	1	VL
Extruding and forming machine setters, operators and tenders	16	VL	3	VL
Furnace, kiln, or kettle operators and tenders	2	VL	0	VL
Laundry and dry cleaning machine operators and tenders[2]	36	VL	9	VL
Motion picture projectionists	1	VL	0	VL
Packaging and filling machine operators and tenders	59	L	6	VL
Painting and coating machine operators	22	-	4	-

[Continued]

★ 232 ★

Job Openings for Machine Setters, Set-up Operators, Operators, and Tenders: 1992-2005

[Continued]

Occupation	Annual average job openings due to growth and total replacement needs		Annual average job openings due to growth and net replacement needs	
	Number	Rank	Number	Rank
Coating, painting, and spraying machine operators, tenders, setters, and set-up operators	15	VL	3	VL
Painters, transportation equipment	6	VL	1	VL
Paper goods machine setters and set-up operators	9	VL	2	VL
Photographic processing machine operators and tenders	10	VL	2	VL
Separating and still machine operators and tenders	2	VL	1	VL
Shoe sewing machine operators and tenders	3	VL	0	VL
Tire building machine operators	1	VL	0	VL
All other machine operators, tenders, setters, and set-up operators	47	L	8	VL

Source: U.S. Department of Labor. Bureau of Labor Statistics. *Occupational Projections and Training Data.* 1994 ed. Bulletin 2451. Washington, DC: U.S. Government Printing Office, May 1994, pp. 26-33. A statistical and research supplement to the 1994-1995 *Occupational Outlook Handbook. Notes:* Rankings are based on all detailed occupations in the National Industry-Occupation Matrix. Codes for describing the ranked variables are: VH - very high; H - high; L - low; or VL - very low. A dash (-) indicates data are not applicable. 1. Including setters. 2. Except pressing.

★ 233 ★

Occupational Outlook: Job Openings

Job Openings for Machinery Mechanics, Installers, and Repairers: 1992-2005

Table shows the average annual job openings due to growth, total replacement, and net replacement needs for 1992 through 2005. Jobs also are ranked by growth expected.

[In thousands]

Occupation	Annual average job openings due to growth and total replacement needs		Annual average job openings due to growth and net replacement needs	
	Number	Rank	Number	Rank
Machinery and related mechanics, installers, and repairers	230	-	57	-
Industrial machinery mechanics	35	VL	11	L
Maintenance repairers, general utility	185	H	43	H
Millwrights	10	VL	3	VL

Source: U.S. Department of Labor. Bureau of Labor Statistics. *Occupational Projections and Training Data.* 1994 ed. Bulletin 2451. Washington, DC: U.S. Government Printing Office, May 1994, pp. 22-23. A statistical and research supplement to the 1994-1995 *Occupational Outlook Handbook. Notes:* Rankings are based on all detailed occupations in the National Industry-Occupation Matrix. Codes for describing the ranked variables are: VH - very high; H - high; L - low; or VL - very low. A dash (-) indicates data are not applicable.

★ 234 ★

Occupational Outlook: Job Openings

Job Openings for Mail Clerks and Messengers: 1992-2005

Table shows the average annual job openings due to growth, total replacement, and net replacement needs for 1992 through 2005. Jobs also are ranked by growth expected.

[In thousands]

Occupation	Annual average job openings due to growth and total replacement needs		Annual average job openings due to growth and net replacement needs	
	Number	Rank	Number	Rank
Mail clerks and messengers	64	-	8	-
Mail clerks[1]	39	VL	6	VL
Messengers	26	VL	3	VL
Postal clerks and mail carriers	11	-	8	-
Postal mail carriers	6	VL	6	VL
Postal service clerks	5	VL	2	VL

Source: U.S. Department of Labor. Bureau of Labor Statistics. *Occupational Projections and Training Data.* 1994 ed. Bulletin 2451. Washington, DC: U.S. Government Printing Office, May 1994, pp. 12-15. A statistical and research supplement to the 1994-1995 *Occupational Outlook Handbook. Notes:* Rankings are based on all detailed occupations in the National Industry-Occupation Matrix. Codes for describing the ranked variables are: VH - very high; H - high; L - low; or VL - very low. A dash (-) indicates data are not applicable. 1. Except mail machine operators and postal service clerks.

★ 235 ★

Occupational Outlook: Job Openings

Job Openings for Management Support Occupations: 1992-2005

Table shows the average annual job openings due to growth, total replacement, and net replacement needs for 1992 through 2005. Jobs also are ranked by growth expected.

[In thousands]

Occupation	Annual average job openings due to growth and total replacement needs		Annual average job openings due to growth and net replacement needs	
	Number	Rank	Number	Rank
Management support occupations	516	-	143	-
Accountants and auditors	138	L	37	H
Budget analysts	9	VL	2	VL
Claims examiners, property and casualty insurance	5	VL	1	VL
Construction and building inspectors	6	VL	3	VL
Cost estimators	24	VL	6	VL
Credit analysts	4	VL	1	VL
Employment interviewers, private or public employment service	9	VL	3	VL
Inspectors and compliance officers[1]	14	VL	6	VL

[Continued]

★ 235 ★

Job Openings for Management Support Occupations: 1992-2005
[Continued]

Occupation	Annual average job openings due to growth and total replacement needs		Annual average job openings due to growth and net replacement needs	
	Number	Rank	Number	Rank
Loan officers and counselors	27	VL	8	VL
Management analysts	43	L	9	L
Personnel, training, and labor relations specialists	37	VL	12	L
Purchasing agents[2]	20	VL	4	VL
Tax examiners, collectors, and revenue agents	5	VL	2	VL
Underwriters	14	VL	4	VL
Wholesale and retail buyers[3]	26	VL	7	VL
All other management support workers	136	L	41	H

Source: U.S. Department of Labor. Bureau of Labor Statistics. *Occupational Projections and Training Data.* 1994 ed. Bulletin 2451. Washington, DC: U.S. Government Printing Office, May 1994, pp. 4-5. A statistical and research supplement to the 1994-1995 *Occupational Outlook Handbook. Notes:* Rankings are based on all detailed occupations in the National Industry-Occupation Matrix. Codes for describing the ranked variables are: VH - very high; H - high; L - low; or VL - very low. A dash (-) indicates data are not applicable. 1. Except construction. 2. Except wholesale, retail, and farm products. 3. Except farm products.

★ 236 ★

Occupational Outlook: Job Openings

Job Openings for Managerial and Administrative Occupations: 1992-2005

Table shows the average annual job openings due to growth, total replacement, and net replacement needs for 1992 through 2005. Jobs also are ranked by growth expected.

[In thousands]

Occupation	Annual average job openings due to growth and total replacement needs		Annual average job openings due to growth and net replacement needs	
	Number	Rank	Number	Rank
Managerial and administrative occupations	860	-	297	-
Administrative services managers	20	VL	6	VL
Communication, transportation, and utilities operations managers	12	VL	3	VL
Construction managers	23	VL	9	L
Education administrators	37	VL	15	L
Engineering, mathematical, and natural science managers	38	VL	14	L
Financial managers	66	L	24	L
Food service and lodging managers	67	L	26	L
Funeral directors and morticians	3	VL	1	VL
General managers and top executives	259	H	75	VH
Government chief executives and legislators	4	VL	2	VL
Industrial production managers	16	VL	4	VL

[Continued]

★ 236 ★

Job Openings for Managerial and Administrative Occupations: 1992-2005
[Continued]

Occupation	Annual average job openings due to growth and total replacement needs		Annual average job openings due to growth and net replacement needs	
	Number	Rank	Number	Rank
Blue-collar worker supervisors	155	H	63	H
Marketing, advertising, and public relations managers	56	L	20	L
Personnel, training, and labor relations managers	20	VL	9	VL
Property and real estate managers	33	VL	10	L
Purchasing managers	13	VL	7	VL
All other managers and administrators	194	H	72	VH

Source: U.S. Department of Labor. Bureau of Labor Statistics. *Occupational Projections and Training Data.* 1994 ed. Bulletin 2451. Washington, DC: U.S. Government Printing Office, May 1994, pp. 4-5. A statistical and research supplement to the 1994-1995 *Occupational Outlook Handbook. Notes:* Rankings are based on all detailed occupations in the National Industry-Occupation Matrix. Codes for describing the ranked variables are: VH - very high; H - high; L - low; or VL - very low. A dash (-) indicates data are not applicable.

★ 237 ★
Occupational Outlook: Job Openings

Job Openings for Material Recording, Scheduling, Dispatching, and Distributing Occupations: 1992-2005

Table shows the average annual job openings due to growth, total replacement, and net replacement needs for 1992 through 2005. Jobs also are ranked by growth expected.

[In thousands]

Occupation	Annual average job openings due to growth and total replacement needs		Annual average job openings due to growth and net replacement needs	
	Number	Rank	Number	Rank
Material recording, scheduling, dispatching, and distributing occupations	742	-	104	-
Dispatchers	30	-	7	-
Dispatchers[1]	20	VL	5	VL
Dispatchers, police, fire, and ambulance	10	VL	2	VL
Meter readers, utilities	9	VL	1	VL
Order fillers, wholesale and retail sales	36	VL	6	VL
Procurement clerks	11	VL	1	VL
Production, planning, and expediting clerks	42	L	8	VL
Stock clerks	371	VH	51	H
Traffic, shipping, and receiving clerks	189	H	22	L
Weighers, measurers, checkers, and samplers, recordkeeping	13	VL	2	VL

[Continued]

★ 237 ★

Job Openings for Material Recording, Scheduling, Dispatching, and Distributing Occupations: 1992-2005
[Continued]

Occupation	Annual average job openings due to growth and total replacement needs		Annual average job openings due to growth and net replacement needs	
	Number	Rank	Number	Rank
All other material recording, scheduling, and distribution workers	42	L	7	VL

Source: U.S. Department of Labor. Bureau of Labor Statistics. *Occupational Projections and Training Data.* 1994 ed. Bulletin 2451. Washington, DC: U.S. Government Printing Office, May 1994, pp. 14-15. A statistical and research supplement to the 1994-1995 *Occupational Outlook Handbook. Notes:* Rankings are based on all detailed occupations in the National Industry-Occupation Matrix. Codes for describing the ranked variables are: VH - very high; H - high; L - low; or VL - very low. A dash (-) indicates data are not applicable. 1. Except police, fire, and ambulance.

★ 238 ★

Occupational Outlook: Job Openings

Job Openings for Mechanics, Installers, and Repairers: 1992-2005

Table shows the average annual job openings due to growth, total replacement, and net replacement needs for 1992 through 2005. Jobs also are ranked by growth expected. See also tables for specific types of mechanics, installers, and repairers; for example, communications equipment mechanics, installers, and repairers.

[In thousands]

Occupation	Annual average job openings due to growth and total replacement needs		Annual average job openings due to growth and net replacement needs	
	Number	Rank	Number	Rank
Mechanics, installers, and repairers	600	-	175	-
Other mechanics, installers, and repairers	118	-	34	-
Bicycle repairers	3	VL	1	VL
Camera and photographic equipment repairers	1	VL	0	VL
Coin and vending machine servicers and repairers	2	VL	0	VL
Electric meter installers and repairers	1	VL	0	VL
Electromedical and biomedical equipment repairers	2	VL	0	VL
Elevator installers and repairers	2	VL	1	VL
Heat, air conditioning, and refrigeration mechanics and installers	20	VL	8	VL
Home appliance and power tool repairers	5	VL	2	VL
Locksmiths and safe repairers	2	VL	1	VL
Musical instrument repairers and tuners	1	VL	0	VL
Office machine and cash register servicers	1	VL	3	VL
Precision instrument repairers	4	VL	1	VL
Riggers	2	VL	0	VL
Tire repairers and changers	35	VL	4	VL

[Continued]

★ 238 ★

Job Openings for Mechanics, Installers, and Repairers: 1992-2005
[Continued]

Occupation	Annual average job openings due to growth and total replacement needs		Annual average job openings due to growth and net replacement needs	
	Number	Rank	Number	Rank
Watchmakers	1	VL	0	VL
All other mechanics, installers, and repairers	35	VL	12	L

Source: U.S. Department of Labor. Bureau of Labor Statistics. *Occupational Projections and Training Data.* 1994 ed. Bulletin 2451. Washington, DC: U.S. Government Printing Office, May 1994, pp. 22-25. A statistical and research supplement to the 1994-1995 *Occupational Outlook Handbook. Notes:* Rankings are based on all detailed occupations in the National Industry-Occupation Matrix. Codes for describing the ranked variables are: VH - very high; H - high; L - low; or VL - very low. A dash (-) indicates data are not applicable.

★ 239 ★

Occupational Outlook: Job Openings

Job Openings for Metal and Plastic Processing Machine Setters, Operators, and Related Workers: 1992-2005

Table shows the average annual job openings due to growth, total replacement, and net replacement needs for 1992 through 2005. Jobs also are ranked by growth expected.

[In thousands]

Occupation	Annual average job openings due to growth and total replacement needs		Annual average job openings due to growth and net replacement needs	
	Number	Rank	Number	Rank
Metal and plastic processing machine setters, operators, and related workers	45	-	12	-
Electrolytic plating machine operators and tenders, setters, and set-up operators, metal and plastic	6	VL	1	VL
Foundry mold assembly and shakeout workers	1	VL	0	VL
Furnace operators and tenders	2	VL	0	VL
Heaters, metal and plastic	0	VL	0	VL
Heating equipment setters and set-up operators, metal and plastic	1	VL	0	VL
Heat treating machine operators and tenders, metal and plastic	3	VL	1	VL
Metal molding machine operators, tenders, setters, and set-up operators	3	VL	1	VL
Nonelectrolytic plating machine operators, tenders, setters, and set-up operators, metal and plastic	1	VL	0	VL
Plastic molding machine operators, tenders, setters, and set-up operators	14	VL	5	VL

[Continued]

★ 239 ★

Job Openings for Metal and Plastic Processing Machine Setters, Operators, and Related Workers: 1992-2005

[Continued]

Occupation	Annual average job openings due to growth and total replacement needs		Annual average job openings due to growth and net replacement needs	
	Number	Rank	Number	Rank
All other metal and plastic machine setters, operators, and related workers	15	VL	3	VL

Source: U.S. Department of Labor. Bureau of Labor Statistics. *Occupational Projections and Training Data.* 1994 ed. Bulletin 2451. Washington, DC: U.S. Government Printing Office, May 1994, pp. 28-29. A statistical and research supplement to the 1994-1995 *Occupational Outlook Handbook. Notes:* Rankings are based on all detailed occupations in the National Industry-Occupation Matrix. Codes for describing the ranked variables are: VH - very high; H - high; L - low; or VL - very low. A dash (-) indicates data are not applicable.

★ 240 ★

Occupational Outlook: Job Openings

Job Openings for Metal Fabricating Machine Setters, Operators, and Related Workers: 1992-2005

Table shows the average annual job openings due to growth, total replacement, and net replacement needs for 1992 through 2005. Jobs also are ranked by growth expected.

[In thousands]

Occupation	Annual average job openings due to growth and total replacement needs		Annual average job openings due to growth and net replacement needs	
	Number	Rank	Number	Rank
Metal fabricating machine setters, operators, and related workers	17	-	4	-
Metal fabricators, structural metal products	6	VL	1	VL
Soldering and brazing machine operators and tenders	1	VL	0	VL
Welding machine setters, operators, and tenders	10	VL	3	VL

Source: U.S. Department of Labor. Bureau of Labor Statistics. *Occupational Projections and Training Data.* 1994 ed. Bulletin 2451. Washington, DC: U.S. Government Printing Office, May 1994, pp. 28-29. A statistical and research supplement to the 1994-1995 *Occupational Outlook Handbook. Notes:* Rankings are based on all detailed occupations in the National Industry-Occupation Matrix. Codes for describing the ranked variables are: VH - very high; H - high; L - low; or VL - very low. A dash (-) indicates data are not applicable.

★ 241 ★

Occupational Outlook: Job Openings

Job Openings for Personal Service Occupations: 1992-2005

Table shows the average annual job openings due to growth, total replacement, and net replacement needs for 1992 through 2005. Jobs also are ranked by growth expected.

[In thousands]

Occupation	Annual average job openings due to growth and total replacement needs		Annual average job openings due to growth and net replacement needs	
	Number	Rank	Number	Rank
Personal service occupations	806	-	148	-
Amusement and recreation attendants	97	L	13	L
Baggage porters and bellhops	12	VL	2	VL
Barbers	4	VL	2	VL
Child care workers	350	VH	39	H
Cosmetologists and related workers	122	-	28	-
Hairdressers, hairstylists, and cosmetologists	113	L	26	L
Manicurists	7	VL	2	VL
Shampooers	2	VL	0	VL
Flight attendants	11	VL	6	VL
Homemaker-home health aides	187	-	55	-
Home health aides	145	H	41	H
Personal and home care aides	41	L	14	L
Ushers, lobby attendants, and ticket takers	24	VL	3	VL

Source: U.S. Department of Labor. Bureau of Labor Statistics. *Occupational Projections and Training Data.(8U* 1994 ed. Bulletin 2451. Washington, DC: U.S. Government Printing Office, May 1994, pp. 18-19. A statistical and research supplement to the 1994-1995 *Occupational Outlook Handbook. Notes:* Rankings are based on all detailed occupations in the National Industry-Occupation Matrix. Codes for describing the ranked variables are: VH - very high; H - high; L - low; or VL - very low. A dash (-) indicates data are not applicable.

★ 242 ★

Occupational Outlook: Job Openings

Job Openings for Physical Scientists: 1992-2005

Table shows the average annual job openings due to growth, total replacement, and net replacement needs for 1992 through 2005. Jobs also are ranked by growth expected.

[In thousands]

Occupation	Annual average job openings due to growth and total replacement needs		Annual average job openings due to growth and net replacement needs	
	Number	Rank	Number	Rank
Physical scientists	17	-	8	-
Chemists	10	VL	4	VL
Geologists, geophysicists, and oceanographers	2	VL	2	VL
Meteorologists	1	VL	0	VL

[Continued]

★ 242 ★

Job Openings for Physical Scientists: 1992-2005
[Continued]

Occupation	Annual average job openings due to growth and total replacement needs		Annual average job openings due to growth and net replacement needs	
	Number	Rank	Number	Rank
Physicists and astronomers	1	VL	1	VL
All other physical scientists	3	VL	2	VL

Source: U.S. Department of Labor. Bureau of Labor Statistics. *Occupational Projections and Training Data.* 1994 ed. Bulletin 2451. Washington, DC: U.S. Government Printing Office, May 1994, pp. 6-7. A statistical and research supplement to the 1994-1995 *Occupational Outlook Handbook.*
Notes: Rankings are based on all detailed occupations in the National Industry-Occupation Matrix. Codes for describing the ranked variables are: VH - very high; H - high; L - low; or VL - very low. A dash (-) indicates data are not applicable.

★ 243 ★

Occupational Outlook: Job Openings

Job Openings for Plant and System Occupations: 1992-2005

Table shows the average annual job openings due to growth, total replacement, and net replacement needs for 1992 through 2005. Jobs also are ranked by growth expected.

[In thousands]

Occupation	Annual average job openings due to growth and total replacement needs		Annual average job openings due to growth and net replacement needs	
	Number	Rank	Number	Rank
Plant and system occupations	17	-	11	-
Chemical plant and system operators	2	VL	1	VL
Electric power generating plant operators, distributors, and dispatchers	2	-	1	-
Power distributors and dispatchers	1	VL	0	VL
Power generating and reactor plant operators	2	VL	1	VL
Gas and petroleum plant and system occupations	1	VL	1	VL
Stationary engineers	1	VL	1	VL
Water and liquid waste treatment plant and system operators	6	VL	3	VL
All other plant and system operators	5	VL	3	VL

Source: U.S. Department of Labor. Bureau of Labor Statistics. *Occupational Projections and Training Data.* 1994 ed. Bulletin 2451. Washington, DC: U.S. Government Printing Office, May 1994, pp. 26-27. A statistical and research supplement to the 1994-1995 *Occupational Outlook Handbook.*
Notes: Rankings are based on all detailed occupations in the National Industry-Occupation Matrix. Codes for describing the ranked variables are: VH - very high; H - high; L - low; or VL - very low. A dash (-) indicates data are not applicable.

★ 244 ★

Occupational Outlook: Job Openings

Job Openings for Precision Assemblers: 1992-2005

Table shows the average annual job openings due to growth, total replacement, and net replacement needs for 1992 through 2005. Jobs also are ranked by growth expected.

[In thousands]

Occupation	Annual average job openings due to growth and total replacement needs		Annual average job openings due to growth and net replacement needs	
	Number	Rank	Number	Rank
Assemblers, precision	40	-	8	-
Aircraft assemblers, precision	2	VL	1	VL
Electrical and electronic equipment assemblers, precision	21	VL	3	VL
Electromechanical equipment assemblers, precision	7	VL	1	VL
Fitters, structural metal, precision	1	VL	0	VL
Machine builders and other precision machine assemblers	5	VL	1	VL
All other precision assemblers	4	VL	1	VL

Source: U.S. Department of Labor. Bureau of Labor Statistics. *Occupational Projections and Training Data.* 1994 ed. Bulletin 2451. Washington, DC: U.S. Government Printing Office, May 1994, pp. 24-25. A statistical and research supplement to the 1994-1995 *Occupational Outlook Handbook. Notes:* Rankings are based on all detailed occupations in the National Industry-Occupation Matrix. Codes for describing the ranked variables are: VH - very high; H - high; L - low; or VL - very low. A dash (-) indicates data are not applicable.

★ 245 ★

Occupational Outlook: Job Openings

Job Openings for Precision Food Workers: 1992-2005

Table shows the average annual job openings due to growth, total replacement, and net replacement needs for 1992 through 2005. Jobs also are ranked by growth expected.

[In thousands]

Occupation	Annual average job openings due to growth and total replacement needs		Annual average job openings due to growth and net replacement needs	
	Number	Rank	Number	Rank
Food workers, precision	47	-	8	-
Bakers, manufacturing	8	VL	1	VL
Butchers and meat cutters	33	VL	6	VL
All other precision food and tobacco workers	7	VL	1	VL

Source: U.S. Department of Labor. Bureau of Labor Statistics. *Occupational Projections and Training Data.* 1994 ed. Bulletin 2451. Washington, DC: U.S. Government Printing Office, May 1994, pp. 24-25. A statistical and research supplement to the 1994-1995 *Occupational Outlook Handbook. Notes:* Rankings are based on all detailed occupations in the National Industry-Occupation Matrix. Codes for describing the ranked variables are: VH - very high; H - high; L - low; or VL - very low. A dash (-) indicates data are not applicable.

★ 246 ★

Occupational Outlook: Job Openings

Job Openings for Precision Metal Workers: 1992-2005

Table shows the average annual job openings due to growth, total replacement, and net replacement needs for 1992 through 2005. Jobs also are ranked by growth expected.

[In thousands]

Occupation	Annual average job openings due to growth and total replacement needs		Annual average job openings due to growth and net replacement needs	
	Number	Rank	Number	Rank
Metal workers, precision	84	-	23	-
Boilermakers	2	VL	1	VL
Jewelers and silversmiths	3	VL	1	VL
Machinists	26	VL	8	VL
Sheet metal workers and duct installers	40	L	8	VL
Shipfitters	1	VL	0	VL
Tool and die makers	5	VL	4	VL
All other precision metal workers	7	VL	2	VL

Source: U.S. Department of Labor. Bureau of Labor Statistics. *Occupational Projections and Training Data.* 1994 ed. Bulletin 2451. Washington, DC: U.S. Government Printing Office, May 1994, pp. 24-25. A statistical and research supplement to the 1994-1995 *Occupational Outlook Handbook. Notes:* Rankings are based on all detailed occupations in the National Industry-Occupation Matrix. Codes for describing the ranked variables are: VH - very high; H - high; L - low; or VL - very low. A dash (-) indicates data are not applicable.

★ 247 ★

Occupational Outlook: Job Openings

Job Openings for Precision Printing Workers: 1992-2005

Table shows the average annual job openings due to growth, total replacement, and net replacement needs for 1992 through 2005. Jobs also are ranked by growth expected.

[In thousands]

Occupation	Annual average job openings due to growth and total replacement needs		Annual average job openings due to growth and net replacement needs	
	Number	Rank	Number	Rank
Printing workers, precision	22	-	6	-
Bookbinders	1	VL	0	VL
Prepress printing workers, precision	17	-	5	-
Camera operators	2	VL	0	VL
Compositors and typesetters, precision	1	VL	0	VL
Electronic pagination systems workers	4	VL	1	VL
Job printers	1	VL	0	VL
Paste-up workers	2	VL	0	VL
Photoengravers	1	VL	0	VL

[Continued]

★ 247 ★

Job Openings for Precision Printing Workers: 1992-2005
[Continued]

Occupation	Annual average job openings due to growth and total replacement needs		Annual average job openings due to growth and net replacement needs	
	Number	Rank	Number	Rank
Platemakers	2	VL	0	VL
Strippers, printing	5	VL	1	VL
All other printing workers, precision	3	VL	1	VL

Source: U.S. Department of Labor. Bureau of Labor Statistics. *Occupational Projections and Training Data.* 1994 ed. Bulletin 2451. Washington, DC: U.S. Government Printing Office, May 1994, pp. 24-27. A statistical and research supplement to the 1994-1995 *Occupational Outlook Handbook. Notes:* Rankings are based on all detailed occupations in the National Industry-Occupation Matrix. Codes for describing the ranked variables are: VH - very high; H - high; L - low; or VL - very low. A dash (-) indicates data are not applicable.

★ 248 ★

Occupational Outlook: Job Openings

Job Openings for Precision Production Occupations: 1992-2005

Table shows the average annual job openings due to growth, total replacement, and net replacement needs for 1992 through 2005. Jobs also are ranked by growth expected. See also tables for specific types of precision production occupations; for example, precision food workers.

[In thousands]

Occupation	Annual average job openings due to growth and total replacement needs		Annual average job openings due to growth and net replacement needs	
	Number	Rank	Number	Rank
Production occupations, precision	353	-	81	-
Inspectors, testers, and graders, precision	80	L	14	L
Precision workers, other	28	-	7	-
Dental lab technicians, precision	4	VL	2	VL
Optical goods workers, precision	2	VL	1	VL
Photographic process workers, precision	3	VL	1	VL
All other precision workers	19	VL	4	VL

Source: U.S. Department of Labor. Bureau of Labor Statistics. *Occupational Projections and Training Data.* 1994 ed. Bulletin 2451. Washington, DC: U.S. Government Printing Office, May 1994, pp. 24-27. A statistical and research supplement to the 1994-1995 *Occupational Outlook Handbook. Notes:* Rankings are based on all detailed occupations in the National Industry-Occupation Matrix. Codes for describing the ranked variables are: VH - very high; H - high; L - low; or VL - very low. A dash (-) indicates data are not applicable.

★ 249 ★

Occupational Outlook: Job Openings

Job Openings for Precision Textile, Apparel, and Furnishings Workers: 1992-2005

Table shows the average annual job openings due to growth, total replacement, and net replacement needs for 1992 through 2005. Jobs also are ranked by growth expected.

[In thousands]

Occupation	Annual average job openings due to growth and total replacement needs		Annual average job openings due to growth and net replacement needs	
	Number	Rank	Number	Rank
Textile, apparel, and furnishings workers, precision	31	-	6	-
Custom tailors and sewers	11	VL	2	VL
Patternmakers and layout workers, fabric and apparel	2	VL	0	VL
Shoe and leather workers and repairers, precision	2	VL	0	VL
Upholsters	6	VL	2	VL
All other precision textile, apparel, and furnishings workers	10	VL	1	VL

Source: U.S. Department of Labor. Bureau of Labor Statistics. *Occupational Projections and Training Data.* 1994 ed. Bulletin 2451. Washington, DC: U.S. Government Printing Office, May 1994, pp. 26-27. A statistical and research supplement to the 1994-1995 *Occupational Outlook Handbook.* *Notes:* Rankings are based on all detailed occupations in the National Industry-Occupation Matrix. Codes for describing the ranked variables are: VH - very high; H - high; L - low; or VL - very low. A dash (-) indicates data are not applicable.

★ 250 ★

Occupational Outlook: Job Openings

Job Openings for Precision Woodworkers: 1992-2005

Table shows the average annual job openings due to growth, total replacement, and net replacement needs for 1992 through 2005. Jobs also are ranked by growth expected.

[In thousands]

Occupation	Annual average job openings due to growth and total replacement needs		Annual average job openings due to growth and net replacement needs	
	Number	Rank	Number	Rank
Woodworkers, precision	21	-	9	-
Cabinetmakers and bench carpenters	6	VL	5	VL
Furniture finishers	8	VL	1	VL
Wood machinists	2	VL	2	VL
All other precision woodworkers	5	VL	1	VL

Source: U.S. Department of Labor. Bureau of Labor Statistics. *Occupational Projections and Training Data.* 1994 ed. Bulletin 2451. Washington, DC: U.S. Government Printing Office, May 1994, pp. 26-27. A statistical and research supplement to the 1994-1995 *Occupational Outlook Handbook. Notes:* Rankings are based on all detailed occupations in the National Industry-Occupation Matrix. Codes for describing the ranked variables are: VH - very high; H - high; L - low; or VL - very low. A dash (-) indicates data are not applicable.

★ 251 ★

Occupational Outlook: Job Openings

Job Openings for Printing, Binding, and Related Workers: 1992-2005

Table shows the average annual job openings due to growth, total replacement, and net replacement needs for 1992 through 2005. Jobs also are ranked by growth expected.

[In thousands]

Occupation	Annual average job openings due to growth and total replacement needs		Annual average job openings due to growth and net replacement needs	
	Number	Rank	Number	Rank
Printing, binding, and related workers	46	-	14	-
Bindery machine operators and set-up operators	10	VL	3	VL
Prepress printing workers, production	3	-	1	-
Photoengraving and lithographic machine operators and tenders	1	VL	0	VL
Typesetting and composing machine operators and tenders	2	VL	0	VL
Printing press operators	24	-	7	-
Letterpress operators	1	VL	0	VL
Offset lithographic press operators	10	VL	4	VL
Printing press machine setters, operators, and tenders	11	VL	3	VL

[Continued]

★ 251 ★

Job Openings for Printing, Binding, and Related Workers: 1992-2005
[Continued]

Occupation	Annual average job openings due to growth and total replacement needs		Annual average job openings due to growth and net replacement needs	
	Number	Rank	Number	Rank
All other printing press setters and set-up operators	2	VL	1	VL
Screen printing machine setters and set-up operators	3	VL	1	VL
All other printing, binding, and related workers	6	VL	2	VL

Source: U.S. Department of Labor. Bureau of Labor Statistics. *Occupational Projections and Training Data.* 1994 ed. Bulletin 2451. Washington, DC: U.S. Government Printing Office, May 1994, pp. 28-31. A statistical and research supplement to the 1994-1995 *Occupational Outlook Handbook. Notes:* Rankings are based on all detailed occupations in the National Industry-Occupation Matrix. Codes for describing the ranked variables are: VH - very high; H - high; L - low; or VL - very low. A dash (-) indicates data are not applicable.

★ 252 ★
Occupational Outlook: Job Openings

Job Openings for Private Household Workers: 1992-2005

Table shows the average annual job openings due to growth, total replacement, and net replacement needs for 1992 through 2005. Jobs also are ranked by growth expected.

[In thousands]

Occupation	Annual average job openings due to growth and total replacement needs		Annual average job openings due to growth and net replacement needs	
	Number	Rank	Number	Rank
Private household workers	239	-	20	-
Child care workers, private household	151	H	13	L
Cleaners and servants, private household	82	L	6	VL
Cooks, private household	2	VL	0	VL
Housekeepers and butlers	5	VL	0	VL

Source: U.S. Department of Labor. Bureau of Labor Statistics. *Occupational Projections and Training Data.* 1994 ed. Bulletin 2451. Washington, DC: U.S. Government Printing Office, May 1994, pp. 18-19. A statistical and research supplement to the 1994-1995 *Occupational Outlook Handbook. Notes:* Rankings are based on all detailed occupations in the National Industry-Occupation Matrix. Codes for describing the ranked variables are: VH - very high; H - high; L - low; or VL - very low. A dash (-) indicates data are not applicable.

★ 253 ★

Occupational Outlook: Job Openings

Job Openings for Protective Service Occupations: 1992-2005

Table shows the average annual job openings due to growth, total replacement, and net replacement needs for 1992 through 2005. Jobs also are ranked by growth expected.

[In thousands]

Occupation	Annual average job openings due to growth and total replacement needs		Annual average job openings due to growth and net replacement needs	
	Number	Rank	Number	Rank
Protective service occupations	743	-	165	-
Firefighting occupations	14	-	14	-
Fire inspection occupations	1	VL	1	VL
Firefighters	13	VL	11	L
Firefighting and prevention supervisors	3	VL	3	VL
Law enforcement occupations	76	-	48	-
Correction officers	48	L	18	L
Police and detectives	30	-	30	-
Police and detective supervisors	5	VL	5	VL
Police detectives and investigators	3	VL	3	VL
Police patrol officers	17	VL	19	L
Sheriffs and deputy sheriffs	3	VL	2	VL
Other law enforcement occupations	4	VL	1	VL
Other protective services workers	357	-	62	-
Crossing guards	17	VL	2	VL
Detectives[1]	21	VL	4	VL
Guards	261	H	46	H
All other protective services workers	57	L	9	L

Source: U.S. Department of Labor. Bureau of Labor Statistics. *Occupational Projections and Training Data.* 1994 ed. Bulletin 2451. Washington, DC: U.S. Government Printing Office, May 1994, pp. 18-19. A statistical and research supplement to the 1994-1995 *Occupational Outlook Handbook. Notes:* Rankings are based on all detailed occupations in the National Industry-Occupation Matrix. Codes for describing the ranked variables are: VH - very high; H - high; L - low; or VL - very low. A dash (-) indicates data are not applicable. 1. Except public.

★ 254 ★

Occupational Outlook: Job Openings

Job Openings for Records Processing Occupations: 1992-2005

Table shows the average annual job openings due to growth, total replacement, and net replacement needs for 1992 through 2005. Jobs also are ranked by growth expected.

[In thousands]

Occupation	Annual average job openings due to growth and total replacement needs		Annual average job openings due to growth and net replacement needs	
	Number	Rank	Number	Rank
Records processing occupations	687	-	97	-
Advertising clerks	4	VL	1	VL
Brokerage clerks	16	VL	2	VL
Correspondence clerks	6	VL	1	VL
File clerks	99	L	12	L
Financial records occupations	456	-	63	-
Billing, cost, and rate clerks	72	L	11	L
Billing, posting, and calculating machine operators	21	VL	3	VL
Bookkeeping, accounting, and auditing clerks	342	H	45	H
Payroll and timekeeping clerks	22	VL	4	VL
Library assistants and bookmobile drivers	34	VL	5	VL
Order clerks, materials, merchandise, and service	52	L	7	VL
Personnel clerks[1]	15	VL	5	VL
Statement clerks	6	VL	1	VL

Source: U.S. Department of Labor. Bureau of Labor Statistics. *Occupational Projections and Training Data.* 1994 ed. Bulletin 2451. Washington, DC: U.S. Government Printing Office, May 1994, pp. 14-15. A statistical and research supplement to the 1994-1995 *Occupational Outlook Handbook. Notes:* Rankings are based on all detailed occupations in the National Industry-Occupation Matrix. Codes for describing the ranked variables are: VH - very high; H - high; L - low; or VL - very low. A dash (-) indicates data are not applicable. 1. Except payroll and timekeeping.

★ 255 ★

Occupational Outlook: Job Openings

Job Openings for Sales Occupations: 1992-2005

Table shows the average annual job openings due to growth, total replacement, and net replacement needs for 1992 through 2005. Jobs also are ranked by growth expected.

[In thousands]

Occupation	Annual average job openings due to growth and total replacement needs		Annual average job openings due to growth and net replacement needs	
	Number	Rank	Number	Rank
Cashiers	1,044	VH	143	VH
Counter and rental clerks	94	L	11	L
Insurance sales workers	40	L	14	L
Marketing and sales worker supervisors	276	H	65	H

[Continued]

★ 255 ★

Job Openings for Sales Occupations: 1992-2005
[Continued]

Occupation	Annual average job openings due to growth and total replacement needs		Annual average job openings due to growth and net replacement needs	
	Number	Rank	Number	Rank
Real estate agents, brokers, and appraisers	68	-	11	-
Brokers, real estate	12	VL	2	VL
Real estate appraisers	9	VL	2	VL
Sales agents, real estate	47	L	7	VL
Salespersons, retail	1,232	VH	167	VH
Securities and financial services sales workers	31	VL	8	VL
Travel agents	46	L	8	VL
All other sales and related workers	642	VH	110	VH

Source: U.S. Department of Labor. Bureau of Labor Statistics. *Occupational Projections and Training Data.* 1994 ed. Bulletin 2451. Washington, DC: U.S. Government Printing Office, May 1994, pp. 12-13. A statistical and research supplement to the 1994-1995 *Occupational Outlook Handbook. Notes:* Rankings are based on all detailed occupations in the National Industry-Occupation Matrix. Codes for describing the ranked variables are: VH - very high; H - high; L - low; or VL - very low. A dash (-) indicates data are not applicable.

★ 256 ★

Occupational Outlook: Job Openings

Job Openings for Secretaries, Stenographers, and Typists: 1992-2005

Table shows the average annual job openings due to growth, total replacement, and net replacement needs for 1992 through 2005. Jobs also are ranked by growth expected.

[In thousands]

Occupation	Annual average job openings due to growth and total replacement needs		Annual average job openings due to growth and net replacement needs	
	Number	Rank	Number	Rank
Secretaries, stenographers, and typists	692	-	118	-
Secretaries	514	-	102	-
Legal secretaries	62	L	18	L
Medical secretaries	48	L	13	L
Secretaries, other[1]	404	VH	70	H
Stenographers	16	VL	2	VL
Typists and word processors	162	H	13	L

Source: U.S. Department of Labor. Bureau of Labor Statistics. *Occupational Projections and Training Data.* 1994 ed. Bulletin 2451. Washington, DC: U.S. Government Printing Office, May 1994, pp. 14-15. A statistical and research supplement to the 1994-1995 *Occupational Outlook Handbook. Notes:* Rankings are based on all detailed occupations in the National Industry-Occupation Matrix. Codes for describing the ranked variables are: VH - very high; H - high; L - low; or VL - very low. A dash (-) indicates data are not applicable. 1. Excludes legal and medical secretaries.

★ 257 ★

Occupational Outlook: Job Openings

Job Openings for Social, Recreational, and Religious Workers: 1992-2005

Table shows the average annual job openings due to growth, total replacement, and net replacement needs for 1992 through 2005. Jobs also are ranked by growth expected.

[In thousands]

Occupation	Annual average job openings due to growth and total replacement needs		Annual average job openings due to growth and net replacement needs	
	Number	Rank	Number	Rank
Social, recreational, and religious workers	174	-	59	-
Clergy	16	VL	7	VL
Directors, religious activities and education	9	VL	2	VL
Human services workers	51	L	22	L
Recreation workers	32	L	8	VL
Social workers	67	L	20	L

Source: U.S. Department of Labor. Bureau of Labor Statistics. *Occupational Projections and Training Data.* 1994 ed. Bulletin 2451. Washington, DC: U.S. Government Printing Office, May 1994, pp. 6-9. A statistical and research supplement to the 1994-1995 *Occupational Outlook Handbook. Notes:* Rankings are based on all detailed occupations in the National Industry-Occupation Matrix. Codes for describing the ranked variables are: VH - very high; H - high; L - low; or VL - very low. A dash (-) indicates data are not applicable.

★ 258 ★

Occupational Outlook: Job Openings

Job Openings for Social Scientists: 1992-2005

Table shows the average annual job openings due to growth, total replacement, and net replacement needs for 1992 through 2005. Jobs also are ranked by growth expected.

[In thousands]

Occupation	Annual average job openings due to growth and total replacement needs		Annual average job openings due to growth and net replacement needs	
	Number	Rank	Number	Rank
Social scientists	34	-	11	-
Economists	12	VL	2	VL
Psychologists	14	VL	6	VL
Urban and regional planners	4	VL	1	VL
All other social scientists	4	VL	1	VL

Source: U.S. Department of Labor. Bureau of Labor Statistics. *Occupational Projections and Training Data.* 1994 ed. Bulletin 2451. Washington, DC: U.S. Government Printing Office, May 1994, pp. 6-7. A statistical and research supplement to the 1994-1995 *Occupational Outlook Handbook. Notes:* Rankings are based on all detailed occupations in the National Industry-Occupation Matrix. Codes for describing the ranked variables are: VH - very high; H - high; L - low; or VL - very low. A dash (-) indicates data are not applicable.

★ 259 ★

Occupational Outlook: Job Openings

Job Openings for Teachers, Librarians, and Counselors: 1992-2005

Table shows the average annual job openings due to growth, total replacement, and net replacement needs for 1992 through 2005. Jobs also are ranked by growth expected.

[In thousands]

Occupation	Annual average job openings due to growth and total replacement needs		Annual average job openings due to growth and net replacement needs	
	Number	Rank	Number	Rank
Teachers, librarians, and counselors	1,017	-	261	-
College and university faculty	132	L	39	H
Teachers, elementary	176	H	52	H
Teachers, preschool and kindergarten	85	L	22	L
Teachers, secondary school	165	H	66	H
Teachers, special education	51	L	25	L
Other teachers and instructors	230	-	24	-
Adult and vocational education teachers	151	-	16	-
Instructors, adult (nonvocational) education	63	L	6	VL
Teachers and instructors, vocational education and training	88	L	10	L
Farm and home management advisors	4	VL	0	VL
Instructors and coaches, sports and physical training	75	L	8	VL
All other teachers and instructors	134	L	22	L
Librarians, archivists, curators, and related workers	19	-	5	-
Curators, archivists, museum technicians, and restorers	2	VL	1	VL
Librarians, professional	17	VL	4	VL
Counselors	25	VL	6	VL

Source: U.S. Department of Labor. Bureau of Labor Statistics. *Occupational Projections and Training Data.* 1994 ed. Bulletin 2451. Washington, DC: U.S. Government Printing Office, May 1994, pp. 8-9. A statistical and research supplement to the 1994-1995 *Occupational Outlook Handbook. Notes:* Rankings are based on all detailed occupations in the National Industry-Occupation Matrix. Codes for describing the ranked variables are: VH - very high; H - high; L - low; or VL - very low. A dash (-) indicates data are not applicable.

★ 260 ★

Occupational Outlook: Job Openings

Job Openings for Technicians: 1992-2005

Table shows the average annual job openings due to growth, total replacement, and net replacement needs for 1992 through 2005. Jobs also are ranked by growth expected. See also tables for health technologists and technicians and for engineering and science technicians and technologists.

[In thousands]

Occupation	Annual average job openings due to growth and total replacement needs		Annual average job openings due to growth and net replacement needs	
	Number	Rank	Number	Rank
Technicians[1]	137	-	46	-
Air traffic controllers	3	VL	1	VL
Aircraft pilots and flight engineers	9	VL	5	VL
Broadcast technicians	4	VL	1	VL
Computer programmers	73	L	26	L
Legal assistants and technicians[2]	32	-	10	-
Paralegals	21	VL	7	VL
Title examiners and searchers	4	VL	1	VL
All other legal assistants[3]	7	VL	2	VL
Programmers, numerical, tool, and process control	1	VL	0	VL
Technical assistants, library	11	VL	3	VL
All other technicians	4	VL	1	VL

Source: U.S. Department of Labor. Bureau of Labor Statistics. *Occupational Projections and Training Data.* 1994 ed. Bulletin 2451. Washington, DC: U.S. Government Printing Office, May 1994, pp. 10-13. A statistical and research supplement to the 1994-1995 *Occupational Outlook Handbook. Notes:* Rankings are based on all detailed occupations in the National Industry-Occupation Matrix. Codes for describing the ranked variables are: VH - very high; H - high; L - low; or VL - very low. A dash (-) indicates data are not applicable. 1. Excludes health, engineering, and science technicians. 2. Except clerical. 3. Includes law clerks.

★ 261 ★

Occupational Outlook: Job Openings

Job Openings for Textile and Related Setters, Operators, and Workers: 1992-2005

Table shows the average annual job openings due to growth, total replacement, and net replacement needs for 1992 through 2005. Jobs also are ranked by growth expected.

[In thousands]

Occupation	Annual average job openings due to growth and total replacement needs		Annual average job openings due to growth and net replacement needs	
	Number	Rank	Number	Rank
Textile and related setters, operators, and related workers	182	-	23	-
Extruding and forming machine operators and tenders, synthetic or glass fibers	2	VL	1	VL

[Continued]

★ 261 ★

Job Openings for Textile and Related Setters, Operators, and Workers: 1992-2005

[Continued]

Occupation	Annual average job openings due to growth and total replacement needs		Annual average job openings due to growth and net replacement needs	
	Number	Rank	Number	Rank
Pressing machine operators and tenders, textile, garment, and related materials	21	VL	3	VL
Sewing machine operators, garment	96	L	12	L
Sewing machine operators, nongarment	24	VL	3	VL
Textile bleaching and dyeing machine operators and tenders	3	VL	1	VL
Textile draw-out and winding machine operators and tenders	30	VL	4	VL
Textile machine setters and set-up operators	6	VL	1	VL

Source: U.S. Department of Labor. Bureau of Labor Statistics. *Occupational Projections and Training Data.* 1994 ed. Bulletin 2451. Washington, DC: U.S. Government Printing Office, May 1994, pp. 30-31. A statistical and research supplement to the 1994-1995 *Occupational Outlook Handbook. Notes:* Rankings are based on all detailed occupations in the National Industry-Occupation Matrix. Codes for describing the ranked variables are: VH - very high; H - high; L - low; or VL - very low. A dash (-) indicates data are not applicable.

★ 262 ★

Occupational Outlook: Job Openings

Job Openings for Transportation and Material Moving Equipment Operators: 1992-2005

Table shows the average annual job openings due to growth, total replacement, and net replacement needs for 1992 through 2005. Jobs also are ranked by growth expected.

[In thousands]

Occupation	Annual average job openings due to growth and total replacement needs		Annual average job openings due to growth and net replacement needs	
	Number	Rank	Number	Rank
Transportation and material moving machine and vehicle operators	723	-	159	-
Motor vehicle operators	574	-	124	-
Bus drivers	111	-	17	-
Bus drivers	29	VL	3	VL
Bus drivers, school	82	L	14	L
Taxi drivers and chauffeurs	30	VL	3	VL
Truck drivers	427	-	103	-
Driver/sales workers	54	L	13	L
Truck drivers, light and heavy	373	VH	90	VH
All other motor vehicle operators	5	VL	1	VL
Rail transportation workers	6	-	3	-
Locomotive engineers	1	VL	0	VL
Railroad brake, signal, and switch operators	1	VL	1	VL

[Continued]

★ 262 ★

Job Openings for Transportation and Material Moving Equipment Operators: 1992-2005

[Continued]

Occupation	Annual average job openings due to growth and total replacement needs		Annual average job openings due to growth and net replacement needs	
	Number	Rank	Number	Rank
Railroad conductors and yardmasters	2	VL	1	VL
Rail yard engineers, dinkey operators, and hostlers	0	VL	0	VL
Subway and streetcar operators	2	VL	1	VL
All other rail vehicle operators	0	VL	0	VL
Water transportation and related workers	19	-	3	-
Able seamen, ordinary seamen, and marine oilers	2	VL	0	VL
Captains and pilots, ship	1	VL	0	VL
Mates, ship, boat, and barge	1	VL	0	VL
Ship engineers	1	VL	0	VL
All other water transportation and related workers	14	VL	2	VL
Material moving equipment operators	122	-	28	-
Crane and tower operators	8	VL	2	VL
Excavation and loading machine operators	4	VL	3	VL
Grader, dozer, and scraper operators	12	VL	4	VL
Hoist and winch operators	1	VL	0	VL
Industrial truck and tractor operators	67	L	11	L
Operating engineers	13	VL	4	VL
All other material moving equipment operators	17	VL	5	VL
All other transportation and material moving equipment operators	3	VL	1	VL

Source: U.S. Department of Labor. Bureau of Labor Statistics. *Occupational Projections and Training Data.* 1994 ed. Bulletin 2451. Washington, DC: U.S. Government Printing Office, May 1994, pp. 32-35. A statistical and research supplement to the 1994-1995 *Occupational Outlook Handbook. Notes:* Rankings are based on all detailed occupations in the National Industry-Occupation Matrix. Codes for describing the ranked variables are: VH - very high; H - high; L - low; or VL - very low. A dash (-) indicates data are not applicable.

★ 263 ★

Occupational Outlook: Job Openings

Job Openings for Vehicle and Mobile Equipment Mechanics and Repairers: 1992-2005

Table shows the average annual job openings due to growth, total replacement, and net replacement needs for 1992 through 2005. Jobs also are ranked by growth expected.

[In thousands]

Occupation	Annual average job openings due to growth and total replacement needs		Annual average job openings due to growth and net replacement needs	
	Number	Rank	Number	Rank
Vehicle and mobile equipment mechanics and repairers	213	-	66	-
Aircraft mechanics and engine specialists	8	-	4	-
Aircraft engine specialists	1	VL	1	VL
Aircraft mechanics	6	VL	3	VL
Automotive body and related repairers	31	VL	9	L
Automotive mechanics	123	L	34	H
Bus and truck mechanics and diesel engine specialists	25	VL	12	L
Farm equipment mechanics	7	VL	2	VL
Mobile heavy equipment mechanics	13	VL	3	VL
Motorcycle, boat, and small engine mechanics	6	-	2	-
Motorcycle repairers	1	VL	0	VL
Small engine specialists	5	VL	2	VL

Source: U.S. Department of Labor. Bureau of Labor Statistics. *Occupational Projections and Training Data.* 1994 ed. Bulletin 2451. Washington, DC: U.S. Government Printing Office, May 1994, pp. 22-23. A statistical and research supplement to the 1994-1995 *Occupational Outlook Handbook. Notes:* Rankings are based on all detailed occupations in the National Industry-Occupation Matrix. Codes for describing the ranked variables are: VH - very high; H - high; L - low; or VL - very low. A dash (-) indicates data are not applicable.

★ 264 ★

Occupational Outlook: Job Openings

Job Openings for Woodworking Machine Setters, Operators, and Other Related Workers: 1992-2005

Table shows the average annual job openings due to growth, total replacement, and net replacement needs for 1992 through 2005. Jobs also are ranked by growth expected.

[In thousands]

Occupation	Annual average job openings due to growth and total replacement needs		Annual average job openings due to growth and net replacement needs	
	Number	Rank	Number	Rank
Woodworking machine setters, operators, and other related workers	18	-	3	-
Head sawyers and sawing machine operators, tenders, setters, and set-up operators	8	VL	2	VL
Woodworking machine operators, tenders, setters, and set-up operators	10	VL	2	VL

Source: U.S. Department of Labor. Bureau of Labor Statistics. *Occupational Projections and Training Data.* 1994 ed. Bulletin 2451. Washington, DC: U.S. Government Printing Office, May 1994, pp. 30-31. A statistical and research supplement to the 1994-1995 *Occupational Outlook Handbook. Notes:* Rankings are based on all detailed occupations in the National Industry-Occupation Matrix. Codes for describing the ranked variables are: VH - very high; H - high; L - low; or VL - very low. A dash (-) indicates data are not applicable.

★ 265 ★

Occupational Outlook: Job Openings

Job Openings for Writers, Artists, and Entertainers: 1992-2005

Table shows the average annual job openings due to growth, total replacement, and net replacement needs for 1992 through 2005. Jobs also are ranked by growth expected.

[In thousands]

Occupation	Annual average job openings due to growth and total replacement needs		Annual average job openings due to growth and net replacement needs	
	Number	Rank	Number	Rank
Writers, artists, and entertainers	266	-	58	-
Artists and commercial artists	46	L	9	L
Athletes, coaches, umpires, and related workers	7	VL	1	VL
Dancers and choreographers	3	VL	1	VL
Designers	47	-	9	-
Designers[1]	37	VL	7	VL
Interior designers	10	VL	2	VL
Musicians	45	L	8	VL
Photographers and camera operators	19	-	5	-
Camera operators, television, motion picture, and video	2	VL	0	VL
Photographers	17	VL	4	VL

[Continued]

★ 265 ★

Job Openings for Writers, Artists, and Entertainers: 1992-2005

[Continued]

Occupation	Annual average job openings due to growth and total replacement needs		Annual average job openings due to growth and net replacement needs	
	Number	Rank	Number	Rank
Producers, directors, actors, and entertainers	28	VL	8	VL
Public relations specialists and publicity writers	17	VL	4	VL
Radio and TV announcers and newscasters	3	VL	3	VL
Reporters and correspondents	8	VL	2	VL
Writers and editors[2]	43	L	9	VL

Source: U.S. Department of Labor. Bureau of Labor Statistics. *Occupational Projections and Training Data.* 1994 ed. Bulletin 2451. Washington, DC: U.S. Government Printing Office, May 1994, pp. 8-11. A statistical and research supplement to the 1994-1995 *Occupational Outlook Handbook. Notes:* Rankings are based on all detailed occupations in the National Industry-Occupation Matrix. Codes for describing the ranked variables are: VH - very high; H - high; L - low; or VL - very low. A dash (-) indicates data are not applicable. 1. Except interior designers. 2. Includes technical writers.

Work Hours and Schedules

★ 266 ★

Flexible Schedules, by Occupation: 1985 and 1991

As of May. For employed persons 16 years old and over who usually work full-time and who were at work during the survey reference week. A flexible schedule allows workers to vary the time they begin and end their work days. Based on Current Population Survey.

[In thousands, except percentages]

Occupation	All workers			Workers with flexible schedules					
				Number			Percent		
	Total	Male	Female	Total	Male	Female	Total	Male	Female
Total, 1985	73,395	43,779	29,616	9,061	5,760	3,300	12.3	13.2	11.1
Total, 1991	80,452	46,308	34,145	12,118	7,168	4,950	15.1	15.5	14.5
Managerial and professional	22,630	12,037	10,593	4,991	3,053	1,937	22.1	25.4	18.3
Technical, sales, administrative	24,116	8,910	15,206	4,258	1,984	2,274	17.7	22.3	15.0
Service occupations	8,389	4,329	4,060	883	432	450	10.5	10.0	11.1
Precision production, craft, and repair	10,270	9,464	807	833	764	69	8.1	8.1	8.6
Operators, fabricators, and laborers	13,514	10,211	3,303	980	783	197	7.3	7.7	6.0
Farming, forestry, and fisheries	1,533	1,355	177	173	151	22	11.3	11.1	12.4

Source: U.S. Bureau of the Census. *Statistical Abstract of the United States, 1994.* 114th ed. Washington, DC: U.S. Government Printing Office, 1994, p. 405. Primary sources: U.S. Bureau of Labor Statistics. *News.* USDL 92-491 (4 August 1992); and unpublished data.

★ 267 ★
Work Hours and Schedules

Shift Schedules, by Occupation: 1985 and 1991

As of May. For employed persons 16 years old and over who usually work full-time and who were at work during the survey reference week. Based on Current Population Survey.

Occupation	Total employed[1]	Regular daytime schedules	Shift workers					
			Total	Evening	Night	Rotating	Irregular[2]	Other
Total, 1985[3]	73,395	84.1	15.9	6.3	2.7	4.3	(NA)	2.6
Total, 1991[3]	80,452	81.8	17.8	5.1	3.7	3.4	3.7	2.0
Managerial and professional	22,630	89.6	10.0	1.6	1.4	1.8	2.8	2.3
Technical, sales, administrative	24,116	85.9	13.8	3.5	2.4	2.7	3.6	1.7
Service occupations	8,389	57.1	42.5	14.7	8.7	7.9	6.6	4.6
Precision production, craft, and repair	10,270	85.3	14.4	4.3	3.7	3.4	2.5	0.5
Operators, fabricators, and laborers	13,514	73.4	26.2	8.6	6.8	4.8	4.2	1.7
Farming, forestry, and fisheries	1,533	89.2	10.4	1.1	1.2	0.7	4.4	3.0

Source: U.S. Bureau of the Census. *Statistical Abstract of the United States, 1994.* 114th ed. Washington, DC: U.S. Government Printing Office, 1994, p. 406. Primary sources: U.S. Bureau of Labor Statistics. *News.* USDL 92-491 (4 August 1992); and unpublished data. *Notes:* "NA" represents "not available." 1. Includes a small number of workers who did not report data on shift worked. 2. Employer arranged. 3. Data for 1985 are not strictly comparable to those for 1991 because of the addition of the "irregular" category in the May 1991 survey.

Workers

★ 268 ★

American Indian and Alaskan Native Occupational Employment, by Sex: 1993

Figures show the number employed, participation rate, and distribution for American Indians and Alaskan Natives in each occupational grouping. Tables shows 1993 data for men and women in U.S. private industry, excluding Hawaii. Data cover all industries, 163,039 units.

Group	Total employment	Officials and managers	Professionals	Technicians	Sales workers	Office and clerical workers	Craft workers	Operatives	Laborers	Service workers
Number employed										
All American Indian and Alaskan Native employees	177,066	12,850	16,440	9,537	19,385	23,294	19,109	33,646	18,998	23,807
Male	100,045	9,045	9,205	5,334	8,157	5,519	17,080	22,004	12,557	11,144
Female	77,021	3,805	7,235	4,203	11,228	17,775	2,029	11,642	6,441	12,663
Participation rate										
All American Indian and Alaskan Native employees	0.5	0.3	0.3	0.4	0.5	0.4	0.6	0.6	0.7	0.6
Male	0.3	0.2	0.2	0.2	0.2	0.1	0.5	0.4	0.5	0.3
Female	0.2	0.1	0.1	0.2	0.3	0.3	0.1	0.2	0.2	0.3
Occupational distribution										
All American Indian and Alaskan Native employees	100.0	7.3	9.3	5.4	10.9	13.2	10.8	19.0	10.7	13.4

[Continued]

226

★ 268 ★

American Indian and Alaskan Native Occupational Employment, by Sex: 1993
[Continued]

Group	Total employment	Officials and managers	Professionals	Technicians	Sales workers	Office and clerical workers	Craft workers	Operatives	Laborers	Service workers
Male	100.0	9.0	9.2	5.3	8.2	5.5	17.1	22.0	12.6	11.1
Female	100.0	4.9	9.4	5.5	14.6	23.1	2.6	15.1	8.4	16.4

Source: U.S. Equal Employment Opportunity Commission. *Job Patterns for Minorities and Women in Private Industry, 1993.* Washington, DC: U.S. Government Printing Office, 1994, p. 1.

★ 269 ★
Workers

Asian and Pacific Islander Occupational Employment, by Sex: 1993

Figures show the number employed, participation rate, and distribution for Asians and Pacific Islanders in each occupational grouping. Tables shows 1993 data for men and women in U.S. private industry, excluding Hawaii. Data cover all industries, 163,039 units.

Group	Total employment	Officials and managers	Professionals	Technicians	Sales workers	Office and clerical workers	Craft workers	Operatives	Laborers	Service workers
Number employed										
All Asian/Pacific Islander employees	1,134,536	84,561	303,279	94,572	80,155	162,276	53,609	152,509	72,422	131,153
Male	579,873	57,992	155,971	54,314	35,381	45,219	41,614	84,161	40,906	64,315
Female	554,663	26,569	147,308	40,258	44,774	117,057	11,995	68,348	31,516	66,838
Participation rate										
All Asian/Pacific Islander employees	3.1	2.1	5.8	4.3	2.1	2.9	1.6	2.8	2.7	3.4
Male	1.6	1.5	3.0	2.4	0.9	0.8	1.2	1.5	1.5	1.7
Female	1.5	0.7	2.8	1.8	1.2	2.1	0.4	1.2	1.2	1.7
Occupational distribution										
All Asian/Pacific Islander employees	100.0	7.5	26.7	8.3	7.1	14.3	4.7	13.4	6.4	11.6
Male	100.0	10.0	26.9	9.4	6.1	7.8	7.2	14.5	7.1	11.1
Female	100.0	4.8	26.6	7.3	8.1	21.1	2.2	12.3	5.7	12.1

Source: U.S. Equal Employment Opportunity Commission. *Job Patterns for Minorities and Women in Private Industry, 1993.* Washington, DC: U.S. Government Printing Office, 1994, p. 1.

★ 270 ★
Workers

Black Occupational Employment, by Sex: 1993

Figures show the number employed, participation rate, and distribution for blacks in each occupational grouping. Tables shows 1993 data for men and women in U.S. private industry, excluding Hawaii. Data cover all industries, 163,039 units.

Group	Total employment	Officials and managers	Professionals	Technicians	Sales workers	Office and clerical workers	Craft workers	Operatives	Laborers	Service workers
Number employed										
All black employees	4,603,282	209,045	291,045	233,294	409,174	779,365	310,167	949,143	496,476	925,573
Male	2,161,798	118,906	101,796	90,516	150,986	140,753	254,822	577,459	317,592	408,968
Female	2,441,484	90,139	189,249	142,778	258,188	638,612	55,345	371,684	178,884	516,605
Participation rate										
All black employees	12.7	5.3	5.5	10.5	10.6	14.0	9.2	17.1	18.7	23.8
Male	6.0	3.0	1.9	4.1	3.9	2.5	7.6	10.4	12.0	10.5
Female	6.7	2.3	3.6	6.4	6.7	11.4	1.6	6.7	6.7	13.3
Occupational distribution										
All black employees	100.0	4.5	6.3	5.1	8.9	16.9	6.7	20.6	10.8	20.1
Male	100.0	5.5	4.7	4.2	7.0	6.5	11.8	26.7	14.7	18.9
Female	100.0	3.7	7.8	5.8	10.6	26.2	2.3	15.2	7.3	21.2

Source: U.S. Equal Employment Opportunity Commission. *Job Patterns for Minorities and Women in Private Industry, 1993.* Washington, DC: U.S. Government Printing Office, 1994, p. 1.

★ 271 ★
Workers

Blacks in Selected Occupations: 1970 and 1990

Table shows the percentage of blacks in selected occupations in 1970 and 1990. The data, according to the source, "clearly show that most blacks have made only modest gains" in employment despite Affirmative Action programs.

Occupation	Percentage of blacks	
	1970	1990
College professors	3.3	4.8
Lawyers	1.3	3.4
Managers[1]	2.6	6.2
Physicians	2.2	3.6

Source: Frank, Robert, and Eleena de Lisser. "Research on Affirmative Action Finds Modest Gains for Blacks Over 30 Years." *Wall Street Journal,* 21 February 1995, p. A2. Primary source: Bureau of the Census. *Note:* 1. Includes executives and administrative managers.

★ 272 ★
Workers

Hispanic Occupational Employment, by Sex: 1993

Figures show the number employed, participation rate, and distribution for Hispanics in each occupational grouping. Tables shows 1993 data for men and women in U.S. private industry, excluding Hawaii. Data cover all industries, 163,039 units.

Group	Total employment	Officials and managers	Professionals	Technicians	Sales workers	Office and clerical workers	Craft workers	Operatives	Laborers	Service workers
Number employed										
All Hispanic employees	2,630,746	121,908	141,708	105,293	262,685	357,871	218,759	507,227	432,335	482,960
Male	1,530,555	82,700	71,806	62,132	117,312	83,881	192,033	346,315	294,129	280,247
Female	1,100,191	39,208	69,902	43,161	145,373	273,990	26,726	160,912	138,206	202,713
Participation rate										
All Hispanic employees	7.2	3.1	2.7	4.7	6.8	6.4	6.5	9.2	16.3	12.4
Male	4.2	2.1	1.4	2.8	3.0	1.5	5.7	6.3	11.1	7.2
Female	3.0	1.0	1.3	1.9	3.8	4.9	0.8	2.9	5.2	5.2
Occupational distribution										
All Hispanic employees	100.0	4.6	5.4	4.0	10.0	13.6	8.3	19.3	16.4	18.4
Male	100.0	5.4	4.7	4.1	7.7	5.5	12.5	22.6	19.2	18.3
Female	100.0	3.6	6.4	3.9	13.2	24.9	2.4	14.6	12.6	18.4

Source: U.S. Equal Employment Opportunity Commission. *Job Patterns for Minorities and Women in Private Industry, 1993.* Washington, DC: U.S. Government Printing Office, 1994, p. 1.

★ 273 ★
Workers

Home Workers, by Occupation: 1991

Table shows workers doing job-related work at home as part of their primary jobs in nonagricultural industries. Data as of May. For persons 16 years old and older.

Occupation	Total at work (1,000)	Persons doing job-related work at home					
		Total (1,000)[1]	Worked at home for pay				Mean hours worked[3] (number)
			Total (1,000)	Worked 8 hours or more		35 hours or more (1,000)	
				Total (1,000)	Rate[2]		
Total[4]	109,126	19,967	7,432	3,651	3.3	1,069	14.1
Managerial and professional	29,971	11,517	3,151	1,511	5.0	360	12.8
Executive, administrative, managerial	14,384	4,729	1,636	749	5.2	191	12.8
Professional	15,587	6,789	1,515	763	4.9	169	12.9
Technical, sales, administrative	34,554	5,611	2,458	1,123	3.2	201	11.2
Sales	13,177	3,528	1,623	813	6.2	133	11.9
Administrative support	17,786	1,617	690	253	1.4	63	10.0
Service occupations	14,955	1,144	733	553	3.7	381	31.7

[Continued]

★ 273 ★

Home Workers, by Occupation: 1991
[Continued]

Occupation	Total at work (1,000)	Persons doing job-related work at home					
		Total (1,000)[1]	Worked at home for pay				Mean hours worked[3] (number)
			Total (1,000)	Worked 8 hours or more			
				Total (1,000)	Rate[2]	35 hours or more (1,000)	
Precision production, craft, repair	12,608	1,070	731	306	2.4	68	11.6
Operators, fabricators, and laborers	16,271	546	312	139	0.9	58	14.9

Source: U.S. Bureau of the Census. *Statistical Abstract of the United States, 1994.* 114th ed. Washington, DC: U.S. Government Printing Office, 1994, p. 406. Primary sources: U.S. Bureau of Labor Statistics. *Monthly Labor Review* (February 1994); and unpublished data. *Notes:* 1. Includes those that did not report pay status and unpaid family members. 2. Persons working at home as a percent of the total at work. 3. An arithmetic mean is derived by summing the individual item values of a particular group and dividing the total by the number of items. The arithmetic mean is often referred to as the "mean" or "average." 4. Excludes unpaid family members.

★ 274 ★
Workers

Minority Occupational Employment, by Sex: 1993

Figures show the number employed, participation rate, and distribution for minorities in each occupational grouping. Tables shows 1993 data for men and women in U.S. private industry, excluding Hawaii. Data cover all industries, 163,039 units. See also tables for specific minorities.

Group	Total employment	Officials and managers	Professionals	Technicians	Sales workers	Office and clerical workers	Craft workers	Operatives	Laborers	Service workers
Number employed										
All minority employees	8,545,630	428,364	752,472	442,696	771,399	1,322,806	601,644	1,642,525	1,020,231	1,563,493
Male	4,372,271	268,643	338,778	212,296	311,836	275,372	505,549	1,029,939	665,184	764,674
Female	4,173,359	159,721	413,694	230,400	459,563	1,047,434	96,095	612,586	355,047	798,819
Participation rate										
All minority employees	23.5	10.8	14.3	19.9	20.0	23.7	17.9	29.7	38.5	40.2
Male	12.0	6.8	6.5	9.5	8.1	4.9	15.0	18.6	25.1	19.6
Female	11.5	4.0	7.9	10.4	11.9	18.8	2.9	11.1	13.4	20.5
Occupational distribution										
All minority employees	100.0	5.0	8.8	5.2	9.0	15.5	7.0	19.2	11.9	18.3
Male	100.0	6.1	7.7	4.9	7.1	6.3	11.6	23.6	15.2	17.5
Female	100.0	3.8	9.9	5.5	11.0	25.1	2.3	14.7	8.5	19.1

Source: U.S. Equal Employment Opportunity Commission. *Job Patterns for Minorities and Women in Private Industry, 1993.* Washington, DC: U.S. Government Printing Office, 1994, p. 1.

★ 275 ★

Workers

Multiple Job Holders, by Occupation: 1991

As of May. Multiple job holders are employed persons who either had jobs as wage or salary workers with two or more employers; were self-employed and also held a wage and salary job; or were unpaid family workers on their primary jobs but also held wage and salary jobs. Based on the Current Population Survey.

Occupation of primary job	Total			Male			Female		
	Employed (1,000)	Multiple job holders		Employed (1,000)	Multiple job holders		Employed (1,000)	Multiple job holders	
		Number (1,000)	Rate[1]		Number (1,000)	Rate[1]		Number (1,000)	Rate[1]
Total, 16 years and over	116,626	7,183	6.2	63,499	4,054	6.4	53,127	3,129	5.9
Managerial and professional specialty	31,154	2,259	7.3	16,678	1,269	7.6	14,476	990	6.8
Technical, sales, and administrative support	36,002	2,154	6.0	12,584	803	6.4	23,418	1,351	5.8
Service occupations	15,534	1,063	6.8	6,252	527	8.4	9,282	536	5.8
Precision production, craft, and repair	13,115	652	5.0	12,019	608	5.1	1,096	44	4.0
Operators, fabricators, and laborers	17,065	851	5.0	12,804	682	5.3	4,261	169	4.0
Farming, forestry, and fishing	3,756	203	5.4	3,162	164	5.2	594	39	6.6

Source: U.S. Bureau of the Census. *Statistical Abstract of the United States, 1994.* 114th ed. Washington, DC: U.S. Government Printing Office, 1994, p. 405. Primary source: U.S. Bureau of Labor Statistics. *News.* USDL 91-547 (28 October 1991). *Notes:* 1. Multiple job holders as a percent of all employed persons in specified group.

★ 276 ★

Workers

Self-Employed Workers, by Occupation: 1970-1993

For civilian noninstitutional population 16 years old and over. Annual averages of monthly figures. Data for 1992 are not fully comparable with data for prior years because of the introduction of the occupational and industrial classification used in the 1990 Census. Based on the Current Population Survey.

[In thousands]

Occupation	1970	1975	1980	1985	1990	1991	1992	1993
Total self-employed	7,031	7,427	8,642	9,269	10,160	10,341	10,017	10,335
Managerial and professional specialty	(NA)	(NA)	(NA)	2,585	3,067	3,117	2,919	3,102
Technical, sales, and administrative support	(NA)	(NA)	(NA)	2,059	2,252	2,245	2,192	2,336
Service	(NA)	(NA)	(NA)	980	1,213	1,273	1,079	1,043
Precision production, craft, and repair	(NA)	(NA)	(NA)	1,611	1,680	1,697	1,803	1,891
Operators, fabricators, and laborers	(NA)	(NA)	(NA)	568	568	584	626	632
Farming, forestry, and fishing	(NA)	(NA)	(NA)	1,465	1,380	1,427	1,390	1,331

Source: U.S. Bureau of the Census. *Statistical Abstract of the United States, 1994.* 114th ed. Washington, DC: U.S. Government Printing Office, 1994, p. 404. Primary sources: U.S. Bureau of Labor Statistics. Bulletin 2307; *Employment and Earnings* (monthly; January issues); and unpublished data. *Note:* "NA" represents "not available."

★ 277 ★
Workers

White Occupational Employment, by Sex: 1993

Figures show the number employed, participation rate, and distribution for whites in each occupational grouping. Tables shows 1993 data for men and women in U.S. private industry, excluding Hawaii. Data cover all industries, 163,039 units.

Group	Total employment	Officials and managers	Professionals	Technicians	Sales workers	Office and clerical workers	Craft workers	Operatives	Laborers	Service workers
Number employed										
All white employees	27,775,606	3,548,244	4,499,412	1,781,941	3,078,474	4,255,981	2,758,689	3,892,354	1,632,347	2,328,164
Male	15,053,016	2,520,475	2,274,476	969,838	1,363,715	683,719	2,470,132	2,720,268	1,075,082	975,311
Female	12,722,590	1,027,769	2,224,936	812,103	1,714,759	3,572,262	288,557	1,172,086	557,265	1,352,853
Participation rate										
All white employees	76.5	89.2	85.7	80.1	80.0	76.3	82.1	70.3	61.5	59.8
Male	41.4	63.4	43.3	43.6	35.4	12.3	73.5	49.1	40.5	25.1
Female	35.0	25.8	42.4	36.5	44.5	64.0	8.6	21.2	21.0	34.8
Occupational distribution										
All white employees	100.0	12.8	16.2	6.4	11.1	15.3	9.9	14.0	5.9	8.4
Male	100.0	16.7	15.1	6.4	9.1	4.5	16.4	18.1	7.1	6.5
Female	100.0	8.1	17.5	6.4	13.5	28.1	2.3	9.2	4.4	10.6

Source: U.S. Equal Employment Opportunity Commission. *Job Patterns for Minorities and Women in Private Industry, 1993.* Washington, DC: U.S. Government Printing Office, 1994, p. 1.

★ 278 ★
Workers

Women in Selected Occupations: 1970 and 1990

Table shows the proportion of women in selected occupations in 1970 and 1990. Occupations are ranked by 1990 data.

[In percentages]

Occupation	1970	1990
Secretary	98	98
Nurse	91	94
Librarian	84	85
Teacher	74	74
Psychologist	43	59
Public official	24	59
Bartender	27	57
Economist	14	44
Chemist	17	29
Industrial engineer	3	27
Lawyer, judge	6	27
Doctor	11	22
Farmer	7	17
Police detective	5	13

Source: Roberts, Sam. "Women's Work: What's New, What Isn't." *New York Times,* 27 April 1995, p. A12. Primary source: Queen's College, Program for Applied Research.

Chapter 3
STATISTICS BY INDUSTRY

This chapter is comprised of nearly 200 tables with industry-specific data on various aspects of the American workplace. Coverage includes compensation, employee benefits, employees and earnings, employment and unemployment, health and safety, industrial relations, production and technology, work hours and schedules, and workers. Complete industry summaries provide comprehensive data for each sector, and employment projections to the year 2005 are presented for 115 occupations employing the largest numbers of workers.

Compensation

★ 279 ★

Compensation and Wages and Salaries, by Industry: 1985-1992

Table reflects the average annual total compensation and wages and salaries per full-time equivalent (FTE) employee in each industry. Wage and salary payments include executives' compensation, bonuses, tips, and payments-in-kind; total compensation includes—in addition to wages and salaries—employer contributions for social insurance, employer contributions to private and welfare funds, director's fees, jury and witness fees, and the like. Through 1985, based on 1972 Standard Industrial Classification Code (SIC); beginning 1988, based on the 1987 SIC.

[In dollars]

Industry	Annual total compensation				Annual wages and salaries			
	1985	1990	1991	1992	1985	1990	1991	1992
Domestic industries	25,263	31,398	32,649	34,536	21,059	26,138	27,178	28,665
Agriculture, forestry, and fisheries	13,084	17,672	16,578	18,976	11,773	15,299	15,646	15,925
Mining	38,883	46,216	48,655	51,811	32,054	37,903	39,756	42,032
Construction	26,721	32,826	34,105	35,005	22,775	27,679	28,487	29,222
Manufacturing	30,145	36,572	38,324	30,342	24,600	29,746	30,942	32,370
Transportation	30,638	35,430	37,107	38,775	25,240	28,916	30,144	31,397
Communication	39,635	47,926	50,063	53,567	31,342	38,382	39,567	42,076
Electric, gas, and sanitary services	39,179	47,936	50,559	53,657	31,653	38,930	40,779	42,998
Wholesale trade	29,195	37,147	38,540	40,408	25,016	31,772	32,760	34,225
Retail trade	15,694	16,588	19,543	20,352	13,603	16,036	16,769	17,406
Finance, insurance, and real estate	27,873	37,049	36,875	42,492	23,724	31,682	33,116	36,159

[Continued]

★ 279 ★

Compensation and Wages and Salaries, by Industry: 1985-1992
[Continued]

Industry	Annual total compensation				Annual wages and salaries			
	1985	1990	1991	1992	1985	1990	1991	1992
Services	21,441	28,381	29,376	31,031	18,698	24,801	25,516	26,869
Government and government enterprises	27,839	35,616	37,686	39,668	21,988	27,772	29,284	30,652

Source: U.S. Bureau of the Census. *Statistical Abstract of the United States, 1994.* 114th ed. Washington, DC: U.S. Government Printing Office, 1994, p. 427. Primary sources: U.S. Bureau of Economic Analysis. *The National Income and Product Accounts of the United States.* Volume 2: 1959-88; and *Survey of Current Business* (July issues).

★ 280 ★

Compensation

Federal Civilian Pay Systems: 1982 and 1992

As of September 30. Covers only on-board employment for Executive Branch agencies participating in Office of Personnel Management (OPM) Central Personnel Data File (CPDF). Excludes foreign nationals abroad and U.S. Postal Service.

Pay system	1982					1992				
		Race/national origin					Race/national origin			
	Total employees (1,000)	Race and origin[1] (1,000)	Percent of total	Black, non-Hispanic (1,000)	Hispanic (1,000)	Total employees (1,000)	Race and origin[1] (1,000)	Percent of total	Black, non-Hispanic (1,000)	Hispanic (1,000)
Total, All pay systems	2,008.6	484.0	24.1	311.1	90.0	2,175.7	604.9	27.8	360.7	120.3
General Schedule and equivalent[2]	1,507.4	336.1	22.3	222.0	59.0	1,680.5	451.9	26.9	277.3	87.9
Grades 1-4 ($11,478-$20,551)	303.6	101.9	33.6	71.0	16.1	198.9	86.0	43.2	56.7	14.2
Grades 5-8 ($17,686-$31,543)	464.9	126.5	27.2	90.2	20.2	517.0	178.8	34.6	120.3	31.7
Grades 9-12 ($26,798-$50,516)	530.0	87.6	16.5	50.1	18.7	654.7	144.7	22.1	79.0	33.1
Grades 13-15 ($46,210-$83,502)	208.9	20.1	9.6	10.7	4.0	309.9	42.4	13.7	21.4	8.9
Executive, total	9.7	0.6	6.2	0.4	0.1	14.9	1.2	8.1	0.7	0.3
Wage pay systems	414.0	134.6	32.5	83.5	28.0	354.0	121.2	34.3	70.0	26.2
Other pay systems[3]	77.5	12.6	16.3	5.2	2.9	126.3	30.6	24.2	12.8	5.9

Source: U.S. Bureau of the Census. *Statistical Abstract of the United States, 1994.* 114th ed. Washington, DC: U.S. Government Printing Office, 1994, p. 346. Primary source: U.S. Office of Personnel Management. Central Personnel Data File. *Notes:* 1. Includes American Indians, Alaska Natives, Asians, and Pacific total. 2. Pay rates as of January 1990 for general schedule. Each grade (except executive) includes several salary steps. Range is from lowest to highest step of grades shown. 3. Includes white-collar employment in other than General Schedule and equivalent.

★ 281 ★

Compensation

Federal General Schedule Employee Pay Increases: 1965-1994

Percent change from prior year shown, except 1965, change from 1964. Represents legislated pay increases. For some years data based on range.

Effective date	Average increase
October 1, 1965	3.6
July 1, 1966	2.9
October 1, 1967	4.5
July 1, 1968	4.9
July 1, 1969	9.1
December 27, 1969	6.0
January 1, 1971	6.0
January 1, 1972	5.5
October 1, 1972	5.1
October 1, 1973	4.8
October 1, 1974	5.5
October 1, 1975	5.0
October 1, 1976	5.2
October 1, 1977	7.0
October 1, 1978	5.5
October 1, 1979	7.0
October 1, 1980	9.1
October 1, 1981	4.8
October 1, 1982	4.0
January 1, 1984	4.0
January 1, 1985	3.5
January 1, 1986	-
January 1, 1987	3.0
January 1, 1988	2.0
January 1, 1989	4.1
January 1, 1990	3.6
January 1, 1991	4.1
January 1, 1992	4.2
January 1, 1993	3.7
January 1, 1994[1]	-

Source: U.S. Bureau of the Census. *Statistical Abstract of the United States, 1994.* 114th ed. Washington, DC: U.S. Government Printing Office, 1994, p. 347. Primary source: U.S. Office of Personnel Management. *Pay Structure of the Federal Civil Service* (annual). *Notes:* "-" represents zero. 1. Estimated.

★ 282 ★

Compensation

Hourly and Weekly Earnings, by Private Industry Group: 1980-1993

Table shows average hourly and weekly earnings in current and constant (1982) dollars. Average earnings include overtime. Data are for production and related workers in mining, manufacturing, and construction, and nonsupervisory employees in other industries. Excludes agriculture.

Private industry group	Current dollars					Constant (1982) dollars[1]				
	1980	1985	1990	1992	1993	1980	1985	1990	1992	1993
Average hourly earnings	6.66	8.57	10.01	10.58	10.83	7.78	7.77	7.52	7.42	7.39
Mining	9.17	11.98	13.68	14.54	14.60	10.71	10.86	10.28	10.20	9.96
Construction	9.94	12.32	13.77	14.15	14.35	11.61	11.17	10.35	9.92	9.79
Manufacturing	7.27	9.54	10.83	11.46	11.76	8.49	8.65	8.14	8.04	8.02
Transportation, public utilities	8.87	11.40	12.97	13.46	13.64	10.36	10.34	9.74	9.44	9.30
Wholesale trade	6.95	9.15	10.79	11.39	11.71	8.12	8.30	8.11	7.99	7.99
Retail trade	4.88	5.94	6.75	7.13	7.29	5.70	5.39	5.07	5.00	4.97
Finance, insurance, real estate	5.79	7.94	9.97	10.82	11.32	6.76	7.20	7.49	7.59	7.72
Services	5.85	7.90	9.83	10.55	10.81	6.83	7.16	7.39	7.40	7.37
Average weekly earnings	235	299	345	364	374	275	271	259	255	255
Mining	397	520	603	638	645	464	471	453	448	440
Construction	368	464	526	538	551	430	421	395	377	376
Manufacturing	289	386	442	470	487	337	350	332	330	332
Transportation, public utilities	351	450	505	524	542	410	408	379	367	369
Wholesale trade	267	351	411	435	447	312	318	309	305	305
Retail trade	147	175	194	205	210	172	158	146	144	143
Finance, insurance, and real estate	210	289	357	387	404	245	262	268	272	276
Services	191	257	319	343	351	223	233	240	240	240

Source: U.S. Bureau of the Census. *Statistical Abstract of the United States, 1994.* 114th ed. Washington, DC: U.S. Government Printing Office, 1994, p. 427. Primary sources: U.S. Bureau of Labor Statistics. Bulletins 2370 and 2429; and *Employment and Earnings* (monthly). *Notes:* 1. Earnings in current dollars divided by the Consumer Price Index (CPI-W) on a 1982 base.

★ 283 ★

Compensation

Minimum Hourly Wage Rates, by Industry: 1991

Figures reflect the effective federal minimum hourly wage rates. The Fair Labor Standards Act of 1938 and subsequent amendments provide for minimum wage coverage applicable to specified nonsupervisory employment categories. Exempt from coverage are executives and administrators or professionals. Employee estimates as of September 1991, except as indicated.

Industry	Nonsupervisory employees, 1991		
	Total (1,000)	Subject to minimum wage rates	
		Total (1,000)	Total Percent of total
Total	91,373	80,540	88.1
Private industry	80,149	69,316	86.5
Agriculture[1]	1,702	653	38.4
Mining	606	603	99.5
Construction	4,452	4,294	96.5
Manufacturing	16,400	15,947	97.2
Transportation, public utilities	5,208	5,175	99.4
Wholesale trade	5,204	4,158	79.9
Retail trade	17,439	15,800	90.6
Finance, insurance, and real estate	5,736	4,349	75.8
Service[2]	22,111	17,466	79.0
Private households	1,291	871	67.5
Government[3]	11,224	11,224	100.0

Source: U.S. Bureau of the Census. *Statistical Abstract of the United States, 1994.* 114th ed. Washington, DC: U.S. Government Printing Office, 1994, p. 432. Primary sources: U.S. Department of Labor. Employment Standards Administration. *Minimum Wage and Maximum Hours Standards Under the Fair Labor Standards Act* (1981; annual); and unpublished data. *Notes:* 1. Estimates based on average employment for the ten-month active season. 2. Estimates for educational services in private industry relate to October. 3. Federal, state, and local employees; estimates for educational services in government relate to October.

★ 284 ★

Compensation

State and Local Government Employee Compensation, by Industry Group: 1993

Table shows employer costs per hour worked for state and local government employee compensation as of March.

[In dollars]

Industry group	Total compensation	Wages and salaries	Benefits						
			Total	Paid leave	Supplemental pay	Insurance	Retirement and savings	Legally required benefits	Other[1]
All state and local government workers	24.44	17.00	7.44	1.86	0.21	2.02	1.87	1.44	0.03
Services	26.02	18.58	7.44	1.74	0.16	2.12	1.95	1.45	0.03
Health services	19.31	12.91	6.41	1.97	0.50	1.56	1.02	1.33	0.02
Hospitals	19.60	13.20	6.40	2.01	0.49	1.53	1.02	1.34	0.02
Educational services	27.68	20.00	7.68	1.69	0.09	2.24	2.15	1.49	0.03
Elementary and secondary education	27.88	20.18	7.70	1.59	0.08	2.32	2.21	1.46	0.04
Higher education	28.13	20.29	7.84	1.97	0.12	2.07	2.06	1.61	(Z)
Public administration	21.35	14.02	7.33	2.10	0.28	1.79	1.80	1.32	0.03

Source: U.S. Bureau of the Census. *Statistical Abstract of the United States, 1994.* 114th ed. Washington, DC: U.S. Government Printing Office, 1994, p. 320. Primary source: U.S. Bureau of Labor Statistics. *News: Employer Costs for Employee Compensation.* USDL 93-220. *Notes:* Data based on a sample. "Z" indicates cost per hour less than one cent. 1. Includes severance pay and supplemental unemployment benefits.

Employee Benefits

★ 285 ★

Health Care Plan Enrollment, by Industry: 1992

Data indicate the percent of employees enrolled in various health care plans for selected industries. Data are for 1992.

	Health care plans			
	Conventional plans[1]	HMOs	PPOs	POS plans
Manufacturing	44	17	32	7
Transportation/communication	37	29	24	9
Retail	53	18	24	4
Finance	36	30	29	5
Services	43	23	19	14
State/local governments	45	31	22	3
Health care	35	28	33	3
High tech	39	34	22	6

Source: "Managed Care Facts." *Hospitals,* 5 April 1993, p. 20. Primary source: KPMG Peat Marwick Survey of 1,057 firms (1992). *Notes:* "HMO" stands for health maintenance organization; "PPO" stands for preferred provider organization; "POS" stands for point-of-service plans. 1. Traditional indemnity plans.

★ 286 ★

Employee Benefits

Workers Without Health Insurance, by Industry

The table below shows the industries that do not offer health insurance coverage to employees.

[In percentages]

Industry	Percent
Retail	43
Services	17
Construction	15
Transportation	6
Wholesale	6
Manufacturing	6
Finance	5

Source: "Health Care Coverage." *San Francisco Examiner,* 28 November 1993, p. E1. Primary source: Lewin-ICF 1991 Retirement Plan Survey.

Employees and Earnings

★ 287 ★

Chemical Manufacturing Employees and Earnings of Production Workers: 1980-1993

Annual averages of monthly figures. Covers all full- and part-time employees who worked during, or received pay for, any part of the pay period, including the 12th of the month. Data refer to production and related workers.

Industry	1987 SIC code[1]	All total employees (1,000)			Production workers					
					Total (1,000)			Average hourly earnings ($)		
		1980	1990	1993	1980	1990	1993	1980	1990	1993
Total	(X)	90,406	109,419	110,178	(NA)	(NA)	(NA)	(NA)	(NA)	(NA)
Private sector[2]	(X)	74,166	91,115	91,336	60,331	73,800	74,353	6.66	10.01	10.83
Manufacturing	(D)	20,285	19,076	17,802	14,214	12,947	12,143	7.27	10.83	11.76
Nondurable goods	(X)	8,127	7,968	7,755	5,798	5,584	5,417	6.56	10.12	11.00
Chemicals and allied products[3]	28	1,107	1,086	1,074	626	600	568	8.30	13.54	14.84
Industrial inorganic chemicals	281	161	138	136	88	70	59	9.07	14.66	16.42
Plastics materials and synthetics	282	205	180	168	137	116	106	8.21	13.97	15.26
Drugs	283	196	237	261	97	105	115	7.69	12.90	14.70
Soap, cleaners, and toilet goods	284	141	159	154	86	98	95	7.67	11.71	12.31
Paints and allied products	285	65	61	58	33	31	31	7.39	11.99	12.69
Industrial organic chemicals	286	174	155	150	88	86	78	9.67	15.97	17.67
Agricultural chemicals	287	72	56	57	45	34	33	8.12	13.73	15.11

Source: U.S. Bureau of the Census. *Statistical Abstract of the United States, 1994.* 114th ed. Washington, DC: U.S. Government Printing Office, 1994, p. 423. Primary sources: U.S. Bureau of Labor Statistics. Bulletins 2370 and 2429; and *Employment and Earnings* (March and June issues). *Notes:* "NA" stands for "not available"; "X" for "not applicable." 1. 1987 Standard Industrial Classification (SIC). 2. Excludes government. 3. Includes industries not shown separately.

★ 288 ★

Employees and Earnings

City Government Employment and Payrolls: 1980-1992

For October. Includes only those school systems operated as part of the city government. 1982, and 1987 based on complete census of all cities; other years based on sample and subject to sampling variation. Minus sign (-) indicates decrease.

Year	All employees, full- and part-time (1,000)		October payrolls (million dollars)		Annual percent change		Full-time equivalent employment[1] (1,000)		Other	Average earnings in October, full-time employees (dollars)	
	Total	Excluding education	Total	Excluding education	All employees	October payroll	Total	Education		Education	Other
1980	2,561	2,130	2,942	2,403	0.3	7.8	2,166	360	1,806	1,501	1,338
1981	2,469	2,056	3,222	2,640	-3.6	9.5	2,111	346	1,765	1,686	1,500
1982	2,396	2,015	3,428	2,861	-2.9	6.4	2,088	317	1,770	1,791	1,625
1983	2,423	2,051	3,640	3,059	1.1	6.2	2,060	300	1,760	1,962	1,739
1984	2,434	2,070	3,872	3,268	0.4	6.4	2,090	300	1,790	2,033	1,831
1985	2,467	2,102	4,191	3,536	1.4	8.2	(NA)	(NA)	(NA)	2,117	1,953
1986	2,494	2,126	4,407	3,724	1.1	5.1	2,181	320	1,860	2,186	2,044
1987	2,493	2,110	4,770	3,977	(Z)	8.2	2,223	337	1,885	2,406	2,163
1988	2,570	2,188	4,979	4,136	3.1	4.4	2,251	342	1,910	2,566	2,220
1989	2,569	2,190	5,274	4,405	(Z)	5.9	2,268	341	1,927	2,669	2,343
1990	2,642	2,237	5,564	4,675	2.8	5.5	2,295	338	1,957	2,683	2,449
1991	2,662	2,324	5,784	4,878	0.7	4.0	2,303	338	1,965	2,739	2,547
1992	2,665	2,312	6,207	5,146	0.1	7.3	2,340	371	1,969	2,931	2,683

Source: U.S. Bureau of the Census. *Statistical Abstract of the United States, 1994.* 114th ed. Washington, DC: U.S. Government Printing Office, 1994, p. 324. Primary source: U.S. Bureau of the Census. *Compendium of Public Employment* and *City Employment,* Series GE, no. 2 (annual). *Notes:* "NA" represents "not available." "Z" is less than .05 percent. 1. Beginning 1986, data not comparable to previous years due to a change in how full-time equivalent is calculated.

★ 289 ★

Employees and Earnings

City Government Employment and Payroll, by Function: 1980-1992

For October.

Item	Employees (1,000)					October payrolls (million dollars)				
	All cities[1]				Cities with 75,000 population or more, 1992[2]	All cities[1]				Cities with 75,000 population or more, 1992[2]
	1980	1990	1991	1992		1980	1990	1991	1992	
Total	2,561	2,642	2,662	2,665	1,568	2,942	5,564	5,784	6,207	4,281
Full-time	2,071	2,149	2,153	2,197	1,418	2,826	5,334	5,543	5,980	4,178
Part-time	489	493	509	468	150	116	229	241	227	103
Full-time equivalent[3]	2,166	2,295	2,303	2,340	1,480	(X)	(X)	(X)	(X)	(X)
Education[4]	360	338	338	371	301	539	889	906	1,061	880

[Continued]

★ 289 ★

City Government Employment and Payroll, by Function: 1980-1992
[Continued]

Item	Employees (1,000)					October payrolls (million dollars)				
	All cities[1]				Cities with 75,000 population or more,	All cities[1]				Cities with 75,000 population or more,
	1980	1990	1991	1992	1992[2]	1980	1990	1991	1992	1992[2]
Percent of total	17	15	15	16	20	18	16	16	17	21
Instructional staff	266	264	262	261	209	436	754	765	848	698
Others	94	74	76	110	92	102	134	141	212	182
Libraries	34	45	45	45	27	38	80	84	86	57
Public welfare	41	57	58	55	49	47	118	116	132	121
Hospitals	131	124	124	125	82	143	282	297	301	217
Health	35	42	41	43	35	47	93	94	104	89
Highways	121	133	132	130	56	141	274	283	301	152
Police protection	365	412	418	423	234	550	1,093	1,162	1,249	783
Fire protection	190	199	201	200	117	300	579	603	642	416
Correction	18	35	36	36	34	27	90	94	108	103
Parks and recreation	103	121	123	123	71	116	211	222	232	141
Housing and community development	44	46	46	45	38	57	104	108	115	97
Sewerage	60	74	75	76	38	74	155	164	172	95
Solid waste management	104	86	85	83	49	118	174	177	193	135
Financial administration	69	74	75	74	35	85	164	169	179	96
Judicial, legal, other gov admin	112	129	129	132	73	147	314	326	345	209
Local utilities[5]	209	226	226	226	144	306	594	619	615	439
Water supply	93	101	103	103	53	116	219	230	240	137
Electric power	44	51	51	51	28	67	142	149	159	101
Transit	66	66	65	64	60	115	217	224	198	191
Other	171	154	152	152	97	208	350	360	372	252

Source: U.S. Bureau of the Census. *Statistical Abstract of the United States, 1994.* 114th ed. Washington, DC: U.S. Government Printing Office, 1994, p. 324. Primary source: U.S. Bureau of the Census. *City Employment.* Series GE, no. 2 (annual). *Notes:* "X" stands for "not applicable." 1. Data are estimates subject to sampling variation. 2. Based on enumerated resident population as of April 1, 1990. 3. 1980 data not directly comparable to previous years due to a change in how full-time equivalent is calculated. 4. City-operated schools and colleges only. 5. Includes gas supply not shown separately.

★ 290 ★

Employees and Earnings

City Government Employment and Payrolls for Largest Cities: 1980 and 1992

Data for October. Cities are ranked by 1990 population.

| City | Total employment (1,000) | | Full-time equivalent employment[1] | | | | October payroll (million dollars) | | Average earnings in October, full-time employees (dollars) | |
| | | | Total (1,000) | | Per 10,000 population[2] | | | | | |
	1980	1992	1980	1992	1980	1992	1980	1992	1980	1992
New York, New York[3]	364	442	319	415	451	557	504	1,307	1,587	3,154
Los Angeles, California	42	50	41	50	138	140	73	188	1,806	3,815
Chicago, Illinois	47	41	45	41	150	148	71	135	1,569	3,269
Houston, Texas	18	21	18	21	111	129	26	51	1,499	2,404
Philadelphia, Pennsylvania	33	31	32	30	189	189	51	92	1,611	3,092
San Diego, California	8	11	7	9	81	93	12	29	1,773	2,894
Detroit, Michigan	22	19	22	19	179	180	40	49	1,852	2,700
Dallas, Texas	14	14	14	14	153	137	20	36	1,465	2,642
Phoenix, Arizona	9	11	9	11	114	110	14	32	1,517	3,104
San Antonio, Texas	10	14	10	13	128	140	13	32	1,282	2,472
San Jose, California	4[4]	7	4[4]	6	60[4]	76	7[4]	24	1,714[4]	4,206
Baltimore, Maryland[5]	44	28	40	27	514	372	47	70	1,172	2,613
Indianapolis, Indiana	13	13	12	13	174	172	13	26	1,098	2,164
San Francisco, California	21	26	21	26	310	354	37	99	1,761	3,881
Jacksonville, Florida	11[6]	11	11[6]	10	202[6]	156	11[6]	27	1,031[6]	2,888
Columbus, Ohio	8	8	7	8	122	125	10	20	1,498	2,607
Milwaukee, Wisconsin	10	9	9	8	145	133	15	23	1,631	2,782
Memphis, Tennessee[7]	25	24	22	22	342	366	29	53	1,335	2,361
Washington, District of Columbia[3]	45	48	42	46	651	763	73	138	1,761	3,022
Boston, Massachusetts[7]	28[4]	21	25[4]	21	444[4]	361	35[4]	61	1,398[4]	2,949
Seattle, Washington	10	11	9	10	188	197	77	35	1,830	3,494
El Paso, Texas	5	5	4	5	104	99	3	11	942	2,220
Cleveland, Ohio	10	9	9	8	160	167	13	20	1,460	2,742
New Orleans, Louisiana	13[8]	10	13[8]	10	225[8]	149	11[8]	12	919[8]	1,623
Nashville-Davidson, Tennessee[7]	18[9]	18	17[9]	17	374[9]	340	22[9]	40	1,295[9]	2,430
Denver, Colorado	13	14	12	12	244	266	18	35	1,540	2,859
Austin, Texas	8	12	7	11	199	246	10	27	1,515	2,496
Fort Worth, Texas	5[6]	5	5[6]	5	120[6]	114	5[6]	11	1,198[6]	2,277
Oklahoma City, Oklahoma	5	5	4	5	104	104	6	12	1,323	2,567
Portland, Oregon	5	5[10]	4	5[10]	115	104[10]	8	15[10]	1,916	3,363[10]
Kansas City, Missouri	7	6[10]	7	6[10]	145	146[10]	9	16[10]	1,368	2,485[10]
Long Beach, California	5[4]	6	4[4]	5	122[4]	123	7[4]	18	1,678[4]	3,627
Tucson, Arizona	4	5	4	5	124	118	6	12	1,474	2,645
St. Louis, Missouri	13	8	13	7	280	188	15	18	1,279	2,405
Charlotte, North Carolina	4	5	4	5	125	115	5	11	1,290	2,436
Atlanta, Georgia	8	8	8	8	187	197	10	18	1,230	2,373
Virginia Beach, Virginia[7]	10	15	9	14	346	356	11	30	1,204	2,275
Albuquerque, New Mexico	4[6]	7	4[6]	6	119[6]	147	4[6]	12	1,135[6]	2,100
Oakland, California	4	6	4	5	109	130	7	17	2,011	3,985
Pittsburgh, Pennsylvania	6[8]	7	6[8]	5	135[8]	145	6[8]	14	1,116[8]	3,092
Sacramento, California	3	4	3	4	119	107	6	13	1,762	3,384

[Continued]

★ 290 ★

City Government Employment and Payrolls for Largest Cities: 1980 and 1992
[Continued]

City	Total employment (1,000)		Full-time equivalent employment[1]				October payroll (million dollars)		Average earnings in October, full-time employees (dollars)	
			Total (1,000)		Per 10,000 popu-lation[2]					
	1980	1992	1980	1992	1980	1992	1980	1992	1980	1992
Minneapolis, Minnesota	6	7	5	6	136	161	9	18	1,821	3,097
Tulsa, Oklahoma	4[4]	4	4[4]	4	115[4]	120	5[4]	11	1,184[4]	2,463
Honolulu, Hawaii	9	11	9	9	117	111	12	29	1,401	3,139
Cincinnati, Ohio	7	8	7	7	174	191	10	20	1,527	3,092
Miami, Florida	4	4	4	4	118	101	6	14	1,408	3,994
Fresno, California	3	3	3	3	115	73	4	8	1,607	3,043
Omaha, Nebraska	3	3	3	3	92	81	5	8	1,684	3,138
Toledo, Ohio	4	3	3	3	96	86	6	9	1,758	2,955
Buffalo, New York[7]	14	14	13	13	348	390	18	36	1,475	2,986
Wichita, Kansas	3	3	3	3	111	97	4	7	1,327	2,429
Santa Ana, California	2	2	1	2	68	64	2	9	1,819	5,162
Mesa, Arizona	1	2	1	2	89	82	2	7	1,592	2,908
Colorado Springs, Colorado	4	5	3	5	158	181	5	13	1,445	2,594
Tampa, Florida	5	4	5	4	165	140	5	11	1,178	2,861
Newark, New Jersey[11]	12	3	12	4	374	139	17	12	1,387	3,220
St. Paul, Minnesota	4	3	3	3	125	119	6	11	1,734	3,429
Louisville, Kentucky	6	4	6	4	186	160	7	8	1,358	1,965
Anaheim, California	2	1	2	3	91	98	3	10	1,616	4,235
Birmingham, Alabama	4	4	4	4	128	145	5	9	1,333	2,293
Arlington, Texas	1[6]	2	1[6]	2	63[6]	73	1[6]	5	1,180[6]	2,721
Norfolk, Virginia[7]	11	11	10	10	380	394	12	24	1,222	2,349

Source: U.S. Bureau of the Census. *Statistical Abstract of the United States, 1994.* 114th ed. Washington, DC: U.S. Government Printing Office, 1994, p. 325. Primary sources: U.S. Bureau of the Census. *City Employment.* Series GE, no. 2 (annual); and unpublished data. *Notes:* 1. 1992 data not comparable with 1980 due to a change in 1986 in how full-time equivalent was calculated. 2. 1980 based on enumerated resident population as of April 1, 1980. 1992 based on enumerated resident population as of April 1, 1990. 3. Includes city-operated elementary and secondary schools and city-operated universities or colleges. 4. 1979 data. 5. Includes city-operated elementary and secondary schools. Prior to 1990, includes data for city operated colleges. 6. 1978 data. 7. Includes city-operated elementary and secondary schools. 8. 1977 data. 9. Noneducation data are for 1979. 10. 1991 data. 11. Prior to 1983, city-operated elementary and secondary schools.

★ 291 ★

Employees and Earnings

Construction Employees and Earnings of Production Workers: 1980-1993

Annual averages of monthly figures. Covers all full- and part-time employees who worked during, or received pay for, any part of the pay period, including the 12th of the month. Data refer to employees engaged in actual construction work.

Industry	1987 SIC code[1]	All total employees (1,000)			Production workers					
					Total (1,000)			Average hourly earnings ($)		
		1980	1990	1993	1980	1990	1993	1980	1990	1993
Total	(X)	90,406	109,419	110,178	(NA)	(NA)	(NA)	(NA)	(NA)	(NA)
Private sector[2]	(X)	74,166	91,115	91,336	60,331	73,800	74,353	6.66	10.01	10.83
Construction	(C)	4,346	5,120	4,574	3,421	3,974	3,524	9.94	13.77	14.35
General building contractors	15	1,173	1,298	1,061	900	938	749	9.22	13.01	13.60
Heavy construction, except building	16	895	770	709	720	643	590	9.20	13.34	14.09
Special trade contractors	17	2,278	3,051	2,804	1,802	2,393	2,185	10.63	14.20	14.68

Source: U.S. Bureau of the Census. *Statistical Abstract of the United States, 1994.* 114th ed. Washington, DC: U.S. Government Printing Office, 1994, p. 422. Primary sources: U.S. Bureau of Labor Statistics. Bulletins 2370 and 2429; and *Employment and Earnings* (March and June issues). *Notes:* "NA" stands for "not available"; "X" for "not applicable." 1. 1987 Standard Industrial Classification (SIC). 2. Excludes government.

★ 292 ★

Employees and Earnings

Electronic and Electrical Equipment Manufacturing Employees and Earnings of Production Workers: 1980-1993

Annual averages of monthly figures. Covers all full- and part-time employees who worked during, or received pay for, any part of the pay period, including the 12th of the month. Data refer to production and related workers.

Industry	1987 SIC code[1]	All total employees (1,000)			Production workers					
					Total (1,000)			Average hourly earnings ($)		
		1980	1990	1993	1980	1990	1993	1980	1990	1993
Total	(X)	90,406	109,419	110,178	(NA)	(NA)	(NA)	(NA)	(NA)	(NA)
Private sector[2]	(X)	74,166	91,115	91,336	60,331	73,800	74,353	6.66	10.01	10.83
Manufacturing	(D)	20,285	19,076	17,802	14,214	12,947	12,143	7.27	10.83	11.76
Durable goods	(X)	12,159	11,109	10,047	8,416	7,363	6,726	7.75	11.35	12.34
Electronic and other electrical equipment[3]	36	1,771	1,673	1,513	(4)	1,055	967	(4)	10.30	11.24
Electric distribution equipment	361	117	97	81	82	67	56	6.96	10.15	10.94
Electrical industrial apparatus	362	232	169	158	163	119	111	(4)	10.00	10.64
Household appliances	363	162	124	121	128	99	97	6.95	10.26	10.48
Electric lighting and wiring equipment	364	211	189	173	157	136	125	6.43	10.12	10.98
Household audio and video equipment	365	109	85	83	79	59	55	6.42	9.68	10.96
Communications equipment	366	(4)	264	231	(4)	133	118	(4)	11.03	11.72
Electronic components and accessories	367	539	582	518	325	329	302	6.05	10.00	11.24

Source: U.S. Bureau of the Census. *Statistical Abstract of the United States, 1994.* 114th ed. Washington, DC: U.S. Government Printing Office, 1994, p. 422. Primary sources: U.S. Bureau of Labor Statistics. Bulletins 2370 and 2429; and *Employment and Earnings* (March and June issues). *Notes:* "NA" stands for "not available"; "X" for "not applicable." 1. 1987 Standard Industrial Classification (SIC). 2. Excludes government. 3. Includes industries not shown separately. 4. Included in totals; not available separately.

★ 293 ★

Employees and Earnings

Federal Civilian Employment and Annual Payroll, by Branch: 1970-1992

Average annual employment for fiscal year ending in year shown. Includes employees in U.S. territories and foreign countries. Data represent employees in active-duty status, including intermittent employees. Annual employment figures are averages of monthly figures. Excludes Central Intelligence Agency, National Security Agency, and, as of November 1984, the Defense Intelligence Agency.

Year	Employment						Payroll (million dollars)				
	Total (1,000)	Percent of U.S. employed[1]	Executive		Legislative (1,000)	Judicial (1,000)	Total	Executive		Legislative	Judicial
			Total (1,000)	Defense (1,000)				Total	Defense		
1970[2]	2,997	3.8	2,961	1,263	29	7	27,322	26,894	11,264	338	89
1975	2,877	3.4	2,830	1,044	37	10	39,126	38,423	13,418	549	154
1980[3]	2,987	3.0	2,933	971	40	14	58,012	56,841	18,795	883	288
1981	2,909	2.9	2,855	986	40	15	63,793	62,510	21,227	922	360
1982	2,871	2.9	2,816	1,019	39	16	65,503	64,125	22,226	980	398
1983	2,878	2.9	2,823	1,033	39	16	69,878	68,420	23,406	1,013	445
1984	2,935	2.8	2,879	1,052	40	17	74,616	73,084	25,253	1,081	451
1985	3,001	2.8	2,944	1,080	39	18	80,599	78,992	28,330	1,098	509
1986	3,047	2.8	2,991	1,089	38	19	82,598	80,941	29,272	1,112	545
1987	3,075	2.7	3,018	1,084	38	19	85,543	83,797	29,786	1,153	593
1988	3,113	2.7	3,054	1,073	38	21	88,841	86,960	29,609	1,226	656
1989	3,133	2.7	3,074	1,067	38	22	92,847	90,870	30,301	1,266	711
1990[4]	3,233	2.7	3,173	1,060	38	23	99,138	97,022	31,990	1,329	787
1991	3,101	2.7	3,038	1,015	38	25	104,273	101,965	32,956	1,434	874
1992	3,106	2.6	3,040	1,004	39	27	108,054	105,402	31,486	1,569	1,083

Source: U.S. Bureau of the Census. *Statistical Abstract of the United States, 1994.* 114th ed. Washington, DC: U.S. Government Printing Office, 1994. p. 347. Primary sources: U.S. Office of Personnel Management. *Federal Civilian Workforce Statistics: Employment and Trends* (bimonthly); and unpublished data. *Notes:* 1. Civilian only. 2. Includes 33,000 temporary census workers. 3. Includes 81,116 temporary census workers. 4. Includes 111,020 temporary census workers.

★ 294 ★

Employees and Earnings

Federal Civilian Full-Time Employment and Earnings: 1990-1993

As of March 31. Covers all areas, but excludes employees of Congress and federal courts, maritime seamen of the Department of Commerce, and small number for whom rates were not reported.

Compensation	Employees (1,000)				Average pay			
	1990	1991	1992	1993	1990	1991	1992	1993
Total	2,697	2,665	2,051	2,017	31,174	33,340	35,357	37,327
General Schedule	1,506	1,499	1,537	1,520	31,239	33,288	35,254	37,332
Wage System	369	328	328	315	26,565	27,543	28,852	30,136
Postal pay system[1]	661	651	(NA)	(NA)	31,992	33,186	(NA)	(NA)
Other	161	187	186	182	41,149	43,926	42,689	49,743

Source: U.S. Bureau of the Census. *Statistical Abstract of the United States, 1994.* 114th ed. Washington, DC: U.S. Government Printing Office, 1994, p. 348. Primary source, except as noted: U.S. Office of Personnel Management. *Pay Structure of the Federal Civil Service* (annual). *Notes:* "NA" stands for "not available." 1. From U.S. Postal Service's *National Payroll Hours* (annual).

★ 295 ★

Employees and Earnings

Finance, Insurance, and Real Estate Employees and Earnings of Production Workers: 1980-1993

Annual averages of monthly figures. Covers all full- and part-time employees who worked during, or received pay for, any part of the pay period, including the 12th of the month. Data refer to nonsupervisory employees and working supervisors.

Industry	1987 SIC code[1]	All total employees (1,000)			Production workers					
					Total (1,000)			Average hourly earnings ($)		
		1980	1990	1993	1980	1990	1993	1980	1990	1993
Total	(X)	90,406	109,419	110,178	(NA)	(NA)	(NA)	(NA)	(NA)	(NA)
Private sector[2]	(X)	74,166	91,115	91,336	60,331	73,800	74,353	6.66	10.01	10.83
Finance, insurance, real estate	(H)	5,160	6,709	6,604	3,907	4,860	4,798	5.79	9.97	11.32
Depository institutions	60	(3)	2,251	2,115	(3)	1,632	1,531	(3)	8.43	9.12
Nondepository institutions	61	(3)	373	410	(3)	270	309	(3)	10.40	12.30
Security and commodity brokers	62	227	424	463	(3)	(3)	(3)	(3)	(3)	(3)
Insurance carriers	63	1,224	1,462	1,465	854	982	1,011	6.29	11.18	13.16
Insurance, agents, brokers, service	64	464	663	647	(3)	(3)	(3)	(3)	(3)	(3)
Real estate	65	989	1,315	1,280	(3)	(3)	(3)	(3)	(3)	(3)
Holding and other investment offices	67	115	221	225	(3)	(3)	(3)	(3)	(3)	(3)

Source: U.S. Bureau of the Census. *Statistical Abstract of the United States, 1994.* 114th ed. Washington, DC: U.S. Government Printing Office, 1994, p. 424. Primary sources: U.S. Bureau of Labor Statistics. Bulletins 2370 and 2429; and *Employment and Earnings* (March and June issues). *Notes:* "NA" stands for "not available"; "X" for "not applicable." 1. 1987 Standard Industrial Classification (SIC). 2. Excludes government. 3. Included in totals; not available separately.

★ 296 ★

Employees and Earnings

Food and Related Manufacturing Employees and Earnings of Production Workers: 1980-1993

Annual averages of monthly figures. Covers all full- and part-time employees who worked during, or received pay for, any part of the pay period, including the 12th of the month. Data refer to production and related workers.

Industry	1987 SIC code[1]	All total employees (1,000)			Production workers					
					Total (1,000)			Average hourly earnings ($)		
		1980	1990	1993	1980	1990	1993	1980	1990	1993
Total	(X)	90,406	109,419	110,178	(NA)	(NA)	(NA)	(NA)	(NA)	(NA)
Private sector[2]	(X)	74,166	91,115	91,336	60,331	73,800	74,353	6.66	10.01	10.83
Manufacturing	(D)	20,285	19,076	17,802	14,214	12,947	12,143	7.27	10.83	11.76
Nondurable goods	(X)	8,127	7,968	7,755	5,798	5,584	5,417	6.56	10.12	11.00
Food and kindred products[3]	20	1,708	1,661	1,650	1,175	1,194	1,205	6.85	9.62	10.43
Meat products	201	358	422	443	298	359	377	6.99	7.94	8.49
Dairy products	202	175	155	151	96	95	95	6.86	10.56	11.66
Preserved fruits and vegetables	203	246	247	242	202	206	202	5.94	8.95	10.05
Grain mill products	204	144	128	123	99	89	88	7.67	11.52	12.61
Bakery products	205	230	213	207	139	133	133	7.14	10.85	11.73
Sugar and confectionery products	206	108	99	101	81	78	78	6.56	10.26	11.26
Fats and oils	207	44	31	31	32	22	21	7.03	10.10	10.90
Beverages	208	234	184	176	105	78	80	8.12	13.51	14.53

Source: U.S. Bureau of the Census. *Statistical Abstract of the United States, 1994.* 114th ed. Washington, DC: U.S. Government Printing Office, 1994, p. 423. Primary sources: U.S. Bureau of Labor Statistics. Bulletins 2370 and 2429; and *Employment and Earnings* (March and June issues). *Notes:* "NA" stands for "not available"; "X" for "not applicable." 1. 1987 Standard Industrial Classification (SIC). 2. Excludes government. 3. Includes industries not shown separately.

★ 297 ★

Employees and Earnings

Government Employees and Earnings of Production Workers: 1980-1993

Annual averages of monthly figures. Covers all full- and part-time employees who worked during, or received pay for, any part of the pay period, including the 12th of the month. Data refer to nonsupervisory employees and working supervisors.

Industry	1987 SIC code[1]	All total employees (1,000)			Production workers					
					Total (1,000)			Average hourly earnings ($)		
		1980	1990	1993	1980	1990	1993	1980	1990	1993
Total	(X)	90,406	109,419	110,178	(NA)	(NA)	(NA)	(NA)	(NA)	(NA)
Government	(J)	16,241	18,304	18,842	(NA)	(NA)	(NA)	(NA)	(NA)	(²)
Federal government	(X)	2,866	3,085	2,915	(NA)	(NA)	(NA)	(NA)	(NA)	(²)
State government	(X)	3,610	4,305	4,467	(NA)	(NA)	(NA)	(NA)	(NA)	(²)
Local government	(X)	9,765	10,914	11,459	(NA)	(NA)	(NA)	(NA)	(NA)	(²)

Source: U.S. Bureau of the Census. *Statistical Abstract of the United States, 1994.* 114th ed. Washington, DC: U.S. Government Printing Office, 1994, p. 424. Primary sources: U.S. Bureau of Labor Statistics. Bulletins 2370 and 2429; and *Employment and Earnings* (March and June issues). *Notes:* "NA" stands for "not available"; "X" for "not applicable." 1. 1987 Standard Industrial Classification (SIC). 2. Included in totals; not available separately.

★ 298 ★

Employees and Earnings

Government Employment and Payroll, by Function: 1992

For October. Covers both full-time and part-time employees in federal, state, and local governments. Local government data are estimates subject to sampling variation.

Function	Employees (1,000)					October payrolls (million dollars)				
	Total	Federal (civilian)[1]	State and local			Total	Federal (civilian)[1]	State and local		
			Total	State	Local			Total	State	Local
Total	18,745	3,047	15,698	4,595	11,103	43,120	9,937	33,183	9,828	23,355
National defense[2]	984	984	(X)	(X)	(X)	2,913	2,913	(X)	(X)	(X)
Postal Service	774	774	(X)	(X)	(X)	2,654	2,654	(X)	(X)	(X)
Space research and technology	25	25	(X)	(X)	(X)	112	112	(X)	(X)	(X)
Education	8,239	14	8,225	2,050	6,174	16,565	45	16,521	3,774	12,747
Highways	565	4	561	261	300	1,271	19	1,252	626	626
Health and hospitals	1,854	310	1,544	721	823	4,292	952	3,340	1,613	1,727
Public welfare	506	10	496	215	281	1,051	36	1,015	471	544
Police protection	858	88	770	87	683	2,396	335	2,061	247	1,814
Fire protection	344	(X)	344	(X)	344	825	(X)	825	(X)	825
Sanitation and sewerage	244	(X)	244	3	241	554	(X)	554	8	547
Parks and recreation	345	27	318	42	276	514	72	441	70	371
Natural resources	436	232	204	164	40	1,249	818	431	355	76
Financial administration	493	138	355	151	205	1,176	425	751	351	400
Government administration, other	399	29	370	52	318	668	100	568	125	443
Judicial and legal	374	51	323	114	209	1,013	181	832	350	482
Other	2,303	360	1,943	734	1,209	5,865	1,273	4,592	1,839	2,753

Source: U.S. Bureau of the Census. *Statistical Abstract of the United States, 1994.* 114th ed. Washington, DC: U.S. Government Printing Office, 1994, p. 319. Primary source: U.S. Bureau of the Census. *Public Employment.* Series GE, no. 1 (annual). *Notes:* "X" stands for "not applicable." 1. Includes employees outside United States. 2. Includes international relations.

★ 299 ★

Employees and Earnings

Industrial Machinery and Equipment Manufacturing Employees and Earnings of Production Workers: 1980-1993

Annual averages of monthly figures. Covers all full- and part-time employees who worked during, or received pay for, any part of the pay period, including the 12th of the month. Data refer to production and related workers.

Industry	1987 SIC code[1]	All total employees (1,000)			Production workers					
					Total (1,000)			Average hourly earnings ($)		
		1980	1990	1993	1980	1990	1993	1980	1990	1993
Total	(X)	90,406	109,419	110,178	(NA)	(NA)	(NA)	(NA)	(NA)	(NA)
Private sector[2]	(X)	74,166	91,115	91,336	60,331	73,800	74,353	6.66	10.01	10.83
Manufacturing	(D)	20,285	19,076	17,802	14,214	12,947	12,143	7.27	10.83	11.76
Durable goods	(X)	12,159	11,109	10,047	8,416	7,363	6,726	7.75	11.35	12.34
Industrial machinery and equipment[3]	35	2,517	2,095	1,900	1,614	1,260	1,150	8.00	11.77	12.73
Engines and turbines	351	135	89	88	87	58	55	9.73	14.55	16.11
Farm and garden machinery	352	169	106	97	116	78	70	8.78	10.99	12.08
Construction and related machinery	353	389	229	207	255	141	127	8.60	11.92	12.92
Metalworking machinery	354	398	330	305	290	236	214	8.13	12.27	13.33
Special industry machinery	355	194	159	146	125	94	84	7.53	11.90	13.14

[Continued]

★ 299 ★

Industrial Machinery and Equipment Manufacturing Employees and Earnings of Production Workers: 1980-1993

[Continued]

Industry	1987 SIC code[1]	All total employees (1,000)			Production workers					
					Total (1,000)			Average hourly earnings ($)		
		1980	1990	1993	1980	1990	1993	1980	1990	1993
General industrial machinery	356	300	247	233	196	158	148	7.95	11.32	12.45
Computer and office equipment	357	420	438	361	181	137	121	6.75	11.51	12.52
Refrigeration and service machinery	358	175	177	175	120	125	123	7.23	10.93	11.48

Source: U.S. Bureau of the Census. Statistical Abstract of the United States, 1994. 114th ed. Washington, DC: U.S. Government Printing Office, 1994, p. 422. Primary sources: U.S. Bureau of Labor Statistics. Bulletins 2370 and 2429; and Employment and Earnings (March and June issues). Notes: "NA" stands for "not available"; "X" for "not applicable." 1. 1987 Standard Industrial Classification (SIC). 2. Excludes government. 3. Includes industries not shown separately.

★ 300 ★

Employees and Earnings

Instrument Manufacturing Employees and Earnings of Production Workers: 1980-1993

Annual averages of monthly figures. Covers all full- and part-time employees who worked during, or received pay for, any part of the pay period, including the 12th of the month. Data refer to production and related workers.

Industry	1987 SIC code[1]	All total employees (1,000)			Production workers					
					Total (1,000)			Average hourly earnings ($)		
		1980	1990	1993	1980	1990	1993	1980	1990	1993
Total	(X)	90,406	109,419	110,178	(NA)	(NA)	(NA)	(NA)	(NA)	(NA)
Private sector[2]	(X)	74,166	91,115	91,336	60,331	73,800	74,353	6.66	10.01	10.83
Manufacturing	(D)	20,285	19,076	17,802	14,214	12,947	12,143	7.27	10.83	11.76
Durable goods	(X)	12,159	11,109	10,047	8,416	7,363	6,726	7.75	11.35	12.34
Instruments and related products	38	1,022	1,006	881	([3])	499	430	([3])	11.29	12.25
Search and navigation equipment	381	([3])	284	201	([3])	94	63	([3])	14.62	16.25
Measuring and controlling devices	382	([3])	323	277	([3])	180	142	([3])	10.68	12.09
Medical instruments and supplies	384	([3])	246	265	([3])	144	153	([3])	9.85	10.86
Ophthalmic goods	385	44	43	38	31	30	26	5.30	8.18	8.77
Photographic equipment and supplies	386	135	100	92	67	43	40	8.83	14.08	14.65
Watches, clocks, watchcases, and parts	387	22	11	8	17	8	7	5.24	7.70	8.22

Source: U.S. Bureau of the Census. Statistical Abstract of the United States, 1994. 114th ed. Washington, DC: U.S. Government Printing Office, 1994, p. 423. Primary sources: U.S. Bureau of Labor Statistics. Bulletins 2370 and 2429; and Employment and Earnings (March and June issues). Notes: "NA" stands for "not available"; "X" for "not applicable." 1. 1987 Standard Industrial Classification (SIC). 2. Excludes government. 3. Included in totals; not available separately.

★ 301 ★

Employees and Earnings

Leather Manufacturing Employees and Earnings of Production Workers: 1980-1993

Annual averages of monthly figures. Covers all full- and part-time employees who worked during, or received pay for, any part of the pay period, including the 12th of the month. Data refer to production and related workers.

Industry	1987 SIC code[1]	All total employees (1,000)			Production workers					
					Total (1,000)			Average hourly earnings ($)		
		1980	1990	1993	1980	1990	1993	1980	1990	1993
Total	(X)	90,406	109,419	110,178	(NA)	(NA)	(NA)	(NA)	(NA)	(NA)
Private sector[2]	(X)	74,166	91,115	91,336	60,331	73,800	74,353	6.66	10.01	10.83
Manufacturing	(D)	20,285	19,076	17,802	14,214	12,947	12,143	7.27	10.83	11.76
Nondurable goods	(X)	8,127	7,968	7,755	5,798	5,584	5,417	6.56	10.12	11.00
Leather and leather products[3]	31	233	133	116	197	109	93	4.58	6.91	7.62
Leather tanning and finishing	311	19	15	15	16	12	13	6.10	9.04	9.92
Footwear, except rubber	314	144	74	62	123	63	51	4.42	6.61	7.18
Luggage	316	16	11	10	12	8	7	4.90	6.91	7.82
Handbags and personal leather goods	317	30	15	12	25	12	8	4.33	6.08	6.84

Source: U.S. Bureau of the Census. *Statistical Abstract of the United States, 1994.* 114th ed. Washington, DC: U.S. Government Printing Office, 1994, p. 423. Primary sources: U.S. Bureau of Labor Statistics. Bulletins 2370 and 2429; and *Employment and Earnings* (March and June issues). *Notes:* "NA" stands for "not available"; "X" for "not applicable." 1. 1987 Standard Industrial Classification (SIC). 2. Excludes government. 3. Includes industries not shown separately.

★ 302 ★

Employees and Earnings

Manufacturing Employees and Earnings of Production Workers: 1980-1993

Data cover miscellaneous manufacturing industries. Annual averages of monthly figures. Covers all full- and part-time employees who worked during, or received pay for, any part of the pay period, including the 12th of the month. Data refer to production and related workers. Also see tables for specific types of manufacturing; for example, instrument or metal manufacturing.

Industry	1987 SIC code[1]	All total employees (1,000)			Production workers					
					Total (1,000)			Average hourly earnings ($)		
		1980	1990	1993	1980	1990	1993	1980	1990	1993
Total	(X)	90,406	109,419	110,178	(NA)	(NA)	(NA)	(NA)	(NA)	(NA)
Private sector[2]	(X)	74,166	91,115	91,336	60,331	73,800	74,353	6.66	10.01	10.83
Manufacturing	(D)	20,285	19,076	17,802	14,214	12,947	12,143	7.27	10.83	11.76
Durable goods	(X)	12,159	11,109	10,047	8,416	7,363	6,726	7.75	11.35	12.34
Miscellaneous manufacturing industries[3]	39	418	375	362	313	272	259	5.46	8.61	9.37
Jewelry, silverware, and plated ware	391	56	52	50	40	37	35	5.76	9.23	9.68
Toys and sporting goods	394	117	104	106	88	76	76	5.01	7.94	8.79
Pens, pencils, office and art supplies	395	37	34	31	27	24	21	5.58	8.89	10.27
Costume jewelry and notions	396	(4)	34	29	(4)	25	22	(4)	7.40	8.10

Source: U.S. Bureau of the Census. *Statistical Abstract of the United States, 1994.* 114th ed. Washington, DC: U.S. Government Printing Office, 1994, p. 423. Primary sources: U.S. Bureau of Labor Statistics. Bulletins 2370 and 2429; and *Employment and Earnings* (March and June issues). *Notes:* "NA" stands for "not available"; "X" for "not applicable." 1. 1987 Standard Industrial Classification (SIC). 2. Excludes government. 3. Includes industries not shown separately. 4. Included in totals; not available separately.

★ 303 ★

Employees and Earnings

Metal Manufacturing Employees and Earnings of Production Workers: 1980-1993

Annual averages of monthly figures. Covers all full- and part-time employees who worked during, or received pay for, any part of the pay period, including the 12th of the month. Data refer to production and related workers.

| Industry | 1987 SIC code[1] | All total employees (1,000) | | | Production workers | | | | | |
| | | | | | Total (1,000) | | | Average hourly earnings ($) | | |
		1980	1990	1993	1980	1990	1993	1980	1990	1993
Total	(X)	90,406	109,419	110,178	(NA)	(NA)	(NA)	(NA)	(NA)	(NA)
Private sector[2]	(X)	74,166	91,115	91,336	60,331	73,800	74,353	6.66	10.01	10.83
Manufacturing	(D)	20,285	19,076	17,802	14,214	12,947	12,143	7.27	10.83	11.76
Durable goods	(X)	12,159	11,109	10,047	8,416	7,363	6,726	7.75	11.35	12.34
Primary metal industries[3]	33	1,142	756	676	878	574	515	9.77	12.92	14.00
Blast furnaces and basic steel products	331	512	276	238	396	212	182	11.39	14.82	16.39
Iron and steel foundries	332	209	132	118	167	105	94	8.20	11.55	12.46
Primary nonferrous metals	333	71	46	43	53	34	32	10.63	14.36	15.19
Nonferrous rolling and drawing	335	211	172	160	151	124	117	8.81	12.29	13.21
Nonferrous foundries (castings)	336	90	84	76	72	66	61	7.30	10.21	11.17
Fabricated metal products[3]	34	1,609	1,419	1,311	1,194	1,045	968	7.45	10.83	11.69
Metal cans and shipping containers	341	75	50	43	63	43	37	9.84	14.27	15.14
Cutlery, handtools, and hardware	342	164	131	123	125	96	91	7.02	10.78	11.59
Plumbing and heating, exc. electric	343	71	60	57	52	43	41	6.59	9.75	10.49
Fabricated structural metal products	344	506	427	386	351	303	274	7.27	10.16	10.88
Screw machine products	345	109	96	90	84	73	69	6.96	10.70	11.54
Metal forgings and stampings	346	260	225	217	205	178	173	8.56	12.70	14.00

Source: U.S. Bureau of the Census. *Statistical Abstract of the United States, 1994.* 114th ed. Washington, DC: U.S. Government Printing Office, 1994, p. 422. Primary sources: U.S. Bureau of Labor Statistics. Bulletins 2370 and 2429; and *Employment and Earnings* (March and June issues). *Notes:* "NA" stands for "not available"; "X" for "not applicable." 1. 1987 Standard Industrial Classification (SIC). 2. Excludes government. 3. Includes industries not shown separately.

★ 304 ★

Employees and Earnings

Mining Employees and Earnings of Production Workers: 1980-1993

Annual averages of monthly figures. Covers all full- and part-time employees who worked during, or received pay for, any part of the pay period, including the 12th of the month. Data refer to production and related workers.

| Industry | 1987 SIC code[1] | All total employees (1,000) | | | Production workers | | | | | |
| | | | | | Total (1,000) | | | Average hourly earnings ($) | | |
		1980	1990	1993	1980	1990	1993	1980	1990	1993
Total	(X)	90,406	109,419	110,178	(NA)	(NA)	(NA)	(NA)	(NA)	(NA)
Private sector[2]	(X)	74,166	91,115	91,336	60,331	73,800	74,353	6.66	10.01	10.83
Mining	(B)	1,027	709	599	762	509	423	9.17	13.68	14.60
Metal mining	10	98	58	51	74	46	41	10.26	14.05	15.31
Coal mining	12	246	147	105	204	119	84	10.86	16.71	17.25
Oil and gas extraction	13	560	395	343	389	261	224	8.59	12.94	14.13
Nonmetallic minerals[3]	14	123	110	100	96	83	75	7.52	11.58	12.70

Source: U.S. Bureau of the Census. *Statistical Abstract of the United States, 1994.* 114th ed. Washington, DC: U.S. Government Printing Office, 1994, p. 422. Primary sources: U.S. Bureau of Labor Statistics. Bulletins 2370 and 2429; and *Employment and Earnings* (March and June issues). *Notes:* "NA" stands for "not available"; "X" for "not applicable." 1. 1987 Standard Industrial Classification (SIC). 2. Excludes government. 3. Except fuels.

★ 305 ★

Employees and Earnings

Paper and Related Manufacturing Employees and Earnings of Production Workers: 1980-1993

Annual averages of monthly figures. Covers all full- and part-time employees who worked during, or received pay for, any part of the pay period, including the 12th of the month. Data refer to production and related workers.

Industry	1987 SIC code[1]	All total employees (1,000)			Production workers					
					Total (1,000)			Average hourly earnings ($)		
		1980	1990	1993	1980	1990	1993	1980	1990	1993
Total	(X)	90,406	109,419	110,178	(NA)	(NA)	(NA)	(NA)	(NA)	(NA)
Private sector[2]	(X)	74,166	91,115	91,336	60,331	73,800	74,353	6.66	10.01	10.83
Manufacturing	(D)	20,285	19,076	17,802	14,214	12,947	12,143	7.27	10.83	11.76
Nondurable goods	(X)	8,127	7,968	7,755	5,798	5,584	5,417	6.56	10.12	11.00
Paper and allied products[3]	26	685	697	680	519	522	513	7.84	12.31	13.42
Papermills	262	178	180	169	133	136	128	9.05	15.10	16.58
Paperboard mills	263	65	52	52	51	40	40	9.28	15.26	16.77
Paperboard containers and boxes	265	205	209	211	157	162	165	6.94	10.39	11.31
Miscellaneous converted paper products	267	220	241	236	163	174	171	6.89	10.79	11.79

Source: U.S. Bureau of the Census. *Statistical Abstract of the United States, 1994.* 114th ed. Washington, DC: U.S. Government Printing Office, 1994, p. 423. Primary sources: U.S. Bureau of Labor Statistics. Bulletins 2370 and 2429; and *Employment and Earnings* (March and June issues). *Notes:* "NA" stands for "not available"; "X" for "not applicable." 1. 1987 Standard Industrial Classification (SIC). 2. Excludes government. 3. Includes industries not shown separately.

★ 306 ★

Employees and Earnings

Petroleum and Coal Product Manufacturing Employees and Earnings of Production Workers: 1980-1993

Annual averages of monthly figures. Covers all full- and part-time employees who worked during, or received pay for, any part of the pay period, including the 12th of the month. Data refer to production and related workers.

Industry	1987 SIC code[1]	All total employees (1,000)			Production workers					
					Total (1,000)			Average hourly earnings ($)		
		1980	1990	1993	1980	1990	1993	1980	1990	1993
Total	(X)	90,406	109,419	110,178	(NA)	(NA)	(NA)	(NA)	(NA)	(NA)
Private sector[2]	(X)	74,166	91,115	91,336	60,331	73,800	74,353	6.66	10.01	10.83
Manufacturing	(D)	20,285	19,076	17,802	14,214	12,947	12,143	7.27	10.83	11.76
Nondurable goods	(X)	8,127	7,968	7,755	5,798	5,584	5,417	6.56	10.12	11.00
Petroleum and coal products[3]	29	198	157	155	125	103	102	10.10	16.24	18.55
Petroleum refining	291	155	118	116	93	75	74	10.94	17.58	20.36
Asphalt paving and roofing materials	295	31	27	28	24	21	21	7.69	12.87	13.77

Source: U.S. Bureau of the Census. *Statistical Abstract of the United States, 1994.* 114th ed. Washington, DC: U.S. Government Printing Office, 1994, p. 423. Primary sources: U.S. Bureau of Labor Statistics. Bulletins 2370 and 2429; and *Employment and Earnings* (March and June issues). *Notes:* "NA" stands for "not available"; "X" for "not applicable." 1. 1987 Standard Industrial Classification (SIC). 2. Excludes government. 3. Includes industries not shown separately.

★ 307 ★

Employees and Earnings

Printing and Publishing Employees and Earnings of Production Workers: 1980-1993

Annual averages of monthly figures. Covers all full- and part-time employees who worked during, or received pay for, any part of the pay period, including the 12th of the month. Data refer to production and related workers.

Industry	1987 SIC code[1]	All total employees (1,000)			Production workers					
					Total (1,000)			Average hourly earnings ($)		
		1980	1990	1993	1980	1990	1993	1980	1990	1993
Total	(X)	90,406	109,419	110,178	(NA)	(NA)	(NA)	(NA)	(NA)	(NA)
Private sector[2]	(X)	74,166	91,115	91,336	60,331	73,800	74,353	6.66	10.01	10.83
Manufacturing	(D)	20,285	19,076	17,802	14,214	12,947	12,143	7.27	10.83	11.76
Nondurable goods	(X)	8,127	7,968	7,755	5,798	5,584	5,417	6.56	10.12	11.00
Printing and publishing[3]	27	1,252	1,569	1,504	699	871	830	7.53	11.24	11.94
Newspapers	271	420	474	452	164	166	157	7.72	11.17	11.86
Periodicals	272	90	129	125	16	47	43	7.16	11.95	13.24
Books	273	101	121	119	52	66	65	6.76	10.10	10.99
Commercial printing	275	410	552	531	304	401	385	7.85	11.52	12.10
Blankbooks and bookbinding	278	62	72	67	51	56	51	5.78	8.83	9.33

Source: U.S. Bureau of the Census. *Statistical Abstract of the United States, 1994.* 114th ed. Washington, DC: U.S. Government Printing Office, 1994, p. 423. Primary sources: U.S. Bureau of Labor Statistics. Bulletins 2370 and 2429; and *Employment and Earnings* (March and June issues). *Notes:* "NA" stands for "not available"; "X" for "not applicable." 1. 1987 Standard Industrial Classification (SIC). 2. Excludes government. 3. Includes industries not shown separately.

★ 308 ★

Employees and Earnings

Rubber and Plastics Manufacturing Employees and Earnings of Production Workers: 1980-1993

Annual averages of monthly figures. Covers all full- and part-time employees who worked during, or received pay for, any part of the pay period, including the 12th of the month. Data refer to production and related workers.

Industry	1987 SIC code[1]	All total employees (1,000)			Production workers					
					Total (1,000)			Average hourly earnings ($)		
		1980	1990	1993	1980	1990	1993	1980	1990	1993
Total	(X)	90,406	109,419	110,178	(NA)	(NA)	(NA)	(NA)	(NA)	(NA)
Private sector[2]	(X)	74,166	91,115	91,336	60,331	73,800	74,353	6.66	10.01	10.83
Manufacturing	(D)	20,285	19,076	17,802	14,214	12,947	12,143	7.27	10.83	11.76
Nondurable goods	(X)	8,127	7,968	7,755	5,798	5,584	5,417	6.56	10.12	11.00
Rubber and misc. plastics products[3]	30	764	888	886	588	687	685	6.58	9.76	10.60
Tires and inner tubes	301	115	84	84	81	62	62	9.74	15.42	17.57
Rubber and plastics footwear	302	22	11	11	20	9	9	4.43	6.66	7.59

Source: U.S. Bureau of the Census. *Statistical Abstract of the United States, 1994.* 114th ed. Washington, DC: U.S. Government Printing Office, 1994, p. 423. Primary sources: U.S. Bureau of Labor Statistics. Bulletins 2370 and 2429; and *Employment and Earnings* (March and June issues). *Notes:* "NA" stands for "not available"; "X" for "not applicable." 1. 1987 Standard Industrial Classification (SIC). 2. Excludes government. 3. Includes industries not shown separately.

★ 309 ★
Employees and Earnings

Services Employees and Earnings of Production Workers: 1980-1993

Annual averages of monthly figures. Covers all full- and part-time employees who worked during, or received pay for, any part of the pay period, including the 12th of the month. Data refer to nonsupervisory employees and working supervisors.

Industry	1987 SIC code[1]	All total employees (1,000)			Production workers					
					Total (1,000)			Average hourly earnings ($)		
		1980	1990	1993	1980	1990	1993	1980	1990	1993
Total	(X)	90,406	109,419	110,178	(NA)	(NA)	(NA)	(NA)	(NA)	(NA)
Private sector[2]	(X)	74,166	91,115	91,336	60,331	73,800	74,353	6.66	10.01	10.83
Services[3]	(I)	17,890	27,934	30,192	15,921	24,387	26,368	5.85	9.83	10.81
Hotels and other lodging places	70	1,076	1,631	1,577	(4)	(4)	(4)	(4)	(4)	(4)
Hotels and motels	701	1,038	1,578	1,524	954	1,398	1,343	4.45	6.98	7.57
Personal services[3]	72	818	1,104	1,109	(4)	(4)	(4)	(4)	(4)	(4)
Laundry, cleaning, garment services	721	356	426	420	318	379	371	4.47	6.82	7.28
Beauty shops	723	284	372	382	264	333	341	4.26	7.10	7.83
Business services[3]	73	2,564	5,139	5,749	(4)	4,522	5,106	(4)	9.48	10.11
Advertising	731	153	235	226	116	169	164	8.07	13.51	14.99
Personnel supply services	736	543	1,535	1,977	(4)	(4)	(4)	(4)	(4)	(4)
Employment agencies	7361	(4)	246	266	(4)	(4)	(4)	(4)	(4)	(4)
Help supply services	7363	(4)	1,288	1,711	(4)	1,245	1,658	(4)	8.09	8.31
Computer and data processing services	737	304	772	882	254	603	716	7.16	15.11	16.35
Prepackaged software	7372	(4)	113	143	(4)	(4)	(4)	(4)	(4)	(4)
Data processing and preparation	7374	(4)	197	214	(4)	(4)	(4)	(4)	(4)	(4)
Auto repair, services, and parking	75	571	914	927	488	756	762	6.10	8.77	9.31
Automotive repair shops	753	350	524	523	297	429	423	6.52	9.67	10.27
Motion pictures	78	(4)	408	421	(4)	344	348	(4)	10.95	12.95
Motion picture theaters	783	124	112	107	(4)	(4)	(4)	(4)	(4)	(4)
Amusement and recreation services	79	(4)	1,076	1,182	(4)	944	1,032	(4)	8.11	8.39
Health services[3]	80	5,278	7,814	8,871	4,712	6,948	7,869	5.68	10.41	11.77
Offices and clinics of medical doctors	801	802	1,338	1,545	(4)	1,105	1,262	(4)	10.58	11.88
Nursing and personal care facilities	805	997	1,415	1,615	898	1,279	1,458	4.17	7.24	8.15
Hospitals	806	2,750	3,549	3,816	2,522	3,248	3,498	6.06	11.79	13.47
Home health care services	808	(4)	291	474	(4)	269	439	(4)	8.72	10.42
Legal services	81	498	908	930	427	748	749	7.35	14.16	15.28
Educational services	82	1,138	1,661	1,747	(4)	(4)	(4)	(4)	(4)	(4)
Social services	83	1,134	1,734	2,068	(4)	1,494	1,790	(4)	7.11	7.86
Membership organizations	86	1,539	1,946	1,960	(4)	(4)	(4)	(4)	(4)	(4)
Engineering and management services	87	(4)	2,478	2,522	(4)	1,886	1,926	(4)	13.56	15.04

Source: U.S. Bureau of the Census. *Statistical Abstract of the United States, 1994.* 114th ed. Washington, DC: U.S. Government Printing Office, 1994, p. 424. Primary sources: U.S. Bureau of Labor Statistics. Bulletins 2370 and 2429; and *Employment and Earnings* (March and June issues). *Notes:* "NA" stands for "not available"; "X" for "not applicable." 1. 1987 Standard Industrial Classification (SIC). 2. Excludes government. 3. Includes industries not shown separately. 4. Included in totals; not available separately.

★ 310 ★
Employees and Earnings

State and Local Government Employment and Earnings, by State: 1986 and 1992

Data are for October.

[Earnings in dollars]

State	Full-time equivalent employment (1,000)				Full-time equivalent employment per 10,000 population[2]				Average October earnings[3] (dollars)			
	State		Local[1]		State		Local[1]		State		Local	
	1986	1992	1986	1992	1986	1992	1986	1992	1986	1992	1986	1992
United States	3,437	3,856	8,415	9,513	143	151	349	373	2,052	2,621	1,992	2,539
Alabama	70	81	131	154	174	196	324	373	1,884	2,243	1,532	1,830
Alaska	21	24	20	22	393	413	377	371	3,228	3,258	3,324	3,590
Arizona	43	54	119	145	128	141	358	379	2,126	2,361	2,185	2,557
Arkansas	39	47	71	82	163	194	299	342	1,724	2,195	1,388	1,724
California	279	323	965	1,108	104	104	358	359	2,751	3,420	2,535	3,281
Colorado	50	53	122	132	155	153	375	381	2,368	3,016	2,017	2,450
Connecticut	56	54	95	97	175	165	297	296	2,336	3,286	2,089	3,160
Delaware	17	20	16	18	272	293	252	254	1,795	2,463	1,991	2,669
District of Columbia	(X)	(X)	51	55	(X)	(X)	817	928	(X)	(X)	2,594	3,175
Florida	124	164	407	500	106	122	348	370	1,748	2,202	1,872	2,294
Georgia	91	114	239	283	149	170	391	419	1,811	2,075	1,589	1,968
Hawaii	41	51	12	14	389	437	113	120	1,844	2,554	2,010	3,031
Idaho	18	20	33	40	175	190	332	373	1,766	2,265	1,535	1,943
Illinois	130	137	385	431	113	117	333	370	2,165	2,642	2,166	2,672
Indiana	75	95	182	202	136	168	330	358	2,056	2,506	1,686	2,199
Iowa	57	47	101	108	199	168	355	386	2,049	2,895	1,735	2,179
Kansas	43	48	96	109	174	190	390	433	1,687	2,191	1,700	2,133
Kentucky	63	76	102	121	170	203	275	322	1,651	2,349	1,596	1,980
Louisiana	86	89	151	161	191	207	337	375	1,673	2,227	1,494	1,800
Maine	20	22	36	43	168	178	307	349	1,714	2,437	1,590	2,101
Maryland	80	82	143	158	178	167	321	321	2,046	2,720	2,233	2,892
Massachusetts	88	85	192	192	151	142	329	321	2,034	2,645	2,082	2,775
Michigan	128	138	315	323	140	146	344	342	2,541	3,134	2,329	2,906
Minnesota	61	67	137	173	145	150	326	385	2,428	3,101	2,318	2,673
Mississippi	42	47	95	108	161	181	364	412	1,430	2,000	1,324	1,608
Missouri	66	74	157	174	130	143	310	334	1,621	2,075	1,826	2,133
Montana	16	17	29	37	192	207	349	451	1,864	2,300	1,727	1,995
Nebraska	29	29	65	71	184	179	407	441	1,509	2,185	1,785	2,198
Nevada	15	19	33	47	154	144	343	353	1,990	2,738	2,140	2,772
New Hampshire	18	16	29	36	172	147	285	320	1,759	2,416	1,701	2,456
New Jersey	96	116	283	302	126	149	372	387	2,278	3,100	2,146	3,062
New Mexico	34	42	49	60	231	267	332	381	1,792	2,253	1,680	1,858
New York	272	267	810	884	153	148	456	488	2,355	3,143	2,266	3,147
North Carolina	93	109	216	260	147	159	341	380	1,935	2,413	1,662	2,092
North Dakota	15	16	22	21	222	259	318	331	1,805	2,231	2,017	2,269
Ohio	122	140	365	399	113	127	340	363	1,984	2,691	1,911	2,417
Oklahoma	64	67	109	121	195	209	329	376	1,733	2,044	1,595	1,903
Oregon	44	50	91	106	163	167	338	354	1,975	2,607	2,018	2,599

[Continued]

★ 310 ★

State and Local Government Employment and Earnings, by State: 1986 and 1992
[Continued]

State	Full-time equivalent employment (1,000)				Full-time equivalent employment per 10,000 population[2]				Average October earnings[3] (dollars)			
	State		Local[1]		State		Local[1]		State		Local	
	1986	1992	1986	1992	1986	1992	1986	1992	1986	1992	1986	1992
Pennsylvania	124	143	340	367	104	119	286	305	1,915	2,696	1,976	2,622
Rhode Island	19	20	24	28	195	198	245	276	2,041	2,817	2,215	2,832
South Carolina	69	78	109	124	204	216	322	344	1,705	2,098	1,558	1,970
South Dakota	13	14	23	26	177	190	330	361	1,684	2,166	1,441	1,833
Tennessee	71	76	157	178	147	151	327	354	1,746	2,153	1,554	2,004
Texas	193	240	633	748	115	136	379	424	1,927	2,351	1,748	2,107
Utah	33	40	47	53	197	219	283	294	1,654	2,100	1,900	2,204
Vermont	11	13	15	18	211	227	270	309	1,842	2,514	1,653	2,240
Virginia	102	116	195	229	177	182	336	359	1,895	2,270	1,787	2,322
Washington	79	98	143	177	177	191	320	345	2,231	2,760	2,134	2,738
West Virginia	34	34	61	59	180	185	317	324	1,574	1,969	1,625	2,002
Wisconsin	74	73	168	189	154	145	351	377	2,128	3,216	2,035	2,594
Wyoming	11	12	25	25	213	242	494	543	1,924	2,055	1,967	2,202

Source: U.S. Bureau of the Census. *Statistical Abstract of the United States, 1994.* 114th ed. Washington, DC: U.S. Government Printing Office, 1994, p. 323. Primary source: U.S. Bureau of the Census. *Public Employment.* Series GE, no. 1 (annual). *Notes:* "X" stands for "not applicable." 1. Estimates subject to sampling variation. 2. Based on enumerated resident population as of July 1. 3. For full-time employees.

★ 311 ★

Employees and Earnings

State and Local Government Full-Time Employee Salaries, by Sex and Race/Ethnicity: 1973-1991

As of June 30. Excludes school systems and educational institutions. Based on reports from state governments (44 in 1973; 48 in 1975, 1976, and 1979; 47 in 1977 and 1983; 45 in 1978; 42 in 1980; 49 in 1981 and 1984 through 1987; and 50 in 1989 through 1991) and a sample of county, municipal, township, and special district jurisdictions employing 15 or more nonelected, nonappointed full-time employees. Data for 1982 and 1988 are not available.

Year	Median annual salary ($1,000)					
	Male	Female	White[1]	Minority		
				Total[2]	Black[1]	Hispanic[3]
1973	9.6	7.0	8.8	7.5	7.4	7.4
1975	11.3	8.2	10.2	8.8	8.6	8.9
1976	11.8	8.6	10.7	9.2	9.1	9.4
1977	12.4	9.1	11.3	9.7	9.5	9.9
1978	13.3	9.7	12.0	10.4	10.1	10.7
1979	14.1	10.4	12.8	10.9	10.6	11.4
1980	15.2	11.4	13.8	11.8	11.5	12.3
1981	17.7	13.1	16.1	13.5	13.3	14.7

[Continued]

★ 311 ★

State and Local Government Full-Time Employee Salaries, by Sex and Race/Ethnicity: 1973-1991

[Continued]

Year	Median annual salary ($1,000)					
	Male	Female	White[1]	Minority		
				Total[2]	Black[1]	Hispanic[3]
1983	20.1	15.3	18.5	15.9	15.6	17.3
1984	21.4	16.2	19.6	17.4	16.5	18.4
1985	22.3	17.3	20.6	18.4	17.5	19.2
1986	23.4	18.1	21.5	19.6	18.7	20.2
1987	24.2	18.9	22.4	20.9	19.3	21.1
1989	26.1	20.6	24.1	22.1	20.7	22.7
1990	27.3	21.8	25.2	23.3	22.0	23.8
1991	28.4	22.7	26.4	23.8	22.7	24.5

Source: U.S. Bureau of the Census. Statistical Abstract of the United States, 1994. 114th ed. Washington, DC: U.S. Government Printing Office, 1994, p. 320. Primary source: U.S. Equal Employment Opportunity Commission. State and Local Government Information Report (annual). Notes: 1. Non-Hispanic. 2. Includes other minority groups not shown separately. 3. Persons of Hispanic origin may be of any race.

★ 312 ★

Employees and Earnings

Stone, Clay, and Glass Manufacturing Employees and Earnings of Production Workers: 1980-1993

Annual averages of monthly figures. Covers all full- and part-time employees who worked during, or received pay for, any part of the pay period, including the 12th of the month. Data refer to production and related workers.

Industry	1987 SIC code[1]	All total employees (1,000)			Production workers					
					Total (1,000)			Average hourly earnings ($)		
		1980	1990	1993	1980	1990	1993	1980	1990	1993
Total	(X)	90,406	109,419	110,178	(NA)	(NA)	(NA)	(NA)	(NA)	(NA)
Private sector[2]	(X)	74,166	91,115	91,336	60,331	73,800	74,353	6.66	10.01	10.83
Manufacturing	(D)	20,285	19,076	17,802	14,214	12,947	12,143	7.27	10.83	11.76
Durable goods	(X)	12,159	11,109	10,047	8,416	7,363	6,726	7.75	11.35	12.34
Stone, clay, and glass products[3]	32	629	556	512	486	432	395	7.50	11.12	11.85
Flat glass	321	18	17	14	14	13	11	9.65	15.15	17.54
Glass and glassware, pressed and blown	322	124	83	78	105	72	66	7.97	12.40	13.32
Products of purchased glass	323	45	60	59	32	46	44	6.50	9.75	10.28
Cement, hydraulic	324	31	18	17	25	14	13	10.55	13.90	15.12
Structural clay products	325	46	36	31	34	28	24	6.14	9.55	10.37
Pottery and related products	326	47	39	38	39	31	30	6.25	9.62	10.23
Concrete, gypsum, and plaster	327	204	206	189	157	157	143	7.45	10.76	11.33

Source: U.S. Bureau of the Census. Statistical Abstract of the United States, 1994. 114th ed. Washington, DC: U.S. Government Printing Office, 1994, p. 422. Primary sources: U.S. Bureau of Labor Statistics. Bulletins 2370 and 2429; and Employment and Earnings (March and June issues). Notes: "NA" stands for "not available"; "X" for "not applicable." 1. 1987 Standard Industrial Classification (SIC). 2. Excludes government. 3. Includes industries not shown separately.

★ 313 ★

Employees and Earnings

Textile Mnaufacturing Employees and Earnings of Production Workers: 1980-1993

Annual averages of monthly figures. Covers all full- and part-time employees who worked during, or received pay for, any part of the pay period, including the 12th of the month. Data refer to production and related workers.

Industry	1987 SIC code[1]	All total employees (1,000)			Production workers					
					Total (1,000)			Average hourly earnings ($)		
		1980	1990	1993	1980	1990	1993	1980	1990	1993
Total	(X)	90,406	109,419	110,178	(NA)	(NA)	(NA)	(NA)	(NA)	(NA)
Private sector[2]	(X)	74,166	91,115	91,336	60,331	73,800	74,353	6.66	10.01	10.83
Manufacturing	(D)	20,285	19,076	17,802	14,214	12,947	12,143	7.27	10.83	11.76
Nondurable goods	(X)	8,127	7,968	7,755	5,798	5,584	5,417	6.56	10.12	11.00
Textile mill products[3]	22	848	691	666	737	593	567	5.07	8.02	8.89
Broadwoven fabric mills, cotton	221	150	91	85	135	82	76	5.25	8.31	9.25
Broadwoven fabric mills, synthetics	222	116	77	69	104	68	58	5.30	8.63	9.69
Broadwoven fabric mills, wool	223	19	17	18	16	14	15	5.21	8.61	9.40
Narrow fabric mills	224	23	24	22	20	20	18	4.63	7.39	8.20
Knitting mills	225	224	205	196	194	179	170	4.77	7.37	8.11
Textile finishing[4]	226	74	62	69	62	50	56	5.39	8.45	9.18
Carpets and rugs	227	54	61	60	44	50	49	5.20	8.25	8.91
Yarn and thread mills	228	125	103	97	113	92	87	4.76	7.68	8.61
Apparel and other textile products[3]	23	1,264	1,036	977	1,079	869	819	4.56	6.57	7.10
Men's and boys' suits and coats	231	77	50	43	67	42	36	5.34	7.34	7.78
Men's and boys' furnishings	232	362	274	273	310	235	236	4.23	6.06	6.70
Women's and misses' outerwear	233	417	328	297	360	274	249	4.61	6.26	6.68
Women's and children's undergarments	234	90	62	55	76	51	46	4.15	6.18	6.84
Girls' and children's outerwear	236	64	56	45	55	47	38	4.20	5.95	6.39

Source: U.S. Bureau of the Census. *Statistical Abstract of the United States, 1994.* 114th ed. Washington, DC: U.S. Government Printing Office, 1994, p. 423. Primary sources: U.S. Bureau of Labor Statistics. Bulletins 2370 and 2429; and *Employment and Earnings* (March and June issues). *Notes:* "NA" stands for "not available"; "X" for "not applicable." 1. 1987 Standard Industrial Classification (SIC). 2. Excludes government. 3. Includes industries not shown separately. 4. Except wool.

★ 314 ★

Employees and Earnings

Tobacco Manufacturing Employees and Earnings of Production Workers: 1980-1993

Annual averages of monthly figures. Covers all full- and part-time employees who worked during, or received pay for, any part of the pay period, including the 12th of the month. Data refer to production and related workers.

Industry	1987 SIC code[1]	All total employees (1,000)			Production workers					
					Total (1,000)			Average hourly earnings ($)		
		1980	1990	1993	1980	1990	1993	1980	1990	1993
Total	(X)	90,406	109,419	110,178	(NA)	(NA)	(NA)	(NA)	(NA)	(NA)
Private sector[2]	(X)	74,166	91,115	91,336	60,331	73,800	74,353	6.66	10.01	10.83
Manufacturing	(D)	20,285	19,076	17,802	14,214	12,947	12,143	7.27	10.83	11.76
Nondurable goods	(X)	8,127	7,968	7,755	5,798	5,584	5,417	6.56	10.12	11.00

[Continued]

★ 314 ★

Tobacco Manufacturing Employees and Earnings of Production Workers: 1980-1993

[Continued]

Industry	1987 SIC code[1]	All total employees (1,000)			Production workers					
					Total (1,000)			Average hourly earnings ($)		
		1980	1990	1993	1980	1990	1993	1980	1990	1993
Tobacco products	21	69	49	47	54	36	35	7.74	16.23	17.04
Cigarettes	211	46	35	33	35	26	25	9.23	19.57	21.03

Source: U.S. Bureau of the Census. *Statistical Abstract of the United States, 1994.* 114th ed. Washington, DC: U.S. Government Printing Office, 1994, p. 423. Primary sources: U.S. Bureau of Labor Statistics. Bulletins 2370 and 2429; and *Employment and Earnings* (March and June issues). *Notes:* "NA" stands for "not available"; "X" for "not applicable." 1. 1987 Standard Industrial Classification (SIC). 2. Excludes government.

★ 315 ★

Employees and Earnings

Transportation and Public Utilities Employees and Earnings of Production Workers: 1980-1993

Annual averages of monthly figures. Covers all full- and part-time employees who worked during, or received pay for, any part of the pay period, including the 12th of the month. Data refer to nonsupervisory employees and working supervisors.

Industry	1987 SIC code[1]	All total employees (1,000)			Production workers					
					Total (1,000)			Average hourly earnings ($)		
		1980	1990	1993	1980	1990	1993	1980	1990	1993
Total	(X)	90,406	109,419	110,178	(NA)	(NA)	(NA)	(NA)	(NA)	(NA)
Private sector[2]	(X)	74,166	91,115	91,336	60,331	73,800	74,353	6.66	10.01	10.83
Transportation and public utilities[3]	(E)	5,146	5,793	5,708	4,293	4,807	4,780	8.87	12.97	13.64
Railroad transportation	40	532	279	250	(4)	(4)	(4)	(4)	(4)	(4)
Class I railroads[5]	4011	482	241	218	(4)	(4)	(4)	9.92[6]	16.08[6]	16.93[6]
Local and interurban passenger transit	41	265	338	367	244	308	336	6.34	9.23	9.99
Trucking and warehousing	42	1,280	1,625	1,629	1,121	1,416	1,419	9.13	11.71	12.34
Water transportation	44	211	177	167	(4)	(4)	(4)	(4)	(4)	(4)
Transportation by air	45	453	745	733	(4)	(4)	(4)	(4)	(4)	(4)
Pipelines, except natural gas	46	21	19	18	15	14	14	10.50	17.04	19.51
Transportation services	47	198	345	347	159	278	273	6.94	10.43	11.05
Communication[3]	48	1,357	1,309	1,252	1,014	978	970	8.50	13.51	14.95
Telephone communication	481	1,072	913	872	779	658	656	8.72	14.13	15.67
Radio and television broadcasting	483	192	234	225	154	193	188	7.44	12.71	14.29
Cable and other pay television services	484	(4)	126	130	(4)	105	110	(4)	10.50	11.44
Electric, gas, and sanitary services[3]	49	829	957	945	678	759	744	8.90	15.23	16.74
Electric services	491	391	454	433	316	351	338	9.12	15.80	17.36
Gas production and distribution	492	168	165	162	138	129	126	8.27	14.25	16.30
Combination utility services	493	197	193	189	162	156	143	9.64	17.58	19.86
Sanitary services	495	50	115	132	44	99	113	7.16	11.55	12.10

Source: U.S. Bureau of the Census. *Statistical Abstract of the United States, 1994.* 114th ed. Washington, DC: U.S. Government Printing Office, 1994, p. 424. Primary sources: U.S. Bureau of Labor Statistics. Bulletins 2370 and 2429; and *Employment and Earnings* (March and June issues). *Notes:* "NA" stands for "not available"; "X" for "not applicable." 1. 1987 Standard Industrial Classification (SIC). 2. Excludes government. 3. Includes industries not shown separately. 4. Included in totals; not available separately. 5. For years prior to 1978, class I railroads were those with annual revenues of $1 million or more for 1950-55; $3 million or more for 1956-64; $5 million or more for 1965-75; and $10 million or more for 1976-77. In 1978, the classifications became: class I, those having more than $50 million gross annual operating revenue; class II, from $10 million to $50 million; and class III, less than $10 million. Effective January 1, 1982, the Interstate Commerce Commission (ICC) adopted a procedure to adjust the threshold for inflation by restating current revenues in constant 1978 dollars. In 1990, the criteria for class I and class II railroads were $94.4 million and $18.9 million, respectively. Also effective January 1, 1982, the ICC adopted a *Carrier Classification Index Survey Form* for carriers not filing annual report form R-1 with the Commission. Class II and class III railroads currently are exempted from filing any financial report with the Commission. The form is used for reclassifying carriers. 6. Includes all employees except executives, officials, and staff assistants who received pay during the month.

★ 316 ★

Employees and Earnings

Transportation Equipment Manufacturing Employees and Earnings of Production Workers: 1980-1993

Annual averages of monthly figures. Covers all full- and part-time employees who worked during, or received pay for, any part of the pay period, including the 12th of the month. Data refer to production and related workers.

Industry	1987 SIC code[1]	All total employees (1,000)			Production workers					
					Total (1,000)			Average hourly earnings ($)		
		1980	1990	1993	1980	1990	1993	1980	1990	1993
Total	(X)	90,406	109,419	110,178	(NA)	(NA)	(NA)	(NA)	(NA)	(NA)
Private sector[2]	(X)	74,166	91,115	91,336	60,331	73,800	74,353	6.66	10.01	10.83
Manufacturing	(D)	20,285	19,076	17,802	14,214	12,947	12,143	7.27	10.83	11.76
Durable goods	(X)	12,159	11,109	10,047	8,416	7,363	6,726	7.75	11.35	12.34
Transportation equipment[3]	37	1,881	1,989	1,727	1,220	1,224	1,099	9.35	14.08	15.84
Motor vehicles and equipment	371	789	812	820	575	617	629	9.85	14.56	16.14
Aircraft and parts	372	633	712	540	344	345	251	9.28	14.79	17.30
Ship and boat building and repairing	373	221	188	157	176	141	122	8.22	10.94	12.34
Railroad equipment	374	71	33	27	53	25	20	9.93	13.41	14.89
Guided missiles, space vehicles, and parts	376	111	185	120	35	57	34	9.22	14.39	16.81

Source: U.S. Bureau of the Census. *Statistical Abstract of the United States, 1994.* 114th ed. Washington, DC: U.S. Government Printing Office, 1994, p. 422. Primary sources: U.S. Bureau of Labor Statistics. Bulletins 2370 and 2429; and *Employment and Earnings* (March and June issues). *Notes:* "NA" stands for "not available"; "X" for "not applicable." 1. 1987 Standard Industrial Classification (SIC). 2. Excludes government. 3. Includes industries not shown separately.

★ 317 ★

Employees and Earnings

Wholesale and Retail Trade Employees and Earnings of Production Workers: 1980-1993

Annual averages of monthly figures. Covers all full- and part-time employees who worked during, or received pay for, any part of the pay period, including the 12th of the month. Data refer to nonsupervisory employees and working supervisors.

Industry	1987 SIC code[1]	All total employees (1,000)			Production workers					
					Total (1,000)			Average hourly earnings ($)		
		1980	1990	1993	1980	1990	1993	1980	1990	1993
Total	(X)	90,406	109,419	110,178	(NA)	(NA)	(NA)	(NA)	(NA)	(NA)
Private sector[2]	(X)	74,166	91,115	91,336	60,331	73,800	74,353	6.66	10.01	10.83
Wholesale trade	(F)	5,292	6,173	6,113	4,328	4,959	4,930	6.95	10.79	11.71
Retail trade[3]	(G)	15,018	19,601	19,743	13,484	17,358	17,386	4.88	6.75	7.29
General merchandise stores	53	2,245	2,540	2,371	2,090	2,380	2,216	4.77	6.83	7.29
Food stores	54	2,384	3,215	3,210	2,202	2,953	2,927	6.24	7.31	7.81
Automotive dealers and service stations	55	1,689	2,063	2,035	1,430	1,718	1,690	5.66	8.92	9.62
Apparel and accessory stores	56	957	1,183	1,141	820	991	939	4.30	6.25	7.03
Furniture and home furnishings stores	57	606	820	843	502	670	684	5.53	8.53	9.44
Eating and drinking places	58	4,626	6,509	6,863	4,256	5,905	6,206	3.69	4.97	5.35

Source: U.S. Bureau of the Census. *Statistical Abstract of the United States, 1994.* 114th ed. Washington, DC: U.S. Government Printing Office, 1994, p. 424. Primary sources: U.S. Bureau of Labor Statistics. Bulletins 2370 and 2429; and *Employment and Earnings* (March and June issues). *Notes:* "NA" stands for "not available"; "X" for "not applicable." 1. 1987 Standard Industrial Classification (SIC). 2. Excludes government. 3. Includes industries not shown separately.

★ 318 ★

Employees and Earnings

Wood Manufacturing Employees and Earnings of Production Workers: 1980- 1993

Annual averages of monthly figures. Covers all full- and part-time employees who worked during, or received pay for, any part of the pay period, including the 12th of the month. Data refer to production and related workers.

Industry	1987 SIC code[1]	All total employees (1,000)			Production workers					
					Total (1,000)			Average hourly earnings ($)		
		1980	1990	1993	1980	1990	1993	1980	1990	1993
Total	(X)	90,406	109,419	110,178	(NA)	(NA)	(NA)	(NA)	(NA)	(NA)
Private sector[2]	(X)	74,166	91,115	91,336	60,331	73,800	74,353	6.66	10.01	10.83
Manufacturing	(D)	20,285	19,076	17,802	14,214	12,947	12,143	7.27	10.83	11.76
Durable goods	(X)	12,159	11,109	10,047	8,416	7,363	6,726	7.75	11.35	12.34
Lumber and wood products[3]	24	704	733	686	587	603	564	6.57	9.08	9.61
Logging	241	88	85	76	71	70	62	8.64	11.22	11.43
Sawmills and planing mills	242	215	198	176	190	172	153	6.70	9.22	9.78
Millwork, plywood, and structural members	243	206	262	246	170	210	197	6.44	9.04	9.64
Wood containers	244	43	45	44	37	38	37	4.95	6.64	7.02
Mobile homes	2451	46	41	46	36	33	38	6.08	8.67	9.39
Furniture and fixtures[3]	25	466	506	481	376	400	380	5.49	8.52	9.27
Household furniture	251	301	289	273	253	241	228	5.12	7.87	8.71
Office furniture	252	51	68	62	40	51	45	5.91	9.64	10.04
Partitions and fixtures	254	63	78	76	47	57	56	6.68	9.77	10.54

Source: U.S. Bureau of the Census. *Statistical Abstract of the United States, 1994.* 114th ed. Washington, DC: U.S. Government Printing Office, 1994, p. 422. Primary sources: U.S. Bureau of Labor Statistics. Bulletins 2370 and 2429; and *Employment and Earnings* (March and June issues). *Notes:* "NA" stands for "not available"; "X" for "not applicable." 1. 1987 Standard Industrial Classification (SIC). 2. Excludes government. 3. Includes industries not shown separately.

Employment and Unemployment

★ 319 ★

Employment, by Industry and Selected Characteristics: 1970-1993

For civilian noninstitutional population, 16 years old and over. Annual averages of monthly figures. Based on Current Population Survey. Data from 1985 to 1991, and also beginning 1992, not strictly comparable with other years due to changes in industrial classification.

[In thousands, except percentages]

Industry	1970	1980	1985	1990	1993			
					Total	Percent		
						Female	Black	Hispanic[1]
Total employed	78,678	99,303	107,150	117,914	119,306	45.8	10.2	7.8
Agriculture	3,463	3,364	3,179	3,186	3,074	20.7	4.6	15.2
Mining	516	979	939	730	669	16.2	3.7	5.0
Construction	4,818	6,215	6,987	7,696	7,220	8.6	6.4	8.7
Manufacturing	20,746	21,942	20,879	21,184	19,557	32.3	10.1	9.0
Transportation, communication, and other public utilities	5,320	6,525	7,548	8,136	8,481	28.5	13.8	7.1
Wholesale and retail trade	15,008	20,191	22,296	24,269	24,769	46.7	8.4	8.4

[Continued]

★ 319 ★

Employment, by Industry and Selected Characteristics: 1970-1993

[Continued]

Industry	1970	1980	1985	1990	1993			
					Total	Percent		
						Female	Black	Hispanic[1]
Wholesale trade	2,672	3,920	4,341	4,651	4,606	28.9	6.0	7.9
Retail trade	12,336	16,270	17,955	19,618	20,163	50.8	8.9	8.5
Finance, insurance, real estate	3,945	5,993	7,005	8,021	7,962	58.6	8.4	6.0
Services[2]	20,385	28,752	33,322	39,084	41,817	61.7	11.4	6.9
Business and repair services[2]	1,403	3,848	5,969	7,409	6,838	35.1	10.4	9.0
Advertising	147	191	263	277	284	52.3	5.3	7.0
Services to dwellings and buildings	(NA)	370	571	813	749	43.5	18.1	17.4
Personnel supply services	(NA)	235	590	704	698	61.0	18.7	7.4
Computer and data processing	(NA)	221	549	799	957	36.3	5.2	3.7
Detective/protective services	(NA)	213	318	373	475	17.8	20.8	7.7
Automobile services	600	952	1,322	1,429	1,477	13.5	8.3	12.4
Personal services[2]	4,276	3,839	4,352	4,667	4,443	70.0	14.1	13.0
Private households	1,782	1,257	1,254	1,023	1,114	86.9	17.8	20.3
Hotels and lodging places	979	1,149	1,451	1,780	1,435	56.7	15.3	14.1
Entertainment and recreation	717	1,047	1,278	1,503	2,060	41.8	9.4	6.8
Professional and related services[2]	12,904	19,853	21,563	25,335	28,293	68.6	11.5	5.5
Hospitals	2,843	4,036	4,269	4,690	5,032	76.2	15.6	5.6
Health services, except hospitals	1,628	3,345	3,641	4,757	5,521	78.2	12.7	6.3
Elementary, secondary schools	6,126	5,550	5,431	6,028	6,372	74.5	11.6	5.9
Colleges and universities	(3)	2,108	2,281	2,609	2,633	52.6	9.1	5.1
Social services	828	1,590	1,682	2,234	2,770	81.6	16.6	6.8
Legal services	429	776	995	1,217	1,253	55.1	5.2	4.1
Public administration[4]	4,476	5,342	4,995	5,608	5,756	42.9	15.0	5.3

Source: U.S. Bureau of the Census. Statistical Abstract of the United States, 1994. 114th ed. Washington, DC: U.S. Government Printing Office, 1994, p. 412. Primary source: U.S. Bureau of Labor Statistics. Employment and Earnings (monthly; January issues). Notes: "NA" represents "not available." 1. Persons of Hispanic origin may be of any race. 2. Includes industries not shown separately. 3. Included with elementary/secondary schools. 4. Includes workers involved in uniquely governmental activities, e.g., judicial and legislative.

★ 320 ★

Employment and Unemployment

Employment in the Federal Government – Accessions to and Separations From: 1992 and 1993

As of end of September 30.

Agency	Accessions				Separations			
	1992		1993		1992		1993	
	Number	Rate	Number	Rate	Number	Rate	Number	Rate
Total, all agencies	555,801	18.2	599,530	20.0	579,422	18.9	659,487	22.0
Legislative Branch, total[1]	1,726	9.3	1,147	6.3	2,247	12.1	2,037	11.2
General Accounting Office	407	7.6	181	3.5	625	11.6	483	9.4
Government Printing Office	404	8.3	92	1.9	381	7.8	245	5.1
Library of Congress	524	10.4	511	10.3	630	12.5	663	13.3
Judicial Branch	31	39.2	14	16.3	17	21.5	9	10.5
Executive Branch, total	554,044	18.2	598,369	20.1	577,158	19.0	657,441	22.1

[Continued]

★ 320 ★

Employment in the Federal Government – Accessions to and Separations From: 1992 and 1993
[Continued]

Agency	Accessions				Separations			
	1992		1993		1992		1993	
	Number	Rate	Number	Rate	Number	Rate	Number	Rate
Executive Office of the President[1]	432	23.5	860	45.3	305	16.6	934	49.2
Executive Departments	401,213	19.6	358,106	17.9	416,999	20.3	397,609	19.8
U.S. Department of State	4,129	15.9	4,166	16.0	3,664	14.1	4,060	15.6
U.S. Department of the Treasury	54,752	32.2	53,484	32.5	63,717	37.5	59,243	36.1
U.S. Department of Defense	175,985	17.5	152,473	16.0	209,177	20.8	197,838	20.8
U.S. Department of Justice	15,316	16.2	9,149	9.3	5,824	6.1	4,481	4.6
U.S. Department of the Interior	23,188	28.8	20,898	25.6	16,890	21.0	17,393	21.3
U.S. Department of Agriculture	41,004	33.5	34,258	28.3	38,117	31.2	39,365	32.6
U.S. Department of Commerce	6,547	17.3	8,013	20.9	9,098	24.1	6,312	16.5
U.S. Department of Labor	1,595	8.9	1,083	6.1	1,625	9.1	1,593	9.0
U.S. Department of Health and Human Services	17,601	13.4	15,702	11.9	12,436	9.4	13,441	10.2
U.S. Department of Housing and Urban Development	547	3.9	971	7.3	1,877	13.3	1,235	9.3
U.S. Department of Transportation	5,795	8.2	3,208	4.6	6,248	8.9	5,469	7.8
U.S. Department of Energy	3,677	17.9	1,570	7.6	2,251	11.0	2,083	10.1
U.S. Department of Education	546	10.8	583	11.6	323	6.4	353	7.0
U.S. Department of Veterans Affairs[2]	50,531	19.6	52,548	19.9	45,752	17.7	44,743	17.0
Independent agencies[1]	152,399	15.5	239,403	24.7	159,854	16.2	258,898	26.7
Board of Governors, Federal Reserve System	189	12.1	249	15.2	157	10.1	167	10.2
Environmental Protection Agency	2,190	12.0	2,196	11.9	2,089	11.4	1,961	10.6
Equal Employment Opportunity Commission	219	7.6	179	6.1	160	5.6	168	5.7
Federal Deposit Insurance Corporation	4,207	18.6	3,280	14.9	3,819	16.9	4,168	18.9
Federal Emergency Management Agency	3,228	87.8	2,759	60.3	982	26.7	2,621	57.3
General Services Administration	2,003	9.5	1,926	9.3	1,816	8.6	1,705	8.2
National Aeronautics and Space Administration	2,685	10.5	2,130	8.5	3,012	11.7	2,669	10.6
National Archives and Records Administration	757	24.5	644	20.4	377	12.2	316	10.0
Nuclear Regulatory Commission	240	6.8	150	4.2	215	6.0	195	5.5
Office of Personnel Management	1,071	15.5	707	10.3	934	13.5	864	12.6
Panama Canal Commission	1,420	16.4	1,388	16.2	1,561	18.0	1,289	15.1
Railroad Retirement Board	137	7.6	92	5.1	106	5.8	131	7.2
Securities and Exchange Commission	603	23.9	349	12.9	296	11.7	278	10.3
U.S. Small Business Administration	2,118	41.6	2,057	36.4	1,088	21.4	2,452	43.4
Smithsonian Institution	1,076	19.7	849	15.4	923	16.9	892	16.2
Tennessee Valley Authority	1,998	9.8	951	5.0	7,450	36.6	1,402	7.3
U.S. Information Agency	658	8.0	529	6.4	547	6.6	556	6.7
U.S. International Development Cooperation Agency	499	10.9	463	10.5	579	12.7	733	16.6
U.S. Postal Service	124,018	15.5	215,964	27.5	131,026	16.4	233,602	29.7

Source: U.S. Bureau of the Census. *Statistical Abstract of the United States, 1994.* 114th ed. Washington, DC: U.S. Government Printing Office, 1994, p. 349. Primary source: U.S. Office of Personnel Management. *Federal Civilian Workforce Statistics: Employment and Trends* (bimonthly). *Notes:* 1. Includes other branches, or other agencies, not shown separately. 2. Formerly Veterans Administration.

★ 321 ★

Employment and Unemployment

Federal Civilian Employment, by Branch and Agency: 1980-1992

Data as of September 30.

Agencies	1980	1985	1989	1990	1991	1992
Total, all agencies	2,875,866	3,020,531	3,123,731	3,128,267	3,111,912	3,085,323
Legislative Branch, total[1]	39,710	38,764	37,690	37,495	38,504	38,509
U.S. Congress[1]	19,096	19,656	19,504	19,474	20,178	20,084
U.S. Senate	7,195	7,294	7,401	7,369	7,571	7,620
U.S. House of Representatives	11,888	12,351	12,090	12,089	12,587	12,446
Architect of the Capitol	2,168	2,145	2,161	2,235	2,316	2,346
Judicial Branch	15,178	18,225	21,915	23,605	25,805	27,987
U.S. Supreme Court	331	337	327	332	343	353
U.S. Courts	14,847	17,888	21,588	23,221	25,392	27,551
Executive Branch, total	2,820,978	2,963,542	3,064,126	3,067,167	3,047,603	3,018,827
Executive Office of the President[1]	1,886	1,526	1,577	1,731	1,758	1,866
White House Office	406	367	371	396	347	392
Office of the Vice-President	16	20	20	21	16	20
Office of Management and Budget	616	566	527	574	609	586
Office of Administration	166	194	202	205	228	247
Council of Economic Advisors	35	30	32	34	34	34
Executive Departments	1,716,970	1,789,270	2,065,038	2,065,542	2,054,094	2,038,675
U.S. Department of State	23,497	25,254	25,327	25,288	25,699	25,734
U.S. Department of the Treasury	124,663	130,084	152,548	158,655	166,433	161,951
U.S. Department of Defense	960,116	1,084,549	1,075,437	1,034,152	1,012,716	982,774
U.S. Department of Justice	56,327	64,433	79,667	83,932	90,821	96,927
U.S. Department of the Interior	77,357	77,485	77,545	77,679	81,683	85,260
U.S. Department of Agriculture	129,139	117,750	122,062	122,594	125,640	128,324
U.S. Department of Commerce	48,563	35,150	45,091	69,920	38,087	38,086
U.S. Department of Labor	23,400	18,260	18,125	17,727	17,938	17,889
U.S. Department of Health and Human Services	155,662	140,151	122,259	123,959	129,483	131,191
U.S. Department of Housing and Urban Development	16,964	12,289	13,544	13,596	14,998	13,701
U.S. Department of Transportation	72,361	62,227	65,615	67,364	69,831	70,558
U.S. Department of Energy	21,557	16,749	17,130	17,731	19,539	20,962
U.S. Department of Education	7,364	4,889	4,696	4,771	5,081	5,113
U.S. Department of Veterans Affairs[2]	228,285	247,156	245,992	248,174	256,145	260,205
Independent agencies[1]	1,102,122	1,172,746	997,511	999,894	991,751	978,286
Environmental Protection Agency	14,715	13,788	15,590	17,123	18,218	18,196
Equal Employment Opportunity Commission	3,515	3,222	2,743	2,880	2,889	2,899
Federal Deposit Insurance Corporation	3,520	6,723	9,031	17,641	22,007	22,467
Federal Emergency Management Agency	3,427	3,133	3,048	3,137	3,130	5,632
General Services Administration[3]	37,654	25,782	20,063	20,277	21,122	20,770
National Aeronautics and Space Administration	23,714	22,562	24,165	24,872	25,737	25,425
Nuclear Regulatory Commission	3,283	3,605	3,288	3,353	3,534	3,528
Office of Personnel Management	8,280	6,353	6,859	6,636	6,757	6,941
U.S. Small Business Administration	5,804	4,960	4,653	5,128	4,867	5,897
Smithsonian Institution	4,403	4,757	5,158	5,092	5,360	5,514
Tennessee Valley Authority	51,714	32,035	26,676	28,392	24,870	19,493
U.S. Information Agency	8,138	8,851	8,723	8,555	8,213	8,342
U.S. International Development Cooperation Agency	6,152	5,054	4,816	4,698	4,575	4,542
U.S. Postal Service	660,014	750,021	826,310	816,886	804,338	791,992

Source: U.S. Bureau of the Census. *Statistical Abstract of the United States, 1994.* 114th ed. Washington, DC: U.S. Government Printing Office, 1994, p. 346. Primary source: U.S. Office of Personnel Management. *Federal Civilian Workforce Statistics: Employment and Trends* (bimonthly). *Notes:* 1. Includes other branches, or other agencies, not shown separately. 2. Formerly Veterans Administration. 3. 1980 figure includes the National Archives and Records Administration, which became an independent agency in 1985.

★ 322 ★

Employment and Unemployment

Federal Civilian Employment Summary: 1980-1992

As of December 31. Excludes U.S. territories and foreign countries, Central Intelligence Agency, National Security Agency, and the Defense Intelligence Agency. Partially estimated.

[In thousands]

Characteristic	United States					Washington, DC[1]				
	1980	1985	1990	1991	1992	1980	1985	1990	1991	1992
Paid employment	2,782	2,902	2,940	2,977	2,983	366	353	358	374	375
Male, estimated	1,806	1,769	1,685	1,688	1,697	202	191	183	189	189
Female, estimated	976	1,133	1,255	1,289	1,286	164	162	175	185	186
Full-time	2,504	2,589	2,632	2,678	2,642	342	335	342	358	359
Other	278	313	308	299	341	24	18	16	16	16
Competitive service	1,692	1,710	1,694	1,732	1,717	258	246	248	260	260
Permanent appointment	1,622	1,628	1,637	1,671	1,658	247	234	241	252	253
Temporary and indefinite appointment	70	82	57	61	59	11	12	7	8	7
Excepted and Senior Executive Services (SES)[2]	1,091	1,191	1,246	1,245	1,266	107	108	109	114	115
Permanent appointment	917	1,015	1,029	1,037	1,005	70	73	76	79	80
Temporary and indefinite appointment	174	176	217	208	261	37	35	33	35	35
White-collar	2,324[3]	2,478	2,576	2,621	2,638	335	327	336	352	354
Blue-collar	458[3]	424	364	356	345	31	26	22	22	21

Source: U.S. Bureau of the Census. *Statistical Abstract of the United States, 1994.* 114th ed. Washington, DC: U.S. Government Printing Office, 1994, p. 347. Primary source: U.S. Office of Personnel Management. *Pay Structure of the Federal Civil Service* (annual). *Notes:* 1. Represents metropilitan statistical area (MSA). 2. Excepted from competitive requirements of Civil Service Act. Prior to 1980 Senior Executive Services (SES) was not included in total. 3. Based on total workforce.

★ 323 ★

Employment and Unemployment

Nonfarm Establishment Employment, by Industry and State: 1980-1993

Based on data from establishment reports. Includes all full- and part-time employees who worked during, or received pay for, any part of the pay period reported. Excludes proprietors, the self-employed, farm workers, unpaid family workers, private household workers, and Armed Forces. National totals differ from the sum of the state figures because of differing benchmarks among states and differing industrial and geographic stratification. Based on 1987 Standard Industrial Classification Manual.

[In thousands]

State	1980	1992	1993							
			Total[1]	Construction	Manufacturing	Transportation and public utilities	Wholesale and retail trade	Finance, insurance, and real estate	Services	Government
United States	90,406	108,519	110,178	4,574	17,802	5,708	25,857	6,604	30,192	18,842
Alabama	1,356	1,675	1,712	78	383	85	376	76	363	341
Alaska	169	247	253	11	17	23	49	11	57	74
Arizona	1,014	1,517	1,571	89	174	78	385	100	448	286
Arkansas	742	963	990	37	243	57	220	40	220	169
California	9,849	12,154	12,000	446	1,804	602	2,787	786	3,463	2,078
Colorado	1,251	1,597	1,666	84	188	104	403	106	468	297
Connecticut	1,427	1,526	1,529	47	294	69	329	139	443	207
Delaware	259	341	348	18	65	15	76	35	89	50
District of Columbia	616	674	670	8	14	21	53	31	255	287
Florida	3,576	5,359	5,567	287	484	286	1,452	357	1,814	882

[Continued]

★ 323 ★

Nonfarm Establishment Employment, by Industry and State: 1980-1993
[Continued]

State	1980	1992	1993							
			Total[1]	Construction	Manufacturing	Transportation and public utilities	Wholesale and retail trade	Finance, insurance, and real estate	Services	Government
Georgia	2,159	2,987	3,106	128	555	202	773	166	729	547
Hawaii	405	543	539	32[2]	19	41	133	39	164	112
Idaho	330	416	437	25	69	21	110	23	98	90
Illinois	4,850	5,235	5,316	198	933	310	1,245	382	1,465	768
Indiana	2,130	2,554	2,589	119	639	134	608	128	562	393
Iowa	1,110	1,253	1,277	48	236	57	320	74	317	223
Kansas	945	1,115	1,135	47	182	66	274	58	269	230
Kentucky	1,210	1,509	1,534	69	292	82	360	63	363	276
Louisiana	1,579	1,627	1,643	97	186	105	382	78	409	341
Maine	418	512	519	21	91	22	130	26	134	95
Maryland	1,712	2,081	2,100	120	180	98	499	129	655	417
Massachusetts	2,652	2,795	2,842	81	454	124	644	199	952	387
Michigan	3,443	3,927	3,982	133	902	156	935	192	1,016	640
Minnesota	1,770	2,185	2,242	79	405	109	537	136	615	354
Mississippi	829	960	998	39	255	46	209	39	196	210
Missouri	1,970	2,334	2,395	95	411	153	569	141	644	377
Montana	280	317	326	14	23	20	87	15	88	74
Nebraska	628	750	763	31	103	47	193	50	188	150
Nevada	400	639	670	46	30	35	133	31	294	89
New Hampshire	385	487	500	17	97	18	128	30	136	74
New Jersey	3,060	3,455	3,493	115	516	235	815	229	1,015	566
New Mexico	465	602	624	36	43	29	147	28	167	159
New York	7,207	7,730	7,736	239	982	401	1,553	728	2,408	1,420
North Carolina	2,380	3,126	3,245	153	846	156	730	138	688	529
North Dakota	245	277	285	12	19	18	75	14	77	67
Ohio	4,367	4,848	4,905	184	1,049	214	1,173	259	1,277	737
Oklahoma	1,138	1,222	1,240	42	168	72	288	61	304	270
Oregon	1,045	1,274	1,310	54	211	66	327	91	327	233
Pennsylvania	4,753	5,076	5,110	197	940	267	1,147	303	1,527	708
Rhode Island	398	425	429	12	88	14	93	25	135	61
South Carolina	1,189	1,528	1,570	82	374	66	351	66	332	297
South Dakota	238	309	318	13	39	15	81	18	83	67
Tennessee	1,747	2,245	2,328	94	528	126	534	104	574	362
Texas	5,851	7,269	7,479	351	987	437	1,808	428	1,926	1,377
Utah	551	769	810	40	111	47	192	41	212	160
Vermont	200	251	256	11	43	11	60	12	74	44
Virginia	2,157	2,848	2,920	153	405	149	648	157	797	598
Washington	1,608	2,222	2,250	118	340	114	545	121	579	429
West Virginia	646	640	652	31	83	39	149	25	167	133
Wisconsin	1,938	2,358	2,407	93	559	113	553	131	595	360
Wyoming	210	206	210	12	10	15	48	8	43	57

Source: U.S. Bureau of the Census. *Statistical Abstract of the United States, 1994.* 114th ed. Washington, DC: U.S. Government Printing Office, 1994, p. 421. Primary source: U.S. Bureau of Labor Statistics. *Employment and Earnings* (monthly, May issues). Compiled from data supplied by cooperating state agencies. *Notes:* "NA" stand for "not available." 1. Includes mining, not shown separately. 2. Hawaii includes mining with construction.

★ 324 ★

Employment and Unemployment

Paid Civilian Employment in the Federal Government: 1992

As of December 31. Excludes members and employees of Congress, Central Intelligence Agency, Defense Intelligence Agency employees overseas, temporary census enumerators, seasonal and on-call employees, temporary Christmas help of the U.S. Postal Service, and National Security Agency.

Division and state	Total (1,000)	Percent defense
United States	2,988	30.1
Northeast United States	481	25.2
New England	126	24.6
Maine	16	56.3
New Hampshire	8	12.5
Vermont	6	16.7
Massachusetts	62	17.7
Rhode Island	10	40.0
Connecticut	24	20.8
Middle Atlantic United States	355	25.4
New York	149	12.1
New Jersey	74	32.4
Pennsylvania	132	36.4
North Central United States	512	23.6
East North Central United States	332	25.3
Ohio	94	37.2
Indiana	43	34.9
Illinois	106	17.9
Michigan	59	20.3
Wisconsin	30	10.0
West North Central United States	180	20.6
Minnesota	34	8.8
Iowa	20	10.0
Missouri	66	27.3
North Dakota	8	25.0
South Dakota	10	10.0
Nebraska	16	25.0
Kansas	26	26.9
Southern United States	1,297	32.8
South Atlantic United States	840	32.4
Delaware	5	40.0
Maryland	136	30.1
District of Columbia	223	7.6
Virginia	168	63.7
West Virginia	17	11.8
North Carolina	51	33.3
South Carolina	33	51.5
Georgia	93	39.8
Florida	114	28.1
East South Central United States	176	33.0

[Continued]

★ 324 ★

Paid Civilian Employment in the Federal Government: 1992

[Continued]

Division and state	Total (1,000)	Percent defense
Kentucky	38	36.8
Tennessee	54	13.0
Alabama	58	44.8
Mississippi	26	42.3
West South Central	281	33.8
Arkansas	21	23.8
Louisiana	35	25.7
Oklahoma	46	47.8
Texas	179	33.0
Western United States	655	35.3
Mountain Region of United States	202	28.7
Montana	12	8.3
Idaho	11	9.1
Wyoming	7	14.3
Colorado	57	24.6
New Mexico	28	32.1
Arizona	40	25.0
Utah	35	57.1
Nevada	12	16.7
Pacific United States	453	38.2
Washington	69	42.0
Oregon	31	9.7
California	312	37.8
Alaska	16	31.3
Hawaii	25	76.0

Source: U.S. Bureau of the Census. *Statistical Abstract of the United States, 1994.* 114th ed. Washington, DC: U.S. Government Printing Office, 1994, p. 348. Primary source: U.S. Office of Personnel Management. *Biennial Report of Employment by Geographic Area.*

★ 325 ★

Employment and Unemployment

Paid Civilian Employment in the Federal Government – Accessions to and Separations From: 1980-1993

For fiscal year ending in year shown. Includes accessions and separations of full-time, part-time, and intermittent employees.

[In thousands, except rate]

Item	United States						Washington, DC[2]					
	1980[1]	1985	1990[1]	1991	1992	October 1992-August 1993	1980[1]	1985	1990[1]	1991	1992	October 1992-August 1993
Accessions, total	995	630	898	573	505	513	94	63	59	63	52	43
Monthly rate[3]	2.9	1.9	2.5	1.6	1.4	1.5	2.3	1.6	1.5	1.5	1.2	1
Separations, total	1,004	530	889	598	518	554	89	58	52	48	45	42
Monthly rate[3]	3.0	1.6	2.4	1.7	1.5	1.6	2.2	1.5	1.3	1.2	1.1	1
Quit[4]	228	218	191	153	136	125	33	25	23	19	18	15

Source: U.S. Bureau of the Census. *Statistical Abstract of the United States, 1994.* 114th ed. Washington, DC: U.S. Government Printing Office, 1994, p. 348. Primary source: U.S. Office of Personnel Management. *Federal Civilian Workforce Statistics: Employment and Trends* (bimonthly). *Notes:* 1. Includes temporary census enumerators. 2. Represents metropolitan statistical area (MSA). 3. Per 100 employees. 4. Represents voluntary resignations by employees or separations by agency if employee declines new assignment, abandons position, joins military, or fails to return from military furlough.

★ 326 ★

Employment and Unemployment

State and Local Government Full-Time Employment, by Sex and Race/Ethnicity: 1973-1991

As of June 30. Excludes school systems and educational institutions. Based on reports from state governments (44 in 1973; 48 in 1975, 1976, and 1979; 47 in 1977 and 1983; 45 in 1978; 42 in 1980; 49 in 1981 and 1984 through 1987; and 50 in 1989 through 1991) and a sample of county, municipal, township, and special district jurisdictions employing 15 or more nonelected, nonappointed full-time employees. Data for 1982 and 1988 are not available.

Year	Employment (1,000)						
	Total	Male	Female	White[1]	Minority		
					Total[2]	Black[1]	Hispanic[3]
1973	3,809	2,486	1,322	3,115	693	523	125
1975	3,899	2,436	1,464	3,102	797	602	147
1976	4,369	2,724	1,645	3,490	880	664	165
1977	4,415	2,737	1,678	3,480	935	705	175
1978	4,447	2,711	1,736	3,481	966	723	181
1979	4,576	2,761	1,816	3,568	1,008	751	192
1980	3,987	2,350	1,637	3,146	842	619	163
1981	4,665	2,740	1,925	3,591	1,074	780	205
1983	4,492	2,674	1,818	3,423	1,069	768	219
1984	4,580	2,700	1,880	3,458	1,121	799	233

[Continued]

★ 326 ★

State and Local Government Full-Time Employment, by Sex and Race/Ethnicity: 1973-1991

[Continued]

Year	Employment (1,000)						
	Total	Male	Female	White[1]	Minority		
					Total[2]	Black[1]	Hispanic[3]
1985	4,742	2,789	1,952	3,563	1,179	835	248
1986	4,779	2,797	1,982	3,549	1,230	865	259
1987	4,849	2,818	2,031	3,600	1,249	872	268
1989	5,257	3,030	2,227	3,863	1,394	961	308
1990	5,374	3,071	2,302	3,918	1,456	994	327
1991	5,459	3,110	2,349	3,965	1,494	1,011	340

Source: U.S. Bureau of the Census. *Statistical Abstract of the United States, 1994.* 114th ed. Washington, DC: U.S. Government Printing Office, 1994, p. 320. Primary source: U.S. Equal Employment Opportunity Commission. *State and Local Government Information Report* (annual). *Notes:* 1. Non-Hispanic. 2. Includes other minority groups not shown separately. 3. Persons of Hispanic origin may be of any race.

★ 327 ★

Employment and Unemployment

State and Local Government Full-Time Equivalent Employment, by Selected Function: 1992

For October. Local government amounts are estimates subject to sampling variation.

[In thousands]

	Education				Health and hospitals		Highways		Police and fire protection		Public welfare	
	Total		Higher education									
	State	Local	State	Local	State	Local	State	Local	State[1]	Local	State	Local
United States	1,412.4	5,243.1	1,285.7	261.3	685.8	736.3	257.3	286.5	86.2	887.7	211.7	261.0
Alabama	34.1	81.7	30.1	-	18.9	21.8	4.3	7.1	1.1	13.8	4.5	1.3
Alaska	9.3	11.8	5.9	-	0.8	0.1	3.0	0.6	0.4	1.7	1.7	0.2
Arizona	21.5	81.0	18.8	7.4	3.4	7.3	3.2	3.7	1.7	13.0	5.0	3.4
Arkansas	17.5	53.7	14.9	-	8.8	4.4	4.0	3.3	0.9	6.4	3.6	0.4
California	111.1	528.8	106.6	63.5	44.7	107.1	19.3	21.1	11.1	108.2	3.1	47.0
Colorado	28.8	68.9	27.3	1.2	6.0	9.5	3.1	4.7	1.0	11.8	1.3	4.1
Connecticut	15.1	61.4	12.4	-	12.7	1.8	3.7	3.6	1.5	11.8	4.2	2.0
Delaware	6.7	12.1	6.4	-	3.6	0.2	1.4	0.6	0.7	1.5	1.6	0.1
District of Columbia	(X)	12.8	(X)	1.5	(X)	7.6	(X)	0.9	(X)	7.0	(X)	1.9
Florida	39.3	252.0	36.7	20.3	28.7	42.2	10.9	13.9	3.8	57.7	9.7	5.3
Georgia	37.5	152.9	32.8	0.6	29.4	44.8	6.2	7.0	2.1	24.7	7.5	0.8
Hawaii	28.9	-	7.1	-	6.2	0.1	0.9	1.1	-	5.1	1.2	0.1
Idaho	7.8	23.9	7.1	0.9	2.0	4.4	1.8	1.5	0.4	3.0	1.6	0.1
Illinois	49.4	228.8	46.5	19.4	23.8	22.6	8.9	11.0	3.8	51.6	12.6	7.4
Indiana	50.1	113.8	45.2	0.0	13.4	23.5	4.8	5.8	1.8	17.0	5.4	2.9
Iowa	19.7	66.7	18.5	5.7	8.8	10.2	2.8	5.7	0.8	7.0	3.3	1.7
Kansas	20.6	67.6	19.9	5.7	8.4	8.3	3.7	5.1	1.0	8.3	1.7	0.7
Kentucky	32.3	80.7	28.1	-	7.7	8.5	5.8	3.0	1.7	8.7	4.9	0.6
Louisiana	31.0	96.1	27.4	0.2	23.9	12.1	5.6	5.0	1.1	15.0	5.9	0.6
Maine	7.1	30.0	5.7	-	2.9	1.2	2.8	1.7	0.6	3.6	1.9	0.2
Maryland	22.1	92.9	20.2	7.3	13.0	3.1	5.1	5.2	2.3	18.4	7.1	1.8
Massachusetts	21.5	105.6	20.7	0.1	20.5	8.9	4.7	5.6	2.0	27.5	7.3	1.8
Michigan	67.2	202.9	65.2	12.4	14.9	21.3	3.9	8.9	3.1	25.0	12.8	2.8
Minnesota	34.8	90.6	33.2	2.6	9.4	17.8	5.1	7.4	0.8	10.7	1.7	10.2

[Continued]

★ 327 ★

State and Local Government Full-Time Equivalent Employment, by Selected Function: 1992

[Continued]

| | Education | | | | Health and hospitals | | Highways | | Police and fire protection | | Public welfare | |
| | Total | | Higher education | | | | | | | | | |
	State	Local	State	Local	State	Local	State	Local	State[1]	Local	State	Local
Mississippi	15.9	67.0	14.5	5.0	10.9	15.2	3.5	4.4	0.9	7.3	3.2	0.3
Missouri	22.5	103.0	20.5	4.6	15.3	11.4	6.3	6.0	1.9	17.8	6.8	2.4
Montana	6.3	26.0	5.6	0.2	1.8	0.8	1.9	1.3	0.4	2.1	1.2	0.9
Nebraska	10.7	38.4	9.9	2.5	4.9	4.6	2.4	3.1	0.7	4.4	2.6	1.3
Nevada	6.3	23.6	6.0	-	1.5	3.9	1.4	1.0	0.5	5.6	1.0	0.3
New Hampshire	5.5	22.3	5.2	-	1.8	0.2	1.9	1.4	0.4	3.9	1.1	2.3
New Jersey	33.9	170.6	27.3	8.6	22.4	10.6	8.3	10.4	3.7	34.4	5.9	11.1
New Mexico	17.6	38.2	16.7	1.8	7.5	2.6	2.7	1.5	0.6	5.3	2.0	0.4
New York	48.3	409.0	42.7	18.9	71.8	85.1	14.9	35.6	5.5	83.2	7.4	57.0
North Carolina	41.8	151.6	38.8	13.4	17.8	28.6	12.1	3.1	3.1	19.8	1.2	11.8
North Dakota	7.1	13.3	6.8	-	3.2	0.2	1.1	1.1	0.2	1.4	0.2	0.9
Ohio	68.3	205.7	66.0	4.3	22.2	30.8	8.9	13.0	2.3	37.3	2.1	23.0
Oklahoma	25.6	75.6	23.6	-	11.6	8.1	3.5	5.4	1.7	10.8	7.9	0.3
Oregon	15.3	64.1	14.1	6.8	7.6	5.1	3.9	3.8	1.1	8.5	4.4	0.7
Pennsylvania	50.8	213.8	48.1	8.1	25.6	5.1	12.7	10.5	5.3	29.3	9.8	21.9
Rhode Island	6.7	17.4	5.8	-	2.8	0.1	1.0	0.9	0.3	4.8	1.6	0.1
South Carolina	29.0	74.6	26.1	-	16.7	14.5	5.2	2.0	1.8	10.0	5.0	0.1
South Dakota	4.7	17.0	4.3	-	2.1	0.7	1.3	1.5	0.3	1.6	1.1	0.3
Tennessee	30.6	87.9	28.6	-	14.2	20.9	4.8	6.7	1.5	16.8	4.7	3.6
Texas	86.7	459.7	81.9	27.2	51.1	58.9	14.3	17.2	3.0	63.1	15.5	2.6
Utah	20.0	33.6	19.2	-	5.5	2.0	1.8	1.4	0.6	4.4	2.6	0.5
Vermont	4.8	13.5	4.5	-	1.0	-	1.1	1.0	0.5	1.0	1.1	0.0
Virginia	45.7	137.3	42.5	-	25.0	8.5	11.3	3.9	2.4	19.7	2.4	8.1
Washington	41.0	89.5	39.3	-	14.2	11.6	6.2	6.4	1.9	15.3	7.5	1.0
West Virginia	13.0	50.8	11.5	-	3.2	4.4	5.8	0.9	0.8	3.1	2.3	-
Wisconsin	37.6	107.4	36.3	9.4	10.1	10.3	2.1	8.7	0.9	16.6	1.2	13.1
Wyoming	3.3	15.5	3.2	1.7	2.1	3.3	1.9	0.8	0.2	1.7	0.3	0.1

Source: U.S. Bureau of the Census. *Statistical Abstract of the United States, 1994.* 114th ed. Washington, DC: U.S. Government Printing Office, 1994, p. 322. Primary source: U.S. Bureau of the Census. *Public Employment.* Series GE, no. 1 (annual). *Notes:* "-" represents or rounds to zero. "X" indicates "not applicable." 1. For state government, represents police protection only.

★ 328 ★

Employment and Unemployment

Unemployment Rates, by Industry: 1975-1993

For civilian noninstitutional population 16 years old and over. Annual averages of monthly figures. Rate represents unemployment as a percent of labor force in each specified group. Data for 1985 through 1991 are not strictly comparable with earlier years due to changes in industrial classification.

[In percentages]

| Industry | 1975 | 1980 | 1985 | 1990 | 1992 | 1993 | Male | | Female | |
							1980	1993	1980	1993
All unemployed[1]	8.5	7.1	7.2	5.5	7.4	6.8	6.9	7.1	7.4	6.5
Industry:[2]										
Agriculture	10.4	11.0	13.2	9.7	12.3	11.6	9.7	11.2	15.1	12.8
Mining	4.1	6.4	9.5	4.8	7.9	7.3	6.7	7.6	4.5	5.6
Construction	18.0	14.1	13.1	11.1	16.7	14.3	14.6	14.8	8.9	9.9
Manufacturing	10.9	8.5	7.7	5.8	7.8	7.2	7.4	6.5	10.8	8.4
Transportation and public utilities	5.6	4.9	5.1	3.8	5.5	5.1	5.1	5.4	4.4	4.3

[Continued]

★ 328 ★

Unemployment Rates, by Industry: 1975-1993
[Continued]

Industry	1975	1980	1985	1990	1992	1993	Male		Female	
							1980	1993	1980	1993
Wholesale and retail trade	8.7	7.4	7.6	6.4	8.4	7.8	6.6	7.3	8.3	8.3
Finance, insurance, and real estate	4.9	3.4	3.5	3.0	4.5	4.1	3.2	3.8	3.5	4.2
Services	7.1	5.9	6.2	5.0	6.5	6.1	6.3	6.6	5.8	5.7
Government	4.1	4.1	3.9	2.6	3.5	3.3	3.9	3.6	4.3	3.0

Source: U.S. Bureau of the Census. *Statistical Abstract of the United States, 1994.* 114th ed. Washington, DC: U.S. Government Printing Office, 1994, p. 417. Primary source: U.S. Bureau of Labor Statistics. *Employment and Earnings* (monthly; January issues). *Notes:* 1. Includes the self-employed, unpaid family workers, and persons with no previous work experience, not shown separately. 2. Covers unemployed wage and salary workers.

Health and Safety

★ 329 ★

Employee Injuries, by Industry: 1992

Figures reflect injuries per 100 full-time workers, as well as the incidence rate of injury, for selected industries. Data provided for 1992.

Industry	Injuries	Rank	Incidence rate	Rank
Eating and drinking places	387.8	1	8.9	7
Hospitals	341.1	2	11.2	5
Grocery stores	252.8	3	12.3	4
Nursing facilities	224.5	4	18.2	2
Trucking/courier services	191.0	5	13.3	3
Department stores	153.8	6	10.4	6
Motor vehicles/equipment	147.2	7	18.3	1

Source: "... And So Are Some Other Things: Overall Injuries Seem to Be on the Upswing." *Restaurant Business,* 20 January 1994, p. 21. Primary source: U.S. Department of Labor. Bureau of Labor Statistics.

★ 330 ★

Health and Safety

Highest Injury and Illness Incidence Rates, by Industry: 1991 and 1992

Table shows the industries with the highest total case incidence rates for injuries and illnesses in 1992. Rates per full-time employees. Rates refer to any occupational injury or illness resulting in (1) fatalities, (2) lost workday cases, or (3) nonfatal cases without lost workdays.

Industry	SIC code[1]	1991	1992[2]
Private sector	(X)	8.4	8.9
Meat packing plants	2011	45.5	44.4
Ship building and repairing	3731	44.1	37.8
Metal sanitary ware	3431	42.0	35.0
Motor vehicles and car bodies	3711	28.3	32.3
Gray and ductile iron foundries	3321	31.3	31.6
Automotive stampings	3465	27.5	29.2
Household appliances, n.e.c.[3]	3639	30.7	27.2
Malt	2083	21.7	26.6
Truck trailers	3715	25.5	25.0
Steel foundries, n.e.c.[3]	3325	24.1	24.4
Poultry slaughtering and processing	2015	23.1	23.2
Mobile homes	2451	22.9	23.0
Household laundry equipment	3633	17.7	22.6
Motorcycles, bicycles, and parts	3751	22.0	22.5
Structural wood members, n.e.c.[3]	2439	22.9	22.4
Truck and bus bodies	3713	23.4	22.3
Prefabricated wood buildings	2452	23.5	21.3
Metal barrels, drums, and pails	3412	22.1	21.3
Iron and steel forgings	3462	20.7	21.1
Flat glass	3211	21.7	21.1
Sausages and other prepared meats	2013	20.8	21.0
Creamery butter	2021	19.8	21.0
Leather tanning and finishing	3111	20.4	20.5
Aluminum die-castings	3363	20.9	20.5
Travel trailers and campers	3792	20.7	20.5
Malleable iron foundries	3322	17.4	20.3
Fresh or frozen prepared fish	2092	21.0	20.3
Aluminum foundries	3365	21.3	20.1
Primary aluminum	3334	23.5	20.0
Railroad equipment	3743	21.1	20.0
Canned and cured fish and seafoods	2091	(NA)	20.0
Prepared flour mixes and doughs	2045	19.0	20.0

Source: U.S. Bureau of the Census. *Statistical Abstract of the United States, 1994.* 114th ed. Washington, DC: U.S. Government Printing Office, 1994, p. 437. Primary source: U.S. Bureau of Labor Statistics. *Occupational Injuries and Illnesses in the United States by Industry* (annual). *Notes:* "X" represents "not applicable." Incidence rates were calculated as: Number of injuries and illnesses divided by total hours worked by all employees during year multiplied by 200,000 as base for 100 full-time equivalent workers (working 40 hours per week, 50 weeks a year). 1. 1987 Standard Industrial Classification (SIC). 2. Data for 1992 exclude fatal work-related injuries and illnesses. Because fatalities account for approximately 4,200 of the 6.8 million cases, the inclusion of fatalities in the survey estimates would marginally impact the estimates. 3. "n.e.c." means "not elsewhere classified."

★ 331 ★

Health and Safety

Lost Workdays Due to Injury and Illness, by Industry

Table shows the lost workdays per 100 full-time workers in selected industries.

Industry	Lost workdays	
	Injury	Illness
Ship and boat building and repairing	337.4	30.5
Logging	274.8	4.7
Iron and steel foundries	184.5	24.9
Railroad equipment	183.0	16.3
Structural clay products	179.5	17.0
Office furniture	131.1	36.5
Millwork[1]	141.9	11.9

Source: "Office Furniture Workers Miss Most Workdays." *Wood and Wood Products* (January 1994), p. 14. Primary source: U.S. Department of Labor. *Note:* 1. Includes cabinetmakers.

★ 332 ★

Health and Safety

Occupational Injury and Illness Incidence Rates, by Selected Industries: 1991 and 1992

Rates per 100 full-time employees. Rates refer to any occupational injury or illness resulting in (1) fatalities, except 1992, (2) lost workday cases, or (3) nonfatal cases without lost workdays.

Industry	SIC code[1]	1991	1992[2]
Private industry[3]	(X)	8.4	8.9
Agriculture, forestry, fishing[3]	A	10.8	11.6
Mining	B	7.4	7.3
Metal mining	10	6.5	6.1
Coal mining	12	11.1	12.5
Oil and gas extraction	13	6.4	6.0
Nonmetallic minerals, exc. fuels	14	7.0	6.5
Construction	C	13.0	13.1
General building contractors	15	12.0	12.2
Heavy construction, except building	16	12.8	12.1
Special trade contractors	17	13.5	13.8
Manufacturing	D	12.7	12.5
Durable goods	(X)	13.6	13.4
Lumber and wood products	24	16.8	16.3
Furniture and fixtures	25	15.9	14.8
Stone, clay, and glass products	32	14.8	13.6
Primary metal industries	33	17.7	17.5
Fabricated metal products	34	17.4	16.8

[Continued]

★ 332 ★

Occupational Injury and Illness Incidence Rates,
by Selected Industries: 1991 and 1992
[Continued]

Industry	SIC code[1]	1991	1992[2]
Industrial machinery and equipment	35	11.2	11.1
Electronic and other electric equipment	36	8.6	8.4
Transportation equipment	37	18.3	18.7
Instruments and related products	38	6.0	5.9
Miscellaneous manufacturing industries	39	11.3	10.7
Nondurable goods	(X)	11.5	11.3
Food and kindred products	20	19.5	18.8
Tobacco products	21	6.4	6.0
Textile mill products	22	10.0	9.9
Apparel and other textile products	23	9.2	9.5
Paper and allied products	26	11.2	11.0
Printing and publishing	27	6.7	7.3
Chemicals and allied products	28	6.4	6.0
Petroleum and coal products	29	6.2	5.9
Rubber and plastics products	30	15.1	14.5
Leather and leather products	31	12.5	12.1
Transportation and public utilities	E	9.3	9.1
Railroad transportation	40	7.6	6.6
Local passenger transit	41	9.5	11.0
Trucking and warehousing	42	14.5	13.4
Water transportation	44	11.6	11.5
Transportation by air	45	14.0	13.8
Pipelines, except natural gas	46	4.0	3.1
Transportation services	47	3.8	3.9
Communications	48	3.2	3.4
Electric, gas, sanitary services	49	7.7	7.6
Wholesale and retail trade	F, G	7.6	8.4
Wholesale trade	F	7.2	7.6
Retail trade	G	7.7	8.7
Finance, insurance, real estate	H	2.4	2.9
Depository institutions	60	1.8	2.1
Nondepository institutions	61	1.1	1.0
Security and commodity brokers	62	(NA)	0.7
Insurance carriers	63	2.4	(NA)
Insurance agents, brokers, and services	64	1.4	1.4
Real estate	65	5.4	6.8
Holding and other investment offices	67	2.6	2.7
Services[4]	I	6.2	7.1
Hotels and other lodging places	70	10.3	11.2
Personal services	72	4.0	5.1
Business services	73	5.2	5.4
Auto repair, services, and parking	75	6.5	7.8
Miscellaneous repair services	76	7.7	8.7
Motion pictures	78	3.6	(NA)
Amusement and recreation services	79	8.8	10.1

[Continued]

★ 332 ★

Occupational Injury and Illness Incidence Rates, by Selected Industries: 1991 and 1992

[Continued]

Industry	SIC code[1]	1991	1992[2]
Health services	80	8.9	10.2
Legal services	81	0.7	1.2
Educational services	82	3.8	5.6
Social services	83	6.6	8.0
Museums, botanical, zoological gardens	84	6.5	7.8
Engineering and management services	87	2.3	2.4
Services, n.e.c.[5]	89	(NA)	2.7

Source: U.S. Bureau of the Census. *Statistical Abstract of the United States, 1994.* 114th ed. Washington, DC: U.S. Government Printing Office, 1994, p. 437. Primary source: U.S. Bureau of Labor Statistics. *Occupational Injuries and Illnesses in the United States by Industry* (annual). *Notes:* "NA" stands for "not available"; "X" represents "not applicable." Incidence rates were calculated as: Number of injuries and illnesses divided by total hours worked by all employees during year multiplied by 200,000 as base for 100 full-time equivalent workers (working 40 hours per week, 50 weeks a year). 1. 1987 Standard Industrial Classification (SIC). 2. Data for 1992 exclude fatal work injuries and illnesses. Because fatalities account for about 4,200 of the 6.8 million cases, the inclusion of fatalities in the survey estimates would marginally impact the estimates. 3. Excludes farms with fewer than 11 employees. 4. Includes categories not shown separately. 5. "n.e.c." stands for "not elsewhere classified."

★ 333 ★

Health and Safety

Violent Crimes in the Workplace, by Industry Sector

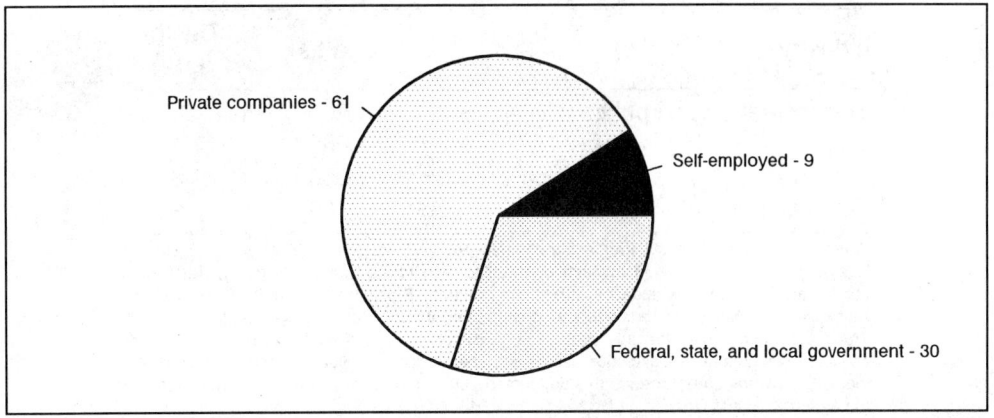

According to the source, government workers comprise 20 percent of the U.S. workforce, yet account for 30 percent of all victims of violent crimes in the workplace. The table below shows the workers victimized in industry sectors.

[In percentages]

Sector	Workplace victims of violent crime
Private companies	61
Federal, state, and local government	30
Self-employed[1]	9

Source: Roberts, Sally. "Violence a Big Threat to Workers, Study Says." *Business Insurance,* 1 August 1994, p. 35. Primary source: Bureau of Justice Statistics. *Note:* 1. Or working without pay.

★ 334 ★

Health and Safety

Work-Related Deaths, by Industry: 1992

Table shows worker deaths and death rates for selected industries.

Industry	Deaths	Death rate[1]
All industries	8,500	7
Agriculture[2]	1,200	37[3]
Mining, quarrying[2]	200	29
Construction	1,300	22
Manufacturing	600	3

[Continued]

★ 334 ★

Work-Related Deaths, by Industry: 1992
[Continued]

Industry	Deaths	Death rate[1]
Transportation and public utilities	1,200	20
Trade[2]	1,000	4
Services[2]	1,300	3
Government	1,700	9

Source: "Work Accidents." *Traffic Safety* (November/December 1993), p. 21. *Notes:* 1. Deaths per 100,000 workers in each division. 2. Agriculture includes forestry and fishing. Mining and quarrying include oil and gas extraction. Preliminary Mine Safety and Health Administration (MSHA) reports show 97 deaths in coal, metal, and nonmetal mining in 1992. Trade includes wholesale and retail trade. Services include finance, insurance, and real estate. 3. Agriculture rate excludes deaths of persons under 14 years of age. Rates for other industry divisions do not require this adjustment. Deaths of persons under 14 are included in the agriculture death total.

Industrial Relations

★ 335 ★

Displaced Workers, by Industry: 1993

According to a Bureau of Labor Statistics study of displaced workers, 9 million lost their jobs between January 1991 and December 1993, usually owing to plant or corporation closures and relocations. The table below shows displaced workers in selected industries. Data are for 1991 through 1993.

Industry	Displaced workers
Manufacturing	1,500,000
Finance, insurance, and real estate	884,000
Wholesale and retail	366,000

Source: "Study Pinpoints Where the Job Losses Were During Early '90s." *HR Focus* (January 1995), p. 18. Primary source: U.S. Bureau of Labor Statisitics.

★ 336 ★
Industrial Relations

Major Collective Bargaining Agreements, by Industry: 1970-1993

Table shows the average percent wage rate changes under all agreements. Data represent all wage rate changes implemented under the terms of private nonfarm industry agreements affecting 1,000 workers or more. Series covers production and related workers in manufacturing and nonsupervisory workers in nonmanufacturing industries. Data measure all wage rate changes effective in the year stemming from settlements reached in the year, deferred from prior year settlements, and cost-of-living adjustment (COLA) clauses.

[In percentages]

Changes	1970	1975	1980	1985	1988	1989	1990	1991	1992	1993
Average wage rate change (prorated over all workers)	8.8	8.7	9.9	3.3	2.6	3.2	3.5	3.6	3.1	3.0
Industry:										
Manufacturing	7.1	8.5	10.2	2.8	2.8	3.5	4.4	3.7	3.1	3.3
Nonmanufacturing	10.5	8.9	9.7	3.6	2.5	3.0	3.0	3.5	3.1	2.8
Construction	(NA)	8.1	9.9	3.0	2.9	3.1	3.4	3.4	3.4	2.7
Transportation and public utilities	(NA)	9.7	10.8	3.6	2.1	2.3	2.2	3.3	2.7	3.0
Wholesale and retail trade	(NA)	9.2	7.6	3.3	2.3	3.2	3.6	3.5	3.5	2.3
Services	(NA)	6.4	8.1	5.1	3.5	5.3	4.3	4.9	3.7	3.4
Nonmanufacturing, excluding construction	(NA)	9.3	9.6	3.7	2.4	3.0	2.9	3.6	3.0	2.8

Source: U.S. Bureau of the Census. *Statistical Abstract of the United States, 1994.* 114th ed. Washington, DC: U.S. Government Printing Office, 1994, p. 435. Primary source: U.S. Bureau of Labor Statistics. *Compensation and Working Conditions* (monthly). *Note:* "NA" stands for "not available."

★ 337 ★
Industrial Relations

Union Members' Weekly Earnings, by Industry: 1983 and 1993

Annual averages of monthly data. Covers employed wage and salary workers 16 years old and over. Excludes self-employed workers whose businesses are incorporated, although they technically qualify as wage and salary workers. Based on Current Population Survey.

Industry	Median usual weekly earnings[1] ($)						Not represented by unions	
	Total		Union members[2]		Represented by unions[3]			
	1983	1993	1983	1993	1983	1993	1983	1993
Total	313	463	388	575	383	569	288	426
Agricultural wage and salary workers	198	277	(B)	(B)	(B)	(B)	195	277
Private nonagricultural wage and salary workers	307	441	389	544	385	538	286	420
Mining	481	645	470	631	470	631	488	657
Construction	348	482	518	692	510	689	296	425
Manufacturing	335	466	370	505	368	505	315	448
Transportation and public utilities	417	570	449	640	445	631	386	516
Wholesale and retail trade, total	252	356	353	465	348	459	242	347
Finance, insurance, and real estate	296	490	284	484	285	481	297	490

[Continued]

★ 337 ★

Union Members' Weekly Earnings, by Industry: 1983 and 1993
[Continued]

| Industry | Median usual weekly earnings[1] ($) | | | | | | Not represented by unions | |
| | Total | | Union members[2] | | Represented by unions[3] | | | |
	1983	1993	1983	1993	1983	1993	1983	1993
Services	272	420	303	482	303	478	268	416
Government	351	547	386	602	381	596	316	498

Source: U.S. Bureau of the Census. *Statistical Abstract of the United States, 1994.* 114th ed. Washington, DC: U.S. Government Printing Office, 1994, p. 439. Primary source: U.S. Bureau of Labor Statistics. *Employment and Earnings* (January issues). *Notes:* "B" represents base less than 50,000. 1. For full-time employed wage and salary workers; 1933 data revised. 2. Members of a labor union or an employee association similar to a labor union. 3. Members of a labor union or an employee association similar to a union as well as workers who report no union affiliations but whose jobs are covered by a union or an employee association contract.

★ 338 ★

Industrial Relations

Union Membership, by Industry: 1983 and 1993

Annual averages of monthly data. Covers employed wage and salary workers 16 years old and over. Excludes self-employed workers whose businesses are incorporated, although they technically qualify as wage and salary workers. Based on Current Population Survey.

| Industry | Employed wage and salary workers | | | | | |
| | Total (1,000) | | Union members[1] (%) | | Represented by unions[2] (%) | |
	1983	1993	1983	1993	1983	1993
Total	88,290	105,067	20.1	15.8	23.3	17.7
Agricultural wage and salary workers	1,446	1,472	3.4	1.6	3.8	2.1
Private nonagricultural wage and salary workers	71,225	84,978	16.8	11.2	18.8	12.3
Mining	869	643	20.7	16.0	23.1	17.6
Construction	4,109	4,638	27.5	20.0	29.4	21.0
Manufacturing	19,066	18,710	27.8	19.2	30.5	20.3
Transportation and public utilities	5,142	6,313	42.4	30.5	46.2	32.5
Wholesale and retail trade, total	18,081	21,655	8.7	6.3	9.8	6.9
Finance, insurance, and real estate	5,559	6,783	2.9	1.9	4.1	2.6
Services	18,400	26,235	7.7	5.8	9.6	7.0
Government	15,618	18,618	36.7	37.7	45.5	43.8

Source: U.S. Bureau of the Census. *Statistical Abstract of the United States, 1994.* 114th ed. Washington, DC: U.S. Government Printing Office, 1994, p. 439. Primary source: U.S. Bureau of Labor Statistics. *Employment and Earnings* (January issues). *Notes:* 1. Members of a labor union or an employee association similar to a union. 2. Members of a labor union or an employee association similar to a union as well as workers who report no union affiliations but whose jobs are covered by a union or by an employee association contract.

Industry Summaries

★ 339 ★

Agriculture, Forestry, and Fishing Establishments, Employment, and Wages, by State: 1993

Data for private industry. Covers establishments primarily engaged in agricultural production (e.g., farms and ranches), forestry (e.g., timber tracts and tree farms), commercial fishing, hunting and trapping, and related services. Figures are 1993 annual averages.

State	Average establish- ments (number)	Annual average employment (number)	Total annual wages (in thousand dollars)	Annual wages per employee (in dollars)	Weekly average wage (in dollars)
Total	173,800	1,539,904	23,498,498	15,260	293
Alabama	1,757	15,984	248,953	15,575	300
Alaska	226	1,604	45,015	28,060	540
Arizona	2,923	37,413	506,936	13,550	261
Arkansas	1,820	14,551	236,362	16,243	312
California	36,536	434,489	6,282,203	14,459	278
Colorado	2,445	21,512	347,351	16,147	311
Connecticut	2,306	13,150	265,630	20,200	388
Delaware	449	2,976	53,778	18,070	348
District of Columbia	52	239	5,324	22,262	428
Florida	11,783	153,116	2,180,607	14,242	274
Georgia	3,379	30,409	480,911	15,815	304
Hawaii	682	11,912	272,403	22,867	440
Idaho	1,601	18,648	267,962	14,370	276
Illinois	4,685	39,313	702,162	17,861	343
Indiana	2,737	22,050	344,828	15,639	301
Iowa	1,913	11,645	183,335	15,743	303
Kansas	1,711	12,193	212,140	17,398	335
Kentucky	1,574	12,283	193,340	15,741	303
Louisiana	1,817	13,587	192,826	14,192	273
Maine	840	5,696	90,371	15,867	305
Maryland	2,648	17,870	319,191	17,862	344
Massachusetts	3,367	16,800	352,358	20,974	403
Michigan	4,418	34,732	535,018	15,404	296
Minnesota	2,603	19,395	325,526	16,784	323
Mississippi	1,713	15,295	220,769	14,434	278
Missouri	2,801	18,793	284,822	15,155	291
Montana	760	3,822	56,612	14,810	285
Nebraska	1,545	10,483	173,975	16,596	319
Nevada	720	5,379	94,141	17,501	337
New Hampshire	642	3,547	59,329	16,727	322
New Jersey	5,028	24,012	468,561	19,514	375
New Mexico	1,034	14,060	151,551	10,779	207
New York	7,060	39,770	735,798	18,501	356
North Carolina	3,967	36,059	560,382	15,541	299
North Dakota	557	2,686	44,934	16,727	322
Ohio	4,781	35,642	566,311	15,889	306

[Continued]

★ 339 ★

Agriculture, Forestry, and Fishing Establishments, Employment, and Wages, by State: 1993
[Continued]

State	Average establishments (number)	Annual average employment (number)	Total annual wages (in thousand dollars)	Annual wages per employee (in dollars)	Weekly average wage (in dollars)
Oklahoma	1,435	10,832	160,316	14,800	285
Oregon	3,365	38,490	552,915	14,365	276
Pennsylvania	4,868	39,688	688,159	17,339	333
Rhode Island	681	2,513	44,882	17,862	343
South Carolina	1,766	14,916	219,737	14,731	283
South Dakota	536	2,448	38,766	15,834	304
Tennessee	1,759	13,623	199,344	14,633	281
Texas	13,340	98,622	1,403,138	14,228	274
Utah	731	5,523	73,654	13,337	256
Vermont	485	2,576	41,057	15,938	307
Virginia	3,167	26,074	416,066	15,957	307
Washington	13,359	85,867	1,130,627	13,167	253
West Virginia	485	3,850	52,134	13,542	260
Wisconsin	2,514	21,050	375,650	17,845	343
Wyoming	433	2,718	40,341	14,842	285

Source: U.S. Department of Labor. Bureau of Labor Statistics. *Employment and Wages Annual Averages, 1993.* Bulletin 2449. Washington, DC: U.S. Government Printing Office, October 1994, p. 32. *Notes:* Data for 1993 are preliminary and subject to revision. Detail may not add to totals due to rounding.

★ 340 ★

Industry Summaries

Construction Establishments, Employment, and Wages, by State: 1993

Data for private industry. Covers establishments primarily engaged in building and heavy construction and special trade contractors; that is, new work, additions, alterations, reconstruction, installations, and repairs. Figures are 1993 annual averages.

State	Average establishments (number)	Annual average employment (number)	Total annual wages (in thousand dollars)	Annual wages per employee (in dollars)	Weekly average wage (in dollars)
Total	636,518	4,589,541	126,485,806	27,560	530
Alabama	8,737	77,874	1,714,786	22,020	423
Alaska	1,735	11,745	516,376	43,966	846
Arizona	9,592	89,417	2,097,939	23,462	451
Arkansas	5,679	38,370	787,441	20,523	395
California	66,494	441,697	13,776,048	31,189	600
Colorado	10,718	85,903	2,375,344	27,651	532
Connecticut	10,620	47,650	1,700,192	35,681	686
Delaware	2,819	17,898	476,069	26,598	512
District of Columbia	690	8,532	277,033	32,471	624

[Continued]

★ 340 ★

Construction Establishments, Employment, and Wages, by State: 1993
[Continued]

State	Average establish- ments (number)	Annual average employment (number)	Total annual wages (in thousand dollars)	Annual wages per employee (in dollars)	Weekly average wage (in dollars)
Florida	35,853	284,256	6,675,720	23,485	452
Georgia	16,254	127,155	3,050,168	23,988	461
Hawaii	2,865	31,926	1,287,540	40,329	776
Idaho	4,378	24,699	618,614	25,046	482
Illinois	26,861	200,319	6,853,529	34,213	658
Indiana	15,059	118,065	3,127,405	26,489	509
Iowa	7,358	48,417	1,180,863	24,390	469
Kansas	6,412	45,708	1,070,963	23,430	451
Kentucky	8,586	70,434	1,613,257	22,904	440
Louisiana	7,226	97,827	2,347,427	23,996	461
Maine	4,367	20,938	487,182	23,268	447
Maryland	16,810	120,914	3,421,853	28,300	544
Massachusetts	14,412	79,069	2,661,261	33,658	647
Michigan	21,749	131,833	3,932,655	29,831	574
Minnesota	12,004	78,478	2,431,105	30,978	596
Mississippi	4,636	39,567	825,201	20,856	401
Missouri	14,364	96,862	2,525,160	26,070	501
Montana	3,014	13,429	321,755	23,959	461
Nebraska	4,569	30,344	698,849	23,031	443
Nevada	3,903	47,024	1,481,110	31,497	606
New Hampshire	3,595	16,805	445,248	26,495	510
New Jersey	23,394	114,502	4,178,701	36,495	702
New Mexico	4,846	35,653	744,641	20,886	402
New York	40,299	241,459	8,231,284	34,090	656
North Carolina	19,154	153,595	3,384,373	22,034	424
North Dakota	2,101	11,726	268,221	22,874	440
Ohio	27,329	187,775	5,218,777	27,793	534
Oklahoma	6,286	42,631	910,275	21,352	411
Oregon	9,707	53,766	1,508,725	28,061	540
Pennsylvania	27,764	196,853	5,683,875	28,874	555
Rhode Island	3,590	12,535	371,763	29,658	570
South Carolina	9,981	82,192	1,872,454	22,782	438
South Dakota	2,454	13,218	274,384	20,759	399
Tennessee	9,784	94,083	2,284,187	24,278	467
Texas	30,341	352,804	9,090,622	25,767	496
Utah	5,295	39,715	893,513	22,498	433
Vermont	2,768	11,568	267,208	23,098	444
Virginia	19,162	153,303	3,700,640	21,139	464
Washington	20,334	112,374	3,114,068	27,712	533
West Virginia	5,077	31,233	751,068	23,047	462

[Continued]

★ 340 ★

Construction Establishments, Employment, and Wages, by State: 1993
[Continued]

State	Average establishments (number)	Annual average employment (number)	Total annual wages (in thousand dollars)	Annual wages per employee (in dollars)	Weekly average wage (in dollars)
Wisconsin	13,405	93,139	2,675,608	28,727	552
Wyoming	2,097	12,266	283,329	23,099	444

Source: U.S. Department of Labor. Bureau of Labor Statistics. *Employment and Wages Annual Averages, 1993.* Bulletin 2449. Washington, DC: U.S. Government Printing Office, October 1994, p. 76. *Notes:* Data for 1993 are preliminary and subject to revision. Detail may not add to totals due to rounding.

★ 341 ★

Industry Summaries

Federal Government Establishments, Employment, and Wages, by State: 1993

Data for total federal government. Covers executive, legislative, judicial, administrative, and regulatory activities of the federal government. Figures are 1993 annual averages.

State	Average establishments (number)	Annual average employment (number)	Total annual wages (in thousand dollars)	Annual wages per employee (in dollars)	Weekly average wage (in dollars)
Total	47,713	3,071,117	113,448,715	36,941	710
Alabama	1,116	59,793	2,263,875	37,862	728
Alaska	451	19,990	746,510	37,345	718
Arizona	343	45,026	1,537,136	34,139	657
Arkansas	1,113	21,450	730,870	34,074	655
California	3,325	330,172	12,000,578	36,346	699
Colorado	852	60,011	2,162,311	36,032	693
Connecticut	635	24,560	963,516	39,231	754
Delaware	96	5,900	206,816	35,051	674
District of Columbia	245	229,463	10,534,855	45,911	883
Florida	1,151	121,661	4,482,422	36,843	709
Georgia	1,335	101,303	3,430,964	33,868	651
Hawaii	222	32,125	1,078,058	33,558	645
Idaho	823	13,572	438,037	32,275	621
Illinois	1,305	103,825	3,962,372	38,164	734
Indiana	557	44,573	1,694,788	38,023	731
Iowa	845	20,228	687,006	33,963	653
Kansas	652	29,376	1,005,846	34,240	658
Kentucky	1,235	42,240	1,316,274	31,162	599
Louisiana	1,080	36,789	1,264,538	34,373	661
Maine	432	16,102	547,089	33,977	653
Maryland	289	133,989	5,350,866	39,935	768
Massachusetts	770	60,145	2,263,844	37,640	724
Michigan	1,676	57,437	2,014,228	35,068	674

[Continued]

★ 341 ★

Federal Government Establishments, Employment, and Wages, by State: 1993
[Continued]

State	Average establish- ments (number)	Annual average employment (number)	Total annual wages (in thousand dollars)	Annual wages per employee (in dollars)	Weekly average wage (in dollars)
Minnesota	1,311	33,891	1,241,309	36,627	704
Mississippi	1,150	27,688	916,111	33,087	636
Missouri	1,610	68,135	2,286,740	33,562	645
Montana	897	13,510	436,804	32,331	622
Nebraska	662	17,145	545,322	31,807	612
Nevada	318	13,313	484,272	36,376	700
New Hampshire	416	7,622	287,199	37,680	725
New Jersey	892	72,954	2,997,275	41,085	790
New Mexico	513	31,730	1,103,593	34,781	669
New York	1,726	150,349	5,763,627	38,335	737
North Carolina	1,747	58,413	1,956,625	33,496	644
North Dakota	576	9,727	286,688	29,472	567
Ohio	1,496	90,977	3,231,175	35,516	683
Oklahoma	1,178	47,274	1,678,216	35,499	683
Oregon	829	32,566	1,178,567	36,190	696
Pennsylvania	2,241	134,079	4,725,608	35,245	678
Rhode Island	100	10,200	356,881	34,988	673
South Carolina	545	34,233	1,185,902	34,642	666
South Dakota	641	11,426	355,836	31,143	599
Tennessee	584	55,882	2,143,772	38,363	738
Texas	1,915	194,001	6,799,510	35,049	674
Utah	515	34,767	1,178,538	33,898	652
Vermont	560	5,530	187,530	33,911	652
Virginia	1,299	178,958	7,018,821	39,221	754
Washington	1,433	71,945	2,549,150	35,432	681
West Virginia	707	17,719	622,702	35,144	676
Wisconsin	914	29,877	1,004,067	33,606	646
Wyoming	396	7,477	244,078	32,644	628

Source: U.S. Department of Labor. Bureau of Labor Statistics. *Employment and Wages Annual Averages, 1993.* Bulletin 2449. Washington, DC: U.S. Government Printing Office, October 1994, p. 529. *Notes:* Data for 1993 are preliminary and subject to revision. Detail may not add to totals due to rounding.

★ 342 ★
Industry Summaries

Finance, Insurance, and Real Estate Establishments, Employment, and Wages, by State: 1993

Data for private industry. Covers establishments operating primarily in the fields of financial services (e.g., depository institutions, holding companies, and security brokers); insurance and insurance agents and brokers; and real estate owners, lessors, lessees, buyers, sellers, agents, and developers. Figures are 1993 annual averages.

State	Average establishments (number)	Annual average employment (number)	Total annual wages (in thousand dollars)	Annual wages per employee (in dollars)	Weekly average wage (in dollars)
Total	558,028	6,561,095	236,287,718	36,013	693
Alabama	7,601	72,693	1,985,136	27,309	525
Alaska	1,029	10,004	302,646	30,253	582
Arizona	9,374	100,573	2,939,938	29,232	562
Arkansas	4,741	38,460	991,017	25,767	496
California	70,682	795,618	29,590,373	37,192	715
Colorado	10,628	104,380	3,341,558	32,013	616
Connecticut	8,486	139,326	6,588,575	47,289	909
Delaware	2,954	35,010	1,046,352	29,887	575
District of Columbia	2,142	28,741	1,317,267	45,833	881
Florida	32,786	356,104	11,106,107	31,188	600
Georgia	14,569	163,456	5,518,162	33,759	649
Hawaii	3,987	38,903	1,214,478	31,218	600
Idaho	2,704	18,975	465,645	24,540	472
Illinois	24,778	373,317	14,528,964	38,919	748
Indiana	11,313	126,633	3,649,189	27,396	527
Iowa	7,362	74,118	2,003,368	27,029	520
Kansas	6,567	58,125	1,573,363	27,069	521
Kentucky	6,699	62,716	1,728,054	27,554	530
Louisiana	8,212	74,411	1,925,549	25,877	498
Maine	2,293	24,688	739,164	29,940	576
Maryland	10,135	129,604	4,513,929	34,829	670
Massachusetts	11,952	196,128	8,161,818	41,615	800
Michigan	14,434	193,414	5,838,541	30,187	581
Minnesota	11,773	134,069	4,683,697	34,935	672
Mississippi	5,301	38,114	923,787	24,237	466
Missouri	12,426	137,725	4,122,747	29,935	576
Montana	2,210	14,514	344,148	23,712	456
Nebraska	4,087	49,043	1,312,676	26,766	515
Nevada	3,990	31,044	886,667	28,562	549
New Hampshire	2,554	27,788	848,279	30,527	587
New Jersey	15,422	221,542	9,403,216	42,444	816
New Mexico	3,346	26,938	656,686	24,378	469
New York	49,859	726,600	43,502,953	59,872	1,151
North Carolina	12,221	135,977	4,064,518	29,891	575
North Dakota	1,909	13,003	305,852	23,521	452
Ohio	20,927	253,106	7,471,194	29,518	568
Oklahoma	7,010	60,294	1,503,651	24,939	480
Oregon	7,618	70,587	1,992,941	28,234	543
Pennsylvania	19,945	300,134	9,860,982	32,855	632

[Continued]

★ 342 ★

Finance, Insurance, and Real Estate Establishments, Employment, and Wages, by State: 1993
[Continued]

State	Average establish-ments (number)	Annual average employment (number)	Total annual wages (in thousand dollars)	Annual wages per employee (in dollars)	Weekly average wage (in dollars)
Rhode Island	1,975	24,231	769,883	31,772	611
South Carolina	6,501	64,081	1,630,859	25,450	489
South Dakota	2,199	17,153	386,858	22,553	434
Tennessee	8,608	99,039	2,958,205	29,869	574
Texas	35,994	411,954	13,314,124	32,319	622
Utah	3,962	41,437	1,082,662	26,128	502
Vermont	1,443	11,637	335,436	28,825	554
Virginia	14,090	154,899	4,928,814	31,820	612
Washington	12,722	119,325	3,714,620	31,130	599
West Virginia	3,171	24,575	553,760	22,533	433
Wisconsin	10,098	129,199	3,642,441	28,192	542
Wyoming	1,242	7,693	196,867	25,590	492

Source: U.S. Department of Labor. Bureau of Labor Statistics. Employment and Wages Annual Averages, 1993. Bulletin 2449. Washington, DC: U.S. Government Printing Office, October 1994, p. 419. Notes: Data for 1993 are preliminary and subject to revision. Detail may not add to totals due to rounding.

★ 343 ★

Industry Summaries

High Technology Establishments: 1992

Figures are for workers on private industry payrolls and exclude the self-employed. Based on surveys of the Occupational Employment Statistics Program and subject to sampling error.

Industry	SIC code[1]	Establishments (1,000)	Employment Total (1,000)	Employment Percent distribution	Average annual pay ($)
All high technology industries[2]	(X)	348.0	9,620	100.0	40,748
Level 1 industries[3]	(X)	312.5	8,358	86.9	41,953
Crude petroleum and natural gas operations	131	9.7	183	1.9	54,439
Cigarettes	211	-	35	0.4	51,105
Industrial inorganic chemicals	281	1.5	136	1.4	45,432
Plastics materials and synthetics	282	1.0	172	1.8	43,370
Drugs	283	1.8	257	2.7	48,327
Soap, cleaners, and toilet goods	284	2.5	154	1.6	40,506
Paints and allied products	285	1.5	58	0.6	35,824
Industrial organic chemicals	286	1.0	153	1.6	49,735
Agricultural chemicals	287	1.2	58	0.6	40,868
Miscellaneous chemical products	289	2.7	93	1.0	39,646
Petroleum refining	291	0.7	120	1.2	52,023

[Continued]

High Technology Establishments: 1992

[Continued]

Industry	SIC code[1]	Establishments (1,000)	Employment		Average annual pay ($)
			Total (1,000)	Percent distribution	
Miscellaneous petroleum and coal products	299	0.5	12	0.1	35,289
Nonferrous rolling and drawing	335	1.2	162	1.7	35,360
Special industry machinery	355	4.1	148	1.5	35,586
Computer and office equipment	357	2.6	387	4.0	48,917
Electrical industrial apparatus	362	1.9	157	1.6	30,784
Communications equipment	366	2.2	238	2.5	40,688
Electronic components and accessories	367	6.4	524	5.4	35,272
Motor vehicles and equipment	371	5.7	819	8.5	40,425
Aircraft and parts	372	2.9	614	6.4	43,743
Guided missiles, space vehicles, parts	376	0.3	144	1.5	48,440
Search and navigation equipment	381	0.9	230	2.4	45,573
Measuring and controlling devices	382	5.1	291	3.0	36,670
Medical instruments and supplies	384	4.1	265	2.8	35,428
Photographic equipment and supplies	386	0.9	95	1.0	45,623
Computer and data-processing services	737	60.5	839	8.7	44,100
Engineering and architectural services	871	65.2	749	7.8	41,209
Research and testing services	873	23.5	562	5.8	38,176
Management and public relations	874	92.4	664	6.9	42,495
Services, n.e.c.[4]	899	8.6	41	0.4	49,211
Level II industries[5]	(X)	35.5	1,262	13.1	32,764
Miscellaneous textile goods	229	0.9	51	0.5	27,113
Pulp mills	261	0.1	14	0.1	45,238
Miscellaneous converted paper products	267	3.1	240	2.5	32,234
Ordinance and accessories, n.e.c.[4]	348	0.4	65	0.7	34,940
Engines and turbines	351	0.5	87	0.9	41,533
General industry machinery	356	4.6	236	2.4	33,429
Industrial machines, n.e.c.[4]	359	21.9	292	3.0	29,654
Household audio and video equipment	365	1.2	81	0.8	35,252
Miscellaneous electrical equipment and supplies	369	1.8	150	1.6	32,767
Miscellaneous transportation equipment	379	1.1	45	0.5	30,173

Source: U.S. Bureau of the Census. *Statistical Abstract of the United States, 1994.* 114th ed. Washington, DC: U.S. Government Printing Office, 1994, p. 414. Primary source: U.S. Bureau of Labor Statistics. *Employment and Wages, Annual Averages 1991.* BLS Bulletin 2419. *Notes:* "X" represents "not applicable." 1. 1987 Standard Industrial Classification (SIC). 2. Those industries whose proportion of R&D employment is at least equal to the average proportion of all industries surveyed. 3. Industries whose proportion of R&D employment is at least 50 percent higher than the average of all industries surveyed. 4. "n.e.c." means "not elsewhere classified." 5. Industries whose proportion of R&D employment is at least equal to the average of all industries surveyed, but less than 50 percent higher than the average.

★ 344 ★

Industry Summaries

Local Government Establishments, Employment, and Wages, by State: 1993

Data for total local government. Covers executive, legislative, judicial, administrative, and regulatory activities of local governments. Figures are 1993 annual averages.

State	Average establish-ments (number)	Annual average employment (number)	Total annual wages (in thousand dollars)	Annual wages per employee (in dollars)	Weekly average wage (in dollars)
Total	118,625	11,056,988	288,481,740	26,090	502
Alabama	2,827	179,706	3,632,423	20,213	389
Alaska	334	29,944	1,078,060	36,002	692
Arizona	1,434	166,313	4,202,179	25,267	486
Arkansas	1,960	88,211	1,687,561	19,131	368
California	4,894	1,322,813	41,148,007	31,106	598
Colorado	1,338	164,847	4,050,506	24,571	473
Connecticut	2,292	112,017	3,780,306	33,748	649
Delaware	79	19,167	538,113	28,075	540
District of Columbia	16	4,392	195,477	44,504	856
Florida	1,257	557,697	14,780,287	26,502	510
Georgia	2,481	311,581	6,650,817	21,345	410
Hawaii	150	15,504	506,461	32,667	628
Idaho	1,431	50,007	937,200	18,741	360
Illinois	6,429	506,711	12,844,432	27,322	525
Indiana	2,006	226,383	5,255,087	23,213	446
Iowa	3,507	141,187	2,898,604	20,530	395
Kansas	2,561	139,978	2,777,438	19,842	382
Kentucky	1,840	138,810	2,997,179	21,592	415
Louisiana	3,011	194,335	3,730,091	19,194	369
Maine	1,853	51,791	1,104,424	21,325	410
Maryland	393	177,233	5,291,204	29,854	574
Massachusetts	3,267	217,463	6,246,830	28,726	552
Michigan	3,008	387,061	10,947,475	28,284	544
Minnesota	4,356	220,389	5,573,901	25,291	486
Mississippi	1,215	120,296	2,117,367	17,601	338
Missouri	5,776	207,841	4,669,519	22,467	432
Montana	864	35,533	710,253	19,989	384
Nebraska	2,129	92,836	1,922,960	20,713	398
Nevada	126	52,565	1,599,771	30,434	585
New Hampshire	671	42,003	1,025,363	24,412	469
New Jersey	1,696	347,698	11,742,320	33,772	649
New Mexico	1,754	69,168	1,438,224	20,793	400
New York	3,525	954,103	30,936,597	32,425	624
North Carolina	3,162	313,659	6,896,951	21,989	423
North Dakota	996	26,850	487,005	18,138	349
Ohio	8,679	472,374	11,600,583	24,558	472
Oklahoma	2,950	140,911	2,792,365	19,817	381
Oregon	1,223	132,652	3,336,324	25,151	484
Pennsylvania	6,480	412,340	11,456,484	27,784	534
Rhode Island	429	29,506	919,942	31,178	600
South Carolina	1,317	153,539	3,341,405	21,763	419

[Continued]

★ 344 ★

Local Government Establishments, Employment, and Wages, by State: 1993

[Continued]

State	Average establish-ments (number)	Annual average employment (number)	Total annual wages (in thousand dollars)	Annual wages per employee (in dollars)	Weekly average wage (in dollars)
South Dakota	741	32,420	566,520	17,475	336
Tennessee	1,590	210,100	4,532,011	21,571	415
Texas	7,698	860,772	19,723,988	22,914	441
Utah	2,224	73,450	1,471,499	20,034	385
Vermont	808	23,311	513,995	22,050	424
Virginia	2,447	267,585	6,458,696	24,137	464
Washington	1,708	231,092	6,351,553	27,485	529
West Virginia	925	69,526	1,486,823	21,385	411
Wisconsin	4,232	228,359	5,837,169	25,561	492
Wyoming	545	32,960	691,990	20,995	404

Source: U.S. Department of Labor. Bureau of Labor Statistics. *Employment and Wages Annual Averages, 1993.* Bulletin 2449. Washington, DC: U.S. Government Printing Office, October 1994, p. 524. *Notes:* Data for 1993 are preliminary and subject to revision. Detail may not add to totals due to rounding.

★ 345 ★

Industry Summaries

Manufacturing Establishments, Employment, and Wages, by State: 1993

Data for private industry. Covers establishments engaged in the mechanical or chemical transformation of materials or substances into new products, establishments engaged in assembling component parts of manufactured products when the new product is neither a structure nor other fixed improvement, or establishments engaged in the blending of materials such as plastics resins or liquors. Figures are 1993 annual averages.

State	Average establish-ments (number)	Annual average employment (number)	Total annual wages (in thousand dollars)	Annual wages per employee (in dollars)	Weekly average wage (in dollars)
Total	390,578	18,063,738	585,344,151	32,404	623
Alabama	6,795	385,385	9,767,176	25,344	487
Alaska	567	17,083	508,421	29,763	572
Arizona	4,858	176,033	5,809,963	33,005	635
Arkansas	4,211	243,729	5,454,565	22,380	430
California	52,907	1,793,222	65,415,952	36,480	702
Colorado	5,513	187,073	6,236,207	33,336	641
Connecticut	6,189	293,660	11,986,276	40,817	785
Delaware	683	65,369	2,744,316	41,982	807
District of Columbia	746	13,691	629,708	45,996	885
Florida	15,654	483,871	14,102,974	29,146	561
Georgia	10,236	555,312	14,754,104	26,569	511
Hawaii	1,056	18,404	510,651	27,747	534

[Continued]

★ 345 ★

Manufacturing Establishments, Employment, and Wages, by State: 1993
[Continued]

State	Average establishments (number)	Annual average employment (number)	Total annual wages (in thousand dollars)	Annual wages per employee (in dollars)	Weekly average wage (in dollars)
Idaho	2,097	69,241	1,949,221	28,151	541
Illinois	19,765	931,242	32,280,107	34,663	667
Indiana	9,646	642,796	21,017,894	32,698	629
Iowa	4,317	235,458	6,793,734	28,853	555
Kansas	3,420	182,619	5,356,009	29,329	564
Kentucky	4,581	293,703	8,265,237	28,141	541
Louisiana	4,362	185,496	5,779,378	31,156	599
Maine	2,313	90,820	2,524,111	27,793	534
Maryland	3,830	179,400	6,081,881	33,901	652
Massachusetts	9,289	453,016	16,939,867	37,394	719
Michigan	16,322	906,132	36,956,453	40,785	784
Minnesota	8,502	405,721	13,505,352	33,287	640
Mississippi	4,032	255,444	5,562,507	21,776	419
Missouri	8,387	410,267	12,461,206	30,373	584
Montana	1,443	23,099	589,010	25,500	490
Nebraska	2,006	103,342	2,627,150	25,422	489
Nevada	1,466	29,479	846,120	28,703	552
New Hampshire	2,456	97,089	3,165,685	32,606	627
New Jersey	12,455	513,662	20,324,802	39,568	761
New Mexico	1,713	42,049	1,076,840	25,609	492
New York	26,650	976,922	36,301,541	37,159	715
North Carolina	11,329	847,067	21,774,530	25,706	494
North Dakota	724	19,477	458,524	23,542	453
Ohio	19,172	1,051,537	36,616,711	34,822	670
Oklahoma	4,937	167,958	4,680,028	27,864	536
Oregon	6,892	212,003	6,447,729	30,413	585
Pennsylvania	18,071	943,839	30,344,871	32,150	618
Rhode Island	2,981	87,994	2,484,755	28,238	543
South Carolina	5,165	374,646	10,091,857	26,937	518
South Dakota	990	39,444	853,891	21,648	416
Tennessee	7,578	525,858	14,270,239	12,137	522
Texas	22,100	986,671	31,818,835	32,249	620
Utah	2,855	109,870	2,970,146	27,033	520
Vermont	1,414	43,592	1,346,779	30,895	594
Virginia	6,424	404,629	11,425,884	28,238	543
Washington	8,840	336,377	11,749,142	34,929	672
West Virginia	1,902	82,804	2,497,423	30,161	580
Wisconsin	10,197	560,579	16,940,955	30,220	581
Wyoming	544	9,568	247,433	25,860	497

Source: U.S. Department of Labor. Bureau of Labor Statistics. Employment and Wages Annual Averages, 1993. Bulletin 2449. Washington, DC: U.S. Government Printing Office, October 1994, p. 89. Notes: Data for 1993 are preliminary and subject to revision. Detail may not add to totals due to rounding.

★ 346 ★

Industry Summaries

Mining Establishments, Employment, and Wages, by State: 1993

Data for private industry. Covers establishments primarily engaged in mining, including the extraction of minerals occurring naturally, quarrying, well operations, milling (e.g., crushing and washing), and other preparation typically conducted at mine sites or as part of mining activities. Figures are 1993 annual averages.

State	Average establishments (number)	Annual average employment (number)	Total annual wages (in thousand dollars)	Annual wages per employee (in dollars)	Weekly average wage (in dollars)
Total	30,750	608,913	25,834,657	42,428	816
Alabama	375	10,677	422,320	39,553	761
Alaska	208	10,028	746,689	74,463	1,432
Arizona	244	12,332	495,698	40,197	773
Arkansas	348	3,539	98,637	27,872	536
California	1,292	33,351	1,721,564	51,620	993
Colorado	1,198	16,048	783,670	48,833	939
Connecticut	88	893	47,006	52,653	1,013
Delaware	6	80	2,436	30,414	585
District of Columbia	19	52	5,820	111,569	2,146
Florida	213	6,589	233,659	35,462	682
Georgia	192	7,511	259,941	34,608	666
Hawaii	9	303	14,252	46,986	904
Idaho	150	2,198	76,477	34,790	669
Illinois	854	15,522	595,313	38,352	738
Indiana	446	6,494	255,493	39,343	757
Iowa	218	2,101	58,661	27,925	537
Kansas	1,267	8,761	243,152	27,754	534
Kentucky	1,199	27,920	1,003,242	35,933	691
Louisiana	1,864	46,444	1,873,133	40,331	776
Maine	36	140	4,564	32,637	628
Maryland	74	1,138	38,508	33,834	651
Massachusetts	83	1,221	42,826	35,063	674
Michigan	461	8,746	319,254	36,505	702
Minnesota	183	7,493	284,106	37,915	729
Mississippi	437	5,193	144,518	27,832	535
Missouri	302	4,465	174,294	39,040	751
Montana	366	5,509	207,895	37,739	726
Nebraska	161	1,443	34,571	23,961	461
Nevada	350	12,620	544,784	43,167	830
New Hampshire	62	422	12,270	29,047	559
New Jersey	99	1,855	75,411	40,660	782
New Mexico	753	15,783	544,586	34,504	664
New York	387	4,979	206,437	41,465	797
North Carolina	184	3,425	107,611	31,423	604
North Dakota	305	3,821	137,967	36,104	694
Ohio	1,123	14,262	478,108	33,523	645
Oklahoma	2,746	36,121	1,404,581	38,885	748
Oregon	144	1,685	61,702	36,615	704
Pennsylvania	1,101	21,790	773,602	35,503	683
Rhode Island	18	174	5,076	29,228	562

[Continued]

★ 346 ★

Mining Establishments, Employment, and Wages, by State: 1993

[Continued]

State	Average establishments (number)	Annual average employment (number)	Total annual wages (in thousand dollars)	Annual wages per employee (in dollars)	Weekly average wage (in dollars)
South Carolina	105	1,786	53,936	30,205	581
South Dakota	77	2,447	81,846	33,451	643
Tennessee	275	4,679	147,284	31,481	605
Texas	7,519	165,622	8,195,501	49,483	952
Utah	395	8,320	327,763	39,396	758
Vermont	62	551	15,225	27,656	532
Virginia	431	12,887	458,412	35,572	684
Washington	215	3,155	118,163	37,459	720
West Virginia	1,164	26,237	1,081,408	41,217	793
Wisconsin	151	2,377	78,628	33,082	636
Wyoming	795	17,729	736,657	41,551	799

Source: U.S. Department of Labor. Bureau of Labor Statistics. *Employment and Wages Annual Averages, 1993.* Bulletin 2449. Washington, DC: U.S. Government Printing Office, October 1994, p. 60. *Notes:* Data for 1993 are preliminary and subject to revision. Detail may not add to totals due to rounding.

★ 347 ★

Industry Summaries

Nonfarm Establishments, by Industry: 1960-1993

Data show the employees, hours, and earnings related to nonfarm establishments in various industries. Based on data from establishment reports. Includes all full- and part-time employees who worked during, or received pay for, any part of the pay period reported. Excludes proprietors, the self-employed, farm workers, unpaid family workers, private household workers, and Armed Forces. Establishment data shown here conform to industry definitions in the 1987 Standard Industrial Classification Manual and are adjusted to March 1991 employment benchmarks; consequently, they may not be comparable with previously published data. Based on the Current Employment Statistics Program.

Item and year	Total	Goods producing				Service producing						
		Total	Mining	Construction	Manufacturing	Total	Transportation and public utilities	Wholesale trade	Retail trade	Finance, insurance, and real estate	Services	Government
Employees (1,000)												
1960	54,189	20,434	712	2,926	16,796	33,755	4,004	3,153	8,238	2,628	7,378	8,353
1965	60,765	21,926	632	3,232	18,062	38,839	4,036	3,477	9,239	2,977	9,036	10,074
1970	70,880	23,578	623	3,588	19,367	47,302	4,515	4,006	11,034	3,645	11,548	12,554
1975	76,945	22,600	752	3,525	18,323	54,345	4,542	4,430	12,630	4,165	13,892	14,686
1980	90,406	25,658	1,027	4,346	20,285	64,748	5,146	5,292	15,018	5,160	17,890	16,241
1985	97,387	24,842	927	4,668	19,248	72,544	5,233	5,727	17,315	5,948	21,927	16,394
1989	107,895	25,254	692	5,171	19,391	82,642	5,625	6,187	19.475	6,668	26,907	17,779
1990	109,419	24,905	709	5,120	19,076	84,514	5,793	6,173	19,601	6,709	27,934	18,304
1991	108,256	23,745	689	4,650	18,406	84,511	5,762	6,081	19,284	6,646	28,336	18,402
1992	108,519	23,142	631	4,471	18,040	85,377	5,709	6,045	19,346	6,571	29,053	18,653
1993	110,178	22,975	599	4,574	17,802	87,203	5,708	6,113	19,743	6,604	30,192	18,842
Percent distribution												
1960	100.0	37.7	1.3	5.4	31.0	62.3	7.4	5.8	15.2	4.9	13.6	15.4
1965	100.0	36.1	1.0	5.3	29.7	63.9	6.6	5.7	15.2	4.9	14.9	16.6
1970	100.0	33.3	0.9	5.1	27.3	66.7	6.4	5.7	15.6	5.1	16.3	17.8
1975	100.0	29.4	1.0	4.6	23.8	70.6	5.9	5.8	16.4	5.4	18.1	19.1
1980	100.0	28.4	1.1	4.8	22.4	71.6	5.7	5.9	16.6	5.7	19.8	18.0
1985	100.0	25.5	1.0	4.8	19.8	74.5	5.4	5.9	17.8	6.1	22.5	16.8
1989	100.0	23.4	0.6	4.8	18.0	76.6	5.2	5.7	18.1	6.2	24.9	16.5
1990	100.0	22.8	0.7	4.7	17.4	77.2	5.3	5.6	17.9	6.1	25.5	16.7
1991	100.0	22.0	0.6	4.3	17.0	78.1	5.3	5.6	17.8	6.1	26.2	17.0
1992	100.0	21.3	0.6	4.1	16.7	78.7	5.3	5.6	17.8	6.1	26.8	17.2

[Continued]

★ 347 ★

Nonfarm Establishments, by Industry: 1960-1993
[Continued]

| Item and year | Total | Goods producing | | | | Service producing | | | | | | |
		Total	Mining	Construction	Manufacturing	Total	Transportation and public utilities	Wholesale trade	Retail trade	Finance, insurance, and real estate	Services	Government
1993	100.0	20.9	0.5	4.2	16.2	79.1	5.2	5.5	17.9	6.0	27.4	17.1
Weekly hours[1]												
1960	38.6	(NA)	40.4	36.7	39.7	(NA)	(NA)	40.5	38.0	37.2	(NA)	(NA)
1965	38.8	(NA)	42.3	37.4	41.2	(NA)	41.3	40.8	36.6	37.2	35.9	(NA)
1970	37.1	(NA)	42.7	37.3	39.8	(NA)	40.5	39.9	33.8	36.7	34.4	(NA)
1975	36.1	(NA)	41.9	36.4	39.5	(NA)	39.7	38.6	32.4	36.5	33.5	(NA)
1980	35.3	(NA)	43.3	37.0	39.7	(NA)	39.6	38.4	30.2	36.2	32.6	(NA)
1985	34.9	(NA)	43.4	37.7	40.5	(NA)	39.5	38.4	29.4	36.4	32.5	(NA)
1989	34.6	(NA)	43.0	37.9	41.0	(NA)	38.9	38.0	28.9	35.8	32.6	(NA)
1990	34.5	(NA)	44.1	38.2	40.8	(NA)	38.9	38.1	28.8	35.8	32.5	(NA)
1991	34.3	(NA)	44.4	38.1	40.7	(NA)	38.7	38.1	28.6	35.7	32.4	(NA)
1992	34.4	(NA)	43.9	38.0	41.0	(NA)	38.9	38.2	28.8	35.8	32.5	(NA)
1993	34.5	(NA)	44.2	38.4	41.4	(NA)	39.7	38.2	28.8	35.7	32.5	(NA)
Hourly earnings[1]												
1960	$2.09	(NA)	$2.60	$3.07	$2.26	(NA)	(NA)	$2.24	$1.52	$2.02	(NA)	(NA)
1965	2.46	(NA)	2.92	3.70	2.61	(NA)	$3.03	2.60	1.82	2.39	$2.05	(NA)
1970	3.23	(NA)	3.85	5.24	3.35	(NA)	3.85	3.43	2.44	3.07	2.81	(NA)
1975	4.53	(NA)	5.95	7.31	4.83	(NA)	5.88	4.72	3.36	4.06	4.02	(NA)
1980	6.66	(NA)	9.17	9.94	7.27	(NA)	8.87	6.95	4.88	5.79	5.85	(NA)
1985	8.57	(NA)	11.98	12.32	9.54	(NA)	11.40	9.15	5.94	7.94	7.90	(NA)
1989	9.66	(NA)	13.26	13.54	10.48	(NA)	12.60	10.39	6.53	9.53	9.38	(NA)
1990	10.01	(NA)	13.68	13.77	10.83	(NA)	12.97	10.79	6.75	9.97	9.83	(NA)
1991	10.32	(NA)	14.19	14.00	11.18	(NA)	13.22	11.15	6.94	10.39	10.23	(NA)
1992	10.58	(NA)	14.54	14.15	11.46	(NA)	13.46	11.39	7.13	10.82	10.55	(NA)
1993	10.83	(NA)	14.60	14.35	11.76	(NA)	13.64	11.71	7.29	11.32	10.81	(NA)
Weekly earnings[1]												
1960	$81	(NA)	$105	$113	$90	(NA)	(NA)	$91	$58	$75	(NA)	(NA)
1965	95	(NA)	124	138	108	(NA)	$125	106	67	89	$74	(NA)
1970	120	(NA)	164	195	133	(NA)	156	137	82	113	97	(NA)
1975	164	(NA)	249	266	191	(NA)	233	182	109	148	135	(NA)
1980	235	(NA)	397	368	289	(NA)	351	267	147	210	191	(NA)
1985	299	(NA)	520	464	386	(NA)	450	351	175	289	257	(NA)
1989	334	(NA)	570	513	430	(NA)	490	395	189	341	306	(NA)
1990	345	(NA)	603	526	442	(NA)	505	411	194	357	319	(NA)
1991	354	(NA)	630	533	455	(NA)	512	425	199	371	331	(NA)
1992	364	(NA)	638	538	470	(NA)	524	435	205	387	343	(NA)
1993	374	(NA)	645	551	487	(NA)	542	447	210	404	351	(NA)

Source: U.S. Bureau of the Census. *Statistical Abstract of the United States, 1994.* 114th ed. Washington, DC: U.S. Government Printing Office, 1994, p. 420. Primary sources: U.S. Bureau of Labor Statistics. Bulletins 2370 and 2429; and *Employment and Earnings* (monthly; March issues). *Notes:* "NA" stands for "not available." 1. Average hours and earnings. Private production and related workers in mining, manufacturing, and construction; nonsupervisory employees in other industries.

★ 348 ★

Industry Summaries

Retail Trade Establishments, Employment, and Wages, by State: 1993

Data for private industry. Covers establishments engaged in selling merchandise for personal or household consumption and in rendering services incidental to the sale of the goods; for example, grocery, drug, or hardware stores. Figures are 1993 annual averages.

State	Average establish-ments (number)	Annual average employment (number)	Total annual wages (in thousand dollars)	Annual wages per employee (in dollars)	Weekly average wage (in dollars)
Total	1,397,229	19,784,961	276,928,974	13,997	269
Alabama	22,196	292,281	3,651,743	12,494	240
Alaska	3,337	40,982	712,339	17,382	334
Arizona	19,261	312,059	4,387,865	14,061	270
Arkansas	14,809	174,986	2,228,807	12,737	245
California	149,489	2,114,234	34,313,140	16,230	312
Colorado	21,900	317,400	4,451,370	14,024	270
Connecticut	20,382	254,660	4,287,522	16,836	324
Delaware	4,407	63,682	847,862	13,314	256
District of Columbia	3,455	46,492	728,505	15,670	301
Florida	76,075	1,159,158	16,651,875	14,365	276
Georgia	37,458	557,757	7,533,693	13,507	260
Hawaii	7,215	110,986	1,775,079	15,994	308
Idaho	6,955	84,430	1,063,978	12,602	242
Illinois	55,888	905,486	13,060,671	14,424	277
Indiana	31,670	488,862	5,920,638	12,111	233
Iowa	19,979	241,587	2,743,488	11,356	218
Kansas	15,980	205,337	2,541,250	12,376	238
Kentucky	20,937	293,036	3,510,182	11,979	230
Louisiana	20,929	300,121	3,626,510	12,083	232
Maine	9,005	106,934	1,395,234	13,048	251
Maryland	27,328	401,136	6,147,141	15,324	295
Massachusetts	35,694	492,974	7,570,587	15,357	295
Michigan	45,042	739,985	9,722,718	13,139	253
Minnesota	27,215	406,801	5,330,894	13,104	252
Mississippi	13,803	167,801	1,961,779	11,691	225
Missouri	30,206	431,703	5,634,844	13,053	251
Montana	6,615	70,637	840,237	11,895	229
Nebraska	10,231	140,525	1,575,147	11,209	216
Nevada	7,342	107,747	1,726,336	16,022	308
New Hampshire	8,161	105,879	1,501,987	14,186	273
New Jersey	46,403	552,611	9,516,645	17,221	331
New Mexico	8,721	122,291	1,544,498	12,630	243
New York	105,145	1,138,681	17,932,613	15,749	303
North Carolina	41,016	565,412	7,293,390	12,899	248
North Dakota	4,774	55,514	599,044	10,791	208
Ohio	58,577	920,453	11,773,763	12,791	246
Oklahoma	17,721	229,460	2,797,550	12,192	234
Oregon	17,607	247,628	3,547,385	14,325	275
Pennsylvania	62,409	891,931	11,909,144	13,352	257
Rhode Island	6,447	75,400	1,055,673	14,001	269

[Continued]

★ 348 ★

Retail Trade Establishments, Employment, and Wages, by State: 1993
[Continued]

State	Average establish-ments (number)	Annual average employment (number)	Total annual wages (in thousand dollars)	Annual wages per employee (in dollars)	Weekly average wage (in dollars)
South Carolina	21,809	294,554	3,673,898	12,473	240
South Dakota	5,393	62,931	694,269	11,032	212
Tennessee	25,486	405,709	5,459,343	13,456	259
Texas	83,442	1,371,321	19,217,381	14,014	270
Utah	9,523	149,768	1,832,159	12,233	235
Vermont	4,964	48,149	630,881	13,103	252
Virginia	34,024	518,267	7,119,107	13,736	264
Washington	28,740	404,589	5,905,739	14,597	281
West Virginia	10,363	119,425	1,383,960	11,589	223
Wisconsin	28,045	433,893	5,123,814	11,809	227
Wyoming	3,658	41,317	475,299	11,504	221

Source: U.S. Department of Labor. Bureau of Labor Statistics. *Employment and Wages Annual Averages, 1993.* Bulletin 2449. Washington, DC: U.S. Government Printing Office, October 1994, p. 387. *Notes:* Data for 1993 are preliminary and subject to revision. Detail may not add to totals due to rounding.

★ 349 ★

Industry Summaries

Service Establishments, Employment, and Wages, by State: 1993

Data for private industry. Covers establishments primarily engaged in providing a variety of services to individuals, businesses, governments, or other organizations; for example, hotels and motels, health care providers, or educational institutions. Figures are 1993 annual averages.

State	Average establish-ments (number)	Annual average employment (number)	Total annual wages (in thousand dollars)	Annual wages per employee (in dollars)	Weekly average wage (in dollars)
Total	2,359,423	28,405,490	700,913,414	24,675	475
Alabama	30,222	335,661	7,471,797	22,260	428
Alaska	5,658	53,671	1,338,930	24,947	480
Arizona	34,745	432,176	9,530,408	22,052	424
Arkansas	18,523	198,766	3,653,926	18,383	354
California	400,304	3,380,654	98,398,208	29,106	560
Colorado	39,291	448,630	10,757,551	23,979	461
Connecticut	36,569	420,224	12,417,721	29,550	568
Delaware	6,499	83,214	1,902,076	22,858	440
District of Columbia	14,722	248,968	9,095,524	36,533	703
Florida	138,720	1,690,714	38,913,646	23,016	443
Georgia	59,060	673,580	16,486,929	24,477	471
Hawaii	10,673	157,200	3,880,019	24,682	475
Idaho	9,620	90,728	1,851,863	20,411	393
Illinois	93,745	1,382,048	35,490,521	25,680	494

[Continued]

★ 349 ★

Service Establishments, Employment, and Wages, by State: 1993
[Continued]

State	Average establish- ments (number)	Annual average employment (number)	Total annual wages (in thousand dollars)	Annual wages per employee (in dollars)	Weekly average wage (in dollars)
Indiana	42,114	537,905	10,934,705	20,328	391
Iowa	25,068	287,298	5,167,236	17,986	346
Kansas	22,546	251,013	5,072,087	20,206	389
Kentucky	27,088	326,268	6,404,625	19,630	378
Louisiana	32,667	381,090	8,032,724	21,078	405
Maine	12,233	125,029	2,539,317	20,310	391
Maryland	53,487	619,518	16,635,933	26,853	516
Massachusetts	57,107	898,083	26,336,801	29,326	564
Michigan	67,967	975,030	23,486,187	24,088	463
Minnesota	39,843	570,632	12,614,482	22,106	425
Mississippi	16,924	177,252	3,296,754	18,599	358
Missouri	44,646	585,233	12,631,860	21,584	415
Montana	9,174	83,427	1,456,565	17,459	336
Nebraska	13,838	179,799	3,450,062	19,188	369
Nevada	12,704	289,375	6,929,838	23,948	461
New Hampshire	11,811	128,189	2,976,095	23,216	446
New Jersey	76,583	943,301	28,446,165	30,156	580
New Mexico	13,817	157,171	3,490,736	22,210	427
New York	172,140	2,313,192	66,489,474	28,744	553
North Carolina	52,040	639,391	13,506,046	21,123	406
North Dakota	5,551	70,455	1,249,543	17,735	341
Ohio	86,391	1,201,821	26,380,816	21,951	422
Oklahoma	25,345	278,271	5,413,095	19,453	374
Oregon	30,327	312,463	6,628,639	21,214	408
Pennsylvania	94,331	1,406,833	34,663,602	24,639	474
Rhode Island	10,272	128,477	2,940,121	22,884	440
South Carolina	27,457	297,046	5,785,306	19,476	375
South Dakota	6,752	74,656	1,298,535	17,394	334
Tennessee	37,560	527,835	11,646,555	22,065	424
Texas	140,224	1,767,616	42,358,823	23,964	461
Utah	14,705	190,119	4,015,578	21,121	406
Vermont	7,122	69,311	1,391,807	20,081	386
Virginia	58,903	742,709	18,989,355	25,568	492
Washington	54,882	541,483	12,546,760	23,171	446
West Virginia	13,228	148,105	2,884,874	19,479	375
Wisconsin	38,817	543,503	10,967,754	20,180	388
Wyoming	5,413	40,360	665,440	16,488	317

Source: U.S. Department of Labor. Bureau of Labor Statistics. Employment and Wages Annual Averages, 1993. Bulletin 2449. Washington, DC: U.S. Government Printing Office, October 1994, p. 444. Notes: Data for 1993 are preliminary and subject to revision. Detail may not add to totals due to rounding.

★ 350 ★

Industry Summaries

State Government Establishments, Employment, and Wages, by State: 1993

Data for total state government. Covers executive, legislative, judicial, administrative, and regulatory activities of state governments. Figures are 1993 annual averages.

State	Average establishments (number)	Annual average employment (number)	Total annual wages (in thousand dollars)	Annual wages per employee (in dollars)	Weekly average wage (in dollars)
Total	59,185	4,088,353	117,094,923	28,641	551
Alabama	1,275	83,730	2,193,534	26,198	504
Alaska	617	19,683	816,910	41,504	798
Arizona	97	77,514	1,480,683	19,102	367
Arkansas	1,034	48,184	1,179,330	24,475	471
California	13,061	339,641	12,759,292	37,567	722
Colorado	677	61,942	1,639,745	26,472	509
Connecticut	887	60,313	2,210,276	36,647	705
Delaware	91	21,625	589,748	27,272	524
District of Columbia	12	49,342	1,688,894	34,228	658
Florida	2,724	188,440	4,263,714	22,626	435
Georgia	1,920	124,820	3,054,863	24,474	471
Hawaii	168	59,991	1,689,226	28,158	542
Idaho	613	21,639	523,043	24,171	465
Illinois	91	130,327	4,204,713	32,263	620
Indiana	1,608	87,110	2,112,271	24,248	466
Iowa	1,048	45,049	1,407,309	31,240	601
Kansas	1,310	45,949	1,152,177	25,075	482
Kentucky	2,755	72,950	1,759,053	24,113	464
Louisiana	1,521	96,019	2,330,380	24,270	467
Maine	357	22,934	570,630	24,882	478
Maryland	491	87,402	2,485,514	28,438	547
Massachusetts	435	93,122	3,207,547	34,445	662
Michigan	122	134,180	4,441,685	33,103	637
Minnesota	1,199	60,920	2,025,425	33,247	639
Mississippi	1,133	46,536	1,009,091	21,684	417
Missouri	1,797	78,287	1,831,956	23,401	450
Montana	593	17,261	427,250	24,753	476
Nebraska	862	32,061	829,020	25,858	497
Nevada	69	22,168	639,126	28,831	554
New Hampshire	687	17,950	464,955	25,903	498
New Jersey	117	110,002	4,089,956	37,181	715
New Mexico	600	37,839	938,163	24,793	477
New York	891	258,181	9,050,292	35,054	674
North Carolina	2,071	137,282	3,666,712	26,709	514
North Dakota	435	16,414	377,098	22,974	442
Ohio	1,643	128,018	3,943,112	30,801	592
Oklahoma	933	76,333	1,654,759	21,678	417
Oregon	852	51,473	1,504,358	29,226	562
Pennsylvania	1,323	134,362	4,152,835	50,908	594
Rhode Island	60	19,785	568,815	28,750	553
South Carolina	798	88,164	2,126,133	24,116	464

[Continued]

★ 350 ★

State Government Establishments, Employment, and Wages, by State: 1993
[Continued]

State	Average establish- ments (number)	Annual average employment (number)	Total annual wages (in thousand dollars)	Annual wages per employee (in dollars)	Weekly average wage (in dollars)
South Dakota	1,014	14,192	329,065	23,186	446
Tennessee	394	79,478	1,895,612	23,851	459
Texas	3,353	288,390	6,999,331	24,270	467
Utah	481	40,978	963,521	23,513	452
Vermont	245	13,286	351,165	26,432	508
Virginia	1,857	127,287	3,179,857	24,982	480
Washington	1,125	104,090	3,199,532	30,738	591
West Virginia	842	36,564	814,085	22,265	428
Wisconsin	413	67,223	2,020,438	30,056	578
Wyoming	489	11,927	282,722	23,705	456

Source: U.S. Department of Labor. Bureau of Labor Statistics. *Employment and Wages Annual Averages, 1993.* Bulletin 2449. Washington, DC: U.S. Government Printing Office, October 1994, p. 520. *Notes:* Data for 1993 are preliminary and subject to revision. Detail may not add to totals due to rounding.

★ 351 ★

Industry Summaries

Transportation and Public Utilities Establishments, Employment, and Wages, by State: 1993

Data for private industry. Covers establishments providing passenger and freight transportation, communications services, and utility or sanitary services (e.g., electricity, gas, steam, and water). U.S. Postal Service establishments are included as well. Figures are 1993 annual averages.

State	Average establish- ments (number)	Annual average employment (number)	Total annual wages (in thousand dollars)	Annual wages per employee (in dollars)	Weekly average wage (in dollars)
Total	262,121	5,546,621	185,537,877	33,451	643
Alabama	4,106	80,819	2,543,828	31,475	605
Alaska	1,322	22,809	869,793	38,133	733
Arizona	3,471	77,077	2,,327,316	30,195	581
Arkansas	3,415	52,679	1,477,612	28,050	539
California	25,290	590,116	21,477,581	36,396	700
Colorado	4,074	99,050	3,461,234	34,944	672
Connecticut	3,264	67,303	2,463,434	36,602	704
Delaware	786	13,371	432,357	32,334	622
District of Columbia	733	17,765	871,778	49,074	944
Florida	13,461	278,503	8,631,646	30,993	596
Georgia	6,908	194,574	7,177,753	36,890	709
Hawaii	1,642	41,836	1,357,934	32,459	624
Idaho	1,836	19,000	505,518	26,606	512
Illinois	11,851	288,462	10,229,831	35,463	682

[Continued]

★ 351 ★

Transportation and Public Utilities Establishments, Employment, and Wages, by State: 1993

[Continued]

State	Average establish- ments (number)	Annual average employment (number)	Total annual wages (in thousand dollars)	Annual wages per employee (in dollars)	Weekly average wage (in dollars)
Indiana	6,057	126,831	3,698,650	29,162	561
Iowa	4,303	53,110	1,420,853	26,753	514
Kansas	3,447	59,369	1,842,990	31,043	597
Kentucky	4,431	78,726	2,325,025	29,533	568
Louisiana	5,081	102,032	3,068,780	30,077	578
Maine	1,935	21,564	586,353	27,191	523
Maryland	4,953	95,741	3,277,488	34,233	658
Massachusetts	5,492	120,631	4,220,817	34,989	673
Michigan	6,642	149,195	5,209,229	34,916	671
Minnesota	5,517	102,850	3,351,824	32,590	627
Mississippi	3,180	44,657	1,260,127	28,218	543
Missouri	6,826	143,948	4,573,813	31,744	611
Montana	1,587	16,929	468,722	27,688	532
Nebraska	2,365	37,277	1,047,873	28,111	541
Nevada	1,479	34,134	1,020,891	29,908	575
New Hampshire	1,256	17,984	567,615	31,563	607
New Jersey	9,633	229,072	8,986,264	39,229	754
New Mexico	1,696	27,949	836,119	29,916	575
New York	17,478	390,333	14,800,508	37,918	729
North Carolina	6,085	154,959	4,836,713	31,213	600
North Dakota	1,454	16,027	441,783	27,564	530
Ohio	9,684	205,175	6,398,131	31,184	600
Oklahoma	3,732	70,599	2,263,615	32,063	617
Oregon	3,849	63,462	1,959,943	30,884	594
Pennsylvania	9,781	252,054	8,407,696	33,357	641
Rhode Island	913	14,078	437,343	31,066	597
South Carolina	2,926	64,221	1,890,522	29,438	566
South Dakota	1,567	14,232	341,453	23,992	461
Tennessee	4,507	121,669	3,615,765	29,718	572
Texas	17,686	416,901	14,181,881	34,017	654
Utah	1,823	44,620	1,401,972	31,421	604
Vermont	858	10,650	306,911	28,818	554
Virginia	6,350	139,848	4,714,280	33,710	648
Washington	5,995	107,206	3,509,413	32,735	630
West Virginia	2,380	35,140	1,071,228	30,484	586
Wisconsin	6,030	108,378	3,002,280	27,702	533
Wyoming	992	11,707	365,392	31,212	600

Source: U.S. Department of Labor. Bureau of Labor Statistics. *Employment and Wages Annual Averages, 1993.* Bulletin 2449. Washington, DC: U.S. Government Printing Office, October 1994, p. 319. *Notes:* Data for 1993 are preliminary and subject to revision. Detail may not add to totals due to rounding.

★ 352 ★

Industry Summaries

Wholesale Trade Establishments, Employment, and Wages, by State: 1993

Data for private industry. Covers establishments or places of business primarily engaged in selling merchandise to retailers; to industrial, commercial, institutional, farm, construction contractors, or professional business users; or to other wholesalers. Also includes establishments acting as agents or brokers in buying merchandise for or in selling merchandise to such persons or companies. Figures are 1993 annual averages.

State	Average establish- ments (number)	Annual average employment (number)	Total annual wages (in thousand dollars)	Annual wages per employee (in dollars)	Weekly average wage (in dollars)
Total	599,677	5,976,127	201,499,508	33,717	648
Alabama	9,381	85,197	2,379,972	27,935	537
Alaska	975	8,009	272,327	34,001	654
Arizona	9,437	77,576	2,368,321	30,529	587
Arkansas	5,749	45,878	1,176,788	25,650	493
California	57,577	680,459	24,454,951	35,939	691
Colorado	10,235	86,372	2,849,450	32,991	634
Connecticut	9,651	75,079	3,327,585	44,321	852
Delaware	1,849	12,560	411,860	32,792	631
District of Columbia	598	6,678	306,406	45,881	882
Florida	34,357	293,249	9,354,681	31,900	613
Georgia	20,509	213,745	7,730,936	36,169	696
Hawaii	2,423	21,920	661,770	30,190	581
Idaho	3,025	24,965	584,783	23,424	450
Illinois	28,024	340,003	12,507,219	36,786	707
Indiana	13,663	127,816	3,780,725	29,579	569
Iowa	9,511	79,580	2,037,831	25,607	492
Kansas	8,121	68,150	1,973,368	28,956	557
Kentucky	7,737	71,994	1,942,009	26,974	519
Louisiana	8,820	85,557	2,363,628	27,627	531
Maine	2,825	23,277	643,836	27,660	532
Maryland	10,572	100,842	3,600,218	35,702	687
Massachusetts	14,774	153,061	6,085,133	39,756	765
Michigan	18,293	199,170	7,319,237	36,749	707
Minnesota	13,568	131,147	4,470,675	34,089	656
Mississippi	4,852	41,895	1,056,833	25,226	485
Missouri	14,251	137,002	4,252,039	31,036	597
Montana	2,236	16,983	412,717	24,302	467
Nebraska	4,984	52,381	1,324,548	25,287	486
Nevada	3,022	24,995	800,140	32,012	616
New Hampshire	3,972	23,427	839,074	35,817	689
New Jersey	23,036	256,943	10,632,227	41,380	796
New Mexico	3,397	26,112	659,773	25,267	486
New York	45,292	416,818	16,844,370	40,412	777
North Carolina	16,746	164,721	5,043,989	30,621	589
North Dakota	2,603	19,301	479,566	24,847	478
Ohio	24,000	257,428	8,438,999	32,782	630
Oklahoma	6,533	59,505	1,592,283	26,759	515
Oregon	8,191	80,079	2,527,031	31,557	607

[Continued]

★ 352 ★

Wholesale Trade Establishments, Employment, and Wages, by State: 1993
[Continued]

State	Average establish- ments (number)	Annual average employment (number)	Total annual wages (in thousand dollars)	Annual wages per employee (in dollars)	Weekly average wage (in dollars)
Pennsylvania	24,127	258,883	8,511,698	32,879	632
Rhode Island	2,965	17,715	568,476	32,089	617
South Carolina	6,230	57,531	1,611,988	28,019	539
South Dakota	2,562	18,663	422,704	22,649	436
Tennessee	11,410	129,253	3,840,415	29,712	571
Texas	39,772	436,043	14,674,211	33,653	647
Utah	4,370	40,296	1,118,758	27,763	534
Vermont	1,505	12,223	342,169	27,993	538
Virginia	12,353	130,369	4,451,144	34,143	657
Washington	13,065	128,305	3,962,251	30,882	594
West Virginia	3,681	29,479	776,134	26,328	506
Wisconsin	11,665	120,654	3,537,189	29,317	564
Wyoming	1,190	6,838	175,074	25,603	492

Source: U.S. Department of Labor. Bureau of Labor Statistics. *Employment and Wages Annual Averages, 1993.* Bulletin 2449. Washington, DC: U.S. Government Printing Office, October 1994, p. 352. *Notes:* Data for 1993 are preliminary and subject to revision. Detail may not add to totals due to rounding.

Occupational Outlook

★ 353 ★

Employment Projections – All Occupations, by Industry: 1992-2005

The National Industry-Occupation Matrix counts jobs, as reflected by data about wage and salary employment collected through the Occupational Employment Statistics surveys. The table below presents total employment figures for all occupations during 1992; the percent of industry employment for all occupations (staffing patterns) in 1992; low, medium, and high employment projections for 2005; and staffing patterns for the 2005 moderate projection. Table shows the industries employing the most occupations in 1992.

Industry	1992		2005 employment			Percent of industry employment for 2005 moderate projection
	Employment	Percent of industry employment	Low	Moderate	High	
Total, all industries	110,746,400	100.00	127,621,398	135,735,330	141,895,701	100.00
Services	38,647,300	100.00	51,593,199	54,152,922	55,693,701	100.00
Wholesale and retail trade	25,391,400	100.00	28,895,400	30,967,669	32,096,601	100.00
Retail trade	19,346,300	100.00	22,254,399	23,776,949	24,336,001	100.00
Manufacturing	18,041,000	100.00	15,980,600	17,522,760	18,866,300	100.00
Durable goods manufacturing	10,235,400	100.00	8,735,241	9,668,646	10,774,791	100.00
Education, public and private	9,718,100	100.00	11,865,500	12,475,522	12,943,300	100.00

[Continued]

★ 353 ★

Employment Projections – All Occupations, by Industry: 1992-2005

[Continued]

Industry	1992		2005 employment			Percent of industry employment for 2005 moderate projection
	Employment	Percent of industry employment	Low	Moderate	High	
Health services	9,612,900	100.00	13,187,599	13,788,740	13,937,300	100.00
Government	9,544,900	100.00	9,827,700	10,457,720	10,965,900	100.00
Nondurable goods manufacturing	7,804,100	100.00	7,242,800	7,850,230	8,078,800	100.00
Eating and drinking places	6,601,700	100.00	8,328,600	8,777,800	8,824,900	100.00
Finance, insurance, and real estate	6,571,200	100.00	7,585,399	7,968,840	8,077,600	100.00
Wholesale trade	6,045,100	100.00	6,641,001	7,190,720	7,760,600	100.00
Transportation and public utilities	5,708,800	100.00	5,908,901	6,497,380	6,763,100	100.00
Business services	5,312,600	100.00	7,798,600	8,370,330	8,664,300	100.00
Hospitals, public and private	4,849,300	100.00	5,990,600	6,289,470	6,353,700	100.00
Construction	4,471,200	100.00	5,407,299	5,632,159	6,643,299	100.00
Local government, except education and hospitals	4,389,700	100.00	4,844,708	5,142,807	5,393,857	100.00
Wholesale trade, other	3,812,400	100.00	4,184,880	4,531,291	4,890,405	100.00
Transportation	3,486,600	100.00	3,865,800	4,309,681	4,506,600	100.00
Food stores	3,179,500	100.00	3,602,892	3,880,590	4,013,042	100.00
Grocery stores	2,842,000	100.00	3,226,652	3,475,351	3,593,971	100.00
Special trade contractors	2,696,200	100.00	3,288,716	3,425,475	4,040,450	100.00
Retail stores, miscellaneous	2,470,200	100.00	2,805,169	3,021,382	3,124,509	100.00
Engineering and management services	2,469,500	100.00	3,439,456	3,685,058	3,951,253	100.00

Source: National Industry-Occupation Matrix, 1992 [data tape]. Prepared by the Bureau of Labor Statistics. Washington, DC: U.S. Department of Labor, Bureau of Labor Statistics, 1992. *Note:* All employment data are wage and salary employment.

★ 354 ★

Occupational Outlook

Employment Projections, by Selected Industry: 1979-2005

Figures may differ from those reported elsewhere since these data exclude establishments not elsewhere classified (SIC 99); in addition, agriculture services (SIC 074, 5, 8) are included in agriculture, not services. Minus sign (-) indicates decrease.

[In thousands, except percentages]

Industry	SIC code[1]	Employment (1,000)			Annual growth rate	
		1979	1992	2005 projections[2]	1979-1992	1992-2005 projections[2]
Total	(X)	101,363	121,093	147,484	1.4	1.5
Nonfarm wage and salary	(X)	89,491	107,888	132,960	1.4	1.6
Goods-producing (excluding agriculture)	(X)	26,461	23,142	23,717	-1.0	0.2
Mining	10-14	958	631	562	-3.2	-0.9
Construction	15,16,17	4,463	4,471	5,632	-	1.8
Manufacturing	20-39	21,040	18,040	17,523	-1.2	-0.2
Durable manufacturing	24,25,32-39	12,730	10,237	9,673	-1.7	-0.4
Lumber and wood products	24	782	674	690	-1.1	0.2
Furniture and fixtures	25	498	476	523	-0.3	0.7
Stone, clay and glass products	32	674	512	437	-2.1	-1.2
Primary metal industries	33	1,254	693	618	-4.5	-0.9
Blast furnaces and basic steel products	331	571	250	224	-6.1	-0.9
Fabricated metal products	34	1,713	1,322	1,196	-2.0	-0.8
Industrial machinery and equipment	35	2,508	1,922	1,868	-2.0	-0.2

[Continued]

★ 354 ★

Employment Projections, by Selected Industry: 1979-2005

[Continued]

Industry	SIC code[1]	Employment (1,000)			Annual growth rate	
		1979	1992	2005 projections[2]	1979-1992	1992-2005 projections[2]
Computer equipment	3571,2,5,7	318	353	237	0.8	-3.0
Electronic and other electric equipment[3]	36	1,793	1,526	1,354	-1.2	-0.9
Telephone and telegraph apparatus	3661	171	108	81	-3.4	-2.3
Semiconductors and related devices	3674	201	218	224	0.6	0.2
Transportation equipment	37	2,059	1,822	1,765	-0.9	-0.2
Motor vehicles and equipment	371	990	809	759	-1.5	-0.5
Instruments and related products[3]	38	1,006	925	887	-0.6	-0.3
Measuring and controlling devices, watches	382	431	300	255	-2.8	-1.2
Medical instruments and supplies	3841-3	144	216	295	3.2	2.4
Miscellaneous manufacturing industries	39	445	363	334	-1.5	-0.6
Nondurable manufacturing	20-23,26-31	8,310	7,804	7,851	-0.5	-
Food and kindred products	20	1,733	1,655	1,648	-0.4	-
Tobacco manufactures	21	70	49	37	-2.7	-2.1
Textile mill products	22	885	671	571	-2.1	-1.2
Apparel and other textile products	23	1,304	1,005	760	-2.0	-2.1
Paper and allied products	26	697	687	729	-0.1	0.4
Printing and publishing	27	1,235	1,504	1,751	1.5	1.2
Chemicals and allied products	28	1,109	1,083	1,090	-0.2	0.1
Petroleum and coal products	29	210	159	128	-2.1	-1.6
Rubber and miscellaneous plastics products	30	821	872	1,066	0.5	1.6
Leather and leather products	31	246	119	71	-5.4	-3.9
Service producing	(X)	63,030	84,746	109,243	2.3	2.0
Transportation, communications, utilities	40-42,44-49	5,136	5,709	6,497	0.8	1.0
Transportation	40-42,44-47	3,019	3,486	4,310	1.1	1.6
Communications	48	1,309	1,268	1,116	-0.2	-1.0
Electric, gas, and sanitary services	49	807	955	1,072	1.3	0.9
Wholesale trade	50,51	5,221	6,045	7,191	1.1	1.3
Retail trade	52-59	14,972	19,346	23,777	2.0	1.6
Eating and drinking places	58	4,513	6,602	8,778	3.0	2.2
Finance, insurance, and real estate	60-67	4,975	6,571	7,969	2.2	1.5
Services	70-87,89	16,779	28,422	41,788	4.1	3.0
Hotels and other lodging places	70	1,060	1,572	2,209	3.1	2.6
Personal services	72	821	1,111	1,382	2.4	1.7
Business services[3]	73	2,410	5,313	8,370	6.3	3.6
Advertising	731	146	226	288	3.4	1.9
Services to buildings	734	487	805	1,000	3.9	1.7
Personnel supply services	736	508	1,649	2,581	9.5	3.5
Computer and data processing services	737	271	831	1,626	9.0	5.3
Auto repair, services, and garages	75	575	878	1,293	3.3	3.0
Miscellaneous repair shops	76	282	345	449	1.6	2.0
Motion pictures	78	228	404	499	4.5	1.6
Videotape rental	784	(NA)	125	107	(NA)	-1.2
Amusement and recreation services	79	751	1,169	1,626	3.5	2.6
Health services	80	4,993	8,523	12,539	4.2	3.0
Offices of health practitioners	801,2,3,4	1,200	2,387	3,617	5.4	3.2
Nursing and personal care facilities	805	951	1,543	2,306	3.8	3.1
Hospitals, private	806	2,608	3,760	5,040	2.9	2.3
Health services, n.e.c.	807,8,9	234	833	1,577	10.3	5.0
Legal services	81	460	915	1,355	5.4	3.1
Educational services	82	1,090	1,700	2,162	3.5	1.9

[Continued]

★ 354 ★

Employment Projections, by Selected Industry: 1979-2005
[Continued]

Industry	SIC code[1]	Employment (1,000)			Annual growth rate	
		1979	1992	2005 projections[2]	1979-1992	1992-2005 projections[2]
Social services	83	1,081	1,958	3,691	4.7	5.0
Museums, zoos, and membership organizations	84,86,8733	1,652	2,164	2,674	2.1	1.6
Engineering, management, and services n.e.c.[4]	87,89	1,341	2,370	3,538	4.5	3.1
Government	(X)	15,947	18,653	22,021	1.2	1.3
Federal government	(X)	2,773	2,969	2,815	0.5	-0.4
State and local government	(X)	13,174	15,683	19,206	1.4	1.6
Agriculture	01,02,07-09	3,398	3,295	3,325	-0.2	0.1
Private households	88	1,264	1,116	802	-1.0	-2.5
Nonagriculture self-employed and unpaid family	(X)	7,210	8,794	10,397	1.5	1.3

Source: U.S. Bureau of the Census. *Statistical Abstract of the United States, 1994.* 114th ed. Washington, DC: U.S. Government Printing Office, 1994, p. 413. Primary source: U.S. Bureau of Labor Statistics. *Monthly Labor Review* (November 1993). *Notes:* "-" represents or rounds to zero. "NA" stands for "not available." "X" represents "not applicable." "n.e.c." means "not elsewhere classified." 1. 1987 Standard Industrial Classification (SIC). 2. Based on assumptions of moderate growth. 3. Includes other industries, not shown separately. 4. Excludes SIC 8733.

★ 355 ★
Occupational Outlook

Employment Projections for Accountants and Auditors, by Industry: 1992-2005

The National Industry-Occupation Matrix counts jobs, as reflected by data about wage and salary employment collected through the Occupational Employment Statistics surveys. The table below presents employment figures for accountants and auditors during 1992; the percent of industry employment for this occupation (staffing patterns) in 1992; low, medium, and high employment projections for 2005; and staffing patterns for the 2005 moderate projection. In 1992, accountants and auditors ranked 27 in terms of total employment for individual occupations and ranked 82 when considering total employment of occupational groups as well as individual occupations. Table shows the industries employing the most accountants and auditors in 1992.

Industry	1992		2005 employment			Percent of industry employment for 2005 moderate projection
	Employment	Percent of industry employment	Low	Moderate	High	
Total, all industries	836,117	0.75	1,058,642	1,130,677	1,181,972	0.83
Services	335,303	0.87	500,185	532,870	553,502	0.98
Engineering and management services	212,602	8.61	321,393	345,128	360,929	9.37
Accounting, auditing, and bookkeeping	192,791	37.72	290,403	311,780	325,444	38.10
Government	131,932	1.38	132,992	140,880	147,093	1.35
Wholesale and retail trade	106,123	0.42	126,535	136,207	143,269	0.44
Finance, insurance, and real estate	103,821	1.58	135,492	142,150	143,656	1.78
Manufacturing	98,314	0.54	96,343	105,888	114,787	0.60
Federal government	63,813	2.93	59,922	63,294	65,710	3.07
Durable goods manufacturing	60,297	0.59	55,435	61,745	69,145	0.64
Retail trade	55,088	0.28	65,690	70,325	72,166	0.30
Wholesale trade	51,036	0.84	60,845	65,882	71,103	0.92
State government, except education and hospitals	41,514	1.90	43,931	46,634	48,911	1.87
Nondurable goods manufacturing	38,022	0.49	40,917	44,148	45,605	0.56
Transportation and public utilities	35,588	0.62	39,619	43,224	44,953	0.67
Wholesale trade, other	33,198	0.87	39,331	42,587	45,962	0.94
Depository institutions	32,506	1.55	36,930	38,462	38,561	1.75
Commercial banks, savings institutions, and credit unions	30,211	1.52	34,267	35,689	35,781	1.73

[Continued]

★ 355 ★

Employment Projections for Accountants and Auditors, by Industry: 1992-2005
[Continued]

Industry	1992		2005 employment			Percent of industry employment for 2005 moderate projection
	Employment	Percent of industry employment	Low	Moderate	High	
Business services	27,232	0.51	45,471	48,901	50,737	0.58
Local government, except education and hospitals	26,167	0.60	28,778	30,549	32,040	0.59
Insurance carriers	24,285	1.64	27,241	29,192	29,205	1.76
Health services	22,719	0.24	32,545	34,040	34,409	0.25
Communications and utilities	20,514	0.92	21,731	23,162	23,971	1.06
Transportation	15,074	0.43	17,888	20,062	20,982	0.47
Membership organizations	14,503	0.74	18,245	18,813	19,036	0.79

Source: National Industry-Occupation Matrix, 1992 [data tape]. Prepared by the Bureau of Labor Statistics. Washington, DC: U.S. Department of Labor, Bureau of Labor Statistics, 1992. Note: All employment data are wage and salary employment.

★ 356 ★
Occupational Outlook

Employment Projections for Adjustment Clerks, by Industry: 1992-2005

The National Industry-Occupation Matrix counts jobs, as reflected by data about wage and salary employment collected through the Occupational Employment Statistics surveys. The table below presents employment figures for adjustment clerks during 1992; the percent of industry employment for this occupation (staffing patterns) in 1992; low, medium, and high employment projections for 2005; and staffing patterns for the 2005 moderate projection. In 1992, adjustment clerks ranked 71 in terms of total employment for individual occupations and ranked 147 when considering total employment of occupational groups as well as individual occupations. Table shows the industries employing the most adjustment clerks in 1992.

Industry	1992		2005 employment			Percent of industry employment for 2005 moderate projection
	Employment	Percent of industry employment	Low	Moderate	High	
Total, all industries	351,790	0.32	412,349	444,917	461,606	0.33
Wholesale and retail trade	107,549	0.42	118,752	128,103	134,178	0.41
Manufacturing	82,105	0.46	86,775	95,230	101,506	0.54
Retail trade	78,098	0.40	83,836	90,296	93,376	0.38
Finance, insurance, and real estate	74,584	1.14	98,338	103,302	103,682	1.30
Transportation and public utilities	54,391	0.95	57,756	64,154	66,344	0.99
Nondurable goods manufacturing	46,603	0.60	53,104	57,636	59,606	0.73
Durable goods manufacturing	35,393	0.35	33,538	37,444	41,694	0.39
Services	31,873	0.08	49,400	52,704	54,364	0.10
General merchandise stores	31,341	1.29	31,960	34,423	35,598	1.32
Depository institutions	31,026	1.48	41,323	43,038	43,149	1.96
Wholesale trade	29,451	0.49	34,916	37,806	40,803	0.53
Department stores	29,396	1.44	30,290	32,625	33,738	1.44
Transportation	29,210	0.84	35,187	39,865	41,425	0.93
Commercial banks, savings institutions, and credit unions	26,519	1.34	36,096	37,593	37,690	1.83
Communications and utilities	25,181	1.13	22,570	24,289	24,918	1.11
Insurance carriers	24,221	1.64	27,371	29,331	29,344	1.77
Wholesale trade, other	23,871	0.63	28,281	30,622	33,048	0.68
Grocery stores	21,952	0.77	23,387	25,189	26,049	0.72

[Continued]

★ 356 ★

Employment Projections for Adjustment Clerks, by Industry: 1992-2005

[Continued]

Industry	1992		2005 employment			Percent of industry employment for 2005 moderate projection
	Employment	Percent of industry employment	Low	Moderate	High	
Communications	21,183	1.67	18,053	19,511	19,946	1.75
Printing and publishing	21,047	1.40	25,772	27,918	28,875	1.59
Business services	19,214	0.36	32,803	35,273	36,635	0.42
Air transportation	17,354	2.38	20,556	23,816	24,520	2.46
Air carriers	17,175	2.72	20,353	23,581	24,277	2.78
Retail stores, miscellaneous	15,674	0.63	17,384	18,724	19,363	0.62

Source: National Industry-Occupation Matrix, 1992 [data tape]. Prepared by the Bureau of Labor Statistics. Washington, DC: U.S. Department of Labor, Bureau of Labor Statistics, 1992. *Note:* All employment data are wage and salary employment.

★ 357 ★

Occupational Outlook

Employment Projections for Administrative Services Managers, by Industry: 1992-2005

The National Industry-Occupation Matrix counts jobs, as reflected by data about wage and salary employment collected through the Occupational Employment Statistics surveys. The table below presents employment figures for administrative services managers during 1992; the percent of industry employment for this occupation (staffing patterns) in 1992; low, medium, and high employment projections for 2005; and staffing patterns for the 2005 moderate projection. In 1992, administrative services managers ranked 109 in terms of total employment for individual occupations and ranked 194 when considering total employment of occupational groups as well as individual occupations. Table shows the industries employing the most administrative services managers in 1992.

Industry	1992		2005 employment			Percent of industry employment for 2005 moderate projection
	Employment	Percent of industry employment	Low	Moderate	High	
Total, all industries	226,495	0.20	240,754	256,083	266,543	0.19
Services	100,049	0.26	126,084	132,877	136,536	0.25
Manufacturing	34,199	0.19	25,436	28,085	30,531	0.16
Government	28,567	0.30	29,593	31,395	32,869	0.30
Finance, insurance, and real estate	27,790	0.42	27,602	29,045	29,353	0.36
Engineering and management services	23,805	0.96	37,376	40,159	41,973	1.09
Durable goods manufacturing	23,412	0.23	16,276	18,168	20,305	0.19
Wholesale and retail trade	21,260	0.08	19,648	21,245	22,703	0.07
Membership organizations	16,824	0.86	17,083	17,589	17,824	0.74
Local government, except education and hospitals	16,448	0.37	17,787	18,882	19,803	0.37
Wholesale trade	16,195	0.27	15,122	16,373	17,671	0.23
Health services	15,792	0.16	18,107	18,915	19,108	0.14
Business services	13,424	0.25	17,258	18,543	19,221	0.22
Wholesale trade, other	12,847	0.34	11,973	12,964	13,991	0.29
Social services	12,395	0.63	17,753	18,304	18,418	0.50
Management and public relations	11,603	1.77	23,403	25,316	26,314	2.28
Nondurable goods manufacturing	10,846	0.14	9,218	9,979	10,285	0.13
Transportation and public utilities	10,563	0.19	8,822	9,640	10,005	0.15
Insurance carriers	8,654	0.58	7,692	8,243	8,247	0.50

[Continued]

★ 357 ★

Employment Projections for Administrative Services Managers, by Industry: 1992-2005
[Continued]

Industry	1992		2005 employment			Percent of industry employment for 2005 moderate projection
	Employment	Percent of industry employment	Low	Moderate	High	
Depository institutions	8,526	0.41	7,617	7,933	7,953	0.36
Commercial banks, savings institutions, and credit unions	8,064	0.41	7,195	7,493	7,513	0.36
Individual and miscellaneous social services	6,986	0.99	9,357	9,633	9,674	0.83
Civic and social associations	6,855	1.63	7,374	7,521	7,608	1.42
Hospitals, public and private	6,717	0.14	6,796	7,136	7,208	0.11
Communications and utilities	6,451	0.29	5,094	5,472	5,644	0.25

Source: National Industry-Occupation Matrix, 1992 [data tape]. Prepared by the Bureau of Labor Statistics. Washington, DC: U.S. Department of Labor, Bureau of Labor Statistics, 1992. Note: All employment data are wage and salary employment.

★ 358 ★
Occupational Outlook

Employment Projections for Adult and Vocational Education Teachers, by Industry: 1992-2005

The National Industry-Occupation Matrix counts jobs, as reflected by data about wage and salary employment collected through the Occupational Employment Statistics surveys. The table below presents employment figures for adult and vocational education teachers during 1992; the percent of industry employment for this occupation (staffing patterns) in 1992; low, medium, and high employment projections for 2005; and staffing patterns for the 2005 moderate projection. In 1992, adult and vocational education teachers ranked 59 in terms of total employment for individual occupations and ranked 130 when considering total employment of occupational groups as well as individual occupations. Table shows the industries employing the most adult and vocational education teachers in 1992.

Industry	1992		2005 employment			Percent of industry employment for 2005 moderate projection
	Employment	Percent of industry employment	Low	Moderate	High	
Total, all industries	421,399	0.38	549,278	576,154	593,849	0.42
Education, public and private	266,831	2.75	354,718	372,954	386,938	2.99
Social services	39,046	1.99	61,717	63,787	64,215	1.73
Membership organizations	27,546	1.41	35,721	36,659	37,032	1.53
Job training and related services	18,793	6.93	23,280	24,228	24,422	5.80
Federal government	15,072	0.69	14,153	14,949	15,520	0.72
Religious organizations	14,525	1.26	18,313	18,851	19,005	1.33
Individual and miscellaneous social services	13,867	1.97	23,614	24,309	24,413	2.09
Amusement and recreation services	13,630	1.17	13,709	13,990	14,157	0.86
Amusement and recreation services, all other	12,107	1.47	11,622	11,836	11,927	0.98
Civic and social associations	10,539	2.51	14,412	14,699	14,868	2.77
Health services	10,310	0.11	14,474	15,146	15,289	0.11
Transportation and public utilities	8,941	0.16	10,237	11,806	12,150	0.18
Personal services	8,290	0.75	10,088	10,207	10,248	0.74

[Continued]

★ 358 ★

Employment Projections for Adult and Vocational Education Teachers, by Industry: 1992-2005

[Continued]

Industry	1992		2005 employment			Percent of industry employment for 2005 moderate projection
	Employment	Percent of industry employment	Low	Moderate	High	
Transportation	8,046	0.23	9,425	10,920	11,243	0.25
Air transportation	8,046	1.10	9,425	10,920	11,243	1.13
Hospitals, public and private	6,567	0.14	8,447	8,869	8,959	0.14
Air carriers	5,845	0.93	6,927	8,025	8,262	0.95
Residential care	5,032	0.94	12,424	12,788	12,910	0.96
Airports, flying fields, and services	2,201	2.25	2,499	2,895	2,981	2.44
Engineering and management services	2,029	0.08	2,900	3,067	3,161	0.08
Health and allied services, n.e.c.	1,995	0.80	3,117	3,246	3,267	0.83
Research and testing services	1,423	0.26	1,889	1,974	2,011	0.26
Child day care services	1,353	0.30	2,399	2,462	2,471	0.32
Nondurable goods manufacturing	1,287	0.02	1,040	1,196	1,209	0.02

Source: National Industry-Occupation Matrix, 1992 [data tape]. Prepared by the Bureau of Labor Statistics. Washington, DC: U.S. Department of Labor, Bureau of Labor Statistics, 1992. *Notes:* All employment data are wage and salary employment. "n.e.c." stands for "not elsewhere classified."

★ 359 ★

Occupational Outlook

Employment Projections for Assemblers and Fabricators, by Industry: 1992-2005

The National Industry-Occupation Matrix counts jobs, as reflected by data about wage and salary employment collected through the Occupational Employment Statistics surveys. The table below presents employment figures for assemblers and fabricators (nonspecific) during 1992; the percent of industry employment for this occupation (staffing patterns) in 1992; low, medium, and high employment projections for 2005; and staffing patterns for the 2005 moderate projection. In 1992, assemblers and fabricators (nonspecific) ranked 23 in terms of total employment for individual occupations and ranked 69 when considering total employment of occupational groups as well as individual occupations. Table shows the industries employing the most assemblers and fabricators (nonspecific) in 1992.

Industry	1992		2005 employment			Percent of industry employment for 2005 moderate projection
	Employment	Percent of industry employment	Low	Moderate	High	
Total, all industries	1,083,372	0.98	890,428	974,633	1,061,501	0.72
Manufacturing	954,155	5.29	770,011	844,684	922,303	4.82
Durable goods manufacturing	801,377	7.83	624,679	686,346	756,605	7.10
Transportation equipment	169,692	9.31	125,613	138,523	147,982	7.85
Nondurable goods manufacturing	154,710	1.98	147,263	160,353	167,108	2.04
Motor vehicles and equipment	127,265	15.74	93,934	103,919	111,815	13.69
Electronic and other electrical equipment	126,328	8.28	85,413	95,173	105,467	7.03
Wholesale and retail trade	121,586	0.48	113,509	122,748	131,144	0.40

[Continued]

★ 359 ★

Employment Projections for Assemblers and Fabricators, by Industry: 1992-2005

[Continued]

Industry	1992		2005 employment			Percent of industry employment for 2005 moderate projection
	Employment	Percent of industry employment	Low	Moderate	High	
Industrial machinery and equipment	108,841	5.66	86,319	96,941	109,860	5.19
Fabricated metal products	103,859	7.85	76,327	82,413	91,851	6.89
Wholesale trade	91,933	1.52	86,088	93,214	100,601	1.30
Instruments and related products	72,014	7.79	63,476	70,638	76,785	7.96
Wholesale trade, other	70,191	1.84	64,938	70,313	75,885	1.55
Rubber and miscellaneous plastics products	69,594	7.98	75,686	82,406	87,001	7.73
Furniture and fixtures	64,232	13.49	57,770	63,355	68,040	12.12
Lumber and wood products	63,337	9.39	60,011	61,390	75,808	8.90
Manufacturing industries, miscellaneous	54,929	15.12	40,079	45,709	46,298	13.67
Plastics products, miscellaneous	52,719	8.52	62,759	67,987	72,370	8.06
Medical instruments and supplies	40,781	15.45	43,686	48,210	52,423	13.67
Refrigeration and service machinery	32,307	18.70	28,114	30,753	34,133	16.67
Fabricated structural metal products	32,291	8.29	22,953	24,467	28,311	7.39
Household furniture	32,002	11.85	27,955	29,863	31,006	10.56
Household appliances	31,751	27.32	22,125	23,370	24,220	24.94
Manufactured products, n.e.c.	30,650	14.79	23,094	25,737	26,178	13.41
Millwork, plywood, and structural members	30,352	12.70	33,186	33,444	42,141	11.55

Source: National Industry-Occupation Matrix, 1992 [data tape]. Prepared by the Bureau of Labor Statistics. Washington, DC: U.S. Department of Labor, Bureau of Labor Statistics, 1992. *Notes:* All employment data are wage and salary employment. "n.e.c." stands for "not elsewhere classified."

★ 360 ★

Occupational Outlook

Employment Projections for Automotive Mechanics, by Industry: 1992-2005

The National Industry-Occupation Matrix counts jobs, as reflected by data about wage and salary employment collected through the Occupational Employment Statistics surveys. The table below presents employment figures for automotive mechanics during 1992; the percent of industry employment for this occupation (staffing patterns) in 1992; low, medium, and high employment projections for 2005; and staffing patterns for the 2005 moderate projection. In 1992, automotive mechanics ranked 44 in terms of total employment for individual occupations and ranked 110 when considering total employment of occupational groups as well as individual occupations. Table shows the industries employing the most automotive mechanics in 1992.

Industry	1992		2005 employment			Percent of industry employment for 2005 moderate projection
	Employment	Percent of industry employment	Low	Moderate	High	
Total, all industries	552,305	0.50	661,923	706,418	745,228	0.52
Wholesale and retail trade	329,782	1.30	362,505	390,611	405,364	1.26
Retail trade	305,113	1.58	333,407	359,105	371,361	1.51
Automotive dealers and service stations	275,693	13.79	302,992	326,346	337,484	14.64

[Continued]

★ 360 ★

Employment Projections for Automotive Mechanics, by Industry: 1992-2005

[Continued]

Industry	1992		2005 employment			Percent of industry employment for 2005 moderate projection
	Employment	Percent of industry employment	Low	Moderate	High	
Motor vehicle dealers	179,053	19.06	203,761	219,466	226,957	20.08
Services	147,808	0.38	220,603	231,324	250,686	0.43
Auto repair, services, and parking	138,194	15.74	208,043	218,024	236,879	16.86
Automotive repair shops	126,229	25.44	191,732	200,622	218,204	26.29
Gasoline service stations	50,722	8.24	44,307	47,722	49,351	7.53
Auto and home supply stores	43,866	13.04	52,729	56,793	58,732	14.70
Government	36,163	0.38	37,619	40,039	42,002	0.38
General merchandise stores	27,172	1.12	27,970	30,126	31,154	1.16
Department stores	27,004	1.32	27,825	29,970	30,993	1.32
Wholesale trade	24,670	0.41	29,098	31,506	34,003	0.44
Transportation and public utilities	21,124	0.37	23,228	25,287	26,326	0.39
Local government, except education and hospitals	20,322	0.46	22,350	23,725	24,883	0.46
Motor vehicles, parts, and supplies	14,893	3.32	17,317	18,751	20,237	3.57
Transportation	12,558	0.36	13,743	15,191	15,851	0.35
Manufacturing	11,698	0.06	11,183	12,096	13,005	0.07
Communications and utilities	8,566	0.39	9,485	10,096	10,475	0.46
Durable goods manufacturing	7,787	0.08	7,402	8,089	8,913	0.08
Trucking and warehousing	7,631	0.48	9,262	10,024	10,572	0.50
Local and long distance trucking and terminals	7,407	0.50	8,990	9,729	10,262	0.52
Automotive rentals, no drivers	7,191	4.51	9,845	10,636	11,316	4.79
Electric, gas, and sanitary services	6,686	0.70	7,773	8,223	8,558	0.77

Source: National Industry-Occupation Matrix, 1992 [data tape]. Prepared by the Bureau of Labor Statistics. Washington, DC: U.S. Department of Labor, Bureau of Labor Statistics, 1992. *Note:* All employment data are wage and salary employment.

★ 361 ★

Occupational Outlook

Employment Projections for Bank Tellers, by Industry: 1992-2005

The National Industry-Occupation Matrix counts jobs, as reflected by data about wage and salary employment collected through the Occupational Employment Statistics surveys. The table below presents employment figures for bank tellers during 1992; the percent of industry employment for this occupation (staffing patterns) in 1992; low, medium, and high employment projections for 2005; and staffing patterns for the 2005 moderate projection. In 1992, bank tellers ranked 47 in terms of total employment for individual occupations and ranked 113 when considering total employment of occupational groups as well as individual occupations. Table shows the industries employing the most bank tellers in 1992.

Industry	1992		2005 employment			Percent of industry employment for 2005 moderate projection
	Employment	Percent of industry employment	Low	Moderate	High	
Total, all industries	525,142	0.47	481,476	501,538	503,233	0.37
Finance, insurance, and real estate	516,950	7.87	474,279	493,899	495,221	6.20
Depository institutions	511,300	24.31	467,402	486,791	488,050	22.18
Commercial banks, savings institutions, and credit unions	501,960	25.33	455,484	474,378	475,606	23.03

[Continued]

★ 361 ★

Employment Projections for Bank Tellers, by Industry: 1992-2005
[Continued]

Industry	1992		2005 employment			Percent of industry employment for 2005 moderate projection
	Employment	Percent of industry employment	Low	Moderate	High	
Banking and closely related functions, n.e.c.	9,340	7.69	11,918	12,412	12,445	9.17
Government	8,192	0.09	7,197	7,639	8,012	0.07
Local government, except education and hospitals	5,562	0.13	4,930	5,233	5,488	0.10
Nondepository institutions	4,300	1.09	5,113	5,270	5,316	0.91
Personal credit institutions	2,883	2.29	3,227	3,327	3,356	1.96
State government, except education and hospitals	2,630	0.12	2,267	2,407	2,524	0.10
Mortgage bankers and brokers	1,077	0.63	1,490	1,536	1,550	0.55
Holding and other investment offices	959	0.44	1,380	1,422	1,435	0.38
Security and commodity brokers	391	0.09	385	416	419	0.07
Federal and business credit institutions	340	0.35	395	407	411	0.31

Source: National Industry-Occupation Matrix, 1992 [data tape]. Prepared by the Bureau of Labor Statistics. Washington, DC: U.S. Department of Labor, Bureau of Labor Statistics, 1992. *Notes:* All employment data are wage and salary employment. "n.e.c." stands for "not elsewhere classified."

★ 362 ★
Occupational Outlook

Employment Projections for Bartenders, by Industry: 1992-2005

The National Industry-Occupation Matrix counts jobs, as reflected by data about wage and salary employment collected through the Occupational Employment Statistics surveys. The table below presents employment figures for bartenders during 1992; the percent of industry employment for this occupation (staffing patterns) in 1992; low, medium, and high employment projections for 2005; and staffing patterns for the 2005 moderate projection. In 1992, bartenders ranked 67 in terms of total employment for individual occupations and ranked 139 when considering total employment of occupational groups as well as individual occupations. Table shows the industries employing the most bartenders in 1992.

Industry	1992		2005 employment			Percent of industry employment for 2005 moderate projection
	Employment	Percent of industry employment	Low	Moderate	High	
Total, all industries	369,586	0.33	325,390	339,847	343,286	0.25
Wholesale and retail trade	250,991	0.99	218,597	230,423	231,710	0.74
Retail trade	250,932	1.30	218,550	230,372	231,654	0.97
Eating and drinking places	248,668	3.77	217,059	228,766	229,994	2.61
Services	118,531	0.31	106,742	109,372	111,522	0.20
Hotels and other lodging places	43,871	2.79	42,759	44,209	45,665	2.00
Membership organizations	40,736	2.09	32,376	33,030	33,413	1.38
Civic and social associations	40,186	9.57	31,910	32,546	32,920	6.13
Amusement and recreation services	33,860	2.90	31,534	32,057	32,368	1.97
Amusement and recreation services, all other	22,221	2.69	22,918	23,340	23,518	1.94
Bowling centers	9,835	11.20	7,039	7,100	7,189	8.35
Retail stores, miscellaneous	1,938	0.08	1,260	1,357	1,403	0.04
Liquor stores	1,811	1.57	1,156	1,245	1,287	1.09

[Continued]

★ 362 ★

Employment Projections for Bartenders, by Industry: 1992-2005

[Continued]

Industry	1992		2005 employment			Percent of industry employment for 2005 moderate projection
	Employment	Percent of industry employment	Low	Moderate	High	
Commercial sports	949	0.84	789	803	818	0.60
Producers, orchestras, and entertainers	856	0.60	788	814	843	0.41
Membership organizations, n.e.c.	326	0.39	297	311	317	0.29
Food stores	164	0.01	122	131	136	0.00
Labor organizations	142	0.10	93	95	96	0.07
General merchandise stores	109	0.00	70	75	78	0.00
Shopping goods stores, miscellaneous	81	0.01	71	77	79	0.01
Social services	63	0.00	73	76	76	0.00
Agriculture, forestry, and fishing	60	0.00	47	49	51	0.00
Wholesale trade	59	0.00	48	52	56	0.00
Individual and miscellaneous social services	51	0.01	58	60	60	0.01

Source: National Industry-Occupation Matrix, 1992 [data tape]. Prepared by the Bureau of Labor Statistics. Washington, DC: U.S. Department of Labor, Bureau of Labor Statistics, 1992. *Notes:* All employment data are wage and salary employment. "n.e.c." stands for "not elsewhere classified."

★ 363 ★

Occupational Outlook

Employment Projections for Bill and Account Collectors, by Industry: 1992-2005

The National Industry-Occupation Matrix counts jobs, as reflected by data about wage and salary employment collected through the Occupational Employment Statistics surveys. The table below presents employment figures for bill and account collectors during 1992; the percent of industry employment for this occupation (staffing patterns) in 1992; low, medium, and high employment projections for 2005; and staffing patterns for the 2005 moderate projection. In 1992, bill and account collectors ranked 107 in terms of total employment for individual occupations and ranked 192 when considering total employment of occupational groups as well as individual occupations. Table shows the industries employing the most bill and account collectors in 1992.

Industry	1992		2005 employment			Percent of industry employment for 2005 moderate projection
	Employment	Percent of industry employment	Low	Moderate	High	
Total, all industries	229,528	0.21	304,512	323,229	333,583	0.24
Services	83,366	0.22	130,855	139,467	143,884	0.26
Wholesale and retail trade	56,068	0.22	61,610	66,563	70,583	0.21
Business services	53,493	1.01	88,307	94,760	98,327	1.13
Credit reporting and collection	35,714	31.19	60,444	64,696	67,024	35.55
Wholesale trade	31,515	0.52	35,800	38,763	41,835	0.54
Depository institutions	28,389	1.35	33,327	34,710	34,800	1.58
Nondepository institutions	26,162	6.62	38,536	39,722	40,072	6.86
Commercial banks, savings institutions, and credit unions	26,124	1.32	30,822	32,100	32,184	1.56
Retail trade	24,554	0.13	25,810	27,799	28,748	0.12
Wholesale trade, other	22,612	0.59	25,543	27,658	29,850	0.61
Health services	21,545	0.22	30,341	31,709	32,059	0.23

[Continued]

★ 363 ★

Employment Projections for Bill and Account Collectors, by Industry: 1992-2005

[Continued]

Industry	1992		2005 employment			Percent of industry employment for 2005 moderate projection
	Employment	Percent of industry employment	Low	Moderate	High	
Transportation and public utilities	15,505	0.27	15,790	16,922	17,516	0.26
Personal credit institutions	15,079	11.97	21,946	22,621	22,821	13.31
Communications and utilities	13,914	0.63	13,949	14,929	15,415	0.68
General merchandise stores	13,542	0.56	13,295	14,320	14,808	0.55
Department stores	13,476	0.66	13,241	14,261	14,748	0.63
Government	9,675	0.10	11,169	11,856	12,435	0.11
Electric, gas, and sanitary services	7,019	0.74	7,656	8,100	8,430	0.76
Local government, except education and hospitals	6,972	0.16	8,111	8,610	9,030	0.17
Communications	6,896	0.54	6,292	6,829	6,985	0.61
Offices of physicians including osteopaths	6,677	0.44	10,420	10,866	11,017	0.46
Federal and business credit institutions	6,393	6.59	8,856	9,128	9,209	7.02
Equipment rental and leasing, miscellaneous	5,884	2.87	8,868	9,681	10,204	2.98
Furniture and homefurnishings stores	5,426	0.67	6,376	6,867	7,102	0.66

Source: *National Industry-Occupation Matrix, 1992* [data tape]. Prepared by the Bureau of Labor Statistics. Washington, DC: U.S. Department of Labor, Bureau of Labor Statistics, 1992. *Note:* All employment data are wage and salary employment.

★ 364 ★

Occupational Outlook

Employment Projections for Billing, Cost, and Rate Clerks, by Industry: 1992-2005

The National Industry-Occupation Matrix counts jobs, as reflected by data about wage and salary employment collected through the Occupational Employment Statistics surveys. The table below presents employment figures for billing, cost, and rate clerks during 1992; the percent of industry employment for this occupation (staffing patterns) in 1992; low, medium, and high employment projections for 2005; and staffing patterns for the 2005 moderate projection. In 1992, billing, cost, and rate clerks ranked 82 in terms of total employment for individual occupations and ranked 161 when considering total employment of occupational groups as well as individual occupations. Table shows the industries employing the most billing, cost, and rate clerks in 1992.

Industry	1992		2005 employment			Percent of industry employment for 2005 moderate projection
	Employment	Percent of industry employment	Low	Moderate	High	
Total, all industries	310,419	0.28	327,430	349,580	362,534	0.26
Services	125,236	0.32	158,805	166,813	170,001	0.31
Health services	90,001	0.94	115,313	120,567	122,014	0.87
Wholesale and retail trade	68,433	0.27	63,793	68,928	73,149	0.22
Transportation and public utilities	49,829	0.87	45,908	50,410	52,905	0.78
Hospitals, public and private	44,660	0.92	45,957	48,250	48,743	0.77
Wholesale trade	40,132	0.66	38,259	41,426	44,709	0.58
Transportation	38,877	1.12	36,713	40,547	42,733	0.94
Manufacturing	32,851	0.18	26,984	29,522	31,457	0.17
Offices of physicians including osteopaths	31,895	2.10	52,203	54,440	55,198	2.30
Retail trade	28,301	0.15	25,534	27,502	28,440	0.12

[Continued]

★ 364 ★

Employment Projections for Billing, Cost, and Rate Clerks, by Industry: 1992-2005
[Continued]

Industry	1992		2005 employment			Percent of industry employment for 2005 moderate projection
	Employment	Percent of industry employment	Low	Moderate	High	
Wholesale trade, other	27,565	0.72	26,125	28,288	30,530	0.62
Trucking and warehousing	21,789	1.36	21,157	22,897	24,150	1.13
Finance, insurance, and real estate	19,604	0.30	19,207	20,435	20,512	0.26
Local and long distance trucking and terminals	19,582	1.32	19,013	20,577	21,703	1.10
Nondurable goods manufacturing	18,232	0.23	15,758	17,091	17,603	0.22
Durable goods manufacturing	14,570	0.14	11,178	12,376	13,780	0.13
Automotive dealers and service stations	13,322	0.67	12,042	12,970	13,413	0.58
Business services	13,086	0.25	17,131	18,416	19,106	0.22
Insurance carriers	13,075	0.88	11,643	12,477	12,482	0.75
Government	11,247	0.12	9,698	10,291	10,784	0.10
Communications and utilities	10,952	0.49	9,195	9,863	10,172	0.45
Motor vehicle dealers	10,943	1.16	9,962	10,730	11,096	0.98
Transportation services	8,681	2.51	9,208	10,343	10,933	2.01
Local government, except education and hospitals	8,444	0.19	7,429	7,886	8,271	0.15

Source: National Industry-Occupation Matrix, 1992 [data tape]. Prepared by the Bureau of Labor Statistics. Washington, DC: U.S. Department of Labor, Bureau of Labor Statistics, 1992. *Note:* All employment data are wage and salary employment.

★ 365 ★
Occupational Outlook

Employment Projections for Blue-Collar Worker Supervisors, by Industry: 1992-2005

The National Industry-Occupation Matrix counts jobs, as reflected by data about wage and salary employment collected through the Occupational Employment Statistics surveys. The table below presents employment figures for blue-collar worker supervisors during 1992; the percent of industry employment for this occupation (staffing patterns) in 1992; low, medium, and high employment projections for 2005; and staffing patterns for the 2005 moderate projection. In 1992, blue-collar worker supervisors ranked 14 in terms of total employment for individual occupations and ranked 50 when considering total employment of occupational groups as well as individual occupations. Table shows the industries employing the most blue-collar worker supervisors in 1992.

Industry	1992		2005 employment			Percent of industry employment for 2005 moderate projection
	Employment	Percent of industry employment	Low	Moderate	High	
Total, all industries	1,588,720	1.43	1,659,901	1,784,146	1,928,338	1.31
Manufacturing	692,073	3.84	622,529	681,084	731,442	3.89
Durable goods manufacturing	379,521	3.71	326,980	360,864	400,790	3.73
Nondurable goods manufacturing	312,564	4.01	295,588	320,216	330,273	4.08
Construction	198,305	4.44	248,794	259,140	305,664	4.60
Wholesale and retail trade	179,433	0.71	209,214	225,957	239,013	0.73
Transportation and public utilities	175,243	3.07	180,970	196,394	205,350	3.02
Services	150,888	0.39	204,295	215,182	224,852	0.40
Government	137,092	1.44	136,865	145,278	152,147	1.39
Special trade contractors	92,268	3.42	117,808	122,707	144,737	3.58

[Continued]

★ 365 ★

Employment Projections for Blue-Collar Worker Supervisors, by Industry: 1992-2005
[Continued]

Industry	1992		2005 employment			Percent of industry employment for 2005 moderate projection
	Employment	Percent of industry employment	Low	Moderate	High	
Wholesale trade	91,687	1.52	109,566	118,635	128,037	1.65
Transportation	90,653	2.60	101,825	111,966	117,909	2.60
Retail trade	87,745	0.45	99,648	107,322	110,975	0.45
Communications and utilities	84,590	3.81	79,145	84,428	87,442	3.86
Local government, except education and hospitals	75,129	1.71	82,656	87,742	92,025	1.71
Food and kindred products	67,186	4.06	64,298	66,718	67,216	4.05
General building contractors	64,281	6.04	79,311	82,609	97,440	6.37
Industrial machinery and equipment	63,275	3.29	56,300	63,824	72,864	3.42
Transportation equipment	60,911	3.34	51,473	56,419	60,295	3.20
Automotive dealers and service stations	59,575	2.98	66,901	72,058	74,517	3.23
Fabricated metal products	58,305	4.41	50,663	55,075	61,070	4.60
Wholesale trade, other	53,320	1.40	63,192	68,423	73,846	1.51
Chemicals and allied products	52,081	4.81	45,914	49,841	51,839	4.57
Trucking and warehousing	51,846	3.23	62,950	68,129	71,857	3.37
Electric, gas, and sanitary services	49,982	5.23	56,923	60,224	62,673	5.62

Source: National Industry-Occupation Matrix, 1992 [data tape]. Prepared by the Bureau of Labor Statistics. Washington, DC: U.S. Department of Labor, Bureau of Labor Statistics, 1992. *Note:* All employment data are wage and salary employment.

★ 366 ★
Occupational Outlook

Employment Projections for Bookkeeping, Accounting, and Auditing Clerks, by Industry: 1992-2005

The National Industry-Occupation Matrix counts jobs, as reflected by data about wage and salary employment collected through the Occupational Employment Statistics surveys. The table below presents employment figures for bookkeeping, accounting, and auditing clerks during 1992; the percent of industry employment for this occupation (staffing patterns) in 1992; low, medium, and high employment projections for 2005; and staffing patterns for the 2005 moderate projection. In 1992, bookkeeping, accounting, and auditing clerks ranked 10 in terms of total employment for individual occupations and ranked 44 when considering total employment of occupational groups as well as individual occupations. Table shows the industries employing the most bookkeeping, accounting, and auditing clerks in 1992.

Industry	1992		2005 employment			Percent of industry employment for 2005 moderate projection
	Employment	Percent of industry employment	Low	Moderate	High	
Total, all industries	1,920,171	1.73	1,891,480	2,011,575	2,110,153	1.48
Services	600,802	1.55	695,175	731,964	755,102	1.35
Wholesale and retail trade	513,460	2.02	473,261	509,603	533,493	1.65
Retail trade	336,624	1.74	312,017	335,012	345,065	1.41
Finance, insurance, and real estate	234,017	3.56	236,504	247,895	251,715	3.11
Manufacturing	199,594	1.11	158,232	173,033	186,305	0.99
Wholesale trade	176,837	2.93	161,244	174,591	188,428	2.43
Government	129,138	1.35	101,976	108,165	113,142	1.03
Construction	120,508	2.70	119,893	124,879	147,298	2.22

[Continued]

★ 366 ★

Employment Projections for Bookkeeping, Accounting, and Auditing Clerks, by Industry: 1992-2005

[Continued]

Industry	1992		2005 employment			Percent of industry employment for 2005 moderate projection
	Employment	Percent of industry employment	Low	Moderate	High	
Health services	112,499	1.17	129,245	134,935	136,529	0.98
Wholesale trade, other	108,857	2.86	98,716	106,887	115,358	2.36
Durable goods manufacturing	105,735	1.03	78,623	86,943	97,354	0.90
Business services	98,252	1.85	123,114	132,241	136,969	1.58
Nondurable goods manufacturing	93,470	1.20	79,245	85,680	88,416	1.09
Transportation and public utilities	89,191	1.56	78,498	86,469	90,024	1.33
Engineering and management services	85,337	3.46	104,382	112,163	119,106	3.04
Automotive dealers and service stations	77,605	3.88	66,511	71,637	74,082	3.21
Depository institutions	77,298	3.67	67,195	69,983	70,164	3.19
Special trade contractors	77,292	2.87	77,875	81,113	95,676	2.37
Education, public and private	73,629	0.76	86,577	91,028	94,441	0.73
Commercial banks, savings institutions, and credit unions	73,000	3.68	63,379	66,009	66,179	3.21
Retail stores, miscellaneous	60,695	2.46	54,425	58,620	60,621	1.94
Food stores	59,121	1.86	63,591	68,492	70,830	1.77
Transportation	56,493	1.62	51,914	58,032	60,686	1.35
Membership organizations	55,868	2.86	54,600	56,266	56,883	2.35

Source: National Industry-Occupation Matrix, 1992 [data tape]. Prepared by the Bureau of Labor Statistics. Washington, DC: U.S. Department of Labor, Bureau of Labor Statistics, 1992. *Note:* All employment data are wage and salary employment.

★ 367 ★

Occupational Outlook

Employment Projections for Bus and Truck Mechanics and Diesel Engine Specialists, by Industry: 1992-2005

The National Industry-Occupation Matrix counts jobs, as reflected by data about wage and salary employment collected through the Occupational Employment Statistics surveys. The table below presents employment figures for bus and truck mechanics and diesel engine specialists during 1992; the percent of industry employment for this occupation (staffing patterns) in 1992; low, medium, and high employment projections for 2005; and staffing patterns for the 2005 moderate projection. In 1992, bus and truck mechanics and diesel engine specialists ranked 101 in terms of total employment for individual occupations and ranked 186 when considering total employment of occupational groups as well as individual occupations. Table shows the industries employing the most bus and truck mechanics and diesel engine specialists in 1992.

Industry	1992		2005 employment			Percent of industry employment for 2005 moderate projection
	Employment	Percent of industry employment	Low	Moderate	High	
Total, all industries	244,649	0.22	289,254	310,632	330,666	0.23
Transportation and public utilities	81,757	1.43	94,997	103,724	108,688	1.60
Transportation	74,471	2.14	85,819	93,971	98,559	2.18
Services	56,437	0.15	78,504	83,014	88,025	0.15
Trucking and warehousing	54,169	3.37	65,743	71,152	75,046	3.52
Local and long distance trucking and terminals	53,808	3.63	65,305	70,677	74,545	3.78
Wholesale and retail trade	52,177	0.21	57,966	62,693	67,071	0.20
Wholesale trade	41,344	0.68	45,852	49,647	53,582	0.69

[Continued]

★ 367 ★

Employment Projections for Bus and Truck Mechanics and Diesel Engine Specialists, by Industry: 1992-2005
[Continued]

Industry	1992		2005 employment			Percent of industry employment for 2005 moderate projection
	Employment	Percent of industry employment	Low	Moderate	High	
Auto repair, services, and parking	30,039	3.42	42,263	44,777	48,283	3.46
Government	23,512	0.25	25,587	27,157	28,475	0.26
Education, public and private	21,616	0.22	29,222	30,724	31,876	0.25
Local government, except education and hospitals	19,210	0.44	21,127	22,427	23,522	0.44
Manufacturing	18,691	0.10	17,917	19,052	20,765	0.11
Automotive repair shops	17,343	3.50	24,898	26,052	28,336	3.41
Motor vehicles, parts, and supplies	16,049	3.58	14,828	16,055	17,327	3.06
Machinery, equipment, and supplies	15,970	2.12	20,140	21,807	23,536	2.30
Automotive rentals, no drivers	11,893	7.47	16,282	17,591	18,715	7.92
Durable goods manufacturing	11,483	0.11	10,700	11,468	13,065	0.12
Local and interurban passenger transit	11,396	3.17	11,020	12,702	12,821	3.32
Retail trade	10,833	0.06	12,114	13,046	13,489	0.05
Automotive dealers and service stations	8,285	0.41	9,315	10,033	10,375	0.45
Construction	7,374	0.16	9,503	9,898	11,675	0.18
Communications and utilities	7,286	0.33	9,177	9,753	10,129	0.45
Nondurable goods manufacturing	7,194	0.09	7,199	7,564	7,676	0.10
Electric, gas, and sanitary services	6,010	0.63	8,039	8,505	8,851	0.79

Source: National Industry-Occupation Matrix, 1992 [data tape]. Prepared by the Bureau of Labor Statistics. Washington, DC: U.S. Department of Labor, Bureau of Labor Statistics, 1992. Note: All employment data are wage and salary employment.

★ 368 ★
Occupational Outlook

Employment Projections for Butchers and Meat Cutters, by Industry: 1992-2005

The National Industry-Occupation Matrix counts jobs, as reflected by data about wage and salary employment collected through the Occupational Employment Statistics surveys. The table below presents employment figures for butchers and meat cutters during 1992; the percent of industry employment for this occupation (staffing patterns) in 1992; low, medium, and high employment projections for 2005; and staffing patterns for the 2005 moderate projection. In 1992, butchers and meat cutters ranked 113 in terms of total employment for individual occupations and ranked 201 when considering total employment of occupational groups as well as individual occupations. Table shows the industries employing the most butchers and meat cutters in 1992.

Industry	1992		2005 employment			Percent of industry employment for 2005 moderate projection
	Employment	Percent of industry employment	Low	Moderate	High	
Total, all industries	217,562	0.20	175,304	186,861	192,523	0.14
Wholesale and retail trade	151,406	0.60	119,506	128,708	133,750	0.42
Retail trade	137,473	0.71	103,514	111,393	115,063	0.47
Food stores	131,502	4.14	98,628	106,230	109,855	2.74
Grocery stores	121,434	4.27	90,610	97,594	100,925	2.81

[Continued]

★ 368 ★

Employment Projections for Butchers and Meat Cutters, by Industry: 1992-2005
[Continued]

Industry	1992		2005 employment			Percent of industry employment for 2005 moderate projection
	Employment	Percent of industry employment	Low	Moderate	High	
Manufacturing	61,773	0.34	50,768	52,913	53,324	0.30
Food and kindred products	61,705	3.73	50,706	52,843	53,246	3.21
Nondurable goods manufacturing	61,705	0.79	50,706	52,843	53,246	0.67
Meat products	59,575	13.74	48,128	50,246	50,642	10.14
Wholesale trade	13,934	0.23	15,991	17,315	18,687	0.24
Groceries and related products	13,836	1.62	15,872	17,186	18,548	1.76
Meat and fish markets	9,202	18.78	7,334	7,899	8,169	16.11
Eating and drinking places	5,116	0.08	4,332	4,566	4,591	0.05
Government	2,091	0.02	1,963	2,074	2,153	0.02
Federal government	2,091	0.10	1,963	2,074	2,153	0.10
Foods and kindred products, miscellaneous	2,009	1.12	2,457	2,472	2,477	1.25
Hotels and other lodging places	1,387	0.09	2,017	2,085	2,154	0.09
Services	1,387	0.00	2,017	2,085	2,154	0.00
Agriculture, forestry, and fishing	905	0.05	1,050	1,081	1,141	0.05
General merchandise stores	625	0.03	386	416	430	0.02
Department stores	337	0.02	225	243	251	0.01
General merchandise stores, n.e.c.	288	0.08	161	173	179	0.05
Retail stores, miscellaneous	145	0.01	105	113	116	0.00
Grain mill products and fats and oils	82	0.05	81	84	85	0.06
Industrial machinery, n.e.c.	68	0.02	63	70	78	0.02

Source: National Industry-Occupation Matrix, 1992 [data tape]. Prepared by the Bureau of Labor Statistics. Washington, DC: U.S. Department of Labor, Bureau of Labor Statistics, 1992. Notes: All employment data are wage and salary employment. "n.e.c." stands for "not elsewhere classified."

★ 369 ★

Occupational Outlook

Employment Projections for Carpenters, by Industry: 1992-2005

The National Industry-Occupation Matrix counts jobs, as reflected by data about wage and salary employment collected through the Occupational Employment Statistics surveys. The table below presents employment figures for carpenters during 1992; the percent of industry employment for this occupation (staffing patterns) in 1992; low, medium, and high employment projections for 2005; and staffing patterns for the 2005 moderate projection. In 1992, carpenters ranked 42 in terms of total employment for individual occupations and ranked 107 when considering total employment of occupational groups as well as individual occupations. Table shows the industries employing the most carpenters in 1992.

Industry	1992		2005 employment			Percent of industry employment for 2005 moderate projection
	Employment	Percent of industry employment	Low	Moderate	High	
Total, all industries	576,131	0.52	668,887	699,158	807,680	0.52
Construction	438,525	9.81	521,954	543,659	641,262	9.65
General building contractors	291,728	27.42	337,514	351,549	414,663	27.11
Residential building construction	176,497	33.96	204,792	213,308	251,603	33.47
Special trade contractors	121,855	4.52	156,167	162,661	191,863	4.75
Nonresidential building construction	112,395	21.74	130,849	136,291	160,759	21.28
Carpentering and floor work	70,907	41.51	95,438	99,407	117,253	43.85
Services	44,852	0.12	56,858	59,994	61,856	0.11
Manufacturing	41,924	0.23	38,621	40,935	47,253	0.23
Durable goods manufacturing	34,342	0.34	31,261	32,915	38,715	0.34
Heavy construction, except building	24,942	3.51	28,273	29,449	34,736	3.24
Heavy construction, except highway and street	20,409	4.11	22,623	23,564	27,794	3.83
Government	16,255	0.17	15,249	16,172	16,920	0.15
Lumber and wood products	15,866	2.35	16,140	16,378	21,047	2.37
Wholesale and retail trade	15,449	0.06	16,070	17,326	18,076	0.06
Masonry, stonework, and plastering	14,793	3.79	18,545	19,316	22,784	3.70
Business services	12,904	0.24	18,389	19,733	20,418	0.24
Concrete work	12,401	6.25	13,370	13,926	16,427	5.90
Retail trade	12,391	0.06	12,799	13,784	14,253	0.06
Special trade contractors, all other	11,786	2.38	13,805	14,379	16,961	2.29
Wood buildings and mobile homes	10,138	18.14	9,459	9,557	12,687	18.88
Transportation equipment	9,717	0.53	7,704	8,350	8,702	0.47
Finance, insurance, and real estate	9,469	0.14	11,016	11,375	11,958	0.14
Real estate	8,860	0.69	10,268	10,589	11,168	0.65
Education, public and private	8,621	0.09	9,535	10,025	10,401	0.08

Source: National Industry-Occupation Matrix, 1992 [data tape]. Prepared by the Bureau of Labor Statistics. Washington, DC: U.S. Department of Labor, Bureau of Labor Statistics, 1992. *Note:* All employment data are wage and salary employment.

★ 370 ★
Occupational Outlook

Employment Projections for Cashiers, by Industry: 1992-2005

The National Industry-Occupation Matrix counts jobs, as reflected by data about wage and salary employment collected through the Occupational Employment Statistics surveys. The table below presents employment figures for cashiers during 1992; the percent of industry employment for this occupation (staffing patterns) in 1992; low, medium, and high employment projections for 2005; and staffing patterns for the 2005 moderate projection. In 1992, cashiers ranked 7 in terms of total employment for individual occupations and ranked 32 when considering total employment of occupational groups as well as individual occupations. Table shows the industries employing the most cashiers in 1992.

Industry	1992		2005 employment			Percent of industry employment for 2005 moderate projection
	Employment	Percent of industry employment	Low	Moderate	High	
Total, all industries	2,711,359	2.45	3,168,854	3,384,287	3,484,843	2.49
Wholesale and retail trade	2,273,827	8.96	2,616,007	2,807,304	2,892,046	9.07
Retail trade	2,224,649	11.50	2,556,456	2,742,823	2,822,455	11.54
Food stores	932,473	29.33	1,100,245	1,185,047	1,225,495	30.54
Grocery stores	895,829	31.52	1,056,542	1,137,976	1,176,817	32.74
Eating and drinking places	377,946	5.72	461,318	486,199	488,808	5.54
Services	348,506	0.90	449,061	467,018	479,053	0.86
Retail stores, miscellaneous	301,677	12.21	349,631	376,580	389,433	12.46
Automotive dealers and service stations	269,789	13.50	274,657	295,827	305,924	13.27
Gasoline service stations	236,470	38.43	236,277	254,489	263,175	40.16
General merchandise stores	204,269	8.43	204,884	220,675	228,207	8.48
Drug stores and proprietary stores	172,469	28.43	192,570	207,413	214,492	29.66
Department stores	136,524	6.67	144,982	156,156	161,486	6.89
Motion pictures	107,502	26.58	96,216	100,393	102,600	20.10
Videotape rental	87,494	70.00	74,576	77,675	79,355	72.40
Shopping goods stores, miscellaneous	67,957	7.98	91,182	98,210	101,562	8.53
General merchandise stores, n.e.c.	67,745	18.02	59,902	64,519	66,721	19.20
Amusement and recreation services	61,642	5.27	90,248	91,911	92,994	5.65
Building materials and garden supplies	57,059	7.74	65,726	70,792	73,209	8.36
Apparel and accessory stores	55,749	4.93	66,410	71,528	73,970	5.17
Wholesale trade	49,178	0.81	59,551	64,480	69,591	0.90
Clothing and accesories stores	46,313	5.47	54,764	58,985	60,998	5.73
Hotels and other lodging places	42,560	2.71	63,805	65,968	68,142	2.99
Government	42,265	0.44	46,924	49,799	52,202	0.48
Amusement and recreation services, all other	36,887	4.47	58,991	60,077	60,536	4.98

Source: National Industry-Occupation Matrix, 1992 [data tape]. Prepared by the Bureau of Labor Statistics. Washington, DC: U.S. Department of Labor, Bureau of Labor Statistics, 1992. *Notes:* All employment data are wage and salary employment. "n.e.c." stands for "not elsewhere classified."

★ 371 ★

Occupational Outlook

Employment Projections for Child Care Workers, by Industry: 1992-2005

The National Industry-Occupation Matrix counts jobs, as reflected by data about wage and salary employment collected through the Occupational Employment Statistics surveys. The table below presents employment figures for child care workers during 1992; the percent of industry employment for this occupation (staffing patterns) in 1992; low, medium, and high employment projections for 2005; and staffing patterns for the 2005 moderate projection. In 1992, child care workers ranked 89 in terms of total employment for individual occupations and ranked 171 when considering total employment of occupational groups as well as individual occupations. Table shows the industries employing the most child care workers in 1992.

Industry	1992		2005 employment			Percent of industry employment for 2005 moderate projection
	Employment	Percent of industry employment	Low	Moderate	High	
Total, all industries	290,469	0.26	487,028	502,564	508,710	0.37
Services	266,952	0.69	459,119	472,867	477,597	0.87
Social services	152,447	7.79	279,025	286,612	288,030	7.76
Child day care services	102,671	22.87	196,513	201,647	202,353	25.96
Membership organizations	55,549	2.85	85,272	87,464	88,290	3.66
Education, public and private	30,960	0.32	51,365	54,006	56,031	0.43
Government	20,765	0.22	24,503	26,011	27,281	0.25
Civic and social associations	17,929	4.27	33,100	33,759	34,147	6.36
Amusement and recreation services	13,854	1.18	21,816	22,179	22,369	1.36
State government, except education and hospitals	13,501	0.62	15,716	16,683	17,498	0.67
Health services	12,265	0.13	19,593	20,499	20,693	0.15
Amusement and recreation services, all other	10,312	1.25	17,643	17,967	18,105	1.49
Individual and miscellaneous social services	9,180	1.31	17,196	17,702	17,778	1.52
Hospitals, public and private	7,810	0.16	11,050	11,601	11,720	0.18
Local government, except education and hospitals	7,263	0.17	8,787	9,328	9,783	0.18
Bowling centers	3,495	3.98	4,107	4,143	4,194	4.87
Home health care services	1,596	0.40	3,582	3,731	3,754	0.41
Agriculture, forestry, and fishing	1,469	0.08	1,999	2,065	2,195	0.10
Local and interurban passenger transit	1,284	0.36	1,406	1,621	1,636	0.42
Transportation	1,284	0.04	1,406	1,621	1,636	0.04
Transportation and public utilities	1,284	0.02	1,406	1,621	1,636	0.02
Nursing and personal care facilities	1,118	0.07	1,878	1,955	1,975	0.08
Private households	1,000	0.09	692	714	759	0.09
Local and suburban transportation	625	0.39	686	791	798	0.45
Hotels and other lodging places	495	0.03	792	819	846	0.04

Source: National Industry-Occupation Matrix, 1992 [data tape]. Prepared by the Bureau of Labor Statistics. Washington, DC: U.S. Department of Labor, Bureau of Labor Statistics, 1992. *Note:* All employment data are wage and salary employment.

★ 372 ★
Occupational Outlook

Employment Projections for Clerical and Administrative Support Workers, by Industry: 1992-2005

The National Industry-Occupation Matrix counts jobs, as reflected by data about wage and salary employment collected through the Occupational Employment Statistics surveys. The table below presents employment figures for miscellaneous clerical and administrative support workers during 1992; the percent of industry employment for this occupation (staffing patterns) in 1992; low, medium, and high employment projections for 2005; and staffing patterns for the 2005 moderate projection. In 1992, clerical and administrative support workers ranked 1 in terms of total employment for individual occupations and ranked 10 when considering total employment of occupational groups as well as individual occupations. Table shows the industries employing the most miscellaneous clerical and administrative support workers in 1992. See also tables on specific clerical and administrative support positions such as secretaries.

Industry	1992		2005 employment			Percent of industry employment for 2005 moderate projection
	Employment	Percent of industry employment	Low	Moderate	High	
Total, all industries	7,132,173	6.44	8,174,570	8,664,252	8,970,857	6.38
Services	2,857,706	7.39	3,794,602	3,997,127	4,116,510	7.38
Finance, insurance, and real estate	1,557,688	23.70	1,650,951	1,728,793	1,740,813	21.69
Education, public and private	1,164,832	11.99	1,475,105	1,550,942	1,609,096	12.43
Depository institutions	939,528	44.67	896,820	934,023	936,440	42.56
Commercial banks, savings institutions, and credit unions	899,240	45.37	853,515	888,920	891,221	43.16
Wholesale and retail trade	835,535	3.29	880,974	949,440	999,062	3.07
Government	769,038	8.06	766,107	814,687	854,254	7.79
Business services	514,434	9.68	772,314	828,856	857,018	9.90
Health services	487,154	5.07	643,135	672,890	680,557	4.88
Transportation and public utilities	477,437	8.36	477,260	520,065	539,456	8.00
Manufacturing	471,073	2.61	422,450	462,795	495,440	2.64
Retail trade	464,145	2.40	482,890	518,405	533,867	2.18
Wholesale trade	371,390	6.14	398,083	431,035	465,196	5.99
Local government, except education and hospitals	360,738	8.22	413,729	439,186	460,626	8.54
Communications and utilities	308,294	13.87	299,588	323,140	332,622	14.77
Hospitals, public and private	264,792	5.46	325,677	341,925	345,417	5.44
Insurance carriers	253,979	17.16	256,749	275,140	275,262	16.57
Wholesale trade, other	246,306	6.46	263,016	284,787	307,357	6.28
Nondurable goods manufacturing	237,841	3.05	226,722	245,554	253,318	3.13
Durable goods manufacturing	233,020	2.28	195,484	216,951	241,634	2.24
Personnel supply services	229,669	13.93	376,155	403,307	414,904	15.62
Communications	209,721	16.55	194,638	212,103	217,070	19.00
State government, except education and hospitals	200,281	9.16	193,569	205,479	215,510	8.22
Engineering and management services	195,609	7.92	257,698	275,622	289,947	7.48

Source: National Industry-Occupation Matrix, 1992 [data tape]. Prepared by the Bureau of Labor Statistics. Washington, DC: U.S. Department of Labor, Bureau of Labor Statistics, 1992. *Note:* All employment data are wage and salary employment.

★ 373 ★

Occupational Outlook

Employment Projections for Clerical Supervisors and Managers, by Industry: 1992-2005

The National Industry-Occupation Matrix counts jobs, as reflected by data about wage and salary employment collected through the Occupational Employment Statistics surveys. The table below presents employment figures for clerical supervisors and managers during 1992; the percent of industry employment for this occupation (staffing patterns) in 1992; low, medium, and high employment projections for 2005; and staffing patterns for the 2005 moderate projection. In 1992, clerical supervisors and managers ranked 19 in terms of total employment for individual occupations and ranked 60 when considering total employment of occupational groups as well as individual occupations. Table shows the industries employing the most clerical supervisors and managers in 1992.

Industry	1992		2005 employment			Percent of industry employment for 2005 moderate projection
	Employment	Percent of industry employment	Low	Moderate	High	
Total, all industries	1,265,597	1.14	1,472,054	1,566,802	1,620,802	1.15
Services	371,228	0.96	496,756	523,096	536,945	0.97
Finance, insurance, and real estate	282,452	4.30	351,710	369,943	372,018	4.64
Wholesale and retail trade	216,595	0.85	239,565	257,598	270,335	0.83
Government	150,241	1.57	148,700	158,858	166,985	1.52
Health services	130,688	1.36	174,177	182,005	184,225	1.32
Depository institutions	130,561	6.21	158,647	165,228	165,655	7.53
Commercial banks, savings institutions, and credit unions	124,165	6.26	151,975	158,279	158,689	7.69
Retail trade	114,768	0.59	130,586	139,598	142,983	0.59
Manufacturing	114,431	0.63	106,011	116,315	124,577	0.66
Transportation and public utilities	111,472	1.95	109,914	120,317	125,066	1.85
Wholesale trade	101,827	1.68	108,979	118,000	127,352	1.64
Business services	70,120	1.32	99,310	106,689	110,698	1.27
Wholesale trade, other	68,645	1.80	73,132	79,185	85,461	1.75
Insurance carriers	68,158	4.61	77,517	83,070	83,107	5.00
Local government, except education and hospitals	62,302	1.42	73,939	78,488	82,320	1.53
Communications and utilities	59,384	2.67	54,060	58,168	59,915	2.66
Nondurable goods manufacturing	57,298	0.73	57,469	62,137	64,096	0.79
Durable goods manufacturing	57,181	0.56	48,598	54,235	60,517	0.56
Education, public and private	53,761	0.55	65,354	68,714	71,290	0.55
Transportation	52,088	1.49	55,853	62,149	65,151	1.44
Offices of physicians, including osteopaths	51,856	3.42	76,321	79,592	80,701	3.37
Hospitals, public and private	47,697	0.98	55,172	57,924	58,516	0.92
Engineering and management services	41,135	1.67	58,372	62,562	65,520	1.70
Communications	38,237	3.02	32,510	35,367	36,187	3.17

Source: National Industry-Occupation Matrix, 1992 [data tape]. Prepared by the Bureau of Labor Statistics. Washington, DC: U.S. Department of Labor, Bureau of Labor Statistics, 1992. *Note:* All employment data are wage and salary employment.

★ 374 ★

Occupational Outlook

Employment Projections for Clinical Lab Technologists and Technicians, by Industry: 1992-2005

The National Industry-Occupation Matrix counts jobs, as reflected by data about wage and salary employment collected through the Occupational Employment Statistics surveys. The table below presents employment figures for clinical lab technologists and technicians during 1992; the percent of industry employment for this occupation (staffing patterns) in 1992; low, medium, and high employment projections for 2005; and staffing patterns for the 2005 moderate projection. In 1992, clinical lab technologists and technicians ranked 96 in terms of total employment for individual occupations and ranked 180 when considering total employment of occupational groups as well as individual occupations. Table shows the industries employing the most clinical lab technologists and technicians in 1992.

Industry	1992		2005 employment			Percent of industry employment for 2005 moderate projection
	Employment	Percent of industry employment	Low	Moderate	High	
Total, all industries	266,675	0.24	322,322	337,549	341,727	0.25
Services	248,371	0.64	305,123	319,333	322,739	0.59
Health services	238,131	2.48	292,450	305,961	308,947	2.22
Hospitals, public and private	150,015	3.09	156,436	164,240	165,918	2.61
Medical and dental laboratories	39,533	21.84	70,448	73,365	73,835	27.17
Offices of physicians, including osteopaths	37,279	2.46	49,463	51,583	52,302	2.18
Government	17,346	0.18	16,184	17,137	17,884	0.16
Federal government	9,460	0.43	8,002	8,452	8,775	0.41
Health and allied services, n.e.c.	9,411	3.75	13,244	13,793	13,881	3.52
Engineering and management services	6,144	0.25	7,917	8,371	8,603	0.23
Research and testing services	4,402	0.79	5,264	5,501	5,603	0.73
State government, except education and hospitals	4,099	0.19	4,196	4,454	4,671	0.18
Education, public and private	4,041	0.04	4,686	4,927	5,112	0.04
Local government, except education and hospitals	3,787	0.09	3,986	4,231	4,438	0.08
Management and public relations	1,647	0.25	2,536	2,743	2,851	0.25
Nursing and personal care facilities	777	0.05	1,069	1,113	1,124	0.05
Chemicals and allied products	753	0.07	770	826	834	0.08
Drugs	753	0.29	770	826	834	0.28
Manufacturing	753	0.00	770	826	834	0.00
Nondurable goods manufacturing	753	0.01	770	826	834	0.01
Offices of other health practitioners	692	0.21	1,090	1,137	1,153	0.20
Agriculture, forestry, and fishing	205	0.01	245	253	270	0.01
Services, n.e.c.	55	0.13	69	75	78	0.13

Source: National Industry-Occupation Matrix, 1992 [data tape]. Prepared by the Bureau of Labor Statistics. Washington, DC: U.S. Department of Labor, Bureau of Labor Statistics, 1992. *Notes:* All employment data are wage and salary employment. "n.e.c." stands for "not elsewhere classified."

★ 375 ★

Occupational Outlook

Employment Projections for College and University Faculty, by Industry: 1992-2005

The National Industry-Occupation Matrix counts jobs, as reflected by data about wage and salary employment collected through the Occupational Employment Statistics surveys. The table below presents employment figures for college and university faculty during 1992; the percent of industry employment for this occupation (staffing patterns) in 1992; low, medium, and high employment projections for 2005; and staffing patterns for the 2005 moderate projection. In 1992, college and university faculty ranked 31 in terms of total employment for individual occupations and ranked 88 when considering total employment of occupational groups as well as individual occupations. Table shows the industries employing the most college and university faculty in 1992.

Industry	1992		2005 employment			Percent of industry employment for 2005 moderate projection
	Employment	Percent of industry employment	Low	Moderate	High	
Total, all industries	811,819	0.73	975,778	1,025,942	1,064,419	0.76
Education, public and private	811,661	8.35	975,575	1,025,731	1,064,191	8.22
Services	811,661	2.10	975,575	1,025,731	1,064,191	1.89
Agriculture, forestry, and fishing	158	0.01	203	211	228	0.01

Source: National Industry-Occupation Matrix, 1992 [data tape]. Prepared by the Bureau of Labor Statistics. Washington, DC: U.S. Department of Labor, Bureau of Labor Statistics, 1992. *Note:* All employment data are wage and salary employment.

★ 376 ★

Occupational Outlook

Employment Projections for Computer Operators, by Industry: 1992-2005

The National Industry-Occupation Matrix counts jobs, as reflected by data about wage and salary employment collected through the Occupational Employment Statistics surveys. The table below presents employment figures for computer operators (excluding peripheral equipment operators) during 1992; the percent of industry employment for this occupation (staffing patterns) in 1992; low, medium, and high employment projections for 2005; and staffing patterns for the 2005 moderate projection. In 1992, computer operators ranked 98 in terms of total employment for individual occupations and ranked 183 when considering total employment of occupational groups as well as individual occupations. Table shows the industries employing the most computer operators in 1992.

Industry	1992		2005 employment			Percent of industry employment for 2005 moderate projection
	Employment	Percent of industry employment	Low	Moderate	High	
Total, all industries	258,690	0.23	144,143	154,322	160,973	0.11
Services	91,708	0.24	62,296	66,362	68,693	0.12
Business services	44,095	0.83	29,144	31,355	32,555	0.37
Finance, insurance, and real estate	41,483	0.63	22,668	23,863	23,971	0.30
Wholesale and retail trade	38,419	0.15	20,077	21,708	23,179	0.07
Manufacturing	36,276	0.20	15,717	17,350	18,744	0.10
Government	32,630	0.34	14,618	15,478	16,150	0.15
Wholesale trade	28,316	0.47	15,010	16,253	17,541	0.23
Computer and data processing services	25,828	3.11	15,825	17,081	17,820	1.05
Durable goods manufacturing	20,525	0.20	8,080	9,068	10,203	0.09

[Continued]

★ 376 ★

Employment Projections for Computer Operators, by Industry: 1992-2005

[Continued]

Industry	1992		2005 employment			Percent of industry employment for 2005 moderate projection
	Employment	Percent of industry employment	Low	Moderate	High	
Wholesale trade, other	19,855	0.52	10,501	11,370	12,271	0.25
Depository institutions	19,194	0.91	9,736	10,140	10,166	0.46
Federal government	17,812	0.82	7,467	7,887	8,188	0.38
Commercial banks, savings institutions, and credit unions	17,730	0.89	8,977	9,350	9,374	0.45
Engineering and management services	16,948	0.69	12,004	12,878	13,598	0.35
Nondurable goods manufacturing	15,761	0.20	7,642	8,288	8,542	0.11
Health services	14,100	0.15	11,693	12,259	12,385	0.09
Transportation and public utilities	13,936	0.24	6,753	7,407	7,673	0.11
Insurance carriers	11,858	0.80	5,909	6,332	6,335	0.38
Hospitals, public and private	11,060	0.23	9,526	10,002	10,104	0.16
Personnel supply services	10,158	0.62	7,445	7,982	8,212	0.31
Retail trade	10,104	0.05	5,067	5,455	5,638	0.02
Education, public and private	8,652	0.09	4,746	4,990	5,178	0.04
Accounting, auditing, and bookkeeping	8,510	1.67	6,358	6,826	7,126	0.83
Communications and utilities	8,487	0.38	3,811	4,095	4,208	0.19

Source: National Industry-Occupation Matrix, 1992 [data tape]. Prepared by the Bureau of Labor Statistics. Washington, DC: U.S. Department of Labor, Bureau of Labor Statistics, 1992. *Note:* All employment data are wage and salary employment.

★ 377 ★

Occupational Outlook

Employment Projections for Computer Programmers, by Industry: 1992-2005

The National Industry-Occupation Matrix counts jobs, as reflected by data about wage and salary employment collected through the Occupational Employment Statistics surveys. The table below presents employment figures for computer programmers during 1992; the percent of industry employment for this occupation (staffing patterns) in 1992; low, medium, and high employment projections for 2005; and staffing patterns for the 2005 moderate projection. In 1992, computer programmers ranked 46 in terms of total employment for individual occupations and ranked 112 when considering total employment of occupational groups as well as individual occupations. Table shows the industries employing the most computer programmers in 1992.

Industry	1992		2005 employment			Percent of industry employment for 2005 moderate projection
	Employment	Percent of industry employment	Low	Moderate	High	
Total, all industries	538,658	0.49	653,627	703,452	737,250	0.52
Services	246,087	0.64	368,482	395,299	412,145	0.73
Business services	158,458	2.98	257,718	277,967	289,709	3.32
Computer and data processing services	140,120	16.86	230,786	249,094	259,870	15.32
Manufacturing	80,798	0.45	65,659	73,194	81,018	0.42
Finance, insurance, and real estate	75,370	1.15	83,947	88,906	89,243	1.12
Wholesale and retail trade	57,041	0.22	61,162	66,126	70,669	0.21
Durable goods manufacturing	56,863	0.56	42,133	47,714	54,700	0.49
Government	50,105	0.52	46,870	49,721	52,035	0.48
Wholesale trade	44,242	0.73	47,311	51,227	55,287	0.71

[Continued]

★ 377 ★

Employment Projections for Computer Programmers, by Industry: 1992-2005
[Continued]

Industry	1992		2005 employment			Percent of industry employment for 2005 moderate projection
	Employment	Percent of industry employment	Low	Moderate	High	
Engineering and management services	40,615	1.64	55,683	59,661	63,335	1.62
Wholesale trade, other	36,137	0.95	38,531	41,721	45,027	0.92
Insurance carriers	34,342	2.32	34,830	37,325	37,341	2.25
Transportation and public utilities	24,125	0.42	22,989	25,222	26,138	0.39
Nondurable goods manufacturing	23,947	0.31	23,540	25,493	26,318	0.32
Education, public and private	21,408	0.22	23,678	24,896	25,829	0.20
Industrial machinery and equipment	20,948	1.09	12,975	15,349	19,083	0.82
Depository institutions	19,617	0.93	20,081	20,914	20,968	0.95
Local government, except education and hospitals	19,489	0.44	19,291	20,478	21,477	0.40
Commercial banks, savings institutions, and credit unions	17,241	0.87	17,601	18,331	18,378	0.89
State government, except education and hospitals	16,547	0.76	15,759	16,729	17,546	0.67
Management and public relations	16,180	2.47	24,892	26,926	27,988	2.43
Life insurance	15,911	2.96	16,880	18,089	18,097	2.93
Communications and utilities	15,521	0.70	13,712	14,754	15,223	0.67
Computer and office equipment	15,085	3.86	7,370	9,017	11,927	3.43

Source: National Industry-Occupation Matrix, 1992 [data tape]. Prepared by the Bureau of Labor Statistics. Washington, DC: U.S. Department of Labor, Bureau of Labor Statistics, 1992. *Note:* All employment data are wage and salary employment.

★ 378 ★

Occupational Outlook

Employment Projections for Construction and Maintenance Painters and Paperhangers, by Industry: 1992-2005

The National Industry-Occupation Matrix counts jobs, as reflected by data about wage and salary employment collected through the Occupational Employment Statistics surveys. The table below presents employment figures for construction and maintenance painters and paperhangers during 1992; the percent of industry employment for this occupation (staffing patterns) in 1992; low, medium, and high employment projections for 2005; and staffing patterns for the 2005 moderate projection. In 1992, construction and maintenance painters and paperhangers ranked 115 in terms of total employment for individual occupations and ranked 203 when considering total employment of occupational groups as well as individual occupations. Table shows the industries employing the most construction and maintenance painters and paperhangers in 1992.

Industry	1992		2005 employment			Percent of industry employment for 2005 moderate projection
	Employment	Percent of industry employment	Low	Moderate	High	
Total, all industries	217,077	0.20	259,151	271,572	307,155	0.20
Construction	129,379	2.89	162,959	169,736	200,209	3.01
Special trade contractors	112,507	4.17	141,382	147,262	173,700	4.30
Painting and paper hanging	100,900	65.52	125,918	131,154	154,700	68.06
Services	33,964	0.09	41,304	43,483	44,837	0.08

[Continued]

★ 378 ★

Employment Projections for Construction and Maintenance Painters and Paperhangers, by Industry: 1992-2005

[Continued]

Industry	1992		2005 employment			Percent of industry employment for 2005 moderate projection
	Employment	Percent of industry employment	Low	Moderate	High	
Manufacturing	18,033	0.10	17,265	18,822	20,446	0.11
General building contractors	15,695	1.48	20,119	20,955	24,717	1.62
Government	15,353	0.16	12,578	13,333	13,933	0.13
Durable goods manufacturing	13,710	0.13	12,793	14,015	15,476	0.14
Finance, insurance, and real estate	13,566	0.21	17,664	18,225	19,203	0.23
Real estate	13,275	1.04	17,309	17,851	18,828	1.10
Residential building construction	9,897	1.90	12,760	13,290	15,676	2.09
Real estate operators and lessors	8,562	1.54	10,741	11,077	11,684	1.67
Business services	7,439	0.14	11,169	11,993	12,413	0.14
Health services	6,749	0.07	8,928	9,364	9,458	0.07
Education, public and private	6,392	0.07	6,284	6,607	6,855	0.05
Federal government	6,382	0.29	4,794	5,064	5,257	0.25
Hospitals, public and private	6,018	0.12	7,741	8,127	8,210	0.13
Private households	6,000	0.54	3,772	3,893	4,141	0.49
Nonresidential building construction	5,546	1.07	7,174	7,472	8,813	1.17
Transportation equipment	5,363	0.29	4,790	5,204	5,457	0.29
Masonry, stonework, and plastering	4,938	1.26	6,701	6,979	8,232	1.34
Special trade contractors, all other	4,927	1.00	6,413	6,680	7,879	1.06
Nondurable goods manufacturing	4,121	0.05	4,222	4,530	4,654	0.06
Real estate agents and managers	4,078	0.70	5,856	6,039	6,370	0.76

Source: *National Industry-Occupation Matrix, 1992* [data tape]. Prepared by the Bureau of Labor Statistics. Washington, DC: U.S. Department of Labor, Bureau of Labor Statistics, 1992. *Note:* All employment data are wage and salary employment.

★ 379 ★

Occupational Outlook

Employment Projections for Construction Trade Helpers, by Industry: 1992-2005

The National Industry-Occupation Matrix counts jobs, as reflected by data about wage and salary employment collected through the Occupational Employment Statistics surveys. The table below presents employment figures for construction trade helpers during 1992; the percent of industry employment for this occupation (staffing patterns) in 1992; low, medium, and high employment projections for 2005; and staffing patterns for the 2005 moderate projection. In 1992, construction trade helpers ranked 52 in terms of total employment for individual occupations and ranked 122 when considering total employment of occupational groups as well as individual occupations. Table shows the industries employing the most construction trade helpers in 1992.

Industry	1992		2005 employment			Percent of industry employment for 2005 moderate projection
	Employment	Percent of industry employment	Low	Moderate	High	
Total, all industries	445,751	0.40	502,800	524,331	617,586	0.39
Construction	410,398	9.18	471,253	490,849	578,971	8.72
Special trade contractors	253,231	9.39	296,132	308,446	363,821	9.00
General building contractors	116,951	10.99	130,921	136,365	160,847	10.52
Masonry, stonework, and plastering	63,733	16.33	75,393	78,528	92,626	15.06
Nonresidential building construction	58,477	11.31	65,945	68,688	81,019	10.72
Residential building construction	56,932	10.95	63,989	66,650	78,616	10.46
Electrical work	55,730	11.21	68,392	71,236	84,025	10.99
Plumbing, heating, and air-conditioning	45,263	7.51	49,128	51,171	60,357	7.17
Heavy construction, except building	40,215	5.65	44,200	46,038	54,303	5.06
Heavy construction, except highway and street	32,596	6.56	35,000	36,456	43,001	5.92
Roofing, siding, and sheet metal work	23,729	12.61	31,889	33,215	39,179	12.86
Concrete work	21,464	10.82	22,417	23,349	27,541	9.89
Special trade contractors, all other	17,048	3.44	19,256	20,057	23,658	3.19
Manufacturing	14,155	0.08	12,310	13,006	14,956	0.07
Painting and paper hanging	13,590	8.82	14,785	15,400	18,165	7.99
Carpentering and floor work	12,673	7.42	14,871	15,489	18,270	6.83
Durable goods manufacturing	12,374	0.12	10,653	11,208	13,038	0.12
Transportation and public utilities	11,131	0.19	11,054	11,700	12,175	0.18
Communications and utilities	10,896	0.49	10,861	11,491	11,958	0.53
Electric, gas, and sanitary services	10,896	1.14	10,861	11,491	11,958	1.07
Mining	9,944	1.58	8,062	8,651	11,351	1.54
Highway and street construction	7,619	3.56	9,199	9,582	11,302	3.25
Electric services	7,340	1.66	7,084	7,495	7,799	1.58
Oil and gas extraction	5,578	1.59	4,361	4,652	7,063	1.55

Source: National Industry-Occupation Matrix, 1992 [data tape]. Prepared by the Bureau of Labor Statistics. Washington, DC: U.S. Department of Labor, Bureau of Labor Statistics, 1992. *Note:* All employment data are wage and salary employment.

★ 380 ★
Occupational Outlook

Employment Projections for Correction Officers, by Industry: 1992-2005

The National Industry-Occupation Matrix counts jobs, as reflected by data about wage and salary employment collected through the Occupational Employment Statistics surveys. The table below presents employment figures for correction officers during 1992; the percent of industry employment for this occupation (staffing patterns) in 1992; low, medium, and high employment projections for 2005; and staffing patterns for the 2005 moderate projection. In 1992, correction officers ranked 91 in terms of total employment for individual occupations and ranked 175 when considering total employment of occupational groups as well as individual occupations. Table shows the industries employing the most correction officers in 1992.

Industry	1992		2005 employment			Percent of industry employment for 2005 moderate projection
	Employment	Percent of industry employment	Low	Moderate	High	
Total, all industries	282,217	0.25	451,678	479,441	502,726	0.35
Government	281,590	2.95	450,608	478,283	501,522	4.57
State government, except education and hospitals	168,854	7.72	268,029	284,521	298,410	11.38
Local government, except education and hospitals	104,807	2.39	172,899	183,538	192,498	3.57
Federal government	7,929	0.36	9,679	10,224	10,614	0.50
Management and public relations	626	0.10	1,071	1,158	1,204	0.10
Services	626	0.00	1,071	1,158	1,204	0.00
Engineering and management services	626	0.03	1,071	1,158	1,204	0.03

Source: National Industry-Occupation Matrix, 1992 [data tape]. Prepared by the Bureau of Labor Statistics. Washington, DC: U.S. Department of Labor, Bureau of Labor Statistics, 1992. *Note:* All employment data are wage and salary employment.

★ 381 ★
Occupational Outlook

Employment Projections for Counter and Rental Clerks, by Industry: 1992-2005

The National Industry-Occupation Matrix counts jobs, as reflected by data about wage and salary employment collected through the Occupational Employment Statistics surveys. The table below presents employment figures for counter and rental clerks during 1992; the percent of industry employment for this occupation (staffing patterns) in 1992; low, medium, and high employment projections for 2005; and staffing patterns for the 2005 moderate projection. In 1992, counter and rental clerks ranked 106 in terms of total employment for individual occupations and ranked 191 when considering total employment of occupational groups as well as individual occupations. Table shows the industries employing the most counter and rental clerks in 1992.

Industry	1992		2005 employment			Percent of industry employment for 2005 moderate projection
	Employment	Percent of industry employment	Low	Moderate	High	
Total, all industries	231,484	0.21	301,503	317,593	327,117	0.23
Services	180,850	0.47	242,934	255,148	261,932	0.47
Personal services	80,464	7.24	97,491	100,850	101,121	7.30
Laundry, cleaning, and garment services	67,134	16.30	79,227	82,205	82,342	17.59
Wholesale and retail trade	39,286	0.15	43,395	46,776	48,689	0.15
Business services	33,909	0.64	54,687	59,226	61,979	0.71

[Continued]

★ 381 ★

Employment Projections for Counter and Rental Clerks, by Industry: 1992-2005
[Continued]

Industry	1992		2005 employment			Percent of industry employment for 2005 moderate projection
	Employment	Percent of industry employment	Low	Moderate	High	
Retail trade	33,830	0.17	36,866	39,706	41,058	0.17
Auto repair, services, and parking	31,847	3.63	44,520	47,887	51,101	3.70
Automotive rentals, no drivers	27,977	17.56	38,304	41,383	44,026	18.64
Amusement and recreation services	27,792	2.38	39,272	39,917	40,278	2.45
Equipment rental and leasing, miscellaneous	20,226	9.88	31,968	34,899	36,786	10.73
Amusement and recreation services, all other	19,238	2.33	30,001	30,554	30,787	2.53
General merchandise stores	16,515	0.68	16,713	18,001	18,615	0.69
Department stores	14,746	0.72	15,195	16,366	16,925	0.72
Personal services, all other	11,664	7.04	15,485	15,811	15,925	7.71
Real estate	10,825	0.84	14,537	14,991	15,812	0.92
Business services, miscellaneous	8,970	0.72	15,007	16,062	16,640	0.80
Bowling centers	7,970	9.08	8,513	8,588	8,695	10.10
Building materials and garden supplies	6,215	0.84	6,970	7,507	7,764	0.89
Wholesale trade	5,456	0.09	6,530	7,070	7,630	0.10
Real estate agents and managers	5,437	0.94	7,808	8,052	8,493	1.01
Real estate operators and lessors	5,157	0.93	6,470	6,672	7,037	1.00
Videotape rental	4,574	3.66	3,783	3,940	4,025	3.67
Motion pictures	4,574	1.13	3,783	3,940	4,025	0.79
Food stores	3,428	0.11	3,917	4,219	4,363	0.11

Source: National Industry-Occupation Matrix, 1992 [data tape]. Prepared by the Bureau of Labor Statistics. Washington, DC: U.S. Department of Labor, Bureau of Labor Statistics, 1992. *Note:* All employment data are wage and salary employment.

★ 382 ★

Occupational Outlook

Employment Projections for Data Entry Keyers, by Industry: 1992-2005

The National Industry-Occupation Matrix counts jobs, as reflected by data about wage and salary employment collected through the Occupational Employment Statistics surveys. The table below presents employment figures for data entry keyers, excluding composing data entry keyers, during 1992; the percent of industry employment for this occupation (staffing patterns) in 1992; low, medium, and high employment projections for 2005; and staffing patterns for the 2005 moderate projection. In 1992, data entry keyers ranked 56 in terms of total employment for individual occupations and ranked 126 when considering total employment of occupational groups as well as individual occupations. Table shows the industries employing the most data entry keyers in 1992.

Industry	1992		2005 employment			Percent of industry employment for 2005 moderate projection
	Employment	Percent of industry employment	Low	Moderate	High	
Total, all industries	429,067	0.39	479,076	512,118	530,321	0.38
Services	205,664	0.53	278,164	296,769	306,296	0.55
Business services	117,699	2.22	176,556	189,588	196,029	2.27
Finance, insurance, and real estate	67,915	1.03	65,787	69,460	69,758	0.87
Wholesale and retail trade	56,855	0.22	51,960	56,125	59,526	0.18
Personnel supply services	54,174	3.29	97,836	104,898	107,914	4.06
Government	45,824	0.48	37,816	40,156	42,052	0.38
Computer and data processing services	38,452	4.63	45,740	49,369	51,504	3.04
Manufacturing	34,022	0.19	28,430	31,162	33,110	0.18
Wholesale trade	32,538	0.54	30,858	33,412	36,060	0.46
Engineering and management services	28,012	1.13	35,639	38,193	40,005	1.04
Insurance carriers	25,707	1.74	22,027	23,605	23,616	1.42
Depository institutions	25,181	1.20	22,902	23,852	23,914	1.09
Retail trade	24,317	0.13	21,102	22,712	23,466	0.10
Health services	23,196	0.24	26,500	27,722	28,003	0.20
Commercial banks, savings institutions, and credit unions	22,635	1.14	20,539	21,391	21,446	1.04
Wholesale trade, other	22,431	0.59	21,260	23,020	24,844	0.51
State government, except education and hospitals	20,105	0.92	17,020	18,067	18,949	0.72
Nondurable goods manufacturing	18,406	0.24	16,530	17,960	18,491	0.23
Business services, miscellaneous	15,833	1.27	21,191	22,682	23,498	1.13
Transportation and public utilities	15,724	0.28	14,174	15,529	16,193	0.24
Durable goods manufacturing	15,622	0.15	11,907	13,207	14,614	0.14
Education, public and private	14,246	0.15	14,007	14,727	15,279	0.12
Hospitals, public and private	13,235	0.27	13,620	14,299	14,445	0.23
Accounting, auditing, and bookkeeping	12,730	2.49	17,044	18,299	19,101	2.24

Source: National Industry-Occupation Matrix, 1992 [data tape]. Prepared by the Bureau of Labor Statistics. Washington, DC: U.S. Department of Labor, Bureau of Labor Statistics, 1992. *Note:* All employment data are wage and salary employment.

★ 383 ★
Occupational Outlook

Employment Projections for Dining Room and Cafeteria Attendants and Bar Helpers, by Industry: 1992-2005

The National Industry-Occupation Matrix counts jobs, as reflected by data about wage and salary employment collected through the Occupational Employment Statistics surveys. The table below presents employment figures for dining room and cafeteria attendants and bar helpers during 1992; the percent of industry employment for this occupation (staffing patterns) in 1992; low, medium, and high employment projections for 2005; and staffing patterns for the 2005 moderate projection. In 1992, dining room and cafeteria attendants and bar helpers ranked 53 in terms of total employment for individual occupations and ranked 123 when considering total employment of occupational groups as well as individual occupations. Table shows the industries employing the most dining room and cafeteria attendants and bar helpers in 1992.

Industry	1992		2005 employment			Percent of industry employment for 2005 moderate projection
	Employment	Percent of industry employment	Low	Moderate	High	
Total, all industries	440,130	0.40	545,301	571,440	578,849	0.42
Wholesale and retail trade	288,405	1.14	338,415	356,791	358,883	1.15
Retail trade	288,131	1.49	338,096	356,445	358,510	1.50
Eating and drinking places	283,523	4.29	333,179	351,149	353,033	4.00
Services	146,345	0.38	200,698	208,085	213,079	0.38
Hotels and other lodging places	51,406	3.27	68,752	71,084	73,426	3.22
Education, public and private	37,124	0.38	45,624	47,970	49,768	0.38
Health services	26,412	0.27	33,344	34,837	35,195	0.25
Amusement and recreation services	16,045	1.37	24,226	24,663	24,872	1.52
Amusement and recreation services, all other	14,111	1.71	21,993	22,398	22,569	1.86
Hospitals, public and private	13,735	0.28	13,955	14,651	14,801	0.23
Nursing and personal care facilities	12,570	0.81	19,195	19,983	20,190	0.87
Social services	8,519	0.44	19,514	20,096	20,275	0.54
Membership organizations	6,765	0.35	9,156	9,350	9,456	0.39
Residential care	6,654	1.24	16,428	16,909	17,070	1.27
Civic and social associations	5,955	1.42	8,144	8,306	8,402	1.56
Government	5,302	0.06	6,092	6,467	6,783	0.06
Local government, except education and hospitals	2,931	0.07	3,410	3,620	3,796	0.07
State government, except education and hospitals	2,371	0.11	2,682	2,847	2,986	0.11
General merchandise stores	2,060	0.09	2,106	2,269	2,346	0.09
Department stores	1,964	0.10	2,023	2,179	2,254	0.10
Retail stores, miscellaneous	1,341	0.05	1,442	1,553	1,606	0.05
Individual and miscellaneous social services	1,255	0.18	2,138	2,201	2,210	0.19
Nonstore retailers	1,087	0.37	1,150	1,239	1,281	0.39
Bowling centers	1,056	1.20	1,128	1,138	1,152	1.34

Source: National Industry-Occupation Matrix, 1992 [data tape]. Prepared by the Bureau of Labor Statistics. Washington, DC: U.S. Department of Labor, Bureau of Labor Statistics, 1992. *Note:* All employment data are wage and salary employment.

★ 384 ★

Occupational Outlook

Employment Projections for Drafters, by Industry: 1992-2005

The National Industry-Occupation Matrix counts jobs, as reflected by data about wage and salary employment collected through the Occupational Employment Statistics surveys. The table below presents employment figures for drafters during 1992; the percent of industry employment for this occupation (staffing patterns) in 1992; low, medium, and high employment projections for 2005; and staffing patterns for the 2005 moderate projection. In 1992, drafters ranked 85 in terms of total employment for individual occupations and ranked 166 when considering total employment of occupational groups as well as individual occupations. Table shows the industries employing the most drafters in 1992.

Industry	1992		2005 employment			Percent of industry employment for 2005 moderate projection
	Employment	Percent of industry employment	Low	Moderate	High	
Total, all industries	302,172	0.27	310,202	335,593	375,887	0.25
Services	144,910	0.37	173,710	186,968	211,138	0.35
Engineering and management services	112,773	4.57	129,919	140,055	162,693	3.80
Engineering and architectural services	105,108	14.09	119,900	129,344	151,633	12.93
Manufacturing	100,107	0.55	81,486	90,160	100,822	0.51
Durable goods manufacturing	90,407	0.88	71,959	79,801	89,862	0.83
Business services	30,626	0.58	42,021	45,050	46,532	0.54
Industrial machinery and equipment	25,711	1.34	21,123	24,037	27,538	1.29
Transportation and public utilities	17,504	0.31	15,647	16,833	17,436	0.26
Construction	15,918	0.36	17,064	17,773	20,964	0.32
Communications and utilities	15,796	0.71	13,875	14,819	15,345	0.68
Transportation equipment	15,727	0.86	12,454	13,622	14,538	0.77
Personnel supply services	14,715	0.89	21,678	23,242	23,911	0.90
Fabricated metal products	14,285	1.08	11,164	12,006	13,598	1.00
Electronic and other electrical equipment	14,234	0.93	9,966	11,400	13,010	0.84
Business services, miscellaneous	12,310	0.99	15,108	16,171	16,753	0.80
Government	11,335	0.12	10,221	10,847	11,369	0.10
Electric, gas, and sanitary services	10,438	1.09	9,765	10,332	10,752	0.96
Special trade contractors	9,470	0.35	10,230	10,656	12,569	0.31
Fabricated structural metal products	8,996	2.31	6,878	7,332	8,484	2.21
Nondurable goods manufacturing	8,537	0.11	8,318	9,024	9,418	0.11
Instruments and related products	8,371	0.91	6,296	7,025	7,717	0.79
Local government, except education and hospitals	6,789	0.15	6,272	6,658	6,983	0.13
Electric services	6,700	1.52	6,230	6,592	6,860	1.39
Wholesale and retail trade	6,553	0.03	6,557	7,088	7,554	0.02

Source: National Industry-Occupation Matrix, 1992 [data tape]. Prepared by the Bureau of Labor Statistics. Washington, DC: U.S. Department of Labor, Bureau of Labor Statistics, 1992. *Note:* All employment data are wage and salary employment.

★ 385 ★

Occupational Outlook

Employment Projections for Driver/Sales Workers, by Industry: 1992-2005

The National Industry-Occupation Matrix counts jobs, as reflected by data about wage and salary employment collected through the Occupational Employment Statistics surveys. The table below presents employment figures for driver/sales workers during 1992; the percent of industry employment for this occupation (staffing patterns) in 1992; low, medium, and high employment projections for 2005; and staffing patterns for the 2005 moderate projection. In 1992, driver/sales workers ranked 83 in terms of total employment for individual occupations and ranked 162 when considering total employment of occupational groups as well as individual occupations. Table shows the industries employing the most driver/sales workers in 1992.

Industry	1992		2005 employment			Percent of industry employment for 2005 moderate projection
	Employment	Percent of industry employment	Low	Moderate	High	
Total, all industries	309,493	0.28	343,719	366,063	379,073	0.27
Wholesale and retail trade	217,962	0.86	254,805	272,587	284,052	0.88
Retail trade	112,179	0.58	143,821	152,417	154,358	0.64
Wholesale trade	105,783	1.75	110,983	120,170	129,694	1.67
Eating and drinking places	75,064	1.14	107,573	113,374	113,983	1.29
Nondurable goods manufacturing	65,216	0.84	57,670	60,761	61,879	0.77
Manufacturing	65,216	0.36	57,670	60,761	61,879	0.35
Groceries and related products	55,775	6.52	57,586	62,353	67,294	6.40
Food and kindred products	44,623	2.70	34,686	36,024	36,211	2.19
Wholesale trade, other	38,111	1.00	40,636	44,000	47,487	0.97
Retail stores, miscellaneous	32,141	1.30	31,101	33,498	34,642	1.11
Services	26,315	0.07	31,244	32,715	33,142	0.06
Printing and publishing	20,592	1.37	22,984	24,737	25,668	1.41
Nonstore retailers	19,459	6.61	18,539	19,968	20,650	6.23
Personal services	18,390	1.65	19,582	20,309	20,345	1.47
Laundry, cleaning, and garment services	18,084	4.39	19,208	19,930	19,963	4.26
Newspapers	16,721	3.71	18,074	19,439	20,187	3.79
Bakery products	16,272	7.85	10,588	11,070	11,119	5.77
Beverages	12,584	7.19	9,867	10,236	10,307	7.46
Dairy products	8,709	5.72	6,541	6,896	6,927	5.15
Motor vehicles, parts, and supplies	6,482	1.45	6,783	7,345	7,927	1.40
Business services	5,391	0.10	8,001	8,595	8,899	0.10
Used merchandise and retail stores, n.e.c.	5,034	1.00	5,568	5,997	6,201	0.94
Foods and kindred products, miscellaneous	4,737	2.63	5,214	5,244	5,257	2.65
Fuel dealers	4,441	4.43	3,738	4,026	4,163	4.16

Source: National Industry-Occupation Matrix, 1992 [data tape]. Prepared by the Bureau of Labor Statistics. Washington, DC: U.S. Department of Labor, Bureau of Labor Statistics, 1992. *Notes:* All employment data are wage and salary employment. "n.e.c." stands for "not elsewhere classified."

★ 386 ★

Occupational Outlook

Employment Projections for Education Administrators, by Industry: 1992-2005

The National Industry-Occupation Matrix counts jobs, as reflected by data about wage and salary employment collected through the Occupational Employment Statistics surveys. The table below presents employment figures for education administrators during 1992; the percent of industry employment for this occupation (staffing patterns) in 1992; low, medium, and high employment projections for 2005; and staffing patterns for the 2005 moderate projection. In 1992, education administrators ranked 79 in terms of total employment for individual occupations and ranked 157 when considering total employment of occupational groups as well as individual occupations. Table shows the industries employing the most education administrators in 1992.

Industry	1992		2005 employment			Percent of industry employment for 2005 moderate projection
	Employment	Percent of industry employment	Low	Moderate	High	
Total, all industries	319,625	0.29	376,498	394,877	408,245	0.29
Services	313,358	0.81	369,921	387,902	400,941	0.72
Social services	20,779	1.06	36,855	37,895	38,065	1.03
Child day care services	14,144	3.15	25,079	25,735	25,825	3.31
Government	6,266	0.07	6,577	6,976	7,304	0.07
Individual and miscellaneous social services	3,342	0.48	5,691	5,858	5,883	0.50
State government, except education and hospitals	3,019	0.14	3,195	3,392	3,557	0.14
Religious organizations	2,643	0.23	3,332	3,430	3,458	0.24
Job training and related services	2,220	0.82	3,434	3,574	3,603	0.86
Civic and social associations	2,105	0.50	2,878	2,936	2,969	0.55
Local government, except education and hospitals	2,071	0.05	2,277	2,417	2,535	0.05
Business and professional organizations	2,070	1.33	2,911	3,055	3,114	1.53
Federal government	1,176	0.05	1,105	1,167	1,211	0.06
Residential care	1,074	0.20	2,651	2,728	2,754	0.20
Membership organizations, n.e.c.	505	0.60	689	720	733	0.66

Source: National Industry-Occupation Matrix, 1992 [data tape]. Prepared by the Bureau of Labor Statistics. Washington, DC: U.S. Department of Labor, Bureau of Labor Statistics, 1992. *Notes:* All employment data are wage and salary employment. "n.e.c." stands for "not elsewhere classified."

★ 387 ★

Occupational Outlook

Employment Projections for Electrical and Electronic Engineers, by Industry: 1992-2005

The National Industry-Occupation Matrix counts jobs, as reflected by data about wage and salary employment collected through the Occupational Employment Statistics surveys. The table below presents employment figures for electrical and electronic engineers during 1992; the percent of industry employment for this occupation (staffing patterns) in 1992; low, medium, and high employment projections for 2005; and staffing patterns for the 2005 moderate projection. In 1992, electrical and electronic engineers ranked 68 in terms of total employment for individual occupations and ranked 141 when considering total employment of occupational groups as well as individual occupations. Table shows the industries employing the most electrical and electronic engineers in 1992.

Industry	1992		2005 employment			Percent of industry employment for 2005 moderate projection
	Employment	Percent of industry employment	Low	Moderate	High	
Total, all industries	363,945	0.33	413,842	451,460	492,417	0.33
Manufacturing	167,576	0.93	146,024	165,353	187,685	0.94
Durable goods manufacturing	160,485	1.57	138,842	157,547	179,566	1.63
Services	78,670	0.20	126,923	135,253	144,530	0.25
Electronic and other electrical equipment	54,632	3.58	46,144	53,462	61,476	3.95
Engineering and management services	53,866	2.18	83,914	89,132	96,622	2.42
Instruments and related products	50,098	5.42	44,643	49,543	54,818	5.58
Government	39,848	0.42	39,409	41,668	43,344	0.40
Wholesale and retail trade	35,545	0.14	55,214	59,770	64,385	0.19
Transportation and public utilities	34,464	0.60	35,820	38,467	39,741	0.59
Wholesale trade	33,655	0.56	52,696	57,058	61,580	0.79
Communications and utilities	33,645	1.51	34,899	37,423	38,657	1.71
Federal government	33,186	1.52	31,987	33,788	35,077	1.64
Wholesale trade, other	31,878	0.84	50,397	54,569	58,894	1.20
Industrial machinery and equipment	30,509	1.59	22,787	26,975	33,541	1.44
Search and navigation equipment	27,918	12.24	26,691	29,400	32,763	16.59
Engineering and architectural services	25,687	3.44	34,071	36,754	43,088	3.67
Research and testing services	23,663	4.24	41,921	43,809	44,627	5.79
Electronic components and accessories	22,881	4.36	23,510	27,823	32,492	5.31
Transportation equipment	20,805	1.14	21,176	23,098	24,854	1.31
Computer and office equipment	20,662	5.28	12,664	15,493	20,494	5.89
Business services	18,814	0.35	34,592	37,297	38,847	0.45
Communications equipment	17,897	7.56	11,122	12,707	14,401	6.47
Electric, gas, and sanitary services	16,972	1.78	19,543	20,676	21,517	1.93
Communications	16,673	1.32	15,356	16,746	17,140	1.50

Source: National Industry-Occupation Matrix, 1992 [data tape]. Prepared by the Bureau of Labor Statistics. Washington, DC: U.S. Department of Labor, Bureau of Labor Statistics, 1992. *Note:* All employment data are wage and salary employment.

★ 388 ★

Occupational Outlook

Employment Projections for Electricians, by Industry: 1992-2005

The National Industry-Occupation Matrix counts jobs, as reflected by data about wage and salary employment collected through the Occupational Employment Statistics surveys. The table below presents employment figures for electricians during 1992; the percent of industry employment for this occupation (staffing patterns) in 1992; low, medium, and high employment projections for 2005; and staffing patterns for the 2005 moderate projection. In 1992, electricians ranked 50 in terms of total employment for individual occupations and ranked 120 when considering total employment of occupational groups as well as individual occupations. Table shows the industries employing the most electricians in 1992.

Industry	1992		2005 employment			Percent of industry employment for 2005 moderate projection
	Employment	Percent of industry employment	Low	Moderate	High	
Total, all industries	459,014	0.41	518,441	546,236	621,139	0.40
Construction	269,307	6.02	338,051	352,108	415,323	6.25
Special trade contractors	252,941	9.38	319,331	332,610	392,324	9.71
Electrical work	244,321	49.16	309,531	322,402	380,284	49.72
Manufacturing	100,874	0.56	86,422	94,395	101,538	0.54
Durable goods manufacturing	67,687	0.66	56,367	61,931	68,052	0.64
Nondurable goods manufacturing	33,367	0.43	30,258	32,683	33,695	0.42
Services	32,436	0.08	40,670	42,926	44,245	0.08
Government	31,992	0.34	30,163	31,989	33,471	0.31
Transportation equipment	22,053	1.21	18,369	20,133	21,435	1.14
Local government, except education and hospitals	18,633	0.42	18,443	19,578	20,534	0.38
Primary metal industries	13,527	1.95	10,798	12,012	13,227	1.95
Motor vehicles and equipment	12,473	1.54	10,611	11,739	12,630	1.55
Transportation and public utilities	11,338	0.20	10,838	11,585	12,139	0.18
General building contractors	10,589	1.00	12,281	12,792	15,088	0.99
Federal government	8,893	0.41	7,516	7,939	8,242	0.38
Chemicals and allied products	8,514	0.79	7,249	7,887	8,200	0.72
Education, public and private	8,282	0.09	9,161	9,632	9,993	0.08
Nonresidential building construction	7,760	1.50	9,034	9,410	11,099	1.47
Industrial machinery and equipment	7,723	0.40	6,797	7,695	8,735	0.41
Communications and utilities	7,510	0.34	7,655	8,104	8,427	0.37
Business services	7,206	0.14	10,254	10,981	11,354	0.13
Electric, gas, and sanitary services	7,198	0.75	7,377	7,805	8,122	0.73
Mining	6,932	1.10	5,620	6,146	6,930	1.09
Fabricated metal products	6,912	0.52	5,771	6,242	6,771	0.52

Source: National Industry-Occupation Matrix, 1992 [data tape]. Prepared by the Bureau of Labor Statistics. Washington, DC: U.S. Department of Labor, Bureau of Labor Statistics, 1992. *Note:* All employment data are wage and salary employment.

★ 389 ★

Occupational Outlook

Employment Projections for Elementary School Teachers, by Industry: 1992-2005

The National Industry-Occupation Matrix counts jobs, as reflected by data about wage and salary employment collected through the Occupational Employment Statistics surveys. The table below presents employment figures for elementary school teachers during 1992; the percent of industry employment for this occupation (staffing patterns) in 1992; low, medium, and high employment projections for 2005; and staffing patterns for the 2005 moderate projection. In 1992, elementary school teachers ranked 16 in terms of total employment for individual occupations and ranked 54 when considering total employment of occupational groups as well as individual occupations. Table shows the industries employing the most elementary school teachers in 1992.

Industry	1992		2005 employment			Percent of industry employment for 2005 moderate projection
	Employment	Percent of industry employment	Low	Moderate	High	
Total, all industries	1,456,156	1.31	1,682,632	1,766,719	1,829,649	1.30
Services	1,456,156	3.77	1,682,632	1,766,719	1,829,649	3.26
Religious organizations	70,853	6.15	87,589	90,162	90,897	6.35
Social services	10,589	0.54	19,411	19,936	20,031	0.54
Child day care services	8,026	1.79	13,954	14,318	14,369	1.84
Residential care	1,575	0.29	3,814	3,925	3,963	0.29
Individual and miscellaneous social services	949	0.13	1,584	1,631	1,638	0.14
Civic and social associations	377	0.09	505	516	521	0.10

Source: National Industry-Occupation Matrix, 1992 [data tape]. Prepared by the Bureau of Labor Statistics. Washington, DC: U.S. Department of Labor, Bureau of Labor Statistics, 1992. *Note:* All employment data are wage and salary employment.

★ 390 ★
Occupational Outlook

Employment Projections for Engineering, Mathematical, and Natural Science Managers, by Industry: 1992-2005

The National Industry-Occupation Matrix counts jobs, as reflected by data about wage and salary employment collected through the Occupational Employment Statistics surveys. The table below presents employment figures for engineering, mathematical, and natural science managers during 1992; the percent of industry employment for this occupation (staffing patterns) in 1992; low, medium, and high employment projections for 2005; and staffing patterns for the 2005 moderate projection. In 1992, engineering, mathematical, and natural science managers ranked 75 in terms of total employment for individual occupations and ranked 151 when considering total employment of occupational groups as well as individual occupations. Table shows the industries employing the most engineering, mathematical, and natural science managers in 1992.

Industry	1992		2005 employment			Percent of industry employment for 2005 moderate projection
	Employment	Percent of industry employment	Low	Moderate	High	
Total, all industries	337,365	0.30	409,953	443,651	476,161	0.33
Manufacturing	132,396	0.73	129,520	144,194	159,096	0.82
Durable goods manufacturing	100,670	0.98	92,921	104,625	118,180	1.08
Services	99,053	0.26	158,548	169,436	180,631	0.31
Engineering and management services	53,607	2.17	80,354	85,865	94,103	2.33
Government	43,426	0.45	45,549	48,239	50,301	0.46
Nondurable goods manufacturing	31,846	0.41	36,761	39,740	41,065	0.51
Industrial machinery and equipment	28,184	1.47	23,772	27,616	33,093	1.48
Business services	27,674	0.52	52,920	57,074	59,488	0.68
Federal government	27,614	1.27	27,579	29,131	30,243	1.41
Engineering and architectural services	26,081	3.50	37,670	40,637	47,640	4.06
Computer and data processing services	23,815	2.87	46,354	50,031	52,195	3.08
Electronic and other electrical equipment	21,042	1.38	19,027	21,953	25,139	1.62
Finance, insurance, and real estate	20,536	0.31	26,582	28,070	28,226	0.35
Transportation equipment	18,905	1.04	19,271	21,055	22,625	1.19
Instruments and related products	18,755	2.03	16,766	18,648	20,472	2.10
Transportation and public utilities	18,417	0.32	20,925	22,593	23,372	0.35
Research and testing services	18,071	3.24	25,517	26,666	27,164	3.52
Wholesale and retail trade	16,138	0.06	20,343	21,995	23,536	0.07
Communications and utilities	15,684	0.71	17,596	18,828	19,443	0.86
Chemicals and allied products	14,100	1.30	15,765	17,060	17,585	1.56
Computer and office equipment	13,533	3.46	7,813	9,559	12,644	3.63
Wholesale trade	12,977	0.21	16,442	17,803	19,214	0.25
Wholesale trade, other	10,578	0.28	13,329	14,432	15,576	0.32
Aircraft and parts	10,287	1.68	10,713	11,674	12,564	1.85

Source: National Industry-Occupation Matrix, 1992 [data tape]. Prepared by the Bureau of Labor Statistics. Washington, DC: U.S. Department of Labor, Bureau of Labor Statistics, 1992. *Note:* All employment data are wage and salary employment.

★ 391 ★

Occupational Outlook

Employment Projections for Engineering Technicians, by Industry: 1992-2005

The National Industry-Occupation Matrix counts jobs, as reflected by data about wage and salary employment collected through the Occupational Employment Statistics surveys. The table below presents employment figures for engineering technicians during 1992; the percent of industry employment for this occupation (staffing patterns) in 1992; low, medium, and high employment projections for 2005; and staffing patterns for the 2005 moderate projection. In 1992, engineering technicians ranked 38 in terms of total employment for individual occupations and ranked 99 when considering total employment of occupational groups as well as individual occupations. Table shows the industries employing the most engineering technicians in 1992.

Industry	1992		2005 employment			Percent of industry employment for 2005 moderate projection
	Employment	Percent of industry employment	Low	Moderate	High	
Total, all industries	684,908	0.62	750,718	816,226	886,821	0.60
Manufacturing	260,066	1.44	233,081	262,515	293,484	1.50
Durable goods manufacturing	231,393	2.26	203,375	230,201	259,920	2.38
Services	161,997	0.42	239,024	255,443	276,054	0.47
Government	117,097	1.23	109,901	116,394	121,460	1.11
Engineering and management services	97,373	3.94	135,576	144,981	161,732	3.93
Wholesale and retail trade	73,517	0.29	90,197	97,645	105,228	0.32
Wholesale trade	70,946	1.17	86,998	94,200	101,665	1.31
Electronic and other electrical equipment	69,929	4.58	63,428	73,629	84,659	5.44
Wholesale trade, other	60,658	1.59	73,753	79,858	86,187	1.76
Engineering and architectural services	60,512	8.11	82,852	89,378	104,780	8.93
Federal government	59,024	2.71	55,969	59,119	61,375	2.86
Transportation and public utilities	52,549	0.92	55,269	59,412	61,438	0.91
Instruments and related products	47,788	5.17	40,678	45,370	49,697	5.11
Communications and utilities	47,601	2.14	49,927	53,397	55,169	2.44
Industrial machinery and equipment	46,266	2.41	35,153	41,075	49,855	2.20
Transportation equipment	45,574	2.50	43,837	47,997	51,557	2.72
Business services	40,941	0.77	72,088	77,574	80,472	0.93
Electronic components and accessories	37,594	7.16	37,401	44,262	51,691	8.44
State government, except education and hospitals	29,781	1.36	22,790	24,192	25,373	0.97
Nondurable goods manufacturing	29,234	0.37	30,411	33,080	34,344	0.42
Research and testing services	28,887	5.18	38,911	40,663	41,422	5.37
Local government, except education and hospitals	27,738	0.63	30,676	32,563	34,153	0.63
Computer and office equipment	25,914	6.62	14,378	17,591	23,268	6.68
Electric, gas, and sanitary services	25,913	2.71	29,189	30,882	32,138	2.88

Source: National Industry-Occupation Matrix, 1992 [data tape]. Prepared by the Bureau of Labor Statistics. Washington, DC: U.S. Department of Labor, Bureau of Labor Statistics, 1992. *Note:* All employment data are wage and salary employment.

★ 392 ★

Occupational Outlook

Employment Projections for Engineers, by Industry: 1992-2005

The National Industry-Occupation Matrix counts jobs, as reflected by data about wage and salary employment collected through the Occupational Employment Statistics surveys. The table below presents employment figures for engineers (nonspecific) during 1992; the percent of industry employment for this occupation (staffing patterns) in 1992; low, medium, and high employment projections for 2005; and staffing patterns for the 2005 moderate projection. In 1992, engineers ranked 90 in terms of total employment for individual occupations and ranked 174 when considering total employment of occupational groups as well as individual occupations. Table shows the industries employing the most engineers in 1992.

Industry	1992		2005 employment			Percent of industry employment for 2005 moderate projection
	Employment	Percent of industry employment	Low	Moderate	High	
Total, all industries	284,543	0.26	337,803	367,016	395,209	0.27
Manufacturing	150,052	0.83	161,774	179,005	195,708	1.02
Durable goods manufacturing	131,063	1.28	140,041	155,466	171,270	1.61
Transportation equipment	74,828	4.11	77,158	84,473	90,859	4.78
Services	53,885	0.14	81,920	87,479	93,552	0.16
Government	39,525	0.41	43,179	45,704	47,622	0.44
Engineering and management services	29,326	1.19	41,401	44,329	49,091	1.20
Federal government	27,476	1.26	28,816	30,438	31,600	1.47
Motor vehicles and equipment	27,030	3.34	23,779	26,306	28,305	3.47
Aircraft and parts	26,090	4.27	30,911	33,684	36,252	5.35
Guided missiles, space vehicles, and parts	19,657	13.55	20,279	22,098	23,783	15.12
Nondurable goods manufacturing	19,400	0.25	22,308	24,163	25,069	0.31
Transportation and public utilities	18,286	0.32	20,477	22,123	22,954	0.34
Engineering and architectural services	17,895	2.40	22,618	24,399	28,604	2.44
Electronic and other electrical equipment	17,687	1.16	20,426	23,290	26,310	1.72
Communications and utilities	16,017	0.72	18,079	19,384	20,039	0.89
Instruments and related products	14,472	1.57	16,834	18,690	20,577	2.11
Business services	14,266	0.27	26,600	28,555	29,463	0.34
Industrial machinery and equipment	13,603	0.71	14,767	17,162	20,703	0.92
Personnel supply services	11,239	0.68	20,609	22,096	22,732	0.86
Wholesale and retail trade	9,451	0.04	12,559	13,591	14,612	0.04
Electric, gas, and sanitary services	8,562	0.90	10,812	11,439	11,905	1.07
Wholesale trade	8,561	0.14	11,402	12,345	13,324	0.17
Chemicals and allied products	8,548	0.79	9,214	10,014	10,379	0.92
Communications	7,455	0.59	7,267	7,945	8,134	0.71

Source: National Industry-Occupation Matrix, 1992 [data tape]. Prepared by the Bureau of Labor Statistics. Washington, DC: U.S. Department of Labor, Bureau of Labor Statistics, 1992. *Note:* All employment data are wage and salary employment.

★ 393 ★
Occupational Outlook

Employment Projections for Farm Workers, by Industry: 1992-2005

The National Industry-Occupation Matrix counts jobs, as reflected by data about wage and salary employment collected through the Occupational Employment Statistics surveys. The table below presents employment figures for farm workers during 1992; the percent of industry employment for this occupation (staffing patterns) in 1992; low, medium, and high employment projections for 2005; and staffing patterns for the 2005 moderate projection. In 1992, farm workers ranked 34 in terms of total employment for individual occupations and ranked 92 when considering total employment of occupational groups as well as individual occupations. Table shows the industries employing the most farm workers in 1992.

Industry	1992		2005 employment			Percent of industry employment for 2005 moderate projection
	Employment	Percent of industry employment	Low	Moderate	High	
Total, all industries	726,000	0.66	626,338	644,396	681,603	0.47
Agriculture, forestry, and fishing	726,000	41.72	626,338	644,396	681,603	32.64

Source: National Industry-Occupation Matrix, 1992 [data tape]. Prepared by the Bureau of Labor Statistics. Washington, DC: U.S. Department of Labor, Bureau of Labor Statistics, 1992. *Note:* All employment data are wage and salary employment.

★ 394 ★
Occupational Outlook

Employment Projections for File Clerks, by Industry: 1992-2005

The National Industry-Occupation Matrix counts jobs, as reflected by data about wage and salary employment collected through the Occupational Employment Statistics surveys. The table below presents employment figures for file clerks during 1992; the percent of industry employment for this occupation (staffing patterns) in 1992; low, medium, and high employment projections for 2005; and staffing patterns for the 2005 moderate projection. In 1992, file clerks ranked 100 in terms of total employment for individual occupations and ranked 185 when considering total employment of occupational groups as well as individual occupations. Table shows the industries employing the most file clerks in 1992.

Industry	1992		2005 employment			Percent of industry employment for 2005 moderate projection
	Employment	Percent of industry employment	Low	Moderate	High	
Total, all industries	254,696	0.23	285,722	303,164	310,853	0.22
Services	135,277	0.35	174,472	184,005	188,053	0.34
Health services	58,655	0.61	86,560	90,395	91,552	0.66
Finance, insurance, and real estate	55,464	0.84	55,008	58,546	58,701	0.73
Business services	35,692	0.67	44,912	48,181	49,700	0.58
Offices of physicians, including osteopaths	30,431	2.00	56,987	59,429	60,257	2.52
Insurance carriers	26,687	1.80	22,982	24,628	24,639	1.48
Personnel supply services	26,485	1.61	33,167	35,561	36,583	1.38
Government	24,484	0.26	24,283	25,781	27,042	0.25
Hospitals, public and private	19,085	0.39	18,725	19,659	19,860	0.31
Local government, except education and hospitals	18,807	0.43	19,722	20,935	21,957	0.41
Legal services	17,028	1.86	17,359	18,386	18,715	1.36

[Continued]

★ 394 ★

Employment Projections for File Clerks, by Industry: 1992-2005

[Continued]

Industry	1992		2005 employment			Percent of industry employment for 2005 moderate projection
	Employment	Percent of industry employment	Low	Moderate	High	
Insurance agents, brokers, and service	14,559	2.23	18,319	19,645	19,657	2.02
Fire, marine, and casualty insurance	13,562	2.45	11,114	11,910	11,915	1.99
Manufacturing	13,151	0.07	10,240	11,261	12,084	0.06
Transportation and public utilities	12,039	0.21	9,390	10,249	10,617	0.16
Wholesale and retail trade	11,804	0.05	10,321	11,149	11,812	0.04
Depository institutions	9,143	0.43	7,920	8,249	8,270	0.38
Engineering and management services	9,086	0.37	10,814	11,598	12,245	0.31
Commercial banks, savings institutions, and credit unions	8,650	0.44	7,484	7,794	7,814	0.38
Communications and utilities	8,404	0.38	6,168	6,682	6,874	0.31
Durable goods manufacturing	7,254	0.07	5,228	5,825	6,471	0.06
Wholesale trade	6,372	0.11	5,797	6,276	6,774	0.09
Communications	6,267	0.49	4,353	4,761	4,875	0.43
Life insurance	6,173	1.15	5,550	5,948	5,950	0.96

Source: National Industry-Occupation Matrix, 1992 [data tape]. Prepared by the Bureau of Labor Statistics. Washington, DC: U.S. Department of Labor, Bureau of Labor Statistics, 1992. *Note:* All employment data are wage and salary employment.

★ 395 ★

Occupational Outlook

Employment Projections for Financial Managers, by Industry: 1992-2005

The National Industry-Occupation Matrix counts jobs, as reflected by data about wage and salary employment collected through the Occupational Employment Statistics surveys. The table below presents employment figures for financial managers during 1992; the percent of industry employment for this occupation (staffing patterns) in 1992; low, medium, and high employment projections for 2005; and staffing patterns for the 2005 moderate projection. In 1992, financial managers ranked 37 in terms of total employment for individual occupations and ranked 98 when considering total employment of occupational groups as well as individual occupations. Table shows the industries employing the most financial managers in 1992.

Industry	1992		2005 employment			Percent of industry employment for 2005 moderate projection
	Employment	Percent of industry employment	Low	Moderate	High	
Total, all industries	693,366	0.63	818,444	865,424	906,162	0.64
Finance, insurance, and real estate	229,308	3.49	270,212	282,488	285,205	3.54
Services	218,421	0.57	293,531	308,601	318,177	0.57
Depository institutions	127,128	6.04	129,789	135,173	135,523	6.16
Commercial banks, savings institutions, and credit unions	122,724	6.19	125,191	130,385	130,722	6.33
Manufacturing	97,803	0.54	87,222	96,185	104,777	0.55
Durable goods manufacturing	64,958	0.63	54,917	61,255	68,707	0.63
Construction	57,573	1.29	67,436	70,240	82,850	1.25
Business services	38,513	0.72	55,978	60,170	62,502	0.72
Health services	38,134	0.40	51,768	54,054	54,664	0.39
Wholesale and retail trade	37,230	0.15	47,720	51,563	54,930	0.17
Engineering and management services	35,566	1.44	50,008	53,739	57,126	1.46

[Continued]

★ 395 ★

Employment Projections for Financial Managers, by Industry: 1992-2005
[Continued]

Industry	1992		2005 employment			Percent of industry employment for 2005 moderate projection
	Employment	Percent of industry employment	Low	Moderate	High	
Special trade contractors	34,707	1.29	41,281	42,998	50,717	1.26
Nondurable goods manufacturing	32,864	0.42	32,329	34,951	36,056	0.45
Membership organizations	27,949	1.43	30,472	31,330	31,696	1.31
Nondepository institutions	26,685	6.76	36,429	37,550	37,882	6.49
Government	26,472	0.28	27,804	29,508	30,899	0.28
Real estate	24,003	1.87	28,744	29,643	31,265	1.83
Wholesale trade	23,571	0.39	33,619	36,402	39,287	0.51
Transportation and public utilities	19,248	0.34	18,737	20,418	21,177	0.31
Social services	17,727	0.91	29,852	30,741	30,925	0.83
Industrial machinery and equipment	17,623	0.92	14,880	17,004	19,721	0.91
Management and public relations	16,236	2.48	24,978	27,020	28,086	2.44
Security and commodity brokers	16,212	3.69	27,045	29,194	29,426	5.12
General building contractors	15,987	1.50	18,269	19,029	22,445	1.47

Source: National Industry-Occupation Matrix, 1992 [data tape]. Prepared by the Bureau of Labor Statistics. Washington, DC: U.S. Department of Labor, Bureau of Labor Statistics, 1992. *Note:* All employment data are wage and salary employment.

★ 396 ★
Occupational Outlook

Employment Projections for Firefighters, by Industry: 1992-2005

The National Industry-Occupation Matrix counts jobs, as reflected by data about wage and salary employment collected through the Occupational Employment Statistics surveys. The table below presents employment figures for firefighters during 1992; the percent of industry employment for this occupation (staffing patterns) in 1992; low, medium, and high employment projections for 2005; and staffing patterns for the 2005 moderate projection. In 1992, firefighters ranked 108 in terms of total employment for individual occupations and ranked 193 when considering total employment of occupational groups as well as individual occupations. Table shows the industries employing the most firefighters in 1992.

Industry	1992		2005 employment			Percent of industry employment for 2005 moderate projection
	Employment	Percent of industry employment	Low	Moderate	High	
Total, all industries	229,166	0.21	251,722	267,142	280,128	0.20
Government	227,967	2.39	250,810	266,196	279,090	2.55
Local government, except education and hospitals	212,164	4.83	235,094	249,559	261,742	4.85
Private households	1,000	0.09	633	654	695	0.08
Services	1,000	0.00	633	654	695	0.00
Agriculture, forestry, and fishing	199	0.01	278	292	343	0.01

Source: National Industry-Occupation Matrix, 1992 [data tape]. Prepared by the Bureau of Labor Statistics. Washington, DC: U.S. Department of Labor, Bureau of Labor Statistics, 1992. *Note:* All employment data are wage and salary employment.

★ 397 ★

Occupational Outlook

Employment Projections for Food Counter, Fountain, and Related Workers, by Industry: 1992-2005

The National Industry-Occupation Matrix counts jobs, as reflected by data about wage and salary employment collected through the Occupational Employment Statistics surveys. The table below presents employment figures for food counter, fountain, and related workers during 1992; the percent of industry employment for this occupation (staffing patterns) in 1992; low, medium, and high employment projections for 2005; and staffing patterns for the 2005 moderate projection. In 1992, food counter, fountain, and related workers ranked 15 in terms of total employment for individual occupations and ranked 52 when considering total employment of occupational groups as well as individual occupations. Table shows the industries employing the most food counter, fountain, and related workers in 1992.

Industry	1992		2005 employment			Percent of industry employment for 2005 moderate projection
	Employment	Percent of industry employment	Low	Moderate	High	
Total, all industries	1,561,112	1.41	1,773,390	1,869,445	1,891,745	1.38
Wholesale and retail trade	1,320,649	5.20	1,458,140	1,541,526	1,556,283	4.98
Retail trade	1,317,756	6.81	1,454,809	1,537,919	1,552,391	6.47
Eating and drinking places	1,171,174	17.74	1,254,076	1,321,714	1,328,807	15.06
Services	227,292	0.59	302,882	314,856	321,900	0.58
Food stores	125,831	3.96	179,132	192,939	199,525	4.97
Grocery stores	80,367	2.83	123,963	133,518	138,075	3.84
Health services	69,392	0.72	79,271	82,976	83,827	0.60
Hospitals, public and private	50,916	1.05	51,007	53,552	54,099	0.85
Education, public and private	50,461	0.52	62,014	65,202	67,647	0.52
Hotels and other lodging places	40,951	2.60	71,485	73,909	76,344	3.35
Amusement and recreation services	37,529	3.21	55,371	56,352	56,858	3.47
Retail bakeries	31,271	19.01	38,273	41,223	42,630	20.92
Amusement and recreation services, all other	29,778	3.61	46,415	47,269	47,630	3.92
Motion pictures	27,284	6.75	32,184	33,787	34,571	6.77
Motion picture theaters	27,067	24.86	31,915	33,504	34,282	28.39
Nursing and personal care facilities	18,302	1.19	27,949	29,096	29,398	1.26
Federal government	13,171	0.60	12,367	13,064	13,562	0.63
Government	13,171	0.14	12,367	13,064	13,562	0.12
Food stores, n.e.c.	11,528	9.30	14,205	15,300	15,822	9.61
Retail stores, miscellaneous	11,327	0.46	12,331	13,282	13,735	0.44
General merchandise stores	8,549	0.35	8,263	8,900	9,203	0.34
Nonstore retailers	7,502	2.55	7,941	8,553	8,845	2.67
Department stores	5,378	0.26	5,542	5,969	6,172	0.26
Bowling centers	3,935	4.48	4,204	4,241	4,294	4.99

Source: National Industry-Occupation Matrix, 1992 [data tape]. Prepared by the Bureau of Labor Statistics. Washington, DC: U.S. Department of Labor, Bureau of Labor Statistics, 1992. *Notes:* All employment data are wage and salary employment. "n.e.c." stands for "not elsewhere classified."

★ 398 ★

Occupational Outlook

Employment Projections for Food Preparation Workers, by Industry: 1992-2005

The National Industry-Occupation Matrix counts jobs, as reflected by data about wage and salary employment collected through the Occupational Employment Statistics surveys. The table below presents employment figures for food preparation workers during 1992; the percent of industry employment for this occupation (staffing patterns) in 1992; low, medium, and high employment projections for 2005; and staffing patterns for the 2005 moderate projection. In 1992, food preparation workers ranked 21 in terms of total employment for individual occupations and ranked 64 when considering total employment of occupational groups as well as individual occupations. Table shows the industries employing the most food preparation workers in 1992.

Industry	1992		2005 employment			Percent of industry employment for 2005 moderate projection
	Employment	Percent of industry employment	Low	Moderate	High	
Total, all industries	1,220,224	1.10	1,658,332	1,744,685	1,771,674	1.29
Wholesale and retail trade	766,436	3.02	1,056,784	1,118,194	1,130,645	3.61
Retail trade	755,093	3.90	1,043,688	1,104,015	1,115,342	4.64
Eating and drinking places	620,647	9.40	869,303	916,188	921,105	10.44
Services	430,734	1.11	576,536	599,943	613,185	1.11
Health services	148,177	1.54	180,213	188,173	190,111	1.36
Food stores	110,359	3.47	148,495	159,941	165,400	4.12
Grocery stores	98,905	3.48	135,607	146,059	151,044	4.20
Nursing and personal care facilities	83,614	5.42	114,916	119,634	120,873	5.19
Hospitals, public and private	63,555	1.31	63,518	66,687	67,368	1.06
Social services	29,089	1.49	61,533	63,353	63,842	1.72
Government	22,953	0.24	24,893	26,425	27,715	0.25
Amusement and recreation services	18,605	1.59	28,335	28,852	29,094	1.77
Amusement and recreation services, all other	16,826	2.04	26,230	26,713	26,917	2.22
Residential care	15,734	2.94	38,845	39,983	40,364	3.00
Local government, except education and hospitals	14,531	0.33	15,981	16,964	17,793	0.33
Religious organizations	13,716	1.19	17,293	17,801	17,946	1.25
Wholesale trade	11,344	0.19	13,095	14,179	15,303	0.20
Civic and social associations	10,459	2.49	14,303	14,587	14,755	2.75
Retail stores, miscellaneous	10,173	0.41	10,840	11,675	12,074	0.39
Automotive dealers and service stations	9,737	0.49	10,789	11,621	12,017	0.52
Gasoline service stations	9,605	1.56	10,644	11,465	11,856	1.81
Groceries and related products	8,937	1.04	10,252	11,101	11,980	1.14
State government, except education and hospitals	8,422	0.39	8,912	9,461	9,923	0.38
Nonstore retailers	7,469	2.54	7,907	8,516	8,807	2.66

Source: National Industry-Occupation Matrix, 1992 [data tape]. Prepared by the Bureau of Labor Statistics. Washington, DC: U.S. Department of Labor, Bureau of Labor Statistics, 1992. *Note:* All employment data are wage and salary employment.

★ 399 ★
Occupational Outlook

Employment Projections for Food Service and Lodging Managers, by Industry: 1992-2005

The National Industry-Occupation Matrix counts jobs, as reflected by data about wage and salary employment collected through the Occupational Employment Statistics surveys. The table below presents employment figures for food service and lodging managers during 1992; the percent of industry employment for this occupation (staffing patterns) in 1992; low, medium, and high employment projections for 2005; and staffing patterns for the 2005 moderate projection. In 1992, food service and lodging managers ranked 76 in terms of total employment for individual occupations and ranked 152 when considering total employment of occupational groups as well as individual occupations. Table shows the industries employing the most food service and lodging managers in 1992.

Industry	1992		2005 employment			Percent of industry employment for 2005 moderate projection
	Employment	Percent of industry employment	Low	Moderate	High	
Total, all industries	336,054	0.30	468,554	491,633	497,179	0.36
Wholesale and retail trade	232,863	0.92	332,079	350,113	352,196	1.13
Retail trade	232,049	1.20	331,131	349,086	351,088	1.47
Eating and drinking places	228,167	3.46	326,982	344,618	346,467	3.93
Services	96,426	0.25	127,620	132,380	135,356	0.24
Hotels and other lodging places	35,974	2.29	39,248	40,578	41,915	1.84
Education, public and private	21,991	0.23	27,026	28,415	29,481	0.23
Health services	16,384	0.17	23,220	24,260	24,509	0.18
Social services	11,547	0.59	23,318	24,000	24,166	0.65
Nursing and personal care facilities	8,454	0.55	12,910	13,440	13,579	0.58
Hospitals, public and private	7,644	0.16	9,833	10,324	10,429	0.16
Finance, insurance, and real estate	6,765	0.10	8,854	9,140	9,628	0.11
Real estate	6,579	0.51	8,634	8,904	9,392	0.55
Membership organizations	5,571	0.29	7,488	7,655	7,743	0.32
Residential care	4,694	0.88	11,589	11,929	12,043	0.89
Amusement and recreation services	4,508	0.39	6,832	6,957	7,017	0.43
Individual and miscellaneous social services	4,458	0.63	7,592	7,815	7,849	0.67
Civic and social associations	4,447	1.06	6,081	6,202	6,273	1.17
Real estate operators and lessors	3,998	0.72	5,016	5,173	5,456	0.78
Amusement and recreation services, all other	3,990	0.48	6,221	6,335	6,384	0.53
Real estate agents and managers	2,300	0.40	3,303	3,406	3,592	0.43
General merchandise stores	1,987	0.08	2,017	2,172	2,246	0.08
Child day care services	1,911	0.43	3,389	3,478	3,490	0.45
Department stores	1,810	0.09	1,865	2,008	2,077	0.09
Retail stores, miscellaneous	869	0.04	956	1,030	1,065	0.03

Source: National Industry-Occupation Matrix, 1992 [data tape]. Prepared by the Bureau of Labor Statistics. Washington, DC: U.S. Department of Labor, Bureau of Labor Statistics, 1992. *Note:* All employment data are wage and salary employment.

★ 400 ★

Occupational Outlook

Employment Projections for Gardeners and Groundskeepers, by Industry: 1992-2005

The National Industry-Occupation Matrix counts jobs, as reflected by data about wage and salary employment collected through the Occupational Employment Statistics surveys. The table below presents employment figures for gardeners and groundskeepers—excluding farm gardeners and groundskeepers—during 1992; the percent of industry employment for this occupation (staffing patterns) in 1992; low, medium, and high employment projections for 2005; and staffing patterns for the 2005 moderate projection. In 1992, gardeners and groundskeepers ranked 35 in terms of total employment for individual occupations and ranked 94 when considering total employment of occupational groups as well as individual occupations. Table shows the industries employing the most gardeners and groundskeepers in 1992.

Industry	1992		2005 employment			Percent of industry employment for 2005 moderate projection
	Employment	Percent of industry employment	Low	Moderate	High	
Total, all industries	702,951	0.63	903,003	938,051	987,083	0.69
Agriculture, forestry, and fishing	278,379	16.00	422,211	437,229	466,425	22.15
Services	249,223	0.64	272,815	282,859	290,276	0.52
Government	80,859	0.85	88,343	93,770	98,329	0.90
Finance, insurance, and real estate	71,981	1.10	93,790	96,759	101,863	1.21
Local government, except education and hospitals	71,745	1.63	78,904	83,759	87,848	1.63
Private households	71,000	6.36	35,707	36,852	39,199	4.60
Real estate	69,458	5.42	89,970	92,784	97,862	5.71
Amusement and recreation services	53,522	4.58	66,766	67,996	68,553	4.18
Amusement and recreation services, all other	50,964	6.17	63,583	64,753	65,248	5.37
Real estate operators and lessors	28,756	5.16	32,483	33,499	35,333	5.04
Membership organizations	23,429	1.20	30,387	31,223	31,529	1.31
Real estate, all other	23,396	16.10	29,514	30,437	32,103	18.45
Real estate agents and managers	17,306	2.99	27,973	28,848	30,427	3.64
Hotels and other lodging places	16,728	1.06	24,334	25,160	25,988	1.14
Religious organizations	15,335	1.33	19,334	19,902	20,064	1.40
Business services	14,197	0.27	21,039	22,544	23,232	0.27
Wholesale and retail trade	12,352	0.05	13,439	14,462	15,012	0.05
Health services	11,944	0.12	16,771	17,537	17,738	0.13
Retail trade	10,891	0.06	11,690	12,569	12,968	0.05
Construction	9,053	0.20	11,290	11,760	13,871	0.21
Building materials and garden supplies	7,506	1.02	7,530	8,110	8,387	0.96
State government, except education and hospitals	7,380	0.34	7,810	8,291	8,695	0.33
Retail nurseries and garden stores	7,153	8.54	7,138	7,689	7,951	6.87
Personnel supply services	7,134	0.43	11,713	12,558	12,919	0.49

Source: National Industry-Occupation Matrix, 1992 [data tape]. Prepared by the Bureau of Labor Statistics. Washington, DC: U.S. Department of Labor, Bureau of Labor Statistics, 1992. *Note:* All employment data are wage and salary employment.

★ 401 ★
Occupational Outlook

Employment Projections for Garment Sewing Machine Operators, by Industry: 1992-2005

The National Industry-Occupation Matrix counts jobs, as reflected by data about wage and salary employment collected through the Occupational Employment Statistics surveys. The table below presents employment figures for garment sewing machine operators during 1992; the percent of industry employment for this occupation (staffing patterns) in 1992; low, medium, and high employment projections for 2005; and staffing patterns for the 2005 moderate projection. In 1992, garment sewing machine operators ranked 45 in terms of total employment for individual occupations and ranked 111 when considering total employment of occupational groups as well as individual occupations. Table shows the industries employing the most garment sewing machine operators in 1992.

Industry	1992		2005 employment			Percent of industry employment for 2005 moderate projection
	Employment	Percent of industry employment	Low	Moderate	High	
Total, all industries	543,536	0.49	328,385	383,168	385,469	0.28
Manufacturing	520,959	2.89	301,012	354,035	355,322	2.02
Nondurable goods manufacturing	519,450	6.66	299,583	352,421	353,686	4.49
Apparel and other textile products	468,750	46.64	257,086	304,025	304,662	39.99
Apparel	447,102	55.42	233,832	278,171	278,186	50.06
Textile mill products	45,926	6.84	38,562	44,047	44,580	7.72
Knitting mills	44,597	22.12	37,360	42,722	43,205	24.66
Fabricated textile products, miscellaneous	21,648	10.92	23,254	25,855	26,476	12.64
Wholesale and retail trade	14,745	0.06	18,151	19,582	20,527	0.06
Retail trade	9,944	0.05	12,463	13,422	13,879	0.06
Apparel and accessory stores	7,578	0.67	9,707	10,455	10,812	0.76
Personal services	6,716	0.60	8,174	8,445	8,472	0.61
Services	6,716	0.02	8,174	8,445	8,472	0.02
Wholesale trade	4,802	0.08	5,689	6,160	6,648	0.09
Leather and leather products	3,222	2.70	2,157	2,388	2,418	3.36
Luggage, handbags, and leather products, n.e.c.	2,562	5.06	1,798	1,966	1,974	6.05
Rubber and miscellaneous plastics products	1,552	0.18	1,778	1,961	2,026	0.18
Durable goods manufacturing	1,509	0.01	1,429	1,614	1,636	0.02
Manufacturing industries, miscellaneous	1,509	0.42	1,429	1,614	1,636	0.48
Retail stores, miscellaneous	1,326	0.05	1,659	1,787	1,848	0.06
Government	1,116	0.01	1,047	1,106	1,149	0.01
Federal government	1,116	0.05	1,047	1,106	1,149	0.05
Rubber products and plastic hose and footwear	1,093	0.64	1,078	1,203	1,220	0.76
Shopping goods stores, miscellaneous	965	0.11	1,257	1,354	1,400	0.12
Weaving, finishing, yarn and thread mills	918	0.25	751	845	855	0.29

Source: National Industry-Occupation Matrix, 1992 [data tape]. Prepared by the Bureau of Labor Statistics. Washington, DC: U.S. Department of Labor, Bureau of Labor Statistics, 1992. *Notes:* All employment data are wage and salary employment. "n.e.c." stands for "not elsewhere classified."

★ 402 ★

Occupational Outlook

Employment Projections for General Managers and Top Executives, by Industry: 1992-2005

The National Industry-Occupation Matrix counts jobs, as reflected by data about wage and salary employment collected through the Occupational Employment Statistics surveys. The table below presents employment figures for general managers and top executives during 1992; the percent of industry employment for this occupation (staffing patterns) in 1992; low, medium, and high employment projections for 2005; and staffing patterns for the 2005 moderate projection. In 1992, general managers and top executives ranked 3 in terms of total employment for individual occupations and ranked 27 when considering total employment of occupational groups as well as individual occupations. Table shows the industries employing the most general managers and top executives in 1992.

Industry	1992		2005 employment			Percent of industry employment for 2005 moderate projection
	Employment	Percent of industry employment	Low	Moderate	High	
Total, all industries	2,871,259	2.59	3,050,253	3,251,134	3,418,076	2.40
Wholesale and retail trade	960,688	3.78	1,037,032	1,115,444	1,169,363	3.60
Services	826,633	2.14	999,800	1,051,637	1,084,996	1.94
Retail trade	624,548	3.23	606,076	648,814	665,752	2.73
Manufacturing	371,859	2.06	300,441	328,819	355,371	1.88
Wholesale trade	336,140	5.56	430,957	466,630	503,611	6.49
Finance, insurance, and real estate	264,878	4.03	280,951	295,433	299,506	3.71
Wholesale trade, other	214,155	5.62	269,694	292,018	315,161	6.44
Durable goods manufacturing	211,274	2.06	161,232	178,116	199,502	1.84
Construction	183,033	4.09	184,289	191,952	226,413	3.41
Business services	167,052	3.14	209,456	225,108	233,687	2.69
Nondurable goods manufacturing	159,492	2.04	138,172	149,541	154,400	1.90
Transportation and public utilities	140,403	2.46	126,229	138,452	144,247	2.13
Eating and drinking places	136,448	2.07	171,783	181,048	182,019	2.06
Retail stores, miscellaneous	121,198	4.91	111,734	120,346	124,454	3.98
Engineering and management services	119,611	4.84	144,716	155,442	165,165	4.22
Special trade contractors	110,621	4.10	113,022	117,722	138,856	3.44
Government	107,575	1.13	110,273	116,985	122,517	1.12
Transportation	95,042	2.73	87,560	97,168	101,718	2.25
Health services	94,699	0.99	137,070	143,126	144,628	1.04
Automotive dealers and service stations	91,832	4.59	79,085	85,181	88,088	3.82
Food stores	84,275	2.65	74,402	80,137	82,872	2.07
Membership organizations	82,720	4.24	81,440	84,063	85,131	3.52
Social services	77,786	3.97	113,416	116,802	117,524	3.16
Grocery stores	71,062	2.50	62,769	67,607	69,914	1.95

Source: National Industry-Occupation Matrix, 1992 [data tape]. Prepared by the Bureau of Labor Statistics. Washington, DC: U.S. Department of Labor, Bureau of Labor Statistics, 1992. *Note:* All employment data are wage and salary employment.

★ 403 ★

Occupational Outlook

Employment Projections for General Office Clerks, by Industry: 1992-2005

The National Industry-Occupation Matrix counts jobs, as reflected by data about wage and salary employment collected through the Occupational Employment Statistics surveys. The table below presents employment figures for general office clerks during 1992; the percent of industry employment for this occupation (staffing patterns) in 1992; low, medium, and high employment projections for 2005; and staffing patterns for the 2005 moderate projection. In 1992, general office clerks ranked 8 in terms of total employment for individual occupations and ranked 33 when considering total employment of occupational groups as well as individual occupations. Table shows the industries employing the most general office clerks in 1992.

Industry	1992		2005 employment			Percent of industry employment for 2005 moderate projection
	Employment	Percent of industry employment	Low	Moderate	High	
Total, all industries	2,671,250	2.41	3,127,907	3,326,497	3,471,992	2.45
Services	1,039,086	2.69	1,397,568	1,473,133	1,514,220	2.72
Wholesale and retail trade	491,916	1.94	522,845	563,833	593,434	1.82
Finance, insurance, and real estate	319,610	4.86	353,067	371,534	375,764	4.66
Government	287,901	3.02	314,817	334,786	351,367	3.20
Retail trade	283,387	1.46	294,450	316,533	326,535	1.33
Health services	275,123	2.86	376,067	393,540	397,996	2.85
Education, public and private	248,640	2.56	280,839	295,277	306,349	2.37
Manufacturing	223,935	1.24	210,471	230,499	247,964	1.32
Business services	219,596	4.13	349,254	374,689	386,759	4.48
Wholesale trade	208,529	3.45	228,394	247,300	266,899	3.44
Transportation and public utilities	176,516	3.09	177,071	193,455	201,767	2.98
Local government, except education and hospitals	165,443	3.77	200,675	213,023	223,422	4.14
Hospitals, public and private	154,424	3.18	200,821	210,840	212,993	3.35
Personnel supply services	136,991	8.31	227,378	243,791	250,801	9.44
Wholesale trade, other	134,196	3.52	146,120	158,215	170,754	3.49
Durable goods manufacturing	122,353	1.20	108,080	119,540	133,414	1.24
Construction	109,580	2.45	130,962	136,408	160,898	2.42
Nondurable goods manufacturing	101,229	1.30	101,996	110,512	113,950	1.41
Transportation	94,550	2.71	101,202	111,768	117,579	2.59
Insurance carriers	93,602	6.32	97,635	104,629	104,675	6.30
State government, except education and hospitals	93,183	4.26	90,629	96,206	100,902	3.85
Depository institutions	90,351	4.30	68,147	70,974	71,157	3.23
Commercial banks, savings institutions, and credit unions	83,766	4.23	61,127	63,662	63,827	3.09
Communications and utilities	81,965	3.69	75,869	81,687	84,188	3.73

Source: National Industry-Occupation Matrix, 1992 [data tape]. Prepared by the Bureau of Labor Statistics. Washington, DC: U.S. Department of Labor, Bureau of Labor Statistics, 1992. *Note:* All employment data are wage and salary employment.

★ 404 ★

Occupational Outlook

Employment Projections for General Utility Maintenance Repairers, by Industry: 1992-2005

The National Industry-Occupation Matrix counts jobs, as reflected by data about wage and salary employment collected through the Occupational Employment Statistics surveys. The table below presents employment figures for general utility maintenance repairers during 1992; the percent of industry employment for this occupation (staffing patterns) in 1992; low, medium, and high employment projections for 2005; and staffing patterns for the 2005 moderate projection. In 1992, general utility maintenance repairers ranked 22 in terms of total employment for individual occupations and ranked 67 when considering total employment of occupational groups as well as individual occupations. Table shows the industries employing the most general utility maintenance repairers in 1992.

Industry	1992		2005 employment			Percent of industry employment for 2005 moderate projection
	Employment	Percent of industry employment	Low	Moderate	High	
Total, all industries	1,104,334	1.00	1,341,434	1,415,955	1,491,101	1.04
Services	379,662	0.98	533,058	557,370	573,249	1.03
Manufacturing	195,676	1.08	179,497	195,132	208,632	1.11
Finance, insurance, and real estate	171,968	2.62	232,177	239,640	252,054	3.01
Real estate	160,788	12.55	218,702	225,542	237,887	13.89
Wholesale and retail trade	141,470	0.56	162,998	175,422	184,694	0.57
Education, public and private	100,769	1.04	148,608	156,248	162,107	1.25
Nondurable goods manufacturing	100,625	1.29	97,045	104,429	107,755	1.33
Real estate operators and lessors	98,270	17.63	123,285	127,141	134,099	19.12
Durable goods manufacturing	95,327	0.93	82,768	91,036	101,147	0.94
Government	88,994	0.93	94,892	100,666	105,439	0.96
Retail trade	72,379	0.37	79,245	84,736	86,821	0.36
Wholesale trade	69,091	1.14	83,753	90,686	97,873	1.26
Construction	63,159	1.41	77,556	80,782	95,284	1.43
Local government, except education and hospitals	61,490	1.40	67,627	71,788	75,292	1.40
Real estate agents and managers	56,654	9.79	89,497	92,296	97,348	11.63
Business services	49,499	0.93	67,609	72,750	75,520	0.87
Transportation and public utilities	48,807	0.85	48,553	53,181	55,604	0.82
Health services	48,483	0.50	64,120	67,024	67,704	0.49
Hotels and other lodging places	47,234	3.00	68,710	71,040	73,380	3.22
Amusement and recreation services	44,453	3.80	62,074	63,150	63,752	3.88
Wholesale trade, other	38,226	1.00	45,287	49,036	52,922	1.08
Special trade contractors	33,152	1.23	38,917	40,535	47,813	1.18
Amusement and recreation services, all other	31,142	3.77	48,486	49,378	49,756	4.10
Membership organizations	28,417	1.46	33,248	34,137	34,482	1.43

Source: National Industry-Occupation Matrix, 1992 [data tape]. Prepared by the Bureau of Labor Statistics. Washington, DC: U.S. Department of Labor, Bureau of Labor Statistics, 1992. *Note:* All employment data are wage and salary employment.

★ 405 ★
Occupational Outlook

Employment Projections for Guards, by Industry: 1992-2005

The National Industry-Occupation Matrix counts jobs, as reflected by data about wage and salary employment collected through the Occupational Employment Statistics surveys. The table below presents employment figures for guards during 1992; the percent of industry employment for this occupation (staffing patterns) in 1992; low, medium, and high employment projections for 2005; and staffing patterns for the 2005 moderate projection. In 1992, guards ranked 32 in terms of total employment for individual occupations and ranked 89 when considering total employment of occupational groups as well as individual occupations. Table shows the industries employing the most guards in 1992.

Industry	1992		2005 employment			Percent of industry employment for 2005 moderate projection
	Employment	Percent of industry employment	Low	Moderate	High	
Total, all industries	802,190	0.72	1,137,427	1,210,117	1,253,714	0.89
Services	599,212	1.55	931,114	990,979	1,024,009	1.83
Business services	445,626	8.39	742,484	794,732	823,261	9.49
Business services, miscellaneous	436,615	34.97	730,550	781,940	810,072	38.81
Finance, insurance, and real estate	57,784	0.88	66,279	68,596	71,537	0.86
Wholesale and retail trade	48,804	0.19	50,900	54,406	55,904	0.18
Manufacturing	45,015	0.25	39,012	42,544	45,675	0.24
Retail trade	44,521	0.23	46,378	49,510	50,620	0.21
Real estate	43,806	3.42	51,186	52,787	55,676	3.25
Health services	39,667	0.41	46,840	49,131	49,634	0.36
Hospitals, public and private	35,882	0.74	41,540	43,612	44,058	0.69
Education, public and private	33,749	0.35	37,328	39,247	40,719	0.31
Government	33,358	0.35	31,948	33,889	35,492	0.32
Real estate operators and lessors	30,768	5.52	34,740	35,826	37,787	5.39
Durable goods manufacturing	27,862	0.27	22,897	25,179	27,809	0.26
Hotels and other lodging places	24,407	1.55	31,954	33,038	34,126	1.50
Local government, except education and hospitals	20,368	0.46	20,161	21,402	22,446	0.42
Amusement and recreation services	18,012	1.54	22,642	23,074	23,380	1.42
Nondurable goods manufacturing	17,159	0.22	16,124	17,373	17,864	0.22
General merchandise stores	17,049	0.70	15,651	16,858	17,433	0.65
Department stores	16,018	0.78	14,855	16,000	16,546	0.71
Membership organizations	12,813	0.66	15,360	15,715	15,899	0.66
Real estate agents and managers	11,603	2.00	14,997	15,466	16,312	1.95
Transportation and public utilities	11,458	0.20	11,592	12,785	13,356	0.20
Depository institutions	9,572	0.46	9,803	10,209	10,236	0.47

Source: National Industry-Occupation Matrix, 1992 [data tape]. Prepared by the Bureau of Labor Statistics. Washington, DC: U.S. Department of Labor, Bureau of Labor Statistics, 1992. *Note:* All employment data are wage and salary employment.

★ 406 ★

Occupational Outlook

Employment Projections for Hairdressers, Hairstylists, and Cosmetologists, by Industry: 1992-2005

The National Industry-Occupation Matrix counts jobs, as reflected by data about wage and salary employment collected through the Occupational Employment Statistics surveys. The table below presents employment figures for hairdressers, hairstylists, and cosmetologists during 1992; the percent of industry employment for this occupation (staffing patterns) in 1992; low, medium, and high employment projections for 2005; and staffing patterns for the 2005 moderate projection. In 1992, hairdressers, hairstylists, and cosmetologists ranked 78 in terms of total employment for individual occupations and ranked 155 when considering total employment of occupational groups as well as individual occupations. Table shows the industries employing the most hairdressers, hairstylists, and cosmetologists in 1992.

Industry	1992		2005 employment			Percent of industry employment for 2005 moderate projection
	Employment	Percent of industry employment	Low	Moderate	High	
Total, all industries	328,050	0.30	446,174	455,700	459,642	0.34
Services	286,797	0.74	382,877	387,534	389,127	0.72
Personal services	283,668	25.52	377,640	382,078	383,610	27.65
Beauty shops	274,643	72.54	368,065	372,358	373,837	73.58
Wholesale and retail trade	41,064	0.16	63,040	67,900	70,232	0.22
Retail trade	40,841	0.21	62,734	67,569	69,875	0.28
General merchandise stores	38,786	1.60	59,996	64,621	66,826	2.48
Department stores	37,420	1.83	58,720	63,246	65,405	2.79
Health services	2,922	0.03	4,878	5,078	5,131	0.04
Nursing and personal care facilities	2,845	0.18	4,726	4,920	4,971	0.21
General merchandise stores, n.e.c.	1,367	0.36	1,276	1,374	1,421	0.41
Retail stores, miscellaneous	1,330	0.05	1,735	1,868	1,932	0.06
Used merchandise and retail stores, n.e.c.	911	0.18	1,217	1,311	1,356	0.21
Apparel and accessory stores	681	0.06	949	1,022	1,057	0.07
Clothing and accesories stores	423	0.05	528	569	588	0.06
Drug stores and proprietary stores	293	0.05	346	372	385	0.05
Wholesale trade	223	0.00	306	331	358	0.00
Motion pictures	208	0.05	359	377	386	0.08
Agriculture, forestry, and fishing	181	0.01	249	257	274	0.01
Machinery, equipment, and supplies	180	0.02	251	272	293	0.03

Source: National Industry-Occupation Matrix, 1992 [data tape]. Prepared by the Bureau of Labor Statistics. Washington, DC: U.S. Department of Labor, Bureau of Labor Statistics, 1992. *Notes:* All employment data are wage and salary employment. "n.e.c." stands for "not elsewhere classified."

★ 407 ★

Occupational Outlook

Employment Projections for Hand Freight, Stock, and Material Movers, by Industry: 1992-2005

The National Industry-Occupation Matrix counts jobs, as reflected by data about wage and salary employment collected through the Occupational Employment Statistics surveys. The table below presents employment figures for hand freight, stock, and material movers during 1992; the percent of industry employment for this occupation (staffing patterns) in 1992; low, medium, and high employment projections for 2005; and staffing patterns for the 2005 moderate projection. In 1992, hand freight, stock, and material movers ranked 29 in terms of total employment for individual occupations and ranked 84 when considering total employment of occupational groups as well as individual occupations. Table shows the industries employing the most hand freight, stock, and material movers in 1992.

Industry	1992		2005 employment			Percent of industry employment for 2005 moderate projection
	Employment	Percent of industry employment	Low	Moderate	High	
Total, all industries	825,528	0.75	866,100	935,216	989,282	0.69
Wholesale and retail trade	406,467	1.60	434,156	468,671	493,897	1.51
Manufacturing	257,667	1.43	233,758	254,435	272,601	1.45
Retail trade	225,275	1.16	244,445	263,256	272,202	1.11
Wholesale trade	181,192	3.00	189,711	205,415	221,694	2.86
Food stores	135,078	4.25	137,137	147,707	152,748	3.81
Grocery stores	134,051	4.72	136,055	146,542	151,544	4.22
Nondurable goods manufacturing	133,104	1.71	123,948	134,515	138,057	1.71
Durable goods manufacturing	124,433	1.22	109,681	119,753	134,154	1.24
Wholesale trade, other	114,831	3.01	120,849	130,852	141,223	2.89
Services	111,520	0.29	154,428	164,602	169,506	0.30
Business services	81,107	1.53	118,181	126,804	130,816	1.51
Personnel supply services	60,601	3.68	88,380	94,759	97,484	3.67
Groceries and related products	45,317	5.30	46,181	50,003	53,966	5.13
Food and kindred products	36,471	2.20	34,261	35,547	35,810	2.16
General merchandise stores	34,955	1.44	50,212	54,082	55,928	2.08
Department stores	32,499	1.59	48,340	52,065	53,842	2.30
Lumber and wood products	25,881	3.84	26,083	27,012	32,169	3.91
Transportation and public utilities	23,716	0.42	14,663	17,126	18,985	0.26
Transportation	23,716	0.68	14,663	17,126	18,985	0.40
Water transportation	23,365	13.47	14,247	16,659	18,491	10.83
Retail stores, miscellaneous	20,570	0.83	20,942	22,556	23,326	0.75
Apparel and other textile products	19,062	1.90	13,940	16,254	16,368	2.14
Furniture and homefurnishings stores	17,614	2.18	18,601	20,034	20,718	1.94
Textile mill products	17,555	2.61	13,488	15,100	15,461	2.65

Source: National Industry-Occupation Matrix, 1992 [data tape]. Prepared by the Bureau of Labor Statistics. Washington, DC: U.S. Department of Labor, Bureau of Labor Statistics, 1992. *Note:* All employment data are wage and salary employment.

★ 408 ★

Occupational Outlook

Employment Projections for Hand Packers and Packagers, by Industry: 1992-2005

The National Industry-Occupation Matrix counts jobs, as reflected by data about wage and salary employment collected through the Occupational Employment Statistics surveys. The table below presents employment figures for hand packers and packagers during 1992; the percent of industry employment for this occupation (staffing patterns) in 1992; low, medium, and high employment projections for 2005; and staffing patterns for the 2005 moderate projection. In 1992, hand packers and packagers ranked 39 in terms of total employment for individual occupations and ranked 100 when considering total employment of occupational groups as well as individual occupations. Table shows the industries employing the most hand packers and packagers in 1992.

Industry	1992		2005 employment			Percent of industry employment for 2005 moderate projection
	Employment	Percent of industry employment	Low	Moderate	High	
Total, all industries	682,035	0.62	711,808	767,058	801,275	0.57
Manufacturing	335,668	1.86	312,680	338,149	353,223	1.93
Nondurable goods manufacturing	240,290	3.08	233,685	251,200	258,181	3.20
Wholesale and retail trade	189,448	0.75	193,024	208,341	219,583	0.67
Services	105,797	0.27	154,445	165,023	169,836	0.30
Durable goods manufacturing	96,837	0.95	80,543	88,619	96,654	0.92
Retail trade	96,064	0.50	107,135	115,342	119,214	0.49
Business services	94,142	1.77	139,309	149,304	154,010	1.78
Wholesale trade	93,384	1.54	85,889	92,999	100,369	1.29
Food stores	81,661	2.57	93,609	100,825	104,266	2.60
Food and kindred products	81,203	4.91	78,378	81,023	81,566	4.92
Grocery stores	76,758	2.70	88,902	95,754	99,022	2.76
Personnel supply services	58,786	3.57	89,682	96,155	98,920	3.73
Wholesale trade, other	51,239	1.34	51,280	55,524	59,925	1.23
Printing and publishing	39,746	2.64	44,343	47,912	49,568	2.74
Transportation	36,120	1.04	37,708	41,092	43,365	0.95
Transportation and public utilities	36,120	0.63	37,708	41,092	43,365	0.63
Groceries and related products	34,240	4.00	26,545	28,742	31,020	2.95
Rubber and miscellaneous plastics products	33,476	3.84	40,935	44,470	47,122	4.17
Trucking and warehousing	29,946	1.86	30,705	33,231	35,049	1.65
Plastics products, miscellaneous	28,756	4.65	37,030	40,115	42,701	4.76
Business services, miscellaneous	26,875	2.15	37,981	40,652	42,115	2.02
Local and long distance trucking and terminals	24,309	1.64	24,923	26,973	28,449	1.44
Apparel and other textile products	23,681	2.36	17,085	19,778	19,967	2.60
Paper and allied products	22,536	3.28	22,707	24,575	25,492	3.37

Source: National Industry-Occupation Matrix, 1992 [data tape]. Prepared by the Bureau of Labor Statistics. Washington, DC: U.S. Department of Labor, Bureau of Labor Statistics, 1992. *Note:* All employment data are wage and salary employment.

★ 409 ★
Occupational Outlook

Employment Projections for Hand Workers, by Industry: 1992-2005

The National Industry-Occupation Matrix counts jobs, as reflected by data about wage and salary employment collected through the Occupational Employment Statistics surveys. The table below presents employment figures for hand workers (nonspecific) during 1992; the percent of industry employment for this occupation (staffing patterns) in 1992; low, medium, and high employment projections for 2005; and staffing patterns for the 2005 moderate projection. In 1992, nonspecific hand workers ranked 69 in terms of total employment for individual occupations and ranked 143 when considering total employment of occupational groups as well as individual occupations. Table shows the industries employing the most hand workers in 1992.

Industry	1992		2005 employment			Percent of industry employment for 2005 moderate projection
	Employment	Percent of industry employment	Low	Moderate	High	
Total, all industries	361,523	0.33	460,242	495,737	519,307	0.37
Manufacturing	197,126	1.09	214,449	234,664	248,779	1.34
Durable goods manufacturing	118,579	1.16	129,806	143,106	155,192	1.48
Services	115,550	0.30	189,206	200,353	205,603	0.37
Nondurable goods manufacturing	79,355	1.02	85,653	92,654	94,702	1.18
Business services	57,121	1.08	101,157	108,450	111,779	1.30
Transportation equipment	54,158	2.97	65,806	72,619	77,882	4.11
Motor vehicles and equipment	44,885	5.55	57,273	63,361	68,175	8.35
Personnel supply services	43,173	2.62	77,969	83,597	86,000	3.24
Social services	34,131	1.74	54,386	56,491	56,919	1.53
Food and kindred products	29,046	1.76	34,449	35,819	36,088	2.17
Job training and related services	28,840	10.64	44,621	46,438	46,811	11.12
Wholesale and retail trade	24,364	0.10	29,082	31,429	33,409	0.10
Meat products	18,203	4.20	22,624	23,619	23,806	4.77
Wholesale trade	15,649	0.26	18,609	20,150	21,747	0.28
Electronic and other electrical equipment	15,360	1.01	13,587	15,125	16,688	1.12
Wholesale trade, other	11,756	0.31	13,927	15,080	16,275	0.33
Rubber and miscellaneous plastics products	10,935	1.25	13,753	15,010	15,799	1.41
Government	10,457	0.11	10,579	11,205	11,698	0.11
Textile mill products	10,322	1.54	8,696	9,897	10,037	1.73
Apparel and other textile products	10,063	1.00	8,387	9,756	9,832	1.28
Business services, miscellaneous	9,741	0.78	16,297	17,444	18,071	0.87
Printing and publishing	9,228	0.61	11,130	12,041	12,412	0.69
Retail trade	8,716	0.05	10,473	11,279	11,663	0.05
Knitting mills	8,614	4.27	7,216	8,252	8,345	4.76

Source: National Industry-Occupation Matrix, 1992 [data tape]. Prepared by the Bureau of Labor Statistics. Washington, DC: U.S. Department of Labor, Bureau of Labor Statistics, 1992. *Note:* All employment data are wage and salary employment.

★ 410 ★

Occupational Outlook

Employment Projections for Health Professionals and Paraprofessionals, by Industry: 1992-2005

The National Industry-Occupation Matrix counts jobs, as reflected by data about wage and salary employment collected through the Occupational Employment Statistics surveys. The table below presents employment figures for health professionals and paraprofessionals (nonspecific) during 1992; the percent of industry employment for this occupation (staffing patterns) in 1992; low, medium, and high employment projections for 2005; and staffing patterns for the 2005 moderate projection. In 1992, health professionals and paraprofessionals ranked 64 in terms of total employment for individual occupations and ranked 136 when considering total employment of occupational groups as well as individual occupations. Table shows the industries employing the most health professionals and paraprofessionals in 1992.

Industry	1992		2005 employment			Percent of industry employment for 2005 moderate projection
	Employment	Percent of industry employment	Low	Moderate	High	
Total, all industries	395,341	0.36	529,015	558,798	573,543	0.41
Services	250,161	0.65	360,579	378,617	385,558	0.70
Health services	139,939	1.46	204,337	214,074	216,299	1.55
Hospitals, public and private	104,061	2.15	146,460	153,767	155,337	2.44
Wholesale and retail trade	69,645	0.27	77,671	83,668	86,912	0.27
Retail trade	61,994	0.32	68,604	73,850	76,316	0.31
Retail stores, miscellaneous	58,671	2.38	64,495	69,467	71,838	2.30
Drug stores and proprietary stores	51,816	8.54	56,138	60,465	62,529	8.65
Government	44,864	0.47	55,640	58,998	61,738	0.56
Business services	22,838	0.43	31,079	33,373	34,430	0.40
Personnel supply services	19,495	1.18	25,605	27,453	28,242	1.06
Engineering and management services	18,931	0.77	29,520	31,560	32,631	0.86
Local government, except education and hospitals	16,496	0.38	27,213	28,887	30,298	0.56
State government, except education and hospitals	15,017	0.69	15,892	16,869	17,693	0.67
Federal government	13,344	0.61	12,530	13,235	13,740	0.64
Social services	11,631	0.59	23,642	24,347	24,524	0.66
Manufacturing	11,455	0.06	11,349	12,420	13,224	0.07
Management and public relations	10,044	1.53	17,170	18,573	19,306	1.67
Finance, insurance, and real estate	9,939	0.15	12,321	12,954	13,212	0.16
Nursing and personal care facilities	9,158	0.59	13,985	14,559	14,710	0.63
Offices of physicians, including osteopaths	8,910	0.59	14,583	15,208	15,420	0.64
Wholesale trade	7,651	0.13	9,068	9,818	10,596	0.14
Wholesale trade, other	7,350	0.19	8,707	9,428	10,175	0.21
Research and testing services	7,197	1.29	9,554	9,984	10,171	1.32
Offices of other health practitioners	6,770	2.07	11,841	12,349	12,520	2.15

Source: National Industry-Occupation Matrix, 1992 [data tape]. Prepared by the Bureau of Labor Statistics. Washington, DC: U.S. Department of Labor, Bureau of Labor Statistics, 1992. *Note:* All employment data are wage and salary employment.

★ 411 ★

Occupational Outlook

Employment Projections for Home Health Aides, by Industry: 1992-2005

The National Industry-Occupation Matrix counts jobs, as reflected by data about wage and salary employment collected through the Occupational Employment Statistics surveys. The table below presents employment figures for home health aides during 1992; the percent of industry employment for this occupation (staffing patterns) in 1992; low, medium, and high employment projections for 2005; and staffing patterns for the 2005 moderate projection. In 1992, home health aides ranked 74 in terms of total employment for individual occupations and ranked 150 when considering total employment of occupational groups as well as individual occupations. Table shows the industries employing the most home health aides in 1992.

Industry	1992		2005 employment			Percent of industry employment for 2005 moderate projection
	Employment	Percent of industry employment	Low	Moderate	High	
Total, all industries	347,085	0.31	793,887	826,560	835,117	0.61
Services	330,141	0.85	765,270	796,181	803,256	1.47
Health services	184,872	1.92	441,524	460,232	463,460	3.34
Home health care services	150,050	37.36	367,391	382,606	385,054	41.81
Social services	101,916	5.20	259,655	267,334	269,213	7.24
Individual and miscellaneous social services	70,830	10.08	120,613	124,164	124,696	10.69
Business services	40,641	0.76	60,065	64,405	66,265	0.77
Personnel supply services	40,414	2.45	59,716	64,027	65,868	2.48
Residential care	26,769	5.00	132,173	136,043	137,340	10.19
Hospitals, public and private	19,269	0.40	49,572	52,045	52,577	0.83
Government	16,943	0.18	28,618	30,378	31,861	0.29
Local government, except education and hospitals	10,526	0.24	15,168	16,101	16,887	0.31
Nursing and personal care facilities	7,287	0.47	11,128	11,584	11,704	0.50
State government, except education and hospitals	6,417	0.29	13,450	14,278	14,975	0.57
Health and allied services, n.e.c.	5,348	2.13	8,356	8,702	8,758	2.22
Job training and related services	3,483	1.29	5,389	5,609	5,654	1.34
Membership organizations	1,632	0.08	2,218	2,265	2,291	0.09
Engineering and management services	1,081	0.04	1,808	1,945	2,026	0.05
Child day care services	834	0.19	1,479	1,518	1,523	0.20
Accounting, auditing, and bookkeeping	718	0.14	1,201	1,290	1,346	0.16
Management and public relations	327	0.05	559	604	628	0.05

Source: National Industry-Occupation Matrix, 1992 [data tape]. Prepared by the Bureau of Labor Statistics. Washington, DC: U.S. Department of Labor, Bureau of Labor Statistics, 1992. *Notes:* All employment data are wage and salary employment. "n.e.c." stands for "not elsewhere classified."

★ 412 ★

Occupational Outlook

Employment Projections for Industrial Machinery Mechanics, by Industry: 1992-2005

The National Industry-Occupation Matrix counts jobs, as reflected by data about wage and salary employment collected through the Occupational Employment Statistics surveys. The table below presents employment figures for industrial machinery mechanics during 1992; the percent of industry employment for this occupation (staffing patterns) in 1992; low, medium, and high employment projections for 2005; and staffing patterns for the 2005 moderate projection. In 1992, industrial machinery mechanics ranked 51 in terms of total employment for individual occupations and ranked 121 when considering total employment of occupational groups as well as individual occupations. Table shows the industries employing the most industrial machinery mechanics in 1992.

Industry	1992		2005 employment			Percent of industry employment for 2005 moderate projection
	Employment	Percent of industry employment	Low	Moderate	High	
Total, all industries	457,300	0.41	407,682	441,924	470,434	0.33
Manufacturing	316,686	1.76	274,674	299,486	318,788	1.71
Nondurable goods manufacturing	170,317	2.18	153,270	165,798	170,341	2.11
Durable goods manufacturing	146,905	1.44	121,998	134,325	149,034	1.39
Government	49,935	0.52	45,067	48,111	50,554	0.46
Food and kindred products	46,554	2.81	43,760	45,362	45,720	2.75
Transportation and public utilities	38,366	0.67	37,681	40,424	42,235	0.62
Textile mill products	33,454	4.98	25,048	28,062	28,659	4.92
Communications and utilities	30,091	1.35	30,251	32,006	33,307	1.46
Electric, gas, and sanitary services	30,091	3.15	30,251	32,006	33,307	2.99
Local government, except education and hospitals	29,708	0.68	28,732	30,500	31,989	0.59
Chemicals and allied products	26,103	2.41	22,725	24,665	25,585	2.26
Fabricated metal products	25,567	1.93	21,138	22,914	24,928	1.92
Primary metal industries	25,297	3.65	19,954	22,188	24,426	3.59
Weaving, finishing, yarn and thread mills	23,328	6.48	16,785	18,886	19,111	6.57
Mining	21,852	3.47	16,898	18,491	21,141	3.29
Industrial machinery and equipment	21,522	1.12	18,779	21,279	24,253	1.14
Rubber and miscellaneous plastics products	19,233	2.21	22,757	24,768	26,180	2.32
Transportation equipment	19,207	1.05	16,094	17,688	18,980	1.00
Electric services	18,178	4.12	17,697	18,724	19,485	3.94
Paper and allied products	17,866	2.60	17,302	18,798	19,329	2.58
Electronic and other electrical equipment	17,494	1.15	13,449	15,285	17,282	1.13
Stone, clay, and glass products	14,079	2.75	9,864	10,571	11,818	2.42
Wholesale and retail trade	13,932	0.05	14,859	16,081	17,290	0.05
Plastics products, miscellaneous	13,568	2.19	18,189	19,704	20,975	2.34

Source: National Industry-Occupation Matrix, 1992 [data tape]. Prepared by the Bureau of Labor Statistics. Washington, DC: U.S. Department of Labor, Bureau of Labor Statistics, 1992. *Note:* All employment data are wage and salary employment.

★ 413 ★

Occupational Outlook

Employment Projections for Industrial Truck and Tractor Operators, by Industry: 1992-2005

The National Industry-Occupation Matrix counts jobs, as reflected by data about wage and salary employment collected through the Occupational Employment Statistics surveys. The table below presents employment figures for industrial truck and tractor operators during 1992; the percent of industry employment for this occupation (staffing patterns) in 1992; low, medium, and high employment projections for 2005; and staffing patterns for the 2005 moderate projection. In 1992, industrial truck and tractor operators ranked 61 in terms of total employment for individual occupations and ranked 132 when considering total employment of occupational groups as well as individual occupations. Table shows the industries employing the most industrial truck and tractor operators in 1992.

Industry	1992		2005 employment			Percent of industry employment for 2005 moderate projection
	Employment	Percent of industry employment	Low	Moderate	High	
Total, all industries	410,458	0.37	407,443	439,407	467,821	0.32
Manufacturing	225,841	1.25	191,006	205,897	220,619	1.18
Durable goods manufacturing	114,424	1.12	91,633	99,570	110,950	1.03
Nondurable goods manufacturing	111,644	1.43	99,610	106,567	109,782	1.36
Wholesale and retail trade	81,029	0.32	83,671	90,498	96,818	0.29
Wholesale trade	61,438	1.02	66,160	71,637	77,314	1.00
Transportation and public utilities	59,017	1.03	71,367	77,497	81,788	1.19
Transportation	56,369	1.62	68,776	74,756	78,935	1.73
Trucking and warehousing	49,934	3.11	63,196	68,395	72,138	3.39
Food and kindred products	39,170	2.37	35,558	36,846	37,147	2.24
Wholesale trade, other	35,501	0.93	42,060	45,541	49,150	1.01
Local and long distance trucking and terminals	28,662	1.93	34,786	37,647	39,708	2.01
Paper and allied products	22,571	3.28	20,413	22,122	22,837	3.04
Public warehousing and storage	21,272	17.42	28,411	30,748	32,430	20.50
Retail trade	19,591	0.10	17,511	18,861	19,504	0.08
Services	19,447	0.05	36,924	39,558	40,790	0.07
Fabricated metal products	18,715	1.42	14,451	15,684	17,188	1.31
Lumber and wood products	18,410	2.73	18,642	19,320	22,967	2.80
Government	17,626	0.18	18,020	19,119	20,030	0.18
Transportation equipment	16,130	0.89	12,238	13,499	14,472	0.76
Groceries and related products	15,788	1.85	14,489	15,688	16,932	1.61
Business services	15,720	0.30	32,537	34,920	35,999	0.42
Primary metal industries	14,756	2.13	10,515	11,670	12,871	1.89
Rubber and miscellaneous plastics products	14,670	1.68	15,191	16,543	17,477	1.55
Stone, clay, and glass products	13,530	2.64	9,480	10,143	11,381	2.32

Source: National Industry-Occupation Matrix, 1992 [data tape]. Prepared by the Bureau of Labor Statistics. Washington, DC: U.S. Department of Labor, Bureau of Labor Statistics, 1992. *Note:* All employment data are wage and salary employment.

★ 414 ★

Occupational Outlook

Employment Projections for Institution or Cafeteria Cooks, by Industry: 1992-2005

The National Industry-Occupation Matrix counts jobs, as reflected by data about wage and salary employment collected through the Occupational Employment Statistics surveys. The table below presents employment figures for institution or cafeteria cooks during 1992; the percent of industry employment for this occupation (staffing patterns) in 1992; low, medium, and high employment projections for 2005; and staffing patterns for the 2005 moderate projection. In 1992, institution or cafeteria cooks ranked 63 in terms of total employment for individual occupations and ranked 134 when considering total employment of occupational groups as well as individual occupations. Table shows the industries employing the most institution or cafeteria cooks in 1992.

Industry	1992		2005 employment			Percent of industry employment for 2005 moderate projection
	Employment	Percent of industry employment	Low	Moderate	High	
Total, all industries	405,218	0.37	447,962	468,804	478,312	0.35
Services	329,096	0.85	332,033	346,447	354,054	0.64
Health services	85,126	0.89	104,617	109,209	110,332	0.79
Wholesale and retail trade	52,969	0.21	91,259	96,256	96,901	0.31
Retail trade	52,411	0.27	90,609	95,553	96,141	0.40
Nursing and personal care facilities	50,638	3.28	69,595	72,452	73,202	3.14
Eating and drinking places	50,125	0.76	88,159	92,914	93,413	1.06
Social services	43,248	2.21	56,862	58,489	58,878	1.58
Hospitals, public and private	33,569	0.69	33,491	35,162	35,521	0.56
Government	21,184	0.22	22,475	23,842	24,972	0.23
Residential care	16,954	3.17	27,207	28,003	28,270	2.10
Child day care services	14,863	3.31	17,131	17,578	17,640	2.26
Religious organizations	12,573	1.09	15,852	16,317	16,450	1.15
Local government, except education and hospitals	10,523	0.24	11,573	12,285	12,885	0.24
Individual and miscellaneous social services	10,166	1.45	11,253	11,584	11,633	1.00
State government, except education and hospitals	7,471	0.34	7,906	8,393	8,802	0.34
Hotels and other lodging places	4,365	0.28	6,350	6,565	6,781	0.30
Federal government	3,190	0.15	2,995	3,164	3,285	0.15
Civic and social associations	2,578	0.61	3,525	3,596	3,637	0.68
Agriculture, forestry, and fishing	1,969	0.11	2,196	2,260	2,385	0.11
Job training and related services	1,265	0.47	1,272	1,324	1,335	0.32
Retail stores, miscellaneous	1,257	0.05	1,350	1,454	1,503	0.05
Nonstore retailers	1,155	0.39	1,223	1,317	1,362	0.41
Wholesale trade	559	0.01	650	703	759	0.01
Health and allied services, n.e.c.	528	0.21	825	859	864	0.22

Source: National Industry-Occupation Matrix, 1992 [data tape]. Prepared by the Bureau of Labor Statistics. Washington, DC: U.S. Department of Labor, Bureau of Labor Statistics, 1992. *Notes:* All employment data are wage and salary employment. "n.e.c." stands for "not elsewhere classified."

★ 415 ★

Occupational Outlook

Employment Projections for Insurance Sales Workers, by Industry: 1992-2005

The National Industry-Occupation Matrix counts jobs, as reflected by data about wage and salary employment collected through the Occupational Employment Statistics surveys. The table below presents employment figures for insurance sales workers during 1992; the percent of industry employment for this occupation (staffing patterns) in 1992; low, medium, and high employment projections for 2005; and staffing patterns for the 2005 moderate projection. In 1992, insurance sales workers ranked 94 in terms of total employment for individual occupations and ranked 178 when considering total employment of occupational groups as well as individual occupations. Table shows the industries employing the most insurance sales workers in 1992.

Industry	1992		2005 employment			Percent of industry employment for 2005 moderate projection
	Employment	Percent of industry employment	Low	Moderate	High	
Total, all industries	276,665	0.25	307,105	328,826	329,335	0.24
Finance, insurance, and real estate	276,665	4.21	307,105	328,826	329,335	4.13
Insurance carriers	154,074	10.41	148,423	159,054	159,125	9.58
Insurance agents, brokers, and service	112,636	17.27	146,809	157,431	157,525	16.21
Life insurance	103,462	19.25	102,660	110,014	110,063	17.83
Fire, marine, and casualty insurance	37,696	6.82	33,750	36,167	36,184	6.03
Medical service and health insurance	10,055	3.75	8,339	8,936	8,940	3.57
Real estate	4,364	0.34	5,390	5,558	5,863	0.34
Pension funds and insurance, n.e.c.	2,861	2.36	3,674	3,937	3,939	2.04
Depository institutions	2,808	0.13	2,869	2,988	2,996	0.14
Commercial banks, savings institutions, and credit unions	2,695	0.14	2,752	2,866	2,873	0.14
Real estate agents and managers	2,216	0.38	2,864	2,953	3,115	0.37
Real estate, all other	1,600	1.10	1,907	1,966	2,074	1.19
Security and commodity brokers	1,275	0.29	1,431	1,544	1,557	0.27
Security and commodity brokers and dealers	1,153	0.33	1,274	1,375	1,386	0.31
Nondepository institutions	1,087	0.28	1,503	1,549	1,563	0.27
Real estate operators and lessors	549	0.10	619	639	674	0.10
Holding and other investment offices	420	0.19	681	702	708	0.19
Mortgage bankers and brokers	402	0.23	625	644	650	0.23
Personal credit institutions	380	0.30	479	494	498	0.29
Federal and business credit institutions	305	0.31	399	412	415	0.32
Security and commodity exchanges and services	123	0.14	157	169	170	0.13
Banking and closely related functions, n.e.c.	113	0.09	118	122	123	0.09

Source: National Industry-Occupation Matrix, 1992 [data tape]. Prepared by the Bureau of Labor Statistics. Washington, DC: U.S. Department of Labor, Bureau of Labor Statistics, 1992. *Notes:* All employment data are wage and salary employment. "n.e.c." stands for "not elsewhere classified."

★ 416 ★
Occupational Outlook

Employment Projections for Janitors, Cleaners, Maids, and Housekeeping Cleaners, by Industry: 1992-2005

The National Industry-Occupation Matrix counts jobs, as reflected by data about wage and salary employment collected through the Occupational Employment Statistics surveys. The table below presents employment figures for janitors, cleaners, maids, and housekeeping cleaners during 1992; the percent of industry employment for this occupation (staffing patterns) in 1992; low, medium, and high employment projections for 2005; and staffing patterns for the 2005 moderate projection. In 1992, janitors, cleaners, maids, and housekeeping cleaners ranked 6 in terms of total employment for individual occupations and ranked 31 when considering total employment of occupational groups as well as individual occupations. Table shows the industries employing the most janitors, cleaners, maids, and housekeeping cleaners in 1992.

Industry	1992		2005 employment			Percent of industry employment for 2005 moderate projection
	Employment	Percent of industry employment	Low	Moderate	High	
Total, all industries	2,732,932	2.47	3,040,707	3,197,506	3,292,669	2.36
Services	2,115,804	5.47	2,462,427	2,584,422	2,651,544	4.77
Business services	635,875	11.97	773,072	825,951	849,934	9.87
Services to buildings	596,870	74.11	721,667	770,801	793,025	77.06
Education, public and private	483,946	4.98	475,795	500,257	519,014	4.01
Hotels and other lodging places	337,065	21.44	420,150	434,398	448,708	19.67
Health services	318,467	3.31	371,320	388,237	392,376	2.82
Wholesale and retail trade	219,724	0.87	209,945	224,346	230,808	0.72
Finance, insurance, and real estate	193,928	2.95	202,299	209,267	218,890	2.63
Retail trade	190,844	0.99	182,449	194,573	198,675	0.82
Hospitals, public and private	174,365	3.60	179,432	188,383	190,307	3.00
Membership organizations	163,787	8.40	201,101	206,786	208,599	8.65
Real estate	160,798	12.55	168,678	173,954	183,475	10.71
Manufacturing	151,097	0.84	124,054	134,881	143,333	0.77
Religious organizations	134,717	11.70	169,850	174,839	176,263	12.31
Real estate operators and lessors	105,312	18.90	105,696	109,001	114,967	16.39
Nursing and personal care facilities	101,272	6.56	137,633	143,283	144,767	6.21
Eating and drinking places	80,347	1.22	83,742	88,258	88,732	1.01
Nondurable goods manufacturing	78,066	1.00	67,244	72,117	73,717	0.92
Durable goods manufacturing	72,912	0.71	56,695	62,631	69,418	0.65
Social services	57,196	2.92	91,573	94,375	95,076	2.56
Real estate agents and managers	52,258	9.03	60,038	61,916	65,305	7.80
Amusement and recreation services	42,310	3.62	48,700	49,558	50,049	3.05
Food stores	37,087	1.17	33,764	36,367	37,608	0.94
Food and kindred products	31,907	1.93	27,843	28,881	29,089	1.75

Source: National Industry-Occupation Matrix, 1992 [data tape]. Prepared by the Bureau of Labor Statistics. Washington, DC: U.S. Department of Labor, Bureau of Labor Statistics, 1992. *Note:* All employment data are wage and salary employment.

★417★

Occupational Outlook

Employment Projections for Lawyers, by Industry: 1992-2005

The National Industry-Occupation Matrix counts jobs, as reflected by data about wage and salary employment collected through the Occupational Employment Statistics surveys. The table below presents employment figures for lawyers during 1992; the percent of industry employment for this occupation (staffing patterns) in 1992; low, medium, and high employment projections for 2005; and staffing patterns for the 2005 moderate projection. In 1992, lawyers ranked 62 in terms of total employment for individual occupations and ranked 133 when considering total employment of occupational groups as well as individual occupations. Table shows the industries employing the most lawyers in 1992.

Industry	1992		2005 employment			Percent of industry employment for 2005 moderate projection
	Employment	Percent of industry employment	Low	Moderate	High	
Total, all industries	409,015	0.37	554,018	586,963	600,412	0.43
Services	300,966	0.78	436,725	462,476	470,859	0.85
Legal services	293,489	32.07	426,489	451,741	459,821	33.33
Government	83,471	0.87	87,319	92,592	96,888	0.89
Local government, except education and hospitals	37,888	0.86	41,670	44,234	46,393	0.86
State government, except education and hospitals	24,007	1.10	25,405	26,968	28,284	1.08
Federal government	21,447	0.99	20,139	21,273	22,085	1.03
Finance, insurance, and real estate	17,901	0.27	23,464	24,769	24,968	0.31
Insurance carriers	8,525	0.58	9,961	10,674	10,679	0.64
Fire, marine, and casualty insurance	4,501	0.81	4,836	5,182	5,184	0.86
Membership organizations	2,872	0.15	3,723	3,863	3,924	0.16
Manufacturing	2,799	0.02	2,718	2,989	3,173	0.02
Depository institutions	2,467	0.12	2,802	2,918	2,926	0.13
Life insurance	2,412	0.45	2,843	3,047	3,049	0.49
Communications and utilities	2,404	0.11	2,540	2,709	2,803	0.12
Transportation and public utilities	2,404	0.04	2,540	2,709	2,803	0.04
Engineering and management services	2,321	0.09	3,672	3,942	4,128	0.11
Commercial banks, savings institutions, and credit unions	2,305	0.12	2,615	2,723	2,730	0.13
Holding and other investment offices	2,188	0.99	3,937	4,058	4,094	1.10
Nondurable goods manufacturing	2,010	0.03	2,051	2,221	2,294	0.03
Chemicals and allied products	1,744	0.16	1,852	2,004	2,063	0.18
Electric, gas, and sanitary services	1,575	0.16	1,745	1,847	1,922	0.17
Real estate	1,541	0.12	2,135	2,202	2,322	0.14
Business and professional organizations	1,458	0.93	2,051	2,152	2,194	1.08
Security and commodity brokers	1,413	0.32	1,839	1,985	2,001	0.35

Source: National Industry-Occupation Matrix, 1992 [data tape]. Prepared by the Bureau of Labor Statistics. Washington, DC: U.S. Department of Labor, Bureau of Labor Statistics, 1992. *Note:* All employment data are wage and salary employment.

★ 418 ★

Occupational Outlook

Employment Projections for Legal Secretaries, by Industry: 1992-2005

The National Industry-Occupation Matrix counts jobs, as reflected by data about wage and salary employment collected through the Occupational Employment Statistics surveys. The table below presents employment figures for legal secretaries during 1992; the percent of industry employment for this occupation (staffing patterns) in 1992; low, medium, and high employment projections for 2005; and staffing patterns for the 2005 moderate projection. In 1992, legal secretaries ranked 92 in terms of total employment for individual occupations and ranked 176 when considering total employment of occupational groups as well as individual occupations. Table shows the industries employing the most legal secretaries in 1992.

Industry	1992		2005 employment			Percent of industry employment for 2005 moderate projection
	Employment	Percent of industry employment	Low	Moderate	High	
Total, all industries	279,806	0.25	414,984	439,475	447,330	0.32
Legal services	270,244	29.53	405,036	429,018	436,691	31.66
Services	270,244	0.70	405,036	429,018	436,691	0.79
Finance, insurance, and real estate	9,542	0.15	9,935	10,442	10,622	0.13
Insurance carriers	4,077	0.28	3,731	3,998	4,000	0.24
Fire, marine, and casualty insurance	2,593	0.47	2,229	2,388	2,389	0.40
Real estate	2,535	0.20	2,833	2,922	3,082	0.18
Real estate agents and managers	1,416	0.24	1,627	1,678	1,770	0.21
Depository institutions	1,152	0.05	1,047	1,091	1,094	0.05
Commercial banks, savings institutions, and credit unions	1,067	0.05	968	1,008	1,011	0.05
Life insurance	798	0.15	752	806	807	0.13
Holding and other investment offices	656	0.30	945	974	982	0.26
Real estate, all other	593	0.41	679	700	738	0.42
Real estate operators and lessors	525	0.09	527	544	574	0.08
Nondepository institutions	447	0.11	556	573	578	0.10
Insurance agents, brokers, and service	440	0.07	581	623	624	0.06
Pension funds and insurance, n.e.c.	373	0.31	519	557	557	0.29
Medical service and health insurance	313	0.12	230	247	247	0.10
Security and commodity brokers	234	0.05	242	261	263	0.05
Federal and business credit institutions	214	0.22	249	257	259	0.20
Mortgage bankers and brokers	176	0.10	244	251	253	0.09
Security and commodity brokers and dealers	157	0.05	155	167	168	0.04
Banking and closely related functions, n.e.c.	86	0.07	79	83	83	0.06
Security and commodity exchanges and services	77	0.09	88	95	95	0.07
Personal credit institutions	56	0.04	63	65	66	0.04

Source: National Industry-Occupation Matrix, 1992 [data tape]. Prepared by the Bureau of Labor Statistics. Washington, DC: U.S. Department of Labor, Bureau of Labor Statistics, 1992. *Notes:* All employment data are wage and salary employment. "n.e.c." stands for "not elsewhere classified."

★ 419 ★

Occupational Outlook

Employment Projections for Licensed Practical Nurses, by Industry: 1992-2005

The National Industry-Occupation Matrix counts jobs, as reflected by data about wage and salary employment collected through the Occupational Employment Statistics surveys. The table below presents employment figures for licensed practical nurses during 1992; the percent of industry employment for this occupation (staffing patterns) in 1992; low, medium, and high employment projections for 2005; and staffing patterns for the 2005 moderate projection. In 1992, licensed practical nurses ranked 40 in terms of total employment for individual occupations and ranked 102 when considering total employment for occupational groups as well as individual occupations. Table shows the industries employing the most licensed practical nurses in 1992.

Industry	1992		2005 employment			Percent of industry employment for 2005 moderate projection
	Employment	Percent of industry employment	Low	Moderate	High	
Total, all industries	653,658	0.59	873,955	914,827	927,506	0.67
Services	610,940	1.58	827,405	865,485	875,904	1.60
Health services	536,346	5.58	713,147	744,991	752,617	5.40
Hospitals, public and private	261,909	5.40	263,930	277,098	279,928	4.41
Nursing and personal care facilities	160,663	10.41	231,212	240,703	243,196	10.44
Offices of physicians, including osteopaths	70,131	4.62	103,305	107,733	109,233	4.56
Government	42,628	0.45	46,437	49,224	51,477	0.47
Business services	39,862	0.75	58,988	63,247	65,076	0.76
Personnel supply services	39,256	2.38	58,004	62,191	63,979	2.41
Home health care services	30,839	7.68	94,386	98,295	98,924	10.74
Social services	20,770	1.06	39,348	40,513	40,852	1.10
Local government, except education and hospitals	15,276	0.35	17,935	19,039	19,968	0.37
Residential care	15,164	2.83	29,896	30,772	31,065	2.31
Federal government	14,185	0.65	13,320	14,070	14,607	0.68
State government, except education and hospitals	13,167	0.60	15,181	16,115	16,902	0.64
Health and allied services, n.e.c.	9,563	3.81	14,941	15,560	15,659	3.97
Individual and miscellaneous social services	4,675	0.67	7,962	8,196	8,231	0.71
Private households	4,000	0.36	2,515	2,595	2,761	0.32
Offices of other health practitioners	2,550	0.78	4,460	4,651	4,716	0.81
Engineering and management services	2,335	0.09	3,896	4,201	4,362	0.11
Management and public relations	1,890	0.29	3,231	3,495	3,633	0.32
Membership organizations	1,545	0.08	1,978	2,038	2,058	0.09
Religious organizations	1,191	0.10	1,501	1,545	1,558	0.11
Job training and related services	708	0.26	1,095	1,140	1,149	0.27
Personal services	494	0.04	663	676	681	0.05

Source: National Industry-Occupation Matrix, 1992 [data tape]. Prepared by the Bureau of Labor Statistics. Washington, DC: U.S. Department of Labor, Bureau of Labor Statistics, 1992. *Notes:* All employment data are wage and salary employment. "n.e.c." stands for "not elsewhere classified."

★ 420 ★

Occupational Outlook

Employment Projections for Machine Feeders and Offbearers, by Industry: 1992-2005

The National Industry-Occupation Matrix counts jobs, as reflected by data about wage and salary employment collected through the Occupational Employment Statistics surveys. The table below presents employment figures for machine feeders and offbearers during 1992; the percent of industry employment for this occupation (staffing patterns) in 1992; low, medium, and high employment projections for 2005; and staffing patterns for the 2005 moderate projection. In 1992, machine feeders and offbearers ranked 99 in terms of total employment for individual occupations and ranked 184 when considering total employment of occupational groups as well as individual occupations. Table shows the industries employing the most machine feeders and offbearers in 1992.

Industry	1992		2005 employment			Percent of industry employment for 2005 moderate projection
	Employment	Percent of industry employment	Low	Moderate	High	
Total, all industries	254,698	0.23	239,117	256,450	273,556	0.19
Manufacturing	234,600	1.30	219,569	235,928	252,686	1.35
Nondurable goods manufacturing	133,850	1.72	130,220	139,993	144,223	1.78
Durable goods manufacturing	103,142	1.01	91,989	98,801	111,385	1.02
Lumber and wood products	38,263	5.67	35,499	36,694	43,831	5.32
Printing and publishing	35,435	2.36	35,914	38,841	40,123	2.22
Food and kindred products	32,605	1.97	32,531	33,760	34,017	2.05
Paper and allied products	26,880	3.91	25,870	27,937	29,000	3.83
Sawmills and planing mills	19,287	10.79	15,929	16,605	19,493	9.96
Commercial printing and business forms	17,357	3.01	16,437	17,610	18,148	2.69
Paperboard containers and boxes	17,004	8.07	16,063	17,265	18,024	7.48
Fabricated metal products	15,829	1.20	13,999	15,295	16,769	1.28
Personal services	14,003	1.26	12,966	13,453	13,475	0.97
Services	14,003	0.04	12,966	13,453	13,475	0.02
Meat products	13,117	3.03	14,385	15,018	15,137	3.03
Textile mill products	12,905	1.92	9,930	11,049	11,356	1.94
Millwork, plywood, and structural members	12,258	5.13	13,461	13,566	17,094	4.69
Rubber and miscellaneous plastics products	11,917	1.37	14,153	15,407	16,279	1.45
Stone, clay, and glass products	10,844	2.12	8,894	9,589	10,495	2.19
Weaving, finishing, yarn and thread mills	9,381	2.61	6,773	7,620	7,711	2.65
Plastics products, miscellaneous	8,378	1.35	11,269	12,208	12,995	1.45
Newspapers	8,232	1.82	8,724	9,383	9,744	1.83
Electronic and other electrical equipment	7,752	0.51	6,021	6,726	7,490	0.50
Primary metal industries	7,258	1.05	5,714	6,360	7,020	1.03
Wood containers and miscellaneous wood products	5,917	4.80	5,457	5,839	6,448	5.08

Source: National Industry-Occupation Matrix, 1992 [data tape]. Prepared by the Bureau of Labor Statistics. Washington, DC: U.S. Department of Labor, Bureau of Labor Statistics, 1992. *Note:* All employment data are wage and salary employment.

★ 421 ★

Occupational Outlook

Employment Projections for Machine Operators, Tenders, Setters, and Set-up Operators, by Industry: 1992-2005

The National Industry-Occupation Matrix counts jobs, as reflected by data about wage and salary employment collected through the Occupational Employment Statistics surveys. The table below presents employment figures for machine operators, tenders, setters, and set-up operators (nonspecific) during 1992; the percent of industry employment for this occupation (staffing patterns) in 1992; low, medium, and high employment projections for 2005; and staffing patterns for the 2005 moderate projection. In 1992, nonspecific machine operators, tenders, setters, and set-up operators ranked 66 in terms of total employment for individual occupations and ranked 138 when considering total employment of occupational groups as well as individual occupations. Table shows the industries employing the most machine operators, tenders, setters, and set-up operators in 1992.

Industry	1992		2005 employment			Percent of industry employment for 2005 moderate projection
	Employment	Percent of industry employment	Low	Moderate	High	
Total, all industries	377,852	0.34	268,492	290,892	306,959	0.21
Manufacturing	273,950	1.52	179,717	196,170	207,230	1.12
Nondurable goods manufacturing	157,363	2.02	106,930	115,664	118,978	1.47
Durable goods manufacturing	119,740	1.17	75,349	83,291	91,127	0.86
Paper and allied products	53,116	7.73	37,861	41,161	42,287	5.65
Services	42,802	0.11	43,149	45,876	47,309	0.08
Wholesale and retail trade	33,232	0.13	25,508	27,581	29,439	0.09
Food and kindred products	30,238	1.83	21,178	21,997	22,156	1.33
Pulp, paper, and paperboard mills	27,846	11.66	17,900	19,585	19,854	8.76
Business services	27,588	0.52	29,453	31,578	32,648	0.38
Transportation equipment	25,202	1.38	15,559	17,204	18,504	0.97
Wholesale trade	24,316	0.40	18,761	20,314	21,924	0.28
Motor vehicles and equipment	23,743	2.94	14,587	16,138	17,364	2.13
Rubber and miscellaneous plastics products	21,952	2.52	15,492	17,016	17,742	1.60
Electronic and other electrical equipment	21,606	1.42	12,337	13,804	15,293	1.02
Wholesale trade, other	21,097	0.55	16,246	17,591	18,985	0.39
Textile mill products	15,394	2.29	8,987	9,965	10,311	1.75
Converted paper products, miscellaneous	15,384	6.47	12,222	13,258	13,749	4.83
Chemicals and allied products	14,695	1.36	10,227	11,087	11,540	1.02
Industrial machinery and equipment	12,814	0.67	8,339	9,448	10,773	0.51
Fabricated metal products	12,682	0.96	7,805	8,501	9,270	0.71
Personnel supply services	11,177	0.68	11,928	12,789	13,156	0.50
Primary metal industries	10,859	1.57	6,223	6,903	7,620	1.12
Agriculture, forestry, and fishing	10,256	0.59	8,138	8,410	9,001	0.43
Instruments and related products	10,250	1.11	6,832	7,625	8,234	0.86

Source: National Industry-Occupation Matrix, 1992 [data tape]. Prepared by the Bureau of Labor Statistics. Washington, DC: U.S. Department of Labor, Bureau of Labor Statistics, 1992. *Note:* All employment data are wage and salary employment.

★ 422 ★

Occupational Outlook

Employment Projections for Machinists, by Industry: 1992-2005

The National Industry-Occupation Matrix counts jobs, as reflected by data about wage and salary employment collected through the Occupational Employment Statistics surveys. The table below presents employment figures for machinists during 1992; the percent of industry employment for this occupation (staffing patterns) in 1992; low, medium, and high employment projections for 2005; and staffing patterns for the 2005 moderate projection. In 1992, machinists ranked 72 in terms of total employment for individual occupations and ranked 148 when considering total employment of occupational groups as well as individual occupations. Table shows the industries employing the most machinists in 1992.

Industry	1992		2005 employment			Percent of industry employment for 2005 moderate projection
	Employment	Percent of industry employment	Low	Moderate	High	
Total, all industries	350,010	0.32	313,559	346,071	379,710	0.25
Manufacturing	273,713	1.52	234,399	261,233	289,027	1.49
Durable goods manufacturing	249,056	2.43	211,531	236,443	263,177	2.45
Industrial machinery and equipment	132,934	6.91	122,181	137,821	155,377	7.38
Industrial machinery, n.e.c.	58,589	20.20	60,601	67,573	75,207	19.24
Fabricated metal products	36,480	2.76	28,802	31,511	34,543	2.63
Transportation equipment	33,860	1.86	26,694	29,156	31,210	1.65
Metalworking machinery	32,848	10.87	29,996	34,243	38,972	10.33
Services	28,755	0.07	35,365	37,567	39,960	0.07
Wholesale and retail trade	28,161	0.11	27,735	30,007	32,177	0.10
Nondurable goods manufacturing	24,847	0.32	23,065	25,002	26,052	0.32
Wholesale trade	23,438	0.39	23,461	25,404	27,417	0.35
Aircraft and parts	17,899	2.93	14,439	15,734	16,934	2.50
Electronic and other electrical equipment	14,728	0.97	10,170	11,670	13,342	0.86
Special industry machinery	12,197	8.26	8,304	9,585	11,159	7.61
Instruments and related products	11,933	1.29	9,030	10,089	11,050	1.14
Primary metal industries	11,800	1.70	8,871	9,843	10,847	1.59
General industrial machinery	11,431	4.85	9,390	10,746	12,309	4.51
Fabricated metal products, miscellaneous	9,639	4.34	7,666	8,495	9,284	4.18
Repair services, miscellaneous	9,477	2.75	10,875	11,591	12,190	2.58
Construction and related machinery	9,211	4.54	7,929	8,953	10,063	4.18
Machinery, equipment, and supplies	9,137	1.21	9,627	10,424	11,250	1.10
Repair shops and related services, all other	8,948	3.78	10,259	10,935	11,522	3.54
Rubber and miscellaneous plastics products	8,350	0.96	9,353	10,193	10,747	0.96
Screw machine products, including bolts	7,987	8.90	6,653	7,425	8,023	8.73

Source: National Industry-Occupation Matrix, 1992 [data tape]. Prepared by the Bureau of Labor Statistics. Washington, DC: U.S. Department of Labor, Bureau of Labor Statistics, 1992. *Notes:* All employment data are wage and salary employment. "n.e.c." stands for "not elsewhere classified."

★ 423 ★

Occupational Outlook

Employment Projections for Management Support Workers, by Industry: 1992-2005

The National Industry-Occupation Matrix counts jobs, as reflected by data about wage and salary employment collected through the Occupational Employment Statistics surveys. The table below presents employment figures for management support workers (nonspecific) during 1992; the percent of industry employment for this occupation (staffing patterns) in 1992; low, medium, and high employment projections for 2005; and staffing patterns for the 2005 moderate projection. In 1992, management support workers (nonspecific) ranked 28 in terms of total employment for individual occupations and ranked 83 when considering total employment of occupational groups as well as individual occupations. Table shows the industries employing the most management support workers (nonspecific) in 1992.

Industry	1992		2005 employment			Percent of industry employment for 2005 moderate projection
	Employment	Percent of industry employment	Low	Moderate	High	
Total, all industries	833,995	0.75	1,092,173	1,166,626	1,214,068	0.86
Services	225,221	0.58	346,671	366,811	379,312	0.68
Finance, insurance, and real estate	178,864	2.72	251,896	266,133	267,449	3.34
Government	167,348	1.75	191,369	203,296	213,048	1.94
Manufacturing	140,990	0.78	145,152	159,554	172,505	0.91
Durable goods manufacturing	93,382	0.91	90,869	101,040	112,185	1.05
Engineering and management services	73,425	2.97	126,185	135,235	141,734	3.67
Depository institutions	67,830	3.22	84,410	87,912	88,139	4.01
Local government, except education and hospitals	65,947	1.50	79,428	84,315	88,431	1.64
State government, except education and hospitals	65,109	2.98	75,455	80,097	84,007	3.20
Commercial banks, savings institutions, and credit unions	62,357	3.15	77,457	80,670	80,879	3.92
Wholesale and retail trade	56,095	0.22	84,231	91,050	97,322	0.29
Transportation and public utilities	54,782	0.96	61,861	67,502	69,784	1.04
Education, public and private	52,929	0.54	64,758	68,087	70,640	0.55
Nondurable goods manufacturing	47,830	0.61	54,588	58,844	60,635	0.75
Insurance carriers	43,978	2.97	53,286	57,103	57,128	3.44
Communications and utilities	42,671	1.92	46,940	50,651	52,205	2.32
Wholesale trade	41,622	0.69	66,094	71,566	77,237	1.00
Accounting, auditing, and bookkeeping	40,834	7.99	74,844	80,353	83,875	9.82
Transportation equipment	37,677	2.07	39,805	43,483	46,768	2.46
Security and commodity brokers	32,596	7.43	52,815	57,011	57,464	10.00
Wholesale trade, other	31,477	0.83	50,121	54,269	58,570	1.20
Health services	31,164	0.32	44,875	47,076	47,562	0.34
Federal government	29,739	1.37	30,582	32,304	33,536	1.57
Hospitals, public and private	28,414	0.59	40,026	42,023	42,452	0.67

Source: National Industry-Occupation Matrix, 1992 [data tape]. Prepared by the Bureau of Labor Statistics. Washington, DC: U.S. Department of Labor, Bureau of Labor Statistics, 1992. *Note:* All employment data are wage and salary employment.

★ 424 ★

Occupational Outlook

Employment Projections for Managers and Administrators, by Industry: 1992-2005

The National Industry-Occupation Matrix counts jobs, as reflected by data about wage and salary employment collected through the Occupational Employment Statistics surveys. The table below presents employment figures for managers and administrators (nonspecific) during 1992; the percent of industry employment for this occupation (staffing patterns) in 1992; low, medium, and high employment projections for 2005; and staffing patterns for the 2005 moderate projection. In 1992, managers and administrators (nonspecific) ranked 24 in terms of total employment for individual occupations and ranked 76 when considering total employment of occupational groups as well as individual occupations. Table shows the industries employing the most managers and administrators (nonspecific) in 1992.

Industry	1992		2005 employment			Percent of industry employment for 2005 moderate projection
	Employment	Percent of industry employment	Low	Moderate	High	
Total, all industries	889,064	0.80	1,052,048	1,117,264	1,159,994	0.82
Services	378,350	0.98	513,746	538,385	548,623	0.99
Health services	207,154	2.15	280,568	293,653	296,623	2.13
Manufacturing	136,757	0.76	121,288	133,445	144,002	0.76
Hospitals, public and private	136,527	2.82	168,759	177,178	178,987	2.82
Government	134,998	1.41	154,586	165,391	174,012	1.58
Durable goods manufacturing	85,813	0.84	70,558	78,639	87,391	0.81
Finance, insurance, and real estate	77,128	1.17	83,331	87,919	88,621	1.10
Wholesale and retail trade	66,971	0.26	82,847	89,439	94,693	0.29
State government, except education and hospitals	52,814	2.42	63,778	67,702	71,007	2.71
Nondurable goods manufacturing	51,270	0.66	51,104	55,210	57,001	0.70
Transportation and public utilities	42,452	0.74	40,796	44,514	46,137	0.69
Education, public and private	40,646	0.42	45,601	47,946	49,743	0.38
Agriculture, forestry, and fishing	36,914	2.12	42,179	43,606	46,551	2.21
Retail trade	35,697	0.18	36,207	38,938	40,189	0.16
Local government, except education and hospitals	35,303	0.80	44,306	47,032	49,328	0.91
Wholesale trade	31,274	0.52	46,641	50,501	54,504	0.70
Insurance carriers	30,295	2.05	31,145	33,376	33,391	2.01
Social services	29,665	1.51	52,858	54,463	54,840	1.48
Communications and utilities	28,442	1.28	26,301	28,287	29,153	1.29
Engineering and management services	28,208	1.14	39,613	42,408	44,538	1.15
U.S. Postal Service	28,177	3.56	26,461	29,487	31,700	3.93
Transportation equipment	26,461	1.45	22,961	25,261	27,139	1.43
Nursing and personal care facilities	25,446	1.65	36,621	38,124	38,519	1.65
Business services	24,284	0.46	35,956	38,664	40,148	0.46

Source: National Industry-Occupation Matrix, 1992 [data tape]. Prepared by the Bureau of Labor Statistics. Washington, DC: U.S. Department of Labor, Bureau of Labor Statistics, 1992. *Note:* All employment data are wage and salary employment.

★ 425 ★
Occupational Outlook

Employment Projections for Marketing, Advertising, and Public Relations Managers, by Industry: 1992-2005

The National Industry-Occupation Matrix counts jobs, as reflected by data about wage and salary employment collected through the Occupational Employment Statistics surveys. The table below presents employment figures for marketing, advertising, and public relations managers during 1992; the percent of industry employment for this occupation (staffing patterns) in 1992; low, medium, and high employment projections for 2005; and staffing patterns for the 2005 moderate projection. In 1992, marketing, advertising, and public relations managers ranked 57 in terms of total employment for individual occupations and ranked 128 when considering total employment of occupational groups as well as individual occupations. Table shows the industries employing the most marketing, advertising, and public relations managers in 1992.

Industry	1992		2005 employment			Percent of industry employment for 2005 moderate projection
	Employment	Percent of industry employment	Low	Moderate	High	
Total, all industries	424,942	0.38	538,934	578,796	606,264	0.43
Services	143,779	0.37	221,100	234,386	242,174	0.43
Manufacturing	117,517	0.65	121,972	134,030	144,329	0.76
Wholesale and retail trade	93,920	0.37	112,412	121,335	128,020	0.39
Durable goods manufacturing	60,426	0.59	55,612	62,498	70,385	0.65
Retail trade	57,930	0.30	59,139	63,652	65,766	0.27
Nondurable goods manufacturing	57,066	0.73	66,331	71,495	73,865	0.91
Business services	54,264	1.02	84,795	91,185	94,809	1.09
Wholesale trade	35,989	0.60	53,273	57,682	62,254	0.80
Finance, insurance, and real estate	33,007	0.50	42,622	44,878	45,297	0.56
Transportation and public utilities	27,978	0.49	31,280	34,008	35,099	0.52
Automotive dealers and service stations	26,561	1.33	24,161	26,023	26,911	1.17
Wholesale trade, other	24,701	0.65	36,590	39,619	42,759	0.87
Engineering and management services	24,562	0.99	41,894	45,008	47,174	1.22
Printing and publishing	22,045	1.47	28,026	30,311	31,391	1.73
Communications and utilities	20,111	0.90	21,820	23,352	23,961	1.07
Motor vehicle dealers	19,998	2.13	16,862	18,161	18,781	1.66
General merchandise stores	19,245	0.79	20,077	21,625	22,363	0.83
Department stores	18,528	0.91	19,450	20,949	21,664	0.92
Advertising	16,976	7.53	19,357	20,787	21,599	7.23
Computer and data processing services	16,415	1.98	30,605	33,032	34,461	2.03
Industrial machinery and equipment	15,986	0.83	12,847	14,920	17,888	0.80
Communications	15,558	1.23	16,488	17,711	18,091	1.59
Management and public relations	15,043	2.30	28,580	30,916	32,136	2.79
Chemicals and allied products	13,905	1.28	15,334	16,590	17,206	1.52

Source: National Industry-Occupation Matrix, 1992 [data tape]. Prepared by the Bureau of Labor Statistics. Washington, DC: U.S. Department of Labor, Bureau of Labor Statistics, 1992. *Note:* All employment data are wage and salary employment.

★ 426 ★

Occupational Outlook

Employment Projections for Marketing and Sales Worker Supervisors, by Industry: 1992-2005

The National Industry-Occupation Matrix counts jobs, as reflected by data about wage and salary employment collected through the Occupational Employment Statistics surveys. The table below presents employment figures for marketing and sales worker supervisors during 1992; the percent of industry employment for this occupation (staffing patterns) in 1992; low, medium, and high employment projections for 2005; and staffing patterns for the 2005 moderate projection. In 1992, marketing and sales worker supervisors ranked 18 in terms of total employment for individual occupations and ranked 59 when considering total employment of occupational groups as well as individual occupations. Table shows the industries employing the most marketing and sales worker supervisors in 1992.

Industry	1992		2005 employment			Percent of industry employment for 2005 moderate projection
	Employment	Percent of industry employment	Low	Moderate	High	
Total, all industries	1,278,700	1.15	1,540,865	1,656,593	1,725,895	1.22
Wholesale and retail trade	956,334	3.77	1,126,560	1,214,542	1,266,498	3.92
Retail trade	773,685	4.00	909,285	979,282	1,012,592	4.12
Food stores	186,327	5.86	232,587	250,514	259,065	6.46
Wholesale trade	182,649	3.02	217,275	235,261	253,905	3.27
Grocery stores	168,842	5.94	212,204	228,560	236,361	6.58
Retail stores, miscellaneous	143,527	5.81	171,775	185,015	191,330	6.12
Services	131,482	0.34	189,712	199,865	207,189	0.37
Apparel and accessory stores	126,128	11.15	155,405	167,382	173,096	12.10
Wholesale trade, other	115,899	3.04	137,309	148,675	160,458	3.28
Automotive dealers and service stations	114,690	5.74	127,998	137,864	142,569	6.18
General merchandise stores	113,438	4.68	111,898	120,522	124,636	4.63
Clothing and accesories stores	90,737	10.72	114,520	123,346	127,556	11.99
Department stores	84,484	4.13	87,055	93,765	96,965	4.13
Manufacturing	77,384	0.43	80,681	87,915	93,720	0.50
Finance, insurance, and real estate	71,201	1.08	95,141	100,573	102,056	1.26
Shopping goods stores, miscellaneous	65,860	7.73	85,746	92,355	95,507	8.02
Motor vehicle dealers	48,314	5.14	54,980	59,218	61,239	5.42
Furniture and homefurnishings stores	47,930	5.95	62,242	67,040	69,328	6.49
Nondurable goods manufacturing	45,496	0.58	50,811	54,539	56,195	0.69
Building materials and garden supplies	38,752	5.26	43,610	46,972	48,575	5.55
Gasoline service stations	37,419	6.08	41,468	44,664	46,189	7.05
Business services	36,812	0.69	60,085	64,671	67,279	0.77
Drug stores and proprietary stores	35,754	5.89	38,736	41,722	43,146	5.97
Transportation and public utilities	32,221	0.56	38,266	42,558	43,973	0.66

Source: National Industry-Occupation Matrix, 1992 [data tape]. Prepared by the Bureau of Labor Statistics. Washington, DC: U.S. Department of Labor, Bureau of Labor Statistics, 1992. *Note:* All employment data are wage and salary employment.

★ 427 ★

Occupational Outlook

Employment Projections for Materials, Merchandise, and Service Order Clerks, by Industry: 1992-2005

The National Industry-Occupation Matrix counts jobs, as reflected by data about wage and salary employment collected through the Occupational Employment Statistics surveys. The table below presents employment figures for materials, merchandise, and service order clerks during 1992; the percent of industry employment for this occupation (staffing patterns) in 1992; low, medium, and high employment projections for 2005; and staffing patterns for the 2005 moderate projection. In 1992, materials, merchandise, and service order clerks ranked 86 in terms of total employment for individual occupations and ranked 167 when considering total employment of occupational groups as well as individual occupations. Table shows the industries employing the most materials, merchandise, and service order clerks in 1992.

Industry	1992		2005 employment			Percent of industry employment for 2005 moderate projection
	Employment	Percent of industry employment	Low	Moderate	High	
Total, all industries	298,634	0.27	288,119	311,903	330,005	0.23
Wholesale and retail trade	152,343	0.60	149,999	162,120	172,551	0.52
Wholesale trade	105,541	1.75	100,621	108,950	117,584	1.52
Manufacturing	81,885	0.45	68,304	75,160	80,263	0.43
Wholesale trade, other	73,399	1.93	69,566	75,324	81,294	1.66
Retail trade	46,803	0.24	49,379	53,170	54,967	0.22
Nondurable goods manufacturing	42,898	0.55	38,521	41,811	43,231	0.53
Services	41,838	0.11	52,393	55,641	57,338	0.10
Durable goods manufacturing	39,018	0.38	29,815	33,381	37,038	0.35
Retail stores, miscellaneous	26,439	1.07	32,029	34,497	35,675	1.14
Business services	22,615	0.43	30,107	32,348	33,566	0.39
Transportation and public utilities	20,505	0.36	15,545	17,008	17,608	0.26
Communications and utilities	16,780	0.76	11,581	12,552	12,902	0.57
Nonstore retailers	15,806	5.37	21,752	23,428	24,228	7.31
Printing and publishing	14,503	0.96	14,347	15,536	16,037	0.89
Machinery, equipment, and supplies	13,982	1.86	14,306	15,490	16,718	1.63
General merchandise stores	13,557	0.56	10,804	11,637	12,034	0.45
Communications	13,518	1.07	8,674	9,476	9,701	0.85
Telephone communications	12,381	1.40	7,681	8,423	8,627	1.19
Groceries and related products	11,802	1.38	10,831	11,728	12,657	1.20
Department stores	10,866	0.53	8,957	9,648	9,977	0.43
Industrial machinery and equipment	10,269	0.53	7,489	8,572	9,976	0.46
Business services, miscellaneous	9,557	0.77	12,791	13,691	14,183	0.68
Commercial printing and business forms	7,735	1.34	7,472	8,004	8,249	1.22
Health services	7,725	0.08	8,508	8,908	8,992	0.06

Source: National Industry-Occupation Matrix, 1992 [data tape]. Prepared by the Bureau of Labor Statistics. Washington, DC: U.S. Department of Labor, Bureau of Labor Statistics, 1992. *Note:* All employment data are wage and salary employment.

Occupational Outlook

Employment Projections for Mechanical Engineers, by Industry: 1992-2005

The National Industry-Occupation Matrix counts jobs, as reflected by data about wage and salary employment collected through the Occupational Employment Statistics surveys. The table below presents employment figures for mechanical engineers during 1992; the percent of industry employment for this occupation (staffing patterns) in 1992; low, medium, and high employment projections for 2005; and staffing patterns for the 2005 moderate projection. In 1992, mechanical engineers ranked 110 in terms of total employment for individual occupations and ranked 196 when considering total employment of occupational groups as well as individual occupations. Table shows the industries employing the most mechanical engineers in 1992.

Industry	1992		2005 employment			Percent of industry employment for 2005 moderate projection
	Employment	Percent of industry employment	Low	Moderate	High	
Total, all industries	222,017	0.20	244,371	267,137	293,582	0.20
Manufacturing	136,583	0.76	139,115	154,700	170,166	0.88
Durable goods manufacturing	113,057	1.10	114,263	127,771	142,151	1.32
Services	52,348	0.14	69,688	74,594	82,598	0.14
Engineering and management services	39,215	1.59	50,392	54,079	61,438	1.47
Industrial machinery and equipment	36,318	1.89	38,230	43,552	49,888	2.33
Engineering and architectural services	29,037	3.89	37,773	40,748	47,770	4.07
Transportation equipment	27,694	1.52	27,418	30,034	32,242	1.70
Nondurable goods manufacturing	23,664	0.30	25,040	27,131	28,203	0.35
Instruments and related products	15,988	1.73	16,510	18,414	20,159	2.07
Electronic and other electrical equipment	15,356	1.01	14,011	16,029	18,242	1.18
Government	13,833	0.14	13,140	13,889	14,435	0.13
Aircraft and parts	12,935	2.12	10,932	11,912	12,821	1.89
Federal government	12,652	0.58	11,881	12,549	13,028	0.61
Fabricated metal products	10,686	0.81	10,759	11,663	12,816	0.98
Research and testing services	7,789	1.40	8,708	9,101	9,270	1.20
Chemicals and allied products	7,781	0.72	7,381	8,036	8,375	0.74
Motor vehicles and equipment	7,734	0.96	9,464	10,471	11,266	1.38
Business services	7,385	0.14	11,871	12,758	13,205	0.15
Wholesale and retail trade	7,063	0.03	8,550	9,254	9,964	0.03
Wholesale trade	6,667	0.11	8,101	8,771	9,467	0.12
General industrial machinery	6,499	2.76	6,991	8,000	9,164	3.36
Rubber and miscellaneous plastics products	5,852	0.67	7,817	8,522	8,981	0.80
Metalworking machinery	5,812	1.92	6,951	7,935	9,031	2.39
Measuring and controlling devices	5,314	1.83	5,788	6,536	7,227	2.62

Source: National Industry-Occupation Matrix, 1992 [data tape]. Prepared by the Bureau of Labor Statistics. Washington, DC: U.S. Department of Labor, Bureau of Labor Statistics, 1992. *Note:* All employment data are wage and salary employment.

★ 429 ★

Occupational Outlook

Employment Projections for Mechanics, Installers, and Repairers, by Industry: 1992-2005

The National Industry-Occupation Matrix counts jobs, as reflected by data about wage and salary employment collected through the Occupational Employment Statistics surveys. The table below presents employment figures for mechanics, installers, and repairers (nonspecific) during 1992; the percent of industry employment for this occupation (staffing patterns) in 1992; low, medium, and high employment projections for 2005; and staffing patterns for the 2005 moderate projection. In 1992, nonspecific mechanics, installers, and repairers ranked 77 in terms of total employment for individual occupations and ranked 154 when considering total employment of occupational groups as well as individual occupations. Table shows the industries employing the most mechanics, installers, and repairers in 1992.

Industry	1992		2005 employment			Percent of industry employment for 2005 moderate projection
	Employment	Percent of industry employment	Low	Moderate	High	
Total, all industries	328,500	0.30	378,324	405,418	430,235	0.30
Services	69,471	0.18	101,621	107,569	111,677	0.20
Manufacturing	65,564	0.36	62,900	68,985	74,959	0.39
Transportation and public utilities	64,552	1.13	62,988	67,794	70,946	1.04
Wholesale and retail trade	58,984	0.23	69,070	74,594	78,894	0.24
Durable goods manufacturing	45,343	0.44	43,010	47,182	52,385	0.49
Government	45,220	0.47	50,410	53,698	56,306	0.51
Communications and utilities	41,609	1.87	40,720	43,261	44,902	1.98
Electric, gas, and sanitary services	31,826	3.33	34,559	36,564	38,050	3.41
Wholesale trade	30,612	0.51	36,019	39,001	42,092	0.54
Retail trade	28,372	0.15	33,050	35,593	36,802	0.15
Transportation	22,943	0.66	22,268	24,533	26,044	0.57
Wholesale trade, other	22,250	0.58	26,360	28,542	30,804	0.63
Local government, except education and hospitals	21,811	0.50	28,785	30,556	32,048	0.59
Business services	21,353	0.40	35,399	38,050	39,505	0.45
Transportation equipment	20,351	1.12	18,963	20,930	22,628	1.19
Nondurable goods manufacturing	20,049	0.26	19,679	21,567	22,279	0.27
Railroad transportation	16,654	6.55	15,116	16,402	17,528	6.50
Electric services	14,833	3.36	16,421	17,374	18,080	3.66
Construction	14,632	0.33	19,507	20,318	23,965	0.36
Automotive dealers and service stations	14,194	0.71	16,409	17,674	18,277	0.79
Motor vehicles and equipment	12,974	1.60	11,037	12,210	13,137	1.61
Special trade contractors	11,582	0.43	15,681	16,333	19,266	0.48
Business services, miscellaneous	10,398	0.83	17,396	18,620	19,290	0.92

Source: National Industry-Occupation Matrix, 1992 [data tape]. Prepared by the Bureau of Labor Statistics. Washington, DC: U.S. Department of Labor, Bureau of Labor Statistics, 1992. *Note:* All employment data are wage and salary employment.

★ 430 ★

Occupational Outlook

Employment Projections for Medical Secretaries, by Industry: 1992-2005

The National Industry-Occupation Matrix counts jobs, as reflected by data about wage and salary employment collected through the Occupational Employment Statistics surveys. The table below presents employment figures for medical secretaries during 1992; the percent of industry employment for this occupation (staffing patterns) in 1992; low, medium, and high employment projections for 2005; and staffing patterns for the 2005 moderate projection. In 1992, medical secretaries ranked 105 in terms of total employment for individual occupations and ranked 190 when considering total employment of occupational groups as well as individual occupations. Table shows the industries employing the most medical secretaries in 1992.

Industry	1992		2005 employment			Percent of industry employment for 2005 moderate projection
	Employment	Percent of industry employment	Low	Moderate	High	
Total, all industries	234,697	0.21	326,287	340,669	345,016	0.25
Health services	234,697	2.44	326,287	340,669	345,016	2.47
Services	234,697	0.61	326,287	340,669	345,016	0.63
Offices of physicians, including osteopaths	130,538	8.60	192,287	200,529	203,321	8.49
Hospitals, public and private	53,133	1.10	61,511	64,580	65,240	1.03
Offices and clinics of dentists	18,620	3.44	23,150	24,142	24,478	3.55
Offices of other health practitioners	16,609	5.07	26,146	27,267	27,647	4.76
Medical and dental laboratories	4,420	2.44	5,907	6,152	6,191	2.28
Nursing and personal care facilities	4,408	0.29	6,058	6,307	6,372	0.27
Health and allied services, n.e.c.	3,649	1.45	5,131	5,343	5,377	1.36
Home health care services	3,320	0.83	6,096	6,349	6,390	0.69

Source: National Industry-Occupation Matrix, 1992 [data tape]. Prepared by the Bureau of Labor Statistics. Washington, DC: U.S. Department of Labor, Bureau of Labor Statistics, 1992. *Notes:* All employment data are wage and salary employment. "n.e.c." stands for "not elsewhere classified."

★ 431 ★

Occupational Outlook

Employment Projections for Nursing Aides, Orderlies, and Attendants, by Industry: 1992-2005

The National Industry-Occupation Matrix counts jobs, as reflected by data about wage and salary employment collected through the Occupational Employment Statistics surveys. The table below presents employment figures for nursing aides, orderlies, and attendants during 1992; the percent of industry employment for this occupation (staffing patterns) in 1992; low, medium, and high employment projections for 2005; and staffing patterns for the 2005 moderate projection. In 1992, nursing aides, orderlies, and attendants ranked 17 in terms of total employment for individual occupations and ranked 58 when considering total employment of occupational groups as well as individual occupations. Table shows the industries employing the most nursing aides, orderlies, and attendants in 1992.

Industry	1992		2005 employment			Percent of industry employment for 2005 moderate projection
	Employment	Percent of industry employment	Low	Moderate	High	
Total, all industries	1,279,471	1.16	1,777,259	1,854,602	1,885,394	1.37
Services	1,180,179	3.05	1,672,342	1,743,339	1,768,871	3.22
Health services	978,675	10.18	1,352,765	1,411,671	1,426,087	10.24
Nursing and personal care facilities	639,161	41.43	919,824	957,584	967,502	41.53
Hospitals, public and private	305,624	6.30	377,779	396,627	400,677	6.31
Government	98,621	1.03	104,076	110,394	115,597	1.06
Private households	86,000	7.71	121,270	125,161	133,132	15.61
Social services	67,715	3.46	130,638	134,500	135,702	3.64
Residential care	57,416	10.73	113,401	116,721	117,834	8.74
Local government, except education and hospitals	43,562	0.99	47,909	50,857	53,340	0.99
State government, except education and hospitals	37,465	1.71	39,646	42,086	44,140	1.68
Business services	34,658	0.65	51,261	54,960	56,546	0.66
Personnel supply services	34,266	2.08	50,631	54,286	55,847	2.10
Federal government	17,593	0.81	16,521	17,451	18,116	0.85
Individual and miscellaneous social services	7,519	1.07	12,803	13,180	13,236	1.13
Religious organizations	7,025	0.61	8,857	9,117	9,191	0.64
Health and allied services, n.e.c.	5,572	2.22	8,706	9,066	9,124	2.31
Offices of physicians, including osteopaths	4,068	0.27	6,658	6,944	7,040	0.29
Job training and related services	2,190	0.81	3,388	3,526	3,555	0.84
Offices of other health practitioners	1,997	0.61	3,493	3,643	3,694	0.64
Agriculture, forestry, and fishing	672	0.04	841	869	926	0.04
Child day care services	590	0.13	1,046	1,073	1,077	0.14

Source: National Industry-Occupation Matrix, 1992 [data tape]. Prepared by the Bureau of Labor Statistics. Washington, DC: U.S. Department of Labor, Bureau of Labor Statistics, 1992. *Notes:* All employment data are wage and salary employment. "n.e.c." stands for "not elsewhere classified."

★ 432 ★

Occupational Outlook

Employment Projections for Packaging and Filling Machine Operators and Tenders, by Industry: 1992-2005

The National Industry-Occupation Matrix counts jobs, as reflected by data about wage and salary employment collected through the Occupational Employment Statistics surveys. The table below presents employment figures for packaging and filling machine operators and tenders during 1992; the percent of industry employment for this occupation (staffing patterns) in 1992; low, medium, and high employment projections for 2005; and staffing patterns for the 2005 moderate projection. In 1992, packaging and filling machine operators and tenders ranked 80 in terms of total employment for individual occupations and ranked 158 when considering total employment of occupational groups as well as individual occupations. Table shows the industries employing the most packaging and filling machine operators and tenders in 1992.

Industry	1992		2005 employment			Percent of industry employment for 2005 moderate projection
	Employment	Percent of industry employment	Low	Moderate	High	
Total, all industries	318,862	0.29	232,379	247,788	256,926	0.18
Manufacturing	246,779	1.37	170,515	181,174	186,811	1.03
Nondurable goods manufacturing	204,999	2.63	144,774	152,905	156,047	1.95
Food and kindred products	120,248	7.27	82,568	85,488	86,112	5.19
Wholesale and retail trade	48,452	0.19	36,676	39,647	42,239	0.13
Chemicals and allied products	45,774	4.23	33,282	35,944	37,113	3.30
Durable goods manufacturing	41,993	0.41	25,915	28,456	30,946	0.29
Wholesale trade	33,198	0.55	25,366	27,465	29,642	0.38
Services	22,825	0.06	24,582	26,339	27,208	0.05
Business services	22,825	0.43	24,582	26,339	27,208	0.31
Wholesale trade, other	19,283	0.51	14,850	16,079	17,353	0.35
Drugs	19,128	7.47	14,876	15,942	16,106	5.37
Meat products	18,995	4.38	15,345	16,020	16,147	3.23
Beverages	18,765	10.72	10,626	11,023	11,100	8.03
Preserved fruits and vegetables	16,066	6.52	12,001	12,415	12,539	4.76
Retail trade	15,253	0.08	11,310	12,182	12,598	0.05
Foods and kindred products, miscellaneous	14,749	8.19	11,726	11,793	11,821	5.95
Bakery products	14,589	7.04	9,493	9,925	9,969	5.18
Food stores	13,805	0.43	10,261	11,052	11,429	0.28
Grain mill products and fats and oils	12,596	8.07	8,082	8,445	8,537	6.06
Dairy products	12,279	8.06	7,493	7,899	7,935	5.90
Sugar and confectionery products	12,210	11.73	7,801	7,967	8,064	8.76
Soap, cleaners, and toilet goods	12,200	7.95	9,199	10,049	10,402	6.02
Grocery stores	11,618	0.41	8,629	9,294	9,611	0.27
Groceries and related products	11,438	1.34	8,529	9,235	9,967	0.95

Source: National Industry-Occupation Matrix, 1992 [data tape]. Prepared by the Bureau of Labor Statistics. Washington, DC: U.S. Department of Labor, Bureau of Labor Statistics, 1992. *Note:* All employment data are wage and salary employment.

★ 433 ★
Occupational Outlook

Employment Projections for Personnel, Training, and Labor Relations Specialists, by Industry: 1992-2005

The National Industry-Occupation Matrix counts jobs, as reflected by data about wage and salary employment collected through the Occupational Employment Statistics surveys. The table below presents employment figures for personnel, training, and labor relations specialists during 1992; the percent of industry employment for this occupation (staffing patterns) in 1992; low, medium, and high employment projections for 2005; and staffing patterns for the 2005 moderate projection. In 1992, personnel, training, and labor relations specialists ranked 95 in terms of total employment for individual occupations and ranked 179 when considering total employment of occupational groups as well as individual occupations. Table shows the industries employing the most personnel, training, and labor relations specialists in 1992.

Industry	1992		2005 employment			Percent of industry employment for 2005 moderate projection
	Employment	Percent of industry employment	Low	Moderate	High	
Total, all industries	272,010	0.25	349,415	371,517	386,413	0.27
Services	104,237	0.27	147,476	154,313	157,960	0.28
Government	56,104	0.59	61,411	65,216	68,165	0.62
Manufacturing	48,197	0.27	55,215	60,886	65,955	0.35
Membership organizations	44,854	2.30	47,355	48,437	49,020	2.03
Labor organizations	39,471	28.38	38,606	39,375	39,827	30.29
Durable goods manufacturing	31,483	0.31	33,887	37,828	42,156	0.39
Federal government	26,393	1.21	29,740	31,414	32,613	1.52
Finance, insurance, and real estate	26,231	0.40	38,724	40,735	40,926	0.51
Nondurable goods manufacturing	16,851	0.22	21,535	23,282	24,021	0.30
Transportation and public utilities	16,491	0.29	20,240	22,037	22,887	0.34
Business services	15,874	0.30	28,410	30,539	31,680	0.36
Wholesale and retail trade	15,348	0.06	19,234	20,749	21,893	0.07
State government, except education and hospitals	14,755	0.67	15,615	16,575	17,384	0.66
Health services	14,436	0.15	23,790	24,922	25,169	0.18
Local government, except education and hospitals	11,467	0.26	12,611	13,387	14,041	0.26
Hospitals, public and private	11,152	0.23	17,214	18,072	18,257	0.29
Depository institutions	11,048	0.53	15,058	15,683	15,723	0.71
Communications and utilities	10,731	0.48	12,286	13,107	13,575	0.60
Commercial banks, savings institutions, and credit unions	10,389	0.52	14,141	14,728	14,766	0.72
Education, public and private	10,161	0.10	12,487	13,129	13,622	0.11
Transportation equipment	9,760	0.54	11,222	12,296	13,209	0.70
Retail trade	8,696	0.04	9,745	10,475	10,804	0.04
Engineering and management services	8,588	0.35	15,955	17,091	17,943	0.46
Insurance carriers	8,573	0.58	11,311	12,121	12,126	0.73

Source: National Industry-Occupation Matrix, 1992 [data tape]. Prepared by the Bureau of Labor Statistics. Washington, DC: U.S. Department of Labor, Bureau of Labor Statistics, 1992. *Note:* All employment data are wage and salary employment.

★ 434 ★

Occupational Outlook

Employment Projections for Physicians, by Industry: 1992-2005

The National Industry-Occupation Matrix counts jobs, as reflected by data about wage and salary employment collected through the Occupational Employment Statistics surveys. The table below presents employment figures for physicians during 1992; the percent of industry employment for this occupation (staffing patterns) in 1992; low, medium, and high employment projections for 2005; and staffing patterns for the 2005 moderate projection. In 1992, physicians ranked 55 in terms of total employment for individual occupations and ranked 125 when considering total employment of occupational groups as well as individual occupations. Table shows the industries employing the most physicians in 1992.

Industry	1992		2005 employment			Percent of industry employment for 2005 moderate projection
	Employment	Percent of industry employment	Low	Moderate	High	
Total, all industries	430,281	0.39	589,440	616,244	625,455	0.45
Services	381,618	0.99	542,039	566,094	573,315	1.05
Health services	379,234	3.95	537,815	561,729	568,910	4.07
Offices of physicians, including osteopaths	262,392	17.28	386,511	403,078	408,691	17.06
Hospitals, public and private	98,918	2.04	127,240	133,588	134,952	2.12
Government	47,158	0.49	45,810	48,450	50,430	0.46
Federal government	36,392	1.67	34,173	36,096	37,474	1.75
Health and allied services, n.e.c.	8,232	3.28	10,290	10,716	10,785	2.73
Local government, except education and hospitals	5,889	0.13	6,477	6,876	7,211	0.13
State government, except education and hospitals	4,876	0.22	5,160	5,478	5,745	0.22
Medical and dental laboratories	3,758	2.08	5,580	5,811	5,848	2.15
Nursing and personal care facilities	2,807	0.18	4,287	4,463	4,509	0.19
Offices of other health practitioners	2,019	0.62	2,295	2,394	2,427	0.42
Social services	1,631	0.08	3,185	3,281	3,303	0.09
Finance, insurance, and real estate	1,418	0.02	1,475	1,580	1,582	0.02
Insurance carriers	1,301	0.09	1,286	1,378	1,378	0.08
Medical service and health insurance	1,013	0.38	933	1,000	1,000	0.40
Individual and miscellaneous social services	922	0.13	1,569	1,616	1,623	0.14
Residential care	555	0.10	1,371	1,411	1,424	0.11
Life insurance	230	0.04	271	290	290	0.05
Job training and related services	128	0.05	198	206	208	0.05
Civic and social associations	108	0.03	148	151	153	0.03
Insurance agents, brokers, and service	105	0.02	173	186	186	0.02
Agriculture, forestry, and fishing	87	0.00	115	120	127	0.01

Source: National Industry-Occupation Matrix, 1992 [data tape]. Prepared by the Bureau of Labor Statistics. Washington, DC: U.S. Department of Labor, Bureau of Labor Statistics, 1992. *Notes:* All employment data are wage and salary employment. "n.e.c." stands for "not elsewhere classified."

★ 435 ★
Occupational Outlook

Employment Projections for Plumbers, Pipefitters, and Steamfitters, by Industry: 1992-2005

The National Industry-Occupation Matrix counts jobs, as reflected by data about wage and salary employment collected through the Occupational Employment Statistics surveys. The table below presents employment figures for plumbers, pipefitters, and steamfitters during 1992; the percent of industry employment for this occupation (staffing patterns) in 1992; low, medium, and high employment projections for 2005; and staffing patterns for the 2005 moderate projection. In 1992, plumbers, pipefitters, and steamfitters ranked 88 in terms of total employment for individual occupationsand ranked 170 when considering total employment of occupational groups as well as individual occupations. Table shows the industries employing the most plumbers, pipefitters, and steamfitters in 1992.

Industry	1992		2005 employment			Percent of industry employment for 2005 moderate projection
	Employment	Percent of industry employment	Low	Moderate	High	
Total, all industries	291,181	0.26	299,744	314,478	359,266	0.23
Construction	198,599	4.44	214,279	223,190	263,259	3.96
Special trade contractors	169,454	6.28	182,591	190,184	224,328	5.55
Plumbing, heating, and air-conditioning	156,162	25.92	167,500	174,466	205,788	24.46
Manufacturing	35,958	0.20	28,040	30,532	32,484	0.17
Durable goods manufacturing	21,906	0.21	16,890	18,426	19,956	0.19
Services	19,357	0.05	22,927	24,219	25,033	0.04
Government	18,588	0.19	16,246	17,209	17,966	0.16
General building contractors	15,000	1.41	16,650	17,342	20,455	1.34
Nondurable goods manufacturing	14,149	0.18	11,254	12,220	12,646	0.16
Heavy construction, except building	14,145	1.99	15,038	15,664	18,476	1.72
Heavy construction, except highway and street	13,932	2.80	14,783	15,398	18,162	2.50
Nonresidential building construction	12,242	2.37	13,643	14,211	16,762	2.22
Transportation equipment	12,116	0.66	9,144	9,899	10,327	0.56
Transportation and public utilities	11,064	0.19	10,114	10,722	11,173	0.17
Communications and utilities	10,350	0.47	9,531	10,084	10,494	0.46
Electric, gas, and sanitary services	10,304	1.08	9,497	10,048	10,456	0.94
Federal government	9,298	0.43	7,522	7,946	8,249	0.38
Special trade contractors, all other	9,245	1.87	10,169	10,592	12,494	1.69
Ship and boat building and repairing	8,086	4.78	5,781	6,198	6,347	4.56
Local government, except education and hospitals	7,492	0.17	7,099	7,535	7,903	0.15
Education, public and private	5,934	0.06	6,282	6,605	6,853	0.05
Gas production and distribution	5,467	3.34	4,318	4,569	4,755	3.11
Chemicals and allied products	4,792	0.44	3,914	4,260	4,430	0.39
Health services	3,882	0.04	4,332	4,547	4,593	0.03

Source: National Industry-Occupation Matrix, 1992 [data tape]. Prepared by the Bureau of Labor Statistics. Washington, DC: U.S. Department of Labor, Bureau of Labor Statistics, 1992. *Note:* All employment data are wage and salary employment.

★ 436 ★

Occupational Outlook

Employment Projections for Police Patrol Officers, by Industry: 1992-2005

The National Industry-Occupation Matrix counts jobs, as reflected by data about wage and salary employment collected through the Occupational Employment Statistics surveys. The table below presents employment figures for police patrol officers during 1992; the percent of industry employment for this occupation (staffing patterns) in 1992; low, medium, and high employment projections for 2005; and staffing patterns for the 2005 moderate projection. In 1992, police patrol officers ranked 60 in terms of total employment for individual occupations and ranked 131 when considering total employment of occupational groups as well as individual occupations. Table shows the industries employing the most police patrol officers in 1992.

Industry	1992		2005 employment			Percent of industry employment for 2005 moderate projection
	Employment	Percent of industry employment	Low	Moderate	High	
Total, all industries	411,088	0.37	441,019	468,159	490,933	0.34
Government	411,088	4.31	441,019	468,159	490,933	4.48
Local government, except education and hospitals	347,373	7.91	375,123	398,204	417,643	7.74
State government, except education and hospitals	52,108	2.38	55,142	58,535	61,393	2.34
Federal government	10,359	0.48	9,727	10,275	10,667	0.50
U.S. Postal Service	1,248	0.16	1,027	1,144	1,230	0.15

Source: National Industry-Occupation Matrix, 1992 [data tape]. Prepared by the Bureau of Labor Statistics. Washington, DC: U.S. Department of Labor, Bureau of Labor Statistics, 1992. *Note:* All employment data are wage and salary employment.

★ 437 ★

Occupational Outlook

Employment Projections for Postal Mail Carriers, by Industry: 1992-2005

The National Industry-Occupation Matrix counts jobs, as reflected by data about wage and salary employment collected through the Occupational Employment Statistics surveys. The table below presents employment figures for postal mail carriers during 1992; the percent of industry employment for this occupation (staffing patterns) in 1992; low, medium, and high employment projections for 2005; and staffing patterns for the 2005 moderate projection. In 1992, postal mail carriers ranked 87 in terms of total employment for individual occupations and ranked 169 when considering total employment of occupational groups as well as individual occupations. Table shows the industries employing the most postal mail carriers in 1992.

Industry	1992		2005 employment			Percent of industry employment for 2005 moderate projection
	Employment	Percent of industry employment	Low	Moderate	High	
Total, all industries	296,917	0.27	268,786	299,522	322,000	0.22
Government	296,917	3.11	268,786	299,522	322,000	2.86
U.S. Postal Service	296,917	37.49	268,786	299,522	322,000	39.89

Source: National Industry-Occupation Matrix, 1992 [data tape]. Prepared by the Bureau of Labor Statistics. Washington, DC: U.S. Department of Labor, Bureau of Labor Statistics, 1992. *Note:* All employment data are wage and salary employment.

★ 438 ★

Occupational Outlook

Employment Projections for Precision Inspectors, Testers, and Graders, by Industry: 1992-2005

The National Industry-Occupation Matrix counts jobs, as reflected by data about wage and salary employment collected through the Occupational Employment Statistics surveys. The table below presents employment figures for precision inspectors, testers, and graders during 1992; the percent of industry employment for this occupation (staffing patterns) in 1992; low, medium, and high employment projections for 2005; and staffing patterns for the 2005 moderate projection. In 1992, precision inspectors, testers, and graders ranked 41 in terms of total employment for individual occupations and ranked 105 when considering total employment of occupational groups as well as individual occupations. Table shows the industries employing the most precision inspectors, testers, and graders in 1992.

Industry	1992		2005 employment			Percent of industry employment for 2005 moderate projection
	Employment	Percent of industry employment	Low	Moderate	High	
Total, all industries	622,770	0.56	509,559	557,279	595,396	0.41
Manufacturing	488,496	2.71	329,422	364,556	393,775	2.08
Durable goods manufacturing	319,626	3.12	208,460	231,822	257,270	2.40
Nondurable goods manufacturing	170,894	2.19	122,733	134,658	138,476	1.72
Electronic and other electrical equipment	65,827	4.31	39,436	45,259	51,567	3.34
Transportation equipment	62,834	3.45	42,217	46,312	49,757	2.62
Services	57,511	0.15	95,769	101,675	104,992	0.19
Industrial machinery and equipment	48,743	2.54	31,913	36,345	41,916	1.95
Instruments and related products	36,366	3.93	24,208	26,997	29,402	3.04
Fabricated metal products	35,386	2.68	24,134	26,320	28,832	2.20
Rubber and miscellaneous plastics products	33,178	3.81	30,323	33,074	34,834	3.10
Apparel and other textile products	32,657	3.25	18,256	21,417	21,521	2.82
Textile mill products	30,848	4.59	18,501	20,794	21,237	3.64
Electronic components and accessories	28,236	5.38	17,986	21,286	24,859	4.06
Business services	27,785	0.52	53,069	56,909	58,775	0.68
Apparel	27,521	3.41	14,393	17,122	17,123	3.08
Motor vehicles and equipment	27,289	3.37	18,056	19,975	21,492	2.63
Food and kindred products	26,206	1.58	20,322	21,053	21,220	1.28
Aircraft and parts	26,055	4.26	17,859	19,462	20,945	3.09
Primary metal industries	24,702	3.56	15,758	17,469	19,265	2.83
Transportation and public utilities	24,315	0.43	25,956	28,521	29,686	0.44
Wholesale and retail trade	23,498	0.09	27,583	29,831	31,906	0.10
Government	21,814	0.23	22,959	24,349	25,489	0.23
Plastics products, miscellaneous	20,790	3.36	22,185	24,033	25,582	2.85
Chemicals and allied products	20,437	1.89	15,056	16,304	16,910	1.50

Source: National Industry-Occupation Matrix, 1992 [data tape]. Prepared by the Bureau of Labor Statistics. Washington, DC: U.S. Department of Labor, Bureau of Labor Statistics, 1992. *Note:* All employment data are wage and salary employment.

★ 439 ★

Occupational Outlook

Employment Projections for Preschool and Kindergarten Teachers, by Industry: 1992-2005

The National Industry-Occupation Matrix counts jobs, as reflected by data about wage and salary employment collected through the Occupational Employment Statistics surveys. The table below presents employment figures for preschool and kindergarten teachers during 1992; the percent of industry employment for this occupation (staffing patterns) in 1992; low, medium, and high employment projections for 2005; and staffing patterns for the 2005 moderate projection. In 1992, preschool and kindergarten teachers ranked 58 in terms of total employment for individual occupations and ranked 129 when considering total employment of occupational groups as well as individual occupations. Table shows the industries employing the most preschool and kindergarten teachers in 1992.

Industry	1992		2005 employment			Percent of industry employment for 2005 moderate projection
	Employment	Percent of industry employment	Low	Moderate	High	
Total, all industries	423,751	0.38	634,432	657,459	668,865	0.48
Services	423,751	1.10	634,432	657,459	668,865	1.21
Social services	173,503	8.86	302,208	310,254	311,404	8.40
Child day care services	153,304	34.14	266,749	273,718	274,677	35.23
Religious organizations	67,579	5.87	85,203	87,705	88,420	6.18
Individual and miscellaneous social services	16,507	2.35	28,110	28,938	29,061	2.49
Civic and social associations	5,128	1.22	7,012	7,152	7,234	1.35
Job training and related services	1,916	0.71	2,965	3,085	3,110	0.74
Residential care	1,776	0.33	4,384	4,513	4,556	0.34

Source: National Industry-Occupation Matrix, 1992 [data tape]. Prepared by the Bureau of Labor Statistics. Washington, DC: U.S. Department of Labor, Bureau of Labor Statistics, 1992. *Note:* All employment data are wage and salary employment.

★ 440 ★

Occupational Outlook

Employment Projections for Private Household Child Care Workers, by Industry: 1992-2005

The National Industry-Occupation Matrix counts jobs, as reflected by data about wage and salary employment collected through the Occupational Employment Statistics surveys. The table below presents employment figures for private household child care workers during 1992; the percent of industry employment for this occupation (staffing patterns) in 1992; low, medium, and high employment projections for 2005; and staffing patterns for the 2005 moderate projection. In 1992, private household child care workers ranked 73 in terms of total employment for individual occupations and ranked 149 when considering total employment of occupational groups as well as individual occupations. Table shows the industries employing the most private household child care workers in 1992.

Industry	1992		2005 employment			Percent of industry employment for 2005 moderate projection
	Employment	Percent of industry employment	Low	Moderate	High	
Total, all industries	350,000	0.32	220,024	227,083	241,545	0.17
Private households	350,000	31.36	220,024	227,083	241,545	28.32
Services	350,000	0.91	220,024	227,083	241,545	0.42

Source: National Industry-Occupation Matrix, 1992 [data tape]. Prepared by the Bureau of Labor Statistics. Washington, DC: U.S. Department of Labor, Bureau of Labor Statistics, 1992. *Note:* All employment data are wage and salary employment.

★ 441 ★

Occupational Outlook

Employment Projections for Private Household Cleaners and Servants, by Industry: 1992-2005

The National Industry-Occupation Matrix counts jobs, as reflected by data about wage and salary employment collected through the Occupational Employment Statistics surveys. The table below presents employment figures for private household cleaners and servants during 1992; the percent of industry employment for this occupation (staffing patterns) in 1992; low, medium, and high employment projections for 2005; and staffing patterns for the 2005 moderate projection. In 1992, private household cleaners and servants ranked 48 in terms of total employment for individual occupations and ranked 117 when considering total employment of occupational groups as well as individual occupations. Table shows the industries employing the most private household cleaners and servants in 1992.

Industry	1992		2005 employment			Percent of industry employment for 2005 moderate projection
	Employment	Percent of industry employment	Low	Moderate	High	
Total, all industries	482,000	0.44	315,097	325,207	345,917	0.24
Private households	482,000	43.19	315,097	325,207	345,917	40.55
Services	482,000	1.25	315,097	325,207	345,917	0.60

Source: National Industry-Occupation Matrix, 1992 [data tape]. Prepared by the Bureau of Labor Statistics. Washington, DC: U.S. Department of Labor, Bureau of Labor Statistics, 1992. *Note:* All employment data are wage and salary employment.

★ 442 ★

Occupational Outlook

Employment Projections for Production, Planning, and Expediting Clerks, by Industry: 1992-2005

The National Industry-Occupation Matrix counts jobs, as reflected by data about wage and salary employment collected through the Occupational Employment Statistics surveys. The table below presents employment figures for production, planning, and expediting clerks during 1992; the percent of industry employment for this occupation (staffing patterns) in 1992; low, medium, and high employment projections for 2005; and staffing patterns for the 2005 moderate projection. In 1992, production, planning, and expediting clerks ranked 104 in terms of total employment for individual occupations and ranked 189 when considering total employment of occupational groups as well as individual occupations. Table shows the industries employing the most production, planning, and expediting clerks in 1992.

Industry	1992		2005 employment			Percent of industry employment for 2005 moderate projection
	Employment	Percent of industry employment	Low	Moderate	High	
Total, all industries	236,370	0.21	244,657	268,531	288,641	0.20
Manufacturing	154,324	0.86	151,997	168,115	182,934	0.96
Durable goods manufacturing	108,737	1.06	100,066	111,735	124,629	1.16
Nondurable goods manufacturing	45,723	0.59	52,105	56,563	58,440	0.72
Transportation equipment	25,053	1.37	25,398	27,769	29,794	1.57

[Continued]

★ 442 ★

Employment Projections for Production, Planning, and Expediting Clerks, by Industry: 1992-2005
[Continued]

Industry	1992		2005 employment			Percent of industry employment for 2005 moderate projection
	Employment	Percent of industry employment	Low	Moderate	High	
Industrial machinery and equipment	24,366	1.27	20,312	23,441	27,763	1.25
Services	22,906	0.06	36,413	39,045	40,714	0.07
Transportation and public utilities	20,689	0.36	16,617	18,503	19,082	0.28
Wholesale and retail trade	18,246	0.07	21,199	22,914	24,398	0.07
Electronic and other electrical equipment	17,488	1.15	14,934	17,137	19,541	1.27
Business services	17,276	0.33	27,921	30,027	31,205	0.36
Government	16,566	0.17	14,551	15,784	16,679	0.15
Instruments and related products	14,745	1.59	12,866	14,321	15,687	1.61
Printing and publishing	14,683	0.98	18,901	20,405	21,074	1.17
Aircraft and parts	13,858	2.27	14,926	16,265	17,505	2.58
Communications	13,840	1.09	8,715	9,505	9,729	0.85
Communications and utilities	13,840	0.62	8,715	9,505	9,729	0.43
Telephone communications	12,588	1.42	7,297	8,001	8,196	1.13
Fabricated metal products	12,181	0.92	11,707	12,723	14,041	1.06
Wholesale trade	12,138	0.20	14,417	15,611	16,848	0.22
Computer and office equipment	9,953	2.54	5,403	6,610	8,744	2.51
Wholesale trade, other	8,685	0.23	10,289	11,141	12,023	0.25
U.S. Postal Service	8,659	1.09	7,126	7,941	8,537	1.06
Federal government	7,908	0.36	7,425	7,843	8,143	0.38
Commercial printing and business forms	7,640	1.32	10,147	10,870	11,203	1.66

Source: *National Industry-Occupation Matrix, 1992* [data tape]. Prepared by the Bureau of Labor Statistics. Washington, DC: U.S. Department of Labor, Bureau of Labor Statistics, 1992. *Note:* All employment data are wage and salary employment.

★ 443 ★

Occupational Outlook

Employment Projections for Purchasing Agents, by Industry: 1992-2005

The National Industry-Occupation Matrix counts jobs, as reflected by data about wage and salary employment collected through the Occupational Employment Statistics surveys. The table below presents employment figures for purchasing agents (excluding wholesale, retail, and farm product purchasing agents) during 1992; the percent of industry employment for this occupation (staffing patterns) in 1992; low, medium, and high employment projections for 2005; and staffing patterns for the 2005 moderate projection. In 1992, purchasing agents ranked 114 in terms of total employment for individual occupations and ranked 202 when considering total employment of occupational groups as well as individual occupations. Table shows the industries employing the most purchasing agents in 1992.

Industry	1992		2005 employment			Percent of industry employment for 2005 moderate projection
	Employment	Percent of industry employment	Low	Moderate	High	
Total, all industries	217,157	0.20	194,002	210,138	225,710	0.15
Manufacturing	100,613	0.56	93,497	103,526	113,774	0.59
Durable goods manufacturing	78,425	0.77	70,096	78,175	87,452	0.81
Government	47,507	0.50	35,267	37,303	38,820	0.36
Federal government	37,393	1.72	27,418	28,962	30,067	1.40
Services	36,859	0.10	37,856	40,064	41,516	0.07
Nondurable goods manufacturing	22,016	0.28	23,198	25,122	26,020	0.32
Industrial machinery and equipment	19,936	1.04	17,424	19,951	23,238	1.07
Transportation equipment	16,422	0.90	15,106	16,525	17,707	0.94
Electronic and other electrical equipment	13,174	0.86	10,753	12,337	14,072	0.91
Instruments and related products	9,523	1.03	8,317	9,279	10,162	1.05
Health services	8,989	0.09	8,772	9,191	9,285	0.07
Wholesale and retail trade	8,856	0.03	7,504	8,106	8,633	0.03
Fabricated metal products	8,745	0.66	7,976	8,640	9,624	0.72
Business services	8,665	0.16	9,655	10,381	10,787	0.12
Aircraft and parts	8,096	1.32	7,631	8,315	8,949	1.32
Transportation and public utilities	7,370	0.13	5,667	6,186	6,429	0.10
Hospitals, public and private	7,023	0.14	6,521	6,847	6,917	0.11
Engineering and management services	6,921	0.28	7,261	7,756	8,319	0.21
Chemicals and allied products	6,612	0.61	6,591	7,143	7,426	0.66
Construction	6,315	0.14	6,143	6,398	7,547	0.11
Wholesale trade	6,131	0.10	5,282	5,719	6,172	0.08
Finance, insurance, and real estate	6,082	0.09	5,482	5,761	5,804	0.07
Local government, except education and hospitals	5,747	0.13	4,563	4,843	5,080	0.09
Computer and office equipment	5,574	1.42	2,913	3,563	4,714	1.35

Source: National Industry-Occupation Matrix, 1992 [data tape]. Prepared by the Bureau of Labor Statistics. Washington, DC: U.S. Department of Labor, Bureau of Labor Statistics, 1992. *Note:* All employment data are wage and salary employment.

★ 444 ★

Occupational Outlook

Employment Projections for Purchasing Managers, by Industry: 1992-2005

The National Industry-Occupation Matrix counts jobs, as reflected by data about wage and salary employment collected through the Occupational Employment Statistics surveys. The table below presents employment figures for purchasing managers during 1992; the percent of industry employment for this occupation (staffing patterns) in 1992; low, medium, and high employment projections for 2005; and staffing patterns for the 2005 moderate projection. In 1992, purchasing managers ranked 111 in terms of total employment for individual occupations and ranked 197 when considering total employment of occupational groups as well as individual occupations. Table shows the industries employing the most purchasing managers in 1992.

Industry	1992		2005 employment			Percent of industry employment for 2005 moderate projection
	Employment	Percent of industry employment	Low	Moderate	High	
Total, all industries	221,328	0.20	233,839	252,172	266,338	0.19
Wholesale and retail trade	143,759	0.57	149,999	161,927	170,701	0.52
Retail trade	80,876	0.42	83,146	89,540	92,578	0.38
Wholesale trade	62,883	1.04	66,853	72,387	78,123	1.01
Wholesale trade, other	40,444	1.06	42,743	46,281	49,949	1.02
Manufacturing	38,003	0.21	36,875	40,568	44,104	0.23
Durable goods manufacturing	24,738	0.24	22,687	25,232	28,261	0.26
Services	23,447	0.06	30,839	32,489	33,421	0.06
Retail stores, miscellaneous	22,739	0.92	24,173	26,036	26,924	0.86
Food stores	21,190	0.67	21,572	23,235	24,028	0.60
Grocery stores	17,885	0.63	18,228	19,633	20,304	0.56
Nondurable goods manufacturing	13,199	0.17	14,109	15,246	15,723	0.19
General merchandise stores	9,920	0.41	8,727	9,400	9,721	0.36
Building materials and garden supplies	9,543	1.30	9,533	10,268	10,619	1.21
Shopping goods stores, miscellaneous	9,415	1.11	10,934	11,777	12,179	1.02
Machinery, equipment, and supplies	9,040	1.20	10,313	11,167	12,052	1.18
Furniture and homefurnishings stores	8,882	1.10	10,034	10,807	11,176	1.05
Health services	7,760	0.08	9,582	10,031	10,132	0.07
Groceries and related products	7,700	0.90	7,880	8,532	9,208	0.88
Apparel and accessory stores	7,558	0.67	7,983	8,599	8,892	0.62
Department stores	7,379	0.36	6,783	7,306	7,555	0.32
Used merchandise and retail stores, n.e.c.	5,751	1.14	6,304	6,790	7,021	1.06
Industrial machinery and equipment	5,575	0.29	4,905	5,623	6,568	0.30
Government	5,559	0.06	5,180	5,491	5,740	0.05
Hospitals, public and private	5,312	0.11	6,150	6,457	6,523	0.10

Source: National Industry-Occupation Matrix, 1992 [data tape]. Prepared by the Bureau of Labor Statistics. Washington, DC: U.S. Department of Labor, Bureau of Labor Statistics, 1992. *Notes:* All employment data are wage and salary employment. "n.e.c." stands for "not elsewhere classified."

★ 445 ★

Occupational Outlook

Employment Projections for Receptionists and Information Clerks, by Industry: 1992-2005

The National Industry-Occupation Matrix counts jobs, as reflected by data about wage and salary employment collected through the Occupational Employment Statistics surveys. The table below presents employment figures for receptionists and information clerks during 1992; the percent of industry employment for this occupation (staffing patterns) in 1992; low, medium, and high employment projections for 2005; and staffing patterns for the 2005 moderate projection. In 1992, receptionists and information clerks ranked 26 in terms of total employment for individual occupations and ranked 78 when considering total employment of occupational groups as well as individual occupations. Table shows the industries employing the most receptionists and information clerks in 1992.

Industry	1992		2005 employment			Percent of industry employment for 2005 moderate projection
	Employment	Percent of industry employment	Low	Moderate	High	
Total, all industries	872,384	0.79	1,123,966	1,183,776	1,217,554	0.87
Services	586,826	1.52	803,113	841,767	858,865	1.55
Health services	274,389	2.85	370,323	386,453	391,452	2.80
Offices of physicians, including osteopaths	132,971	8.76	193,984	202,299	205,116	8.56
Finance, insurance, and real estate	105,155	1.60	131,854	138,084	141,233	1.73
Business services	95,041	1.79	143,247	153,705	158,668	1.84
Wholesale and retail trade	76,772	0.30	85,393	92,306	98,424	0.30
Personnel supply services	60,064	3.64	96,159	103,100	106,065	3.99
Wholesale trade	55,329	0.92	61,232	66,301	71,555	0.92
Offices and clinics of dentists	54,723	10.10	60,643	63,243	64,123	9.29
Personal services	49,460	4.45	63,007	63,974	64,349	4.63
Manufacturing	41,230	0.23	39,545	43,146	46,000	0.25
Real estate	40,791	3.18	50,854	52,445	55,315	3.23
Wholesale trade, other	39,570	1.04	45,671	49,452	53,371	1.09
Hospitals, public and private	38,264	0.79	43,871	46,060	46,530	0.73
Legal services	37,248	4.07	52,061	55,144	56,130	4.07
Engineering and management services	34,052	1.38	47,821	51,355	54,449	1.39
Membership organizations	28,759	1.47	34,252	35,350	35,825	1.48
Government	25,526	0.27	24,627	26,143	27,410	0.25
Offices of other health practitioners	25,143	7.68	39,200	40,880	41,449	7.13
Nondurable goods manufacturing	24,168	0.31	25,077	27,088	27,981	0.35
Real estate agents and managers	22,861	3.95	32,404	33,418	35,247	4.21
Retail trade	21,443	0.11	24,161	26,005	26,868	0.11
Beauty shops	21,282	5.62	28,045	28,372	28,485	5.61
Social services	21,061	1.08	35,008	36,082	36,312	0.98

Source: National Industry-Occupation Matrix, 1992 [data tape]. Prepared by the Bureau of Labor Statistics. Washington, DC: U.S. Department of Labor, Bureau of Labor Statistics, 1992. *Note:* All employment data are wage and salary employment.

★ 446 ★

Occupational Outlook

Employment Projections for Registered Nurses, by Industry: 1992-2005

The National Industry-Occupation Matrix counts jobs, as reflected by data about wage and salary employment collected through the Occupational Employment Statistics surveys. The table below presents employment figures for registered nurses during 1992; the percent of industry employment for this occupation (staffing patterns) in 1992; low, medium, and high employment projections for 2005; and staffing patterns for the 2005 moderate projection. In 1992, registered nurses ranked 11 in terms of total employment for individual occupations and ranked 45 when considering total employment of occupational groups as well as individual occupations. Table shows the industries employing the most registered nurses in 1992.

Industry	1992		2005 employment			Percent of industry employment for 2005 moderate projection
	Employment	Percent of industry employment	Low	Moderate	High	
Total, all industries	1,820,427	1.64	2,463,655	2,584,510	2,620,358	1.90
Services	1,691,027	4.38	2,311,577	2,423,268	2,452,024	4.47
Health services	1,541,458	16.04	2,091,590	2,191,590	2,214,109	15.89
Hospitals, public and private	1,201,650	24.78	1,548,044	1,625,276	1,641,873	25.84
Offices of physicians, including osteopaths	137,670	9.07	202,792	211,484	214,429	8.95
Government	121,784	1.28	143,881	152,511	159,454	1.46
Nursing and personal care facilities	96,740	6.27	147,729	153,794	155,386	6.67
Home health care services	71,349	17.77	131,021	136,447	137,320	14.91
Business services	55,865	1.05	77,777	83,407	85,843	1.00
Personnel supply services	54,393	3.30	75,362	80,802	83,125	3.13
Education, public and private	50,556	0.52	62,131	65,325	67,774	0.52
Federal government	48,277	2.22	45,333	47,885	49,712	2.32
Local government, except education and hospitals	39,193	0.89	50,196	53,285	55,886	1.04
State government, except education and hospitals	33,971	1.55	48,069	51,027	53,517	2.04
Social services	28,266	1.44	58,336	60,104	60,568	1.63
Health and allied services, n.e.c.	25,629	10.22	48,052	50,042	50,362	12.77
Residential care	13,961	2.61	34,467	35,476	35,814	2.66
Individual and miscellaneous social services	10,265	1.46	17,479	17,994	18,071	1.55
Offices of other health practitioners	6,386	1.95	11,169	11,648	11,810	2.03
Finance, insurance, and real estate	6,029	0.09	6,471	6,888	6,956	0.09
Engineering and management services	5,782	0.23	9,218	9,887	10,238	0.27
Insurance carriers	4,724	0.32	4,633	4,964	4,967	0.30
Management and public relations	3,935	0.60	6,727	7,277	7,564	0.66
Medical service and health insurance	3,582	1.34	3,301	3,537	3,539	1.42
Job training and related services	3,430	1.27	5,307	5,524	5,568	1.32

Source: National Industry-Occupation Matrix, 1992 [data tape]. Prepared by the Bureau of Labor Statistics. Washington, DC: U.S. Department of Labor, Bureau of Labor Statistics, 1992. *Notes:* All employment data are wage and salary employment. "n.e.c." stands for "not elsewhere classified."

★ 447 ★

Occupational Outlook

Employment Projections for Restaurant Cooks, by Industry: 1992-2005

The National Industry-Occupation Matrix counts jobs, as reflected by data about wage and salary employment collected through the Occupational Employment Statistics surveys. The table below presents employment figures for restaurant cooks during 1992; the percent of industry employment for this occupation (staffing patterns) in 1992; low, medium, and high employment projections for 2005; and staffing patterns for the 2005 moderate projection. In 1992, restaurant cooks ranked 43 in terms of total employment for individual occupations and ranked 108 when considering total employment of occupational groups as well as individual occupations. Table shows the industries employing the most restaurant cooks in 1992.

Industry	1992		2005 employment			Percent of industry employment for 2005 moderate projection
	Employment	Percent of industry employment	Low	Moderate	High	
Total, all industries	566,411	0.51	793,883	833,556	840,817	0.61
Wholesale and retail trade	474,305	1.87	663,849	699,762	703,693	2.26
Retail trade	473,670	2.45	663,112	698,964	702,831	2.94
Eating and drinking places	470,162	7.12	659,340	694,901	698,630	7.92
Services	92,106	0.24	130,034	133,794	137,124	0.25
Hotels and other lodging places	62,012	3.94	85,989	88,905	91,833	4.03
Amusement and recreation services	21,616	1.85	32,894	33,491	33,766	2.06
Amusement and recreation services, all other	19,739	2.39	30,751	31,317	31,556	2.60
Membership organizations	7,661	0.39	9,419	9,615	9,726	0.40
Civic and social associations	7,270	1.73	8,906	9,084	9,188	1.71
General merchandise stores	1,439	0.06	1,438	1,549	1,602	0.06
Bowling centers	1,213	1.38	1,296	1,307	1,324	1.54
Department stores	1,180	0.06	1,216	1,310	1,355	0.06
Social services	817	0.04	1,732	1,784	1,798	0.05
Automotive dealers and service stations	701	0.04	776	836	865	0.04
Wholesale trade	636	0.01	737	798	862	0.01
Food stores	581	0.02	656	706	730	0.02
Retail stores, miscellaneous	518	0.02	572	616	637	0.02
Commercial sports	496	0.44	616	627	638	0.46
Residential care	456	0.09	1,125	1,158	1,169	0.09
Groceries and related products	356	0.04	409	442	477	0.05
General merchandise stores, n.e.c.	259	0.07	222	239	247	0.07
Religious organizations	214	0.02	270	278	280	0.02
Apparel and accessory stores	197	0.02	240	259	267	0.02
Nonstore retailers	184	0.06	194	209	217	0.07

Source: National Industry-Occupation Matrix, 1992 [data tape]. Prepared by the Bureau of Labor Statistics. Washington, DC: U.S. Department of Labor, Bureau of Labor Statistics, 1992. *Notes:* All employment data are wage and salary employment. "n.e.c." stands for "not elsewhere classified."

★ 448 ★

Occupational Outlook

Employment Projections for Restaurant, Lounge, or Coffee Shop Hosts and Hostesses, by Industry: 1992-2005

The National Industry-Occupation Matrix counts jobs, as reflected by data about wage and salary employment collected through the Occupational Employment Statistics surveys. The table below presents employment figures for restaurant, lounge, or coffee shop hosts and hostesses during 1992; the percent of industry employment for this occupation (staffing patterns) in 1992; low, medium, and high employment projections for 2005; and staffing patterns for the 2005 moderate projection. In 1992, restaurant, lounge, or coffee shop hosts and hostesses ranked 112 in terms of total employment for individual occupations and ranked 198 when considering total employment of occupational groups as well as individual occupations. Table shows the industries employing the most restaurant, lounge, or coffee shop hosts and hostesses in 1992.

Industry	1992		2005 employment			Percent of industry employment for 2005 moderate projection
	Employment	Percent of industry employment	Low	Moderate	High	
Total, all industries	218,562	0.20	283,107	297,540	300,924	0.22
Wholesale and retail trade	158,009	0.62	205,164	216,300	217,557	0.70
Retail trade	157,968	0.82	205,114	216,246	217,499	0.91
Eating and drinking places	155,144	2.35	202,122	213,023	214,166	2.43
Services	56,228	0.15	72,976	75,967	77,837	0.14
Hotels and other lodging places	17,399	1.11	20,248	20,935	21,624	0.95
Education, public and private	17,048	0.18	21,848	22,971	23,833	0.18
Health services	15,645	0.16	21,742	22,736	22,969	0.16
Hospitals, public and private	8,799	0.18	11,416	11,986	12,108	0.19
Nursing and personal care facilities	6,845	0.44	10,326	10,750	10,861	0.47
Amusement and recreation services	4,509	0.39	6,634	6,756	6,817	0.42
Government	4,326	0.05	4,967	5,273	5,530	0.05
Amusement and recreation services, all other	3,875	0.47	5,881	5,990	6,035	0.50
Local government, except education and hospitals	2,270	0.05	2,641	2,803	2,940	0.05
State government, except education and hospitals	2,056	0.09	2,326	2,469	2,590	0.10
Retail stores, miscellaneous	1,145	0.05	1,219	1,313	1,358	0.04
General merchandise stores	1,129	0.05	1,147	1,235	1,278	0.05
Nonstore retailers	1,071	0.36	1,134	1,221	1,263	0.38
Membership organizations	1,007	0.05	1,153	1,180	1,192	0.05
Civic and social associations	700	0.17	766	781	790	0.15
Social services	621	0.03	1,350	1,390	1,401	0.04
Food stores	452	0.01	515	554	573	0.01
Residential care	386	0.07	952	980	989	0.07
Bowling centers	289	0.33	309	311	315	0.37
Individual and miscellaneous social services	220	0.03	374	385	387	0.03

Source: National Industry-Occupation Matrix, 1992 [data tape]. Prepared by the Bureau of Labor Statistics. Washington, DC: U.S. Department of Labor, Bureau of Labor Statistics, 1992. *Note:* All employment data are wage and salary employment.

★ 449 ★

Occupational Outlook

Employment Projections for Retail Salespersons, by Industry: 1992-2005

The National Industry-Occupation Matrix counts jobs, as reflected by data about wage and salary employment collected through the Occupational Employment Statistics surveys. The table below presents employment figures for retail salespersons during 1992; the percent of industry employment for this occupation (staffing patterns) in 1992; low, medium, and high employment projections for 2005; and staffing patterns for the 2005 moderate projection. In 1992, retail salespersons ranked 2 in terms of total employment for individual occupations and ranked 20 when considering total employment of occupational groups as well as individual occupations. Table shows the industries employing the most retail salespersons in 1992.

Industry	1992		2005 employment			Percent of industry employment for 2005 moderate projection
	Employment	Percent of industry employment	Low	Moderate	High	
Total, all industries	3,462,672	3.13	3,939,668	4,242,035	4,393,086	3.13
Wholesale and retail trade	3,403,888	13.41	3,873,625	4,171,877	4,320,322	13.47
Retail trade	3,272,907	16.92	3,717,552	4,002,885	4,137,937	16.84
General merchandise stores	965,538	39.86	973,506	1,048,541	1,084,330	40.27
Department stores	840,514	41.08	866,219	932,984	964,829	41.14
Retail stores, miscellaneous	686,508	27.79	847,396	912,710	943,863	30.21
Apparel and accessory stores	657,488	58.13	759,106	817,615	845,522	59.09
Clothing and accesories stores	489,281	57.80	561,388	604,658	625,296	58.76
Shopping goods stores, miscellaneous	407,097	47.81	530,013	570,864	590,349	49.58
Automotive dealers and service stations	261,100	13.06	298,150	321,131	332,091	14.40
Furniture and homefurnishings stores	244,449	30.32	313,724	337,905	349,439	32.70
Food stores	235,468	7.41	270,470	291,317	301,261	7.51
Motor vehicle dealers	196,674	20.93	223,851	241,105	249,334	22.06
Building materials and garden supplies	182,490	24.77	203,253	218,919	226,391	25.85
Grocery stores	152,908	5.38	174,737	188,205	194,629	5.42
Used merchandise and retail stores, n.e.c.	132,942	26.46	163,387	175,980	181,987	27.54
Wholesale trade	130,981	2.17	156,073	168,992	182,385	2.35
Shoe stores	127,291	62.25	135,750	146,213	151,203	63.81
General merchandise stores, n.e.c.	125,024	33.25	107,287	115,557	119,501	34.38
Furniture and homefurnishings stores	123,057	28.04	140,925	151,787	156,968	30.21
Appliance, radio, television, and music stores	121,392	33.04	172,799	186,118	192,471	35.06
Drug stores and proprietary stores	91,869	15.14	99,550	107,223	110,882	15.33
Wholesale trade, other	87,566	2.30	103,760	112,349	121,253	2.48
Lumber and other building materials	86,746	20.20	100,057	107,769	111,448	21.63
Hardware stores	57,016	36.71	58,147	62,629	64,767	38.52

Source: National Industry-Occupation Matrix, 1992 [data tape]. Prepared by the Bureau of Labor Statistics. Washington, DC: U.S. Department of Labor, Bureau of Labor Statistics, 1992. *Notes:* All employment data are wage and salary employment. "n.e.c." stands for "not elsewhere classified."

★ 450 ★
Occupational Outlook

Employment Projections for Sales and Related Workers, by Industry: 1992- 2005

The National Industry-Occupation Matrix counts jobs, as reflected by data about wage and salary employment collected through the Occupational Employment Statistics surveys. The table below presents employment figures for sales and related workers during 1992; the percent of industry employment for this occupation (staffing patterns) in 1992; low, medium, and high employment projections for 2005; and staffing patterns for the 2005 moderate projection. In 1992, sales and related workers ranked 4 in terms of total employment for individual occupations and ranked 28 when considering total employment of occupational groups as well as individual occupations. Table shows the industries employing the most nonspecific sales and related workers in 1992. See also tables for specific sales workers such as retail salespersons.

Industry	1992		2005 employment			Percent of industry employment for 2005 moderate projection
	Employment	Percent of industry employment	Low	Moderate	High	
Total, all industries	2,808,058	2.54	3,010,810	3,242,549	3,437,917	2.39
Wholesale and retail trade	1,543,252	6.08	1,630,397	1,762,484	1,878,681	5.69
Wholesale trade	1,117,317	18.48	1,150,763	1,246,019	1,344,769	17.33
Wholesale trade, other	723,574	18.98	740,480	801,775	865,317	17.69
Manufacturing	489,857	2.72	402,162	439,561	471,360	2.51
Services	487,696	1.26	632,934	672,199	696,047	1.24
Retail trade	425,936	2.20	479,634	516,465	533,912	2.17
Nondurable goods manufacturing	263,505	3.38	234,280	252,648	261,457	3.22
Business services	260,674	4.91	354,306	380,560	394,957	4.55
Durable goods manufacturing	226,125	2.21	167,676	186,668	209,473	1.93
Machinery, equipment, and supplies	164,664	21.89	181,910	196,968	212,578	20.75
Transportation and public utilities	142,324	2.49	159,990	174,175	180,307	2.68
Automotive dealers and service stations	139,120	6.96	154,675	166,597	172,284	7.47
Printing and publishing	132,054	8.78	126,268	136,181	141,028	7.78
Groceries and related products	130,898	15.30	129,711	140,448	151,579	14.42
General merchandise stores	96,987	4.00	98,629	106,231	109,857	4.08
Business services, miscellaneous	94,693	7.58	132,055	141,344	146,430	7.02
Department stores	89,396	4.37	92,116	99,216	102,603	4.38
Motor vehicles, parts, and supplies	86,141	19.21	86,519	93,680	101,105	17.86
Communications and utilities	85,718	3.86	91,097	97,570	99,945	4.46
Retail stores, miscellaneous	84,767	3.43	97,248	104,744	108,319	3.47
Communications	73,653	5.81	76,796	82,439	84,199	7.39
Finance, insurance, and real estate	65,513	1.00	86,515	91,124	92,469	1.14
Auto and home supply stores	64,038	19.04	69,980	75,374	77,946	19.52
Motor vehicle dealers	61,759	6.57	70,282	75,699	78,282	6.93

Source: National Industry-Occupation Matrix, 1992 [data tape]. Prepared by the Bureau of Labor Statistics. Washington, DC: U.S. Department of Labor, Bureau of Labor Statistics, 1992. *Note:* All employment data are wage and salary employment.

★ 451 ★

Occupational Outlook

Employment Projections for School Bus Drivers, by Industry: 1992-2005

The National Industry-Occupation Matrix counts jobs, as reflected by data about wage and salary employment collected through the Occupational Employment Statistics surveys. The table below presents employment figures for school bus drivers during 1992; the percent of industry employment for this occupation (staffing patterns) in 1992; low, medium, and high employment projections for 2005; and staffing patterns for the 2005 moderate projection. In 1992, school bus drivers ranked 65 in terms of total employment for individual occupations and ranked 137 when considering total employment of occupational groups as well as individual occupations. Table shows the industries employing the most school bus drivers in 1992.

| Industry | 1992 | | 2005 employment | | | Percent of industry employment for 2005 moderate projection |
	Employment	Percent of industry employment	Low	Moderate	High	
Total, all industries	394,650	0.36	470,822	503,586	518,928	0.37
Services	306,233	0.79	381,847	401,025	415,405	0.74
Education, public and private	294,780	3.03	362,269	380,894	395,175	3.05
Transportation	88,417	2.54	88,975	102,561	103,523	2.38
Transportation and public utilities	88,417	1.55	88,975	102,561	103,523	1.58
Local and interurban passenger transit	88,417	24.61	88,975	102,561	103,523	26.79
School buses	81,885	68.35	82,926	95,589	96,485	69.37
Social services	10,188	0.52	17,932	18,441	18,523	0.50
Child day care services	6,015	1.34	10,665	10,944	10,982	1.41
Local and interurban transportation, all other	3,664	4.57	3,341	3,851	3,887	5.50
Local and suburban transportation	2,867	1.80	2,708	3,121	3,151	1.78
Individual and miscellaneous social services	2,779	0.40	4,733	4,872	4,893	0.42
Membership organizations	1,266	0.06	1,647	1,690	1,706	0.07
Job training and related services	985	0.36	1,523	1,585	1,598	0.38
Civic and social associations	447	0.11	611	623	630	0.12
Residential care	409	0.08	1,010	1,040	1,050	0.08

Source: *National Industry-Occupation Matrix, 1992* [data tape]. Prepared by the Bureau of Labor Statistics. Washington, DC: U.S. Department of Labor, Bureau of Labor Statistics, 1992. *Note:* All employment data are wage and salary employment.

★ 452 ★
Occupational Outlook

Employment Projections for Science and Mathematics Technicians, by Industry: 1992-2005

The National Industry-Occupation Matrix counts jobs, as reflected by data about wage and salary employment collected through the Occupational Employment Statistics surveys. The table below presents employment figures for science and mathematics technicians during 1992; the percent of industry employment for this occupation (staffing patterns) in 1992; low, medium, and high employment projections for 2005; and staffing patterns for the 2005 moderate projection. In 1992, science and mathematics technicians ranked 102 in terms of total employment for individual occupations and ranked 187 when considering total employment of occupational groups as well as individual occupations. Table shows the industries employing the most science and mathematics technicians in 1992.

Industry	1992		2005 employment			Percent of industry employment for 2005 moderate projection
	Employment	Percent of industry employment	Low	Moderate	High	
Total, all industries	240,063	0.22	281,561	300,145	314,027	0.22
Services	93,438	0.24	128,382	134,987	139,367	0.25
Manufacturing	89,293	0.49	92,788	100,582	105,231	0.57
Nondurable goods manufacturing	71,849	0.92	75,948	81,775	84,496	1.04
Education, public and private	47,375	0.49	55,188	58,025	60,201	0.47
Chemicals and allied products	47,122	4.35	50,125	54,289	56,257	4.98
Engineering and management services	33,529	1.36	54,576	57,313	59,120	1.56
Government	32,389	0.34	31,972	33,851	35,315	0.32
Federal government	18,853	0.87	16,781	17,726	18,402	0.86
Durable goods manufacturing	17,495	0.17	16,907	18,879	20,811	0.20
Drugs	14,054	5.49	17,532	18,789	18,982	6.33
Food and kindred products	11,937	0.72	12,882	13,353	13,457	0.81
Industrial organic chemicals	10,493	6.83	9,621	10,519	10,935	7.54
Mining	9,537	1.51	8,676	9,870	12,109	1.76
State government, except education and hospitals	7,594	0.35	8,380	8,895	9,329	0.36
Oil and gas extraction	7,413	2.12	6,336	7,309	9,381	2.43
Plastics materials and synthetics	7,162	4.13	6,698	7,339	7,753	4.65
Health services	6,967	0.07	9,836	10,303	10,406	0.07
Local government, except education and hospitals	5,937	0.14	6,808	7,227	7,580	0.14
Crude petroleum, natural gas, and gas liquids	5,752	3.08	4,754	5,649	6,778	3.45
Instruments and related products	5,317	0.58	5,644	6,279	6,792	0.71
Hospitals, public and private	5,182	0.11	6,950	7,297	7,371	0.12
Agriculture, forestry, and fishing	5,172	0.30	6,792	7,022	7,488	0.36
Industrial inorganic chemicals	4,978	3.65	4,332	4,737	4,924	4.09
Petroleum and coal products	4,370	2.75	3,504	3,815	4,080	2.98

Source: National Industry-Occupation Matrix, 1992 [data tape]. Prepared by the Bureau of Labor Statistics. Washington, DC: U.S. Department of Labor, Bureau of Labor Statistics, 1992. *Note:* All employment data are wage and salary employment.

★ 453 ★

Occupational Outlook

Employment Projections for Secondary School Teachers, by Industry: 1992- 2005

The National Industry-Occupation Matrix counts jobs, as reflected by data about wage and salary employment collected through the Occupational Employment Statistics surveys. The table below presents employment figures for secondary school teachers during 1992; the percent of industry employment for this occupation (staffing patterns) in 1992; low, medium, and high employment projections for 2005; and staffing patterns for the 2005 moderate projection. In 1992, secondary school teachers ranked 20 in terms of total employment for individual occupations and ranked 61 when considering total employment of occupational groups as well as individual occupations. Table shows the industries employing the most secondary school teachers in 1992.

Industry	1992		2005 employment			Percent of industry employment for 2005 moderate projection
	Employment	Percent of industry employment	Low	Moderate	High	
Total, all industries	1,262,861	1.14	1,640,133	1,724,454	1,789,114	1.27
Education, public and private	1,262,861	12.99	1,640,133	1,724,454	1,789,114	13.82
Services	1,262,861	3.27	1,640,133	1,724,454	1,789,114	3.18

Source: National Industry-Occupation Matrix, 1992 [data tape]. Prepared by the Bureau of Labor Statistics. Washington, DC: U.S. Department of Labor, Bureau of Labor Statistics, 1992. *Note:* All employment data are wage and salary employment.

★ 454 ★

Occupational Outlook

Employment Projections for Secretaries, by Industry: 1992-2005

The National Industry-Occupation Matrix counts jobs, as reflected by data about wage and salary employment collected through the Occupational Employment Statistics surveys. The table below presents employment figures for secretaries, excluding legal and medical secretaries, during 1992; the percent of industry employment for this occupation (staffing patterns) in 1992; low, medium, and high employment projections for 2005; and staffing patterns for the 2005 moderate projection. In 1992, secretaries, excluding legal and medical secretaries, ranked 5 in terms of total employment for individual occupations and ranked 30 when considering total employment of occupational groups as well as individual occupations. Table shows the industries employing the most secretaries, excluding legal and medical secretaries, in 1992.

Industry	1992		2005 employment			Percent of industry employment for 2005 moderate projection
	Employment	Percent of industry employment	Low	Moderate	High	
Total, all industries	2,739,900	2.47	2,697,669	2,859,287	2,991,718	2.11
Services	1,273,444	3.30	1,421,064	1,496,348	1,544,682	2.76
Education, public and private	408,649	4.21	501,422	527,200	546,968	4.23
Finance, insurance, and real estate	343,362	5.23	329,021	345,871	350,937	4.34
Government	290,067	3.04	271,922	288,339	301,670	2.76
Manufacturing	284,046	1.57	204,193	224,272	242,601	1.28
Wholesale and retail trade	279,492	1.10	237,611	256,418	271,844	0.83
Business services	198,799	3.74	232,292	249,354	257,744	2.98
Wholesale trade	169,702	2.81	145,681	157,740	170,241	2.19
Health services	168,785	1.76	170,622	178,511	180,478	1.29
Durable goods manufacturing	166,489	1.63	111,576	124,089	139,106	1.28
Membership organizations	165,184	8.47	150,951	155,696	157,357	6.51

[Continued]

★ 454 ★

Employment Projections for Secretaries, by Industry: 1992-2005
[Continued]

Industry	1992		2005 employment			Percent of industry employment for 2005 moderate projection
	Employment	Percent of industry employment	Low	Moderate	High	
Engineering and management services	153,149	6.20	169,229	181,461	193,426	4.92
Construction	135,081	3.02	126,273	131,524	155,137	2.34
Nondurable goods manufacturing	117,273	1.50	92,369	99,900	103,100	1.27
Wholesale trade, other	115,919	3.04	98,728	106,901	115,373	2.36
Religious organizations	110,762	9.62	100,393	103,342	104,183	7.28
Local government, except education and hospitals	109,923	2.50	120,946	128,388	134,656	2.50
Retail trade	109,790	0.57	91,930	98,677	101,602	0.42
Personnel supply services	106,272	6.45	125,430	134,484	138,351	5.21
Federal government	101,077	4.64	68,233	72,074	74,824	3.49
Hospitals, public and private	95,354	1.97	88,178	92,577	93,522	1.47
Transportation and public utilities	90,215	1.58	73,093	79,793	83,064	1.23
Depository institutions	87,149	4.14	71,163	74,115	74,307	3.38
Commercial banks, savings institutions, and credit unions	81,730	4.12	66,644	69,409	69,588	3.37

Source: *National Industry-Occupation Matrix, 1992* [data tape]. Prepared by the Bureau of Labor Statistics. Washington, DC: U.S. Department of Labor, Bureau of Labor Statistics, 1992. *Note:* All employment data are wage and salary employment.

★ 455 ★
Occupational Outlook

Employment Projections for Short Order and Fast Food Cooks, by Industry: 1992-2005

The National Industry-Occupation Matrix counts jobs, as reflected by data about wage and salary employment collected through the Occupational Employment Statistics surveys. The table below presents employment figures for short order and fast food cooks during 1992; the percent of industry employment for this occupation (staffing patterns) in 1992; low, medium, and high employment projections for 2005; and staffing patterns for the 2005 moderate projection. In 1992, short order and fast food cooks ranked 36 in terms of total employment for individual occupations and ranked 95 when considering total employment of occupational groups as well as individual occupations. Table shows the industries employing the most short order and fast food cooks in 1992.

Industry	1992		2005 employment			Percent of industry employment for 2005 moderate projection
	Employment	Percent of industry employment	Low	Moderate	High	
Total, all industries	702,829	0.63	908,490	957,534	964,355	0.71
Wholesale and retail trade	679,143	2.67	875,049	923,203	929,453	2.98
Retail trade	678,892	3.51	874,756	922,886	929,111	3.88
Eating and drinking places	647,137	9.80	833,676	878,640	883,354	10.01
Services	23,667	0.06	33,421	34,310	34,880	0.06
Food stores	17,910	0.56	25,952	27,953	28,907	0.72
Grocery stores	13,972	0.49	21,551	23,212	24,004	0.67
Amusement and recreation services	12,715	1.09	17,934	18,228	18,393	1.12
Amusement and recreation services, all other	8,674	1.05	13,525	13,774	13,879	1.14
Automotive dealers and service stations	8,480	0.42	9,396	10,120	10,465	0.45
Gasoline service stations	8,303	1.35	9,201	9,911	10,249	1.56
Health services	3,723	0.04	5,114	5,351	5,407	0.04

[Continued]

★ 455 ★

Employment Projections for Short Order and Fast Food Cooks, by Industry: 1992-2005

[Continued]

Industry	1992		2005 employment			Percent of industry employment for 2005 moderate projection
	Employment	Percent of industry employment	Low	Moderate	High	
Bowling centers	3,506	3.99	3,745	3,778	3,825	4.44
Retail stores, miscellaneous	3,149	0.13	3,537	3,810	3,940	0.13
Hospitals, public and private	2,434	0.05	3,131	3,287	3,321	0.05
General merchandise stores	2,146	0.09	2,114	2,277	2,355	0.09
Retail bakeries	1,798	1.09	2,001	2,155	2,229	1.09
Department stores	1,583	0.08	1,631	1,757	1,817	0.08
Nursing and personal care facilities	1,209	0.08	1,846	1,922	1,942	0.08
Food stores, n.e.c.	1,078	0.87	1,328	1,431	1,479	0.90
Meat and fish markets	1,062	2.17	1,072	1,155	1,194	2.36
Nonstore retailers	862	0.29	913	983	1,017	0.31
Shopping goods stores, miscellaneous	833	0.10	1,085	1,168	1,208	0.10
Drug stores and proprietary stores	707	0.12	766	825	853	0.12
General merchandise stores, n.e.c.	563	0.15	483	520	538	0.15

Source: National Industry-Occupation Matrix, 1992 [data tape]. Prepared by the Bureau of Labor Statistics. Washington, DC: U.S. Department of Labor, Bureau of Labor Statistics, 1992. *Notes:* All employment data are wage and salary employment. "n.e.c." stands for "not elsewhere classified."

★ 456 ★

Occupational Outlook

Employment Projections for Social Workers, by Industry: 1992-2005

The National Industry-Occupation Matrix counts jobs, as reflected by data about wage and salary employment collected through the Occupational Employment Statistics surveys. The table below presents employment figures for social workers during 1992; the percent of industry employment for this occupation (staffing patterns) in 1992; low, medium, and high employment projections for 2005; and staffing patterns for the 2005 moderate projection. In 1992, social workers ranked 49 in terms of total employment for individual occupations and ranked 119 when considering total employment of occupational groups as well as individual occupations. Table shows the industries employing the most social workers in 1992.

Industry	1992		2005 employment			Percent of industry employment for 2005 moderate projection
	Employment	Percent of industry employment	Low	Moderate	High	
Total, all industries	474,176	0.43	634,593	664,547	680,798	0.49
Services	282,474	0.73	406,805	422,769	427,268	0.78
Government	191,671	2.01	227,749	241,738	253,487	2.31
Social services	126,546	6.46	167,522	172,569	173,627	4.67
Health services	123,372	1.28	192,000	200,840	202,789	1.46
State government, except education and hospitals	98,501	4.51	113,110	120,070	125,931	4.80
Local government, except education and hospitals	88,171	2.01	110,008	116,776	122,477	2.27
Individual and miscellaneous social services	81,235	11.56	95,523	98,335	98,756	8.46
Hospitals, public and private	67,022	1.38	102,056	107,147	108,242	1.70
Residential care	31,988	5.98	50,639	52,121	52,619	3.90

[Continued]

★ 456 ★

Employment Projections for Social Workers, by Industry: 1992-2005
[Continued]

Industry	1992		2005 employment			Percent of industry employment for 2005 moderate projection
	Employment	Percent of industry employment	Low	Moderate	High	
Health and allied services, n.e.c.	25,013	9.97	38,553	40,149	40,406	10.24
Education, public and private	22,572	0.23	34,206	35,965	37,313	0.29
Nursing and personal care facilities	14,200	0.92	21,391	22,269	22,500	0.97
Membership organizations	9,983	0.51	13,077	13,395	13,539	0.56
Job training and related services	8,721	3.22	13,311	13,853	13,964	3.32
Offices of physicians, including osteopaths	7,025	0.46	11,342	11,828	11,993	0.50
Civic and social associations	5,993	1.43	8,085	8,246	8,340	1.55
Offices of other health practitioners	5,805	1.77	10,016	10,446	10,591	1.82
Federal government	4,999	0.23	4,631	4,892	5,078	0.24
Child day care services	4,601	1.02	8,049	8,259	8,288	1.06
Home health care services	4,257	1.06	8,568	8,923	8,980	0.98
Religious organizations	3,453	0.30	4,294	4,420	4,457	0.31
Membership organizations, n.e.c.	263	0.31	354	370	377	0.34
Business and professional organizations	188	0.12	261	274	279	0.14
Labor organizations	86	0.06	83	84	85	0.06

Source: National Industry-Occupation Matrix, 1992 [data tape]. Prepared by the Bureau of Labor Statistics. Washington, DC: U.S. Department of Labor, Bureau of Labor Statistics, 1992. *Notes:* All employment data are wage and salary employment. "n.e.c." stands for "not elsewhere classified."

★ 457 ★
Occupational Outlook

Employment Projections for Special Education Teachers, by Industry: 1992-2005

The National Industry-Occupation Matrix counts jobs, as reflected by data about wage and salary employment collected through the Occupational Employment Statistics surveys. The table below presents employment figures for special education teachers during 1992; the percent of industry employment for this occupation (staffing patterns) in 1992; low, medium, and high employment projections for 2005; and staffing patterns for the 2005 moderate projection. In 1992, special education teachers ranked 70 in terms of total employment for individual occupations and ranked 146 when considering total employment of occupational groups as well as individual occupations. Table shows the industries employing the most special education teachers in 1992.

Industry	1992		2005 employment			Percent of industry employment for 2005 moderate projection
	Employment	Percent of industry employment	Low	Moderate	High	
Total, all industries	358,127	0.32	594,161	624,708	648,131	0.46
Education, public and private	358,127	3.69	594,161	624,708	648,131	5.01
Services	358,127	0.93	594,161	624,708	648,131	1.15

Source: National Industry-Occupation Matrix, 1992 [data tape]. Prepared by the Bureau of Labor Statistics. Washington, DC: U.S. Department of Labor, Bureau of Labor Statistics, 1992. *Note:* All employment data are wage and salary employment.

★ 458 ★

Occupational Outlook

Employment Projections for Sports and Physical Training Instructors and Coaches, by Industry: 1992-2005

The National Industry-Occupation Matrix counts jobs, as reflected by data about wage and salary employment collected through the Occupational Employment Statistics surveys. The table below presents employment figures for sports and physical training instructors and coaches during 1992; the percent of industry employment for this occupation (staffing patterns) in 1992; low, medium, and high employment projections for 2005; and staffing patterns for the 2005 moderate projection. In 1992, sports and physical training instructors and coaches ranked 97 in terms of total employment for individual occupations and ranked 182 when considering total employment of occupational groups as well as individual occupations. Table shows the industries employing the most sports and physical training instructors and coaches in 1992.

Industry	1992		2005 employment			Percent of industry employment for 2005 moderate projection
	Employment	Percent of industry employment	Low	Moderate	High	
Total, all industries	260,385	0.24	342,703	354,580	362,670	0.26
Services	260,385	0.67	342,703	354,580	362,670	0.65
Amusement and recreation services	95,485	8.17	131,596	134,008	135,067	8.24
Amusement and recreation services, all other	92,470	11.20	128,057	130,415	131,411	10.82
Membership organizations	24,475	1.26	33,403	34,094	34,489	1.43
Civic and social associations	23,302	5.55	31,866	32,500	32,874	6.12
Personal services	6,118	0.55	6,955	7,092	7,145	0.51
Social services	2,134	0.11	3,842	3,957	3,979	0.11
Individual and miscellaneous social services	1,351	0.19	2,300	2,368	2,378	0.20
Bowling centers	1,327	1.51	1,417	1,430	1,447	1.68
Religious organizations	619	0.05	781	804	810	0.06
Membership organizations, n.e.c.	526	0.62	717	749	763	0.69
Child day care services	288	0.06	511	525	527	0.07
Residential care	287	0.05	709	730	736	0.05
Job training and related services	208	0.08	322	335	338	0.08

Source: National Industry-Occupation Matrix, 1992 [data tape]. Prepared by the Bureau of Labor Statistics. Washington, DC: U.S. Department of Labor, Bureau of Labor Statistics, 1992. *Notes:* All employment data are wage and salary employment. "n.e.c." stands for "not elsewhere classified."

★ 459 ★

Occupational Outlook

Employment Projections for Stock Clerks, by Industry: 1992-2005

The National Industry-Occupation Matrix counts jobs, as reflected by data about wage and salary employment collected through the Occupational Employment Statistics surveys. The table below presents employment figures for stock clerks during 1992; the percent of industry employment for this occupation (staffing patterns) in 1992; low, medium, and high employment projections for 2005; and staffing patterns for the 2005 moderate projection. In 1992, stock clerks ranked 12 in terms of total employment for individual occupations and ranked 46 when considering total employment of occupational groups as well as individual occupations. Table shows the industries employing the most stock clerks in 1992.

Industry	1992		2005 employment			Percent of industry employment for 2005 moderate projection
	Employment	Percent of industry employment	Low	Moderate	High	
Total, all industries	1,780,041	1.61	1,798,717	1,937,555	2,021,702	1.43
Wholesale and retail trade	1,398,107	5.51	1,440,407	1,552,497	1,615,184	5.01
Retail trade	1,186,859	6.13	1,239,901	1,335,394	1,380,875	5.62
Food stores	642,912	20.22	683,674	736,369	761,503	18.98
Grocery stores	623,597	21.94	662,699	713,778	738,140	20.54
Wholesale trade	21,248	3.49	200,506	217,103	234,309	3.02
General merchandise stores	182,500	7.53	166,338	179,159	185,274	6.88
Retail stores, miscellaneous	168,373	6.82	182,016	196,046	202,737	6.49
Wholesale trade, other	136,825	3.59	129,680	140,415	151,543	3.10
Department stores	129,055	6.31	123,688	133,221	137,768	5.87
Manufacturing	128,385	0.71	99,820	110,280	119,247	0.63
Services	118,662	0.31	139,180	147,424	151,559	0.27
Durable goods manufacturing	85,723	0.84	63,600	70,934	78,752	0.73
Building materials and garden supplies	64,004	8.69	66,616	71,750	74,199	8.47
Drug stores and proprietary stores	60,760	10.02	61,227	65,947	68,197	9.43
Apparel and accessory stores	60,245	5.33	64,639	69,621	71,997	5.03
Government	58,094	0.61	46,224	48,984	51,119	0.47
Shopping goods stores, miscellaneous	57,792	6.79	69,982	75,376	77,949	6.55
General merchandise stores, n.e.c.	53,445	14.21	42,650	45,937	47,505	13.67
Business services	45,692	0.86	59,843	64,205	66,352	0.77
Transportation and public utilities	45,310	0.79	41,449	45,248	47,236	0.70
Clothing and accesories stores	44,828	5.30	47,839	51,527	53,285	5.01
Nondurable goods manufacturing	42,785	0.55	36,345	39,478	40,597	0.50
Furniture and homefurnishings stores	41,906	5.20	48,292	52,014	53,789	5.03
Lumber and other building materials	36,892	8.59	39,572	42,622	44,076	8.56

Source: National Industry-Occupation Matrix, 1992 [data tape]. Prepared by the Bureau of Labor Statistics. Washington, DC: U.S. Department of Labor, Bureau of Labor Statistics, 1992. *Notes:* All employment data are wage and salary employment. "n.e.c." stands for "not elsewhere classified."

★ 460 ★

Occupational Outlook

Employment Projections for Switchboard Operators, by Industry: 1992-2005

The National Industry-Occupation Matrix counts jobs, as reflected by data about wage and salary employment collected through the Occupational Employment Statistics surveys. The table below presents employment figures for switchboard operators during 1992; the percent of industry employment for this occupation (staffing patterns) in 1992; low, medium, and high employment projections for 2005; and staffing patterns for the 2005 moderate projection. In 1992, switchboard operators ranked 103 in terms of total employment for individual occupations and ranked 188 when considering total employment of occupational groups as well as individual occupations. Table shows the industries employing the most switchboard operators in 1992.

Industry	1992		2005 employment			Percent of industry employment for 2005 moderate projection
	Employment	Percent of industry employment	Low	Moderate	High	
Total, all industries	239,159	0.22	177,199	188,121	194,121	0.14
Services	141,403	0.37	121,504	128,228	131,399	0.24
Business services	52,974	1.00	45,546	48,794	50,489	0.58
Health services	47,985	0.50	45,304	47,449	47,965	0.34
Business services, miscellaneous	35,048	2.81	30,293	32,424	33,591	1.61
Hospitals, public and private	32,735	0.68	30,123	31,625	31,948	0.50
Manufacturing	25,401	0.14	13,452	14,757	15,865	0.08
Wholesale and retail trade	22,626	0.09	12,956	13,984	14,726	0.05
Finance, insurance, and real estate	22,251	0.34	14,669	15,415	15,607	0.19
Transportation and public utilities	14,551	0.25	7,428	8,113	8,373	0.12
Retail trade	13,776	0.07	7,512	8,090	8,365	0.03
Durable goods manufacturing	13,441	0.13	6,559	7,304	8,156	0.08
Personnel supply services	12,408	0.75	10,525	11,285	11,609	0.44
Nondurable goods manufacturing	11,899	0.15	6,855	7,410	7,655	0.09
Hotels and other lodging places	11,601	0.74	8,719	9,015	9,312	0.41
Government	10,933	0.11	6,004	6,370	6,671	0.06
Communications and utilities	10,807	0.49	5,336	5,791	5,944	0.26
General merchandise stores	9,399	0.39	4,870	5,246	5,425	0.20
Communications	9,223	0.73	4,419	4,821	4,935	0.43
Wholesale trade	8,850	0.15	5,444	5,894	6,361	0.08
Department stores	7,905	0.39	4,208	4,533	4,687	0.20
Offices of physicians, including osteopaths	7,884	0.52	9,231	9,627	9,761	0.41
Depository institutions	7,693	0.37	4,511	4,698	4,711	0.21
Commercial banks, savings institutions, and credit unions	7,442	0.38	4,361	4,542	4,554	0.22
Engineering and management services	6,825	0.28	5,522	5,927	6,265	0.16

Source: National Industry-Occupation Matrix, 1992 [data tape]. Prepared by the Bureau of Labor Statistics. Washington, DC: U.S. Department of Labor, Bureau of Labor Statistics, 1992. *Note:* All employment data are wage and salary employment.

★ 461 ★

Occupational Outlook

Employment Projections for Systems Analysts, by Industry: 1992-2005

The National Industry-Occupation Matrix counts jobs, as reflected by data about wage and salary employment collected through the Occupational Employment Statistics surveys. The table below presents employment figures for systems analysts during 1992; the percent of industry employment for this occupation (staffing patterns) in 1992; low, medium, and high employment projections for 2005; and staffing patterns for the 2005 moderate projection. In 1992, systems analysts ranked 54 in terms of total employment for individual occupations and ranked 124 when considering total employment of occupational groups as well as individual occupations. Table shows the industries employing the most systems analysts in 1992.

Industry	1992		2005 employment			Percent of industry employment for 2005 moderate projection
	Employment	Percent of industry employment	Low	Moderate	High	
Total, all industries	431,106	0.39	852,099	916,127	958,641	0.67
Services	139,620	0.36	365,838	392,053	408,425	0.72
Manufacturing	90,581	0.50	135,194	149,552	163,021	0.85
Government	81,285	0.85	127,853	135,410	141,192	1.29
Business services	78,626	1.48	228,346	246,370	256,896	2.94
Computer and data processing services	73,588	8.86	215,475	232,568	242,629	14.30
Finance, insurance, and real estate	64,969	0.99	126,775	134,115	134,585	1.68
Durable goods manufacturing	64,113	0.63	88,816	99,400	111,336	1.03
Federal government	52,235	2.40	78,480	82,897	86,060	4.02
Insurance carriers	28,860	1.95	51,364	55,043	55,068	3.32
Wholesale and retail trade	26,527	0.10	49,791	53,804	57,266	0.17
Nondurable goods manufacturing	26,509	0.34	46,463	50,241	51,756	0.64
Engineering and management services	25,823	1.05	64,105	68,762	72,774	1.87
Transportation and public utilities	24,136	0.42	40,743	44,564	46,143	0.69
Transportation equipment	22,060	1.21	34,094	37,231	40,046	2.11
Depository institutions	20,016	0.95	36,413	37,924	38,022	1.73
Commercial banks, savings institutions, and credit unions	17,899	0.90	32,484	33,831	33,919	1.64
Wholesale trade	17,784	0.29	33,763	36,558	39,455	0.51
Communications and utilities	17,145	0.77	27,538	29,559	30,543	1.35
State government, except education and hospitals	16,561	0.76	28,041	29,766	31,219	1.19
Aircraft and parts	15,387	2.52	24,107	26,270	28,273	4.17
Wholesale trade, other	14,971	0.39	28,379	30,728	33,163	0.68
Life insurance	14,188	2.64	26,757	28,674	28,687	4.65
Industrial machinery and equipment	14,153	0.74	16,368	19,188	23,415	1.03
Health services	12,764	0.13	27,087	28,406	28,696	0.21

Source: National Industry-Occupation Matrix, 1992 [data tape]. Prepared by the Bureau of Labor Statistics. Washington, DC: U.S. Department of Labor, Bureau of Labor Statistics, 1992. *Note:* All employment data are wage and salary employment.

★ 462 ★

Occupational Outlook

Employment Projections for Teacher Aides and Educational Assistants, by Industry: 1992-2005

The National Industry-Occupation Matrix counts jobs, as reflected by data about wage and salary employment collected through the Occupational Employment Statistics surveys. The table below presents employment figures for teacher aides and educational assistants during 1992; the percent of industry employment for this occupation (staffing patterns) in 1992; low, medium, and high employment projections for 2005; and staffing patterns for the 2005 moderate projection. In 1992, teacher aides and educational assistants ranked 25 in terms of total employment for individual occupations and ranked 77 when considering total employment of occupational groups as well as individual occupations. Table shows the industries employing the most teacher aides and educational assistants in 1992.

Industry	1992		2005 employment			Percent of industry employment for 2005 moderate projection
	Employment	Percent of industry employment	Low	Moderate	High	
Total, all industries	884,176	0.80	1,207,790	1,265,484	1,306,806	0.93
Services	877,641	2.27	1,201,915	1,259,248	1,300,266	2.33
Education, public and private	742,288	7.64	1,013,600	1,065,711	1,105,670	8.54
Social services	94,698	4.84	138,943	142,749	143,344	3.87
Child day care services	72,203	16.08	105,374	108,127	108,505	13.92
Membership organizations	39,655	2.03	48,854	50,254	50,683	2.10
Religious organizations	35,349	3.07	44,018	45,311	45,680	3.19
Individual and miscellaneous social services	13,772	1.96	19,301	19,870	19,955	1.71
Government	6,522	0.07	5,864	6,225	6,529	0.06
Local government, except education and hospitals	5,351	0.12	4,844	5,142	5,393	0.10
Job training and related services	4,558	1.68	5,805	6,041	6,090	1.45
Residential care	4,165	0.78	8,464	8,711	8,794	0.65
Civic and social associations	3,898	0.93	4,388	4,475	4,527	0.84
State government, except education and hospitals	1,171	0.05	1,020	1,083	1,136	0.04
Private households	1,000	0.09	517	534	568	0.07
Membership organizations, n.e.c.	330	0.39	371	387	394	0.36

Source: National Industry-Occupation Matrix, 1992 [data tape]. Prepared by the Bureau of Labor Statistics. Washington, DC: U.S. Department of Labor, Bureau of Labor Statistics, 1992. *Notes:* All employment data are wage and salary employment. "n.e.c." stands for "not elsewhere classified."

★ 463 ★
Occupational Outlook

Employment Projections for Telephone Operators, by Industry: 1992-2005

The National Industry-Occupation Matrix counts jobs, as reflected by data about wage and salary employment collected through the Occupational Employment Statistics surveys. The table below presents employment figures for telephone operators during 1992; the percent of industry employment for this occupation (staffing patterns) in 1992; low, medium, and high employment projections for 2005; and staffing patterns for the 2005 moderate projection. In 1992, telephone operators ranked 81 in terms of total employment for individual occupations and ranked 160 when considering total employment of occupational groups as well as individual occupations. Table shows the industries employing the most telephone operators in 1992.

Industry	1992		2005 employment			Percent of industry employment for 2005 moderate projection
	Employment	Percent of industry employment	Low	Moderate	High	
Total, all industries	313,897	0.28	211,005	225,184	232,082	0.17
Services	141,403	0.37	121,504	128,228	131,399	0.24
Transportation and public utilities	89,288	1.56	41,235	45,175	46,333	0.70
Communications and utilities	85,545	3.85	39,142	42,853	43,905	1.96
Communications	83,960	6.62	38,225	41,884	42,896	3.75
Telephone communications	82,300	9.28	37,201	40,792	41,782	5.75
Business services	52,974	1.00	45,546	48,794	50,489	0.58
Health services	47,985	0.50	45,304	47,449	47,965	0.34
Business services, miscellaneous	35,048	2.81	30,293	32,424	33,591	1.61
Hospitals, public and private	32,735	0.68	30,123	31,625	31,948	0.50
Manufacturing	25,401	0.14	13,452	14,757	15,865	0.08
Wholesale and retail trade	22,626	0.09	12,956	13,984	14,726	0.05
Finance, insurance, and real estate	22,251	0.34	14,669	15,415	15,607	0.19
Retail trade	13,776	0.07	7,512	8,090	8,365	0.03
Durable goods manufacturing	13,441	0.13	6,559	7,304	8,156	0.08
Personnel supply services	12,408	0.75	10,525	11,285	11,609	0.44
Nondurable goods manufacturing	11,899	0.15	6,855	7,410	7,655	0.09
Hotels and other lodging places	11,601	0.74	8,719	9,015	9,312	0.41
Government	10,933	0.11	6,004	6,370	6,671	0.06
General merchandise stores	9,399	0.39	4,870	5,246	5,425	0.20
Wholesale trade	8,850	0.15	5,444	5,894	6,361	0.08
Department stores	7,905	0.39	4,208	4,533	4,687	0.20
Offices of physicians including osteopaths	7,884	0.52	9,231	9,627	9,761	0.41
Depository institutions	7,693	0.37	4,511	4,698	4,711	0.21
Commercial banks, savings institutions, and credit unions	7,442	0.38	4,361	4,542	4,554	0.22

Source: National Industry-Occupation Matrix, 1992 [data tape]. Prepared by the Bureau of Labor Statistics. Washington, DC: U.S. Department of Labor, Bureau of Labor Statistics, 1992. *Note:* All employment data are wage and salary employment.

★ 464 ★

Occupational Outlook

Employment Projections for Traffic, Shipping, and Receiving Clerks, by Industry: 1992-2005

The National Industry-Occupation Matrix counts jobs, as reflected by data about wage and salary employment collected through the Occupational Employment Statistics surveys. The table below presents employment figures for traffic, shipping, and receiving clerks during 1992; the percent of industry employment for this occupation (staffing patterns) in 1992; low, medium, and high employment projections for 2005; and staffing patterns for the 2005 moderate projection. In 1992, traffic, shipping, and receiving clerks ranked 30 in terms of total employment for individual occupations and ranked 85 when considering total employment for occupational groups as well as individual occupations. Table shows the industries employing the most traffic, shipping, and receiving clerks in 1992.

Industry	1992		2005 employment			Percent of industry employment for 2005 moderate projection
	Employment	Percent of industry employment	Low	Moderate	High	
Total, all industries	823,294	0.74	888,404	969,991	1,032,576	0.71
Wholesale and retail trade	297,920	1.17	366,724	396,234	420,470	1.28
Manufacturing	224,635	1.25	229,446	252,560	270,709	1.44
Government	221,996	2.33	183,723	204,464	219,647	1.96
U.S. Postal Service	217,345	27.44	178,866	199,319	214,278	26.55
Wholesale trade	171,474	2.84	219,439	237,604	256,434	3.30
Retail trade	126,446	0.65	147,284	158,630	164,036	0.67
Durable goods manufacturing	122,378	1.20	119,066	132,286	146,684	1.37
Wholesale trade, other	115,255	3.02	150,200	162,633	175,522	3.59
Nondurable goods manufacturing	102,090	1.31	110,183	120,040	123,627	1.53
General merchandise stores	46,432	1.92	51,257	55,208	57,092	2.12
Services	43,459	0.11	66,609	70,837	73,181	0.13
Department stores	41,452	2.03	46,985	50,606	52,333	2.23
Transportation and public utilities	33,158	0.58	39,327	43,233	45,647	0.67
Transportation	30,256	0.87	36,369	40,058	42,376	0.93
Retail stores, miscellaneous	24,735	1.00	29,462	31,733	32,816	1.05
Industrial machinery and equipment	24,442	1.27	23,465	26,739	30,840	1.43
Machinery, equipment, and supplies	21,782	2.90	27,857	30,163	32,554	3.18
Fabricated metal products	21,380	1.62	21,143	23,042	25,597	1.93
Groceries and related products	19,465	2.28	22,330	24,178	26,095	2.48
Food and kindred products	19,312	1.17	20,586	21,372	21,517	1.30
Electronic and other electrical equipment	18,738	1.23	16,002	18,238	20,678	1.35
Apparel and other textile products	18,612	1.85	15,227	17,777	17,894	2.34
Business services	18,090	0.34	30,712	33,006	34,221	0.39
Food stores	17,144	0.54	21,440	23,092	23,880	0.60

Source: National Industry-Occupation Matrix, 1992 [data tape]. Prepared by the Bureau of Labor Statistics. Washington, DC: U.S. Department of Labor, Bureau of Labor Statistics, 1992. *Note:* All employment data are wage and salary employment.

★ 465 ★

Occupational Outlook

Employment Projections for Truck Drivers, by Industry: 1992-2005

The National Industry-Occupation Matrix counts jobs, as reflected by data about wage and salary employment collected through the Occupational Employment Statistics surveys. The table below presents employment figures for truck drivers during 1992; the percent of industry employment for this occupation (staffing patterns) in 1992; low, medium, and high employment projections for 2005; and staffing patterns for the 2005 moderate projection. In 1992, truck drivers ranked 9 in terms of total employment for individual occupations and ranked 40 when considering total employment of occupational groups as well as individual occupations. Table shows the industries employing the most truck drivers (light and heavy) in 1992.

Industry	1992		2005 employment			Percent of industry employment for 2005 moderate projection
	Employment	Percent of industry employment	Low	Moderate	High	
Total, all industries	2,160,517	1.95	2,615,335	2,810,748	2,991,860	2.07
Transportation and public utilities	842,411	14.76	1,023,291	1,110,910	1,170,125	17.10
Transportation	822,198	23.58	995,671	1,081,643	1,139,691	25.10
Trucking and warehousing	765,499	47.66	929,064	1,005,494	1,060,521	49.79
Local and long distance trucking and terminals	758,869	51.14	921,014	996,782	1,051,333	53.32
Wholesale and retail trade	691,766	2.72	845,392	910,277	960,283	2.94
Wholesale trade	392,450	6.49	466,260	504,855	544,866	7.02
Retail trade	299,316	1.55	379,132	405,421	415,417	1.71
Manufacturing	252,756	1.40	257,867	274,559	299,132	1.57
Wholesale trade, other	197,558	5.18	234,052	253,426	273,511	5.59
Services	144,188	0.37	216,058	229,109	238,334	0.42
Durable goods manufacturing	138,859	1.36	135,100	144,032	165,108	1.49
Nondurable goods manufacturing	114,011	1.46	122,918	130,676	134,057	1.66
Construction	110,533	2.47	143,776	149,755	176,640	2.66
Groceries and related products	98,048	11.46	112,479	121,789	131,441	12.50
Eating and drinking places	72,066	1.09	126,748	133,585	134,301	1.52
Retail stores, miscellaneous	67,090	2.72	73,736	79,419	82,130	2.63
Stone, clay, and glass products	62,429	12.20	58,011	60,759	71,811	13.90
Concrete, gypsum, and plaster products	58,261	31.21	54,199	56,639	67,293	33.87
Business services	57,010	1.07	92,121	99,308	103,338	1.19
Food and kindred products	56,023	3.39	57,976	60,285	60,692	3.66
Special trade contractors	54,880	2.04	71,015	73,969	87,248	2.16
Building materials and garden supplies	50,975	6.92	53,673	57,810	59,784	6.83
Heavy construction, except building	44,277	6.23	58,134	60,551	71,422	6.65
Lumber and other building materials	43,821	10.20	45,483	48,989	50,661	9.83

Source: National Industry-Occupation Matrix, 1992 [data tape]. Prepared by the Bureau of Labor Statistics. Washington, DC: U.S. Department of Labor, Bureau of Labor Statistics, 1992. *Note:* All employment data are wage and salary employment.

★ 466 ★

Occupational Outlook

Employment Projections for Typists and Word Processors, by Industry: 1992-2005

The National Industry-Occupation Matrix counts jobs, as reflected by data about wage and salary employment collected through the Occupational Employment Statistics surveys. The table below presents employment figures for typists and word processors during 1992; the percent of industry employment for this occupation (staffing patterns) in 1992; low, medium, and high employment projections for 2005; and staffing patterns for the 2005 moderate projection. In 1992, typists and word processors ranked 33 in terms of total employment for individual occupations and ranked 91 when considering total employment of occupational groups as well as individual occupations. Table shows the industries employing the most typists and word processors in 1992.

Industry	1992		2005 employment			Percent of industry employment for 2005 moderate projection
	Employment	Percent of industry employment	Low	Moderate	High	
Total, all industries	772,141	0.70	611,216	649,210	671,747	0.48
Services	410,678	1.06	366,413	388,113	399,803	0.72
Government	200,297	2.10	126,840	134,575	140,958	1.29
Business services	143,423	2.70	141,745	151,997	156,584	1.82
Personnel supply services	122,168	7.41	120,343	129,030	132,740	5.00
State government, except education and hospitals	86,687	3.97	55,041	58,428	61,280	2.34
Local government, except education and hospitals	81,387	1.85	53,706	57,010	59,793	1.11
Finance, insurance, and real estate	81,027	1.23	64,807	68,767	69,332	0.86
Health services	79,068	0.82	70,706	73,898	74,784	0.54
Engineering and management services	46,323	1.88	42,624	45,740	49,003	1.24
Manufacturing	37,971	0.21	23,798	26,023	27,691	0.15
Insurance carriers	37,078	2.51	26,333	28,219	28,231	1.70
Offices of physicians, including osteopaths	34,518	2.27	33,898	35,350	35,843	1.50
Hospitals, public and private	31,687	0.65	24,456	25,676	25,938	0.41
Federal government	31,341	1.44	17,658	18,652	19,364	0.90
Membership organizations	28,553	1.46	21,912	22,588	22,827	0.95
Wholesale and retail trade	25,318	0.10	17,956	19,422	20,791	0.06
Legal services	22,780	2.49	18,267	19,349	19,695	1.43
Wholesale trade	20,175	0.33	14,468	15,665	16,907	0.22
Nondurable goods manufacturing	20,127	0.26	13,889	15,008	15,516	0.19
Fire, marine, and casualty insurance	19,017	3.44	12,259	13,137	13,143	2.19
Durable goods manufacturing	17,806	0.17	9,880	10,982	12,135	0.11
Insurance agents, brokers, and service	17,314	2.65	17,137	18,377	18,388	1.89
Wholesale trade, other	13,949	0.37	9,915	10,736	11,587	0.24
Engineering and architectural services	13,181	1.77	10,740	11,586	13,582	1.16

Source: National Industry-Occupation Matrix, 1992 [data tape]. Prepared by the Bureau of Labor Statistics. Washington, DC: U.S. Department of Labor, Bureau of Labor Statistics, 1992. *Note:* All employment data are wage and salary employment.

★ 467 ★

Occupational Outlook

Employment Projections for Vocational Education and Training Teachers and Instructors, by Industry: 1992-2005

The National Industry-Occupation Matrix counts jobs, as reflected by data about wage and salary employment collected through the Occupational Employment Statistics surveys. The table below presents employment figures for vocational education and training teachers and instructors during 1992; the percent of industry employment for this occupation (staffing patterns) in 1992; low, medium, and high employment projections for 2005; and staffing patterns for the 2005 moderate projection. In 1992, vocational education and training teachers and instructors ranked 84 in terms of total employment for individual occupations and ranked 164 when considering total employment of occupational groups as well as individual occupations. Table shows the industries employing the most vocational education and training teachers and instructors in 1992.

Industry	1992		2005 employment			Percent of industry employment for 2005 moderate projection
	Employment	Percent of industry employment	Low	Moderate	High	
Total, all industries	305,065	0.28	395,688	416,381	430,399	0.31
Services	252,980	0.65	341,599	357,987	369,581	0.66
Education, public and private	207,952	2.14	282,359	296,876	308,007	2.38
Social services	18,566	0.95	25,542	26,412	26,591	0.72
Federal government	15,072	0.69	14,153	14,949	15,520	0.72
Job training and related services	10,705	3.95	10,765	11,204	11,294	2.68
Membership organizations	10,134	0.52	12,814	13,177	13,307	0.55
Transportation and public utilities	8,941	0.16	10,237	11,806	12,150	0.18
Personal services	8,290	0.75	10,088	10,207	10,248	0.74
Transportation	8,046	0.23	9,425	10,920	11,243	0.25
Air transportation	8,046	1.10	9,425	10,920	11,243	1.13
Health services	8,038	0.08	10,796	11,315	11,428	0.08
Hospitals, public and private	6,567	0.14	8,447	8,869	8,959	0.14
Air carriers	5,845	0.93	6,927	8,025	8,262	0.95
Individual and miscellaneous social services	5,730	0.82	9,757	10,044	10,087	0.86
Airports, flying fields, and services	2,201	2.25	2,499	2,895	2,981	2.44
Civic and social associations	1,843	0.44	2,521	2,571	2,600	0.48
Residential care	1,782	0.33	4,399	4,528	4,571	0.34
Nondurable goods manufacturing	1,287	0.02	1,040	1,196	1,209	0.02
Labor organizations	897	0.65	878	895	905	0.69
Communications	895	0.07	812	886	907	0.08
Communications and utilities	895	0.04	812	886	907	0.04
Telephone communications	737	0.08	664	728	746	0.10
Textile mill products	634	0.09	530	598	607	0.10
Apparel and other textile products	603	0.06	482	565	568	0.07

Source: National Industry-Occupation Matrix, 1992 [data tape]. Prepared by the Bureau of Labor Statistics. Washington, DC: U.S. Department of Labor, Bureau of Labor Statistics, 1992. *Note:* All employment data are wage and salary employment.

★ 468 ★
Occupational Outlook

Employment Projections for Waiters and Waitresses, by Industry: 1992-2005

The National Industry-Occupation Matrix counts jobs, as reflected by data about wage and salary employment collected through the Occupational Employment Statistics surveys. The table below presents employment figures for waiters and waitresses during 1992; the percent of industry employment for this occupation (staffing patterns) in 1992; low, medium, and high employment projections for 2005; and staffing patterns for the 2005 moderate projection. In 1992, waiters and waitresses ranked 13 in terms of total employment for individual occupations and ranked 47 when considering total employment of occupational groups as well as individual occupations. Table shows the industries employing the most waiters and waitresses in 1992.

Industry	1992		2005 employment			Percent of industry employment for 2005 moderate projection
	Employment	Percent of industry employment	Low	Moderate	High	
Total, all industries	1,745,403	1.58	2,268,922	2,382,709	2,403,258	1.76
Wholesale and retail trade	1,461,540	5.76	1,895,218	1,998,554	2,010,805	6.45
Retail trade	1,460,905	7.55	1,894,476	1,997,751	2,009,938	8.40
Eating and drinking places	1,417,778	21.48	1,847,087	1,946,709	1,957,155	22.18
Services	283,432	0.73	373,234	383,661	391,926	0.71
Hotels and other lodging places	164,755	10.48	191,731	198,233	204,764	8.98
Amusement and recreation services	73,748	6.31	109,207	111,130	112,079	6.83
Amusement and recreation services, all other	61,641	7.47	95,765	97,528	98,273	8.09
Membership organizations	26,130	1.34	35,509	36,253	36,665	1.52
Civic and social associations	23,704	5.65	32,416	33,061	33,441	6.23
Food stores	17,657	0.56	19,997	21,538	22,273	0.56
Automotive dealers and service stations	12,520	0.63	13,869	14,938	15,448	0.67
Gasoline service stations	12,305	2.00	13,636	14,687	15,188	2.32
Social services	10,050	0.51	24,238	24,950	25,182	0.68
Bowling centers	9,625	10.96	10,282	10,372	10,501	12.20
Residential care	9,323	1.74	23,018	23,692	23,918	1.77
Grocery stores	9,008	0.32	10,292	11,086	11,464	0.32
Health services	8,266	0.09	12,052	12,575	12,705	0.09
General merchandise stores	7,499	0.31	7,328	7,893	8,162	0.30
Retail bakeries	6,379	3.88	7,097	7,644	7,905	3.88
Nursing and personal care facilities	5,775	0.37	8,820	9,182	9,277	0.40
Department stores	5,186	0.25	5,344	5,756	5,952	0.25
Retail stores, miscellaneous	4,954	0.20	5,584	6,014	6,220	0.20
Hospitals, public and private	2,440	0.05	3,139	3,295	3,329	0.05
General merchandise stores, n.e.c.	2,313	0.62	1,984	2,137	2,210	0.64

Source: National Industry-Occupation Matrix, 1992 [data tape]. Prepared by the Bureau of Labor Statistics. Washington, DC: U.S. Department of Labor, Bureau of Labor Statistics, 1992. *Notes:* All employment data are wage and salary employment. "n.e.c." stands for "not elsewhere classified."

★ 469 ★

Occupational Outlook

Employment Projections for Welders and Cutters, by Industry: 1992-2005

The National Industry-Occupation Matrix counts jobs, as reflected by data about wage and salary employment collected through the Occupational Employment Statistics surveys. The table below presents employment figures for welders and cutters during 1992; the percent of industry employment for this occupation (staffing patterns) in 1992; low, medium, and high employment projections for 2005; and staffing patterns for the 2005 moderate projection. In 1992, welders and cutters ranked 93 in terms of total employment for individual occupations and ranked 177 when considering total employment of occupational groups as well as individual occupations. Table shows the industries employing the most welders and cutters in 1992.

Industry	1992		2005 employment			Percent of industry employment for 2005 moderate projection
	Employment	Percent of industry employment	Low	Moderate	High	
Total, all industries	277,756	0.25	299,265	324,222	357,928	0.24
Manufacturing	163,718	0.91	155,899	171,770	190,091	0.98
Durable goods manufacturing	156,653	1.53	148,416	163,587	181,332	1.69
Transportation equipment	47,103	2.58	41,006	44,914	47,627	2.54
Industrial machinery and equipment	45,772	2.38	48,117	54,231	61,217	2.90
Fabricated metal products	37,828	2.86	35,159	37,744	42,978	3.16
Services	33,254	0.09	48,783	52,001	54,912	0.10
Construction	30,953	0.69	39,462	41,103	48,482	0.73
Fabricated structural metal products	27,343	7.02	24,889	26,531	30,698	8.01
Wholesale and retail trade	22,742	0.09	27,552	29,829	32,170	0.10
Wholesale trade	22,316	0.37	27,061	29,301	31,623	0.41
Repair services, miscellaneous	20,778	6.02	28,925	30,831	32,484	6.87
Motor vehicles and equipment	19,017	2.35	16,177	17,896	19,256	2.36
Ship and boat building and repairing	17,248	10.21	12,882	13,811	14,142	10.16
Construction and related machinery	14,718	7.26	15,378	17,364	19,517	8.12
Wholesale trade, other	12,981	0.34	15,378	16,651	17,971	0.37
Heavy construction, except building	12,884	1.81	16,028	16,695	19,692	1.83
Special trade contractors	12,405	0.46	16,117	16,787	19,801	0.49
Heavy construction, except highway and street	11,846	2.38	14,590	15,196	17,925	2.47
Special trade contractors, all other	11,404	2.30	14,810	15,426	18,195	2.45
Transportation and public utilities	11,270	0.20	12,231	13,270	13,971	0.20
Primary metal industries	8,623	1.24	7,598	8,434	9,296	1.37
Mining	7,620	1.21	7,019	7,544	9,178	1.34
Industrial machinery, n.e.c.	7,563	2.61	9,496	10,588	11,784	3.02
Transportation equipment, all other	7,429	8.41	8,631	9,593	10,340	10.12

Source: National Industry-Occupation Matrix, 1992 [data tape]. Prepared by the Bureau of Labor Statistics. Washington, DC: U.S. Department of Labor, Bureau of Labor Statistics, 1992. *Notes:* All employment data are wage and salary employment. "n.e.c." stands for "not elsewhere classified."

Production and Technology

★ 470 ★

Output Per Hour, by Industry: 1975-1992

Table shows indexes of output per hour for all employees in selected industries. Output per hour measures labor productivity for the business sector and major subsectors.

Industry	1987 SIC code[1]	Indexes (1987 = 100)						Average annual percent change[2]	
		1975	1980	1985	1990	1991	1992 preliminary	1975-1991	1991-1992
Mining:	(B)								
Coal mining	12	57.9	61.9	85.2	118.6	122.2	134.1	4.8	9.7
Crude petroleum and natural gas	1311	142.9	97.5	83.4	96.9	98.0	102.5	-2.3	4.6
Nonmetallic minerals[3]	14	79.4	84.6	93.9	108.3	103.4	110.9	1.7	7.3
Manufacturing:	(D)								
Red meat products	2011,13	69.1	87.6	99.7	92.3	93.5	(NA)	1.9	(NA)
Poultry dressing and processing	2015	64.6	77.8	98.2	106.1	112.5	(NA)	3.5	(NA)
Dairy products	202	66.3	77.4	93.3	104.5	106.8	112.1	3.0	5.0
Preserved fruits and vegetables	203	77.8	83.7	94.6	97.7	99.9	(NA)	1.6	(NA)
Grain mill products	204	58.4	70.4	93.8	104.1	104.6	(NA)	3.7	(NA)
Bakery products	2051,52	81.2	81.5	95.5	93.8	90.5	89.9	0.7	-0.7
Bottled and canned soft drinks	2086	55.7	66.6	85.1	126.6	135.1	143.5	5.7	6.2
Cotton and synthetic broadwoven fabrics	2211,21	65.2	79.0	94.1	106.1	114.0	120.8	3.6	6.0
Hosiery	2251,52	81.5	92.9	101.3	105.7	111.4	117.6	2.0	5.6
Yarn spinning mills	2281	65.3	64.3	87.5	107.1	106.9	114.8	3.1	7.4
Sawmills and planing mills, general	2421	67.4	70.9	92.3	100.3	102.9	110.5	2.7	7.4
Millwork	2431	103.8	97.0	95.5	98.3	96.2	96.2	-0.5	0.0
Wood kitchen cabinets	2434	83.6	95.0	85.2	94.3	92.5	(NA)	0.6	(NA)
Household furniture	251	82.4	84.5	94.6	100.8	104.3	106.2	1.5	1.8
Office furniture	252	71.8	94.1	98.6	95.6	95.0	97.6	1.8	2.7
Pulp, paper, and paperboard mills	2611,21,31	62.8	76.1	89.1	103.2	105.2	112.9	3.3	7.3
Corrugated and solid fiber boxes	2653	78.1	90.1	99.3	100.3	100.0	101.1	1.6	1.1
Industrial inorganic chemicals	281	69.6	75.9	86.1	90.3	85.4	(NA)	1.3	(NA)
Industrial inorganic chemicals, n.e.c.[4]	2819 (pt)	74.3	79.9	87.4	86.5	81.3	(NA)	0.6	(NA)
Synthetic fibers	2823,24	53.7	73.4	86.2	99.1	101.9	108.3	4.1	6.3
Cosmetics and other toiletries	2844	94.7	84.2	88.9	100.3	102.5	(NA)	0.5	(NA)
Industrial organic chemicals, n.e.c.[4]	2869	64.9	75.4	85.7	98.0	91.8	90.4	2.2	-1.5
Petroleum refining	2911	77.0	81.6	84.3	109.9	107.4	111.6	2.1	3.9
Tires and inner tubes	3011	53.1	59.2	88.1	108.3	109.8	116.7	4.6	6.3
Miscellaneous plastics products, n.e.c.[4]	308	67.0	74.3	88.0	100.1	100.8	100.5	2.6	-0.3
Footwear	314	94.6	92.5	100.3	92.6	92.8	93.6	-0.1	0.9
Concrete products	3271,72	88.7	87.2	97.3	105.8	107.5	109.9	1.2	2.2
Ready-mixed concrete	3273	93.3	89.0	93.2	99.7	96.1	97.9	0.2	1.9
Steel	331	61.3	67.5	91.4	110.4	106.3	116.2	3.5	9.3
Gray and ductile iron foundries	3321	90.3	84.5	96.1	103.7	99.0	104.5	0.6	5.6
Fabricated structural metal	3441	82.4	86.4	99.6	97.2	99.5	(NA)	1.2	(NA)
Metal doors, sash, and trim	3442	86.2	87.3	102.5	98.3	96.0	(NA)	0.7	(NA)
Metal stampings	3465,66,69	80.8	86.7	90.6	98.3	100.5	(NA)	1.4	(NA)
Valves and pipe fittings	3491,92,94	83.0	92.5	94.4	102.1	102.1	(NA)	1.3	(NA)
Farm and garden machinery	352	90.4	86.3	93.3	117.7	112.6	118.8	1.4	5.5
Construction machinery	3531	85.8	89.1	96.7	114.5	99.8	(NA)	0.9	(NA)
Pumps and compressors	3561,63,94	75.1	82.4	89.6	105.9	106.1	(NA)	2.2	(NA)
Refrigeration and heating equipment	3585	85.0	88.7	98.2	106.0	103.1	(NA)	1.2	(NA)
Motors and generators	3621	82.7	85.7	95.9	102.6	105.3	104.6	1.5	-0.7
Major household appliances	3631,32,33,39	70.0	79.0	93.0	102.6	104.5	112.9	2.5	8.0
Lighting fixtures and equipment	3645,46,47,48	79.9	83.5	96.4	94.4	92.4	93.0	0.9	0.6
Motor vehicles and equipment	371	69.6	71.9	95.0	102.0	96.3	104.1	2.1	8.1
Aircraft	3721	84.0	101.0	92.4	106.2	124.5	125.2	2.5	0.6
Instruments to measure electricity	3825	72.0	81.6	98.3	108.0	111.6	(NA)	2.8	(NA)
Photographic equipment and supplies	3861	71.2	84.4	90.3	109.5	110.6	(NA)	2.8	(NA)

[Continued]

★ 470 ★

Output Per Hour, by Industry: 1975-1992
[Continued]

Industry	1987 SIC code[1]	Indexes (1987 = 100)						Average annual percent change[2]	
		1975	1980	1985	1990	1991	1992 preliminary	1975-1991	1991-1992
Service producing:	(E,G,H,I)								
Railroad transportation, revenue traffic	4011	43.4	52.0	78.4	122.4	132.7	140.2	7.2	5.7
Air transportation[5]	4512,13,22 (pt)	59.9	72.8	93.6	89.6	90.9	94.1	2.6	3.5
Telephone communications	481	50.0	68.6	90.4	110.7	116.2	122.0	5.4	5.0
Gas and electric utilities	491,2,3	101.6	103.2	97.4	106.3	108.4	109.9	0.4	1.4
Hardware stores	5251	84.0	95.9	96.0	110.5	102.4	109.9	1.2	7.3
Department stores	5311	64.3	74.5	93.1	95.0	98.9	103.2	2.7	4.3
Variety stores	5331	143.3	126.1	129.1	131.8	130.0	117.8	-0.6	-9.4
Food stores	54	106.0	107.5	102.4	94.6	93.8	94.5	-0.8	0.7
New and used car dealers	5511	83.9	87.9	99.8	107.1	105.5	106.2	1.4	0.7
Auto and home supply stores	5531	70.8	84.0	95.0	114.2	114.6	114.0	3.1	-0.5
Gasoline service stations	5541	58.8	72.3	93.8	101.1	102.1	106.6	3.5	4.4
Apparel and accessory stores	56	72.6	81.4	102.0	101.6	102.3	109.4	2.2	6.9
Home furniture, furnishings, equipment stores	57	64.6	75.3	92.4	113.5	118.1	128.7	3.8	9.0
Eating and drinking places	581	107.5	106.5	96.2	104.6	106.1	104.6	-0.1	-1.4
Drug stores and proprietary stores	5912	89.5	101.5	101.4	106.6	109.6	108.0	1.3	-1.5
Liquor stores	5921	89.9	95.2	101.6	110.6	112.3	126.6	1.4	12.7
Commercial banks	602	76.3	78.6	94.3	108.5	112.3	117.3	2.4	4.5
Hotels and motels	7011	100.2	103.8	101.1	90.6	91.3	97.8	-0.6	7.1
Laundry, cleaning, and garment services	721	112.5	105.9	103.2	99.0	96.6	97.1	-0.9	0.5
Beauty and barber shops	7231,41	83.2	86.8	94.7	92.2	88.4	92.8	0.4	5.0
Automotive repair shops	753	107.0	100.7	99.4	106.4	99.9	103.2	-0.4	3.3

Source: U.S. Bureau of the Census. *Statistical Abstract of the United States, 1994.* 114th ed. Washington, DC: U.S. Government Printing Office, 1994, p. 425. Primary sources: U.S. Bureau of Labor Statistics. *Productivity Measures for Selected Industries and Government Services.* Bulletin 2440 (March 1993); and unpublished data. *Notes:* "NA" stands for "not available"; "pt" represents "partial." Minus sign (-) indicates decrease. 1. 1987 Standard Industrial Classification. 2. Average annual percent change based on compound rate formula. 3. Except fuels. 4. "n.e.c." means "not elsewhere classified." 5. Refers to output per employee.

★ 471 ★

Production and Technology

Productivity, by Industry

Mining and oil and gas drilling - 242.5

Utilities - 204.3

Transportation and communication - 76.7

Manufacturing - 66.9

Finance, insurance, and real estate - 45.2

Agriculture, forestry, and fisheries - 42.7

Wholesale and retail sales, hotels and restaurants - 41.2

Construction - 38.7

Table shows productivity in terms of dollar value of goods produced per worker.

[In thousands of 1991 dollars]

Industry	Total productivity
Mining and oil and gas drilling	242.5
Utilities	204.3
Transportation and communication	76.7
Manufacturing	66.9
Finance, insurance, and real estate	45.2
Agriculture, forestry, and fisheries	42.7
Wholesale and retail sales, hotels and restaurants	41.2
Construction	38.7

Source: Nasar, Sylvia. "Cars and VCRs Aren't Necessarily the First Domino." *New York Times,* 3 May 1992, p. 6R. Primary source: Edward N. Wolff, professor of economics, New York University. *Notes:* Data based on gross domestic product and labor figures from 1988, the most recent year available when source compiled table.

Work Hours and Schedules

★ 472 ★

Flexible Schedules, by Industry: 1985 and 1991

As of May. For employed persons 16 years old and over who usually work full-time and who were at work during the survey reference week. A flexible schedule allows workers to vary the time they begin and end their work days. Based on Current Population Survey.

[In thousands, except percentages]

Industry	All workers			Workers with flexible schedules					
				Number			Percent		
	Total	Male	Female	Total	Male	Female	Total	Male	Female
Total, 1985	73,395	43,779	29,616	9,061	5,760	3,300	12.3	13.2	11.1
Total, 1991	80,452	46,308	34,145	12,118	7,168	4,950	15.1	15.5	14.5
Private sector	65,556	38,909	26,647	10,010	6,018	3,992	15.3	15.5	15.0
Goods producing[1]	24,057	17,776	6,281	2,815	2,060	755	11.7	11.6	12.0
Service producing	41,499	21,132	20,367	7,196	3,959	3,237	17.3	18.7	15.9
Public sector	14,896	7,399	7,497	2,108	1,150	958	14.2	15.5	12.8
Federal government	3,007	1,868	1,140	812	481	331	27.0	25.7	29.0
State government	3,616	1,801	1,814	655	351	304	18.1	19.5	16.8
Local government	8,274	3,730	4,543	640	319	322	7.7	8.6	7.1

Source: U.S. Bureau of the Census. *Statistical Abstract of the United States, 1994.* 114th ed. Washington, DC: U.S. Government Printing Office, 1994, p. 405. Primary sources: U.S. Bureau of Labor Statistics. *News.* USDL 92-491 (4 August 1992); and unpublished data. *Note:* 1. Includes agriculture, mining, construction, and manufacturing.

★ 473 ★

Work Hours and Schedules

Work Week, by Industry

```
Mining - 45.4
Manufacturing - 42.3
Services - 32.4
Retail trade - 29.0
```

Table shows the average number of hours worked each week by nonsupervisory employees in private industry.

Industry	Hours
Mining	45.4
Manufacturing	42.3
Services	32.4
Retail trade	29.0

Source: "How Many Hours in a Week?" *USA TODAY,* 12 October 1994, p. B1. Primary source: Bureau of Labor Statistics.

Workers

★ 474 ★

Multiple Job Holders, by Industry: 1991

As of May. Multiple job holders are employed persons who either had jobs as wage or salary workers with two or more employers; were self-employed and also held a wage and salary job; or were unpaid family workers on their primary jobs but also held wage and salary jobs. Based on the Current Population Survey.

Industry and class of worker by primary job	Total			Male			Female		
	Employed (1,000)	Multiple job holders		Employed (1,000)	Multiple job holders		Employed (1,000)	Multiple job holders	
		Number (1,000)	Rate[1]		Number (1,000)	Rate[1]		Number (1,000)	Rate[1]
Total, 16 years and over	116,626	7,183	6.2	63,499	4,054	6.4	53,127	3,129	5.9
Industry and class of worker of primary job:									
Agriculture	3,466	179	5.2	2,737	139	5.1	728	41	5.6
Nonagricultural industries	113,160	7,003	6.2	60,762	3,915	6.4	52,399	3,088	5.9
Wage and salary workers	104,193	6,691	6.4	55,063	3,733	6.8	49,129	2,958	6.0
Mining	737	25	3.4	592	17	2.8	145	8	5.8
Construction	5,745	271	4.7	5,231	239	4.6	514	33	6.4
Manufacturing	19,993	1,044	5.2	13,497	798	5.9	6,496	245	3.8
Transportation and public utilities	7,848	487	6.2	5,526	356	6.4	2,321	131	5.6
Wholesale trade	4,255	261	6.1	3,010	190	6.3	1,245	70	5.7
Retail trade	17,250	914	5.3	8,354	444	5.3	8,896	470	5.3
Finance, insurance, and real estate	7,066	414	5.9	2,860	187	6.5	4,206	227	5.4
Services	35,592	2,747	7.7	12,719	1,125	8.8	22,873	1,622	7.1
Public administration	5,709	528	9.3	3,274	376	11.5	2,434	152	6.2

[Continued]

★ 474 ★

Multiple Job Holders, by Industry: 1991
[Continued]

Industry and class of worker by primary job	Total			Male			Female		
	Employed (1,000)	Multiple job holders		Employed (1,000)	Multiple job holders		Employed (1,000)	Multiple job holders	
		Number (1,000)	Rate[1]		Number (1,000)	Rate[1]		Number (1,000)	Rate[1]
Self-employed workers	8,733	306	3.5	5,663	182	3.2	3,070	123	4.0
Unpaid family workers	235	7	2.9	36	-	-	199	7	3.4

Source: U.S. Bureau of the Census. *Statistical Abstract of the United States, 1994.* 114th ed. Washington, DC: U.S. Government Printing Office, 1994, p. 405. Primary source: U.S. Bureau of Labor Statistics. *News.* USDL 91-547 (28 October 1991). *Notes:* "-" represents or rounds to zero. 1. Multiple job holders as a percent of all employed persons in specified group.

★ 475 ★

Workers

Self-Employed Workers, by Industry: 1970-1993

For civilian noninstitutional population 16 years old and over. Annual averages of monthly figures. Data for 1992 are not fully comparable with data for prior years because of the introduction of the occupational and industrial classification used in the 1990 Census. Based on the Current Population Survey.

[In thousands]

Industry	1970	1975	1980	1985	1990	1991	1992	1993
Total self-employed	7,031	7,427	8,642	9,269	10,160	10,341	10,017	10,335
Agriculture	1,810	1,722	1,642	1,458	1,400	1,442	1,398	1,332
Nonagriculture	5,221	5,705	7,000	7,811	8,760	8,899	8,619	9,003
Mining	14	16	28	20	24	23	23	17
Construction	687	839	1,173	1,301	1,463	1,447	1,466	1,555
Manufacturing	264	273	358	347	429	420	392	442
Transportation and public utilities	196	223	282	315	302	318	337	372
Trade	1,667	1,709	1,899	1,792	1,859	1,879	1,776	1,890
Finance, insurance, and real estate	254	335	458	558	635	619	630	664
Services	2,140	2,310	2,804	3,477	4,048	4,193	3,995	4,062

Source: U.S. Bureau of the Census. *Statistical Abstract of the United States, 1994.* 114th ed. Washington, DC: U.S. Government Printing Office, 1994, p. 404. Primary sources: U.S. Bureau of Labor Statistics. Bulletin 2307; *Employment and Earnings* (monthly; January issues); and unpublished data.

Chapter 4
EMPLOYMENT AND UNEMPLOYMENT

The United Nations and the Organization for Economic Cooperation and Development identified 2.8 billion workers in the world in 1994, more than 49 percent of the global population. Another 120 million people were job hunting that year. About 120 million workers were employed members of the U.S. labor force in 1993, and according to Bureau of Economic Analysis summary projections, by the year 2000, the United States should see 19 million new job openings, mostly in the top 54 metropolitan areas; for example, Los Angeles, Washington, Anaheim, Atlanta, San Diego, Phoenix, Boston, and Philadelphia to name a few. The 118 tables in this chapter offer a picture of employment in the United States. Coverage includes employers, job growth, labor force participation, recruiting and placement, unemployment, work hours and schedules, and workers, particularly special classes in the workforce such as minorities, women, and workers with disabilities. Data on the employment status of the civilian noninstitutionalized population of each state is reported fully as well.

Employers

★ 476 ★

Employers in South Africa

Sara Lee - 4,703	
Caltex Petroleum - 2,168	
CPC International - 2,000	
	International Paper - 1,534
	Johnson & Johnson - 1,232

Table shows the top five U.S. employers in South Africa.

Employer	Number employed
Sara Lee	4,703
Caltex Petroleum	2,168
CPC International	2,000
International Paper	1,534
Johnson & Johnson	1,232

Source: "Largest U.S. Employers in South Africa." *USA TODAY,* 6 June 1994, p. 1A. Primary source: Investor Responsibility Research Center Inc.

★ 477 ★

Employers

Employment at Foreign Affiliates: 1991

Estimates suggest that by 1991 4.6 million American workers were employed by foreign companies at affiliates and branch offices in the United States. Major countries of origin for these employers include Britain, Canada, Japan, Germany, Netherlands, and France.

Source: Hoerr, John, Leah Nathans Spiro, Larry Armstrong, and James B. Treece. "Culture Shock at Home: Working for a Foreign Boss." *Business Week,* 17 December 1990, p. 84.

★ 478 ★

Employers

Fastest Growing Employers: 1993

Table shows the 25 companies with the fastest employment growth from 1992 to 1993.

[In percentages]

Company	Increase
Blockbuster Entertainment Corp.	105
Gateway 2000 Inc.	93
Intelligent Electronics Inc.	69
Foundation Health Corp.	62
Office Depot Inc.	60
CompUSA Inc.	57
Best Buy Co.	50
Novell Inc.	44
Microsoft Corp.	44
Oracle Systems Corp.	43
Amgen Inc.	42
Sun Microsystems Inc.	35
PacifiCare Health Systems Inc.	35
Seagate Technology Inc.	34
First Flnancial Management Corp.	34
AST Research Inc.	33
Home Depot Inc.	33
Maxtor Corp.	32
Price/Costco Inc.	31
Reebok International Ltd.	29
MacAndrews & Forbes Holdings Inc.	29
Compaq Computer Corp.	26
First Union Corp.	26
Conner Peripherals Inc.	26
Silicon Graphics Inc.	26

Source: "Healthy Payrolls." *Wall Street Journal,* 27 February 1995, p. R5. Primary source: *Hoover's Handbook of American Business, 1995. Notes:* Figures based on total company employment and may reflect acquisitions in addition to internal growth.

Employment Status

★479★

Employment Status: 1950-1993

Annual averages of monthly figures for the noninstitutionalized population 16 years of age and older. Based on Current Population Survey.

[In thousands, except as indicated]

Year	Noninsti-tutional popula-tion	Labor force								Not in labor force
		Employed						Unemployed		
		Number	Total	Resi-dent Armed Forces	Civilian			Number	Percent of labor force[1]	
					Total	Agri-culture	Nonagri-culture			
1950	106,164	63,377	60,087	1,169	58,918	7,160	51,758	3,288	5.2	42,787
1960	119,106	71,489	67,639	1,861	65,778	5,458	60,318	3,852	5.4	47,617
1965	128,459	76,401	73,034	1,946	71,088	4,361	66,726	3,366	4.4	52,058
1970	139,203	84,889	80,796	2,118	78,678	3,463	75,215	4,093	4.8	54,315
1975	154,831	95,453	87,524	1,678	85,846	3,408	82,438	7,929	8.3	59,377
1976	157,818	97,826	90,420	1,668	88,752	3,331	85,421	7,406	7.6	59,991
1977	160,689	100,665	93,673	1,656	92,017	3,283	88,734	6,991	6.9	60,025
1978	163,541	103,882	97,679	1,631	96,048	3,387	92,661	6,202	6.0	59,659
1979	166,460	106,559	100,421	1,597	98,824	3,347	95,477	6,137	5.8	59,900
1980	169,349	108,544	100,907	1,604	99,303	3,364	95,938	7,637	7.0	60,806
1981	171,775	110,315	102,042	1,645	100,397	3,368	97,030	8,273	7.5	61,460
1982	173,939	111,872	101,194	1,668	99,526	3,401	96,125	10,678	9.5	62,067
1983	175,891	113,226	102,510	1,676	100,834	3,383	97,450	10,717	9.5	62,665
1984	178,080	115,241	106,702	1,697	105,005	3,321	101,685	8,539	7.4	62,839
1985	179,912	117,167	108,856	1,706	107,150	3,179	103,971	8,312	7.1	62,744
1986	182,293	119,540	111,303	1,706	109,597	3,163	106,434	8,237	6.9	62,752
1987	184,490	121,602	114,177	1,737	112,440	3,208	109,232	7,425	6.1	62,888
1988	186,322	123,378	116,677	1,709	114,968	3,169	111,800	6,701	5.4	62,944
1989	188,081	125,557	119,030	1,688	117,342	3,199	114,142	6,528	5.2	62,523
1990	189,686	126,424	119,550	1,637	117,914	3,186	114,728	6,874	5.4	63,262
1991	191,329	126,867	118,440	1,564	116,877	3,233	113,644	8,426	6.6	64,462
1992	193,142	128,548	119,164	1,566	117,598	3,207	114,391	9,384	7.3	64,593
1993	195,034	129,525	120,791	1,485	119,306	3,074	116,232	8,734	6.7	65,509
Percent distribution										
1950	100.0	59.7	56.6	1.1	55.5	6.7	48.8	3.1	(X)	40.3
1960	100.0	60.0	56.8	1.6	55.2	4.6	50.6	3.2	(X)	40.0
1970	100.0	61.0	58.0	1.5	56.5	2.5	54.0	2.9	(X)	39.0
1980	100.0	64.1	59.6	0.9	58.6	2.0	56.7	4.5	(X)	35.9
1985	100.0	65.1	60.5	0.9	59.6	1.8	57.8	4.6	(X)	34.9
1988	100.0	66.2	62.6	0.9	61.7	1.7	60.0	3.6	(X)	33.8
1989	100.0	66.8	63.3	0.9	62.4	1.7	60.7	3.5	(X)	33.2
1990	100.0	66.6	63.0	0.9	62.2	1.7	60.5	3.6	(X)	33.4
1991	100.0	66.3	61.9	0.8	61.1	1.7	59.4	4.4	(X)	33.7

[Continued]

★ 479 ★

Employment Status: 1950-1993
[Continued]

Year	Noninsti-tutional popula-tion	Labor force								Not in labor force
		Number	Employed					Unemployed		
			Total	Resi-dent Armed Forces	Civilian			Number	Percent of labor force[1]	
					Total	Agri-culture	Nonagri-culture			
1992	100.0	66.6	61.7	0.8	60.9	1.7	59.2	4.9	(X)	33.4
1993	100.0	66.4	61.9	0.8	61.2	1.6	59.6	4.5	(X)	33.6

Source: U.S. Bureau of the Census. *Statistical Abstract of the United States, 1994.* 114th ed. Washington, DC: U.S. Government Printing Office, 1994, p. 395. Primary sources: U.S. Bureau of Labor Statistics. Bulletin 2307; and *Employment and Earnings* (monthly). *Notes:* "X" indicates "not applicable." 1. Unemployment as a percent of the labor force, including resident Armed Forces.

★ 480 ★
Employment Status

Employment Status – Civilians: 1960-1993

Table shows data for the total civilian noninstitutionalized population 16 years old and older. See also tables for specific groups such as women and Hispanics. Annual averages of monthly figures. Based on Current Population Survey.

[In thousands, except as indicated]

Year	Civilian noninsti-tutional popula-tion	Civilian labor force						Not in labor force	
		Total	Per-cent of popu-lation	Employed	Employ-ment/ popula-tion ratio[1]	Unemployed			
						Number	Percent of labor force	Number	Percent of popu-lation
1960	117,245	69,628	59.4	65,778	56.1	3,852	5.5	47,617	40.6
1970	137,085	82,771	60.4	78,678	57.4	4,093	4.9	54,315	39.6
1980	167,745	106,940	63.8	99,303	59.2	7,637	7.1	60,806	36.2
1985	178,206	115,461	64.8	107,150	60.1	8,312	7.2	62,744	35.2
1989	186,393	123,869	66.5	117,342	63.0	6,528	5.3	62,523	33.5
1990	188,049	124,787	66.4	117,914	62.7	6,874	5.5	63,262	33.6
1991	189,765	125,303	66.0	116,877	61.6	8,426	6.7	64,462	34.0
1992	191,576	126,982	66.3	117,598	61.4	9,384	7.4	64,593	33.7
1993	193,550	128,040	66.2	119,306	61.6	8,734	6.8	65,509	33.8

Source: U.S. Bureau of the Census. *Statistical Abstract of the United States, 1994.* 114th ed. Washington, DC: U.S. Government Printing Office, 1994, p. 396. Primary sources: U.S. Bureau of Labor Statistics. Bulletin 2307; and *Employment and Earnings* (monthly; January issues). *Notes:* 1. Civilian employed as a percent of the civilian noninstitutional population.

★ 481 ★
Employment Status

Employment Status in Alabama: 1993

Data show the employment status of the civilian noninstitutionalized population by sex, age, race, and marital status. Figures are 1993 annual averages.

[Numbers in thousands]

Population group	Civilian non-institutional population	Civilian labor force		Employment		Unemployment		
		Number	Percent of population	Number	Percent of population	Number	Rate	Error range of rate[1]
Total	3,190	1,990	62.4	1,840	57.7	149	7.5	6.8-8.2
Men	1,508	1,089	72.2	1,011	67.0	78	7.1	6.2-8.1
Women	1,682	901	53.6	830	49.3	71	7.9	6.9-9.0
Both sexes, 16-19 years old	239	115	48.3	89	37.2	27	23.0	19.1-27.0
White	2,395	1,508	63.0	1,437	60.0	71	4.7	4.1-5.4
Men	1,150	850	74.0	811	70.6	39	4.6	3.7-5.4
Women	1,245	658	52.8	626	50.2	32	4.9	3.9-5.9
Both sexes, 16-19 years old	159	81	51.1	70	44.3	11	13.3	9.1-17.5
Black	775	471	60.8	393	50.8	77	16.5	14.3-18.6
Men	351	234	66.6	196	55.7	39	16.4	13.4-19.5
Women	423	236	55.9	197	46.7	39	16.5	13.4-19.5
Single (never married)	701	459	65.5	389	55.5	70	15.3	13.4-17.2
Married (spouse present)	1,866	1,225	65.7	1,175	63.0	50	4.1	3.4-4.8
Other marital status[2]	623	306	49.1	277	44.4	29	9.5	7.5-11.4

Source: U.S. Department of Labor. Bureau of Labor Statistics. *Geographic Profile of Employment and Unemployment, 1993.* Bulletin 2446. Washington, DC: U.S. Government Printing Office, September 1994, p. 37. *Notes:* Data for demographic groups are not shown when they do not meet Bureau of Labor Statistics publication standards of reliability for the particular area based on the sample in that area. Items may not add to totals or compute to displayed percentages because of rounding. Detail for race and Hispanic origin groups will not add totals because data for the "other races" group are not presented and because Hispanics are included in both the white and black population groups. 1. Error ranges are calculated at the 90 percent confidence interval, which means that if repeated samples were drawn from the same population and an error range constructed around each sample estimate, in 9 of 10 cases the true value based on a complete census of the population would be contained within these error ranges. 2. "Other marital status" includes divorced, widowed, separated, and married with spouse absent.

★ 482 ★
Employment Status

Employment Status in Alaska: 1993

Data show the employment status of the civilian noninstitutionalized population by sex, age, race, and marital status. Figures are 1993 annual averages.

[Numbers in thousands]

Population group	Civilian non-institutional population	Civilian labor force		Employment		Unemployment		
		Number	Percent of population	Number	Percent of population	Number	Rate	Error range of rate[1]
Total	405	298	73.6	276	68.0	23	7.6	6.7-8.5
Men	201	163	81.2	149	74.1	14	8.8	7.4-10.1
Women	204	135	66.2	126	62.1	8	6.1	4.9-7.4
Both sexes, 16-19 years old	29	15	50.5	12	40.1	3	20.7	14.9-26.5

[Continued]

★ 482 ★

Employment Status in Alaska: 1993

[Continued]

Population group	Civilian non-institutional population	Civilian labor force		Employment		Unemployment		
		Number	Percent of population	Number	Percent of population	Number	Rate	Error range of rate[1]
White	319	244	76.6	228	71.3	17	6.9	5.9-7.9
Men	162	136	84.0	125	77.3	11	8.0	6.6-9.4
Women	157	108	69.0	102	65.1	6	5.6	4.2-6.9
Both sexes, 16-19 years old	22	12	56.1	10	45.0	2	19.8	13.5-26.1
Black	16	12	80.5	12	75.4	1	6.3	3.8-8.8
Single (never married)	106	78	73.0	69	64.5	9	11.7	9.5-13.8
Married (spouse present)	224	169	75.2	160	71.2	9	5.3	4.3-6.4
Other marital status[2]	74	52	69.7	47	63.5	5	8.9	6.5-11.3

Source: U.S. Department of Labor. Bureau of Labor Statistics. *Geographic Profile of Employment and Unemployment, 1993.* Bulletin 2446. Washington, DC: U.S. Government Printing Office, September 1994, p. 37. *Notes:* Data for demographic groups are not shown when they do not meet Bureau of Labor Statistics publication standards of reliability for the particular area based on the sample in that area. Items may not add to totals or compute to displayed percentages because of rounding. Detail for race and Hispanic origin groups will not add totals because data for the "other races" group are not presented and because Hispanics are included in both the white and black population groups. 1. Error ranges are calculated at the 90 percent confidence interval, which means that if repeated samples were drawn from the same population and an error range constructed around each sample estimate, in 9 of 10 cases the true value based on a complete census of the population would be contained within these error ranges. 2. "Other marital status" includes divorced, widowed, separated, and married with spouse absent.

★ 483 ★

Employment Status

Employment Status in Arizona: 1993

Data show the employment status of the civilian noninstitutionalized population by sex, age, race, Hispanic origin, and marital status. Figures are 1993 annual averages.

[Numbers in thousands]

Population group	Civilian non-institutional population	Civilian labor force		Employment		Unemployment		
		Number	Percent of population	Number	Percent of population	Number	Rate	Error range of rate[1]
Total	2,956	1,837	62.1	1,723	58.3	114	6.2	5.5-6.9
Men	1,404	1,008	71.8	945	67.3	63	6.3	5.3-7.3
Women	1,552	829	53.4	779	50.2	50	6.0	5.0-7.1
Both sexes, 16-19 years old	166	84	50.6	71	43.1	12	14.7	10.2-19.3
White	2,794	1,734	62.1	1,634	58.5	100	5.7	5.0-6.5
Men	1,335	958	71.8	901	67.5	57	6.0	5.0-6.9
Women	1,459	776	53.2	733	50.3	42	5.5	4.4-6.5
Both sexes, 16-19 years old	152	80	52.2	68	44.7	11	14.4	9.7-19.1
Hispanic origin	495	310	62.6	282	56.9	28	9.2	6.5-11.8
Men	243	187	77.2	168	69.4	19	10.1	6.5-13.7
Women	253	123	48.7	113	44.9	9	7.7	3.8-11.6
Single (never married)	606	435	71.9	388	64.1	47	10.9	9.1-12.7

[Continued]

★ 483 ★

Employment Status in Arizona: 1993
[Continued]

Population group	Civilian non-institutional population	Civilian labor force		Employment		Unemployment		
		Number	Percent of population	Number	Percent of population	Number	Rate	Error range of rate[1]
Married (spouse present)	1,769	1,075	60.8	1,033	58.4	42	3.9	3.1-4.7
Other marital status[2]	582	326	56.1	302	52.0	24	7.4	5.6-9.2

Source: U.S. Department of Labor. Bureau of Labor Statistics. *Geographic Profile of Employment and Unemployment, 1993.* Bulletin 2446. Washington, DC: U.S. Government Printing Office, September 1994, p. 37. *Notes:* Data for demographic groups are not shown when they do not meet Bureau of Labor Statistics publication standards of reliability for the particular area based on the sample in that area. Items may not add to totals or compute to displayed percentages because of rounding. Detail for race and Hispanic origin groups will not add totals because data for the "other races" group are not presented and because Hispanics are included in both the white and black population groups. 1. Error ranges are calculated at the 90 percent confidence interval, which means that if repeated samples were drawn from the same population and an error range constructed around each sample estimate, in 9 of 10 cases the true value based on a complete census of the population would be contained within these error ranges. 2. "Other marital status" includes divorced, widowed, separated, and married with spouse absent.

★ 484 ★
Employment Status

Employment Status in Arkansas: 1993

Data show the employment status of the civilian noninstitutionalized population by sex, age, race, and marital status. Figures are 1993 annual averages.

[Numbers in thousands]

Population group	Civilian non-institutional population	Civilian labor force		Employment		Unemployment		
		Number	Percent of population	Number	Percent of population	Number	Rate	Error range of rate[1]
Total	1,841	1,163	63.2	1,091	59.3	72	6.2	5.6-6.8
Men	875	630	72.0	592	67.7	37	5.9	5.1-6.7
Women	966	533	55.2	499	51.7	34	6.4	5.5-7.4
Both sexes, 16-19 years old	149	74	49.8	62	41.4	13	16.9	13.2-20.6
White	1,545	988	64.0	939	60.8	49	5.0	4.4-5.6
Men	732	536	73.2	512	69.9	24	4.4	3.7-5.2
Women	813	453	55.7	428	52.6	25	5.6	4.6-6.5
Both sexes, 16-19 years old	117	62	52.7	55	46.5	7	11.8	8.2-15.3
Black	270	157	58.2	137	50.6	21	13.1	10.6-15.6
Men	131	85	64.6	73	55.6	12	14.0	10.5-17.5
Women	139	72	52.2	64	45.9	9	12.1	8.5-15.7
Single (never married)	339	217	64.1	188	55.4	29	13.5	11.5-15.5
Married (spouse present)	1,122	751	67.0	724	64.5	27	3.6	3.0-4.2
Other marital status[2]	380	195	51.2	180	47.3	15	7.7	6.0-9.4

Source: U.S. Department of Labor. Bureau of Labor Statistics. *Geographic Profile of Employment and Unemployment, 1993.* Bulletin 2446. Washington, DC: U.S. Government Printing Office, September 1994, p. 37. *Notes:* Data for demographic groups are not shown when they do not meet Bureau of Labor Statistics publication standards of reliability for the particular area based on the sample in that area. Items may not add to totals or compute to displayed percentages because of rounding. Detail for race and Hispanic origin groups will not add totals because data for the "other races" group are not presented and because Hispanics are included in both the white and black population groups. 1. Error ranges are calculated at the 90 percent confidence interval, which means that if repeated samples were drawn from the same population and an error range constructed around each sample estimate, in 9 of 10 cases the true value based on a complete census of the population would be contained within these error ranges. 2. "Other marital status" includes divorced, widowed, separated, and married with spouse absent.

★ 485 ★

Employment Status

Employment Status in California: 1993

Data show the employment status of the civilian noninstitutionalized population by sex, age, race, Hispanic origin, and marital status. Figures are 1993 annual averages.

[Numbers in thousands]

Population group	Civilian non-institutional population	Civilian labor force		Employment		Unemployment		
		Number	Percent of population	Number	Percent of population	Number	Rate	Error range of rate[1]
Total	23,288	15,259	65.5	13,853	59.5	1,407	9.2	8.9-9.5
Men	11,326	8,590	75.8	7,761	68.5	829	9.7	9.2-10.1
Women	11,962	6,670	55.8	6,092	50.9	577	8.7	8.2-9.1
Both sexes, 16-19 years old	1,593	737	46.2	544	34.1	193	26.2	24.3-28.1
White	19,437	12,853	66.1	11,713	60.3	1,139	8.9	8.5-9.2
Men	9,534	7,323	76.8	6,651	69.8	672	9.2	8.8-9.6
Women	9,904	5,529	55.8	5,062	51.1	467	8.4	8.0-8.9
Both sexes, 16-19 years old	1,303	628	48.2	473	36.3	155	24.7	22.6-26.7
Black	1,398	825	59.0	702	50.2	123	14.9	13.4-16.4
Men	641	419	65.3	347	54.1	71	17.1	14.8-19.3
Women	756	406	53.7	355	46.9	51	12.6	10.6-14.7
Hispanic origin	5,660	3,783	66.8	3,315	58.6	468	12.4	11.7-13.1
Men	2,865	2,331	81.3	2,053	71.6	277	11.9	11.0-12.8
Women	2,795	1,452	52.0	1,262	45.1	191	13.1	12.0-14.3
Both sexes, 16-19 years old	577	246	42.7	178	30.8	68	27.8	24.0-31.6
Single (never married)	6,143	4,325	70.4	3,740	60.9	586	13.5	12.9-14.2
Married (spouse present)	12,680	8,490	67.0	7,921	62.5	569	6.7	6.4-7.0
Other marital status[2]	4,465	2,444	54.7	2,192	49.1	252	10.3	9.5-11.1

Source: U.S. Department of Labor. Bureau of Labor Statistics. *Geographic Profile of Employment and Unemployment, 1993.* Bulletin 2446. Washington, DC: U.S. Government Printing Office, September 1994, p. 38. *Notes:* Data for demographic groups are not shown when they do not meet Bureau of Labor Statistics publication standards of reliability for the particular area based on the sample in that area. Items may not add to totals or compute to displayed percentages because of rounding. Detail for race and Hispanic origin groups will not add totals because data for the "other races" group are not presented and because Hispanics are included in both the white and black population groups. 1. Error ranges are calculated at the 90 percent confidence interval, which means that if repeated samples were drawn from the same population and an error range constructed around each sample estimate, in 9 of 10 cases the true value based on a complete census of the population would be contained within these error ranges. 2. "Other marital status" includes divorced, widowed, separated, and married with spouse absent.

★ 486 ★

Employment Status

Employment Status in Colorado: 1993

Data show the employment status of the civilian noninstitutionalized population by sex, age, race, Hispanic origin, and marital status. Figures are 1993 annual averages.

[Numbers in thousands]

Population group	Civilian non-institutional population	Civilian labor force		Employment		Unemployment		
		Number	Percent of population	Number	Percent of population	Number	Rate	Error range of rate[1]
Total	2,685	1,904	70.9	1,805	67.2	99	5.2	4.6-5.8
Men	1,306	1,024	78.5	964	73.8	60	5.9	5.1-6.7
Women	1,379	879	63.7	841	61.0	39	4.4	3.6-5.2
Both sexes, 16-19 years old	168	104	61.5	86	50.8	18	17.4	14.1-20.6
White	2,461	1,745	70.9	1,659	67.4	86	4.9	4.3-5.5
Men	1,201	944	78.6	890	74.1	54	5.7	4.9-6.6
Women	1,260	801	63.6	769	61.1	32	3.9	3.2-4.7
Both sexes, 16-19 years old	145	92	63.3	76	52.4	16	17.2	13.8-20.7
Black	118	81	68.7	73	62.2	8	9.5	6.2-12.7
Hispanic origin	229	163	71.0	151	65.8	12	7.3	4.9-9.7
Men	116	91	78.1	85	73.3	6	6.1	3.2-9.1
Women	113	72	63.7	66	58.1	6	8.8	4.9-12.7
Single (never married)	657	508	77.3	465	70.8	43	8.4	7.1-9.7
Married (spouse present)	1,507	1,081	71.7	1,043	69.2	38	3.5	2.9-4.1
Other marital status[2]	521	314	60.3	296	56.9	18	5.8	4.4-7.2

Source: U.S. Department of Labor. Bureau of Labor Statistics. *Geographic Profile of Employment and Unemployment, 1993*. Bulletin 2446. Washington, DC: U.S. Government Printing Office, September 1994, p. 38. *Notes:* Data for demographic groups are not shown when they do not meet Bureau of Labor Statistics publication standards of reliability for the particular area based on the sample in that area. Items may not add to totals or compute to displayed percentages because of rounding. Detail for race and Hispanic origin groups will not add totals because data for the "other races" group are not presented and because Hispanics are included in both the white and black population groups. 1. Error ranges are calculated at the 90 percent confidence interval, which means that if repeated samples were drawn from the same population and an error range constructed around each sample estimate, in 9 of 10 cases the true value based on a complete census of the population would be contained within these error ranges. 2. "Other marital status" includes divorced, widowed, separated, and married with spouse absent.

★ 487 ★
Employment Status

Employment Status in Connecticut: 1993

Data show the employment status of the civilian noninstitutionalized population by sex, age, race, Hispanic origin, and marital status. Figures are 1993 annual averages.

[Numbers in thousands]

Population group	Civilian non-institutional population	Civilian labor force		Employment		Unemployment		
		Number	Percent of population	Number	Percent of population	Number	Rate	Error range of rate[1]
Total	2,542	1,788	70.3	1,678	66.0	111	6.2	5.5-6.9
Men	1,228	966	78.7	894	72.8	72	7.5	6.5-8.5
Women	1,314	822	62.6	783	59.6	38	4.7	3.8-5.6
Both sexes, 16-19 years old	177	92	51.9	85	48.2	7	7.2	4.1-10.3
White	2,315	1,624	70.1	1,530	66.1	94	5.8	5.1-6.5
Men	1,115	873	78.3	813	73.0	60	6.9	5.9-7.9
Women	1,201	751	62.5	717	59.7	34	4.5	3.6-5.4
Both sexes, 16-19 years old	157	85	53.7	79	50.4	5	6.3	3.2-9.4
Black	187	140	74.8	124	66.2	16	11.5	8.5-14.5
Men	96	79	83.0	68	71.0	12	14.5	10.2-18.8
Women	91	60	66.1	56	61.1	5	7.5	3.6-11.4
Hispanic origin	115	79	68.6	67	58.2	12	15.2	10.6-19.7
Single (never married)	654	461	70.5	422	64.5	39	8.6	7.1-10.1
Married (spouse present)	1,484	1,104	74.4	1,054	71.0	51	4.6	3.8-5.3
Other marital status[2]	405	223	55.1	202	50.0	21	9.2	7.0-11.4

Source: U.S. Department of Labor. Bureau of Labor Statistics. *Geographic Profile of Employment and Unemployment, 1993.* Bulletin 2446. Washington, DC: U.S. Government Printing Office, September 1994, p. 38. *Notes:* Data for demographic groups are not shown when they do not meet Bureau of Labor Statistics publication standards of reliability for the particular area based on the sample in that area. Items may not add to totals or compute to displayed percentages because of rounding. Detail for race and Hispanic origin groups will not add totals because data for the "other races" group are not presented and because Hispanics are included in both the white and black population groups. 1. Error ranges are calculated at the 90 percent confidence interval, which means that if repeated samples were drawn from the same population and an error range constructed around each sample estimate, in 9 of 10 cases the true value based on a complete census of the population would be contained within these error ranges. 2. "Other marital status" includes divorced, widowed, separated, and married with spouse absent.

★ 488 ★

Employment Status

Employment Status in Delaware: 1993

Data show the employment status of the civilian noninstitutionalized population by sex, age, race, and marital status. Figures are 1993 annual averages.

[Numbers in thousands]

Population group	Civilian non-institutional population	Civilian labor force		Employment		Unemployment		
		Number	Percent of population	Number	Percent of population	Number	Rate	Error range of rate[1]
Total	533	373	70.1	354	66.3	20	5.3	4.7-5.9
Men	266	206	77.5	194	73.2	11	5.5	4.6-6.4
Women	267	168	62.7	159	59.5	9	5.2	4.2-6.1
Both sexes, 16-19 years old	34	16	47.3	14	41.0	2	13.3	8.9-17.7
White	426	298	70.1	285	66.9	14	4.6	3.9-5.2
Men	213	166	77.8	158	74.1	8	4.7	3.8-5.6
Women	213	133	62.3	127	59.6	6	4.3	3.3-5.3
Both sexes, 16-19 years old	24	13	54.3	11	47.6	2	12.3	7.5-17.1
Black	92	64	70.0	58	63.4	6	9.5	7.5-11.4
Men	44	33	74.5	29	66.7	3	10.4	7.6-13.3
Women	48	32	65.9	29	60.4	3	8.5	5.8-11.1
Single (never married)	143	106	74.0	97	67.9	9	8.3	6.8-9.7
Married (spouse present)	296	211	71.2	203	68.5	8	3.8	3.0-4.5
Other marital status[2]	94	57	60.4	54	57.0	3	5.7	4.0-7.3

Source: U.S. Department of Labor. Bureau of Labor Statistics. *Geographic Profile of Employment and Unemployment, 1993.* Bulletin 2446. Washington, DC: U.S. Government Printing Office, September 1994, p. 39. *Notes:* Data for demographic groups are not shown when they do not meet Bureau of Labor Statistics publication standards of reliability for the particular area based on the sample in that area. Items may not add to totals or compute to displayed percentages because of rounding. Detail for race and Hispanic origin groups will not add totals because data for the "other races" group are not presented and because Hispanics are included in both the white and black population groups. 1. Error ranges are calculated at the 90 percent confidence interval, which means that if repeated samples were drawn from the same population and an error range constructed around each sample estimate, in 9 of 10 cases the true value based on a complete census of the population would be contained within these error ranges. 2. "Other marital status" includes divorced, widowed, separated, and married with spouse absent.

★ 489 ★

Employment Status

Employment Status in District of Columbia: 1993

Data show the employment status of the civilian noninstitutionalized population by sex, age, race, Hispanic origin, and marital status. Figures are 1993 annual averages.

[Numbers in thousands]

Population group	Civilian non-institutional population	Civilian labor force		Employment		Unemployment		
		Number	Percent of population	Number	Percent of population	Number	Rate	Error range of rate[1]
Total	458	306	66.8	280	61.2	26	8.5	7.7-9.3
Men	211	154	73.1	141	66.8	13	8.6	7.4-9.7
Women	247	152	61.5	139	56.3	13	8.4	7.3-9.6
White	162	128	79.2	123	76.0	5	4.1	3.2-5.0
Men	78	67	85.9	64	82.3	3	4.2	2.9-5.5
Women	84	61	72.9	59	70.0	2	3.9	2.6-5.2
Black	285	169	59.2	148	52.0	21	12.2	11.0-13.5
Men	128	83	64.8	72	56.7	10	12.5	10.7-14.3
Women	158	86	54.8	76	48.2	10	11.9	10.2-13.7
Hispanic origin	24	19	79.4	17	72.7	2	8.4	5.2-11.7
Men	11	10	88.8	9	80.6	1	9.2	4.5-13.9
Women	13	9	71.4	8	66.0	1	7.6	3.1-12.1
Single (never married)	217	154	71.1	137	63.1	17	11.2	9.9-12.5
Married (spouse present)	137	97	70.4	92	66.9	5	4.9	3.8-6.1
Other marital status[2]	104	56	53.4	52	49.5	4	7.2	5.4-9.0

Source: U.S. Department of Labor. Bureau of Labor Statistics. *Geographic Profile of Employment and Unemployment, 1993.* Bulletin 2446. Washington, DC: U.S. Government Printing Office, September 1994, p. 39. *Notes:* Data for demographic groups are not shown when they do not meet Bureau of Labor Statistics publication standards of reliability for the particular area based on the sample in that area. Items may not add to totals or compute to displayed percentages because of rounding. Detail for race and Hispanic origin groups will not add totals because data for the "other races" group are not presented and because Hispanics are included in both the white and black population groups. 1. Error ranges are calculated at the 90 percent confidence interval, which means that if repeated samples were drawn from the same population and an error range constructed around each sample estimate, in 9 of 10 cases the true value based on a complete census of the population would be contained within these error ranges. 2. "Other marital status" includes divorced, widowed, separated, and married with spouse absent.

★ 490 ★

Employment Status

Employment Status in Florida: 1993

Data show the employment status of the civilian noninstitutionalized population by sex, age, race, Hispanic origin, and marital status. Figures are 1993 annual averages.

[Numbers in thousands]

Population group	Civilian non-institutional population	Civilian labor force		Employment		Unemployment		
		Number	Percent of population	Number	Percent of population	Number	Rate	Error range of rate[1]
Total	10,688	6,628	62.0	6,166	57.7	462	7.0	6.7-7.3
Men	5,062	3,567	70.5	3,315	65.5	252	7.1	6.6-7.5
Women	5,626	3,061	54.4	2,851	50.7	209	6.8	6.4-7.3
Both sexes, 16-19 years old	618	311	50.4	248	40.2	63	20.3	18.3-22.4
White	9,069	5,577	61.5	5,239	57.8	337	6.0	5.7-6.4
Men	4,321	3,049	70.6	2,859	66.2	190	6.2	5.8-6.7
Women	4,748	2,527	53.2	2,380	50.1	147	5.8	5.3-6.3
Both sexes, 16-19 years old	461	252	54.6	210	45.5	42	16.7	14.5-18.9
Black	1,425	924	64.8	807	56.7	116	12.6	11.5-13.7
Men	654	452	69.0	395	60.4	57	12.5	10.9-14.1
Women	770	472	61.2	412	53.5	60	12.6	11.1-14.2
Both sexes, 16-19 years old	144	54	37.7	34	23.5	20	37.7	32.9-42.5
Hispanic origin	1,463	948	64.8	866	59.2	82	8.7	7.7-9.6
Men	709	565	79.7	518	73.0	48	8.4	7.2-9.6
Women	754	383	50.8	348	46.2	35	9.1	7.6-10.6
Both sexes, 16-19 years old	111	59	52.9	45	40.7	13	23.0	17.6-28.3
Single (never married)	2,352	1,687	71.7	1,491	63.4	196	11.6	10.8-12.4
Married (spouse present)	6,015	3,706	61.6	3,533	58.7	174	4.7	4.3-5.1
Other marital status[2]	2,322	1,234	53.2	1,142	49.2	92	7.5	6.7-8.3

Source: U.S. Department of Labor. Bureau of Labor Statistics. *Geographic Profile of Employment and Unemployment, 1993.* Bulletin 2446. Washington, DC: U.S. Government Printing Office, September 1994, p. 39. *Notes:* Data for demographic groups are not shown when they do not meet Bureau of Labor Statistics publication standards of reliability for the particular area based on the sample in that area. Items may not add to totals or compute to displayed percentages because of rounding. Detail for race and Hispanic origin groups will not add totals because data for the "other races" group are not presented and because Hispanics are included in both the white and black population groups. 1. Error ranges are calculated at the 90 percent confidence interval, which means that if repeated samples were drawn from the same population and an error range constructed around each sample estimate, in 9 of 10 cases the true value based on a complete census of the population would be contained within these error ranges. 2. "Other marital status" includes divorced, widowed, separated, and married with spouse absent.

★ 491 ★

Employment Status

Employment Status in Georgia: 1993

Data show the employment status of the civilian noninstitutionalized population by sex, age, race, and marital status. Figures are 1993 annual averages.

[Numbers in thousands]

Population group	Civilian non-institutional population	Civilian labor force		Employment		Unemployment		
		Number	Percent of population	Number	Percent of population	Number	Rate	Error range of rate[1]
Total	5,181	3,467	66.9	3,267	63.1	200	5.8	5.2-6.4
Men	2,404	1,812	75.4	1,709	71.1	104	5.7	4.9-6.5
Women	2,777	1,655	59.6	1,558	56.1	96	5.8	4.9-6.7
Both sexes, 16-19 years old	359	176	49.1	145	40.5	31	17.5	13.5-21.5
White	3,564	2,422	68.0	2,320	65.1	102	4.2	3.6-4.8
Men	1,700	1,322	77.8	1,271	74.7	51	3.9	3.1-4.7
Women	1,863	1,100	59.0	1,049	56.3	51	4.6	3.7-5.6
Both sexes, 16-19 years old	219	119	54.2	104	47.7	14	12.1	7.7-16.4
Black	1,509	981	65.0	888	58.8	93	9.5	8.1-10.9
Men	658	454	69.0	404	61.4	50	11.1	8.9-13.3
Women	851	527	61.9	484	56.8	43	8.2	6.4-10.0
Single (never married)	1,256	875	69.7	788	62.7	88	10.0	8.5-11.5
Married (spouse present)	2,829	1,968	69.6	1,896	67.0	72	3.7	3.0-4.3
Other marital status[2]	1,096	624	56.9	584	53.3	40	6.4	4.9-7.8

Source: U.S. Department of Labor. Bureau of Labor Statistics. *Geographic Profile of Employment and Unemployment, 1993.* Bulletin 2446. Washington, DC: U.S. Government Printing Office, September 1994, p. 40. *Notes:* Data for demographic groups are not shown when they do not meet Bureau of Labor Statistics publication standards of reliability for the particular area based on the sample in that area. Items may not add to totals or compute to displayed percentages because of rounding. Detail for race and Hispanic origin groups will not add totals because data for the "other races" group are not presented and because Hispanics are included in both the white and black population groups. 1. Error ranges are calculated at the 90 percent confidence interval, which means that if repeated samples were drawn from the same population and an error range constructed around each sample estimate, in 9 of 10 cases the true value based on a complete census of the population would be contained within these error ranges. 2. "Other marital status" includes divorced, widowed, separated, and married with spouse absent.

★ 492 ★

Employment Status

Employment Status in Hawaii: 1993

Data show the employment status of the civilian noninstitutionalized population by sex, age, race, and marital status. Figures are 1993 annual averages.

[Numbers in thousands]

Population group	Civilian non-institutional population	Civilian labor force		Employment		Unemployment		
		Number	Percent of population	Number	Percent of population	Number	Rate	Error range of rate[1]
Total	854	583	68.2	558	65.4	25	4.2	3.6-4.8
Men	405	305	75.4	292	72.0	14	4.5	3.7-5.3
Women	449	277	61.8	266	59.4	11	3.9	3.1-4.7
Both sexes, 16-19 years old	46	19	41.7	17	36.0	3	13.9	8.7-19.0

[Continued]

★ 492 ★

Employment Status in Hawaii: 1993

[Continued]

Population group	Civilian non-institutional population	Civilian labor force		Employment		Unemployment		
		Number	Percent of population	Number	Percent of population	Number	Rate	Error range of rate[1]
White	275	194	70.7	185	67.1	10	5.1	4.0-6.2
Men	133	106	79.7	100	75.5	6	5.3	3.8-6.8
Women	142	89	62.2	84	59.2	4	4.8	3.3-6.4
Single (never married)	207	151	72.8	142	68.7	8	5.6	4.3-6.9
Married (spouse present)	502	350	69.7	337	67.2	13	3.6	2.9-4.3
Other marital status[2]	146	82	56.7	79	54.3	3	4.2	2.7-5.7

Source: U.S. Department of Labor. Bureau of Labor Statistics. *Geographic Profile of Employment and Unemployment, 1993.* Bulletin 2446. Washington, DC: U.S. Government Printing Office, September 1994, p. 40. *Notes:* Data for demographic groups are not shown when they do not meet Bureau of Labor Statistics publication standards of reliability for the particular area based on the sample in that area. Items may not add to totals or compute to displayed percentages because of rounding. Detail for race and Hispanic origin groups will not add totals because data for the "other races" group are not presented and because Hispanics are included in both the white and black population groups. 1. Error ranges are calculated at the 90 percent confidence interval, which means that if repeated samples were drawn from the same population and an error range constructed around each sample estimate, in 9 of 10 cases the true value based on a complete census of the population would be contained within these error ranges. 2. "Other marital status" includes divorced, widowed, separated, and married with spouse absent.

★ 493 ★

Employment Status

Employment Status in Idaho: 1993

Data show the employment status of the civilian noninstitutionalized population by sex, age, race, Hispanic origin, and marital status. Figures are 1993 annual averages.

[Numbers in thousands]

Population group	Civilian non-institutional population	Civilian labor force		Employment		Unemployment		
		Number	Percent of population	Number	Percent of population	Number	Rate	Error range of rate[1]
Total	799	545	68.2	512	64.0	34	6.1	5.5-6.7
Men	391	303	77.6	284	72.8	19	6.2	5.4-7.1
Women	408	242	59.2	227	55.7	15	6.0	5.1-6.9
Both sexes, 16-19 years old	65	42	64.3	36	55.0	6	14.4	11.4-17.4
White	782	535	68.3	502	64.1	33	6.2	5.5-6.8
Men	383	298	77.7	279	72.9	19	6.2	5.4-7.1
Women	399	236	59.3	222	55.7	14	6.1	5.2-7.0
Both sexes, 16-19 years old	63	41	64.3	35	54.9	6	14.6	11.6-17.6
Hispanic origin	37	29	78.4	27	71.8	2	8.4	5.4-11.4
Men	20	18	87.2	17	81.9	1	6.1	2.7-9.5
Women	17	12	67.9	10	59.7	1	12.0	6.4-17.6
Single (never married)	148	111	75.0	100	67.5	11	10.0	8.4-11.7

[Continued]

★ 493 ★

Employment Status in Idaho: 1993
[Continued]

Population group	Civilian non-institutional population	Civilian labor force		Employment		Unemployment		
		Number	Percent of population	Number	Percent of population	Number	Rate	Error range of rate[1]
Married (spouse present)	511	354	69.1	337	65.9	16	4.7	4.0-5.3
Other marital status[2]	140	81	57.7	75	53.5	6	7.3	5.6-9.0

Source: U.S. Department of Labor. Bureau of Labor Statistics. *Geographic Profile of Employment and Unemployment, 1993*. Bulletin 2446. Washington, DC: U.S. Government Printing Office, September 1994, p. 40. *Notes:* Data for demographic groups are not shown when they do not meet Bureau of Labor Statistics publication standards of reliability for the particular area based on the sample in that area. Items may not add to totals or compute to displayed percentages because of rounding. Detail for race and Hispanic origin groups will not add totals because data for the "other races" group are not presented and because Hispanics are included in both the white and black population groups. 1. Error ranges are calculated at the 90 percent confidence interval, which means that if repeated samples were drawn from the same population and an error range constructed around each sample estimate, in 9 of 10 cases the true value based on a complete census of the population would be contained within these error ranges. 2. "Other marital status" includes divorced, widowed, separated, and married with spouse absent.

★ 494 ★
Employment Status

Employment Status in Illinois: 1993

Data show the employment status of the civilian noninstitutionalized population by sex, age, race, Hispanic origin, and marital status. Figures are 1993 annual averages.

[Numbers in thousands]

Population group	Civilian non-institutional population	Civilian labor force		Employment		Unemployment		
		Number	Percent of population	Number	Percent of population	Number	Rate	Error range of rate[1]
Total	8,830	5,983	67.8	5,538	62.7	444	7.4	7.0-7.8
Men	4,226	3,249	76.9	2,992	70.8	257	7.9	7.4-8.4
Women	4,604	2,734	59.4	2,547	55.3	187	6.8	6.3-7.4
Both sexes, 16-19 years old	626	335	53.5	272	43.5	63	18.8	16.8-20.9
White	7,263	5,024	69.2	4,726	65.1	298	5.9	5.6-6.3
Men	3,530	2,773	78.6	2,599	73.6	173	6.3	5.8-6.7
Women	3,733	2,251	60.3	2,127	57.0	125	5.5	5.0-6.1
Both sexes, 16-19 years old	478	282	58.9	241	50.5	40	14.3	12.2-16.4
Black	1,307	784	60.0	654	50.1	130	16.6	15.2-17.9
Men	570	380	66.6	306	53.7	74	19.5	17.5-21.4
Women	737	404	54.9	349	47.3	56	13.8	12.1-15.5
Both sexes, 16-19 years old	127	45	35.4	24	19.0	21	46.3	40.7-51.9
Hispanic origin	655	468	71.4	433	66.0	35	7.5	6.2-8.7
Men	330	289	87.5	267	81.0	21	7.4	5.9-9.0
Women	325	179	55.0	166	50.9	13	7.5	5.5-9.5
Single (never married)	2,411	1,717	71.2	1,501	62.2	216	12.6	11.8-13.4

[Continued]

★ 494 ★

Employment Status in Illinois: 1993
[Continued]

Population group	Civilian non-institutional population	Civilian labor force		Employment		Unemployment		
		Number	Percent of population	Number	Percent of population	Number	Rate	Error range of rate[1]
Married (spouse present)	4,815	3,434	71.3	3,266	67.8	167	4.9	4.5-5.3
Other marital status[2]	1,604	832	51.9	771	48.1	61	7.3	6.4-8.2

Source: U.S. Department of Labor. Bureau of Labor Statistics. *Geographic Profile of Employment and Unemployment, 1993.* Bulletin 2446. Washington, DC: U.S. Government Printing Office, September 1994, pp. 40-41. *Notes:* Data for demographic groups are not shown when they do not meet Bureau of Labor Statistics publication standards of reliability for the particular area based on the sample in that area. Items may not add to totals or compute to displayed percentages because of rounding. Detail for race and Hispanic origin groups will not add totals because data for the "other races" group are not presented and because Hispanics are included in both the white and black population groups. 1. Error ranges are calculated at the 90 percent confidence interval, which means that if repeated samples were drawn from the same population and an error range constructed around each sample estimate, in 9 of 10 cases the true value based on a complete census of the population would be contained within these error ranges. 2. "Other marital status" includes divorced, widowed, separated, and married with spouse absent.

★ 495 ★

Employment Status

Employment Status in Indiana: 1993

Data show the employment status of the civilian noninstitutionalized population by sex, age, race, and marital status. Figures are 1993 annual averages.

[Numbers in thousands]

Population group	Civilian non-institutional population	Civilian labor force		Employment		Unemployment		
		Number	Percent of population	Number	Percent of population	Number	Rate	Error range of rate[1]
Total	4,317	2,937	68.0	2,780	64.4	157	5.3	4.7-5.9
Men	2,010	1,562	77.7	1,483	73.8	79	5.1	4.2-5.9
Women	2,307	1,375	59.6	1,297	56.2	77	5.6	4.7-6.6
Both sexes, 16-19 years old	347	211	60.9	180	52.0	31	14.6	11.3-17.9
White	3,896	2,710	69.6	2,582	66.3	128	4.7	4.1-5.3
Men	1,836	1,466	79.8	1,402	76.4	64	4.4	3.6-5.2
Women	2,060	1,244	60.4	1,180	57.3	64	5.2	4.2-6.1
Both sexes, 16-19 years old	306	200	65.2	172	56.2	27	13.8	10.4-17.1
Black	390	208	53.4	180	46.1	29	13.7	10.5-17.0
Men	160	86	53.5	70	43.9	15	18.0	12.5-23.5
Women	230	123	53.3	109	47.5	13	10.8	6.9-14.6
Single (never married)	1,022	742	72.7	674	66.0	68	9.2	7.6-10.7
Married (spouse present)	2,440	1,742	71.4	1,685	69.1	57	3.3	2.6-3.9
Other marital status[2]	856	453	52.9	421	49.2	32	7.0	5.2-8.7

Source: U.S. Department of Labor. Bureau of Labor Statistics. *Geographic Profile of Employment and Unemployment, 1993.* Bulletin 2446. Washington, DC: U.S. Government Printing Office, September 1994, p. 41. *Notes:* Data for demographic groups are not shown when they do not meet Bureau of Labor Statistics publication standards of reliability for the particular area based on the sample in that area. Items may not add to totals or compute to displayed percentages because of rounding. Detail for race and Hispanic origin groups will not add totals because data for the "other races" group are not presented and because Hispanics are included in both the white and black population groups. 1. Error ranges are calculated at the 90 percent confidence interval, which means that if repeated samples were drawn from the same population and an error range constructed around each sample estimate, in 9 of 10 cases the true value based on a complete census of the population would be contained within these error ranges. 2. "Other marital status" includes divorced, widowed, separated, and married with spouse absent.

★ 496 ★

Employment Status

Employment Status in Iowa: 1993

Data show the employment status of the civilian noninstitutionalized population by sex, age, race, and marital status. Figures are 1993 annual averages.

[Numbers in thousands]

Population group	Civilian non-institutional population	Civilian labor force		Employment		Unemployment		
		Number	Percent of population	Number	Percent of population	Number	Rate	Error range of rate[1]
Total	2,115	1,550	73.3	1,488	70.4	62	4.0	3.5-4.5
Men	1,036	848	81.8	813	78.4	35	4.2	3.5-4.8
Women	1,079	702	65.1	676	62.6	26	3.8	3.1-4.5
Both sexes, 16-19 years old	155	105	68.0	93	60.1	12	11.5	8.6-14.4
White	2,057	1,511	73.5	1,453	70.6	58	3.9	3.4-4.3
Men	1,006	826	82.1	792	78.7	34	4.1	3.4-4.7
Women	1,051	685	65.2	661	62.9	25	3.6	2.9-4.3
Both sexes, 16-19 years old	149	103	68.9	91	61.3	11	11.0	8.1-13.9
Single (never married)	488	387	79.3	361	73.9	26	6.7	5.5-7.9
Married (spouse present)	1,296	981	75.7	958	73.9	23	2.4	1.9-2.9
Other marital status[2]	331	182	54.9	169	51.2	12	6.8	5.0-8.6

Source: U.S. Department of Labor. Bureau of Labor Statistics. *Geographic Profile of Employment and Unemployment, 1993.* Bulletin 2446. Washington, DC: U.S. Government Printing Office, September 1994, p. 41. *Notes:* Data for demographic groups are not shown when they do not meet Bureau of Labor Statistics publication standards of reliability for the particular area based on the sample in that area. Items may not add to totals or compute to displayed percentages because of rounding. Detail for race and Hispanic origin groups will not add totals because data for the "other races" group are not presented and because Hispanics are included in both the white and black population groups. 1. Error ranges are calculated at the 90 percent confidence interval, which means that if repeated samples were drawn from the same population and an error range constructed around each sample estimate, in 9 of 10 cases the true value based on a complete census of the population would be contained within these error ranges. 2. "Other marital status" includes divorced, widowed, separated, and married with spouse absent.

★ 497 ★

Employment Status

Employment Status in Kansas: 1993

Data show the employment status of the civilian noninstitutionalized population by sex, age, race, Hispanic origin, and marital status. Figures are 1993 annual averages.

[Numbers in thousands]

Population group	Civilian non-institutional population	Civilian labor force		Employment		Unemployment		
		Number	Percent of population	Number	Percent of population	Number	Rate	Error range of rate[1]
Total	1,858	1,318	71.0	1,253	67.4	66	5.0	4.4-5.6
Men	912	717	78.6	683	74.9	35	4.8	4.1-5.6
Women	946	601	63.6	570	60.3	31	5.2	4.3-6.1
Both sexes, 16-19 years old	127	78	61.4	66	52.2	12	15.0	11.5-18.5
White	1,696	1,210	71.3	1,158	68.3	52	4.3	3.7-4.8
Men	835	661	79.1	632	75.6	29	4.4	3.6-5.1
Women	861	549	63.8	526	61.1	23	4.2	3.4-5.0
Both sexes, 16-19 years old	111	70	62.8	60	53.9	10	14.1	10.5-17.8

[Continued]

★ 497 ★

Employment Status in Kansas: 1993

[Continued]

Population group	Civilian non-institutional population	Civilian labor force		Employment		Unemployment		
		Number	Percent of population	Number	Percent of population	Number	Rate	Error range of rate[1]
Black	130	87	66.9	75	57.8	12	13.6	10.0-17.2
Men	64	47	72.6	42	65.0	5	10.6	6.1-15.0
Women	66	41	61.3	34	50.9	7	17.1	11.3-22.8
Hispanic origin	49	37	77.0	35	72.2	2	6.2	2.2-10.3
Single (never married)	393	294	74.8	266	67.7	28	9.5	7.9-11.1
Married (spouse present)	1,162	844	72.7	817	70.3	27	3.2	2.6-3.8
Other marital status[2]	303	180	59.4	169	55.8	11	6.0	4.3-7.6

Source: U.S. Department of Labor. Bureau of Labor Statistics. *Geographic Profile of Employment and Unemployment, 1993.* Bulletin 2446. Washington, DC: U.S. Government Printing Office, September 1994, p. 41. *Notes:* Data for demographic groups are not shown when they do not meet Bureau of Labor Statistics publication standards of reliability for the particular area based on the sample in that area. Items may not add to totals or compute to displayed percentages because of rounding. Detail for race and Hispanic origin groups will not add totals because data for the "other races" group are not presented and because Hispanics are included in both the white and black population groups. 1. Error ranges are calculated at the 90 percent confidence interval, which means that if repeated samples were drawn from the same population and an error range constructed around each sample estimate, in 9 of 10 cases the true value based on a complete census of the population would be contained within these error ranges. 2. "Other marital status" includes divorced, widowed, separated, and married with spouse absent.

★ 498 ★

Employment Status

Employment Status in Kentucky: 1993

Data show the employment status of the civilian noninstitutionalized population by sex, age, race, and marital status. Figures are 1993 annual averages.

[Numbers in thousands]

Population group	Civilian non-institutional population	Civilian labor force		Employment		Unemployment		
		Number	Percent of population	Number	Percent of population	Number	Rate	Error range of rate[1]
Total	2,883	1,794	62.2	1,684	58.4	110	6.2	5.5-6.9
Men	1,383	985	71.2	923	66.8	61	6.2	5.4-7.1
Women	1,500	810	54.0	761	50.7	49	6.1	5.1-7.0
Both sexes, 16-19 years old	192	95	49.5	80	41.7	15	15.8	12.0-19.6
White	2,686	1,682	62.6	1,588	59.1	94	5.6	4.9-6.2
Men	1,288	921	71.6	870	67.6	51	5.6	4.7-6.4
Women	1,398	761	54.4	718	51.3	43	5.6	4.7-6.6
Both sexes, 16-19 years old	177	89	50.5	76	42.9	13	15.0	11.2-18.9
Black	173	97	56.4	81	47.1	16	16.6	12.3-20.9
Men	83	52	63.0	42	50.9	10	19.2	13.1-25.3
Single (never married)	529	349	66.0	310	58.6	39	11.1	9.3-13.0

[Continued]

★ 498 ★

Employment Status in Kentucky: 1993
[Continued]

Population group	Civilian non-institutional population	Civilian labor force		Employment		Unemployment		
		Number	Percent of population	Number	Percent of population	Number	Rate	Error range of rate[1]
Married (spouse present)	1,763	1,161	65.9	1,115	63.2	47	4.0	3.4-4.7
Other marital status[2]	591	283	48.0	259	43.8	25	8.7	6.9-10.6

Source: U.S. Department of Labor. Bureau of Labor Statistics. Geographic Profile of Employment and Unemployment, 1993. Bulletin 2446. Washington, DC: U.S. Government Printing Office, September 1994, pp. 41-42. Notes: Data for demographic groups are not shown when they do not meet Bureau of Labor Statistics publication standards of reliability for the particular area based on the sample in that area. Items may not add to totals or compute to displayed percentages because of rounding. Detail for race and Hispanic origin groups will not add totals because data for the "other races" group are not presented and because Hispanics are included in both the white and black population groups. 1. Error ranges are calculated at the 90 percent confidence interval, which means that if repeated samples were drawn from the same population and an error range constructed around each sample estimate, in 9 of 10 cases the true value based on a complete census of the population would be contained within these error ranges. 2. "Other marital status" includes divorced, widowed, separated, and married with spouse absent.

★ 499 ★

Employment Status

Employment Status in Louisiana: 1993

Data show the employment status of the civilian noninstitutionalized population by sex, age, race, and marital status. Figures are 1993 annual averages.

[Numbers in thousands]

Population group	Civilian non-institutional population	Civilian labor force		Employment		Unemployment		
		Number	Percent of population	Number	Percent of population	Number	Rate	Error range of rate[1]
Total	3,138	1,879	59.9	1,740	55.5	139	7.4	6.6-8.2
Men	1,478	1,046	70.8	970	65.7	76	7.2	6.2-8.3
Women	1,660	833	50.2	770	46.4	63	7.5	6.3-8.7
Both sexes, 16-19 years old	271	105	38.7	78	28.7	27	25.8	20.9-30.8
White	2,260	1,415	62.6	1,338	59.2	77	5.4	4.6-6.2
Men	1,097	811	73.9	759	69.3	51	6.3	5.2-7.4
Women	1,164	605	52.0	579	49.7	26	4.3	3.2-5.3
Both sexes, 16-19 years old	178	79	44.6	63	35.5	16	20.4	15.0-25.9
Black	832	438	52.7	379	45.6	59	13.5	11.4-15.6
Men	357	219	61.5	196	54.9	23	10.7	8.0-13.3
Women	475	219	46.1	183	38.6	36	16.3	13.1-19.5
Single (never married)	797	453	56.9	384	48.2	69	15.3	13.2-17.4
Married (spouse present)	1,723	1,117	64.9	1,067	62.0	50	4.5	3.7-5.3
Other marital status[2]	618	308	49.9	289	46.8	19	6.2	4.4-8.0

Source: U.S. Department of Labor. Bureau of Labor Statistics. Geographic Profile of Employment and Unemployment, 1993. Bulletin 2446. Washington, DC: U.S. Government Printing Office, September 1994, p. 42. Notes: Data for demographic groups are not shown when they do not meet Bureau of Labor Statistics publication standards of reliability for the particular area based on the sample in that area. Items may not add to totals or compute to displayed percentages because of rounding. Detail for race and Hispanic origin groups will not add totals because data for the "other races" group are not presented and because Hispanics are included in both the white and black population groups. 1. Error ranges are calculated at the 90 percent confidence interval, which means that if repeated samples were drawn from the same population and an error range constructed around each sample estimate, in 9 of 10 cases the true value based on a complete census of the population would be contained within these error ranges. 2. "Other marital status" includes divorced, widowed, separated, and married with spouse absent.

★ 500 ★

Employment Status

Employment Status in Maine: 1993

Data show the employment status of the civilian noninstitutionalized population by sex, age, race, and marital status. Figures are 1993 annual averages.

[Numbers in thousands]

Population group	Civilian non-institutional population	Civilian labor force		Employment		Unemployment		
		Number	Percent of population	Number	Percent of population	Number	Rate	Error range of rate[1]
Total	950	631	66.4	581	61.1	50	7.9	7.1-8.7
Men	464	335	72.3	306	66.0	29	8.7	7.6-9.8
Women	486	296	60.8	275	56.5	21	7.0	5.9-8.0
Both sexes, 16-19 years old	65	35	54.2	29	44.2	7	18.5	14.4-22.5
White	935	622	66.6	573	61.3	49	7.9	7.2-8.7
Men	456	330	72.5	302	66.1	29	8.7	7.6-9.8
Women	479	292	60.9	271	56.7	20	7.0	6.0-8.1
Both sexes, 16-19 years old	64	35	55.3	29	45.1	7	18.5	14.4-22.5
Single (never married)	209	146	69.8	127	60.9	19	12.7	10.9-14.6
Married (spouse present)	560	391	69.9	370	66.1	21	5.4	4.6-6.2
Other marital status[2]	181	94	51.7	84	46.2	10	10.7	8.6-12.9

Source: U.S. Department of Labor. Bureau of Labor Statistics. *Geographic Profile of Employment and Unemployment, 1993.* Bulletin 2446. Washington, DC: U.S. Government Printing Office, September 1994, p. 42. *Notes:* Data for demographic groups are not shown when they do not meet Bureau of Labor Statistics publication standards of reliability for the particular area based on the sample in that area. Items may not add to totals or compute to displayed percentages because of rounding. Detail for race and Hispanic origin groups will not add totals because data for the "other races" group are not presented and because Hispanics are included in both the white and black population groups. 1. Error ranges are calculated at the 90 percent confidence interval, which means that if repeated samples were drawn from the same population and an error range constructed around each sample estimate, in 9 of 10 cases the true value based on a complete census of the population would be contained within these error ranges. 2. "Other marital status" includes divorced, widowed, separated, and married with spouse absent.

★ 501 ★

Employment Status

Employment Status in Maryland: 1993

Data show the employment status of the civilian noninstitutionalized population by sex, age, race, Hispanic origin, and marital status. Figures are 1993 annual averages.

[Numbers in thousands]

Population group	Civilian non-institutional population	Civilian labor force		Employment		Unemployment		
		Number	Percent of population	Number	Percent of population	Number	Rate	Error range of rate[1]
Total	3,797	2,672	70.4	2,507	66.0	165	6.2	5.5-6.9
Men	1,804	1,385	76.8	1,289	71.5	95	6.9	6.0-7.8
Women	1,993	1,287	64.6	1,218	61.1	69	5.4	4.5-6.3
Both sexes, 16-19 years old	213	108	50.6	83	39.1	24	22.7	17.8-27.5
White	2,639	1,839	69.7	1,751	66.4	88	4.8	4.1-5.5
Men	1,261	972	77.1	921	73.0	51	5.3	4.3-6.3
Women	1,378	867	62.9	830	60.2	36	4.2	3.2-5.1
Both sexes, 16-19 years old	117	66	56.2	56	47.9	10	14.9	9.2-20.5

[Continued]

★ 501 ★

Employment Status in Maryland: 1993

[Continued]

Population group	Civilian non-institutional population	Civilian labor force		Employment		Unemployment		
		Number	Percent of population	Number	Percent of population	Number	Rate	Error range of rate[1]
Black	1,026	741	72.2	668	65.1	72	9.8	8.3-11.2
Men	474	358	75.6	316	66.7	42	11.7	9.5-14.0
Women	552	383	69.2	352	63.8	30	7.9	6.1-9.8
Hispanic origin	80	63	78.3	57	71.0	6	9.4	4.4-14.3
Single (never married)	1,003	766	76.3	688	68.5	78	10.2	8.7-11.7
Married (spouse present)	2,077	1,476	71.0	1,418	68.3	58	3.9	3.2-4.6
Other marital status[2]	716	430	60.1	402	56.1	29	6.7	5.0-8.3

Source: U.S. Department of Labor. Bureau of Labor Statistics. *Geographic Profile of Employment and Unemployment, 1993.* Bulletin 2446. Washington, DC: U.S. Government Printing Office, September 1994, p. 42. *Notes:* Data for demographic groups are not shown when they do not meet Bureau of Labor Statistics publication standards of reliability for the particular area based on the sample in that area. Items may not add to totals or compute to displayed percentages because of rounding. Detail for race and Hispanic origin groups will not add totals because data for the "other races" group are not presented and because Hispanics are included in both the white and black population groups. 1. Error ranges are calculated at the 90 percent confidence interval, which means that if repeated samples were drawn from the same population and an error range constructed around each sample estimate, in 9 of 10 cases the true value based on a complete census of the population would be contained within these error ranges. 2. "Other marital status" includes divorced, widowed, separated, and married with spouse absent.

★ 502 ★

Employment Status

Employment Status in Massachusetts: 1993

Data show the employment status of the civilian noninstitutionalized population by sex, age, race, Hispanic origin, and marital status. Figures are 1993 annual averages.

[Numbers in thousands]

Population group	Civilian non-institutional population	Civilian labor force		Employment		Unemployment		
		Number	Percent of population	Number	Percent of population	Number	Rate	Error range of rate[1]
Total	4,663	3,170	68.0	2,953	63.3	217	6.9	6.6-7.2
Men	2,229	1,702	76.4	1,570	70.5	132	7.8	7.3-8.2
Women	2,434	1,468	60.3	1,383	56.8	85	5.8	5.3-6.3
Both sexes, 16-19 years old	255	135	52.9	109	42.9	26	19.0	16.8-21.1
White	4,330	2,954	68.2	2,762	63.8	192	6.5	6.1-6.8
Men	2,068	1,585	76.7	1,467	71.0	117	7.4	6.9-7.9
Women	2,262	1,369	60.5	1,295	57.2	74	5.4	5.0-5.9
Both sexes, 16-19 years old	224	122	54.7	102	45.4	21	16.9	14.7-19.2
Black	209	143	68.6	124	59.4	19	13.3	11.4-15.3
Men	100	77	76.5	65	65.4	11	14.5	11.7-17.3
Women	109	67	61.3	59	54.0	8	12.0	9.2-14.8
Hispanic origin	131	79	60.8	70	53.5	10	12.0	9.4-14.7
Men	61	47	75.9	41	66.5	6	12.4	8.9-16.0
Women	69	33	47.4	29	42.0	4	11.4	7.4-15.4
Single (never married)	1,372	1,015	74.0	916	66.8	98	9.7	9.0-10.4

[Continued]

★ 502 ★

Employment Status in Massachusetts: 1993

[Continued]

Population group	Civilian non-institutional population	Civilian labor force		Employment		Unemployment		
		Number	Percent of population	Number	Percent of population	Number	Rate	Error range of rate[1]
Married (spouse present)	2,494	1,746	70.0	1,658	66.5	88	5.0	4.6-5.4
Other marital status[2]	797	409	51.3	379	47.5	31	7.5	6.6-8.5

Source: U.S. Department of Labor. Bureau of Labor Statistics. *Geographic Profile of Employment and Unemployment, 1993.* Bulletin 2446. Washington, DC: U.S. Government Printing Office, September 1994, p. 43. *Notes:* Data for demographic groups are not shown when they do not meet Bureau of Labor Statistics publication standards of reliability for the particular area based on the sample in that area. Items may not add to totals or compute to displayed percentages because of rounding. Detail for race and Hispanic origin groups will not add totals because data for the "other races" group are not presented and because Hispanics are included in both the white and black population groups. 1. Error ranges are calculated at the 90 percent confidence interval, which means that if repeated samples were drawn from the same population and an error range constructed around each sample estimate, in 9 of 10 cases the true value based on a complete census of the population would be contained within these error ranges. 2. "Other marital status" includes divorced, widowed, separated, and married with spouse absent.

★ 503 ★

Employment Status

Employment Status in Michigan: 1993

Data show the employment status of the civilian noninstitutionalized population by sex, age, race, Hispanic origin, and marital status. Figures are 1993 annual averages.

[Numbers in thousands]

Population group	Civilian non-institutional population	Civilian labor force		Employment		Unemployment		
		Number	Percent of population	Number	Percent of population	Number	Rate	Error range of rate[1]
Total	7,132	4,702	65.9	4,374	61.3	328	7.0	6.6-7.4
Men	3,446	2,591	75.2	2,407	69.8	183	7.1	6.6-7.6
Women	3,686	2,111	57.3	1,967	53.4	145	6.9	6.3-7.4
Both sexes, 16-19 years old	507	297	58.5	246	48.5	51	17.1	15.2-18.9
White	6,041	4,053	67.1	3,809	63.1	244	6.0	5.7-6.4
Men	2,955	2,260	76.5	2,123	71.8	137	6.1	5.6-6.6
Women	3,086	1,793	58.1	1,686	54.7	107	6.0	5.4-6.5
Both sexes, 16-19 years old	414	256	61.8	220	53.1	36	14.2	12.2-16.1
Black	955	559	58.5	482	50.5	77	13.7	12.4-15.0
Men	423	277	65.6	236	55.9	41	14.7	12.9-16.5
Women	532	282	52.9	246	46.2	36	12.7	11.0-14.4
Both sexes, 16-19 years old	80	34	42.5	21	26.5	13	37.8	31.9-43.6
Hispanic origin	110	76	69.2	69	62.5	7	9.7	6.6-12.8
Men	53	42	79.2	38	72.0	4	9.0	5.0-13.0
Women	56	34	59.8	30	53.5	4	10.6	5.8-15.4
Single (never married)	1,865	1,356	72.7	1,200	64.4	156	11.5	10.7-12.3

[Continued]

★ 503 ★

Employment Status in Michigan: 1993
[Continued]

Population group	Civilian non-institutional population	Civilian labor force		Employment		Unemployment		
		Number	Percent of population	Number	Percent of population	Number	Rate	Error range of rate[1]
Married (spouse present)	3,945	2,659	67.4	2.543	64.5	116	4.4	4.0-4.7
Other marital status[2]	1,322	687	51.9	631	47.7	56	8.2	7.2-9.1

Source: U.S. Department of Labor. Bureau of Labor Statistics. *Geographic Profile of Employment and Unemployment, 1993.* Bulletin 2446. Washington, DC: U.S. Government Printing Office, September 1994, p. 43. *Notes:* Data for demographic groups are not shown when they do not meet Bureau of Labor Statistics publication standards of reliability for the particular area based on the sample in that area. Items may not add to totals or compute to displayed percentages because of rounding. Detail for race and Hispanic origin groups will not add totals because data for the "other races" group are not presented and because Hispanics are included in both the white and black population groups. 1. Error ranges are calculated at the 90 percent confidence interval, which means that if repeated samples were drawn from the same population and an error range constructed around each sample estimate, in 9 of 10 cases the true value based on a complete census of the population would be contained within these error ranges. 2. "Other marital status" includes divorced, widowed, separated, and married with spouse absent.

★ 504 ★

Employment Status

Employment Status in Minnesota: 1993

Data show the employment status of the civilian noninstitutionalized population by sex, age, race, and marital status. Figures are 1993 annual averages.

[Numbers in thousands]

Population group	Civilian non-institutional population	Civilian labor force		Employment		Unemployment		
		Number	Percent of population	Number	Percent of population	Number	Rate	Error range of rate[1]
Total	3,351	2,466	73.6	2,341	69.9	125	5.1	4.5-5.7
Men	1,620	1,312	81.0	1,232	76.0	80	6.1	5.3-6.9
Women	1,731	1,155	66.7	1,110	64.1	45	3.9	3.2-4.6
Both sexes, 16-19 years old	229	163	71.0	145	63.3	18	10.9	8.0-13.8
White	3,162	2,353	74.4	2,242	70.9	111	4.7	4.1-5.3
Men	1,522	1,242	81.6	1,172	77.0	70	5.6	4.8-6.5
Women	1,640	1,111	67.8	1,071	65.3	41	3.7	2.9-4.4
Both sexes, 16-19 years old	206	150	72.8	136	65.8	15	9.7	6.8-12.6
Single (never married)	963	783	81.3	720	74.8	62	8.0	6.8-9.2
Married (spouse present)	1,829	1,379	75.4	1,337	73.1	41	3.0	2.4-3.6
Other marital status[2]	559	305	54.5	284	50.8	21	6.9	5.1-8.7

Source: U.S. Department of Labor. Bureau of Labor Statistics. *Geographic Profile of Employment and Unemployment, 1993.* Bulletin 2446. Washington, DC: U.S. Government Printing Office, September 1994, p. 43. *Notes:* Data for demographic groups are not shown when they do not meet Bureau of Labor Statistics publication standards of reliability for the particular area based on the sample in that area. Items may not add to totals or compute to displayed percentages because of rounding. Detail for race and Hispanic origin groups will not add totals because data for the "other races" group are not presented and because Hispanics are included in both the white and black population groups. 1. Error ranges are calculated at the 90 percent confidence interval, which means that if repeated samples were drawn from the same population and an error range constructed around each sample estimate, in 9 of 10 cases the true value based on a complete census of the population would be contained within these error ranges. 2. "Other marital status" includes divorced, widowed, separated, and married with spouse absent.

★ 505 ★

Employment Status

Employment Status in Mississippi: 1993

Data show the employment status of the civilian noninstitutionalized population by sex, age, race, and marital status. Figures are 1993 annual averages.

[Numbers in thousands]

Population group	Civilian non-institutional population	Civilian labor force		Employment		Unemployment		
		Number	Percent of population	Number	Percent of population	Number	Rate	Error range of rate[1]
Total	1,948	1,212	62.2	1,135	58.3	77	6.3	5.7-6.9
Men	943	680	72.1	645	68.4	35	5.2	4.4-5.9
Women	1,005	532	52.9	490	48.8	42	7.8	6.8-8.9
Both sexes, 16-19 years old	161	63	39.1	51	31.7	12	19.0	14.9-23.0
White	1,271	800	63.0	770	60.6	30	3.8	3.2-4.4
Men	628	469	74.7	455	72.5	14	2.9	2.2-3.6
Women	644	332	51.5	315	48.9	17	5.0	3.9-6.1
Both sexes, 16-19 years old	84	40	46.8	38	44.4	2	5.0	1.9-8.2
Black	668	406	60.9	360	53.9	46	11.4	10.0-12.9
Men	311	208	66.8	186	59.9	21	10.3	8.3-12.2
Women	356	199	55.7	174	48.7	25	12.6	10.4-14.7
Single (never married)	470	284	60.4	249	53.0	35	12.3	10.6-14.0
Married (spouse present)	1,081	729	67.5	706	65.3	23	3.2	2.6-3.8
Other marital status[2]	397	199	50.0	180	45.3	19	9.5	7.6-11.3

Source: U.S. Department of Labor. Bureau of Labor Statistics. *Geographic Profile of Employment and Unemployment, 1993.* Bulletin 2446. Washington, DC: U.S. Government Printing Office, September 1994, p. 44. *Notes:* Data for demographic groups are not shown when they do not meet Bureau of Labor Statistics publication standards of reliability for the particular area based on the sample in that area. Items may not add to totals or compute to displayed percentages because of rounding. Detail for race and Hispanic origin groups will not add totals because data for the "other races" group are not presented and because Hispanics are included in both the white and black population groups. 1. Error ranges are calculated at the 90 percent confidence interval, which means that if repeated samples were drawn from the same population and an error range constructed around each sample estimate, in 9 of 10 cases the true value based on a complete census of the population would be contained within these error ranges. 2. "Other marital status" includes divorced, widowed, separated, and married with spouse absent.

★ 506 ★

Employment Status

Employment Status in Missouri: 1993

Data show the employment status of the civilian noninstitutionalized population by sex, age, race, and marital status. Figures are 1993 annual averages.

[Numbers in thousands]

Population group	Civilian non-institutional population	Civilian labor force		Employment		Unemployment		
		Number	Percent of population	Number	Percent of population	Number	Rate	Error range of rate[1]
Total	3,926	2,650	67.5	2,481	63.2	169	6.4	5.7-7.1
Men	1,867	1,409	75.5	1,333	71.4	76	5.4	4.5-6.2
Women	2,059	1,241	60.3	1,148	55.7	94	7.5	6.5-8.6
Both sexes, 16-19 years old	279	171	61.4	145	51.9	26	15.4	12.0-18.9

[Continued]

★ 506 ★

Employment Status in Missouri: 1993
[Continued]

Population group	Civilian non-institutional population	Civilian labor force		Employment		Unemployment		
		Number	Percent of population	Number	Percent of population	Number	Rate	Error range of rate[1]
White	3,513	2,397	68.2	2,274	64.7	123	5.1	4.5-5.8
Men	1,684	1,286	76.3	1,230	73.0	55	4.3	3.5-5.1
Women	1,829	1,112	60.8	1,044	57.1	68	6.1	5.1-7.1
Both sexes, 16-19 years old	239	151	63.5	135	56.5	17	11.0	7.6-14.3
Black	355	218	61.3	173	48.9	44	20.3	17.1-23.5
Men	154	102	66.4	83	53.7	20	19.1	14.5-23.7
Women	201	115	57.4	91	45.1	25	21.4	16.9-25.8
Single (never married)	906	673	74.3	597	65.9	76	11.4	9.7-13.0
Married (spouse present)	2,232	1,536	68.8	1,478	66.2	57	3.7	3.1-4.4
Other marital status[2]	788	442	56.0	406	51.5	35	8.0	6.3-9.8

Source: U.S. Department of Labor. Bureau of Labor Statistics. *Geographic Profile of Employment and Unemployment, 1993.* Bulletin 2446. Washington, DC: U.S. Government Printing Office, September 1994, p. 44. *Notes:* Data for demographic groups are not shown when they do not meet Bureau of Labor Statistics publication standards of reliability for the particular area based on the sample in that area. Items may not add to totals or compute to displayed percentages because of rounding. Detail for race and Hispanic origin groups will not add totals because data for the "other races" group are not presented and because Hispanics are included in both the white and black population groups. 1. Error ranges are calculated at the 90 percent confidence interval, which means that if repeated samples were drawn from the same population and an error range constructed around each sample estimate, in 9 of 10 cases the true value based on a complete census of the population would be contained within these error ranges. 2. "Other marital status" includes divorced, widowed, separated, and married with spouse absent.

★ 507 ★

Employment Status

Employment Status in Montana: 1993

Data show the employment status of the civilian noninstitutionalized population by sex, age, race, and marital status. Figures are 1993 annual averages.

[Numbers in thousands]

Population group	Civilian non-institutional population	Civilian labor force		Employment		Unemployment		
		Number	Percent of population	Number	Percent of population	Number	Rate	Error range of rate[1]
Total	629	427	67.9	401	63.8	26	6.0	5.3-6.7
Men	315	234	74.5	219	69.7	15	6.4	5.4-7.4
Women	314	193	61.3	182	57.8	11	5.6	4.6-6.7
Both sexes, 16-19 years old	50	25	50.6	22	43.9	3	13.4	9.3-17.4
White	595	407	68.3	384	64.5	23	5.7	4.9-6.4
Men	298	224	74.9	210	70.5	13	5.9	5.0-6.9
Women	297	183	61.7	173	58.4	10	5.3	4.3-6.4
Both sexes, 16-19 years old	46	24	52.7	21	45.7	3	13.4	9.2-17.6
Single (never married)	140	97	69.7	87	62.5	10	10.4	8.5-12.2

[Continued]

★ 507 ★

Employment Status in Montana: 1993
[Continued]

Population group	Civilian non-institutional population	Civilian labor force		Employment		Unemployment		
		Number	Percent of population	Number	Percent of population	Number	Rate	Error range of rate[1]
Married (spouse present)	377	265	70.4	254	67.6	11	4.0	3.2-4.7
Other marital status[2]	112	64	57.2	59	52.6	5	8.0	5.9-10.1

Source: U.S. Department of Labor. Bureau of Labor Statistics. *Geographic Profile of Employment and Unemployment, 1993*. Bulletin 2446. Washington, DC: U.S. Government Printing Office, September 1994, p. 44. *Notes:* Data for demographic groups are not shown when they do not meet Bureau of Labor Statistics publication standards of reliability for the particular area based on the sample in that area. Items may not add to totals or compute to displayed percentages because of rounding. Detail for race and Hispanic origin groups will not add totals because data for the "other races" group are not presented and because Hispanics are included in both the white and black population groups. 1. Error ranges are calculated at the 90 percent confidence interval, which means that if repeated samples were drawn from the same population and an error range constructed around each sample estimate, in 9 of 10 cases the true value based on a complete census of the population would be contained within these error ranges. 2. "Other marital status" includes divorced, widowed, separated, and married with spouse absent.

★ 508 ★
Employment Status

Employment Status in Nebraska: 1993

Data show the employment status of the civilian noninstitutionalized population by sex, age, race, and marital status. Figures are 1993 annual averages.

[Numbers in thousands]

Population group	Civilian non-institutional population	Civilian labor force		Employment		Unemployment		
		Number	Percent of population	Number	Percent of population	Number	Rate	Error range of rate[1]
Total	1,184	853	72.0	830	70.1	22	2.6	2.2-3.0
Men	562	443	78.8	434	77.2	9	2.0	1.5-2.5
Women	622	410	65.8	396	63.7	13	3.2	2.6-3.9
Both sexes, 16-19 years old	90	58	64.7	53	58.7	5	9.4	6.6-12.1
White	1,131	818	72.3	798	70.5	20	2.5	2.1-2.9
Men	541	429	79.3	420	77.8	8	2.0	1.5-2.5
Women	590	389	66.0	377	63.9	12	3.1	2.4-3.7
Both sexes, 16-19 years old	83	55	66.6	50	60.7	5	8.9	6.1-11.6
Black	42	27	64.2	25	60.4	2	5.9	2.9-9.0
Single (never married)	268	205	76.4	194	72.3	11	5.4	4.2-6.5
Married (spouse present)	732	548	74.9	540	73.7	8	1.5	1.1-1.9
Other marital status[2]	184	100	54.2	97	52.6	3	3.0	1.8-4.3

Source: U.S. Department of Labor. Bureau of Labor Statistics. *Geographic Profile of Employment and Unemployment, 1993*. Bulletin 2446. Washington, DC: U.S. Government Printing Office, September 1994, p. 44. *Notes:* Data for demographic groups are not shown when they do not meet Bureau of Labor Statistics publication standards of reliability for the particular area based on the sample in that area. Items may not add to totals or compute to displayed percentages because of rounding. Detail for race and Hispanic origin groups will not add totals because data for the "other races" group are not presented and because Hispanics are included in both the white and black population groups. 1. Error ranges are calculated at the 90 percent confidence interval, which means that if repeated samples were drawn from the same population and an error range constructed around each sample estimate, in 9 of 10 cases the true value based on a complete census of the population would be contained within these error ranges. 2. "Other marital status" includes divorced, widowed, separated, and married with spouse absent.

★ 509 ★

Employment Status

Employment Status in Nevada: 1993

Data show the employment status of the civilian noninstitutionalized population by sex, age, race, Hispanic origin, and marital status. Figures are 1993 annual averages.

[Numbers in thousands]

Population group	Civilian non-institutional population	Civilian labor force		Employment		Unemployment		
		Number	Percent of population	Number	Percent of population	Number	Rate	Error range of rate[1]
Total	1,064	745	70.0	692	65.0	54	7.2	6.5-7.9
Men	532	411	77.3	383	71.9	28	6.9	6.0-7.8
Women	532	334	62.8	309	58.1	25	7.5	6.6-8.5
Both sexes, 16-19 years old	64	36	55.3	29	44.5	7	19.5	15.7-23.3
White	952	668	70.2	624	65.5	45	6.7	6.0-7.4
Men	476	369	77.5	345	72.4	24	6.6	5.7-7.5
Women	476	299	62.9	279	58.7	20	6.8	5.8-7.8
Both sexes, 16-19 years old	57	33	57.8	27	47.2	6	18.3	14.3-22.2
Black	60	41	67.7	34	56.8	7	16.0	12.4-19.6
Men	31	23	75.5	21	66.7	3	11.7	7.4-16.0
Hispanic origin	103	79	77.5	73	71.0	7	8.3	6.3-10.4
Men	57	50	87.3	46	79.7	4	8.7	6.0-11.4
Women	45	29	65.0	27	59.9	2	7.8	4.4-11.1
Single (never married)	234	179	76.6	159	67.9	20	11.4	9.9-13.0
Married (spouse present)	580	405	69.8	385	66.4	20	4.9	4.2-5.7
Other marital status[2]	250	161	64.5	148	59.1	13	8.2	6.8-9.7

Source: U.S. Department of Labor. Bureau of Labor Statistics. *Geographic Profile of Employment and Unemployment, 1993.* Bulletin 2446. Washington, DC: U.S. Government Printing Office, September 1994, p. 45. *Notes:* Data for demographic groups are not shown when they do not meet Bureau of Labor Statistics publication standards of reliability for the particular area based on the sample in that area. Items may not add to totals or compute to displayed percentages because of rounding. Detail for race and Hispanic origin groups will not add totals because data for the "other races" group are not presented and because Hispanics are included in both the white and black population groups. 1. Error ranges are calculated at the 90 percent confidence interval, which means that if repeated samples were drawn from the same population and an error range constructed around each sample estimate, in 9 of 10 cases the true value based on a complete census of the population would be contained within these error ranges. 2. "Other marital status" includes divorced, widowed, separated, and married with spouse absent.

★ 510 ★

Employment Status

Employment Status in New Hampshire: 1993

Data show the employment status of the civilian noninstitutionalized population by sex, age, race, and marital status. Figures are 1993 annual averages.

[Numbers in thousands]

Population group	Civilian non-institutional population	Civilian labor force		Employment		Unemployment		
		Number	Percent of population	Number	Percent of population	Number	Rate	Error range of rate[1]
Total	859	620	72.1	579	67.4	41	6.6	5.9-7.3
Men	422	338	80.0	314	74.4	24	7.0	6.0-8.0
Women	437	282	64.5	265	60.6	17	6.1	5.0-7.1
Both sexes, 16-19 years old	53	30	57.0	26	49.5	4	13.2	9.1-17.3
White	845	609	72.0	569	67.3	40	6.6	5.8-7.3
Men	415	332	79.9	308	74.3	23	7.0	6.0-8.0
Women	430	277	64.4	260	60.6	17	6.0	5.0-7.0
Both sexes, 16-19 years old	52	30	56.9	26	49.8	4	12.5	8.4-16.6
Single (never married)	201	154	76.9	141	70.0	14	9.0	7.4-10.6
Married (spouse present)	504	376	74.6	356	70.7	20	5.2	4.4-6.1
Other marital status[2]	154	89	57.9	82	53.3	7	8.0	6.0-10.0

Source: U.S. Department of Labor. Bureau of Labor Statistics. *Geographic Profile of Employment and Unemployment, 1993.* Bulletin 2446. Washington, DC: U.S. Government Printing Office, September 1994, p. 45. *Notes:* Data for demographic groups are not shown when they do not meet Bureau of Labor Statistics publication standards of reliability for the particular area based on the sample in that area. Items may not add to totals or compute to displayed percentages because of rounding. Detail for race and Hispanic origin groups will not add totals because data for the "other races" group are not presented and because Hispanics are included in both the white and black population groups. 1. Error ranges are calculated at the 90 percent confidence interval, which means that if repeated samples were drawn from the same population and an error range constructed around each sample estimate, in 9 of 10 cases the true value based on a complete census of the population would be contained within these error ranges. 2. "Other marital status" includes divorced, widowed, separated, and married with spouse absent.

★ 511 ★

Employment Status

Employment Status in New Jersey: 1993

Data show the employment status of the civilian noninstitutionalized population by sex, age, race, Hispanic origin, and marital status. Figures are 1993 annual averages.

[Numbers in thousands]

Population group	Civilian non-institutional population	Civilian labor force		Employment		Unemployment		
		Number	Percent of population	Number	Percent of population	Number	Rate	Error range of rate[1]
Total	6,107	4,001	65.5	3,706	60.7	295	7.4	7.0-7.8
Men	2,908	2,198	75.6	2,021	69.5	177	8.1	7.6-8.6
Women	3,199	1,803	56.4	1,685	52.7	118	6.5	6.0-7.0
Both sexes, 16-19 years old	383	158	41.4	127	33.3	31	19.6	17.1-22.0
White	5,079	3,310	65.2	3,095	60.9	215	6.5	6.1-6.9
Men	2,423	1,840	75.9	1,709	70.5	131	7.1	6.6-7.6
Women	2,656	1,470	55.4	1,386	52.2	84	5.7	5.2-6.2
Both sexes, 16-19 years old	284	128	45.0	107	37.6	21	16.4	13.8-19.0

[Continued]

★ 511 ★

Employment Status in New Jersey: 1993

[Continued]

Population group	Civilian non-institutional population	Civilian labor force		Employment		Unemployment		
		Number	Percent of population	Number	Percent of population	Number	Rate	Error range of rate[1]
Black	790	522	66.0	454	57.5	67	12.9	11.7-14.1
Men	368	266	72.1	227	61.6	39	14.6	12.9-16.4
Women	422	256	60.7	227	53.9	28	11.1	9.5-12.7
Both sexes, 16-19 years old	76	23	31.0	14	18.4	9	40.6	33.4-47.7
Hispanic origin	559	375	67.2	330	59.0	46	12.2	10.8-13.6
Men	263	221	84.0	193	73.5	28	12.5	10.6-14.3
Women	296	155	52.2	137	46.1	18	11.7	9.6-13.9
Single (never married)	1,684	1,158	68.7	1,027	61.0	131	11.3	10.5-12.1
Married (spouse present)	3,353	2,303	68.7	2,190	65.3	113	4.9	4.5-5.3
Other marital status[2]	1,070	539	50.4	488	45.6	51	9.5	8.4-10.5

Source: U.S. Department of Labor. Bureau of Labor Statistics. *Geographic Profile of Employment and Unemployment, 1993.* Bulletin 2446. Washington, DC: U.S. Government Printing Office, September 1994, p. 45. *Notes:* Data for demographic groups are not shown when they do not meet Bureau of Labor Statistics publication standards of reliability for the particular area based on the sample in that area. Items may not add to totals or compute to displayed percentages because of rounding. Detail for race and Hispanic origin groups will not add totals because data for the "other races" group are not presented and because Hispanics are included in both the white and black population groups. 1. Error ranges are calculated at the 90 percent confidence interval, which means that if repeated samples were drawn from the same population and an error range constructed around each sample estimate, in 9 of 10 cases the true value based on a complete census of the population would be contained within these error ranges. 2. "Other marital status" includes divorced, widowed, separated, and married with spouse absent.

★ 512 ★

Employment Status

Employment Status in New Mexico: 1993

Data show the employment status of the civilian noninstitutionalized population by sex, age, race, Hispanic origin, and marital status. Figures are 1993 annual averages.

[Numbers in thousands]

Population group	Civilian non-institutional population	Civilian labor force		Employment		Unemployment		
		Number	Percent of population	Number	Percent of population	Number	Rate	Error range of rate[1]
Total	1,186	756	63.8	700	59.0	57	7.5	6.7-8.3
Men	576	423	73.5	389	67.6	34	7.9	6.9-8.9
Women	610	333	54.6	310	50.9	23	6.9	5.8-8.0
Both sexes, 16-19 years old	93	44	46.9	35	38.1	8	18.8	14.9-22.8
White	1,057	678	64.1	634	60.0	44	6.5	5.8-7.3
Men	516	382	74.1	356	69.0	26	6.9	5.9-7.9
Women	541	296	54.7	278	51.4	18	6.0	4.9-7.1
Both sexes, 16-19 years old	78	38	48.9	32	40.7	6	16.7	12.5-20.9
Hispanic origin	373	227	60.8	207	55.5	20	8.8	7.3-10.4
Men	179	128	71.7	116	64.5	13	10.1	7.9-12.2
Women	194	98	50.8	91	47.1	7	7.3	5.1-9.4
Single (never married)	284	188	66.2	162	57.3	26	13.6	11.7-15.4

[Continued]

★512★

Employment Status in New Mexico: 1993
[Continued]

Population group	Civilian non-institutional population	Civilian labor force		Employment		Unemployment		
		Number	Percent of population	Number	Percent of population	Number	Rate	Error range of rate[1]
Married (spouse present)	674	444	65.9	423	62.8	21	4.8	4.0-5.6
Other marital status[2]	229	124	54.3	115	50.1	10	7.7	5.9-9.5

Source: U.S. Department of Labor. Bureau of Labor Statistics. *Geographic Profile of Employment and Unemployment, 1993.* Bulletin 2446. Washington, DC: U.S. Government Printing Office, September 1994, p. 45. *Notes:* Data for demographic groups are not shown when they do not meet Bureau of Labor Statistics publication standards of reliability for the particular area based on the sample in that area. Items may not add to totals or compute to displayed percentages because of rounding. Detail for race and Hispanic origin groups will not add totals because data for the "other races" group are not presented and because Hispanics are included in both the white and black population groups. 1. Error ranges are calculated at the 90 percent confidence interval, which means that if repeated samples were drawn from the same population and an error range constructed around each sample estimate, in 9 of 10 cases the true value based on a complete census of the population would be contained within these error ranges. 2. "Other marital status" includes divorced, widowed, separated, and married with spouse absent.

★513★
Employment Status

Employment Status in New York: 1993

Data show the employment status of the civilian noninstitutionalized population by sex, age, race, Hispanic origin, and marital status. Figures are 1993 annual averages.

[Numbers in thousands]

Population group	Civilian non-institutional population	Civilian labor force		Employment		Unemployment		
		Number	Percent of population	Number	Percent of population	Number	Rate	Error range of rate[1]
Total	14,034	8,649	61.6	7,985	56.9	664	7.7	7.4-8.0
Men	6,586	4,663	70.8	4,271	64.9	392	8.4	8.0-8.8
Women	7,448	3,986	53.5	3,714	49.9	272	6.8	6.4-7.2
Both sexes, 16-19 years old	956	370	38.7	287	30.0	83	22.5	20.9-24.2
White	11,315	7,047	62.3	6,572	58.1	475	6.7	6.4-7.0
Men	5,349	3,838	71.7	3,563	66.6	275	7.2	6.8-7.6
Women	5,966	3,209	53.8	3,009	50.4	200	6.2	5.8-6.7
Both sexes, 16-19 years old	717	321	44.7	254	35.3	67	21.0	19.2-22.7
Black	2,134	1,223	57.3	1,066	50.0	157	12.9	12.0-13.7
Men	949	607	64.0	511	53.8	96	15.8	14.6-17.1
Women	1,184	616	52.0	555	46.8	61	9.9	8.8-11.0
Both sexes, 16-19 years old	196	38	19.2	24	12.1	14	37.0	32.4-41.7
Hispanic origin	1,503	817	54.4	712	47.4	105	12.9	11.8-14.0
Men	687	473	68.8	408	59.3	65	13.7	12.3-15.2
Women	816	345	42.3	304	37.3	41	11.8	10.2-13.4
Single (never married)	4,127	2,614	63.3	2,297	55.6	317	12.1	11.5-12.7

[Continued]

★ 513 ★

Employment Status in New York: 1993
[Continued]

Population group	Civilian non-institutional population	Civilian labor force		Employment		Unemployment		
		Number	Percent of population	Number	Percent of population	Number	Rate	Error range of rate[1]
Married (spouse present)	7,284	4,801	65.9	4,563	62.6	238	5.0	4.7-5.3
Other marital status[2]	2,623	1,235	47.1	1,125	42.9	109	8.9	8.1-9.6

Source: U.S. Department of Labor. Bureau of Labor Statistics. *Geographic Profile of Employment and Unemployment, 1993.* Bulletin 2446. Washington, DC: U.S. Government Printing Office, September 1994, p. 46. *Notes:* Data for demographic groups are not shown when they do not meet Bureau of Labor Statistics publication standards of reliability for the particular area based on the sample in that area. Items may not add to totals or compute to displayed percentages because of rounding. Detail for race and Hispanic origin groups will not add totals because data for the "other races" group are not presented and because Hispanics are included in both the white and black population groups. 1. Error ranges are calculated at the 90 percent confidence interval, which means that if repeated samples were drawn from the same population and an error range constructed around each sample estimate, in 9 of 10 cases the true value based on a complete census of the population would be contained within these error ranges. 2. "Other marital status" includes divorced, widowed, separated, and married with spouse absent.

★ 514 ★
Employment Status

Employment Status in North Carolina: 1993

Data show the employment status of the civilian noninstitutionalized population by sex, age, race, Hispanic origin, and marital status. Figures are 1993 annual averages.

[Numbers in thousands]

Population group	Civilian non-institutional population	Civilian labor force		Employment		Unemployment		
		Number	Percent of population	Number	Percent of population	Number	Rate	Error range of rate[1]
Total	5,290	3,555	67.2	3,383	63.9	173	4.9	4.6-5.2
Men	2,504	1,873	74.8	1,792	71.5	81	4.3	4.0-4.7
Women	2,786	1,682	60.4	1,591	57.1	91	5.4	5.0-5.9
Both sexes, 16-19 years old	346	186	53.9	152	44.0	34	18.3	16.2-20.4
White	4,038	2,739	67.8	2,638	65.3	101	3.7	3.4-4.0
Men	1,930	1,467	76.0	1,419	73.5	48	3.3	2.9-3.6
Women	2,108	1,272	60.4	1,219	57.8	53	4.2	3.7-4.6
Both sexes, 16-19 years old	233	134	57.5	116	49.9	18	13.2	11.0-15.4
Black	1,160	751	64.8	684	59.0	67	8.9	8.1-9.7
Men	528	368	69.8	337	63.9	31	8.4	7.3-9.5
Women	632	383	60.6	347	54.9	36	9.4	8.3-10.6
Both sexes, 16-19 years old	104	48	46.4	33	31.8	15	31.5	27.0-36.0
Hispanic origin	55	40	73.0	37	66.2	4	9.3	5.7-12.8
Men	35	30	85.5	27	79.1	2	7.5	3.7-11.2
Single (never married)	1,189	847	71.3	765	64.4	82	9.7	8.9-10.5

[Continued]

★ 514 ★

Employment Status in North Carolina: 1993
[Continued]

Population group	Civilian non-institutional population	Civilian labor force		Employment		Unemployment		
		Number	Percent of population	Number	Percent of population	Number	Rate	Error range of rate[1]
Married (spouse present)	3,049	2,137	70.1	2,078	68.2	59	2.7	2.5-3.0
Other marital status[2]	1,052	572	54.3	539	51.3	32	5.7	4.9-6.4

Source: U.S. Department of Labor. Bureau of Labor Statistics. *Geographic Profile of Employment and Unemployment, 1993.* Bulletin 2446. Washington, DC: U.S. Government Printing Office, September 1994, p. 46. *Notes:* Data for demographic groups are not shown when they do not meet Bureau of Labor Statistics publication standards of reliability for the particular area based on the sample in that area. Items may not add to totals or compute to displayed percentages because of rounding. Detail for race and Hispanic origin groups will not add totals because data for the "other races" group are not presented and because Hispanics are included in both the white and black population groups. 1. Error ranges are calculated at the 90 percent confidence interval, which means that if repeated samples were drawn from the same population and an error range constructed around each sample estimate, in 9 of 10 cases the true value based on a complete census of the population would be contained within these error ranges. 2. "Other marital status" includes divorced, widowed, separated, and married with spouse absent.

★ 515 ★
Employment Status

Employment Status in North Dakota: 1993

Data show the employment status of the civilian noninstitutionalized population by sex, age, race, and marital status. Figures are 1993 annual averages.

[Numbers in thousands]

Population group	Civilian non-institutional population	Civilian labor force		Employment		Unemployment		
		Number	Percent of population	Number	Percent of population	Number	Rate	Error range of rate[1]
Total	463	318	68.7	305	65.8	14	4.3	3.6-5.0
Men	222	169	76.3	161	72.7	8	4.7	3.7-5.7
Women	241	149	61.8	143	59.5	6	3.8	2.8-4.7
Both sexes, 16-19 years old	38	23	60.3	20	52.7	3	12.6	8.6-16.7
White	441	306	69.3	294	66.7	11	3.7	3.1-4.4
Men	213	163	76.8	157	73.6	7	4.1	3.2-5.0
Women	229	142	62.3	138	60.3	5	3.2	2.3-4.1
Both sexes, 16-19 years old	35	22	61.9	19	55.1	2	11.1	7.1-15.0
Single (never married)	115	83	72.6	77	67.2	6	7.4	5.7-9.1
Married (spouse present)	277	199	71.9	194	70.0	5	2.6	2.0-3.3
Other marital status[2]	72	36	50.3	34	47.2	2	6.0	3.7-8.4

Source: U.S. Department of Labor. Bureau of Labor Statistics. *Geographic Profile of Employment and Unemployment, 1993.* Bulletin 2446. Washington, DC: U.S. Government Printing Office, September 1994, p. 46. *Notes:* Data for demographic groups are not shown when they do not meet Bureau of Labor Statistics publication standards of reliability for the particular area based on the sample in that area. Items may not add to totals or compute to displayed percentages because of rounding. Detail for race and Hispanic origin groups will not add totals because data for the "other races" group are not presented and because Hispanics are included in both the white and black population groups. 1. Error ranges are calculated at the 90 percent confidence interval, which means that if repeated samples were drawn from the same population and an error range constructed around each sample estimate, in 9 of 10 cases the true value based on a complete census of the population would be contained within these error ranges. 2. "Other marital status" includes divorced, widowed, separated, and married with spouse absent.

★516★
Employment Status

Employment Status in Ohio: 1993

Data show the employment status of the civilian noninstitutionalized population by sex, age, race, and marital status. Figures are 1993 annual averages.

[Numbers in thousands]

Population group	Civilian non-institutional population	Civilian labor force		Employment		Unemployment		
		Number	Percent of population	Number	Percent of population	Number	Rate	Error range of rate[1]
Total	8,397	5,488	65.4	5,132	61.1	357	6.5	6.2-6.8
Men	3,982	2,975	74.7	2,771	69.6	203	6.8	6.4-7.3
Women	4,415	2,514	56.9	2,360	53.5	153	6.1	5.6-6.6
Both sexes, 16-19 years old	580	317	54.7	259	44.8	58	18.2	16.4-20.0
White	7,464	4,927	66.0	4,642	62.2	286	5.8	5.5-6.1
Men	3,556	2,689	75.6	2,525	71.0	164	6.1	5.6-6.5
Women	3,909	2,238	57.3	2,116	54.1	122	5.5	5.0-5.9
Both sexes, 16-19 years old	482	284	58.9	237	49.2	47	16.4	14.5-18.3
Black	847	505	59.6	438	51.7	67	13.3	11.9-14.7
Men	384	253	66.0	216	56.2	38	14.8	12.9-16.8
Women	463	252	54.4	222	48.0	30	11.8	9.9-13.6
Single (never married)	1,919	1,363	71.0	1,209	63.0	154	11.3	10.5-12.1
Married (spouse present)	4,901	3,333	68.0	3,187	65.0	146	4.4	4.0-4.7
Other marital status[2]	1,578	792	50.2	735	46.6	57	7.2	6.3-8.1

Source: U.S. Department of Labor. Bureau of Labor Statistics. *Geographic Profile of Employment and Unemployment, 1993.* Bulletin 2446. Washington, DC: U.S. Government Printing Office, September 1994, pp. 46-47. *Notes:* Data for demographic groups are not shown when they do not meet Bureau of Labor Statistics publication standards of reliability for the particular area based on the sample in that area. Items may not add to totals or compute to displayed percentages because of rounding. Detail for race and Hispanic origin groups will not add totals because data for the "other races" group are not presented and because Hispanics are included in both the white and black population groups. 1. Error ranges are calculated at the 90 percent confidence interval, which means that if repeated samples were drawn from the same population and an error range constructed around each sample estimate, in 9 of 10 cases the true value based on a complete census of the population would be contained within these error ranges. 2. "Other marital status" includes divorced, widowed, separated, and married with spouse absent.

★517★
Employment Status

Employment Status in Oklahoma: 1993

Data show the employment status of the civilian noninstitutionalized population by sex, age, race, Hispanic origin, and marital status. Figures are 1993 annual averages.

[Numbers in thousands]

Population group	Civilian non-institutional population	Civilian labor force		Employment		Unemployment		
		Number	Percent of population	Number	Percent of population	Number	Rate	Error range of rate[1]
Total	2,403	1,524	63.4	1,432	59.6	92	6.0	5.4-6.6
Men	1,137	842	74.0	793	69.7	49	5.8	5.0-6.7
Women	1,266	683	53.9	640	50.5	43	6.3	5.3-7.3
Both sexes, 16-19 years old	180	89	49.6	73	40.4	16	18.5	14.6-22.4

[Continued]

★ 517 ★

Employment Status in Oklahoma: 1993
[Continued]

Population group	Civilian non-institutional population	Civilian labor force		Employment		Unemployment		
		Number	Percent of population	Number	Percent of population	Number	Rate	Error range of rate[1]
White	2,053	1,316	64.1	1,250	60.9	66	5.0	4.4-5.7
Men	979	738	75.4	701	71.6	37	5.0	4.1-5.8
Women	1,074	578	53.9	549	51.1	30	5.1	4.1-6.1
Both sexes, 16-19 years old	148	77	52.0	65	43.8	12	15.8	11.7-19.8
Black	171	100	58.3	84	49.1	16	15.7	12.0-19.4
Men	78	48	61.8	41	52.5	7	15.1	9.9-20.3
Women	93	51	55.3	43	46.3	8	16.3	11.1-21.4
Hispanic origin	56	36	64.5	33	59.2	3	8.2	3.0-13.4
Single (never married)	453	286	63.2	253	55.8	33	11.7	9.7-13.6
Married (spouse present)	1,499	1,009	67.3	972	64.8	38	3.8	3.1-4.4
Other marital status[2]	451	229	50.8	208	46.1	21	9.1	7.2-11.0

Source: U.S. Department of Labor. Bureau of Labor Statistics. *Geographic Profile of Employment and Unemployment, 1993.* Bulletin 2446. Washington, DC: U.S. Government Printing Office, September 1994, p. 47. *Notes:* Data for demographic groups are not shown when they do not meet Bureau of Labor Statistics publication standards of reliability for the particular area based on the sample in that area. Items may not add to totals or compute to displayed percentages because of rounding. Detail for race and Hispanic origin groups will not add totals because data for the "other races" group are not presented and because Hispanics are included in both the white and black population groups. 1. Error ranges are calculated at the 90 percent confidence interval, which means that if repeated samples were drawn from the same population and an error range constructed around each sample estimate, in 9 of 10 cases the true value based on a complete census of the population would be contained within these error ranges. 2. "Other marital status" includes divorced, widowed, separated, and married with spouse absent.

★ 518 ★

Employment Status

Employment Status in Oregon: 1993

Data show the employment status of the civilian noninstitutionalized population by sex, age, race, Hispanic origin, and marital status. Figures are 1993 annual averages.

[Numbers in thousands]

Population group	Civilian non-institutional population	Civilian labor force		Employment		Unemployment		
		Number	Percent of population	Number	Percent of population	Number	Rate	Error range of rate[1]
Total	2,327	1,587	68.2	1,473	63.3	114	7.2	6.5-7.9
Men	1,153	869	75.4	800	69.4	69	7.9	6.9-8.9
Women	1,174	718	61.1	672	57.3	45	6.3	5.3-7.3
Both sexes, 16-19 years old	139	75	54.3	62	44.6	13	17.9	13.3-22.5
White	2,210	1,503	68.0	1,394	63.1	109	7.2	6.5-8.0
Men	1,093	822	75.2	756	69.2	66	8.0	6.9-9.0
Women	1,117	681	60.9	638	57.1	43	6.4	5.3-7.4
Both sexes, 16-19 years old	133	72	54.2	60	44.8	13	17.4	12.7-22.0
Hispanic origin	90	69	77.2	62	68.9	7	10.7	6.0-15.4
Men	54	50	91.4	44	81.0	6	11.4	5.7-17.1
Single (never married)	492	362	73.7	315	64.1	47	13.0	11.1-14.8

[Continued]

★518★

Employment Status in Oregon: 1993
[Continued]

Population group	Civilian non-institutional population	Civilian labor force		Employment		Unemployment		
		Number	Percent of population	Number	Percent of population	Number	Rate	Error range of rate[1]
Married (spouse present)	1,375	957	69.6	914	66.5	42	4.4	3.7-5.2
Other marital status[2]	460	268	58.2	243	52.8	25	9.3	7.4-11.3

Source: U.S. Department of Labor. Bureau of Labor Statistics. *Geographic Profile of Employment and Unemployment, 1993.* Bulletin 2446. Washington, DC: U.S. Government Printing Office, September 1994, p. 47. *Notes:* Data for demographic groups are not shown when they do not meet Bureau of Labor Statistics publication standards of reliability for the particular area based on the sample in that area. Items may not add to totals or compute to displayed percentages because of rounding. Detail for race and Hispanic origin groups will not add totals because data for the "other races" group are not presented and because Hispanics are included in both the white and black population groups. 1. Error ranges are calculated at the 90 percent confidence interval, which means that if repeated samples were drawn from the same population and an error range constructed around each sample estimate, in 9 of 10 cases the true value based on a complete census of the population would be contained within these error ranges. 2. "Other marital status" includes divorced, widowed, separated, and married with spouse absent.

★519★

Employment Status

Employment Status in Pennsylvania: 1993

Data show the employment status of the civilian noninstitutionalized population by sex, age, race, Hispanic origin, and marital status. Figures are 1993 annual averages.

[Numbers in thousands]

Population group	Civilian non-institutional population	Civilian labor force		Employment		Unemployment		
		Number	Percent of population	Number	Percent of population	Number	Rate	Error range of rate[1]
Total	9,284	5,893	63.5	5,479	59.0	414	7.0	6.6-7.4
Men	4,414	3,229	73.2	2,986	67.6	243	7.5	7.0-8.0
Women	4,870	2,664	54.7	2,494	51.2	170	6.4	5.9-6.9
Both sexes, 16-19 years old	583	312	53.6	253	43.4	59	18.9	16.7-21.2
White	8,412	5,387	64.0	5,040	59.9	347	6.4	6.1-6.8
Men	4,024	2,973	73.9	2,766	68.7	207	7.0	6.5-7.4
Women	4,388	2,414	55.0	2,274	51.8	140	5.8	5.3-6.3
Both sexes, 16-19 years old	515	288	55.8	238	46.3	49	17.1	14.9-19.3
Black	728	409	56.1	351	48.2	58	14.1	12.4-15.8
Men	317	202	63.8	172	54.3	30	14.9	12.4-17.4
Women	410	206	50.2	179	43.6	27	13.3	10.9-15.6
Hispanic origin	124	77	61.8	63	50.5	14	18.2	13.7-22.6
Men	59	43	72.7	36	60.3	7	17.2	11.3-23.0
Women	66	34	51.9	27	41.8	7	19.4	12.6-26.3
Single (never married)	2,316	1,615	69.7	1,432	61.9	183	11.3	10.5-12.1

[Continued]

★ 519 ★

Employment Status in Pennsylvania: 1993
[Continued]

Population group	Civilian non-institutional population	Civilian labor force		Employment		Unemployment		
		Number	Percent of population	Number	Percent of population	Number	Rate	Error range of rate[1]
Married (spouse present)	5,269	3,484	66.1	3,324	63.1	160	4.6	4.2-5.0
Other marital status[2]	1,699	793	46.7	722	42.5	71	8.9	7.9-10.0

Source: U.S. Department of Labor. Bureau of Labor Statistics. *Geographic Profile of Employment and Unemployment, 1993.* Bulletin 2446. Washington, DC: U.S. Government Printing Office, September 1994, p. 47. *Notes:* Data for demographic groups are not shown when they do not meet Bureau of Labor Statistics publication standards of reliability for the particular area based on the sample in that area. Items may not add to totals or compute to displayed percentages because of rounding. Detail for race and Hispanic origin groups will not add totals because data for the "other races" group are not presented and because Hispanics are included in both the white and black population groups. 1. Error ranges are calculated at the 90 percent confidence interval, which means that if repeated samples were drawn from the same population and an error range constructed around each sample estimate, in 9 of 10 cases the true value based on a complete census of the population would be contained within these error ranges. 2. "Other marital status" includes divorced, widowed, separated, and married with spouse absent.

★ 520 ★

Employment Status

Employment Status in Rhode Island: 1993

Data show the employment status of the civilian noninstitutionalized population by sex, age, race, Hispanic origin, and marital status. Figures are 1993 annual averages.

[Numbers in thousands]

Population group	Civilian non-institutional population	Civilian labor force		Employment		Unemployment		
		Number	Percent of population	Number	Percent of population	Number	Rate	Error range of rate[1]
Total	761	512	67.2	472	62.0	40	7.7	6.9-8.5
Men	359	268	74.7	245	68.4	23	8.5	7.4-9.6
Women	402	244	60.6	227	56.4	17	6.9	5.9-8.0
Both sexes, 16-19 years old	45	25	56.0	22	48.3	3	13.7	9.5-17.9
White	719	484	67.3	448	62.3	36	7.4	6.6-8.2
Men	338	253	74.7	232	68.6	21	8.2	7.1-9.3
Women	381	231	60.7	216	56.8	15	6.5	5.5-7.6
Both sexes, 16-19 years old	43	24	56.1	21	48.7	3	13.1	8.9-17.4
Black	23	16	72.0	14	60.6	3	15.8	10.3-21.4
Hispanic origin	36	26	74.1	22	61.7	4	16.7	12.1-21.3
Men	16	14	87.1	12	71.4	3	18.1	11.7-24.5
Women	19	12	62.8	10	53.3	2	15.1	8.5-21.6
Single (never married)	203	150	74.1	133	65.9	17	11.1	9.5-12.7
Married (spouse present)	415	291	70.1	274	66.0	17	5.8	5.0-6.7
Other marital status[2]	143	71	49.3	65	45.2	6	8.4	6.3-10.5

Source: U.S. Department of Labor. Bureau of Labor Statistics. *Geographic Profile of Employment and Unemployment, 1993.* Bulletin 2446. Washington, DC: U.S. Government Printing Office, September 1994, p. 48. *Notes:* Data for demographic groups are not shown when they do not meet Bureau of Labor Statistics publication standards of reliability for the particular area based on the sample in that area. Items may not add to totals or compute to displayed percentages because of rounding. Detail for race and Hispanic origin groups will not add totals because data for the "other races" group are not presented and because Hispanics are included in both the white and black population groups. 1. Error ranges are calculated at the 90 percent confidence interval, which means that if repeated samples were drawn from the same population and an error range constructed around each sample estimate, in 9 of 10 cases the true value based on a complete census of the population would be contained within these error ranges. 2. "Other marital status" includes divorced, widowed, separated, and married with spouse absent.

★ 521 ★

Employment Status

Employment Status in South Carolina: 1993

Data show the employment status of the civilian noninstitutionalized population by sex, age, race, and marital status. Figures are 1993 annual averages.

[Numbers in thousands]

Population group	Civilian non-institutional population	Civilian labor force		Employment		Unemployment		
		Number	Percent of population	Number	Percent of population	Number	Rate	Error range of rate[1]
Total	2,733	1,823	66.7	1,685	61.7	138	7.5	6.9-8.1
Men	1,273	977	76.8	907	71.3	70	7.2	6.4-8.0
Women	1,460	845	57.9	778	53.3	68	8.0	7.1-8.9
Both sexes, 16-19 years old	214	104	48.6	80	37.4	24	23.0	19.5-26.4
White	1,891	1,284	67.9	1,227	64.8	57	4.5	3.9-5.0
Men	908	704	77.5	674	74.2	30	4.3	3.6-5.1
Women	983	580	58.9	553	56.2	27	4.6	3.8-5.5
Both sexes, 16-19 years old	119	67	55.7	57	48.1	9	13.7	9.8-17.6
Black	803	512	63.7	432	53.8	80	15.6	14.0-17.2
Men	345	257	74.4	217	63.0	39	15.3	13.1-17.6
Women	459	255	55.7	215	46.8	41	15.9	13.6-18.2
Both sexes, 16-19 years old	90	35	39.2	21	22.9	15	41.5	34.3-48.6
Single (never married)	666	440	66.0	375	56.3	65	14.7	13.1-16.2
Married (spouse present)	1,555	1,116	71.8	1,064	68.4	52	4.7	4.1-5.3
Other marital status[2]	512	267	52.1	246	48.1	21	7.8	6.2-9.4

Source: U.S. Department of Labor. Bureau of Labor Statistics. *Geographic Profile of Employment and Unemployment, 1993.* Bulletin 2446. Washington, DC: U.S. Government Printing Office, September 1994, p. 48. *Notes:* Data for demographic groups are not shown when they do not meet Bureau of Labor Statistics publication standards of reliability for the particular area based on the sample in that area. Items may not add to totals or compute to displayed percentages because of rounding. Detail for race and Hispanic origin groups will not add totals because data for the "other races" group are not presented and because Hispanics are included in both the white and black population groups. 1. Error ranges are calculated at the 90 percent confidence interval, which means that if repeated samples were drawn from the same population and an error range constructed around each sample estimate, in 9 of 10 cases the true value based on a complete census of the population would be contained within these error ranges. 2. "Other marital status" includes divorced, widowed, separated, and married with spouse absent.

★ 522 ★

Employment Status

Employment Status in South Dakota: 1993

Data show the employment status of the civilian noninstitutionalized population by sex, age, race, and marital status. Figures are 1993 annual averages.

[Numbers in thousands]

Population group	Civilian non-institutional population	Civilian labor force		Employment		Unemployment		
		Number	Percent of population	Number	Percent of population	Number	Rate	Error range of rate[1]
Total	513	360	70.1	347	67.7	12	3.5	2.9-4.1
Men	252	197	78.1	191	75.7	6	3.0	2.3-3.7
Women	261	163	62.4	156	59.9	7	4.0	3.1-4.9
Both sexes, 16-19 years old	37	24	64.3	21	56.1	3	12.7	8.8-16.5

[Continued]

★ 522 ★

Employment Status in South Dakota: 1993
[Continued]

Population group	Civilian non-institutional population	Civilian labor force		Employment		Unemployment		
		Number	Percent of population	Number	Percent of population	Number	Rate	Error range of rate[1]
White	480	341	71.0	330	68.8	11	3.1	2.6-3.6
Men	235	186	78.9	181	76.8	5	2.6	1.9-3.3
Women	245	155	63.4	149	61.1	6	3.7	2.8-4.5
Both sexes, 16-19 years old	34	23	68.1	20	60.0	3	11.8	8.0-15.7
Single (never married)	115	87	76.2	82	71.2	6	6.5	5.0-8.1
Married (spouse present)	311	228	73.3	224	72.0	4	1.9	1.4-2.4
Other marital status[2]	87	44	50.5	41	47.6	2	5.7	3.7-7.7

Source: U.S. Department of Labor. Bureau of Labor Statistics. *Geographic Profile of Employment and Unemployment, 1993.* Bulletin 2446. Washington, DC: U.S. Government Printing Office, September 1994, p. 48. *Notes:* Data for demographic groups are not shown when they do not meet Bureau of Labor Statistics publication standards of reliability for the particular area based on the sample in that area. Items may not add to totals or compute to displayed percentages because of rounding. Detail for race and Hispanic origin groups will not add totals because data for the "other races" group are not presented and because Hispanics are included in both the white and black population groups. 1. Error ranges are calculated at the 90 percent confidence interval, which means that if repeated samples were drawn from the same population and an error range constructed around each sample estimate, in 9 of 10 cases the true value based on a complete census of the population would be contained within these error ranges. 2. "Other marital status" includes divorced, widowed, separated, and married with spouse absent.

★ 523 ★

Employment Status

Employment Status in Tennessee: 1993

Data show the employment status of the civilian noninstitutionalized population by sex, age, race, and marital status. Figures are 1993 annual averages.

[Numbers in thousands]

Population group	Civilian non-institutional population	Civilian labor force		Employment		Unemployment		
		Number	Percent of population	Number	Percent of population	Number	Rate	Error range of rate[1]
Total	3,925	2,500	63.7	2,358	60.1	142	5.7	5.1-6.3
Men	1,819	1,316	72.3	1,248	68.6	67	5.1	4.4-5.9
Women	2,106	1,185	56.2	1,110	52.7	74	6.3	5.4-7.2
Both sexes, 16-19 years old	278	140	50.5	112	40.2	29	20.4	16.6-24.2
White	3,207	2,077	64.8	1,975	61.6	103	4.9	4.3-5.6
Men	1,522	1,123	73.8	1,069	70.3	54	4.8	4.0-5.6
Women	1,685	954	56.6	905	53.7	49	5.1	4.2-6.1
Both sexes, 16-19 years old	202	110	54.6	93	45.9	18	16.0	11.9-20.1
Black	677	396	58.5	358	52.9	38	9.5	7.7-11.3
Men	273	174	64.0	161	59.1	13	7.7	5.2-10.1
Women	404	221	54.7	197	48.7	24	10.9	8.4-13.5
Single (never married)	864	567	65.6	504	58.4	63	11.0	9.4-12.7

[Continued]

★ 523 ★

Employment Status in Tennessee: 1993
[Continued]

Population group	Civilian non-institutional population	Civilian labor force		Employment		Unemployment		
		Number	Percent of population	Number	Percent of population	Number	Rate	Error range of rate[1]
Married (spouse present)	2,220	1,492	67.2	1,440	64.9	52	3.5	2.9-4.1
Other marital status[2]	841	441	52.5	414	49.2	27	6.2	4.7-7.6

Source: U.S. Department of Labor. Bureau of Labor Statistics. *Geographic Profile of Employment and Unemployment, 1993.* Bulletin 2446. Washington, DC: U.S. Government Printing Office, September 1994, p. 48. *Notes:* Data for demographic groups are not shown when they do not meet Bureau of Labor Statistics publication standards of reliability for the particular area based on the sample in that area. Items may not add to totals or compute to displayed percentages because of rounding. Detail for race and Hispanic origin groups will not add totals because data for the "other races" group are not presented and because Hispanics are included in both the white and black population groups. 1. Error ranges are calculated at the 90 percent confidence interval, which means that if repeated samples were drawn from the same population and an error range constructed around each sample estimate, in 9 of 10 cases the true value based on a complete census of the population would be contained within these error ranges. 2. "Other marital status" includes divorced, widowed, separated, and married with spouse absent.

★ 524 ★

Employment Status

Employment Status in Texas: 1993

Data show the employment status of the civilian noninstitutionalized population by sex, age, race, Hispanic origin, and marital status. Figures are 1993 annual averages.

[Numbers in thousands]

Population group	Civilian non-institutional population	Civilian labor force		Employment		Unemployment		
		Number	Percent of population	Number	Percent of population	Number	Rate	Error range of rate[1]
Total	13,302	9,149	68.8	8,508	64.0	642	7.0	6.7-7.4
Men	6,450	5,095	79.0	4,749	73.6	346	6.8	6.3-7.2
Women	6,852	4,054	59.2	3,758	54.9	296	7.3	6.8-7.8
Both sexes, 16-19 years old	984	508	51.6	399	40.5	109	21.5	19.8-23.3
White	11,404	7,821	68.6	7,351	64.5	471	6.0	5.7-6.4
Men	5,557	4,404	79.2	4,142	74.5	262	5.9	5.5-6.4
Women	5,847	3,418	58.5	3,209	54.9	209	6.1	5.6-6.6
Both sexes, 16-19 years old	814	439	53.9	354	43.4	85	19.4	17.5-21.3
Black	1,510	1,058	70.1	910	60.3	148	14.0	12.8-15.2
Men	703	539	76.7	466	66.3	73	13.6	11.9-15.2
Women	807	519	64.3	444	55.0	75	14.5	12.7-16.2
Hispanic origin	3,163	2,112	66.8	1,923	60.8	189	8.9	8.1-9.8
Men	1,581	1,269	80.2	1,162	73.5	106	8.4	7.3-9.5
Women	1,582	844	53.3	761	48.1	83	9.8	8.4-11.2
Both sexes, 16-19 years old	319	156	48.9	117	36.6	39	25.1	20.7-29.5
Single (never married)	2,970	2,137	71.9	1,868	62.9	269	12.6	11.7-13.4

[Continued]

★ 524 ★

Employment Status in Texas: 1993
[Continued]

Population group	Civilian non-institutional population	Civilian labor force		Employment		Unemployment		
		Number	Percent of population	Number	Percent of population	Number	Rate	Error range of rate[1]
Married (spouse present)	7,750	5,455	70.4	5,206	67.2	248	4.6	4.2-4.9
Other marital status[2]	2,582	1,558	60.3	1,433	55.5	125	8.0	7.2-8.9

Source: U.S. Department of Labor. Bureau of Labor Statistics. *Geographic Profile of Employment and Unemployment, 1993.* Bulletin 2446. Washington, DC: U.S. Government Printing Office, September 1994, p. 49. *Notes:* Data for demographic groups are not shown when they do not meet Bureau of Labor Statistics publication standards of reliability for the particular area based on the sample in that area. Items may not add to totals or compute to displayed percentages because of rounding. Detail for race and Hispanic origin groups will not add totals because data for the "other races" group are not presented and because Hispanics are included in both the white and black population groups. 1. Error ranges are calculated at the 90 percent confidence interval, which means that if repeated samples were drawn from the same population and an error range constructed around each sample estimate, in 9 of 10 cases the true value based on a complete census of the population would be contained within these error ranges. 2. "Other marital status" includes divorced, widowed, separated, and married with spouse absent.

★ 525 ★
Employment Status

Employment Status in Utah: 1993

Data show the employment status of the civilian noninstitutionalized population by sex, age, race, Hispanic origin, and marital status. Figures are 1993 annual averages.

[Numbers in thousands]

Population group	Civilian non-institutional population	Civilian labor force		Employment		Unemployment		
		Number	Percent of population	Number	Percent of population	Number	Rate	Error range of rate[1]
Total	1,261	910	72.2	875	69.4	35	3.9	3.3-4.5
Men	619	502	81.2	484	78.3	18	3.6	2.9-4.4
Women	642	408	63.5	391	60.8	17	4.2	3.3-5.1
Both sexes, 16-19 years old	132	89	67.9	79	60.0	10	11.5	8.7-14.4
White	1,232	889	72.2	855	69.4	34	3.9	3.3-4.4
Men	605	491	81.1	473	78.2	18	3.6	2.9-4.4
Women	627	398	63.5	382	60.9	16	4.1	3.2-5.0
Both sexes, 16-19 years old	128	87	68.1	77	60.2	10	11.6	8.8-14.5
Hispanic origin	54	41	75.9	37	68.3	4	9.9	6.3-13.6
Single (never married)	283	222	78.4	206	72.6	16	7.4	5.9-8.9
Married (spouse present)	797	580	72.8	567	71.1	14	2.4	1.8-2.9
Other marital status[2]	180	108	59.7	103	56.9	5	4.7	2.9-6.5

Source: U.S. Department of Labor. Bureau of Labor Statistics. *Geographic Profile of Employment and Unemployment, 1993.* Bulletin 2446. Washington, DC: U.S. Government Printing Office, September 1994, p. 49. *Notes:* Data for demographic groups are not shown when they do not meet Bureau of Labor Statistics publication standards of reliability for the particular area based on the sample in that area. Items may not add to totals or compute to displayed percentages because of rounding. Detail for race and Hispanic origin groups will not add totals because data for the "other races" group are not presented and because Hispanics are included in both the white and black population groups. 1. Error ranges are calculated at the 90 percent confidence interval, which means that if repeated samples were drawn from the same population and an error range constructed around each sample estimate, in 9 of 10 cases the true value based on a complete census of the population would be contained within these error ranges. 2. "Other marital status" includes divorced, widowed, separated, and married with spouse absent.

★ 526 ★

Employment Status

Employment Status in Vermont: 1993

Data show the employment status of the civilian noninstitutionalized population by sex, age, race, and marital status. Figures are 1993 annual averages.

[Numbers in thousands]

Population group	Civilian non-institutional population	Civilian labor force		Employment		Unemployment		
		Number	Percent of population	Number	Percent of population	Number	Rate	Error range of rate[1]
Total	440	316	71.8	299	67.9	17	5.4	4.7-6.1
Men	212	164	77.7	152	72.0	12	7.3	6.2-8.3
Women	228	152	66.4	146	64.1	5	3.5	2.7-4.2
Both sexes, 16-19 years old	24	15	62.4	13	55.4	2	11.3	7.3-15.3
White	436	313	71.9	296	68.0	17	5.4	4.7-6.0
Men	209	163	77.8	151	72.2	12	7.2	6.2-8.3
Women	226	150	66.5	145	64.2	5	3.4	2.6-4.1
Both sexes, 16-19 years old	23	15	62.5	13	56.4	1	9.8	5.9-13.7
Single (never married)	102	78	75.8	71	69.7	6	8.1	6.5-9.7
Married (spouse present)	260	198	75.9	189	72.8	8	4.2	3.4-4.9
Other marital status[2]	77	41	52.7	38	49.3	3	6.4	4.4-8.4

Source: U.S. Department of Labor. Bureau of Labor Statistics. *Geographic Profile of Employment and Unemployment, 1993.* Bulletin 2446. Washington, DC: U.S. Government Printing Office, September 1994, p. 49 *Notes:* Data for demographic groups are not shown when they do not meet Bureau of Labor Statistics publication standards of reliability for the particular area based on the sample in that area. Items may not add to totals or compute to displayed percentages because of rounding. Detail for race and Hispanic origin groups will not add totals because data for the "other races" group are not presented and because Hispanics are included in both the white and black population groups. 1. Error ranges are calculated at the 90 percent confidence interval, which means that if repeated samples were drawn from the same population and an error range constructed around each sample estimate, in 9 of 10 cases the true value based on a complete census of the population would be contained within these error ranges. 2. "Other marital status" includes divorced, widowed, separated, and married with spouse absent.

★ 527 ★

Employment Status

Employment Status in Virginia: 1993

Data show the employment status of the civilian noninstitutionalized population by sex, age, race, Hispanic origin, and marital status. Figures are 1993 annual averages.

[Numbers in thousands]

Population group	Civilian non-institutional population	Civilian labor force		Employment		Unemployment		
		Number	Percent of population	Number	Percent of population	Number	Rate	Error range of rate[1]
Total	4,863	3,376	69.4	3,208	66.0	168	5.0	4.5-5.5
Men	2,331	1,793	76.9	1,707	73.2	87	4.8	4.1-5.5
Women	2,532	1,583	62.5	1,502	59.3	82	5.2	4.4-5.9
Both sexes, 16-19 years old	346	175	50.5	142	40.9	33	19.1	15.7-22.5
White	3,840	2,655	69.1	2,557	66.6	98	3.7	3.2-4.2
Men	1,841	1,426	77.5	1,380	74.9	46	3.2	2.6-3.9
Women	1,999	1,229	61.5	1,178	58.9	52	4.2	3.4-5.0
Both sexes, 16-19 years old	253	133	52.7	117	46.3	16	12.1	8.5-15.7

[Continued]

★ 527 ★

Employment Status in Virginia: 1993

[Continued]

Population group	Civilian non-institutional population	Civilian labor force		Employment		Unemployment		
		Number	Percent of population	Number	Percent of population	Number	Rate	Error range of rate[1]
Black	874	619	70.9	559	63.9	61	9.8	8.2-11.3
Men	424	321	75.8	287	67.7	34	10.6	8.4-12.8
Women	450	298	66.2	272	60.3	26	8.8	6.7-11.0
Hispanic origin	114	94	82.3	90	78.3	5	4.8	1.9-7.7
Single (never married)	1,192	866	72.7	778	65.3	88	10.2	8.8-11.5
Married (spouse present)	2,817	2,000	71.0	1,943	69.0	57	2.8	2.3-3.4
Other marital status[2]	854	510	59.7	487	57.0	24	4.7	3.4-6.0

Source: U.S. Department of Labor. Bureau of Labor Statistics. *Geographic Profile of Employment and Unemployment, 1993.* Bulletin 2446. Washington, DC: U.S. Government Printing Office, September 1994, p. 49. *Notes:* Data for demographic groups are not shown when they do not meet Bureau of Labor Statistics publication standards of reliability for the particular area based on the sample in that area. Items may not add to totals or compute to displayed percentages because of rounding. Detail for race and Hispanic origin groups will not add totals because data for the "other races" group are not presented and because Hispanics are included in both the white and black population groups. 1. Error ranges are calculated at the 90 percent confidence interval, which means that if repeated samples were drawn from the same population and an error range constructed around each sample estimate, in 9 of 10 cases the true value based on a complete census of the population would be contained within these error ranges. 2. "Other marital status" includes divorced, widowed, separated, and married with spouse absent.

★ 528 ★

Employment Status

Employment Status in Washington: 1993

Data show the employment status of the civilian noninstitutionalized population by sex, age, race, and marital status. Figures are 1993 annual averages.

[Numbers in thousands]

Population group	Civilian non-institutional population	Civilian labor force		Employment		Unemployment		
		Number	Percent of population	Number	Percent of population	Number	Rate	Error range of rate[1]
Total	3,940	2,693	68.3	2,490	63.2	203	7.5	6.7-8.3
Men	1,924	1,465	76.2	1,344	69.9	121	8.3	7.2-9.3
Women	2,016	1,228	60.9	1,146	56.8	82	6.7	5.6-7.7
Both sexes, 16-19 years old	234	134	57.1	114	48.8	20	14.7	10.3-19.1
White	3,605	2,486	69.0	2,311	64.1	176	7.1	6.3-7.8
Men	1,776	1,357	76.4	1,254	70.6	103	7.6	6.5-8.6
Women	1,830	1,129	61.7	1,056	57.7	73	6.5	5.4-7.5
Both sexes, 16-19 years old	212	125	59.1	107	50.7	18	14.2	9.7-18.7
Single (never married)	924	712	77.0	638	69.1	73	10.3	8.6-12.0

[Continued]

★ 528 ★

Employment Status in Washington: 1993
[Continued]

Population group	Civilian non-institutional population	Civilian labor force		Employment		Unemployment		
		Number	Percent of population	Number	Percent of population	Number	Rate	Error range of rate[1]
Married (spouse present)	2,289	1,548	67.6	1,456	63.6	92	5.9	5.1-6.8
Other marital status[2]	727	434	59.6	396	54.5	38	8.7	6.7-10.6

Source: U.S. Department of Labor. Bureau of Labor Statistics. *Geographic Profile of Employment and Unemployment, 1993.* Bulletin 2446. Washington, DC: U.S. Government Printing Office, September 1994, p. 50. *Notes:* Data for demographic groups are not shown when they do not meet Bureau of Labor Statistics publication standards of reliability for the particular area based on the sample in that area. Items may not add to totals or compute to displayed percentages because of rounding. Detail for race and Hispanic origin groups will not add totals because data for the "other races" group are not presented and because Hispanics are included in both the white and black population groups. 1. Error ranges are calculated at the 90 percent confidence interval, which means that if repeated samples were drawn from the same population and an error range constructed around each sample estimate, in 9 of 10 cases the true value based on a complete census of the population would be contained within these error ranges. 2. "Other marital status" includes divorced, widowed, separated, and married with spouse absent.

★ 529 ★
Employment Status

Employment Status in West Virginia: 1993

Data show the employment status of the civilian noninstitutionalized population by sex, age, race, and marital status. Figures are 1993 annual averages.

[Numbers in thousands]

Population group	Civilian non-institutional population	Civilian labor force		Employment		Unemployment		
		Number	Percent of population	Number	Percent of population	Number	Rate	Error range of rate[1]
Total	1,431	786	55.0	702	49.0	85	10.8	9.9-11.7
Men	679	448	66.0	391	57.5	57	12.8	11.6-14.0
Women	752	338	45.0	311	41.3	27	8.1	6.9-9.3
Both sexes, 16-19 years old	98	37	37.9	24	24.6	13	35.1	31.4-38.7
White	1,373	755	55.0	673	49.1	81	10.8	9.9-11.7
Men	652	430	66.0	375	57.5	55	12.9	11.6-14.1
Women	721	325	45.0	299	41.4	26	8.0	6.8-9.2
Both sexes, 16-19 years old	94	37	38.7	24	25.2	13	34.8	31.1-38.5
Black	51	27	53.6	24	47.3	3	11.6	7.2-16.1
Single (never married)	276	163	59.1	131	47.6	32	19.5	17.4-21.7
Married (spouse present)	872	511	58.5	473	54.3	37	7.3	6.4-8.3
Other marital status[2]	282	112	39.8	97	34.3	15	13.8	11.4-16.2

Source: U.S. Department of Labor. Bureau of Labor Statistics. *Geographic Profile of Employment and Unemployment, 1993.* Bulletin 2446. Washington, DC: U.S. Government Printing Office, September 1994, p. 50. *Notes:* Data for demographic groups are not shown when they do not meet Bureau of Labor Statistics publication standards of reliability for the particular area based on the sample in that area. Items may not add to totals or compute to displayed percentages because of rounding. Detail for race and Hispanic origin groups will not add totals because data for the "other races" group are not presented and because Hispanics are included in both the white and black population groups. 1. Error ranges are calculated at the 90 percent confidence interval, which means that if repeated samples were drawn from the same population and an error range constructed around each sample estimate, in 9 of 10 cases the true value based on a complete census of the population would be contained within these error ranges. 2. "Other marital status" includes divorced, widowed, separated, and married with spouse absent.

★ 530 ★

Employment Status

Employment Status in Wisconsin: 1993

Data show the employment status of the civilian noninstitutionalized population by sex, age, race, and marital status. Figures are 1993 annual averages.

[Numbers in thousands]

Population group	Civilian non-institutional population	Civilian labor force		Employment		Unemployment		
		Number	Percent of population	Number	Percent of population	Number	Rate	Error range of rate[1]
Total	3,773	2,715	72.0	2,589	68.6	127	4.7	4.2-5.2
Men	1,836	1,439	78.4	1,366	74.4	74	5.1	4.4-5.8
Women	1,937	1,276	65.9	1,223	63.1	53	4.2	3.5-4.8
Both sexes, 16-19 years old	276	185	67.1	158	57.3	27	14.6	11.8-17.4
White	3,532	2,565	72.6	2,461	69.7	104	4.0	3.6-4.5
Men	1,733	1,370	79.0	1,307	75.4	63	4.6	3.9-5.3
Women	1,798	1,195	66.4	1,154	64.2	41	3.4	2.8-4.1
Both sexes, 16-19 years old	247	172	69.6	152	61.4	20	11.8	9.1-14.6
Black	162	102	63.3	85	52.7	17	16.6	12.8-20.5
Single (never married)	944	735	77.8	675	71.4	60	8.2	7.0-9.4
Married (spouse present)	2,177	1,608	73.9	1,562	71.7	46	2.9	2.4-3.4
Other marital status[2]	652	372	57.1	352	54.0	20	5.4	4.0-6.8

Source: U.S. Department of Labor. Bureau of Labor Statistics. *Geographic Profile of Employment and Unemployment, 1993.* Bulletin 2446. Washington, DC: U.S. Government Printing Office, September 1994, p. 50. *Notes:* Data for demographic groups are not shown when they do not meet Bureau of Labor Statistics publication standards of reliability for the particular area based on the sample in that area. Items may not add to totals or compute to displayed percentages because of rounding. Detail for race and Hispanic origin groups will not add totals because data for the "other races" group are not presented and because Hispanics are included in both the white and black population groups. 1. Error ranges are calculated at the 90 percent confidence interval, which means that if repeated samples were drawn from the same population and an error range constructed around each sample estimate, in 9 of 10 cases the true value based on a complete census of the population would be contained within these error ranges. 2. "Other marital status" includes divorced, widowed, separated, and married with spouse absent.

★ 531 ★

Employment Status

Employment Status in Wyoming: 1993

Data show the employment status of the civilian noninstitutionalized population by sex, age, race, Hispanic origin, and marital status. Figures are 1993 annual averages.

[Numbers in thousands]

Population group	Civilian non-institutional population	Civilian labor force		Employment		Unemployment		
		Number	Percent of population	Number	Percent of population	Number	Rate	Error range of rate[1]
Total	343	239	69.7	226	66.0	13	5.4	4.7-6.1
Men	168	131	77.6	123	73.0	8	5.9	4.9-6.9
Women	175	108	62.2	103	59.2	5	4.8	3.8-5.8
Both sexes, 16-19 years old	29	17	57.3	14	47.1	3	17.8	13.9-21.7
White	334	234	69.9	221	66.2	12	5.3	4.6-6.0
Men	164	128	78.0	120	73.6	7	5.7	4.7-6.7

[Continued]

★ 531 ★

Employment Status in Wyoming: 1993
[Continued]

Population group	Civilian non-institutional population	Civilian labor force		Employment		Unemployment		
		Number	Percent of population	Number	Percent of population	Number	Rate	Error range of rate[1]
Women	171	106	62.1	101	59.1	5	4.9	3.9-5.9
Both sexes, 16-19 years old	28	16	57.5	13	47.7	3	17.2	13.2-21.1
Hispanic origin	13	9	70.2	8	65.3	1	7.0	2.9-11.2
Single (never married)	65	46	71.6	40	62.6	6	12.6	10.5-14.8
Married (spouse present)	214	155	72.3	150	70.3	4	2.8	2.2-3.5
Other marital status[2]	64	38	59.3	35	55.1	3	7.1	5.1-9.0

Source: U.S. Department of Labor. Bureau of Labor Statistics. *Geographic Profile of Employment and Unemployment, 1993.* Bulletin 2446. Washington, DC: U.S. Government Printing Office, September 1994, p. 50. *Notes:* Data for demographic groups are not shown when they do not meet Bureau of Labor Statistics publication standards of reliability for the particular area based on the sample in that area. Items may not add to totals or compute to displayed percentages because of rounding. Detail for race and Hispanic origin groups will not add totals because data for the "other races" group are not presented and because Hispanics are included in both the white and black population groups. 1. Error ranges are calculated at the 90 percent confidence interval, which means that if repeated samples were drawn from the same population and an error range constructed around each sample estimate, in 9 of 10 cases the true value based on a complete census of the population would be contained within these error ranges. 2. "Other marital status" includes divorced, widowed, separated, and married with spouse absent.

Job Growth

★ 532 ★

Employment Projections of CEOs

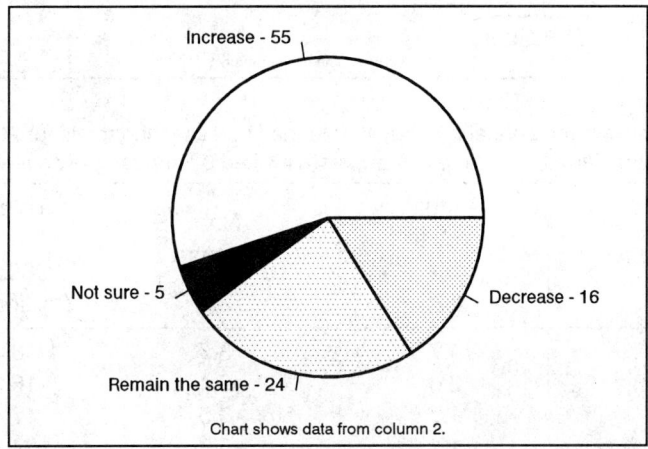

Chart shows data from column 2.

When polled in 1993, top executives indicated that job growth at their companies would slow due to increased automation and productivity. Table shows the job creation expected by Fortune 500 and Service 500 chief executive officers (CEOs).

[In percentages]

Number of full-time employees expected to:	Regular employees		Management only	
	Next 12 months	Next 3 years	Next 12 months	Next 3 years
Increase	34	55	20	33
Decrease	28	16	33	27
Remain the same	38	24	47	37
Not sure	0	5	0	3

Source: Richman, Louis S. "CEOs to Workers: Help Not Wanted." *Fortune,* 12 July 1993, p. 42. Primary source: *Fortune* CEO poll conducted by Clark Martire & Bartolomeo.

★ 533 ★

Job Growth

Job Growth Rate, by Race/Ethnicity: 2005

```
┌─────────────────────────────────────────────────┐
│  ┌─────────────────────────────────────────────┐ │
│  │ Asian - 4.7                                  │ │
│  ├───────────────────────────────────┐         │ │
│  │ Hispanic - 3.9                     │         │ │
│  ├──────────────────┐                 │         │ │
│  │ Black - 1.7       │                 │         │ │
│  ├──────────┐        │                 │         │ │
│  │ White - 1.1│       │                 │         │ │
│  └──────────┘                                   │ │
│              Chart shows data from column 1.     │ │
└─────────────────────────────────────────────────┘
```

Table shows the annual job growth rate, net increase, and totals for 2005 for various racial/ethnic groups. Groups are ranked by annual growth rates.

Group	Annual growth rate (%)	Net increase (millions)	Total in 2005 (millions)
Asian	4.7	3.7	8.3
Hispanic	3.9	6.4	16.6
Black	1.7	3.5	17.4
White	1.1	16.3	124.8

Source: "Job Demographics for the Next Decade." *Manufacturing Engineering* (March 1994), p. 38. Primary source: Bureau of the Census. *Current Population Reports.*

★ 534 ★

Job Growth

Professional Job Growth, by Sex and Race: 1982-1992

According to the source, black women professionals comprised the fastest growing—125 percent increase from 1982 to 1992—group of American workers. Their number remains "miniscule compared with the number of white professionals—male and female," the source reported. "But it is nearly twice the number of black male professionals" (p. A1). Table shows the compound annual growth rate in professional jobs for white and black men and women.

[In percentages]

Worker	Growth
Black females	8.4
White females	6.4
Black males	4.2
White males	2.0

Source: Gaiter, Dorothy J. "The Gender Divide: Black Women's Gains in Corporate America Outstrip Black Men's." *Wall Street Journal*, 8 March 1994, p. A1. Primary source: *Wall Street Journal* study.

Labor Force Participation

★ 535 ★

Civilian Labor Force and Participation Rates, by Educational Attainment, Sex, and Race: 1970-1991

As of March, except as noted. For civilian noninstitutional population 25 to 64 years of age.

Item	Civilian labor force Total (1,000)	Percent distribution Less than high school	High school graduate	College 1-3 years	College 4 years or more	Participation rate[1] Total	Less than high school	High school graduate	College 1-3 years	College 4 years or more
Total[2]:										
1970	61,765	36.1	38.1	11.8	14.1	70.3	65.5	70.2	73.8	82.3
1980	78,010	20.6	39.8	17.6	22.0	73.9	60.7	74.2	79.5	86.1
1985	88,424	15.9	40.2	19.0	24.9	76.2	59.9	75.9	81.6	87.7
1990[3]	99,981	13.3	39.4	20.8	26.5	78.9	61.4	78.4	83.5	88.6
1991[3]	101,171	12.8	39.2	21.3	26.7	78.8	61.0	78.2	83.4	88.3
Male:										
1970	39,303	37.5	34.5	12.2	15.7	93.5	89.3	96.3	95.8	96.1
1980	45,417	22.2	35.7	17.7	24.3	89.4	78.8	91.9	92.4	95.3
1985	49,647	17.7	36.9	18.3	27.1	88.6	72.2	90.0	91.2	94.6
1990[3]	55,049	14.9	37.3	19.8	28.0	89.3	76.4	90.1	92.1	94.6
1991[3]	55,554	14.5	37.1	20.3	28.2	88.9	75.9	89.4	91.9	94.3
Female:										
1970	22,462	33.5	44.3	10.9	11.2	49.0	43.0	51.3	50.9	60.9
1980	32,593	18.4	45.4	17.4	18.7	59.5	43.7	61.2	66.4	73.4
1985	38,779	13.7	44.4	19.9	22.0	64.7	44.3	65.0	72.5	78.6
1990[3]	44,932	11.2	42.1	22.1	24.6	69.1	46.5	68.8	75.7	81.3
1991[3]	45,617	10.7	41.8	22.5	25.0	69.3	46.0	68.9	75.8	81.3
White:										
1970	55,044	33.7	39.3	12.2	14.8	70.1	65.2	69.7	73.3	81.9
1980	68,509	19.1	40.2	17.7	22.9	74.2	61.4	73.7	79.2	86.0
1985	76,739	14.7	40.7	19.1	25.6	76.6	60.7	75.8	81.1	87.7
1990[3]	85,882	12.5	39.4	20.8	27.3	79.5	63.0	78.6	83.4	88.6
1991[3]	86,776	12.1	39.1	21.3	27.5	79.5	62.6	78.5	83.4	88.5
Black:										
1970	6,721	55.5	28.2	8.0	8.3	72.0	67.1	76.8	81.0	87.4
1980	7,731	34.7	38.1	16.3	11.0	71.5	58.1	79.2	82.0	90.1
1985	9,157	26.2	39.5	19.2	15.0	73.4	57.0	77.2	85.6	89.9
1990[3]	10,711	19.4	43.0	21.8	15.8	75.4	55.7	78.6	84.6	91.0
1991[3]	10,863	18.4	43.0	22.5	16.0	75.0	55.1	77.4	84.6	90.4

Source: U.S. Bureau of the Census. *Statistical Abstract of the United States, 1994.* 114th ed. Washington, DC: U.S. Government Printing Office, 1994, p. 397. Primary sources: U.S. Bureau of Labor Statistics. Bulletin 2307; and unpublished data. *Notes:* 1. Percent of the civilian population in each group in the civilian labor force. 2. Includes other races, not shown separately. For 1970, white and black races only. 3. Not strictly comparable with previous years. Annual averages of monthly figures.

★ 536 ★

Labor Force Participation

Civilian Labor Force and Participation Rates, by Educational Attainment, Sex, and Race: 1992 and 1993

Tables reflects the employment status of the civilian noninstitutional population 25 years old or older. Data are annual averages of monthly figures presented by sex and race. Based on Current Population Survey.

[In thousands, except rate]

Year, sex, race	Civlian labor force (1,000)					Participation rate[1]				
	Total	Less than a high school diploma	High school graduates, no college	Less than a bachelor's degree	College graduates	Total	Less than a high school diploma	High school graduates, no college	Less than a bachelor's degree	College graduates
Total[2]:										
1992	106,530	13,191	37,993	27,089	28,257	66.3	40.7	66.2	75.1	81.2
1993	107,657	12,360	37,821	28,413	29,062	66.2	39.7	65.4	75.0	81.0
Male:										
1992	58,393	8,105	19,914	14,038	16,336	76.6	53.8	78.0	83.6	86.8
1993	58,904	7,669	19,916	14,668	16,652	76.2	52.8	77.0	83.4	86.3
Female:										
1992	48,138	5,086	18,080	13,051	11,920	57.0	29.4	56.7	67.7	74.7
1993	48,753	4,692	17,906	13,745	12,410	57.1	28.3	56.0	67.7	74.9
White:										
1992	91,242	10,543	32,488	23,273	24,938	66.3	40.8	65.4	74.5	80.9
1993	92,168	9,960	32,273	24,345	25,590	66.3	40.1	64.8	74.4	80.8
Black:										
1992	11,422	2,110	4,505	3,004	1,803	65.7	39.7	72.3	80.5	85.6
1993	11,477	1,873	4,492	3,216	1,896	64.7	37.1	69.9	79.7	84.8
Hispanic[3]:										
1992	7,993	3,124	2,358	1,592	919	67.9	55.9	75.2	82.1	83.0
1993	8,261	3,130	2,411	1,756	963	67.6	55.7	73.2	81.6	83.7

Source: U.S. Bureau of the Census. *Statistical Abstract of the United States, 1994.* 114th ed. Washington, DC: U.S. Government Printing Office, 1994, p. 397. Primary source: U.S. Bureau of Labor Statistics. Unpublished data. *Notes:* 1. Percent of civilian population in each group in the civilian labor force. 2. Includes other races, not shown separately. 3. Persons of Hispanic origin may be of any race.

★ 537 ★

Labor Force Participation

Civilian Labor Force, by Age and Class of Worker: 1970-1993

For civilian noninstitutional population 16 years old and over. Annual averages of monthly figures. Based on Current Population Survey.

[In thousands, except as indicated]

Age and class of worker	1970	1980	1985	1989	1990	1991	1992	1993
Total employed	78,678	99,303	107,150	117,342	117,914	116,877	117,598	119,306
Age:								
16 to 19 years old	6,144	7,710	6,434	6,759	6,261	5,628	5,398	5,530
20 to 24 years old	9,731	14,087	13,980	12,962	12,622	12,233	12,157	12,137
25 to 34 years old	16,318	27,204	31,208	34,045	33,831	32,914	32,441	32,107
35 to 44 years old	15,922	19,523	24,732	29,443	30,543	31,286	31,662	32,402

[Continued]

★ 537 ★

Civilian Labor Force, by Age and Class of Worker: 1970-1993

[Continued]

Age and class of worker	1970	1980	1985	1989	1990	1991	1992	1993
45 to 54 years old	16,473	16,234	16,509	19,279	19,765	20,164	21,246	22,412
55 to 64 years old	10,974	11,586	11,474	11,499	11,464	11,268	11,267	11,311
65 years old and over	3,118	2,960	2,813	3,355	3,428	3,384	3,427	3,409
Class of worker:								
Nonagriculture	75,215	95,938	103,971	114,142	114,728	113,644	114,391	116,232
Wage and salary workers	69,491	88,525	95,871	105,259	105,715	104,520	105,540	107,011
Self-employed	5,221	7,000	7,811	8,605	8,760	8,899	8,619	9,003
Unpaid family workers	502	413	289	279	252	225	232	218
Agriculture	3,463	3,364	3,179	3,199	3,186	3,233	3,207	3,074
Wage and salary workers	1,154	1,425	1,535	1,665	1,679	1,673	1,696	1,637
Self-employed	1,810	1,642	1,458	1,403	1,400	1,442	1,398	1,332
Unpaid family workers	499	297	185	131	107	118	113	105

Source: U.S. Bureau of the Census. *Statistical Abstract of the United States, 1994.* 114th ed. Washington, DC: U.S. Government Printing Office, 1994, p. 403. Primary sources: U.S. Bureau of Labor Statistics. *Employment and Earnings* (monthly; January issues); and unpublished data.

★ 538 ★

Labor Force Participation

Civilian Labor Force Characteristics: 1993

Data show the employment status of the civilian noninstitutional population 16 years old and older. Annual averages of monthly figures. Based on Current Population Survey.

Age and race	Total (1,000)	Male (1,000)			Female (1,000)			Percent of labor force			
								Employed		Unemployed	
		Total	Employed	Unemployed	Total	Employed	Unemployed	Male	Female	Male	Female
All workers[1]	128,040	69,633	64,700	4,932	58,407	54,606	3,801	92.9	93.5	7.1	6.5
16 to 19 years	6,826	3,564	2,836	728	3,261	2,694	568	79.6	82.6	20.4	17.4
20 to 24 years	13,558	7,164	6,356	808	6,393	5,780	613	88.7	90.4	11.3	9.6
25 to 34 years	34,465	19,053	17,734	1,319	15,412	14,373	1,038	93.1	93.3	6.9	6.7
35 to 44 years	34,264	18,537	17,508	1,029	15,727	14,894	833	94.4	94.7	5.6	5.3
45 to 54 years	23,542	12,634	11,997	638	10,907	10,415	492	95.0	95.5	5.0	4.5
55 to 64 years	11,867	6,639	6,294	345	5,228	5,017	211	94.8	96.0	5.2	4.0
65 years and over	3,520	2,041	1,976	65	1,479	1,433	46	96.8	96.9	3.2	3.1
White	109,359	60,150	56,397	3,753	49,208	46,415	2,793	93.8	94.3	6.2	5.7
16 to 19 years	5,831	3,035	2,500	535	2,795	2,387	408	82.4	85.4	17.6	14.6
20 to 24 years	11,360	6,021	5,448	573	5,339	4,921	418	90.5	92.2	9.5	7.8
25 to 34 years	28,996	16,217	15,211	1,006	12,779	12,045	734	93.8	94.3	6.2	5.7
35 to 44 years	29,190	16,043	15,248	795	13,148	12,529	619	95.0	95.3	5.0	4.7
45 to 54 years	20,407	11,099	10,584	516	9,308	8,907	400	95.4	95.7	4.6	4.3
55 to 64 years	10,385	5,861	5,588	274	4,524	4,349	175	95.3	96.1	4.7	3.9
65 years and over	3,189	1,873	1,818	55	1,316	1,277	39	97.1	97.0	2.9	3.0
Black	13,943	6,911	5,957	954	7,031	6,189	842	86.2	88.0	13.8	12.0
16 to 19 years	776	413	247	166	363	227	136	59.8	62.5	40.2	37.5
20 to 24 years	1,689	854	658	196	835	661	174	77.0	79.2	23.0	20.8
25 to 34 years	4,168	2,115	1,854	261	2,053	1,789	264	87.7	87.1	12.3	12.9
35 to 44 years	3,738	1,788	1,600	188	1,950	1,783	167	89.5	91.4	10.5	8.6
45 to 54 years	2,213	1,050	964	85	1,163	1,096	67	91.9	94.2	8.1	5.8
55 to 64 years	1,102	566	515	51	536	508	28	91.0	94.8	9.0	5.2
65 years and over	257	126	119	7	131	126	5	94.4	96.2	5.6	3.8
Hispanic[2]	10,377	6,256	5,603	653	4,120	3,669	451	89.6	89.1	10.4	10.9
16 to 19 years	660	385	285	101	274	202	72	73.8	73.7	26.2	26.3

[Continued]

★ 538 ★

Civilian Labor Force Characteristics: 1993
[Continued]

Age and race	Total (1,000)	Male (1,000)			Female (1,000)			Percent of labor force			
								Employed		Unemployed	
		Total	Employed	Unemployed	Total	Employed	Unemployed	Male	Female	Male	Female
20 to 24 years	1,456	895	782	113	561	482	79	87.4	85.9	12.6	14.1
25 to 34 years	3,365	2,119	1,930	189	1,246	1,123	123	91.1	90.1	8.9	9.9
35 to 44 years	2,671	1,562	1,424	138	1,109	1,003	106	91.2	90.4	8.8	9.6
45 to 54 years	1,442	842	768	74	600	550	50	91.2	91.7	8.8	8.3
55 to 64 years	646	369	338	31	277	257	20	91.6	92.8	8.4	7.2
65 years and over	137	84	76	8	53	52	1	90.5	98.1	9.5	1.9

Source: U.S. Bureau of the Census. Statistical Abstract of the United States, 1994. 114th ed. Washington, DC: U.S. Government Printing Office, 1994, p. 403. Primary source: U.S. Bureau of Labor Statistics. Employment and Earnings (monthly; January 1994). Notes: 1. Includes other races not shown separately. 2. Persons of Hispanic origin may be of any race.

★ 539 ★
Labor Force Participation

Civilian Labor Force Characteristics, by State: 1993

For civilian noninstitutional population, 16 years old and over. Annual averages of monthly figures. Because of separate processing and weighting procedures, the totals the United States may differ from results obtained by aggregating totals for regions and states.

[In thousands, except ratio and rate]

State	Total		Employed		Employed/ popula-tion ratio[1]	Total		Rate[2]			Participation rate[3]	
	Number	Female	Total	Female		Number	Female	Total	Male	Female	Male	Female
United States	128,040	58,407	119,306	54,606	61.6	8,734	3,801	6.8	7.1	6.5	75.2	57.9
Alabama	1,990	901	1,840	830	57.7	149	71	7.5	7.1	7.9	72.2	53.6
Alaska	298	135	276	126	68.1	23	8	7.6	8.8	6.1	81.2	66.2
Arizona	1,837	829	1,723	779	58.3	114	50	6.2	6.3	6.0	71.8	53.4
Arkansas	1,163	533	1,091	499	59.3	72	34	6.2	5.9	6.4	72.0	55.2
California	15,259	6,670	13,853	6,092	59.5	1,407	577	9.2	9.7	8.7	75.8	55.8
Colorado	1,904	879	1,805	841	67.2	99	39	5.2	5.9	4.4	78.5	63.7
Connecticut	1,788	822	1,678	783	66.0	111	38	6.2	7.5	4.7	78.7	62.6
Delaware	373	168	354	159	66.4	20	9	5.3	5.5	5.2	77.5	62.7
District of Columbia	306	152	280	139	61.1	26	13	8.5	8.6	8.4	73.1	61.5
Florida	6,628	3,061	6,166	2,851	57.7	462	209	7.0	7.1	6.8	70.5	54.4
Georgia	3,467	1,655	3,267	1,558	63.1	200	96	5.8	5.7	5.8	75.4	59.6
Hawaii	583	277	558	266	65.3	25	11	4.2	4.5	3.9	75.4	61.8
Idaho	545	242	512	227	64.1	34	15	6.1	6.2	6.0	77.6	59.2
Illinois	5,983	2,734	5,538	2,547	62.7	444	187	7.4	7.9	6.8	76.9	59.4
Indiana	2,937	1,375	2,780	1,297	64.4	157	77	5.3	5.1	5.6	77.7	59.6
Iowa	1,550	702	1,488	676	70.4	62	26	4.0	4.2	3.8	81.8	65.1
Kansas	1,318	601	1,253	570	67.4	66	31	5.0	4.8	5.2	78.6	63.6
Kentucky	1,794	810	1,684	761	58.4	110	49	6.2	6.2	6.1	71.2	54.0
Louisiana	1,879	833	1,740	770	55.4	139	63	7.4	7.2	7.5	70.8	50.2
Maine	631	296	581	275	61.2	50	21	7.9	8.7	7.0	72.3	60.8
Maryland	2,672	1,287	2,507	1,218	66.0	165	69	6.2	6.9	5.4	76.8	64.6
Massachusetts	3,170	1,468	2,953	1,383	63.3	217	85	6.9	7.8	5.8	76.4	60.3
Michigan	4,702	2,111	4,374	1,967	61.3	328	145	7.0	7.1	6.9	75.2	57.3
Minnesota	2,466	1,155	2,341	1,110	69.9	125	45	5.1	6.1	3.9	81.0	66.7
Mississippi	1,212	532	1,135	490	58.3	77	42	6.3	5.2	7.8	72.1	52.9
Missouri	2,650	1,241	2,481	1,148	63.2	169	94	6.4	5.4	7.5	75.5	60.3
Montana	427	193	401	182	63.8	26	11	6.0	6.4	5.6	74.5	61.3
Nebraska	853	410	830	396	70.1	22	13	2.6	2.0	3.2	78.8	65.8
Nevada	745	334	692	309	65.0	54	25	7.2	6.9	7.5	77.3	62.8

[Continued]

★ 539 ★

Civilian Labor Force Characteristics, by State: 1993

[Continued]

State	Total		Employed		Employed/ population ratio[1]	Total		Rate[2]			Participation rate[3]	
	Number	Female	Total	Female		Number	Female	Total	Male	Female	Male	Female
New Hampshire	620	282	579	265	67.4	41	17	6.6	7.0	6.1	80.0	64.5
New Jersey	4,001	1,803	3,706	1,685	60.7	295	118	7.4	8.1	6.5	75.6	56.4
New Mexico	756	333	700	310	59.0	57	23	7.5	7.9	6.9	73.5	54.6
New York	8,649	3,986	7,985	3,714	56.9	664	272	7.7	8.4	6.8	70.8	53.5
North Carolina	3,555	1,682	3,383	1,591	64.0	173	91	4.9	4.3	5.4	74.8	60.4
North Dakota	318	149	305	143	65.9	14	6	4.3	4.7	3.8	76.3	61.8
Ohio	5,488	2,514	5,132	2,360	61.1	357	153	6.5	6.8	6.1	74.7	56.9
Oklahoma	1,524	683	1,432	640	59.6	92	43	6.0	5.8	6.3	74.0	53.9
Oregon	1,587	718	1,473	672	63.3	114	45	7.2	7.9	6.3	75.4	61.1
Pennsylvania	5,893	2,664	5,479	2,494	59.0	414	170	7.0	7.5	6.4	73.2	54.7
Rhode Island	512	244	472	227	62.0	40	17	7.7	8.5	6.9	74.7	60.6
South Carolina	1,823	845	1,685	778	61.7	138	68	7.5	7.2	8.0	76.8	57.9
South Dakota	360	163	347	156	67.6	12	7	3.5	3.0	4.0	78.1	62.4
Tennessee	2,500	1,185	2,358	1,110	60.1	142	74	5.7	5.1	6.3	72.3	56.2
Texas	9,149	4,054	8,508	3,758	64.0	642	296	7.0	6.8	7.3	79.0	59.2
Utah	910	408	875	391	69.4	35	17	3.9	3.6	4.2	81.2	63.5
Vermont	316	152	299	146	68.0	17	5	5.4	7.3	3.5	77.7	66.4
Virginia	3,376	1,583	3,208	1,502	66.0	168	82	5.0	4.8	5.2	76.9	62.5
Washington	2,693	1,228	2,490	1,146	63.2	203	82	7.5	8.3	6.7	76.2	60.9
West Virginia	786	338	702	311	49.1	85	27	10.8	12.8	8.1	66.0	45.0
Wisconsin	2,715	1,276	2,589	1,223	68.6	127	53	4.7	5.1	4.2	78.4	65.9
Wyoming	239	108	226	103	65.9	13	5	5.4	5.9	4.8	77.6	62.2

Source: U.S. Bureau of the Census. *Statistical Abstract of the United States, 1994.* 114th ed. Washington, DC: U.S. Government Printing Office, 1994, p. 399. Primary source: U.S. Bureau of Labor Statistics. *Geographic Profile Employment and Unemployment, 1993. Notes:* 1. Civilian employment as a percent of civilian noninstitutional population. 2. Percent unemployed of the civilian labor force. 3. Percent of civilian noninstitutional population of each specified group in the civilian labor force.

★ 540 ★

Labor Force Participation

Civilian Labor Force Participation Rates and Projections, by Race, Sex, and Age: 1970-2005

For civilian noninstitutional population 16 years old and over. Annual averages of monthly figures. Rates are based on annual average civilian noninstitutional population of each specified group and represent proportion of each specified group in the civilian labor force. Based on Current Population Survey.

Race, sex, and age	Civilian labor force (millions)						Participation rate (percent)					
	1970	1980	1990	1993	2000 projected	2005 projected	1970	1980	1990	1993	2000 projected	2005 projected
Total[1]	82.8	106.9	124.8	128.0	141.8	150.5	60.4	63.8	66.4	66.2	68.2	68.8
White	73.6	93.6	107.2	109.4	118.8	124.8	60.2	64.1	66.8	66.7	68.7	69.3
Male	46.0	54.5	59.3	60.2	63.8	66.0	80.0	78.2	76.9	76.1	76.0	75.3
Female	27.5	39.1	47.9	49.2	55.1	58.8	42.6	51.2	57.5	58.0	61.8	63.6
Black[2]	9.2	10.9	13.5	13.9	16.0	17.4	61.8	61.0	63.3	62.4	65.5	66.2
Male	5.2	5.6	6.7	6.9	7.8	8.3	76.5	70.3	70.1	68.6	70.8	70.5
Female	4.0	5.3	6.8	7.0	8.2	9.0	49.5	53.1	57.8	57.4	61.2	62.6
Hispanic[3]	(NA)	6.1	9.6	10.4	14.3	16.6	(NA)	64.0	67.0	65.9	68.0	68.4
Male	(NA)	3.8	5.8	6.3	8.7	9.6	(NA)	81.4	81.2	80.0	80.2	79.5

[Continued]

★ 540 ★

Civilian Labor Force Participation Rates and Projections, by Race, Sex, and Age: 1970-2005

[Continued]

Race, sex, and age	Civilian labor force (millions)						Participation rate (percent)					
	1970	1980	1990	1993	2000 projected	2005 projected	1970	1980	1990	1993	2000 projected	2005 projected
Female	(NA)	2.3	3.8	4.1	5.8	7.0	(NA)	47.4	53.0	52.0	55.8	57.3
Male	51.2	61.5	68.2	69.6	75.3	78.7	79.7	77.4	76.1	75.2	75.3	74.7
16 to 19 years	4.0	5.0	3.9	3.6	4.4	4.6	56.1	60.5	55.7	53.1	55.4	55.5
20 to 24 years	5.7	8.6	7.3	7.2	7.2	8.1	83.3	85.9	84.3	83.1	84.0	84.4
25 to 34 years	11.3	17.0	19.8	19.1	17.2	16.5	96.4	95.2	94.2	93.5	73.1	93.5
35 to 44 years	10.5	11.8	17.3	18.5	20.7	19.6	96.9	95.5	94.4	93.5	93.7	93.5
45 to 54 years	10.4	9.9	11.2	12.6	15.8	18.1	94.3	91.2	90.7	90.1	90.4	90.2
55 to 64 years	7.1	7.2	6.8	6.6	7.7	9.6	83.0	72.1	67.7	66.5	69.1	69.7
65 years and over	2.2	1.9	2.0	2.0	2.1	2.2	26.8	19.0	16.4	15.6	15.0	14.7
Female	31.5	45.5	56.6	58.4	66.6	71.8	43.3	51.5	57.5	57.9	61.6	63.2
16 to 19 years	3.2	4.4	3.5	3.3	4.0	4.2	44.0	52.9	51.8	49.9	52.0	52.4
20 to 24 years	4.9	7.3	6.6	6.4	6.4	7.2	57.7	68.9	71.6	71.3	72.5	73.6
25 to 34 years	5.7	12.3	16.0	15.4	14.9	14.8	45.0	65.5	73.6	73.6	78.1	80.7
35 to 44 years	6.0	8.6	14.6	15.7	18.8	18.6	51.1	65.5	76.5	76.7	83.0	86.2
45 to 54 years	6.5	7.0	9.3	10.9	14.7	17.4	54.4	59.9	71.2	73.5	79.7	82.8
55 to 64 years	4.2	4.7	5.1	5.2	6.2	7.8	43.0	41.3	45.3	47.3	50.3	52.4
65 years and over	1.1	1.2	1.5	1.5	1.6	1.7	9.7	8.1	8.7	8.2	8.5	8.8

Source: U.S. Bureau of the Census. *Statistical Abstract of the United States, 1994.* 114th ed. Washington, DC: U.S. Government Printing Office, 1994, p. 395. Primary sources: U.S. Bureau of Labor Statistics, Bulletin 2307; *Employment and Earnings* (monthly; January issues); *Monthly Labor Review* (November 1991); and unpublished data. *Notes:* "NA" indicates "not available." 1. Beginning 1975, includes other races not shown separately. 2. For 1970, black and other races. 3. Persons of Hispanic origin may be of any race.

★ 541 ★

Labor Force Participation

Civilian Labor Force Percent Distribution, by Sex and Age: 1960-1993

For civilian noninstitutional population 16 years old and over. Annual averages of monthly figures. Based on Current Population Survey.

Year and sex	Civilian labor force (1,000)	Percent distribution						
		16 to 19 years	20 to 24 years	25 to 34 years	35 to 44 years	45 to 54 years	55 to 64 years	65 years and over
Total:								
1960	69,628	7.0	9.6	20.7	23.4	21.3	13.5	4.6
1970	82,771	8.8	12.8	20.6	19.9	20.5	13.6	3.9
1980	106,940	8.8	14.9	27.3	19.1	15.8	11.2	2.9
1985	115,461	6.8	13.6	29.1	22.6	15.0	10.4	2.5
1989	123,869	6.4	11.4	29.0	24.7	16.1	9.6	2.8
1990	124,787	5.9	11.1	28.7	25.5	16.4	9.5	2.8
1991	125,303	5.5	10.9	28.2	26.3	16.9	9.4	2.8
1992	126,982	5.3	10.8	27.6	26.5	17.6	9.3	2.8
1993	128,040	5.3	10.6	26.9	26.8	18.4	9.3	2.7

[Continued]

★ 541 ★

Civilian Labor Force Percent Distribution, by Sex and Age: 1960-1993
[Continued]

Year and sex	Civilian labor force (1,000)	Percent distribution						
		16 to 19 years	20 to 24 years	25 to 34 years	35 to 44 years	45 to 54 years	55 to 64 years	65 years and over
Male:								
1960	46,388	6.0	8.9	22.1	23.6	20.6	13.8	4.9
1970	51,228	7.8	11.2	22.1	20.4	20.3	13.9	4.2
1980	61,453	8.1	14.0	27.6	19.3	16.1	11.8	3.1
1985	64,411	6.4	12.9	29.2	22.5	15.3	11.0	2.7
1989	67,840	6.1	11.0	29.3	24.5	16.1	10.0	3.0
1990	68,234	5.7	10.7	29.0	25.3	16.4	9.9	3.0
1991	68,411	5.2	10.6	28.6	26.1	16.8	9.8	2.9
1992	69,184	5.1	10.5	28.0	26.3	17.5	9.7	3.0
1993	69,633	5.1	10.3	27.4	26.6	18.1	9.5	2.9
Female:								
1960	23,240	8.8	11.1	17.8	22.8	22.7	12.8	3.9
1970	31,543	10.3	15.5	18.1	18.9	20.7	13.2	3.3
1980	45,487	9.6	16.1	26.9	19.0	15.4	10.4	2.6
1985	51,050	7.4	14.6	28.9	22.7	14.6	9.7	2.3
1989	56,030	6.8	12.0	28.5	25.0	16.1	9.1	2.6
1990	56,554	6.3	11.6	28.3	25.8	16.5	9.0	2.7
1991	56,893	5.9	11.3	27.7	26.6	17.0	8.9	2.7
1992	57,798	5.5	11.2	27.2	26.7	17.8	8.9	2.6
1993	58,407	5.6	10.9	26.4	26.9	18.7	9.0	2.5

Source: U.S. Bureau of the Census. *Statistical Abstract of the United States, 1994.* 114th ed. Washington, DC: U.S. Government Printing Office, 1994, p. 398. Primary sources: U.S. Bureau of Labor Statistics. Bulletin 2307; *Employment and Earnings* (monthly; January issues).

★ 542 ★
Labor Force Participation

Civilian Labor Force Status, by Selected Metropolitan Area: 1993

Table shows metropolitan areas ranked by size of labor force in 1993. Data are for civilian noninstitutional population 16 years old and over. Annual averages of monthly figures. Except as noted, data are derived from the Local Area Unemployment Statistics Program.

[In thousands, except rate]

Metropolitan area	Civilian labor force	Unemployment rate[1]
U.S. total	128,040	6.8
Los Angeles, California; Long Beach, California[2]	4,411.0	9.7
Chicago, Illinois	3,951.9	7.1

[Continued]

★ 542 ★

Civilian Labor Force Status, by Selected Metropolitan Area: 1993
[Continued]

Metropolitan area	Civilian labor force	Unemployment rate[1]
New York, New York	3,901.6	9.4
Washington, D.C.	2,550.3	4.5
Philadelphia, Pennsylvania	2,452.4	6.8
Detroit, Michigan	2,114.8	7.1
Houston, Texas	1,923.4	7.2
Atlanta, Georgia	1,773.1	5.2
Boston, Massachusetts	1,745.4	6.0
Dallas, Texas	1,617.4	6.0
Minneapolis, Minnesota; St. Paul, Minnesota	1,509.9	4.3
Nassau, New York; Suffolk, New York	1,359.1	6.4
Orange County, California	1,315.5	6.7
St. Louis, Missouri[3]	1,270.3	6.5
Riverside, California; San Bernardino, California	1,245.2	10.5
Baltimore, Maryland	1,215.0	7.3
San Diego, California	1,208.8	7.8
Seattle, Washington; Bellevue, Washington; Everett, Washington	1,194.7	6.4
Phoneix, Arizona; Mesa, Arizona	1,165.6	5.1
Pittsburgh, Pennsylvania	1,153.8	6.8
Oakland, California	1,109.9	6.6
Cleveland, Ohio; Lorain, Ohio; Elyria, Ohio	1,082.1	6.7
Tampa, Florida; St. Petersburg, Florida; Clearwater, Florida	1,031.9	6.5
Miami, Florida	1,019.8	7.7
Newark, New Jersey	994.3	7.6
Denver, Colorado	974.3	4.7
Portland, Oregon; Vancouver, Washington	915.8	6.1
San Francisco, California	899.5	6.1
Kansas City, Missouri	873.9	5.4
San Jose, California	838.8	6.8
Cincinnati, Ohio	797.6	5.6
Fort Worth, Texas; Arlington, Texas	789.3	6.4
Indianapolis, Indiana	757.4	4.4
Columbus, Ohio	756.7	4.9

[Continued]

★ 542 ★

Civilian Labor Force Status, by Selected Metropolitan Area: 1993
[Continued]

Metropolitan area	Civilian labor force	Unemployment rate[1]
Milwaukee, Wisconsin;		
Waukesha, Wisconsin	755.5	4.4
Orlando, Florida	719.7	6.2
Fort Lauderdale, Florida	693.9	6.8
Norfolk, Virginia;		
Virginia Beach, Virginia;		
Newport News, Virginia	692.0	5.4
Sacramento, California	684.6	8.3
San Antonio, Texas	681.6	5.6
Charlotte, North Carolina;		
Gastonia, North Carolina;		
Rock Hill, South Carolina	673.2	4.6
Bergen, New Jersey;		
Passaic, New Jersey	655.0	7.7
Hartford, Connecticut	627.6	6.6
Greensboro, North Carolina;		
Winston-Salem, North Carolina;		
High Point, North Carolina	599.6	4.1
Providence, Rhode Island;		
Fall River, Massachusetts;		
Warwick, Rhode Island	588.1	8.4
Salt Lake City, Utah;		
Ogden, Utah	587.8	3.6
New Orleans, Louisiana	585.6	6.8
Middlesex, New Jersey;		
Somerset, New Jersey;		
Hunterdon, New Jersey	581.1	6.0
Buffalo, New York;		
Niagra Falls, New York	577.2	6.6
Rochester, New York	568.2	4.9
Nashville, Tennessee	555.3	4.2
Raleigh, North Carolina;		
Durham, North Carolina;		
Chapel Hill, North Carolina	551.4	3.2
Austin, Texas;		
San Marcos, Texas	547.7	4.0
Las Vegas, Nevada	533.8	7.3

[Continued]

★ 542 ★

Civilian Labor Force Status, by Selected Metropolitan Area: 1993

[Continued]

Metropolitan area	Civilian labor force	Unemploy- ment rate[1]
Grand Rapids, Michigan; Muskegon, Michigan; Holland, Michigan	515.3	5.7
Louisville, Kentucky	506.0	4.9

Source: U.S. Bureau of the Census. *Statistical Abstract of the United States, 1994.* 114th ed. Washington, DC: U.S. Government Printing Office, 1994, p. 398. Primary source: U.S. Bureau of Labor Statistics. *Employment and Earnings* (May issues). *Notes:* 1. Percent unemployed of the civilian labor force. 2. Derived from the Current Population Survey. 3. Excludes part of Sullivan City in Crawford County, Missouri.

Recruiting and Placement

★ 543 ★

Job Openings and Placements: 1970-1992

Openings 1970 and 1980 for years ending September 30; beginning 1985, for years ending June 30.

Item	1970	1980	1985	1987	1988	1989	1990	1991	1992
Job openings[1]									
Received (1,000)	6,130	8,122	7,529	6,968	7,240	6,998	5,651	5,635	5,752
Average per month	511	677	627	581	603	583	471	470	479
Nonagricultural placements (1,000)[1]	4,604	5,610	3,270	4,516	4,503	4,284	3,714	3,507	3,396

Source: U.S. Bureau of the Census. *Statistical Abstract of the United States, 1994.* 114th ed. Washington, DC: U.S. Government Printing Office, 1994, p. 419. Primary source: U.S. Employment and Training Administration. Unpublished data. *Notes:* 1. As reported by state employment agencies. Beginning 1985, all placements. Placements include duplication for individuals placed more than once.

★ 544 ★

Recruiting and Placement

Recruitment Methods

Table shows the strategies used by human resources professionals when recruiting new hires. Data are based on a survey of more than 475 human resources executives.

[In percentages]

Method	Use
Help-wanted ads	89
Referrals from current employees	77
Temporary help services	63
Networking with associations	57
Employment/recruiting firms	51
College placement offices	48
Job fairs	35

Source: Rose, Robert L. "A Foot in the Door." *Wall Street Journal,* 27 February 1995, p. R7. Primary source: Olsten Corp.

Unemployment

★ 545 ★

Duration of Unemployment, by Race: 1993

Table shows the percent distribution of unemployed men and women and the duration of unemployment in various Census regions and divisions of the United States. Data are 1993 annual averages.

[In percentages]

Population group and area	Total unemployed		Duration of unemployment						
	Number (in thousands)	Percent	Less than 5 weeks	5-14 weeks	15 weeks and over	15-26 weeks	27 weeks and over	27-51 weeks	52 weeks and over
Total									
Northeast	1,848	100.0	28.9	27.9	43.2	15.8	27.4	10.5	16.8
New England	475	100.0	27.9	27.2	44.9	16.3	28.6	10.5	18.1
Middle Atlantic	1,372	100.0	29.2	28.2	42.6	15.7	26.9	10.5	16.4
Midwest	1,883	100.0	39.0	28.9	32.0	14.4	17.6	8.0	9.6
East North Central	1,414	100.0	38.4	28.7	32.9	14.4	18.5	8.0	10.5
West North Central	469	100.0	40.9	29.7	29.5	14.3	15.2	8.3	6.9
South	2,857	100.0	39.6	29.4	31.0	13.6	17.4	8.2	9.2
South Atlantic	1,436	100.0	36.9	29.6	33.5	14.5	18.9	8.5	10.4
East South Central	478	100.0	42.2	30.0	27.8	13.7	14.1	6.3	7.8
West South Central	943	100.0	42.3	28.8	28.9	12.2	16.8	8.8	8.0
West	2,202	100.0	35.6	29.0	35.5	14.9	20.6	8.4	12.2

[Continued]

★ 545 ★

Duration of Unemployment, by Race: 1993
[Continued]

Population group and area	Total unemployed		Duration of unemployment						
	Number (in thousands)	Percent	Less than 5 weeks	5-14 weeks	15 weeks and over	15-26 weeks	27 weeks and over	27-51 weeks	52 weeks and over
Mountain	430	100.0	41.9	29.9	28.2	13.9	14.3	5.7	8.5
Pacific	1,772	100.0	34.1	28.7	37.2	15.1	22.1	9.0	13.1
White									
Northeast	1,465	100.0	30.1	27.9	42.1	15.6	26.4	10.5	15.9
New England	428	100.0	28.3	27.6	44.1	16.5	27.6	10.5	17.1
Middle Atlantic	1,037	100.0	30.8	28.0	41.2	15.2	26.0	10.6	15.4
Midwest	1,446	100.0	39.1	29.1	31.8	14.8	17.0	8.3	8.7
East North Central	1,060	100.0	38.4	28.7	32.9	14.9	18.0	8.3	9.6
West North Central	386	100.0	41.3	30.0	28.7	14.4	14.3	8.0	6.3
South	1,847	100.0	40.9	29.3	29.8	13.1	16.6	8.1	8.5
South Atlantic	887	100.0	38.5	29.3	32.3	13.8	18.5	8.6	9.9
East South Central	298	100.0	43.0	29.7	27.3	13.9	13.4	6.2	7.3
West South Central	662	100.0	43.1	29.2	27.6	12.0	15.6	8.4	7.2
West	1,829	100.0	36.0	29.3	34.6	15.0	19.7	8.1	11.5
Mountain	377	100.0	41.5	30.0	28.5	14.4	14.1	5.8	8.2
Pacific	1,452	100.0	34.6	29.2	36.2	15.1	21.1	8.7	12.4
Black									
Northeast	319	100.0	23.4	28.1	48.5	16.7	31.8	10.9	20.9
New England	38	100.0	24.2	22.1	53.7	13.9	39.8	11.4	28.4
Middle Atlantic	281	100.0	23.3	28.9	47.8	17.1	30.7	10.8	19.9
Midwest	390	100.0	37.8	28.5	33.7	13.3	20.4	7.5	12.9
East North Central	320	100.0	37.8	28.8	33.4	13.2	20.2	6.9	13.4
West North Central	70	100.0	37.9	27.1	35.0	14.1	20.9	10.2	10.7
South	938	100.0	36.9	29.8	33.3	14.8	18.5	8.4	10.1
South Atlantic	516	100.0	34.5	30.0	35.5	16.3	19.2	8.2	11.0
East South Central	178	100.0	40.6	30.7	28.8	13.6	15.1	6.6	8.5
West South Central	244	100.0	39.4	28.7	31.9	12.6	19.4	10.1	9.3
West	163	100.0	31.5	25.6	42.9	15.1	27.8	10.1	17.7
Pacific	137	100.0	29.1	25.8	45.1	15.5	29.6	10.7	19.0
Hispanic origin									
Northeast	190	100.0	28.0	27.0	45.0	17.3	27.7	10.6	17.1
Middle Atlantic	164	100.0	27.2	27.7	45.1	18.0	27.1	11.0	16.1
Midwest	62	100.0	42.3	29.5	28.3	15.5	12.8	8.3	4.5
East North Central	50	100.0	43.8	28.3	27.9	13.9	14.0	9.1	4.9
South	298	100.0	46.1	26.8	27.1	13.2	13.8	6.5	7.3
South Atlantic	104	100.0	38.8	29.3	31.9	14.7	17.2	8.1	9.1
West South Central	192	100.0	50.2	25.5	24.4	12.5	11.9	5.7	6.2
West	564	100.0	38.3	29.0	32.7	14.5	18.2	7.8	10.4

[Continued]

★ 545 ★

Duration of Unemployment, by Race: 1993

[Continued]

Population group and area	Total unemployed		Duration of unemployment						
	Number (in thousands)	Percent	Less than 5 weeks	5-14 weeks	15 weeks and over	15-26 weeks	27 weeks and over	27-51 weeks	52 weeks and over
Mountain	75	100.0	44.1	29.0	26.9	11.7	15.1	7.3	7.8
Pacific	489	100.0	37.4	29.0	33.6	15.0	18.6	7.8	10.8

Source: U.S. Department of Labor. Bureau of Labor Statistics. *Geographic Profile of Employment and Unemployment, 1993.* Bulletin 2446. Washington, DC: U.S. Government Printing Office, September 1994, pp. 33-34. *Notes:* East North Central region includes Illinois, Indiana, Ohio, Michigan, Wisconsin. East South Central region includes Alabama, Kentucky, Mississippi, Tennessee. Middle Atlantic region includes New Jersey, New York, Pennsylvania. Mountain region includes Arizona, Colorado, Idaho, Montana, Nevada, New Mexico, Utah, Wyoming. New England region includes Connecticut, Maine, Massachusetts, New Hampshire, Rhode Island, Vermont. Pacific region includes Alaska, California, Hawaii, Oregon, Washington. South Atlantic region includes Delaware, District of Columbia, Florida, Georgia, Maryland, North Carolina, South Carolina, Virginia, West Virginia. West North Central region includes Iowa, Kansas, Minnesota, Missouri, Nebraska, North Dakota, South Dakota. West South Central region includes Arkansas, Louisiana, Oklahoma, Texas. Data for demographic groups are not shown when they do not meet Bureau of Labor Statistics publication standards of reliability for the particular area based on the sample in that area. Items may not add to totals or compute to displayed percentages because of rounding. Detail for race and Hispanic origin groups will not add totals because data for the "other races" group are not presented and because Hispanics are included in both the white and black population groups.

★ 546 ★

Unemployment

Duration of Unemployment, by Sex and Region: 1993

Table shows the percent distribution of unemployed men and women and the duration of unemployment in various Census regions and divisions of the United States. Data are 1993 annual averages.

[In percentages]

Population group and area	Total unemployed		Duration of unemployment						
	Number (in thousands)	Percent	Less than 5 weeks	5-14 weeks	15 weeks and over	15-26 weeks	27 weeks and over	27-51 weeks	52 weeks and over
Total									
Northeast	1,848	100.0	28.9	27.9	43.2	15.8	27.4	10.5	16.8
New England	475	100.0	27.9	27.2	44.9	16.3	28.6	10.5	18.1
Middle Atlantic	1,372	100.0	29.2	28.2	42.6	15.7	26.9	10.5	16.4
Midwest	1,883	100.0	39.0	28.9	32.0	14.4	17.6	8.0	9.6
East North Central	1,414	100.0	38.4	28.7	32.9	14.4	18.5	8.0	10.5
West North Central	469	100.0	40.9	29.7	29.5	14.3	15.2	8.3	6.9
South	2,857	100.0	39.6	29.4	31.0	13.6	17.4	8.2	9.2
South Atlantic	1,436	100.0	36.9	29.6	33.5	14.5	18.9	8.5	10.4
East South Central	478	100.0	42.2	30.0	27.8	13.7	14.1	6.3	7.8
West South Central	943	100.0	42.3	28.8	28.9	12.2	16.8	8.8	8.0
West	2,202	100.0	35.6	29.0	35.5	14.9	20.6	8.4	12.2
Mountain	430	100.0	41.9	29.9	28.2	13.9	14.3	5.7	8.5
Pacific	1,772	100.0	34.1	28.7	37.2	15.1	22.1	9.0	13.1
Men									
Northeast	1,104	100.0	26.3	27.7	46.0	16.8	29.2	10.7	18.5
New England	292	100.0	25.5	26.8	47.7	17.3	30.4	11.0	19.5
Middle Atlantic	812	100.0	26.5	28.0	45.4	16.7	28.7	10.6	18.1
Midwest	1,046	100.0	35.7	29.0	35.3	15.3	20.0	8.7	11.3
East North Central	798	100.0	35.6	28.4	36.0	14.8	21.2	8.8	12.4

[Continued]

★ 546 ★

Duration of Unemployment, by Sex and Region: 1993
[Continued]

Population group and area	Total unemployed		Duration of unemployment						
	Number (in thousands)	Percent	Less than 5 weeks	5-14 weeks	15 weeks and over	15-26 weeks	27 weeks and over	27-51 weeks	52 weeks and over
West North Central	248	100.0	36.0	30.8	33.1	16.7	16.4	8.6	7.8
South	1,521	100.0	36.5	28.5	35.0	15.1	19.9	8.9	11.0
South Atlantic	771	100.0	32.7	29.1	38.2	16.1	22.1	9.2	12.8
East South Central	242	100.0	38.6	29.1	32.2	16.7	15.6	7.0	8.6
West South Central	508	100.0	41.1	27.4	31.5	12.8	18.7	9.3	9.4
West	1,293	100.0	32.3	29.4	38.3	15.4	22.9	8.9	14.0
Mountain	246	100.0	38.8	29.8	31.4	14.8	16.5	5.9	10.7
Pacific	1,048	100.0	30.7	29.3	40.0	15.6	24.4	9.6	14.8
Women									
Northeast	744	100.0	32.8	28.2	39.0	14.4	24.7	10.3	14.4
New England	184	100.0	31.8	27.8	40.4	14.7	25.7	9.8	16.0
Middle Atlantic	560	100.0	33.1	28.3	38.6	14.3	24.3	10.5	13.9
Midwest	837	100.0	43.1	28.9	28.0	13.3	14.7	7.2	7.5
East North Central	616	100.0	42.0	29.1	28.9	14.0	15.0	6.9	8.1
West North Central	221	100.0	46.3	28.3	25.4	11.6	13.8	8.0	5.8
South	1,336	100.0	43.1	30.4	26.5	12.0	14.5	7.4	7.1
South Atlantic	664	100.0	41.9	30.2	28.0	12.7	15.3	7.6	7.7
East South Central	236	100.0	45.9	30.9	23.3	10.8	12.5	5.6	6.9
West South Central	435	100.0	43.6	30.4	26.0	11.5	14.5	8.1	6.4
West	909	100.0	40.3	28.3	31.4	14.1	17.2	7.6	9.6
Mountain	185	100.0	45.9	30.0	24.0	12.7	11.3	5.6	5.7
Pacific	724	100.0	38.9	27.9	33.2	14.5	18.8	8.2	10.6

Source: U.S. Department of Labor. Bureau of Labor Statistics. *Geographic Profile of Employment and Unemployment, 1993.* Bulletin 2446. Washington, DC: U.S. Government Printing Office, September 1994, p. 33. *Notes:* East North Central region includes Illinois, Indiana, Ohio, Michigan, Wisconsin. East South Central region includes Alabama, Kentucky, Mississippi, Tennessee. Middle Atlantic region includes New Jersey, New York, Pennsylvania. Mountain region includes Arizona, Colorado, Idaho, Montana, Nevada, New Mexico, Utah, Wyoming. New England region includes Connecticut, Maine, Massachusetts, New Hampshire, Rhode Island, Vermont. Pacific region includes Alaska, California, Hawaii, Oregon, Washington. South Atlantic region includes Delaware, District of Columbia, Florida, Georgia, Maryland, North Carolina, South Carolina, Virginia, West Virginia. West North Central region includes Iowa, Kansas, Minnesota, Missouri, Nebraska, North Dakota, South Dakota. West South Central region includes Arkansas, Louisiana, Oklahoma, Texas. Data for demographic groups are not shown when they do not meet Bureau of Labor Statistics publication standards of reliability for the particular area based on the sample in that area. Items may not add to totals or compute to displayed percentages because of rounding.

★ 547 ★
Unemployment

State Unemployment Insurance: 1980-1992

Includes unemployment compensation for state and local government employees where covered by state law.

Item	Unit	1980	1984	1985	1986	1987	1988	1989	1990	1991	1992
Insured unemployment, avg. weekly	1,000	3,350	2,476	2,611	2,641	2,330	2,081	2,158	2,522	3,342	3,245
Percent of covered employment[1]	Percent	3.9	2.8	2.9	2.8	2.3	2.0	2.1	2.4	3.3	3.1
Percent of civilian unemployed	Percent	43.9	29.0	31.4	32.1	31.4	31.0	33.0	36.0	40.0	34.0
Unemployment benefits, avg. weekly	$	99	123	127	135	140	145	152	162	170	174
Percent of weekly wage	Percent	37.5	35.8	35.3	35.8	35.3	34.9	35.4	36.2	36.4	35.4
Weeks compensated	Million	149.0	111.6	119.3	121.4	105.2	94.2	97.6	116.0	155.1	150.2

[Continued]

★ 547 ★

State Unemployment Insurance: 1980-1992
[Continued]

Item	Unit	1980	1984	1985	1986	1987	1988	1989	1990	1991	1992
Beneficiaries, first payments	1,000	10,001	7,765	8,350	8,361	7,205	6,861	7,369	8,629	10,075	9,243
Average duration of benefits[2]	Weeks	14.9	14.4	14.3	14.5	14.6	13.7	13.2	13.4	15.4	16.2
Claimants exhausting benefits	1,000	3,072	2,600	2,575	2,688	2,409	1,979	1,940	2,323	3,472	3,821
Percent of first payment[3]	Percent	33.2	34.1	31.3	32.1	30.6	28.5	28.0	29.4	34.8	39.7
Contributions collected[4]	Billion $	11.4	18.8	19.3	18.1	17.6	17.7	16.5	15.2	14.5	16.9
Benefits paid	Billion $	13.8	12.6	14.0	15.4	14.2	13.2	14.3	18.1	25.4	25.2
Funds available for benefits[5]	Billion $	11.4	11.6	16.0	19.6	23.2	31.1	37.5	38.4	31.9	27.9
Average employer contribution rate[6]	Percent	2.5	3.2	3.1	2.7	2.6	2.5	2.2	2.0	2.1	2.3

Source: U.S. Bureau of the Census. *Statistical Abstract of the United States, 1994.* 114th ed. Washington, DC: U.S. Government Printing Office, 1994, p. 380. Primary source: U.S. Employment and Training Administration. *Unemployment Insurance Data Summary* (annual). *Notes:* 1. Insured unemployment as percent of average covered employment in preceding year. 2. Weeks compensated divided by first payment. 3. Based on first payments for 12-month period ending June 30. 4. Contributions from employers; also employees in states which tax workers. 5. End of year. Sum of balances in state clearing accounts, benefit-payment accounts, and state accounts in federal unemployment trust funds. 6. As percent of taxable wages.

★ 548 ★

Unemployment

State Unemployment Insurance, by State and Other Areas: 1992

Includes unemployment compensation for state and local government employees where covered by state law.

State or area	Beneficiaries, first payments (1,000)	Benefits paid (million $)	Average weekly unemployment benefits ($)
Total	9,243	25,153	174
Alabama	157	209	121
Alaska	44	117	170
Arizona	90	211	147
Arkansas	100	185	151
California	1,444	3,852	152
Colorado	79	179	178
Connecticut	157	587	211
Delaware	29	72	181
District of Columbia	27	128	228
Florida	339	861	158
Georgia	232	381	148
Hawaii	39	138	240
Idaho	46	84	156
Illinois	391	1,339	183
Indiana	150	217	126
Iowa	89	195	170
Kansas	71	189	179
Kentucky	127	228	144
Louisiana	110	210	118

[Continued]

★ 548 ★

State Unemployment Insurance, by State and Other Areas: 1992

[Continued]

State or area	Beneficiaries, first payments (1,000)	Benefits paid (million $)	Average weekly unemployment benefits ($)
Maine	59	146	167
Maryland	145	461	180
Massachusetts	249	1,036	226
Michigan	487	1,288	211
Minnesota	134	409	198
Mississippi	79	129	123
Missouri	184	380	146
Montana	25	45	135
Nebraska	33	50	133
Nevada	60	155	168
New Hampshire	40	61	136
New Jersey	340	1,429	225
New Mexico	32	73	138
New York	673	2,635	197
North Carolina	244	378	158
North Dakota	15	30	146
Ohio	357	972	180
Oklahoma	66	148	159
Oregon	142	382	172
Pennsylvania	518	1,751	201
Rhode Island	61	196	206
South Carolina	125	215	143
South Dakota	9	12	128
Tennessee	190	289	124
Texas	430	1,181	176
Utah	38	82	174
Vermont	26	66	155
Virginia	138	288	164
Washington	219	661	176
West Virginia	61	148	163
Wisconsin	216	463	175
Wyoming	12	29	163
Puerto Rico	113	179	84
Virgin Islands	3	6	161

Source: U.S. Bureau of the Census. *Statistical Abstract of the United States, 1994.* 114th ed. Washington, DC: U.S. Government Printing Office, 1994, p. 380. Primary source: U.S. Employment and Training Administration. *Unemployment Insurance Data Summary* (annual).

★ 549 ★

Unemployment

Unemployed and Insured Unemployed, by State: 1980-1992

For civilian noninstitutional population 16 years old and over. Annual averages of monthly figures. Total unemployment estimates based on the Current Population Survey (CPS). U.S. totals derived by independent population controls; therefore state data may not add to U.S. totals.

| Division and state | Total unemployed | | | | | | | | Insured unemployed[2] | | | |
| | Number (1,000) | | | | Percent[1] | | | | Number (1,000) | | Percent[3] | |
	1980	1985	1990	1992	1980	1985	1990	1992	1991	1992	1991	1992
United States	7,637	8,312	6,874	9,384	7.1	7.2	5.5	7.4	3,342[4]	3,245[4]	3.1[4]	3.2[4]
Alabama	147	160	127	143	8.8	8.9	6.8	7.3	41.7	38.8	2.5	2.5
Alaska	18	24	19	26	9.7	9.7	6.9	9.1	13.2	13.9	6.4	6.4
Arizona	83	96	96	135	6.7	6.5	5.3	7.4	34.1	34.2	2.3	2.3
Arkansas	76	91	77	83	7.6	8.7	6.9	7.2	31.7	31.5	3.6	3.6
California	790	931	850	1,393	6.8	7.2	5.6	9.1	528.4	552.5	4.5	4.5
Colorado	88	101	87	108	5.9	5.9	4.9	5.9	26.2	26.4	1.8	1.8
Connecticut	94	83	93	137	5.9	4.9	5.1	7.5	61.0	57.3	3.8	3.8
Delaware	22	17	18	19	7.7	5.3	5.1	5.3	7.8	7.9	2.3	2.3
District of Columbia	24	27	21	26	7.3	8.4	6.6	8.4	12.0	11.0	2.5	3.2
Florida	251	319	384	533	5.9	6.0	5.9	8.2	120.8	127.0	2.4	2.4
Georgia	163	187	179	232	6.4	6.5	5.4	6.9	66.3	56.4	2.0	2.0
Hawaii	21	27	15	26	4.9	5.6	2.8	4.5	7.9	11.6	2.3	2.3
Idaho	34	37	29	34	7.9	7.9	5.8	6.5	14.0	14.3	3.7	3.7
Illinois	458	513	363	451	8.3	9.0	6.2	7.5	156.5	156.0	3.1	3.1
Indiana	252	215	147	185	9.6	7.9	5.3	6.5	46.9	42.3	1.9	1.8
Iowa	82	113	61	70	5.8	8.0	4.2	4.6	24.9	24.8	2.1	2.1
Kansas	53	62	56	55	4.5	5.0	4.4	4.2	22.9	22.7	2.2	2.2
Kentucky	133	161	102	122	8.0	9.5	5.8	6.9	40.6	33.9	2.5	2.5
Louisiana	121	229	114	156	6.7	11.5	6.2	8.1	35.2	40.9	2.7	2.7
Maine	39	30	32	46	7.8	5.4	5.1	7.1	25.7	19.3	5.0	4.0
Maryland	140	103	121	176	6.5	4.6	4.6	6.6	63.5	59.9	3.1	3.1
Massachusetts	162	121	193	267	5.6	3.9	6.0	8.5	127.3	100.8	4.4	3.7
Michigan	534	433	345	408	12.4	9.9	7.1	8.8	154.9	133.7	4.0	3.6
Minnesota	125	133	115	124	5.9	6.0	4.8	5.1	48.0	44.2	2.2	2.2
Mississippi	79	115	88	97	7.5	10.3	7.5	8.1	28.2	27.3	3.1	3.1
Missouri	167	159	149	151	7.2	6.4	5.7	5.7	66.1	61.7	2.8	2.8
Montana	23	31	23	28	6.1	7.7	5.8	6.7	8.7	8.8	3.1	3.1
Nebraska	31	44	18	25	4.1	5.5	2.2	3.0	9.1	9.3	1.3	1.3
Nevada	27	41	33	47	6.2	8.0	4.9	6.6	20.2	20.2	3.3	3.3
New Hampshire	22	21	35	46	4.7	3.9	5.6	7.5	14.7	10.7	3.0	2.3
New Jersey	259	218	202	337	7.2	5.7	5.0	8.4	135.6	131.7	3.9	3.9
New Mexico	42	57	44	51	7.5	8.8	6.3	6.8	12.9	13.5	2.5	2.5
New York	597	544	458	734	7.5	6.5	5.2	8.5	292.6	281.2	3.7	3.7
North Carolina	187	167	141	210	6.6	5.4	4.1	5.9	80.3	60.8	2.0	2.0
North Dakota	15	20	12	15	5.0	5.9	3.9	4.9	4.6	4.7	2.0	2.0
Ohio	426	455	305	397	8.4	8.9	5.7	7.2	132.1	127.5	2.8	2.8
Oklahoma	66	112	84	86	4.8	7.1	5.6	5.7	20.8	22.8	2.0	2.0
Oregon	108	117	82	116	8.3	8.8	5.5	7.5	50.5	51.1	4.3	4.3
Pennsylvania	425	442	311	442	7.8	8.0	5.4	7.5	199.2	195.5	4.1	4.1
Rhode Island	34	25	35	46	7.2	4.9	6.7	8.9	23.9	20.5	5.5	5.0
South Carolina	96	107	82	112	6.9	6.8	4.7	6.2	41.0	37.6	2.6	2.6
South Dakota	16	18	13	11	4.9	5.1	3.7	3.1	2.4	2.6	0.9	0.9

[Continued]

★ 549 ★

Unemployed and Insured Unemployed, by State: 1980-1992
[Continued]

Division and state	Total unemployed								Insured unemployed[2]			
	Number (1,000)				Percent[1]				Number (1,000)		Percent[3]	
	1980	1985	1990	1992	1980	1985	1990	1992	1991	1992	1991	1992
Tennessee	152	180	124	156	7.3	8.0	5.2	6.4	63.0	55.4	2.7	2.7
Texas	352	564	531	675	5.2	7.0	6.2	7.5	135.8	152.3	2.2	2.2
Utah	40	43	35	42	6.3	5.9	4.3	4.9	10.3	10.7	1.6	1.6
Vermont	16	13	15	21	6.4	4.8	5.0	6.6	10.6	9.5	4.3	4.0
Virginia	128	161	138	216	5.0	5.6	4.3	6.4	45.3	41.8	1.6	1.6
Washington	157	171	124	198	7.9	8.1	4.9	7.5	80.3	83.9	4.0	4.0
West Virginia	74	100	63	87	9.4	13.0	8.3	11.3	22.9	21.4	3.7	3.7
Wisconsin	167	171	113	135	7.2	7.2	4.4	5.1	65.2	62.0	2.8	2.8
Wyoming	9	18	13	13	4.0	7.1	5.4	5.6	3.7	4.2	2.3	2.3

Source: U.S. Bureau of the Census. Statistical Abstract of the United States, 1994. 114th ed. Washington, DC: U.S. Government Printing Office, 1994, p. 419. Primary source, except as noted: U.S. Bureau of Labor Statistics. Geographic Profile of Employment and Unemployment (annual). Notes: 1. Total unemployment as percent of civilian labor force. 2. Source: U.S. Employment and Training Administration. Unemployment Insurance, Financial Data (annual updates). 3. Insured unemployment as percent of average covered employment in the previous year. 4. Includes 50,400 in Puerto Rico and the Virgin Islands in 1991 and 55,100 in 1992.

★ 550 ★

Unemployment

Unemployed, by Sex and Reason: 1970-1993

For civilian noninstitutional population 16 years old and over. Annual averages of monthly figures.

[In thousands]

Unemployed	1970	1980	1984	1985	1986	1987	1988	1989	1990	1991	1992	1993
Male, total	2,238	4,267	4,744	4,521	4,530	4,101	3,655	3,525	3,799	4,817	5,380	4,932
Job losers	1,199	2,649	2,976	2,749	2,725	2,432	2,078	1,975	2,208	3,105	3,518	3,091
Job leavers	282	438	375	409	520	494	503	495	511	492	479	490
Reentrants	533	776	867	876	805	761	697	726	782	865	950	914
New entrants	224	405	526	487	480	413	376	328	298	356	433	437
Female, total	1,855	3,370	3,794	3,791	3,707	3,324	3,046	3,003	3,075	3,609	4,005	3,801
Job losers	614	1,297	1,445	1,390	1,308	1,134	1,014	1,008	1,114	1,503	1,773	1,677
Job leavers	267	453	449	468	494	471	480	529	503	487	496	456
Reentrants	696	1,152	1,317	1,380	1,355	1,213	1,112	1,117	1,101	1,222	1,278	1,230
New entrants	279	468	584	552	549	506	440	349	357	398	457	438

Source: U.S. Bureau of the Census. Statistical Abstract of the United States, 1994. 114th ed. Washington, DC: U.S. Government Printing Office, 1994, p. 417. Primary sources: U.S. Bureau of Labor Statistics. Employment and Earnings (monthly; January issues); Bulletin 2307; and unpublished data.

★ 551 ★

Unemployment

Unemployed Workers: 1980-1993

For civilian noninstitutional population 16 years old and over. Annual averages of monthly figures.

[In thousands, except as indicated]

Age, type of worker, and length of unemployment	1980	1985	1988	1989	1990	1991	1992	1993
				Unemployed				
Total	7,637	8,312	6,701	6,528	6,874	8,426	9,384	8,734
16 to 19 years old	1,669	1,468	1,226	1,194	1,149	1,290	1,352	1,296
20 to 24 years old	1,835	1,738	1,261	1,218	1,221	1,477	1,546	1,421
25 to 44 years old	2,964	3,681	3,095	3,010	3,273	4,106	4,603	4,220
45 to 64 years old	1,075	1,331	1,032	1,016	1,124	1,437	1,748	1,686
65 years and over	94	93	87	91	107	116	135	111
Full-time workers	6,269	6,793	5,357	5,211	5,541	6,932	7,746	7,146
Part-time workers	1,369	1,519	1,343	1,317	1,332	1,494	1,638	1,588
				Unemployment rate (percent)[1]				
Total	7.1	7.2	5.5	5.3	5.5	6.7	7.4	6.8
16 to 19 years old	17.8	18.6	15.3	15.0	15.5	18.6	20.0	19.0
20 to 24 years old	11.5	11.1	8.7	8.6	8.8	10.8	11.3	10.5
25 to 44 years old	6.0	6.2	4.8	4.5	4.8	6.0	6.7	6.1
45 to 64 years old	3.7	4.5	3.3	3.2	3.5	4.4	5.1	4.8
65 years and over	3.1	3.2	2.7	2.6	3.0	3.3	3.8	3.2
Experienced workers[2]	6.9	6.8	5.2	5.0	5.3	6.5	7.1	6.5
				Duration of unemployment				
Percent without work for –								
Less than 5 weeks	43.1	42.1	46.0	48.6	46.1	40.1	34.8	36.2
5 to 10 weeks	23.4	22.2	22.2	22.2	23.5	22.9	20.9	20.6
11 to 14 weeks	9.0	8.0	7.8	8.1	8.6	9.5	8.5	8.3
15 to 26 weeks	13.8	12.3	12.0	11.2	11.8	14.5	15.2	14.6
27 weeks and over	10.7	15.4	12.1	9.9	10.1	13.0	20.6	20.4
Average unemployment duration (weeks)	11.9	15.6	13.5	11.9	12.1	13.8	17.9	18.1

Source: U.S. Bureau of the Census. *Statistical Abstract of the United States, 1994.* 114th ed. Washington, DC: U.S. Government Printing Office, 1994, p. 416. Primary sources: U.S. Bureau of Labor Statistics. *Employment and Earnings* (monthly; January issues); and unpublished data. *Notes:* 1. Unemployed as percent of civilian labor force in specified group. 2. Wage and salary workers.

★ 552 ★
Unemployment

Unemployment, by Educational Attainment: 1992-1993

Annual averages of monthly figures for civilian noninstitutional population 25 years old and over. Based on Current Population Survey.

Year and characteristics	Unemployed (1,000)					Unemployment rate[1]				
	Total	Less than high school diploma	High school graduates, no degree	Less than bachelor's degree	College graduate	Total	Less than high school diploma	High school graduates, no degree	Less than bachelor's degree	College graduate
Total:[2]										
1992	6,491	1,502	2,577	1,519	893	6.1	11.4	6.8	5.6	3.2
1993	6,017	1,328	2,354	1,480	855	5.6	10.7	6.2	5.2	2.9
Male										
1992	3,735	922	1,454	825	533	6.4	11.4	7.3	5.9	3.3
1993	3,396	817	1,320	773	485	5.8	10.7	6.6	5.3	2.9
Female										
1992	2,756	580	1,123	694	360	5.7	11.4	6.2	5.3	3.0
1993	2,621	510	1,035	707	370	5.4	10.9	5.8	5.1	3.0
White										
1992	4,982	1,126	1,936	1,168	751	5.5	10.7	6.0	5.0	3.0
1993	4,612	975	1,791	1,136	711	5.0	9.8	5.5	4.7	2.8
Black										
1992	1,246	318	555	294	79	10.9	15.1	12.3	9.8	4.4
1993	1,124	285	485	281	73	9.8	15.2	10.8	8.7	3.8
Hispanic[3]										
1992	781	400	213	122	46	9.8	12.8	9.0	7.7	5.0
1993	740	377	202	123	38	9.0	12.1	8.4	7.0	3.9

Source: U.S. Bureau of the Census. *Statistical Abstract of the United States, 1994.* 114th ed. Washington, DC: U.S. Government Printing Office, 1994, p. 418. Primary source: U.S. Bureau of Labor Statistics. Unpublished data. *Notes:* 1. Percent unemployed of the civilian labor force. 2. Includes other races not shown separately. 3. Persons of Hispanic origin may be of any race.

★ 553 ★

Unemployment

Unemployment Measures: 1970-1992

Table shows the range of unemployment measures based on varying definitions of unemployment and the labor force. Annual averages of monthly figures. Based on Current Population Survey.

[In percentages]

Measure	1970	1975	1980	1985	1986	1987	1988	1989	1990	1991	1992
Persons unemployed 15 weeks or longer as a percent of the civilian labor force	0.8	2.7	1.7	2.0	1.9	1.7	1.3	1.1	1.2	1.9	2.6
Job losers as a percent of the civilian labor force	2.2	4.7	3.7	3.6	3.4	3.0	2.5	2.4	2.7	3.7	4.2
Unemployed persons 25 years and over as a percent of the 25 and over civilian labor force	3.3	6.0	5.1	5.6	5.4	4.8	4.3	4.0	4.4	5.4	6.1
Unemployed full-time jobseekers as a percent of the full-time civilian labor force	4.5	8.1	6.9	6.8	6.6	5.8	5.2	4.9	5.2	6.5	7.1
Total unemployed as a percent of the labor force, including the resident Armed Forces[1]	4.8	8.3	7.0	7.1	6.9	6.1	5.4	5.2	5.4	6.6	7.3
Total unemployed as a percent of the civilian labor force[1]	4.9	8.5	7.1	7.2	7.0	6.2	5.5	5.3	5.5	6.7	7.4
Total full-time jobseekers plus 1/2 part-time jobseekers plus 1/2 total on part-time for economic reasons as a percent of the civilian labor force less 1/2 of the part-time labor force	6.3	10.5	9.2	9.6	9.4	8.5	7.6	7.2	7.6	9.2	10.0
Total full-time jobseekers plus 1/2 part-time jobseekers plus 1/2 total on part-time for economic reasons plus discouraged workers as a percent of the civilian labor force plus discouraged workers less 1/2 of the part-time labor force	7.1	11.6	10.1	10.6	10.3	9.3	8.4	7.9	8.2	10.0	10.8

Source: U.S. Bureau of the Census. *Statistical Abstract of the United States, 1993.* 113th ed. Washington, DC: U.S. Government Printing Office, 1993, p. 415. Primary sources: U.S. Bureau of Labor Statistics. Bulletin 2307; and unpublished data. *Note:* 1. Current unemployment rate definition.

★ 554 ★

Unemployment

Unemployment Rates, by Educational Attainment, Sex, and Race: 1970-1991

As of March, except as indicated. Civilian noninstitutional population 25 to 64 years of age. Due to a change in the method of reporting educational attainment, 1992 data are not comparable with data for earlier years. See separate table for 1992-1993 data. Based on the Current Population Survey.

[In percentages]

Item	1970	1975	1980	1984	1985	1986	1987	1988	1989	1990[1]	1991[1]
Total	3.3	6.9	5.0	6.6	6.1	6.1	5.7	4.7	4.4	4.4	5.5
Less than 4 years of high school[2]	4.6	10.7	8.4	12.1	11.4	11.6	11.1	9.6	9.1	8.5	11.0
4 years of high school, only	2.9	6.9	5.1	7.2	6.9	6.9	6.3	5.4	4.8	4.9	5.9
College: 1-3 years	2.9	5.5	4.3	5.3	4.7	4.7	4.5	3.7	3.4	3.7	4.8
4 years or more	1.3	2.5	1.9	2.7	2.4	2.3	2.3	1.7	2.2	2.2	2.8
Male:											
Total	2.9	6.7	4.9	6.9	6.1	6.2	6.0	5.1	4.7	4.4	5.8
Less than 4 years of high school[2]	4.0	10.5	8.2	12.3	11.2	11.7	11.2	10.1	9.7	8.2	11.0

[Continued]

493

★ 554 ★

Unemployment Rates, by Educational Attainment, Sex, and Race: 1970-1991
[Continued]

Item	1970	1975	1980	1984	1985	1986	1987	1988	1989	1990[1]	1991[1]
4 years of high school, only	2.4	6.7	5.3	8.1	7.2	7.4	6.7	6.2	5.4	5.1	6.4
College: 1-3 years	2.7	5.1	4.4	5.2	4.5	4.7	5.0	3.9	3.2	3.7	4.9
4 years or more	1.1	2.2	1.7	2.7	2.4	2.3	2.5	1.6	2.3	2.1	2.8
Female:											
Total	4.0	7.4	5.0	6.1	6.0	5.8	5.2	4.2	4.0	4.4	5.2
Less than 4 years of high school[2]	5.7	10.5	8.9	11.7	11.7	11.4	10.9	8.9	8.4	9.0	10.9
4 years of high school, only	3.6	7.1	5.0	6.3	6.5	6.3	5.8	4.6	4.2	4.6	5.4
College: 1-3 years	3.1	6.3	4.1	5.3	4.8	4.8	4.0	3.4	3.7	3.7	4.7
4 years or more	1.9	3.4	2.2	2.7	2.5	2.4	2.1	1.9	2.0	2.3	2.8
White:											
Total	3.1	6.5	4.4	5.7	5.3	5.5	5.0	4.0	3.8	3.8	5.0
Less than 4 years of high school[2]	4.5	10.1	7.8	10.9	10.6	10.9	10.2	8.3	7.4	7.6	10.3
4 years of high school, only	2.7	6.5	4.6	6.4	6.1	6.2	5.5	4.6	4.2	4.2	5.4
College: 1-3 years	2.8	5.1	3.9	4.6	3.9	4.2	4.1	3.2	3.0	3.2	4.2
4 years or more	1.3	2.4	1.8	2.4	2.1	2.2	2.2	1.5	2.0	2.1	2.7
Black:											
Total[3]	4.7	10.9	9.6	13.3	12.0	10.7	10.6	10.0	9.2	8.6	9.6
Less than 4 years of high school[2]	5.2	13.5	11.7	17.4	15.3	15.3	14.8	15.7	15.9	13.3	14.7
4 years of high school, only	5.2	10.7	9.5	14.5	13.0	11.7	11.7	11.2	9.2	9.5	9.9
College: 1-3 years	3.5	9.8	9.0	9.7	10.6	8.7	7.6	7.4	6.9	6.8	8.8
4 years or more	0.9	3.9	4.0	6.2	5.4	3.2	4.2	3.3	4.7	3.0	4.1

Source: U.S. Bureau of the Census. *Statistical Abstract of the United States, 1994.* 114th ed. Washington, DC: U.S. Government Printing Office, 1994, p. 418. Primary sources: U.S. Bureau of Labor Statistics. Bulletin 2307; and unpublished data. *Notes:* 1. Not strictly comparable with data for earlier years. Annual averages of monthly figures. 2. Includes persons reporting no school years completed. 3. For 1970 and 1975, data refer to black and other workers.

Work Hours and Schedules

★ 555 ★

Flexible Schedules, by Worker Characteristics: 1985 and 1991

As of May. For employed persons 16 years old and over who usually work full-time and who were at work during the survey reference week. A flexible schedule allows workers to vary the time they begin and end their work days. Based on Current Population Survey.

[In thousands, except percentages]

Characteristic	All workers			Workers with flexible schedules					
				Number			Percent		
	Total	Male	Female	Total	Male	Female	Total	Male	Female
Total, 1985	73,395	43,779	29,616	9,061	5,760	3,300	12.3	13.2	11.1
Total, 1991	80,452	46,308	34,145	12,118	7,168	4,950	15.1	15.5	14.5
Age:									
16 to 19 years	1,413	855	558	150	82	67	10.6	9.6	12.0
20 to 24 years	8,332	4,694	3,638	999	542	456	12.0	11.5	12.5
25 to 34 years	25,523	14,917	10,606	4,008	2,358	1,650	15.7	15.8	15.6
35 to 44 years	22,749	13,001	9,749	3,744	2,213	1,531	16.5	17.0	15.7
45 to 54 years	14,306	8,003	6,302	2,184	1,299	885	15.3	16.2	14.0
55 to 64 years	7,197	4,286	2,910	880	574	306	12.2	13.4	10.5
65 years and over	933	552	382	153	99	54	16.4	17.9	14.1
Race:									
White	68,795	40,267	28,528	10,630	6,416	4,214	15.5	15.9	14.8
Black	8,943	4,522	4,421	1,083	525	558	12.1	11.6	12.6
Hispanic[1]	6,598	4,172	2,425	702	427	275	10.6	10.2	11.3
Marital status:									
Single	18,420	10,621	7,799	2,887	1,606	1,281	15.7	15.1	16.4
Married, spouse present	49,101	30,510	18,591	7,195	4,794	2,401	14.7	15.7	12.9
Other	12,932	5,177	7,755	2,035	768	1,267	15.7	14.8	16.3

Source: U.S. Bureau of the Census. *Statistical Abstract of the United States, 1994.* 114th ed. Washington, DC: U.S. Government Printing Office, 1994, p. 405. Primary sources: U.S. Bureau of Labor Statistics. *News.* USDL 92-491 (4 August 1992); and unpublished data. *Note:* 1. Persons of Hispanic origin may be of any race.

★ 556 ★

Work Hours and Schedules

Hours of Work, by Race/Ethnicity: 1993

Table shows the hours of work for men and women in various Census regions and divisions of the United States. Data are 1993 annual averages.

[In thousands, except average hours]

Area	Total at work	\multicolumn{6}{c}{Hours of work}						\multicolumn{2}{c}{Average hours}	
		1 to 14	15 to 29	30 to 34	35 or more hours					Total	Full-time schedules[1]
					Total	35 to 39	40	41 to 48	49 or more		
\multicolumn{12}{c}{Total}											
Northeast	22,457	1,068	2,939	1,639	16,811	2,107	8,565	2,117	4,022	38.6	46.4
New England	6,212	319	843	533	4,517	492	2,191	627	1,207	38.6	47.2
Middle Atlantic	16,245	749	2,096	1,105	12,294	1,615	6,373	1,491	2,815	38.6	46.1
Midwest	28,002	1,504	3,431	2,085	20,982	1,622	9,957	3,230	6,173	39.7	47.7
East North Central	19,356	982	2,354	1,395	14,625	1,130	7,144	2,238	4,114	39.6	47.3
West North Central	8,646	522	1,077	690	6,357	492	2,814	992	2,059	39.9	48.8
South	39,308	1,604	4,465	2,922	30,318	2,390	15,770	4,035	8,123	40.0	47.2
South Atlantic	20,501	814	2,306	1,561	15,821	1,283	8,364	2,041	4,132	39.9	47.1
East South Central	6,668	271	775	495	5,127	434	2,677	697	1,319	39.8	47.0
West South Central	12,139	519	1,384	866	9,370	674	4,728	1,296	2,672	40.3	47.5
West	24,256	1,172	3,105	2,086	17,892	1,294	9,535	2,295	4,768	39.0	47.2
Mountain	6,588	340	857	565	4,826	359	2,363	687	1,416	39.4	48.1
Pacific	17,668	832	2,249	1,521	13,066	935	7,172	1,,608	3,352	38.9	46.9
\multicolumn{12}{c}{White}											
Northeast	19,768	994	2,646	1,477	14,652	1,736	7,271	1,949	3,696	38.6	46.7
New England	5,852	307	799	503	4,245	467	2,018	600	1,161	38.6	47.3
Middle Atlantic	13,916	687	1,847	975	10,407	1,270	5,253	1,349	2,535	38.6	46.5
Midwest	25,454	1,401	3,114	1,889	19,050	1,461	8,718	3,026	5,846	39.9	48.0
East North Central	17,284	901	2,098	1,242	13,044	997	6,129	2,068	3,850	39.8	47.5
West North Central	8,170	499	1,016	648	6,006	464	2,588	958	1,997	40.1	49.0
South	31,805	1,326	3,559	2,315	24,605	1,862	12,116	3,475	7,152	40.3	47.6
South Atlantic	15,987	654	1,788	1,194	12,352	965	6,116	1,715	3,556	40.2	47.5
East South Central	5,485	223	625	389	4,248	345	2,116	610	1,177	40.2	47.3
West South Central	10,333	449	1,147	733	8,004	552	3,883	1,149	2,419	40.6	47.9
West	21,170	1,048	2,724	1,831	15,567	1,154	8,016	2,082	4,315	39.1	47.4
Mountain	6,187	325	807	527	4,528	334	2,172	659	1,363	39.5	48.3
Pacific	14,983	723	1,917	1,304	11,039	820	5,844	1,422	2,953	39.0	47.1
\multicolumn{12}{c}{Black}											
Northeast	2,013	49	225	125	1,614	300	995	113	206	38.2	43.8
New England	249	7	31	23	189	19	122	18	31	38.2	45.4
Middle Atlantic	1,763	42	195	102	1,425	281	873	96	175	38.2	43.6
Midwest	2,063	78	253	167	1,565	138	1,025	162	241	38.1	44.9
East North Central	1,732	64	210	135	1,322	119	866	138	200	38.1	44.9
West North Central	331	14	43	32	242	19	159	24	41	37.8	45.3
South	6,633	247	797	546	5,044	479	3,276	480	808	38.3	45.2
South Atlantic	4,067	143	462	333	3,129	292	2,053	290	494	38.5	45.2
East South Central	1,131	47	144	102	838	86	542	80	129	37.7	45.3
West South Central	1,435	56	191	110	1,077	101	681	110	186	38.2	45.2
West	927	39	113	77	698	45	476	60	116	38.0	45.5
Mountain	156	5	18	12	121	9	80	11	21	38.6	44.9
Pacific	771	34	95	65	577	36	397	49	95	37.8	45.6
\multicolumn{12}{c}{Hispanic origin}											
Northeast	1,201	29	129	73	971	152	570	99	151	38.8	44.1
New England	153	4	18	13	119	13	77	14	15	38.1	44.6
Middle Atlantic	1,048	25	111	60	853	139	493	85	136	38.9	44.1
Midwest	676	18	65	44	549	36	359	69	85	39.3	44.4
East North Central	568	14	51	35	468	28	316	57	67	39.4	44.2
West North Central	108	4	15	8	81	9	44	11	17	38.8	45.4
South	3,024	99	352	254	2,319	198	1,391	264	466	39.1	45.7

[Continued]

★ 556 ★

Hours of Work, by Race/Ethnicity: 1993
[Continued]

| Area | Total at work | Hours of work | | | | | | | | Average hours | |
| | | 1 to 14 | 15 to 29 | 30 to 34 | 35 or more hours | | | | | Total | Full-time schedules[1] |
					Total	35 to 39	40	41 to 48	49 or more		
South Atlantic	1,115	32	130	84	869	62	568	68	171	39.1	45.1
West South Central	1,889	67	220	170	1,432	136	816	194	286	39.0	46.0
West	4,043	154	559	356	2,973	234	1,957	326	457	37.5	44.7
Mountain	755	29	97	70	560	50	343	62	104	38.3	45.7
Pacific	3,287	125	462	286	2,414	184	1,614	264	352	37.4	44.4

Source: U.S. Department of Labor. Bureau of Labor Statistics. *Geographic Profile of Employment and Unemployment, 1993.* Bulletin 2446. Washington, DC: U.S. Government Printing Office, September 1994, pp. 25-26. *Notes:* East North Central region includes Illinois, Indiana, Ohio, Michigan, Wisconsin. East South Central region includes Alabama, Kentucky, Mississippi, Tennessee. Middle Atlantic region includes New Jersey, New York, Pennsylvania. Mountain region includes Arizona, Colorado, Idaho, Montana, Nevada, New Mexico, Utah, Wyoming. New England region includes Connecticut, Maine, Massachusetts, New Hampshire, Rhode Island, Vermont. Pacific region includes Alaska, California, Hawaii, Oregon, Washington. South Atlantic region includes Delaware, District of Columbia, Florida, Georgia, Maryland, North Carolina, South Carolina, Virginia, West Virginia. West North Central region includes Iowa, Kansas, Minnesota, Missouri, Nebraska, North Dakota, South Dakota. West South Central region includes Arkansas, Louisiana, Oklahoma, Texas. Data for demographic groups are not shown when they do not meet Bureau of Labor Statistics publication standards of reliability for the particular area based on the sample in that area. Items may not add to totals or compute to displayed percentages because of rounding. Detail for race and Hispanic origin groups will not add to totals because data for the "other races" group are not presented and because Hispanics are included in both the white and black population groups. 1. Refers to persons who worked 35 hours or more during survey week.

★ 557 ★

Work Hours and Schedules

Hours of Work, by Sex and Region: 1993

Table shows the hours of work for men and women in various Census regions and divisions of the United States. Data are 1993 annual averages.

[In thousands, except average hours]

| Area | Total at work | Hours of work | | | | | | | | Average hours | |
| | | 1 to 14 | 15 to 29 | 30 to 34 | 35 or more hours | | | | | Total | Full-time schedules[1] |
					Total	35 to 39	40	41 to 48	49 or more		
					Total						
Northeast	22,457	1,068	2,939	1,639	16,811	2,107	8,565	2,117	4,022	38.6	46.4
New England	6,212	319	843	533	4,517	492	2,191	627	1,207	38.6	47.2
Middle Atlantic	16,245	749	2,096	1,105	12,294	1,615	6,373	1,491	2,815	38.6	46.1
Midwest	28,002	1,504	3,431	2,085	20,982	1,622	9,957	3,230	6,173	39.7	47.7
East North Central	19,356	982	2,354	1,395	14,625	1,130	7,144	2,238	4,114	39.6	47.3
West North Central	8,646	522	1,077	690	6,357	492	2,814	992	2,059	39.9	48.8
South	39,308	1,604	4,465	2,922	30,318	2,390	15,770	4,035	8,123	40.0	47.2
South Atlantic	20,501	814	2,306	1,561	15,821	1,283	8,364	2,041	4,132	39.9	47.1
East South Central	6,668	271	775	495	5,127	434	2,677	697	1,319	39.8	47.0
West South Central	12,139	519	1,384	866	9,370	674	4,728	1,296	2,672	40.3	47.5
West	24,256	1,172	3,105	2,086	17,892	1,294	9,535	2,295	4,768	39.0	47.2
Mountain	6,588	340	857	565	4,826	359	2,363	687	1,416	39.4	48.1
Pacific	17,668	832	2,249	1,521	13,066	935	7,172	1,608	3,352	38.9	46.9
					Men						
Northeast	12,179	395	1,021	673	10,091	752	4,940	1,356	3,043	41.7	47.4
New England	3,318	115	280	211	2,712	173	1,240	391	907	41.9	48.2
Middle Atlantic	8,861	280	741	462	7,379	579	3,700	965	2,136	41.6	47.1
Midwest	15,184	569	1,220	803	12,592	570	5,397	2,006	4,619	43.1	49.0
East North Central	10,521	370	819	531	8,802	378	3,927	1,412	3,085	42.9	48.4
West North Central	4,664	200	401	273	3,790	192	1,470	594	1,534	43.5	50.5
South	21,445	658	1,803	1,267	17,717	909	8,427	2,427	5,954	42.5	48.4
South Atlantic	10,985	328	904	671	9,082	467	4,411	1,230	2,973	42.4	48.2

[Continued]

★ 557 ★

Hours of Work, by Sex and Region: 1993

[Continued]

Area	Total at work	Hours of work								Average hours	
		1 to 14	15 to 29	30 to 34	35 or more hours					Total	Full-time schedules[1]
					Total	35 to 39	40	41 to 48	49 or more		
East South Central	3,661	115	320	215	3,011	154	1,443	417	996	42.3	48.4
West South Central	6,799	216	578	381	5,624	287	2,572	780	1,985	42.9	48.8
West	13,499	475	1,236	893	10,895	555	5,403	1,425	3,512	41.7	48.0
Mountain	3,629	131	325	240	2,934	149	1,315	423	1,047	42.4	49.2
Pacific	9,869	344	911	653	7,961	406	4,088	1,002	2,465	41.4	47.6
					Women						
Northeast	10,278	673	1,919	966	6,720	1,355	3,625	762	979	35.0	45.0
New England	2,895	204	563	322	1,805	318	951	236	300	34.8	45.8
Middle Atlantic	7,383	469	1,356	644	4,915	1,037	2,674	526	679	35.1	44.7
Midwest	12,818	935	2,211	1,282	8,389	1,052	4,560	1,224	1,554	35.8	45.8
East North Central	8,835	613	1,535	864	5,823	753	3,216	826	1,028	35.8	45.5
West North Central	3,982	322	676	418	2,566	299	1,344	398	525	35.8	46.4
South	17,863	946	2,662	1,654	12,601	1,482	7,343	1,608	2,169	36.9	45.5
South Atlantic	9,516	486	1,402	889	6,739	816	3,953	811	1,159	37.0	45.6
East South Central	3,007	156	454	280	2,116	279	1,234	280	323	36.7	45.1
West South Central	5,340	303	806	485	3,746	387	2,156	517	687	36.9	45.7
West	10,757	697	1,869	1,193	6,998	739	4,132	871	1,256	35.8	46.0
Mountain	2,959	209	531	325	1,893	211	1,048	264	369	35.7	46.5
Pacific	7,799	488	1,338	868	5,105	528	3,084	606	887	35.8	45.8

Source: U.S. Department of Labor. Bureau of Labor Statistics. *Geographic Profile of Employment and Unemployment, 1993.* Bulletin 2446. Washington, DC: U.S. Government Printing Office, September 1994, p. 25. *Notes:* East North Central region includes Illinois, Indiana, Ohio, Michigan, Wisconsin. East South Central region includes Alabama, Kentucky, Mississippi, Tennessee. Middle Atlantic region includes New Jersey, New York, Pennsylvania. Mountain region includes Arizona, Colorado, Idaho, Montana, Nevada, New Mexico, Utah, Wyoming. New England region includes Connecticut, Maine, Massachusetts, New Hampshire, Rhode Island, Vermont. Pacific region includes Alaska, California, Hawaii, Oregon, Washington. South Atlantic region includes Delaware, District of Columbia, Florida, Georgia, Maryland, North Carolina, South Carolina, Virginia, West Virginia. West North Central region includes Iowa, Kansas, Minnesota, Missouri, Nebraska, North Dakota, South Dakota. West South Central region includes Arkansas, Louisiana, Oklahoma, Texas. Data for demographic groups are not shown when they do not meet Bureau of Labor Statistics publication standards of reliability for the particular area based on the sample in that area. Items may not add to totals or compute to displayed percentages because of rounding. 1. Refers to persons who worked 35 hours or more during survey week.

★ 558 ★

Work Hours and Schedules

Shift Schedules, by Worker Characteristics: 1985 and 1991

As of May. For employed persons 16 years old and over who usually work full-time and who were at work during the survey reference week. Based on Current Population Survey.

Characteristic	Total employed[1]	Work schedules (percent distribution)						
		Regular daytime schedules	Shift workers					
			Total	Evening	Night	Rotating	Irregular[2]	Other
Total, 1985[3]	73,395	84.1	15.9	6.3	2.7	4.3	(NA)	2.6
Total, 1991[3]	80,452	81.8	17.8	5.1	3.7	3.4	3.7	2.0
Age:								
16 to 19 years old	1,413	70.6	28.6	12.0	5.5	3.2	6.4	1.5
20 to 24 years old	8,332	74.8	25.0	8.5	4.7	4.6	5.5	1.7
25 to 34 years old	25,523	81.3	18.3	5.0	3.9	3.8	3.7	1.9
35 to 44 years old	22,749	83.7	16.0	4.1	3.5	3.2	3.2	2.0
45 to 54 years old	14,306	83.6	16.2	4.6	2.9	2.9	3.4	2.3

[Continued]

★ 558 ★

Shift Schedules, by Worker Characteristics: 1985 and 1991
[Continued]

| Characteristic | Total employed[1] | Work schedules (percent distribution) | | | | | | |
| | | Regular daytime schedules | Shift workers | | | | | |
			Total	Evening	Night	Rotating	Irregular[2]	Other
55 to 64 years old	7,197	84.1	15.3	4.2	3.4	2.4	3.0	2.3
65 years old and over	933	88.1	11.7	2.3	2.7	1.1	2.4	3.3
Sex:								
Male	46,308	79.5	20.2	5.4	4.2	4.0	4.2	2.3
Female	34,145	85.0	14.6	4.6	2.9	2.6	2.9	1.7
Race and Hispanic origin:								
White	68,795	82.6	17.1	4.6	3.4	3.3	3.8	2.1
Black	8,943	76.0	23.3	8.4	5.6	4.7	2.9	1.8
Hispanic[4]	6,598	80.3	19.1	6.4	4.6	2.7	3.1	2.4
Marital status:								
Single	18,420	77.6	22.0	7.0	4.0	4.0	4.7	2.2
Married, spouse present	49,101	83.9	15.8	4.2	3.3	3.2	3.3	1.9
Other	12,932	80.1	19.4	5.8	4.4	3.4	3.5	2.4

Source: U.S. Bureau of the Census. *Statistical Abstract of the United States, 1994.* 114th ed. Washington, DC: U.S. Government Printing Office, 1994, p. 406. Primary sources: U.S. Bureau of Labor Statistics. *News.* USDL 92-491 (4 August 1992); and unpublished data. *Notes:* "NA" represents "not available." 1. Includes a small number of workers who did not report data on shift worked. 2. Employer arranged. 3. Data for 1985 are not strictly comparable to those for 1991 because of the addition of the "irregular" category in the May 1991 survey. Includes other races, not shown separately. 4. Persons of Hispanic origin may be of any race.

★ 559 ★

Work Hours and Schedules

Weekly Hours of Employed Civilians, by Class of Worker: 1970-1993

For civilian noninstitutional population 16 years old and over. Annual averages of monthly figures. Based on Current Population Survey.

[In thousands, except as indicated]

Weekly hours	1970	1980	1985	1989	1990	1991	1992	1993
Nonagriculture:								
Wage and salary workers	38.3	38.1	38.7	39.3	39.2	39.0	38.8	39.3
Self-employed	45.0	41.2	41.1	41.1	40.8	40.4	40.1	40.5
Unpaid family workers	37.9	34.7	35.1	35.1	33.9	35.4	34.5	34.2
Agriculture:								
Wage and salary workers	40.0	41.6	40.8	41.8	41.3	41.0	40.6	40.8
Self-employed	51.0	49.3	48.2	47.9	46.9	46.8	47.1	46.5
Unpaid family workers	40.0	38.6	38.5	39.4	38.5	40.3	40.5	36.9

Source: U.S. Bureau of the Census. *Statistical Abstract of the United States, 1994.* 114th ed. Washington, DC: U.S. Government Printing Office, 1994, p. 403. Primary sources: U.S. Bureau of Labor Statistics. *Employment and Earnings* (monthly; January issues); and unpublished data.

★ 560 ★
Work Hours and Schedules

Work Hours of Students: 1992

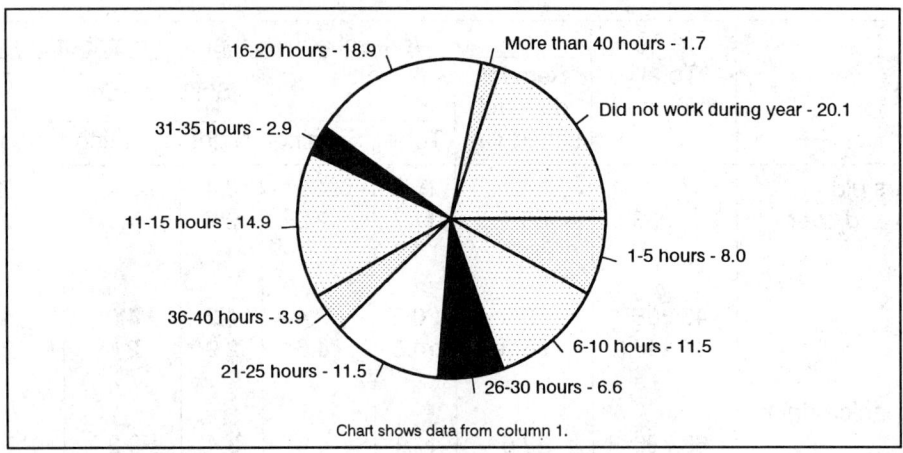

Chart shows data from column 1.

Table shows the average hours worked per week by seniors in high school during 1992. Data are by selected student characteristics.

[In percentages]

Work hours	Total	Sex		Race/Ethnicity				
		Male	Female	White	Black	Hispanic	Asian	American Indian
Did not work during year	20.1	22.0	18.3	19.1	26.6	20.4	24.2	28.9
1-5 hours	8.0	7.0	8.9	7.9	6.9	7.9	12.4	12.9
6-10 hours	11.5	10.4	12.6	12.5	9.1	6.9	9.1	7.0
11-15 hours	14.9	12.9	17.0	15.8	10.0	14.8	12.4	9.4
16-20 hours	18.9	17.5	20.3	19.3	16.6	17.5	18.2	17.6
21-25 hours	11.5	11.9	11.1	11.1	12.3	13.5	10.8	8.6
26-30 hours	6.6	7.5	5.6	6.1	8.9	8.6	6.0	5.7
31-35 hours	2.9	3.6	2.3	2.9	3.3	3.2	1.1	7.6
36-40 hours	3.9	4.9	2.8	3.6	4.0	5.4	5.0	1.4
More than 40 hours	1.7	2.3	1.1	1.7	2.4	1.9	0.9	1.0

Source: U.S. Department of Education. Office of Educational Research and Improvement. National Center for Education Statistics. *Digest of Education Statistics, 1994.* NCES 94-115. Lanham, MD: Bernan, November 1994, p. 403. Primary source: U.S. Department of Education. National Center for Education Statistics. "National Education Longitudinal Study of 1988." Second Follow-up Survey. (Table prepared February 1994.).

Work Hours and Schedules

Work Schedules of Employed and Unemployed Workers: 1980-1993

For civilian noninstitutional population 16 years old and over. Annual averages of monthly figures. Based on Current Population Survey.

[In thousands]

Characteristic	1980	1990	1993
	Employed		
Total	99,303	117,914	119,306
Full-time[1]	82,562	97,994	98,439
Male	51,717	57,982	57,643
16 to 19 years old	2,017	1,343	1,042
20 to 24 years old	6,533	5,452	4,968
25 to 54 years old	35,644	44,229	44,946
55 years and over	7,521	6,959	6,688
Female	30,845	40,011	40,796
16 to 19 years old	1,456	975	744
20 to 24 years old	5,098	4,386	3,955
25 to 54 years old	20,395	30,485	31,889
55 years and over	3,897	4,166	4,208
Part-time[1]	16,740	19,920	20,868
Male	5,471	6,452	7,057
16 to 19 years old	2,068	1,894	1,794
20 to 24 years old	999	1,174	1,388
25 to 54 years old	1,092	1,842	2,293
55 years and over	1,314	1,543	1,582
Female	11,270	13,468	13,810
16 to 19 years old	2,169	2,049	1,950
20 to 24 years old	1,456	1,611	1,825
25 to 54 years old	5,827	7,584	7,793
55 years and over	1,815	2,224	2,243
	Unemployed		
Total	7,637	6,874	8,734
Looking for full-time work	6,269	5,541	7,146
Male	3,703	3,264	4,277
16 to 19 years old	537	328	343
20 to 24 years old	994	582	704
25 to 54 years old	1,923	2,098	2,884
55 years and over	250	255	346
Female	2,564	2,277	2,869
16 to 19 years old	430	233	246
20 to 24 years old	636	439	476
25 to 54 years old	1,363	1,491	1,968
55 years and over	135	115	179
Looking for part-time work	1,369	1,332	1,588
Male	563	535	655
16 to 19 years old	377	301	385
20 to 24 years old	81	84	103

[Continued]

★ 561 ★

Work Schedules of Employed and Unemployed Workers: 1980-1993
[Continued]

Characteristic	1980	1990	1993
25 to 54 years old	54	89	102
55 years and over	52	61	64
Female	806	797	933
16 to 19 years old	326	286	322
20 to 24 years old	124	116	137
25 to 54 years old	299	323	396
55 years and over	57	72	78

Source: U.S. Bureau of the Census. *Statistical Abstract of the United States, 1994.* 114th ed. Washington, DC: U.S. Government Printing Office, 1994, p. 404. Primary sources: U.S. Bureau of Labor Statistics. Bulletin 2307; and *Employment and Earnings* (monthly; January issues). *Notes:* 1. Full-time workers include employed persons on full-time (35 hours or more per week) schedules and those working part-time (between 1 and 34 hours) for economic reasons who usually work full-time. Part-time workers include employed persons working part-time voluntarily and those working part-time for economic reasons, who usually work part-time. Employed persons with a job but not at work are distributed according to whether they usually work full- or part-time.

Workers

★ 562 ★

Full-Time Wage and Salary Workers, by Selected Characteristics: 1983- 1993

Tables shows the number of workers and median salary earnings for selected occupations. Data represent annual averages of quarterly data. Based on Current Population Survey.

[In current dollars of usual weekly earnings]

Characteristic	Number of workers (1,000)				Median weekly earnings ($)			
	1983	1985	1990	1993	1983	1985	1990	1993
All workers[1]	70,976	77,002	85,082	85,211	313	343	415	463
Male	42,309	45,589	49,015	48,384	378	406	485	514
16 to 24 years old	6,702	6,956	6,313	5,556	223	240	283	289
25 years old and over	35,607	38,632	42,702	42,828	406	442	514	559
Female	28,667	31,414	36,068	36,827	252	277	348	396
16 to 24 years old	5,345	5,621	5,001	4,324	197	210	254	274
25 years old and over	23,322	25,793	31,066	32,503	267	296	370	416
White	61,739	66,481	72,637	72,395	319	355	427	478
Male	37,378	40,030	42,563	41,825	387	417	497	531
Female	24,361	26,452	30,075	30,571	254	281	355	403
Black	7,373	8,393	9,642	9,729	261	277	329	370
Male	3,883	4,367	4,909	4,855	293	304	360	392
Female	3,490	4,026	4,733	4,873	231	252	308	349
Hispanic origin[2]	(NA)	(NA)	6,993	7,106	(NA)	(NA)	307	335

[Continued]

★ 562 ★

Full-Time Wage and Salary Workers, by Selected Characteristics: 1983- 1993
[Continued]

Characteristic	Number of workers (1,000)				Median weekly earnings ($)			
	1983	1985	1990	1993	1983	1985	1990	1993
Male	(NA)	(NA)	4,410	4,495	(NA)	(NA)	322	352
Female	(NA)	(NA)	2,583	2,611	(NA)	(NA)	280	314
Family relationship:								
Husbands	28,720	30,260	31,326	31,061	410	455	532	587
Wives	14,884	16,270	18,666	19,570	257	285	363	412
Women who maintain families	3,948	4,333	5,007	5,279	256	278	339	379
Men who maintain families	1,331	1,313	1,786	1,827	377	396	444	482
Other persons in families:								
Men	5,518	6,173	6,434	5,908	219	238	296	307
Women	4,032	4,309	4,475	4,003	201	213	271	295
All other men[3]	6,740	7,841	9,468	9,587	350	380	442	479
All other women[3]	5,803	6,503	7,920	7,975	274	305	376	419

Source: U.S. Bureau of the Census. *Statistical Abstract of the United States, 1994.* 114th ed. Washington, DC: U.S. Government Printing Office, 1994, p. 429. Primary sources: U.S. Bureau of Labor Statistics. Bulletin 2307; and *Employment and Earnings* (monthly, January issues). *Notes:* "NA" stands for "not available." The median of a group of numbers is the middle number or value when each item in the group is arranged according to size, either from lowest to highest or highest to lowest. The median generally has the same number of items above it and below it. If there is an even number of items in the group, the median is taken to be the average of the two middle numbers. 1. Includes other races, not shown separately. 2. Persons of Hispanic origin may be of any race. 3. The majority of these persons are living alone or with nonrelatives. Also included are persons in families where the husband, wife or other person maintaining the family is in the Armed Forces, and persons in unrelated subfamilies.

★ 563 ★

Workers

Home Workers, by Selected Characteristics: 1991

Table shows workers doing job-related work at home as part of their primary jobs in nonagricultural industries. Data as of May. For persons 16 years old and older.

Characteristic	Total at work (1,000)	Persons doing job-related work at home					
		Total (1,000)[1]	Worked at home for pay				Mean hours worked[3] (number)
			Total (1,000)	Worked 8 hours or more			
				Total (1,000)	Rate[2]	35 hours or more (1,000)	
Total[4]	109,126	19,967	7,432	3,651	3.3	1,069	14.1
Age:							
16 to 24 years old	16,268	862	329	122	0.7	40	12.3
25 to 34 years old	31,248	5,290	1,798	839	2.7	259	13.7
35 to 44 years old	29,500	6,755	2,430	1,144	3.9	297	13.0
45 to 54 years old	18,842	4,368	1,567	876	4.6	264	15.4
55 to 64 years old	10,291	1,995	865	462	4.5	161	16.8
65 years old and over	2,977	697	445	207	7.0	47	13.3

[Continued]

★ 563 ★

Home Workers, by Selected Characteristics: 1991
[Continued]

Characteristic	Total at work (1,000)	Persons doing job-related work at home					
		Total (1,000)[1]	Worked at home for pay				Mean hours worked[3] (number)
			Total (1,000)	Worked 8 hours or more		35 hours or more (1,000)	
				Total (1,000)	Rate[2]		
Sex:							
Male	58,794	10,731	4,210	1,894	3.2	438	12.0
Female	50,332	9,236	3,222	1,757	3.5	632	16.8
Race and Hispanic origin:							
White	94,387	18,520	7,022	3,403	3.6	966	13.8
Black	11,020	970	239	147	1.3	76	22.8
Hispanic[5]	7,977	667	255	137	1.7	36	13.7

Source: U.S. Bureau of the Census. *Statistical Abstract of the United States, 1994.* 114th ed. Washington, DC: U.S. Government Printing Office, 1994, p. 406. Primary sources: U.S. Bureau of Labor Statistics. *Monthly Labor Review* (February 1994); and unpublished data. *Notes:* 1. Includes those that did not report pay status and unpaid family members. 2. Persons working at home as a percent of the total at work. 3. An arithmetic mean is derived by summing the individual item values of a particular group and dividing the total by the number of items. The arithmetic mean is often referred to as the "mean" or "average." 4. Excludes unpaid family members. 5. Persons of Hispanic origin may be of any race.

★ 564 ★
Workers

Job Holders Not at Work: 1970-1993

Data show reasons persons with jobs are not at work. For civilian noninstitutional population 16 years old and over. Annual averages of monthly figures. Based on Current Population Survey.

[In thousands, except percentages]

Reason for not working	1970	1975	1980	1985	1987	1988	1989	1990	1991	1992	1993
All industries, number	4,645	5,221	5,881	5,789	5,910	5,831	6,170	6,157	5,909	6,082	6,028
Percent of employed	5.9	6.1	5.9	5.4	5.3	5.1	5.3	5.2	5.1	5.2	5.1
Reason for not working:											
Vacation	2,341	2,815	3,320	3,338	3,421	3,236	3,437	3,531	3,297	3,414	3,330
Illness	1,324	1,343	1,426	1,308	1,320	1,364	1,405	1,341	1,302	1,258	1,290
Bad weather	128	139	155	141	92	122	133	89	118	126	151
Industrial dispute	156	95	105	42	34	30	63	24	17	19	24
All other	696	829	876	960	1,043	1,080	1,132	1,172	1,175	1,265	1,233

Source: U.S. Bureau of the Census. *Statistical Abstract of the United States, 1994.* 114th ed. Washington, DC: U.S. Government Printing Office, 1994, p. 404. Primary sources: U.S. Bureau of Labor Statistics. *Employment and Earnings* (monthly; January issues); and unpublished data.

★ 565 ★

Workers

Multiple Job Holders, by Job Type: 1994

There are roughly 7 million multiple job holders in the United States. The table below profiles those holding more than one job as of July 1994.

Job type	Men	Women
One full-time and one part-time job	2,400,000	1,600,000
Two part-time jobs	497,000	1,000,000
Two full-time jobs	204,000	80,000

Source: "When One Job Is Not Enough." *Washington Post,* 12 September 1994, p. A10. Primary source: Bureau of Labor Statistics.

Workers: Blacks

★ 566 ★

Employment Status of Blacks: 1973-1993

Table shows data for the civilian noninstitutionalized population 16 years old and older. Annual averages of monthly figures. Based on Current Population Survey.

[In thousands, except as indicated]

Year	Civilian noninstitutional population	Civilian labor force						Not in labor force	
		Total	Percent of population	Employed	Employment/population ratio[1]	Unemployed			
						Number	Percent of labor force	Number	Percent of population
1973	14,917	8,976	60.2	8,128	54.5	846	9.4	5,941	39.8
1980	17,824	10,865	61.0	9,313	52.2	1,553	14.3	6,959	39.0
1985	19,664	12,364	62.9	10,501	53.4	1,864	15.1	7,299	37.1
1989	21,021	13,497	64.2	11,953	56.9	1,544	11.4	7,524	35.8
1990	21,300	13,493	63.3	11,966	56.2	1,527	11.3	7,808	36.7
1991	21,615	13,542	62.6	11,863	54.9	1,679	12.4	8,074	37.4
1992	21,958	13,891	63.3	11,933	54.3	1,958	14.1	8,067	36.7
1993	22,329	13,943	62.4	12,146	54.4	1,796	12.9	8,386	37.6

Source: U.S. Bureau of the Census. *Statistical Abstract of the United States, 1994.* 114th ed. Washington, DC: U.S. Government Printing Office, 1994, p. 396. Primary sources: U.S. Bureau of Labor Statistics. Bulletin 2307; and *Employment and Earnings* (monthly; January issues). *Note:* 1. Civilian employed as a percent of the civilian noninstitutional population.

★ 567 ★

Workers: Blacks

Unemployed Black Workers: 1980-1993

For civilian noninstitutional population 16 years old and over. Annual averages of monthly figures.

[In thousands, except as indicated]

Age	1980	1985	1988	1989	1990	1991	1992	1993
Unemployment[1]	1,553	1,864	1,547	1,544	1,527	1,679	1,958	1,796
16 to 19 years old	343	357	288	300	258	270	313	302
20 to 24 years old	426	455	349	322	335	362	401	371
Unemployment rate (percent)[2]	14.3	15.1	11.7	11.4	11.3	12.4	14.1	12.9
16 to 19 years old	38.5	40.2	32.4	32.4	31.1	36.3	39.8	38.9
20 to 24 years old	23.6	24.5	19.6	18.0	19.9	21.6	23.9	22.0

Source: U.S. Bureau of the Census. *Statistical Abstract of the United States, 1994.* 114th ed. Washington, DC: U.S. Government Printing Office, 1994. p. 416. Primary sources: U.S. Bureau of Labor Statistics. *Employment and Earnings* (monthly; January issues); and unpublished data. *Notes:* 1. Includes other ages not shown separately. 2. Unemployed as percent of civilian labor force in specified group. Includes other ages not shown separately.

Workers: Disabled

★ 568 ★

Men With Work Disabilities – Employed, by State: 1990

Figures show males in the civilian noninstitutionalized population 16 years and over who have work disabilities and who are employed.

State	Number	Percent of all persons 16 years old and older
U.S. Total	2,671,515	1.4
Alabama	41,119	1.3
Alaska	6,582	1.7
Arizona	40,298	1.4
Arkansas	28,233	1.6
California	297,384	1.3
Colorado	42,136	1.7
Connecticut	35,193	1.3
Delaware	7,405	1.4
D.C.	5,440	1.1
Florida	146,067	1.4
Georgia	74,119	1.5
Hawaii	11,042	1.3

[Continued]

★ 568 ★

Men With Work Disabilities – Employed, by State: 1990
[Continued]

State	Number	Percent of all persons 16 years old and older
Idaho	14,545	2.0
Illinois	100,899	1.1
Indiana	59,900	1.4
Iowa	33,463	1.6
Kansas	27,404	1.5
Kentucky	42,144	1.5
Louisiana	40,569	1.3
Maine	18,208	1.9
Maryland	53,612	1.4
Massachusetts	61,299	1.3
Michigan	100,973	1.4
Minnesota	57,947	1.7
Mississippi	26,058	1.4
Missouri	56,894	1.4
Montana	11,093	1.8
Nebraska	19,032	1.6
Nevada	17,527	1.9
New Hampshire	13,517	1.6
New Jersey	68,044	1.1
New Mexico	16,561	1.5
New York	154,144	1.1
North Carolina	76,369	1.5
North Dakota	6,933	1.4
Ohio	121,344	1.5
Oklahoma	42,841	1.8
Oregon	45,704	2.1
Pennsylvania	119,302	1.3
Rhode Island	11,719	1.5
South Carolina	36,550	1.4
South Dakota	8,701	1.7
Tennessee	52,936	1.4
Texas	178,428	1.4
Utah	20,284	1.8
Vermont	7,700	1.8
Virginia	65,791	1.4
Washington	69,591	1.9
West Virginia	19,138	1.4
Wisconsin	53,846	1.4
Wyoming	5,487	1.7

Source: Census of Population and Housing, 1990: Summary Tape File 3C on CD-ROM [machine-readable datafiles]. Prepared by Bureau of the Census. Washington, DC: The Bureau, 1992.

★ 569 ★

Workers: Disabled

Men With Work Disabilities – Not Working, by State: 1990

Figures show males in the civilian noninstitutionalized population 16 years and over who are prevented from working due to work disabilities.

State	Number	Percent of all persons 16 years old and older
U.S. Total	3,158,993	1.65
Alabama	72,094	2.32
Alaska	3,791	0.96
Arizona	46,431	1.67
Arkansas	46,720	2.60
California	335,049	1.47
Colorado	33,416	1.33
Connecticut	26,551	1.01
Delaware	6,998	1.35
D.C.	8,394	1.67
Florida	172,256	1.66
Georgia	93,470	1.89
Hawaii	10,382	1.21
Idaho	11,051	1.51
Illinois	119,013	1.35
Indiana	64,004	1.51
Iowa	25,860	1.21
Kansas	22,609	1.20
Kentucky	86,015	3.03
Louisiana	83,027	2.66
Maine	18,966	1.99
Maryland	46,585	1.25
Massachusetts	68,746	1.43
Michigan	130,507	1.84
Minnesota	36,484	1.10
Mississippi	52,874	2.77
Missouri	67,806	1.72
Montana	11,610	1.94
Nebraska	13,529	1.13
Nevada	14,323	1.53
New Hampshire	10,542	1.23
New Jersey	69,325	1.13
New Mexico	22,662	2.04
New York	219,816	1.55
North Carolina	93,231	1.79
North Dakota	5,492	1.14
Ohio	156,136	1.87
Oklahoma	46,852	1.95
Oregon	34,902	1.59
Pennsylvania	157,563	1.68
Rhode Island	13,407	1.67

[Continued]

★ 569 ★

Men With Work Disabilities – Not Working, by State: 1990
[Continued]

State	Number	Percent of all persons 16 years old and older
South Carolina	54,138	2.03
South Dakota	6,593	1.28
Tennessee	85,512	2.25
Texas	198,416	1.57
Utah	13,319	1.15
Vermont	6,201	1.43
Virginia	74,397	1.54
Washington	57,222	1.53
West Virginia	50,864	3.62
Wisconsin	49,417	1.32
Wyoming	4,425	1.33

Source: Census of Population and Housing, 1990: Summary Tape File 3C on CD-ROM [machine-readable datafiles]. Prepared by Bureau of the Census. Washington, DC: The Bureau, 1992.

★ 570 ★
Workers: Disabled

Persons With Work Disabilities, by Selected Characteristics: 1992

As of March. Covers civilian noninstitutional population and members of Armed Forces living off posts or with their families on posts. Persons are classified as having a work disability if they (1) have a health problem or disability that prevents them from working or that limits the kind or amount of work they can perform; (2) have a service-connected disability or ever retired from or left a job for health reasons; (3) did not work in survey reference week or previous year because of long-term illness or disability; or (4) are under age 65 and are covered by Medicare or receive Supplemental Security Income. Based on Current Population Survey.

[In thousands, except percentages]

Age and participation status in assistance programs	Total[1]	Male	Female	White	Black	Hispanic[2]
Persons with work disability	14,959	7,573	7,386	11,819	2,670	1,192
16 to 24 years old	1,196	553	643	916	237	123
25 to 34 years old	2,727	1,412	1,315	2,057	562	208
35 to 44 years old	3,226	1,748	1,478	2,568	560	288
45 to 54 years old	3,154	1,547	1,607	2,508	560	254
55 to 64 years old	4,656	2,313	2,343	3,769	751	318
Percent work disabled of total population	9.3	9.6	9.0	8.7	13.8	8.5
16 to 24 years old	3.9	3.6	4.1	3.6	5.2	3.5
25 to 34 years old	6.4	6.7	6.2	5.8	10.4	4.9
35 to 44 years old	8.2	9.0	7.4	7.7	12.6	9.1
45 to 54 years old	11.7	11.8	11.6	10.8	20.1	14.0

[Continued]

★ 570 ★

Persons With Work Disabilities, by Selected Characteristics: 1992
[Continued]

Age and participation status in assistance programs	Total[1]	Male	Female	White	Black	Hispanic[2]
55 to 64 years old	22.0	23.1	21.1	20.6	34.7	25.4
Percent of work disabled –						
Receiving Social Security income	28.2	29.3	27.1	28.3	28.2	24.2
Receiving food stamps	22.8	18.4	27.4	19.1	39.1	31.7
Covered by Medicaid	29.7	23.8	35.8	25.6	47.2	44.1
Residing in public housing	4.8	3.1	6.5	3.2	12.1	7.0
Residing in subsidized housing	3.9	2.6	5.2	3.2	7.1	5.5

Source: U.S. Bureau of the Census. *Statistical Abstract of the United States, 1994.* 114th ed. Washington, DC: U.S. Government Printing Office, 1994, p. 382. Primary source: U.S. Bureau of the Census. Unpublished data. *Notes:* 1. Includes other races not shown separately. 2. Hispanic persons may be of any race.

★ 571 ★
Workers: Disabled

Women With Work Disabilities – Employed, by State: 1990

Figures show female civilian noninstitutionalized population 16 years and over who have work disabilities and who are employed.

State	Number	Percent of all persons 16 years old or older
U.S. Total	1,700,526	0.89
Alabama	22,845	0.74
Alaska	3,719	0.95
Arizona	25,401	0.91
Arkansas	16,717	0.93
California	197,300	0.87
Colorado	28,266	1.12
Connecticut	24,126	0.92
Delaware	6,008	1.16
D.C.	5,464	1.09
Florida	89,025	0.86
Georgia	44,464	0.90
Hawaii	7,042	0.82
Idaho	8,515	1.17
Illinois	67,391	0.77
Indiana	40,588	0.96
Iowa	21,092	0.99
Kansas	17,247	0.92
Kentucky	22,692	0.80
Louisiana	22,514	0.72

[Continued]

★ 571 ★

Women With Work Disabilities – Employed, by State: 1990
[Continued]

State	Number	Percent of all persons 16 years old or older
Maine	11,250	1.18
Maryland	34,907	0.93
Massachusetts	41,822	0.87
Michigan	69,962	0.99
Minnesota	40,557	1.22
Mississippi	14,097	0.74
Missouri	35,686	0.91
Montana	6,569	1.10
Nebraska	11,748	0.98
Nevada	10,068	1.08
New Hampshire	9,426	1.10
New Jersey	46,701	0.76
New Mexico	9,192	0.83
New York	107,710	0.76
North Carolina	48,030	0.92
North Dakota	4,019	0.84
Ohio	80,147	0.96
Oklahoma	24,962	1.04
Oregon	29,964	1.37
Pennsylvania	75,939	0.81
Rhode Island	8,764	1.09
South Carolina	22,418	0.84
South Dakota	5,918	1.14
Tennessee	31,723	0.83
Texas	99,925	0.79
Utah	11,405	0.99
Vermont	4,407	1.01
Virginia	40,151	0.83
Washington	43,609	1.17
West Virginia	9,797	0.70
Wisconsin	36,074	0.97
Wyoming	3,163	0.95

Source: Census of Population and Housing, 1990: Summary Tape File 3C on CD-ROM [machine-readable datafiles]. Prepared by Bureau of the Census. Washington, DC: The Bureau, 1992.

★572★

Workers: Disabled

Women With Work Disabilities – Not Working, by State: 1990

Figures show female civilian noninstitutionalized population 16 years and over who have work disabilities that prevent them from working.

State	Number	Percent of all persons 16 years old or older
U.S. Total	3,435,036	1.8
Alabama	77,462	2.5
Alaska	4,137	1.1
Arizona	46,886	1.7
Arkansas	47,169	2.6
California	382,270	1.7
Colorado	36,011	1.4
Connecticut	30,159	1.2
Delaware	8,168	1.6
D.C.	10,140	2.0
Florida	170,465	1.6
Georgia	108,241	2.2
Hawaii	9,948	1.2
Idaho	11,288	1.5
Illinois	137,578	1.6
Indiana	71,858	1.7
Iowa	28,292	1.3
Kansas	24,509	1.3
Kentucky	82,849	2.9
Louisiana	82,162	2.6
Maine	18,550	1.9
Maryland	55,632	1.5
Massachusetts	72,617	1.5
Michigan	145,474	2.0
Minnesota	36,575	1.1
Mississippi	57,400	3.0
Missouri	71,376	1.8
Montana	10,361	1.7
Nebraska	14,191	1.2
Nevada	13,809	1.5
New Hampshire	10,643	1.2
New Jersey	83,887	1.4
New Mexico	20,798	1.9
New York	257,918	1.8
North Carolina	108,389	2.1
North Dakota	5,568	1.2
Ohio	171,634	2.1
Oklahoma	49,564	2.1
Oregon	37,552	1.7
Pennsylvania	174,353	1.9
Rhode Island	14,002	1.7

[Continued]

★ 572 ★

Women With Work Disabilities – Not Working, by State: 1990

[Continued]

State	Number	Percent of all persons 16 years old or older
South Carolina	62,238	2.3
South Dakota	6,458	1.2
Tennessee	96,770	2.5
Texas	209,403	1.7
Utah	14,884	1.3
Vermont	6,368	1.5
Virginia	78,175	1.6
Washington	62,814	1.7
West Virginia	43,456	3.1
Wisconsin	50,634	1.4
Wyoming	3,951	1.2

Source: Census of Population and Housing, 1990: Summary Tape File 3C on CD-ROM [machine-readable datafiles]. Prepared by Bureau of the Census. Washington, DC: The Bureau, 1992.

★ 573 ★

Workers: Disabled

Work Disabilities, by State: 1990

Table shows the states with the highest and lowest incidence of work disability.

[Rate per 1,000 people]

State	Disability rate
States with highest disability rates	
West Virginia	126.2
Kentucky	114.3
Arkansas	111.7
Mississippi	109.8
Louisiana	102.9
Oklahoma	101.6
Maine	101.5
Oregon	100.1
Tennessee	97.3
Montana	97.0
States with lowest disability rates	
Kansas	72.0
Massachusetts	72.0
Nebraska	71.4

[Continued]

★ 573 ★

Work Disabilities, by State: 1990

[Continued]

State	Disability rate
Maryland	70.5
North Dakota	69.7
Illinois	68.9
Alaska	66.3
Hawaii	65.9
Connecticut	63.8
New Jersey	61.8

Source: "The State of Affairs in Work Disability." Small Business Reports 19, no. 1 (January 1994), p. 35. Primary source: Morbidity and Mortality Weekly Report.

Workers: Hispanics

★ 574 ★

Employment Status of Hispanics: 1980-1993

Table shows data for the civilian noninstitutionalized population 16 years old and older. Annual averages of monthly figures. Based on Current Population Survey.

[In thousands, except as indicated]

Year and Hispanic origin	Civilian noninstitutional population	Civilian labor force				Unemployed		Not in labor force	
		Total	Percent of population	Employed	Employment/ population ratio[1]	Number	Percent of labor force	Number	Percent of population
Hispanic:[2]									
1980	9,598	6,146	64.0	5,527	57.6	620	10.1	3,451	36.0
1985	11,915	7,698	64.6	6,888	57.8	811	10.5	4,217	35.4
1986	12,344	8,076	65.4	7,219	58.5	857	10.6	4,268	34.6
1990	14,297	9,576	67.0	8,808	61.6	769	8.0	4,721	33.0
1991	14,770	9,762	66.1	8,799	59.6	963	9.9	5,008	33.9
1992	15,244	10,131	66.5	8,971	58.9	1,160	11.4	5,113	33.5
1993	15,753	10,377	65.9	9,272	58.9	1,104	10.6	5,377	34.1
Mexican:									
1986	7,377	4,941	67.0	4,387	59.5	555	11.2	2,436	33.0
1990	8,742	5,970	68.3	5,478	62.7	492	8.2	2,773	31.7
1991	8,947	5,984	66.9	5,363	59.9	621	10.4	2,963	33.1
1992	9,368	6,319	67.5	5,581	59.6	739	11.7	3,049	32.5
1993	9,693	6,499	67.0	5,805	59.9	693	10.7	3,194	33.0
Puerto Rican:									
1986	1,494	804	53.8	691	46.3	113	14.0	690	46.2

[Continued]

★ 574 ★

Employment Status of Hispanics: 1980-1993

[Continued]

Year and Hispanic origin	Civilian noninstitutional population	Civilian labor force						Not in labor force	
		Total	Percent of population	Employed	Employment/population ratio[1]	Unemployed		Number	Percent of population
						Number	Percent of labor force		
1990	1,546	859	55.6	780	50.5	79	9.1	687	44.4
1991	1,629	930	57.1	822	50.5	108	11.6	699	42.9
1992	1,628	934	57.4	802	49.2	132	14.1	694	42.6
1993	1,676	950	56.7	828	49.4	122	12.8	725	43.3
Cuban:									
1986	842	570	67.7	533	63.3	36	6.4	272	32.3
1990	847	552	65.1	512	60.4	40	7.2	295	34.8
1991	849	543	63.9	499	58.8	44	8.1	306	36.0
1992	867	529	61.1	488	56.3	42	7.9	337	38.9
1993	927	554	59.8	511	55.1	43	7.8	373	40.2

Source: U.S. Bureau of the Census. *Statistical Abstract of the United States, 1994.* 114th ed. Washington, DC: U.S. Government Printing Office, 1994, p. 396. Primary sources: U.S. Bureau of Labor Statistics. Bulletin 2307; and *Employment and Earnings* (monthly; January issues). *Notes:* 1. Civilian employed as a percent of the civilian noninstitutional population. 2. Persons of Hispanic origin may be of any race. Includes persons of other Hispanic origin, not shown separately.

★ 575 ★

Workers: Hispanics

Hispanic Participation in Civilian Labor Force: 1992-1993

For civilian noninstitutional population, 16 years old and over. Annual averages of monthly figures. Based on Current Population Survey.

Item	1992					1993				
	Total	Mexican	Puerto Rican	Cuban	Other Hispanic origin[1]	Total	Mexican	Puerto Rican	Cuban	Other Hispanic origin[1]
Total (1,000)	15,244	9,368	1,628	867	3,381	15,753	9,693	1,676	927	3,457
Percent in labor force:										
Male	80.5	82.0	69.9	73.2	82.5	80.0	81.5	70.6	73.3	81.2
Female	52.6	52.1	47.1	50.3	57.4	52.0	51.9	45.3	47.9	56.7
Employed (1,000)	8,971	5,581	802	488	2,100	9,272	5,805	828	511	2,128
Percent by occupation	100.0	100.0	100.0	100.0	100.0	100.0	100.0	100.0	100.0	100.0
Managerial and professional	13.4	10.8	18.2	25.1	16.0	14.1	11.5	19.1	25.0	16.6
Technical, sales, and administrative support	24.8	23.2	31.8	32.5	24.8	24.9	23.3	32.1	32.9	24.3
Services	20.3	19.2	19.7	12.1	25.2	19.9	19.1	19.9	12.9	23.8
Precision production, craft, and repair	13.4	14.2	11.0	13.0	12.4	13.2	14.4	9.8	10.2	12.0
Operators, fabricators, and laborers	22.2	24.4	18.1	15.4	19.6	22.2	23.7	17.9	17.0	20.9
Farming, forestry, and fishing	5.8	8.3	1.1	1.9	1.9	5.8	8.0	1.2	2.2	2.3
Percent of labor force unemployed:										
Male	11.5	11.7	15.6	7.1	10.5	10.4	10.2	14.4	7.8	10.1
Female	11.3	11.7	12.3	8.9	10.5	10.9	11.4	10.8	7.7	10.8

Source: U.S. Bureau of the Census. *Statistical Abstract of the United States, 1994.* 114th ed. Washington, DC: U.S. Government Printing Office, 1994, p. 400. Primary source: U.S. Bureau of Labor Statistics. *Employment and Earnings* (monthly, January issues). *Note:* 1. Includes Central or South American and other Hispanic origin.

★ 576 ★

Workers: Hispanics

Unemployed Hispanic Workers: 1980-1993

For civilian noninstitutional population 16 years old and over. Annual averages of monthly figures.

[In thousands, except as indicated]

Age	1980	1985	1988	1989	1990	1991	1992	1993
Unemployed[1]	620	811	732	750	769	963	1,160	1,104
16 to 19 years old	145	141	148	132	131	149	185	173
20 to 24 years old	138	171	145	158	135	172	193	191
Unemployment rate (percent)[2]	10.1	10.5	8.2	8.0	8.0	9.9	11.4	10.6
16 to 19 years old	22.5	24.3	22.0	19.4	19.5	22.9	27.5	26.2
20 to 24 years old	12.1	12.6	9.8	10.7	9.1	11.6	13.2	13.1

Source: U.S. Bureau of the Census. *Statistical Abstract of the United States, 1994.* 114th ed. Washington, DC: U.S. Government Printing Office, 1994. p. 416. Primary sources: U.S. Bureau of Labor Statistics. *Employment and Earnings* (monthly; January issues); and unpublished data. *Notes:* 1. Persons of Hispanic origin may be of any race. Includes other ages not shown separately. 2. Unemployed as percent of civilian labor force in specified group. Persons of Hispanic origin may be of any race. Includes other ages not shown separately.

Workers: Men

★ 577 ★

Employment Status of Men: 1960-1993

Table shows data for the civilian noninstitutionalized population 16 years old and older. Annual averages of monthly figures. Based on Current Population Survey.

[In thousands, except as indicated]

Year	Civilian noninsti-tutional popula-tion	Civilian labor force						Not in labor force	
		Total	Per-cent of popu-lation	Employed	Employ-ment/popula-tion ratio[1]	Unemployed			
						Number	Percent of labor force	Number	Percent of popu-lation
1960	55,662	46,388	83.3	43,904	78.9	2,486	5.4	9,274	16.7
1970	64,304	51,228	79.7	48,990	76.2	2,238	4.4	13,076	20.3
1980	79,398	61,453	77.4	57,186	72.0	4,267	6.9	17,945	22.6
1985	84,469	64,411	76.3	59,891	70.9	4,521	7.0	20,058	23.7
1989	88,762	67,840	76.4	64,315	72.5	3,525	5.2	20,923	23.6
1990	89,650	68,234	76.1	64,435	71.9	3,799	5.6	21,417	23.9
1991	90,552	68,411	75.5	63,593	70.2	4,817	7.0	22,141	24.5

[Continued]

★ 577 ★

Employment Status of Men: 1960-1993

[Continued]

Year	Civilian noninsti-tutional popula-tion	Civilian labor force						Not in labor force	
		Total	Per-cent of popu-lation	Employed	Employ-ment/ popula-tion ratio[1]	Unemployed		Number	Percent of popu-lation
						Number	Percent of labor force		
1992	91,541	69,184	75.6	63,805	69.7	5,380	7.8	22,356	24.4
1993	92,620	69,633	75.2	64,700	69.9	4,932	7.1	22,987	24.8

Source: U.S. Bureau of the Census. Statistical Abstract of the United States, 1994. 114th ed. Washington, DC: U.S. Government Printing Office, 1994, p. 396. Primary sources: U.S. Bureau of Labor Statistics. Bulletin 2307; and Employment and Earnings (monthly; January issues). Notes: 1. Civilian employed as a percent of the civilian noninstitutional population.

★ 578 ★

Workers: Men

Labor Force Participation Rates of Men, by Marital Status and Age: 1960-1993

Annual averages of monthly figures. Based on Current Population Survey.

Marital status and year	Total	16-19 years	20-24 years	25-34 years	35-44 years	45-64 years	65 and over
Single:							
1960	69.8	42.6	80.3	91.5	88.6	80.1	31.2
1970	65.5	54.6	73.8	87.9	86.2	75.7	25.2
1975	68.7	57.9	77.9	86.7	83.2	69.9	21.0
1980	72.6	59.9	81.3	89.2	82.2	66.9	16.8
1985	73.8	56.3	81.5	89.4	84.6	65.5	15.6
1989	75.5	57.4	82.5	90.0	84.6	64.6	18.2
1990	74.9	55.1	81.5	89.9	84.6	67.1	15.7
1991	74.2	52.6	80.6	89.6	84.8	66.8	14.0
1992	74.6	52.9	80.7	89.8	84.9	67.6	16.3
1993	74.2	52.5	80.5	89.2	84.5	68.2	15.0
Married:[1]							
1960	89.2	91.5	97.1	98.8	98.6	93.7	36.6
1970	86.1	92.3	94.7	98.0	98.1	91.2	29.9
1975	83.0	92.9	95.3	97.4	97.1	86.8	23.3
1980	80.9	91.3	96.9	97.5	97.2	84.3	20.5
1985	78.7	91.0	95.6	97.4	96.8	81.7	16.8
1989	78.5	93.7	95.9	97.2	96.8	82.4	17.8
1990	78.2	92.3	95.6	96.9	96.8	82.5	17.6
1991	77.8	93.2	95.4	96.6	96.6	82.3	16.8
1992	77.6	90.2	94.8	96.6	96.2	82.7	17.2
1993	77.3	91.2	95.0	96.6	96.1	82.5	16.6
Other:[2]							
1960	63.1	(B)	96.9	95.2	94.4	83.2	22.7

[Continued]

★578★

Labor Force Participation Rates of Men, by Marital Status and Age: 1960-1993
[Continued]

Marital status and year	Total	16-19 years	20-24 years	25-34 years	35-44 years	45-64 years	65 and over
1970	60.7	(B)	90.4	93.7	91.1	78.5	19.3
1975	63.4	(B)	88.8	92.4	89.4	73.4	15.4
1980	67.5	(B)	92.6	94.1	91.9	73.3	13.7
1985	68.7	(B)	95.1	93.7	91.8	72.8	11.4
1989	67.9	(B)	91.1	93.6	90.9	74.2	11.7
1990	68.3	(B)	93.1	93.0	90.8	74.6	12.0
1991	67.7	(B)	93.9	92.1	90.5	73.5	12.3
1992	68.0	(B)	91.8	93.5	90.3	74.7	12.2
1993	67.4	(B)	91.7	91.9	89.6	74.2	12.0

Source: U.S. Bureau of the Census. *Statistical Abstract of the United States, 1994.* 114th ed. Washington, DC: U.S. Government Printing Office, 1994, p. 401. Primary sources: U.S. Bureau of Labor Statistics. Bulletins 2217 and 2340; and unpublished data. *Notes:* "B" represents the following: for 1960, percentage not shown where base is less than 50,000; beginning 1970, 35,000. 1. Spouse present. 2. Widowed, divorced, and married (spouse absent).

★579★

Workers: Men

Unemployed Men: 1980-1993

For civilian noninstitutional population 16 years old and over. Annual averages of monthly figures.

[In thousands, except as indicated]

Age and marital status	1980	1985	1988	1989	1990	1991	1992	1993
Unemployed	4,267	4,521	3,655	3,525	3,799	4,817	5,380	4,932
16 to 19 years old	913	806	667	658	629	709	761	728
20 to 24 years old	1,076	944	676	660	666	849	884	808
25 to 44 years old	1,619	1,950	1,657	1,572	1,774	2,331	2,603	2,348
45 to 64 years old	600	766	606	585	668	862	1,062	983
65 years and over	58	55	49	49	61	66	69	65
Unemployment rate (percent)[1]	6.9	7.0	5.5	5.2	5.6	7.0	7.8	7.1
16 to 19 years old	18.3	19.5	16.0	15.9	16.3	19.8	21.5	20.4
20 to 24 years old	12.5	11.4	8.9	8.8	9.1	11.7	12.2	11.3
25 to 44 years old	5.6	5.9	4.6	4.3	4.8	6.2	6.9	6.2
45 to 64 years old	3.5	4.5	3.5	3.3	3.7	4.7	5.6	5.1
65 years and over	3.1	3.1	2.5	2.4	3.0	3.3	3.3	3.2
Marital status								
Married men, wife present[2]	4.2	4.3	3.3	3.0	3.4	4.4	5.0	4.4

[Continued]

★ 579 ★

Unemployed Men: 1980-1993
[Continued]

Age and marital status	1980	1985	1988	1989	1990	1991	1992	1993
White	3.9	4.0	3.0	2.8	3.1	4.2	4.7	4.1
Black	7.4	8.0	5.8	5.8	6.2	6.5	8.3	7.2

Source: U.S. Bureau of the Census. *Statistical Abstract of the United States, 1994.* 114th ed. Washington, DC: U.S. Government Printing Office, 1994, p. 416. Primary sources: U.S. Bureau of Labor Statistics. *Employment and Earnings* (monthly; January issues); and unpublished data. *Notes:* 1. Unemployed as percent of civilian labor force in specified group. 2. Includes other races not shown separately.

Workers: Older Americans

★ 580 ★

Recruitment of Older Americans

Bureau of Labor Statistics reported that 12 percent of the workforce in 1990 was 55 years old or older. Projections suggest that by 2005 older Americans will comprise 15 percent of the workforce. Table shows the reasons why surveyed firms recruit older workers.

[In percentages]

Reason	Firms
Skill	88
Scheduling flexibility	81
Low absenteeism	69
Motivation	67
Loyalty	66
Mentoring	58
Respect	50

Source: "Golden Years: Golden Opportunities." *Black Enterprise* (December 1993), p. 37. Primary source: American Association of Retired Persons (AARP) and Society for Human Resource Management. *The Older Workforce: Recruitment and Retention* (Alexandria, VA; 1993).

★ 581 ★

Workers: Older Americans

Retention of Older Americans

Table shows the reasons why surveyed firms retain older workers.

[In percentages]

Reason	Firms
Skill	87
Scheduling flexibility	67
Low absenteeism	65
Motivation	62
Mentoring	60

Source: "Golden Years: Golden Opportunities." *Black Enterprise* (December 1993), p. 37. Primary source: American Association of Retired Persons (AARP) and Society for Human Resource Management. *The Older Workforce: Recruitment and Retention* (Alexandria, VA; 1993).

Workers: Whites

★ 582 ★

Employment Status of Whites: 1960-1993

Table shows data for the civilian noninstitutionalized population 16 years old and older. Annual averages of monthly figures. Based on Current Population Survey.

[In thousands, except as indicated]

Year	Civilian noninstitutional population	Civilian labor force						Not in labor force	
		Total	Percent of population	Employed	Employment/population ratio[1]	Unemployed		Number	Percent of population
						Number	Percent of labor force		
1960	105,282	61,915	58.8	58,850	55.9	3,065	5.0	43,367	41.2
1970	122,174	73,556	60.2	70,217	57.5	3,339	4.5	48,618	39.8
1980	146,122	93,600	64.1	87,715	60.0	5,884	6.3	52,523	35.9
1985	153,679	99,926	65.0	93,736	61.0	6,191	6.2	53,753	35.0
1989	159,338	106,355	66.7	101,584	63.8	4,770	4.5	52,983	33.3
1990	160,415	107,177	66.8	102,087	63.6	5,091	4.7	53,237	33.2
1991	161,511	107,486	66.6	101,039	62.6	6,447	6.0	54,025	33.4
1992	162,658	108,526	66.7	101,479	62.4	7,047	6.5	54,132	33.3
1993	163,921	109,359	66.7	102,812	62.7	6,547	6.0	54,562	33.3

Source: U.S. Bureau of the Census. *Statistical Abstract of the United States, 1994.* 114th ed. Washington, DC: U.S. Government Printing Office, 1994, p. 396. Primary sources: U.S. Bureau of Labor Statistics. Bulletin 2307; and *Employment and Earnings* (monthly; January issues). *Note:* 1. Civilian employed as a percent of the civilian noninstitutional population.

★ 583 ★

Workers: Whites

Unemployed White Workers: 1980-1993

For civilian noninstitutional population 16 years old and over. Annual averages of monthly figures.

[In thousands, except as indicated]

Age	1980	1985	1988	1989	1990	1991	1992	1993
Unemployed[1]	5,884	6,191	4,944	4,770	5,091	6,447	7,047	6,547
16 to 19 years old	1,291	1,074	910	863	856	977	983	943
20 to 24 years old	1,364	1,235	874	856	844	1,063	1,084	991
Unemployment rate (percent)[2]	6.3	6.2	4.7	4.5	4.7	6.0	6.5	6.0
16 to 19 years old	15.5	15.7	13.1	12.7	13.4	16.4	17.1	16.2
20 to 24 years old	9.9	9.2	7.1	7.2	7.2	9.2	9.4	8.7

Source: U.S. Bureau of the Census. *Statistical Abstract of the United States, 1994.* 114th ed. Washington, DC: U.S. Government Printing Office, 1994, p. 416. Primary sources: U.S. Bureau of Labor Statistics. *Employment and Earnings* (monthly; January issues); and unpublished data. *Notes:* 1. Includes other ages not shown separately. 2. Unemployed as percent of civilian labor force in specified group. Includes other ages not shown separately.

Workers: Women

★ 584 ★

Employment Status of Women: 1960-1993

Table shows data for the civilian noninstitutionalized population 16 years old and older. Annual averages of monthly figures. Based on Current Population Survey.

[In thousands, except as indicated]

Year	Civilian noninstitutional population	Civilian labor force				Unemployed		Not in labor force	
		Total	Percent of population	Employed	Employment/ population ratio[1]	Number	Percent of labor force	Number	Percent of population
1960	61,582	23,240	37.7	21,874	35.5	1,366	5.9	38,343	62.3
1970	72,782	31,543	43.3	29,688	40.8	1,855	5.9	41,239	56.7
1980	88,348	45,487	51.5	42,117	47.7	3,370	7.4	42,861	48.5
1985	93,736	51,050	54.5	47,259	50.4	3,791	7.4	42,686	45.5
1989	97,630	56,030	57.4	53,027	54.3	3,003	5.4	41,601	42.6
1990	98,399	56,554	57.5	53,479	54.3	3,075	5.4	41,845	42.5
1991	99,214	56,893	57.3	53,284	53.7	3,609	6.3	42,321	42.7

[Continued]

★ 584 ★

Employment Status of Women: 1960-1993

[Continued]

Year	Civilian noninstitutional population	Civilian labor force						Not in labor force	
		Total	Percent of population	Employed	Employment/population ratio[1]	Unemployed		Not in labor force	
						Number	Percent of labor force	Number	Percent of population
1992	100,035	57,798	57.8	53,793	53.8	4,005	6.9	42,237	42.2
1993	100,930	58,407	57.9	54,606	54.1	3,801	6.5	42,522	42.1

Source: U.S. Bureau of the Census. Statistical Abstract of the United States, 1994. 114th ed. Washington, DC: U.S. Government Printing Office, 1994, p. 396. Primary sources: U.S. Bureau of Labor Statistics. Bulletin 2307; and Employment and Earnings (monthly; January issues). Notes: 1. Civilian employed as a percent of the civilian noninstitutional population.

★ 585 ★

Workers: Women

Labor Force Participation Rates of Women, by Marital Status and Age: 1960-1993

Annual averages of monthly figures. Based on Current Population Survey.

Marital status and year	Total	16-19 years	20-24 years	25-34 years	35-44 years	45-64 years	65 and over
Single:							
1960	58.6	30.2	77.2	83.4	82.9	79.8	24.3
1970	56.8	44.7	73.0	81.4	78.6	73.0	19.7
1975	59.8	49.6	72.5	80.8	78.6	68.3	15.8
1980	64.4	53.6	75.2	83.3	76.9	65.6	13.9
1985	66.6	52.3	76.3	82.4	80.8	67.9	9.8
1989	68.0	54.1	76.4	82.2	81.6	66.3	11.4
1990	66.9	51.8	74.7	81.2	81.0	66.1	12.2
1991	66.5	50.3	73.5	80.3	81.2	68.4	12.7
1992	66.4	49.2	73.7	80.5	80.6	68.2	11.3
1993	66.4	49.8	74.2	79.1	79.1	68.8	12.5
Married:[1]							
1960	31.9	27.2	31.7	28.8	37.2	36.0	6.7
1970	40.5	37.8	47.9	38.8	46.8	44.0	7.3
1975	44.3	46.2	57.0	48.4	52.0	43.8	7.0
1980	49.8	49.3	61.4	58.8	61.8	46.9	7.3
1985	53.8	49.6	65.7	65.8	68.1	49.4	6.6
1989	57.8	51.9	65.7	69.0	73.5	55.5	8.1
1990	58.4	50.0	66.5	69.8	74.0	56.5	8.5
1991	58.5	48.7	65.0	70.1	74.3	57.1	8.3
1992	59.2	49.0	66.3	70.9	74.8	58.6	7.9
1993	59.4	50.1	65.6	70.8	74.7	60.0	7.6
Other:[2]							
1960	41.6	43.5	58.0	63.1	70.0	60.0	11.4

[Continued]

★ 585 ★

Labor Force Participation Rates of Women, by Marital Status and Age: 1960-1993
[Continued]

Marital status and year	Total	16-19 years	20-24 years	25-34 years	35-44 years	45-64 years	65 and over
1970	40.3	48.6	60.3	64.6	68.8	61.9	10.0
1975	40.1	47.6	65.3	68.6	69.2	59.0	8.3
1980	43.6	50.0	68.4	76.5	77.1	60.2	8.2
1985	45.1	51.9	66.2	76.9	81.6	61.0	7.5
1989	47.0	48.2	65.8	78.3	82.2	64.7	8.3
1990	47.2	54.4	65.6	77.3	82.3	65.0	8.5
1991	46.8	45.8	63.3	74.8	82.1	65.2	8.4
1992	47.0	47.8	66.9	75.7	81.6	66.4	8.4
1993	47.1	53.3	65.2	75.2	81.6	66.9	8.2

Source: U.S. Bureau of the Census. *Statistical Abstract of the United States, 1994.* 114th ed. Washington, DC: U.S. Government Printing Office, 1994, p. 401. Primary sources: U.S. Bureau of Labor Statistics. Bulletins 2217 and 2340; and unpublished data. *Notes:* 1. Spouse present. 2. Widowed, divorced, and married (spouse absent).

★ 586 ★

Workers: Women

Unemployed Women: 1980-1993

For civilian noninstitutional population 16 years old and over. Annual averages of monthly figures.

[In thousands, except as indicated]

Age and family status	1980	1985	1988	1989	1990	1991	1992	1993
Unemployed	3,370	3,791	3,046	3,003	3,075	3,609	4,005	3,801
16 to 19 years old	755	661	558	536	519	581	591	568
20 to 24 years old	760	794	585	558	555	628	662	613
25 to 44 years old	1,345	1,732	1,439	1,437	1,498	1,775	1,999	1,871
45 to 64 years old	473	566	427	430	456	575	686	703
65 years and over	36	39	38	41	46	50	66	46
Unemployment rate (percent)[1]	7.4	7.4	5.6	5.4	5.4	6.3	6.9	6.5
16 to 19 years old	17.2	17.6	14.4	14.0	14.7	17.4	18.5	17.4
20 to 24 years old	10.4	10.7	8.5	8.3	8.5	9.8	10.2	9.6
25 to 44 years old	6.4	6.6	4.9	4.8	4.9	5.7	6.4	6.0
45 to 64 years old	4.0	4.6	3.2	3.1	3.2	3.9	4.4	4.4
65 years and over	3.1	3.3	2.9	2.9	3.1	3.3	4.5	3.1
Women maintaining families[2]	9.2	10.5	8.2	8.1	8.2	9.1	9.9	9.5

[Continued]

★ 586 ★

Unemployed Women: 1980-1993
[Continued]

Age and family status	1980	1985	1988	1989	1990	1991	1992	1993
White	7.3	8.1	6.0	6.1	6.3	7.2	7.8	7.7
Black	14.0	16.4	13.7	13.0	13.1	13.9	14.7	13.7

Source: U.S. Bureau of the Census. *Statistical Abstract of the United States, 1994.* 114th ed. Washington, DC: U.S. Government Printing Office, 1994, p. 416. Primary sources: U.S. Bureau of Labor Statistics. *Employment and Earnings* (monthly; January issues); and unpublished data. *Notes:* 1. Unemployed as percent of civilian labor force in specified group. 2. Includes other races, not shown separately.

★ 587 ★

Workers: Women

Wives in the Labor Force: 1975-1993

Table shows the labor force participation rates of wives with husbands present by age of own youngest child. As of March. For civilian noninstitutional population, 16 years old and over.

Presence and age of child	Total			White			Black		
	1975	1985	1993	1975	1985	1993	1975	1985	1993
Wives, total	44.4	54.2	59.4	43.6	53.3	58.9	54.1	63.8	64.8
No children under 18	43.8	48.2	52.4	43.6	47.5	52.2	47.6	55.2	53.8
With children under 18	44.9	60.8	67.5	43.6	59.9	66.9	58.4	71.7	75.3
Under 6, total	36.7	53.4	59.6	34.7	52.1	58.6	54.9	69.6	70.9
Under 3	32.7	50.5	57.3	30.7	49.4	56.7	50.1	66.2	65.6
1 year or under	30.8	49.4	57.5	29.2	48.6	56.8	50.0	63.7	64.8
2 years	37.1	54.0	58.1	35.1	52.7	56.5	56.4	69.9	74.5
3 to 5 years	42.2	58.4	63.1	40.1	56.6	61.6	61.2	73.8	78.1
3 years	41.2	55.1	61.6	39.0	52.7	60.2	62.7	72.3	79.4
4 years	41.2	59.7	65.7	38.7	58.4	64.3	64.9	70.6	79.3
5 years	44.4	62.1	63.1	43.8	59.9	61.4	56.3	79.1	77.5
6 to 13 years	51.8	68.2	74.7	50.7	67.7	74.5	65.7	73.3	80.6
14 to 17 years	53.5	67.0	75.6	53.4	66.6	75.6	52.3	74.4	75.7

Source: U.S. Bureau of the Census. *Statistical Abstract of the United States, 1994.* 114th ed. Washington, DC: U.S. Government Printing Office, 1994, p. 402. Primary sources: U.S. Bureau of Labor Statistics. Bulletin 2340; and unpublished data.

★ 588 ★
Workers: Women

Women in Management, by Company: 1990

Wells Fargo - 66.1	
BankAmerica - 61.2	
Aetna Life and Casualty - 48.9	
Chemical Bank - 44.4	
Citicorp - 41.5	
Sara Lee - 36.2	
PepsiCo. - 31.8	
Johnson & Johnson - 27.9	
H. J. Heinz Co. - 27.6	
Monsanto Co. - 15.9	
Weyerhaeuser - 13.8	
Ralston-Purina - 12.6	
Dow Chemical - 9.6	
DuPont Co. - 9.3	
Nucor - 2.6	

Table shows the female officers and managers at selected companies. Data are for 1990 unless otherwise noted.

[In percentages]

Company	Female officers and managers
Wells Fargo	66.1
BankAmerica	61.2
Aetna Life and Casualty	48.9
Chemical Bank	44.4
Citicorp	41.5
Sara Lee	36.2
PepsiCo.	31.8
Johnson & Johnson	27.9
H. J. Heinz Co.	27.6
Monsanto Co.	15.9
Weyerhaeuser	13.8
Ralston-Purina	12.6
Nucor[1]	2.6
Dow Chemical	9.6
DuPont Co.	9.3

Source: Sharpe, Rochelle. "Family Friendly Firms Don't Always Promote Females." *Wall Street Journal,* 29 March 1994, p. B1. Primary sources: Families and Work Institute; *Wall Street Journal* study. *Note:* 1. 1993.

Women in the Civilian Labor Force, by Marital Status: 1960-1993

Annual averages of monthly figures. For civilian noninstitutional population 16 years old and over. Based on Current Population Survey.

Year	Female labor force (1,000)				Female participation rate[3]			
	Total	Single	Married[1]	Other[2]	Total	Single	Married[1]	Other[2]
1960	23,240	5,410	12,893	4,937	37.7	58.6	31.9	41.6
1965	26,200	5,976	14,829	5,396	39.3	54.5	34.9	40.7
1970	31,543	7,265	18,475	5,804	43.3	56.8	40.5	40.3
1975	37,475	9,125	21,484	6,866	46.3	59.8	44.3	40.1
1978	42,631	11,067	23,539	8,025	50.0	63.7	47.8	42.8
1979	44,235	11,597	24,378	8,260	50.9	64.6	49.0	43.1
1980	45,487	11,865	24,980	8,643	51.5	64.4	49.9	43.6
1981	46,696	12,124	25,428	9,144	52.1	64.5	50.5	44.6
1982	47,755	12,460	25,971	9,324	52.6	65.1	51.1	44.8
1983	48,503	12,659	26,468	9,376	52.9	65.0	51.8	44.4
1984	49,709	12,867	27,199	9,644	53.6	65.6	52.8	44.7
1985	51,050	13,163	27,894	9,993	54.5	66.6	53.8	45.1
1986	52,413	13,512	28,623	10,277	55.3	67.2	54.9	45.6
1987	53,658	13,885	29,381	10,393	56.0	67.4	55.9	45.7
1988	54,742	14,194	29,921	10,627	56.6	67.7	56.7	46.2
1989	56,030	14,377	30,548	11,104	57.4	68.0	57.8	47.0
1990	56,554	14,229	30,970	11,354	57.5	66.9	58.4	47.2
1991	56,893	14,295	31,175	11,423	57.3	66.5	58.5	46.8
1992	57,798	14,477	31,720	11,601	57.8	66.4	59.2	47.0
1993	58,407	14,624	31,978	11,805	57.9	66.4	59.4	47.1

Source: U.S. Bureau of the Census. *Statistical Abstract of the United States, 1994.* 114th ed. Washington, DC: U.S. Government Printing Office, 1994. p. 401. Primary sources: U.S. Bureau of Labor Statistics. Bulletin 2307; and unpublished data. *Notes:* 1. Husband present. 2. Widowed, divorced, or separated. 3. Percent of female civilian noninstitutional population in the civilian labor force.

Women in the Civilian Labor Force, by Marital Status and Presence and Age of Children: 1960-1993

As of March. For 1960, civilian noninstitutional persons 14 years old and over, thereafter 16 years old and over. Based on Current Population Survey.

Women	Total			With any children								
				Total			Children 6 to 17 only			Children under 6		
	Single	Married[1]	Other[2]	Single	Married[1]	Other[2]	Single	Married[1]	Other[2]	Single	Married[1]	Other[2]
In labor force (million)												
1960	5.4	12.3	4.9	(NA)	6.6	1.5	(NA)	4.1	1.0	(NA)	2.5	0.4
1970	7.0	18.4	5.9	(NA)	10.2	1.9	(NA)	6.3	1.3	(NA)	3.9	0.6

[Continued]

★ 590 ★

Women in the Civilian Labor Force, by Marital Status and Presence and Age of Children: 1960-1993
[Continued]

Women	Total			With any children								
				Total			Children 6 to 17 only			Children under 6		
	Single	Married[1]	Other[2]	Single	Married[1]	Other[2]	Single	Married[1]	Other[2]	Single	Married[1]	Other[2]
1980	11.2	24.9	8.8	0.6	13.7	3.6	0.2	8.4	2.6	0.3	5.2	1.0
1985	12.9	27.7	10.3	1.1	14.9	4.0	0.4	8.5	2.9	0.7	6.4	1.1
1989	14.0	30.5	10.7	1.5	16.4	4.0	0.6	9.4	2.8	1.0	7.0	1.1
1990	14.0	31.0	11.2	1.5	16.5	4.2	0.6	9.3	3.0	0.9	7.2	1.2
1991	14.1	31.1	11.1	1.7	16.6	4.1	0.6	9.1	3.0	1.1	7.4	1.2
1992	14.1	31.7	11.5	1.7	16.8	4.2	0.7	9.5	3.0	1.0	7.3	1.2
1993	14.1	32.2	11.3	1.9	16.9	4.2	0.7	9.7	3.0	1.1	7.3	1.2
Participation rate[3]												
1960	44.1	30.5	40.0	(NA)	27.6	56.0	(NA)	39.0	65.9	(NA)	18.6	40.5
1970	53.0	40.8	39.1	(NA)	39.7	60.7	(NA)	49.2	66.9	(NA)	30.3	52.2
1980	61.5	50.1	44.0	52.0	54.1	69.4	67.6	61.7	74.6	44.1	45.1	60.3
1985	65.2	54.2	45.6	51.6	60.8	71.9	64.1	67.8	77.8	46.5	53.4	59.7
1989	66.0	57.6	46.0	54.7	65.6	72.0	69.0	73.4	78.2	48.9	57.4	60.1
1990	66.4	58.2	46.8	55.2	66.3	74.2	69.7	73.6	79.7	48.7	58.9	63.6
1991	65.1	58.5	46.2	53.6	66.8	72.7	64.8	73.6	79.5	48.8	59.9	59.8
1992	64.7	59.3	46.7	52.5	67.8	73.2	67.2	75.4	80.0	45.8	59.9	60.5
1993	64.5	59.4	45.9	54.4	67.5	72.1	70.2	74.9	78.3	47.4	59.6	60.0
Employment (million)												
1960	5.1	11.6	4.6	(NA)	6.2	1.3	(NA)	3.9	0.9	(NA)	2.3	0.4
1970	6.5	17.5	5.6	(NA)	9.6	1.8	(NA)	6.0	1.2	(NA)	3.6	0.6
1980	10.1	23.6	8.2	0.4	12.8	3.3	0.2	8.1	2.4	0.2	4.8	0.9
1985	11.6	26.1	9.4	0.9	13.9	3.5	0.3	8.1	2.6	0.5	5.9	0.9
1989	12.8	29.4	10.1	1.2	15.8	3.6	0.5	9.1	2.6	0.7	6.7	1.0
1990	12.9	29.9	10.5	1.2	15.8	3.8	0.5	8.9	2.7	0.7	6.9	1.1
1991	12.9	29.7	10.4	1.4	15.7	3.7	0.5	8.8	2.7	0.8	6.9	1.0
1992	12.8	30.1	10.6	1.4	15.9	3.7	0.6	9.1	2.7	0.8	6.8	1.0
1993	12.7	30.8	10.5	1.5	16.1	3.9	0.6	9.3	2.8	0.9	6.8	1.1
Unemployment rate[4]												
1960	6.0	5.4	6.2	(NA)	6.0	8.4	(NA)	4.9	6.8	(NA)	7.8	12.5
1970	7.1	4.8	4.8	(NA)	6.0	7.2	(NA)	4.8	5.9	(NA)	7.9	9.8
1980	10.3	5.3	6.4	23.2	5.9	9.2	15.6	4.4	7.9	29.2	8.3	12.8
1985	10.2	5.7	8.5	23.8	6.6	12.1	15.4	5.5	10.6	28.5	8.0	16.1
1989	8.1	3.4	5.7	21.3	3.8	8.4	14.3	3.7	7.2	25.3	4.1	11.3
1990	8.2	3.5	5.7	18.4	4.2	8.5	14.5	3.8	7.7	20.8	4.8	10.2
1991	8.8	4.6	6.8	17.9	5.3	9.1	10.7	4.2	7.7	22.0	6.7	12.7
1992	9.1	4.9	7.6	17.3	5.7	10.8	14.1	4.6	8.6	19.4	7.0	16.3
1993	9.8	4.4	6.9	19.2	4.8	8.5	13.7	3.8	7.0	22.8	6.2	12.5

Source: U.S. Bureau of the Census. Statistical Abstract of the United States, 1994. 114th ed. Washington, DC: U.S. Government Printing Office, 1994, p. 402. Primary sources: U.S. Bureau of Labor Statistics. Bulletin 2307; and unpublished data. Notes: "NA" represents "not available." 1. Husband present. 2. Widowed, divorced or separated. 3. Percent of women in each specific category in the labor force. 4. Unemployed as a percent of civilian labor force in specified group.

★ 591 ★

Workers: Women

Working Women, by Metropolitan Area: 1990

```
┌─────────────────────────────────────────────────┐
│  ┌─────────────────────────────────────────────┐ │
│  │ Anchorage, Alaska - 69.9                     │ │
│  └─────────────────────────────────────────────┘ │
│  ┌──────────────────────────────────────────┐    │
│  │ Madison, Wisconsin - 69.4                  │    │
│  └──────────────────────────────────────────┘    │
│  ┌──────────────────────────────────────────┐    │
│  │ Washington, District of Columbia - 68.8    │    │
│  └──────────────────────────────────────────┘    │
│  ┌──────────────────────────────────────────┐    │
│  │ Nashua, New Hampshire - 68.5               │    │
│  └──────────────────────────────────────────┘    │
│  ┌──────────────────────────────────────────┐    │
│  │ Iowa City, Iowa - 68.2                     │    │
│  └──────────────────────────────────────────┘    │
│  ┌──────────────────────────────────────────┐    │
│  │ Rochester, Minnesota - 67.9                │    │
│  └──────────────────────────────────────────┘    │
│  ┌──────────────────────────────────────────┐    │
│  │ Sioux Falls, South Dakota - 67.7           │    │
│  └──────────────────────────────────────────┘    │
│  ┌──────────────────────────────────────────┐    │
│  │ Minneapolis, Minnesota - 67.3              │    │
│  └──────────────────────────────────────────┘    │
│  ┌──────────────────────────────────────────┐    │
│  │ Middletown, Connecticut - 67.0             │    │
│  └──────────────────────────────────────────┘    │
│  ┌──────────────────────────────────────────┐    │
│  │ Reno, Nevada - 67.0                        │    │
│  └──────────────────────────────────────────┘    │
└─────────────────────────────────────────────────┘
```

Table shows the metropolitan areas reporting the most working women in 1990.

[In percentages]

Metropolitan area	Working women
Anchorage, Alaska	69.9
Madison, Wisconsin	69.4
Washington, District of Columbia	68.8
Nashua, New Hampshire	68.5
Iowa City, Iowa	68.2
Rochester, Minnesota	67.9
Sioux Falls, South Dakota	67.7
Minneapolis, Minnesota	67.3
Middletown, Connecticut	67.0
Reno, Nevada	67.0

Source: "Ethics in the News." *Business & Society Review* (winter 1994), p. 5.

Chapter 5
EARNINGS AND COSTS OF EMPLOYMENT

This chapter consists of more than 60 tables detailing employment costs and employee earnings in the American workplace. Tables profile compensation costs; that is, dollars required for employers to pay wages and salaries, plus employee benefits. Compensation and cost control strategies are covered as well. Tables have been prepared for specific business costs such as business travel, health and safety, health care, relocation, Social Security, and taxes. In addition, tables show the earnings of men and women, and indicate pay disparities by sex, sexual preference, location, and other characterisitics. Tables also cover pay increases and wage rates, including minimum wage.

Compensation

★ 592 ★

Benefit Costs: 1993

From the source: "Employee benefit costs hit a record high in 1993, driven largely by corporate restructuring and rising health insurance premiums" (p. 36). According to a U.S. Chamber of Commerce survey—on an average—employers spent $14,807 per worker for employee benefits during 1993. The table shows the cost of selected benefits as a percentage of payroll costs.

Benefit	Percent of payroll costs
Medical and related benefits	26.7
Payments for time not worked[1]	25.2
Payments required by law[2]	21.1
Retirement and savings plans	16.0
Paid rest periods	5.6

[Continued]

★ 592 ★

Benefit Costs: 1993
[Continued]

Benefit	Percent of payroll costs
Miscellaneous[3]	3.9
Life insurance	1.5

Source: Thompson, Roger. "Benefit Costs Hit Record High." *Nation's Business* (February 1995), p. 36. Primary source: U.S. Chamber of Commerce. *Notes:* 1. Vacations, holidays, and like time off. 2. Social Security, workers' compensation, and like requirements. 3. Discounts, educational assistance, and like benefits.

★ 593 ★

Compensation

Compensation and Earning Changes: 1980-1993

Table shows the annual percent changes in earnings and compensation from immediate prior year. Minus sign (-) indicates decrease.

Item	1980	1985	1987	1988	1989	1990	1991	1992	1993
Current dollars:									
Hourly earnings, total[1]	8.1	3.0	2.5	3.3	4.1	3.6	3.1	2.5	2.4
Hourly earnings, manufacturing	8.5	3.8	1.8	2.8	2.8	3.3	3.2	2.5	2.6
Compensation per employee-hour[1]	10.7	4.1	3.5	4.2	3.3	5.5	5.0	5.1	3.6
Constant (1982) dollars:									
Hourly earnings, total[1]	-4.8	-0.4	-1.0	-0.5	-0.7	-1.6	-0.9	-0.4	-0.4
Hourly earnings, manufacturing	-4.5	0.3	-1.6	-1.2	-1.9	-1.7	-0.9	-0.4	-0.2
Compensation per employee-hour[1]	-2.5	0.6	-0.2	0.1	-1.4	0.1	0.8	2.0	0.6
Consumer Price Index	13.5	3.6	3.6	4.1	4.8	5.4	4.2	3.0	3.0

Source: U.S. Bureau of the Census. *Statistical Abstract of the United States, 1994.* 114th ed. Washington, DC: U.S. Government Printing Office, 1994, p. 427. Primary sources: U.S. Bureau of Labor Statistics. *Monthly Labor Review;* and unpublished data. *Note:* 1. Nonfarm business sector.

★ 594 ★

Compensation

Compensation Costs for Self-Employed

Nearly 8 percent of the workforce (excluding those in agriculture) is self-employed and without corporate-sponsored employee benefit programs. "The cost of replacing employer-provided benefits could be hefty," warns the source, since benefits and legally required taxes comprise about 22 percent of an average employer's expenses for each worker. The table below profiles a typical compensation package.

[In percentages]

Item	Compensation
Salary	71.4
Mandatory contributions[1]	9.3
Insurance	7.2
Paid leave	6.6
Retirement and savings	2.9
Supplemental pay	2.5
Other benefits	0.2

Source: Birnbaum, Jane. "Benefits Pose Challenge for Entrepreneurs." *St. Louis Post-Dispatch,* 23 December 1994, p. 5C. Primary source: Employee Benefits Reasearch Institute. *Notes:* Figures do not add to total due to rounding. 1. Employer's share of Social Security taxes, worker's compensation, and unemployment insurance.

★ 595 ★

Compensation

Employee Compensation Costs: 1989-1993

Table shows employer costs for employee compensation for each hour worked, as of March, for private industry workers. Based on a sample of establishments.

[In dollars]

Compensation component	1989	1990	1991	1992	1993 Total	1993 Goods producing[1]	1993 Service producing[2]	1993 Manufacturing	1993 Non-manufacturing
Total compensation	14.28	14.96	15.40	16.14	16.70	20.22	15.51	20.09	15.85
Wages and salaries	10.38	10.84	11.14	11.58	11.90	13.54	11.34	13.35	11.54
Total benefits	3.90	4.13	4.27	4.55	4.80	6.67	4.17	6.74	4.31
Paid leave	1.00	1.03	1.05	1.09	1.11	1.38	1.01	1.52	1.00
Vacation	0.50	0.51	0.52	0.54	0.54	0.72	0.48	0.78	0.48
Holiday	0.34	0.34	0.35	0.37	0.38	0.50	0.34	0.56	0.33
Sick	0.12	0.13	0.13	0.14	0.14	0.11	0.15	0.13	0.14
Other	0.04	0.04	0.05	0.05	0.05	0.05	0.05	0.06	0.05
Supplemental pay	0.34	0.37	0.36	0.39	0.42	0.67	0.34	0.71	0.35
Premium pay	0.17	0.17	0.17	0.18	0.19	0.39	0.12	0.39	0.14
Nonproduction bonuses	0.12	0.16	0.13	0.15	0.19	0.21	0.18	0.23	0.18
Shift pay	0.05	0.05	0.05	0.05	0.05	0.08	0.04	0.10	0.04
Insurance	0.85	0.92	1.01	1.12	1.19	1.74	1.01	1.86	1.03
Health insurance	(NA)	(NA)	(NA)	1.02	1.10	1.59	0.93	1.69	0.95

[Continued]

★ 595 ★

Employee Compensation Costs: 1989-1993
[Continued]

Compensation component	1989	1990	1991	1992	1993				
					Total	Goods producing[1]	Service producing[2]	Manufacturing	Non-manufacturing
Retirement and savings	0.42	0.45	0.44	0.46	0.48	0.77	0.39	0.72	0.43
Pensions	0.34	0.36	0.35	0.36	0.38	0.60	0.31	0.55	0.34
Savings and thrift	0.08	0.09	0.10	0.10	0.10	0.17	0.08	0.17	0.09
Legally required[3]	1.27	1.35	1.40	1.47	1.55	1.99	1.40	1.79	1.49
Social Security	0.84	0.89	0.92	0.96	0.99	1.17	0.93	1.16	0.95
Federal unemployment	0.03	0.03	0.03	0.03	0.03	0.03	0.03	0.03	0.03
State unemployment	0.11	0.09	0.09	0.10	0.11	0.15	0.10	0.14	0.11
Workers' compensation	0.27	0.31	0.33	0.36	0.39	0.63	0.31	0.44	0.38
Other benefits[4]	0.02	(Z)	(Z)	0.02	0.04	0.12	(NA)	0.14	0.02

Source: U.S. Bureau of the Census. Statistical Abstract of the United States, 1994. 114th ed. Washington, DC: U.S. Government Printing Office, 1994, p. 433. Primary sources: U.S. Bureau of Labor Statistics. News, Employer Costs for Employee Compensation. USDL 89-295, 90-317, 91-292, 92-391, and 93-220. Notes: "NA" represents "not available." "Z" represents or rounds to zero. 1. Mining, construction, and manufacturing. 2. Transportation, communications, public utilities, wholesale trade, retail trade, finance, insurance, real estate, and services. 3. Includes railroad retirement, railroad unemployment, railroad supplemental unemployment, and other legally required benefits, not shown separately. 4. Includes severance pay and supplemental unemployment benefits.

★ 596 ★
Compensation

Employment Cost Index: 1982-1993

As of December. The Employment Cost Index (ECI) is a measure of the rate of change in compensation (wages, salaries, and employer costs for employee benefits). Data are not seasonally adjusted: 1982-1985 based on fixed employment counts from 1970 Census of Population; thereafter, based on fixed employment counts from the 1980 Census of Population.

Item	Indexes (June 1989 = 100)						Percent change for 12 month ending:				
	1982	1985	1990	1991	1992	1993	1985	1990	1991	1992	1993
Civilian workers[1]	74.8	86.8	107.6	112.2	116.1	120.2	4.3	4.9	4.3	3.5	3.5
Workers, by occupational group:											
White-collar workers	72.9	85.8	108.3	112.8	116.6	120.6	4.9	5.2	4.2	3.4	3.4
Blue-collar workers	78.2	88.4	106.5	111.1	115.2	119.4	3.3	4.4	4.3	3.7	3.6
Service workers	74.3	87.2	108.0	113.1	116.7	120.5	3.9	5.1	4.7	3.2	3.3
Workers, by industry division:											
Manufacturing	76.9	87.8	107.2	112.2	116.5	121.3	3.3	5.1	4.7	3.8	4.1
Nonmanufacturing	73.9	86.4	107.8	112.3	116.0	119.8	4.7	4.9	4.2	3.3	3.3
Services	70.5	84.1	110.2	114.6	119.2	122.9	4.7	6.3	4.0	4.0	3.1
Public administration[2]	71.9	85.4	108.7	112.6	116.3	120.0	4.9	5.3	3.6	3.3	3.2
Private industry workers[3]	75.8	87.3	107.0	111.7	115.6	119.8	3.9	4.6	4.4	3.5	3.6
Workers, by occupational group:											
White-collar workers	73.7	86.4	107.4	112.2	115.9	120.2	4.9	4.9	4.5	3.3	3.7
Blue-collar workers	78.4	88.5	106.4	111.0	115.0	119.3	3.1	4.4	4.3	3.6	3.7
Service workers	76.3	88.4	107.3	112.4	115.9	119.5	3.0	4.7	4.8	3.1	3.1
Workers, by industry division:											
Manufacturing	76.9	87.8	107.2	112.2	116.5	121.3	3.3	5.1	4.7	3.8	4.1
Nonmanufacturing	75.1	87.0	106.9	111.5	115.1	119.0	4.3	4.5	4.3	3.2	3.4
Services	(NA)	84.1	109.3	114.0	118.9	123.1	(NA)	6.2	4.3	4.3	3.5
Business services	(NA)	(NA)	107.4	111.1	115.9	118.6	(NA)	6.0	3.4	4.3	2.3
Health services	(NA)	83.7	110.8	116.5	121.8	126.0	(NA)	6.8	5.1	4.5	3.4

[Continued]

★ 596 ★

Employment Cost Index: 1982-1993
[Continued]

Item	Indexes (June 1989 = 100)						Percent change for 12 month ending:				
	1982	1985	1990	1991	1992	1993	1985	1990	1991	1992	1993
Hospitals	(NA)	(NA)	110.7	116.1	121.6	125.6	(NA)	7.0	4.9	4.7	3.3
Workers by bargaining status:											
Union	79.6	90.1	106.2	111.1	115.9	120.9	2.6	4.3	4.6	4.3	4.3
Nonunion	74.3	86.3	107.3	111.9	115.5	119.5	4.6	4.8	4.3	3.2	3.5
State and local government workers	70.8	84.6	110.4	114.4	118.6	121.9	5.6	5.8	3.6	3.7	2.8
Workers, by occupational group:											
White-collar workers	70.4	84.2	110.9	114.6	118.9	121.9	5.8	6.0	3.3	3.8	2.5
Blue-collar workers	73.9	86.7	108.7	112.9	117.8	121.4	5.3	4.8	3.9	4.3	3.1
Workers, by industry division:											
Services	70.0	84.0	111.3	115.3	119.6	122.6	5.9	6.3	3.6	3.7	2.5
Schools	69.0	83.6	111.6	115.6	119.9	122.9	6.2	6.0	3.6	3.7	2.5
Elementary and secondary	68.6	83.6	112.1	116.2	120.7	123.6	6.4	6.3	3.7	3.9	2.4
Colleges and universities	(NA)	(NA)	110.2	113.5	117.2	120.7	(NA)	5.3	3.0	3.3	3.0
Services, excluding schools[4]	73.1	85.2	110.2	114.4	118.6	121.9	4.7	6.8	3.8	3.7	2.8
Public administration[2]	71.9	85.4	108.7	112.6	116.3	120.0	4.9	5.3	3.6	3.3	3.2

Source: U.S. Bureau of the Census. *Statistical Abstract of the United States, 1994.* 114th ed. Washington, DC: U.S. Government Printing Office, 1994, p. 431. Primary source: U.S. Bureau of Labor Statistics. *News, Employment Cost Index* (quarterly). *Notes:* "NA" stands for "not available." 1. Includes private industry and state and local government workers and excludes farm, household, and federal government workers. 2. Consists of legislative, judicial, administrative, and regulatory activities. 3. Excludes farm and household workers. 4. Includes library, social, and health services. Formerly called "hospitals and other services."

★ 597 ★
Compensation

Paid Leave Costs

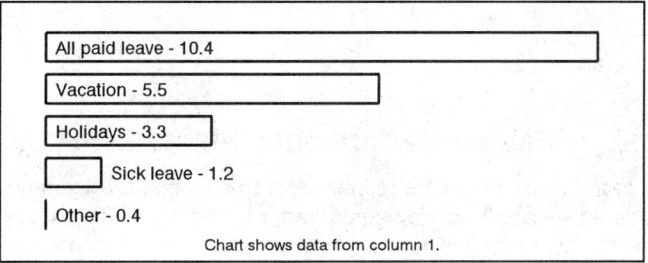

All paid leave - 10.4
Vacation - 5.5
Holidays - 3.3
Sick leave - 1.2
Other - 0.4

Chart shows data from column 1.

Table shows paid leave time as a percentage of total payroll costs.

[In percentages]

Leave	All employers	Manufacturing	Non-manufacturing
All paid leave	10.4	10.8	10.4
Vacation	5.5	5.7	5.4
Holidays	3.3	3.4	3.3
Sick leave	1.2	1.2	1.3
Other	0.4	0.5	0.4

Source: Leonard, Bill. "The Employee's Favorite, the Employer's Quandry." *HR Magazine* (November 1994), p. 53. Primary source: Bureau of Labor Statistics.

Compensation Methods

★ 598 ★

Broadbanding

Survey respondents most often cited flatter organizations and new corporate cultures as reasons for adopting broadbanding as a compensation strategy. The table below shows reasons listed by respondents for broadbanding.

Reason	Companies
Supports flatter organizations	71
Nurtures new organizational culture	71
Promotes widely skilled workforce	57
Facilitates career development	57
Minimizes administrative effort	55
Reduces job evaluations	55
Addresses compensation faults	45
Downplays promotions	40
Emphasizes individual performance	36
Responds to request from a top executive	26
Supports changes in job structure	26
Supports decentralized administration	14
Responds to changes in employee demographics	7
Other	16

Source: "Companies Cite Reasons for Broadbanding." *Personnel Journal* (June 1994), p. 20. Primary source: Hewitt Associates. *Note:* Total exceeds 100 percent due to multiple responses.

★ 599 ★
Compensation Methods

Pay-for-Performance Plans: 1994

More than 30 percent of the respondents to a Coopers & Lybrand survey considered a pay-for-performance program in 1994. The table below shows the types of pay-for-performance plans under consideration by survey respondents.

[In percentages]

Pay-for-performance plan	Companies
Team/group incentives	19.6
Merit-based pay	13.7
Miscellaneous plans	11.8
Variable pay plan	9.8
Bonuses	7.8
Gainsharing	7.8

[Continued]

★ 599 ★

Pay-for-Performance Plans: 1994
[Continued]

Pay-for-performance plan	Companies
Job and pay banding	3.9
Salary commission	3.9

Source: "Pay-for-Performance Plans Become More Popular." *Personnel Journal* (February 1994), p. 22. Primary source: Coopers & Lybrand Human Resource Advisory Group. *Notes:* Percentages based on 30.5 percent of 187 surveyed companies indicating that they were considering the implementation of a pay-for-performance plan in 1994.

★ 600 ★
Compensation Methods

Variable Pay Programs, by Region

Table shows the organizations with variable pay programs. Data are presented by region of the United States.

[In percentages]

Region	Organizations
North Central	50.0
Northeast	48.5
South Central	47.2
United States	46.9
West Coast	43.8
Southeast	41.2

Source: "Percent of Organziations With Variable Pay Programs." *HR Focus* (July 1994), p. 14. Primary source: 1994-1995 ECS Survey of Supervisory Management Compensation; Wyatt Data Services.

Cost Control

★ 601 ★

Flexible Benefit Plan Cost Reductions

Table shows some of the reasons for cost reductions when employers adopted flexible benefit plans. Data taken from a survey of more than 1,300 companies employing 1,000 or more employees. More than 25 percent of these employers maintained flexible plans.

[In percentages]

Reason for cost reduction	Employers
Reduced benefits	73
Increased contributions	71
Employees waiving coverage	55
Higher HMO enrollment	22

Source: Lissy, William E. "Currents in Compensation and Benefits." *Compensation & Benefits Review* 26, no. 2 (March-April 1994), p. 19. Primary source: Foster Higgins. *Note:* "HMO" stands for "health maintenance organization."

★ 602 ★

Cost Control

Payroll Cost Control

From the source: "Reducing payroll costs remains a priority for most companies" (p. 2). The table below shows some measures taken by surveyed employers to ease payroll costs.

[In percentages]

Action	Employers
Cross-training	71
Streamlining	61
Reduce overtime	41
Layoffs	39
New technologies	38
Hiring freeze	36
Flexible staffing	35

Source: "Optimism for Workforce Growth Varies Among Regions." *HR Focus* 70, no. 9 (September 1993), p. 2. Primary source: Olsten Corporation's *Forum on Human Resource Issues and Trends.*

★ 603 ★

Cost Control

Travel Spending Restraints

According to the source, "U.S. firms spent about $136 billion on travel in 1993" (p. 20BP). The table below shows measures surveyed companies plan to use to control travel costs.

[In percentages]

Action	Companies
Require travelers to take the lowest logical airfare	81
Provide a corporate card	73
Create a travel policy	71
Enforce existing policies more strictly	68
Refuse to reimburse employees for disallowed expenses	64
Tighten receipt requirements	64

Source: Flannery, William. "Companies Keep Reins Tight on Travel Money." *St. Louis Post-Dispatch,* 7 November 1994, p. 20BP. Primary source: 1994 American Express Survey of Business Travel Management.

Costs: Business Travel

★ 604 ★

Business Travel Per Diem Costs, by City

Table shows the average costs for breakfast, lunch, dinner, and single-rate lodging in business-class hotels, motels, and restaurants in major U.S. cities.

[In dollars]

City	Per diem costs
New York[1]	338
Washington, DC	260
Chicago	229
Boston	216
San Francisco	208

Source: "Cheaper in the 'Burbs." *USA TODAY,* 8 December 1994, p. 1B. Primary source: Runzheimer International Meal-Lodging Cost Index. *Note:* 1. Manhattan.

★ 605 ★

Costs: Business Travel

Business Travel Reimbursements for Personal Expenses

Laundry - 32	
Excess baggage fees - 27	
In-room movie - 14	
Liquor - 12	
	Travel insurance - 9
	Reading material - 6
	Grooming items - 5
	Child care - 4
	Traffic fines - 3
	Pet care - 2

Table shows the personal expenses for which companies reimburse business travelers.

[In percentages]

Item	Companies
Laundry	32
Excess baggage fees	27
In-room movie	14
Liquor[1]	12
Travel insurance	9
Reading material	6
Grooming items	5
Child care	4
Traffic fines	3
Pet care	2

Source: "Companies Increase Allowable Expenses." *USA TODAY,* 3 January 1995, p. 6B. Primary source: Runzheimer International. *Note:* 1. On airline.

★ 606 ★

Costs: Business Travel

Business Travelers' Expenses: 1993

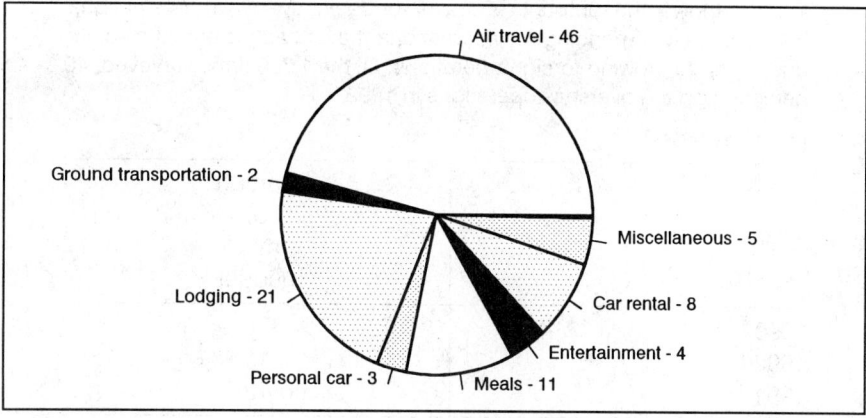

Table shows the expenses incurred during business travel. Data are for 1993.

[In percentages]

Item	1993
Air travel	46
Lodging	21
Meals	11
Car rental	8
Miscellaneous	5
Entertainment	4
Personal car	3
Ground transportation	2

Source: "Dial 'E' for Efficient." *Sales & Marketing Management* (September 1994), p. 52. Primary source: Runzheimer International. *Survey and Analysis of Business Travel Policies and Costs* (1994).

★ 607 ★

Costs: Business Travel

International Business Travel

Tables shows the amount of travel budgets spent on international business travel. Spending for international travel has increased steadily, due in part to growing foreign operations. Of the 1,700 firms surveyed, 40 percent reported overseas operations in 1992.

[In percentages]

Year	Portion of travel budget
1990	8
1992	10
1994	13

Source: Craig, Charlotte W. "Budget-wise Business Travel." *Detroit Free Press,* 19 December 1994, p. 10F. Primary source: 1994 American Express travel survey.

Costs: Health and Safety

★ 608 ★

High Risk Health Behavior Costs

| Drinking alcohol - 597 |
| Physical activity - 488 |
| Blood pressure - 327 |
| Smoking - 285 |
| Relative body weight - 222 |
| Seat belt usage - 196 |
| Cholesterol - 189 |
| Job satisfaction - 150 |

Employees engaging in high risk health behaviors such as smoking cost employers more than workers with healthier lifestyles. The table shows the average annual additional costs per employee for selected high risk behaviors.

[In 1993 dollars]

Health-related measure	Additional cost
Drinking alcohol	597
Physical activity	488
Blood pressure	327
Smoking	285
Relative body weight	222
Seat belt usage	196
Cholesterol	189
Job satisfaction	150

Source: "Costly Health Risks." *Workplace Vitality* (June 1994), p. 14. Primary sources: University of Michigan; Grand Rapids and Steelcase Inc.; *Business & Health.*

★ 609 ★

Motor Vehicle Accident-Related Business Losses

The Network of Employers for Traffic Safety (NETS) found that on-the-job motor vehicle accidents cost companies billions of dollars in lost work time and compensation.

[In thousand dollars]

Loss	Cost
Lost work time	16,400,000.0
Workers' compensation for each fatality[1]	110.5
Compensation for each injury[1]	2.4

Source: "Safety First." *Business Week,* 2 November 1992, p. 37. *Note:* 1. Average compensation.

Costs: Health Care

★ 610 ★

Health Care Benefit Cost Increases, by Region: 1993

Data are based on responses to a survey of nearly 2,400 employers. According the survey, in 1993, the average cost of health care benefits was $3,781 per employee.

[In dollars, except as noted]

Region of the United States	Average cost	Percent increase[1]
Nationwide average	3,781	8.0
Eastern	4,260	10.0
Midwestern	4,020	9.4
Southern	3,262	6.6
Western	3,620	5.3

Source: "Costs of Health-care Benefits Rise in 1993." *Personnel Journal* (June 1994), p. 18. Primary source: Foster Higgins. *Note:* 1. Increase from cost in 1992.

★ 611 ★

Costs: Health Care

Health Care Cost Containment Methods

Financial accounting standard (FAS) 106 requires companies to plan ahead for retiree medical benefit costs. In response to the rule, effective January 1, 1993, companies began taking measures to limit their FAS 106 liability. Figures below represent percentages of companies adopting particular cost containment methods. Data are based on a survey of 780 employers.

Cost containment method	Percent
Increase retiree contributions	48
Increase deductible or copayment	44
Use managed care	38
Tighten eligibility	29
Cap employer contributions	23

Source: "At a Glance: Snapshots of the Workplace Health Industry." *Workplace Health* (March 1993), p. 15. Primary source: William M. Mercer, Inc.

★ 612 ★

Costs: Health Care

Health Care Costs as a Percentage of Company Earnings

According to a survey of 1,955 businesses and governments conducted by the A. Foster Higgins & Co. benefits consulting firm, health care costs consumed 26 percent of the average employer's net earnings.

Source: Freudenheim, Milt. "Health Care: A Growing Burden." *New York Times,* 29 January 1991, p. D1.

★ 613 ★

Costs: Health Care

Health Care Plan Costs, by Region: 1991 and 1993

The data below indicate the annual health costs per employee at employers in various regions of the United States. Data are from 1992 and 1994 surveys of previous year's health costs of 1,455 employers nationwide.

[In dollars]

Region	Costs	
	1994 survey	1992 survey
Nationwide	3,020	2,873
Central/Southwest	2,662	2,691
East Central	2,973	2,739
Northeast	2,873	2,642
South	2,679	2,448

Source: "Cost Containment Is Helping to Cure Some Ailing Budgets." *HR Focus* (September 1994), p. 16. Primary source: Business & Legal Reports. *1994 Survey of Employee Benefits.*

★ 614 ★

Costs: Health Care

Health Care Plan Coverage Costs, by Metropolitan Area: 1992

The table below presents the cost per employee for traditional (indemnity plan), health maintenance organization (HMO), and preferred provider organization (PPO) medical coverage in selected U.S. cities.

City	Indemnity plans	HMOs	PPOs
Atlanta, Georgia	3,729	3,311	3,363
Chicago, Illinois	4,245	3,088	3,684
Cleveland, Ohio	4,027	3,727	3,459
Dallas-Fort Worth, Texas	3,917	3,330	3,837
Houston, Texas	3,627	3,575	[1]
Los Angeles, California	4,350	3,189	4,457
Minneapolis-St. Paul, Minnesota	3,347	2,969	3,121
New York, New York	4,852	3,448	3,871
Orange County, California	4,276	3,124	4,315
Philadelphia, Pennsylvania	4,696	3,319	3,708
San Francisco, California	4,531	3,092	4,459
Seattle, Washington	3,554	3,092	3,114

Source: "Indemnity Plan Costs vs. Managed-Care Plan Costs in Selected U.S. Cities, 1992." *Modern Healthcare,* 8 March 1993, p. 12. "Health Care Coverage in the '90s." *Los Angeles Times,* 8 March 1993, p. D2. "Shifting Health Traditions." *Miami Herald,* 2 March 1993, p. C1. Primary source: A. Foster Higgins. *Foster Higgins 1992 Health Care Benefits Survey. Note:* 1. Not reported.

★ 615 ★

Costs: Health Care

Health Expenditures of U.S. Businesses: 1965-1991

This table profiles the expenditures of businessess for health services and supplies. Where businesses pay dedicated funds into government health programs (e.g., Medicare), costs are assigned to businesses accordingly. Estimates of national health care expenditures by source of funds aim to track government-sponsored health programs over time, and do not delineate the role of business employers in paying for health care. Data also indicate the percent distribution of businesses' health-related expenditures for selected years.

Type of payer	1965	1967	1970	1975	1980	1985	1987	1988	1989	1990	1991
					Amount in billion dollars[1]						
Total[1]	38.2	47.9	69.1	124.7	238.9	407.2	476.9	526.2	583.6	652.4	728.6
Private	30.3	35.0	50.1	86.2	162.0	279.0	327.5	362.5	398.3	436.6	474.1
Private business	6.0	8.3	13.7	27.8	64.3	113.5	131.8	151.0	167.0	187.9	205.4
Private employer share of private health insurance premiums	4.9	5.6	9.8	19.9	47.9	83.9	95.0	110.9	122.8	140.2	152.7
Private employer contribution to Medicare hospital insurance trust fund[2]	0.0	1.4	2.1	5.0	10.5	20.3	24.6	26.2	28.1	29.5	32.8
Workers' compensation and temporary disability insurance medical benefits and administration	0.8	1.0	1.4	2.4	5.1	7.8	10.5	12.0	14.1	16.0	17.5
Industrial inplant health services	0.2	0.2	0.3	0.5	0.9	1.4	1.7	1.9	2.1	2.2	2.4
					Percent distribution						
Total	100.0	100.0	100.0	100.0	100.0	100.0	100.0	100.0	100.0	100.0	100.0
Private	79.3	73.2	72.6	69.2	67.8	68.5	68.7	68.9	68.2	66.9	65.1
Private business	15.6	17.3	19.8	22.3	26.9	27.9	27.6	28.7	28.6	28.8	28.2
Private employer share of private health insurance premiums	12.9	11.7	14.2	16.0	20.0	20.6	19.9	21.1	21.0	21.5	21.0
Private employer contribution to Medicare hospital insurance trust fund[2]	0.0	2.9	3.0	4.0	4.4	5.0	5.2	5.0	4.8	4.5	4.5
Workers' compensation and temporary disability insurance medical benefits and administration	2.2	2.2	2.1	2.0	2.1	1.9	2.2	2.3	2.4	2.4	2.4
Industrial inplant health services	0.6	0.5	0.5	0.4	0.4	0.4	0.4	0.4	0.4	0.3	0.3

Source: U.S. Department of Health and Human Services. Public Health Service. Centers for Disease Control and Prevention. National Center for Health Statistics. *Health, United States, 1992.* Hyattsville, MD: Public Health Service, 1993, p. 170. Primary source: Health Care Financing Administration. Office of National Health Statistics. Office of the Actuary. "Business, Households, and Governments—Health Spending 1991." *Health Care Financing Review* 14, no.3 (winter 1993). *Notes:* Data are compiled by the Health Care Financing Administration. 1. Excludes research and construction. 2. Includes one-half of self-employment contribution to Medicare hospital insurance trust fund.

★ 616 ★

Costs: Health Care

Health Insurance Costs, by Company Size: 1992

Data note cost of health insurance per employee by size of company.

Size of company	Average cost per employee
Fewer than 500	$3,500
500-999	3,628
1,000-2,499	3,599
2,500-4,999	3,579
5,000-9,999	3,714
10,000-19,000	3,847

[Continued]

★ 616 ★

Health Insurance Costs, by Company Size: 1992
[Continued]

Size of company	Average cost per employee
20,000-39,000	4,003
40,000 +	3,775

Source: "Company Health Costs Soar." *USA TODAY,* 27 April 1993, p. 2A. Primary sources: Employee Benefit Research Institute; A. Foster Higgins & Co., Inc.

★ 617 ★

Costs: Health Care

Health Insurance Costs, by Employee Characteristics: 1994

Figures show the estimated costs to employers for health insurance coverage for male and female employees. Data provided by worker ages.

[In dollars]

Age	Men	Women
18-24 years old	710	900
25-34 years old	1,500	1,780
35-44 years old	2,380	2,410
45-54 years old	3,200	2,580
55-64 years old	3,960	2,300

Source: Stevens, Carol. "Who Will Pay Health Bill for Early Retirees?" *Detroit News,* 27 February 1994, p. 1A. Primary sources: Employee Benefit Research Institute; Lewin-VHI health consultants.

★ 618 ★

Costs: Health Care

Health Insurance Plan Costs, by Plan Type: 1990-1992

Figures represent the average medical plan cost per employee. Data provided by plan type.

[In dollars]

Plan	Cost per employee		
	1990	1991	1992
Traditional indemnity plans	3,161	3,573	4,080
Preferred Provider Organizations	2,952	3,355	3,708
Point-of-Service plans	-	3,291	3,566
Health Maintenance Organizations	2,683	3,046	3,313

Source: "Benefits." *Personnel Journal* (November 1993), p. 48B. Primary source: A. Foster Higgins & Co. Inc. *Note:* "-" indicates "not available or applicable."

★ 619 ★

Costs: Health Care

Health-Related Spending on Retirees, by Selected Major Corporations

The institution of financial accounting standard (FAS) 106 in 1993 required companies to reserve funds for health care coverage of their retirees, to report their health care obligations to retirees, and to forecast future spending increases for retirees in financial statements. The table below shows the amounts set aside for health care spending for retirees by selected large corporations.

[In billion dollars]

Company	Amount
Fortune top 50 companies	115.2
General Motors	35.6
Ford Motor Company	12.7
Chrysler Corporation	7.5
IBM	6.9
DuPont	5.5

Source: "Health Care Write-Down." *American Medical News,* 1 November 1993, p. 30. Primary source: 1992 annual reports.

★ 620 ★

Costs: Health Care

Self-Funded Health Insurance, by Size of Company

The table below shows the percent of companies that self-fund health insurance benefits for their employees. Data are provided by number of employees.

Number of employees	Percent that self-fund medical indemnity plans
10-49	6
50-199	37
200-499	60
500-999	52
1,000-4,999	69
5,000-9,999	86
10,000-19,999	84
20,000+	89

Source: Schachner, Michael. "Large Companies Still See Self-Funding as Health Care Cure." *Business Insurance,* 7 February 1994, p. 3. Primary source: A. Foster Higgins & Co. Inc.

Costs: Relocation

★ 621 ★

Relocation Costs

In 1993, executive relocation activity increased after a decline the preceding year. According to the source, average domestic relocations cost more than $31,000, while international relocations averaged in excess of $130,000. The table below compares the costs of domestic relocation for existing employees and new hires.

Employee	Homeowner	Renter
Existing employee	50,793	16,859
New Hire	30,383	9,999

Source: "Executive Relocation Reverses Its Downward Trend." *HR Focus* (September 1994), p. 14. Primary source: Coldwell Banker Relocation Inc. *Corporate Mobility Survey.*

★ 622 ★

Costs: Relocation

Relocations, by Region

Data are from a survey of more than 1,250 ASM International members. Table shows the average salaries for survey respondents in various regions of the United States and the relocations to and from each region. Figures suggest that relocation moves most often occur within the same region or between adjacent regions.

[Average salary among respondents was $51,395.]

	Moved to:									
	New England ($58,013)	Northeast ($49,827)	Mid-Atlantic ($48,250)	Southeast ($48,162)	Midwest ($48,848)	Northern ($49,026)	Central ($50,958)	South ($51,688)	West ($51,378)	West Coast ($58,766)
N =	62	95	47	38	166	29	41	66	24	87
Percent	10	15	7	6	25	4	6	10	4	13
	Percent moved from:									
New England ($58,013)	76	12	6	-	2	10	-	6	4	-
Northeast ($49,827)	15	80	-	3	4	-	7	5	4	2
Mid-Atlantic ($48,250)	3	1	77	5	3	-	-	2	-	2
Southeast ($48,162)	-	-	2	63	2	3	2	2	-	-
Midwest ($48,848)	3	4	9	11	78	3	17	5	13	2
Northern ($49,026)	2	-	-	-	1	76	5	-	4	2
Central ($50,958)	-	1	6	8	4	-	59	2	4	3
South ($51,688)	2	1	-	3	1	-	2	68	-	2
West ($51,378)	-	-	-	-	1	4	-	5	71	1
West Coast ($58,766)	-	1	-	8	5	3	7	8	-	84

Source: "1992 Salary Survey Results." *Advanced Materials & Processes* 145, no. 3 (March 1994), pp. 52-53. Primary source: 1992 ASM salary survey. ASM International (formerly the American Society for Metals) gathers, processes, and shares technical information, particularly in the understanding and application of engineered materials. *Note:* "-" indicates "not applicable."

Costs: Social Security

★ 623 ★

Social Insurance Programs – Covered Payrolls: 1980-1991

Figures show the estimated payrolls of covered employment for selected social insurance programs in relation to wages and salaries. Data for federal civilian and military personnel cover all areas. Gross amount before deduction of social insurance contributions.

[In billions of dollars, except percentages]

Program	1980	1983	1984	1985	1986	1987	1988	1989	1990	1991
Total earnings[1]	1,553	1,867	2,073	2,232	2,377	2,573	2,767	2,934	3,110	3,180
All wages and salaries[1]	1,372	1,676	1,839	1,975	2,094	2,250	2,443	2,586	2,743	2,812
Civilian	1,342	1,634	1,794	1,928	2,044	2,198	2,390	2,531	2,685	2,751
Payrolls covered by –										
Retirement programs[2]	1,318	1,614	1,775	1,896	2,011	2,149	2,360	2,469	2,641	2,716
OASDHI[3]	1,229	1,502	1,665	1,782	1,896	2,042	2,225	2,368	2,507	2,579
Railroad retirement[4]	13	12	13	13	12	12	12	12	12	12
Federal civil service	52	62	65	70	72	74	80	83	88	92

[Continued]

★ 623 ★

Social Insurance Programs – Covered Payrolls: 1980-1991

[Continued]

Program	1980	1983	1984	1985	1986	1987	1988	1989	1990	1991
State and local government	123	153	162	175	190	195	210	225	239	254
Unemployment insurance[4]	1,303	1,583	1,739	1,870	1,983	2,046	2,205	2,336	2,479	2,537
Workers' compensation program[5]	1,136	1,382	1,516	1,618	1,725	1,845	1,997	2,115	2,250	2,300
Net earnings in self-employment covered by OASDHI	98	109	117	130	139	156	208	221	213	213
Percent of civilian payrolls covered by –										
OASDHI[6]	92.6	92.6	92.9	92.4	92.8	92.9	93.1	93.6	93.4	93.7
Railroad retirement[4]	1.0	0.7	0.7	0.7	0.6	0.5	0.5	0.5	0.4	0.4
Federal civil service retirement	3.9	3.8	3.7	3.6	3.5	3.4	3.3	3.3	3.3	3.3
State and local government retirement	9.2	9.4	9.0	9.1	9.3	9.2	8.8	8.9	8.9	9.2
Unemployment insurance[4]	97.1	96.9	97.0	97.0	97.0	93.1	92.3	92.3	92.3	92.2
Workers' compensation programs[5]	84.6	84.6	84.5	83.9	84.4	84.0	83.6	83.6	83.9	83.6

Source: U.S. Bureau of the Census. *Statistical Abstract of the United States, 1994.* 114th ed. Washington, DC: U.S. Government Printing Office, 1994, p. 374. Primary sources: U.S. Social Security Administration. *Annual Statistical Supplement to the Social Security Bulletin;* and unpublished data. *Notes:* "OASDHI" is the acronym for Old-Age, Survivors, Disability, and Health Insurance programs under Social Security Act 1. Data from U.S. Bureau of Economic Analysis. Earnings include self-employed; wages and salaries represent civilian and military pay in cash and in kind. 2. Adjusted for duplication in coverage by both OASDHI and state and local government retirement systems. 3. Taxable plus estimated nontaxable wages and salaries. Includes Armed Forces in all areas. 4. Taxable plus estimated nontaxable wages and salaries. 5. Payrolls of employers insured with private carriers, state funds, or self-insured, and pay covered by federal programs in all areas. 6. Taxable plus estimated nontaxable wages and salaries. Percent computed after excluding Armed Forces payroll covered by OASDHI.

★ 624 ★

Costs: Social Security

Social Insurance Programs – Covered Workers: 1970-1991

Estimated number of workers covered under social insurance programs, as of December (except as noted).

[In millions]

Employment and coverage status	1970	1980	1983	1984	1985	1986	1987	1988	1989	1990	1991
Total labor force[1]	86.3	109.1	113.5	115.7	117.5	119.8	122.0	123.8	125.7	126.2	126.7
Paid civilian population	77.8	98.9	102.2	105.5	107.7	110.2	113.3	115.6	117.4	117.0	116.2
Unpaid family workers	0.9	0.6	0.6	0.5	0.4	0.3	0.4	0.4	0.3	0.3	0.3
Unemployed	4.7	7.4	9.0	8.0	7.7	7.5	6.5	6.1	6.3	7.3	8.6
Armed Forces[2]	3.0	2.1	1.7	1.7	1.7	1.8	1.8	1.7	1.7	1.6	1.6
Civilian population covered by:											
Public retirement programs	75.2	96.4	99.5	104.4	106.6	109.3	113.5	116.0	117.9	117.7	117.9
OASDHI[3]	69.1	89.3	92.7	98.0	100.3	102.9	106.3	108.7	110.5	110.2	110.5
Railroad retirement	0.6	0.5	0.4	0.4	0.3	0.3	0.3	0.3	0.3	0.3	0.3
Public employees retirement[4]	5.5	6.6	6.4	6.0	6.0	6.2	6.9	7.0	7.1	7.2	7.1
Unemployment insurance	55.8	87.2	91.3	95.8	98.2	100.2	103.7	106.9	108.8	109.5	106.0
Workers' compensation	59.0	79.1	80.5	83.4	85.1	87.2	90.0	92.8	95.3	96.7	95.1
Temporary disability insurance	14.6	18.4	18.7	19.3	19.8	20.3	21.6	21.8	22.2	(NA)	(NA)

Source: U.S. Bureau of the Census. *Statistical Abstract of the United States, 1993.* 113th ed. Washington, DC: U.S. Government Printing Office, 1993, p. 372. Primary source: U.S. Social Security Administration. *Annual Statistical Supplement to the Social Security Bulletin. Notes:* "NA" represents "not available." 1. Data from U.S. Bureau of Labor Statistics and based on U.S. Bureau of the Census' Current Population Survey. Excludes Armed Forces overseas beginning 1983. 2. Excludes Armed Forces overseas beginning 1983. 3. "OASDHI" represents Old-Age, Survivors, Disability, and Health Insurance. Excludes members of Armed Forces and railroad employees. 4. Data represent yearly averages. Excludes state and local government employees covered by both OASDHI and their own retirement programs.

★ 625 ★

Costs: Social Security

Social Security Beneficiaries, Payments, and Benefits, by State and Other Areas: 1980-1992

Table reflects the number of beneficiaries in current-payment status and average monthly benefits as of December. A person eligible to receive more than one type of benefit is generally classified or counted only once as a retired-worker beneficiary. Also shows annual payments. Includes Puerto Rico, Virgin Islands, American Samoa, and Guam.

Year, division, state or other area	Number of beneficiaries (1,000)[1]				Annual payments (million dollars)				Average monthly benefit (dollars)		
	Total	Retired workers and dependents[2]	Survivors	Disabled workers and dependents	Total	Retired workers and dependents[2]	Survivors[3]	Disabled workers and dependents	Retires workers[4]	Disabled workers	Widows and widowers[5]
1980	35,585	23,309	7,598	4,678	120,472	78,025	27,010	15,437	341	371	311
1985	37,058	25,989	7,162	3,907	186,195	128,536	38,824	18,836	479	484	433
1990	39,832	28,369	7,197	4,266	247,796	172,042	50,951	24,803	603	587	557
1991	40,592	28,824	7,255	4,513	268,098	185,545	54,891	27,662	629	609	584
1992, total[6]	41,497	29,296	7,297	4,903	285,980	196,688	58,203	31,089	653	626	608
United States	40,524	28,711	7,077	4,735	281,673	194,301	57,052	30,020	(NA)	(NA)	(NA)
New England	2,231	1,656	336	239	15,913	11,544	2,852	1,517	(NA)	(NA)	(NA)
Maine	224	159	36	28	1,436	991	281	164	601	567	574
New Hampshire	172	129	25	18	1,210	885	211	114	655	627	630
Vermont	92	65	15	12	624	432	121	71	640	601	608
Massachusetts	1,011	743	155	114	7,144	5,103	1,314	727	655	612	638
Rhode Island	186	140	27	20	1,314	969	222	123	652	596	633
Connecticut	546	420	78	47	4,185	3,164	703	318	718	636	679
Middle Atlantic	6,470	4,735	1,088	648	48,001	34,175	9,361	4,465	(NA)	(NA)	(NA)
New York	2,910	2,111	475	324	21,642	15,377	4,030	2,235	698	658	653
New Jersey	1,267	946	201	120	9,720	7,100	1,778	842	716	654	670
Pennsylvania	2,293	1,678	412	204	16,639	11,698	3,553	1,388	672	648	640
East North Central	7,006	4,953	1,261	794	50,976	34,900	10,773	5,303	(NA)	(NA)	(NA)
Ohio	1,859	1,289	357	213	13,259	8,813	3,032	1,414	669	652	637
Indiana	938	661	164	113	6,799	4,661	1,405	733	679	644	644
Illinois	1,800	1,293	320	188	13,267	9,299	2,706	1,262	692	651	656
Michigan	1,546	1,079	280	188	11,478	7,748	2,430	1,300	697	685	654
Wisconsin	863	631	140	92	6,173	4,379	1,200	594	669	632	639
West North Central	3,105	2,251	541	313	21,263	14,893	4,411	1,959	(NA)	(NA)	(NA)
Minnesota	689	510	117	62	4,706	3,346	964	396	637	610	608
Iowa	532	391	92	49	3,706	2,622	772	312	653	617	620
Missouri	941	661	165	115	6,402	4,360	1,316	726	638	615	600
North Dakota	114	82	22	10	736	508	168	60	615	590	575
South Dakota	132	94	24	13	836	576	185	75	602	567	573
Nebraska	276	203	48	26	1,891	1,338	399	154	643	605	624
Kansas	421	310	73	38	2,986	2,143	607	236	669	601	632
South Atlantic	7,548	5,332	1,295	923	50,714	34,934	9,933	5,847	(NA)	(NA)	(NA)
Delaware	112	82	18	12	813	581	152	80	680	642	638
Maryland	641	462	118	61	4,501	3,124	958	419	652	643	619
District of Columbia	79	55	15	8	477	325	101	51	556	562	510
Virginia	883	608	162	114	5,810	3,875	1,225	710	619	614	564
West Virginia	376	231	82	63	2,542	1,488	648	406	644	672	578
North Carolina	1,143	775	202	167	7,394	4,929	1,447	1,018	612	590	535
South Carolina	575	380	106	90	3,686	2,407	727	552	611	604	528
Georgia	937	599	184	154	6,010	3,777	1,309	924	610	602	542
Florida	2,802	2,140	408	254	19,481	14,428	3,366	1,687	651	638	627
East South Central	2,752	1,732	559	461	17,253	10,590	3,971	2,692	(NA)	(NA)	(NA)
Kentucky	674	412	139	123	4,238	2,501	1,010	727	602	623	543
Tennessee	870	567	167	135	5,581	3,556	1,220	805	611	592	548
Alabama	739	468	156	116	4,674	2,874	1,114	686	604	601	536
Mississippi	469	285	97	87	2,760	1,659	627	474	569	577	491
West South Central	4,032	2,679	831	525	26,151	16,826	6,229	3,096	(NA)	(NA)	(NA)
Arkansas	482	313	90	79	2,975	1,881	637	457	588	594	524
Louisiana	679	405	159	116	4,263	2,447	1,150	666	607	631	555
Oklahoma	552	386	104	63	3,636	2,451	800	385	622	609	578
Texas	2,319	1,575	478	267	15,277	10,047	3,642	1,588	633	616	588
Mountain	2,098	1,506	336	257	14,207	9,911	2,673	1,623	(NA)	(NA)	(NA)
Montana	146	101	25	20	974	654	195	125	633	640	610
Idaho	166	121	27	18	1,113	785	217	111	634	626	612
Wyoming	66	47	11	8	455	316	90	49	651	633	620
Colorado	453	318	76	59	3,045	2,059	613	373	635	622	610
New Mexico	235	158	44	33	1,468	966	313	189	612	609	572
Arizona	635	468	93	74	4,416	3,168	757	491	660	655	634
Utah	205	149	33	23	1,392	992	267	133	658	611	638
Nevada	192	144	27	22	1,344	971	221	152	658	659	634
Pacific	5,279	3,871	830	579	37,195	26,528	6,849	3,818	(NA)	(NA)	(NA)
Washington	747	553	113	81	5,377	3,866	970	541	677	639	646
Oregon	521	392	78	52	3,675	2,684	653	338	663	632	637
California	3,819	2,779	611	429	26,852	19,008	5,010	2,834	667	627	635
Alaska	37	24	7	5	250	163	56	31	653	620	575
Hawaii	155	123	21	12	1,041	807	160	74	643	625	583
Puerto Rico	581	321	117	144	2,504	1,276	563	665	418	519	377
Guam	6	3	2	1	25	13	9	3	459	542	442
American Samoa	4	2	2	1	14	5	6	3	388	441	344

[Continued]

★ 625 ★

Social Security Beneficiaries, Payments, and Benefits, by State and Other Areas: 1980-1992
[Continued]

Year, division, state or other area	Number of beneficiaries (1,000) [1]				Annual payments (million dollars)				Average monthly benefit (dollars)		
	Total	Retired workers and dependents[2]	Survivors	Disabled workers and dependents	Total	Retired workers and dependents[2]	Survivors[3]	Disabled workers and dependents	Retires workers[4]	Disabled workers	Widows and widowers[5]
Virgin Islands	11	7	2	1	59	37	14	8	548	584	489
Abroad	350	243	91	16	1,705	1,056	559	90	452	544	456

Source: U.S. Bureau of the Census. *Statistical Abstract of the United States, 1994.* 114th ed. Washington, DC: U.S. Government Printing Office, 1994, p. 377. Primary source: U.S. Social Security Administration. *Social Security Bulletin* (quarterly). *Notes:* "NA" stands for "not available." 1. Data for 1992 based on 10-percent sample. 2. Includes special benefits; for example, benefits for persons aged 72 and over not insured under regular or transitional provisions of Social Security Act. 3. Includes lump-sum payments to survivors of deceased workers. 4. Excludes persons with special benefits. 5. Nondisabled only. 6. Number of beneficiaries includes those with state or area unknown.

★ 626 ★

Costs: Social Security

Social Security Benefits, by Type of Beneficiary: 1970-1992

Table shows beneficiaries of Old-Age, Survivors, and Disability Insurance (OASDI) programs. A person eligible to receive more than one type of benefit is generally classified or counted only once as a retired-worker beneficiary. Includes Puerto Rico, Virgin Islands, American Samoa, and Guam. Represents all reported employment. Data are estimated.

Type of beneficiary	1970	1980	1985	1986	1987	1988	1989	1990	1991	1992
	Benefits in current-payment status [1] (end of year)									
Number of benefits (1,000)	26,229	35,585	37,058	37,703	38,190	38,627	39,151	39,832	40,592	41,507
Retired workers[2] (1,000)	13,349	19,562	22,432	22,980	23,440	23,858	24,327	24,838	25,289	25,758
Disabled workers[3] (1,000)	1,493	2,859	2,657	2,728	2,786	2,830	2,895	3,011	3,195	3,468
Wives and husbands[4] (1,000)	2,952	3,477	3,375	3,387	3,381	3,367	3,365	3,367	3,370	3,382
Children (1,000)	4,122	4,607	3,319	3,295	3,244	3,204	3,165	3,187	3,268	3,391
Under age 18	3,315	3,423	2,699	2,665	2,604	2,534	2,488	2,497	2,558	2,664
Disabled children[5]	271	450	526	545	561	574	586	600	616	637
Students[6]	537	733	94	84	79	96	91	89	95	90
Of retired workers	546	639	457	450	439	432	423	422	426	432
Of deceased workers	2,688	2,610	1,917	1,878	1,837	1,809	1,780	1,776	1,791	1,808
Of disabled workers	889	1,358	945	966	968	963	962	989	1,052	1,151
Widowed mothers[7] (1,000)	523	562	372	351	329	318	312	304	301	294
Widows and widowers[8] (1,000)	3,227	4,411	4,863	4,928	4,984	5,029	5,071	5,111	5,158	5,205
Parents[2] (1,000)	29	15	10	9	8	7	6	6	5	5
Special benefits[9] (1,000)	534	93	32	25	19	14	10	7	5	4
Average monthly benefit, current dollars:										
Retired workers[2]	118	341	479	489	513	537	567	603	629	653
Retired worker and wife[2]	199	567	814	831	873	914	966	1,027	1,072	1,111
Disabled workers[3]	131	371	484	488	508	530	556	587	609	626
Wives and husbands[4]	59	164	236	241	253	265	281	298	311	322
Children of retired workers	45	140	198	204	216	228	242	259	273	285
Children of deceased workers	82	240	330	337	352	368	385	406	420	432
Children of disabled workers	39	110	142	141	146	151	157	164	168	170
Widowed mothers[7]	87	246	332	338	353	368	388	409	424	438
Widows and widowers, nondisabled[2]	102	311	433	444	468	493	522	557	584	608
Parents[2]	103	276	378	386	407	428	454	482	506	526

[Continued]

★ 626 ★

Social Security Benefits, by Type of Beneficiary: 1970-1992

[Continued]

Type of beneficiary	1970	1980	1985	1986	1987	1988	1989	1990	1991	1992
Special benefits[9]	45	105	138	140	145	151	158	167	173	178
Average monthly benefit, constant (1992) dollars:[10]										
Retired workers[2]	421	561	622	627	631	632	638	640	647	653
Retired worker and wife[2]	710	932	1,057	1,067	1,073	1,076	1,087	1,089	1,103	1,111
Disabled workers[3]	467	610	628	627	625	624	626	623	627	626
Wives and husbands[4]	210	270	306	309	311	312	316	316	320	322
Children of deceased workers	292	395	430	433	433	433	433	431	432	432
Widowed mothers[7]	310	404	431	434	434	433	437	434	436	438
Widows and widowers, nondisabled[2]	364	511	562	570	575	581	587	590	600	608
Benefits awarded during year (1,000)										
Number of benefits	3,722	4,215	3,796	3,853	3,734	3,681	3,646	3,717	3,865	4,051
Retired workers[2]	1,338	1,620	1,690	1,734	1,682	1,654	1,657	1,665	1,695	1,708
Disabled workers[3]	350	389	377	417	416	409	426	468	536	637
Wives and husbands[4]	436	469	440	441	411	391	380	379	380	383
Children	1,091	1,174	714	701	685	706	675	695	727	795
Widowed mothers[7]	112	108	72	69	65	63	60	58	58	56
Widows and widowers[8]	363	452	502	491	475	458	449	452	469	472
Parents[2]	2	1	(Z)	(Z)	(Z)	(Z)	(Z)	(Z)	(Z)	(Z)
Special benefits[9]	30	1	1	(Z)	(Z)	(Z)	(Z)	(Z)	(Z)	(Z)
Benefit payments during year (billion dollars)										
Total amount[11]	31.9	120.5	186.2	196.7	204.2	217.2	230.9	247.8	268.1	286.0
Monthly benefits[12]	31.6	120.1	186.0	196.5	204.0	217.0	230.6	247.6	267.9	285.8
Retired workers[2]	18.4	70.4	116.8	123.6	128.5	137.0	146.0	156.8	169.1	179.4
Disabled workers[3]	2.4	12.8	16.5	17.4	18.1	19.2	20.3	22.1	24.7	27.9
Wives and husbands[4]	2.2	7.0	11.1	11.7	12.1	12.8	13.6	14.5	15.5	16.4
Children	3.5	10.5	10.7	10.9	11.0	11.3	11.5	12.0	12.8	13.6
Under age 18	2.7	7.4	8.5	8.7	8.5	8.7	8.7	9.0	9.5	10.1
Disabled children[5]	0.3	1.0	1.8	2.0	2.0	2.2	2.3	2.5	2.8	3.0
Students[6]	0.6	2.1	0.4	0.3	0.4	0.5	0.5	0.5	0.5	0.5
Of retired workers	0.3	1.1	1.1	1.2	1.2	1.2	1.2	1.3	1.4	1.5
Of deceased workers	2.8	7.4	7.8	7.8	7.8	8.1	8.3	8.6	9.0	9.4
Of disabled workers	0.5	2.0	1.8	1.9	1.9	2.0	2.0	2.2	2.4	2.7
Widowed mothers[7]	0.6	1.6	1.5	1.5	1.4	1.4	1.4	1.4	1.5	1.5
Widows and widowers[8]	4.1	17.6	29.3	31.3	32.8	35.2	37.7	40.7	44.1	47.1
Parents[2]	(Z)	0.1	0.1	(Z)	(Z)	(Z)	(Z)	(Z)	(Z)	(Z)

[Continued]

Earnings and Costs of Employment

★ 626 ★

Social Security Benefits, by Type of Beneficiary: 1970-1992
[Continued]

Type of beneficiary	1970	1980	1985	1986	1987	1988	1989	1990	1991	1992
Special benefits[9]	0.3	0.1	0.1	(Z)	(Z)	(Z)	(Z)	(Z)	(Z)	(Z)
Lump sum	0.3	0.4	0.2	0.2	0.2	0.2	0.2	0.2	0.2	0.2

Source: U.S. Bureau of the Census. Statistical Abstract of the United States, 1994. 114th ed. Washington, DC: U.S. Government Printing Office, 1994, p. 376. Primary sources: U.S. Social Security Administration. Annual Statistical Supplement to the Social Security Bulletin; and unpublished data. Notes: "Z" represents fewer than 500 or less than $50 million. 1. Benefit payment actually being made at a specified time with no deductions or with deductions amounting to less than a month's benefits; i.e., the benefits actually being received. 2. 62 years and over. 3. Disabled workers under age 65. 4. 62 years and over. Includes wife beneficiaries with entitled children in their care and entitled divorced wives. 5. 18 years old and over. Disability began before age 18 and, beginning 1973, before age 22. 6. Full-time students aged 18-21 through 1984 and aged 18 and 19 beginning 1985. 7. Includes surviving divorced mothers with entitled children in their care and, beginning 1980, widowed fathers with entitled children in their care. 8. 62 years and over. Includes widows aged 60-61, surviving divorced wives aged 60 and over, disabled widows and widowers aged 50 and over; and beginning 1980, widowers aged 60-61. 9. Benefits for persons aged 72 and over not insured under regular or transitional provisions of Social Security Act. 10. Constant dollar figures are based on the consumer price index for December as published by the U.S. Bureau of Labor Statistics. 11. Represents total disbursements of benefit checks by the U.S. Department of the Treasury during the years specified. 12. Distribution by type estimated.

★ 627 ★

Costs: Social Security

Social Security-Covered Employment, Earnings, and Contribution Rates: 1970-1992

Includes Puerto Rico, Virgin Islands, American Samoa, and Guam. Represents all reported employment. Data are estimated.

Item	Unit	1970	1980	1985	1986	1987	1988	1989	1990	1991	1992
Workers with insured status[1]	Million	105.7	137.4	148.7	150.6	152.7	155.4	158.0	161.2	163.6	166.0
Male	Million	61.9	75.4	79.7	80.7	81.5	82.6	83.7	85.1	86.1	87.2
Female	Million	43.8	62.0	69.0	69.9	71.2	72.8	74.5	76.1	77.5	78.8
Under 25 years old	Million	17.7	25.5	22.3	21.9	21.3	21.3	21.3	21.3	21.2	21.0
25-34 years old	Million	22.3	34.9	39.9	40.0	40.6	41.0	41.4	41.5	41.5	41.2
35-44 years old	Million	19.0	22.4	28.5	29.8	31.2	32.3	33.5	34.9	36.2	37.2
45-54 years old	Million	19.0	18.6	19.0	19.3	19.8	20.5	21.4	22.1	22.8	23.9
55-59 years old	Million	7.8	9.2	9.1	9.0	8.9	8.8	8.7	8.7	8.7	8.8
60-64 years old	Million	6.3	7.9	8.7	8.8	8.7	8.7	8.6	8.7	8.7	8.7
65-69 years old	Million	5.1	6.7	7.3	7.5	7.6	7.7	7.8	8.1	8.2	8.2
70 years old and over	Million	8.5	12.1	13.9	14.3	14.7	15.0	15.5	15.8	16.3	16.8
Workers reported with –											
Taxable earnings[2]	Million	93	113	120	123	126	130	132	133	132	132
Maximum earnings[2]	Million	24	10	8	8	8	8	8	8	8	8
Earnings in covered employment[2]	Billion $	532	1,329	1,937	2,082	2,237	2,433	2,583	2,703	2,780	2,960
Reported taxable[2]	Billion $	416	1,181	1,723	1,844	1,960	2,089	2,239	2,363	2,423	2,541
Percent of total	Percent	78.2	88.9	88.9	88.6	87.6	85.9	86.7	87.4	87.2	85.8
Annual maximum taxable earnings[3]	$	7,800	25,900	39,600	42,000	43,800	45,000	48,000	51,300	53,400	55,500
Maximum tax	$	374	1,588	2,792	3,003	3,132	3,380	3,605	3,924	5,123	5,329
Contribution rates for OASDHI:[4]											
Each employer and employee	Percent	4.80	6.13	7.05	7.15	7.15	7.51	7.51	7.65	7.65	7.65

[Continued]

★ 627 ★

Social Security-Covered Employment, Earnings, and Contribution Rates: 1970-1992
[Continued]

Item	Unit	1970	1980	1985	1986	1987	1988	1989	1990	1991	1992
Self-employed[5]	Percent	6.90	8.10	14.10	14.30	14.30	15.02	15.02	15.30	15.30	15.30
SMI, monthly premium[6]	$	5.30	9.60	15.50	15.50	17.90	24.80	31.90	28.60	29.90	31.80

Source: U.S. Bureau of the Census. *Statistical Abstract of the United States, 1994.* 114th ed. Washington, DC: U.S. Government Printing Office, 1994, p. 375. Primary sources: U.S. Social Security Administration. *Annual Statistical Supplement to the Social Security Bulletin;* and unpublished data. *Notes:* "OASDHI" is an acronym for Old-Age, Survivors, Disability, and Health Insurance; "SMI" for Supplementary Medical Insurance. 1. Fully insured for retirement and/or survivor benefits as of beginning of year. 2. Includes self-employment. 3. The maximum taxable earnings for Health Insurance (HI) were $125,000 in 1991 and $130,200 in 1992. 4. As of January 1, 1993 and 1994, each employee and employer pays 7.65 percent and the self-employed pay 15.3 percent. 5. Self-employed pays 11.8 percent in 1985, 12.3 percent in 1986 and 1987, and 13.02 percent in 1988 and 1989. The additional amount is supplied from general revenues. Beginning 1990, self-employed pays 15.3 percent, and half of the tax is deductible for income tax purposes and for computing self-employment income subject to Social Security tax. 6. 1970-1982, as of July 1; beginning 1985, as of January 1. As of January 1, 1993, the monthly premium is $36.60 and as of January 1, 1994, the monthly premium is $41.10.

Costs: Taxes

★ 628 ★

Health Insurance Benefit Taxes

Table shows the simulated effects of taxing employee health insurance benefits.

Policy	Percentage annual increase in federal personal income tax revenue			
	Aggregate	Average worker in		
		Low-wage industry[1]	Medium-wage industry[2]	High-wage industry[3]
Tax all health insurance contributions	8.3	7.7	6.8	10.8
Tax health insurance contributions above $1,125 per year (1982 dollars)	1.5	0.2	0.6	4.3
Tax all employee benefits	17.6	14.5	13.9	25.9

Source: U.S. Department of Labor. Pension and Welfare Benefits Administration. *Trends in Health Benefits.* Washington, DC: U.S. Government Printing Office, 1993, p. 98. Primary source: Woodbury, Stephen A., and Wei-Jang Huang. *The Tax Treatment of Fringe Benefits.* W.E. Upjohn Institute, 1991. *Notes:* Figures are simulated average annual revenue effects between 1969 and 1982 of policy changes relative to current tax law, based upon econometric estimates of the demand for health insurance and other employee benefits. 1. Average wage between $11,630 and $17,041. 2. Average wage between $17,643 and $22,550. 3. Average wage between $23,103 and $39,498.

★ 629 ★

Costs: Taxes

Health Insurance Tax Expenditures: 1975-1995

Table shows the tax expenditures of employers for health insurance.

Fiscal year	Exclusion of contributions for medical insurance premiums and medical care (billions of dollars)	Total of tax expenditure items for individuals (billions of dollars)	Net exclusion of medical insurance and care as a percentage of total tax expenditures for individuals (percent)
1975	3.3	70.6	4.7
1976	4.5	72.7	6.2
1977	5.6	87.5	6.4
1978	7.1	92.6	7.7
1979	11.1	112.2	9.9
1980	12.1	139.1	8.7
1981	14.1	179.8	7.8
1982	16.4	198.4	8.3
1983[1]	18.7	239.1	6.4
1984	19.1	248.0	7.7
1985	21.1	270.3	7.8
1986	23.4	304.6	7.7
1987	24.6	353.4	7.0
1988	24.7	259.1	9.5
1989	26.6	255.4	10.4
1990	29.8	279.9	10.6
1991	33.3	277.6	12.0
1992	38.0	297.0	12.8
1993	42.4	316.4	13.4
1994	46.8	337.1	13.9
1995	49.5	357.0	13.9

Source: U.S. Department of Labor. Pension and Welfare Benefits Administration. *Trends in Health Benefits.* Washington, DC: U.S. Government Printing Office, 1993, p. 96. Primary sources: U.S. House of Representatives Committee on Ways and Means. *Overview of the Federal Tax System,* 1976-1990 editions; U.S. Office of Management and Budget. *Special Analyses, Budget of the United States Government* (annual). *Note:* 1. The methodology for estimating tax expenditures changed in 1983.

★ 630 ★

Costs: Taxes

Tax Bite: 1993

The Tax Foundation labeled the amount of time in each 8-hour workday needed to pay for a worker's tax obligations as the "tax bite." In 1993, a worker devoted 2 hours and 42 minutes in each 8-hour day to paying taxes: 1 hour and 43 minutes for federal taxes, and 59 minutes for state and local taxes. The table below shows the time worked to pay for taxes and selected personal obligations.

[In hours and minutes]

Obligation	Portion of 8-hour day
Federal taxes	1:43
Health and medical care	1:22
State and local taxes	0:59
Housing and household operations	0:57
Food and tobacco	0:53
All other	0:47
Transportation	0:35
Recreation	0:24
Clothing	0:21

Source: "Tax Bite in the 8-Hour Day." *Tax Features* (April 1993), p. 7.

★ 631 ★

Costs: Taxes

Tax Freedom Day: 1944-1994

Tax Freedom Day is the calendar date in a given year when the average worker has paid all his or her federal, state, and local taxes. The table below shows Tax Freedom days from 1944 through 1994 and indicates the length of time required to work for each year.

Year	Date	Number of days
1944[1]	March 30	90
1949	March 24	83
1954	April 6	96
1959	April 13	103
1964[1]	April 13	104
1969	April 30	120
1974	May 2	122
1979	May 1	121
1984[1]	April 28	119

[Continued]

★ 631 ★

Tax Freedom Day: 1944-1994
[Continued]

Year	Date	Number of days
1989	May 4	124
1994	May 5	124

Source: Lohse, Deborah. "Feeding Uncle Sam." *Wall Street Journal,* 9 December 1994, p. R10. Primary source: Tax Foundation. *Note:* 1. Tax Freedom Day appears one day earlier due to leap year.

Earnings

★ 632 ★

Earnings of Families, by Selected Characteristics: 1980-1993

Table shows the median weekly earnings of families with wage and salary earners by type of family, number of earners, and race/ethnicity. Annual averages of quarterly figures based on Current Population Survey.

[In current dollars of usual weekly earnings]

Characteristic	Number of families (1,000)				Median weekly earnings ($)			
	1980	1985	1990	1993	1980	1985	1990	1993
Total								
Total families with earners[1]	41,162	41,616	43,759	44,383	400	522	653	707
Married-couple families	33,825	33,459	34,219	34,257	433	582	732	804
One earner	14,797	13,347	12,166	12,185	303	385	455	481
Husband	12,127	10,346	8,994	8,643	336	440	520	565
Wife	2,059	2,243	2,407	2,773	159	217	267	314
Other family member	611	758	764	769	163	204	280	282
Two or more earners[2]	19,028	20,112	22,053	22,071	535	715	880	973
Husband and wife only	12,990	14,019	15,934	16,349	507	684	844	944
Husband and other family member(s)	2,369	2,159	1,751	1,509	557	689	825	875
Wife and other family member(s)	426	514	527	574	350	454	557	613
Other family members only	139	176	176	150	356	468	554	605
Families maintained by women	5,690	6,470	7,323	7,792	222	297	363	393
One earner	4,022	4,397	4,983	5,452	184	234	288	307
Householder	3,104	3,432	3,937	4,402	188	243	296	315
Other family member	918	965	1,045	1,050	168	200	254	263
Two or more earners	1,668	2,073	2,340	2,340	370	487	607	655
Families maintained by men	1,647	1,688	2,218	2,334	360	450	514	523
One earner	1,016	1,031	1,352	1,523	283	346	396	429
Two or more earners	631	656	866	811	502	625	778	763

[Continued]

★ 632 ★

Earnings of Families, by Selected Characteristics: 1980-1993
[Continued]

Characteristic	Number of families (1,000)				Median weekly earnings ($)			
	1980	1985	1990	1993	1980	1985	1990	1993
White								
Total families with earners[1]	35,786	35,848	37,239	37,458	411	543	681	739
Married-couple families	30,316	29,899	30,361	30,288	438	589	745	816
One earner[2]	13,437	12,097	10,856	10,790	311	395	473	492
Husband	11,152	9,496	8,162	7,755	343	452	535	583
Wife	1,740	1,925	2,044	3,383	160	218	270	313
Two or more earners	16,878	17,802	19,505	19,497	542	723	892	984
Husband and wife only	11,448	12,394	14,148	14,546	511	691	855	954
Families maintained by women	4,140	4,616	5,127	5,355	233	311	382	415
Families maintained by men	1,331	1,333	1,751	1,816	374	475	539	547
Black								
Total families with earners[1]	4,503	4,668	5,082	5,268	299	378	459	490
Married-couple families	2,802	2,671	2,724	2,698	366	487	601	674
One earner[2]	1,103	902	893	909	210	257	304	344
Husband	769	580	527	539	244	292	345	381
Wife	279	257	290	287	151	206	243	321
Two or more earners	1,700	1,769	1,831	1,789	472	622	748	846
Husband and wife only	1,238	1,258	1,297	1,285	461	603	713	819
Families maintained by women	1,438	1,703	1,986	2,168	192	259	314	334
Families maintained by men	263	294	372	403	307	360	397	413
Hispanic origin[3]								
Total families with earners[1]	(NA)	(NA)	3,624	3,879	(NA)	(NA)	496	505
Married-couple families	(NA)	(NA)	2,599	2,800	(NA)	(NA)	555	566
One earner[2]	(NA)	(NA)	1,050	1,177	(NA)	(NA)	322	334
Husband	(NA)	(NA)	814	912	(NA)	(NA)	356	365
Wife	(NA)	(NA)	164	183	(NA)	(NA)	236	262
Two or more earners	(NA)	(NA)	1,549	1,622	(NA)	(NA)	716	744
Husband and wife only	(NA)	(NA)	924	1,032	(NA)	(NA)	672	733
Families maintained by women	(NA)	(NA)	691	749	(NA)	(NA)	326	353
Families maintained by men	(NA)	(NA)	334	330	(NA)	(NA)	468	432

Source: U.S. Bureau of the Census. *Statistical Abstract of the United States, 1994.* 114th ed. Washington, DC: U.S. Government Printing Office, 1994, p. 430. Primary sources: U.S. Bureau of Labor Statistics. Bulletin 2307; and *Employment and Earnings* (monthly, January issues). *Notes:* "NA" represents "not available." The median of a group of numbers is the middle number or value when each item in the group is arranged according to size, either from lowest to highest or highest to lowest. The median generally has the same number of items above it and below it. If there is an even number of items in the group, the median is taken to be the average of the two middle numbers. 1. Excludes families in which there is no wage or salary earner or in which the husband, wife, or other person maintaining the family is either self-employed or in the Armed Forces. 2. Includes other earners, not shown separately. 3. Persons of Hispanic origin may be of any race.

★ 633 ★

Earnings

Earnings of Men, by Age: 1992

Table shows the total annual money earnings of male full-time and part-time employees 25 years old and older by age. Data are median earnings for 1992.

[In dollars]

Age	Total	Less than 9th grade	Some high school (no diploma)	High school graduates[1]	Some college (no degree)	Associate's degree	College				
								Bachelor's degree or more			
							Total	Bachelor's degree	Master's degree	Professional degree	Doctorate degree
All ages, 25 and over	26,472	12,206	15,928	22,765	26,873	30,052	40,590	36,691	43,371	70,728	52,285
25 to 34 years	21,692	10,235	13,449	20,016	21,537	25,489	31,973	31,119	35,555	39,342	36,485
35 to 44 years	30,306	14,366	16,606	25,587	30,536	31,270	44,211	40,903	45,831	85,870	54,527
45 to 54 years	32,817	15,317	20,674	28,084	34,243	36,542	48,783	41,898	51,104	78,822	59,155
55 to 64 years	26,703	15,971	20,352	23,934	29,633	30,462	42,344	40,467	37,429	80,185	55,179
65 years and over	9,093	4,817	6,941	8,307	9,257	11,247	19,554	16,333	12,406	48,318	37,440

Source: U.S. Department of Education. Office of Educational Research and Improvement. National Center for Education Statistics. *Digest of Education Statistics, 1994.* NCES 94-115. Lanham, MD: Bernan, November 1994, p. 400. Primary source: U.S. Department of Commerce. Bureau of the Census. *Current Population Reports: Money Income of Households, Families, and Persons in the United States, 1992.* Series P-60. Table prepared August 1994. *Notes:* Details may not add to totals because of rounding. 1. Includes equivalency.

★ 634 ★

Earnings

Earnings of Men, by Educational Attainment: 1992

Table shows the total annual money earnings of male full-time and part-time employees 25 years old and older. Data are for 1992.

Earnings	Total	Less than 9th grade	Some high school (no diploma)	High school graduates[1]	Some college (no degree)	Associate's degree	College				
								Bachelor's degree or more			
							Total	Bachelor's degree	Master's degree	Professional degree	Doctorate degree
Men, total	77,644	7,302	7,820	25,766	12,920	4,601	19,234	12,154	4,368	1,652	1,060
With earnings	60,356	3,230	4,983	20,268	10,831	4,072	16,975	10,667	3,887	1,505	916
Percent distribution of men with earnings											
$1 to $2,499 or loss	4.6	11.8	7.5	4.4	4.4	3.4	2.8	3.0	2.8	1.5	2.6
$2,500 to $7,499	7.6	19.1	14.3	8.3	7.2	5.1	3.5	4.0	3.4	0.5	2.1
$7,500 to $12,499	9.4	20.5	18.5	10.7	7.9	6.5	4.8	5.4	4.1	2.7	4.6
$12,500 to $14,999	3.9	8.0	6.8	4.8	3.2	2.9	2.0	2.4	1.7	1.0	0.4
$15,000 to $17,499	6.1	8.9	7.9	7.7	6.9	5.5	2.9	3.6	1.8	0.9	1.9
$17,500 to $19,999	4.4	5.1	5.5	5.6	4.6	4.7	2.3	2.7	1.9	0.7	2.0
$20,000 to $22,499	6.5	7.1	9.1	8.1	6.6	6.7	3.6	4.2	2.8	1.9	2.2
$22,500 to $24,999	3.9	3.6	4.5	4.8	3.9	4.2	2.4	3.0	1.8	0.9	1.6
$25,000 to $29,999	9.7	5.5	8.1	12.1	10.7	10.7	7.1	8.3	5.8	4.0	3.7
$30,000 to $34,499	9.1	3.3	5.8	10.2	10.5	11.6	8.3	9.3	7.6	5.6	4.4
$35,000 to $39,999	7.9	2.4	3.8	8.0	9.0	9.9	8.7	9.4	8.2	5.6	8.2
$40,000 to $44,999	6.4	1.6	2.6	5.1	8.2	7.9	8.5	8.8	9.8	4.9	5.9
$45,000 to $49,999	4.2	1.0	2.1	3.3	4.1	6.0	6.2	6.4	7.3	2.7	4.1
$50,000 to $64,999	8.3	1.1	2.6	4.5	8.2	9.3	15.6	14.4	18.8	12.8	21.6
$65,000 to $74,999	2.4	0.4	0.3	1.1	1.4	2.2	5.8	4.4	7.7	8.3	9.6

[Continued]

★ 634 ★

Earnings of Men, by Educational Attainment: 1992

[Continued]

Earnings	Total	Less than 9th grade	Some high school (no diploma)	High school graduates[1]	Some college (no degree)	Associate's degree	College				
							Bachelor's degree or more				
							Total	Bachelor's degree	Master's degree	Professional degree	Doctorate degree
$75,000 to $99,999	2.8	0.2	0.1	0.8	1.6	2.1	7.5	5.8	7.9	16.1	11.8
$100,000 and over	2.7	0.3	0.3	0.5	1.5	1.2	7.9	4.8	6.4	29.8	13.4

Source: U.S. Department of Education. Office of Educational Research and Improvement. National Center for Education Statistics. *Digest of Education Statistics, 1994.* NCES 94-115. Lanham, MD: Bernan, November 1994, p. 400. Primary source: U.S. Department of Commerce. Bureau of the Census. *Current Population Reports: Money Income of Households, Families, and Persons in the United States, 1992.* Series P-60. Table prepared August 1994. *Notes:* Details may not add to totals because of rounding. 1. Includes equivalency.

★ 635 ★

Earnings

Earnings of Women: 1994

Of the more than 1,500 women surveyed by Louis Harris Associates for a study conducted by the Families and Work Institute and the Whirlpool Foundation, two-thirds were employed outside of the home and 55 percent earned at least half of their households' incomes. The table below shows the contributions of women's earnings to their households.

[In percentagegs]

Contribution to household income	Women
Sole earner	18
Provides more than half of family's income	11
Provides about half of family's income	26

Source: Walters, Donna K. H. "Earnings Clout Grows for Women, Study Shows." *Detroit News,* 11 May 1995, p. 1A. Primary source: Louis Harris Associates.

★ 636 ★

Earnings

Earnings of Women, by Age: 1992

Table shows the total annual money earnings of female full-time and part-time employees 25 years old and older by age. Data are median earnings for 1992.

[In dollars]

Age	Total	Less than 9th grade	Some high school (no diploma)	High school graduates[1]	Some college (no degree)	Associate's degree	College				
							Bachelor's degree or more				
							Total	Bachelor's degree	Master's degree	Professional degree	Doctorate degree
All ages, 25 and over	16,227	7,942	9,784	13,266	16,611	19,642	26,417	24,126	30,934	37,249	39,901
25 to 34 years	16,022	7,503	9,205	12,261	15,588	18,427	24,748	23,604	27,088	35,667	-
35 to 44 years	17,286	8,392	9,558	14,145	17,174	20,415	27,551	25,245	30,850	40,000	40,218
45 to 54 years	17,977	9,845	11,395	15,240	19,324	21,112	30,454	25,818	34,669	44,824	41,490
55 to 64 years	14,017	7,906	10,064	12,805	16,825	20,227	27,240	21,757	33,037	-	-
65 years and over	6,292	4,665	4,993	6,768	6,010	6,894	7,807	6,593	9,078	-	-

Source: U.S. Department of Education. Office of Educational Research and Improvement. National Center for Education Statistics. *Digest of Education Statistics, 1994.* NCES 94-115. Lanham, MD: Bernan, November 1994, p. 400. Primary source: U.S. Department of Commerce. Bureau of the Census. *Current Population Reports: Money Income of Households, Families, and Persons in the United States, 1992.* Series P-60. Table prepared August 1994. *Notes:* Details may not add to totals because of rounding. "-" indicates "not available." 1. Includes equivalency.

★ 637 ★

Earnings

Earnings of Women, by Educational Attainment: 1992

Table shows the total annual money earnings of female full-time and part-time employees 25 years old and older. Data are for 1992.

Earnings	Total	Less than 9th grade	Some high school (no diploma)	High school graduates[1]	Some college (no degree)	Associate's degree	College				
							Bachelor's degree or more				
							Total	Bachelor's degree	Master's degree	Professional degree	Doctorate degree
Women, total	85,181	7,826	9,246	31,823	14,175	5,755	16,356	11,465	3,942	584	366
With earnings	51,246	1,649	3,507	18,882	9,918	4,391	12,898	8,824	3,247	498	329
Percent distribution of women with earnings											
$1 to $2,499 or loss	10.0	19.8	16.5	11.0	9.6	7.9	6.7	7.7	5.2	2.6	2.7
$2,500 to $7,499	14.2	27.5	23.3	17.0	13.9	9.8	7.6	8.3	6.1	5.2	7.6
$7,500 to $12,499	16.1	28.2	27.4	19.8	15.2	13.9	7.7	8.7	5.5	5.6	3.3
$12,500 to $14,999	5.9	7.3	7.5	7.2	6.0	5.5	3.3	3.8	2.3	2.6	1.2
$15,000 to $17,499	7.7	5.9	8.8	9.6	8.3	7.3	4.7	5.6	3.0	0.6	1.8
$17,500 to $19,999	5.6	3.0	3.5	6.6	6.7	6.5	4.0	4.7	2.9	0.6	1.2
$20,000 to $22,499	7.4	3.0	3.9	7.7	8.9	9.3	6.7	7.6	4.6	5.8	3.9
$22,500 to $24,999	4.4	1.6	2.0	4.3	4.9	5.4	5.1	5.6	4.1	2.2	4.5
$25,000 to $29,999	9.3	2.1	3.8	7.4	10.6	12.0	12.6	12.9	12.8	8.9	6.1
$30,000 to $34,499	6.6	0.5	1.2	4.5	6.7	8.0	11.3	10.6	14.2	7.8	7.0
$35,000 to $39,999	4.3	0.6	0.7	2.2	3.5	6.1	8.9	7.7	11.2	13.5	10.3
$40,000 to $44,999	3.0	0.4	0.5	1.3	2.5	3.1	6.9	5.6	10.2	6.0	12.1
$45,000 to $49,999	1.7	0.0	0.5	0.4	1.2	2.7	4.2	3.6	5.2	5.8	6.7
$50,000 to $64,999	1.3	0.0	0.3	0.2	0.9	1.0	3.6	2.9	4.6	5.6	8.5
$65,000 to $74,999	1.6	0.0	0.1	0.6	0.7	1.3	4.4	3.1	6.0	9.9	15.8

[Continued]

★ 637 ★

Earnings of Women, by Educational Attainment: 1992

[Continued]

Earnings	Total	Less than 9th grade	Some high school (no diploma)	High school graduates[1]	Some college (no degree)	Associate's degree	College				
							Bachelor's degree or more				
							Total	Bachelor's degree	Master's degree	Professional degree	Doctorate degree
$75,000 to $99,999	0.5	0.1	0.1	0.2	0.2	0.3	1.4	1.1	1.3	6.8	4.2
$100,000 and over	0.3	0.0	0.1	0.0	0.2	0.1	1.0	0.5	0.9	10.3	3.0

Source: U.S. Department of Education. Office of Educational Research and Improvement. National Center for Education Statistics. *Digest of Education Statistics, 1994.* NCES 94-115. Lanham, MD: Bernan, November 1994, p. 400. Primary source: U.S. Department of Commerce. Bureau of the Census. *Current Population Reports: Money Income of Households, Families, and Persons in the United States, 1992.* Series P-60. Table prepared August 1994. *Notes:* Details may not add to totals because of rounding. 1. Includes equivalency.

★ 638 ★

Earnings

Earnings of Workers, by Educational Level: 1992

Table shows the median annual earnings of year-round, full-time workers in 1992. Data are provided by highest education level achieved.

Highest education level	Median annual earnings ($)	Premium over high school graduates (%)
All degree levels	37,359	76
Professional degree	67,131	216
Ph.D. degree	52,403	147
Master's degree	40,666	91
Bachelor's degree	34,385	62
High school diploma	21,241	-

Source: Hecker, Daniel E. "Further Analysis of Labor Market for College Graduates." *Monthly Labor Review* 118, no. 2 (February 1995), p. 40. *Note:* "-" indicates "not applicable."

★ 639 ★
Earnings

Earnings of Workers, by Field of Study: 1991

Table shows the average salary of class of 1990 graduates who were employed full time one year after graduation (1991). Figures also reflect the relation of the graduates' jobs with their major fields of study.

Field of study	Average salary ($)	Those in jobs related to field of study (%)
All majors	23,600	76
Health professions	31,500	95
Engineering	30,900	89
Mathematics, computer and physical sciences	27,200	86
Business and management	24,700	81
Social sciences	22,200	53
History	21,300	30
Biological sciences	21,100	73
Public affairs	20,800	71
Psychology	19,200	65
Education	19,100	87
Humanities	19,100	57

Source: Hecker, Daniel E. "Further Analysis of Labor Market for College Graduates." *Monthly Labor Review* 118, no. 2 (February 1995), p. 40.

★ 640 ★

Earnings

Pay, by Selected Metropolitan Areas: 1991 and 1992

Table shows the average annual pay in metropolitan areas, ranked by 1992 figures. Data are for metropolitan statistical areas (MSAs) and primary metropolitan statistical areas (PMSAs), except for New England. Data for this region are for New England county metropolitan areas (NECMAs). Also see related table on annual pay by state.

[In dollars]

Metropolitan area	1991	1992[1]
Metropolitan areas	25,729	27,173
Bridgeport, Connecticut;		
Stamford, Connecticut;		
Norwalk, Connecticut;		
Danbury, Connecticut	35,998	39,006
New York, New York	35,073	38,802
San Jose, California	34,462	37,068
Middlesex, New Jersey;		
Somerset, New Jersey;		
Hunterdon, New Jersey	32,523	34,826
Newark, New Jersey	32,231	34,712
San Francisco, California	32,031	34,358
Trenton, New Jersey	31,888	33,960
Bergen, New Jersey;		
Passaic, New Jersey	31,292	33,592
Anchorage, Alaska	31,828	33,007
Washington, District of Columbia	31,057	32,899
Hartford, Connecticut;		
New Britain, Connecticut;		
Middletown, Connecticut;		
Bristol, Connecticut	30,375	31,967
Boston, Massachusetts;		
Lawrence, Massachusetts;		
Salem, Massachusetts;		
Lowell, Massachusetts;		
Brockton, Massachusetts	29,968	31,872
Jersey City, New Jersey	29,045	31,628
Los Angeles, California;		
Long Beach, California	29,697	31,267
Chicago, Illinois	28,711	30,692
Oakland, California	29,111	30,622
Lake County, Illinois	28,521	30,461
Detroit, Michigan	28,664	30,408
Houston, Texas	28,026	29,802
Nassau, New York;		
Suffolk, New York	28,167	29,708
Flint, Michigan	29,318	29,672
Seattle, Washington	27,327	29,586
Philadelphia, Pennsylvania	27,607	29,355
Anaheim, California;		
Santa Ana, California	27,852	29,353

[Continued]

★ 640 ★

Pay, by Selected Metropolitan Areas: 1991 and 1992

[Continued]

Metropolitan area	1991	1992[1]
New Haven, Connecticut; Waterbury, Connecticut; Meriden, Connecticut	27,729	29,347
Poughkeepsie, New York	28,382	29,262
Wilmington, Delaware	27,766	29,047
Dallas, Texas	27,364	28,988
Ann Arbor, Michigan	27,503	28,714
Kokomo, Indiana	27,918	28,676
Huntsville, Alabama	26,625	28,432
Manchester, New Hampshire; Nashua, New Hampshire	26,448	28,372
Atlanta, Georgia	26,636	28,159
Minneapolis, Minnesota; St. Paul, Minnesota	26,423	28,035
Brazoria, Texas	27,027	27,979
New London, Connecticut; Norwich, Connecticut	26,821	27,926
Denver, Colorado	26,526	27,734
Rochester, New York	26,572	27,562
Monmouth, New Jersey; Ocean, New Jersey	25,784	27,468
Rochester, Minnesota	26,189	27,416
Sacramento, California	25,658	26,999
Cleveland, Ohio	25,462	26,857
Baltimore, Maryland	25,708	26,795
Saginaw, Michigan; Bay City, Michigan; Midland, Michigan	25,706	26,650
Honolulu, Hawaii	25,014	26,638
Lansing, Michigan; East Lansing, Michigan	25,681	26,548
Midland, Texas	25,726	26,321
Worcester, Massachusetts; Fitchburg, Massachusetts; Leominster, Massachusetts	25,077	26,309
St. Louis, Missouri	25,209	26,285
Oxnard, California; Ventura, California	25,124	26,267
Cincinnati, Ohio	24,763	26,187
Pittsburgh, Pennsylvania	24,733	26,163
San Diego, California	25,002	26,153
Kalamazoo, Michigan	25,170	26,143
Raleigh, North Carolina; Durham, North Carolina	24,789	26,140

[Continued]

★ 640 ★

Pay, by Selected Metropolitan Areas: 1991 and 1992

[Continued]

Metropolitan area	1991	1992[1]
West Palm Beach, Florida; Boca Raton, Florida; Delray Beach, Florida	24,564	25,050
Melbourne, Florida; Titusville, Florida; Palm Bay, Florida	24,473	26,032
Albany, New York; Schenectady, New York; Troy, New York	24,817	26,020
Portland, Oregon	24,555	26,007
Battle Creek, Michigan	24,743	25,969

Source: U.S. Bureau of the Census. *Statistical Abstract of the United States, 1994.* 114th ed. Washington, DC: U.S. Government Printing Office, 1994, p. 428. Primary source: U.S. Bureau of Labor Statistics. *Average Annual Pay Levels in Metropolitan Areas, 1992.* USDL News Release 93-428. *Note:* 1. Preliminary.

★ 641 ★

Earnings

Pay, by Sex: 1992

From the source: "Even though the earnings gap between men and women is slowly closing, women earn only 71 cents for every dollar earned by men" (p. 1). The table below compares the earnings of men and women of various ethnic/racial backgrounds.

[In dollars]

Race/ethnicity	Men	Women
Black	22,369	19,819
Hispanic	20,049	17,138
White	31,012	21,659

Source: "Who Are the Working Poor?" *National Consumers League Bulletin* 55, no. 6 (November/December 1993), p. 1.

★ 642 ★

Earnings

Pay, by Sexual Preference

Table compares the average incomes of persons by sexual preferences. Data are based on a nationwide survey conducted from 1989 through 1991 by economist Lee Badgett of the University of Maryland. Survey findings show that "both gay men and lesbians earn less on average than similarly qualified heterosexual men and women" (p. F25).

Full-time employees	Percent earning $30,000 or more annually	Average income
Lesbians	5.9	15,068
Heterosexual women	16.7	18,341
Gay men	38.3	26,321
Heterosexual men	42.5	28,312

Source: Noble, Barbara Presley. "Linking Gay Rights and Unionism." *New York Times,* 4 December 1994, p. F25. Primary source: Lee Badgett, University of Maryland; University of Chicago.

★ 643 ★

Earnings

Pay, by State

Table shows the average annual pay in each state for workers covered by state unemployment insurance laws and for federal civilian workers covered by unemployment compensation for federal employees, approximately 90 percent of total civilian employment. Excludes most agricultural workers on small farms, all Armed Forces, elected officials in most states, railroad employees, most domestic workers, employees of certain nonprofit organizations, and most self-employed individuals. Pay includes bonuses, cash value of meals and lodging, and tips and other gratuities.

[In dollars, except percentage changes]

State	Average annual pay		Precent change, 1991-1992[1]
	1991	1992[1]	
United States	24,758	25,903	5.4
Alabama	21,287	22,340	4.9
Alaska	30,830	31,825	3.2
Arizona	22,207	23,161	4.3
Arkansas	19,008	20,108	5.8
California	27,513	28,934	5.2
Colorado	23,981	25,040	4.4
Connecticut	30,689	32,587	6.2
Delaware	25,647	26,596	3.7
District of Columbia	35,570	37,971	6.8

[Continued]

★ 643 ★

Pay, by State

[Continued]

State	Average annual pay		Precent change, 1991-1992[1]
	1991	1992[1]	
Florida	21,992	23,144	5.2
Georgia	23,165	24,373	5.2
Hawaii	24,104	25,613	6.3
Idaho	19,688	20,649	4.9
Illinois	26,317	27,910	6.1
Indiana	22,522	23,570	4.7
Iowa	19,810	20,937	5.7
Kansas	21,002	21,982	4.7
Kentucky	20,730	21,858	5.4
Louisiana	21,503	22,340	3.9
Maine	20,870	21,808	4.5
Maryland	25,962	27,145	4.6
Massachusetts	28,041	29,664	5.8
Michigan	26,125	27,463	5.1
Minnesota	23,962	25,315	5.6
Mississippi	18,411	19,237	4.5
Missouri	22,574	23,550	4.3
Montana	18,648	19,378	3.9
Nebraska	19,372	20,355	5.1
Nevada	23,083	24,743	7.2
New Hampshire	23,600	24,925	5.6
New Jersey	29,991	32,125	7.1
New Mexico	20,272	21,051	3.8
New York	30,011	32,399	8.0
North Carolina	21,095	22,248	5.5
North Dakota	18,132	18,945	4.5
Ohio	23,602	24,846	5.3
Oklahoma	20,968	21,699	3.5
Oregon	22,338	23,514	5.3
Pennsylvania	24,393	25,785	5.7
Rhode Island	23,082	24,315	5.3
South Carolina	20,439	21,423	4.8
South Dakota	17,143	18,016	5.1
Tennessee	21,541	22,807	5.9
Texas	23,760	25,080	5.6
Utah	20,874	21,976	5.3
Vermont	21,355	22,347	4.6
Virginia	23,805	24,937	4.8
Washington	23,942	25,553	6.7
West Virginia	21,356	22,169	3.8
Wisconsin	21,838	23,022	5.4
Wyoming	20,591	21,215	3.0

Source: U.S. Bureau of the Census. *Statistical Abstract of the United States, 1994.* 114th ed. Washington, DC: U.S. Government Printing Office, 1994, p. 428. Primary sources: U.S. Bureau of Labor Statistics. *Employment and Wages Annual Averages, 1992;* and USDL News Release 93-371, *Average Annual Pay by State and Industry, 1992. Note:* 1. Preliminary.

Earnings: Pay Increases

★ 644 ★

Bonuses and Incentives: 1994

Table shows the average bonus and incentive pay outs as a percentage of base pay for non-sales employees. Data are based on a survey of Fortune 1,000 companies.

[In percentages]

Employee	Bonus
Executives	31.2
Exempt employees	12.4
Nonexempt employees	5.3

Source: "Merit Increases, Alternative Pay Are More Popular." *HR Focus* (December 1994), p. 11. Primary source: Buck Consultants.

★ 645 ★

Earnings: Pay Increases

General Pay Increases

According to one compensation budget survey, few companies adjust pay using general increases or through combined merit and general pay increases. In fact, 90 percent of more than 300 Fortune 1,000 companies surveyed offered only merit increases.

Source: "Merit Increases, Alternative Pay Are More Popular." *HR Focus* (December 1994), p. 11. Primary source: Buck Consultants. 1994-1995 compensation budget survey.

★ 646 ★

Earnings: Pay Increases

Merit Increases: 1994

Table shows the average merit pay increases budgeted for 1994. Data are from a survey of 480 companies.

[In percentages]

Position	Average merit increase
Executive	5.2
Middle management	4.5
Exempt	4.4
Sales	4.4
Nonexempt	4.2
Hourly nonunion	4.1

Source: "Recession Still Puts Pressure on Pay Plans." *Sales & Marketing Management* (October 1993), p. 42. Primary source: Coopers & Lybrand Human Resource Advisory Group.

★ 647 ★

Earnings: Pay Increases

Salary Increases, by Country: 1994

Table shows the average total salary increases in relation to Consumer Price Indices (CPI) for management and nonmanagement positions in selected countries. Data are for 1994.

[In percentages]

Country	Management	Nonmanagement	Consumer Price Indices
Argentina	10.0-11.0	11.0-12.0	10.0-11.0
Brazil	4.0-6.0[1]	4.0-6.0[1]	1,200.0-1,300.0
Canada	2.7-2.9	2.7-2.9	2.0-2.2
China	17.0-19.0	12.0-15.0	15.0-16.0
Hong Kong	10.0-10.5	10.5-11.0	8.5-9.0
Korea	3.5-4.0	6.5-7.0	5.0-5.5
Mexico	8.0-9.0	7.0-8.0	7.0-8.0
Singapore	6.0-6.5	6.0-6.5	2.5-3.0
Taiwan	7.0-7.5	7.5-8.0	3.0-3.5
Thailand	14.0-16.0	12.0-13.0	2.0-3.0
United Kingdom	3.3-3.5	3.0-3.3	3.3-3.6
United States	4.5-4.6	4.3-4.4	3.0-3.5

Source: "Asian Managers Expected to Receive Highest Increases." *HR Focus* (May 1994), p. 14. Primary source: William M. Mercer Inc. *Note:* 1. Percentages indicate increases in excess of inflation.

★ 648 ★

Earnings: Pay Increases

Wage Increases, by Region: 1993

Table shows the median first-year wage increases by region of the United States. Figures reflect median percentage changes for the first 3 quarters of 1993.

Region	Increase
New England	2.7
Middle Atlantic	2.7
Southwest	2.8
Southeast	2.9
North Central	3.0
Midwest	3.0
West	3.0

Source: Lissy, William E. "Currents in Compensation and Benefits." *Compensation & Benefits Review* 26, no. 2 (March/April 1994), p. 15. Primary sources: CBNC Database.

Earnings: Wage Rates and Workers

★ 649 ★

Hourly Rate Workers, by Selected Characteristics: 1993

Annual average of monthly figures for employed wage and salary workers paid hourly rates. Based on Current Population Survey.

Characteristic	Number of workers[1] (1,000)				Percent of all workers paid hourly rates At or below $4.25			Median earnings hourly of workers paid hourly rates[2]
	Total paid hourly rates	At or below $4.25			Total	At $4.25	Below $4.25	
		Total	At $4.25	Below $4.25				
Total, 16 years and over[3]	63,316	4,186	2,518	1,668	6.6	4.0	2.6	7.92
16 to 24 years	14,331	2,241	1,434	807	15.6	10.0	5.6	5.50
16 to 19 years	5,021	1,308	928	380	26.1	18.5	7.6	4.79
25 years and over	48,984	1,946	1,085	861	4.0	2.2	1.8	8.97
Male, 16 years and over	31,699	1,583	1,032	551	5.0	3.3	1.7	8.96
16 to 24 years	7,385	966	678	288	13.1	9.2	3.9	5.75
16 to 19 years	2,532	599	462	137	23.7	18.2	5.4	4.86
25 years and over	24,314	618	355	263	2.5	1.5	1.1	10.21
Women, 16 years and over	31,617	2,603	1,486	1,117	8.2	4.7	3.5	7.15
16 to 24 years	6,946	1,275	756	519	18.4	10.9	7.5	5.27
16 to 19 years	2,489	709	465	244	28.5	18.7	9.8	4.73
25 years and over	24,671	1,328	730	598	5.4	3.0	2.4	7.88
White	52,971	3,467	2,036	1,431	6.5	3.8	2.7	8.03
Black	8,078	572	392	180	7.1	4.9	2.2	7.19

[Continued]

★ 649 ★

Hourly Rate Workers, by Selected Characteristics: 1993
[Continued]

Characteristic	Number of workers[1] (1,000)				Percent of all workers paid hourly rates At or below $4.25			Median earnings hourly of workers paid hourly rates[2]
	Total paid hourly rates	At or below $4.25			Total	At $4.25	Below $4.25	
		Total	At $4.25	Below $4.25				
Hispanic origin[4]	6,047	544	427	117	9.0	7.1	1.9	6.87
Full-time workers	47,125	1,448	835	613	3.1	1.8	1.3	8.89
Part-time workers[5]	16,191	2,739	1,684	1,055	16.9	10.4	6.5	5.55
Private sector	54,862	3,874	2,294	1,580	7.1	4.2	2.9	7.66
Goods-producing industries[6]	17,596	422	300	122	2.4	1.7	0.7	9.22
Service-producing industries[7]	37,266	3,452	1,994	1,458	9.3	5.4	3.9	6.92
Public sector	8,454	313	225	88	3.7	2.7	1.0	9.96

Source: U.S. Bureau of the Census. *Statistical Abstract of the United States, 1994.* 114th ed. Washington, DC: U.S. Government Printing Office, 1994, p. 432. Primary source: U.S. Bureau of Labor Statistics. Unpublished data. *Notes:* 1. Excludes the incorporated self-employed. 2. The median of a group of numbers is the middle number or value when each item in the group is arranged according to size, either from lowest to highest or highest to lowest. The median generally has the same number of items above it and below it. If there is an even number of items in the group, the median is taken to be the average of the two middle numbers. 3. Includes races not shown separately. 4. Persons of Hispanic origin may be of any race. 5. Working fewer than 35 hours per week. 6. Includes agriculture, mining, construction, and manufacturing. 7. Includes transportation and public utilities; wholesale trade; finance, insurance, and real estate; private households; and other service industries, not shown separately.

★ 650 ★

Earnings: Wage Rates and Workers

Minimum Hourly Wage Rates: 1950-1993

Figures reflect the effective federal minimum hourly wage rates. The Fair Labor Standards Act of 1938 and subsequent amendments provide for minimum wage coverage applicable to specified nonsupervisory employment categories. Exempt from coverage are executives and administrators or professionals. Employee estimates as of September 1991, except as indicated.

In effect	Minimum rates for nonfarm workers			Minimum rates for farm workers[4]
	Laws prior to 1966[1]	Percent average earnings[2]	1966 and later[3]	
January 25, 1950	$0.75	54	(X)	(X)
March 1, 1956	1.00	52	(X)	(X)
September 3, 1961	1.15	50	(X)	(X)
September 3, 1963	1.25	51	(X)	(X)
February 1, 1967	1.40	50	$1.00	$1.00
February 1, 1968	1.60	54	1.15	1.15
February 1, 1969	([5])	51	1.30	1.30
February 1, 1970	([5])	49	1.45	([5])
February 1, 1971	([5])	46	1.60	([5])
May 1, 1974	2.00	46	1.90	1.60
January 1, 1975	2.10	45	2.00	1.80

[Continued]

★ 650 ★

Minimum Hourly Wage Rates: 1950-1993
[Continued]

| In effect | Minimum rates for nonfarm workers | | | Minimum rates for farm workers[4] |
	Laws prior to 1966[1]	Percent average earnings[2]	1966 and later[3]	
January 1, 1976	2.30	46	2.20	2.00
January 1, 1977	(5)	42	2.30	2.20
January 1, 1978	2.65	44	2.65	2.65
January 1, 1979	2.90	45	2.90	2.90
January 1, 1980	3.10	44	3.10	3.10
January 1, 1981	3.35	43	3.35	3.35
April 1, 1990	3.80	35	3.80	3.80
April 1, 1991	4.25	38	4.25	4.25
April 1, 1992	(5)	37	(5)	(5)
April 1, 1993	(5)	36	(5)	(5)

Source: U.S. Bureau of the Census. *Statistical Abstract of the United States, 1994.* 114th ed. Washington, DC: U.S. Government Printing Office, 1994, p. 432. Primary sources: U.S. Department of Labor. Employment Standards Administration. *Minimum Wage and Maximum Hours Standards Under the Fair Labor Standards Act* (1981; annual); and unpublished data. *Notes:* "X" represents "not applicable." 1. Applies to workers covered prior to 1961 amendments and, after September 1965, to workers covered by 1961 amendments. Rates set by 1961 amendments were: September 1961, $1.00; September 1964, $1.15; and September 1965, $1.25. 2. Percent of gross average hourly earnings of production workers in manufacturing. 3. Applies to workers newly covered by amendments of 1966, 1974, and 1977, and Title IX of Education Amendments of 1972. 4. Included in coverage as of 1966, 1974, and 1977 amendments. 5. No change in rate.

★ 651 ★

Earnings: Wage Rates and Workers

Minimum Hourly Wage Workers, by Age: 1993

Ages 25 and older - 43.1

Ages 16-19 - 36.9

Ages 20-24 - 20.0

Most of the 2.5 million minimum wage workers earning $4.25 an hour are young. In fact, nearly 57 percent are under 25 years old. The table below shows the age breakdown of minimum wage workers.

[In percentages]

Age	Workers
Ages 16-19	36.9
Ages 20-24	20.0
Ages 25 and older	43.1

Source: Kilborn, Peter T. "A City Built on $4.25 an Hour." *New York Times,* 12 February 1995, sec. 3, p. 5. Primary source: Bureau of Labor Statistics.

★ 652 ★

Earnings: Wage Rates and Workers

Minimum Hourly Wage Workers, by Race/Ethnicity: 1993

More than 7 percent of the workers in private industry earned hourly minimum wages ($4.25) or less in 1993. Similarly, more than 3.5 percent of the public sector's workers earned $4.25 an hour or less. The table below shows the racial and/or ethnic characteristics of minimum wage earners in 1993.

[In percentages]

Race/ethnicity	Workers
White	6.5
Black	7.1
Hispanic	9.0

Source: Chavez, Linda. "Minimum Wage Hurts the Poor." *USA TODAY,* 8 February 1995, p. 11A. Primary source: Bureau of Labor Statistics.

★ 653 ★

Earnings: Wage Rates and Workers

Student Wages: 1992

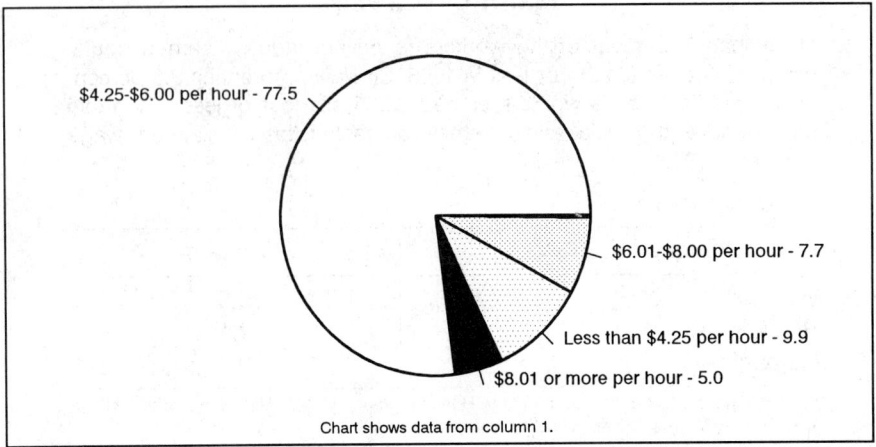

Chart shows data from column 1.

Table shows the most recent hourly wages reported by employed seniors in high school during 1992. Data are by selected student characteristics.

[In percentages]

Hourly wage	Total	Sex		Race/Ethnicity				
		Male	Female	White	Black	Hispanic	Asian	American Indian
Less than $4.25 per hour	9.9	7.2	12.4	10.3	8.3	8.8	7.9	5.8
$4.25-$6.00 per hour	77.5	75.6	79.2	76.7	80.9	81.1	77.0	79.3
$6.01-$8.00 per hour	7.7	10.3	5.3	8.0	5.8	6.1	10.7	6.7
$8.01 or more per hour	5.0	6.9	3.2	5.1	5.0	4.0	4.5	8.3

Source: U.S. Department of Education. Office of Educational Research and Improvement. National Center for Education Statistics. *Digest of Education Statistics, 1994.* NCES 94-115. Lanham, MD: Bernan, November 1994, p. 403. Primary source: U.S. Department of Education. National Center for Education Statistics. "National Education Longitudinal Study of 1988." Second Follow-up Survey. (Table prepared February 1994.).

Chapter 6
EMPLOYEE BENEFITS

"Historically," wrote work and family consultant Barbara P. Adolf, "employer benefits have provided employees with protection against financial devastation due to illness, disability, loss of work, retirement, and death. Benefit programs, specifically, financial accumulation plans, have also served as a reward for service to the organization" ("Life Cycle Benefits," *Employee Benefits Journal,* March 1993, p. 13). While employees still look for these traditional benefits, evolution of the workplace has refocused benefit plans. In order to face the demands of the changing workplace—for example, increased numbers of women in the workforce, competition for qualified workers, reemphasis on productivity, and the need for low absenteeism—more employers offer benefits that assist employees in dealing with routine responsibilities such as child care or eldercare. The 61 tables in this chapter profile the various benefits packages offered by small, medium-sized, and large private industry employers and by the public sector to full- and part-time employees. Work and family (or "life cycle") benefits are covered in detail. Other topics include health care, incentives, insurance, pension plans, retirement plans, benefits to retirees, paid and unpaid time off from work, and miscellaneous benefits.

Benefit Programs and Packages

★ 654 ★

Employee Benefits of Large Employers

According to the source, employees of companies with more than 1,000 workers can be considered the "benefit elite" because they most often receive the widest variety of benefits. The table below shows the prevalence of selected employee benefits at large companies.

[In percentages]

Benefit	Prevalence of benefit
Death and disability	
Employee life	100
Long-term disability	100
Dependent life	64

[Continued]

★ 654 ★

Employee Benefits of Large Employers
[Continued]

Benefit	Prevalence of benefit
Health care	
Medical coverage	100
Dental coverage	96
Health care FSA	69
Choice of plans	55
Paid time off	
Vacation	100
Holidays	100
Buy/sell additional days	11
Retirement	
401(k)	96
Matched savings	87
Pension	84
Retiree medical	81
Work and family	
Dependent care FSA	74
Flex time	44
Part-time employment	40
Resource and referral	31

Source: Jenner, Lisa. "Large Employers Support the 'Benefit Elite.'" *HR Focus* (May 1994), p. 3. Primary source: Hewitt Associates. *Salaried Employee Benefits Provided by Major U.S. Employers in 1993,* a survey of 1,034 companies. *Note:* "FSA" stands for "flexible spending account."

★ 655 ★

Benefit Programs and Packages

Employee Benefits of Medium and Large Private Establishments – Full-Time Workers: 1991

Table shows participation of full-time employees in private industry in miscellaneous benefits in medium and large establishments. Medium and large establishments exclude establishments with fewer than 100 workers, executive and traveling operating employees, and Alaska and Hawaii. Covers only benefits for which the employer pays part or all of the premium or expenses involved, except unpaid parental leave and long-term care insurance. Based on a sample survey of establishments. See also tables for specific benefits such as time off or insurance plans.

[In percentages]

Benefit	Employees			
	All	Professional, technical, and related	Clerical and sales	Production and service
Parking	88	86	85	92
Educational assistance	72	87	73	64
Employee assistance programs	56	64	56	51
Travel accident insurance	42	55	47	32
Severance pay	41	55	48	30
Reimbursement accounts[1]	36	48	40	26
Nonproduction bonuses, cash	35	33	36	35
Wellness programs	35	47	34	28
Relocation allowance	31	50	30	21
Recreation facilities	26	34	25	23
Flexible benefits plans	10	16	10	6
Eldercare	9	11	12	6
Child care	8	11	9	5
Long-term care insurance	4	6	5	2

Source: U.S. Bureau of the Census. *Statistical Abstract of the United States, 1994.* 114th ed. Washington, DC: U.S. Government Printing Office, 1994, p. 434. Primary source: U.S. Bureau of Labor Statistics. *Employee Benefits in Medium and Large Private Establishments, 1991.* Bulletin 2422. *Notes:* 1. Account which is used throughout the year to pay for plan premiums or to reimburse the employee for benefit-related expenses. Account may be financed by employer, employee, or both.

★ 656 ★

Benefit Programs and Packages

Employee Benefits of Medium and Large Private Establishments – Part-Time: 1991

Table shows the part-time employees eligible for special benefits at medium and large private establishments. Data are for 1991.

[In percentages]

Benefit	All employees	Professional, technical, and related employees	Clerical and sales employees	Production and service employees
Family benefits				
Employer assistance for child care	5	12	5	4
Adoption financial assistance	1	1	2	1
Eldercare	4	7	6	2
Long-term care insurance	1	4	(1)	1
Financial and legal services				
Financial counseling	8	9	11	4
Prepaid legal services	2	(1)	3	2
Gifts and cash bonuses				
Gifts	15	21	18	12
Nonproduction bonuses	19	14	23	16
Health promotion programs				
Inhouse infirmary	11	43	7	6
Wellness programs	16	35	18	10
Employee assistance programs	31	51	36	22
Income continuation plans				
Severance pay	13	13	20	8
Supplemental unemployment benefits	2	1	1	3
Miscellaneous benefits				
Employee discounts	50	48	62	41
Employer subsidized recreation facilities	13	31	14	8
Subsidized meals	20	51	12	18
Sabbatical leave	3	12	3	1
Relocation allowance	5	7	6	5
Education assistance				
Job related	31	53	34	23
Not job related	6	10	7	3
Transportation benefits				
Free or subsidized employee parking	84	86	84	83
Subsidized commuting	4	8	2	4
Job-related travel accident insurance	18	17	24	13

Source: U.S. Department of Labor. Bureau of Labor Statistics. *Employee Benefits in Medium and Large Private Establishments, 1991.* Bulletin 2422. Washington, DC: U.S. Government Printing Office, May 1993, p. 128. *Note:* 1. Less than 0.5 percent.

★ 657 ★
Benefit Programs and Packages

Employee Benefits of Small Establishments: 1991

Table shows participation of full-time employees in private industry in miscellaneous benefits at small establishments. Small establishments include those with fewer than 100 employees. Covers only benefits for which the employer pays part or all of the premium or expenses involved, except unpaid parental leave and long-term care insurance. Based on a sample survey of establishments. See also tables for specific benefits such as time off or insurance plans.

[In percentages]

| Benefit | Employees | | | |
	All	Professional, technical, and related	Clerical and sales	Production and service
Parking[1]	86	84	85	88
Recreation facilities	77	13	7	4
Nonproduction bonuses, cash	47	52	50	43
Educational assistance	36	51	43	26
Employee assistance programs	17	24	21	12
Wellness programs	17	24	21	12
Travel accident insurance	16	24	19	11
Severance pay	15	26	21	8
Reimbursement accounts[2]	14	24	20	7
Relocation allowance[1]	12	22	15	6
Eldercare	3	4	5	2
Child care	2	3	3	(Z)
Flexible benefits plans	2	4	4	(Z)
Long-term care insurance	1	2	1	1

Source: U.S. Bureau of the Census. *Statistical Abstract of the United States, 1994.* 114th ed. Washington, DC: U.S. Government Printing Office, 1994, p. 434. Primary source: U.S. Bureau of Labor Statistics. *Employee Benefits in Small Private Establishments, 1992. Notes:* "Z" represents or rounds to zero. 1. 1990 data. 2. Account which is used throughout the year to pay for plan premiums or to reimburse the employee for benefit-related expenses. Account may be financed by employer, employee, or both.

★ 658 ★

Benefit Programs and Packages

Employee Benefits of Small, Medium, and Large Firms – A Comparison

Table comparess benefits of employees at small firms (establishments with fewer than 100 employees) and at medium and large establishments.

[In percentages]

Benefit	Employees at:	
	Small firms	Larger firms
Child care	2	8
Dental care	33	60
Flexible benefits	2	10
Life insurance	64	94
Long-term disability	23	40
Medical care	71	83
Reimbursement accounts	14	36
Retirement plan	45	78
Sickness and accident	26	45

Source: "BLS Releases Its Second Survey of Employee Benefits in Small Firms." Employee Benefit Plan Review (May 1994), p. 27. Primary source: Bureau of Labor Statistics.

★ 659 ★

Benefit Programs and Packages

Employee Benefits of State and Local Governments: 1992

For January through July. Covers full-time employees in state and local governments. Covers only benefits for which the employer pays part or all of the premium or expenses involved. Based on sample survey of establishments.

[In percentages]

Benefit	All employees	White-collar employees[1]	Teachers[2]	Blue-collar employees[3]
Child care	8	10	6	7
Educational assistance:				
Job related	66	73	57	64
Not job related	18	20	14	18
Eldercare	13	14	15	11
Employee assistance programs	63	70	47	68
Flexible benefits plans	5	5	7	4
In-house infirmary	17	18	16	14
Long-term care insurance	5	6	5	3
Nonproduction bonuses, cash	38	43	26	44
Prepaid legal services	7	8	7	7
Recreation facilities	15	15	19	12
Reimbursement accounts[4]	50	55	44	48

[Continued]

★ 659 ★

Employee Benefits of State and Local Governments: 1992
[Continued]

Benefit	All employees	White-collar employees[1]	Teachers[2]	Blue-collar employees[3]
Severance pay	32	30	31	35
Travel accident insurance	15	17	13	13
Wellness programs	30	34	23	30

Source: U.S. Bureau of the Census. *Statistical Abstract of the United States, 1994.* 114th ed. Washington, DC: U.S. Government Printing Office, 1994, p. 321. Primary source: U.S. Bureau of Labor Statistics. *Employee Benefits in State and Local Governments, 1992. Notes:* 1. Includes all professional, administrative, technical, and clerical employees except teachers. 2. Includes all personnel in primary and secondary schools, junior colleges, and universities whose primary duty is teaching or closely related activities. 3. Includes police, firefighters, and all production and service employees. 4. Account which is used throughout the year to pay for plan premiums or to reimburse the employee for benefit related expenses. Account may be financed by employer, employee, or both.

★ 660 ★

Benefit Programs and Packages

Employee Benefits of Women-Owned Firms: 1992

Table shows the benefits offered to employees by women-owned small businesses.

[In percentages]

Benefit	Women-owned businesses offering benefit
Paid vacation	59
Health/medical	48
Flex time	40
Tuition reimbursement	21
Dental	21
Retirement/401(k)	19
Profit sharing	16
Paid personal leave	15
No benefits	16

Source: Rowland, Mary. "Get More From Your Benefits Package." *Working Woman* (October 1994), p. 23. Primary sources: National Foundation for Women Business Owners; National Small Business United; Arthur Andersen's Enterprise Group.

★ 661 ★

Benefit Programs and Packages

Executive Perks: 1985-1993

According to the source, large employers have decreased the fringe benfits offered to senior executives: "The world of visible status perks isn't what it used to be. Shareholder revolts over high executive pay, together with corporate retrenchments and significant tax-law changes, have forced many companies to rethink the high level of perquisites granted to senior management for decades" (p. R4). The table below shows perks offered to executives from 1985 through 1993.

[In percentages]

Perk	1993	1991	1989	1987	1985	Percent change 1985-1993
Executive dining rooms	20	26	30	34	35	-42.9
Company planes	53	56	63	67	66	-19.7
Reserved parking	29	29	32	37	36	-19.4
Airline VIP clubs	30	32	34	38	37	-18.9
Chauffeur services	35	36	40	42	43	-18.6
Loans	6	7	9	8	7	-14.3
First-class air travel	57	60	62	66	66	-13.6
Club memberships	62	63	71	73	70	-11.4
Company cars	63	63	68	70	71	-11.3
Physical exams	85	89	91	93	94	-9.6
Financial counseling	70	70	74	73	68	2.9
Personal liability insurance	47	46	50	48	42	11.9
Home security systems	26	27	25	28	22	18.2
Home computers	9	7	6	5	6	50.0
Cellular telephones	45	37	22	N/A	N/A	N/A

Source: Schellhardt, Timothy D. "Passing of Perks." *Wall Street Journal,* 13 April 1994, p. R4. Primary source: Hewitt Associates. *Note:* "N/A" indicates "not applicable or available."

Health Care

★ 662 ★

COBRA Coverage: 1987-1991

The Consolidated Onmibus Budget Reconcilliation Act (COBRA) became law in 1985 and ensures the temporary continuation of health plan coverage for former (and certain current) employees, their spouses, and their dependent children. Qualifying individuals may purchase coverage from their former employers at group rates. The table below reflects the characteristics of those obtaining coverage through COBRA, as well the average number of months they were on COBRA, from 1987-1991.

Characteristics	All events	Qualifying events		
		Work related	Disability	Family related
Average number of months on COBRA				
Ages				
All ages	7	7	13	9
18-24 years old	5	4	0	6
25-40 years old	6	5	5	10
41-60 years old	8	7	15	15
61-64 years old	12	12	14	18
65 years old or older	11	10	0	14
Females	7	6	8	9
Males	7	7	17	7
Total	7	7	13	9

Source: U.S. Department of Labor. Pension and Welfare Benefits Administration. *Health Benefits and the Workforce.* Washington, DC: U.S. Government Printing Office, 1992, p. 114. Primary source: 1987-1991 CobraServ.

★ 663 ★

Health Care

Group Health Plans Provided by Employers or Unions, by Selected Characteristic: 1992

Table shows the number of employees and percentages with employer- or union-provided group health plans. Data are for wage and salary workers 15 years old and over as of March 1993. Based on Current Population Survey.

[In thousands, except percentages]

Characteristic	Total	Percent with group health plan
Age		
Total	134,516	50.8
15 to 24 years	22,797	21.7
25 to 44 years	70,336	56.3
45 to 64 years	36,818	60.0
65 years and over	4,564	36.2
Work experience		
Worked	134,516	50.8
Full-time	104,919	60.6
50 weeks or more	81,545	68.2
27 to 49 weeks	13,589	43.5
26 weeks or fewer	9,784	20.9
Part-time	29,597	16.0
50 weeks or more	12,393	23.1
27 to 49 weeks	6,887	14.9
26 weeks or fewer	10,317	8.2
Employer size		
Under 25	40,489	24.6
25 to 99	18,110	50.2
100 to 499	19,100	61.2
500 to 999	7,422	64.9
Over 1,000	49,396	66.2

Source: U.S. Bureau of the Census. *Statistical Abstract of the United States, 1994.* 114th ed. Washington, DC: U.S. Government Printing Office, 1994, p. 433. Primary source: U.S. Bureau of the Census. Unpublished data.

★ 664 ★

Health Care

Health Insurance Sources, by Company Size

Table shows sources of health insurance for employed persons.

[In percentages]

Employer size	Sources of health insurance				No health insurance
	Own employer	Spouse's employer	Other private[1]	Public source[2]	
Self-employed	22.7	25.8	26.0	4.2	22.9
Fewer than 10 employees	22.1	23.4	15.5	7.9	33.0
10-24 employees	36.7	20.2	10.0	6.9	27.6
25-99 employees	51.7	16.0	7.5	6.4	20.7
100-499 employees	62.8	14.1	5.4	5.6	14.4
500-999 employees	66.5	14.4	5.6	4.7	11.0
1,000 or more employees	69.3	12.4	5.1	6.3	10.0

Source: "Ranks of the Uninsured Increase." *Nation's Business* (May 1994), p. 59. Primary source: Employee Benefit Research Institute. *Notes:* 1. Purchased by individuals. 2. Including Medicare and Medicaid.

★ 665 ★

Health Care

Health Plans: 1992-1994

Table shows the employees in various health plans from 1992 through 1994. Data reflect a movement from high cost indemnity plans to more cost effective managed care programs.

[In percentages]

Health plan	Enrolled employees		
	1992	1993	1994
Traditional indemnity	52	48	37
PPO	23	27	25
Point-of-service	5	7	15
HMO	20	19	23

Source: Schwartz, Matthew P. "Employer Health Costs Fell 1.1% in '94." *Underwriter,* 20 February 1995, p. 1. Primary source: Foster Higgins survey of 2,097 employers. *Notes:* "PPO" represents "preferred provider organization." "HMO" represents "health maintenance organization."

★ 666 ★
Health Care

Medical Care Benefits of Full-Time Employees: 1989 and 1990

The table below shows the percent of full-time participants by type of plan and coverage for selected special medical care benefits; for example, well-baby care or organ transplants. Data are provided by type of employer and type of plan.

Employer and benefit	All plans combined	Plans	
		HMO	non-HMO
Medium and large firms[1]			
Hearing care[2]	26	93	12
Orthoptics[3]	3	[4]	4
Physical examinations (routine)	28	97	14
Organ transplants	26	23	26
Well-baby care	34	95	22
Immunization and innoculation	28	98	14
Small firms[5]			
Hearing care[2]	16	92	4
Orthoptics[3]	1	-	1
Physical examinations (routine)	26	98	15
Organ transplants	28	13	31
Well-baby care	32	97	22
Immunization and innoculation	23	96	12
Dental care (preventive)[6]	2	9	[4]
Vision examinations[7]	12	71	3
State and local governments[8]			
Hearing care[2]	27	84	11
Orthoptics[3]	1	[4]	1
Physical examinations (routine)	36	97	19
Organ transplants	32	20	36
Well-baby care	39	96	23
Immunization and innoculation	33	95	16

[Continued]

★ 666 ★

Medical Care Benefits of Full-Time Employees: 1989 and 1990
[Continued]

Employer and benefit	All plans combined	Plans	
		HMO	non-HMO
Dental care (preventive)[6]	2	10	4
Vision examinations[7]	19	73	4

Source: U.S. Congress. Office of Technology Assessment. *Does Health Insurance Make a Difference? Background Paper.* OTA-BP-H-99. Washington, DC: U.S. Government Printing Office, September 1992, p. 53. Primary sources: U.S. Department of Labor. Bureau of Labor Statistics. *Employee Benefits in Medium and Large Firms, 1989.* Bulletin 2363. Washington, DC: U.S. Government Printing Office, June 1990; U.S. Department of Labor. Bureau of Labor Statistics. *Employee Benefits in Small Private Establishments, 1990.* Bulletin 2388. Washington, DC: U.S. Government Printing Office, June 1990; U.S. Department of Labor. Bureau of Labor Statistics. *Employee Benefits in State and Local Governments, 1990.* Washington, DC: U.S. Government Printing Office, 1991. *Notes:* "HMO" stands for health maintenance organization. Where applicable, "-" indicates no employees in the category. 1. Data from 1989. Medium and large firms are establishments with 100 workers or more in all private nonfarm industries, excluding (in the 1989 survey) firms in Alaska and Hawaii. According to the Bureau of Labor Statistics (BLS), its survey of these firms provides representative data on 32.4 million full-time employees. 2. Plan provides, as a minimum, coverage for hearing examination expenses. 3. Exercises to improve the function of eye muscles. 4. Less than 0.5 percent. 5. Data for 1990. Small firms are defined as those private nonfarm firms with fewer than 100 workers. According to the Bureau of Labor Statistics (BLS), its survey of these firms provided representative data on 40.8 million full- and part-time employees. Data shown in this table are for full-time employees only. According to the BLS, insurance benefits—sickness and accident insurance, long-term disability insurance, medical care, dental care, and life insurance—were available to one-tenth or fewer part-time workers. No further details were provided on benefits available to part-time workers in the BLS report. 6. Includes plans that provide only examinations and x-rays. 7. Includes plans that provide examinations only. 8. Data for 1990. According to the Bureau of Labor Statistics (BLS), these data represent about 13 million full-time employees in all state and local governments in the 50 states and the District of Columbia. Detailed data for 1.6 million part-time workers were not provided.

Incentives

★ 667 ★

Incentive Programs

The table below shows the areas in which 623 surveyed companies award incentives to employees.

Area	Companies
Sales	85
Profits	70
Service	68
Customer satisfaction	53
Employee product knowledge	49

[Continued]

★ 667 ★

Incentive Programs
[Continued]

Area	Companies
Customer retention	47
Quality measures	62

Source: Eisman, Regina. "Incentives: There's More to Measure." *Incentive* (February 1995), p. 11. Primary sources: Northwestern University and Society of Incentive Travel Executives Foundation.

★ 668 ★

Incentives

Incentives

Table shows the leading nonmonetary rewards used as employee incentives at manufacturing companies.

[In percentages]

Incentive	Companies awarding incentive
Special lunches	77
Plaques	47
Employee-of-the-month award	20

Source: "Rewarding Workers." *USA TODAY,* 12 January 1995, p. B1. Primary sources: Sibson & Co.; Association for Manufacturing Excellence.

Insurance Plans

★ 669 ★

Insurance Plans of Medium and Large Private Establishments – Full-Time Workers: 1991

Table shows participation of full-time employees in private industry in benefits relating to insurance plans in medium and large establishments. Medium and large establishments exclude establishments with fewer than 100 workers, executive and traveling operating employees, and Alaska and Hawaii. Covers only benefits for which the employer pays part or all of the premium or expenses involved, except unpaid parental leave and long-term care insurance. Based on a sample survey of establishments.

[In percentages]

Benefit	Employees			
	All	Professional, technical, and related	Clerical and sales	Production and service
Insurance plans:				
Medical care	83	85	81	84
Noncontributory	41	38	35	46
Hospital/room and board	83	85	81	84
Inpatient surgery	83	85	81	84
Mental health care	81	83	79	82
Inpatient	81	83	79	82
Outpatient	80	82	78	81
Dental	60	67	60	57
Extended care facility	66	70	66	66
Home health care	67	71	66	66
Hospice care	46	48	45	45
Vision	23	21	21	25
In HMO's	14	15	15	12
Alcohol abuse treatment	82	83	80	82
Inpatient detoxification	81	82	79	81
Inpatient rehabilitation	64	63	63	66
Outpatient	64	66	63	64
Drug abuse treatment	81	83	79	80
Inpatient detoxification	80	82	79	80
Inpatient rehabilitation	63	62	62	65
Outpatient	62	65	62	61
Life	94	98	95	92
Noncontributory	80	83	82	77
Accident/sickness	45	32	35	57
Noncontributory	33	19	23	46

[Continued]

★ 669 ★

Insurance Plans of Medium and Large Private Establishments – Full-Time Workers: 1991

[Continued]

Benefit	Employees			
	All	Professional, technical, and related	Clerical and sales	Production and service
Long-term disability	40	61	49	24
Noncontributory	31	46	38	20

Source: U.S. Bureau of the Census. *Statistical Abstract of the United States, 1994.* 114th ed. Washington, DC: U.S. Government Printing Office, 1994, p. 434. Primary source: U.S. Bureau of Labor Statistics. *Employee Benefits in Medium and Large Private Establishments, 1991.* Bulletin 2422.

★ 670 ★

Insurance Plans

Insurance Plans of Medium and Large Private Establishments – Part-Time Workers: 1991

Table shows the part-time employees participating in employee benefit programs related to insurance plans at medium and large private establishments. Participants are workers covered by paid time off, insurance, retirement, or capital accumulation plans. Employees subject to a minimum service requirement before they are eligible for benefit coverage are counted as participants even if they have not met the requirement at the time of the survey. If employees are required to pay part of the cost a benefit, only those who elect the coverage and pay their share are counted as participants. Benefits for which the employee must pay the full premium are outside the scope of the survey. Only current employees are counted as participants; retirees are excluded. Data are for 1991.

[In percentages]

Employee benefit program	All employees	Professional, technical, and related employees	Clerical and sales employees	Production and service employees
Sickness and accident insurance	19	20	20	18
Wholly employer financed	12	13	11	13
Partly employer financed	7	7	9	5
Long-term disability insurance	3	16	2	1
Wholly employer financed	3	15	2	1
Partly employer financed	1	2	(¹)	(¹)
Medical care	28	42	26	26
Employee coverage				
Wholly employer financed	12	10	11	14
Partly employer financed	16	32	16	12
Family coverage				
Wholly employer financed	10	3	10	12

[Continued]

★ 670 ★

Insurance Plans of Medium and Large Private Establishments – Part-Time Workers: 1991
[Continued]

Employee benefit program	All employees	Professional, technical, and related employees	Clerical and sales employees	Production and service employees
Partly employer financed	18	39	17	14
Dental care	18	35	18	14
Employee coverage				
Wholly employer financed	10	11	11	9
Partly employer financed	8	24	8	5
Family coverage				
Wholly employer financed	9	8	10	8
Partly employer financed	9	26	9	6
Life insurance	31	41	36	24
Wholly employer financed	22	39	26	15
Partly employer financed	9	1	11	10

Source: U.S. Department of Labor. Bureau of Labor Statistics. *Employee Benefits in Medium and Large Private Establishments, 1991.* Bulletin 2422. Washington, DC: U.S. Government Printing Office, May 1993, p. 127. *Notes:* Because of rounding, sums of individual items may not equal totals. 1. Less than 0.5 percent.

★ 671 ★
Insurance Plans

Insurance Plans of Small Private Establishments: 1992

Table shows participation of full-time employees in private industry in benefits relating to time off in small establishments. Small establishments include those with fewer than 100 employees. Covers only benefits for which the employer pays part or all of the premium or expenses involved, except unpaid parental leave and long-term care insurance. Based on a sample survey of establishments.

[In percentages]

Benefit	Employees			
	All	Professional, technical, and related	Clerical and sales	Production and service
Insurance plans:				
Medical care	71	83	78	61
Noncontributory	37	43	40	34
Hospital/room and board	71	83	78	61
Inpatient surgery	71	83	78	61
Mental health care				
Inpatient	68	80	76	57
Outpatient	67	80	74	57

[Continued]

★ 671 ★

Insurance Plans of Small Private Establishments: 1992
[Continued]

| Benefit | Employees | | | |
	All	Professional, technical, and related	Clerical and sales	Production and service
Dental	33	43	37	27
Extended care facility	60	72	66	49
Home health care	57	69	66	46
Hospice care	40	50	44	34
Vision	10	9	10	10
In HMO's	14	14	13	16
Alcohol abuse treatment				
Inpatient detoxification	67	79	74	59
Inpatient rehabilitation	50	58	52	43
Outpatient	50	61	55	43
Drug abuse treatment				
Inpatient detoxification	66	78	71	58
Inpatient rehabilitation	48	57	50	41
Outpatient	49	60	53	41
Life	64	77	73	53
Noncontributory	53	66	62	42
Accident/sickness	26	24	27	27
Noncontributory	17	17	16	18
Long-term disability	23	43	31	10
Noncontributory	18	38	26	6

Source: U.S. Bureau of the Census. *Statistical Abstract of the United States, 1994.* 114th ed. Washington, DC: U.S. Government Printing Office, 1994, p. 434. Primary source: U.S. Bureau of Labor Statistics. *Employee Benefits in Small Private Establishments, 1992.*

★ 672 ★

Insurance Plans

Insurance Plans of State and Local Government: 1992

For January through July. Covers full-time employees in state and local governments. Covers only benefits for which the employer pays part or all of the premium or expenses involved, except long-term care insurance. Based on sample survey of establishments.

[In percentages]

Insurance plans	All employees	White-collar employees[1]	Teachers[2]	Blue-collar employees[3]
Medical	90	91	90	89
Dental	65	65	65	64
Extended care facility	76	76	75	75
Home health care	78	79	77	77
Hospital/room & board	90	91	90	89
In HMO's	27	25	25	30
Inpatient surgery	90	91	90	89

[Continued]

★ 672 ★

Insurance Plans of State and Local Government: 1992
[Continued]

Insurance plans	All employees	White-collar employees[1]	Teachers[2]	Blue-collar employees[3]
Mental health care:				
Inpatient	89	90	88	88
Outpatient	83	85	83	84
Vision	35	34	33	38
Alcohol abuse treatment:				
Inpatient detox	89	90	89	89
Inpatient rehab	65	66	64	65
Outpatient	67	67	65	67
Drug abuse treatment:				
Inpatient detox	89	90	88	88
Inpatient rehab	64	65	62	64
Outpatient	66	66	63	66
Life	89	89	87	89
Noncontributory	75	76	73	77
Accident/sickness	22	25	15	23
Noncontributory	16	18	13	17
Long-term disability	28	30	33	22
Noncontributory	22	23	27	18

Source: U.S. Bureau of the Census. *Statistical Abstract of the United States, 1994.* 114th ed. Washington, DC: U.S. Government Printing Office, 1994, p. 321. Primary source: U.S. Bureau of Labor Statistics. *Employee Benefits in State and Local Governments, 1992. Notes:* 1. Includes all professional, administrative, technical, and clerical employees except teachers. 2. Includes all personnel in primary and secondary schools, junior colleges, and universities whose primary duty is teaching or closely related activities. 3. Includes police, firefighters, and all production and service employees.

★ 673 ★
Insurance Plans

Long-term Care Insurance Plans: 1987-1991

The table below reflects the number of long-term care insurance plans sold to employers between 1987 and 1991.

Year	Each year	Cumulative
1987	2	-
1988	5	7
1989	47	54
1990	81	135
1991	51	186

Source: U.S. Department of Labor. Pension and Welfare Benefits Administration. *Trends in Health Benefits.* Washington, DC: U.S. Government Printing Office, 1993, p. 221. Primary source: Health Insurance Association of America. Unpublished data.

★ 674 ★

Insurance Plans

Short-Term Sickness Income Loss Protection: 1980-1992

"Short-term sickness" refers to a short-term or temporary nonwork-connected disability (lasting not more than 6 months) and the first 6 months of long-term disability.

[In millions of dollars, except percentages]

Item	1980	1985	1986	1987	1988	1989	1990	1991	1992
Short-term sickness: Income loss	38,529	59,145	62,981	68,166	73,841	77,917	82,601	84,722	89,417
Total protection provided[1]	14,426	19,587	20,285	22,466	23,964	25,417	27,276	28,332	30,141
Protection as percent of loss	37.4	33.1	32.2	32.9	32.6	32.5	33.1	34.4	33.7
Benefits provided by protection:									
Individual insurance	1,280	1,796	1,774	2,062	2,057	2,451	2,701	2,588	2,479
Group benefits to workers in private employment	7,634	9,896	10,018	11,357	12,239	12,680	13,426	14,001	15,056
Private cash insurance[2]	3,271	2,601	2,275	2,692	2,903	2,732	2,711	2,590	2,475
Publicly operated cash sickness funds[3]	770	1,179	1,255	1,696	1,779	1,907	2,269	2,810	3,482
Sick leave	3,593	6,116	6,488	6,969	7,557	8,041	8,446	8,601	9,099
Sick leave for government employees	5,338	7,700	8,299	8,827	9,462	10,062	10,875	11,432	11,901

Source: U.S. Bureau of the Census. *Statistical Abstract of the United States, 1994.* 114th ed. Washington, DC: U.S. Government Printing Office, 1994, p. 382. Primary sources: Social Security Administration. *Social Security Bulletin* (fall 1992); and unpublished data. *Notes:* 1. Provided by individual insurance, group benefits to workers in private employment, and sick leave for government employees. Includes benefits for the sixth month of disability payable under Old-Age, Survivors, Disability, and Health Insurance program, not shown separately. 2. Group accident and sickness insurance and self-insurance privately written either on a voluntary basis or in compliance with state temporary disability insurance laws in California, Hawaii, New Jersey, and New York. Includes a small but undetermined amount of group disability insurance benefits paid to government workers and to self-employed persons through farm, trade, or professional associations. 3. Includes state-operated plans in Rhode Island, California, and New Jersey; State Insurance Fund and special fund for disabled unemployed in New York; and provisions of Railroad Unemployment Insurance Act.

★ 675 ★

Insurance Plans

Uninsured Workers, by Company Size: 1992

The table below reflects the percentage of working Americans, ages 18 to 64, without insurance coverage. Data are provided by size of employer for 1992.

[In percentages]

Company size	Uninsured
Total	17
Self-employed	23
Under 10 employees	33
10-24 employees	28
25-99 employees	21
100-499 employees	14
500-999 employees	11
1,000 or more employees	10

Source: "Percentage of Uninsured Workers Aged 18-64 by Firm Size, 1992." *HR Focus* (May 1994), p. 13. Primary source: Employee Benefit Research Institute Analysis of March 1993 Current Population Survey.

Pension and Retirement Plans

★ 676 ★

401(k) Investment

Table shows the investment options offered by companies to employees through 401(k) plans.

[In percentages]

Investment option	Companies offering option
Stock mutual funds	88
Money market mutual funds	61
Balanced mutual funds	57
Guaranteed investment contracts	56
Bond mutual funds	52
Company stock	26
Real estate	2
Other	13

Source: "401(k) Is Too Good a Deal to Pass Up." *USA TODAY,* 31 May 1994, p. 7B. Primary source: Foster Higgins.

★ 677 ★

Pension and Retirement Plans

Defined Contribution Retirement Plans: 1992 and 1993

Table shows the funds into which defined contribution retirement plan participants are putting their money. The source defines defined benefit plans as those in which "employees are promised a specified payout upon retirement based primarily on their earnings and years of service" (p. R19). Data are for 1992 and 1993.

Fund	1992	1993
Stock or equity fund	42	56
GIC fund	47	39
Company stock	40	36
Money market fund	37	32
Corporate bond fund	27	28
Treasury bond fund	18	19
Balanced fund	9	15

Source: Gottschalk, Earl C., Jr. "On Your Own." *Wall Street Journal,* 9 December 1994, p. R19. Primary source: John Hancock Financial Services. *Note:* "GIC" stands for "guaranteed income or investment contract."

★ 678 ★

Pension and Retirement Plans

Federal Civil Service Retirement: 1980-1992

As of September 30 or for year ending September 30 in year shown. Covers both Civil Service Retirement System and Federal Employees Retirement System.

Item	Unit	1980	1985	1986	1987	1988	1989	1990	1991	1992
Employees covered[1]	1,000	2,720	2,750	2,800	2,810	2,800	2,880	2,945	2,885	2,902
Annuitants, total	1,000	1,675	1,955	2,008	2,032	2,089	2,120	2,143	2,184	2,185
Age and service	1,000	905	1,122	1,166	1,186	1,237	1,267	1,288	1,325	1,322
Disability	1,000	343	332	326	318	311	305	297	289	282
Survivors	1,000	427	501	516	528	541	548	558	570	581
Receipts, total[2]	Million $	24,389	40,790	43,216	43,640	46,696	49,249	52,689	56,815	60,003
Employee contributions	Million $	3,686	4,679	4,714	4,641	4,544	4,491	4,501	4,563	4,713
Federal government contributions	Million $	15,562	22,301	22,980	23,144	24,258	25,367	27,368	29,509	31,050
Disbursements, total[3]	Million $	14,977	23,203	24,694	25,772	28,306	29,713	31,416	33,209	33,187
Age and service annuitants[4]	Million $	12,639	19,414	20,702	21,678	23,889	25,095	26,495	27,997	27,693
Survivors	Million $	1,912	3,158	3,304	3,485	3,749	4,033	4,366	4,716	5,065
Average monthly benefit:										
Age and service	$	992	1,189	1,197	1,267	1,263	1,310	1,369	1,439	1,493
Disability	$	723	881	881	893	930	966	1,008	1,059	1,094
Survivors	$	392	528	536	552	583	616	653	698	731
Cash and security holdings	Billion $	73.7	142.3	160.8	178.7	197.1	216.7	238.0	258.6	288.4

Source: U.S. Bureau of the Census. *Statistical Abstract of the United States, 1994.* 114th ed. Washington, DC: U.S. Government Printing Office, 1994, p. 378. Primary source: U.S. Office of Personnel Management. *Compensation Report* (annual). *Notes:* 1. Excludes employees in Leave Without Pay status. 2. Includes interest on investments. 3. Includes refunds, death claims, and administration. 4. Includes disability annuitants.

★ 679 ★

Pension and Retirement Plans

Lump-Sum Distributions From Retirement Accounts

Withdrawing funds from 401(k) and other retirement accounts is not supposed to occur until the employee is of retirement age. Nevertheless, early withdrawals—with a 10 percent penalty—are allowed for certain hardships, such as medical expenses and college costs. The table shows the uses employees have for lump-sum distributions taken from company retirement plans prior to retirement.

[In percentages]

Use	Employees
Consumer products or household expenses	29
Spending on business or house; pay debts	23
Retirement account	21
Savings or investment account	12

[Continued]

★ 679 ★

Lump-Sum Distributions From Retirement Accounts
[Continued]

Use	Employees
Combination of options	11
Other	4

Source: Waggoner, John. "Dipping Into Funds Early Carries Price." *USA TODAY,* 20 February 1995, p. 4B. Primary source: Department of Labor.

★ 680 ★
Pension and Retirement Plans

Pension Coverage and Participation, by State: 1990

Table shows employment, pension coverage, and pension participation of the civilian, nonagricultural wage and salary workforce by state or territory for 1990.

[Employment in millions]

State or territory	Employment	Employer sponsors a plan[1] (%)	Included in employer's plan[2] (%)
Total	119.3	55.3	42.9
Alabama	1.7	56.1	44.6
Alaska	0.2	54.9	42.2
Arizona	1.6	57.0	40.1
Arkansas	1.0	53.2	40.7
California	13.4	48.8	36.8
Colorado	1.6	56.1	42.7
Connecticut	1.7	59.3	46.9
Delaware	0.4	53.7	42.4
District of Columbia	0.3	56.0	43.0
Florida	6.1	49.2	35.5
Georgia	3.1	53.9	42.8
Hawaii	0.5	59.3	48.8
Idaho	0.5	52.8	38.4
Illinois	5.9	58.2	46.8
Indiana	2.8	58.4	47.2
Iowa	1.4	55.3	44.3
Kansas	1.2	60.0	44.0
Kentucky	1.7	54.8	41.9
Louisiana	1.8	51.7	36.6
Maine	0.6	49.3	40.5
Maryland	2.5	63.6	52.2
Massachusetts	3.1	56.1	43.5
Michigan	4.5	57.8	46.1

[Continued]

★ 680 ★

Pension Coverage and Participation, by State:
1990
[Continued]

State or territory	Employment	Employer sponsors a plan[1] (%)	Included in employer's plan[2] (%)
Minnesota	2.3	62.6	46.2
Mississippi	1.1	48.2	37.7
Missouri	2.6	57.8	41.3
Montana	0.4	51.0	40.2
Nebraska	0.8	55.3	42.4
Nevada	0.6	49.8	35.6
New Hampshire	0.6	56.6	43.7
New Jersey	4.0	58.0	48.6
New Mexico	0.7	49.5	36.4
New York	8.4	55.4	45.7
North Carolina	3.3	57.0	43.7
North Dakota	0.3	58.2	40.5
Ohio	5.3	59.6	47.6
Oklahoma	1.4	55.3	40.5
Oregon	1.4	56.5	40.6
Pennsylvania	5.7	58.4	46.7
Rhode Island	0.5	54.2	41.9
South Carolina	1.7	56.3	46.4
South Dakota	0.3	49.3	36.9
Tennessee	2.4	56.1	41.7
Texas	8.0	52.0	39.4
Utah	0.8	62.7	42.5
Vermont	0.3	56.2	41.4
Virginia	3.2	56.0	44.1
Washington	2.4	57.2	42.5
West Virginia	0.8	54.1	41.2
Wisconsin	2.4	62.0	48.9
Wyoming	0.2	49.2	38.0

Source: Anzick, Michael A. "Pensions: An Important Component of Retirement Income." *Benefits Quarterly* (second quarter 1993), p. 46. Primary source: Piacentini, Joseph, and Jill D. Foley. *EBRI Databook on Employee Benefits.* 2nd ed. Washington, DC: Employee Benefit Research Institute, 1992. *Notes:* 1. Employees reporting that their employers had a pension plan or a retirement plan for any employees at any job held in 1990. 2. Employees reporting that they participated in a pension plan or a retirement plan at any job held in 1990.

★ 681 ★

Pension and Retirement Plans

Pension Coverage of Workers, by Selected Characteristics: 1992

Covers workers as of March of following year who had earnings in year shown. Based on Current Population Survey.

Sex and age	Number with coverage (1,000)				Percent of total workers			
	Total[1]	White	Black	Hispanic[2]	Total[1]	White	Black	Hispanic[2]
Total	53,899	46,628	5,519	2,586	40	40	39	25
Male	30,197	26,607	2,624	1,499	42	43	37	24
Under 65 years old	29,617	26,097	2,572	1,486	43	43	38	24
15 to 24 years old	1,411	1,223	140	91	12	12	10	7
25 to 44 years old	17,428	15,186	1,628	952	46	47	42	27
45 to 64 years old	10,777	9,688	804	443	54	55	50	36
65 years old and over	579	509	52	14	22	21	31	16
Female	23,703	20,021	2,896	1,087	38	38	41	26
Under 65 years old	23,287	19,657	2,850	1,074	39	39	41	26
15 to 24 years old	1,206	1,044	129	67	11	11	11	8
25 to 44 years old	13,857	11,561	1,796	701	43	43	45	29
45 to 64 years old	8,224	7,052	925	306	48	48	54	34
65 years old and over	416	364	46	12	21	21	26	20

Source: U.S. Bureau of the Census. *Statistical Abstract of the United States, 1994.* 114th ed. Washington, DC: U.S. Government Printing Office, 1994, p. 379. Primary source: U.S. Bureau of the Census. Unpublished data. *Notes:* 1. Includes other races, not shown separately. 2. Hispanic persons may be of any race.

★ 682 ★

Pension and Retirement Plans

Pension Incomes: 1992

Table shows the 25 Standard and Poor's 500 plan sponsors with the highest pension incomes in 1992.

[In million dollars]

Company	Income
General Electric	494.00
AT&T	441.00
USX-US Steel	231.00
GTE	168.00
Ameritech	110.50
US West	108.40
McDonnell Douglas	99.00
DuPont	83.00
Rockwell International	54.86
Unocal	51.00
International Paper	51.00
Unisys	43.10
Conrail	38.00
Westvaco	37.96

[Continued]

★ 682 ★

Pension Incomes: 1992
[Continued]

Company	Income
Teledyne	37.90
Chevron	35.00
Northrop	35.00
Atlantic Richfield	34.00
USX-Marathon	30.00
Household International	25.70
American General	22.00
Rohm & Haas	21.00
Ohio Edison	20.82
W. R. Grace	19.60
Panhandle Eastern	19.10

Source: Burr, Barry B. "A Nasty Surprise in Store for Funds." *Pensions & Investments* 21, no. 3 (15 November 1993), p. 3. Primary source: Goldman, Sachs & Co. (New York).

★ 683 ★

Pension and Retirement Plans

Pension Plans Provided by Employers or Unions, by Selected Characteristic: 1992

Table shows the number of employees and percentages with employer- or union-provided pension plans. Data are for wage and salary workers 15 years old and over as of March 1993. Based on Current Population Survey.

[In thousands, except percentages]

Characteristic	Total	Percent with pension plan
Age		
Total	134,516	40.1
15 to 24 years	22,797	11.5
25 to 44 years	70,336	44.5
45 to 64 years	36,818	51.6
65 years and over	4,564	21.8
Work experience		
Worked	134,516	40.1
Full-time	104,919	48.2
50 weeks or more	81,545	55.1
27 to 49 weeks	13,589	30.2
26 weeks or fewer	9,784	15.4
Part-time	29,597	11.2
50 weeks or more	12,393	17.0
27 to 49 weeks	6,887	11.6

[Continued]

★ 683 ★

Pension Plans Provided by Employers or Unions, by Selected Characteristic: 1992

[Continued]

Characteristic	Total	Percent with pension plan
26 weeks or fewer	10,317	4.0
Employer size		
Under 25	40,489	12.0
25 to 99	18,110	30.4
100 to 499	19,100	47.2
500 to 999	7,422	54.9
Over 1,000	49,396	61.6

Source: U.S. Bureau of the Census. *Statistical Abstract of the United States, 1994.* 114th ed. Washington, DC: U.S. Government Printing Office, 1994, p. 433. Primary source: U.S. Bureau of the Census. Unpublished data.

★ 684 ★

Pension and Retirement Plans

Private Pension Plans, by Type of Plan: 1975-1990

"Pension plan" is defined by the Employee Retirement Income Security Act (ERISA) as "any plan, fund, or program which was heretofore or is hereafter established or maintained by an employer or an employee organization, or by both, to the extent that such plan (a) provides retirement income to employees, or (b) results in a deferral of income by employees for periods extending to the termination of covered employment or beyond, regardless of the method of calculating the contributions made to the plan, the method of calculating the benefits under the plan, or the method of distributing benefits from the plan." A defined benefit plan provides a definite benefit formula for calculating benefit amounts—such as a flat amount per year of service or a percentage of salary times years of service. A defined contribution plan is a pension plan in which the contributions are made to an individual account for each employee. The retirement benefit is dependent upon the account balance at retirement. The balance depends upon amounts contributed, investment experience, and, in the case of profit sharing plans, amounts which may be allocated to the account due to forfeitures by terminating employees. Employee Stock Ownership Plans (ESOP) and 401(k) plans are included among defined contribution plans. Data are based on Form 5500 series reports filed with the Internal Revenue Service.

Item	Total				Defined contribution plan				Defined benefit plan			
	1975	1980	1985	1990	1975	1980	1985	1990	1975	1980	1985	1990
Number of plans (1,000)[1]	311.1	488.9	632.1	712.3	207.7	340.8	462.0	599.2	103.3	148.1	170.2	113.1
Total participants (million)[2]	44.5	57.9	74.7	76.9	11.5	19.9	35.0	38.1	33.0	38.0	39.7	38.8
Active participants (million)[3]	38.4	49.0	62.3	61.8	11.2	18.9	33.2	35.5	27.2	30.1	29.0	26.3
Contributions (billion dollars)[4]	37.1	66.2	95.1	98.8	12.8	23.5	53.1	75.8	24.2	42.6	42.0	23.0
Benefits (billion dollars)[5]	19.1	35.3	101.9	124.4	6.2	13.1	47.4	63.0	12.9	22.1	54.5	66.4

Source: U.S. Bureau of the Census. *Statistical Abstract of the United States, 1994.* 114th ed. Washington, DC: U.S. Government Printing Office, 1994, p. 379. Primary source: U.S. Department of Labor. Pension and Welfare Benefits Administration. *Private Pension Plan Bulletin* (summer 1993). *Notes:* 1. Excludes all plans covering only one participant. 2. Includes double counting of workers in more than one plan. Total participants include active participants, vested separated workers, and retirees. 3. Includes double counting of workers in more than one plan. Any workers currently in employment covered by a plan and who are earning or retaining credited service under a plan. Includes any nonvested former employees who have not yet incurred breaks in service. 4. Includes both employer and employee contributions. 5. Benefits paid directly from trust and premium payments made from plan to insurance carriers. Excludes benefits paid directly by insurance carriers.

★ 685 ★

Pension and Retirement Plans

Retirement and Savings Plans of Medium and Large Private Establishments – Full-Time Workers: 1991

Table shows participation of full-time employees in private industry in benefits relating to retirement and savings plans in medium and large establishments. Medium and large establishments exclude establishments with fewer than 100 workers, executive and traveling operating employees, and Alaska and Hawaii. Covers only benefits for which the employer pays part or all of the premium or expenses involved, except unpaid parental leave and long-term care insurance. Based on a sample survey of establishments.

[In percentages]

Benefit	Employees			
	All	Professional, technical, and related	Clerical and sales	Production and service
Retirement and savings plans:				
Defined benefit pension	59	60	56	59
Earnings-based formula[1]	41	52	46	32
Defined contribution	48	57	53	39
Savings and thrift	29	38	35	20
Employee stock owner- ship	3	4	4	2
Deferred profit sharing	16	13	16	18
Money purchase pension	7	11	7	5

Source: U.S. Bureau of the Census. *Statistical Abstract of the United States, 1994.* 114th ed. Washington, DC: U.S. Government Printing Office, 1994, p. 434. Primary source: U.S. Bureau of Labor Statistics. *Employee Benefits in Medium and Large Private Establishments, 1991.* Bulletin 2422. *Notes:* 1. Earnings-based formulas pay a percent of employee's annual earnings (usually earnings in the final years of employment) per year of service.

★ 686 ★

Pension and Retirement Plans

Retirement and Savings Plans of Medium and Large Private Establishments – Part-Time Workers: 1991

Table shows the part-time employees participating in employee benefit programs related to retirement and savings plans at medium and large private establishments. Participants are workers covered by paid time off, insurance, retirement, or capital accumulation plans. Employees subject to a minimum service requirement before they are eligible for benefit coverage are counted as participants even if they have not met the requirement at the time of the survey. If employees are required to pay part of the cost a benefit, only those who elect the coverage and pay their share are counted as participants. Benefits for which the employee must pay the full premium are outside the scope of the survey. Only current employees are counted as participants; retirees are excluded. Data are for 1991.

[In percentages]

Employee benefit program	All employees	Professional, technical, and related employees	Clerical and sales employees	Production and service employees
All retirement[1]	40	46	44	36
Defined benefit pension	28	35	31	23
Wholly employer financed	27	35	30	22
Partly employer financed	1	(²)	1	1
Defined contribution[3]	20	21	23	17
Uses of funds:				
Retirement[4]	18	19	20	16
Wholly employer financed[5]	10	6	8	13
Partly employer financed	7	13	12	3
Capital accumulation[6]	2	2	3	1
Wholly employer financed[5]	(²)	1	(²)	(²)
Partly employer financed	2	(²)	3	1
Types of plans				
Savings and thrift	8	14	12	3
Deferred profit sharing	10	1	12	10
Employee stock ownership	(²)	1	1	-
Money purchase pension	4	11	1	5
Stock bonus	-	-	-	-
Stock option	-	-	-	-
Stock purchase	1	-	1	(²)
Cash only profit sharing	-	-	-	-

[Continued]

★ 686 ★

Retirement and Savings Plans of Medium and Large Private Establishments – Part-Time Workers: 1991

[Continued]

Employee benefit program	All employees	Professional, technical, and related employees	Clerical and sales employees	Production and service employees
Flexible benefit plans	2	6	1	2
Reimbursement accounts	11	31	11	5

Source: U.S. Department of Labor. Bureau of Labor Statistics. *Employee Benefits in Medium and Large Private Establishments, 1991.* Bulletin 2422. Washington, DC: U.S. Government Printing Office, May 1993, p. 127. *Notes:* Because of rounding, sums of individual items may not equal totals. "-" indicates no employees in this category. 1. Includes defined benefit pension plans and defined contribution retirement plans. The total is less that the sum of the individual items because many employees participated in both types of plans. 2. Less than 0.5 percent. 3. The total is less that the sum of the individual items because many employees participated in both retirement and capital accumulation plans and in more than one type of plan. 4. Plans were counted as retirement plans if employer contributions had to remain in the participant's account until retirement age, death, disability, separation from service, age 59 1/2, or hardship. 5. Employees participating in two or more plans were counted as participants in wholly employer financed plans only if plans were noncontributory. 6. Includes plans in which employer contributions may be withdrawn from participant's account prior to retirement age, death, disability, separation from service, age 59 1/2, or hardship. Excludes pure cash profit sharing, stock option, and stock purchase plans.

★ 687 ★

Pension and Retirement Plans

Retirement and Savings Plans of Small Private Establishments: 1992

Table shows participation of full-time employees in private industry in benefits relating to time off in small establishments. Small establishments include those with fewer than 100 employees. Covers only benefits for which the employer pays part or all of the premium or expenses involved, except unpaid parental leave and long-term care insurance. Based on a sample survey of establishments.

[In percentages]

Benefit	Employees			
	All	Professional, technical, and related	Clerical and sales	Production and service
Retirement and savings plans:				
Defined benefit pension	22	21	25	20
Earnings-based formula[1]	15	19	20	9
Defined contribution	33	43	38	26
Savings and thrift	14	20	17	9
Employee stock owner-ship	1	1	1	1

[Continued]

★ 687 ★

Retirement and Savings Plans of Small Private Establishments: 1992
[Continued]

Benefit	Employees			
	All	Professional, technical, and related	Clerical and sales	Production and service
Deferred profit sharing	16	18	19	14
Money purchase pension	5	99	5	4

Source: U.S. Bureau of the Census. *Statistical Abstract of the United States, 1994.* 114th ed. Washington, DC: U.S. Government Printing Office, 1994, p. 434. Primary source: U.S. Bureau of Labor Statistics. *Employee Benefits in Small Private Establishments, 1992.* Notes: 1. Earnings-based formulas pay a percent of employee's annual earnings (usually earnings in the final years of employment) per year of service.

★ 688 ★

Pension and Retirement Plans

Retirement and Savings Plans of State and Local Government: 1992

For January through July. Covers full-time employees in state and local governments. Covers only benefits for which the employer pays part or all of the premium or expenses involved. Based on sample survey of establishments.

[In percentages]

Retirement and savings plans	All employees	White-collar employees[1]	Teachers[2]	Blue-collar employees[3]
Defined benefit pensions	87	86	89	87
Noncontributory	24	25	22	24
Defined contributions	9	10	8	9
Money purchase pensions[4]	7	7	7	8

Source: U.S. Bureau of the Census. *Statistical Abstract of the United States, 1994.* 114th ed. Washington, DC: U.S. Government Printing Office, 1994, p. 321. Primary source: U.S. Bureau of Labor Statistics. *Employee Benefits in State and Local Governments, 1992.* Notes: 1. Includes all professional, administrative, technical, and clerical employees except teachers. 2. Includes all personnel in primary and secondary schools, junior colleges, and universities whose primary duty is teaching or closely related activities. 3. Includes police, firefighters, and all production and service employees. 4. Fixed contributions are periodically placed in an employee's account and benefits are based on how much money has accumulated at retirement.

★ 689 ★

Pension and Retirement Plans

State and Local Government Retirement System Beneficiaries and Finances: 1980-1991

For fiscal years closed during the 12 months ending June 30.

[In millions of dollars, except as indicated]

Year and level of government	Number of beneficiaries (1,000)	Receipts					Benefits and withdrawals			Cash and security holdings
		Total	Employee contri-butions	Government contributions		Earnings on invest-ments	Total	Benefits	Withdrawals	
				State	Local					
1980: All systems	(NA)	37,313	6,466	7,581	9,951	13,315	14,008	12,207	1,801	185,226
State-administered	(NA)	28,603	5,285	7,399	5,611	10,308	10,257	8,809	1,448	144,682
Locally administered	(NA)	8,710	1,180	181	4,340	3,008	3,752	3,399	353	40,544
1985: All systems	3,378	71,411	9,468	12,227	15,170	34,546	24,413	21,999	2,414	374,433
State-administered	2,661	55,960	7,901	11,976	8,944	27,139	18,230	16,183	2,047	296,951
Locally administered	716	15,451	1,567	251	6,226	7,407	6,183	5,816	367	77,481
1990: All systems	4,026	111,339	13,853	13,994	18,583	64,907	38,396	35,966	2,430	703,772
State-administered	3,232	89,162	11,648	13,964	11,538	52,012	29,603	27,562	2,041	565,641
Locally administered	794	22,177	2,205	32	7,045	12,895	8,793	8,404	389	138,131
1991: All systems	4,179	108,240	16,268	14,473	18,691	58,808	42,028	39,421	2,607	783,405
State-administered	3,357	85,576	12,563	14,455	11,553	47,006	32,323	30,167	2,156	630,551
Locally administered	822	22,664	3,705	18	7,138	11,803	9,706	9,255	451	152,854

Source: U.S. Bureau of the Census. *Statistical Abstract of the United States, 1994.* 114th ed. Washington, DC: U.S. Government Printing Office, 1994, p. 379. Primary source: U.S. Bureau of the Census. *Finances of Employee-Retirement Systems of State and Local Governments.* Series GF, no. 2 (annual). *Note:* "NA" stands for "not available."

Retirees

★ 690 ★

Health Benefit Modifications for Retirees

A survey of 230 companies revealed that 90 percent of those offering medical benefits to retirees are altering or planning to alter those programs in response to rising costs and changing accounting practices. The table below shows modifications to retiree health benefits.

Status of modifications	Percent
No modifications made or considered	10
Modifications considered	16
Modifications to address:	
New accounting rules	43
Costs	20
New accounting rules and costs	37
Modifications made[1]	74

[Continued]

★ 690 ★

Health Benefit Modifications for Retirees
[Continued]

Status of modifications	Percent
Modifications to address:	
New accounting rules	25
Costs	22
New accounting rules and costs	53

Source: "By the Numbers: Why Retiree Medical Benefits Are Changing." *Journal of Accountancy* (September 1993), p. 20. Primary source: Buck Consultants. *Notes:* 1. Includes those having made modifications and considering additional changes.

★ 691 ★
Retirees

Health Care Benefits for Retirees, by Company Size: 1991-1992

Figures reflect the decline of U.S. firms offering health care benefits to retirees.

[In percentages]

Company size	1991	1992
200-999 employees	44	37
1,000-4,999 employees	56	52
5,000 or more employees	72	72

Source: Rose, Robert L. "Retiree Health Coverage Erodes at Small, Midsize Firms." *Wall Street Journal,* 16 April 1993, p. B2. Primary source: KPMG Peat Marwick survey.

★ 692 ★

Retirees

Health Care Plans for Retirees – Expectations, by Company Size

The table below reflects expectations of employees surveyed in 1993 concerning the availability of employer health care plan coverage for retired private wage and salary workers. Data are for currently covered workers aged 46 years or older.

[In percentages, except as noted]

Company size	Number of workers[1] (in thousands)	Coverage available throughout retirement	Coverage available until age 65	No coverage during retirement	Don't know or no response
1-9 employees	250	26	10	28	36
10-24 employees	201	28	8	28	35
25-99 employees	380	27	8	25	40
100-499 employees	413	35	9	26	30
500-999 employees	185	34	8	25	34
1,000 or more employees	1,456	55	7	13	25

Source: "Employer-Provider Health Care Insurance." New York Times, 19 June 1994, p. F21. Primary source: Employee Benefits Supplement to the April 1993 Current Population Survey. Note: 1. Nationally.

★ 693 ★

Retirees

Health Insurance Benefit Cutbacks for Retirees: 1989-1991

Table below presents the percent of companies who have ended or restricted their health care insurance coverage for retired employees. Data are based on a survey of 2,000 companies conducted by the consulting firm of A. Foster Higgins. Survey samples were not necessarily representative of all companies.

Year	Number of companies surveyed	Have ended[1] or plan to end[2] benefits	Have reduced[1] or plan to reduce[2] benefits
1989	1,380	3.0	43.0
1990	1,180	5.0	58.0
1991	1,114	7.0	65.0

Source: Freudenheim, Milt. "Retirees Threatened With Loss of Insurance." New York Times, 28 June 1992, sec. 1, pp. 1, 20. Primary source: A. Foster Higgins, a consulting firm. Notes: 1. In 1990 or 1991. 2. In 1992 or 1993.

★ 694 ★

Retirees

Health Insurance Sources of Early Retirees

The table below shows the sources of health insurance for workers retiring early.

[In thousands]

Source of coverage	Number of retirees covered
Employer coverage	1,700
Other[1]	870
Uninsured	349.2

Source: Stevens, Carol. "Who Will Pay Health Bill for Early Retirees?" *Detroit News,* 27 February 1994, p. 1A. Primary sources: Employee Benefit Research Institute; Lewin-VHI health consultants. *Notes:* 1. Includes insurance purchased privately and public programs for the poor and disabled.

Time Off

★ 695 ★

Funeral Leave: 1991

Table shows the full-time employees by number of paid funeral leave days available per occurrence at medium and large private establishments. Data are for 1991.

[In percentages]

Number of days	All employees	Professional, technical, and related employees	Clerical and sales employees	Production and service employees
Total	100	100	100	100
Provided paid funeral leave	80	84	82	77
1 day	1	(¹)	1	1
2 days	3	1	2	3
3 days	59	58	57	61
4 days	3	4	2	3
5 days	10	14	15	6
More than 5 days	(¹)	1	(¹)	(¹)
No maximum specified[2]	3	5	4	2
Varies by length of service	1	(¹)	1	(¹)
Number of days not available	(¹)	(¹)	(¹)	(¹)

[Continued]

★ 695 ★

Funeral Leave: 1991
[Continued]

Number of days	All employees	Professional, technical, and related employees	Clerical and sales employees	Production and service employees
Not provided paid funeral leave	20	16	18	13
Number of days varies by relationship to deceased[3]	17	21	19	13

Source: U.S. Department of Labor. Bureau of Labor Statistics. *Employee Benefits in Medium and Large Private Establishments, 1991.* Bulletin 2422. Washington, DC: U.S. Government Printing Office, May 1993, p. 14. *Notes:* Because of rounding, sums of individual items may not equal totals. 1. Less than 0.5 percent. 2. Workers were provided as much funeral leave as needed. 3. The maximum number of days provided for any occurrence was included in the distribution of funeral leave days.

★ 696 ★
Time Off

Holidays and Vacations: 1991

Table shows the average number of paid holidays and vacation days for full-time participants at medium and large private establishments. Data are for 1991.

[In percentages]

Item	All employees	Professional, technical, and related employees	Clerical and sales employees	Production and service employees
Paid holidays	10.2	10.6	10.1	10.1
Paid vacation:[1]				
After 1 year[2]	9.3	11.8	9.4	7.8
After 3 years	11.1	12.8	10.9	10.2
After 5 years	13.4	15.4	13.5	12.2
After 10 years	16.5	18.5	16.4	15.5
After 15 years	18.7	20.3	18.9	17.7
After 20 years	20.4	21.9	20.4	19.5
After 25 years	21.5	22.9	21.5	20.8
After 30 years[3]	21.9	23.4	21.9	21.1

Source: U.S. Department of Labor. Bureau of Labor Statistics. *Employee Benefits in Medium and Large Private Establishments, 1991.* Bulletin 2422. Washington, DC: U.S. Government Printing Office, May 1993, p. 9. *Notes:* Computation of average included partial days and excluded workers with zero holidays or vacation days and those with informal plans. 1. By minimum length of service requirement. Employees either are granted a specified number of days after completion of the indicated length of service or accrue days during the next 12-month period. The total number of days are assumed available for use immediately upon completion of the described length of service interval. 2. Employees receiving vacation days, but none at 1 year of service, were included only for the service periods for which they receive vacations. 3. The average (mean) was essentially the same for longer lengths of service.

★ 697 ★

Time Off

Jury Duty: 1991

Table shows the full-time employees by number of paid jury duty leave days available per occurrence at medium and large private establishments. Data are for 1991.

[In percentages]

Number of days	All employees	Professional, technical, and related employees	Clerical and sales employees	Production and service employees
Total	100	100	100	100
Provided paid jury duty leave	86	92	88	82
Under 10 days	1	1	(¹)	1
10 days	6	7	6	5
11-19 days	1	1	1	1
20 days	1	2	2	1
21 days	(¹)	(¹)	(¹)	(¹)
22-30 days	2	2	2	1
More than 30 days	1	1	1	1
No maximum specified[2]	74	79	75	71
Number of days not available	1	1	1	1
Not provided paid jury duty leave	14	8	12	18

Source: U.S. Department of Labor. Bureau of Labor Statistics. *Employee Benefits in Medium and Large Private Establishments, 1991.* Bulletin 2422. Washington, DC: U.S. Government Printing Office, May 1993, p. 14. *Notes:* Because of rounding, sums of individual items may not equal totals. 1. Less than 0.5 percent. 2. Jury duty leave provided as needed.

★ 698 ★

Time Off

Jury Duty Pay

From the source: "Federal and state laws prohibit employers from firing workers who are selected for jury duty.... But only a few states, including Alabama and Nebraska, require employers to pay their employees wages for a specified number of days or for the entire time they serve on a jury" (p. 7B). Hence, financial losses of a juror on a long trial can be high. The table below shows amounts paid by state courts for jurors. Figures are per day amounts unless otherwise noted.

[In dollars]

State	Pay per day
Alabama	10
Alaska[1]	25
Arizona	12
Arkansas	20
California	5
Colorado	50
Connecticut	50
Delaware	15
District of Columbia	30
Florida	15
Georgia	35
Hawaii	30
Idaho[1]	10
Illinois	15
Indiana	50
Iowa	10
Kansas	10
Kentucky	12.50
Louisiana	12
Maine	10
Maryland	15
Massachusetts	15
Michigan	15
Minnesota	15
Mississippi	15
Missouri	6
Montana	25
Nebraska	20
Nevada	30
New Hampshire	30
New Jersey	5
New Mexico[2]	4.25
New York	50
North Carolina	30
North Dakota	25
Ohio	10
Oklahoma	12.50
Oregon	10

[Continued]

★ 698 ★

Jury Duty Pay
[Continued]

State	Pay per day
Pennsylvania	25
Rhode Island	15
South Carolina	10
South Dakota	40
Tennessee	10
Texas	30
Utah	17
Vermont	30
Virginia	30
Washington	25
West Virginia	15
Wisconsin	16
Wyoming	50

Source: Overstreet, James. "Most Employers Honor Jury Duty." *USA TODAY,* 29 September 1994, p. 7B. Primary source: National Center for State Courts. *State Court Organization. Notes:* Pay of state courts can vary by county. Federal courts pay jurors $40 per day. 1. Half day. 2. Per hour.

★ 699 ★

Time Off

Lunch Time: 1991

Table shows the full-time employees by minutes of paid lunch time per day at medium and large private establishments. Data are for 1991.

[In percentages]

Minutes per day	All employees	Professional, technical, and related employees	Clerical and sales employees	Production and service employees
Total	100	100	100	100
Provided paid lunch time	8	5	4	11
Under 20 minutes	(¹)	(¹)	(¹)	1
20 minutes	2	(¹)	(¹)	4
Over 20 minutes and under 30 minutes	(¹)	-	-	(¹)
30 minutes	4	3	1	5
Over 30 minutes	1	1	2	1

[Continued]

★ 699 ★
Lunch Time: 1991
[Continued]

Minutes per day	All employees	Professional, technical, and related employees	Clerical and sales employees	Production and service employees
Number of minutes not available	(¹)	(¹)	(¹)	(¹)
Not provided paid lunch time	92	95	96	89

Source: U.S. Department of Labor. Bureau of Labor Statistics. *Employee Benefits in Medium and Large Private Establishments, 1991.* Bulletin 2422. Washington, DC: U.S. Government Printing Office, May 1993, p. 9. *Notes:* Because of rounding, sums of individual items may not equal totals. "-" indicates no employees in this category. 1. Less than 0.5 percent.

★ 700 ★
Time Off
Military Leave: 1991

Table shows the full-time employees by number of paid military leave days available per year at medium and large private establishments. Data are for 1991.

[In percentages]

Number of days	All employees	Professional, technical, and related employees	Clerical and sales employees	Production and service employees
Total	100	100	100	100
Provided paid military leave	54	63	56	48
Less than 10 days	(¹)	1	1	(¹)
10 days	27	32	29	23
11-14 days	4	4	5	4
15 days	5	5	3	6
16-19 days	1	1	1	1
20 days	1	1	1	1
21-29 days	(¹)	(¹)	(¹)	(¹)
30 days	1	2	1	1
More than 30 days	2	2	2	1
No maximum specified[2]	12	14	13	11
Number of days not available	1	1	(¹)	1
Not provided paid military leave	46	37	44	52

Source: U.S. Department of Labor. Bureau of Labor Statistics. *Employee Benefits in Medium and Large Private Establishments, 1991.* Bulletin 2422. Washington, DC: U.S. Government Printing Office, May 1993, p. 14. *Notes:* Because of rounding, sums of individual items may not equal totals. 1. Less than 0.5 percent. 2. Military leave is provided as needed.

★ 701 ★

Time Off

Personal Leave: 1991

Table shows the full-time employees by number of paid personal leave days provided per year at medium and large private establishments. Data are for 1991.

[In percentages]

Number of days	All employees	Professional, technical, and related employees	Clerical and sales employees	Production and service employees
Total	100	100	100	100
Provided personal leave	21	29	26	13
1 day	2	2	4	2
2 days	5	6	7	4
3 days	5	7	6	2
4 days	4	7	5	3
5 days	2	3	2	1
More than 5 days	1	1	2	1
No maximum specified[1]	1	2	([2])	([2])
Varies by length of service[3]	2	2	3	1
Not provided personal leave	79	71	74	87

Source: U.S. Department of Labor. Bureau of Labor Statistics. *Employee Benefits in Medium and Large Private Establishments, 1991.* Bulletin 2422. Washington, DC: U.S. Government Printing Office, May 1993, p. 14. *Notes:* Because of rounding, sums of individual items may not equal totals. 1. Workers provided as much personal leave as needed. 2. Less than 0.5 percent. 3. The maximum number of days provided was included in the distribution of personal leave days.

★ 702 ★

Time Off

Rest Time: 1991

Table shows the full-time employees by minutes of paid rest time per day at medium and large private establishments. Data are for 1991.

[In percentages]

Minutes per day	All employees	Professional, technical, and related employees	Clerical and sales employees	Production and service employees
Total	100	100	100	100
Provided paid rest time	67	58	67	71
Under 15 minutes	1	1	1	2

[Continued]

★ 702 ★

Rest Time: 1991
[Continued]

Minutes per day	All employees	Professional, technical, and related employees	Clerical and sales employees	Production and service employees
15 minutes	6	6	7	6
20 minutes	20	15	16	24
Over 20 minutes and under 30 minutes	1	(¹)	1	2
30 minutes	36	35	41	34
Over 30 minutes and under 40 minutes	(¹)	(¹)	(¹)	(¹)
40 minutes	(¹)	(¹)	(¹)	1
Over 40 minutes	1	(¹)	(¹)	3
Number of minutes not available	1	1	1	1
Not provided paid rest time	33	42	33	29

Source: U.S. Department of Labor. Bureau of Labor Statistics. *Employee Benefits in Medium and Large Private Establishments, 1991.* Bulletin 2422. Washington, DC: U.S. Government Printing Office, May 1993, p. 9. *Notes:* Because of rounding, sums of individual items may not equal totals. 1. Less than 0.5 percent.

★ 703 ★
Time Off

Time Off at Medium and Large Private Establishments – Full-Time Workers: 1991

Table shows participation of full-time employees in private industry in benefits relating to time off in medium and large establishments. Medium and large establishments exclude establishments with fewer than 100 workers, executive and traveling operating employees, and Alaska and Hawaii. Covers only benefits for which the employer pays part or all of the premium or expenses involved, except unpaid parental leave and long-term care insurance. Based on a sample survey of establishments.

[In percentages]

Benefit	Employees			
	All	Professional, technical, and related	Clerical and sales	Production and service
Paid:				
Vacations	96	97	98	95
Holidays	92	93	94	90
Jury duty leave	86	92	88	82
Funeral leave	80	84	82	77
Rest time	67	58	67	71
Military leave	54	63	56	48
Sick leave	67	87	82	48
Personal leave	21	29	26	13

[Continued]

★ 703 ★

Time Off at Medium and Large Private Establishments – Full-Time Workers: 1991
[Continued]

Benefit	Employees			
	All	Professional, technical, and related	Clerical and sales	Production and service
Lunch time	8	5	4	11
Maternity leave	2	3	2	1
Paternity leave	1	1	1	(Z)
Unpaid:				
Maternity leave	37	43	38	33
Paternity leave	26	31	26	23

Source: U.S. Bureau of the Census. *Statistical Abstract of the United States, 1994.* 114th ed. Washington, DC: U.S. Government Printing Office, 1994, p. 434. Primary source: U.S. Bureau of Labor Statistics. *Employee Benefits in Medium and Large Private Establishments, 1991.* Bulletin 2422. *Note:* "Z" represents or rounds to zero.

★ 704 ★
Time Off

Time Off at Medium and Large Private Establishments – Part-Time Workers: 1991

Table shows the part-time employees participating in employee benefit programs related to time off at medium and large private establishments. Participants are workers covered by paid time off, insurance, retirement, or capital accumulation plans. Employees subject to a minimum service requirement before they are eligible for benefit coverage are counted as participants even if they have not met the requirement at the time of the survey. If employees are required to pay part of the cost a benefit, only those who elect the coverage and pay their share are counted as participants. Benefits for which the employee must pay the full premium are outside the scope of the survey. Only current employees are counted as participants; retirees are excluded. Data are for 1991.

[In percentages]

Employee benefit program	All employees	Professional, technical, and related employees	Clerical and sales employees	Production and service employees
Paid:				
Holidays	47	45	62	37
Vacations	55	55	66	47
Personal leave	10	15	11	7
Lunch period	2	5	1	2
Rest time	56	56	62	50
Funeral leave	39	46	49	29
Jury duty leave	45	57	47	39
Military leave	14	20	19	10

[Continued]

★ 704 ★

Time Off at Medium and Large Private Establishments – Part-Time Workers: 1991

[Continued]

Employee benefit program	All employees	Professional, technical, and related employees	Clerical and sales employees	Production and service employees
Sick leave	30	41	37	22
Maternity leave	1	3	(^{1})	(^{1})
Paternity leave	(^{1})	1	(^{1})	(^{1})
Unpaid:				
Maternity leave	19	33	20	14
Paternity leave	14	22	15	11

Source: U.S. Department of Labor. Bureau of Labor Statistics. *Employee Benefits in Medium and Large Private Establishments, 1991.* Bulletin 2422. Washington, DC: U.S. Government Printing Office, May 1993, p. 127. *Notes:* Because of rounding, sums of individual items may not equal totals. 1. Less than 0.5 percent.

★ 705 ★
Time Off

Time Off at Small Private Establishments: 1992

Table shows participation of full-time employees in private industry in benefits relating to time off in small establishments. Small establishments include those with fewer than 100 employees. Covers only benefits for which the employer pays part or all of the premium or expenses involved, except unpaid parental leave and long-term care insurance. Based on a sample survey of establishments.

[In percentages]

Benefit	Employees			
	All	Professional, technical, and related	Clerical and sales	Production and service
Paid:				
Vacations	88	94	94	81
Holidays	82	94	90	74
Jury duty leave	58	76	65	47
Funeral leave	50	60	56	43
Rest time	49	40	43	56
Military leave	21	33	27	13
Sick leave	53	74	70	35
Personal leave	12	19	16	7
Lunch time	9	12	8	8
Maternity leave	2	3	2	1
Paternity leave	1	1	(Z)	(Z)

[Continued]

★ 705 ★

Time Off at Small Private Establishments: 1992
[Continued]

Benefit	Employees			
	All	Professional, technical, and related	Clerical and sales	Production and service
Unpaid:				
Maternity leave	18	27	20	13
Paternity leave	86	13	99	6

Source: U.S. Bureau of the Census. *Statistical Abstract of the United States, 1994.* 114th ed. Washington, DC: U.S. Government Printing Office, 1994, p. 434. Primary source: U.S. Bureau of Labor Statistics. *Employee Benefits in Small Private Establishments, 1992. Note:* "Z" represents or rounds to zero.

★ 706 ★
Time Off

Time Off in State and Local Government: 1992

For January through July. Covers full-time employees in state and local governments. Covers only benefits for which the employer pays part or all of the premium or expenses involved, except unpaid maternity and paternity leave. Based on sample survey of establishments.

[In percentages]

Benefit	All employees	White-collar employees[1]	Teachers[2]	Blue-collar employees[3]
Paid:				
Vacations	67	87	10	91
Holidays	75	88	38	91
Jury duty leave	97	97	98	97
Funeral leave	65	64	61	70
Rest time	53	68	20	64
Military leave	83	87	76	85
Sick leave	95	94	97	94
Personal leave	38	31	55	33
Lunch time	10	6	14	13
Unpaid:				
Maternity leave	59	59	63	54
Paternity leave	44	46	44	40

Source: U.S. Bureau of the Census. *Statistical Abstract of the United States, 1994.* 114th ed. Washington, DC: U.S. Government Printing Office, 1994, p. 321. Primary source: U.S. Bureau of Labor Statistics. *Employee Benefits in State and Local Governments, 1992. Notes:* 1. Includes all professional, administrative, technical, and clerical employees except teachers. 2. Includes all personnel in primary and secondary schools, junior colleges, and universities whose primary duty is teaching or closely related activities. 3. Includes police, firefighters, and all production and service employees.

Work and Family

★ 707 ★

Child Care Assistance

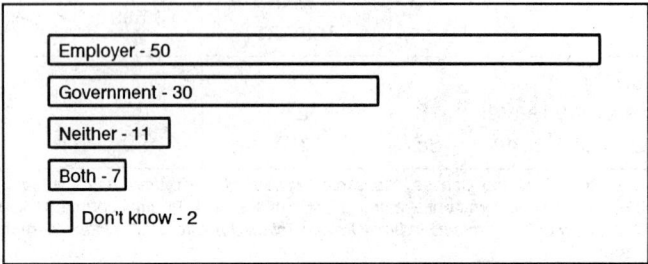

Table shows the results of an Employee Benefit Research Institute (EBRI)/ Gallup Organization survey about public attitudes toward child care and family leave. Data show the parties respondents cited as having primary responsibility for assisting working parents with child care.

[In percentages]

Responsible party	Respondents
Employer	50
Government	30
Neither	11
Both	7
Don't know	2

Source: "Survey: Employers, Not Government, Should Provide Childcare." *HR Focus* (April 1994), p. 6. Primary source: Employee Benefit Research Institute (EBRI)/ Gallup Organization report (1993).

★ 708 ★

Work and Family

Child Care Benefits

Table shows the most common child care-related benefits offered by employers. Data are based on a survey of more than 1,000 employers nationwide. Survey was conducted in 1993 and 1994.

[In percentages]

Benefit	Firms
Dependent care spending accounts	95
Resource and referral services	40
Sick/emergency child care	12
Child care centers	9

Source: Elmer, Vickie. "The Holistic Workplace." *Detroit Free Press*, 28 November 1994, p. 11F. Primary source: Hewitt Associates.

★ 709 ★
Work and Family

Eldercare Programs

By 1997, roughly 40 percent of surveyed employees expect to be responsible for an aging relative, double those responsible for an elderly person in 1992. The table below shows the eldercare programs that large employers are providing to their workforces.

[In percentages]

Program	Employers offering program
Dependent care spending account	88
Resource and referral service	30
Counseling	10
Long-term care insurance	7
Other	3

Source: Lissy William E. "Currents in Compensation and Benefits." *Compensation & Benefits Review* (November-December 1993), p. 16. Primary source: Hewitt Associates (Illinois).

★ 710 ★
Work and Family

Employee Assistance Program Counseling, by Area: 1990-1994

Table shows the employers offering counseling to exempt administrative, professional, and executive employees through employee assistance programs from 1990 through 1994.

[In percentages]

Area	1990	1992	1994
Alcohol abuse	35	42	46
Drug abuse	35	42	46
Emotional problems	29	36	43
Marital/family problems	-	32	40
AIDS	-	26	33
Outplacement	14	18	23
Personal finances	12	17	22
Retirement	-	17	22
Legal matters	9	13	17

Source: "Employee Assistance Programs: Percent of Employers Offering Counseling in Specified Areas." *HR Focus* (September 1994), p. 6. Primary source: Business & Legal Reports, Inc. 1994 Survey of Employee Benefits. *Note:* "-" indicates "not reported."

★ 711 ★
Work and Family

Flexible Work Arrangements

Table shows the employees eligible for flexible work arrangements as indicated by a survey conducted by Work/Family Directions. The survey reported that few employees (2 percent) take advantage of flexibile work arrangements such as job sharing and part-time work, although flextime was more popular with employees.

[In percentages]

Flexible work arrangement	Eligible employees utilizing flexible arrangements
Flextime	24.00
Part-time	1.70
Telecommuting	0.60
Job sharing	0.06

Source: Fierman, Jaclyn. "Are Companies Less Family-Friendly?" *Fortune,* 21 March 1994, pp. 64+. Primary source: Work/Family Directions.

★ 712 ★
Work and Family

Job Sharing Advantages

Data taken from a Conference Board survey of more than 130 companies indicates that job sharing can be beneficial to an employer. According to the source: "Job sharing increases employee motivation, loyalty, and commitment" (p. 13). The table below shows some of the advantages of job sharing noted by survey respondents.

Advantage	Percent
Employee retention	79
Increased productivity	48
Increased motivation and loyalty	40
Responsiveness to employee requests	31
Staffing continuity	26

Source: Boyd, Malia. "Job Sharers Are More Motivated." *Incentive* (February 1995), p. 13. Primary source: The Conference Board.

★ 713 ★

Work and Family

Work and Family Benefits: 1992-1993

Employee assistance programs - 81

Child care - 78

Flexible scheduling - 60

Eldercare - 20

Adoption benefits - 18

Chart shows data from column 2.

Table shows the work and family-related benefits provided by major U.S. employers for 1992 and 1993. Data are ranked by 1993 figures.

[In percentages]

Benefit	1992	1993
Employee assistance programs	79	81
Child care	74	78
Flexible scheduling	58	60
Eldercare	16	20
Adoption benefits	15	18

Source: "Child Care and Flextime Are Prevalent Work and Family Programs." *Employee Benefit Plan Review* (August 1994), p. 37. Primary source: Hewitt Associates.

★ 714 ★

Work and Family

Work-Life Programs

Work-Life assistance programs such as dependent care spending accounts, wellness programs, and preretirement planning can benefit an employer as well as employees. The table below shows the results of a survey that polled 100 companies. Sixty-five percent of the participants demonstrated a high level of committment to work-life programs. The data below reflect the affect of work-life initiatives on workforces of employers with high levels of commitment.

Contributions of work-life programs	Employers
Assist with recruiting	60
Enhance employee job satisfaction	56

Source: "Small Investments in Work-Life Programs Pay Off Big." *Personnel Journal* (May 1995), p. 22. Primary source: Towers Perrin survey.

Chapter 7
SKILLS, TRAINING, AND EDUCATION

In a *St. Louis Post-Dispatch* column, Bill Bradley wrote that "the only sure way America will guarantee its workers higher wages is if they have higher skills. The more American workers with superior talents, the higher productivity will be, and the higher worker productivity, the faster the economy will grow" ("U.S. Needs Economic Security Platform," *St. Louis Post-Dispatch,* 31 October 1993, p. 3B). Tables in this chapter reflect the formal and informal training of the American workforce. Coverage includes tables on academic awards and degrees, basic skills of job applicants and adults, job training and retraining, school enrollment, and schools. This chapter also provides an overview of educational attainment of each state's population by age, sex, and race/ethnicity.

Academic Awards and Degrees

★ 715 ★

Awards and Degrees, by Field of Study: 1991-1992

Table shows the number of academic awards and degrees granted during 1991-1992. Data are shown by instructional program titles.

Classification of Instructional Programs (CIP) title	Awards curriculums of under 1 year	1- to 4-year awards	Associate degrees	Bachelor's degrees requiring 4 or 5 years	Master's degrees	Doctoral degrees	First professional degrees
Total, all programs	567,273	422,780	529,392	1,158,895	356,414	41,545	75,688
Agricultural business and production	3,360	2,681	3,123	4,707	699	176	-
Agricultural sciences	263	1,574	1,008	5,843	1,602	773	-
Architecture[1]	724	201	456	8,878	3,653	132	-
Area and ethnic studies	129	162	29	5,371	1,399	155	-
Business management and administrative services	160,342	70,050	102,874	254,557	84,633	1,295	-
Communications	2,908	774	1,942	54,666	4,201	252	-
Communications technologies	2,750	472	1,866	775	284	3	-
Computer and information sciences	18,131	11,694	10,343	24,875	9,534	776	-
Conservation and renewable natural resources	585	196	1,259	4,649	1,456	265	-
Construction	13,539	7,625	1,646	67	0	0	-
Education	3,498	1,492	10,308	110,510	93,189	6,925	-
Engineering	200	584	2,976	62,069	25,071	5,495	-
Engineering and engineering-related technology	7,793	18,324	38,404	16,339	994	11	-

[Continued]

626

★ 715 ★

Awards and Degrees, by Field of Study: 1991-1992
[Continued]

Classification of Instructional Programs (CIP) title	Awards curriculums of under 1 year	1- to 4-year awards	Associate degrees	Bachelor's degrees requiring 4 or 5 years	Master's degrees	Doctoral degrees	First professional degrees
English language, literature, and letters	5,037	592	1,020	55,020	7,469	1,273	-
Foreign languages and literature	818	77	433	13,961	2,944	854	-
Health[2]	78,954	78,629	82,914	62,921	23,360	1,817	28,352
Home economics	584	179	589	14,227	2,455	291	-
Law and legal studies	6,562	5,532	8,084	2,189	2,383	81	39,579
Liberal arts and sciences[3]	159	1,048	154,993	32,334	2,412	123	-
Library science	77	50	103	97	4,920	50	-
Life sciences	170	265	1,378	43,848	4,816	4,246	-
Marketing and distribution	47,889	7,462	8,844	7,704	595	4	-
Mathematics	0	143	744	14,857	4,019	1,082	-
Mechanics and repair	26,214	46,554	11,623	78	0	0	-
Military technologies	2	0	172	184	0	0	-
Multi/interdisciplinary studies	59	105	7,859	20,864	2,134	250	-
Parks, recreation, and leisure studies	98	122	620	8,446	1,358	61	-
Personal and miscellaneous services	34,732	72,671	5,208	155	3	0	-
Philosophy and religion	10	1,036	63	7,581	1,159	498	-
Physical sciences	358	17	1,229	17,078	5,352	4,384	-
Precision production	17,552	17,409	9,507	378	0	0	-
Protective services	8,874	5,202	15,217	19,069	1,269	24	-
Psychology	33	294	1,209	64,046	10,381	3,493	-
Public administration and services	94	333	3,232	16,333	19,438	439	-
Science technologies	59	368	894	97	35	13	-
Social sciences and history	12	122	3,203	134,567	12,727	3,231	-
Theology studies and religious vocations	231	2,497	736	5,483	5,456	1,310	5,544
Transportation and material moving	49,099	2,102	2,503	3,617	385	0	-
Visual and performing arts	10,236	8,952	12,759	46,879	9,363	906	-
Vocational home economics	10,193	10,676	6,014	801	23	5	-

Source: U.S. Department of Labor. Bureau of Labor Statistics. *Occupational Projections and Training Data.* 1994 ed. Bulletin 2451. Washington, DC: U.S. Government Printing Office, May 1994, pp. 46-67. A statistical and research supplement to the 1994-1995 *Occupational Outlook Handbook. Notes:* "-" indicates data not available. 1. Includes related programs. 2. Health professions and related sciences. 3. Includes general studies and humanities.

★ 716 ★

Academic Awards and Degrees

Bachelor's Degree Recipients Pursuing Further Education: 1991

Table shows the recipients of bachelor's degrees in 1989-1990 who pursued further education within one year (1991) of their graduations. Data are by type of enrollment and by undergraduate major.

[In percentages]

Undergraduate major field of study	Ever enrolled since graduation	Ever enrolled full-time	Ever enrolled and employed	Ever enrolled and not employed	Enrolled in degree program beyond bachelor's
All bachelor's graduates	35	17	24	11	24
Professional/technical fields	28	17	22	6	18
Engineering	32	18	23	9	23

[Continued]

★716★

Bachelor's Degree Recipients Pursuing Further Education: 1991
[Continued]

Undergraduate major field of study	Ever enrolled since graduation	Ever enrolled full-time	Ever enrolled and employed	Ever enrolled and not employed	Enrolled in degree program beyond bachelor's
Business and management	21	13	16	5	12
Health professions	27	16	22	5	20
Education	38	27	33	5	29
Public affairs and social services	35	13	28	7	22
Arts and sciences fields	46	17	28	18	34
Biological sciences	64	17	30	34	47
Physical sciences, mathematics, and computer sciences	40	17	24	16	30
Psychology	50	19	31	20	40
Social sciences	42	16	28	14	30
Humanities	43	17	28	15	28
Other[1]	29	15	21	9	18
Highest degree graduate expects to obtain:					
Bachelor's degree	15	10	13	3	3
Master's degree	31	18	24	6	20
Doctor's degree	58	21	36	22	49
First professional degree	68	9	27	41	61

Source: U.S. Department of Education. Office of Educational Research and Improvement. National Center for Education Statistics. *Digest of Education Statistics, 1994.* NCES 94-115. Lanham, MD: Bernan, November 1994, p. 406. Primary source: U.S. Department of Education. National Center for Education Statistics. "Recent College Graduates, 1991" (survey). Table was prepared May 1993. *Notes:* Data are from a sample survey of recent college graduates. Data exclude bachelor's degree recipients from U.S. Service Schools. Deceased graduates and graduates living at foreign addresses at the time of the survey are not included. 1. Includes agriculture and natural resources, architecture and environmental design, area and ethnic studies, consumer/personal/miscellaneous services, home economics, industrial arts, law, liberal/general studies, library and archival sciences, military sciences, multi/interdisciplinary studies, personal and social development, and trade and industrial.

★ 717 ★

Academic Awards and Degrees

Degrees Earned by Latinos: 1991

Table shows the academic degrees earned by Latinos in 1991. According to the source, Latinos earned 5 percent of associate, 3.5 percent of bachelor's and master's, 2 percent of doctoral, and 4 percent of first professional degrees.

Degree	Men	Women
Associate	10,213	14,042
Bachelor's	16,157	20,455
Master's	3,667	4,715
Doctoral	387	345
First professional	1,506	1,021

Source: "Latinos in Higher Ed." *Manpower Comments* (March 1994), p. 16. Primary source: O'Brien, Eileen M. *Latinos in Higher Education.* ACE Research Brief Series, vol. 4, no. 4 (1993).

★ 718 ★

Academic Awards and Degrees

Doctoral Degree Recipients: 1991

Table shows the total number of doctoral degrees earned by field of study for 1991, as well as the percentage of degrees earned by women.

Field	Total	Percentage of women
All fields	37,451	36.7
Business and management	1,164	25.0
Education	6,397	58.1
Engineering	5,212	8.7
Humanities	4,094	46.5
American and English language and literature	853	56.6
Foreign language and literature	498	60.0
History	658	37.5
Other humanities	2,085	41.9
Life sciences	6,928	38.5
Agricultural sciences	1,237	19.8
Biological sciences	4,642	37.8
Health sciences	1,049	63.8
Physical sciences	6,276	18.3
Chemistry	2,194	23.1
Computer science	797	14.5
Earth, atmosphere, and marine	837	22.1
Mathematics	1,040	18.6
Physics and astronomy	1,408	10.7
Social sciences	6,127	49.3

[Continued]

★ 718 ★

Doctoral Degree Recipients: 1991
[Continued]

Field	Total	Percentage of women
Anthropology and sociology	806	45.4
Economics	852	20.3
Political science and international relations	522	27.2
Psychology	3,240	61.2
Other social sciences	707	51.0
Other professional fields	829	41.9
Other fields	81	49.3

Source: Baxter, Neal. "Is There Another Degree in Your Future?" *Occupational Outlook Quarterly* 37, no. 4 (winter 1993-1994), p. 26.

★ 719 ★

Academic Awards and Degrees

Fields of Study, by Degree: 1994

Table shows the academic majors expected to be most in demand by employers during 1994.

Major	Total	Bachelor's degree	Master's degree
Accounting	2,891	2,425	466
Business administration/management	2,547	1,710	837
Secondary education	2,184	1,574	610
Electrical engineering	1,863	1,249	614
Elementary education	1,482	1,147	335
Computer programming	1,492	1,139	353
Liberal arts	1,069	739	330
Mechanical engineering	1,059	867	192
Marketing/retail/merchandising	1,341	1,195	146
Management information systems	849	715	134
Computer engineering	701	427	274
Hospitality/hotel management	605	605	0
Finance/banking	559	343	216
Chemical engineering	527	407	120
Math/actuarial science	369	334	35
Chemistry	363	262	101
Architecture	324	269	55
Sales	317	263	54
Biology	286	235	51
Social sciences	251	220	31
Human resources	168	116	52
Industrial engineering	168	116	52
Environmental engineering	163	153	10
Systems engineering	140	125	15
Psychology	138	136	2

[Continued]

★ 719 ★

Fields of Study, by Degree: 1994
[Continued]

Major	Total	Bachelor's degree	Master's degree
Communications	134	125	9
Physics	131	55	76
Aeronautical engineering	121	111	10
Civil engineering	113	91	22

Source: "Who's Hiring?" *Manpower Comments* (December 1993), p. 10. Primary source: *The Black Collegian* (November/December 1993).

Basic Skills

★ 720 ★

Basic Skill Deficiency Rates of Job Applicants: 1989-1992

According to the source, 40 percent of 1992's job applicants did not have the necessary math and reading skills required of the jobs for which they were applying. The table shows the job deficiency rates of job applicants from 1989 to 1992.

[In percentages]

Year	Deficiency rate
1989	26.1
1990	26.3
1991	35.5
1992	39.3

Source: "Increased Skills Testing Uncovers Higher Deficiency Rates." *HR Focus* 70, no. 9 (September 1993), p. 14. Primary source: American Management Association.

★ 721 ★

Basic Skills

Basic Skills Testing: 1989-1994

Despite five years of increased use since 1989, basic skills testing of employees declined in 1994. The table below shows the use of literacy and math skills testing since 1989.

[In percentages]

Year	Testing	
	Literacy	Math
1989	5.0	5.0
1990	9.8	9.9
1991	15.6	19.9
1992	22.3	27.3
1993	28.7	31.9
1994	22.0	25.9

Source: "Basic Skills Testing on the Decline." *Personnel Journal* (November 1994), p. 18. Primary source: 1994 American Management Survey on Basic Skills Testing and Training.

★ 722 ★

Basic Skills

Literacy Skills of Adults: 1992

Table shows the average scores of adults, 16 years old and older, by selected characteristics. Data are from 1992 and cover prose, document, and quantitative literacy skills.

Characteristic	Average score		
	Prose literacy[1]	Document literacy[2]	Quantitative literacy[3]
Total	272	267	271
Sex			
Male	272	269	277
Female	273	265	266
Age			
16 to 18 years old	271	274	268
19 to 24 years old	280	280	277
25 to 39 years old	284	282	283
40 to 54 years old	286	278	286
55 to 64 years old	260	249	261
65 years old and older	230	217	227
Race/ethnicity			
White	286	280	287
Black	237	230	224
Asian or Pacific Islander	242	245	256

[Continued]

★ 722 ★

Literacy Skills of Adults: 1992
[Continued]

Characteristic	Average score		
	Prose literacy[1]	Document literacy[2]	Quantitative literacy[3]
American Indian	254	254	250
Hispanic, Mexican	206	205	205
Hispanic, Cuban	211	212	223
Hispanic, Puerto Rican	218	215	212
Hispanic, Central/South American	207	206	203
Hispanic, other	260	254	246
Highest level of education			
Still in high school	271	274	269
0 to 8 years	177	170	169
9 to 12 years	231	227	227
GED	268	264	268
High school diploma	270	264	270
Some college	294	290	295
Associate's degree	308	299	307
Bachelor's degree	322	314	322
Graduate studies/degree	336	326	334
Region			
Northeast	270	264	267
Midwest	279	274	280
South	267	262	265
West	276	271	276
Prison population	246	240	236

Source: U.S. Department of Education. Office of Educational Research and Improvement. National Center for Education Statistics. *Digest of Education Statistics, 1994.* NCES 94-115. Lanham, MD: Bernan, November 1994, p. 408. Primary source: U.S. Department of Education. National Center for Education Statistics. *National Adult Literacy Survey: Adult Literacy in America, 1992.* Prepared by Educational Testing Service. Table was prepared February 1994. *Notes:* "GED" stands for General Educational Development. 1. Prose literacy is the ability to understand and use information contained in various kinds of textual material. A score of 0 to 225 requires the reader to locate a single piece of information in a short text. A score of 226 to 275 requires the reader to locate a single piece of information in the text with several distractors or to make low-level inferences. A score of 276 to 325 requires the reader to make literal or synonymous matches between the text and information given in the task, or to make low-level inferences. A score of 326 to 375 requires the reader to perform multiple feature matches and to integrate or synthesize information from complex passages. A score of 376 to 500 requires the reader to search for information in dense text that contains a number of distractors. 2. Document literacy reflects the knowledge and skills used to process information from documents. A score of 0 to 225 requires the reader to locate pieces of information based on a literal match. A score of 226 to 275 requires the reader to match a single piece of information among several distractors. A score of 276 to 325 requires the reader to integrate multiple pieces of information from one or more documents. A score of 326 to 375 requires the performance of multiple feature matches, cycling through documents, and integrating information. A score of 376 to 500 requires the reader to search through complex displays that contain multiple distractors to make high-level text-based inferences. 3. Quantitative literacy is the ability to perform numerical operations in everyday life. A score of 0 to 225 requires the reader to perform a single, relatively simple, arithmetic operation. A score of 226 to 275 requires the reader to perform a single operation using numbers that are either stated in the task or easily located in the material. A score of 276 to 325 requires the reader to use two or more numbers to solve the problem. A score of 326 to 375 requires the reader to perform two or more sequential operations or a single operation in which the quantities are found in different types of displays. A score of 376 to 500 requires the reader to perform multiple operations sequentially. They must extract the features of the problem from the text or rely on background knowledge to determine the quantities or operations needed.

Educational Attainment

★ 723 ★

Educational Attainment in Alabama, by Selected Characteristics

Table presents the number of civilians 16 years old or older who reported their educational backgrounds during the 1990 Census. Data show the number of individuals achieving various levels of education. Figures are reported by sex, age, and race.

Characteristic	Not high school graduate	High school graduate	Some college or associate's degree	Bachelor's degree	Graduate or professional degree
16 to 19 years old					
Men					
White	26,341	8,335	7,764	51	0
Black	8,359	2,899	1,507	0	0
American Indian, Eskimo, and Aleut	276	94	20	0	0
Asian or Pacific Islander	185	34	10	0	0
Other race	49	0	38	0	0
Women					
White	17,539	8,507	9,514	3	4
Black	6,418	3,555	3,041	19	0
American Indian, Eskimo, and Aleut	93	89	66	0	0
Asian or Pacific Islander	133	34	72	0	0
Other race	41	17	28	0	0
20 to 24 years old					
Men					
White	18,424	27,426	31,404	6,706	354
Black	6,750	10,166	7,310	641	7
American Indian, Eskimo, and Aleut	152	239	145	10	0
Asian or Pacific Islander	86	76	222	96	37
Other race	111	34	49	36	0
Women					
White	9,123	21,245	32,245	8,846	451
Black	4,571	9,101	12,675	1,350	65
American Indian, Eskimo, and Aleut	48	116	127	26	0
Asian or Pacific Islander	20	60	284	38	5
Other race	18	47	67	4	0
25 to 29 years old					
Men					
White	19,385	34,043	29,864	18,229	3,853
Black	6,685	11,666	7,401	2,094	237
American Indian, Eskimo, and Aleut	141	165	149	55	12
Asian or Pacific Islander	136	49	222	256	251
Other race	103	83	117	22	16
Women					
White	10,095	24,081	28,448	16,673	3,756
Black	5,360	10,450	13,403	3,924	401
American Indian, Eskimo, and Aleut	97	169	135	20	0
Asian or Pacific Islander	74	86	187	183	105

[Continued]

★ 723 ★

Educational Attainment in Alabama, by Selected Characteristics
[Continued]

Characteristic	Not high school graduate	High school graduate	Some college or associate's degree	Bachelor's degree	Graduate or professional degree
Other race	17	49	24	52	14
30 to 34 years old					
Men					
White	19,897	38,261	29,629	17,909	7,302
Black	7,418	11,544	7,805	2,423	632
American Indian, Eskimo, and Aleut	247	232	146	62	3
Asian or Pacific Islander	98	74	95	161	425
Other race	32	62	55	3	25
Women					
White	10,596	27,983	27,820	14,164	6,225
Black	6,629	10,320	13,400	4,372	1,292
American Indian, Eskimo, and Aleut	103	193	194	81	12
Asian or Pacific Islander	153	168	146	77	207
Other race	38	41	64	63	0
35 to 39 years old					
Men					
White	15,580	29,712	30,224	18,088	9,234
Black	6,635	9,051	7,669	2,384	1,037
American Indian, Eskimo, and Aleut	106	225	257	71	23
Asian or Pacific Islander	134	35	94	106	369
Other race	62	7	22	24	31
Women					
White	10,129	28,598	24,958	12,110	7,896
Black	6,129	10,231	9,825	3,735	1,840
American Indian, Eskimo, and Aleut	69	204	238	83	45
Asian or Pacific Islander	156	180	161	142	204
Other race	31	33	23	0	20
40 to 69 years old					
Men					
White	79,196	99,821	83,010	50,646	36,721
Black	29,791	18,533	11,670	3,631	3,125
American Indian, Eskimo, and Aleut	422	494	534	195	153
Asian or Pacific Islander	227	181	287	349	877
Other race	100	67	66	51	39
Women					
White	53,672	101,934	65,190	22,252	21,691
Black	26,428	21,529	15,027	5,039	5,168
American Indian, Eskimo, and Aleut	294	394	386	76	80
Asian or Pacific Islander	480	427	382	258	205
Other race	35	140	76	8	7
70 years old and older					
Men					
White	4,852	2,546	1,923	1,017	1,133
Black	1,554	272	176	68	102

[Continued]

★ 723 ★

Educational Attainment in Alabama, by Selected Characteristics
[Continued]

Characteristic	Not high school graduate	High school graduate	Some college or associate's degree	Bachelor's degree	Graduate or professional degree
American Indian, Eskimo, and Aleut	10	0	0	8	5
Asian or Pacific Islander	9	9	0	0	12
Other race	1	0	0	0	0
Women					
White	2,939	2,256	1,119	330	258
Black	1,555	275	146	40	91
American Indian, Eskimo, and Aleut	10	0	7	0	0
Asian or Pacific Islander	0	0	0	8	0
Other race	0	0	0	0	0

Source: Census of Population and Housing, 1990: Equal Employment Opportunity (EEO) File on CD-ROM [machine-readable datafiles]. Prepared by the Bureau of the Census. Washington, DC: The Bureau, 1992.

★ 724 ★
Educational Attainment

Educational Attainment in Alaska, by Selected Characteristics

Table presents the number of civilians 16 years old or older who reported their educational backgrounds during the 1990 Census. Data show the number of individuals achieving various levels of education. Figures are reported by sex, age, and race.

Characteristic	Not high school graduate	High school graduate	Some college or associate's degree	Bachelor's degree	Graduate or professional degree
16 to 19 years old					
Men					
White	3,787	1,373	642	9	0
Black	227	102	16	0	0
American Indian, Eskimo, and Aleut	698	246	87	0	0
Asian or Pacific Islander	126	31	12	0	0
Other race	112	17	4	0	0
Women					
White	3,037	1,249	930	0	0
Black	169	90	80	6	0
American Indian, Eskimo, and Aleut	636	340	134	0	0
Asian or Pacific Islander	155	51	41	0	0
Other race	12	38	22	0	0
20 to 24 years old					
Men					
White	1,206	3,406	3,888	743	38
Black	21	248	171	0	0
American Indian, Eskimo, and Aleut	432	1,299	488	4	0
Asian or Pacific Islander	114	219	224	10	0

[Continued]

★ 724 ★

Educational Attainment in Alaska, by Selected Characteristics
[Continued]

Characteristic	Not high school graduate	High school graduate	Some college or associate's degree	Bachelor's degree	Graduate or professional degree
Other race	78	93	73	3	0
Women					
White	643	2,685	4,184	831	39
Black	71	162	271	29	0
American Indian, Eskimo, and Aleut	224	1,031	608	76	0
Asian or Pacific Islander	50	148	220	41	4
Other race	9	41	88	7	0
25 to 29 years old					
Men					
White	1,469	5,134	5,486	2,352	367
Black	63	193	219	11	16
American Indian, Eskimo, and Aleut	577	1,568	605	59	24
Asian or Pacific Islander	172	196	444	96	13
Other race	157	103	133	22	0
Women					
White	730	4,007	4,828	2,554	466
Black	80	238	360	104	15
American Indian, Eskimo, and Aleut	303	1,193	670	128	9
Asian or Pacific Islander	104	252	193	108	3
Other race	66	104	105	30	7
30 to 34 years old					
Men					
White	1,393	6,402	7,645	3,558	1,465
Black	89	223	337	48	16
American Indian, Eskimo, and Aleut	593	1,334	492	48	19
Asian or Pacific Islander	119	182	266	113	34
Other race	58	106	123	48	1
Women					
White	916	4,275	7,019	3,476	1,091
Black	36	232	393	114	6
American Indian, Eskimo, and Aleut	350	907	751	99	11
Asian or Pacific Islander	150	233	263	201	34
Other race	82	49	127	39	0
35 to 39 years old					
Men					
White	961	5,348	7,929	4,081	2,668
Black	19	171	361	60	46
American Indian, Eskimo, and Aleut	374	1,178	722	81	40
Asian or Pacific Islander	103	234	235	171	41
Other race	31	71	105	13	5
Women					
White	583	3,747	6,545	3,718	1,635
Black	24	106	383	131	4
American Indian, Eskimo, and Aleut	373	722	857	163	45

[Continued]

★ 724 ★

Educational Attainment in Alaska, by Selected Characteristics

[Continued]

Characteristic	Not high school graduate	High school graduate	Some college or associate's degree	Bachelor's degree	Graduate or professional degree
Asian or Pacific Islander	173	279	309	207	24
Other race	50	44	68	4	4
40 to 69 years old					
Men					
White	4,088	11,468	16,881	9,561	8,124
Black	133	368	577	199	115
American Indian, Eskimo, and Aleut	1,829	1,618	1,267	186	151
Asian or Pacific Islander	401	585	357	390	123
Other race	110	132	206	23	42
Women					
White	2,235	8,546	13,156	6,806	4,613
Black	145	191	474	136	122
American Indian, Eskimo, and Aleut	1,418	1,327	1,380	197	116
Asian or Pacific Islander	607	552	423	313	141
Other race	80	128	101	56	14
70 years old and older					
Men					
White	134	106	217	82	109
Black	25	0	8	0	0
American Indian, Eskimo, and Aleut	22	5	2	3	0
Asian or Pacific Islander	5	3	8	5	0
Other race	5	0	0	0	0
Women					
White	53	52	130	56	25
Black	6	0	0	0	0
American Indian, Eskimo, and Aleut	29	0	14	0	0
Asian or Pacific Islander	0	0	2	2	0
Other race	0	0	0	0	0

Source: Census of Population and Housing, 1990: Equal Employment Opportunity (EEO) File on CD-ROM [machine-readable datafiles]. Prepared by the Bureau of the Census. Washington, DC: The Bureau, 1992.

★ 725 ★

Educational Attainment

Educational Attainment in Arizona, by Selected Characteristics

Table presents the number of civilians 16 years old or older who reported their educational backgrounds during the 1990 Census. Data show the number of individuals achieving various levels of education. Figures are reported by sex, age, and race.

Characteristic	Not high school graduate	High school graduate	Some college or associate's degree	Bachelor's degree	Graduate or professional degree
16 to 19 years old					
Men					
White	27,416	9,242	8,444	62	0
Black	1,158	240	261	0	0
American Indian, Eskimo, and Aleut	1,492	430	214	0	0
Asian or Pacific Islander	546	173	207	0	0
Other race	4,897	1,292	664	0	0
Women					
White	20,729	9,483	10,673	9	0
Black	646	349	307	0	0
American Indian, Eskimo, and Aleut	1,279	463	379	0	0
Asian or Pacific Islander	377	128	129	0	0
Other race	2,955	1,223	916	0	0
20 to 24 years old					
Men					
White	15,402	24,335	37,804	6,406	356
Black	621	909	1,447	118	0
American Indian, Eskimo, and Aleut	2,192	2,117	1,156	54	0
Asian or Pacific Islander	255	417	941	258	33
Other race	6,453	3,911	3,280	233	64
Women					
White	8,381	18,997	38,679	7,486	507
Black	500	909	1,571	148	9
American Indian, Eskimo, and Aleut	1,153	1,801	1,522	44	5
Asian or Pacific Islander	210	332	760	143	15
Other race	2,593	3,198	3,755	290	12
25 to 29 years old					
Men					
White	15,782	28,802	41,791	20,425	4,245
Black	539	1,122	2,040	417	117
American Indian, Eskimo, and Aleut	1,978	2,497	1,520	208	32
Asian or Pacific Islander	209	293	672	586	370
Other race	6,792	4,516	3,689	692	138
Women					
White	7,906	21,408	38,359	19,947	3,476
Black	430	683	1,726	531	62
American Indian, Eskimo, and Aleut	1,382	1,946	1,882	210	40
Asian or Pacific Islander	200	268	732	537	157
Other race	3,136	3,277	3,586	805	112
30 to 34 years old					
Men					
White	12,749	28,313	44,159	23,337	8,740

[Continued]

★ 725 ★

Educational Attainment in Arizona, by Selected Characteristics

[Continued]

Characteristic	Not high school graduate	High school graduate	Some college or associate's degree	Bachelor's degree	Graduate or professional degree
Black	617	946	1,783	582	140
American Indian, Eskimo, and Aleut	1,737	2,270	1,617	121	37
Asian or Pacific Islander	189	258	637	616	812
Other race	5,550	3,985	3,267	601	314
Women					
White	7,674	23,769	39,473	17,832	6,001
Black	316	750	1,731	416	124
American Indian, Eskimo, and Aleut	1,116	1,813	1,936	263	59
Asian or Pacific Islander	256	394	675	645	203
Other race	3,199	2,404	3,176	506	301
35 to 39 years old					
Men					
White	9,684	21,070	41,628	21,139	11,070
Black	258	707	1,761	449	274
American Indian, Eskimo, and Aleut	1,342	1,546	1,197	278	130
Asian or Pacific Islander	162	167	529	610	693
Other race	4,548	2,907	3,043	582	221
Women					
White	6,488	20,961	37,169	15,636	8,304
Black	370	665	1,647	360	170
American Indian, Eskimo, and Aleut	921	1,393	1,628	302	178
Asian or Pacific Islander	461	359	612	467	209
Other race	3,070	2,225	2,292	404	144
40 to 69 years old					
Men					
White	40,217	68,645	108,491	56,879	44,122
Black	1,535	1,547	3,351	1,005	682
American Indian, Eskimo, and Aleut	4,510	2,708	2,351	430	374
Asian or Pacific Islander	706	632	1,103	916	1,188
Other race	12,097	4,457	4,161	902	580
Women					
White	30,614	73,951	97,918	33,843	23,464
Black	1,317	1,759	2,847	741	500
American Indian, Eskimo, and Aleut	2,730	2,607	2,270	415	410
Asian or Pacific Islander	1,282	1,002	1,059	692	471
Other race	7,248	3,687	3,086	273	226
70 years old and older					
Men					
White	2,638	2,570	2,612	1,377	1,284
Black	40	59	12	33	37
American Indian, Eskimo, and Aleut	101	13	5	0	0
Asian or Pacific Islander	16	6	5	0	21
Other race	167	31	11	0	0

[Continued]

★ 725 ★

Educational Attainment in Arizona, by Selected Characteristics
[Continued]

Characteristic	Not high school graduate	High school graduate	Some college or associate's degree	Bachelor's degree	Graduate or professional degree
Women					
White	1,559	1,938	1,943	631	531
Black	72	3	19	16	16
American Indian, Eskimo, and Aleut	63	3	15	23	2
Asian or Pacific Islander	0	0	10	0	0
Other race	206	10	25	0	0

Source: Census of Population and Housing, 1990: Equal Employment Opportunity (EEO) File on CD-ROM [machine-readable datafiles]. Prepared by the Bureau of the Census. Washington, DC: The Bureau, 1992.

★ 726 ★

Educational Attainment

Educational Attainment in Arkansas, by Selected Characteristics

Table presents the number of civilians 16 years old or older who reported their educational backgrounds during the 1990 Census. Data show the number of individuals achieving various levels of education. Figures are reported by sex, age, and race.

Characteristic	Not high school graduate	High school graduate	Some college or associate's degree	Bachelor's degree	Graduate or professional degree
16 to 19 years old					
Men					
White	17,489	7,375	3,977	0	0
Black	2,820	1,366	560	10	0
American Indian, Eskimo, and Aleut	176	43	4	0	0
Asian or Pacific Islander	156	63	28	0	0
Other race	111	30	28	0	0
Women					
White	13,350	7,046	5,726	29	0
Black	2,677	1,414	1,128	0	0
American Indian, Eskimo, and Aleut	76	59	40	0	0
Asian or Pacific Islander	60	8	7	0	0
Other race	26	54	10	0	0
20 to 24 years old					
Men					
White	10,151	21,134	17,458	3,192	148
Black	1,989	3,598	2,387	246	7
American Indian, Eskimo, and Aleut	140	171	119	7	0
Asian or Pacific Islander	65	44	164	60	0
Other race	331	96	106	25	0
Women					
White	5,250	16,200	19,213	4,350	274

[Continued]

641

Educational Attainment in Arkansas, by Selected Characteristics
[Continued]

Characteristic	Not high school graduate	High school graduate	Some college or associate's degree	Bachelor's degree	Graduate or professional degree
Black	1,445	3,740	3,688	519	14
American Indian, Eskimo, and Aleut	47	176	133	22	2
Asian or Pacific Islander	132	76	125	15	0
Other race	57	61	53	22	0
25 to 29 years old					
Men					
White	13,019	26,338	16,519	8,221	1,942
Black	1,951	4,435	2,117	601	48
American Indian, Eskimo, and Aleut	182	243	145	39	14
Asian or Pacific Islander	165	80	86	33	41
Other race	219	65	54	28	11
Women					
White	6,565	20,173	16,373	8,598	1,677
Black	1,996	4,488	3,787	1,205	167
American Indian, Eskimo, and Aleut	88	205	119	34	0
Asian or Pacific Islander	108	118	91	21	33
Other race	24	81	35	7	0
30 to 34 years old					
Men					
White	12,734	26,908	16,526	8,385	3,558
Black	2,697	4,380	2,318	815	197
American Indian, Eskimo, and Aleut	151	149	182	45	22
Asian or Pacific Islander	162	73	121	50	48
Other race	175	30	51	4	19
Women					
White	6,942	21,903	16,185	7,618	2,775
Black	2,431	4,838	3,998	1,330	316
American Indian, Eskimo, and Aleut	67	104	162	20	21
Asian or Pacific Islander	144	171	98	70	42
Other race	40	51	74	11	5
35 to 39 years old					
Men					
White	10,050	22,491	17,605	8,977	4,743
Black	2,401	3,858	2,081	888	299
American Indian, Eskimo, and Aleut	65	169	180	32	37
Asian or Pacific Islander	136	115	144	34	69
Other race	163	52	81	29	13
Women					
White	6,456	19,979	15,454	7,480	3,875
Black	2,232	3,923	2,964	1,390	601
American Indian, Eskimo, and Aleut	96	144	130	42	28
Asian or Pacific Islander	165	101	70	147	8
Other race	87	65	10	9	0

[Continued]

★ 726 ★

Educational Attainment in Arkansas, by Selected Characteristics

[Continued]

Characteristic	Not high school graduate	High school graduate	Some college or associate's degree	Bachelor's degree	Graduate or professional degree
40 to 69 years old					
Men					
White	52,400	70,072	47,443	26,050	17,474
Black	10,013	5,516	3,679	1,634	901
American Indian, Eskimo, and Aleut	401	291	424	121	90
Asian or Pacific Islander	279	170	107	132	305
Other race	255	77	72	6	11
Women					
White	36,111	71,376	40,024	14,975	10,813
Black	9,139	7,062	3,616	1,597	1,380
American Indian, Eskimo, and Aleut	307	455	308	62	91
Asian or Pacific Islander	487	303	182	142	80
Other race	84	78	52	3	5
70 years old and older					
Men					
White	3,498	1,953	1,276	507	552
Black	814	118	69	27	32
American Indian, Eskimo, and Aleut	27	0	0	0	6
Asian or Pacific Islander	0	0	0	0	0
Other race	0	0	7	0	0
Women					
White	2,171	1,353	851	256	135
Black	643	150	22	25	32
American Indian, Eskimo, and Aleut	6	0	0	0	0
Asian or Pacific Islander	12	0	0	0	0
Other race	0	0	0	0	0

Source: Census of Population and Housing, 1990: Equal Employment Opportunity (EEO) File on CD-ROM [machine-readable datafiles]. Prepared by the Bureau of the Census. Washington, DC: The Bureau, 1992.

★ 727 ★

Educational Attainment

Educational Attainment in California, by Selected Characteristics

Table presents the number of civilians 16 years old or older who reported their educational backgrounds during the 1990 Census. Data show the number of individuals achieving various levels of education. Figures are reported by sex, age, and race.

Characteristic	Not high school graduate	High school graduate	Some college or associate's degree	Bachelor's degree	Graduate or professional degree
16 to 19 years old					
Men					
White	166,181	59,810	51,835	346	36
Black	13,550	5,789	4,366	0	7
American Indian, Eskimo, and Aleut	2,613	942	584	6	0
Asian or Pacific Islander	16,768	7,593	7,407	113	8
Other race	67,228	16,160	6,928	33	7
Women					
White	124,295	59,809	65,004	208	19
Black	11,439	6,751	6,350	48	0
American Indian, Eskimo, and Aleut	1,908	769	622	0	0
Asian or Pacific Islander	14,005	7,607	8,795	76	8
Other race	36,562	13,434	9,007	36	0
20 to 24 years old					
Men					
White	152,602	168,793	239,355	53,306	3,956
Black	12,253	20,368	23,508	2,590	171
American Indian, Eskimo, and Aleut	2,795	2,702	2,856	296	34
Asian or Pacific Islander	10,173	17,549	37,546	10,594	1,279
Other race	131,533	52,102	39,037	3,494	632
Women					
White	66,944	128,259	253,313	64,475	3,370
Black	6,866	17,155	28,386	4,288	389
American Indian, Eskimo, and Aleut	1,121	1,821	2,998	269	39
Asian or Pacific Islander	6,134	13,839	36,911	13,577	761
Other race	49,850	34,497	38,121	3,335	573
25 to 29 years old					
Men					
White	158,640	200,807	279,756	171,223	42,993
Black	12,410	21,977	32,761	8,878	1,742
American Indian, Eskimo, and Aleut	2,222	3,235	3,699	848	136
Asian or Pacific Islander	12,981	16,810	37,604	30,200	11,237
Other race	126,617	46,154	42,634	8,987	2,677
Women					
White	73,163	138,491	254,484	160,354	32,797
Black	6,716	16,529	37,316	11,468	2,010
American Indian, Eskimo, and Aleut	1,223	2,074	3,631	581	167
Asian or Pacific Islander	9,234	13,802	32,668	32,282	7,366
Other race	55,334	29,146	36,360	7,934	1,603
30 to 34 years old					
Men					
White	133,443	200,062	314,715	184,298	84,549

[Continued]

★ 727 ★

Educational Attainment in California, by Selected Characteristics

[Continued]

Characteristic	Not high school graduate	High school graduate	Some college or associate's degree	Bachelor's degree	Graduate or professional degree
Black	9,477	20,279	34,420	11,654	3,762
American Indian, Eskimo, and Aleut	2,113	2,672	3,754	734	202
Asian or Pacific Islander	13,765	16,397	38,325	31,750	18,735
Other race	103,458	34,775	37,898	8,500	3,621
Women					
White	70,611	139,155	275,487	144,846	55,328
Black	6,587	15,821	39,357	11,751	3,420
American Indian, Eskimo, and Aleut	1,251	2,026	3,593	891	311
Asian or Pacific Islander	10,831	15,179	33,138	32,405	10,723
Other race	56,685	24,296	27,584	5,570	2,238
35 to 39 years old					
Men					
White	93,243	139,974	293,548	170,201	106,971
Black	7,264	14,062	29,814	10,372	4,241
American Indian, Eskimo, and Aleut	1,391	2,195	3,928	972	498
Asian or Pacific Islander	12,612	14,368	32,471	30,162	20,055
Other race	77,095	21,780	27,160	5,958	3,552
Women					
White	57,527	125,797	260,914	127,053	67,867
Black	5,542	13,934	33,183	10,167	4,330
American Indian, Eskimo, and Aleut	1,063	1,957	3,701	794	381
Asian or Pacific Islander	13,196	14,332	29,635	32,433	10,594
Other race	47,514	18,539	20,031	3,790	1,880
40 to 69 years old					
Men					
White	316,127	424,864	781,369	483,561	410,267
Black	31,275	38,729	67,196	22,371	16,251
American Indian, Eskimo, and Aleut	5,383	5,359	9,048	2,307	1,684
Asian or Pacific Islander	42,576	42,658	74,597	79,396	50,050
Other race	164,750	35,875	38,934	9,069	6,186
Women					
White	230,864	463,781	703,877	305,916	196,474
Black	25,984	40,473	73,182	19,141	15,317
American Indian, Eskimo, and Aleut	4,369	5,178	7,493	1,498	1,292
Asian or Pacific Islander	48,744	50,255	65,394	69,880	22,067
Other race	104,681	31,968	28,137	4,717	3,244
70 years old and older					
Men					
White	18,228	19,146	24,009	12,600	14,170
Black	1,780	815	822	203	316
American Indian, Eskimo, and Aleut	190	62	51	31	49
Asian or Pacific Islander	2,216	1,631	1,299	778	583
Other race	2,095	379	183	76	88

[Continued]

★ 727 ★

Educational Attainment in California, by Selected Characteristics

[Continued]

Characteristic	Not high school graduate	High school graduate	Some college or associate's degree	Bachelor's degree	Graduate or professional degree
Women					
White	13,408	17,691	17,451	6,011	4,502
Black	1,745	860	938	344	230
American Indian, Eskimo, and Aleut	137	72	97	34	8
Asian or Pacific Islander	1,129	949	657	420	163
Other race	1,371	347	199	73	46

Source: Census of Population and Housing, 1990: Equal Employment Opportunity (EEO) File on CD-ROM [machine-readable datafiles]. Prepared by the Bureau of the Census. Washington, DC: The Bureau, 1992.

★ 728 ★

Educational Attainment

Educational Attainment in Colorado, by Selected Characteristics

Table presents the number of civilians 16 years old or older who reported their educational backgrounds during the 1990 Census. Data show the number of individuals achieving various levels of education. Figures are reported by sex, age, and race.

Characteristic	Not high school graduate	High school graduate	Some college or associate's degree	Bachelor's degree	Graduate or professional degree
16 to 19 years old					
Men					
White	25,700	8,471	6,239	40	0
Black	1,001	452	266	0	0
American Indian, Eskimo, and Aleut	419	48	62	0	0
Asian or Pacific Islander	554	129	174	0	0
Other race	2,623	555	353	0	0
Women					
White	22,350	8,647	8,493	10	0
Black	885	434	154	0	0
American Indian, Eskimo, and Aleut	269	137	71	0	0
Asian or Pacific Islander	464	136	178	0	0
Other race	1,741	602	442	0	0
20 to 24 years old					
Men					
White	9,298	22,765	33,881	8,170	393
Black	374	1,199	1,385	129	0
American Indian, Eskimo, and Aleut	252	263	361	29	0
Asian or Pacific Islander	242	297	829	226	0
Other race	2,771	2,084	1,489	97	0
Women					
White	5,766	20,204	35,636	10,528	389

[Continued]

★ 728 ★

Educational Attainment in Colorado, by Selected Characteristics
[Continued]

Characteristic	Not high school graduate	High school graduate	Some college or associate's degree	Bachelor's degree	Graduate or professional degree
Black	336	1,146	1,619	204	16
American Indian, Eskimo, and Aleut	160	248	486	52	0
Asian or Pacific Islander	275	330	608	209	0
Other race	1,256	1,689	1,480	127	6
25 to 29 years old					
Men					
White	11,388	30,638	37,321	25,168	5,216
Black	627	1,346	1,825	769	118
American Indian, Eskimo, and Aleut	230	411	416	88	23
Asian or Pacific Islander	246	417	664	509	318
Other race	3,034	2,578	1,583	375	78
Women					
White	6,675	24,666	37,091	26,291	3,985
Black	349	1,175	2,093	607	94
American Indian, Eskimo, and Aleut	149	358	430	171	19
Asian or Pacific Islander	201	404	597	503	225
Other race	1,329	2,039	1,443	531	77
30 to 34 years old					
Men					
White	10,473	34,744	45,479	30,797	11,823
Black	546	1,460	2,046	878	222
American Indian, Eskimo, and Aleut	216	339	394	98	41
Asian or Pacific Islander	300	420	791	490	382
Other race	2,711	2,433	2,028	493	163
Women					
White	7,217	28,454	41,499	26,618	8,561
Black	498	1,260	2,209	780	209
American Indian, Eskimo, and Aleut	167	310	373	94	34
Asian or Pacific Islander	399	647	677	491	321
Other race	1,468	1,868	1,794	476	107
35 to 39 years old					
Men					
White	7,555	25,939	45,330	31,888	16,715
Black	566	855	1,765	760	305
American Indian, Eskimo, and Aleut	156	427	404	65	101
Asian or Pacific Islander	187	320	542	526	479
Other race	1,919	1,782	1,770	445	208
Women					
White	4,891	24,292	41,846	24,065	11,730
Black	423	1,049	1,879	683	212
American Indian, Eskimo, and Aleut	140	247	460	54	67
Asian or Pacific Islander	551	460	575	489	301
Other race	1,408	1,877	1,389	236	105

[Continued]

★ 728 ★

Educational Attainment in Colorado, by Selected Characteristics

[Continued]

Characteristic	Not high school graduate	High school graduate	Some college or associate's degree	Bachelor's degree	Graduate or professional degree
40 to 69 years old					
Men					
White	32,678	74,324	102,018	74,824	58,166
Black	1,833	2,926	4,444	1,526	1,010
American Indian, Eskimo, and Aleut	633	581	738	204	222
Asian or Pacific Islander	570	927	1,107	1,049	1,173
Other race	5,796	3,123	2,790	675	469
Women					
White	24,362	80,628	95,178	48,511	30,849
Black	1,479	3,093	3,530	1,180	882
American Indian, Eskimo, and Aleut	505	565	687	183	120
Asian or Pacific Islander	1,432	1,642	1,142	789	468
Other race	4,145	3,013	1,952	343	267
70 years old and older					
Men					
White	2,642	2,385	2,151	1,366	1,294
Black	76	43	62	22	8
American Indian, Eskimo, and Aleut	10	3	7	0	0
Asian or Pacific Islander	55	46	53	21	24
Other race	79	9	18	2	0
Women					
White	1,657	2,005	1,558	640	397
Black	50	21	68	8	6
American Indian, Eskimo, and Aleut	3	4	6	0	0
Asian or Pacific Islander	52	33	0	0	1
Other race	48	0	7	0	1

Source: Census of Population and Housing, 1990: Equal Employment Opportunity (EEO) File on CD-ROM [machine-readable datafiles]. Prepared by the Bureau of the Census. Washington, DC: The Bureau, 1992.

★ 729 ★

Educational Attainment

Educational Attainment in Connecticut, by Selected Characteristics

Table presents the number of civilians 16 years old or older who reported their educational backgrounds during the 1990 Census. Data show the number of individuals achieving various levels of education. Figures are reported by sex, age, and race.

Characteristic	Not high school graduate	High school graduate	Some college or associate's degree	Bachelor's degree	Graduate or professional degree
16 to 19 years old					
Men					
White	25,386	8,539	5,993	38	0
Black	2,462	1,222	505	5	0
American Indian, Eskimo, and Aleut	70	16	0	0	0
Asian or Pacific Islander	406	215	172	0	0
Other race	1,381	283	213	0	0
Women					
White	22,489	9,317	8,577	105	0
Black	2,218	1,165	689	0	0
American Indian, Eskimo, and Aleut	47	26	5	0	0
Asian or Pacific Islander	481	137	181	5	0
Other race	903	355	187	0	0
20 to 24 years old					
Men					
White	9,947	30,764	27,102	13,035	757
Black	1,639	3,753	2,849	615	18
American Indian, Eskimo, and Aleut	121	81	50	53	10
Asian or Pacific Islander	177	445	615	304	74
Other race	1,574	1,565	742	80	18
Women					
White	5,077	22,487	33,220	16,614	849
Black	995	3,624	3,824	666	64
American Indian, Eskimo, and Aleut	30	100	108	9	7
Asian or Pacific Islander	154	275	510	323	39
Other race	760	1,130	892	129	34
25 to 29 years old					
Men					
White	10,698	36,857	28,878	28,524	6,923
Black	2,004	4,039	2,625	1,118	288
American Indian, Eskimo, and Aleut	75	150	97	11	0
Asian or Pacific Islander	282	248	461	526	728
Other race	1,443	1,320	1,034	249	156
Women					
White	5,392	24,436	31,103	30,078	6,951
Black	1,446	3,728	3,509	1,347	318
American Indian, Eskimo, and Aleut	91	48	102	16	0
Asian or Pacific Islander	177	298	384	703	387
Other race	735	857	963	351	44
30 to 34 years old					
Men					
White	11,224	34,779	32,692	29,515	14,936

[Continued]

★ 729 ★

Educational Attainment in Connecticut, by Selected Characteristics
[Continued]

Characteristic	Not high school graduate	High school graduate	Some college or associate's degree	Bachelor's degree	Graduate or professional degree
Black	1,845	3,516	2,635	1,193	528
American Indian, Eskimo, and Aleut	63	121	102	5	44
Asian or Pacific Islander	327	392	550	632	747
Other race	1,147	1,215	731	206	141
Women					
White	5,777	26,284	31,512	24,382	11,903
Black	1,446	3,428	3,485	1,346	553
American Indian, Eskimo, and Aleut	25	86	84	17	42
Asian or Pacific Islander	330	261	318	442	429
Other race	785	852	671	219	101
35 to 39 years old					
Men					
White	8,396	25,389	30,717	25,867	18,999
Black	1,691	2,319	2,533	1,007	532
American Indian, Eskimo, and Aleut	60	105	83	41	14
Asian or Pacific Islander	273	252	303	490	846
Other race	1,141	727	457	158	98
Women					
White	5,402	23,269	28,206	18,818	15,690
Black	1,226	2,590	2,915	1,088	637
American Indian, Eskimo, and Aleut	40	102	115	23	0
Asian or Pacific Islander	287	239	307	461	408
Other race	800	498	407	202	108
40 to 69 years old					
Men					
White	56,753	92,339	78,999	72,525	69,706
Black	8,925	7,804	3,981	1,594	1,836
American Indian, Eskimo, and Aleut	146	168	107	73	59
Asian or Pacific Islander	760	540	778	1,031	2,292
Other race	3,665	1,213	476	194	284
Women					
White	41,077	108,461	80,176	40,129	43,392
Black	7,846	9,901	5,974	1,610	2,047
American Indian, Eskimo, and Aleut	147	238	187	47	66
Asian or Pacific Islander	841	603	664	883	810
Other race	2,867	1,048	562	96	138
70 years old and older					
Men					
White	4,835	4,267	2,499	1,856	2,014
Black	392	171	41	7	29
American Indian, Eskimo, and Aleut	6	0	0	0	0
Asian or Pacific Islander	12	5	15	6	16
Other race	17	14	0	0	0

[Continued]

★ 729 ★

Educational Attainment in Connecticut, by Selected Characteristics
[Continued]

Characteristic	Not high school graduate	High school graduate	Some college or associate's degree	Bachelor's degree	Graduate or professional degree
Women					
White	3,578	4,074	1,735	771	700
Black	402	215	77	17	16
American Indian, Eskimo, and Aleut	11	33	0	0	0
Asian or Pacific Islander	20	23	21	9	8
Other race	9	15	0	0	0

Source: Census of Population and Housing, 1990: Equal Employment Opportunity (EEO) File on CD-ROM [machine-readable datafiles]. Prepared by the Bureau of the Census. Washington, DC: The Bureau, 1992.

★ 730 ★
Educational Attainment

Educational Attainment in Delaware, by Selected Characteristics

Table presents the number of civilians 16 years old or older who reported their educational backgrounds during the 1990 Census. Data show the number of individuals achieving various levels of education. Figures are reported by sex, age, and race.

Characteristic	Not high school graduate	High school graduate	Some college or associate's degree	Bachelor's degree	Graduate or professional degree
16 to 19 years old					
Men					
White	4,949	1,674	1,367	0	0
Black	1,117	415	284	0	0
American Indian, Eskimo, and Aleut	10	0	0	0	0
Asian or Pacific Islander	67	21	16	2	0
Other race	122	24	0	0	0
Women					
White	4,077	2,140	1,895	33	0
Black	844	509	296	0	0
American Indian, Eskimo, and Aleut	35	17	6	0	0
Asian or Pacific Islander	40	17	16	0	0
Other race	56	71	8	0	0
20 to 24 years old					
Men					
White	2,347	6,304	5,474	1,841	61
Black	728	1,516	793	203	0
American Indian, Eskimo, and Aleut	0	16	20	9	0
Asian or Pacific Islander	28	8	103	59	11
Other race	251	108	85	0	0
Women					
White	1,052	5,686	6,695	2,579	93

[Continued]

★ 730 ★

Educational Attainment in Delaware, by Selected Characteristics

[Continued]

Characteristic	Not high school graduate	High school graduate	Some college or associate's degree	Bachelor's degree	Graduate or professional degree
Black	407	1,657	1,309	216	6
American Indian, Eskimo, and Aleut	13	15	0	0	0
Asian or Pacific Islander	10	32	100	33	8
Other race	19	59	125	0	0
25 to 29 years old					
Men					
White	2,801	7,924	5,203	4,388	999
Black	819	1,686	889	324	40
American Indian, Eskimo, and Aleut	10	46	0	0	0
Asian or Pacific Islander	18	26	30	125	103
Other race	261	43	58	23	18
Women					
White	1,348	6,040	6,341	4,633	750
Black	692	1,907	1,227	468	72
American Indian, Eskimo, and Aleut	3	49	6	1	0
Asian or Pacific Islander	44	55	77	80	50
Other race	70	146	134	33	5
30 to 34 years old					
Men					
White	2,383	7,650	6,156	4,209	2,155
Black	847	1,475	846	320	183
American Indian, Eskimo, and Aleut	13	56	28	15	0
Asian or Pacific Islander	28	36	49	112	167
Other race	173	36	59	22	7
Women					
White	1,243	5,490	6,083	4,004	1,453
Black	756	1,513	1,397	409	167
American Indian, Eskimo, and Aleut	17	37	45	14	0
Asian or Pacific Islander	51	70	56	75	52
Other race	43	99	57	6	10
35 to 39 years old					
Men					
White	1,611	5,883	5,571	3,972	2,304
Black	651	1,285	1,030	333	146
American Indian, Eskimo, and Aleut	25	30	56	0	0
Asian or Pacific Islander	35	33	26	88	144
Other race	183	44	65	0	0
Women					
White	1,046	5,894	5,250	3,134	1,710
Black	805	1,494	1,223	359	166
American Indian, Eskimo, and Aleut	0	6	17	8	0
Asian or Pacific Islander	20	61	78	119	62
Other race	65	96	22	0	15

[Continued]

★ 730 ★

Educational Attainment in Delaware, by Selected Characteristics
[Continued]

Characteristic	Not high school graduate	High school graduate	Some college or associate's degree	Bachelor's degree	Graduate or professional degree
40 to 69 years old					
Men					
White	10,856	18,623	14,818	10,154	9,651
Black	3,447	2,680	1,532	706	647
American Indian, Eskimo, and Aleut	121	49	66	16	52
Asian or Pacific Islander	90	81	69	177	619
Other race	311	106	53	35	18
Women					
White	7,146	20,568	13,841	6,938	4,249
Black	2,900	3,257	2,431	835	560
American Indian, Eskimo, and Aleut	71	116	62	6	18
Asian or Pacific Islander	198	225	107	238	213
Other race	230	42	38	0	25
70 years old and older					
Men					
White	743	401	397	275	290
Black	230	47	2	6	13
American Indian, Eskimo, and Aleut	5	0	0	0	0
Asian or Pacific Islander	5	0	0	12	0
Other race	8	0	0	0	0
Women					
White	419	462	304	212	70
Black	162	44	60	9	3
American Indian, Eskimo, and Aleut	0	0	0	0	0
Asian or Pacific Islander	0	6	7	0	0
Other race	0	0	0	0	0

Source: Census of Population and Housing, 1990: Equal Employment Opportunity (EEO) File on CD-ROM [machine-readable datafiles]. Prepared by the Bureau of the Census. Washington, DC: The Bureau, 1992.

★ 731 ★
Educational Attainment

Educational Attainment in District of Columbia, by Selected Characteristics

Table presents the number of civilians 16 years old or older who reported their educational backgrounds during the 1990 Census. Data show the number of individuals achieving various levels of education. Figures are reported by sex, age, and race.

Characteristic	Not high school graduate	High school graduate	Some college or associate's degree	Bachelor's degree	Graduate or professional degree
16 to 19 years old					
Men					
White	554	344	784	0	0
Black	2,743	965	638	0	0
American Indian, Eskimo, and Aleut	38	9	0	0	0
Asian or Pacific Islander	30	72	67	0	0
Other race	300	71	68	0	0
Women					
White	313	543	1,287	0	0
Black	2,369	1,252	1,003	0	0
American Indian, Eskimo, and Aleut	0	6	0	0	0
Asian or Pacific Islander	46	89	69	0	0
Other race	248	22	15	0	0
20 to 24 years old					
Men					
White	492	393	2,219	3,373	410
Black	2,693	3,769	3,073	379	73
American Indian, Eskimo, and Aleut	29	12	21	6	0
Asian or Pacific Islander	38	25	182	183	0
Other race	580	187	172	31	10
Women					
White	247	690	2,910	4,891	178
Black	2,030	4,478	4,301	1,069	101
American Indian, Eskimo, and Aleut	0	11	0	7	0
Asian or Pacific Islander	35	25	156	254	12
Other race	179	99	130	48	0
25 to 29 years old					
Men					
White	518	340	1,357	4,846	3,167
Black	3,236	4,606	4,064	1,551	470
American Indian, Eskimo, and Aleut	26	16	0	0	0
Asian or Pacific Islander	124	18	123	197	154
Other race	561	218	129	78	39
Women					
White	254	287	851	5,579	2,925
Black	2,284	4,544	4,634	2,353	563
American Indian, Eskimo, and Aleut	8	0	0	21	0
Asian or Pacific Islander	26	44	62	249	114
Other race	388	38	96	156	19
30 to 34 years old					
Men					
White	436	484	1,064	3,113	4,476

[Continued]

★ 731 ★

Educational Attainment in District of Columbia, by Selected Characteristics

[Continued]

Characteristic	Not high school graduate	High school graduate	Some college or associate's degree	Bachelor's degree	Graduate or professional degree
Black	3,126	3,838	3,593	1,586	917
American Indian, Eskimo, and Aleut	11	14	11	20	0
Asian or Pacific Islander	69	37	62	67	209
Other race	578	103	84	85	147
Women					
White	281	291	970	3,235	3,433
Black	2,295	4,178	4,991	2,474	1,051
American Indian, Eskimo, and Aleut	0	19	35	0	9
Asian or Pacific Islander	54	82	120	214	170
Other race	411	74	90	55	64
35 to 39 years old					
Men					
White	379	350	1,174	2,281	3,829
Black	2,799	3,386	2,960	1,242	1,150
American Indian, Eskimo, and Aleut	14	26	22	5	0
Asian or Pacific Islander	93	21	97	76	163
Other race	257	81	42	83	94
Women					
White	214	283	807	2,143	3,358
Black	2,112	3,893	4,204	1,857	1,596
American Indian, Eskimo, and Aleut	13	23	8	0	7
Asian or Pacific Islander	98	59	106	105	113
Other race	324	96	65	71	53
40 to 69 years old					
Men					
White	1,010	1,017	2,156	5,037	13,572
Black	11,774	10,127	6,769	3,351	3,634
American Indian, Eskimo, and Aleut	44	29	38	15	28
Asian or Pacific Islander	146	143	149	216	365
Other race	682	242	122	70	48
Women					
White	962	1,366	3,595	5,640	8,349
Black	11,443	13,281	9,311	3,900	4,172
American Indian, Eskimo, and Aleut	70	19	114	6	27
Asian or Pacific Islander	309	252	196	310	342
Other race	627	101	163	29	101
70 years old and older					
Men					
White	125	33	195	262	554
Black	674	378	122	122	177
American Indian, Eskimo, and Aleut	0	0	0	0	0
Asian or Pacific Islander	9	9	0	15	14
Other race	16	27	5	0	0

[Continued]

★ 731 ★

Educational Attainment in District of Columbia, by Selected Characteristics

[Continued]

Characteristic	Not high school graduate	High school graduate	Some college or associate's degree	Bachelor's degree	Graduate or professional degree
Women					
White	118	215	296	206	191
Black	864	481	193	66	79
American Indian, Eskimo, and Aleut	0	0	0	0	0
Asian or Pacific Islander	16	10	20	11	0
Other race	10	10	0	7	0

Source: Census of Population and Housing, 1990: Equal Employment Opportunity (EEO) File on CD-ROM [machine-readable datafiles]. Prepared by the Bureau of the Census. Washington, DC: The Bureau, 1992.

★ 732 ★

Educational Attainment

Educational Attainment in Florida, by Selected Characteristics

Table presents the number of civilians 16 years old or older who reported their educational backgrounds during the 1990 Census. Data show the number of individuals achieving various levels of education. Figures are reported by sex, age, and race.

Characteristic	Not high school graduate	High school graduate	Some college or associate's degree	Bachelor's degree	Graduate or professional degree
16 to 19 years old					
Men					
White	90,471	28,372	21,555	31	0
Black	16,168	4,442	2,229	0	5
American Indian, Eskimo, and Aleut	411	156	62	0	0
Asian or Pacific Islander	1,274	423	450	7	0
Other race	4,015	808	413	0	0
Women					
White	67,744	31,015	29,365	73	26
Black	13,484	5,957	4,523	21	0
American Indian, Eskimo, and Aleut	312	192	48	0	10
Asian or Pacific Islander	1,074	386	398	7	0
Other race	2,760	893	591	9	0
20 to 24 years old					
Men					
White	61,822	88,752	96,981	21,232	1,614
Black	12,170	16,866	11,577	1,364	102
American Indian, Eskimo, and Aleut	570	504	519	23	0
Asian or Pacific Islander	653	821	1,739	674	33
Other race	5,130	2,912	2,320	257	12
Women					
White	30,872	76,219	110,171	28,024	2,220

[Continued]

★ 732 ★

Educational Attainment in Florida, by Selected Characteristics

[Continued]

Characteristic	Not high school graduate	High school graduate	Some college or associate's degree	Bachelor's degree	Graduate or professional degree
Black	9,426	17,137	18,190	2,625	231
American Indian, Eskimo, and Aleut	284	383	369	32	0
Asian or Pacific Islander	535	925	1,896	753	75
Other race	1,915	2,074	3,023	393	49
25 to 29 years old					
Men					
White	64,989	121,168	121,596	62,511	14,327
Black	14,590	20,033	13,324	4,307	570
American Indian, Eskimo, and Aleut	599	679	548	182	61
Asian or Pacific Islander	680	1,053	1,837	1,441	742
Other race	5,194	3,045	3,384	974	416
Women					
White	31,533	92,227	123,763	62,326	12,783
Black	12,453	19,920	20,650	6,501	943
American Indian, Eskimo, and Aleut	420	379	479	92	24
Asian or Pacific Islander	677	1,143	1,565	1,328	470
Other race	2,228	2,075	3,181	1,077	295
30 to 34 years old					
Men					
White	60,108	119,195	126,310	70,533	28,485
Black	16,886	20,553	14,708	5,079	1,482
American Indian, Eskimo, and Aleut	458	714	557	152	42
Asian or Pacific Islander	766	1,030	1,581	1,495	1,109
Other race	4,155	2,051	3,029	955	449
Women					
White	33,095	97,071	122,108	57,360	19,066
Black	14,064	20,386	22,672	7,319	1,962
American Indian, Eskimo, and Aleut	314	407	806	164	59
Asian or Pacific Islander	1,122	955	1,487	1,647	598
Other race	2,231	1,624	2,305	711	314
35 to 39 years old					
Men					
White	44,250	89,942	119,356	66,540	36,644
Black	15,955	14,792	12,769	4,498	1,881
American Indian, Eskimo, and Aleut	392	519	645	217	62
Asian or Pacific Islander	801	1,121	1,482	1,248	1,394
Other race	3,794	1,651	2,001	699	457
Women					
White	28,973	87,928	109,082	49,548	24,492
Black	13,687	16,414	17,305	6,383	2,820
American Indian, Eskimo, and Aleut	232	444	555	178	67
Asian or Pacific Islander	1,323	1,615	1,631	1,628	762
Other race	2,442	1,637	1,892	726	317

[Continued]

★ 732 ★

Educational Attainment in Florida, by Selected Characteristics
[Continued]

Characteristic	Not high school graduate	High school graduate	Some college or associate's degree	Bachelor's degree	Graduate or professional degree
40 to 69 years old					
Men					
White	220,579	304,821	336,765	197,832	143,122
Black	65,176	31,313	22,649	8,252	6,559
American Indian, Eskimo, and Aleut	1,318	1,042	1,373	505	369
Asian or Pacific Islander	2,513	2,767	3,232	3,013	3,889
Other race	12,300	3,787	3,079	1,566	1,113
Women					
White	164,368	347,544	298,042	111,043	73,790
Black	53,033	38,766	28,930	10,747	8,013
American Indian, Eskimo, and Aleut	1,007	1,070	1,114	197	215
Asian or Pacific Islander	4,343	3,947	3,029	2,650	1,539
Other race	7,992	3,980	2,507	851	586
70 years old and older					
Men					
White	18,440	15,219	13,692	7,189	7,627
Black	2,778	582	178	127	176
American Indian, Eskimo, and Aleut	50	7	11	9	0
Asian or Pacific Islander	81	45	54	31	40
Other race	392	57	55	12	30
Women					
White	11,220	13,670	7,903	2,598	1,805
Black	2,823	741	364	110	154
American Indian, Eskimo, and Aleut	20	23	12	0	8
Asian or Pacific Islander	63	19	4	8	8
Other race	89	23	58	27	17

Source: Census of Population and Housing, 1990: Equal Employment Opportunity (EEO) File on CD-ROM [machine-readable datafiles]. Prepared by the Bureau of the Census. Washington, DC: The Bureau, 1992.

★ 733 ★

Educational Attainment

Educational Attainment in Georgia, by Selected Characteristics

Table presents the number of civilians 16 years old or older who reported their educational backgrounds during the 1990 Census. Data show the number of individuals achieving various levels of education. Figures are reported by sex, age, and race.

Characteristic	Not high school graduate	High school graduate	Some college or associate's degree	Bachelor's degree	Graduate or professional degree
16 to 19 years old					
Men					
White	47,998	14,668	10,324	19	0
Black	16,597	5,211	2,213	0	0
American Indian, Eskimo, and Aleut	171	74	7	0	0
Asian or Pacific Islander	640	147	116	0	0
Other race	913	107	71	0	0
Women					
White	35,765	16,019	14,041	35	0
Black	13,980	6,775	4,154	15	0
American Indian, Eskimo, and Aleut	69	19	26	0	0
Asian or Pacific Islander	536	221	122	0	0
Other race	329	108	78	0	0
20 to 24 years old					
Men					
White	29,577	48,551	44,682	14,034	800
Black	11,458	21,641	12,145	1,567	42
American Indian, Eskimo, and Aleut	161	174	167	5	0
Asian or Pacific Islander	367	703	753	229	71
Other race	2,467	687	369	57	6
Women					
White	15,326	41,008	49,343	19,162	1,114
Black	8,572	20,980	20,182	3,673	173
American Indian, Eskimo, and Aleut	80	98	160	57	0
Asian or Pacific Islander	261	471	508	397	47
Other race	294	315	390	169	9
25 to 29 years old					
Men					
White	32,186	59,968	48,198	38,068	8,045
Black	12,823	25,831	15,581	5,812	791
American Indian, Eskimo, and Aleut	180	271	166	31	24
Asian or Pacific Islander	448	593	523	652	547
Other race	1,884	502	565	255	95
Women					
White	16,209	46,084	45,903	38,648	7,115
Black	10,190	23,967	22,760	10,218	1,342
American Indian, Eskimo, and Aleut	130	227	175	82	17
Asian or Pacific Islander	491	459	575	546	243
Other race	332	265	419	127	58
30 to 34 years old					
Men					
White	30,104	57,553	49,307	38,330	14,891

[Continued]

★ 733 ★

Educational Attainment in Georgia, by Selected Characteristics
[Continued]

Characteristic	Not high school graduate	High school graduate	Some college or associate's degree	Bachelor's degree	Graduate or professional degree
Black	13,813	23,204	14,223	6,063	1,810
American Indian, Eskimo, and Aleut	187	178	144	27	76
Asian or Pacific Islander	657	487	827	848	876
Other race	1,291	385	465	227	66
Women					
White	17,394	50,224	46,898	29,327	11,923
Black	11,796	24,377	20,988	9,647	2,695
American Indian, Eskimo, and Aleut	92	182	170	56	2
Asian or Pacific Islander	537	681	533	722	354
Other race	417	276	307	131	41
35 to 39 years old					
Men					
White	24,064	46,731	47,517	35,624	19,525
Black	13,377	18,245	11,733	5,024	2,429
American Indian, Eskimo, and Aleut	75	161	276	85	33
Asian or Pacific Islander	468	358	510	913	794
Other race	693	214	236	89	147
Women					
White	15,408	48,125	42,771	24,481	16,000
Black	12,324	21,642	17,046	7,376	3,805
American Indian, Eskimo, and Aleut	136	160	262	63	24
Asian or Pacific Islander	782	836	538	617	397
Other race	233	188	173	37	17
40 to 69 years old					
Men					
White	111,962	148,354	132,264	97,001	66,348
Black	53,322	33,740	19,943	8,041	6,404
American Indian, Eskimo, and Aleut	404	428	577	150	130
Asian or Pacific Islander	1,209	1,227	1,170	1,840	2,153
Other race	1,296	390	430	155	90
Women					
White	80,525	162,418	109,754	48,923	36,832
Black	50,703	39,501	23,506	9,745	9,185
American Indian, Eskimo, and Aleut	207	354	399	84	78
Asian or Pacific Islander	1,711	1,683	918	1,226	646
Other race	480	305	339	101	64
70 years old and older					
Men					
White	6,834	3,411	2,849	1,841	1,608
Black	2,603	472	140	90	132
American Indian, Eskimo, and Aleut	0	0	7	0	0
Asian or Pacific Islander	47	18	0	2	15
Other race	3	0	0	0	0

[Continued]

★ 733 ★

Educational Attainment in Georgia, by Selected Characteristics

[Continued]

Characteristic	Not high school graduate	High school graduate	Some college or associate's degree	Bachelor's degree	Graduate or professional degree
Women					
White	4,837	3,438	1,951	842	514
Black	2,588	635	226	103	130
American Indian, Eskimo, and Aleut	30	0	0	0	0
Asian or Pacific Islander	24	4	2	0	3
Other race	2	0	0	0	0

Source: Census of Population and Housing, 1990: Equal Employment Opportunity (EEO) File on CD-ROM [machine-readable datafiles]. Prepared by the Bureau of the Census. Washington, DC: The Bureau, 1992.

★ 734 ★

Educational Attainment

Educational Attainment in Hawaii, by Selected Characteristics

Table presents the number of civilians 16 years old or older who reported their educational backgrounds during the 1990 Census. Data show the number of individuals achieving various levels of education. Figures are reported by sex, age, and race.

Characteristic	Not high school graduate	High school graduate	Some college or associate's degree	Bachelor's degree	Graduate or professional degree
16 to 19 years old					
Men					
White	2,074	1,155	609	0	0
Black	100	24	36	0	0
American Indian, Eskimo, and Aleut	57	13	8	0	0
Asian or Pacific Islander	5,081	3,037	1,726	11	0
Other race	146	80	43	0	0
Women					
White	1,721	874	908	7	0
Black	52	39	36	0	0
American Indian, Eskimo, and Aleut	15	26	0	0	0
Asian or Pacific Islander	4,175	2,857	2,312	21	0
Other race	110	59	65	0	0
20 to 24 years old					
Men					
White	740	3,397	3,062	582	32
Black	55	214	171	25	0
American Indian, Eskimo, and Aleut	25	63	39	0	0
Asian or Pacific Islander	1,968	8,606	7,506	1,401	35
Other race	58	317	184	0	0
Women					
White	375	3,069	4,096	845	47

[Continued]

★ 734 ★

Educational Attainment in Hawaii, by Selected Characteristics

[Continued]

Characteristic	Not high school graduate	High school graduate	Some college or associate's degree	Bachelor's degree	Graduate or professional degree
Black	58	277	299	49	9
American Indian, Eskimo, and Aleut	6	33	95	0	0
Asian or Pacific Islander	954	5,908	8,480	1,796	95
Other race	36	150	262	11	0
25 to 29 years old					
Men					
White	824	4,052	4,362	2,341	562
Black	27	286	319	35	7
American Indian, Eskimo, and Aleut	28	72	52	50	4
Asian or Pacific Islander	2,271	8,747	8,181	4,068	686
Other race	109	286	126	65	19
Women					
White	468	2,925	4,544	2,670	649
Black	31	260	589	122	17
American Indian, Eskimo, and Aleut	39	59	92	8	0
Asian or Pacific Islander	1,416	6,005	8,087	5,063	896
Other race	36	222	248	93	7
30 to 34 years old					
Men					
White	918	3,721	4,965	3,102	1,534
Black	55	202	377	62	37
American Indian, Eskimo, and Aleut	24	66	95	15	17
Asian or Pacific Islander	2,560	7,984	8,630	4,538	1,861
Other race	115	286	287	79	14
Women					
White	580	2,933	5,357	2,465	920
Black	41	106	393	113	30
American Indian, Eskimo, and Aleut	29	60	57	5	10
Asian or Pacific Islander	2,001	5,961	9,000	5,365	1,251
Other race	53	191	279	48	5
35 to 39 years old					
Men					
White	816	2,802	6,311	3,016	1,841
Black	21	167	245	69	28
American Indian, Eskimo, and Aleut	25	79	99	10	33
Asian or Pacific Islander	2,623	6,116	8,342	5,247	1,957
Other race	65	299	307	69	0
Women					
White	482	2,912	5,202	3,108	1,455
Black	7	107	183	96	42
American Indian, Eskimo, and Aleut	26	20	104	68	22
Asian or Pacific Islander	2,420	5,234	8,099	5,888	1,689
Other race	73	202	191	82	49

[Continued]

★ 734 ★

Educational Attainment in Hawaii, by Selected Characteristics
[Continued]

Characteristic	Not high school graduate	High school graduate	Some college or associate's degree	Bachelor's degree	Graduate or professional degree
40 to 69 years old					
Men					
White	3,334	7,765	12,587	8,909	8,543
Black	66	186	405	165	138
American Indian, Eskimo, and Aleut	57	38	174	81	72
Asian or Pacific Islander	13,773	24,705	19,716	12,880	5,809
Other race	452	483	297	100	87
Women					
White	2,235	7,350	11,235	6,532	4,665
Black	19	132	197	120	99
American Indian, Eskimo, and Aleut	77	118	195	50	50
Asian or Pacific Islander	15,269	24,765	18,216	11,461	4,027
Other race	289	343	260	31	10
70 years old and older					
Men					
White	246	330	378	189	341
Black	6	0	13	0	0
American Indian, Eskimo, and Aleut	5	0	0	0	0
Asian or Pacific Islander	1,729	935	273	261	249
Other race	31	0	12	0	0
Women					
White	118	168	274	94	130
Black	0	0	6	0	0
American Indian, Eskimo, and Aleut	0	0	7	0	0
Asian or Pacific Islander	1,074	464	129	82	55
Other race	0	4	0	0	0

Source: Census of Population and Housing, 1990: Equal Employment Opportunity (EEO) File on CD-ROM [machine-readable datafiles]. Prepared by the Bureau of the Census. Washington, DC: The Bureau, 1992.

★ 735 ★

Educational Attainment

Educational Attainment in Idaho, by Selected Characteristics

Table presents the number of civilians 16 years old or older who reported their educational backgrounds during the 1990 Census. Data show the number of individuals achieving various levels of education. Figures are reported by sex, age, and race.

Characteristic	Not high school graduate	High school graduate	Some college or associate's degree	Bachelor's degree	Graduate or professional degree
16 to 19 years old					
Men					
White	11,456	3,099	2,228	0	4
Black	24	5	9	0	0
American Indian, Eskimo, and Aleut	178	67	22	0	0
Asian or Pacific Islander	160	42	0	0	0
Other race	625	130	46	0	0
Women					
White	8,870	3,286	3,521	18	0
Black	30	12	0	0	0
American Indian, Eskimo, and Aleut	125	17	49	0	0
Asian or Pacific Islander	60	42	14	0	0
Other race	343	77	30	0	0
20 to 24 years old					
Men					
White	3,783	8,258	10,385	1,135	63
Black	6	10	81	17	0
American Indian, Eskimo, and Aleut	220	205	156	0	0
Asian or Pacific Islander	44	68	135	20	2
Other race	927	404	173	14	5
Women					
White	1,840	6,654	10,786	1,487	90
Black	7	20	46	30	0
American Indian, Eskimo, and Aleut	70	101	181	7	0
Asian or Pacific Islander	41	51	109	0	0
Other race	319	298	188	0	0
25 to 29 years old					
Men					
White	3,961	9,969	11,054	3,722	701
Black	6	27	99	37	0
American Indian, Eskimo, and Aleut	180	280	122	4	2
Asian or Pacific Islander	45	38	135	60	49
Other race	1,381	309	156	21	12
Women					
White	2,573	7,804	9,311	3,391	393
Black	18	24	33	9	7
American Indian, Eskimo, and Aleut	129	166	163	32	0
Asian or Pacific Islander	26	68	74	66	8
Other race	415	249	85	36	0
30 to 34 years old					
Men					
White	4,666	11,163	11,959	5,642	1,867

[Continued]

★ 735 ★

Educational Attainment in Idaho, by Selected Characteristics
[Continued]

Characteristic	Not high school graduate	High school graduate	Some college or associate's degree	Bachelor's degree	Graduate or professional degree
Black	7	27	75	9	10
American Indian, Eskimo, and Aleut	140	164	162	33	15
Asian or Pacific Islander	63	48	82	66	112
Other race	1,005	214	252	40	20
Women					
White	2,620	8,937	11,410	3,918	1,059
Black	14	44	28	12	0
American Indian, Eskimo, and Aleut	102	138	165	20	6
Asian or Pacific Islander	106	66	69	54	9
Other race	363	225	182	11	0
35 to 39 years old					
Men					
White	2,678	8,949	14,074	6,483	3,295
Black	0	15	85	31	9
American Indian, Eskimo, and Aleut	89	166	116	46	7
Asian or Pacific Islander	12	84	90	112	73
Other race	643	185	116	32	12
Women					
White	1,860	7,916	12,292	4,514	1,627
Black	0	38	14	4	20
American Indian, Eskimo, and Aleut	47	175	170	13	0
Asian or Pacific Islander	86	81	119	89	12
Other race	339	166	101	10	0
40 to 69 years old					
Men					
White	14,937	28,082	32,992	17,469	11,538
Black	24	94	64	39	17
American Indian, Eskimo, and Aleut	323	311	369	81	53
Asian or Pacific Islander	102	144	151	136	80
Other race	1,549	187	205	78	62
Women					
White	9,576	26,592	28,348	10,261	4,532
Black	15	57	48	12	5
American Indian, Eskimo, and Aleut	188	308	375	58	14
Asian or Pacific Islander	146	226	186	28	49
Other race	766	245	64	23	14
70 years old and older					
Men					
White	1,563	1,129	1,043	351	337
Black	0	0	0	0	0
American Indian, Eskimo, and Aleut	18	2	14	0	0
Asian or Pacific Islander	22	25	9	0	0
Other race	14	7	0	0	0

[Continued]

★ 735 ★

Educational Attainment in Idaho, by Selected Characteristics

[Continued]

Characteristic	Not high school graduate	High school graduate	Some college or associate's degree	Bachelor's degree	Graduate or professional degree
Women					
White	550	588	567	221	81
Black	0	0	0	0	0
American Indian, Eskimo, and Aleut	4	2	7	0	8
Asian or Pacific Islander	12	7	0	0	0
Other race	0	0	0	0	0

Source: Census of Population and Housing, 1990: Equal Employment Opportunity (EEO) File on CD-ROM [machine-readable datafiles]. Prepared by the Bureau of the Census. Washington, DC: The Bureau, 1992.

★ 736 ★

Educational Attainment

Educational Attainment in Illinois, by Selected Characteristics

Table presents the number of civilians 16 years old or older who reported their educational backgrounds during the 1990 Census. Data show the number of individuals achieving various levels of education. Figures are reported by sex, age, and race.

Characteristic	Not high school graduate	High school graduate	Some college or associate's degree	Bachelor's degree	Graduate or professional degree
16 to 19 years old					
Men					
White	78,484	30,029	26,526	68	8
Black	15,763	5,281	3,041	23	0
American Indian, Eskimo, and Aleut	283	102	42	0	0
Asian or Pacific Islander	2,083	655	941	14	0
Other race	9,124	2,409	990	0	0
Women					
White	67,864	30,003	31,787	65	14
Black	12,302	5,892	5,122	6	6
American Indian, Eskimo, and Aleut	264	93	89	0	0
Asian or Pacific Islander	1,656	617	1,065	6	0
Other race	5,382	1,642	1,309	4	0
20 to 24 years old					
Men					
White	32,578	80,968	103,604	39,047	2,073
Black	10,394	15,851	15,236	1,981	183
American Indian, Eskimo, and Aleut	251	320	409	42	15
Asian or Pacific Islander	634	1,202	3,483	1,649	269
Other race	14,292	7,444	4,997	572	38
Women					
White	16,517	63,805	111,166	45,953	2,350

[Continued]

★ 736 ★

Educational Attainment in Illinois, by Selected Characteristics

[Continued]

Characteristic	Not high school graduate	High school graduate	Some college or associate's degree	Bachelor's degree	Graduate or professional degree
Black	6,717	12,641	20,868	3,313	245
American Indian, Eskimo, and Aleut	170	204	219	31	0
Asian or Pacific Islander	466	1,160	3,323	1,551	137
Other race	4,760	4,169	5,089	527	72
25 to 29 years old					
Men					
White	36,871	102,494	106,035	85,042	22,413
Black	10,457	16,511	16,896	5,046	902
American Indian, Eskimo, and Aleut	186	359	285	78	38
Asian or Pacific Islander	849	1,137	2,659	3,312	2,243
Other race	13,995	6,479	5,050	1,167	470
Women					
White	19,007	75,507	102,238	79,387	17,081
Black	6,489	13,008	24,322	8,003	1,482
American Indian, Eskimo, and Aleut	140	196	340	114	17
Asian or Pacific Islander	659	1,079	2,331	3,298	1,242
Other race	5,881	3,610	3,716	1,163	326
30 to 34 years old					
Men					
White	37,988	111,502	117,323	74,453	35,931
Black	10,323	15,117	17,924	5,721	1,865
American Indian, Eskimo, and Aleut	246	260	392	77	87
Asian or Pacific Islander	1,039	1,511	2,855	3,501	3,254
Other race	13,737	4,958	4,245	886	396
Women					
White	20,708	86,015	100,549	60,470	25,875
Black	8,404	14,561	26,634	7,739	2,486
American Indian, Eskimo, and Aleut	195	253	343	48	30
Asian or Pacific Islander	1,084	1,242	2,291	3,201	1,613
Other race	6,119	2,994	3,322	735	167
35 to 39 years old					
Men					
White	30,077	85,984	110,470	69,329	43,763
Black	8,378	12,736	16,414	5,232	2,315
American Indian, Eskimo, and Aleut	188	259	339	169	29
Asian or Pacific Islander	1,082	1,305	2,582	3,949	2,850
Other race	10,762	3,361	2,481	618	406
Women					
White	18,545	79,460	91,892	51,149	29,275
Black	6,841	13,680	21,907	7,310	3,525
American Indian, Eskimo, and Aleut	129	223	265	108	83
Asian or Pacific Islander	1,420	1,518	2,123	4,173	1,672
Other race	6,244	2,378	2,035	502	393

[Continued]

★ 736 ★

Educational Attainment in Illinois, by Selected Characteristics
[Continued]

Characteristic	Not high school graduate	High school graduate	Some college or associate's degree	Bachelor's degree	Graduate or professional degree
40 to 69 years old					
Men					
White	171,467	313,323	274,586	171,940	144,153
Black	41,697	34,304	33,680	9,564	7,748
American Indian, Eskimo, and Aleut	617	662	795	174	229
Asian or Pacific Islander	3,552	3,749	6,185	10,969	10,683
Other race	24,965	5,186	3,560	706	743
Women					
White	111,672	320,793	238,751	107,975	77,227
Black	33,505	39,940	47,369	12,183	11,128
American Indian, Eskimo, and Aleut	497	643	549	176	157
Asian or Pacific Islander	4,294	4,556	5,369	9,994	4,362
Other race	12,676	4,245	2,702	746	425
70 years old and older					
Men					
White	12,087	10,374	7,839	4,216	5,295
Black	1,728	498	389	107	154
American Indian, Eskimo, and Aleut	13	15	0	0	0
Asian or Pacific Islander	161	121	126	77	67
Other race	351	34	17	0	16
Women					
White	8,972	9,979	5,308	2,071	1,707
Black	1,671	729	555	169	203
American Indian, Eskimo, and Aleut	9	7	5	0	0
Asian or Pacific Islander	82	54	43	49	8
Other race	178	24	55	8	19

Source: Census of Population and Housing, 1990: Equal Employment Opportunity (EEO) File on CD-ROM [machine-readable datafiles]. Prepared by the Bureau of the Census. Washington, DC: The Bureau, 1992.

★ 737 ★

Educational Attainment

Educational Attainment in Indiana, by Selected Characteristics

Table presents the number of civilians 16 years old or older who reported their educational backgrounds during the 1990 Census. Data show the number of individuals achieving various levels of education. Figures are reported by sex, age, and race.

Characteristic	Not high school graduate	High school graduate	Some college or associate's degree	Bachelor's degree	Graduate or professional degree
16 to 19 years old					
Men					
White	55,248	18,623	10,819	37	0
Black	4,605	1,538	677	0	0
American Indian, Eskimo, and Aleut	210	58	26	0	0
Asian or Pacific Islander	245	144	87	0	0
Other race	697	240	115	0	0
Women					
White	45,272	19,126	14,638	40	8
Black	3,747	1,806	1,411	0	0
American Indian, Eskimo, and Aleut	144	65	17	0	0
Asian or Pacific Islander	280	114	93	10	0
Other race	513	236	157	0	0
20 to 24 years old					
Men					
White	23,428	59,326	51,548	14,133	853
Black	2,435	4,203	3,477	281	27
American Indian, Eskimo, and Aleut	205	184	121	35	8
Asian or Pacific Islander	96	195	558	310	25
Other race	567	638	606	103	8
Women					
White	14,046	48,699	58,077	15,962	801
Black	1,862	4,245	5,001	529	44
American Indian, Eskimo, and Aleut	84	152	172	24	0
Asian or Pacific Islander	45	199	536	170	40
Other race	196	350	621	99	7
25 to 29 years old					
Men					
White	26,669	73,209	49,618	30,321	6,916
Black	2,618	5,232	3,978	1,068	171
American Indian, Eskimo, and Aleut	98	278	146	13	7
Asian or Pacific Islander	52	130	267	426	542
Other race	485	545	478	147	42
Women					
White	14,693	57,535	48,490	26,853	6,092
Black	2,141	4,907	6,167	1,622	253
American Indian, Eskimo, and Aleut	172	158	109	20	21
Asian or Pacific Islander	116	140	251	312	344
Other race	207	503	414	124	26
30 to 34 years old					
Men					
White	25,354	80,848	52,540	28,082	11,323

[Continued]

★ 737 ★

Educational Attainment in Indiana, by Selected Characteristics
[Continued]

Characteristic	Not high school graduate	High school graduate	Some college or associate's degree	Bachelor's degree	Graduate or professional degree
Black	2,461	5,346	4,441	1,233	331
American Indian, Eskimo, and Aleut	143	243	133	46	26
Asian or Pacific Islander	124	174	194	382	667
Other race	577	777	559	92	65
Women					
White	16,651	66,498	47,819	20,553	10,312
Black	2,239	5,614	6,348	1,416	490
American Indian, Eskimo, and Aleut	88	279	145	25	27
Asian or Pacific Islander	144	254	205	323	300
Other race	207	432	347	97	23
35 to 39 years old					
Men					
White	20,644	68,841	53,444	27,537	16,459
Black	2,281	4,018	3,940	1,101	572
American Indian, Eskimo, and Aleut	112	132	115	51	31
Asian or Pacific Islander	178	197	224	256	598
Other race	647	471	229	83	50
Women					
White	13,606	61,668	46,195	16,620	14,828
Black	1,918	4,304	5,680	1,188	777
American Indian, Eskimo, and Aleut	59	185	120	72	44
Asian or Pacific Islander	217	210	233	297	210
Other race	254	488	257	79	4
40 to 69 years old					
Men					
White	107,683	214,564	128,184	63,680	60,254
Black	10,519	10,591	7,984	2,174	1,686
American Indian, Eskimo, and Aleut	531	470	294	94	77
Asian or Pacific Islander	312	485	311	680	1,829
Other race	1,561	766	399	94	138
Women					
White	74,933	204,205	107,924	28,716	43,422
Black	9,453	12,055	9,222	1,611	2,851
American Indian, Eskimo, and Aleut	327	436	269	67	38
Asian or Pacific Islander	723	782	488	587	666
Other race	864	595	323	80	39
70 years old and older					
Men					
White	5,900	6,214	2,942	1,441	1,828
Black	451	235	121	22	49
American Indian, Eskimo, and Aleut	14	11	0	0	0
Asian or Pacific Islander	8	0	0	10	76
Other race	25	6	4	0	0

[Continued]

★ 737 ★

Educational Attainment in Indiana, by Selected Characteristics
[Continued]

Characteristic	Not high school graduate	High school graduate	Some college or associate's degree	Bachelor's degree	Graduate or professional degree
Women					
White	4,358	4,803	1,860	627	604
Black	515	206	105	14	40
American Indian, Eskimo, and Aleut	24	21	10	0	0
Asian or Pacific Islander	9	0	8	0	6
Other race	2	9	0	0	0

Source: Census of Population and Housing, 1990: Equal Employment Opportunity (EEO) File on CD-ROM [machine-readable datafiles]. Prepared by the Bureau of the Census. Washington, DC: The Bureau, 1992.

★ 738 ★
Educational Attainment

Educational Attainment in Iowa, by Selected Characteristics

Table presents the number of civilians 16 years old or older who reported their educational backgrounds during the 1990 Census. Data show the number of individuals achieving various levels of education. Figures are reported by sex, age, and race.

Characteristic	Not high school graduate	High school graduate	Some college or associate's degree	Bachelor's degree	Graduate or professional degree
16 to 19 years old					
Men					
White	28,620	9,394	8,051	33	5
Black	498	192	309	0	0
American Indian, Eskimo, and Aleut	143	15	0	0	0
Asian or Pacific Islander	282	51	102	10	0
Other race	180	43	33	0	0
Women					
White	25,218	9,705	10,333	22	2
Black	436	181	182	0	0
American Indian, Eskimo, and Aleut	57	53	10	0	0
Asian or Pacific Islander	274	96	132	0	0
Other race	193	59	64	0	0
20 to 24 years old					
Men					
White	6,303	26,457	35,101	7,448	270
Black	235	496	786	104	11
American Indian, Eskimo, and Aleut	80	95	45	0	0
Asian or Pacific Islander	220	180	406	215	34
Other race	368	218	265	15	0
Women					
White	3,212	19,929	38,726	8,832	341

[Continued]

★ 738 ★

Educational Attainment in Iowa, by Selected Characteristics
[Continued]

Characteristic	Not high school graduate	High school graduate	Some college or associate's degree	Bachelor's degree	Graduate or professional degree
Black	149	323	817	138	0
American Indian, Eskimo, and Aleut	59	61	61	18	0
Asian or Pacific Islander	110	195	377	99	16
Other race	107	157	174	18	0
25 to 29 years old					
Men					
White	7,983	36,056	28,534	15,615	2,602
Black	232	531	428	246	7
American Indian, Eskimo, and Aleut	92	95	69	0	0
Asian or Pacific Islander	101	160	174	274	356
Other race	242	182	146	23	47
Women					
White	4,349	26,831	31,002	15,221	2,461
Black	172	531	614	195	15
American Indian, Eskimo, and Aleut	57	59	80	29	2
Asian or Pacific Islander	153	91	222	229	126
Other race	45	135	163	29	25
30 to 34 years old					
Men					
White	8,911	42,026	30,394	15,714	5,117
Black	122	559	552	179	77
American Indian, Eskimo, and Aleut	45	100	84	53	0
Asian or Pacific Islander	134	126	97	127	594
Other race	263	195	90	39	34
Women					
White	4,970	32,010	31,863	14,088	3,702
Black	155	451	614	91	82
American Indian, Eskimo, and Aleut	40	51	118	17	0
Asian or Pacific Islander	151	89	117	104	135
Other race	72	88	94	22	20
35 to 39 years old					
Men					
White	5,884	34,525	32,198	17,765	8,280
Black	119	450	415	236	100
American Indian, Eskimo, and Aleut	42	91	72	32	21
Asian or Pacific Islander	131	77	89	70	293
Other race	142	140	122	21	7
Women					
White	3,932	30,276	30,595	14,859	5,077
Black	116	449	419	113	102
American Indian, Eskimo, and Aleut	34	80	43	13	11
Asian or Pacific Islander	195	126	133	83	121
Other race	62	135	59	14	17

[Continued]

★ 738 ★

Educational Attainment in Iowa, by Selected Characteristics
[Continued]

Characteristic	Not high school graduate	High school graduate	Some college or associate's degree	Bachelor's degree	Graduate or professional degree
40 to 69 years old					
Men					
White	48,265	123,256	67,953	38,792	30,383
Black	1,016	962	855	276	303
American Indian, Eskimo, and Aleut	180	217	156	33	29
Asian or Pacific Islander	347	204	225	203	589
Other race	408	192	127	44	23
Women					
White	28,508	112,976	67,353	29,260	13,997
Black	767	955	935	224	147
American Indian, Eskimo, and Aleut	165	145	94	56	29
Asian or Pacific Islander	507	248	172	149	292
Other race	204	226	58	30	37
70 years old and older					
Men					
White	5,219	4,829	1,949	961	960
Black	83	24	10	6	0
American Indian, Eskimo, and Aleut	8	0	8	0	0
Asian or Pacific Islander	0	0	0	0	0
Other race	22	11	0	0	0
Women					
White	2,776	3,487	1,490	531	338
Black	62	34	21	11	0
American Indian, Eskimo, and Aleut	5	0	0	0	0
Asian or Pacific Islander	3	9	0	0	0
Other race	5	0	0	0	7

Source: Census of Population and Housing, 1990: Equal Employment Opportunity (EEO) File on CD-ROM [machine-readable datafiles]. Prepared by the Bureau of the Census. Washington, DC: The Bureau, 1992.

★ 739 ★

Educational Attainment

Educational Attainment in Kansas, by Selected Characteristics

Table presents the number of civilians 16 years old or older who reported their educational backgrounds during the 1990 Census. Data show the number of individuals achieving various levels of education. Figures are reported by sex, age, and race.

Characteristic	Not high school graduate	High school graduate	Some college or associate's degree	Bachelor's degree	Graduate or professional degree
16 to 19 years old					
Men					
White	21,854	6,515	5,980	31	0
Black	1,149	480	387	0	0
American Indian, Eskimo, and Aleut	281	77	117	0	0
Asian or Pacific Islander	399	124	85	0	6
Other race	748	211	109	0	9
Women					
White	18,228	6,394	8,056	0	0
Black	1,071	433	390	0	0
American Indian, Eskimo, and Aleut	241	117	100	0	0
Asian or Pacific Islander	225	66	99	0	0
Other race	417	243	78	0	0
20 to 24 years old					
Men					
White	6,260	18,972	26,947	6,422	296
Black	783	1,139	1,347	134	11
American Indian, Eskimo, and Aleut	266	232	332	36	0
Asian or Pacific Islander	236	159	463	238	36
Other race	993	639	538	92	4
Women					
White	4,143	14,982	28,418	8,098	339
Black	491	1,310	1,768	188	5
American Indian, Eskimo, and Aleut	81	206	245	7	7
Asian or Pacific Islander	108	189	449	119	5
Other race	376	522	493	12	6
25 to 29 years old					
Men					
White	8,280	27,003	25,533	16,407	3,199
Black	722	1,496	1,546	448	43
American Indian, Eskimo, and Aleut	189	351	133	27	11
Asian or Pacific Islander	235	205	207	345	401
Other race	1,141	792	477	142	22
Women					
White	4,237	19,357	24,416	16,602	2,632
Black	646	1,527	1,834	545	49
American Indian, Eskimo, and Aleut	71	250	376	42	0
Asian or Pacific Islander	182	142	232	307	127
Other race	388	409	483	158	36
30 to 34 years old					
Men					
White	7,804	29,881	27,029	16,572	6,120

[Continued]

★ 739 ★

Educational Attainment in Kansas, by Selected Characteristics

[Continued]

Characteristic	Not high school graduate	High school graduate	Some college or associate's degree	Bachelor's degree	Graduate or professional degree
Black	702	1,611	1,563	586	211
American Indian, Eskimo, and Aleut	160	305	297	90	23
Asian or Pacific Islander	182	192	242	128	314
Other race	1,125	751	450	123	43
Women					
White	4,640	22,400	26,896	14,785	4,810
Black	717	1,559	1,874	494	201
American Indian, Eskimo, and Aleut	105	284	331	86	0
Asian or Pacific Islander	197	191	169	165	94
Other race	522	487	354	92	12
35 to 39 years old					
Men					
White	5,362	23,377	27,473	17,847	8,822
Black	413	1,401	1,309	415	218
American Indian, Eskimo, and Aleut	73	249	381	58	48
Asian or Pacific Islander	181	135	122	163	275
Other race	687	462	410	94	21
Women					
White	3,780	20,041	26,135	13,276	6,294
Black	425	1,353	1,624	437	202
American Indian, Eskimo, and Aleut	97	253	303	66	26
Asian or Pacific Islander	318	151	169	190	106
Other race	347	315	292	75	20
40 to 69 years old					
Men					
White	32,851	80,589	66,273	43,871	32,041
Black	2,568	2,583	2,961	768	548
American Indian, Eskimo, and Aleut	363	709	536	219	193
Asian or Pacific Islander	374	277	335	407	951
Other race	1,771	727	524	130	95
Women					
White	22,438	76,919	64,270	25,558	17,561
Black	2,179	3,171	2,724	723	972
American Indian, Eskimo, and Aleut	362	658	578	108	168
Asian or Pacific Islander	765	415	383	339	304
Other race	1,048	831	244	51	49
70 years old and older					
Men					
White	4,564	3,976	2,512	1,291	1,025
Black	156	83	27	11	19
American Indian, Eskimo, and Aleut	19	16	5	2	6
Asian or Pacific Islander	11	0	0	19	7
Other race	48	0	0	0	0

[Continued]

★ 739 ★

Educational Attainment in Kansas, by Selected Characteristics
[Continued]

Characteristic	Not high school graduate	High school graduate	Some college or associate's degree	Bachelor's degree	Graduate or professional degree
Women					
White	2,173	2,755	1,826	582	438
Black	156	86	47	39	8
American Indian, Eskimo, and Aleut	2	8	0	13	0
Asian or Pacific Islander	0	8	3	7	0
Other race	22	5	4	0	0

Source: Census of Population and Housing, 1990: Equal Employment Opportunity (EEO) File on CD-ROM [machine-readable datafiles]. Prepared by the Bureau of the Census. Washington, DC: The Bureau, 1992.

★ 740 ★
Educational Attainment

Educational Attainment in Kentucky, by Selected Characteristics

Table presents the number of civilians 16 years old or older who reported their educational backgrounds during the 1990 Census. Data show the number of individuals achieving various levels of education. Figures are reported by sex, age, and race.

Characteristic	Not high school graduate	High school graduate	Some college or associate's degree	Bachelor's degree	Graduate or professional degree
16 to 19 years old					
Men					
White	29,777	12,449	8,085	22	5
Black	2,428	859	480	10	0
American Indian, Eskimo, and Aleut	49	30	11	0	0
Asian or Pacific Islander	86	36	29	0	0
Other race	65	18	14	0	0
Women					
White	21,179	12,987	11,618	40	0
Black	1,909	1,032	865	0	0
American Indian, Eskimo, and Aleut	58	19	6	0	0
Asian or Pacific Islander	119	42	55	0	0
Other race	42	7	18	0	0
20 to 24 years old					
Men					
White	19,594	40,090	30,812	6,337	408
Black	1,324	2,803	1,946	149	0
American Indian, Eskimo, and Aleut	46	90	53	0	5
Asian or Pacific Islander	63	40	211	162	36
Other race	57	46	32	5	0
Women					
White	8,628	30,117	35,624	9,272	621

[Continued]

★ 740 ★

Educational Attainment in Kentucky, by Selected Characteristics
[Continued]

Characteristic	Not high school graduate	High school graduate	Some college or associate's degree	Bachelor's degree	Graduate or professional degree
Black	889	2,336	3,199	266	26
American Indian, Eskimo, and Aleut	17	102	107	0	4
Asian or Pacific Islander	56	103	215	131	24
Other race	31	38	52	12	0
25 to 29 years old					
Men					
White	23,838	47,621	27,046	15,737	3,498
Black	1,377	3,015	1,947	540	84
American Indian, Eskimo, and Aleut	60	82	63	15	0
Asian or Pacific Islander	52	60	109	143	191
Other race	90	66	31	29	26
Women					
White	11,438	33,972	30,740	15,690	4,413
Black	1,122	2,803	3,299	841	154
American Indian, Eskimo, and Aleut	40	87	121	12	5
Asian or Pacific Islander	99	96	127	104	57
Other race	46	24	64	14	15
30 to 34 years old					
Men					
White	25,991	50,467	28,071	14,774	7,037
Black	1,714	3,148	2,310	586	164
American Indian, Eskimo, and Aleut	106	43	52	21	7
Asian or Pacific Islander	35	100	150	133	221
Other race	13	41	87	36	7
Women					
White	11,244	39,852	30,614	12,033	7,523
Black	1,488	3,359	3,838	776	342
American Indian, Eskimo, and Aleut	79	54	53	11	0
Asian or Pacific Islander	137	84	126	117	101
Other race	36	12	41	25	2
35 to 39 years old					
Men					
White	21,961	42,052	28,160	15,759	9,775
Black	1,272	2,591	1,996	539	310
American Indian, Eskimo, and Aleut	47	60	57	7	12
Asian or Pacific Islander	110	63	95	133	191
Other race	22	29	43	12	0
Women					
White	10,668	36,922	28,086	9,750	10,980
Black	1,147	2,721	3,110	631	482
American Indian, Eskimo, and Aleut	38	72	98	20	24
Asian or Pacific Islander	129	103	68	119	49
Other race	14	75	19	0	11

[Continued]

★ 740 ★

Educational Attainment in Kentucky, by Selected Characteristics
[Continued]

Characteristic	Not high school graduate	High school graduate	Some college or associate's degree	Bachelor's degree	Graduate or professional degree
40 to 69 years old					
Men					
White	103,468	106,949	69,325	37,483	33,027
Black	6,778	6,040	3,654	1,057	753
American Indian, Eskimo, and Aleut	188	200	126	44	30
Asian or Pacific Islander	145	152	179	342	763
Other race	85	48	53	18	43
Women					
White	58,306	102,890	61,140	18,549	25,576
Black	6,188	6,812	5,187	782	993
American Indian, Eskimo, and Aleut	143	147	138	22	38
Asian or Pacific Islander	403	353	221	243	256
Other race	21	45	41	0	5
70 years old and older					
Men					
White	5,461	2,142	1,589	780	978
Black	579	84	89	31	54
American Indian, Eskimo, and Aleut	6	0	3	0	0
Asian or Pacific Islander	7	0	11	0	0
Other race	0	0	0	0	0
Women					
White	2,960	1,840	1,190	405	367
Black	414	136	70	23	8
American Indian, Eskimo, and Aleut	0	9	0	0	0
Asian or Pacific Islander	5	0	0	0	0
Other race	0	0	0	0	0

Source: Census of Population and Housing, 1990: Equal Employment Opportunity (EEO) File on CD-ROM [machine-readable datafiles]. Prepared by the Bureau of the Census. Washington, DC: The Bureau, 1992.

★ 741 ★

Educational Attainment

Educational Attainment in Louisiana, by Selected Characteristics

Table presents the number of civilians 16 years old or older who reported their educational backgrounds during the 1990 Census. Data show the number of individuals achieving various levels of education. Figures are reported by sex, age, and race.

Characteristic	Not high school graduate	High school graduate	Some college or associate's degree	Bachelor's degree	Graduate or professional degree
16 to 19 years old					
Men					
White	20,122	9,753	6,593	0	7
Black	9,596	3,146	1,685	0	0
American Indian, Eskimo, and Aleut	211	84	51	0	0
Asian or Pacific Islander	156	101	110	0	0
Other race	207	94	36	0	0
Women					
White	13,873	8,852	9,430	38	0
Black	7,033	3,786	3,427	14	0
American Indian, Eskimo, and Aleut	115	104	54	0	0
Asian or Pacific Islander	184	123	98	0	0
Other race	125	68	88	10	0
20 to 24 years old					
Men					
White	15,831	28,378	27,258	6,156	376
Black	9,355	11,789	7,786	763	134
American Indian, Eskimo, and Aleut	299	195	109	3	3
Asian or Pacific Islander	166	182	337	82	23
Other race	289	234	378	50	0
Women					
White	6,497	22,321	29,041	7,761	515
Black	6,351	11,267	12,975	1,406	147
American Indian, Eskimo, and Aleut	66	167	101	21	0
Asian or Pacific Islander	127	158	331	125	33
Other race	55	195	316	14	5
25 to 29 years old					
Men					
White	18,984	38,655	23,626	14,899	4,355
Black	10,598	13,796	8,052	2,008	201
American Indian, Eskimo, and Aleut	389	218	186	11	8
Asian or Pacific Islander	294	227	342	226	198
Other race	205	220	287	132	18
Women					
White	6,701	28,725	23,169	16,329	3,363
Black	7,184	13,089	12,825	4,010	796
American Indian, Eskimo, and Aleut	94	199	98	20	7
Asian or Pacific Islander	150	199	149	253	53
Other race	71	137	316	144	15
30 to 34 years old					
Men					
White	17,821	40,378	27,229	18,637	7,363

[Continued]

Educational Attainment in Louisiana, by Selected Characteristics
[Continued]

Characteristic	Not high school graduate	High school graduate	Some college or associate's degree	Bachelor's degree	Graduate or professional degree
Black	10,344	14,260	8,780	2,538	740
American Indian, Eskimo, and Aleut	233	218	121	42	7
Asian or Pacific Islander	369	243	211	190	365
Other race	232	263	293	111	70
Women					
White	7,016	29,432	23,898	15,471	5,398
Black	7,584	13,632	13,634	5,402	1,213
American Indian, Eskimo, and Aleut	125	250	136	24	33
Asian or Pacific Islander	346	266	183	143	201
Other race	117	166	204	100	57
35 to 39 years old					
Men					
White	13,792	30,673	28,618	18,252	9,587
Black	8,931	11,508	7,406	3,055	1,126
American Indian, Eskimo, and Aleut	233	130	160	26	24
Asian or Pacific Islander	384	300	348	260	531
Other race	273	123	189	79	54
Women					
White	6,534	26,472	22,420	13,228	7,092
Black	7,397	12,229	10,468	4,743	2,279
American Indian, Eskimo, and Aleut	94	169	139	7	14
Asian or Pacific Islander	331	281	222	242	157
Other race	124	184	171	63	59
40 to 69 years old					
Men					
White	58,954	92,364	72,065	47,962	35,510
Black	36,742	22,035	12,150	4,643	4,222
American Indian, Eskimo, and Aleut	722	395	249	65	64
Asian or Pacific Islander	845	461	472	424	1,090
Other race	826	409	399	151	167
Women					
White	32,358	85,095	55,225	26,108	20,405
Black	30,577	25,894	16,171	6,681	7,157
American Indian, Eskimo, and Aleut	293	296	298	20	44
Asian or Pacific Islander	893	546	506	442	254
Other race	632	429	367	38	72
70 years old and older					
Men					
White	3,329	2,080	1,882	1,170	1,167
Black	1,484	245	89	30	98
American Indian, Eskimo, and Aleut	5	0	8	0	0
Asian or Pacific Islander	13	29	0	0	0
Other race	11	0	0	0	0

[Continued]

★ 741 ★

Educational Attainment in Louisiana, by Selected Characteristics

[Continued]

Characteristic	Not high school graduate	High school graduate	Some college or associate's degree	Bachelor's degree	Graduate or professional degree
Women					
White	1,865	1,916	1,029	608	506
Black	1,385	338	212	35	63
American Indian, Eskimo, and Aleut	16	0	0	9	0
Asian or Pacific Islander	22	0	12	0	0
Other race	13	15	0	0	0

Source: Census of Population and Housing, 1990: Equal Employment Opportunity (EEO) File on CD-ROM [machine-readable datafiles]. Prepared by the Bureau of the Census. Washington, DC: The Bureau, 1992.

★ 742 ★

Educational Attainment

Educational Attainment in Maine, by Selected Characteristics

Table presents the number of civilians 16 years old or older who reported their educational backgrounds during the 1990 Census. Data show the number of individuals achieving various levels of education. Figures are reported by sex, age, and race.

Characteristic	Not high school graduate	High school graduate	Some college or associate's degree	Bachelor's degree	Graduate or professional degree
16 to 19 years old					
Men					
White	11,853	4,733	2,272	15	0
Black	36	8	16	0	0
American Indian, Eskimo, and Aleut	57	15	0	0	0
Asian or Pacific Islander	93	16	17	0	0
Other race	16	11	6	0	0
Women					
White	10,272	4,411	3,239	0	0
Black	38	45	17	0	0
American Indian, Eskimo, and Aleut	72	33	12	0	0
Asian or Pacific Islander	107	24	36	0	0
Other race	18	8	0	0	0
20 to 24 years old					
Men					
White	4,726	14,868	10,680	2,300	81
Black	30	43	73	14	0
American Indian, Eskimo, and Aleut	39	145	42	6	0
Asian or Pacific Islander	47	48	36	14	0
Other race	9	35	0	2	0
Women					
White	2,396	12,147	12,627	3,356	134

[Continued]

681

★ 742 ★

Educational Attainment in Maine, by Selected Characteristics

[Continued]

Characteristic	Not high school graduate	High school graduate	Some college or associate's degree	Bachelor's degree	Graduate or professional degree
Black	0	32	86	4	0
American Indian, Eskimo, and Aleut	35	85	80	35	0
Asian or Pacific Islander	5	64	76	6	0
Other race	10	16	35	7	0
25 to 29 years old					
Men					
White	4,949	18,428	10,573	6,227	784
Black	21	85	81	32	0
American Indian, Eskimo, and Aleut	55	171	21	12	0
Asian or Pacific Islander	41	70	56	6	35
Other race	0	21	18	0	0
Women					
White	2,535	14,313	11,960	7,270	1,086
Black	5	24	44	36	5
American Indian, Eskimo, and Aleut	38	118	71	23	5
Asian or Pacific Islander	42	73	64	58	6
Other race	1	20	15	2	0
30 to 34 years old					
Men					
White	4,825	20,385	12,647	6,958	2,550
Black	0	65	114	38	19
American Indian, Eskimo, and Aleut	59	74	77	21	3
Asian or Pacific Islander	66	52	32	91	35
Other race	10	25	41	7	8
Women					
White	2,448	15,434	12,644	7,110	2,172
Black	19	20	39	6	13
American Indian, Eskimo, and Aleut	9	115	74	6	0
Asian or Pacific Islander	36	66	76	41	8
Other race	0	21	2	10	0
35 to 39 years old					
Men					
White	3,861	15,946	13,357	8,221	3,946
Black	0	12	44	32	20
American Indian, Eskimo, and Aleut	31	106	50	25	7
Asian or Pacific Islander	66	97	41	44	38
Other race	30	7	21	0	3
Women					
White	2,285	14,376	12,609	7,544	3,356
Black	8	16	29	11	26
American Indian, Eskimo, and Aleut	19	26	43	19	10
Asian or Pacific Islander	60	76	67	63	11
Other race	6	8	14	6	2

[Continued]

★ 742 ★

Educational Attainment in Maine, by Selected Characteristics
[Continued]

Characteristic	Not high school graduate	High school graduate	Some college or associate's degree	Bachelor's degree	Graduate or professional degree
40 to 69 years old					
Men					
White	25,556	46,049	28,334	19,462	15,073
Black	47	144	106	70	40
American Indian, Eskimo, and Aleut	186	169	117	23	25
Asian or Pacific Islander	80	139	100	55	143
Other race	26	15	10	0	13
Women					
White	15,715	45,102	27,190	14,270	8,854
Black	32	67	19	11	47
American Indian, Eskimo, and Aleut	69	129	57	48	2
Asian or Pacific Islander	238	155	136	63	82
Other race	23	16	6	11	10
70 years old and older					
Men					
White	1,293	1,343	702	516	399
Black	0	16	0	0	0
American Indian, Eskimo, and Aleut	6	2	0	0	0
Asian or Pacific Islander	5	5	5	0	0
Other race	0	0	0	0	21
Women					
White	854	1,213	755	207	130
Black	0	8	0	0	0
American Indian, Eskimo, and Aleut	5	6	2	0	0
Asian or Pacific Islander	0	0	0	1	0
Other race	0	0	0	0	0

Source: Census of Population and Housing, 1990: Equal Employment Opportunity (EEO) File on CD-ROM [machine-readable datafiles]. Prepared by the Bureau of the Census. Washington, DC: The Bureau, 1992.

★ 743 ★

Educational Attainment

Educational Attainment in Maryland, by Selected Characteristics

Table presents the number of civilians 16 years old or older who reported their educational backgrounds during the 1990 Census. Data show the number of individuals achieving various levels of education. Figures are reported by sex, age, and race.

Characteristic	Not high school graduate	High school graduate	Some college or associate's degree	Bachelor's degree	Graduate or professional degree
16 to 19 years old					
Men					
White	27,644	11,280	8,836	23	0
Black	10,267	4,343	2,035	11	0
American Indian, Eskimo, and Aleut	163	56	27	0	0
Asian or Pacific Islander	843	427	372	20	0
Other race	787	142	60	0	0
Women					
White	23,058	11,627	11,052	13	0
Black	7,751	5,333	3,140	13	0
American Indian, Eskimo, and Aleut	91	56	36	0	0
Asian or Pacific Islander	921	392	463	0	0
Other race	466	145	136	0	0
20 to 24 years old					
Men					
White	13,928	35,517	34,663	13,831	658
Black	7,797	15,841	9,942	1,897	156
American Indian, Eskimo, and Aleut	154	255	155	14	0
Asian or Pacific Islander	281	725	1,551	969	149
Other race	1,342	674	691	107	20
Women					
White	6,641	28,637	40,202	19,176	853
Black	4,598	14,730	15,140	3,083	184
American Indian, Eskimo, and Aleut	53	221	177	34	0
Asian or Pacific Islander	234	840	1,625	967	65
Other race	576	441	712	58	14
25 to 29 years old					
Men					
White	16,097	43,188	36,936	34,693	9,654
Black	8,239	16,568	13,462	5,625	1,005
American Indian, Eskimo, and Aleut	129	138	132	68	66
Asian or Pacific Islander	353	623	1,272	1,509	1,095
Other race	1,361	594	753	299	164
Women					
White	7,433	32,187	38,975	35,913	8,255
Black	4,992	15,844	18,836	9,355	1,732
American Indian, Eskimo, and Aleut	55	203	187	76	7
Asian or Pacific Islander	310	577	1,110	2,033	733
Other race	649	401	598	254	76
30 to 34 years old					
Men					
White	14,843	42,322	39,278	32,914	18,292

[Continued]

★ 743 ★

Educational Attainment in Maryland, by Selected Characteristics

[Continued]

Characteristic	Not high school graduate	High school graduate	Some college or associate's degree	Bachelor's degree	Graduate or professional degree
Black	7,706	15,233	13,789	6,317	2,425
American Indian, Eskimo, and Aleut	191	148	183	71	49
Asian or Pacific Islander	445	819	1,178	1,436	2,089
Other race	954	456	550	305	175
Women					
White	7,159	33,062	38,527	27,678	14,565
Black	6,040	15,997	20,106	8,753	2,625
American Indian, Eskimo, and Aleut	100	137	218	68	40
Asian or Pacific Islander	546	862	1,189	1,595	1,103
Other race	627	437	547	230	83
35 to 39 years old					
Men					
White	10,983	32,952	36,290	29,219	23,163
Black	6,328	12,364	12,080	4,984	2,743
American Indian, Eskimo, and Aleut	61	135	197	65	54
Asian or Pacific Islander	398	612	1,020	1,476	2,177
Other race	631	374	415	143	122
Women					
White	7,079	30,167	33,511	22,512	18,225
Black	5,357	15,131	16,980	7,163	3,880
American Indian, Eskimo, and Aleut	51	198	207	105	40
Asian or Pacific Islander	734	996	1,004	1,667	1,023
Other race	426	297	449	198	113
40 to 69 years old					
Men					
White	67,533	101,680	91,587	81,241	89,825
Black	32,435	30,853	23,911	10,461	9,893
American Indian, Eskimo, and Aleut	458	329	430	172	169
Asian or Pacific Islander	1,754	1,931	2,850	3,872	6,836
Other race	1,405	670	593	255	306
Women					
White	44,154	114,690	92,347	49,564	46,892
Black	26,028	35,796	32,988	11,782	11,699
American Indian, Eskimo, and Aleut	304	297	424	182	118
Asian or Pacific Islander	2,669	2,673	2,676	3,779	2,861
Other race	1,322	791	456	154	126
70 years old and older					
Men					
White	4,521	2,675	2,430	1,990	3,241
Black	1,458	301	232	80	146
American Indian, Eskimo, and Aleut	22	0	0	7	0
Asian or Pacific Islander	76	26	27	26	61
Other race	54	3	0	6	0

[Continued]

★ 743 ★

Educational Attainment in Maryland, by Selected Characteristics

[Continued]

Characteristic	Not high school graduate	High school graduate	Some college or associate's degree	Bachelor's degree	Graduate or professional degree
Women					
White	2,803	2,832	1,389	751	669
Black	1,305	584	200	81	89
American Indian, Eskimo, and Aleut	14	0	7	0	0
Asian or Pacific Islander	29	9	10	42	8
Other race	50	21	0	0	0

Source: Census of Population and Housing, 1990: Equal Employment Opportunity (EEO) File on CD-ROM [machine-readable datafiles]. Prepared by the Bureau of the Census. Washington, DC: The Bureau, 1992.

★ 744 ★

Educational Attainment

Educational Attainment in Massachusetts, by Selected Characteristics

Table presents the number of civilians 16 years old or older who reported their educational backgrounds during the 1990 Census. Data show the number of individuals achieving various levels of education. Figures are reported by sex, age, and race.

Characteristic	Not high school graduate	High school graduate	Some college or associate's degree	Bachelor's degree	Graduate or professional degree
16 to 19 years old					
Men					
White	47,416	20,793	15,249	76	7
Black	2,996	1,007	770	21	0
American Indian, Eskimo, and Aleut	104	32	41	0	0
Asian or Pacific Islander	796	462	485	7	0
Other race	2,113	524	180	0	0
Women					
White	42,467	22,316	22,040	103	5
Black	2,295	1,389	1,142	0	0
American Indian, Eskimo, and Aleut	77	68	30	0	0
Asian or Pacific Islander	924	580	869	20	0
Other race	1,638	656	429	0	0
20 to 24 years old					
Men					
White	21,376	60,901	61,299	29,546	1,560
Black	2,361	3,392	3,150	831	53
American Indian, Eskimo, and Aleut	110	107	94	42	16
Asian or Pacific Islander	575	1,038	1,728	1,091	159
Other race	2,602	2,012	1,346	285	47
Women					
White	10,554	45,314	76,374	40,458	1,954

[Continued]

★ 744 ★

Educational Attainment in Massachusetts, by Selected Characteristics

[Continued]

Characteristic	Not high school graduate	High school graduate	Some college or associate's degree	Bachelor's degree	Graduate or professional degree
Black	1,175	3,164	4,033	1,018	60
American Indian, Eskimo, and Aleut	72	103	152	40	6
Asian or Pacific Islander	430	726	1,883	1,312	135
Other race	1,151	1,511	1,657	318	25
25 to 29 years old					
Men					
White	20,351	69,320	58,087	61,671	14,655
Black	1,929	3,807	3,546	1,965	433
American Indian, Eskimo, and Aleut	82	129	115	25	31
Asian or Pacific Islander	994	898	1,101	1,853	1,749
Other race	2,530	1,950	1,288	435	186
Women					
White	10,506	45,880	61,901	66,434	14,531
Black	1,387	3,167	4,539	1,716	460
American Indian, Eskimo, and Aleut	69	139	111	46	24
Asian or Pacific Islander	597	655	928	1,827	1,049
Other race	1,067	1,499	1,377	479	203
30 to 34 years old					
Men					
White	18,704	65,853	59,149	53,474	27,869
Black	2,118	3,475	3,392	1,856	610
American Indian, Eskimo, and Aleut	136	139	164	52	4
Asian or Pacific Islander	955	878	948	1,383	2,320
Other race	2,207	1,606	1,111	286	286
Women					
White	11,473	44,861	60,483	49,196	23,314
Black	1,849	2,740	3,593	1,562	767
American Indian, Eskimo, and Aleut	83	248	166	50	20
Asian or Pacific Islander	789	842	851	1,444	1,302
Other race	1,398	1,154	951	446	220
35 to 39 years old					
Men					
White	16,287	49,287	55,393	45,935	33,288
Black	1,899	2,293	2,852	1,396	1,085
American Indian, Eskimo, and Aleut	56	81	126	41	66
Asian or Pacific Islander	1,068	808	844	1,017	1,930
Other race	2,019	1,111	811	190	290
Women					
White	11,309	43,258	52,318	38,139	27,932
Black	1,645	2,394	2,783	1,208	941
American Indian, Eskimo, and Aleut	67	117	217	63	38
Asian or Pacific Islander	1,032	703	741	965	838
Other race	1,081	927	662	248	150

[Continued]

★ 744 ★

Educational Attainment in Massachusetts, by Selected Characteristics

[Continued]

Characteristic	Not high school graduate	High school graduate	Some college or associate's degree	Bachelor's degree	Graduate or professional degree
40 to 69 years old					
Men					
White	102,144	160,754	144,123	111,657	118,283
Black	6,791	6,587	5,178	2,456	2,607
American Indian, Eskimo, and Aleut	305	375	297	134	101
Asian or Pacific Islander	2,868	1,649	1,552	1,915	4,307
Other race	4,172	1,515	956	347	254
Women					
White	72,339	191,648	145,332	79,032	69,585
Black	6,830	7,669	6,100	2,500	2,278
American Indian, Eskimo, and Aleut	228	252	247	67	71
Asian or Pacific Islander	2,853	1,497	1,518	1,814	1,731
Other race	3,466	1,606	809	268	261
70 years old and older					
Men					
White	7,057	7,379	4,575	2,809	3,770
Black	272	176	122	49	67
American Indian, Eskimo, and Aleut	11	0	7	0	17
Asian or Pacific Islander	35	22	28	36	52
Other race	56	16	0	0	6
Women					
White	4,968	7,980	3,478	1,411	1,433
Black	234	177	88	57	33
American Indian, Eskimo, and Aleut	0	29	0	10	7
Asian or Pacific Islander	84	30	0	32	0
Other race	61	28	0	0	0

Source: Census of Population and Housing, 1990: Equal Employment Opportunity (EEO) File on CD-ROM [machine-readable datafiles]. Prepared by the Bureau of the Census. Washington, DC: The Bureau, 1992.

★ 745 ★

Educational Attainment

Educational Attainment in Michigan, by Selected Characteristics

Table presents the number of civilians 16 years old or older who reported their educational backgrounds during the 1990 Census. Data show the number of individuals achieving various levels of education. Figures are reported by sex, age, and race.

Characteristic	Not high school graduate	High school graduate	Some college or associate's degree	Bachelor's degree	Graduate or professional degree
16 to 19 years old					
Men					
White	82,316	25,052	23,569	54	13
Black	14,358	3,992	2,073	0	0
American Indian, Eskimo, and Aleut	836	176	179	0	0
Asian or Pacific Islander	936	188	384	0	0
Other race	1,383	364	218	0	0
Women					
White	67,271	26,446	32,650	38	1
Black	11,913	4,825	4,588	2	0
American Indian, Eskimo, and Aleut	823	182	206	0	0
Asian or Pacific Islander	759	259	428	0	0
Other race	1,023	382	312	0	0
20 to 24 years old					
Men					
White	30,032	80,464	98,953	22,400	923
Black	9,797	11,974	9,812	1,136	36
American Indian, Eskimo, and Aleut	751	729	697	37	5
Asian or Pacific Islander	279	456	1,331	551	139
Other race	1,246	1,206	860	140	6
Women					
White	14,280	63,550	108,917	26,129	1,222
Black	5,596	10,704	15,992	1,758	108
American Indian, Eskimo, and Aleut	375	622	691	69	0
Asian or Pacific Islander	238	376	1,200	605	49
Other race	533	957	896	108	0
25 to 29 years old					
Men					
White	32,058	98,748	95,991	53,111	11,616
Black	7,532	11,103	12,116	2,978	698
American Indian, Eskimo, and Aleut	603	842	705	134	23
Asian or Pacific Islander	291	356	731	1,130	1,203
Other race	1,211	1,217	984	323	155
Women					
White	16,415	72,360	90,594	48,110	8,179
Black	4,577	9,299	17,662	4,168	766
American Indian, Eskimo, and Aleut	321	751	757	159	23
Asian or Pacific Islander	210	380	559	910	539
Other race	474	824	912	153	87
30 to 34 years old					
Men					
White	32,975	106,401	108,392	48,081	21,827

[Continued]

★ 745 ★

Educational Attainment in Michigan, by Selected Characteristics
[Continued]

Characteristic	Not high school graduate	High school graduate	Some college or associate's degree	Bachelor's degree	Graduate or professional degree
Black	7,374	11,206	14,417	3,378	1,174
American Indian, Eskimo, and Aleut	439	1,054	673	96	39
Asian or Pacific Islander	301	448	562	930	1,851
Other race	1,423	993	977	139	88
Women					
White	17,312	84,173	92,630	38,498	14,635
Black	4,829	10,685	19,672	5,014	1,697
American Indian, Eskimo, and Aleut	322	637	728	107	65
Asian or Pacific Islander	399	410	570	780	627
Other race	600	805	777	164	133
35 to 39 years old					
Men					
White	25,302	85,249	107,014	47,484	29,144
Black	5,819	9,746	12,708	3,484	1,712
American Indian, Eskimo, and Aleut	433	656	564	140	48
Asian or Pacific Islander	392	407	573	794	1,568
Other race	1,000	896	740	237	81
Women					
White	15,236	76,330	88,281	34,463	20,427
Black	4,688	10,219	17,062	4,623	2,753
American Indian, Eskimo, and Aleut	298	597	630	142	111
Asian or Pacific Islander	565	428	555	881	651
Other race	584	759	670	94	94
40 to 69 years old					
Men					
White	142,189	253,236	248,834	120,037	106,919
Black	27,712	26,198	24,084	6,431	6,206
American Indian, Eskimo, and Aleut	1,538	1,489	1,227	277	287
Asian or Pacific Islander	986	762	1,295	2,373	4,920
Other race	3,027	1,266	985	218	233
Women					
White	82,523	259,766	197,554	71,958	60,630
Black	20,363	28,718	32,182	7,503	8,446
American Indian, Eskimo, and Aleut	854	1,350	1,304	244	124
Asian or Pacific Islander	1,523	1,231	1,426	2,145	1,791
Other race	1,713	986	826	235	131
70 years old and older					
Men					
White	7,077	5,621	4,235	2,397	2,694
Black	926	268	258	80	82
American Indian, Eskimo, and Aleut	30	14	6	8	0
Asian or Pacific Islander	41	6	13	26	12
Other race	40	2	0	0	0

[Continued]

★ 745 ★

Educational Attainment in Michigan, by Selected Characteristics
[Continued]

Characteristic	Not high school graduate	High school graduate	Some college or associate's degree	Bachelor's degree	Graduate or professional degree
Women					
White	5,044	5,058	3,272	826	946
Black	1,090	519	380	84	54
American Indian, Eskimo, and Aleut	22	25	18	0	0
Asian or Pacific Islander	15	17	24	12	0
Other race	15	4	0	0	0

Source: Census of Population and Housing, 1990: Equal Employment Opportunity (EEO) File on CD-ROM [machine-readable datafiles]. Prepared by the Bureau of the Census. Washington, DC: The Bureau, 1992.

★ 746 ★
Educational Attainment

Educational Attainment in Minnesota, by Selected Characteristics

Table presents the number of civilians 16 years old or older who reported their educational backgrounds during the 1990 Census. Data show the number of individuals achieving various levels of education. Figures are reported by sex, age, and race.

Characteristic	Not high school graduate	High school graduate	Some college or associate's degree	Bachelor's degree	Graduate or professional degree
16 to 19 years old					
Men					
White	43,004	13,080	11,761	21	18
Black	1,187	326	182	0	0
American Indian, Eskimo, and Aleut	611	129	27	0	0
Asian or Pacific Islander	1,017	173	185	0	0
Other race	360	55	70	0	0
Women					
White	39,030	12,574	15,940	22	10
Black	782	375	251	0	0
American Indian, Eskimo, and Aleut	395	198	87	0	0
Asian or Pacific Islander	831	181	251	5	0
Other race	211	136	73	0	0
20 to 24 years old					
Men					
White	9,764	37,972	59,349	13,908	485
Black	603	910	1,131	239	21
American Indian, Eskimo, and Aleut	474	638	383	9	7
Asian or Pacific Islander	216	566	1,216	410	57
Other race	277	260	266	53	0
Women					
White	5,024	30,748	66,150	17,519	506

[Continued]

★ 746 ★

Educational Attainment in Minnesota, by Selected Characteristics
[Continued]

Characteristic	Not high school graduate	High school graduate	Some college or associate's degree	Bachelor's degree	Graduate or professional degree
Black	401	855	1,044	182	4
American Indian, Eskimo, and Aleut	194	430	540	34	2
Asian or Pacific Islander	211	479	899	211	35
Other race	125	212	223	19	0
25 to 29 years old					
Men					
White	11,067	53,506	58,032	37,792	5,815
Black	535	1,181	1,531	487	131
American Indian, Eskimo, and Aleut	400	623	414	87	14
Asian or Pacific Islander	368	583	720	568	500
Other race	274	381	324	91	125
Women					
White	5,780	42,206	57,719	38,549	4,682
Black	228	905	1,322	567	156
American Indian, Eskimo, and Aleut	226	413	500	66	0
Asian or Pacific Islander	371	467	533	471	257
Other race	64	186	260	112	5
30 to 34 years old					
Men					
White	11,841	62,364	60,088	36,277	12,887
Black	600	1,141	1,214	939	240
American Indian, Eskimo, and Aleut	431	719	564	76	11
Asian or Pacific Islander	392	384	568	642	674
Other race	242	268	223	125	51
Women					
White	6,298	48,204	57,982	33,552	8,582
Black	234	810	1,157	480	158
American Indian, Eskimo, and Aleut	211	385	610	123	42
Asian or Pacific Islander	538	415	475	399	299
Other race	98	174	227	77	52
35 to 39 years old					
Men					
White	7,635	51,051	56,102	35,070	15,674
Black	518	927	1,080	644	380
American Indian, Eskimo, and Aleut	285	398	417	83	31
Asian or Pacific Islander	280	306	561	452	599
Other race	277	210	206	24	26
Women					
White	4,723	44,779	52,443	28,863	10,562
Black	155	674	967	364	90
American Indian, Eskimo, and Aleut	134	348	527	147	61
Asian or Pacific Islander	342	307	440	398	166
Other race	59	150	106	58	19

[Continued]

★ 746 ★

Educational Attainment in Minnesota, by Selected Characteristics

[Continued]

Characteristic	Not high school graduate	High school graduate	Some college or associate's degree	Bachelor's degree	Graduate or professional degree
40 to 69 years old					
Men					
White	63,259	149,408	117,684	80,884	56,196
Black	1,110	1,555	1,628	957	653
American Indian, Eskimo, and Aleut	744	1,014	769	236	189
Asian or Pacific Islander	736	567	716	597	1,344
Other race	429	281	327	90	93
Women					
White	36,553	156,201	110,030	58,243	26,071
Black	975	1,476	1,586	609	350
American Indian, Eskimo, and Aleut	648	887	767	256	120
Asian or Pacific Islander	928	927	637	697	491
Other race	363	231	198	56	53
70 years old and older					
Men					
White	6,242	3,702	2,434	1,233	1,307
Black	22	39	22	6	0
American Indian, Eskimo, and Aleut	49	13	0	0	0
Asian or Pacific Islander	12	17	24	15	8
Other race	10	0	0	0	0
Women					
White	3,683	3,255	2,023	758	392
Black	36	46	5	0	0
American Indian, Eskimo, and Aleut	38	19	10	2	0
Asian or Pacific Islander	12	0	7	1	0
Other race	1	0	0	0	0

Source: Census of Population and Housing, 1990: Equal Employment Opportunity (EEO) File on CD-ROM [machine-readable datafiles]. Prepared by the Bureau of the Census. Washington, DC: The Bureau, 1992.

★ 747 ★
Educational Attainment

Educational Attainment in Mississippi, by Selected Characteristics

Table presents the number of civilians 16 years old or older who reported their educational backgrounds during the 1990 Census. Data show the number of individuals achieving various levels of education. Figures are reported by sex, age, and race.

Characteristic	Not high school graduate	High school graduate	Some college or associate's degree	Bachelor's degree	Graduate or professional degree
16 to 19 years old					
Men					
White	13,338	4,939	4,590	27	3
Black	6,883	2,578	1,514	12	0
American Indian, Eskimo, and Aleut	75	27	0	0	0
Asian or Pacific Islander	137	4	67	0	0
Other race	43	0	0	0	0
Women					
White	9,259	4,690	6,175	14	0
Black	5,513	2,895	2,833	7	0
American Indian, Eskimo, and Aleut	20	32	0	0	0
Asian or Pacific Islander	91	31	9	0	0
Other race	4	0	0	0	0
20 to 24 years old					
Men					
White	8,934	14,505	16,649	3,819	221
Black	6,524	8,307	6,167	716	52
American Indian, Eskimo, and Aleut	117	106	22	0	0
Asian or Pacific Islander	31	97	28	79	7
Other race	27	41	28	0	0
Women					
White	4,049	10,326	17,949	4,556	445
Black	5,058	8,054	10,204	1,265	86
American Indian, Eskimo, and Aleut	80	74	57	34	0
Asian or Pacific Islander	17	126	135	48	0
Other race	5	17	2	0	0
25 to 29 years old					
Men					
White	10,956	17,713	16,050	8,566	1,798
Black	7,427	9,223	6,358	1,480	189
American Indian, Eskimo, and Aleut	108	149	22	15	0
Asian or Pacific Islander	107	81	37	62	96
Other race	52	11	25	38	0
Women					
White	4,771	13,432	16,066	8,593	1,844
Black	6,313	9,320	10,763	3,109	443
American Indian, Eskimo, and Aleut	85	76	35	21	0
Asian or Pacific Islander	31	47	54	83	50
Other race	46	31	32	28	0
30 to 34 years old					
Men					
White	11,295	18,992	17,581	8,796	3,618

[Continued]

★ 747 ★

Educational Attainment in Mississippi, by Selected Characteristics
[Continued]

Characteristic	Not high school graduate	High school graduate	Some college or associate's degree	Bachelor's degree	Graduate or professional degree
Black	8,563	8,896	5,781	1,709	300
American Indian, Eskimo, and Aleut	116	160	17	29	9
Asian or Pacific Islander	107	65	77	84	149
Other race	57	11	55	0	5
Women					
White	5,435	13,945	15,733	7,731	3,025
Black	7,585	9,048	9,797	3,390	847
American Indian, Eskimo, and Aleut	38	76	90	31	0
Asian or Pacific Islander	89	63	68	87	36
Other race	15	7	31	26	5
35 to 39 years old					
Men					
White	9,247	14,320	16,456	9,177	5,199
Black	8,301	7,064	5,169	1,765	815
American Indian, Eskimo, and Aleut	80	42	45	19	9
Asian or Pacific Islander	115	25	29	54	165
Other race	79	5	25	18	8
Women					
White	4,906	13,737	15,300	6,605	4,491
Black	6,800	7,244	7,295	2,940	1,300
American Indian, Eskimo, and Aleut	67	79	80	36	2
Asian or Pacific Islander	152	111	81	57	55
Other race	29	16	14	22	8
40 to 69 years old					
Men					
White	41,306	52,044	48,793	26,501	18,778
Black	28,926	10,049	7,004	3,542	2,765
American Indian, Eskimo, and Aleut	216	148	170	38	31
Asian or Pacific Islander	241	91	110	153	315
Other race	114	25	42	6	20
Women					
White	26,930	52,316	40,106	14,535	11,231
Black	24,571	13,956	9,268	4,197	4,642
American Indian, Eskimo, and Aleut	211	125	174	28	25
Asian or Pacific Islander	259	159	172	144	125
Other race	71	41	25	5	7
70 years old and older					
Men					
White	2,504	1,504	1,123	735	646
Black	1,411	188	60	63	40
American Indian, Eskimo, and Aleut	9	0	0	0	0
Asian or Pacific Islander	8	6	3	8	0
Other race	0	0	0	0	0

[Continued]

★ 747 ★

Educational Attainment in Mississippi, by Selected Characteristics
[Continued]

Characteristic	Not high school graduate	High school graduate	Some college or associate's degree	Bachelor's degree	Graduate or professional degree
Women					
White	1,590	1,513	926	340	152
Black	1,312	281	136	86	33
American Indian, Eskimo, and Aleut	0	8	0	0	0
Asian or Pacific Islander	11	0	0	0	0
Other race	0	0	0	0	0

Source: Census of Population and Housing, 1990: Equal Employment Opportunity (EEO) File on CD-ROM [machine-readable datafiles]. Prepared by the Bureau of the Census. Washington, DC: The Bureau, 1992.

★ 748 ★
Educational Attainment

Educational Attainment in Missouri, by Selected Characteristics

Table presents the number of civilians 16 years old or older who reported their educational backgrounds during the 1990 Census. Data show the number of individuals achieving various levels of education. Figures are reported by sex, age, and race.

Characteristic	Not high school graduate	High school graduate	Some college or associate's degree	Bachelor's degree	Graduate or professional degree
16 to 19 years old					
Men					
White	42,765	15,584	11,445	38	0
Black	5,552	1,546	931	0	0
American Indian, Eskimo, and Aleut	374	70	55	0	0
Asian or Pacific Islander	320	97	126	0	0
Other race	272	84	68	0	0
Women					
White	35,996	14,503	15,372	8	0
Black	4,574	2,154	1,501	0	0
American Indian, Eskimo, and Aleut	183	57	55	0	0
Asian or Pacific Islander	267	101	129	0	0
Other race	266	123	67	14	0
20 to 24 years old					
Men					
White	17,949	45,103	46,377	12,628	576
Black	3,679	5,357	4,597	505	24
American Indian, Eskimo, and Aleut	196	259	228	10	0
Asian or Pacific Islander	137	256	548	148	43
Other race	248	180	255	58	15
Women					
White	10,405	35,819	52,286	16,610	927

[Continued]

★ 748 ★

Educational Attainment in Missouri, by Selected Characteristics

[Continued]

Characteristic	Not high school graduate	High school graduate	Some college or associate's degree	Bachelor's degree	Graduate or professional degree
Black	2,479	5,572	6,338	901	68
American Indian, Eskimo, and Aleut	87	180	203	27	7
Asian or Pacific Islander	81	179	597	186	40
Other race	69	176	287	67	17
25 to 29 years old					
Men					
White	22,516	60,584	44,348	31,805	6,326
Black	3,130	6,224	4,890	1,527	228
American Indian, Eskimo, and Aleut	278	295	259	64	14
Asian or Pacific Islander	196	168	447	464	414
Other race	299	252	256	212	53
Women					
White	12,932	44,654	45,903	30,898	5,787
Black	2,770	6,409	6,914	2,416	388
American Indian, Eskimo, and Aleut	136	225	128	47	3
Asian or Pacific Islander	137	165	307	349	234
Other race	69	230	223	134	25
30 to 34 years old					
Men					
White	20,742	65,363	48,009	30,339	12,941
Black	3,207	5,950	5,713	1,966	557
American Indian, Eskimo, and Aleut	247	354	357	83	16
Asian or Pacific Islander	154	205	216	338	541
Other race	227	265	326	78	32
Women					
White	13,353	48,936	46,840	26,089	9,669
Black	2,994	6,545	7,701	2,423	797
American Indian, Eskimo, and Aleut	186	242	274	41	18
Asian or Pacific Islander	203	211	300	348	208
Other race	135	245	229	66	66
35 to 39 years old					
Men					
White	15,637	50,431	48,384	28,732	16,339
Black	2,508	4,636	5,310	1,542	741
American Indian, Eskimo, and Aleut	161	251	266	121	60
Asian or Pacific Islander	129	154	276	268	532
Other race	285	158	157	63	50
Women					
White	11,637	45,205	41,990	22,205	11,810
Black	2,655	5,742	6,725	2,453	876
American Indian, Eskimo, and Aleut	127	208	218	81	33
Asian or Pacific Islander	203	273	314	365	212
Other race	123	213	164	66	22

[Continued]

★ 748 ★

Educational Attainment in Missouri, by Selected Characteristics
[Continued]

Characteristic	Not high school graduate	High school graduate	Some college or associate's degree	Bachelor's degree	Graduate or professional degree
40 to 69 years old					
Men					
White	92,393	164,741	117,405	72,543	57,364
Black	12,588	11,906	9,734	3,395	2,349
American Indian, Eskimo, and Aleut	562	652	609	274	208
Asian or Pacific Islander	470	324	467	595	1,612
Other race	573	508	420	96	149
Women					
White	66,612	165,874	103,282	42,514	31,633
Black	12,089	14,343	13,900	3,645	3,596
American Indian, Eskimo, and Aleut	437	476	579	144	85
Asian or Pacific Islander	837	642	524	627	730
Other race	474	501	221	49	59
70 years old and older					
Men					
White	7,739	5,174	3,229	1,502	1,958
Black	742	185	171	38	96
American Indian, Eskimo, and Aleut	16	19	16	0	8
Asian or Pacific Islander	25	0	0	2	23
Other race	12	2	0	0	0
Women					
White	5,123	3,645	2,141	847	795
Black	953	297	182	33	40
American Indian, Eskimo, and Aleut	10	19	7	0	0
Asian or Pacific Islander	8	30	0	0	10
Other race	0	0	7	0	0

Source: Census of Population and Housing, 1990: Equal Employment Opportunity (EEO) File on CD-ROM [machine-readable datafiles]. Prepared by the Bureau of the Census. Washington, DC: The Bureau, 1992.

★ 749 ★

Educational Attainment

Educational Attainment in Montana, by Selected Characteristics

Table presents the number of civilians 16 years old or older who reported their educational backgrounds during the 1990 Census. Data show the number of individuals achieving various levels of education. Figures are reported by sex, age, and race.

Characteristic	Not high school graduate	High school graduate	Some college or associate's degree	Bachelor's degree	Graduate or professional degree
16 to 19 years old					
Men					
White	7,593	1,899	1,308	6	0
Black	20	8	0	0	0
American Indian, Eskimo, and Aleut	423	82	59	0	0
Asian or Pacific Islander	46	18	17	0	0
Other race	54	13	6	0	0
Women					
White	6,083	1,939	2,189	6	0
Black	0	0	0	0	0
American Indian, Eskimo, and Aleut	389	102	62	0	0
Asian or Pacific Islander	48	13	7	0	0
Other race	42	15	9	0	0
20 to 24 years old					
Men					
White	1,577	5,677	7,332	1,113	75
Black	0	6	46	0	9
American Indian, Eskimo, and Aleut	371	520	290	27	0
Asian or Pacific Islander	14	45	54	33	0
Other race	56	47	56	0	0
Women					
White	1,246	4,880	7,582	1,382	47
Black	0	25	31	0	0
American Indian, Eskimo, and Aleut	315	308	312	8	0
Asian or Pacific Islander	14	52	41	13	0
Other race	20	36	22	0	0
25 to 29 years old					
Men					
White	2,228	8,532	6,758	3,421	485
Black	4	17	22	13	0
American Indian, Eskimo, and Aleut	399	423	507	29	6
Asian or Pacific Islander	6	25	35	44	0
Other race	77	79	28	15	5
Women					
White	1,379	6,454	6,358	3,613	275
Black	7	0	12	23	0
American Indian, Eskimo, and Aleut	238	347	534	81	17
Asian or Pacific Islander	14	34	38	33	16
Other race	28	45	47	15	0
30 to 34 years old					
Men					
White	2,483	11,165	8,478	4,809	1,422

[Continued]

★ 749 ★

Educational Attainment in Montana, by Selected Characteristics
[Continued]

Characteristic	Not high school graduate	High school graduate	Some college or associate's degree	Bachelor's degree	Graduate or professional degree
Black	5	7	8	8	0
American Indian, Eskimo, and Aleut	387	702	485	68	26
Asian or Pacific Islander	18	30	6	41	19
Other race	38	49	54	7	7
Women					
White	1,334	8,192	8,397	4,946	1,119
Black	6	6	48	21	6
American Indian, Eskimo, and Aleut	223	548	652	141	41
Asian or Pacific Islander	10	46	31	25	32
Other race	25	23	27	6	0
35 to 39 years old					
Men					
White	1,769	8,893	9,978	6,084	2,611
Black	18	6	27	7	0
American Indian, Eskimo, and Aleut	251	415	571	149	31
Asian or Pacific Islander	17	30	16	39	27
Other race	61	27	34	8	6
Women					
White	1,262	7,522	8,899	5,992	1,655
Black	0	5	20	7	2
American Indian, Eskimo, and Aleut	133	305	473	122	21
Asian or Pacific Islander	32	59	31	25	6
Other race	15	46	33	9	0
40 to 69 years old					
Men					
White	11,752	26,763	21,907	14,674	10,463
Black	11	47	37	11	2
American Indian, Eskimo, and Aleut	778	931	847	209	164
Asian or Pacific Islander	28	64	56	43	80
Other race	122	72	52	17	13
Women					
White	7,313	23,535	20,164	10,330	4,173
Black	0	15	34	3	0
American Indian, Eskimo, and Aleut	676	647	882	268	118
Asian or Pacific Islander	114	93	118	71	18
Other race	63	36	41	9	0
70 years old and older					
Men					
White	1,711	1,041	625	247	260
Black	0	5	0	0	0
American Indian, Eskimo, and Aleut	34	3	0	0	0
Asian or Pacific Islander	2	0	0	0	0
Other race	0	2	0	0	0

[Continued]

★ 749 ★

Educational Attainment in Montana, by Selected Characteristics

[Continued]

Characteristic	Not high school graduate	High school graduate	Some college or associate's degree	Bachelor's degree	Graduate or professional degree
Women					
White	751	667	562	161	85
Black	0	0	0	0	0
American Indian, Eskimo, and Aleut	20	0	14	0	0
Asian or Pacific Islander	0	0	6	0	0
Other race	0	0	0	0	0

Source: Census of Population and Housing, 1990: Equal Employment Opportunity (EEO) File on CD-ROM [machine-readable datafiles]. Prepared by the Bureau of the Census. Washington, DC: The Bureau, 1992.

★ 750 ★

Educational Attainment

Educational Attainment in Nebraska, by Selected Characteristics

Table presents the number of civilians 16 years old or older who reported their educational backgrounds during the 1990 Census. Data show the number of individuals achieving various levels of education. Figures are reported by sex, age, and race.

Characteristic	Not high school graduate	High school graduate	Some college or associate's degree	Bachelor's degree	Graduate or professional degree
16 to 19 years old					
Men					
White	16,041	4,845	4,425	19	0
Black	574	176	74	0	0
American Indian, Eskimo, and Aleut	180	74	24	0	0
Asian or Pacific Islander	232	21	19	0	0
Other race	176	86	38	0	0
Women					
White	14,439	4,785	6,276	9	0
Black	479	252	97	0	0
American Indian, Eskimo, and Aleut	141	33	21	0	0
Asian or Pacific Islander	127	33	72	0	0
Other race	149	88	70	0	0
20 to 24 years old					
Men					
White	3,278	12,436	20,768	3,969	160
Black	278	628	504	89	0
American Indian, Eskimo, and Aleut	94	162	61	0	4
Asian or Pacific Islander	49	71	207	53	9
Other race	234	261	296	19	0
Women					
White	2,049	9,822	21,801	5,185	224

[Continued]

★ 750 ★

Educational Attainment in Nebraska, by Selected Characteristics

[Continued]

Characteristic	Not high school graduate	High school graduate	Some college or associate's degree	Bachelor's degree	Graduate or professional degree
Black	171	562	696	103	6
American Indian, Eskimo, and Aleut	76	151	142	19	0
Asian or Pacific Islander	87	88	221	31	5
Other race	88	127	127	24	0
25 to 29 years old					
Men					
White	3,906	17,380	19,135	9,694	1,623
Black	321	680	596	222	41
American Indian, Eskimo, and Aleut	119	187	85	25	17
Asian or Pacific Islander	121	104	111	144	140
Other race	274	271	166	38	18
Women					
White	2,276	13,266	18,905	10,316	1,666
Black	198	701	1,014	234	61
American Indian, Eskimo, and Aleut	61	173	105	24	2
Asian or Pacific Islander	48	89	154	106	47
Other race	73	195	189	53	19
30 to 34 years old					
Men					
White	4,127	21,240	20,020	10,392	3,270
Black	278	498	696	201	94
American Indian, Eskimo, and Aleut	77	142	116	0	3
Asian or Pacific Islander	61	55	102	116	133
Other race	343	153	203	40	0
Women					
White	2,449	16,558	18,738	9,141	2,611
Black	192	674	945	207	50
American Indian, Eskimo, and Aleut	79	85	109	23	3
Asian or Pacific Islander	73	68	136	187	48
Other race	97	157	171	53	14
35 to 39 years old					
Men					
White	3,042	15,900	19,817	10,648	4,779
Black	121	432	662	182	48
American Indian, Eskimo, and Aleut	57	118	131	29	18
Asian or Pacific Islander	32	46	147	45	130
Other race	197	144	127	31	20
Women					
White	2,041	15,053	18,748	8,868	3,507
Black	129	643	669	215	82
American Indian, Eskimo, and Aleut	44	124	139	11	0
Asian or Pacific Islander	96	142	60	45	70
Other race	163	146	92	21	0

[Continued]

★ 750 ★

Educational Attainment in Nebraska, by Selected Characteristics
[Continued]

Characteristic	Not high school graduate	High school graduate	Some college or associate's degree	Bachelor's degree	Graduate or professional degree
40 to 69 years old					
Men					
White	23,969	61,167	41,436	23,886	18,386
Black	973	1,207	1,042	428	207
American Indian, Eskimo, and Aleut	160	232	219	68	34
Asian or Pacific Islander	101	137	109	120	353
Other race	573	267	192	46	31
Women					
White	14,676	55,634	41,827	16,507	9,028
Black	993	1,361	1,216	314	234
American Indian, Eskimo, and Aleut	152	226	172	52	31
Asian or Pacific Islander	339	221	184	129	114
Other race	343	256	142	8	0
70 years old and older					
Men					
White	3,773	2,828	1,134	509	496
Black	47	10	20	16	0
American Indian, Eskimo, and Aleut	8	0	2	12	0
Asian or Pacific Islander	2	4	0	0	0
Other race	4	0	0	0	0
Women					
White	1,852	1,877	1,210	348	213
Black	48	21	12	5	0
American Indian, Eskimo, and Aleut	15	23	1	0	0
Asian or Pacific Islander	0	5	0	0	0
Other race	0	0	0	0	0

Source: Census of Population and Housing, 1990: Equal Employment Opportunity (EEO) File on CD-ROM [machine-readable datafiles]. Prepared by the Bureau of the Census. Washington, DC: The Bureau, 1992.

★ 751 ★

Educational Attainment

Educational Attainment in Nevada, by Selected Characteristics

Table presents the number of civilians 16 years old or older who reported their educational backgrounds during the 1990 Census. Data show the number of individuals achieving various levels of education. Figures are reported by sex, age, and race.

Characteristic	Not high school graduate	High school graduate	Some college or associate's degree	Bachelor's degree	Graduate or professional degree
16 to 19 years old					
Men					
White	9,147	3,271	1,792	8	0
Black	785	377	142	0	0
American Indian, Eskimo, and Aleut	154	99	57	0	0
Asian or Pacific Islander	396	129	36	0	0
Other race	897	300	61	0	0
Women					
White	7,259	3,317	2,781	0	0
Black	622	319	195	0	0
American Indian, Eskimo, and Aleut	135	50	4	0	0
Asian or Pacific Islander	319	161	99	0	0
Other race	676	182	82	0	0
20 to 24 years old					
Men					
White	6,024	11,368	10,518	1,484	72
Black	561	1,011	770	36	0
American Indian, Eskimo, and Aleut	245	276	150	0	0
Asian or Pacific Islander	159	421	571	55	24
Other race	2,177	828	489	25	0
Women					
White	3,496	9,200	11,614	1,842	119
Black	282	1,065	914	99	25
American Indian, Eskimo, and Aleut	209	223	223	10	3
Asian or Pacific Islander	154	225	508	82	2
Other race	660	445	508	8	0
25 to 29 years old					
Men					
White	7,262	14,915	14,355	5,089	949
Black	517	1,197	1,019	233	35
American Indian, Eskimo, and Aleut	316	413	343	39	2
Asian or Pacific Islander	234	386	605	267	120
Other race	2,050	933	737	157	18
Women					
White	4,300	10,028	12,687	4,354	646
Black	417	773	1,361	266	90
American Indian, Eskimo, and Aleut	58	223	293	56	23
Asian or Pacific Islander	256	407	418	271	40
Other race	989	524	491	58	7
30 to 34 years old					
Men					
White	5,974	13,887	15,829	4,939	2,213

[Continued]

★ 751 ★

Educational Attainment in Nevada, by Selected Characteristics
[Continued]

Characteristic	Not high school graduate	High school graduate	Some college or associate's degree	Bachelor's degree	Graduate or professional degree
Black	553	1,120	1,115	219	8
American Indian, Eskimo, and Aleut	195	274	268	25	16
Asian or Pacific Islander	287	282	409	260	141
Other race	1,565	690	539	115	101
Women					
White	3,601	11,298	14,462	4,067	1,493
Black	407	1,070	1,159	230	90
American Indian, Eskimo, and Aleut	109	225	394	70	8
Asian or Pacific Islander	321	473	449	313	63
Other race	685	306	396	63	33
35 to 39 years old					
Men					
White	4,030	11,378	15,608	6,148	3,299
Black	392	716	868	211	157
American Indian, Eskimo, and Aleut	155	254	227	41	30
Asian or Pacific Islander	195	370	582	259	138
Other race	1,059	467	371	93	48
Women					
White	3,267	9,885	13,089	4,216	1,953
Black	428	903	999	124	234
American Indian, Eskimo, and Aleut	81	214	287	35	4
Asian or Pacific Islander	509	478	582	386	76
Other race	684	466	256	35	4
40 to 69 years old					
Men					
White	19,491	37,166	45,519	17,786	12,602
Black	2,019	1,841	2,165	414	267
American Indian, Eskimo, and Aleut	550	546	543	161	115
Asian or Pacific Islander	789	723	1,007	701	402
Other race	2,396	963	732	252	71
Women					
White	15,860	35,560	34,459	9,278	6,513
Black	1,706	2,019	1,498	353	303
American Indian, Eskimo, and Aleut	498	442	617	117	59
Asian or Pacific Islander	1,438	1,398	1,177	740	280
Other race	1,528	644	495	110	91
70 years old and older					
Men					
White	1,352	1,241	1,000	361	250
Black	39	15	48	9	35
American Indian, Eskimo, and Aleut	0	3	15	0	17
Asian or Pacific Islander	50	47	8	0	6
Other race	63	2	0	0	11

[Continued]

★ 751 ★

Educational Attainment in Nevada, by Selected Characteristics

[Continued]

Characteristic	Not high school graduate	High school graduate	Some college or associate's degree	Bachelor's degree	Graduate or professional degree
Women					
White	910	1,020	685	185	152
Black	37	21	21	0	8
American Indian, Eskimo, and Aleut	10	0	0	0	7
Asian or Pacific Islander	44	21	10	0	17
Other race	24	0	13	0	0

Source: Census of Population and Housing, 1990: Equal Employment Opportunity (EEO) File on CD-ROM [machine-readable datafiles]. Prepared by the Bureau of the Census. Washington, DC: The Bureau, 1992.

★ 752 ★

Educational Attainment

Educational Attainment in New Hampshire, by Selected Characteristics

Table presents the number of civilians 16 years old or older who reported their educational backgrounds during the 1990 Census. Data show the number of individuals achieving various levels of education. Figures are reported by sex, age, and race.

Characteristic	Not high school graduate	High school graduate	Some college or associate's degree	Bachelor's degree	Graduate or professional degree
16 to 19 years old					
Men					
White	11,861	4,019	2,286	18	0
Black	70	19	16	0	0
American Indian, Eskimo, and Aleut	11	13	12	0	0
Asian or Pacific Islander	81	17	4	0	0
Other race	77	0	0	0	0
Women					
White	10,659	4,411	3,442	6	0
Black	35	61	90	0	0
American Indian, Eskimo, and Aleut	16	26	9	0	0
Asian or Pacific Islander	87	26	52	0	0
Other race	25	8	3	0	0
20 to 24 years old					
Men					
White	5,164	12,796	10,737	3,236	168
Black	30	114	143	9	0
American Indian, Eskimo, and Aleut	12	41	13	0	0
Asian or Pacific Islander	38	56	111	48	30
Other race	60	36	36	8	0
Women					
White	3,106	10,836	13,309	4,673	158

[Continued]

★ 752 ★

Educational Attainment in New Hampshire, by Selected Characteristics
[Continued]

Characteristic	Not high school graduate	High school graduate	Some college or associate's degree	Bachelor's degree	Graduate or professional degree
Black	18	82	84	26	0
American Indian, Eskimo, and Aleut	21	35	21	0	0
Asian or Pacific Islander	104	57	121	71	0
Other race	14	56	42	0	0
25 to 29 years old					
Men					
White	5,059	15,274	12,682	9,150	1,554
Black	22	125	189	81	37
American Indian, Eskimo, and Aleut	14	11	36	2	0
Asian or Pacific Islander	41	39	51	184	131
Other race	52	50	47	19	0
Women					
White	2,789	12,483	13,129	9,167	1,342
Black	12	70	88	45	13
American Indian, Eskimo, and Aleut	38	12	39	12	0
Asian or Pacific Islander	28	77	75	101	52
Other race	36	54	56	13	15
30 to 34 years old					
Men					
White	4,864	16,453	14,624	10,377	3,702
Black	19	69	111	71	33
American Indian, Eskimo, and Aleut	40	7	45	8	20
Asian or Pacific Islander	24	57	47	98	185
Other race	50	64	56	8	10
Women					
White	2,821	13,425	14,199	8,530	2,968
Black	22	52	96	71	21
American Indian, Eskimo, and Aleut	33	39	44	21	12
Asian or Pacific Islander	52	62	113	111	82
Other race	14	13	52	47	9
35 to 39 years old					
Men					
White	4,059	12,304	14,267	10,032	5,147
Black	24	35	72	51	53
American Indian, Eskimo, and Aleut	26	0	35	18	0
Asian or Pacific Islander	54	44	40	105	181
Other race	43	28	64	9	16
Women					
White	2,661	12,056	12,484	7,875	3,741
Black	27	49	62	31	20
American Indian, Eskimo, and Aleut	28	37	20	6	20
Asian or Pacific Islander	114	67	65	77	75
Other race	19	30	48	15	20

[Continued]

★ 752 ★

Educational Attainment in New Hampshire, by Selected Characteristics
[Continued]

Characteristic	Not high school graduate	High school graduate	Some college or associate's degree	Bachelor's degree	Graduate or professional degree
40 to 69 years old					
Men					
White	20,782	34,445	32,122	22,992	17,172
Black	83	154	187	93	48
American Indian, Eskimo, and Aleut	71	52	90	63	40
Asian or Pacific Islander	86	119	123	142	236
Other race	37	42	25	15	39
Women					
White	14,274	38,870	28,945	15,081	9,240
Black	90	89	160	71	58
American Indian, Eskimo, and Aleut	16	60	81	18	0
Asian or Pacific Islander	174	235	84	85	94
Other race	8	37	7	4	16
70 years old and older					
Men					
White	1,311	1,149	779	349	535
Black	7	6	11	0	0
American Indian, Eskimo, and Aleut	0	0	4	0	0
Asian or Pacific Islander	10	0	0	8	0
Other race	0	0	0	0	0
Women					
White	781	1,143	602	347	161
Black	0	0	0	0	0
American Indian, Eskimo, and Aleut	0	0	0	0	0
Asian or Pacific Islander	6	0	0	0	0
Other race	0	0	0	0	0

Source: Census of Population and Housing, 1990: Equal Employment Opportunity (EEO) File on CD-ROM [machine-readable datafiles]. Prepared by the Bureau of the Census. Washington, DC: The Bureau, 1992.

★ 753 ★
Educational Attainment

Educational Attainment in New Jersey, by Selected Characteristics

Table presents the number of civilians 16 years old or older who reported their educational backgrounds during the 1990 Census. Data show the number of individuals achieving various levels of education. Figures are reported by sex, age, and race.

Characteristic	Not high school graduate	High school graduate	Some college or associate's degree	Bachelor's degree	Graduate or professional degree
16 to 19 years old					
Men					
White	44,733	19,263	12,588	45	0
Black	8,606	3,945	1,526	0	0
American Indian, Eskimo, and Aleut	214	103	16	0	0
Asian or Pacific Islander	1,289	520	508	0	6
Other race	3,761	1,050	481	0	0
Women					
White	41,621	18,533	15,457	55	0
Black	8,326	3,991	2,904	6	0
American Indian, Eskimo, and Aleut	151	50	41	0	0
Asian or Pacific Islander	1,455	504	548	9	13
Other race	2,667	1,140	771	0	0
20 to 24 years old					
Men					
White	20,552	63,914	58,172	27,273	1,377
Black	7,956	12,953	8,403	1,440	74
American Indian, Eskimo, and Aleut	132	198	125	20	0
Asian or Pacific Islander	627	1,371	1,977	1,448	200
Other race	5,042	4,275	2,765	409	68
Women					
White	10,886	52,926	64,675	31,838	1,748
Black	4,733	11,249	12,680	2,836	274
American Indian, Eskimo, and Aleut	80	138	143	17	7
Asian or Pacific Islander	445	1,113	2,198	1,800	201
Other race	2,254	3,439	3,039	633	49
25 to 29 years old					
Men					
White	24,519	76,290	61,013	62,678	14,401
Black	6,554	13,901	10,726	4,692	910
American Indian, Eskimo, and Aleut	147	278	283	56	46
Asian or Pacific Islander	802	1,427	1,866	3,300	2,468
Other race	5,114	5,045	3,503	917	259
Women					
White	11,525	56,525	60,818	61,330	11,532
Black	5,255	12,461	13,738	6,025	1,155
American Indian, Eskimo, and Aleut	88	109	203	63	22
Asian or Pacific Islander	636	896	1,791	3,654	1,258
Other race	2,643	3,227	3,007	1,170	249
30 to 34 years old					
Men					
White	24,052	76,317	66,514	62,280	30,154

[Continued]

Educational Attainment in New Jersey, by Selected Characteristics
[Continued]

Characteristic	Not high school graduate	High school graduate	Some college or associate's degree	Bachelor's degree	Graduate or professional degree
Black	6,598	11,485	10,093	5,001	1,667
American Indian, Eskimo, and Aleut	135	157	138	99	45
Asian or Pacific Islander	947	1,313	2,172	4,177	4,626
Other race	5,040	3,689	2,712	903	606
Women					
White	12,413	55,719	57,735	48,944	18,614
Black	5,779	11,705	13,176	6,056	1,893
American Indian, Eskimo, and Aleut	118	142	193	83	40
Asian or Pacific Islander	721	1,348	1,794	4,779	2,025
Other race	2,657	2,783	2,317	972	382
35 to 39 years old					
Men					
White	20,654	58,410	60,078	57,932	35,593
Black	5,670	9,006	8,616	4,331	2,188
American Indian, Eskimo, and Aleut	79	151	110	69	38
Asian or Pacific Islander	796	1,176	2,058	4,308	4,441
Other race	3,995	2,695	1,797	711	360
Women					
White	12,566	54,483	50,202	41,125	23,216
Black	5,036	10,538	11,136	5,029	2,323
American Indian, Eskimo, and Aleut	52	168	159	116	55
Asian or Pacific Islander	1,034	1,396	1,782	4,546	2,166
Other race	2,947	2,024	1,526	336	314
40 to 69 years old					
Men					
White	137,424	219,967	165,584	149,600	128,581
Black	32,719	28,751	18,434	8,099	6,356
American Indian, Eskimo, and Aleut	612	453	350	165	93
Asian or Pacific Islander	3,008	3,433	4,617	11,687	13,056
Other race	14,513	4,865	2,545	818	548
Women					
White	95,969	258,613	143,644	92,232	64,255
Black	28,569	36,839	24,722	9,959	6,798
American Indian, Eskimo, and Aleut	398	505	328	72	104
Asian or Pacific Islander	3,738	3,944	4,385	8,874	4,795
Other race	10,199	4,583	2,298	786	468
70 years old and older					
Men					
White	10,760	7,808	5,670	3,706	4,413
Black	1,680	637	396	87	104
American Indian, Eskimo, and Aleut	25	19	0	0	6
Asian or Pacific Islander	70	71	46	133	65
Other race	211	24	15	6	0

[Continued]

★ 753 ★

Educational Attainment in New Jersey, by Selected Characteristics
[Continued]

Characteristic	Not high school graduate	High school graduate	Some college or associate's degree	Bachelor's degree	Graduate or professional degree
Women					
White	7,885	8,020	2,930	1,423	1,167
Black	1,747	638	321	101	75
American Indian, Eskimo, and Aleut	12	13	25	0	0
Asian or Pacific Islander	89	67	61	85	16
Other race	118	53	32	0	0

Source: Census of Population and Housing, 1990: Equal Employment Opportunity (EEO) File on CD-ROM [machine-readable datafiles]. Prepared by the Bureau of the Census. Washington, DC: The Bureau, 1992.

★ 754 ★

Educational Attainment

Educational Attainment in New Mexico, by Selected Characteristics

Table presents the number of civilians 16 years old or older who reported their educational backgrounds during the 1990 Census. Data show the number of individuals achieving various levels of education. Figures are reported by sex, age, and race.

Characteristic	Not high school graduate	High school graduate	Some college or associate's degree	Bachelor's degree	Graduate or professional degree
16 to 19 years old					
Men					
White	10,096	3,785	2,449	16	0
Black	157	68	52	0	0
American Indian, Eskimo, and Aleut	933	267	110	0	0
Asian or Pacific Islander	104	21	36	0	0
Other race	2,301	657	247	0	0
Women					
White	7,283	3,629	3,029	0	0
Black	212	109	69	0	0
American Indian, Eskimo, and Aleut	678	425	218	0	0
Asian or Pacific Islander	75	40	34	0	0
Other race	1,515	785	478	0	2
20 to 24 years old					
Men					
White	4,918	9,496	10,866	1,590	214
Black	63	314	303	25	8
American Indian, Eskimo, and Aleut	998	1,689	1,011	27	13
Asian or Pacific Islander	34	102	120	40	11
Other race	2,010	2,602	1,512	184	0
Women					
White	2,689	7,624	11,258	2,283	137

[Continued]

★ 754 ★

Educational Attainment in New Mexico, by Selected Characteristics
[Continued]

Characteristic	Not high school graduate	High school graduate	Some college or associate's degree	Bachelor's degree	Graduate or professional degree
Black	61	199	245	51	0
American Indian, Eskimo, and Aleut	598	1,524	925	77	0
Asian or Pacific Islander	46	50	128	99	0
Other race	941	2,329	1,929	213	18
25 to 29 years old					
Men					
White	6,077	13,087	11,547	5,526	1,588
Black	89	258	375	104	25
American Indian, Eskimo, and Aleut	1,274	2,084	1,287	165	33
Asian or Pacific Islander	52	52	89	68	146
Other race	2,298	3,704	2,101	571	163
Women					
White	3,106	9,334	11,499	5,407	1,390
Black	34	308	378	68	19
American Indian, Eskimo, and Aleut	627	1,460	1,369	151	29
Asian or Pacific Islander	47	109	156	121	61
Other race	1,203	2,535	1,813	453	116
30 to 34 years old					
Men					
White	5,925	13,765	12,635	6,702	3,484
Black	85	343	557	109	60
American Indian, Eskimo, and Aleut	1,102	1,558	1,065	169	70
Asian or Pacific Islander	79	97	97	143	180
Other race	2,134	3,275	2,020	575	186
Women					
White	3,199	10,631	12,439	6,190	2,587
Black	103	244	386	131	40
American Indian, Eskimo, and Aleut	824	1,401	1,367	111	56
Asian or Pacific Islander	78	165	148	131	60
Other race	1,106	2,743	2,073	544	235
35 to 39 years old					
Men					
White	4,148	9,792	13,254	8,336	5,247
Black	63	201	396	166	97
American Indian, Eskimo, and Aleut	706	1,241	1,021	200	121
Asian or Pacific Islander	99	57	104	76	236
Other race	1,702	2,346	1,666	639	221
Women					
White	2,820	8,926	11,857	6,331	4,319
Black	77	168	446	87	55
American Indian, Eskimo, and Aleut	717	993	1,214	248	138
Asian or Pacific Islander	142	53	216	172	57
Other race	963	2,182	1,510	415	320

[Continued]

★ 754 ★

Educational Attainment in New Mexico, by Selected Characteristics
[Continued]

Characteristic	Not high school graduate	High school graduate	Some college or associate's degree	Bachelor's degree	Graduate or professional degree
40 to 69 years old					
Men					
White	19,997	29,438	33,682	21,740	22,270
Black	594	584	762	243	219
American Indian, Eskimo, and Aleut	2,478	2,299	1,749	476	354
Asian or Pacific Islander	132	176	204	171	417
Other race	5,526	4,070	2,410	696	691
Women					
White	13,133	29,259	29,753	14,226	12,939
Black	478	463	515	153	143
American Indian, Eskimo, and Aleut	2,083	1,980	1,825	361	285
Asian or Pacific Islander	310	397	246	170	219
Other race	3,758	3,580	1,761	402	420
70 years old and older					
Men					
White	1,576	1,132	773	508	650
Black	21	0	22	0	0
American Indian, Eskimo, and Aleut	47	32	15	0	2
Asian or Pacific Islander	0	0	0	4	0
Other race	126	36	12	0	14
Women					
White	750	779	656	162	221
Black	55	17	9	0	13
American Indian, Eskimo, and Aleut	113	0	17	9	3
Asian or Pacific Islander	6	7	5	4	0
Other race	113	34	2	0	0

Source: Census of Population and Housing, 1990: Equal Employment Opportunity (EEO) File on CD-ROM [machine-readable datafiles]. Prepared by the Bureau of the Census. Washington, DC: The Bureau, 1992.

★ 755 ★

Educational Attainment

Educational Attainment in New York, by Selected Characteristics

Table presents the number of civilians 16 years old or older who reported their educational backgrounds during the 1990 Census. Data show the number of individuals achieving various levels of education. Figures are reported by sex, age, and race.

Characteristic	Not high school graduate	High school graduate	Some college or associate's degree	Bachelor's degree	Graduate or professional degree
16 to 19 years old					
Men					
White	92,174	37,273	33,224	225	29
Black	18,722	7,909	3,652	20	0
American Indian, Eskimo, and Aleut	677	224	113	0	0
Asian or Pacific Islander	3,094	1,483	1,176	71	0
Other race	9,844	2,973	1,167	18	0
Women					
White	78,616	40,264	43,486	311	2
Black	17,623	8,557	6,569	36	11
American Indian, Eskimo, and Aleut	315	146	185	0	0
Asian or Pacific Islander	2,638	1,297	1,762	32	0
Other race	6,716	2,612	1,995	63	9
20 to 24 years old					
Men					
White	48,644	120,980	139,536	59,711	3,380
Black	20,772	26,981	22,690	3,873	430
American Indian, Eskimo, and Aleut	658	643	492	65	10
Asian or Pacific Islander	2,429	3,854	6,261	3,668	426
Other race	14,902	11,529	8,159	972	96
Women					
White	22,554	95,968	156,000	75,729	5,158
Black	14,178	24,343	32,014	7,680	589
American Indian, Eskimo, and Aleut	334	538	722	146	15
Asian or Pacific Islander	1,803	3,368	6,246	4,726	298
Other race	7,344	7,570	9,982	1,778	96
25 to 29 years old					
Men					
White	53,767	145,623	142,926	119,164	40,238
Black	20,773	29,454	29,279	10,321	2,334
American Indian, Eskimo, and Aleut	524	747	606	232	54
Asian or Pacific Islander	4,562	5,285	6,206	8,118	4,956
Other race	15,482	11,962	10,381	2,720	902
Women					
White	23,413	103,386	134,535	118,896	40,471
Black	13,395	26,063	38,059	16,545	2,822
American Indian, Eskimo, and Aleut	248	618	551	167	25
Asian or Pacific Islander	2,894	3,650	4,392	9,037	3,519
Other race	6,473	7,800	10,095	3,229	782
30 to 34 years old					
Men					
White	50,863	150,785	154,551	114,300	69,115

[Continued]

★ 755 ★

Educational Attainment in New York, by Selected Characteristics
[Continued]

Characteristic	Not high school graduate	High school graduate	Some college or associate's degree	Bachelor's degree	Graduate or professional degree
Black	20,204	24,944	27,788	10,876	4,213
American Indian, Eskimo, and Aleut	797	656	661	207	119
Asian or Pacific Islander	6,288	6,680	7,077	8,012	7,406
Other race	13,426	10,404	8,214	2,503	1,164
Women					
White	24,940	106,811	129,988	88,637	58,263
Black	17,295	25,509	37,270	14,280	5,721
American Indian, Eskimo, and Aleut	443	567	719	191	154
Asian or Pacific Islander	3,675	4,327	4,654	8,640	3,745
Other race	7,500	6,845	8,325	2,633	1,005
35 to 39 years old					
Men					
White	45,008	119,061	144,062	101,555	79,263
Black	18,063	20,780	23,398	8,720	5,034
American Indian, Eskimo, and Aleut	550	514	501	268	151
Asian or Pacific Islander	6,260	4,864	5,666	7,458	7,045
Other race	12,286	6,842	6,289	1,893	992
Women					
White	24,661	104,820	116,755	71,373	66,864
Black	15,639	25,276	29,917	11,628	6,920
American Indian, Eskimo, and Aleut	333	453	746	243	139
Asian or Pacific Islander	5,349	3,868	3,827	5,844	3,541
Other race	7,341	5,928	5,475	1,310	876
40 to 69 years old					
Men					
White	275,380	434,730	371,939	257,293	282,333
Black	84,953	72,766	51,911	19,057	16,538
American Indian, Eskimo, and Aleut	1,558	1,226	1,100	470	388
Asian or Pacific Islander	22,470	13,135	12,170	17,730	20,142
Other race	43,448	15,576	8,312	2,550	1,896
Women					
White	177,964	487,380	322,664	164,922	193,825
Black	82,446	93,152	71,907	25,378	21,599
American Indian, Eskimo, and Aleut	1,369	1,626	1,391	502	376
Asian or Pacific Islander	21,881	11,974	9,857	13,508	9,672
Other race	30,333	13,705	7,904	2,078	1,891
70 years old and older					
Men					
White	19,476	16,596	12,275	8,263	13,574
Black	2,978	1,371	860	258	349
American Indian, Eskimo, and Aleut	49	3	4	4	2
Asian or Pacific Islander	571	187	116	206	219
Other race	557	164	44	50	6

[Continued]

★ 755 ★

Educational Attainment in New York, by Selected Characteristics
[Continued]

Characteristic	Not high school graduate	High school graduate	Some college or associate's degree	Bachelor's degree	Graduate or professional degree
Women					
White	14,368	17,860	8,618	4,399	4,854
Black	3,518	1,857	805	364	324
American Indian, Eskimo, and Aleut	61	31	53	19	7
Asian or Pacific Islander	415	131	96	87	105
Other race	387	164	99	16	53

Source: Census of Population and Housing, 1990: Equal Employment Opportunity (EEO) File on CD-ROM [machine-readable datafiles]. Prepared by the Bureau of the Census. Washington, DC: The Bureau, 1992.

★ 756 ★

Educational Attainment

Educational Attainment in North Carolina, by Selected Characteristics

Table presents the number of civilians 16 years old or older who reported their educational backgrounds during the 1990 Census. Data show the number of individuals achieving various levels of education. Figures are reported by sex, age, and race.

Characteristic	Not high school graduate	High school graduate	Some college or associate's degree	Bachelor's degree	Graduate or professional degree
16 to 19 years old					
Men					
White	51,426	16,394	11,323	10	0
Black	15,928	4,731	1,874	10	0
American Indian, Eskimo, and Aleut	1,059	255	138	0	0
Asian or Pacific Islander	550	160	139	0	0
Other race	344	92	26	0	0
Women					
White	38,692	16,602	16,489	12	32
Black	12,725	5,471	4,294	33	0
American Indian, Eskimo, and Aleut	805	349	267	0	0
Asian or Pacific Islander	277	187	182	0	0
Other race	192	48	41	0	0
20 to 24 years old					
Men					
White	29,095	53,569	52,741	14,351	615
Black	9,664	17,975	10,402	1,640	98
American Indian, Eskimo, and Aleut	1,022	1,184	520	132	0
Asian or Pacific Islander	243	298	497	398	67
Other race	1,232	412	245	70	0
Women					
White	14,789	42,129	62,297	20,046	880

[Continued]

★ 756 ★

Educational Attainment in North Carolina, by Selected Characteristics

[Continued]

Characteristic	Not high school graduate	High school graduate	Some college or associate's degree	Bachelor's degree	Graduate or professional degree
Black	6,235	17,051	17,752	3,264	117
American Indian, Eskimo, and Aleut	545	865	599	54	0
Asian or Pacific Islander	283	228	594	395	17
Other race	108	225	207	39	2
25 to 29 years old					
Men					
White	33,217	62,475	52,695	35,667	7,028
Black	10,529	19,935	11,142	3,872	471
American Indian, Eskimo, and Aleut	1,146	1,170	576	125	8
Asian or Pacific Islander	327	316	418	525	558
Other race	931	400	374	126	28
Women					
White	17,956	46,988	56,722	37,914	6,619
Black	8,420	18,954	18,557	6,535	827
American Indian, Eskimo, and Aleut	546	963	790	315	55
Asian or Pacific Islander	318	305	448	498	198
Other race	205	216	314	126	11
30 to 34 years old					
Men					
White	33,480	59,718	55,592	34,789	13,641
Black	11,651	19,676	11,838	4,286	1,013
American Indian, Eskimo, and Aleut	959	1,080	525	137	75
Asian or Pacific Islander	357	255	264	405	804
Other race	868	176	283	111	62
Women					
White	17,883	50,486	56,222	31,408	11,139
Black	9,981	19,406	18,659	7,156	1,367
American Indian, Eskimo, and Aleut	736	906	676	297	95
Asian or Pacific Islander	555	330	441	362	253
Other race	145	186	254	109	47
35 to 39 years old					
Men					
White	26,570	49,252	55,530	34,204	17,169
Black	10,992	16,350	11,074	3,985	1,318
American Indian, Eskimo, and Aleut	1,007	837	568	176	91
Asian or Pacific Islander	237	231	397	360	573
Other race	554	172	213	47	17
Women					
White	16,953	50,044	53,016	26,829	13,951
Black	10,105	18,399	16,029	5,479	2,451
American Indian, Eskimo, and Aleut	628	1,094	629	153	131
Asian or Pacific Islander	418	365	429	298	206
Other race	98	141	195	78	46

[Continued]

★ 756 ★

Educational Attainment in North Carolina, by Selected Characteristics

[Continued]

Characteristic	Not high school graduate	High school graduate	Some college or associate's degree	Bachelor's degree	Graduate or professional degree
40 to 69 years old					
Men					
White	150,875	164,027	147,320	86,904	57,597
Black	50,791	29,525	19,714	6,163	4,485
American Indian, Eskimo, and Aleut	4,108	1,573	1,177	386	239
Asian or Pacific Islander	593	551	689	868	1,613
Other race	575	152	265	77	105
Women					
White	103,042	183,046	138,004	54,326	32,554
Black	43,949	37,798	23,955	9,230	5,491
American Indian, Eskimo, and Aleut	2,656	1,842	1,152	418	218
Asian or Pacific Islander	1,258	1,085	805	663	544
Other race	289	160	207	54	23
70 years old and older					
Men					
White	9,363	4,309	3,326	2,217	1,559
Black	3,040	344	154	41	95
American Indian, Eskimo, and Aleut	35	0	0	9	0
Asian or Pacific Islander	41	0	7	2	0
Other race	5	0	6	0	0
Women					
White	5,834	3,899	2,437	743	466
Black	2,732	596	299	59	135
American Indian, Eskimo, and Aleut	116	0	6	0	0
Asian or Pacific Islander	19	0	5	9	0
Other race	6	0	0	0	0

Source: Census of Population and Housing, 1990: Equal Employment Opportunity (EEO) File on CD-ROM [machine-readable datafiles]. Prepared by the Bureau of the Census. Washington, DC: The Bureau, 1992.

★ 757 ★

Educational Attainment

Educational Attainment in North Dakota, by Selected Characteristics

Table presents the number of civilians 16 years old or older who reported their educational backgrounds during the 1990 Census. Data show the number of individuals achieving various levels of education. Figures are reported by sex, age, and race.

Characteristic	Not high school graduate	High school graduate	Some college or associate's degree	Bachelor's degree	Graduate or professional degree
16 to 19 years old					
Men					
White	5,685	1,770	1,735	0	0
Black	35	15	18	0	0
American Indian, Eskimo, and Aleut	230	62	71	0	0
Asian or Pacific Islander	8	0	3	0	0
Other race	18	2	0	0	0
Women					
White	5,182	1,826	2,326	0	0
Black	25	3	0	0	0
American Indian, Eskimo, and Aleut	138	94	59	0	0
Asian or Pacific Islander	39	12	11	0	0
Other race	11	12	6	0	0
20 to 24 years old					
Men					
White	943	4,274	9,502	1,584	25
Black	0	27	36	16	0
American Indian, Eskimo, and Aleut	129	206	202	3	0
Asian or Pacific Islander	6	21	38	0	10
Other race	8	19	6	0	0
Women					
White	510	3,217	9,857	2,246	104
Black	11	39	41	0	0
American Indian, Eskimo, and Aleut	161	173	240	3	0
Asian or Pacific Islander	20	56	52	20	0
Other race	3	15	12	0	0
25 to 29 years old					
Men					
White	1,471	6,380	8,389	3,461	548
Black	0	69	63	36	10
American Indian, Eskimo, and Aleut	146	233	289	17	4
Asian or Pacific Islander	0	2	37	19	5
Other race	22	20	32	20	6
Women					
White	706	4,819	7,853	4,343	488
Black	13	27	67	40	0
American Indian, Eskimo, and Aleut	124	179	250	87	0
Asian or Pacific Islander	14	17	33	24	0
Other race	6	21	25	0	0
30 to 34 years old					
Men					
White	1,702	7,956	8,378	3,997	1,238

[Continued]

★ 757 ★

Educational Attainment in North Dakota, by Selected Characteristics
[Continued]

Characteristic	Not high school graduate	High school graduate	Some college or associate's degree	Bachelor's degree	Graduate or professional degree
Black	3	16	17	6	6
American Indian, Eskimo, and Aleut	153	224	311	43	6
Asian or Pacific Islander	19	14	66	39	40
Other race	12	21	6	0	0
Women					
White	737	5,994	8,721	4,046	837
Black	0	7	21	31	0
American Indian, Eskimo, and Aleut	103	122	278	75	18
Asian or Pacific Islander	32	25	36	6	2
Other race	17	15	35	8	0
35 to 39 years old					
Men					
White	1,310	5,938	9,231	4,855	1,491
Black	5	27	36	10	6
American Indian, Eskimo, and Aleut	125	124	223	63	2
Asian or Pacific Islander	1	7	6	2	43
Other race	0	31	8	0	0
Women					
White	661	4,636	8,032	4,243	955
Black	5	21	24	0	0
American Indian, Eskimo, and Aleut	59	191	229	106	15
Asian or Pacific Islander	19	26	34	4	7
Other race	18	11	10	6	0
40 to 69 years old					
Men					
White	14,022	18,236	16,524	9,786	5,989
Black	0	30	23	4	10
American Indian, Eskimo, and Aleut	488	352	369	83	62
Asian or Pacific Islander	26	16	15	7	116
Other race	36	6	11	0	0
Women					
White	6,890	16,973	15,558	6,994	2,362
Black	6	8	19	7	0
American Indian, Eskimo, and Aleut	374	364	458	123	41
Asian or Pacific Islander	65	41	38	21	13
Other race	37	19	27	0	2
70 years old and older					
Men					
White	1,978	525	412	215	165
Black	0	0	0	0	0
American Indian, Eskimo, and Aleut	15	2	0	0	0
Asian or Pacific Islander	0	0	0	0	0
Other race	0	0	0	0	0

[Continued]

★ 757 ★

Educational Attainment in North Dakota, by Selected Characteristics

[Continued]

Characteristic	Not high school graduate	High school graduate	Some college or associate's degree	Bachelor's degree	Graduate or professional degree
Women					
White	731	474	285	147	71
Black	0	0	0	0	7
American Indian, Eskimo, and Aleut	7	1	11	3	0
Asian or Pacific Islander	0	0	0	0	0
Other race	0	0	0	0	0

Source: Census of Population and Housing, 1990: Equal Employment Opportunity (EEO) File on CD-ROM [machine-readable datafiles]. Prepared by the Bureau of the Census. Washington, DC: The Bureau, 1992.

★ 758 ★

Educational Attainment

Educational Attainment in Ohio, by Selected Characteristics

Table presents the number of civilians 16 years old or older who reported their educational backgrounds during the 1990 Census. Data show the number of individuals achieving various levels of education. Figures are reported by sex, age, and race.

Characteristic	Not high school graduate	High school graduate	Some college or associate's degree	Bachelor's degree	Graduate or professional degree
16 to 19 years old					
Men					
White	94,731	32,456	20,855	35	9
Black	9,749	3,425	1,872	0	0
American Indian, Eskimo, and Aleut	234	82	46	0	0
Asian or Pacific Islander	555	231	271	0	0
Other race	680	212	196	0	0
Women					
White	77,974	36,441	29,040	31	0
Black	8,720	4,252	3,027	0	0
American Indian, Eskimo, and Aleut	170	59	59	0	0
Asian or Pacific Islander	724	235	298	0	0
Other race	558	341	178	0	0
20 to 24 years old					
Men					
White	36,219	110,799	102,147	26,824	1,031
Black	6,483	11,437	8,537	1,045	102
American Indian, Eskimo, and Aleut	197	310	238	32	0
Asian or Pacific Islander	216	454	1,189	714	140
Other race	581	781	587	64	20
Women					
White	18,226	89,722	109,792	32,710	1,724

[Continued]

★ 758 ★

Educational Attainment in Ohio, by Selected Characteristics

[Continued]

Characteristic	Not high school graduate	High school graduate	Some college or associate's degree	Bachelor's degree	Graduate or professional degree
Black	3,562	10,035	12,464	1,601	91
American Indian, Eskimo, and Aleut	115	288	110	26	0
Asian or Pacific Islander	158	417	1,075	526	110
Other race	301	643	566	108	0
25 to 29 years old					
Men					
White	41,362	133,718	93,581	60,465	13,816
Black	6,103	11,928	9,529	3,144	610
American Indian, Eskimo, and Aleut	245	266	298	48	14
Asian or Pacific Islander	342	300	512	881	1,086
Other race	741	1,010	577	196	98
Women					
White	22,730	98,688	93,828	58,517	11,273
Black	4,175	10,915	15,316	3,907	768
American Indian, Eskimo, and Aleut	78	256	239	55	18
Asian or Pacific Islander	283	266	590	930	664
Other race	375	548	654	156	75
30 to 34 years old					
Men					
White	43,068	149,359	103,765	59,062	25,719
Black	6,212	12,034	11,336	3,267	963
American Indian, Eskimo, and Aleut	287	411	257	94	34
Asian or Pacific Islander	230	361	545	779	1,811
Other race	668	815	531	191	77
Women					
White	25,321	112,365	94,942	45,269	17,366
Black	4,758	11,489	17,818	3,964	993
American Indian, Eskimo, and Aleut	105	309	224	45	15
Asian or Pacific Islander	465	380	422	660	765
Other race	394	654	487	177	82
35 to 39 years old					
Men					
White	33,171	122,592	102,613	57,950	34,816
Black	4,949	10,382	10,770	3,039	1,467
American Indian, Eskimo, and Aleut	125	332	344	34	43
Asian or Pacific Islander	365	362	605	773	1,451
Other race	584	495	461	126	49
Women					
White	22,001	106,124	85,752	42,638	23,385
Black	4,407	10,660	14,630	3,494	2,133
American Indian, Eskimo, and Aleut	99	289	297	31	75
Asian or Pacific Islander	558	449	429	671	553
Other race	354	524	281	98	56

[Continued]

★ 758 ★

Educational Attainment in Ohio, by Selected Characteristics
[Continued]

Characteristic	Not high school graduate	High school graduate	Some college or associate's degree	Bachelor's degree	Graduate or professional degree
40 to 69 years old					
Men					
White	195,956	367,053	242,014	147,903	116,787
Black	26,619	28,401	20,192	5,988	4,624
American Indian, Eskimo, and Aleut	702	622	521	141	100
Asian or Pacific Islander	803	1,065	995	1,961	5,004
Other race	2,080	790	555	174	226
Women					
White	124,605	362,672	207,115	91,056	62,464
Black	24,097	31,917	26,949	6,130	5,203
American Indian, Eskimo, and Aleut	434	456	511	159	55
Asian or Pacific Islander	1,613	1,395	1,280	1,624	1,774
Other race	1,084	698	395	87	98
70 years old and older					
Men					
White	9,468	9,671	5,598	3,304	3,895
Black	1,136	457	384	105	123
American Indian, Eskimo, and Aleut	7	20	10	0	0
Asian or Pacific Islander	0	35	11	17	26
Other race	13	0	5	0	0
Women					
White	6,147	7,836	3,856	1,498	1,131
Black	1,248	549	343	76	71
American Indian, Eskimo, and Aleut	42	13	6	0	0
Asian or Pacific Islander	10	21	0	16	31
Other race	1	0	0	0	0

Source: Census of Population and Housing, 1990: Equal Employment Opportunity (EEO) File on CD-ROM [machine-readable datafiles]. Prepared by the Bureau of the Census. Washington, DC: The Bureau, 1992.

★ 759 ★
Educational Attainment

Educational Attainment in Oklahoma, by Selected Characteristics

Table presents the number of civilians 16 years old or older who reported their educational backgrounds during the 1990 Census. Data show the number of individuals achieving various levels of education. Figures are reported by sex, age, and race.

Characteristic	Not high school graduate	High school graduate	Some college or associate's degree	Bachelor's degree	Graduate or professional degree
16 to 19 years old					
Men					
White	22,399	8,251	6,477	17	6
Black	2,098	760	459	0	0
American Indian, Eskimo, and Aleut	2,471	1,150	650	0	0
Asian or Pacific Islander	284	98	107	0	0
Other race	651	134	101	0	0
Women					
White	19,007	7,881	8,835	0	0
Black	1,559	786	683	10	0
American Indian, Eskimo, and Aleut	2,071	1,138	787	0	0
Asian or Pacific Islander	262	65	102	0	0
Other race	278	118	87	11	0
20 to 24 years old					
Men					
White	9,429	22,976	28,306	5,214	263
Black	950	2,228	2,019	228	49
American Indian, Eskimo, and Aleut	1,640	2,832	2,324	197	8
Asian or Pacific Islander	130	228	566	217	23
Other race	865	401	392	65	0
Women					
White	5,961	17,338	27,674	6,874	261
Black	828	1,938	2,843	435	31
American Indian, Eskimo, and Aleut	1,002	1,992	2,237	231	2
Asian or Pacific Islander	84	175	419	96	6
Other race	343	338	271	59	0
25 to 29 years old					
Men					
White	13,095	30,773	27,652	13,841	3,116
Black	958	2,599	2,628	778	74
American Indian, Eskimo, and Aleut	2,127	3,305	2,135	426	61
Asian or Pacific Islander	284	174	317	336	228
Other race	1,114	407	460	70	23
Women					
White	7,409	22,152	24,220	14,114	2,467
Black	962	2,620	3,151	881	153
American Indian, Eskimo, and Aleut	1,149	2,285	2,171	681	89
Asian or Pacific Islander	179	168	188	166	73
Other race	506	322	271	147	24
30 to 34 years old					
Men					
White	11,947	32,738	29,941	16,516	5,797

[Continued]

★ 759 ★

Educational Attainment in Oklahoma, by Selected Characteristics

[Continued]

Characteristic	Not high school graduate	High school graduate	Some college or associate's degree	Bachelor's degree	Graduate or professional degree
Black	1,238	2,630	2,537	930	287
American Indian, Eskimo, and Aleut	1,956	2,884	2,499	628	150
Asian or Pacific Islander	117	181	355	211	304
Other race	1,311	323	328	175	27
Women					
White	8,057	24,482	26,291	13,705	4,703
Black	910	2,421	3,306	986	220
American Indian, Eskimo, and Aleut	1,203	2,504	2,513	592	226
Asian or Pacific Islander	233	246	331	223	125
Other race	431	258	270	30	35
35 to 39 years old					
Men					
White	9,535	23,979	30,257	17,140	8,388
Black	659	1,898	2,129	732	474
American Indian, Eskimo, and Aleut	1,071	2,418	2,548	880	396
Asian or Pacific Islander	211	162	246	220	323
Other race	873	338	271	112	35
Women					
White	6,813	23,170	25,319	12,305	6,270
Black	773	2,278	2,768	957	408
American Indian, Eskimo, and Aleut	893	2,176	2,253	726	332
Asian or Pacific Islander	354	286	316	139	161
Other race	290	255	203	73	0
40 to 69 years old					
Men					
White	48,902	80,477	82,091	48,300	33,419
Black	3,651	4,864	4,268	1,505	804
American Indian, Eskimo, and Aleut	4,982	5,339	5,866	2,106	1,398
Asian or Pacific Islander	399	362	562	423	855
Other race	1,646	489	437	135	81
Women					
White	36,550	82,960	70,996	25,109	19,030
Black	4,023	5,650	4,353	1,235	1,081
American Indian, Eskimo, and Aleut	3,804	6,201	5,193	1,512	991
Asian or Pacific Islander	874	737	668	394	281
Other race	878	471	270	42	16
70 years old and older					
Men					
White	4,861	2,611	2,422	1,267	1,293
Black	246	72	75	23	21
American Indian, Eskimo, and Aleut	132	118	40	19	33
Asian or Pacific Islander	11	0	0	0	16
Other race	20	0	1	0	0

[Continued]

★ 759 ★

Educational Attainment in Oklahoma, by Selected Characteristics
[Continued]

Characteristic	Not high school graduate	High school graduate	Some college or associate's degree	Bachelor's degree	Graduate or professional degree
Women					
White	2,527	2,685	1,569	503	293
Black	307	115	124	52	29
American Indian, Eskimo, and Aleut	164	163	65	20	14
Asian or Pacific Islander	6	7	11	0	0
Other race	16	4	0	0	0

Source: Census of Population and Housing, 1990: Equal Employment Opportunity (EEO) File on CD-ROM [machine-readable datafiles]. Prepared by the Bureau of the Census. Washington, DC: The Bureau, 1992.

★ 760 ★
Educational Attainment

Educational Attainment in Oregon, by Selected Characteristics

Table presents the number of civilians 16 years old or older who reported their educational backgrounds during the 1990 Census. Data show the number of individuals achieving various levels of education. Figures are reported by sex, age, and race.

Characteristic	Not high school graduate	High school graduate	Some college or associate's degree	Bachelor's degree	Graduate or professional degree
16 to 19 years old					
Men					
White	24,120	8,278	5,560	8	0
Black	564	127	168	0	0
American Indian, Eskimo, and Aleut	506	129	35	0	0
Asian or Pacific Islander	666	172	279	0	0
Other race	1,219	159	50	0	0
Women					
White	19,505	8,321	8,048	4	0
Black	388	187	178	2	0
American Indian, Eskimo, and Aleut	441	137	96	0	0
Asian or Pacific Islander	536	217	203	0	0
Other race	579	169	145	7	0
20 to 24 years old					
Men					
White	12,264	23,408	26,442	4,832	243
Black	232	535	611	28	28
American Indian, Eskimo, and Aleut	439	553	304	22	0
Asian or Pacific Islander	226	570	1,099	323	12
Other race	2,053	757	465	47	0
Women					
White	6,691	16,303	29,855	6,351	335

[Continued]

★ 760 ★

Educational Attainment in Oregon, by Selected Characteristics
[Continued]

Characteristic	Not high school graduate	High school graduate	Some college or associate's degree	Bachelor's degree	Graduate or professional degree
Black	158	315	510	117	0
American Indian, Eskimo, and Aleut	265	391	385	34	0
Asian or Pacific Islander	143	456	945	343	12
Other race	529	421	381	28	0
25 to 29 years old					
Men					
White	13,191	27,159	29,500	14,344	2,522
Black	288	484	663	143	15
American Indian, Eskimo, and Aleut	414	525	455	47	0
Asian or Pacific Islander	352	437	1,006	594	276
Other race	2,165	541	427	128	27
Women					
White	7,227	19,848	27,413	13,576	2,198
Black	165	370	655	104	36
American Indian, Eskimo, and Aleut	194	457	452	77	7
Asian or Pacific Islander	211	286	813	605	175
Other race	604	352	314	79	9
30 to 34 years old					
Men					
White	12,468	29,660	36,611	16,304	6,258
Black	224	465	651	236	78
American Indian, Eskimo, and Aleut	451	512	400	101	27
Asian or Pacific Islander	297	463	887	722	506
Other race	2,079	469	425	147	49
Women					
White	7,447	23,428	33,758	14,018	4,813
Black	170	409	614	230	64
American Indian, Eskimo, and Aleut	276	417	619	117	11
Asian or Pacific Islander	348	484	818	589	218
Other race	498	354	343	98	5
35 to 39 years old					
Men					
White	8,426	25,340	42,968	19,711	11,078
Black	146	355	556	298	147
American Indian, Eskimo, and Aleut	250	508	556	75	65
Asian or Pacific Islander	344	410	1,108	626	469
Other race	1,179	301	415	78	62
Women					
White	5,849	22,071	37,961	16,699	7,900
Black	197	286	527	141	67
American Indian, Eskimo, and Aleut	230	402	590	132	31
Asian or Pacific Islander	450	463	742	517	283
Other race	526	289	387	88	21

[Continued]

★ 760 ★

Educational Attainment in Oregon, by Selected Characteristics
[Continued]

Characteristic	Not high school graduate	High school graduate	Some college or associate's degree	Bachelor's degree	Graduate or professional degree
40 to 69 years old					
Men					
White	36,598	77,629	100,523	52,811	40,927
Black	715	1,004	1,316	465	358
American Indian, Eskimo, and Aleut	843	834	1,376	241	231
Asian or Pacific Islander	834	975	1,458	1,374	965
Other race	2,088	478	570	167	127
Women					
White	24,892	75,256	89,072	35,115	20,865
Black	448	767	1,081	384	200
American Indian, Eskimo, and Aleut	673	950	1,070	264	120
Asian or Pacific Islander	1,339	1,375	1,494	994	518
Other race	760	374	360	58	37
70 years old and older					
Men					
White	3,278	2,749	2,322	1,190	1,063
Black	19	20	32	0	11
American Indian, Eskimo, and Aleut	60	15	1	14	10
Asian or Pacific Islander	50	33	34	19	15
Other race	20	6	4	0	0
Women					
White	1,283	1,913	1,901	525	399
Black	29	12	42	20	0
American Indian, Eskimo, and Aleut	11	3	15	0	7
Asian or Pacific Islander	38	40	13	0	4
Other race	0	0	0	0	0

Source: Census of Population and Housing, 1990: Equal Employment Opportunity (EEO) File on CD-ROM [machine-readable datafiles]. Prepared by the Bureau of the Census. Washington, DC: The Bureau, 1992.

★ 761 ★

Educational Attainment

Educational Attainment in Pennsylvania, by Selected Characteristics

Table presents the number of civilians 16 years old or older who reported their educational backgrounds during the 1990 Census. Data show the number of individuals achieving various levels of education. Figures are reported by sex, age, and race.

Characteristic	Not high school graduate	High school graduate	Some college or associate's degree	Bachelor's degree	Graduate or professional degree
16 to 19 years old					
Men					
White	87,574	38,071	22,195	44	0
Black	8,559	3,643	1,573	0	0
American Indian, Eskimo, and Aleut	261	71	38	0	0
Asian or Pacific Islander	1,033	390	416	0	0
Other race	1,454	387	218	0	0
Women					
White	74,463	39,937	30,898	86	9
Black	6,602	3,848	2,915	0	13
American Indian, Eskimo, and Aleut	115	74	71	0	0
Asian or Pacific Islander	852	268	474	7	0
Other race	970	363	344	0	0
20 to 24 years old					
Men					
White	33,743	127,450	90,170	35,710	1,795
Black	6,810	12,438	7,649	1,364	108
American Indian, Eskimo, and Aleut	192	292	217	54	0
Asian or Pacific Islander	415	874	1,450	934	145
Other race	1,923	1,399	728	144	7
Women					
White	16,767	102,781	105,384	44,055	2,786
Black	4,441	10,887	10,149	2,399	152
American Indian, Eskimo, and Aleut	64	148	236	22	0
Asian or Pacific Islander	322	796	1,276	908	109
Other race	725	886	889	202	14
25 to 29 years old					
Men					
White	38,185	159,036	83,752	69,437	16,401
Black	6,944	12,990	8,028	3,252	616
American Indian, Eskimo, and Aleut	175	328	113	73	5
Asian or Pacific Islander	460	688	859	1,265	1,233
Other race	1,661	1,477	739	238	70
Women					
White	18,291	116,036	84,554	68,924	15,558
Black	4,070	11,553	10,893	4,680	981
American Indian, Eskimo, and Aleut	46	198	164	41	7
Asian or Pacific Islander	413	672	760	1,260	663
Other race	731	1,140	714	237	83
30 to 34 years old					
Men					
White	38,831	174,028	94,358	71,923	31,560

[Continued]

★ 761 ★

Educational Attainment in Pennsylvania, by Selected Characteristics
[Continued]

Characteristic	Not high school graduate	High school graduate	Some college or associate's degree	Bachelor's degree	Graduate or professional degree
Black	5,742	12,203	8,568	3,697	1,320
American Indian, Eskimo, and Aleut	107	236	159	38	16
Asian or Pacific Islander	819	583	956	809	2,005
Other race	1,862	1,121	719	185	191
Women					
White	20,993	129,201	86,546	56,521	25,562
Black	4,920	12,813	13,239	4,395	1,364
American Indian, Eskimo, and Aleut	54	138	102	69	23
Asian or Pacific Islander	639	844	735	885	793
Other race	748	934	570	179	79
35 to 39 years old					
Men					
White	31,077	140,655	96,136	71,735	43,077
Black	5,142	10,396	8,038	3,232	1,353
American Indian, Eskimo, and Aleut	91	137	295	74	50
Asian or Pacific Islander	838	755	763	889	1,733
Other race	1,641	813	546	231	148
Women					
White	19,557	120,761	77,809	50,683	33,161
Black	4,251	12,354	10,131	4,082	2,163
American Indian, Eskimo, and Aleut	68	171	123	75	59
Asian or Pacific Islander	954	858	699	796	666
Other race	752	789	360	155	121
40 to 69 years old					
Men					
White	225,110	453,693	232,685	171,181	144,913
Black	27,794	29,056	16,210	5,456	4,879
American Indian, Eskimo, and Aleut	487	484	328	123	126
Asian or Pacific Islander	2,309	1,816	1,688	2,760	5,540
Other race	4,288	1,278	464	237	272
Women					
White	144,553	456,124	191,519	94,172	82,632
Black	23,498	37,701	21,265	6,425	6,029
American Indian, Eskimo, and Aleut	332	495	321	52	99
Asian or Pacific Islander	2,759	2,422	1,753	2,183	2,058
Other race	2,041	1,211	554	179	121
70 years old and older					
Men					
White	16,442	11,254	6,404	3,945	5,377
Black	1,547	688	352	80	130
American Indian, Eskimo, and Aleut	8	5	0	0	0
Asian or Pacific Islander	52	20	49	16	108
Other race	64	6	0	0	0

[Continued]

★ 761 ★

Educational Attainment in Pennsylvania, by Selected Characteristics
[Continued]

Characteristic	Not high school graduate	High school graduate	Some college or associate's degree	Bachelor's degree	Graduate or professional degree
Women					
White	10,417	10,617	3,886	1,954	1,737
Black	1,764	850	305	156	102
American Indian, Eskimo, and Aleut	5	7	0	0	0
Asian or Pacific Islander	18	28	12	0	6
Other race	63	14	0	0	0

Source: Census of Population and Housing, 1990: Equal Employment Opportunity (EEO) File on CD-ROM [machine-readable datafiles]. Prepared by the Bureau of the Census. Washington, DC: The Bureau, 1992.

★ 762 ★
Educational Attainment

Educational Attainment in Rhode Island, by Selected Characteristics

Table presents the number of civilians 16 years old or older who reported their educational backgrounds during the 1990 Census. Data show the number of individuals achieving various levels of education. Figures are reported by sex, age, and race.

Characteristic	Not high school graduate	High school graduate	Some college or associate's degree	Bachelor's degree	Graduate or professional degree
16 to 19 years old					
Men					
White	8,803	3,249	3,008	16	0
Black	398	145	88	0	0
American Indian, Eskimo, and Aleut	29	20	0	0	0
Asian or Pacific Islander	172	66	148	0	0
Other race	363	49	39	0	0
Women					
White	8,046	3,810	4,353	0	0
Black	317	111	126	5	0
American Indian, Eskimo, and Aleut	52	18	15	0	0
Asian or Pacific Islander	142	118	37	0	0
Other race	335	148	116	0	0
20 to 24 years old					
Men					
White	4,682	9,447	10,681	3,686	144
Black	264	343	446	77	0
American Indian, Eskimo, and Aleut	69	88	99	7	0
Asian or Pacific Islander	104	135	197	31	0
Other race	423	342	257	48	0
Women					
White	2,580	8,286	13,234	5,020	145

[Continued]

★ 762 ★

Educational Attainment in Rhode Island, by Selected Characteristics

[Continued]

Characteristic	Not high school graduate	High school graduate	Some college or associate's degree	Bachelor's degree	Graduate or professional degree
Black	187	419	468	92	0
American Indian, Eskimo, and Aleut	31	72	28	21	0
Asian or Pacific Islander	59	133	124	68	17
Other race	284	314	273	30	0
25 to 29 years old					
Men					
White	4,941	11,107	9,454	6,916	1,529
Black	400	488	360	162	32
American Indian, Eskimo, and Aleut	69	23	48	14	0
Asian or Pacific Islander	188	131	138	105	102
Other race	527	587	321	12	0
Women					
White	2,287	8,281	10,248	7,252	1,511
Black	298	531	294	176	12
American Indian, Eskimo, and Aleut	15	36	20	28	0
Asian or Pacific Islander	186	94	122	120	100
Other race	312	269	235	61	42
30 to 34 years old					
Men					
White	4,922	11,504	9,877	7,571	3,106
Black	325	443	467	180	125
American Indian, Eskimo, and Aleut	18	41	50	17	7
Asian or Pacific Islander	214	126	70	66	145
Other race	525	137	234	24	27
Women					
White	2,906	8,725	9,997	6,869	2,573
Black	268	384	416	132	30
American Indian, Eskimo, and Aleut	32	33	21	0	0
Asian or Pacific Islander	142	114	91	114	25
Other race	395	217	178	30	5
35 to 39 years old					
Men					
White	3,623	8,521	9,342	7,193	3,852
Black	232	430	419	134	125
American Indian, Eskimo, and Aleut	28	69	25	0	0
Asian or Pacific Islander	182	121	133	87	42
Other race	514	94	147	47	12
Women					
White	2,994	8,225	8,714	5,061	3,498
Black	240	356	396	125	49
American Indian, Eskimo, and Aleut	29	68	38	7	6
Asian or Pacific Islander	235	108	90	73	59
Other race	331	166	34	8	5

[Continued]

★ 762 ★

Educational Attainment in Rhode Island, by Selected Characteristics

[Continued]

Characteristic	Not high school graduate	High school graduate	Some college or associate's degree	Bachelor's degree	Graduate or professional degree
40 to 69 years old					
Men					
White	23,104	26,351	22,366	17,338	14,415
Black	853	772	490	305	206
American Indian, Eskimo, and Aleut	95	75	69	32	15
Asian or Pacific Islander	517	140	159	214	409
Other race	933	327	185	22	63
Women					
White	19,021	33,482	20,611	9,178	9,377
Black	793	879	606	174	169
American Indian, Eskimo, and Aleut	45	81	133	26	7
Asian or Pacific Islander	426	90	154	231	147
Other race	912	367	209	41	35
70 years old and older					
Men					
White	1,943	1,155	635	444	499
Black	53	41	3	0	0
American Indian, Eskimo, and Aleut	0	0	0	0	0
Asian or Pacific Islander	6	0	0	0	8
Other race	16	4	10	0	0
Women					
White	1,172	858	426	187	176
Black	28	0	6	14	0
American Indian, Eskimo, and Aleut	5	0	12	0	0
Asian or Pacific Islander	6	8	0	0	9
Other race	44	0	0	0	0

Source: Census of Population and Housing, 1990: Equal Employment Opportunity (EEO) File on CD-ROM [machine-readable datafiles]. Prepared by the Bureau of the Census. Washington, DC: The Bureau, 1992.

★ 763 ★

Educational Attainment

Educational Attainment in South Carolina, by Selected Characteristics

Table presents the number of civilians 16 years old or older who reported their educational backgrounds during the 1990 Census. Data show the number of individuals achieving various levels of education. Figures are reported by sex, age, and race.

Characteristic	Not high school graduate	High school graduate	Some college or associate's degree	Bachelor's degree	Graduate or professional degree
16 to 19 years old					
Men					
White	22,869	8,331	5,721	29	0
Black	10,431	3,426	1,126	6	0
American Indian, Eskimo, and Aleut	121	27	1	0	0
Asian or Pacific Islander	179	45	51	0	0
Other race	94	23	10	0	0
Women					
White	17,360	8,325	8,111	6	0
Black	9,549	4,680	2,410	12	0
American Indian, Eskimo, and Aleut	54	25	11	0	0
Asian or Pacific Islander	140	48	100	0	0
Other race	79	33	43	0	0
20 to 24 years old					
Men					
White	14,271	24,014	23,591	7,277	210
Black	7,262	12,965	5,502	960	28
American Indian, Eskimo, and Aleut	130	112	78	13	0
Asian or Pacific Islander	33	169	125	110	6
Other race	172	117	55	48	0
Women					
White	7,237	19,987	27,868	9,365	549
Black	5,046	12,795	11,003	2,035	101
American Indian, Eskimo, and Aleut	31	97	49	6	16
Asian or Pacific Islander	95	126	301	101	8
Other race	7	93	91	8	0
25 to 29 years old					
Men					
White	15,794	28,003	24,986	16,658	3,196
Black	7,949	15,089	5,991	1,720	130
American Indian, Eskimo, and Aleut	88	218	79	46	6
Asian or Pacific Islander	107	194	190	196	143
Other race	225	120	118	12	18
Women					
White	8,386	21,823	25,254	16,253	3,618
Black	6,239	14,054	11,546	3,572	474
American Indian, Eskimo, and Aleut	82	70	66	20	0
Asian or Pacific Islander	37	156	171	145	73
Other race	44	50	43	88	16
30 to 34 years old					
Men					
White	15,977	28,197	27,266	16,210	5,758

[Continued]

★ 763 ★

Educational Attainment in South Carolina, by Selected Characteristics
[Continued]

Characteristic	Not high school graduate	High school graduate	Some college or associate's degree	Bachelor's degree	Graduate or professional degree
Black	9,086	14,174	6,804	2,197	462
American Indian, Eskimo, and Aleut	120	184	73	54	9
Asian or Pacific Islander	72	108	146	79	175
Other race	159	73	97	29	5
Women					
White	9,058	23,663	25,013	13,682	5,654
Black	7,663	14,465	11,128	3,698	1,023
American Indian, Eskimo, and Aleut	66	78	154	54	6
Asian or Pacific Islander	145	216	208	190	65
Other race	43	26	80	44	25
35 to 39 years old					
Men					
White	13,090	23,125	26,111	16,013	8,456
Black	8,947	11,747	6,697	1,937	721
American Indian, Eskimo, and Aleut	115	84	86	9	19
Asian or Pacific Islander	43	91	160	151	157
Other race	133	61	86	28	11
Women					
White	8,579	24,640	23,008	10,396	7,914
Black	7,971	14,082	9,107	3,104	1,422
American Indian, Eskimo, and Aleut	74	98	66	41	0
Asian or Pacific Islander	300	269	141	187	95
Other race	55	89	41	19	32
40 to 69 years old					
Men					
White	64,978	78,114	69,007	43,615	29,613
Black	37,164	19,586	11,714	3,033	2,360
American Indian, Eskimo, and Aleut	357	226	233	102	67
Asian or Pacific Islander	261	302	486	311	658
Other race	214	136	114	18	81
Women					
White	47,888	83,983	58,471	21,963	17,190
Black	33,568	25,556	11,249	4,549	3,564
American Indian, Eskimo, and Aleut	190	242	141	31	9
Asian or Pacific Islander	692	539	312	382	251
Other race	46	92	42	28	9
70 years old and older					
Men					
White	3,358	1,901	1,649	1,294	786
Black	1,717	169	139	54	31
American Indian, Eskimo, and Aleut	0	0	19	0	0
Asian or Pacific Islander	11	0	0	0	0
Other race	0	0	10	0	0

[Continued]

★ 763 ★

Educational Attainment in South Carolina, by Selected Characteristics

[Continued]

Characteristic	Not high school graduate	High school graduate	Some college or associate's degree	Bachelor's degree	Graduate or professional degree
Women					
White	2,405	1,848	1,113	365	182
Black	1,557	322	176	117	68
American Indian, Eskimo, and Aleut	0	0	0	0	0
Asian or Pacific Islander	0	0	0	0	0
Other race	6	0	0	0	0

Source: Census of Population and Housing, 1990: Equal Employment Opportunity (EEO) File on CD-ROM [machine-readable datafiles]. Prepared by the Bureau of the Census. Washington, DC: The Bureau, 1992.

★ 764 ★

Educational Attainment

Educational Attainment in South Dakota, by Selected Characteristics

Table presents the number of civilians 16 years old or older who reported their educational backgrounds during the 1990 Census. Data show the number of individuals achieving various levels of education. Figures are reported by sex, age, and race.

Characteristic	Not high school graduate	High school graduate	Some college or associate's degree	Bachelor's degree	Graduate or professional degree
16 to 19 years old					
Men					
White	7,024	2,016	1,549	0	0
Black	41	0	21	0	0
American Indian, Eskimo, and Aleut	383	116	39	0	0
Asian or Pacific Islander	29	0	0	0	0
Other race	36	7	22	0	0
Women					
White	6,074	2,046	2,458	0	0
Black	35	0	0	0	0
American Indian, Eskimo, and Aleut	429	164	67	0	0
Asian or Pacific Islander	74	14	7	0	0
Other race	8	21	0	0	0
20 to 24 years old					
Men					
White	1,472	5,689	7,517	1,525	50
Black	0	13	67	6	0
American Indian, Eskimo, and Aleut	369	545	218	4	0
Asian or Pacific Islander	11	53	38	11	0
Other race	8	28	14	9	2
Women					
White	833	4,569	8,378	1,974	111

[Continued]

★ 764 ★

Educational Attainment in South Dakota, by Selected Characteristics
[Continued]

Characteristic	Not high school graduate	High school graduate	Some college or associate's degree	Bachelor's degree	Graduate or professional degree
Black	0	11	38	14	0
American Indian, Eskimo, and Aleut	227	333	388	26	0
Asian or Pacific Islander	36	11	48	7	0
Other race	10	13	17	12	0
25 to 29 years old					
Men					
White	1,946	7,935	6,722	3,878	524
Black	0	33	34	27	0
American Indian, Eskimo, and Aleut	386	603	457	46	16
Asian or Pacific Islander	48	24	9	9	12
Other race	21	37	6	5	0
Women					
White	1,258	6,149	7,362	4,168	458
Black	7	14	18	8	0
American Indian, Eskimo, and Aleut	250	396	447	75	7
Asian or Pacific Islander	9	43	29	40	12
Other race	5	4	23	0	0
30 to 34 years old					
Men					
White	2,306	9,929	6,845	4,010	1,224
Black	36	36	65	20	13
American Indian, Eskimo, and Aleut	388	439	362	61	7
Asian or Pacific Islander	28	14	5	7	15
Other race	5	13	13	6	15
Women					
White	1,218	7,260	7,924	3,872	792
Black	7	22	36	2	0
American Indian, Eskimo, and Aleut	176	414	416	98	16
Asian or Pacific Islander	20	56	11	32	0
Other race	13	21	18	0	0
35 to 39 years old					
Men					
White	1,618	8,348	7,441	4,442	1,772
Black	5	7	8	44	0
American Indian, Eskimo, and Aleut	257	337	310	41	46
Asian or Pacific Islander	8	7	14	29	8
Other race	28	10	26	7	7
Women					
White	905	6,677	7,575	3,853	1,067
Black	13	25	17	0	0
American Indian, Eskimo, and Aleut	136	268	452	130	72
Asian or Pacific Islander	44	28	3	7	5
Other race	4	24	19	0	0

[Continued]

★ 764 ★

Educational Attainment in South Dakota, by Selected Characteristics
[Continued]

Characteristic	Not high school graduate	High school graduate	Some college or associate's degree	Bachelor's degree	Graduate or professional degree
40 to 69 years old					
Men					
White	14,340	24,721	15,021	9,449	7,192
Black	54	15	63	43	18
American Indian, Eskimo, and Aleut	766	736	837	136	135
Asian or Pacific Islander	19	35	32	3	73
Other race	57	17	22	5	9
Women					
White	7,569	22,586	16,315	6,991	3,241
Black	18	10	7	31	15
American Indian, Eskimo, and Aleut	558	707	861	216	108
Asian or Pacific Islander	97	87	52	41	37
Other race	23	13	20	14	0
70 years old and older					
Men					
White	2,473	1,163	524	234	256
Black	6	0	0	0	0
American Indian, Eskimo, and Aleut	31	26	20	3	10
Asian or Pacific Islander	0	0	0	0	4
Other race	0	0	0	0	0
Women					
White	914	634	471	213	57
Black	0	0	0	0	0
American Indian, Eskimo, and Aleut	22	13	3	7	0
Asian or Pacific Islander	0	0	0	0	0
Other race	0	0	0	0	0

Source: Census of Population and Housing, 1990: Equal Employment Opportunity (EEO) File on CD-ROM [machine-readable datafiles]. Prepared by the Bureau of the Census. Washington, DC: The Bureau, 1992.

Educational Attainment in Tennessee, by Selected Characteristics

Table presents the number of civilians 16 years old or older who reported their educational backgrounds during the 1990 Census. Data show the number of individuals achieving various levels of education. Figures are reported by sex, age, and race.

Characteristic	Not high school graduate	High school graduate	Some college or associate's degree	Bachelor's degree	Graduate or professional degree
16 to 19 years old					
Men					
White	38,500	14,206	9,527	0	0
Black	7,441	2,430	1,201	0	0
American Indian, Eskimo, and Aleut	160	53	14	0	0
Asian or Pacific Islander	261	72	57	0	0
Other race	66	53	41	0	0
Women					
White	28,194	14,982	12,621	31	12
Black	5,896	2,842	2,464	6	0
American Indian, Eskimo, and Aleut	105	41	37	0	0
Asian or Pacific Islander	161	110	39	0	0
Other race	73	18	27	0	0
20 to 24 years old					
Men					
White	24,601	46,165	39,400	9,248	341
Black	4,834	8,722	6,071	725	24
American Indian, Eskimo, and Aleut	122	151	145	25	0
Asian or Pacific Islander	126	182	287	177	27
Other race	176	140	120	17	6
Women					
White	13,736	36,546	42,348	12,443	773
Black	3,476	8,732	10,176	1,261	100
American Indian, Eskimo, and Aleut	67	71	153	12	0
Asian or Pacific Islander	70	268	315	99	17
Other race	29	58	127	43	0
25 to 29 years old					
Men					
White	28,167	52,854	36,708	23,348	5,296
Black	5,081	9,901	7,163	2,020	215
American Indian, Eskimo, and Aleut	159	144	135	22	6
Asian or Pacific Islander	151	204	219	275	247
Other race	165	76	169	26	35
Women					
White	15,731	40,535	39,977	23,860	5,096
Black	4,087	8,607	11,043	3,452	543
American Indian, Eskimo, and Aleut	49	95	135	22	14
Asian or Pacific Islander	146	198	278	213	119
Other race	29	48	84	80	26
30 to 34 years old					
Men					
White	28,823	53,363	39,413	24,081	9,846

[Continued]

★ 765 ★

Educational Attainment in Tennessee, by Selected Characteristics

[Continued]

Characteristic	Not high school graduate	High school graduate	Some college or associate's degree	Bachelor's degree	Graduate or professional degree
Black	5,411	9,624	6,765	2,151	570
American Indian, Eskimo, and Aleut	162	169	100	36	6
Asian or Pacific Islander	213	121	234	218	483
Other race	125	109	82	101	45
Women					
White	16,317	44,198	38,998	20,420	7,654
Black	4,440	10,279	10,898	3,711	1,217
American Indian, Eskimo, and Aleut	69	169	175	49	8
Asian or Pacific Islander	277	164	175	200	122
Other race	59	93	155	27	2
35 to 39 years old					
Men					
White	24,373	44,520	37,709	24,939	13,598
Black	4,803	8,028	6,804	2,341	827
American Indian, Eskimo, and Aleut	115	228	115	66	16
Asian or Pacific Islander	110	214	160	300	414
Other race	71	59	99	29	29
Women					
White	14,703	42,808	35,201	18,088	10,834
Black	4,449	8,537	8,567	3,006	1,515
American Indian, Eskimo, and Aleut	104	222	160	23	42
Asian or Pacific Islander	245	218	229	195	145
Other race	39	41	74	25	27
40 to 69 years old					
Men					
White	125,463	136,111	102,397	65,419	47,573
Black	20,996	14,717	10,485	3,479	2,655
American Indian, Eskimo, and Aleut	363	303	356	94	136
Asian or Pacific Islander	262	428	300	566	1,375
Other race	228	54	131	89	53
Women					
White	84,039	141,884	89,401	33,313	25,449
Black	20,853	18,274	13,053	4,352	4,280
American Indian, Eskimo, and Aleut	372	302	300	84	48
Asian or Pacific Islander	741	612	477	445	415
Other race	135	72	65	51	16
70 years old and older					
Men					
White	6,601	3,272	2,399	1,413	1,641
Black	1,173	191	104	84	56
American Indian, Eskimo, and Aleut	10	0	0	0	0
Asian or Pacific Islander	8	0	0	8	13
Other race	6	0	0	0	0

[Continued]

★ 765 ★

Educational Attainment in Tennessee, by Selected Characteristics

[Continued]

Characteristic	Not high school graduate	High school graduate	Some college or associate's degree	Bachelor's degree	Graduate or professional degree
Women					
White	4,200	2,847	1,798	550	435
Black	1,181	415	161	29	48
American Indian, Eskimo, and Aleut	13	0	0	0	0
Asian or Pacific Islander	5	0	0	0	9
Other race	0	0	0	4	0

Source: Census of Population and Housing, 1990: Equal Employment Opportunity (EEO) File on CD-ROM [machine-readable datafiles]. Prepared by the Bureau of the Census. Washington, DC: The Bureau, 1992.

★ 766 ★

Educational Attainment

Educational Attainment in Texas, by Selected Characteristics

Table presents the number of civilians 16 years old or older who reported their educational backgrounds during the 1990 Census. Data show the number of individuals achieving various levels of education. Figures are reported by sex, age, and race.

Characteristic	Not high school graduate	High school graduate	Some college or associate's degree	Bachelor's degree	Graduate or professional degree
16 to 19 years old					
Men					
White	115,233	32,328	29,483	86	11
Black	17,415	5,236	3,112	12	0
American Indian, Eskimo, and Aleut	721	211	173	0	0
Asian or Pacific Islander	2,272	632	875	42	0
Other race	27,434	6,045	2,906	6	0
Women					
White	86,492	32,549	38,082	35	7
Black	15,260	6,632	5,403	46	0
American Indian, Eskimo, and Aleut	606	127	128	0	0
Asian or Pacific Islander	1,891	617	691	4	0
Other race	17,309	5,894	3,778	23	0
20 to 24 years old					
Men					
White	72,966	105,092	143,452	30,923	2,041
Black	12,334	21,759	18,507	1,653	179
American Indian, Eskimo, and Aleut	655	750	758	82	6
Asian or Pacific Islander	1,347	1,902	3,711	1,404	270
Other race	40,052	21,838	16,670	1,418	152
Women					
White	36,616	82,773	146,129	41,241	1,880

[Continued]

★ 766 ★

Educational Attainment in Texas, by Selected Characteristics

[Continued]

Characteristic	Not high school graduate	High school graduate	Some college or associate's degree	Bachelor's degree	Graduate or professional degree
Black	7,994	21,269	26,070	3,465	200
American Indian, Eskimo, and Aleut	371	568	587	112	11
Asian or Pacific Islander	889	1,341	3,472	1,221	135
Other race	16,524	17,473	17,283	1,506	188
25 to 29 years old					
Men					
White	86,370	134,974	153,922	97,870	22,817
Black	13,536	25,826	22,608	6,768	1,075
American Indian, Eskimo, and Aleut	1,057	858	1,208	234	112
Asian or Pacific Islander	1,765	1,969	3,307	3,753	2,247
Other race	47,416	23,029	17,481	4,538	955
Women					
White	43,237	102,543	141,009	98,142	15,880
Black	10,469	23,659	30,706	9,943	1,353
American Indian, Eskimo, and Aleut	509	712	844	332	53
Asian or Pacific Islander	1,294	1,665	2,603	3,284	1,083
Other race	18,885	17,063	15,434	4,322	614
30 to 34 years old					
Men					
White	84,083	143,282	165,981	109,681	41,228
Black	11,762	24,247	24,370	9,357	2,257
American Indian, Eskimo, and Aleut	694	930	1,196	316	113
Asian or Pacific Islander	2,057	1,564	3,571	3,997	3,639
Other race	42,564	19,293	14,845	3,757	1,390
Women					
White	45,919	108,519	145,186	89,012	26,997
Black	10,609	23,197	28,923	11,420	2,550
American Indian, Eskimo, and Aleut	455	657	1,140	214	60
Asian or Pacific Islander	2,055	2,008	2,769	3,342	1,489
Other race	19,905	14,450	12,103	3,347	1,010
35 to 39 years old					
Men					
White	62,968	103,874	157,938	102,794	53,235
Black	10,568	18,454	19,223	8,284	3,318
American Indian, Eskimo, and Aleut	590	620	1,062	231	211
Asian or Pacific Islander	1,711	1,725	3,216	3,392	4,230
Other race	32,087	13,246	11,549	3,064	1,496
Women					
White	40,578	99,193	133,047	74,560	34,750
Black	9,192	20,722	24,446	9,079	3,811
American Indian, Eskimo, and Aleut	423	505	1,008	306	106
Asian or Pacific Islander	2,608	2,201	2,617	3,466	1,806
Other race	17,667	11,676	8,680	2,523	1,118

[Continued]

★ 766 ★

Educational Attainment in Texas, by Selected Characteristics
[Continued]

Characteristic	Not high school graduate	High school graduate	Some college or associate's degree	Bachelor's degree	Graduate or professional degree
40 to 69 years old					
Men					
White	265,705	312,802	402,551	278,156	182,439
Black	46,898	41,240	37,182	12,530	8,152
American Indian, Eskimo, and Aleut	1,808	1,686	2,128	1,169	596
Asian or Pacific Islander	4,849	4,247	5,997	7,440	9,058
Other race	80,859	18,726	16,274	4,220	2,460
Women					
White	178,508	332,569	343,384	148,707	92,849
Black	44,511	47,266	41,636	12,649	11,206
American Indian, Eskimo, and Aleut	1,293	1,660	2,032	569	482
Asian or Pacific Islander	5,930	5,447	5,097	5,435	3,382
Other race	46,619	17,725	11,594	2,283	1,545
70 years old and older					
Men					
White	18,664	10,296	10,185	6,012	6,053
Black	2,628	511	385	124	204
American Indian, Eskimo, and Aleut	54	22	48	10	21
Asian or Pacific Islander	56	50	39	39	43
Other race	1,465	159	110	8	10
Women					
White	11,994	9,831	7,054	2,454	1,638
Black	3,153	1,068	525	131	112
American Indian, Eskimo, and Aleut	32	29	27	0	0
Asian or Pacific Islander	63	29	8	27	18
Other race	876	118	24	5	3

Source: Census of Population and Housing, 1990: Equal Employment Opportunity (EEO) File on CD-ROM [machine-readable datafiles]. Prepared by the Bureau of the Census. Washington, DC: The Bureau, 1992.

★ 767 ★

Educational Attainment

Educational Attainment in Utah, by Selected Characteristics

Table presents the number of civilians 16 years old or older who reported their educational backgrounds during the 1990 Census. Data show the number of individuals achieving various levels of education. Figures are reported by sex, age, and race.

Characteristic	Not high school graduate	High school graduate	Some college or associate's degree	Bachelor's degree	Graduate or professional degree
16 to 19 years old					
Men					
White	22,474	6,128	5,236	10	6
Black	149	17	54	0	0
American Indian, Eskimo, and Aleut	275	85	15	0	0
Asian or Pacific Islander	370	83	116	0	0
Other race	565	167	9	5	0
Women					
White	18,352	6,162	8,623	16	0
Black	35	24	21	0	0
American Indian, Eskimo, and Aleut	325	88	80	0	0
Asian or Pacific Islander	255	95	190	0	0
Other race	478	94	170	0	0
20 to 24 years old					
Men					
White	6,265	13,258	28,331	2,163	101
Black	40	115	127	25	0
American Indian, Eskimo, and Aleut	203	341	218	9	0
Asian or Pacific Islander	259	260	397	103	0
Other race	742	542	342	26	6
Women					
White	3,928	11,212	27,930	3,767	250
Black	13	111	113	7	0
American Indian, Eskimo, and Aleut	197	209	303	6	17
Asian or Pacific Islander	101	155	437	80	8
Other race	379	364	331	24	0
25 to 29 years old					
Men					
White	6,248	14,063	24,778	10,215	1,975
Black	36	92	213	68	44
American Indian, Eskimo, and Aleut	254	343	254	21	16
Asian or Pacific Islander	154	250	530	377	180
Other race	828	559	422	108	35
Women					
White	3,959	11,466	19,135	7,920	1,075
Black	22	50	177	42	6
American Indian, Eskimo, and Aleut	152	267	262	60	0
Asian or Pacific Islander	161	274	324	361	75
Other race	377	337	346	51	28
30 to 34 years old					
Men					
White	5,715	14,910	22,724	12,012	4,726

[Continued]

★ 767 ★

Educational Attainment in Utah, by Selected Characteristics
[Continued]

Characteristic	Not high school graduate	High school graduate	Some college or associate's degree	Bachelor's degree	Graduate or professional degree
Black	46	96	245	122	24
American Indian, Eskimo, and Aleut	238	265	246	30	13
Asian or Pacific Islander	140	206	508	251	223
Other race	692	377	475	82	29
Women					
White	3,626	13,053	17,969	7,110	1,945
Black	27	66	176	62	10
American Indian, Eskimo, and Aleut	242	158	241	23	24
Asian or Pacific Islander	184	223	366	165	112
Other race	470	377	290	93	18
35 to 39 years old					
Men					
White	3,134	11,211	22,394	11,034	6,643
Black	83	68	247	63	24
American Indian, Eskimo, and Aleut	138	213	245	38	28
Asian or Pacific Islander	180	119	442	240	231
Other race	427	387	328	141	48
Women					
White	2,458	11,530	18,078	7,681	2,594
Black	4	33	121	22	20
American Indian, Eskimo, and Aleut	83	199	188	45	3
Asian or Pacific Islander	191	199	322	212	80
Other race	242	391	270	68	20
40 to 69 years old					
Men					
White	13,047	30,136	51,091	29,679	22,195
Black	129	173	237	79	107
American Indian, Eskimo, and Aleut	447	314	430	86	56
Asian or Pacific Islander	415	553	556	313	435
Other race	1,316	419	535	108	139
Women					
White	10,993	35,599	42,246	16,825	6,759
Black	76	141	171	52	28
American Indian, Eskimo, and Aleut	389	231	225	73	29
Asian or Pacific Islander	664	802	473	275	164
Other race	738	667	411	51	14
70 years old and older					
Men					
White	1,251	1,282	1,337	763	696
Black	0	7	0	0	6
American Indian, Eskimo, and Aleut	25	9	0	0	0
Asian or Pacific Islander	9	44	17	0	2
Other race	19	0	0	0	0

[Continued]

★ 767 ★

Educational Attainment in Utah, by Selected Characteristics
[Continued]

Characteristic	Not high school graduate	High school graduate	Some college or associate's degree	Bachelor's degree	Graduate or professional degree
Women					
White	558	920	736	261	176
Black	13	10	0	0	0
American Indian, Eskimo, and Aleut	0	0	0	0	0
Asian or Pacific Islander	0	23	12	0	0
Other race	19	0	0	0	0

Source: Census of Population and Housing, 1990: Equal Employment Opportunity (EEO) File on CD-ROM [machine-readable datafiles]. Prepared by the Bureau of the Census. Washington, DC: The Bureau, 1992.

★ 768 ★

Educational Attainment

Educational Attainment in Vermont, by Selected Characteristics

Table presents the number of civilians 16 years old or older who reported their educational backgrounds during the 1990 Census. Data show the number of individuals achieving various levels of education. Figures are reported by sex, age, and race.

Characteristic	Not high school graduate	High school graduate	Some college or associate's degree	Bachelor's degree	Graduate or professional degree
16 to 19 years old					
Men					
White	5,647	2,152	1,541	6	1
Black	24	14	14	0	0
American Indian, Eskimo, and Aleut	57	31	0	0	0
Asian or Pacific Islander	28	16	7	0	0
Other race	22	0	0	0	0
Women					
White	4,814	2,247	1,954	25	0
Black	7	8	39	0	0
American Indian, Eskimo, and Aleut	28	11	12	0	0
Asian or Pacific Islander	38	28	16	0	0
Other race	0	0	29	0	0
20 to 24 years old					
Men					
White	2,248	7,104	5,788	1,358	80
Black	0	16	30	5	0
American Indian, Eskimo, and Aleut	52	28	16	0	0
Asian or Pacific Islander	8	31	76	7	0
Other race	7	0	14	0	0
Women					
White	1,287	5,384	6,621	2,275	80

[Continued]

★ 768 ★

Educational Attainment in Vermont, by Selected Characteristics
[Continued]

Characteristic	Not high school graduate	High school graduate	Some college or associate's degree	Bachelor's degree	Graduate or professional degree
Black	6	0	52	14	0
American Indian, Eskimo, and Aleut	0	26	25	9	0
Asian or Pacific Islander	43	8	65	43	0
Other race	0	2	0	9	0
25 to 29 years old					
Men					
White	2,496	9,012	4,939	3,381	606
Black	25	25	22	43	8
American Indian, Eskimo, and Aleut	19	46	27	9	6
Asian or Pacific Islander	11	15	45	44	33
Other race	0	7	0	0	0
Women					
White	1,227	6,407	5,269	3,852	844
Black	0	26	32	17	0
American Indian, Eskimo, and Aleut	10	29	18	6	0
Asian or Pacific Islander	7	9	13	36	20
Other race	0	2	11	6	7
30 to 34 years old					
Men					
White	2,376	9,593	5,383	3,931	1,863
Black	13	16	40	22	0
American Indian, Eskimo, and Aleut	48	42	14	16	0
Asian or Pacific Islander	8	14	10	26	16
Other race	0	11	0	0	0
Women					
White	1,249	6,889	5,745	4,116	1,699
Black	5	13	19	36	2
American Indian, Eskimo, and Aleut	9	11	30	10	0
Asian or Pacific Islander	6	20	17	31	11
Other race	0	9	10	0	0
35 to 39 years old					
Men					
White	2,010	7,837	5,981	4,776	2,464
Black	18	9	40	29	23
American Indian, Eskimo, and Aleut	21	24	14	10	5
Asian or Pacific Islander	0	41	15	13	50
Other race	7	0	15	0	0
Women					
White	1,130	6,600	5,719	4,329	2,315
Black	6	20	37	2	26
American Indian, Eskimo, and Aleut	9	41	18	2	4
Asian or Pacific Islander	7	7	0	38	47
Other race	8	10	8	0	2

[Continued]

★ 768 ★

Educational Attainment in Vermont, by Selected Characteristics
[Continued]

Characteristic	Not high school graduate	High school graduate	Some college or associate's degree	Bachelor's degree	Graduate or professional degree
40 to 69 years old					
Men					
White	11,956	20,364	11,961	10,012	9,457
Black	21	18	57	30	20
American Indian, Eskimo, and Aleut	74	77	33	0	12
Asian or Pacific Islander	19	37	25	25	109
Other race	0	0	11	13	26
Women					
White	6,705	19,688	13,194	8,609	6,266
Black	3	19	13	4	14
American Indian, Eskimo, and Aleut	12	23	28	17	10
Asian or Pacific Islander	64	75	22	44	31
Other race	0	8	0	5	6
70 years old and older					
Men					
White	731	659	333	232	271
Black	0	4	0	0	2
American Indian, Eskimo, and Aleut	0	0	0	0	0
Asian or Pacific Islander	0	0	0	8	0
Other race	0	0	0	0	0
Women					
White	453	512	434	225	199
Black	0	0	0	0	0
American Indian, Eskimo, and Aleut	0	0	0	0	0
Asian or Pacific Islander	0	0	0	0	0
Other race	0	0	0	0	0

Source: Census of Population and Housing, 1990: Equal Employment Opportunity (EEO) File on CD-ROM [machine-readable datafiles]. Prepared by the Bureau of the Census. Washington, DC: The Bureau, 1992.

★ 769 ★

Educational Attainment

Educational Attainment in Virginia, by Selected Characteristics

Table presents the number of civilians 16 years old or older who reported their educational backgrounds during the 1990 Census. Data show the number of individuals achieving various levels of education. Figures are reported by sex, age, and race.

Characteristic	Not high school graduate	High school graduate	Some college or associate's degree	Bachelor's degree	Graduate or professional degree
16 to 19 years old					
Men					
White	41,192	14,309	10,300	34	0
Black	10,057	3,272	1,426	0	0
American Indian, Eskimo, and Aleut	224	41	46	5	0
Asian or Pacific Islander	1,489	449	340	7	0
Other race	876	156	68	0	0
Women					
White	32,703	15,679	14,249	60	0
Black	7,826	4,299	3,368	0	0
American Indian, Eskimo, and Aleut	115	69	76	0	0
Asian or Pacific Islander	1,165	381	418	0	0
Other race	438	94	100	0	0
20 to 24 years old					
Men					
White	23,288	46,237	48,303	18,824	1,061
Black	8,162	12,837	8,369	1,261	36
American Indian, Eskimo, and Aleut	149	173	125	38	19
Asian or Pacific Islander	478	990	1,755	757	153
Other race	2,166	823	578	105	5
Women					
White	11,258	41,412	54,054	26,323	1,237
Black	4,769	13,057	12,740	2,809	131
American Indian, Eskimo, and Aleut	136	175	197	33	0
Asian or Pacific Islander	447	801	2,095	1,093	89
Other race	772	509	614	221	13
25 to 29 years old					
Men					
White	27,168	56,507	49,370	44,277	11,115
Black	8,658	16,183	9,529	3,894	616
American Indian, Eskimo, and Aleut	82	304	129	69	22
Asian or Pacific Islander	863	1,019	1,662	1,966	1,003
Other race	1,971	893	890	320	110
Women					
White	12,621	43,269	53,568	49,129	9,865
Black	6,034	14,655	15,563	5,850	832
American Indian, Eskimo, and Aleut	79	183	162	89	11
Asian or Pacific Islander	587	934	1,684	1,899	620
Other race	874	611	692	371	90
30 to 34 years old					
Men					
White	26,818	53,596	51,535	40,638	19,777

[Continued]

★ 769 ★

Educational Attainment in Virginia, by Selected Characteristics
[Continued]

Characteristic	Not high school graduate	High school graduate	Some college or associate's degree	Bachelor's degree	Graduate or professional degree
Black	9,909	14,589	10,251	3,538	948
American Indian, Eskimo, and Aleut	159	206	202	96	25
Asian or Pacific Islander	851	1,103	1,499	1,480	1,350
Other race	1,457	639	819	320	168
Women					
White	13,757	44,032	53,237	38,292	15,469
Black	7,659	15,223	15,931	6,368	1,824
American Indian, Eskimo, and Aleut	98	304	242	51	6
Asian or Pacific Islander	945	1,295	1,470	1,709	597
Other race	810	532	743	202	121
35 to 39 years old					
Men					
White	21,319	40,529	49,517	37,318	26,158
Black	8,771	11,476	9,372	3,902	1,610
American Indian, Eskimo, and Aleut	165	100	189	89	39
Asian or Pacific Islander	625	1,101	1,163	1,481	1,364
Other race	1,176	357	454	244	131
Women					
White	11,818	40,887	49,534	32,709	19,096
Black	7,443	12,751	12,906	5,082	2,278
American Indian, Eskimo, and Aleut	119	127	278	55	29
Asian or Pacific Islander	1,151	1,386	1,779	1,835	953
Other race	567	418	404	139	88
40 to 69 years old					
Men					
White	109,491	129,692	128,290	102,728	105,642
Black	40,729	23,685	17,988	6,092	5,382
American Indian, Eskimo, and Aleut	501	450	515	147	216
Asian or Pacific Islander	1,844	2,652	3,764	4,182	4,883
Other race	1,507	538	559	379	376
Women					
White	69,633	143,441	132,921	70,405	47,731
Black	35,248	28,576	21,005	7,700	6,260
American Indian, Eskimo, and Aleut	282	448	590	132	100
Asian or Pacific Islander	3,315	3,904	3,569	4,025	2,034
Other race	987	637	542	177	135
70 years old and older					
Men					
White	6,415	3,410	2,897	2,241	2,477
Black	1,814	318	186	58	99
American Indian, Eskimo, and Aleut	0	0	0	0	10
Asian or Pacific Islander	69	35	29	47	32
Other race	29	15	0	0	0

[Continued]

★ 769 ★

Educational Attainment in Virginia, by Selected Characteristics
[Continued]

Characteristic	Not high school graduate	High school graduate	Some college or associate's degree	Bachelor's degree	Graduate or professional degree
Women					
White	3,306	2,988	2,074	959	534
Black	2,146	466	254	35	41
American Indian, Eskimo, and Aleut	6	0	0	0	7
Asian or Pacific Islander	19	21	11	8	0
Other race	33	10	10	0	0

Source: Census of Population and Housing, 1990: Equal Employment Opportunity (EEO) File on CD-ROM [machine-readable datafiles]. Prepared by the Bureau of the Census. Washington, DC: The Bureau, 1992.

★ 770 ★

Educational Attainment

Educational Attainment in Washington, by Selected Characteristics

Table presents the number of civilians 16 years old or older who reported their educational backgrounds during the 1990 Census. Data show the number of individuals achieving various levels of education. Figures are reported by sex, age, and race.

Characteristic	Not high school graduate	High school graduate	Some college or associate's degree	Bachelor's degree	Graduate or professional degree
16 to 19 years old					
Men					
White	39,937	11,906	9,896	28	0
Black	1,298	404	277	0	0
American Indian, Eskimo, and Aleut	1,042	322	101	0	0
Asian or Pacific Islander	2,100	525	555	0	0
Other race	2,069	284	190	0	0
Women					
White	33,977	13,584	13,351	40	0
Black	1,226	455	340	0	0
American Indian, Eskimo, and Aleut	682	329	211	0	0
Asian or Pacific Islander	1,596	715	1,003	0	0
Other race	1,408	344	280	0	0
20 to 24 years old					
Men					
White	17,127	38,608	48,871	10,428	296
Black	680	1,695	1,622	181	0
American Indian, Eskimo, and Aleut	750	1,033	762	66	19
Asian or Pacific Islander	625	1,521	2,934	786	64
Other race	3,576	1,121	754	143	10
Women					
White	8,558	29,952	53,641	13,055	397

[Continued]

★ 770 ★

Educational Attainment in Washington, by Selected Characteristics
[Continued]

Characteristic	Not high school graduate	High school graduate	Some college or associate's degree	Bachelor's degree	Graduate or professional degree
Black	415	1,183	2,013	306	0
American Indian, Eskimo, and Aleut	338	797	837	92	7
Asian or Pacific Islander	467	1,042	3,213	994	44
Other race	1,173	768	978	119	11
25 to 29 years old					
Men					
White	17,977	48,580	53,484	32,168	5,063
Black	640	1,711	2,019	723	56
American Indian, Eskimo, and Aleut	745	1,259	958	188	27
Asian or Pacific Islander	932	1,222	2,663	2,137	769
Other race	3,372	1,129	1,209	254	63
Women					
White	9,172	33,330	51,353	29,950	4,418
Black	415	1,163	1,976	614	22
American Indian, Eskimo, and Aleut	490	804	1,155	177	8
Asian or Pacific Islander	694	1,273	2,588	1,996	439
Other race	1,457	823	977	205	35
30 to 34 years old					
Men					
White	16,288	51,194	64,489	35,066	12,631
Black	567	1,686	2,798	710	308
American Indian, Eskimo, and Aleut	553	1,042	917	208	68
Asian or Pacific Islander	890	1,393	2,514	2,094	905
Other race	3,092	1,098	1,098	173	163
Women					
White	8,991	37,164	58,998	29,517	9,047
Black	380	1,374	2,502	708	166
American Indian, Eskimo, and Aleut	374	748	1,227	184	58
Asian or Pacific Islander	1,162	1,634	2,264	1,946	599
Other race	1,301	829	972	235	81
35 to 39 years old					
Men					
White	10,584	39,675	67,227	37,764	18,897
Black	229	1,182	2,507	691	310
American Indian, Eskimo, and Aleut	319	765	1,104	190	167
Asian or Pacific Islander	897	1,085	2,433	1,874	1,073
Other race	2,202	561	1,009	224	125
Women					
White	7,275	35,265	61,449	29,065	12,627
Black	286	1,001	2,069	678	229
American Indian, Eskimo, and Aleut	281	612	1,221	181	82
Asian or Pacific Islander	1,330	1,492	2,391	2,219	689
Other race	946	492	708	184	52

[Continued]

★ 770 ★

Educational Attainment in Washington, by Selected Characteristics
[Continued]

Characteristic	Not high school graduate	High school graduate	Some college or associate's degree	Bachelor's degree	Graduate or professional degree
40 to 69 years old					
Men					
White	48,253	118,739	165,104	99,067	69,362
Black	1,495	2,998	4,823	1,909	951
American Indian, Eskimo, and Aleut	1,463	1,758	1,982	678	329
Asian or Pacific Islander	2,646	3,107	4,955	4,583	3,169
Other race	4,401	1,033	1,275	395	255
Women					
White	33,776	111,573	148,235	61,360	32,234
Black	1,148	2,099	3,956	1,102	743
American Indian, Eskimo, and Aleut	1,017	1,653	2,076	441	225
Asian or Pacific Islander	4,545	4,614	4,457	3,923	1,463
Other race	2,120	708	875	266	124
70 years old and older					
Men					
White	3,474	3,414	3,172	2,184	1,397
Black	116	45	22	15	4
American Indian, Eskimo, and Aleut	72	30	29	0	0
Asian or Pacific Islander	145	83	62	56	24
Other race	61	0	0	4	0
Women					
White	1,895	2,835	2,786	860	554
Black	122	30	52	20	18
American Indian, Eskimo, and Aleut	60	8	10	0	11
Asian or Pacific Islander	82	93	60	14	0
Other race	34	8	0	0	0

Source: Census of Population and Housing, 1990: Equal Employment Opportunity (EEO) File on CD-ROM [machine-readable datafiles]. Prepared by the Bureau of the Census. Washington, DC: The Bureau, 1992.

★ 771 ★
Educational Attainment

Educational Attainment in West Virginia, by Selected Characteristics

Table presents the number of civilians 16 years old or older who reported their educational backgrounds during the 1990 Census. Data show the number of individuals achieving various levels of education. Figures are reported by sex, age, and race.

Characteristic	Not high school graduate	High school graduate	Some college or associate's degree	Bachelor's degree	Graduate or professional degree
16 to 19 years old					
Men					
White	11,059	5,768	3,640	15	9
Black	344	160	131	0	0
American Indian, Eskimo, and Aleut	9	9	10	0	0
Asian or Pacific Islander	65	11	14	0	0
Other race	7	9	11	0	0
Women					
White	8,419	5,835	4,806	0	0
Black	252	236	109	0	0
American Indian, Eskimo, and Aleut	11	12	15	0	0
Asian or Pacific Islander	33	41	20	0	0
Other race	14	13	6	0	0
20 to 24 years old					
Men					
White	8,039	19,617	12,096	2,675	230
Black	172	633	487	56	0
American Indian, Eskimo, and Aleut	35	48	41	7	0
Asian or Pacific Islander	6	41	71	68	0
Other race	18	0	17	0	0
Women					
White	3,013	12,971	14,214	3,587	282
Black	93	396	501	64	0
American Indian, Eskimo, and Aleut	16	42	19	0	0
Asian or Pacific Islander	17	4	88	12	1
Other race	0	6	41	15	10
25 to 29 years old					
Men					
White	9,356	23,608	9,604	5,865	1,617
Black	184	567	381	119	37
American Indian, Eskimo, and Aleut	43	38	9	0	0
Asian or Pacific Islander	0	0	34	76	59
Other race	34	7	24	7	0
Women					
White	3,626	14,628	11,400	5,325	1,561
Black	145	466	468	183	15
American Indian, Eskimo, and Aleut	11	2	59	0	0
Asian or Pacific Islander	0	6	46	36	22
Other race	0	7	14	13	2
30 to 34 years old					
Men					
White	10,588	27,334	11,790	6,415	2,749

[Continued]

★ 771 ★

Educational Attainment in West Virginia, by Selected Characteristics
[Continued]

Characteristic	Not high school graduate	High school graduate	Some college or associate's degree	Bachelor's degree	Graduate or professional degree
Black	284	589	529	154	81
American Indian, Eskimo, and Aleut	21	60	18	0	18
Asian or Pacific Islander	0	12	18	26	125
Other race	16	18	6	3	7
Women					
White	4,508	17,846	12,316	5,546	3,043
Black	153	649	486	153	69
American Indian, Eskimo, and Aleut	10	61	43	0	8
Asian or Pacific Islander	7	76	27	71	25
Other race	3	10	3	5	0
35 to 39 years old					
Men					
White	9,487	25,043	14,503	7,661	4,309
Black	184	657	491	223	95
American Indian, Eskimo, and Aleut	29	23	16	16	0
Asian or Pacific Islander	6	20	23	58	162
Other race	0	11	14	15	4
Women					
White	3,872	18,007	12,064	5,516	4,754
Black	119	641	617	198	86
American Indian, Eskimo, and Aleut	8	47	17	0	9
Asian or Pacific Islander	31	9	24	47	89
Other race	0	12	18	0	5
40 to 69 years old					
Men					
White	43,610	66,409	33,208	17,414	14,487
Black	874	1,240	819	254	240
American Indian, Eskimo, and Aleut	87	66	53	11	22
Asian or Pacific Islander	17	59	28	88	772
Other race	9	0	8	0	6
Women					
White	21,567	54,442	28,408	9,985	9,849
Black	775	1,408	912	253	246
American Indian, Eskimo, and Aleut	55	87	15	0	14
Asian or Pacific Islander	72	83	96	170	216
Other race	14	31	20	0	9
70 years old and older					
Men					
White	1,823	1,073	725	409	464
Black	84	23	11	0	2
American Indian, Eskimo, and Aleut	0	0	0	0	0
Asian or Pacific Islander	0	0	0	0	0
Other race	0	0	0	0	0

[Continued]

★ 771 ★

Educational Attainment in West Virginia, by Selected Characteristics

[Continued]

Characteristic	Not high school graduate	High school graduate	Some college or associate's degree	Bachelor's degree	Graduate or professional degree
Women					
White	1,186	1,134	476	224	166
Black	77	23	24	7	8
American Indian, Eskimo, and Aleut	0	0	0	0	0
Asian or Pacific Islander	0	0	0	2	13
Other race	0	0	0	0	0

Source: Census of Population and Housing, 1990: Equal Employment Opportunity (EEO) File on CD-ROM [machine-readable datafiles]. Prepared by the Bureau of the Census. Washington, DC: The Bureau, 1992.

★ 772 ★

Educational Attainment

Educational Attainment in Wisconsin, by Selected Characteristics

Table presents the number of civilians 16 years old or older who reported their educational backgrounds during the 1990 Census. Data show the number of individuals achieving various levels of education. Figures are reported by sex, age, and race.

Characteristic	Not high school graduate	High school graduate	Some college or associate's degree	Bachelor's degree	Graduate or professional degree
16 to 19 years old					
Men					
White	47,514	16,418	12,141	23	0
Black	2,895	768	349	0	0
American Indian, Eskimo, and Aleut	535	131	38	0	0
Asian or Pacific Islander	538	116	126	0	0
Other race	731	151	84	0	0
Women					
White	40,765	17,285	16,975	6	0
Black	2,593	905	764	6	0
American Indian, Eskimo, and Aleut	515	165	90	0	0
Asian or Pacific Islander	352	133	116	0	0
Other race	538	132	159	0	2
20 to 24 years old					
Men					
White	14,326	52,262	58,235	12,200	391
Black	1,968	2,335	1,893	171	0
American Indian, Eskimo, and Aleut	374	513	381	13	4
Asian or Pacific Islander	151	236	617	255	41
Other race	809	522	378	52	0
Women					
White	7,659	42,183	64,809	16,399	716

[Continued]

★ 772 ★

Educational Attainment in Wisconsin, by Selected Characteristics

[Continued]

Characteristic	Not high school graduate	High school graduate	Some college or associate's degree	Bachelor's degree	Graduate or professional degree
Black	1,230	2,135	2,401	273	13
American Indian, Eskimo, and Aleut	226	429	498	14	4
Asian or Pacific Islander	175	286	586	226	25
Other race	255	523	371	61	9
25 to 29 years old					
Men					
White	17,307	68,661	51,896	29,134	5,223
Black	1,803	2,312	2,043	522	29
American Indian, Eskimo, and Aleut	281	570	474	60	5
Asian or Pacific Islander	236	195	448	365	469
Other race	757	592	335	49	67
Women					
White	9,497	53,541	51,750	30,489	4,687
Black	1,558	2,167	2,854	619	116
American Indian, Eskimo, and Aleut	250	560	442	78	8
Asian or Pacific Islander	193	198	272	323	277
Other race	328	373	278	84	22
30 to 34 years old					
Men					
White	16,808	75,261	55,934	28,148	10,852
Black	1,600	2,576	2,190	678	153
American Indian, Eskimo, and Aleut	365	606	422	26	8
Asian or Pacific Islander	160	203	412	266	543
Other race	931	421	371	123	54
Women					
White	9,302	62,233	51,275	26,052	7,575
Black	1,879	2,335	3,256	733	176
American Indian, Eskimo, and Aleut	204	418	452	90	20
Asian or Pacific Islander	210	206	247	311	208
Other race	306	401	339	72	8
35 to 39 years old					
Men					
White	12,132	61,750	55,316	30,683	15,497
Black	1,315	2,105	2,089	638	318
American Indian, Eskimo, and Aleut	293	452	360	49	41
Asian or Pacific Islander	158	183	249	213	480
Other race	772	428	267	65	66
Women					
White	7,213	54,350	48,320	25,862	10,088
Black	1,338	2,212	2,834	689	299
American Indian, Eskimo, and Aleut	173	337	366	65	28
Asian or Pacific Islander	335	187	162	316	184
Other race	311	195	219	51	38

[Continued]

★ 772 ★

Educational Attainment in Wisconsin, by Selected Characteristics
[Continued]

Characteristic	Not high school graduate	High school graduate	Some college or associate's degree	Bachelor's degree	Graduate or professional degree
40 to 69 years old					
Men					
White	82,506	190,064	117,547	71,068	54,842
Black	4,976	3,957	3,515	825	732
American Indian, Eskimo, and Aleut	799	980	750	149	84
Asian or Pacific Islander	440	246	416	480	1,272
Other race	1,274	410	363	65	76
Women					
White	49,332	190,229	101,847	51,821	27,412
Black	4,531	4,622	3,877	1,306	641
American Indian, Eskimo, and Aleut	658	919	825	143	116
Asian or Pacific Islander	684	463	471	556	398
Other race	839	278	210	50	55
70 years old and older					
Men					
White	7,086	4,753	2,757	1,382	1,448
Black	75	63	31	12	27
American Indian, Eskimo, and Aleut	14	12	2	0	3
Asian or Pacific Islander	8	7	0	2	34
Other race	9	0	0	0	0
Women					
White	4,015	3,818	1,884	816	527
Black	104	56	52	10	0
American Indian, Eskimo, and Aleut	42	15	5	0	2
Asian or Pacific Islander	17	6	0	0	2
Other race	22	2	0	0	0

Source: Census of Population and Housing, 1990: Equal Employment Opportunity (EEO) File on CD-ROM [machine-readable datafiles]. Prepared by the Bureau of the Census. Washington, DC: The Bureau, 1992.

★ 773 ★

Educational Attainment

Educational Attainment in Wyoming, by Selected Characteristics

Table presents the number of civilians 16 years old or older who reported their educational backgrounds during the 1990 Census. Data show the number of individuals achieving various levels of education. Figures are reported by sex, age, and race.

Characteristic	Not high school graduate	High school graduate	Some college or associate's degree	Bachelor's degree	Graduate or professional degree
16 to 19 years old					
Men					
White	4,615	1,465	950	0	0
Black	15	16	0	0	0
American Indian, Eskimo, and Aleut	84	34	13	0	0
Asian or Pacific Islander	63	4	7	0	0
Other race	70	53	6	0	0
Women					
White	3,680	1,395	1,309	7	0
Black	20	8	6	0	0
American Indian, Eskimo, and Aleut	98	17	5	0	0
Asian or Pacific Islander	11	11	8	0	0
Other race	101	52	2	0	0
20 to 24 years old					
Men					
White	869	3,176	4,058	679	39
Black	23	35	44	8	0
American Indian, Eskimo, and Aleut	97	137	36	16	0
Asian or Pacific Islander	9	10	73	0	0
Other race	83	183	77	7	0
Women					
White	740	2,467	4,286	792	59
Black	0	5	45	0	0
American Indian, Eskimo, and Aleut	34	68	88	4	0
Asian or Pacific Islander	0	24	49	13	0
Other race	48	127	102	17	0
25 to 29 years old					
Men					
White	1,527	5,066	4,259	2,089	291
Black	31	26	31	14	0
American Indian, Eskimo, and Aleut	40	119	86	25	0
Asian or Pacific Islander	15	24	29	32	34
Other race	213	155	92	10	0
Women					
White	972	3,762	4,367	1,974	239
Black	0	32	49	0	8
American Indian, Eskimo, and Aleut	48	62	128	28	0
Asian or Pacific Islander	20	52	23	26	0
Other race	71	106	108	28	0
30 to 34 years old					
Men					
White	1,616	6,785	5,979	2,631	1,089

[Continued]

★ 773 ★

Educational Attainment in Wyoming, by Selected Characteristics
[Continued]

Characteristic	Not high school graduate	High school graduate	Some college or associate's degree	Bachelor's degree	Graduate or professional degree
Black	13	30	46	0	8
American Indian, Eskimo, and Aleut	61	156	72	0	13
Asian or Pacific Islander	15	18	16	27	20
Other race	167	280	94	37	8
Women					
White	957	4,455	5,526	2,578	699
Black	7	28	69	0	0
American Indian, Eskimo, and Aleut	34	120	67	9	0
Asian or Pacific Islander	5	20	38	8	0
Other race	69	157	113	29	13
35 to 39 years old					
Men					
White	1,125	5,646	7,132	3,306	1,707
Black	0	18	57	16	2
American Indian, Eskimo, and Aleut	22	87	158	3	0
Asian or Pacific Islander	0	26	23	8	28
Other race	101	122	111	7	10
Women					
White	764	4,061	6,051	2,895	825
Black	6	14	54	0	0
American Indian, Eskimo, and Aleut	58	66	73	28	0
Asian or Pacific Islander	36	22	28	29	0
Other race	60	103	101	5	0
40 to 69 years old					
Men					
White	6,325	15,747	13,859	7,369	5,818
Black	22	64	75	15	9
American Indian, Eskimo, and Aleut	267	159	223	33	34
Asian or Pacific Islander	33	20	29	30	19
Other race	471	144	190	26	8
Women					
White	4,361	12,674	12,828	5,351	2,180
Black	23	73	56	32	5
American Indian, Eskimo, and Aleut	114	131	227	23	33
Asian or Pacific Islander	71	74	52	40	0
Other race	284	121	135	3	14
70 years old and older					
Men					
White	639	571	259	180	108
Black	5	0	0	0	0
American Indian, Eskimo, and Aleut	13	0	5	5	0
Asian or Pacific Islander	0	8	0	0	0
Other race	17	0	0	0	0

[Continued]

★ 773 ★

Educational Attainment in Wyoming, by Selected Characteristics
[Continued]

Characteristic	Not high school graduate	High school graduate	Some college or associate's degree	Bachelor's degree	Graduate or professional degree
Women					
White	292	361	252	80	40
Black	7	0	0	0	0
American Indian, Eskimo, and Aleut	5	0	0	0	0
Asian or Pacific Islander	0	0	0	0	0
Other race	0	0	0	0	0

Source: Census of Population and Housing, 1990: Equal Employment Opportunity (EEO) File on CD-ROM [machine-readable datafiles]. Prepared by the Bureau of the Census. Washington, DC: The Bureau, 1992.

Job Training and Retraining

★ 774 ★

Training Sources: 1991

Table shows the workers reporting that training was needed to obtain their jobs. Data are for 1991.

[Numbers in thousands]

Source of training	Workers needing training	
	Number	Percent
Total, all workers	65,276	57
High school vocational programs	4,488	4
Post-high school vocational programs	3,141	3
Junior college or technical institute	8,868	8
4-year or longer college program	21,637	20
Formal company training	13,948	12
Informal on-the-job training	31,260	27
Armed Forces	2,434	2
Friends, relatives, or other nonwork-related experience	8,490	7

Source: Amirault, Thomas. "Job Training: Who Needs It and Where They Get It." Occupational Outlook Quarterly (winter 1992-1993), p. 22.

★ 775 ★

Job Training and Retraining

Vocational Rehabilitation: 1980-1992

Vocational rehabilitation of the disabled is defined as restoration, preservation, or development of the ability to function in productive activity. Rehabilitation services provided by state vocational rehabilitation agencies with matching state and federal funds include medical restoration, training, counseling, guidance, and placement services.

Item	Unit	1980	1985	1986	1987	1988	1989	1990	1991	1992
Federal and state expenditures[1]	Million $	1,076[2]	1,452	1,506	1,649	1,776	1,867	1,910	2,092	2,240
Federal expenditures	Million $	817[2]	1,100	1,144	1,275	1,373	1,446	1,525	1,622	1,731
Applicants processed for program eligibility	1,000	717	594	594	597	606	623	625	619	713
Percent accepted into program	Percent	58	60	58	58	58	58	57	57	57
Total persons rehabilitated[3]	1,000	277	228	223	220	218	220	216	203	192
Rehabilitation rate[4]	Percent	64	64	64	63	63	63	62	60	58
Severely disabled persons rehabilitated[5]	1,000	143	135	135	136	141	147	146	140	134
Rehabilitation rate[4]	Percent	61	62	62	62	62	62	62	59	57
Percent of total persons rehabilitated	Percent	51	59	61	62	65	67	68	69	70
Persons served, total[6]	1,000	1,095	932	924	917	919	929	938	942	950
Persons served, severely disabled[7]	1,000	606	581	580	584	604	625	640	654	667
Percent of total persons served	Percent	55	62	63	64	66	67	68	69	70

Source: U.S. Bureau of the Census. *Statistical Abstract of the United States, 1994.* 114th ed. Washington, DC: U.S. Government Printing Office, 1994, p. 382. Primary source: U.S. Department of Education. Rehabilitation Services Administration. *Caseload Statistics of State Vocational Rehabilitation Agencies in Fiscal Years* (annual) and *State Vocational Rehabilitation Agency Program Data in Fiscal Years* (annual). *Notes:* For fiscal years ending in year shown. Includes Puerto Rico, Guam, Virgin Islands, American Samoa, Northern Mariana Islands, and Trust Territory of the Pacific Islands. 1. Includes expenditures only under the basic support provisions of the Rehabilitation Act. 2. Estimates based on amounts appropriated. 3. Persons successfully placed into gainful employment. 4. Persons rehabilitated as a percent of all active case closures (whether rehabilitated or not). 5. Persons successfully placed into gainful employment. Severely disabled individuals fall into any of the following three categories: (a) clients with specified major disabling conditions such as blindness and deafness; (b) clients who at any time in the vocational rehabilitation process had been Social Security disability beneficiaries or recipients of Supplemental Security Income; and (c) other individuals with substantial loss in conducting certain specified activities. 6. Includes active cases accepted for rehabilitation services during year plus active cases on hand at beginning of year. 7. Severely disabled individuals fall into any of the following three categories: (a) clients with specified major disabling conditions such as blindness and deafness; (b) clients who at any time in the vocational rehabilitation process had been Social Security disability beneficiaries or recipients of Supplemental Security Income; and (c) other individuals with substantial loss in conducting certain specified activities. Includes active cases accepted for rehabilitation services during year plus active cases on hand at beginning of year.

★ 776 ★

Job Training and Retraining

Work-Related Training, by Selected Characteristics of Recipients: 1990

Data show persons 18 to 64 years old who received work-related training as of spring 1990. Based on Survey of Income and Program Participation.

[In thousands, except as indicated]

Characteristic	Total	Sex		Race		Hispanic origin[1]	Education		
		Male	Female	White	Black		Less than 9 years	9 to 12 years	More than 12 years
All persons	152,815	74,828	77,987	129,575	17,891	12,463	9,714	77,599	65,502
Persons ever receiving work training	39,238	19,950	19,288	33,984	4,241	2,218	1,050	20,447	17,742
Uses training on current or most recent job	26,563	14,073	12,489	23,595	2,316	1,486	580	12,671	13,311
Location:									
Apprenticeship	1,749	1,411	338	1,616	76	114	70	999	680
Business/vo-tech school	10,213	4,388	5,825	8,659	1,301	537	192	6,562	3,460

[Continued]

★ 776 ★

Work-Related Training, by Selected Characteristics of Recipients: 1990
[Continued]

Characteristic	Total	Sex		Race		Hispanic origin[1]	Education		
		Male	Female	White	Black		Less than 9 years	9 to 12 years	More than 12 years
Community college	4,077	1,664	2,413	3,722	275	220	92	1,838	2,147
Four-year college	2,738	1,396	1,341	2,488	198	89	22	355	2,360
High school vo-tech program	2,158	1,068	1,090	1,875	250	183	36	1,798	324
Training program at work	13,330	7,393	5,936	11,774	1,164	598	270	5,903	7,156
Military	2,229	1,990	238	1,968	180	139	12	1,151	1,065
Previous job	1,821	968	853	1,636	134	134	87	705	1,029
Other	9,720	4,874	4,845	8,304	1,169	497	413	4,524	4,783
Program paid for by –									
Self or family	11,540	4,708	6,832	10,348	914	588	215	6,014	5,311
Employer	17,834	10,019	7,815	16,059	1,379	880	426	7,885	9,524
Federal, state, or local government	10,429	5,543	4,886	8,079	2,010	748	387	6,675	3,366
Someone else	1,000	553	447	859	99	84	41	586	373
Length of training program (average number of weeks)	22	25	20	23	21	22	20	25	19

Source: U.S. Bureau of the Census. *Statistical Abstract of the United States, 1994.* 114th ed. Washington, DC: U.S. Government Printing Office, 1994, p. 426. Primary source: U.S. Bureau of the Census. *Current Population Reports.* Series P70-32. *Note:* 1. Persons of Hispanic origin may be of any race.

School Enrollment

★ 777 ★

High School Dropouts in the Labor Force: 1992-1993

Table shows the labor force status of 1992-1993 high school dropouts, 16 to 24 years old, by sex and race/ethnicity. Data from October 1993.

[Numbers in thousands]

Sex and race/ethnicity[1]	Dropouts		Dropouts in civilian labor force[2]						Not in labor force
	Number	Percent of total	Number	Labor force participation rate	Employed		Unemployed		
					Number	Percent of dropouts	Number	Unemployment rate	
All dropouts	399	100.0	254	63.8	187	47.0	67	26.3	145
Men	213	53.4	156	73.5	132	61.8	25	15.9	57
Women	186	46.6	98	52.6	56	30.1	42	42.9	88
White[3]	304	76.2	209	68.8	159	52.2	50	24.1	95

[Continued]

★ 777 ★

High School Dropouts in the Labor Force: 1992-1993

[Continued]

Sex and race/ethnicity[1]	Dropouts		Dropouts in civilian labor force[2]						Not in labor force
	Number	Percent of total	Number	Labor force participation rate	Employed		Unemployed		
					Number	Percent of dropouts	Number	Unemployment rate	
Black[3]	80	20.1	34	42.9	21	26.2	13	([4])	46
Hispanic[5]	60	15.0	43	([4])	28	([4])	15	([4])	17

Source: U.S. Department of Education. Office of Educational Research and Improvement. National Center for Education Statistics. *Digest of Education Statistics, 1994.* NCES 94-115. Lanham, MD: Bernan, November 1994, p. 402. Primary source: U.S. Department of Labor. Bureau of Labor Statistics. *College Enrollment of 1993 High School Graduates.* Table prepared June 1994. *Notes:* Data are based upon sample surveys of the civilian noninstitutional population. Percents are only shown when the base is 75,000 or greater. Even though the standard errors are large, smaller estimates are shown to permit users to combine categories in various ways. Because of rounding, details may not add to totals. 1. Persons who dropped out of school between October 1992 and October 1993. 2. The labor force includes all employed persons plus those seeking employment. The labor force participation rate is the percentage of persons either employed or seeking employment. 3. Includes persons of Hispanic origin. 4. Data not shown where base is less than 75,000. 5. Persons of Hispanic origin may be of any race.

★ 778 ★

School Enrollment

High School Graduates Enrolling in College: 1993

Table shows the college enrollment and labor force status of 1993 high school graduates, 16 to 24 years old, by sex and race/ethnicity. Data are for October 1993.

[Numbers in thousands]

High school graduates[1]	Civilain noninstitutionalized population			Civilian labor force[2]					Not in labor force
	Number	Percent	Percent of high school graduates	Number	Labor force participation rate	Employed	Unemployed		
							Number	Unemployment rate	
Total	2,338	100.0	100.0	1,413	60.5	1,144	268	19.1	925
Men	1,118	47.8	47.8	693	62.0	558	135	19.5	425
Women	1,219	52.1	52.1	720	59.0	586	134	18.6	500
White[3]	1,910	81.7	81.7	1,217	63.7	1,002	215	17.7	693
Black[3]	302	12.9	12.9	149	49.2	102	47	31.6	154
Hispanic origin[4]	200	8.6	8.6	131	65.7	86	46	34.8	68
Enrolled in college[5]	1,464	100.0	62.6	677	46.3	580	97	14.3	787
Men	668	45.6	28.6	305	45.7	252	54	17.6	362
Women	797	54.4	34.1	372	46.7	329	43	11.6	425
2-year	534	36.5	22.8	351	65.7	305	46	13.2	183
4-year	930	63.5	39.8	326	35.1	276	51	15.5	604
Full-time students	1,314	89.8	56.2	567	43.1	473	93	16.5	748
Part-time students	150	10.2	6.4	111	73.6	107	3	3.2	40
White[3]	1,200	82.0	51.3	585	48.7	511	74	12.6	615
Black[3]	168	11.5	7.2	62	37.1	45	17	([6])	106
Hispanic origin[4]	125	8.5	5.3	70	56.2	53	17	([6])	54
Not enrolled in college[5]	873	100.0	37.3	736	84.3	563	173	23.5	137
Men	451	51.7	19.3	388	86.1	306	82	21.1	63
Women	422	48.3	18.0	348	82.3	257	91	26.1	75

[Continued]

★ 778 ★

High School Graduates Enrolling in College: 1993

[Continued]

High school graduates[1]	Civilain noninstitutionalized population			Civilian labor force[2]						Not in labor force
	Number	Percent	Percent of high school graduates	Number	Labor force participation rate	Employed	Unemployed			
							Number	Unemployment rate		
White[3]	710	81.3	30.4	632	89.1	491	141	22.4		77
Black[3]	134	15.3	5.7	86	64.3	57	30	34.4		48
Hispanic origin[4]	75	8.6	3.2	61	81.1	33	28	([6])		14

Source: U.S. Department of Education. Office of Educational Research and Improvement. National Center for Education Statistics. *Digest of Education Statistics, 1994.* NCES 94-115. Lanham, MD: Bernan, November 1994, p. 401. Primary source: U.S. Department of Labor. Bureau of Labor Statistics. *College Enrollment of 1993 High School Graduates.* Table prepared June 1994. *Notes:* Data are based upon sample surveys of the civilian noninstitutional population. Percents are only shown when the base is 75,000 or greater. Even though the standard errors are large, smaller estimates are shown to permit users to combine categories in various ways. Because of rounding, details may not add to totals. 1. Includes persons who graduated from high school between January and October 1993. 2. The labor force includes all employed persons plus those seeking employment. The labor force participation rate is the percentage of persons either employed or seeking employment. 3. Includes persons of Hispanic origin. 4. Persons of Hispanic origin may be of any race. 5. October 1993. 6. Data not shown where base is less than 75,000.

★ 779 ★

School Enrollment

Higher Education Enrollment, by Race/Ethnicity: 1992

Table shows the number of enrollees in higher education for each state and the District of Columbia. Data are provided by race/ethnicity for 1992.

State	Total	Race/ethnicity of enrollee					
		American Indian	Asian	Black	Hispanic	White	Foreign
Alabama[1]	264,831	1,186	2,918	53,189	3,986	198,556	4,996
Alaska	30,902	2,852	799	1,143	730	24,682	696
Arizona	275,599	9,244	7,065	8,616	34,443	208,688	7,543
Arkansas	97,435	578	1,024	14,014	511	79,602	1,706
California[1]	1,979,079	21,936	287,552	139,748	315,485	1,116,323	98,035
Colorado	244,520	2,680	6,760	8,044	20,336	201,220	5,480
Connecticut	166,820	414	5,006	11,069	6,486	138,933	4,912
Delaware	42,763	113	881	5,156	569	35,230	814
District of Columbia	81,909	202	3,742	25,156	2,648	40,934	9,227
Florida	618,285	2,287	15,205	72,750	75,270	435,987	16,786
Georgia	293,162	762	5,785	65,261	3,838	211,081	6,435
Hawaii	61,162	225	36,112	1,446	1,229	17,075	5,075
Idaho	57,798	630	833	333	1,305	52,914	1,783
Illinois	748,033	2,428	36,270	93,641	54,582	543,108	18,004
Indiana	296,912	1,015	4,600	17,466	5,354	280,263	8,214
Iowa	177,813	552	3,051	5,179	2,534	158,393	8,104
Kansas	169,527	2,270	3,152	7,890	4,189	145,875	6,351
Kentucky	188,320	592	1,589	12,026	977	170,235	2,901
Louisiana	204,379	1,054	3,446	50,181	4,348	139,873	5,477
Maine	57,977	854	632	666	352	54,777	696
Maryland	273,449	903	13,515	51,961	5,530	192,807	8,733
Massachusetts[1]	422,976	1,709	20,299	20,491	15,146	342,585	22,746

[Continued]

★ 779 ★

Higher Education Enrollment, by Race/Ethnicity: 1992
[Continued]

State	Total	Race/ethnicity of enrollee					
		American Indian	Asian	Black	Hispanic	White	Foreign
Michigan	559,729	4,147	12,060	57,086	9,996	480,953	15,487
Minnesota	272,920	2,548	7,062	5,588	2,919	248,519	6,284
Mississippi	123,754	398	849	34,496	454	85,331	2,226
Missouri	296,617	1,253	5,496	25,484	4,030	252,664	7,690
Montana	39,644	4,240	214	133	371	33,501	1,185
Nebraska[1]	122,603	800	1,644	3,820	2,336	111,388	2,615
Nevada	63,877	995	3,338	3,222	4,104	50,783	1,435
New Hampshire	63,924	238	1,539	722	926	59,521	978
New Jersey	342,446	837	17,075	38,001	25,702	247,458	13,373
New Mexico	99,276	5,675	1,462	2,933	28,577	58,534	2,095
New York	1,074,928	3,595	56,668	129,232	87,915	758,093	39,425
North Carolina	383,453	3,338	7,015	71,533	3,552	291,861	6,154
North Dakota	40,470	2,019	281	311	213	35,923	1,723
Ohio	574,064	1,829	8,880	49,944	6,733	490,826	15,852
Oklahoma	182,105	11,832	3,306	12,843	3,292	143,732	7,100
Oregon	167,415	2,184	8,285	2,651	4,033	143,921	6,341
Pennsylvania	629,832	1,326	17,951	46,317	11,109	536,620	16,509
Rhode Island	79,165	273	2,289	2,976	2,295	68,636	2,696
South Carolina	171,443	397	1,917	36,268	1,310	128,445	3,106
South Dakota[1]	37,596	2,063	270	290	146	33,998	829
Tennessee	242,970	612	2,895	35,459	1,969	197,783	4,252
Texas	938,526	3,762	33,423	89,213	168,644	616,515	26,969
Utah	133,083	1,301	2,489	766	2,905	119,979	5,643
Vermont	37,377	97	522	429	406	35,108	815
Virginia	354,172	1,127	14,128	52,881	5,963	273,589	6,484
Washington	276,484	4,435	18,701	9,350	7,528	230,176	6,294
West Virginia	90,252	155	829	3,384	451	83,673	1,760
Wisconsin	307,902	2,429	5,720	12,354	5,545	274,875	6,979
Wyoming	31,548	454	268	371	1,150	28,691	614
Total	14,491,226	118,845	696,812	1,393,483	954,422	10,870,037	457,627

Source: "Enrollment in Higher Education by State and Race, 1992." *Manpower Comments* (March 1994), p. 21. Primary source: U.S. Department of Education. *Notes:* 1. Significant proportions of enrollment figures for public two-year institutions were imputed because institutions did not provide complete data for 1992.

★ 780 ★

School Enrollment

School Enrollment and Labor Force Status, by Age, Sex, and Race: 1980 and 1992

As of October. Covers civilian noninstitutional population 16 to 24 years old. Based on Current Population Survey.

[In thousands, except percentages]

Characteristic	Population		Civilian labor force			Employed		Unemployed		
			1980 total	1992				1980 total	1992	
	1980	1992		Total	Percent[1]	1980	1992		Total	Rate[2]
Total, 16 to 24 years[3]	37,103	30,969	24,918	19,950	64.4	21,454	17,335	3,464	2,615	13.1
Enrolled in school[3]	15,713	15,868	7,454	7,737	48.8	6,433	6,718	1,021	1,019	13.2
16 to 19 years	11,126	10,276	4,836	4,318	42.0	4,029	3,574	807	744	17.2
20 to 24 years	4,587	5,592	2,618	3,419	61.1	2,404	3,144	214	275	8.0
Sex:										
Male	7,997	7,917	3,825	3,871	48.9	3,259	3,322	566	549	14.2
Female	7,716	7,951	3,629	3,866	48.6	3,174	3,396	455	469	12.1
College level	7,664	8,524	3,996	4,931	57.9	3,632	4,534	364	397	8.1
Full-time	6,396	7,165	2,854	3,710	51.8	2,554	3,400	300	309	8.3
Race:										
White	13,242	12,777	6,687	6,631	51.9	5,889	5,900	798	731	11.0
Below college	6,566	5,720	3,095	2,399	41.9	2,579	1,950	516	449	18.7
College level	6,678	7,057	3,592	4,232	60.0	3,310	3,950	282	282	6.7
Black	2,028	2,199	595	751	34.2	406	522	189	229	30.5
Below college	1,282	1,288	294	323	25.0	174	172	120	151	46.8
College level	747	911	300	428	47.0	230	350	70	78	18.3
Not enrolled[3]	21,390	15,101	17,464	12,213	80.9	15,021	10,617	2,443	1,597	13.1
White	18,103	12,207	15,121	10,149	83.1	13,318	9,092	1,803	1,057	10.4
Black	2,864	2,393	2,055	1,677	70.1	1,451	1,204	604	474	28.2

Source: U.S. Bureau of the Census. *Statistical Abstract of the United States, 1994.* 114th ed. Washington, DC: U.S. Government Printing Office, 1994, p. 400. Primary sources: U.S. Bureau of Labor Statistics. Bulletin 2307; *News.* USDL 93-226 (22 June 1993); and unpublished data. *Notes:* 1. Percent of civilian noninstitutional population. 2. Percent of civilian labor force in each category. 3. Includes other races, not shown separately.

Schools

★ 781 ★

Top Business Schools

A survey of more than 4,600 Master's of Business Administration (MBA) students graduating in 1994 showed that nearly 13 percent of them expected to earn at least $100,000 in their first year of work. The table shows the schools of the respondents expecting this salary upon graduation.

[In percentages]

School	Salaries of $100,000 or more
Stanford	53.7
Harvard	52.1
Dartmouth	39.2
Wharton	33.3
Northwestern	30.8

Source: Bongiorno, Lori, and John A. Byrne. "Is There an MBA Glut? If You Answered No, You Pass." *Business Week,* 24 October 1994, p. 72. Primary source: *Business Week* survey.

★ 782 ★

Schools

Undergraduate Schools of MBA Candidates

A survey of more than 4,600 Master's of Business Administration (MBA) students graduating in 1994 showed that nearly 13 percent of them expected to earn at least $100,000 in their first year of work. The table shows the undergraduate schools of the respondents expecting this salary upon graduation.

[In percentages]

School	Salaries of $100,000 or more
University of California – Berkeley	3.2
University of Pennsylvania	2.9
Dartmouth	2.7
Harvard	2.7
Stanford	2.7

Source: Bongiorno, Lori, and John A. Byrne. "Is There an MBA Glut? If You Answered No, You Pass." *Business Week,* 24 October 1994, p. 72. Primary source: *Business Week* survey.

Chapter 8
HEALTH AND SAFETY

This chapter is comprised of 43 tables on occupational health and safety. Some tables focus on more traditional topics such as work-related illnesses, injuries, and deaths; others profile current issues such as AIDS and violence in the workplace or employer-sponsored health promotions and initiatives. Other topics include ergonomics, lost work time due to occupational illness or injury, Occupational Safety and Health Administration, stress, substance abuse, and workers' compensation.

AIDS

★ 783 ★

AIDS Programs in the Workplace – Availability

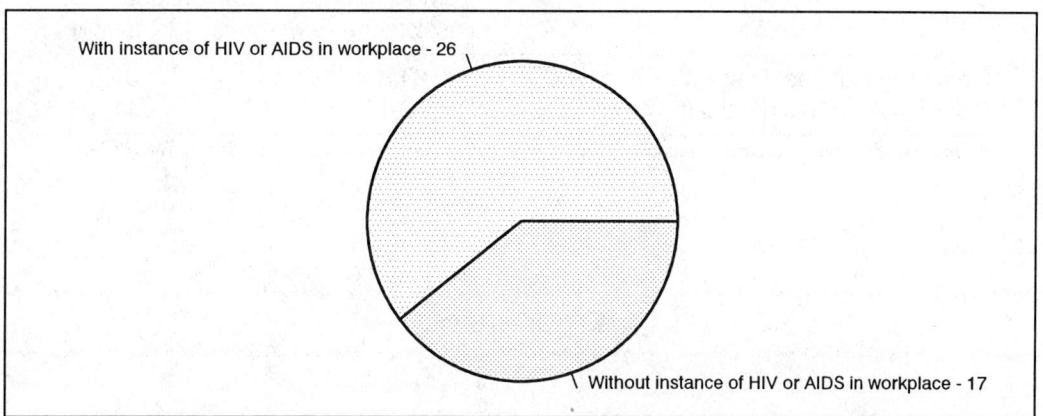

With instance of HIV or AIDS in workplace - 26

Without instance of HIV or AIDS in workplace - 17

Table shows the results of the American Management Association's 1994 Survey on HIV- and AIDS-Related Policies. According to the source: "There's no doubt about it: AIDS is rapidly becoming a top workplace issue." For example, of the 794 participating companies, 38 percent addressed one or more HIV cases during 1994. Yet many of the companies surveyed had no AIDS program or policies established.

[In percentages]

Company	Companies with AIDS policies or programs
With instance of HIV or AIDS in workplace	26
Without instance of HIV or AIDS in workplace	17

Source: Jacobs, Heidi. "Corporate Response to AIDS." *American Management Association* (January 1995), p. 6.

★ 784 ★

AIDS

AIDS Programs in the Workplace – Types

Tables shows the types of AIDS programs offered by polled companies. Data taken from the American Management Association's 1994 Survey on HIV- and AIDS-Related Policies.

[In percentages]

Company	Employee assistance	AIDS awareness	Supervisory training
Company that has dealt with HIV or AIDS	64.8	48.4	34.4
Company that has not dealt with HIV or AIDS	43.1	25.2	11.5

Source: Jacobs, Heidi. "Corporate Response to AIDS." *American Management Association* (January 1995), p. 6.

Ergonomics

★ 785 ★

Work Environment and Health Problems

Twenty-five percent of those surveyed by the Gallup Organization for a U.S. News/CNN poll indicated that their work environments somehow adversely affected their physical well being. Both men (34 percent) and women (38 percent) cited back injuriess as the most common work-related health problem.

Source: "Sore Workers." *U.S. News & World Report,* 24 April 1995, n.p. Primary source: Gallup Organization, U.S. News/CNN poll.

★ 786 ★

Ergonomics

Workplace Ergonomics

Ergonomists evaluate workplace comfort levels and effectiveness. The table below shows measures employed by ergonomists to make work areas more comfortable and efficient.

Measure	Percent
Redesign/replacement of machinery or tools	45
Monitor certain jobs or employees	43
Redesign/replacement of furniture	40
Mechanization of certain work functions	38

[Continued]

★ 786 ★

Workplace Ergonomics
[Continued]

Measure	Percent
Job duty rotation	34
Alternation of work tasks	34
Ergonomics training programs	31
Longer/more frequent breaks	13

Source: Hansen, Marc D. "Engineering Design for Safety." *Professional Safety* 38, no. 10 (October 1993), p. 38.

Fatalities

★ 787 ★

Fatal Work Injuries: 1991

Figures show percent distribution of 3,465 fatal work injuries in 31 states. Data provided by demographic characteristics.

Characteristics	Fatal occupational injuries
Employment status	
Wage and salary workers	81
Self-employed[1]	19
Sex and age	
Men	92
Women	8
Both sexes:	
Under 20 years old	5
20-24 years old	7
25-34 years old	26
35-44 years old	25
45-54 years old	17
55-64 years old	13
65 years old and older	7
Race/Origin	
Asian or Pacific Islander	3
Black	9
Hispanic	9

[Continued]

★ 787 ★

Fatal Work Injuries: 1991
[Continued]

Characteristics	Fatal occupational injuries
White	84
Other or unknown	4

Source: U.S. Department of Labor. Bureau of Labor Statistics. *Fatal Workplace Injuries in 1991: A Collection of Data and Analysis.* Report 845. Washington, DC: U.S. Government Printing Office, April 1993, p. 3. Primary source: 31 participating states in the 1991 Census of Fatal Occupational Injuries (CFOI) program. *Notes:* Percentages may not add to total due to rounding. Participating states include Arizona, California, Colorado, Connecticut, Delaware, Georgia, Hawaii, Idaho, Indiana, Iowa, Kansas, Kentucky, Maine, Maryland, Massachusetts, Michigan, Minnesota, Montana, Nebraska, Nevada, New Hampshire, New Jersey, North Carolina, Oklahoma, Oregon, Tennessee, Texas, Utah, Washington, Wisconsin, and Wyoming. 1. May include unpaid family workers, owners of incorporated businesses, or members of partnerships.

★ 788 ★

Fatalities

Occupational Disease-Related Deaths: 1980-1990

Table shows the number of deaths from selected occupational diseases for males by underlying and nonunderlying causes. Data are for 1978 through 1990.

Year	By underlying cause				By nonunderlying cause			
	Malignant neoplasm of perioneum and pleura (mesothelioma)	Coal workers pneumoconiosis	Asbestosis	Silicosis	Malignant neoplasm of perioneum and pleura (mesothelioma)	Coal workers pneumoconiosis	Asbestosis	Silicosis
1980	552	977	96	202	135	1,587	228	232
1983	584	926	128	149	115	1,758	321	205
1984	584	923	131	160	124	1,742	298	210
1985	571	947	130	138	102	1,652	382	187
1986	564	884	180	135	106	1,536	494	175
1987	575	823	195	153	111	1,419	488	173
1988	556	757	206	128	104	1,445	536	162
1989	565	725	261	130	83	1,402	588	156
1990	629	727	282	146	105	1,248	619	152

Source: Executive Office of the President of the United States. *Environmental Quality 24: The Twenty-fourth Annual Report of the Council on Environmental Quality.* Prepared by Ray Clark. Written by Carroll Curtis. Edited by Barry Walsh. Washington, DC: U.S. Government Printing Office, 1994, p. 516. Primary source: U.S. Department of Health and Human Services. National Center for Health Statistics. *Health United States, 1992.* Hyattsville, MD: Public Health Service, 1993, p. 82, table 46.

★ 789 ★
Fatalities

Work Fatalities – Number: 1992

Table shows causes of fatal work injuries for the 50 states and the District of Columbia. Based on the 1992 Census of Fatal Occupational Injuries.

Cause	Number of fatalities
Total	6,083
Transportation accidents[1]	2,441
Highway accidents[1]	1,121
Collision between vehicles, mobile equipment	553
Noncollision accidents	292
Nonhighway accidents[2]	436
Aircraft accidents	350
Workers struck by vehicles	342
Water vehicle accidents	110
Railway accidents	66
Assaults and violent acts[1]	1,216
Homicides[1]	1,004
Shooting	822
Stabbing	82
Self-inflicted injury	183
Contacts with objects and equipment[1]	1,001
Struck by object[1]	558
Struck by falling objects	360
Struck by flying objects	79
Caught in or compressed by:	
Equipment or objects	312
Collapsing material	110
Falls[1]	590
Fall to lower level	500
Fall on same level	60
Exposure to harmful substances or environments[1]	593
Contact with electrical current	334
Exposure to caustic, noxious, or allergenic substances	118
Oxygen deficiency	109
Drowning, submersion	76
Fire and explosions	167
Other events and exposures	75

Source: U.S. Bureau of the Census. *Statistical Abstract of the United States, 1994.* 114th ed. Washington, DC: U.S. Government Printing Office, 1994, p. 436. Primary source: U.S. Bureau of Labor Statistics. *Monthly Labor Report* (October 1993). *Notes:* 1. Includes other causes not shown separately. 2. Farm, industrial premises.

★ 790 ★
Fatalities

Work Fatalities – Percent Distribution: 1992

Data reflect findings from the first national census of occupational fatalities conducted by the Bureau of Labor Statistics. The survey identified 6,083 worker fatalities in 1992.

Cause of fatality	Percent
Transportation accidents	40
Assaults and violent acts	20
Homicides	17
Suicides	3
Highway accidents	18
Contact with objects	16
Exposure to harmful substances	10
Falls	10
Nonhighway accidents	7
Aircraft accidents	6
Struck by vehicle	6

Source: Laabs, Jennifer J. "Danger at Work: Fatalities and Injuries on the Rise." *Personnel Journal* (February 1994), p. 12.

Lost Work Time

★ 791 ★

Lost Work Time, by Reason

The table below presents the most frequent reasons given for work time lost due to illness. Data include the average number of sick days taken per year for selected illnesses and conditions.

Reason	Days off per year
Flu	76
Sprains	30
Fractures	23
Colds	21

Source: "Hello Boss...." *Detroit Free Press,* 14 March 1993, p. 3A. Primary source: National Center for Health Statistics.

★ 792 ★
Lost Work Time

Occupational Injury and Illness Cases and Lost Work Time: 1972-1991

Figures show the occupational injury and illness incidence rates for private industry during 1972 through 1991. The incidence rates represent the number of injuries and illnesses or lost workdays per 100 full-time workers.

Year[1]	Total cases	Lost workday cases	Nonfatal cases without lost workdays	Lost workdays
1972	10.9	3.3	7.6	47.9
1973	11.0	3.4	7.5	53.3
1974	10.4	3.5	6.9	54.6
1975	9.1	3.3	5.8	56.1
1976	9.2	3.5	5.7	60.5
1977	9.3	3.8	5.5	61.6
1978[2]	9.4	4.1	5.3	63.5
1979[2]	9.5	4.3	5.2	67.7
1980	8.7	4.0	4.7	65.2
1981	8.3	3.8	4.5	61.7
1982	7.7	3.5	4.2	58.7
1983[2]	7.6	3.4	4.2	58.5
1984[2]	8.0	3.7	4.3	63.4
1985	7.9	3.6	4.3	64.9
1986	7.9	3.6	4.3	65.8
1987	8.3	3.8	4.4	69.9
1988	8.6	4.0	4.6	76.1
1989	8.6	4.0	4.6	78.7
1990	8.8	4.1	4.7	84.0
1991	8.4	3.9	4.5	86.5

Source: U.S. Department of Labor. Bureau of Labor Statistics. *Occupational Injuries and Illnesses in the United States by Industry, 1991.* Bulletin 2424. Washington, DC: U.S. Government Printing Office, May 1993, p. 1. *Notes:* Data for 1976-1991 exclude farms with fewer than 11 employees. 1. Data for 1972-1975 are based on the *Standard Industrial Classification Manual* (1967 edition); data for 1976-1987 are based on the *Standard Industrial Classification Manual* (1972 edition); and data for 1988-1991 are based on the *Standard Industrial Classification Manual* (1987 edition). 2. In 1978, 1979, 1983, and 1984, small nonfarm employers in low-risk industries were not surveyed. To maintain comparability with the other data, a statistical method was developed to provide estimates for those employers.

★ 793 ★

Lost Work Time

Sick Days, by Metropolitan Area

The table below presents the frequency with which employees call in sick. Data are provided by selected cities.

City	Sick days
Atlanta, Georgia	6
Baltimore, Maryland	8
Boston, Massachusetts	6
Chicago, Illinois	6
Cincinnati, Ohio	6
Dallas, Texas	5
Denver, Colorado	4
Detroit, Michigan	4
Houston, Texas	6
Indianapolis, Indiana	6
Los Angeles-Long Beach, California	6
Miami-Hialeah, Florida	4
Minneapolis-St. Paul, Minnesota	5
Newark, New Jersey	5
New Orleans, Louisiana	7
New York, New York	5
Philadelphia, Pennsylvania	4
Phoenix, Arizona	6
Portland, Oregon	5
Riverside-San Bernardino, California	9
San Diego, California	5
San Francisco-Oakland, California	6
Seattle, Washington	4
St. Louis, Missouri	5
Washington, District of Columbia	5

Source: "Something's in the Air." *Small Business Reports* 19, no. 3 (March 1994), p. 64. Primary source: National Center for Health Statistics.

Occupational Illnesses and Injuries

★ 794 ★

Americans With Disabilities Act Complaints: July 1992-July 1993

Figures below represent percentages of Americans With Disabilities Act (ADA) charges filed with the Equal Employment Opportunity Commission (EEOC) between July 26, 1992, and July 31, 1993. Data reflect complaints for specific, alleged diseases and disorders. In total, 12,962 charges were filed with the EEOC during this time period.

Problem	Percent
Back impairment	18.5
Mental illness	9.8
Retaliation	7.3
Heart impairment	4.3
Neurological disorder	3.7
Diabetes	3.6
Vision impairment	3.3
Hearing impairment	3.3
Arthritis	2.8
Cancer	2.7
All other	40.8

Source: Hansen, Mark. "The ADA's Wide Reach: Little League and Health Insurers Among Those Covered by Act." *ABA Journal* (December 1993), p. 14. Primary source: Equal Employment Opportunity Commission.

★ 795 ★

Occupational Illnesses and Injuries

Migrant Worker Protection Standards

The National Advisory Council on Migrant Health reported that "basic worker protection standards which were enacted in the early part of this century exempt agricultural workers" (p. 65). In particular, unsanitary working conditions and long-term exposure to pesticides threaten the well being of migrant farm workers. Farms with less than 11 workers are not required to adhere to field sanitation laws. Among those farms legally bound by the laws in 1990, 69 percent were found to be in violation during Occupational Safety and Health Administration field inspections. Similarly, the Environmental Protection Agency attributes the illnesses and injuries of 300,000 farm workers annually to pesticides.

Source: National Advisory Council on Migrant Health. *1993 Recommendations of the National Advisory Council on Migrant Health.* Rockville, MD: National Advisory Council on Migrant Health, May 1993, pp. 65-66.

★ 796 ★

Occupational Illnesses and Injuries

Occupational Illnesses – New Cases: 1981-1991

Figures show the percent distribution of new cases of reported occupational illnesses by category of illness. Data are for private industry from 1981 through 1991.

Illness category	1981	1982	1983	1984	1985	1986	1987	1988	1989	1990	1991
Total illness cases	100	100	100	100	100	100	100	100	100	100	100
Skin diseases or disorders	41	40	37	34	33	30	28	24	22	18	16
Dust diseases of the lungs	2	2	2	1	1	2	2	1	1	1	1
Respiratory conditions due to toxic agents	9	8	7	9	9	9	8	7	7	6	5
Poisoning	4	3	3	4	3	3	3	2	2	2	2
Disorders due to physical agents	9	8	8	7	7	7	7	7	6	6	5
Disorders associated with repeated trauma	18	21	25	28	29	33	38	48	52	56	61
All other occupational illnesses	17	18	17	17	16	15	14	11	10	11	11

Source: U.S. Department of Labor. Bureau of Labor Statistics. *Occupational Injuries and Illnesses in the United States by Industry, 1991.* Bulletin 2424. Washington, DC: U.S. Government Printing Office, May 1993, p. 5.

★ 797 ★

Occupational Illnesses and Injuries

Repetitive Motion Injuries: 1992

Of the 90,000 repetitive motion injuries studied by the U.S. Department of Labor in 1992, 65 percent of those afflicted were women; 34 percent were men. More than 50 percent of the cases involved wrist injuries. The table below shows the various types of repetitive motion, disabling conditions, and workdays lost.

[In percentages]

Item	Cases
Type of repetitive motion	
Placing, grasping, or moving objects[1]	31
Repetitive use of tools	18
Other motions	14
Typing or key entry	12
Type of motion not reported	25
Disabling condition	
Carpal tunnel symdrome	36
Sprains and strains	18
All other conditions	46
Workdays lost	
1-10	37
11-20	14

[Continued]

★ 797 ★

Repetitive Motion Injuries: 1992
[Continued]

Item	Cases
21-30	10
31 or more	39

Source: Litvan, Laura M. "Controlling Wrist and Back Injuries." *Nation's Business* (August 1994), p. 45. Primary source: U.S. Department of Labor. *Notes:* Some totals do not equal 100 percent due to rounding. 1. Except tools.

★ 798 ★

Occupational Illnesses and Injuries

Returning to Work After Injuries, by Disorder

Table shows the success rate for returning to work following an injury or illness.

[In percentages]

Ailment	Success rate
Back/spine	61
Musculoskeletal	60
Neurological	49
Cancer	44
Mental illness	43

Source: "Getting 'Back' to Work." *USA TODAY,* 19 October 1994, p. B1. Primary source: Northwestern National Life. 1987-1993 claims data.

★ 799 ★

Occupational Illnesses and Injuries

Returning to Work After Injuries, by Worker Characteristic

Table shows the success rate for returning to work following a disabling injury or illness by sex, age, and marital status of workers. Data are from a study of more than 2,700 group disability claims.

[In percentages]

Characteristic	Success rate
Sex:	
Men	54
Female	63
Age:	
18-24 years old	100
25-34 years old	82
35-44 years old	69
45-54 years old	54
55-64 years old	41
65 years old or older	91
Marital status	
Never married	66
Married	59
Widowed/divorced	56

Source: "Returning to Work After Illness or Injury." *HR Focus* (October 1994), p. 11. Primary sources: Fortis Benefits Insurance Co.; Menninger Return to Work Centers.

★ 800 ★

Occupational Illnesses and Injuries

Work Injuries, by Affected Body Part: 1993

In 1993, 3.2 billion disabling work injuries were reported. The table below shows the number of injuries for selected body parts.

[In thousands]

Body part	Number
Back	770
Legs	420
Arms	380
Fingers	350
Trunk	350
Multiple	320
Hands	160
Eyes	130

[Continued]

★ 800 ★

Work Injuries, by Affected Body Part: 1993

[Continued]

Body part	Number
Feet	130
Head[1]	130
Body systems	100
Neck	60
Toes	30

Source: Sabir, Nadirah Z. "Watch That Last Step!" *Black Enterprise* (May 1995), p. 28. Primary source: National Safety Council. *Note:* 1. Except eyes.

★ 801 ★

Occupational Illnesses and Injuries

Work Injury Rates: 1993

In 1993 the work-related unintentional death rate was at a record low. Nevertheless, that year work injury expenses included nearly $112 billion and 65 percent of all lost workdays. The table below shows the number and various rates of occurrence for work-related deaths and injuries.

Incident	Number	Rate				
		Per 1 million hours exposure	One every:	Number per:		
				Hour	Day	Week
Death	9,100	.04	58 minutes	1	25	180
Injury	3,200,000[1]	12.5	10 seconds	370	8,800	61,500

Source: Sabir, Nadirah Z. "Watch That Last Step!" *Black Enterprise* (May 1995), p. 28. Primary source: National Safety Council. *Note:* 1. Disabling injuries.

Occupational Safety and Health Administration

★ 802 ★

OSHA Star Certification

Table shows the companies and number of sites that have received Star certifications from the Occupational Safety and Health Administration (OSHA) in recognition of their safety and health management practices. Injuries and lost workdays due to injuries at listed sites meet or fall below that of the national average for their industries.

Company	Number of sites
Amoco Foam Products	1
BASF	2
Ciba Chemical	2
Corning	1
Dow Chemical	4
DuPont	3
Exxon	1
GE Plastics	2
Georgia Pacific	2
Hoechst Celanese	2
Huntsman Design	1
IBM	2
Kerr-McGee	4
Lyondell Petrochemical	1
Mobil Chemical	18
Mobil Mining & Minerals	1
Mobil Oil	1
Monsanto Chemical	2
Motorola	2
Ortho Diagnostic Systems	1
OxyChem Petrochemicals	6
Pioneer Chlor Alkali	1
Star Enterprise	1
Texaco	4
U.S. Paint	1
Weyerhaeuser Paper	1

Source: "OSHA Star: Seal of Approval." *C&EN*, 29 November 1993, p. 35.

★ 803 ★

Occupational Safety and Health Administration

OSHA Violations of Federal Contractors: 1988-1992

Lockheed - 349	
General Motors - 209	
Chevron - 112	
Chrysler - 101	
	General Electric - 43
	Johnson Controls - 38
	United Technologies - 29
	Tenneco - 22
	Olin - 22

Chart shows data from column 1.

Table shows the large federal contractors cited for multiple "willful" safety violations by the Occupational Safety and Health Administration (OSHA) from 1988 through 1992. Data include value of contracts awarded.

Company	Citations	Awards (billion dollars)
Lockheed	349	7.0
General Motors	209	4.8
Chevron	112	0.3
Chrysler	101	0.3
General Electric	43	3.7
Johnson Controls	38	0.4
United Technologies	29	3.5
Tenneco	22	0.9
Olin	22	0.4

Source: Stipp, David. "Officials Reject Contract Bids on Proof of Poor Safety Records." *Wall Street Journal,* 6 February 1995, p. B1. Primary sources: U.S. Occupational Safety and Health Administration; Eagle Eye Publishers, Inc.

Stress

★ 804 ★

Heart Attacks and Monday Mornings

Results of a Harvard Medical School study identified Monday from 7:00 a.m. until 10:00 a.m. as the time when employed people are at greatest risk of heart attacks. The study suggests that stress associated with returning to work after the weekend make Monday mornings the peak risk period.

Source: "Monday Tops List for Risk." *Detroit News,* 20 July 1994, p. E1.

★ 805 ★
Stress

Job Burnout

According to a national Families and Work Institute study, 59 percent of the 3,700 respondents reported job burnout or stress.

Source: Hammonds, Keith H. "Work: More Complex Than We Thought." *Business Week,* 13 September 1993, p. 42.

★ 806 ★
Stress

Work Stress of Women

Table shows the causes of work stress for more than 500 women who responded to a survey by the New York Business Group on Health (NYBGH). Forty-two percent reported frequent stress on the job. Data show work stress by managerial status of women workers.

[In percentages]

Cause of stress	Managerial status of women	
	Manager	Nonmanager
Perceived job stress	50	34
Work load too heavy	29	17
Pay equity	35	23
Major job change	40	39

Source: "Study Pinpoints the Causes of Stress for Working Women." *HR Focus* 70, no. 9 (September 1993), p. 24. Primary source: *Stress Among Working Women,* a survey.

Substance Abuse

★ 807 ★

Drug Use of Workers: 1987-1993

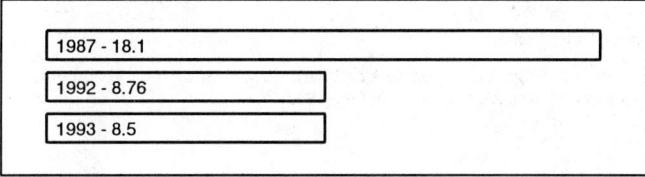

In the first 6 months of 1993, SmithKline Beecham Clinical Laboratories conducted drug tests of 1.5 million U.S. workers. For the sixth consecutive year, the tests showed a decrease in the number of workers testing positive for illegal drugs.

[In percentages]

Year	Tested positive for illegal drugs
1987	18.1
1992	8.76
1993	8.5

Source: Castelli, Jim. "A Digest of Developments in Occupational Safety and Health." *Safety + Health* (February 1994), p. 89.

★ 808 ★

Substance Abuse

Workplace Drug Testing and Programs

Data are from a 1993 survey in which respondents indicated various drug testing methods and substance abuse programs used at their companies.

[In percentages]

Program	Companies
Urine tests	97
Employee assistance programs	68
Blood tests	38
Fitness-for-duty programs	29
Search of property	18
Breathalizer	14
Employee surveillance	14
Search of employees	11

[Continued]

★ 808 ★

Workplace Drug Testing and Programs

[Continued]

Program	Companies
Preemployment psychological tests	9
Saliva analysis	4
Rapid eye tests	2
Lie detection tests	1

Source: "Fighting Drug Abuse." *Workplace Vitality* (September 1994), p. 5. Primary source: *Human Resource Executive* magazine survey (1993).

Wellness

★ 809 ★

Fitness and Exercise Facilities at Work: 1992

Table reflects the private work sites with 50 or more employees that offer facilities or programs (information or activities) that promote health, exercise, and physical fitness.

[In percentages]

Wellness promotion facility	Work sites offering
Locker room with showers	24
Indoor exercise area	12
Aerobics equipment	10
Strength training equipment	9
Other[1]	41

Source: "How Employers Are Helping Workers Stay Healthy." *Washington Post,* 18 May 1993, final edition, p. Z5. *Note:* 1. For example, counseling, classes, or videos.

★ 810 ★

Wellness

Health and Fitness Benefits: 1991-1993

The table below reflects the health-enhancing benefits provided by employers during 1991, 1992, and 1993. Data are from a survey of 600 U.S. businesses.

[In percentages]

Benefit	1991	1992	1993
Gym facilities	14	12	10
Sports teams	28	20	24
Stress management programs	N/A	N/A	16
Wellness programs	N/A	21	20

Source: Peters, Shannon. "Employers Provide More Parties, Fewer Gym Facilities in 1993." *Personnel Journal* (May 1994), p. 13. Primary source: Tempforce Inc. *Note:* "N/A" indicates "not available" or "not applicable."

★ 811 ★

Wellness

Health Promotion Initiatives

Figures compare corporate health promotion initiatives in 1992 and 1993.

[In percentages]

Health promotion initiative	1992[1]	1993[2]
Education/training	83	80
Health risk appraisals	29	30
Health risk assessments	66	74
Incentives/disincentives	14	18
Other	38	44

Source: "More Companies Adopt the Notion That an Ounce of Prevention...." *HR Focus* (December 1994), p. 14. Primary source: Hewitt Associates. "Health Promotion Initiatives/Managed Health Provided by Major U.S. Employers in 1993." *Notes:* 1. 661 employers. 2. 786 employers.

★ 812 ★

Wellness

Physical Activity at Work: 1990

Table reflects the percent of persons in the United States 18 years of age and older whose job or main daily activity requires at least a moderate amount of physical work. Data provided by sex, age, and selected characteristics.

[In percentages]

Characteristic	Both sexes 18 years and over	Male					Female				
		Total	18-29 years	30-44 years	45-64 years	65 years and over	Total	18-29 years	30-44 years	45-64 years	65 years and over
All persons[1]	39.3	43.6	54.2	47.6	39.1	23.3	35.3	36.5	37.4	37.0	27.5
Education level											
Less than 12 years	44.2	49.1	63.6	65.2	52.3	22.9	39.9	46.1	52.1	46.2	25.7
12 years	46.7	56.5	64.8	65.1	49.8	26.1	38.9	39.9	42.7	38.8	30.3
More than 12 years	29.7	30.4	39.1	31.6	23.8	21..3	28.9	29.2	29.5	28.3	26.6
13-15 years	37.8	44.2	50.0	48.8	36.1	22.0	32.0	30.6	34.7	30.6	29.6
16 years or more	21.4	18.3	20.3	18.5	16.0	20.7	25.2	26.8	24.6	26.0	22.4
Income											
Less than $10,000	35.3	37.1	42.1	50.2	30.9	21.1	34.4	35.8	46.6	39.5	23.8
$10,000-$19,999	46.7	50.2	60.2	64.9	45.8	26.4	43.8	46.6	50.0	45.1	34.5
$20,000-$34,999	45.9	53.2	59.3	59.6	53.1	25.1	38.9	36.3	40.7	43.4	31.8
$35,000-$49,999	41.2	46.1	55.8	45.0	43.9	30.5	35.7	33.0	36.0	39.3	29.2
$50,000 or more	29.5	30.5	49.2	28.4	24.9	18.1	28.4	31.0	28.6	28.1	20.5
Race											
White	38.7	43.2	55.3	46.8	38.2	23.6	34.6	36.1	36.2	36.1	27.8
Black	44.1	48.2	52.7	54.8	44.9	22.8	40.8	40.5	43.8	46.4	24.1
Hispanic origin											
Hispanic	45.0	54.3	53.0	60.6	54.6	23.6	37.1	35.5	40.5	38.7	25.2
Non-Hispanic	38.8	42.7	54.4	46.4	38.2	23.3	35.2	36.7	37.2	37.0	27.6
Geographic region											
Northeast	37.9	41.5	51.0	45.3	35.7	27.0	34.6	36.3	37.8	35.7	26.4
Midwest	41.6	45.3	56.8	48.5	41.2	24.9	38.2	40.2	40.4	39.0	30.8
South	39.4	44.1	56.2	49.0	39.2	20.4	35.2	36.0	37.8	38.3	25.1
West	37.6	42.7	50.9	46.3	39.7	22.8	32.7	33.5	33.1	33.7	29.1
Marital status											
Currently married	40.3	42.8	57.1	47.8	39.6	24.7	37.6	39.7	37.6	37.4	35.1
Formerly married	33.2	39.0	65.5	48.6	37.8	18.1	30.8	35.2	39.7	37.0	21.8
Never married	41.3	48.4	51.6	45.6	34.7	19.5	32.6	33.1	32.5	31.8	27.2
Employment status											
Currently employed	43.7	50.2	59.2	49.3	43.8	37.6	35.9	36.7	34.9	36.6	34.3

[Continued]

★ 812 ★

Physical Activity at Work: 1990
[Continued]

Characteristic	Both sexes 18 years and over	Male					Female				
		Total	18-29 years	30-44 years	45-64 years	65 years and over	Total	18-29 years	30-44 years	45-64 years	65 years and over
Unemployed	41.3	42.6	48.1	42.5	32.1	43.9[2]	39.9	34.5	45.1	43.4	29.0[2]
Not in labor force	29.8	20.6	23.8	20.3	19.3	20.3	34.2	36.3	44.4	37.4	26.8

Source: U.S. Department of Health and Human Services. Public Health Service. Centers for Disease Control and Prevention. National Center for Health Statistics. *Health Promotion and Disease Prevention: United States, 1990.* Vital and Health Statistics, Series 10, no. 185. Hyattsville, MD: U.S. Department of Health and Human Services, Public Health Service, Centers for Disease Control and Prevention, National Center for Health Statistics, n.d., p. 43. *Notes:* Data are based on household interviews of the civilian noninstitutionalized population. The survey design, general qualifications, and information on the reliability of the estimates are given in Appendix 1 in the original source. Denominator for each cell excludes unknowns. 1. Includes persons with unknown sociodemographic characteristics. 2. Figure does not meet standard of reliability or precision (more than 30 percent relative standard error in numerator of percent or rate).

★ 813 ★

Wellness

Preventive Health Programs

Many companies offer preventive health programs as a method of reducing overall health care costs. The table below shows popular health promotion plans offered by employers. Data are from a survey of more than 925 employers. Respondents indicated programs that they currently offered or planned to offer in 1994 to employees.

[In percentages]

Programs	Currently offer	Plan to offer in 1994
Smoking cessation	41	10
Annual physicals[1]	23	7
Weight control	23	9
Stress management	20	12
Health risk appraisals	18	12

Source: Flynn, Gillian. "Preventive Health Programs Soar." *Personnel Journal* (September 1994), p. 16. Primary source: Wyatt Co. *Note:* 1. For all employees.

★ 814 ★

Wellness

Workplace Wellness Issues, by Company Size

Data reflect the percentages of organizations with policies or programs dedicated to wellness issues in the workplace.

Issue and program	All organizations	Number of employees				
		100-499	500-999	1,000-2,499	2,500-9,999	10,000 or more
Drugs						
Test employees for drug use (with probable cause)	38	36	48	46	49	50
Test employees for drug use (without probable cause)	11	10	15	16	16	25
Test job applicants for drug use	37	31	54	55	58	62
Have formal policy on substance abuse	86	84	93	92	90	98
Conduct or sponsor training about substance abuse	33	29	47	44	50	60
Have an Employee Assistance Program (EAP)[1]	52	47	65	72	79	88
AIDS						
AIDS antibody testing of employees	1	1	3	1	1	2
AIDS antibody testing of job applicants	1	1	2	0	2	3
Have formal AIDS policy	20	19	29	24	27	26
Have AIDS education program	21	19	34	25	28	28
Smoking						
Have policy limiting smoking at work	77	76	80	76	79	87
Have policy banning smoking at work	56	57	53	55	49	51
Do not hire smokers	2	1	2	2	2	2

Source: "Social Issues at Work." *Training* (October 1993), p. 55. *Note:* 1. Handles substance abuse problems.

Workers' Compensation

★ 815 ★

Workers' Compensation Benefit Payments, by Program: 1987-1990

Table reflects the estimated workers' compensation benefit payment amounts for 1987 through 1990. Data provided by type of benefit.

[In million dollars]

Benefit	1987	1988	1989	1990
Regular program	25,773	29,234	32,837	36,804
Medical and hospitalization	9,794	11,401	13,299	15,067
Compensation	15,979	17,833	19,538	21,737
Disability	15,046	16,956	18,553	20,635
Survivor	933	877	985	1,102
Black lung program	1,545	1,499	1,479	1,434
Medical and hospitalization	118	117	125	120
Compensation	1,426	1,381	1,354	1,314
Disability	698	657	618	577

[Continued]

★ 815 ★

Workers' Compensation Benefit Payments, by Program: 1987-1990

[Continued]

Benefit	1987	1988	1989	1990
Survivor	729	725	736	737
Total[1]	27,318	30,733	34,316	38,238
Medical and hospitalization	9,912	11,518	13,424	15,187
Compensation	17,406	19,215	20,892	23,051
Disability	15,775	17,613	19,171	21,212
Survivor	1,631	1,602	1,721	1,839

Source: U.S. House Committee on Ways and Means. *Overview of Entitlement Programs, 1993 Green Book: Background Material and Data Programs Within the Jurisdiction of the Committee on Ways and Means.* 103d Cong., 1st sess., 7 July 1993. Washington, DC: U.S. Government Printing Office, 1993, p. 1706. Primary sources: *Social Security Bulletin* 55, no. 1 (spring 1992); Social Security Adminstration. *Note:* 1. Regular and black lung programs combined.

★ 816 ★

Workers' Compensation

Workers' Compensation Claims and Costs: 1990-1992

Data reflect the percentages and costs of workers' compensation claims per body part injured. Data cover April 1990 through May 1992.

Body part	Percent of claims	Cost
Back and chest	45	$211,242
Upper extremity	25	$116,305
Head, eye, neck	7	$33,293
Lower extremity	5	$25,615
Other	18	$85,124

Source: "Workers' Compensation Claims." *Occupational Health and Safety* 62, no. 10 (October 1993), p. 76.

★ 817 ★

Workers' Compensation

Workers' Compensation Medical Costs

Table shows the distribution of medical costs for workers' compensation by type of treatment or by service provider.

[In percentages]

Treatment or service	Medical benefits
Physicians	54.2
Hospitals	36.0
Medicine	22.7
Surgery	17.6
Drugs and other	9.8
Radiology	8.5
Physical medicine	3.6
Other physician	1.8

Source: "Workers' Compensation Medical Cost Distribution." *Risk Management* (October 1994), p. 44. Primary source: NCCI and David Durbin. "The Cost of Treating Injured Workers: The Changing Workers' Compensation Landscape." *Benefits Quarterly* 9, no. 4 (1993), pp. 9-21.

★ 818 ★

Workers' Compensation

Workers' Compensation Payments: 1980-1991

Calendar-year data, except fiscal-year data for federal civilian and other programs and for a few states with state funds. Payments represent cash and medical benefits and include insurance losses paid by private insurance carriers [compiled from the *Spectator (Insurance by States ... of Casualty Lines)*, from reports of state insurance commissions, and from A. M. Best Co.]; net disbursements of state funds [from the *Spectator,* from *Argus Casualty and Surety Chart,* and from state reports], estimated for some states; and self-insurance payments, estimated from available state data. Includes benefit payments under Longshoremen's and Harbor Workers' Compensation Act and Defense Bases Compensation Act for states in which such payments are made.

[In billions of dollars, except as indicated]

Item	1980	1982	1983	1984	1985	1986	1987	1988	1989	1990	1991
Workers covered[1] (million)	79	77	78	82	84	86	88	91	94	95	94
Premium amounts paid	22.3	22.8	23.0	25.1	29.2	34.0	38.1	43.3	48.0	53.1	55.2
Private carriers	15.7	15.4	15.4	16.6	19.5	22.8	25.4	28.5	31.9	35.1	35.7
State funds	3.0	2.6	2.7	3.0	3.5	4.5	5.3	6.7	7.2	8.0	8.7
Federal programs[2]	1.1	1.5	1.5	1.6	1.7	1.8	1.8	1.9	2.0	2.2	2.1
Self-insurers	2.4	3.2	3.5	3.9	4.5	4.9	5.5	6.2	6.9	7.9	8.7
Annual benefits paid	13.6	16.4	17.6	19.7	22.2	24.6	27.3	30.7	34.3	38.2	42.2
By private carriers[3]	7.0	8.6	9.3	10.6	12.3	13.8	15.5	17.5	19.9	22.2	24.5
From state funds[4]	4.3	4.8	5.1	5.4	5.7	6.2	6.8	7.5	8.0	8.7	9.7
Employers' self-insurance[5]	2.3	3.0	3.2	3.7	4.1	4.5	5.1	5.7	6.4	7.4	7.9

[Continued]

★ 818 ★

Workers' Compensation Payments: 1980-1991
[Continued]

Item	1980	1982	1983	1984	1985	1986	1987	1988	1989	1990	1991
Type of benefit:											
Medical/hospitalization	3.9	5.1	5.7	6.4	7.5	8.6	9.9	11.5	13.4	15.2	16.8
Compensation payments	9.7	11.3	11.9	13.3	14.7	16.0	17.4	19.2	20.9	23.1	25.3
Disability	8.4	9.9	10.4	11.7	13.1	14.3	15.8	17.6	19.2	21.2	23.3
Survivor	1.3	1.5	1.5	1.6	1.7	1.6	1.6	1.6	1.7	1.8	2.0
Percent of covered payroll:											
Workers' compensation costs[6]	1.96	1.75	1.67	1.66	1.82	1.99	2.07	2.16	2.27	2.36	2.40
Benefits[7]	1.07	1.16	1.17	1.21	1.30	1.37	1.43	1.49	1.58	1.70	1.79

Source: U.S. Bureau of the Census. *Statistical Abstract of the United States, 1994.* 114th ed. Washington, DC: U.S. Government Printing Office, 1994, p. 381. Primary source: U.S. Social Security Administration. *Annual Statistical Supplement to the Social Security Bulletin. Notes:* 1. Estimated per month. 2. Includes federal employer compensation program and that portion of federal black lung benefits program financed from employer contributions. 3. Net cash and medical benefits paid under standard workers' compensation policies. 4. Net cash and medical benefits paid by competitive and exclusive state funds and by federal workers' compensation programs, including black lung benefit program. 5. Cash and medical benefits paid by self-insurers, plus value of medical benefits paid by employers carrying workers' compensation policies that exclude standard medical coverage. 6. Premiums written by private carriers and state funds, and benefits paid by self-insurers increased by 5-10 percent to allow for administrative costs. Also includes benefits paid and administrative costs of federal system for government employees. Excludes programs financed from general revenue-black lung benefits and supplemental pensions in some states. 7. Excludes programs financed from general revenue-black lung benefits and supplemental pensions in some states.

★ 819 ★

Workers' Compensation

Workers' Compensation Payments, by State: 1980-1991

Calendar-year data, except fiscal-year data for federal civilian and other programs and for a few states with state funds. Payments represent cash and medical benefits and include insurance losses paid by private insurance carriers [compiled from the *Spectator (Insurance by States ... of Casualty Lines),* from reports of state insurance commissions, and from A. M. Best Co.]; net disbursements of state funds [from the *Spectator,* from *Argus Casualty and Surety Chart,* and from state reports], estimated for some states; and self-insurance payments, estimated from available state data. Includes benefit payments under Longshoremen's and Harbor Workers' Compensation Act and Defense Bases Compensation Act for states in which such payments are made.

[In millions of dollars]

State	1980	1985	1989	1990	1991
Total	13,618	22,224	34,316	38,238	42,169
Alabama	112	203	380	444	472
Alaska	60	109	113	113	124
Arizona	120	198	324	371	368
Arkansas	83	129	196	229	251
California	1,628	3,243	5,242	6,065	7,248
Colorado	114	284	532	595	657
Connecticut	147	305	587	694	773
Delaware	21	41	68	75	80
District of Columbia	69	74	84	86	91
Florida	362	815	1,732	1,976	1,961

[Continued]

★ 819 ★

Workers' Compensation Payments, by State: 1980-1991
[Continued]

State	1980	1985	1989	1990	1991
Georgia	185	360	661	735	791
Hawaii	60	133	180	216	250
Idaho	37	66	93	105	115
Illinois	699	912	1,432	1,607	1,745
Indiana	110	152	297	350	380
Iowa	99	121	190	231	241
Kansas	84	142	220	266	295
Kentucky	161	225	326	383	432
Louisiana	301	466	586	575	560
Maine	81	194	342	380	419
Maryland	187	306	437	505	523
Massachusetts	296	510	1,078	1,235	1,276
Michigan	626	769	1,120	1,205	1,286
Minnesota	260	453	497	582	646
Mississippi	60	98	171	198	203
Missouri	124	237	423	496	557
Montana	41	102	153	150	168
Nebraska	42	68	112	137	146
Nevada	69	123	250	339	392
New Hampshire	48	91	154	169	203
New Jersey	316	501	761	844	916
New Mexico	54	140	226	228	232
New York	637	985	1,528	1,752	2,014
North Carolina	131	236	386	480	545
North Dakota	17	33	50	60	73
Ohio	776	1,387	1,816	1,960	2,195
Oklahoma	127	289	313	369	434
Oregon	275	396	576	573	587
Pennsylvania	572	998	1,820	2,019	2,329
Rhode Island	55	97	200	219	214
South Carolina	79	152	240	277	292
South Dakota	13	26	44	56	64
Tennessee	129	204	390	463	515
Texas	701	1,564	2,843	2,896	3,264
Utah	39	80	142	187	183
Vermont	15	30	55	61	67
Virginia	182	276	465	507	545
Washington	324	619	811	883	949
West Virginia	176	285	375	389	417
Wisconsin	170	287	487	561	627
Wyoming	22	47	47	49	59
Federal programs: Civilian employees	776	1,055	1,274	1,448	1,595

[Continued]

★ 819 ★

Workers' Compensation Payments, by State: 1980-1991

[Continued]

State	1980	1985	1989	1990	1991
Black lung benefits[1]	1,739	1,603	1,479	1,435	1,391
Other[2]	8	7	8	11	11

Source: U.S. Bureau of the Census. *Statistical Abstract of the United States, 1994.* 114th ed. Washington, DC: U.S. Government Printing Office, 1994, p. 381. Primary sources: U.S. Social Security Administration. *Social Security Bulletin* (fall 1993 and selected prior issues); and unpublished data. *Notes:* 1. Includes payments by Social Security Administration and by Department of Labor. 2. Primarily payments made to dependents of reservists who died while on active duty in the Armed Forces.

Workplace Violence

★ 820 ★

Murder in the Workplace

An employee who murders at his or her workplace stands a 1 in 4 chance of ending the violent episode by committing suicide.

Source: "Just the Facts." *Detroit News,* 12 April 1994, p. 7D. Primary source: *Harper's Magazine.*

★ 821 ★

Workplace Violence

Violent Crime in the Workplace

Approximately 1 million violent crime occur annually to workers on the job. A handgun is used in 10 percent of these crimes. The table below shows the types of violent crime that occur in the workplace.

Crime	Percent occurring at work
Assault	16
Rape	8
Robbery	7
Homicide[1]	4

Source: "Workplace Violence Taking Toll on Quality of Life, Report Says." *St. Louis Post-Dispatch*, 25 July 1994, p. 3A. Primary source: Data from 1987-1992 as reported in the National Criminal Victimization Survey, unless otherwise noted. *Notes:* 1. Data from Bureau of Labor Statistics, Centers for Disease Control, and National Institute for Occupational Safety and Health.

★ 822 ★

Workplace Violence

Workplace Attacks, by Perpetrators

From the source: "As an increasing number of American workers have discovered, violence is something that can't be escaped" (p. 66). The table below shows perpetrators of violent attacks on workers.

[In percentages]

Perpetrator	Attacks
Customers or clients	44
Strangers	24
Co-workers	20
Bosses	7
Former employees	3
Someone else	3

Source: Anfuso, Dawn. "Deflecting Workplace Violence." *Personnel Journal* (October 1994), p. 70. Primary source: Northwestern National Life Insurance Co.

★ 823 ★

Workplace Violence

Workplace Violence, by Method of Attack

Sixty-seven percent of nearly 480 Society for Human Resource Management survey participants experienced workplace violence. The table below indicates the violent acts reported by respondent companies.

[In percentages]

Incident	Companies
Fistfights/altercations	75
Shootings	17
Stabbings	8
Sexual assaults	6

Source: "The Violent Workplace." *Small Business Reports* (March 1994), p. 38. Primary source: Society for Human Resource Management (Alexandria, Virginia).

★ 824 ★

Workplace Violence

Workplace Violence, by Reason

According to the source, 30,000 people experience violence and harassment at work annually. The table below shows reasons why individuals commit violent acts in the workplace.

Reason	Percent
Irrational behavior	26
Dissatisfied with service	19
Interpersonal conflict	15
Upset at being disciplined	12
Criminal behavior	10
Personal problems	8
Firing or layoff	2
Prejudice	1
Unknown	7

Source: Manigan, Colleen. "The Graveyard Shift." *Public Management* (April 1994), p. 13. Primary source: Northwestern National Life Insurance Co.

★ 825 ★

Workplace Violence

Workplaces at Risk

```
Taxicabs/dispatch offices - 26.9
Liquor stores - 8.0
[ ] Gas stations - 5.6
[ ] Detective/protective agencies - 5.0
[ ] Courthouses, prisons, police and fire departments - 3.4
[ ] Grocery stores - 3.2
[ ] Jewelry stores - 3.2
[ ] Hotels/motels - 1.5
[ ] Restaurants/bars - 1.5
```

According to the source, 2 million workers were victims of workplace violence in 1993. The table below shows the riskiest workplaces for on-the-job murders.

[In percentages]

Workplace	Murders per 100,000 workers
Taxicabs/dispatch offices	26.9
Liquor stores	8.0
Gas stations	5.6
Detective/protective agencies	5.0
Courthouses, prisons, police and fire departments	3.4
Grocery stores	3.2
Jewelry stores	3.2
Hotels/motels	1.5
Restaurants/bars	1.5

Source: Castelli, Jim. "A Digest of Developments in Occupational Safety and Health." *Safety + Health* (February 1994), p. 88. Primary source: National Institute of Occupational Safety and Health (NIOSH).

Chapter 9
LEGAL AND ETHICAL ISSUES

According to Gary Edwards, president of the Ethics Resource Center in Washington, D.C., workers frequently witness unethical behavior on the job, including lying, stealing, theft, sexual harassment, and substance abuse. Although many recognize unethical behavior, few report it—less than half, based on Edwards' poll of 4,035 workers. The tables in this chapter provide an overview of legal, social, and ethical concerns affecting the American workplace. Coverage includes Affirmative Action, Americans With Disabilities Act, discrimination, business ethics, Family and Medical Leave Act, corporate director and officer liability, sexual harassment, commuting, charitable giving, domestic violence, political action committees, workplace attire, and worker satisfaction.

Affirmative Action

★ 826 ★

Affirmative Action Support

Table shows the percentage of respondents agreeing that there should be special considerations afforded to minority groups to increase their opportunities for admission to colleges, for hiring, or for promotions.

Minority group	Respondents	
	Blacks	Whites
Asians	48	18
Blacks	62	25
Hispanics	57	22
Native Americans	65	34
Women	62	26

Source: Klein, Joe. "The End of Affirmative Action." *Newsweek,* 13 February 1995, p. 37. Primary source: *Newsweek* poll, February 1-3, 1995.

★ 827 ★

Affirmative Action

Hiring Practices and Workforce Diversity

According to the source, "Diversity is taking people from different backgrounds, with different expectations and at different stages of life and melding them into a force that will drive the company's profitability and competitiveness" (p. F27). Yet the source also notes that companies seldom view workforce diversity in this way. Rather, they interpret diversity to mean compliance with Affirmative Action guidelines and the Americans With Disabilities Act. The table below presents the reasons given by surveyed companies for hiring from certain minority or other "targeted" groups.

[In percentages]

Reason	Affirmative Action concerns[1]	Regulations	Community relations	Other	Productivity
Part-time workers	72.9	2.5	5.9	5.1	13.6
Family caretakers	68.4	9.6	4.4	6.6	11.0
Women	56.9	23.5	4.9	7.8	6.9
Minorities	56.8	21.6	4.3	10.1	7.2
Skill-deficient workers	52.3	3.7	6.4	8.2	29.4
Domestic partners	47.1	5.9	11.8	23.4	11.8
People with HIV or chronic illness	37.7	13.1	16.4	23.0	9.8
Disabled workers	22.1	68.5	4.7	3.0	1.7

Source: Noble, Barbara Presley. "Still in the Dark on Diversity." *New York Times,* 6 November 1994, p. F27. Primary source: Survey of 300 companies with 250 or more employees in New York, New Jersey, and Connecticut by Center for the New American Workforce. *Note:* 1. Recruitment and retention.

★ 828 ★

Affirmative Action

Minority Hiring and College Enrollment

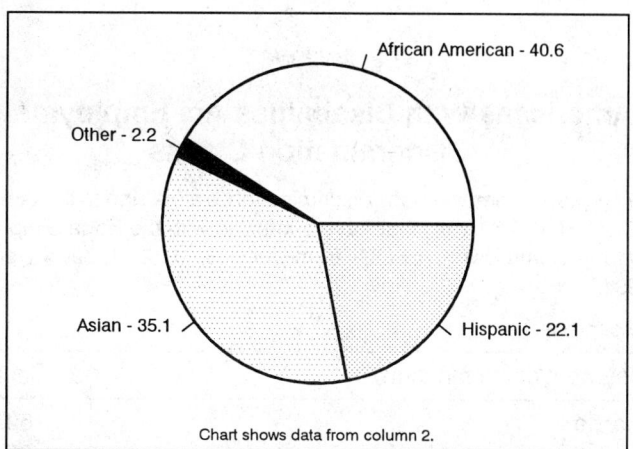

Chart shows data from column 2.

Table shows data from a survey of 100 companies that found that 1993 hires of ethnic minorities did not reflect each group's percentage of enrollment in colleges and universities during 1991, thus disproving arguments that a shortage of qualified minority candidates confounds recruiting and hiring minorities.

[In percentages]

Ethnic group	1991 enrollment	1993 hiring
African American	48.2	40.6
Asian	24.2	35.1
Hispanic	24.3	22.1
Other	3.0	2.2

Source: Smith, Bob. "Recruitment Insights for Strategic Workforce Diversity." *HR Focus* (January 1994), p. 7. Primary sources: U.S. Department of Education; Hanigan Consulting Group.

Americans With Disabilities Act

★ 829 ★

Americans With Disabilities Act Employment Discrimination Claims

Table shows the employment discrimination claims under the Americans With Disabilities Act (ADA) that have been filed with the Equal Employment Opportuny Commission (EEOC) from July 26, 1992, through December 31, 1994.

[In percentages]

Employment discrimination	Claims
Discharge	50.5
Failure to provide reasonable accomodations	25.7
Hiring	10.9
Harassment	10.8
Discipline	7.4
Layoff	5.2
Benefits	3.9
Promotion	3.7
Rehiring	3.7
Wages	3.5
Suspension	2.3

Source: "On the Job." Wall Street Journal, 17 February 1995, p. B12. Primary source: Equal Employment Opportunity Commission.

★ 830 ★

Americans With Disabilities Act

Americans With Disabilities Act Employment Discrimination Claims – Bases for Filing Charges

```
┌─────────────────────────────────────────────────────────┐
│  ┌────────────────────────────────────────┐              │
│  │ Discharge - 49.0                        │              │
│  └────────────────────────────────────────┘              │
│  ┌──────────────────────┐                                │
│  │                      │ Reasonable accomodation - 22.7  │
│  └──────────────────────┘                                │
│  ┌──────────────┐                                        │
│  │ Hiring - 13.0│                                        │
│  └──────────────┘                                        │
│  ┌──────────┐                                            │
│  │          │ Harassment - 9.9                           │
│  └──────────┘                                            │
│  ┌──────┐                                                │
│  │      │ Other - 5.4                                    │
│  └──────┘                                                │
└─────────────────────────────────────────────────────────┘
```

Table shows the reasons behind the the 16,054 discrimination complaints filed under the Americans With Disabilities Act from August 1992 through October 1993. Most of the filings were prompted by firings. "This," noted Judy Young, a coordinator for the National Center for Disability Services, "may reflect the state of the economy" (p. 8D).

[In percentages]

Reason	Claims
Discharge	49.0
Reasonable accomodation	22.7
Hiring	13.0
Harassment	9.9
Other	5.4

Source: Flannery, William. "Rights Act Generates Few Suits." *St. Louis Post-Dispatch,* 6 April 1994, p. 8D.

Discrimination

★ 831 ★

Civil Rights Complaint Outcomes: 1993

Title VII of the Civil Rights Act of 1964 prohibits discrimination in the workplace. More than 50,000 alleged violations of this act were filed with the Equal Employment Opportunities Commission (EEOC) in 1993, approximately 60 percent of all the EEOC's discrimination cases. The table below shows the outcome of the filings.

Result or status	Complaints
Not resolved in worker's favor	73
EEOC finds insufficient evidence of discrimination	50
Case closed for administrative reasons[1]	23
Resolved in workers favor	14

[Continued]

★ 831 ★

Civil Rights Complaint Outcomes: 1993

[Continued]

Result or status	Complaints
Worker received payment or other settlement without formal finding of discrimination	12
Worker has "reasonable cause" to sue	2
Backlog to be resolved in a later year	13

Source: Kilborn, Peter T. "In Rare Move, Agency Acts Swiftly in a Sexual Harassment Case." *New York Times,* 10 January 1995, p. C18. Primary source: Equal Employment Opportunity Commission. *Notes:* 1. Case falls outside of EEOC's jurisdiction; worker withdraws charge or refuses to cooperate with investigation.

★ 832 ★

Discrimination

Discrimination Claims, by Type

Table below shows the types of job discrimination claims filed in fiscal year 1993. In total, more than 85,000 claims were filed.

[In percentages]

Type of discrimination	Percent of total claims[1]
Race	36
Sex	27
Age	23
Disability	17
National origin	9
Religion	2
Equal pay	2

Source: "Many Faces of Discrimination." *USA TODAY,* 23 June 1994, p. B1. Primary source: Equal Employment Opportunity Commission (EEOC). *Notes:* 1. Exceeds 100 percent since more than one form of discrimination may be alleged in some cases.

★ 833 ★

Discrimination

Discrimination Complaints, by State: 1993-1994

Texas - 14,239
California - 10,998
Florida - 8,735
New York - 7,841
Pennsylvania - 7,215

Table shows the number of complaints filed with the Equal Employment Opportunity Commission and related state and local government agencies. Data are for the most populated states and cover the period from October 1, 1993, through September 30, 1994.

State	Complaints filed
Texas	14,239
California	10,998
Florida	8,735
New York	7,841
Pennsylvania	7,215

Source: Abrahamson, Vicki Lafer. "No: Hunting for Dishonest Undercuts Discrimination Laws." *ABA Journal* (December 1994), p. 45.

★ 834 ★

Discrimination

Racial Discrimination

In a national survey of more than 3,700 individuals, 27 percent of the respondents reported experiencing racially motivated discrimination at work.

Source: Hammonds, Keith H. "Work: More Complex Than We Thought." *Business Week,* 13 September 1993, p. 42. Primary source: Families & Work Institute.

Ethics

★ 835 ★

Computer Security Risks

Ex-employees - 95

Unauthorized E-mail - 92

Instrusion by hackers - 91

PBX fraud - 82

Data show survey responses indicating the various threats to a corporation's computer security.

Threat	Percent of responses
Ex-employees	95
Unauthorized E-mail	92
Instrusion by hackers	91
PBX fraud	82

Source: "How Safe Is Your System?" *InformationWeek,* 26 December 1994, p. 56. Primary source: Security Dynamics (Cambridge, Massachusetts).

★ 836 ★

Ethics

Employee Theft

According to the source, part-time employees steal 39 percent more cash and merchandise from their employers than full-time workers. The table below shows the average amounts of cash and merchandise stolen by full- and part-time workers.

[In dollars]

| Employees | Amount stolen | |
	Cash	Merchandise
Part-time	414	368
Full-time	311	251

Source: Szwergold, Jack. "Part-timers Are More Apt to Have Their Hands in the Cookie Jar." *Management Review* (December 1994), p. 5.

★ 837 ★

Ethics

Phone Fraud: 1994

"Shoulder surfers" obtain corporate toll-free phone numbers, authorization and access codes, or PIN numbers, thus giving fraud artists access to private branch exchanges that allow them to charge their phone calls to an unsuspecting corporation. Corporations usually are liable for fraudulent calls. The estimated total cost of phone fraud for 1994 is reported in the source as $3.3 billion. The table below shows the various types of phone fraud and their costs.

[In million dollars]

Type of fraud	Cost
Corporate switchboard toll	1,300
Service	475
Calling card	400
Cellular	400
Direct hits to switches/networks	190
800 calls by hackers	115
800/900 calls charged to a company	100
Pay phone	90
Call forwarding	85
Other	170

Source: DePompa, Barbara. "Fighting Telephone Fraud." *InformationWeek,* 1 August 1994, p. 74. Primary source: Telecommunications Advisors Inc.

★ 838 ★

Ethics

Unethical Behavior of Employees

Industry Week surveyed 1,500 subscribers regarding employee actions that cause leaders to distrust workers. The table below presents respondents—91 percent of whom were top or middle managers—answers.

[In percentages]

Unethical behavior	Respondents
Abuse of sick days	42
Laziness	37
Leaking information	25
Abuse of specific corporate policies	23
Abuse of expense reporting	11
Stealing	7

Source: Moskal, Brian S. "Hide This Report Card!" *Industry Week* 243, no. 17 (19 September 1994), p. 27. Primary source: *Industry Week* survey.

Family and Medical Leave Act

★ 839 ★

Family and Medical Leave Act

The Family and Medical Leave Act (FMLA) became effective August 1, 1993. It was enacted to protect workers on sick leaves. As the source explains: "Before the law, employers could fire workers for getting sick, and the Department of Labor could do little." Provisions of the law include: 12 weeks of unpaid leave for workers to care for new babies, sick relatives, or themselves during illnesses; continuation of an employee's health insurance while on leave; and a guarantee that the worker will return to the same or an equivalent job upon termination of the leave. From August 1, 1993, through March 31, 1994, the Wage and Hour Division received 564 complaints against employers. Sixty percent (338 claims) were uphelp as FMLA violations upon investigation.

Source: Hick, Virginia Baldwin. "Ex-Child Laborer Is in Charge of Enforcing Laws." *St. Louis Post-Dispatch*, 10 June 1994, p. 5C. Primary source: U.S. Department of Labor, Wage and Hour Division.

★ 840 ★

Family and Medical Leave Act

Family and Medical Leave Act Complaints

The table below shows a breakdown of complaints based on provisions of the Family and Medical Leave Act (FMLA) that the U.S. Department of Labor received in the first few months after the law's enactment. Data are based on two-month figures.

Allegations	Percent
Refusal to grant leave	41
Failure to restore employee to former position	33
Discrimination	12
Health benefits	10
Failure to restore employee to equivalent position	4

Source: "Few FMLA Complaints in Initial Months." *Employee Benefit Plan Review* (May 1994), p. 36. Primary source: U.S. Department of Labor, Wage and Hour Division.

★ 841 ★

Family and Medical Leave Act

Family and Medical Leave Act Costs

From the source: "Although businesses campaigned loudly against the Family and Medical Leave Act [FMLA], their fears of excessive costs and administrative burdens haven't materialized" (p. 2). The table below shows the responses of approximately 300 survey participants when asked about the anticipated affect of the law.

[In percentages]

Concern	Respondents
Administrative burdens:	
Companies expecting little administrative difficulty complying	47.1
Companies expecting no administrative difficulty complying	11.8
Small companies expecting little administrative difficulty complying[1]	51.4
Small companies expecting no administrative difficulty complying[1]	20.0
Costs	
Companies expecting to incur major costs for compliance	4.2
Companies expecting to incur minor costs for compliance	49.5
Companies expecting to incur insignificant costs for compliance	13.9

Source: Zolkos, Rodd. "Employer Survey Dispels Fears Over Family Leaves." *Business Insurance,* 7 March 1994, pp. 2, 50. Primary sources: William M. Mercer Inc.; University of California at Berkeley. *Note:* 1. Less than 200 employees.

★ 842 ★

Family and Medical Leave Act

Family and Medical Leave Act Noncompliance

Forty percent of the 300 medium-sized companies polled by William M. Mercer and the University of California at Berkeley reported not being in compliance with the Family and Medical Leave Act. The table below shows areas of admitted noncompliance.

[In percentages]

Area of noncompliance	Respondents
Lack formal leave system	15
Discontinue health care coverage	10
Do not guarantee employee's job	9
Provide less than 12 weeks leave	5

Source: Hermelin, Francine G. "How Well Is Family Leave Really Working?" *Working Woman* (September 1994), p. 9. Primary sources: William M. Mercer Inc.; University of California at Berkeley.

Lawsuits

★ 843 ★

Corporate Director and Officer Liability Claims, by Company: 1993

The table below shows the average number of liability claims per company against directors and officers. Data are based on a 1993 survey of more than 1,200 U.S. companies across a variety of industries. More than 300 respondents listed 712 claims over a 9 year period. Of that number, 468 claims were resolved, with the claimant dropping his or her claim in 100 instances. Though most of the remaining resolved cased did not result in an indemnity payment, according to the source, the average cost of defending claims was $750,000.

Company	Claims
Large banking	1.50
Transportation and communications	0.96
Utilities	0.76
Nonbanking financial services	0.76
Construction and real estate	0.31
Middle market banking	0.10

Source: Henry, Shannon. "Big-Bank Officers Sued Most Often, Poll Says." *American Banker,* 9 June 1994, p. 9. Primary source: Wyatt Co.

★ 844 ★

Lawsuits

Corporate Director and Officer Liability Claims, by Plaintiff: 1993

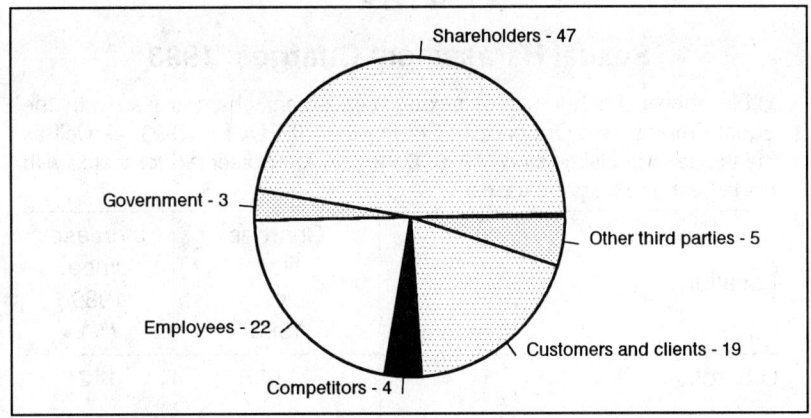

Table reflects the liability claims filed against directors and officers by the type of claimant.

[In percentages]

Claimant	Claims
Shareholders	47
Employees	22
Customers and clients	19
Other third parties	5
Competitors	4
Government	3

Source: "Who Sues Officers and Directors?" *Wall Street Journal,* 11 March 1994, p. B5. Primary source: Wyatt Co. 1993 Directors and Officers Liability Survey.

Sexual Harassment

★ 845 ★

Sexual Harassment Charges: 1993

Table shows the number of sexual harassment charges filed with the Equal Employment Opportunity Commission (EEOC) in 1993, as well as the increase in claims since 1989. Data also are presented for states with the largest and least increases.

Location	Charges filed in 1993	Increase since 1989 (%)
U.S. total	11,908	112
States with largest increases:		
Illinois	616	433
Wyoming	37	429
New Hampshire	59	386
States with smallest increases:		
Hawaii	51	14
Rhode Island	29	10
California	656	1

Source: "Highly Harassed." *Workplace Vitality* (October 1994), p. 15. Primary sources: EEOC; State University of New York at Albany.

★ 846 ★
Sexual Harassment

Sexual Harassment Claim Outcomes

Table shows the types of action taken in sexual harassment claims.

[In percentages]

Action	Companies
Counseling for involved parties	38.3
Offender issued formal reprimand	26.5
Allegation dismissed without action	17.2
Offender put on probation	14.3
Offender dismissed	13.7
Mediation for involved parties	6.4

[Continued]

★ 846 ★

Sexual Harassment Claim Outcomes

[Continued]

Action	Companies
Offender transferred to new position	5.5
Claimant transferred to new position	2.9

Source: "Effective Policies for Prevention and Investigation." *HR Focus* (February 1992), p. 11. Primary source: American Management Association.

Social Issues

★ 847 ★

Charitable Giving

Table compares workplace giving to United Way and other charities.

[In million dollars]

Charity	1991	1992
United Way charities	3,170	3,040
Non-United Way charities	276	290

Source: "Charitable Giving in the Workplace." *Business and Society Review* (winter 1994), p. 72. Primary source: National Committee for Responsive Philanthropy.

★ 848 ★

Social Issues

Domestic Violence

According to the Bureau of National Affairs, domestic violence costs American businesses $3 to $5 billion annually (excluding health care expenses) and 1 million lost workdays.

Source: Genasci, Lisa. "Domestic Violence Often Causes Havoc at Work." *Detroit News,* 27 January 1995, p. 2A.

★ 849 ★

Social Issues

Emissions-to-Jobs Ratios, by State: 1990

Emissions-to-jobs ratio measures relative risk of environmental pollution by comparing the number of jobs in manufacturing industries with annual level of emissions as reported in the *Toxic Release Inventory,* compiled by the Environmental Protection Agency. According to the source, "it is simply not true that jobs and environmental protection are antithetical" (p. 1). In fact, the source's author goes on to say that "a diminished ecosystem reduces long-term economic welfare" (p. 1). The table below shows the emissions-to-jobs ratio for each state. High ratios typically indicate higher pollution levels.

State	Ratio
Alabama	264-471
Alaska	1513
Arizona	264-471
Arkansas	264-471
California	23-100
Colorado	23-100
Connecticut	23-100
Delaware	23-100
Florida	105-214
Georgia	105-214
Hawaii	23-100
Idaho	105-214
Illinois	105-214
Indiana	264-471
Iowa	105-214
Kansas	264-471
Kentucky	105-214
Louisiana	2496
Maine	105-214
Maryland	23-100
Massachusetts	23-100
Michigan	105-214
Minnesota	-
Mississippi	264-471
Missouri	105-214
Montana	-
Nebraska	105-214
Nevada	105-214
New Hampshire	23-100
New Jersey	23-100
New Mexico	818
New York	23-100
North Carolina	105-214
North Dakota	105-214
Ohio	105-214
Oklahoma	105-214
Oregon	105-214
Pennsylvania	23-100
Rhode Island	23-100
South Carolina	105-214

[Continued]

★ 849 ★

Emissions-to-Jobs Ratios, by State: 1990
[Continued]

State	Ratio
South Dakota	23-100
Tennessee	264-471
Texas	264-471
Utah	1236
Vermont	23-100
Virginia	105-214
Washington	105-214
West Virginia	264-471
Wisconsin	23-100
Wyoming	1135

Source: Templet, Paul H. "Jobs and a Clean Environment: Having Them Both." *Environment and Development* (October 1993), pp. 1-2. *Note:* "-" indicates data not available.

★ 850 ★
Social Issues

Political Action Committee Contributions: 1991-1992

Tables shows the political action committee (PAC) contributions of employers and unions in federal elections during the 1991-1992 cycle.

[In percentages]

Contributor	Contribution
Employers	73.1
Unions	25.1
Other	1.8

Source: "Vote for NAFTA Earns Edge in Political $$$." *AFL-CIO News,* 13 December 1993, p. 4. Primary source: Center for Responsive Politics.

★ 851 ★

Social Issues

Transportation to Work, by State: 1990

Table below shows the various means of transportation used by employees to reach their workplaces. Data are for 1990 for workers 16 years old and older.

[In percentages]

State or area	Workers who:		
	Drove alone	Rode in a carpool	Used public trans- portation[1]
United States	73.2	13.4	5.3
Alabama	79.2	15.4	.8
Alaska	62.5	15.3	2.4
Arizona	73.6	14.9	2.1
Arkansas	77.3	15.5	.5
California	71.6	14.6	4.9
Colorado	74.3	12.8	2.9
Connecticut	77.7	11.2	3.9
Delaware	77.2	12.9	2.4
District of Columbia	35.0	12.0	36.6
Florida	77.1	14.1	2.0
Georgia	76.6	15.1	2.8
Hawaii	60.5	20.5	7.4
Idaho	74.8	12.0	1.9
Illinois	69.9	12.2	10.1
Indiana	78.9	12.8	1.3
Iowa	73.4	11.9	1.2
Kansas	78.8	11.5	.6
Kentucky	76.3	14.6	1.6
Louisiana	75.3	15.0	3.0
Maine	74.3	14.0	.9
Maryland	69.8	15.2	8.1
Massachusetts	72.1	10.7	8.3
Michigan	81.5	10.5	1.6
Minnesota	73.8	11.4	3.6
Mississippi	75.6	17.9	.8
Missouri	77.4	13.3	2.0
Montana	71.7	11.9	.6
Nebraska	76.1	11.2	1.2
Nevada	73.4	15.5	2.7
New Hampshire	78.2	12.3	.7
New Jersey	71.6	12.4	8.8
New Mexico	74.6	15.2	1.0
New York	54.3	10.5	24.8
North Carolina	76.6	16.1	1.0
North Dakota	71.4	10.7	.6
Ohio	80.3	10.8	2.5
Oklahoma	78.5	13.9	.6
Oregon	73.3	12.8	3.4
Pennsylvania	71.4	12.9	6.4

[Continued]

★ 851 ★

Transportation to Work, by State: 1990

[Continued]

State or area	Workers who:		
	Drove alone	Rode in a carpool	Used public trans-portation[1]
Rhode Island	78.1	12.1	2.5
South Carolina	75.5	16.9	1.1
South Dakota	72.0	10.1	.3
Tennessee	78.7	14.5	1.3
Texas	76.5	14.9	2.2
Utah	73.9	15.2	2.3
Vermont	72.2	12.9	.7
Virginia	72.5	15.9	4.0
Washington	73.9	12.3	4.5
West Virginia	74.8	16.2	1.1
Wisconsin	74.5	11.5	2.5
Wyoming	73.8	13.5	1.4

Source: U.S. Department of Commerce. *County and City Data Book, 1994.* 12th ed. Washington, DC: U.S. Government Printing Office, 1994, p. 9. *Notes:* 1. Includes bus or trolley bus, streetcar or trolley car, subway or elevated railroad, ferryboat, or taxicab.

★ 852 ★

Social Issues

Travel Time to Work, by State: 1990

Table below shows average amount of time needed for employees to reach their workplaces. Data are for 1990 for workers 16 years old and older who did not work at home.

[In minutes]

State or area	Average travel time to work
United States	22.4
Alabama	21.2
Alaska	16.7
Arizona	21.6
Arkansas	19.0
California	24.6
Colorado	20.7
Connecticut	21.1
Delaware	20.0
District of Columbia	27.1
Florida	21.8
Georgia	22.7

[Continued]

★ 852 ★

Travel Time to Work, by State: 1990
[Continued]

State or area	Average travel time to work
Hawaii	23.8
Idaho	17.3
Illinois	25.1
Indiana	20.4
Iowa	16.2
Kansas	17.2
Kentucky	20.7
Louisiana	22.3
Maine	19.0
Maryland	27.0
Massachusetts	22.7
Michigan	21.2
Minnesota	19.1
Mississippi	20.6
Missouri	21.6
Montana	14.8
Nebraska	15.8
Nevada	19.8
New Hampshire	21.9
New Jersey	25.3
New Mexico	19.1
New York	28.6
North Carolina	19.8
North Dakota	13.0
Ohio	20.7
Oklahoma	19.3
Oregon	19.6
Pennsylvania	21.6
Rhode Island	19.2
South Carolina	20.5
South Dakota	13.8
Tennessee	21.5
Texas	22.2
Utah	18.9
Vermont	18.0
Virginia	24.0
Washington	22.0
West Virginia	21.0
Wisconsin	18.3
Wyoming	15.4

Source: U.S. Department of Commerce. *County and City Data Book, 1994.* 12th ed. Washington, DC: U.S. Government Printing Office, 1994, p. 9.

★ 853 ★

Social Issues

Workplace Attire

An NPD Group survey of employers and workers found general acceptance of casual business clothing. Seventy-four percent of the respondents thought that performance did not decline due to casual clothing in the workplace. In fact, 51 percent noted productivity increases. The table below shows the types of clothing worn by workers while on the job.

[In percentages]

Clothing type	Worn by:	
	Men	Women
Casual[1]	18	42
Everyday casual[2]	36	26
Formal[3]	21	19
Uniforms	25	13

Source: Van Hoof, Kari. "Casual Clothes Are Workplace Trend." *Brandweek,* 18 July 1994, p. 17. Primary source: NPD Group Inc. *Notes:* 1. Casual pants with or without jacket or tie, sweaters, separates, pantsuits. 2. Jeans, shorts, T-shirts, athletic footwear, jacket or tie optional, and pantyhose optional. 3. Suit or sportcoat with dress pants, dresses, skirts with jackets, no slacks for women, pantyhose required.

Worker Satisfaction

★ 854 ★

Employee Morale and Management Behavior

Table shows the behaviors of supervisors and managers that are most detrimental to employee morale. Data are from a survey of 150 executives from large U.S. companies.

[In percentages]

Behavior	Responses
Criticizing in front of others	38
Dishonesty	38
Taking credit for another's work	12
Being inaccessible	6
Showing favoritism	4

Source: "Survey Identifies Top Morale-Damaging Actions in the Workplace." *HR Focus* (May 1994), p. 11. Primary source: Accountemps.

★ 855 ★

Worker Satisfaction

Job Satisfaction

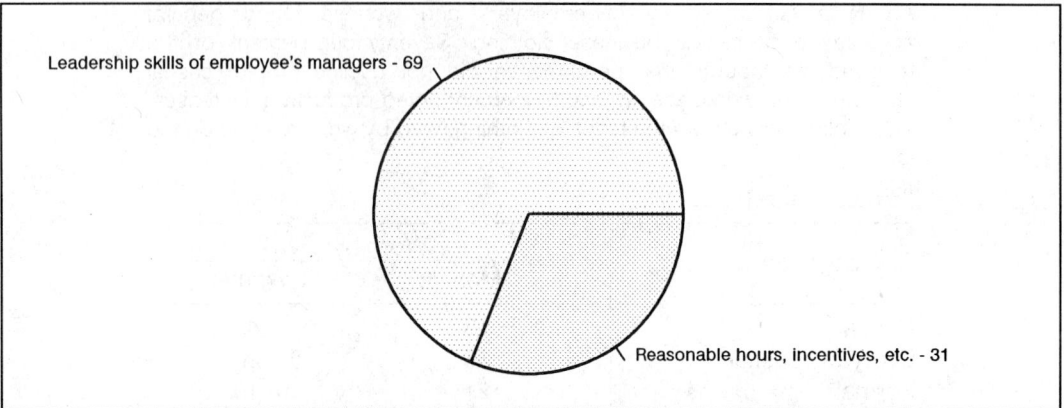

Leadership skills of employee's managers - 69

Reasonable hours, incentives, etc. - 31

Table show the responses to a survey of more than 25,000 employees from a cross-section of industries. Respondents were asked to indicate factors contributing to their satisfaction on the job.

Factor	Percent of responses
Leadership skills of employee's managers	69
Reasonable hours, incentives, etc.	31

Source: "Work Satisfaction Linked to Manager." *HR Magazine* (May 1994), p. 27. Primary source: Wilson Learning Corp.

★ 856 ★

Worker Satisfaction

Success

The National Study of the Changing Workforce by the Families and Work Institute surveyed a nationally representative sample of nearly 3,000 workers on a variety of issues. The table below shows the ways in which respondents defined success.

[In percentages]

Factor	Responses
Personal satisfaction from doing a good job	52
Earning the respect and recognition of others	30
Getting ahead or advancing in job or career	22
Making a good income	21
Feeling work is important	12
Having control over work content and schedule	6

Source: Shellenbarger, Sue. "Work-Force Study Finds Loyalty Is Weak, Divisions of Race and Gender Are Deep." *Wall Street Journal,* 3 September 1993, p. B1.

★ 857 ★

Worker Satisfaction

Worker Resignation, by Reason

| Limited recognition and praise - 34 |
| Compensation - 29 |
| Limited authority - 13 |
| Personality conflicts - 8 |

Table shows the reasons why people leave their jobs. Data are based on a survey of 150 executives from 1,000 large companies.

[In percentages]

Reason	Resignations
Limited recognition and praise	34
Compensation	29
Limited authority	13
Personality conflicts	8

Source: "How to Keep Employees." *Agri Finance* (November 1994), p. 7. Primary source: Robert Half International.

Chapter 10
PRODUCTION AND TECHNOLOGY

According to *Personnel Journal,* "the average U.S. employee works approximately 160 more hours each year" than 20 years ago ("Work Till You Drop," *Personnel Journal,* June 1993, p. 34). The average workday is about 10 hours long and highly stressful. So stressful, in fact, that 50 percent of American workers reported reductions in their productivity due to job pressures. This translates to lost sleep for some, guilt at neglecting homelife for others. Still others feel imprisoned by the daily grind. Nevertheless, American workers remain more productive than employees elsewhere in the world. (See table on labor productivity by country in this chapter.) The 30 tables in this chapter profile current productivity and technology issues in the American workplace. Coverage includes productivity measures, quality and reengineering, specific technologies, and telecommuting.

Productivity Measures

★ 858 ★

Labor Productivity, by Country: 1990

The table below reflects the gross domestic product (GDP) per person employed for selected countries during 1990. Data show the production of U.S. workers surpasses that of workers elsewhere.

[In thousand dollars]

Country	GDP per person employed
France	47.0
Germany[1]	44.2
Japan	38.2
United Kingdom	37.1
United States	49.6

Source: "Labor Productivity." *Christian Science Monitor,* 11 January 1993, p. 7. Primary sources: McKinsey Global Institute; Organization for Economic Cooperation and Development (OECD). *Notes:* Part-time employees counted as 0.5 full-time employee. Currencies were converted at parity according to 1990 purchasing power. 1. West.

★ 859 ★

Productivity Measures

Manufacturing Productivity Indexes, by Country: 1970-1993

Table shows the annual indexes of manufacturing productivity for 12 countries during selected years.

[1982 = 100]

Country	Output per hour				Output				Total hours			
	1970	1985	1990	1993	1970	1985	1990	1993	1970	1985	1990	1993
Belgium	44.3	117.2	133.9	-	70.9	109.6	126.4	-	159.9	93.5	94.4	-
Canada	76.9	119.8	122.6	131.8	78.5	127.0	137.5	136.1	102.1	106.0	112.2	103.3
Denmark	57.2	105.0	105.5	113.9	75.7	115.3	112.4	113.2	132.3	109.8	106.6	99.4
France	59.6	108.2	127.6	132.3	72.7	99.1	112.4	106.3	122.0	91.5	88.1	80.4
Germany	67.1	113.4	125.4	131.1	87.0	108.4	121.7	114.9	129.7	95.6	97.0	87.7
Italy	54.6	122.3	139.3	160.3	58.4	108.9	132.3	129.6	107.0	89.0	95.0	80.8
Japan	52.0	112.0	144.5	149.6	55.1	121.2	160.6	160.7	105.9	108.2	111.2	107.4
Netherlands	52.9	118.7	130.1	133.8	80.3	111.1	129.3	125.8	152.0	93.6	99.4	94.0
Norway	74.5	116.0	129.1	135.2	88.4	108.8	104.5	105.9	118.6	93.8	80.9	78.4
Sweden	69.0	113.2	124.9	147.9	91.1	115.7	124.3	118.5	131.9	102.2	99.5	80.1

[Continued]

★ 859 ★

Manufacturing Productivity Indexes, by Country: 1970-1993
[Continued]

Country	Output per hour				Output				Total hours			
	1970	1985	1990	1993	1970	1985	1990	1993	1970	1985	1990	1993
United Kingdom	72.1	116.4	140.1	160.1	110.5	108.9	128.9	123.1	153.3	93.5	92.0	76.9
United States	-	106.7	122.1	134.5	-	114.0	130.6	138.0	106.5	106.8	107.0	102.6

Source: "Current Labor Statistics." *Monthly Labor Review* 118, no. 2 (February 1995), p. 102. *Note:* "-" indicates data not available.

★ 860 ★

Productivity Measures

Manufacturing Productivity Percent Changes: 1992-1993

Table shows the annual percent changes in manufacturing productivity, unit labor costs, and related measures for 14 countries or areas.

Country or area	Output per hour	Output	Total hours	Employment	Hourly compensation	Unit labor costs		Exchange rate
						National currency	U.S. dollars	
United States	3.2	4.1	0.8	-0.3	3.3	0.1	0.1	-
Canada	2.3	5.0	2.6	0.6	0.5	-1.7	-7.9	-6.3
Japan	0.3	-4.2	-4.4	-2.1	2.7	2.4	16.9	14.1
Korea	[1]	5.0	[1]	[1]	[1]	1.4	-1.3	-2.7
Taiwan	[1]	2.8	[1]	[1]	[1]	3.2	-1.7	-4.8
Belgium	2.9	-4.2	-6.9	-5.4	3.8	0.9	-6.2	-7.0
Denmark	5.7	0.6	-4.8	-4.1	2.5	-3.0	-9.7	-6.9
France	1.1	-3.2	-4.2	-3.9	3.3	2.2	-4.5	-6.6
Germany	1.6	-7.7	-9.1	-5.9	7.4	5.7	-0.2	-5.6
Italy	5.6	-2.1	-7.3	-5.4	6.6	0.9	-21.0	-21.7
Netherlands	1.2	-2.5	-3.6	-3.6	2.9	1.7	-3.8	-5.4
Norway	2.1	1.7	-0.4	-0.7	1.0	-1.1	-13.4	-12.5
Sweden	6.6	1.6	-4.7	-7.3	-1.5	-7.6	-30.9	-25.3
United Kingdom	4.8	1.4	-3.3	-2.6	7.5	2.5	-12.8	-15.0

Source: Greiner, Mary, Christopher Kask, and Christopher Sparks. "Comparative Manufacturing Productivity and Unit Labor Costs." *Monthly Labor Review* 118, no. 2 (February 1995), p. 28. *Notes:* "-" indicates "not applicable." 1. Data not available.

★ 861 ★
Productivity Measures
Overtime

According to the source, 95 percent of all employees work in excess of the standard 40-hour work week. The table below shows the extra hours workers spend on the job each week.

Overtime hours[1]	Percent of workers
6-20 hours more	57
20 hours or more	6

Source: Filipowski, Diane. "Work Till You Drop." *Personnel Journal* (June 1993), p. 34. *Note:* 1. 40 hours is considered the standard work week.

★ 862 ★
Productivity Measures
Productivity Indexes – Annual: 1982-1993

Table shows the annual indexes of productivity, hourly compensation, unit costs, and prices for selected years.

[1982 = 100]

Item	1982	1984	1986	1987	1988	1989	1990	1991	1992	1993
Business:										
Output per hour of all persons	100.0	104.8	108.5	109.6	110.7	109.9	110.7	112.1	115.5	117.2
Compensation per hour	100.0	108.3	118.8	123.1	128.5	133.0	140.6	147.4	154.9	160.5
Real compensation per hour	100.0	100.6	104.6	104.6	104.8	103.5	103.8	104.4	106.6	107.2
Unit labor costs	100.0	103.4	109.5	112.3	116.0	121.0	127.1	131.5	134.2	136.9
Unit nonlabor payments	100.0	116.5	122.0	125.5	130.6	136.6	139.8	144.9	148.3	150.9
Implicit price deflator	100.0	107.7	113.6	116.6	120.8	126.1	131.2	135.9	138.8	141.5
Nonfarm business:										
Output per hour of all persons	100.0	104.7	107.7	108.6	109.6	108.6	109.1	110.7	113.7	115.4
Compensation per hour	100.0	108.3	118.4	122.5	127.7	132.0	139.2	146.2	153.7	158.7
Real compensation per hour	100.0	100.6	104.3	104.1	104.2	102.7	102.8	103.6	105.7	106.0
Unit labor costs	100.0	103.4	110.0	112.8	116.5	121.5	127.6	132.1	135.2	137.5
Unit nonlabor payments	100.0	116.5	123.2	126.6	131.8	137.1	140.6	146.5	149.7	153.3
Implicit price deflator	100.0	107.6	114.2	117.2	121.4	126.5	131.8	136.7	139.9	142.6
Nonfinancial corporations:										
Output per hour of all employees	100.0	105.4	109.3	111.2	113.3	111.5	112.7	115.0	118.5	122.0
Compensation per hour	100.0	107.6	117.2	120.9	125.9	130.2	137.1	143.8	150.4	154.9
Real compensation per hour	100.0	99.9	103.2	102.7	102.7	101.3	101.2	101.9	103.5	103.5
Total unit costs	100.0	101.1	105.9	107.0	109.8	115.7	120.1	123.7	124.4	123.8
Unit labor costs	100.0	102.0	107.2	108.8	111.1	116.8	121.7	125.0	126.9	127.0
Unit nonlabor costs	100.0	98.8	102.4	102.5	106.4	112.9	116.3	120.5	118.0	115.8
Unit profits	100.0	168.4	150.0	172.1	183.5	168.5	167.5	164.7	177.2	201.9
Unit nonlabor payments	100.0	111.9	111.4	115.6	120.9	123.3	125.9	128.8	129.1	132.0

[Continued]

★ 862 ★

Productivity Indexes – Annual: 1982-1993

[Continued]

Item	1982	1984	1986	1987	1988	1989	1990	1991	1992	1993
Implicit price deflator	100.0	105.3	108.6	111.0	114.3	119.0	123.1	126.3	127.7	128.6
Manufacturing:										
Output per hour of all persons	100.0	103.5	109.5	116.6	119.2	119.9	122.1	124.9	127.5	131.6
Compensation per hour	100.0	106.0	115.8	118.4	123.1	127.9	134.7	141.9	147.9	152.8
Real compensation per hour	100.0	98.4	102.0	100.6	100.4	99.5	99.5	100.5	101.7	102.0
Unit labor costs	100.0	102.4	105.8	101.6	103.2	106.7	110.4	113.7	116.0	116.1
Unit nonlabor payments	100.0	122.3	127.4	134.5	147.4	153.3	153.7	157.0	-	-
Implicit price deflator	100.0	107.4	111.2	109.8	114.3	118.4	121.2	124.5	-	-

Source: "Current Labor Statistics." Monthly Labor Review 118, no. 2 (February 1995), p. 97. Note: "-" indicates data not available.

★ 863 ★

Productivity Measures

Productivity Indexes – Quarterly: 1992-1993

Table shows quarterly indexes of productivity, hourly compensation, and unit costs for 1992 and 1993. Data are seasonally adjusted.

[1982 = 100]

Item	Quarterly indexes							
	1992				1993			
	I	II	III	IV	I	II	III	IV
Business:								
Output per hour of all persons	114.5	114.8	115.9	116.8	116.2	116.4	117.3	119.0
Compensation per hour	152.2	153.7	156.0	157.7	158.8	160.0	161.2	162.1
Real compensation per hour	105.9	106.1	106.8	107.1	107.0	107.0	107.3	107.2
Unit labor costs	133.0	133.9	134.7	135.1	136.6	137.5	137.4	136.3
Unit nonlabor payments	148.4	148.8	145.8	150.2	149.5	149.6	150.4	153.8
Implicit price deflator	138.0	138.8	138.3	140.1	140.8	141.4	141.6	142.1
Nonfarm business:								
Output per hour of all persons	112.6	113.1	113.9	115.0	114.4	114.5	115.6	117.0
Compensation per hour	150.9	152.6	154.7	156.4	157.2	158.2	159.3	160.2
Real compensation per hour	105.0	105.3	106.0	106.3	106.0	105.8	106.1	105.9
Unit labor costs	134.0	134.9	135.9	136.1	137.5	138.1	137.7	136.9
Unit nonlabor payments	149.5	150.4	147.0	152.1	151.5	151.8	153.5	156.1
Implicit price deflator	139.0	139.9	139.5	141.2	142.0	142.5	142.8	143.1
Nonfinancial corporations:								
Output per hour of all employees	116.8	117.6	119.1	120.6	120.0	121.3	122.7	124.1
Compensation per hour	147.7	149.4	151.5	153.1	154.0	154.5	155.4	155.9
Real compensation per hour	102.7	103.1	103.7	104.0	103.8	103.4	103.5	103.1
Total unit costs	124.5	124.5	124.9	123.8	125.0	124.1	123.6	122.6
Unit labor costs	126.5	127.1	127.2	127.0	128.3	127.3	126.7	125.7
Unit nonlabor costs	119.3	118.0	119.0	115.7	116.8	115.8	115.8	114.8

[Continued]

★ 863 ★

Productivity Indexes – Quarterly: 1992-1993

[Continued]

Item	Quarterly indexes							
	1992				1993			
	I	II	III	IV	I	II	III	IV
Unit profits	170.4	175.6	171.0	191.2	183.7	199.4	202.5	220.9
Unit nonlabor payments	128.9	128.8	128.8	129.9	129.4	131.5	132.1	134.8
Implicit price deflator	127.3	127.6	127.7	127.9	128.7	128.7	128.5	128.7
Manufacturing:								
Output per hour of all persons	126.4	126.8	127.6	128.8	130.0	130.7	131.7	133.6
Compensation per hour	145.2	146.8	148.4	150.7	150.0	152.1	153.6	155.1
Real compensation per hour	101.0	101.3	101.6	102.4	101.1	101.8	102.3	102.5
Unit labor costs	114.9	115.8	116.3	117.0	115.4	116.4	116.6	116.1

Source: "Current Labor Statistics." Monthly Labor Review 118, no. 2 (February 1995), p. 96.

★ 864 ★

Productivity Measures

Productivity Measures: 1970-1990

Table shows labor productivity as measured by output per hour, as well as other related measures.

Item	1970	1975	1980	1985	1989	1990	1991	1992	1993
	Indexes (1982 = 100)								
Output per hour, business sector	87.0	95.5	98.6	106.3	109.9	110.7	111.8	115.5	117.6
Nonfarm business	88.5	96.7	99.0	105.6	108.6	109.1	110.3	113.7	115.7
Manufacturing	(NA)	(NA)	92.9	106.8	120.0	122.2	124.5	129.8	136.4
Output[1], business sector	75.8	85.0	100.5	116.7	132.3	133.3	131.6	135.4	140.3
Nonfarm business	75.7	84.9	100.8	116.8	132.7	133.5	131.8	135.4	140.6
Manufacturing	(NA)	(NA)	102.0	114.0	131.2	130.6	127.8	131.7	138.0
Hours[2], business sector	87.2	89.0	101.9	109.8	120.4	120.5	117.7	117.3	119.4
Nonfarm business	85.6	87.9	101.8	110.7	122.2	122.4	119.5	119.1	121.5
Manufacturing	(NA)	(NA)	109.8	106.7	109.3	106.9	102.6	101.5	101.1
Compensation per hour[3], business sector	36.7	54.5	85.0	113.2	133.0	140.6	147.4	154.9	160.8
Nonfarm business	37.0	54.9	84.9	112.8	131.9	139.2	146.2	153.7	159.2
Manufacturing	(NA)	(NA)	83.3	111.2	127.9	134.7	141.9	148.2	152.3
Real hourly compensation[3], business sector	91.3	97.8	99.5	101.5	103.5	103.8	104.5	106.5	107.4
Nonfarm business	92.0	98.4	99.4	101.2	102.7	102.8	103.6	105.7	106.3
Manufacturing	(NA)	(NA)	97.5	99.8	99.5	99.4	100.5	101.9	101.7
Unit labor costs[4], business sector	42.2	57.1	86.2	106.5	121.0	127.1	131.9	134.1	136.8
Nonfarm business	41.8	56.8	85.7	106.8	121.5	127.6	132.6	135.1	137.6
Manufacturing	(NA)	(NA)	89.6	104.2	106.6	110.3	114.0	114.1	111.6
	Annual percent change[5]								
Output per hour, business sector	1.4	2.4	-0.8	1.4	-0.7	0.7	1.0	3.3	1.8
Nonfarm business	1.0	2.3	-0.9	0.8	-0.9	0.4	1.1	3.1	1.7

[Continued]

★ 864 ★

Productivity Measures: 1970-1990
[Continued]

Item	1970	1975	1980	1985	1989	1990	1991	1992	1993
Manufacturing	(NA)	(NA)	-2.2	3.2	0.6	1.8	1.9	4.2	5.1
Output[1], business sector	-0.5	-1.9	-1.6	3.6	1.7	0.7	-1.3	2.9	3.6
Nonfarm business	-0.6	-2.0	-1.7	3.4	1.7	0.6	-1.3	2.7	3.8
Manufacturing	(NA)	(NA)	-6.7	2.4	0.9	-0.4	-2.2	3.1	4.7
Hours[2], business sector	-1.8	-4.2	-0.9	2.1	2.5	0.1	-2.3	-0.4	1.8
Nonfarm business	-1.5	-4.2	-0.8	2.5	2.6	0.2	-2.4	-0.4	2.1
Manufacturing	(NA)	(NA)	-4.6	-0.7	0.3	-2.2	-4.1	-1.1	-0.3
Compensation per hour[3], business sector	7.5	10.0	10.7	4.5	3.5	5.7	4.9	5.0	3.8
Nonfarm business	7.2	10.0	10.7	4.1	3.3	5.5	5.0	5.1	3.6
Manufacturing	(NA)	(NA)	11.9	5.0	3.9	5.3	5.4	4.4	2.8
Real hourly compensation[3], business sector	1.7	0.8	-2.5	0.9	-1.3	0.3	0.6	2.0	0.8
Nonfarm business	1.4	0.8	-2.5	0.6	-1.4	0.1	0.8	2.0	0.6
Manufacturing	(NA)	(NA)	-1.4	1.4	-0.9	-0.1	1.1	1.3	-0.2
Unit labor costs[4], business sector	6.1	7.5	11.5	3.0	4.3	5.0	3.8	1.7	2.0
Nonfarm business	6.2	7.5	11.7	3.3	4.3	5.1	3.9	2.0	1.8
Manufacturing	(NA)	(NA)	14.4	1.8	3.3	3.5	3.4	0.2	-2.2

Source: U.S. Bureau of the Census. *Statistical Abstract of the United States, 1994.* 114th ed. Washington, DC: U.S. Government Printing Office, 1994, p. 426. Primary sources: U.S. Bureau of Labor Statistics. *Employment and Earnings* (monthly); and unpublished data. *Notes:* "NA" represents "not available." Minus sign (-) indicates decrease. 1. Refers to gross domestic product originating in the sector, in 1987 prices. 2. Hours at work of all persons engaged in the business and nonfarm business sectors (employees, proprietors, and unpaid family workers); employees' and proprietors' hours in manufacturing. 3. Wages and salaries of employees plus employers' contributions for social insurance and private benefit plans. Also includes an estimate of same for self-employed. Real compensation deflated by the consumer price index for all urban consumers. 4. Hourly compensation divided by output per hour. 5. All changes are from the immediate prior year.

★ 865 ★

Productivity Measures

Worker Productivity and Downsizing

The table below shows the affect of downsizing on worker productivity. Data are from a survey of human resources managers at companies that downsized from 1984 through 1994.

[In percentages]

Affect of downsizing on worker productivity	Change
Remained constant	35.5
Increased	34.4
Declined	30.1

Source: Belsie, Laurent. "New Employer-Employee Contract Replaces Loyalty and Job Security." *Christian Science Monitor,* 21 February 1995, p. 8. Primary source: American Management Association's July 1994 survey.

Quality and Reengineering

★ 866 ★

Quality Programs, by Organization Type

The table shows the results of an annual survey conducted jointly by the American Society for Quality Control (ASQC) and the Gallup Organization in 1994. Data reflect the organizations that have instituted formal quality programs and the length of time such programs have been in place.

[In percentages]

Organization	Percent with formal quality program	Age of quality program[1]
General business sector	58	67
Hospitals	94	48
Motor vehicle departments	28	90
Schools	66	70

Source: Ryan, John. "Alternate Routes on the Quality Journey." *Quality Progress* 27, no. 12 (December 1994), p. 38. Primary source: ASQC/Gallup Survey Report (1994). *Note:* 1. Mean number of months program has been established.

★ 867 ★

Quality and Reengineering

Reengineering Obstacles

The table below presents the results of a Deloitte & Touche survey of chief information officers (CIOs). The survey found most executives pleased with the outcome of business process reengineering efforts. Nevertheless, they noted difficulties with reengineering. Data reflect the number of executives indicating that a particular condition is an obstacle to reeingineering's success.

Condition	CIOs citing as an obstacle
Resistance to change	59
Limitations of existing system	40
Lack of executive consensus	38
Lack of senior executive champion	37
Unrealistic expectations	27
Lack of cross-functional project team skills	26
Inadequate project team skills	24

[Continued]

★ 867 ★

Reengineering Obstacles

[Continued]

Condition	CIOs citing as an obstacle
Information system staff involved too late	16
Project charter too narrow	12

Source: "Reeingineering Succeeds Despite Tight Budgets." *HR Focus* (July 1994), p. 24. Primary source: Deloitte & Touche.

★ 868 ★

Quality and Reengineering

Reengineering Technology Issues

CSC Index Inc. surveyed 500 chief executives and chief operating officers at North American companies with sales totalling $200 million or more. More than 50 percent of the respondents thought that establishing the information technology (IT) infrastructure was "the most difficult aspect of reengineering." In fact, 11 percent claimed that IT was the foremost obstacle to reengineering. Only 1 percent of those surveyed viewed IT as the "key facilitator" in their reengineering programs.

Source: Bartholomew, Doug. "Technology: A Hurdle?" *InformationWeek,* 7 November 1994, p. 18. Primary source: CSC Index survey.

Technologies

★ 869 ★

Business Travel Communication

Tables shows the various communication technologies used by business travelers to maintain contact with their offices.

[In percentages]

Communication method	Business travelers
Call secretary	25
Have someone call them	16
Cellular phone	16
Voice mail	15

[Continued]

★ 869 ★

Business Travel Communication
[Continued]

Communication method	Business travelers
Beeper/pager	12
Fax	10
E-mail	5
Laptop computer	3
Other	6

Source: "Phoning Home." *USA TODAY,* 31 May 1994, p. 5B. Primary sources: Sprint; Visa.

★ 870 ★

Technologies

Client Server Costs: 1995

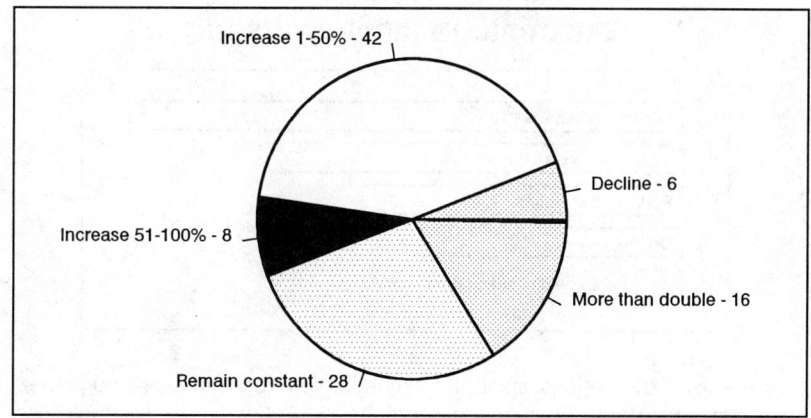

Table shows the expectations of survey respondents regarding client server expenses in 1995.

[In percentages]

Client server spending	Change
Increase 1-50%	42
Increase 51-100%	8
More than double	16
Remain constant	28
Decline	6

Source: "Client Server Can Cost You." *InformationWeek,* 7 November 1994, p. 80. Primary source: Forrester Research Inc. (Cambridge, Massachusetts).

★ 871 ★

Technologies

Communications Technologies

Table shows the percentages of companies using selected technologies to communicate. Data reflect midsize companies with 100 to 1,000 employees.

Technology	Use
Fax	97
800 number	75
Voice mail	57
Computer E-mail	49
Video conference	20

Source: "Business Reaches Out." *USA TODAY,* 14 September 1994, p. B1. Primary source: Sprint Business Survey.

★ 872 ★

Technologies

Electronic Technology Users

```
┌─────────────────────────────────────────────────┐
│  ┌───────────────────────────────────────────┐  │
│  │ Pagers or beepers - 12.1                  │  │
│  └───────────────────────────────────────────┘  │
│  ┌───────────────────────────────────────┐      │
│  │ Cellular phones - 8.7                 │      │
│  └───────────────────────────────────────┘      │
│  ┌─────────────────────────────────┐            │
│  │ Portable computers - 7.3        │            │
│  └─────────────────────────────────┘            │
│  ┌──────────────────────────┐                   │
│  │ On-line services - 5.9   │                   │
│  └──────────────────────────┘                   │
│  ┌────┐                                          │
│  │    │ Personal digital assistant - 0.8         │
│  └────┘                                          │
│            Chart shows data from column 1.        │
└─────────────────────────────────────────────────┘
```

Table shows the various electronic technologies used for work purposes. Data are from a national survey of more than 76,000 workers. Technologies are ranked in order of use by all workers.

[In percentages]

Technology	All workers	Tele- commuters	Home workers[1]	Mobile workers[2]
Pagers or beepers	12.1	23.8	13.1	33.3
Cellular phones	8.7	28.5	16.0	37.8
Portable computers	7.3	24.0	7.4	16.0
On-line services	5.9	18.7	6.7	7.8
Personal digital assistant	0.8	2.6	0.9	2.1

Source: "Work-at-Homers Work Habits." *Advertising Age,* 14 March 1994, p. S-2. Primary source: Market Facts. *Notes:* 1. Workers in home-based businesses. 2. Those who work from cars or on the road.

★ 873 ★

Technologies

Information Superhighway

A survey of chief executive officers (CEOs), senior marketing executives, and chief information officers (CIOs) asked about the affects of the Information Superhighway on their companies. The table below shows the responses of 300 executives to the survey question: "Is the Information Superhighway a resource that your company will use?"

[In percentages]

Executive	Use of Information Superhighway as a company resource				
	Current	6-11 months	12-23 months	24-48 months	5 years
CEOs	23	12	17	29	18
Marketers	28	8	20	21	8
CIOs	20	10	12	15	18

Source: "Survey Said...." *Business Marketing* (June 1994), p. 42. Primary source: Survey conducted by *Business Marketing, Advertising Age,* and USA Chicago, Inc. (marketing consultants).

★ 874 ★

Technologies

Information Technology Investment

Table shows the results of a Grant Thornton survey of executives at 253 midsize manufacturing companies. Findings indicate that investment in information systems and technology is expected to slow.

[In percentages]

Investment	1991-1993	1994-1996
Acquire new or upgrade existing computer platforms to client server technology, open systems, or proprietary architecture	64	36
Install one or more major software applications	60	38
Invest significantly in technology support[1]	52	42

Source: "Companies Spending Less on Information Technology." *T&D* (July 1994), p. 78. Primary source: Grant Thornton (Chicago, Illinois). *Note:* 1. Consulting services, training, or technology assistance.

★ 875 ★

Technologies

Internet Uses

Data show the leading purposes for which users access the Internet and the topics they search frequently.

[In percentages]

Uses and topics	Users
Purpose	
Browsing	79
Entertainment	66
Educational	59
Work-related	47
Academic research	41
Business research	26
Shopping	8
Subjects	
Computer hardware	70
Computer software	66
Books	46
Movies and videos	42
Home electronics	36
Music	35
Vacations	31

Source: Smith, Joel J. "Business Is Blooming on the Net." *Detroit News,* 14 March 1995, p. E1. Primary source: University of Michigan Business School survey of 3,500 users.

★ 876 ★

Technologies

LAN E-Mail Costs

Table presents a cost breakdown for LAN-based E-mail packages.

[In percentages]

Component	Costs
Networking platform	43
Hardware and software products	26
Technical support	24
Communications lines	7

Source: Stahl, Stephanie, and Jospeh C. Panettieri. "MS Mail Disappoints." *InformationWeek,* 7 November 1994, p. 15. Primary source: Ferris Networks.

★ 877 ★

Technologies

Online Service Uses

The table below shows the purposes for which chief executives use online services. Data are the results of a The Executive Committee (TEC) survey of small company chief executive officers.

[In percentages]

Use	Executives using service
Business research	72
Personal information	54
Electronic mail	47
Travel plans	32
Transferring files	23
Investments	22
Government updates	9

Source: "How Chief Executives Use On-Line Services." *Inc.* (February 1995), p. 120. Primary source: May 1994 survey of 226 members of The Executive Committee (TEC).

★ 878 ★

Technologies

Online Services

The table below shows the use of online services by chief executives. Data are the results of a The Executive Committee (TEC) survey of small company chief executive officers.

[In percentages]

Service	Executives using service
CompuServe	58
Prodigy	51
America Online	25
Internet	16
Dow Jones News/Retrieval	9
Lexis/Nexis	8
Dialog	7
Genie	3
Delphi	1

Source: "How Chief Executives Use On-Line Services." *Inc.* (February 1995), p. 120. Primary source: May 1994 survey of 226 members of The Executive Committee (TEC).

★ 879 ★

Technologies

Resume Databases

```
┌──────────────────────────────────────────────────┐
│ ┌──────────────────────────────────────────┐      │
│ │ Datamation Databank - 200,000            │      │
│ └──────────────────────────────────────────┘      │
│ ┌─────────────┐                                    │
│ │             │ University ProNet - 50,000         │
│ └─────────────┘                                    │
│ ┌────────┐                                         │
│ │        │ SkillSearch - 35,000                    │
│ └────────┘                                         │
│ ┌──────┐                                           │
│ │      │ Job Bank USA - 25,000                     │
│ └──────┘                                           │
│ ┌───┐                                              │
│ │   │ HispanData - 10,000                          │
│ └───┘                                              │
│ ┌─┐                                                │
│ │ │ National Employee Database - 6,000             │
│ └─┘                                                │
│ ▌ Career Net Online - 3,000                        │
│ │ MedSearch America - 400                          │
│         Chart shows data from column 2.            │
└──────────────────────────────────────────────────┘
```

Table profiles selected online resume services for job hunters. Services are ranked by number of resumes on file.

Service	Cost[1]	Size[2]	Clients[3]
Datamation Databank	$0	200,000	600-700
University ProNet	$35/lifetime	50,000	250
SkillSearch	$65/two years	35,000	500
Job Bank USA	$75/year	25,000	720
HispanData	$15/lifetime	10,000	60
National Employee Database	$25/year	6,000	600
Career Net Online	$42/year	3,000	900+
MedSearch America	$0	400	50

Source: Keeton, Laura E. "Net-Working." *Wall Street Journal,* 27 February 1995, p. R9. Primary source: *National Business Employment Weekly. Notes:* 1. The amount paid by individual job hunters. 2. Resumes in a database or file. 3. Employers and recruiters using the service.

★ 880 ★

Technologies

Technologies That Increase Competitiveness

Data shows the results of a 1993 IBM Consulting Group survey of insurance company executives. Respondents indicated that technology was of critical importance to their companies' ability to compete. Figures reflect the ratings given to the various technologies that respondents thought would have high potential in improving competitiveness.

[In percentages]

Technology	Respondents
Client server/LAN	87
Electronic data interchange (EDI)	74
Expert systems	53
Image processing	51
Mobile computing	49

[Continued]

★ 880 ★

Technologies That Increase Competitiveness
[Continued]

Technology	Respondents
Voice-grade/data-grade telecommunications	47
Pen-based computers	23
Multimedia	23

Source: Ingrassia, Paula V. "Harnessing Technology to Remain Competitive." *Best's Review* (May 1994), p. 84. Primary source: IBM Consulting Group.

Telecommuting

★ 881 ★

Telecommuters, by Sex

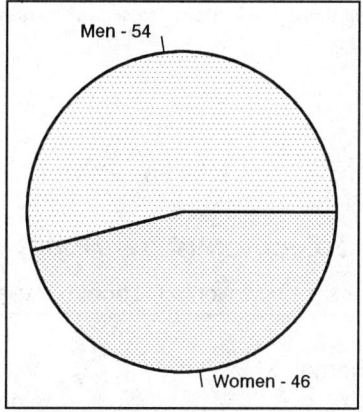

More than 7 million Americans telecommute; that is, work at home using new technologies such as personal computers and fax machines. The table below shows men and women telecommuters.

Sex	Percent of telecommuters
Men	54
Women	46

Source: "Who Works From Home." *USA TODAY,* 21 September 1994, p. B1. Primary source: LINK Resources.

★ 882 ★

Telecommuting

Telecommuters' Equipment

```
PCs - 55
Modems - 27
Cellular phones - 21
        Fax machines - 14
```

The table below shows the equipment used by home workers to "telecommute."

[In percentages]

Equipment	Telecommuters owning
PCs	55
Modems	27
Cellular phones	21
Fax machines	14

Source: "Who Works From Home." *USA TODAY,* 21 September 1994, p. B1. Primary source: LINK Resources.

★ 883 ★

Telecommuting

Telecommuters' Hours

Table below presents the hours worked at home by telecommuters.

Hours worked at home[1]	Percent of telecommuters
Less than 8 hours	26.1
8-34 hours	52.9
35 or more hours	15.9
Varies	5.1

Source: "Who Are the Telecommuters?" *HR Focus* (November 1994), p. 19. Primary source: LINK Resources. *Note:* 1. Per week.

★ 884 ★

Telecommuting

Telecommuters' Income

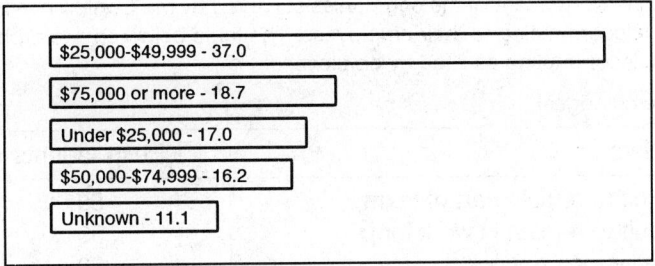

Data show the annual incomes of telecommuters.

Income	Percent of telecommuters
Under $25,000	17.0
$25,000-$49,999	37.0
$50,000-$74,999	16.2
$75,000 or more	18.7
Unknown	11.1

Source: "Who Are the Telecommuters?" *HR Focus* (November 1994), p. 19. Primary source: LINK Resources.

★ 885 ★

Telecommuting

Telecommuters' Selection Criteria

Table shows the job criteria and employee character traits that managers consider when selecting telecommuters.

[In percentages]

Criterion	Managers
Type of job or position	85
Ability to work autonomously	83
Dependability; ability to meet deadlines	75
Performance evaluations	62
Type of department	44
Communication skills	28
Supervisory responsibilities	21
Length of service	14
No special requirements	11
Job grade and level	9

Source: Barnes, Kathleen. "The New Workforce: Tips for Managing Telecommuters." *HR Focus* (November 1994), p. 10. Primary source: Conference Board, Work-Family Roundtable—Telecommuting.

★ 886 ★

Telecommuting

Telecommuting Challenges for Employees

Seventy-two percent of the companies surveyed by the Conference Board offer telecommuting to their employees. The table below shows problems with telecommuting as cited by employees.

[In percentages]

Problem	Respondents
Difficult to remain part of team	58
Difficult to remain in work loop	55
Negative perceptions	52
Hindered career advancement	51
Household distractions	44

Source: "Conference Board Discovers Pros and Cons of Telecommuting." *HR Focus* (November 1994), p. 20. Primary source: Conference Board.

★ 887 ★

Telecommuting

Telecommuting Challenges for Employers

Seventy-two percent of the companies surveyed by the Conference Board offer telecommuting to their employees. The table below shows problems with telecommuting as cited by employers.

[In percentages]

Problem	Respondents
Management resistance and skepticism	75
Control; difficult to supervise	67
Equity[1]	45
Culture change	41
Customer needs	32
Difficult to schedule meetings	26

Source: "Conference Board Discovers Pros and Cons of Telecommuting." *HR Focus* (November 1994), p. 20. Primary source: Conference Board. *Note:* 1. Telecommuting not available to all employees.

Chapter 11
INDUSTRIAL RELATIONS

In 1869 suffragist Susan B. Anthony advised her audience to "join the union, girls, and together say *Equal Pay for Equal Work.*" Nearly 125 years later, a Bureau of Labor Statistics study found Anthony's words still rang true. Pay of unionized women and minority workers far exceeded that of their nonunion counterparts—$130 more each week for women and $160-170 each week for minorities. (Union men received $128 more each week than nonunion workers.) The tables in this chapter profile union worker earnings, among other aspects of the labor situation in the United States. Coverage includes collective bargaining, labor disputes, unions, and worker displacement.

Collective Bargaining

★ 888 ★

Collective Bargaining Agreements: 1970-1993

Table shows the average percent wage rate changes under all major collective bargaining agreements. Data represent all wage rate changes implemented under the terms of private nonfarm industry agreements affecting 1,000 workers or more. Series covers production and related workers in manufacturing and nonsupervisory workers in nonmanufacturing industries. Data measure all wage rate changes effective in the year stemming from settlements reached in the year, deferred from prior year settlements, and cost-of-living adjustment (COLA) clauses.

[In percentages, except as indicated]

Changes	1970	1975	1980	1985	1988	1989	1990	1991	1992	1993
Average wage rate change (prorated over all workers)	8.8	8.7	9.9	3.3	2.6	3.2	3.5	3.6	3.1	3.0
Source:										
Current settlements	5.1	2.8	3.6	0.7	0.7	1.2	1.3	1.1	0.8	0.9
Prior settlements	3.1	3.7	3.5	1.8	1.3	1.3	1.5	1.9	1.9	1.9
COLA provisions	0.6	2.2	2.8	0.7	0.6	0.7	0.7	0.5	0.4	0.2
Average wage rate increase for workers receiving an increase	9.4	9.0	10.1	4.2	3.4	4.0	4.2	4.0	3.7	3.5
Source:										
Current settlements	11.9	10.2	9.4	4.1	3.3	4.2	4.1	4.2	3.6	3.2
Prior settlements	5.8	5.2	5.6	3.7	3.1	3.4	3.3	3.7	3.8	3.4

[Continued]

★ 888 ★

Collective Bargaining Agreements: 1970-1993
[Continued]

Changes	1970	1975	1980	1985	1988	1989	1990	1991	1992	1993
COLA provisions	3.7	4.8	7.7	2.2	2.7	3.3	2.7	2.0	2.0	1.3
Total number of workers receiving a wage rate increase (million)	10.2	9.7	8.9	5.5	4.7	4.8	4.9	5.1	4.7	4.8
Source (million):										
Current settlements	4.7	2.7	3.5	1.4	1.4	1.7	1.9	1.5	1.3	1.7
Prior settlements	5.7	7.3	5.6	3.4	2.6	2.3	2.7	3.0	2.8	3.0
COLA provisions	1.8	4.7	3.4	2.3	1.3	1.3	1.4	1.3	1.0	0.9
Number of workers not receiving a wage rate increase (million)	0.6	0.4	0.2	1.5	1.3	1.2	1.0	0.5	0.9	0.7

Source: U.S. Bureau of the Census. *Statistical Abstract of the United States, 1994.* 114th ed. Washington, DC: U.S. Government Printing Office, 1994, p. 435. Primary source: U.S. Bureau of Labor Statistics. *Compensation and Working Conditions* (monthly).

★ 889 ★

Collective Bargaining

Collective Bargaining Settlements: 1970-1993

Table shows the average percent changes in wage and compensation rates negotiated from 1970 through 1993 in major collective bargaining settlements. Data represent private nonfarm industry settlements affecting production and related workers in manufacturing and nonsupervisory workers in nonmanufacturing industries. Wage data cover units with 1,000 workers or more. Compensation data relate to units of 5,000 or more. Data relate to contracts negotiated in each calendar year but exclude possible changes in wage rates under cost-of-living adjustment (COLA) clauses, except increases guaranteed by the contract. Includes all settlements, whether wage and benefit rates were changed or not. Minus sign (-) indicates decrease.

[In percentages, except as indicated]

Changes	1970	1975	1980	1985	1987	1988	1989	1990	1991	1992	1993
Compensation rates:											
First year	13.1	11.4	10.4	2.6	3.0	3.1	4.5	4.6	4.1	3.0	3.0
Over life of contract[1]	9.1	8.1	7.1	2.7	2.6	2.5	3.4	3.2	3.4	3.1	2.4
Wage rates:											
All industries:											
First year	11.9	10.2	9.5	2.3	2.2	2.5	4.0	4.0	3.6	2.7	2.3
Contracts with COLA	(NA)	12.2	8.0	1.6	2.3	2.4	3.9	3.4	3.4	2.7	2.8
Contracts without COLA	(NA)	9.1	11.7	2.7	2.1	2.7	4.0	4.4	3.7	2.7	2.1
Over life of contract[1]	8.9	7.8	7.1	2.7	2.1	2.4	3.4	3.2	3.2	3.0	2.1
Contracts with COLA	(NA)	7.1	5.0	2.5	1.5	1.8	2.8	1.9	3.0	2.5	1.4
Contracts without COLA	(NA)	8.3	10.3	2.8	2.5	2.8	3.5	4.0	3.3	3.1	2.5
Manufacturing:											
First year	8.1	9.8	7.4	0.8	2.1	2.2	3.9	3.7	3.9	2.6	2.7
Over life of contract[1]	6.0	8.0	5.4	1.8	1.3	2.1	3.2	2.1	3.1	2.6	1.5
Nonmanufacturing:											
First year	15.2	10.4	10.9	3.3	2.3	2.8	4.0	4.3	3.4	2.7	2.1

[Continued]

★ 889 ★

Collective Bargaining Settlements: 1970-1993

[Continued]

Changes	1970	1975	1980	1985	1987	1988	1989	1990	1991	1992	1993
Over life of contract[1]	11.5	7.8	8.3	3.3	2.7	2.5	3.4	4.0	3.3	3.0	2.5
Number of workers affected (million)	4.7	2.9	3.8	2.2	2.0	1.8	1.9	2.0	1.8	1.6	2.1
Manufacturing (million)	2.2	0.8	1.6	0.9	0.9	0.7	0.4	0.9	0.6	0.3	0.8
Nonmanufacturing (million)	2.5	2.1	2.2	1.3	1.1	1.1	1.5	1.1	1.2	1.3	1.3

Source: U.S. Bureau of the Census. *Statistical Abstract of the United States, 1994.* 114th ed. Washington, DC: U.S. Government Printing Office, 1994, p. 435. Primary source: U.S. Bureau of Labor Statistics. *Compensation and Working Conditions* (monthly). *Notes:* "NA" stands for "not available." 1. Average annual rate of change.

★ 890 ★

Collective Bargaining

Cost-of-Living Adjustment Clauses in Collective Bargaining Agreements: 1968-1994

According to the source, "COLA clauses are designed to protect the purchasing power of workers against rising prices by tying wages to the BLS [Bureau of Labor Statistics] Consumer Price Index (CPI). Payments generated under these clauses are usually added to the wage rates, commonly at the end of the contract term and before implementation of the new contract" (p. 7). The table below shows workers under cost-of-living adjustment (COLA) clauses in major collective bargaining agreements between 1968 and 1994.

[Numbers in millions]

Year[1]	Workers covered	With COLA coverage	
		Number	Percent[2]
1968	10.6	2.7	25
1969	10.8	2.8	26
1970	10.8	3.0	28
1971	10.6	4.3	41
1972	10.4	4.1	39
1973	10.2	4.0	39
1974	10.3	5.3	51
1975	10.1	6.0	59
1976	9.8	6.0	61
1977	9.6	5.8	60
1978	9.5	5.6	59
1979	9.3	5.4	58
1980	9.1	5.3	58
1981	8.8	5.0	57
1982	8.3	5.0	60
1983	7.7	4.4	57
1984	7.3	4.1	56
1985	7.0	3.4	48
1986	6.5	2.6	40
1987	6.3	2.4	38
1988	6.1	2.4	40

[Continued]

★ 890 ★

Cost-of-Living Adjustment Clauses in Collective Bargaining Agreements: 1968-1994
[Continued]

Year[1]	Workers covered	With COLA coverage	
		Number	Percent[2]
1989	6.0	2.4	39
1990	5.9	2.3	39
1991	5.6	1.7	30
1992	5.5	1.5	28
1993	5.5	1.3	24
1994[3]	5.4	1.3	24

Source: Sleemi, Fehmida. "Collective Bargaining Outlook for 1995." *Monthly Labor Review* 118, no. 1 (January 1995), pp. 7, 11. *Notes:* 1. Data relate to December 31. 2. Percent coverage was computed on actual rather than rounded employment numbers. 3. Preliminary. Data relate to information available as of September 30.

★ 891 ★

Collective Bargaining

Lump-Sum Payment Provisions in Collective Bargaining Agreements: 1987- 1994

According to the source, lump-sum payments "emerged in the mid-1980's as a method of controlling labor costs because the payments generally do not become a part of the employee's wage rate and thus are often excluded from calculations of employee benefits such as vacations, penions, and holidays" (p. 7). The table below shows workers with lump-sum payment provisions in major collective bargaining agreements between 1987 and 1994.

[Numbers in millions]

Year[1]	Workers covered	With lump-sum payment provisions	
		Number	Percent[2]
Total:			
1987	8.8	2.8	32
1988	8.7	2.8	32
1989	8.6	2.7	32
1990	8.5	2.5	30
1991	8.5	2.2	27
1992	8.2	2.2	26
1993	8.2	2.5	31
1994[3]	8.1	2.7	33
Private industry:			
1987	6.3	2.7	42
1988	6.1	2.6	43
1989	6.0	2.6	44
1990	5.9	2.4	41
1991	5.6	2.1	37

[Continued]

★ 891 ★

Lump-Sum Payment Provisions in Collective Bargaining Agreements: 1987- 1994

[Continued]

Year[1]	Workers covered	With lump-sum payment provisions	
		Number	Percent[2]
1992	5.5	2.0	36
1993	5.5	2.1	39
1994[3]	5.4	2.3	42
State and local government:			
1987	2.3	0.2	7
1988	2.4	0.2	7
1989	2.5	0.1	5
1990	2.5	0.1	4
1991	2.6	0.1	4
1992	2.7	0.2	7
1993	2.7	0.4	14
1994[3]	2.8	0.4	14

Source: Sleemi, Fehmida. "Collective Bargaining Outlook for 1995." *Monthly Labor Review* 118, no. 1 (January 1995), p. 7. *Notes:* 1. Data relate to December 31. 2. Percent coverage was computed on actual rather than rounded employment numbers. 3. Preliminary. Data relate to information available as of September 30.

★ 892 ★

Collective Bargaining

State and Local Government Major Collective Bargaining Agreements: 1986- 1993

Table shows the average changes in wage and compensation rates negotiated through collective bargaining agreements. Averages presented are means.

[In percentages, except as indicated]

Item	1986	1987	1988	1989	1990	1991	1992	1993
Compensation rate changes, all settlements:[1]								
First year	6.2	4.9	5.4	5.1	5.1	1.8	0.6	0.9
Over life of contract[2]	6.0	4.8	5.3	4.9	5.1	2.9	1.9	1.9
State government:								
First year	6.8	4.3	5.3	4.9	4.4	1.9	0.2	1.2
Over life of contract[2]	6.0	4.3	4.9	4.6	3.9	2.8	2.0	2.2
Local government:								
First year	5.6	5.4	5.5	5.6	5.4	1.6	1.2	0.7
Over life of contract[2]	6.0	5.1	5.8	5.5	5.8	2.9	1.5	1.7
Wage rate changes, all settlements:[3]								
First year	5.7	4.9	5.1	5.1	4.9	2.3	1.1	1.1
Over life of contract[2]	5.7	5.1	5.3	5.1	5.0	2.8	2.1	2.1

[Continued]

★ 892 ★

State and Local Government Major Collective Bargaining Agreements: 1986-1993

[Continued]

Item	1986	1987	1988	1989	1990	1991	1992	1993
State government:								
First year	6.3	4.1	5.3	5.0	4.7	2.0	0.5	1.3
Over life of contract[2]	6.0	4.2	5.0	4.7	4.2	3.0	2.0	2.5
Local government:								
First year	5.3	5.3	5.0	5.2	5.0	2.5	1.7	1.0
Over life of contract[2]	5.6	5.5	5.5	5.4	5.2	2.7	2.1	1.9
Number of workers affected (million)[4]	0.9	1.3	1.1	1.1	0.9	0.8	1.2	1.6
State government	0.3	0.5	0.4	0.5	0.2	0.4	0.6	0.5
Local government	0.6	0.8	0.7	0.6	0.7	0.4	0.6	1.1
Wage rate changes, all agreements[5]	5.5	4.9	4.7	5.1	4.6	2.6	1.9	2.7
Source:								
Current settlements	2.4	2.7	2.3	2.5	2.0	0.6	0.8	1.5
Prior settlements	3.0	2.2	2.4	2.6	2.6	1.8	1.1	1.1
Cost-of-living adjustments	(Z)	(Z)	(Z)	(Z)	(Z)	0.1	(Z)	(Z)
State government	5.6	4.3	4.1	4.0	4.7	2.5	1.6	3.4
Local government	5.4	5.3	5.1	5.9	4.6	2.6	2.1	2.2

Source: U.S. Bureau of the Census. *Statistical Abstract of the United States, 1994.* 114th ed. Washington, DC: U.S. Government Printing Office, 1994, p. 321. Primary source: U.S. Bureau of Labor Statistics. *Current Wage Developments* (monthly). *Notes:* "Z" is less than .05 percent. 1. Data relate to settlements of 5,000 workers or more in each calendar year, whether wages and benefits were changed or not. 2. Average annual rate of change. 3. Data relate to settlements covering 1,000 workers or more in each calendar year but exclude possible changes in wages under cost-of-living adjustment (COLA) clauses, except increases guaranteed by the contract. Includes all settlements, whether wages were changed or not. 4. Number of workers covered by settlements reached in each calendar year. 5. Data relate to all wage changes implemented in the year stemming from settlements reached in the year, deferred from prior year agreements, and cost-of-living clauses.

★ 893 ★

Collective Bargaining

Workers in Collective Bargaining Agreements: 1985-1995

Table shows the workers in collective bargaining agreements covering 1,000 or more workers with contract expirations or reopenings from 1985 through 1995.

[In thousands]

Year	Workers covered	Workers with contract expirations or reopenings	Percent of workers covered by expirations or reopenings
Total:			
1985	9,448	3,532	37.4
1986	9,100	3,800	41.8
1987	8,793	3,103	35.3
1988	8,697	3,415	39.3

[Continued]

★ 893 ★

Workers in Collective Bargaining Agreements: 1985-1995
[Continued]

Year	Workers covered	Workers with contract expirations or reopenings	Percent of workers covered by expirations or reopenings
1989	8,567	3,068	35.8
1990	8,482	3,008	35.5
1991	8,483	2,820	33.2
1992	8,291	2,720	32.8
1993	8,184	2,795	34.2
1994	8,191	2,145	26.2
1995	8,141	3,447	42.3
Private industry:			
1985	7,404	2,410	32.5
1986	6,981	3,029	43.4
1987	6,539	1,988	30.4
1988	6,327	2,408	38.1
1989	6,080	2,100	34.5
1990	5,959	2,124	35.6
1991	5,907	1,470	24.9
1992	5,681	1,859	32.7
1993	5,509	2,060	37.4
1994	5,492	1,381	25.1
1995	5,359	1,887	35.2
State and local government:			
1985	2,044	1,122	54.9
1986	2,149	741	34.5
1987	2,253	1,115	49.5
1988	2,370	1,006	42.4
1989	2,487	968	38.9
1990	2,523	884	35.0
1991	2,576	1,349	52.4
1992	2,610	860	33.0
1993	2,675	735	27.5
1994	2,699	764	28.3
1995	2,782	1,559	56.0

Source: Sleemi, Fehmida. "Collective Bargaining Outlook for 1995." *Monthly Labor Review* 118, no. 1 (January 1995), p. 4. *Notes:* Data for 1985 through 1994 were published each year in the January issue of the *Monthly Labor Review.*

Labor Disputes

★ 894 ★

Baseball Strike Salary Losses: 1995

Barry Bonds - 42,350	
Cecil Fielder - 39,344	
Frank Thomas - 39,071	
Ken Griffey, Jr. - 38,251	
Joe Carter - 35,519	
Jeff Bagwell - 32,787	
Cal Ripkin, Jr. - 32,787	
Will Clark - 31,421	
Lenny Dykstra - 31,148	
Gary Sheffield - 30,738	

Chart shows data from column 2.

Table below presents leading major league baseball players' pay and daily pay losses due to the 1994-1995 baseball strike. Data reflect salaries for the 1995 season.

[In dollars]

Player	Salary	Pay loss per day
Barry Bonds	7,750,000	42,350
Cecil Fielder	7,200,000	39,344
Frank Thomas	7,150,000	39,071
Ken Griffey, Jr.	7,000,000	38,251
Joe Carter	6,500,000	35,519
Jeff Bagwell	6,000,000	32,787
Cal Ripkin, Jr.	6,000,000	32,787
Will Clark	5,750,000	31,421
Lenny Dykstra	5,700,000	31,148
Gary Sheffield	5,625,000	30,738

Source: "Salaries and Strike Losses." *Detroit News,* 1 March 1995, p. 1D. Primary sources: Associated Press. Data from management and player sources. *Notes:* Figures show only base salaries, excluding shares of signing bonuses or incentive bonus opportunities.

★ 895 ★
Labor Disputes

Strikes: 1993-1994

| Teamsters - 131 |
| Steelworkers - 62 |
| Machinists - 42 |
| United Auto Workers - 37 |
| United Food and Commercial Workers - 24 |
| National Education Association - 20 |
| Electronic Workers - 17 |
| Operating Engineers - 16 |
| Service Employees International Union - 15 |
| Retail/Wholesale - 15 |

Chart shows data from column 1.

Tables shows the labor disputes resulting in strikes for the leading unions. Data include the number of strikes and workers affected. The total number of strikes for all unions was reported as 601, with 321,395 workers affected. Figures are for September 1, 1993, through August 31, 1994.

Union	Number of strikes	Workers affected
Teamsters	131	87,563
Steelworkers	62	20,442
Machinists	42	26,177
United Auto Workers	37	60,692
United Food and Commercial Workers	24	28,365
National Education Association	20	4,284
Electronic Workers	17	2,262
Operating Engineers	16	1,273
Service Employees International Union	15	1,448
Retail/Wholesale	15	832

Source: Sunoo, Brenda Paik. "Managing Strikes, Minimizing Loss." *Personnel Journal* (January 1995), p. 52.

★ 896 ★

Labor Disputes

Work Days Lost to Strikes, by Country: 1985-1991

Table shows the number of working days lost because of strikes in selected countries throughout the world. Data are annual averages for 1985 through 1991, unless otherwise noted.

[Per 1,000 people employed]

Country	Lost work days
Spain	588
Ireland	308
Italy	271
Denmark	187
United Kingdom	145
United States	78
France	67
Netherlands	11
Japan[1]	5
Germany	4

Source: "Evaluation of Investment Opportunities in North Rhine-Westphalia." *North Rhine-Westphalia/Site Selection* (October 1993), p. 15. Primary source: *Information World. Note:* 1. Annual average 1985-1990.

★ 897 ★

Labor Disputes

Work Stoppages: 1960-1993

Excludes work stoppages involving fewer than 1,000 workers and lasting less than 1 day.

Year	Number of work stoppages[1]	Workers involved[2] (1,000)	Days idle	
			Number[3] (1,000)	Percent estimated working time[4]
1960	222	896	13,260	0.09
1965	268	999	15,140	0.10
1969	412	1,576	29,397	0.16
1970	381	2,468	52,761	0.29
1971	298	2,516	35,538	0.19
1972	250	975	16,764	0.09
1973	317	1,400	16,260	0.08
1974	424	1,796	31,809	0.16
1975	235	965	17,563	0.09
1976	231	1,519	23,962	0.12
1977	298	1,212	21,258	0.10

[Continued]

★ 897 ★

Work Stoppages: 1960-1993
[Continued]

Year	Number of work stop-pages[1]	Workers involved[2] (1,000)	Days idle	
			Number[3] (1,000)	Percent estimated working time[4]
1978	219	1,006	23,774	0.11
1979	235	1,021	20,409	0.09
1980	187	795	20,844	0.09
1981	145	729	16,908	0.07
1982	96	656	9,061	0.04
1983	81	909	17,461	0.08
1984	62	376	8,499	0.04
1985	54	324	7,079	0.03
1986	69	533	11,861	0.05
1987	46	174	4,481[5]	0.02
1988	40	118	4,481[5]	0.02
1989	51	452	16,996	0.07
1990	44	185	5,926	0.02
1991	40	392	4,584	0.02
1992	35	364	3,989	0.01
1993	35	182	3,981	0.01

Source: U.S. Bureau of the Census. *Statistical Abstract of the United States, 1994.* 114th ed. Washington, DC: U.S. Government Printing Office, 1994, p. 438. Primary source: U.S. Bureau of Labor Statistics. *Compensation and Working Conditions* (monthly). Information is based on reports of labor disputes appearing in daily newspapers, trade journals, and other public sources. The parties to the disputes are contacted by telephone, when necessary, to clarify details of the stoppages. *Notes:* 1. Beginning in year indicated. 2. Workers counted more than once if involved in more than one stoppage during the year. 3. Resulting from all stoppages in effect in a year, including those that began in an earlier year. 4. Agricultural and government employees are included in the total working time; private household and forestry and fishery employees are excluded. 5. Revised data.

Unions

★ 898 ★

ACTWU Representation: 1993

Table shows the workers that elected to be represented by the Amalgamated Clothing and Textile Workers Union (ACTWU) during 1993.

Company	Number of workers
Courtlauds Fibers Inc. (Mobile, Alabama)	60
JK Dawson Shirtmakers Inc. (Miami, Florida)	60
Crown Textile Co. (Talladega, Alabama)	450
Polyfelt Inc. (Evergreen, Alabama)	75
Londontown Distribution Center (Savannah, Georgia)	160
Mr. T's Apparel Inc. (Crystal Springs, Mississippi)	330
Chipman-Union Inc. (Greensboro, North Carolina; Union Point, Georgia)	560
Brooks Brothers Inc. (Garland, North Carolina; Kingston, North Carolina)	350
K Mart Distribution Center (Greensboro, North Carolina)	450
Springs Industries, Inc. (Nashville, Tennessee)	660
Thomson Co. Inc. (Thomson, Georgia)	275

Source: Cooper, Muriel H. "ACTWU on Win Streak in the South." *AFL-CIO News,* 1 November 1993, p. 12. Primary source: Amalgamated Clothing and Textile Workers Union.

★ 899 ★

Unions

AFL-CIO Affiliated Unions: 1979-1993

Data show U.S. membership in American Federation of Labor-Congress of Industrial Organizations (AFL-CIO)- affiliated unions. Figures represent the labor organizations as constituted in 1989 and reflect past merger activity. Membership figures based on average per capita paid membership to the AFL-CIO for the 2-year period ending in June of the year shown and reflect only actively employed members. Labor unions shown had a membership of 50,000 or more in 1993.

[In thousands]

Labor organization	1979	1989	1993
Total[1]	13,621	14,100	13,299
Associated Actors and Artistes of America	75	97	93
International Union, United Automobile, Aerospace and Agricultural Implement Workers of America (UAW)	(X)	917	771
Bakery, Confectionery and Tobacco Workers International Union	131	103	99
International Brotherhood of Boiler Makers, Iron Shipbuilders, Blacksmiths, Forgers, and Helpers[2]	129	75	58

[Continued]

★ 899 ★

AFL-CIO Affiliated Unions: 1979-1993
[Continued]

Labor organization	1979	1989	1993
International Union of Bricklayers and Allied Craftsmen	106	84	84
United Brotherhood of Carpenters and Joiners of America[2]	626	613	408
Amalgamated Clothing and Textile Workers Union (ACTWU)[2]	308	180	143
Communication Workers of America (CWA)	485	492	472
International Brotherhood of Electrical Workers (IBEW)	825	744	710
International Union of Electronic, Electrical, Salaried, Machine, and Furniture Workers[2]	243	171	143
International Union of Operating Engineers	313	330	305
International Association of Firefighters	150	142	151
United Food and Commercial Workers International Union (UFCW)[2]	1,123	999	997
International Ladies' Garment Workers' Union (ILGWU)	314	153	133
Glass, Molders, Pottery, Plastics, and Allied Workers International Union[2]	50	86	73
American Federation of Government Employees (AFGE)	236	156	149
Graphic Communications International Union[2]	171	124	95
Hotel Employees and Restaurant Employees International Union	373	278	258
International Association of Bridge, Structural, and Ornamental Ironworkers	146	111	91
Laborers' International Union of North America	475	406	408
National Association of Letter Carriers (NALC)	151	201	210
International Longshoremen's Association	63	62	58
International Association of Machinists and Aerospace Workers (IAM)[2]	688	517	474
Marine Engineers Beneficial Association/National Maritime Union	23	48	52
United Mine Workers of America	(X)	(X)	75
Office and Professional Employees International Union	83	84	89
Oil, Chemical, and Atomic Workers International Union (OCAW)	146	71	86
International Brotherhood of Painters and Allied Trades	160	128	106
United Paperworkers International Union	262	210	188
United Association of Journeymen and Apprentices of the Plumbing and Pipefitting Industry of the United States and Canada	228	220	220
American Postal Workers Union	245	213	249
Retail, Wholesale, and Department Store Union	122	137	80
United Rubber, Cork, Linoleum, and Plastic Workers of America	158	92	81
Seafarers International Union of North America	84	80	80
Service Employees International Union (SEIU)[3]	537	762	919
Sheet Metal Workers' International Association	120	108	108

[Continued]

★ 899 ★

AFL-CIO Affiliated Unions: 1979-1993
[Continued]

Labor organization	1979	1989	1993
International Alliance of Theatrical Stage Employees and Moving Picture Machine Operators of the United States and Canada	50	50	51
American Federation of State, County, and Municipal Employees (AFSCME)[5]	889	1,090	1,167
United Steelworkers of America	964	481	421
American Federation of Teachers (AFT)	423	544	574
International Brotherhood of Teamsters, Chauffers, Warehousemen, and Helpers of America	(X)	1,161	1,316
Amalgamated Transit Union	94	96	94
Transport Workers Union of America	85	85	78
United Transportation Union	121	(X)	60

Source: U.S. Bureau of the Census. *Statistical Abstract of the United States, 1994.* 114th ed. Washington, DC: U.S. Government Printing Office, 1994, p. 438. Primary source: American Federation of Labor and Congress of Industrial Organizations. *Report of the AFL-CIO Executive Council* (Washington, DC; biannual). *Notes:* "X" represents "not applicable." 1. Includes other AFL-CIO affiliated unions, not shown separately. 2. Figures reflect mergers with one or more unions since 1979. 3. Figures reflect mergers with one or more unions since 1979. Excludes Hospital and Health Care Employees, which merged into both unions on June 1, 1989 (membership of 23,000 in 1985; 60,000 in 1987; and 58,000 in 1989).

★ 900 ★
Unions

Anti-Union Campaigns: 1991-1992

According to a 1991-1992 study of union elections, anti-union campaigns were more prevalent in the private than public sector. The table below shows the employers engaging in anti-union campaigns, as well as the successful union certification elections, during the survey years.

[In percentages]

Employers	Anti-union campaigns	Successful certification elections
Private sector	38	48
Public sector	7	85

Source: Geddes, Darryl. "Survey: Private Sector Firms More Likely to Wage Anti-Union Campaigns." *Cornell Chronicle,* 10 November 1994. Primary source: National survey conducted by researchers at Cornell and at University of Massachusetts.

★ 901 ★

Unions

Union Members' Weekly Earnings, by Selected Characteristics: 1983 and 1993

Annual averages of monthly data. Covers employed wage and salary workers 16 years old and over. Excludes self-employed workers whose businesses are incorporated, although they technically qualify as wage and salary workers. Based on Current Population Survey.

| Characteristic | Median usual weekly earnings[1] ($) | | | | | | Not represented by unions | |
| | Total | | Union members[2] | | Represented by unions[3] | | | |
	1983	1993	1983	1993	1983	1993	1983	1993
Total	313	463	388	575	383	569	288	426
Age								
16 to 24 years old	210	283	281	377	275	366	203	277
25 to 34 years old	321	439	382	520	376	514	304	420
35 to 44 years old	369	519	411	595	407	593	339	499
45 to 54 years old	366	543	404	622	402	620	335	507
55 to 64 years old	346	492	392	576	390	573	316	462
65 years and over	260	394	338	467	330	462	238	381
Sex								
Men	378	514	416	608	414	606	349	490
Women	252	395	309	504	307	500	237	374
Race								
White	319	478	396	589	391	585	295	444
Men	387	531	423	619	421	618	362	505
Women	254	403	314	514	313	510	240	382
Black	261	370	331	490	324	485	222	330
Men	293	392	366	514	360	510	244	345
Women	231	349	292	454	287	447	209	320
Hispanic[4]	(NA)	335	(NA)	481	(NA)	478	(NA)	311
Men	(NA)	352	(NA)	511	(NA)	509	(NA)	318
Women	(NA)	314	(NA)	413	(NA)	415	(NA)	297
Work status								
Full-time workers	313	463	388	575	383	569	288	426
Part-time workers	(X)	(X)	(X)	(X)	(X)	(X)	(X)	(X)

Source: U.S. Bureau of the Census. *Statistical Abstract of the United States, 1994.* 114th ed. Washington, DC: U.S. Government Printing Office, 1994, p. 439. Primary source: U.S. Bureau of Labor Statistics. *Employment and Earnings* (January issues). *Notes:* "NA" stands for "not available. "X" indicates "not applicable." 1. For full-time employed wage and salary workers; 1983 data revised. 2. Members of a labor union or an employee association similar to a labor union. 3. Members of a labor union or an employee association similar to a union as well as workers who report no union affiliation but whose jobs are covered by a union or an employee association contract. 4. Persons of Hispanic origin may be of any race.

★ 902 ★
Unions

Union Membership, by Selected Characteristics: 1983 and 1993

Annual averages of monthly data. Covers employed wage and salary workers 16 years old and over. Excludes self-employed workers whose businesses are incorporated, although they technically qualify as wage and salary workers. Based on Current Population Survey.

Characteristic	Employed wage and salary workers					
	Total (1,000)		Union members[1] (%)		Represented by unions[2] (%)	
	1983	1993	1983	1993	1983	1993
Total	88,290	105,067	20.1	15.8	23.3	17.7
Age						
16 to 24 years old	19,305	17,193	9.1	5.9	11.1	6.8
25 to 34 years old	25,978	29,479	19.6	13.0	23.1	14.9
35 to 44 years old	18,722	28,144	24.8	18.8	28.6	21.1
45 to 54 years old	13,150	18,885	27.0	23.1	30.5	25.7
55 to 64 years old	9,201	9,064	26.9	20.8	30.3	23.0
65 years and over	1,934	2,303	10.1	8.6	12.1	10.0
Sex						
Men	47,856	54,776	24.7	18.4	27.7	20.2
Women	40,433	50,292	14.6	13.0	18.0	15.1
Race						
White	77,046	89,643	19.3	15.2	22.3	17.0
Men	42,168	47,186	24.0	18.0	26.9	19.7
Women	34,877	42,458	13.5	12.1	16.7	14.1
Black	8,979	11,612	27.2	21.0	31.7	23.9
Men	4,477	5,588	31.7	23.2	36.1	25.8
Women	4,502	6,024	22.7	18.9	27.4	22.0
Hispanic[3]	(NA)	8,575	(NA)	15.1	(NA)	16.6
Men	(NA)	5,085	(NA)	16.3	(NA)	17.5
Women	(NA)	3,490	(NA)	13.3	(NA)	15.4
Work status						
Full-time workers	70,976	85,211	22.9	17.8	26.4	19.9
Part-time workers	17,314	19,856	8.4	7.2	10.3	8.3

Source: U.S. Bureau of the Census. *Statistical Abstract of the United States, 1994.* 114th ed. Washington, DC: U.S. Government Printing Office, 1994, p. 439. Primary source: U.S. Bureau of Labor Statistics. *Employment and Earnings* (January issues). *Notes:* "NA" represents "not available." 1. Members of a labor union or an employee association similar to a labor union. 2. Members of a labor union or an employee association similar to a union as well as workers who report no union affiliation but whose jobs are covered by a union or an employee association contract. 3. Persons of Hispanic origin may be of any race.

★ 903 ★

Unions

Union Mergers: 1956-1994

From the source: "Union membership declined by nearly 4.4 million between 1979 (when union membership reached its peak) and 1994. The decrease was widespread in the private sector, particularly in the primary metals, automobile and aerospace equipment manufacturing, transportation and communication industries, which have large numbers of unionized workers.... One of the strategies unions have employed to cope with declining membership is to merge" (p. 18). The table below shows union mergers from 1956 through 1994. Data cover both AFL-CIO and independent unions.

Year	Total mergers	AFL-CIO only	AFL-CIO and independent	Independent only
Total, 1956-1994	133	70	51	12
1956	3	3	0	0
1957	2	1	0	1
1958	1	1	0	0
1959	3	2	1	0
1960	4	1	2	1
1961	3	2	1	0
1962	3	0	1	2
1963	0	0	0	0
1964	1	0	1	0
1965	1	1	0	0
1966	1	0	0	1
1967	1	0	1	0
1968	4	3	0	1
1969	6	2	4	0
1970	1	0	1	0
1971	3	2	1	0
1972	5	3	2	0
1973	2	1	1	0
1974	1	1	0	0
1975	3	1	1	1
1976	3	2	1	0
1977	3	2	0	1
1978	3	2	1	0
1979	5	3	2	0
1980	6	4	1	1
1981	3	2	1	0
1982	6	3	3	0
1983	5	2	3	0
1984	5	2	3	0
1985	6	2	3	1
1986	5	3	2	0
1987	3	1	2	0
1988	4	3	1	0
1989	5	4	1	0
1990	1	0	1	0
1991	5	2	3	0
1992	5	3	2	0

[Continued]

★ 903 ★

Union Mergers: 1956-1994

[Continued]

Year	Total mergers	AFL-CIO only	AFL-CIO and independent	Independent only
1993	7	2	3	2
1994[1]	5	4	1	0

Source: Williamson, Lisa. "Union Mergers: 1985-94 Update." *Monthly Labor Review* 118, no. 2 (February 1995), pp. 18-19. *Notes:* "AFL-CIO" stands for American Federation of Labor-Congress of Industrial Organizations. 1. Includes Service Employees International Union and International Brotherhood of Firemen and Oilers merger, effective February 1995.

Worker Displacement

★ 904 ★

Displaced Workers, by Selected Characteristics: 1992

As of January. For persons 20 years old and older with tenure of 3 years or more who lost or left a job between January 1987 and January 1992 because of plant closings or moves, slack work, or the abolishment of their positions. Based on Current Population Survey and subject to sampling error.

[In percentages, except total]

Sex, age, race, and Hispanic origin	Total (1,000)	Employment status			Reason for job loss		
		Employed	Unemployed	Not in labor force	Plant or company closed or moved	Slack work	Position or shift abolished
Total[1]	5,584	64.9	22.2	12.9	52.1	31.6	16.3
Males	3,447	66.6	24.5	8.9	49.4	34.7	15.9
20 to 24 years old	127	55.6	32.5	11.8	45.0	49.4	5.6
25 to 54 years old	2,728	71.6	24.5	3.9	49.5	34.0	16.5
55 to 64 years old	488	52.3	24.2	23.5	49.0	34.6	16.4
65 years old and over	103	15.8	15.3	68.9	53.3	35.7	11.0
Females	2,137	62.2	18.6	19.2	56.6	26.4	17.0
20 to 24 years old	76	72.7	7.3	20.1	43.8	46.1	10.0
25 to 54 years old	1,688	65.8	19.9	14.3	54.4	26.7	18.9
55 to 64 years old	262	51.4	17.4	31.2	70.5	19.4	10.1
65 years old and over	111	26.5	8.7	64.8	66.3	25.1	8.6
White	4,828	65.7	21.2	13.0	52.5	30.6	16.9
Male	3,003	67.6	23.3	9.1	49.4	34.1	16.5
Female	1,825	62.7	17.8	19.5	57.6	24.8	17.6
Black	626	58.7	28.6	12.7	51.3	36.3	12.4

[Continued]

★ 904 ★

Displaced Workers, by Selected Characteristics: 1992
[Continued]

Sex, age, race, and Hispanic origin	Total (1,000)	Employment status			Reason for job loss		
		Employed	Unemployed	Not in labor force	Plant or company closed or moved	Slack work	Position or shift abolished
Male	356	58.9	33.4	7.7	52.3	36.6	11.1
Female	270	58.5	22.2	19.3	50.0	35.9	14.1
Hispanic origin[2]	511	60.4	27.4	12.3	57.0	34.5	8.5
Male	323	64.6	27.2	8.2	57.6	35.7	6.7
Female	188	53.0	27.7	19.3	56.0	32.5	11.6

Source: U.S. Bureau of the Census. *Statistical Abstract of the United States, 1994.* 114th ed. Washington, DC: U.S. Government Printing Office, 1994, p. 415. Primary source: U.S. Bureau of Labor Statistics. *News.* USDL 92-530. *Notes:* 1. Includes other races, not shown separately. 2. Persons of Hispanic origin may be of any race.

★ 905 ★

Worker Displacement

Downsizing, by Company: 1994

Downsizing—that is, laying off workers to streamline production and increase profits, has become the norm instead of an emergency measure during slack economies that it once was. According to one outplacement firm cited in the source, 700 companies dismissed in excess of 500,000 workers in 1994, and one of four companies surveyed by the American Management Association in 1994 expected to lower its headcount. The table shows the ten leading companies that reduced staffs in 1994.

Corporation	Staff reduction
Digital Equipment Corporation	26,000
GTE Corporation	17,000
Nynex Corporation	16,800
AT&T Corporation	15,000
Delta Airlines	15,000
Scott Paper Company	10,500
Boeing Company	10,100
Ameritech	10,000
Pacific Bell	10,000
Sara Lee Corporation	9,900

Source: Tyson, James L. "'Ready-Fire-Aim' Layoff Strategy Backfires on Corporate America." *Christian Science Monitor,* 6 February 1995, pp. 10-11. Primary source: Challenger, Gray, and Christmas Inc. (Chicago, Illinois), an outplacement firm.

★ 906 ★

Worker Displacement

Job Loss Relief: 1989-1994

The table below shows the actions taken by employers to reduce job losses. Actions are ranked by 1994 data.

[In percentages]

Action	July 1989-June 1990	July 1990-June 1991	July 1991-June 1992	July 1992-June 1993	July 1993-June 1994
Transfers and downgrades	44	70	44	45	44
Early retirement	19	27	34	28	34
Voluntary separation	20	23	29	29	31
Salary freeze/reduction	46	36	35	29	27
Job sharing	11	12	16	8	13
Short work week/days	24	19	15	11	10
Furloughs	NA	13	14	10	8

Source: "Downsizing Turns More Systematic in Corporate America." *HR Focus* (January 1995), p. 20. Primary source: American Management Association. *Note:* "NA" indicates "not available or applicable."

★ 907 ★

Worker Displacement

Outplacement Time Limits

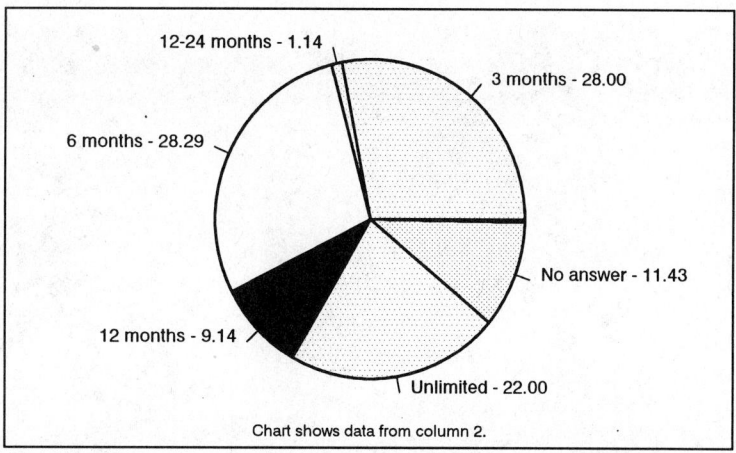

Chart shows data from column 2.

The table below shows the time limits of employers for outplacement for individuals. Average time is 5.9 months, based on 233 employers with time limits.

Period allowed	Number of employees	Percentage
Unlimited	77	22.00
3 months	98	28.00
6 months	99	28.29
12 months	32	9.14
12-24 months	4	1.14
No answer	40	11.43

Source: Lublin, Joann S. "Turned Tables: The Layoff Industry Learns That the Ax Can Be a Real Grind." *Wall Street Journal,* 28 November 1994, Midwest edition, pp. A1, A8. Primary source: American Management Association survey of 564 employers (1994).

Glossary

The Glossary includes statistical terms, labor-related definitions, and descriptions of geographic regions to assist users in better understanding and analyzing tabular data in *Statistical Handbood of Working America*. Items in italic type within definitions indicate terms explained in their own citations in the Glossary.

Adjustments for price changes: Data adjusted to eliminate the effect of changes in price. These adjustments are made by dividing current dollar values by the Consumer Price Index or the appropriate component of the index, then multiplying by 100.

Arithmetic mean: A type of average derived by summing the individual item values of a particular group and then dividing the total by the number of items. Often referred to as simply the "mean" or "average."

Averages: A single number or value that is often used to represent the "typical value" of a group of numbers. It is regarded as a measure of "location" or "central tendency" of a group of numbers. See also *arithmetic mean; median;* and *per capita.*

Basic skills: The ability to read, write, and do arithmetic at a level sufficient to perform common tasks.

Benefits: Cost to employers for paid leave, supplemental pay (including nonproduction bonuses), insurance, retirement and savings plans, and legally required benefits such as Social Security, workers' compensation, and unemployment insurance. See also *employer-provided benefits.*

Capital productivity: Value of goods and services in constant dollars produced per unit of capital services input.

Capital services: The flow of services from the capital stock used in production. Capital services is developed from the measures of the net stock of physical assets (equipment, land, and inventories) weighted by rental prices for each type of asset.

Cash payments: Wages and *lump-sum payments..*

Civilian labor force: All persons classified as employed or unemployed in the *civilian noninstitutional population.*

Civilian labor force participation rate: The proportion of the *civilian noninstitional population* that is in the labor force.

Civilian noninstitutional population: All persons 16 years old and older who are not inmates of penal or mental institutions, sanitariums, or homes for the aged, infirmed, or needy.

Collective bargaining settlements: Statistical measures of negotiated changes (increases, decreases, and zero changes) in wage rates alone and in *compensation* (wages and benefits), quarterly for nonagricultural industries and semiannually for state and local governments.

Combined units of labor and capital inputs: Derived by combining changes in labor and capital input with weights that represent each component's share of total output. The indexes for capital services and combined units of labor and capital are based on changing weights that are averages of the shares in the current and preceeding years.

Compensation: All payments in cash or kind made directly to employees plus employer expenditures for legally required insurance programs and contractual and private benefit plans.

Compensation costs: Includes items covered by *compensation rates* plus specified *lump-sum payments,* the cost of contractually required training programs that are not a cost of doing business, and the additional costs of changes in legally required insurance.

Compensation per hour: The sum of wages and salaries of employees plus employers' contributions for social insurance and private benefits plans and the wages, salaries, and supplementary payments for the self-employed divided by work hours. Wages, salaries, and supplementary payments for the self-employed exclude nonfinancial corporations in which there are no self-employed.

Compensation rates: Includes wage rate, premium pay (overtime and holidays), paid leave, insurance (life, health, and sickness and accident), pension and retirement plans, severance pay, and legally required benefits.

Compound interest formula: A method of computing rates of change; for example, average annual percent changes. This formula assumes that the rate of change is constant throughout a specified compounding period (one year for average annual rates of change). By the end of the compounding period, the amount of

accrued change is added to the amount that existed at the beginning of the period. As a result, the same rate of change is applied to a larger figure over time. See also *exponential formula.*

Constant dollars: Estimates representing an effort to remove the effects of price changes from statistical series reported in dollar terms. Generally, constant dollars are derived by dividing current dollar estimates by the appropriate price index for a given period. The result is a series presumably as it would exist if prices were the same throughout as in the base year; that is, as if the dollar had constant purchasing power. Any changes in this constant dollar series would reflect only changes in real volume of output, income, expenditures, or other measures. See also *current dollars* and *index numbers.*

Consumer Price Index: Measure of the average change in the prices paid by urban consumers for a fixed market basket of goods and services.

Cost-of-living adjustment: Clauses designed to protect the purchasing power of workers against rising prices by linking wages to the *Consumer Price Index.*

Contingent pay provisions: Clauses that could provide compensation changes beyond those specified in a collective bargaining settlement.

Current dollars: Actual prices or costs prevailing during specified years or time periods.

Days idle: Aggregate number of workdays lost by workers involved in stoppages.

Defined benefit pension plans: Plans using predetermined formulas to calculate a retirement benefit, obligating the employer to provide those benefits. Generally benefits are based on salary or years of service or both.

Defined contribution plans: Plans specifying the level of employer and employee contributions, but not the formula for determining eventual benefits. Individual accounts are estalished for *participants,* and benefits are based on amounts credited to these accounts.

Duration of unemployment: Length of time during which unemployed persons have been continuously looking for work. For persons laid off, duration of unemployment represents the number of full weeks since the termination of their most recent employment.

Earnings: Payment production or nonsupervisory workers receive, including premium pay for *overtime* or late shift work but excluding irregular bonuses and other special payments. See also *real earnings.*

East North Central states: Illinois, Indiana, Ohio, Michigan, Wisconsin.

East South Central states: Alabama, Kentucky, Mississippi, Tennessee.

Employed: All persons who worked in any capacity as paid employees or in their own businesses, or who worked 15 hours or more as unpaid workers in enterprises operated by family members. Persons temporarily absent from a job because of illness, bad weather, labor strikes, or personal reasons are counted among the employed whether they were paid by their employers or were seeking other jobs.

Employer-provided benefits: *Benefits* financed either wholly or partly by the employer.

Employment Cost Index: A quarterly measure of the rate of change in *compensation per hour* worked and includes wages, salaries, and employer costs of employee benefits.

Employment-population ratio: Number of employed as a percent of the *civilian noninstitutional population.*

Establishment: An economic unit that produces goods or services (such as a factory or store) at a single location and is engaged in one type of economic activity.

Exponential formula: A method of computing rates of change, usually population change. This method is based on ongoing compounding, applying the amount of change continuously to the base instead of at the end of each compounding period. See also *compound interest formula.*

Flexible benefit plans: Plans allowing employees to choose among several *benefits,* such as life insurance, medical care, and vacations days, and among several levels of care within a given benefit.

Full-time equivalents: Persons working 35 or more hours in a week.

Hispanics or Hispanic origin: Persons who identify themselves as Mexican, Puerto Rican, Cuban, Central or South American, or of other Hispanic descent. Persons of Hispanic origin may be of any race, thus they are included in white, black, or other population groups.

Hours of all persons: Total hours at work of payroll workers, the self-employed, and unpaid family workers.

Hours of work: Actual number of hours worked during a week, or average weekly hours of production or nonsupervisory workers for which pay was received. For persons working more than one job, the figures relate to the number of hours worked in all jobs, with all hours credited to their major jobs.

Incidence rates: The number of injuries, illnesses, lost workdays, or whatever per a given number of a defined population; for example, the number of occupational injuries per 100 full-time workers.

Index number: An index number is the measure of difference or change, usually expressed as a percent, relating one quantity (the "variable") of a specified kind to another quantity of the same kind.

International Price Program: Monthly and quarterly export and import price indexes for nonmilitary goods traded between the United States and the rest of the world. The export price index provides a measure of price change for all products sold by U.S. residents (national income accounts such as corporations, businesses, or individuals) to foreign buyers. The import price index provides a measure of price change for goods purchased from other countries by U.S. residents.

Job leavers: Persons who voluntarily ended their employment (e.g., quit) and began looking for work.

Job losers: Persons whose employment ended involuntarily and who began looking for work. Includes laid off workers.

Job openings due to growth and net replacement needs: The estimated number of *new entrants* needed annually for an occupation.

Job openings due to growth and total replacement needs: The broadest measure of job opportunities. Identifies the total number of employees needed annually to enter an occupation.

Labor cost See *Compensation.*

Labor productivity: The value of goods and services in constant prices produced per hour of labor input.

Lost workday cases: Occupational illness and injury cases involving days away from work, days of restricted activity, or both.

Lost workday cases involving restricted work activity: Occupational illness and injury cases resulting in restricted work activity only.

Lost workdays away from work: Number of workdays (consecutive or not) on which an employee would have worked but could not because of *occupational injuries* or *occupational illnesses.*

Lost workdays--restricted work activity: Number of workdays (consecutive or not) on which, because of injury or illness, the employee was assigned to another job on a temporary basis; the employee worked at a permanent job less than full time; or the employee worked at a permanently assigned job but could not perform all duties normally connected with it.

Lump-sum payments: Provision to control labor costs by giving a worker a payment that does not become part of his or her *wage rate* and that is often excluded from calculations of *employee benefits* such as vacations, pensions, and holidays.

Mean See *Arithmetic mean.*

Median: The middle number or value in a group of numbers when each item in the group is arranged according to size (lowest to highest or highest to lowest). Generally, the median has the same number of items above it as below it. If there is an even number of items in the group, the median is taken to be the average of the two middle numbers.

Middle Atlantic states: New Jersey, New York, Pennsylvania.

Midwest: Comprised of *East North Central* and *West North Central* states.

Mountain states: Arizona, Colorado, Idaho, Montana, Nevada, New Mexico, Utah, Wyoming.

Multifactor productivity: The value of goods and services in constant prices produced per combined unit of labor and capital inputs. Changes in this measure reflect changes in a number of factors that affect the production process, such as changes in technology, shifts in the composition of the labor force, or skill and effort of the workforce.

New England: Connecticut, Maine, Massachusetts, New Hampshire, Rhode Island, Vermont.

New entrants: People who have never worked.

Northeast states: Comprised of *New England* and *Middle Atlantic* states.

Occupational illnesses: Abnormal conditions or disorders caused by exposure to environmental factors associated with employment. Includes acute and chronic illness or disease that may be caused by inhalation, absorption, ingestion, or direct contact. Excludes disorders and conditions from *occupational injuries.*

Occupational injuries: Any injury--such as a cut, fracture, sprain, or amputation--that results from a work accident or from exposure involving a single incident in the work environment.

Output: Refers to the value added in manufacturing (gross product originating) in constant prices from the national accounts of each country.

Output per hour of all persons See *Labor productivity.*

Output per unit of capital services See *Capital productivity.*

Overtime hours: Portion of average weekly hours in excess of regular hours and for which overtime premiums were paid.

Pacific states: Alaska, California, Hawaii, Oregon, Washington.

Part-time equivalents: Persons working between 1 and 34 hours in a week.

Participants: Workers covered by an employee benefit, whether or not they use the benefit.

Participation rate: Ratio of the *civilian labor force* to the *civilian noninstitutional population.*

Per capita: Per person quantities. Per capita figures represent an average computed for every person in a specified group or population. It is derived by taking the total for an item (such as income, taxes, or retail sales) and dividing it by the number of persons in the specified population.

Persons not in the labor force: Retirees, housewives and househusbands, full-time students who do not work, those unable to work due to long-term illnesses, those who chose not to work, and others falling outside the classifications of *employed* and *unemployed.*

Producer Price Index: Measures average changes in prices received by domestic producers of all commodities in all stages of processing.

Production workers: Manufacturing workers, including working supervisors and nonsupervisory workers closely associated with production operations.

Real compensation per hour: *Compensation per hour* deflated by the change in the *Consumer Price Index* for all urban consumers.

Real earnings: Payment production or nonsupervisory workers receive--including premium pay for overtime or late shift work but excluding irregular bonuses and other special payments--adjusted to reflect the effects of changes in consumer prices.

Recordable occupational injuries and illnesses: Occupational deaths, regardless of the time between injury and death or the length of the illness; nonfatal *occupational illnesses;* or nonfatal *occupational injuries* that involve loss of consciousness, restriction of work or motion, trasfer to another job, and/or medical treatment other than first aid.

Reentrants: Persons who previously worked but were out of the labor force before beginning to look for employment.

Seasonal adjustment: Certain monthly and quarterly data are adjusted to eliminate the effect of such factors as climatic conditions, industry production schedules, openings and closings of schools, buying periods, and vacation practices that might prevent short-term evaluation of the statistical series. Tables containing data that have been adjusted are identified as "seasonally adjusted."

South: Comprised of *East South Central, South Atlantic,* and *West South Central* states.

South Atlantic states: Delaware, District of Columbia, Florida, Georgia, Maryland, North Carolina, South Carolina, Virginia, West Virginia.

Tax-deferred savings plans: A type of *defined contribution plan* that allows *participants* to to contribute a portion of their salaries to an employer- sponsored plan and defer income taxes until withdrawal.

Tornquist Index-Number Formula See *Combined units of labor and capital inputs.*

Total compensation costs: Wages, salaries, and employer costs for employee benefits.

Unemployed: All persons who do not work, are making specific efforts to find work, and are available to work (excluding temporary illness). Persons waiting to be recalled to a job from which they have been laid off need not be looking for work to be classified as unemployed.

Unemployment rate: The number of *unemployed* as a percent of the civilian labor force.

Unit labor costs: Labor *compensation costs* expended in the production of a unit of output. Unit labor costs are derived by dividing compensation by output.

Unit nonlabor costs: All components of unit nonlabor payments except *unit profits.*

Unit nonlabor payments: Items such as profits, depreciation, interest, and indirect taxes per unit of output. Unit nonlabor payments are computed by subtracting compensation of all persons from current dollar value of output and dividing by output.

Unit profits: Corporate profits with inventory valuation and capital consumption adjustments per unit of output.

Wage rate: Average straight time hourly wage rate plus shift premiums.

Wage rate changes under all major agreements: Measures all wage increases, decreases, and zero changes under collective bargaining agreements covering 1,000 or more workers.

Wages and salaries: *Earnings* before payroll deductions, including production bonuses, incentive earnings, commissions, and *cost-of-living adjustments.*

West: Comprised of Mountain and Pacific states.

West North Central states: Iowa, Kansas, Minnesota, Missouri, Nebraska, North Dakota, South Dakota.

West South Central states: Arkansas, Louisiana, Oklahoma, Texas.

Work stoppages: Strikes and lockouts, usually involving 1,000 or more workers and lasting a full shift or longer.

Workplace literacy See *Basic skills.*

Sources

Thousands of work-related statistics are produced by a variety of reliable sources each year. Data were selected for inclusion in *SHWA* on the basis of their timeliness, interest or value to researchers and the general public, and their ability to contribute to the comprehensive coverage of the field. This list contains complete bibliographic citations for material from which tables were compiled or from which data were selected. Tables appear in the list by table number. Tables can be accessed by reference number or by page number using the Table of Contents, the Occupation Index, or the Keyword Index.

"... And So Are Some Other Things: Overall Injuries Seem to Be on the Upswing." *Restaurant Business,* 20 January 1994. Table: 329

"1992 Salary Survey Results." *Advanced Materials & Processes* 145, no. 3 (March 1994). Table: 622

"401(k) Is Too Good a Deal to Pass Up." *USA TODAY,* 31 May 1994. Table: 676

Abrahamson, Vicki Lafer. "No: Hunting for Dishonest Undercuts Discrimination Laws." *ABA Journal* (December 1994). Table: 833

Amirault, Thomas. "Job Training: Who Needs It and Where They Get It." *Occupational Outlook Quarterly* (winter 1992-1993). Table: 774

Anfuso, Dawn. "Deflecting Workplace Violence." *Personnel Journal* (October 1994). Table: 822

Anzick, Michael A. "Pensions: An Important Component of Retirement Income." *Benefits Quarterly* (second quarter 1993). Table: 680

"Asian Managers Expected to Receive Highest Increases." *HR Focus* (May 1994). Table: 647

"At a Glance: Snapshots of the Workplace Health Industry." *Workplace Health* (March 1993). Table: 611

Balagopal, Sudha Sethu. "Life From Square One." *India Today,* 31 March 1994. Table: 84

Barnes, Kathleen. "The New Workforce: Tips for Managing Telecommuters." *HR Focus* (November 1994). Table: 885

Bartholomew, Doug. "Technology: A Hurdle?" *InformationWeek,* 7 November 1994. Table: 868

"Basic Skills Testing on the Decline." *Personnel Journal* (November 1994). Table: 721

Baxter, Neal. "Is There Another Degree in Your Future?" *Occupational Outlook Quarterly* 37, no. 4 (winter 1993-1994). Table: 718

Belsie, Laurent. "New Employer-Employee Contract Replaces Loyalty and Job Security." *Christian Science Monitor,* 21 February 1995. Table: 865

"Benefits." *Personnel Journal* (November 1993). Table: 618

"The Best Jobs in America? How *Money* Ranks Today's Occupations." *Career Opportunities News* 12, no. 4 (January-February 1995). Tables: 16-28

Birnbaum, Jane. "Benefits Pose Challenge for Entrepreneurs." *St. Louis Post-Dispatch,* 23 December 1994. Table: 594

"BLS Releases Its Second Survey of Employee Benefits in Small Firms." *Employee Benefit Plan Review* (May 1994). Table: 658

Bongiorno, Lori, and John A. Byrne. "Is There an MBA Glut? If You Answered No, You Pass." *Business Week,* 24 October 1994. Tables: 781-782

Boyd, Malia. "Job Sharers Are More Motivated." *Incentive* (February 1995). Table: 712

Burr, Barry B. "A Nasty Surprise in Store for Funds." *Pensions & Investments* 21, no. 3 (15 November 1993). Table: 682

"Business Reaches Out." *USA TODAY,* 14 September 1994. Table: 871

"By the Numbers: Why Retiree Medical Benefits Are Changing." *Journal of Accountancy* (September 1993). Table: 690

Castelli, Jim. "A Digest of Developments in Occupational Safety and Health." *Safety + Health* (February 1994). Tables: 87, 807, 825

Census of Population and Housing, 1990: Equal Employment Opportunity (EEO) File on CD-ROM [machine-readable datafiles]. Prepared by the Bureau of the Census. Washington, DC: The Bureau, 1992. Tables: 91-203, 723-773

Census of Population and Housing, 1990: Summary Tape File 3C on CD-ROM [machine-readable datafiles]. Prepared by Bureau of the Census. Washington, DC: The Bureau, 1992. Tables: 568-569, 571-572

"Charitable Giving in the Workplace." *Business and Society Review* (winter 1994). Table: 847

Chavez, Linda. "Minimum Wage Hurts the Poor." *USA TODAY,* 8 February 1995. Table: 652

"Cheaper in the 'Burbs." *USA TODAY,* 8 December 1994. Table: 604

"Child Care and Flextime Are Prevalent Work and Family Programs." *Employee Benefit Plan Review* (August 1994). Table: 713

"Client Server Can Cost You." *InformationWeek,* 7 November 1994. Table: 870

"Companies Cite Reasons for Broadbanding." *Personnel Journal* (June 1994). Table: 598

"Companies Increase Allowable Expenses." *USA TODAY,* 3 January 1995. Table: 605

"Companies Spending Less on Information Technology." *T&D* (July 1994). Table: 874

"Company Health Costs Soar." *USA TODAY,* 27 April 1993. Table: 616

"Conference Board Discovers Pros and Cons of Telecommuting." *HR Focus* (November 1994). Tables: 886-887

Cooper, Muriel H. "ACTWU on Win Streak in the South." *AFL-CIO News,* 1 November 1993. Table: 898

"Cost Containment Is Helping to Cure Some Ailing Budgets." *HR Focus* (September 1994). Table: 613

"Costly Health Risks." *Workplace Vitality* (June 1994). Table: 608

"Costs of Health-care Benefits Rise in 1993." *Personnel Journal* (June 1994). Table: 610

Craig, Charlotte W. "Budget-wise Business Travel." *Detroit Free Press,* 19 December 1994. Table: 607

"Current Labor Statistics." *Monthly Labor Review* 118, no. 2 (February 1995). Tables: 859, 862-863

DePompa, Barbara. "Fighting Telephone Fraud." *InformationWeek,* 1 August 1994. Table: 837

"Dial 'E' for Efficient." *Sales & Marketing Management* (September 1994). Table: 606

"Downsizing Turns More Systematic in Corporate America." *HR Focus* (January 1995). Table: 906

"Effective Policies for Prevention and Investigation." *HR Focus* (February 1992). Table: 846

Eisman, Regina. "Incentives: There's More to Measure." *Incentive* (February 1995). Table: 667

Elmer, Vickie. "The Holistic Workplace." *Detroit Free Press,* 28 November 1994. Table: 708

"Employee Assistance Programs: Percent of Employers Offering Counseling in Specified Areas." *HR Focus* (September 1994). Table: 710

"Employer-Provider Health Care Insurance." *New York Times,* 19 June 1994. Table: 692

"Enrollment in Higher Education by State and Race, 1992." *Manpower Comments* (March 1994). Table: 779

"Ethics in the News." *Business & Society Review* (winter 1994). Table: 591

"Evaluation of Investment Opportunities in North Rhine-Westphalia." *North Rhine-Westphalia/Site Selection* (October 1993). Table: 896

Executive Office of the President of the United States. *Environmental Quality 24: The Twenty-fourth Annual Report of the Council on Environmental Quality.* Prepared by Ray Clark. Written by Carroll Curtis. Edited by Barry Walsh. Washington, DC: U.S.Government Printing Office, 1994. Table: 788

"Executive Relocation Reverses Its Downward Trend." *HR Focus* (September 1994). Table: 621

"Few FMLA Complaints in Initial Months." *Employee Benefit Plan Review* (May 1994). Table: 840

Fierman, Jaclyn. "Are Companies Less Family-Friendly?" *Fortune,* 21 March 1994. Table: 711

"Fighting Drug Abuse." *Workplace Vitality* (September 1994). Table: 808

Filipowski, Diane. "Work Till You Drop." *Personnel Journal* (June 1993). Table: 861

Flannery, William. "Companies Keep Reins Tight on Travel Money." *St. Louis Post-Dispatch,* 7 November 1994. Table: 603

Flannery, William. "Rights Act Generates Few Suits." *St. Louis Post-Dispatch,* 6 April 1994. Table: 830

Flynn, Gillian. "Preventive Health Programs Soar." *Personnel Journal* (September 1994). Table: 813

Frank, Robert, and Eleena de Lisser. "Research on Affirmative Action Finds Modest Gains for Blacks Over 30 Years." *Wall Street Journal,* 21 February 1995. Table: 271

Freudenheim, Milt. "Health Care: A Growing Burden." *New York Times,* 29 January 1991. Table: 612

Freudenheim, Milt. "Retirees Threatened With Loss of Insurance." *New York Times,* 28 June 1992. Table: 693

Gaiter, Dorothy J. "The Gender Divide: Black Women's Gains in Corporate America Outstrip Black Men's." *Wall Street Journal,* 8 March 1994. Table: 534

Geddes, Darryl. "Survey: Private Sector Firms More Likely to Wage Anti-Union Campaigns." *Cornell Chronicle,* 10 November 1994. Table: 900

Genasci, Lisa. "Domestic Violence Often Causes Havoc at Work." *Detroit News,* 27 January 1995. Table: 848

"Getting 'Back' to Work." *USA TODAY,* 19 October 1994. Table: 798

"Golden Years: Golden Opportunities." *Black Enterprise* (December 1993). Tables: 580-581

Gottschalk, Earl C., Jr. "On Your Own." *Wall Street Journal,* 9 December 1994. Table: 677

Greiner, Mary, Christopher Kask, and Christopher Sparks. "Comparative Manufacturing Productivity and Unit Labor Costs." *Monthly Labor Review* 118, no. 2 (February 1995). Table: 860

Hammonds, Keith H. "Work: More Complex Than We Thought." *Business Week,* 13 September 1993. Tables: 805, 834

Hansen, Marc D. "Engineering Design for Safety." *Professional Safety* 38, no. 10 (October 1993). Table: 786

Hansen, Mark. "The ADA's Wide Reach: Little League and Health Insurers Among Those Covered by Act." *ABA Journal* (December 1993). Table: 794

"Health Care Coverage." *San Francisco Examiner,* 28 November 1993. Table: 286

"Health Care Coverage in the '90s." *Los Angeles Times,* 8 March 1993. Table: 614

"Health Care Write-Down." *American Medical News,* 1 November 1993. Table: 619

"Healthy Payrolls." *Wall Street Journal,* 27 February 1995. Table: 478

Hecker, Daniel E. "Further Analysis of Labor Market for College Graduates." *Monthly Labor Review* 118, no. 2 (February 1995). Tables: 638-639

"Hello Boss...." *Detroit Free Press,* 14 March 1993. Table: 791

Henry, Shannon. "Big-Bank Officers Sued Most Often, Poll Says." *American Banker,* 9 June 1994. Table: 843

Hermelin, Francine G. "How Well Is Family Leave Really Working?" *Working Woman* (September 1994). Table: 842

Hick, Virginia Baldwin. "Ex-Child Laborer Is in Charge of Enforcing Laws." *St. Louis Post-Dispatch,* 10 June 1994. Table: 839

"Highly Harassed." *Workplace Vitality* (October 1994). Table: 845

Hoerr, John, Leah Nathans Spiro, Larry Armstrong, and James B. Treece. "Culture Shock at Home: Working for a Foreign Boss." *Business Week,* 17 December 1990. Table: 477

"How Chief Executives Use On-Line Services." *Inc.* (February 1995). Tables: 877-878

"How Employers Are Helping Workers Stay Healthy." *Washington Post,* 18 May 1993, final edition. Table: 809

"How Many Hours in a Week?" *USA TODAY,* 12 October 1994. Table: 473

"How Safe Is Your System?" *InformationWeek,* 26 December 1994. Table: 835

"How to Keep Employees." *Agri Finance* (November 1994). Table: 857

"Increased Skills Testing Uncovers Higher Deficiency Rates." *HR Focus* 70, no. 9 (September 1993). Table: 720

"Indemnity Plan Costs vs. Managed-Care Plan Costs in Selected U.S. Cities, 1992." *Modern Healthcare,* 8 March 1993. Table: 614

Ingrassia, Paula V. "Harnessing Technology to Remain Competitive." *Best's Review* (May 1994). Table: 880

Jacobs, Heidi. "Corporate Response to AIDS." *American Management Association* (January 1995). Tables: 783-784

Jenner, Lisa. "Large Employers Support the 'Benefit Elite.'" *HR Focus* (May 1994). Table: 654

"Job Demographics for the Next Decade." *Manufacturing Engineering* (March 1994). Table: 533

"Just the Facts." *Detroit News,* 12 April 1994. Table: 820

Keeton, Laura E. "Net-Working." *Wall Street Journal,* 27 February 1995. Table: 879

Kilborn, Peter T. "A City Built on $4.25 an Hour." *New York Times,* 12 February 1995. Table: 651

Kilborn, Peter T. "In Rare Move, Agency Acts Swiftly in a Sexual Harassment Case." *New York Times,* 10 January 1995. Table: 831

Klein, Joe. "The End of Affirmative Action." *Newsweek,* 13 February 1995. Table: 826

Laabs, Jennifer J. "Danger at Work: Fatalities and Injuries on the Rise." *Personnel Journal* (February 1994). Table: 790

"Labor Productivity." *Christian Science Monitor,* 11 January 1993. Table: 858

"Largest U.S. Employers in South Africa." *USA TODAY,* 6 June 1994. Table: 476

"Latinos in Higher Ed." *Manpower Comments* (March 1994). Table: 717

Leonard, Bill. "The Employee's Favorite, the Employer's Quandry." *HR Magazine* (November 1994). Table: 597

Levine, Chester. "Employee Benefits: Growing in Diversity and Cost." *Occupational Outlook Quarterly* (winter 1993-1994). Table: 11

Lissy William E. "Currents in Compensation and Benefits." *Compensation & Benefits Review* (November-December 1993). Table: 709

Lissy, William E. "Currents in Compensation and Benefits." *Compensation & Benefits Review* (March-April 1994). Tables: 601, 648

Litvan, Laura M. "Controlling Wrist and Back Injuries." *Nation's Business* (August 1994). Table: 797

Lohse, Deborah. "Feeding Uncle Sam." *Wall Street Journal,* 9 December 1994. Table: 631

Lublin, Joann S. "Turned Tables: The Layoff Industry Learns That the Ax Can Be a Real Grind." *Wall Street Journal,* 28 November 1994, Midwest edition. Table: 907

"Managed Care Facts." *Hospitals,* 5 April 1993. Table: 285

Manigan, Colleen. "The Graveyard Shift." *Public Management* (April 1994). Table: 824

"Many Faces of Discrimination." *USA TODAY,* 23 June 1994. Table: 832

"Merit Increases, Alternative Pay Are More Popular." *HR Focus* (December 1994). Tables: 644-645

"Monday Tops List for Risk." *Detroit News,* 20 July 1994. Table: 804

"More Companies Adopt the Notion That an Ounce of Prevention...." *HR Focus* (December 1994). Table: 811

Moskal, Brian S. "Hide This Report Card!" *Industry Week* 243, no. 17 (19 September 1994). Table: 838

Nasar, Sylvia. "Cars and VCRs Aren't Necessarily the First Domino." *New York Times,* 3 May 1992. Table: 471

National Advisory Council on Migrant Health. *1993 Recommendations of the National Advisory Council on Migrant Health.* Rockville, MD: National Advisory Council on Migrant Health, May 1993. Table: 795

National Industry-Occupation Matrix, 1992 [data tape]. Prepared by the Bureau of Labor Statistics. Washington, DC: U.S. Department of Labor, Bureau of Labor Statistics, 1992. Tables: 353, 355-469

Noble, Barbara Presley. "Linking Gay Rights and Unionism." *New York Times,* 4 December 1994. Table: 642

Noble, Barbara Presley. "Still in the Dark on Diversity." *New York Times,* 6 November 1994. Table: 827

"Office Furniture Workers Miss Most Workdays." *Wood and Wood Products* (January 1994). Table: 331

"On the Job." *Wall Street Journal,* 17 February 1995. Table: 829

"Optimism for Workforce Growth Varies Among Regions." *HR Focus* 70, no. 9 (September 1993). Table: 602

"OSHA Star: Seal of Approval." *C&EN,* 29 November 1993. Table: 802

Overstreet, James. "Most Employers Honor Jury Duty." *USA TODAY,* 29 September 1994. Table: 698

"Pay-for-Performance Plans Become More Popular." *Personnel Journal* (February 1994). Table: 599

"Percent of Organziations With Variable Pay Programs." *HR Focus* (July 1994). Table: 600

"Percentage of Uninsured Workers Aged 18-64 by Firm Size, 1992." *HR Focus* (May 1994). Table: 675

Peters, Shannon. "Employers Provide More Parties, Fewer Gym Facilities in 1993." *Personnel Journal* (May 1994). Table: 810

"Phoning Home." *USA TODAY,* 31 May 1994. Table: 869

"Ranks of the Uninsured Increase." *Nation's Business* (May 1994). Table: 664

"Recession Still Puts Pressure on Pay Plans." *Sales & Marketing Management* (October 1993). Table: 646

"Reeingineering Succeeds Despite Tight Budgets." *HR Focus* (July 1994). Table: 867

"Returning to Work After Illness or Injury." *HR Focus* (October 1994). Table: 799

"Rewarding Workers." *USA TODAY,* 12 January 1995. Table: 668

Richman, Louis S. "CEOs to Workers: Help Not Wanted." *Fortune,* 12 July 1993. Table: 532

Roberts, Sally. "Violence a Big Threat to Workers, Study Says." *Business Insurance,* 1 August 1994. Table: 333

Roberts, Sam. "Women's Work: What's New, What Isn't." *New York Times,* 27 April 1995. Table: 278

Rose, Robert L. "A Foot in the Door." *Wall Street Journal,* 27 February 1995. Table: 544

Rose, Robert L. "Retiree Health Coverage Erodes at Small, Midsize Firms." *Wall Street Journal,* 16 April 1993. Table: 691

Rowland, Mary. "Get More From Your Benefits Package." *Working Woman* (October 1994). Table: 660

Ryan, John. "Alternate Routes on the Quality Journey." *Quality Progress* 27, no. 12 (December 1994). Table: 866

Sabir, Nadirah Z. "Watch That Last Step!" *Black Enterprise* (May 1995). Tables: 800-801

"Safety First." *Business Week,* 2 November 1992. Table: 609

"Salaries and Strike Losses." *Detroit News,* 1 March 1995. Table: 894

Schachner, Michael. "Large Companies Still See Self-Funding as Health Care Cure." *Business Insurance,* 7 February 1994. Table: 620

Schellhardt, Timothy D. "Passing of Perks." *Wall Street Journal,* 13 April 1994. Table: 661

Schwartz, Matthew P. "Employer Health Costs Fell 1.1% in '94." *Underwriter,* 20 February 1995. Table: 665

Sharpe, Rochelle. "Family Friendly Firms Don't Always Promote Females." *Wall Street Journal,* 29 March 1994. Table: 588

Shellenbarger, Sue. "Work-Force Study Finds Loyalty Is Weak, Divisions of Race and Gender Are Deep." *Wall Street Journal,* 3 September 1993. Table: 856

Shelley, Kristina J. "More Job Openings—Even More New Entrants: The Outlook for College Graduates, 1992-2005." *Occupational Outlook Quarterly* 38, no. 2 (summer 1994). Table: 81

"Shifting Health Traditions." *Miami Herald,* 2 March 1993. Table: 614

Sleemi, Fehmida. "Collective Bargaining Outlook for 1995." *Monthly Labor Review* 118, no. 1 (January 1995). Tables: 890-891, 893

"Small Investments in Work-Life Programs Pay Off Big." *Personnel Journal* (May 1995). Table: 714

Smith, Bob. "Recruitment Insights for Strategic Workforce Diversity." *HR Focus* (January 1994). Table: 828

Smith, Joel J. "Business Is Blooming on the Net." *Detroit News,* 14 March 1995. Table: 875

"Social Issues at Work." *Training* (October 1993). Table: 814

"Something's in the Air." *Small Business Reports* 19, no. 3 (March 1994). Table: 793

"Sore Workers." *U.S. News & World Report,* 24 April 1995. Table: 785

Stahl, Stephanie, and Jospeh C. Panettieri. "MS Mail Disappoints." *InformationWeek,* 7 November 1994. Table: 876

"The State of Affairs in Work Disability." *Small Business Reports* 19, no. 1 (January 1994). Table: 573

Stevens, Carol. "Who Will Pay Health Bill for Early Retirees?" *Detroit News,* 27 February 1994. Tables: 617, 694

Stipp, David. "Officials Reject Contract Bids on Proof of Poor Safety Records." *Wall Street Journal,* 6 February 1995. Table: 803

"Study Pinpoints the Causes of Stress for Working Women." *HR Focus* 70, no. 9 (September 1993). Table: 806

"Study Pinpoints Where the Job Losses Were During Early '90s." *HR Focus* (January 1995). Table: 335

Sunoo, Brenda Paik. "Managing Strikes, Minimizing Loss." *Personnel Journal* (January 1995). Table: 895

"Survey Identifies Top Morale-Damaging Actions in the Workplace." *HR Focus* (May 1994). Table: 854

"Survey Said...." *Business Marketing* (June 1994). Table: 873

"Survey: Employers, Not Government, Should Provide Childcare." *HR Focus* (April 1994). Table: 707

Szwergold, Jack. "Part-timers Are More Apt to Have Their Hands in the Cookie Jar." *Management Review* (December 1994). Table: 836

"Tax Bite in the 8-Hour Day." *Tax Features* (April 1993). Table: 630

Templet, Paul H. "Jobs and a Clean Environment: Having Them Both." *Environment and Development* (October 1993). Table: 849

Thompson, Roger. "Benefit Costs Hit Record High." *Nation's Business* (February 1995). Table: 592

"To Have and to Have Not." *The Economist,* 12 March 1994. Table: 13

Tyson, James L. "'Ready-Fire-Aim' Layoff Strategy Backfires on Corporate America." *Christian Science Monitor,* 6 February 1995. Table: 905

U.S. Bureau of the Census. *Statistical Abstract of the United States, 1993.* 113th ed. Washington, DC: U.S. Government Printing Office, 1993. Tables: 553, 624

U.S. Bureau of the Census. *Statistical Abstract of the United States, 1994.* 114th ed. Washington, DC: U.S. Government Printing Office, 1994. Tables: 12, 14-15, 29, 31, 33-80, 85-86, 88, 90, 204-206, 266-267, 273, 275-276, 279-284, 287-328, 330, 332, 336-338, 343, 347, 354, 470, 472, 474-475, 479-480, 535-543, 547-552, 554-555, 558-559, 561-564, 566-567, 570, 574-579, 582-587, 589-590, 593, 595-596, 623, 625-627, 632, 640, 643, 649-650, 655, 657, 659, 663, 669, 671-672, 674, 678, 681, 683-685, 687-689, 703, 705-706, 775-776, 780, 789, 818-819, 864, 888-889, 892, 897, 899, 901-902, 904

U.S. Congress. Office of Technology Assessment. *Does Health Insurance Make a Difference? Background Paper.* OTA-BP-H-99. Washington, DC: U.S. Government Printing Office, September 1992. Table: 666

U.S. Department of Commerce. *County and City Data Book, 1994.* 12th ed. Washington, DC: U.S. Government Printing Office, 1994. Tables: 851-852

U.S. Department of Education. Office of Educational Research and Improvement. National Center for Education Statistics. *Digest of Education Statistics, 1994.* NCES 94-115. Lanham, MD: Bernan, November 1994. Tables: 83, 560, 633-634, 636-637, 653, 716, 722, 777-778

U.S. Department of Health and Human Services. Public Health Service. Centers for Disease Control and Prevention. National Center for Health Statistics. *Health Promotion and Disease Prevention: United States, 1990.* Vital and Health Statistics, Series 10, no. 185. Hyattsville, MD: U.S. Department of Health and Human Services, Public Health Service, Centers for Disease Control and Prevention, National Center for Health Statistics, n.d. Table: 812

U.S. Department of Health and Human Services. Public Health Service. Centers for Disease Control and Prevention. National Center for Health Statistics. *Health, United States, 1992.* Hyattsville, MD: Public Health Service, 1993. Table: 615

U.S. Department of Labor. Bureau of Labor Statistics. *Employee Benefits in Medium and Large Private Establishments, 1991.* Bulletin 2422. Washington, DC:

U.S. Government Printing Office, May 1993. Tables: 30, 32, 656, 670, 686, 695-697, 699-702, 704

U.S. Department of Labor. Bureau of Labor Statistics. *Employment and Wages Annual Averages, 1993.* Bulletin 2449. Washington, DC: U.S. Government Printing Office, October 1994. Tables: 339-342, 344-346, 348-352

U.S. Department of Labor. Bureau of Labor Statistics. *Fatal Workplace Injuries in 1991: A Collection of Data and Analysis.* Report 845. Washington, DC: U.S. Government Printing Office, April 1993. Table: 787

U.S. Department of Labor. Bureau of Labor Statistics. *Geographic Profile of Employment and Unemployment, 1993.* Bulletin 2446. Washington, DC: U.S. Government Printing Office, September 1994. Tables: 481-531, 545-546, 556-557

U.S. Department of Labor. Bureau of Labor Statistics. *Occupational Injuries and Illnesses in the United States by Industry, 1991.* Bulletin 2424. Washington, DC: U.S. Government Printing Office, May 1993. Tables: 792, 796

U.S. Department of Labor. Bureau of Labor Statistics. *Occupational Projections and Training Data.* 1994 ed. Bulletin 2451. Washington, DC: U.S. Government Printing Office, May 1994. Tables: 207-265, 715

U.S. Department of Labor. Bureau of Labor Statistics. *Working for US in the 1990's.* Washington, DC: U.S. Department of Labor. Bureau of Labor Statistics, 1993. Table: 82

U.S. Department of Labor. Pension and Welfare Benefits Administration. *Health Benefits and the Workforce.* Washington, DC: U.S. Government Printing Office, 1992. Table: 662

U.S. Department of Labor. Pension and Welfare Benefits Administration. *Trends in Health Benefits.* Washington, DC: U.S. Government Printing Office, 1993. Tables: 628-629, 673

U.S. Equal Employment Opportunity Commission. *Job Patterns for Minorities and Women in Private Industry, 1993.* Washington, DC: U.S. Government Printing Office, 1994. Tables: 89, 268-270, 272, 274, 277

U.S. House Committee on Ways and Means. *Overview of Entitlement Programs, 1993 Green Book: Background Material and Data Programs Within the Jurisdiction of the Committee on Ways and Means.* 103d Cong., 1st sess., 7 July 1993. Washington, DC: U.S. Government Printing Office, 1993. Table: 815

Van Hoof, Kari. "Casual Clothes Are Workplace Trend." *Brandweek,* 18 July 1994. Table: 853

"The Violent Workplace." *Small Business Reports* (March 1994). Table: 823

"Vote for NAFTA Earns Edge in Political $$$." *AFL-CIO News,* 13 December 1993. Table: 850

Waggoner, John. "Dipping Into Funds Early Carries Price." *USA TODAY,* 20 February 1995. Table: 679

Walters, Donna K. H. "Earnings Clout Grows for Women, Study Shows." *Detroit News,* 11 May 1995. Table: 635

"When One Job Is Not Enough." *Washington Post,* 12 September 1994. Table: 565

"Who Are the Telecommuters?" *HR Focus* (November 1994). Tables: 883-884

"Who Are the Working Poor?" *National Consumers League Bulletin* 55, no. 6 (November/December 1993). Table: 641

"Who Sues Officers and Directors?" *Wall Street Journal,* 11 March 1994. Table: 844

"Who Works From Home." *USA TODAY,* 21 September 1994. Tables: 881-882

"Who's Hiring?" *Manpower Comments* (December 1993). Table: 719

Williamson, Lisa. "Union Mergers: 1985-94 Update." *Monthly Labor Review* 118, no. 2 (February 1995). Table: 903

"Work Accidents." *Traffic Safety* (November/December 1993). Table: 334

"Work Satisfaction Linked to Manager." *HR Magazine* (May 1994). Table: 855

"Work-at-Homers Work Habits." *Advertising Age,* 14 March 1994. Table: 872

"Workers' Compensation Claims." *Occupational Health and Safety* 62, no. 10 (October 1993). Table: 816

"Workers' Compensation Medical Cost Distribution." *Risk Management* (October 1994). Table: 817

"Workplace Violence Taking Toll on Quality of Life, Report Says." *St. Louis Post-Dispatch,* 25 July 1994. Table: 821

Zolkos, Rodd. "Employer Survey Dispels Fears Over Family Leaves." *Business Insurance,* 7 March 1994. Table: 841

Occupation Index

This index presents all occupations covered in *SHWA* by their official Bureau of Labor Statistics job titles, alternate career names, occupation names contained within job titles, popular names, and synonymous or related names. Each citation is followed by table and page reference numbers. Page references do not necessarily identify the page on which a table begins. In the cases where tables span two or more pages, references point to the page on which the index term appears—which may be the second or subsequent page of a table. Cross-references have been added to index citations to facilitate the location of related topics and tables.

Numbers following p. or pp. are page references. Numbers in [ ] are table references.

Numbers following p. or pp. are page references. Numbers in [ ] are table references.

Numbers following p. or pp. are page references. Numbers in [ ] are table references.

Numbers following p. or pp. are page references. Numbers in [ ] are table references.

Occupation Index

883

Numbers following p. or pp. are page references. Numbers in [ ] are table references.

Numbers following p. or pp. are page references. Numbers in [ ] are table references.

Occupation Index

Conservation workers *See:* Forest and conservation workers
Construction and building inspectors
— job openings, p. 201 [235]
Construction and maintenance painters and paperhangers *See:* Painters and paperhangers, construction and maintenance
Construction laborers
— earnings, p. 20 [23]
— employment by metropolitan area, p. 83 [111]
— unemployment, p. 52 [79]
Construction managers
— job openings, p. 202 [236]
Construction supervisors
— earnings, p. 20 [23]
— employment by metropolitan area, p. 84 [112]
Construction trade helpers *See:* Helpers, construction trades
Construction trades
See also: specific construction trades
— blacks, p. 33 [41]
— employed, p. 33 [41]
— Hispanics, p. 33 [41]
— job openings, p. 188 [217]
— median weekly earnings, p. 11 [14]
— unemployment, p. 52 [79]
— women, p. 33 [41]
Consultants *See:* Management consultants
Contracting specialists
— college graduates hired by federal government, p. 55 [82]
Cooking and roasting machine operators and tenders, food and tobacco
— job openings, p. 199 [232]
Cooks
See also: specific types of cooks
— blacks, p. 38 [51]
— employed, p. 38 [51]
— employment by metropolitan area, p. 85 [113]
— Hispanics, p. 38 [51]
— job growth, p. 181 [206]
— job openings, p. 192 [222]
— women, p. 38 [51]
Cooks, institution or cafeteria
— employment by industry, p. 364 [414]
— job openings, p. 192 [222]
Cooks, private household
— job openings, p. 214 [252]
Cooks, restaurant
— earnings, p. 23 [26]
— employment by industry, p. 396 [447]
— job openings, p. 192 [222]
Cooks, short order and fast food
— employment by industry, p. 403 [455]
— job openings, p. 192 [222]
Copy markers *See:* Proofreaders and copy markers
Correction officers
— blacks, p. 47 [68]
— employed, p. 47 [68]

Correction officers continued:
— employment by industry, p. 331 [380]
— growth, p. 180 [205]
— Hispanics, p. 47 [68]
— job openings, p. 215 [253]
— women, p. 47 [68]
Correctional institution officers *See:* Correction officers
Corrective therapy assistants and aides *See:* Physical and corrective therapy assistants and aides
Correspondence clerks
— job openings, p. 216 [254]
Correspondents *See:* Reporters and correspondents
Cosmetologists *See:* Hairdressers, hairstylists, and cosmetologists
Cost and rate clerks *See:* Billing, cost, and rate clerks
Cost estimators
— job openings, p. 201 [235]
Counselors
— job openings, p. 219 [259]
Counselors, loan *See:* Loan officers and counselors
Counter clerks, sales *See:* Sales counter clerks
Court clerks
— job openings, p. 185 [212]
Court reporters *See:* Stenographers
Craft artists *See:* Painters, sculptors, craft artists, and artist printmakers
Craft occupations, precision *See:* Precision production, craft, and repair occupations
Crane and tower operators
— job openings, p. 221 [262]
— occupational and employer tenure, p. 60 [88]
Credit analysts
— job openings, p. 201 [235]
Credit authorizers
— job openings, p. 185 [212]
Credit checkers
— blacks, p. 34 [42]
— employed, p. 34 [42]
— Hispanics, p. 34 [42]
— job openings, p. 185 [212]
— women, p. 34 [42]
Credit clerks *See:* Loan and credit clerks
Criminal investigators
— college graduates hired by federal government, p. 55 [82]
Crossing guards
— job openings, p. 215 [253]
Crushing and mixing machine operators and tenders
— job openings, p. 199 [232]
Curators, archivists, museum technicians, and restorers
— blacks, p. 34 [42]
— employed, p. 34 [42]
— Hispanics, p. 34 [42]
— job openings, p. 219 [259]
— women, p. 34 [42]
Custom tailors and sewers
— earnings, p. 20 [23]
— job openings, p. 212 [249]
Customer service representatives, utilities
— job openings, p. 185 [212]

Numbers following p. or pp. are page references. Numbers in [ ] are table references.

Numbers following p. or pp. are page references. Numbers in [ ] are table references.

Occupation Index

Numbers following p. or pp. are page references. Numbers in [ ] are table references.

Numbers following p. or pp. are page references. Numbers in [ ] are table references.

Numbers following p. or pp. are page references. Numbers in [ ] are table references.

Numbers following p. or pp. are page references. Numbers in [ ] are table references.

Numbers following p. or pp. are page references. Numbers in [ ] are table references.

Numbers following p. or pp. are page references. Numbers in [ ] are table references.

Numbers following p. or pp. are page references. Numbers in [ ] are table references.

Numbers following p. or pp. are page references. Numbers in [ ] are table references.

Occupation Index

Numbers following p. or pp. are page references. Numbers in [ ] are table references.

Occupation Index

Numbers following p. or pp. are page references. Numbers in [ ] are table references.

897

Numbers following p. or pp. are page references. Numbers in [ ] are table references.

Mathematical science managers *See:* Engineering, mathematical, and natural science managers
Mathematical scientists *See:* Mathematicians and mathematical scientists
Mathematicians and mathematical scientists
— bachelor's degree recipients, p. 56 [83]
— blacks, p. 44 [62]
— earnings, p. 22 [25]
— employed, p. 44 [62]
— Hispanics, p. 44 [62]
— job openings, p. 188 [216]
— women, p. 44 [62]
Mathematics technicians *See:* Science and mathematics technicians
Mayors
— earnings, p. 10 [13]
Measurers, recordkeeping *See:* Weighers, measurers, checkers, and samplers, recordkeeping
Measuring opticians *See:* Opticians, dispensing and measuring
Meat cutters *See:* Butchers and meat cutters
Meat, poultry, and fish cutters and trimmers, hand
See also: Butchers and meat cutters
— job openings, p. 193 [224]
Mechanic and repairer supervisors
— employment by metropolitan area, p. 136 [162]
Mechanical engineers
— blacks, p. 31 [36]
— employed, p. 31 [36]
— employment by industry, p. 378 [428]
— Hispanics, p. 31 [36]
— job openings, p. 191 [220]
— women, p. 31 [36]
Mechanics, installers, and repairers
See also: specific types of mechanics, installers, and repairers
— blacks, p. 44 [63]
— employed, p. 44 [63]
— employment by industry, p. 379 [429]
— Hispanics, p. 44 [63]
— job openings, p. 204 [238]
— median weekly earnings, p. 11 [14]
— unemployment, p. 52 [79]
— women, p. 44 [63]
Medical appliance technicians *See:* Dental laboratory and medical appliance technicians
Medical assistants
— growth, p. 180 [205]
— job openings, p. 196 [227]
Medical laboratory technologists and technicians *See:* Clinical lab technologists and technicians
Medical officers
— college graduates hired by federal government, p. 55 [82]
Medical records technicians
See also: Records processing occupations
— blacks, p. 41 [56]
— employed, p. 41 [56]
— growth, p. 180 [205]

Medical records technicians continued:
— Hispanics, p. 41 [56]
— job openings, p. 196 [228]
— women, p. 41 [56]
Medical scientists
— job openings, p. 198 [231]
Medical secretaries
— employment by industry, p. 380 [430]
— job openings, p. 217 [256]
Medical technolgists *See:* Health technicians and technologists
Medicine and health managers
See also: Hospital administrators
— blacks, p. 36 [46]
— employed, p. 36 [46]
— Hispanics, p. 36 [46]
— women, p. 36 [46]
Merchandise order clerks *See:* Order clerks, materials, merchandise, and service
Messengers
— blacks, p. 42 [59]
— employed, p. 42 [59]
— Hispanics, p. 42 [59]
— job openings, p. 201 [234]
— women, p. 42 [59]
Metal and plastic drilling and boring machine tool setters and set-up operators *See:* Drilling and boring machine tool setters and set-up operators, metal and plastic
Metal and plastic machine setters, operators, and related workers
— job openings, p. 205 [239]
Metal and plastic processing machine setters, operators, and related workers
See also: specific types of metal and plastic processing machine setters, operators, and related workers
— job openings, p. 205 [239]
Metal electrolytic plating machine operators, tenders, setters, and set-up operators *See:* Electrolytic plating machine operators, tenders, setters, and set-up operators, metal and plastic
Metal fabricating machine setters, operators, and related workers
See also: specific types of metal fabricating machine setters, operators, and related workers
— job openings, p. 206 [240]
Metal fabricators, structural metal products
— job openings, p. 206 [240]
Metal grinding machine setters and set-up operators *See:* Grinding machine setters and set-up operators, metal and plastic
Metal heat treating machine operators and tenders *See:* Heat treating machine operators and tenders, metal and plastic
Metal heaters *See:* Heaters, metal and plastic
Metal heating equipment setters and set-up operators *See:* Heating equipment setters and set-up operators, metal and plastic
Metal lathe and turning machine tool setters and set-up operators *See:* Lathe and turning machine tool setters and set-up operators, metal and plastic

Numbers following p. or pp. are page references. Numbers in [ ] are table references.

899

Occupation Index

Numbers following p. or pp. are page references. Numbers in [ ] are table references.

Occupation Index

Numbers following p. or pp. are page references. Numbers in [ ] are table references.

901

Numbers following p. or pp. are page references. Numbers in [ ] are table references.

Occupation Index

Numbers following p. or pp. are page references. Numbers in [ ] are table references.

904

Numbers following p. or pp. are page references. Numbers in [ ] are table references.

Occupation Index

Private household workers continued:
— unemployment, p. 52 [79]
— women, p. 46 [67]
Process programmers See: Programmers, numerical, tool, and process control
Procurement clerks
— job openings, p. 203 [237]
Producers, directors, actors, and entertainers
— blacks, pp. 31, 35, 53 [37, 45, 80]
— earnings, pp. 10, 14 [13, 17]
— employed, pp. 31, 35, 53 [37, 45, 80]
— growth, p. 180 [205]
— Hispanics, pp. 31, 35, 53 [37, 45, 80]
— job openings, p. 224 [265]
— women, pp. 31, 35, 53 [37, 45, 80]
Production coordinators
— blacks, p. 43 [61]
— employed, p. 43 [61]
— Hispanics, p. 43 [61]
— women, p. 43 [61]
Production inspectors, checkers, and examiners
— blacks, p. 42 [58]
— employed, p. 42 [58]
— employment by metropolitan area, p. 151 [176]
— Hispanics, p. 42 [58]
— women, p. 42 [58]
Production managers, industrial See: Industrial production managers
Production occupation supervisors
— employment by metropolitan area, p. 152 [177]
Production occupations, precision
See also: specific precision production occupations
— blacks, p. 46 [66]
— employed, p. 46 [66]
— Hispanics, p. 46 [66]
— job openings, p. 211 [248]
— women, p. 46 [66]
Production, planning, and expediting clerks
— employment by industry, p. 390 [442]
— job openings, p. 203 [237]
Production prepress printing workers See: Prepress printing workers, production
Production samplers and weighers
— blacks, p. 42 [58]
— employed, p. 42 [58]
— Hispanics, p. 42 [58]
— women, p. 42 [58]
Production testers
— blacks, p. 42 [58]
— employed, p. 42 [58]
— Hispanics, p. 42 [58]
— women, p. 42 [58]
Production workers See: Precision production, craft, and repair occupations
Professional specialty occupations
See also: Managerial and administrative occupations; specific occupations
— American Indians and Alaskan Natives, p. 226 [268]

Professional specialty occupations continued:
— Asians and Pacific Islanders, p. 227 [269]
— benefits, p. 8 [11]
— benefits of part-time workers, p. 580 [656]
— blacks, pp. 43, 228 [60, 270]
— college graduates in the labor force, p. 54 [81]
— displaced workers, p. 57 [84]
— earnings, p. 12 [15]
— earnings of union members, p. 57 [85]
— employed, p. 43 [60]
— employee benefit financing sources, p. 26 [30]
— employee benefits, pp. 28, 579, 581 [32, 655, 657]
— employment, p. 61 [90]
— employment by industry, p. 374 [424]
— employment growth, p. 472 [534]
— flexible work schedules, p. 225 [266]
— group health plans, p. 27 [31]
— Hispanics, pp. 43, 229 [60, 272]
— holidays, p. 612 [696]
— home workers, p. 229 [273]
— insurance plans, pp. 591, 593 [669, 671]
— insurance plans of part-time workers, p. 592 [670]
— job openings, p. 182 [207]
— jury duty leave, p. 613 [697]
— local government employee salaries, p. 25 [29]
— local government employees, p. 50 [75]
— local government employer costs per hour worked, p. 9 [12]
— median weekly earnings, p. 11 [14]
— men, pp. 61, 226-230, 232 [89, 268-270, 272, 274, 277]
— minorities, p. 230 [274]
— multiple job holders, p. 231 [275]
— paid funeral leave, p. 611 [695]
— paid lunch time, p. 615 [699]
— paid military leave, p. 616 [700]
— paid personal leave days, p. 617 [701]
— paid rest time, p. 617 [702]
— pension plans, p. 29 [33]
— retirement and savings plans, pp. 604, 606 [685, 687]
— retirement and savings plans of part-time workers, p. 605 [686]
— self-employed, p. 231 [276]
— state government employee salaries, p. 25 [29]
— state government employees, p. 50 [75]
— state government employer costs per hour worked, p. 9 [12]
— time off, p. 620 [705]
— time off of full-time workers, p. 618 [703]
— time off of part-time workers, p. 619 [704]
— unemployment, p. 52 [79]
— union membership or representation, p. 58 [86]
— vacation days, p. 612 [696]
— wages and salaries, p. 8 [11]
— whites, p. 232 [277]
— women, pp. 43, 61, 226-230, 232 [60, 89, 268-270, 272, 274, 277]
— workers on shift schedules, p. 226 [267]
Professional workers See: Professional specialty occupations
Professors See: College and university faculty

Numbers following p. or pp. are page references. Numbers in [ ] are table references.

906

Numbers following p. or pp. are page references. Numbers in [ ] are table references.

Occupation Index

Numbers following p. or pp. are page references. Numbers in [ ] are table references.

Numbers following p. or pp. are page references. Numbers in [ ] are table references.

Occupation Index

Numbers following p. or pp. are page references. Numbers in [ ] are table references.

Numbers following p. or pp. are page references. Numbers in [ ] are table references.

Occupation Index

Numbers following p. or pp. are page references. Numbers in [ ] are table references.

Numbers following p. or pp. are page references. Numbers in [ ] are table references.

Occupation Index

Numbers following p. or pp. are page references. Numbers in [ ] are table references.

Numbers following p. or pp. are page references. Numbers in [ ] are table references.

Numbers following p. or pp. are page references. Numbers in [ ] are table references.

Keyword Index

This index allows users to access all subjects, issues, government agencies, companies, unions, programs, associations, schools, educational institutions, personal names, and locations cited in the tables of *SHWA*. Each citation is followed by table and page reference numbers. Page references do not necessarily identify the page on which a table begins. In the cases where tables span two or more pages, references point to the page on which the index term appears—which may be the second or subsequent page of a table. Cross-references have been added to index citations to facilitate the location of related topics and tables.

Numbers following p. or pp. are page references. Numbers in [ ] are table references.

Numbers following p. or pp. are page references. Numbers in [ ] are table references.

Keyword Index

Numbers following p. or pp. are page references. Numbers in [ ] are table references.

Numbers following p. or pp. are page references. Numbers in [ ] are table references.

Keyword Index

Numbers following p. or pp. are page references. Numbers in [ ] are table references.

Numbers following p. or pp. are page references. Numbers in [ ] are table references.

Numbers following p. or pp. are page references. Numbers in [ ] are table references.

Keyword Index

Numbers following p. or pp. are page references. Numbers in [ ] are table references.

Numbers following p. or pp. are page references. Numbers in [ ] are table references.

Numbers following p. or pp. are page references. Numbers in [ ] are table references.

Keyword Index

Numbers following p. or pp. are page references. Numbers in [ ] are table references.

Numbers following p. or pp. are page references. Numbers in [ ] are table references.

Numbers following p. or pp. are page references. Numbers in [ ] are table references.

Numbers following p. or pp. are page references. Numbers in [ ] are table references.

Keyword Index

Numbers following p. or pp. are page references. Numbers in [ ] are table references.

Numbers following p. or pp. are page references. Numbers in [ ] are table references.

Keyword Index

Blood pressure
— cost of high risk health behaviors, p. 541 [608]
Blood tests
— drug testing, p. 787 [808]
Boat building and repairing *See:* Ship and boat building and repairing
Boca Raton, Florida
— annual pay, p. 567 [640]
— farm workers, p. 98 [126]
— groundskeepers and gardeners, p. 110 [138]
— private household cleaners and servants, p. 150 [175]
— real estate sales occupations, p. 156 [181]
— securities and financial services sales occupations, p. 163 [188]
Body systems
— work injuries, p. 782 [800]
Boeing Company
— downsizing, p. 861 [905]
Bond mutual funds
— 401(k) investment options, p. 597 [676]
Bonds, Barry
— strike-related pay losses, p. 850 [894]
Bonuses
   See also: Incentives
— employee benefits in state and local government, p. 582 [659]
— employer costs, p. 531 [595]
— full-time workers, p. 579 [655]
— part-time workers, pp. 580, 605 [656, 686]
— pay-for-performanace program use, p. 534 [599]
— pay outs, p. 570 [644]
— small establishments, p. 581 [657]
— state and local government, p. 582 [659]
Bookbinding *See:* Blankbooks and bookbinding
Bookkeeping *See:* Accounting, auditing, and bookeeping
Books and magazines
— business travel reimbursement, p. 538 [605]
— employees and earnings, p. 253 [307]
Boston, Massachusetts
— accountants and auditors, p. 63 [91]
— administrative support occupations, p. 64 [92]
— annual pay, p. 565 [640]
— apparel sales workers, p. 65 [93]
— assemblers, p. 66 [94]
— automobile mechanics, p. 67 [95]
— bank tellers, p. 68 [96]
— bartenders, p. 69 [97]
— bookkeeping, accounting, and auditing clerks, p. 70 [98]
— bus drivers, p. 71 [99]
— business service sales occupations, p. 72 [100]
— business travel per diem costs, p. 537 [604]
— butchers and meat cutters, p. 73 [101]
— carpenters, p. 74 [102]
— cashiers, p. 75 [103]
— city government employment and payroll, p. 242 [290]
— civilian labor force, p. 480 [542]
— clergy, p. 76 [104]
— clinical laboratory technologists and technicians, p. 77

Boston, Massachusetts continued:
   [105]
— commodity sales workers, p. 78 [106]
— computer operators, p. 79 [107]
— computer programmers, p. 80 [108]
— computer systems analysts and scientists, p. 81 [109]
— construction and maintenance painters, p. 82 [110]
— construction laborers, p. 83 [111]
— construction supervisors, p. 84 [112]
— cooks, p. 85 [113]
— data entry keyers, p. 86 [114]
— designers, p. 87 [115]
— drafting occupations, p. 88 [116]
— early childhood teachers' assistants, p. 89 [117]
— education administrators, p. 90 [118]
— electrical and electronic engineers, p. 91 [119]
— electrical and electronic equipment assemblers, p. 92 [120]
— electrical and electronic technicians, p. 93 [121]
— electricians, p. 94 [122]
— elementary school teachers, p. 95 [123]
— employee sick days, p. 778 [793]
— engineers, p. 96 [124]
— experienced unemployed, p. 175 [200]
— family child care providers, p. 97 [125]
— financial managers, p. 100 [128]
— financial officers, p. 101 [129]
— food preparation and service occupation supervisors, p. 102 [130]
— food preparation occupations, p. 103 [131]
— food service and lodging managers, p. 104 [132]
— freight, stock, and material handlers, p. 105 [133]
— garage and service station occupations, p. 106 [134]
— general maintenance mechanics and repairers, p. 107 [135]
— general office clerks, p. 108 [136]
— general office supervisors, p. 109 [137]
— groundskeepers and gardeners, p. 110 [138]
— guards and police, p. 111 [139]
— hairdressers, hairstylists, and cosmetologists, p. 112 [140]
— hand packers and packagers, p. 113 [141]
— health technologists and technicians, p. 114 [142]
— industrial machinery repairers, p. 116 [143]
— industrial truck and tractor equipment operators, p. 117 [144]
— insurance adjusters, examiners, and investigators, p. 118 [145]
— insurance sales occupations, p. 119 [146]
— investigators and adjusters, p. 120 [147]
— janitors, cleaners, maids, and housekeeping cleaners, p. 121 [148]
— laborers, p. 122 [149]
— lawyers, p. 123 [150]
— licensed practical nurses, p. 124 [151]
— machine operators, pp. 125-127 [152-154]
— machinists, p. 129 [155]
— maids and housemen, p. 130 [156]
— management analysts, p. 131 [157]
— management-related occupations, p. 132 [158]
— managers and administrators, pp. 133-134 [159-160]
— marketing, advertising, and public relations managers, p. 135

Numbers following p. or pp. are page references. Numbers in [ ] are table references.

Keyword Index

Numbers following p. or pp. are page references. Numbers in [ ] are table references.

937

Numbers following p. or pp. are page references. Numbers in [ ] are table references.

938

Numbers following p. or pp. are page references. Numbers in [ ] are table references.

Keyword Index

Numbers following p. or pp. are page references. Numbers in [ ] are table references.

940

Keyword Index

Numbers following p. or pp. are page references. Numbers in [ ] are table references.

Numbers following p. or pp. are page references. Numbers in [ ] are table references.

942

Keyword Index

Numbers following p. or pp. are page references. Numbers in [ ] are table references.

943

Numbers following p. or pp. are page references. Numbers in [ ] are table references.

Keyword Index

Numbers following p. or pp. are page references. Numbers in [ ] are table references.

945

Numbers following p. or pp. are page references. Numbers in [ ] are table references.

Numbers following p. or pp. are page references. Numbers in [ ] are table references.

Numbers following p. or pp. are page references. Numbers in [ ] are table references.

Keyword Index

Numbers following p. or pp. are page references. Numbers in [ ] are table references.

Numbers following p. or pp. are page references. Numbers in [ ] are table references.

Communications, telephone *See:* Telephone communications
Community colleges
— job training, p. 762 [776]
Community development *See:* Housing and community development
Commuting
See also: Carpools; Local and interurban passenger transit
— means of transportation, pp. 818-819 [851-852]
— part-time workers, p. 580 [656]
Company cars
— executive perks, p. 584 [661]
Company planes
— executive perks, p. 584 [661]
Company stock
— 401(k) investment options, p. 597 [676]
— defined contribution retirement plans, p. 597 [677]
Compaq Computer Corp.
— employment growth, p. 426 [478]
Compensation
See also: Earnings
— broadbanding, p. 534 [598]
— collective bargaining settlements, p. 844 [889]
— compensation per hour, pp. 826-829 [860, 862-864]
— cost to self-employed, p. 531 [594]
— local government employer costs per hour worked, pp. 9, 238 [12, 284]
— real compensation per hour, pp. 827-828 [862-863]
— real hourly compensation, p. 829 [864]
— state government employer costs per hour worked, pp. 9, 238 [12, 284]
— variable pay programs, p. 535 [600]
— worker resignations, p. 823 [857]
Competitors
— liability claims against directors and officers, p. 813 [844]
Compression
— fatal work injuries, p. 775 [789]
Compressors *See:* Pumps and compressors
CompUSA Inc.
— employment growth, p. 426 [478]
CompuServe
— use by executives, p. 837 [878]
Computer and data processing services
— computer operators, p. 326 [376]
— computer programmers, p. 327 [377]
— data entry keyers, p. 333 [382]
— employees and earnings, p. 254 [309]
— employment, pp. 262, 304 [319, 354]
— employment projections, p. 304 [354]
— engineering, mathematical, and natural science managers, p. 341 [390]
— marketing, advertising, and public relations managers, p. 375 [425]
— systems analysts, p. 409 [461]
Computer and information sciences
— academic awards and degrees, p. 626 [715]
— bachelor's degree recipients, p. 56 [83]
— doctoral degree recipients, p. 629 [718]

Computer and information sciences continued:
— earnings, p. 564 [639]
— further education of bachelor's degree recipients, p. 627 [716]
Computer and office equipment
See also: specific types of computers and office equipment
— computer programmers, p. 328 [377]
— electrical and electronic engineers, p. 338 [387]
— employees and earnings, p. 249 [299]
— employment, p. 304 [354]
— employment projections, p. 304 [354]
— engineering, mathematical, and natural science managers, p. 341 [390]
— engineering technicians, p. 342 [391]
— production, planning, and expediting clerks, p. 391 [442]
— purchasing agents, p. 392 [443]
— security, p. 808 [835]
Computer engineering
— academic awards and degrees, p. 630 [719]
Computer programming
— academic awards and degrees, p. 630 [719]
Concrete, gypsum, and plaster products
— employees and earnings, p. 257 [312]
— output per hour, p. 418 [470]
— truck drivers, p. 413 [465]
Concrete work
— carpenters, p. 320 [369]
— construction trade helpers, p. 330 [379]
Confectionery products *See:* Sugar and confectionery products
Confidentiality
— abuse, p. 809 [838]
Congress *See:* U.S. Congress; U.S. House of Representatives
Congress of Industrial Organizations (CIO)
— membership of affiliated unions, p. 854 [899]
— mergers, p. 859 [903]
Connecticut
— agriculture, p. 281 [339]
— average annual pay, p. 568 [643]
— civilian labor force, p. 434 [487]
— civilian labor force characteristics, p. 476 [539]
— civilian noninstitutionalized population, p. 434 [487]
— construction, p. 282 [340]
— construction employees, p. 265 [323]
— earnings in state and local government, p. 255 [310]
— educational attainment, p. 649 [729]
— employed men with work disabilities, p. 506 [568]
— employed women with work disabilities, p. 510 [571]
— employment, p. 434 [487]
— employment in state and local government, p. 255 [310]
— employment status of blacks, p. 434 [487]
— employment status of Hispanics, p. 434 [487]
— employment status of married persons, p. 434 [487]
— employment status of men, p. 434 [487]
— employment status of single persons, p. 434 [487]
— employment status of teens, p. 434 [487]
— employment status of whites, p. 434 [487]
— employment status of women, p. 434 [487]

Keyword Index

Numbers following p. or pp. are page references. Numbers in [ ] are table references.

Connecticut continued:
— enrollment in higher education, p. 765 [779]
— federal government, p. 284 [341]
— financial services, p. 286 [342]
— financial services employees, p. 265 [323]
— fishing, p. 281 [339]
— forestry, p. 281 [339]
— government employees, p. 265 [323]
— insurance, p. 286 [342]
— insurance industry employees, p. 265 [323]
— jury duty pay, p. 614 [698]
— local government, p. 289 [344]
— manufacturing, p. 290 [345]
— manufacturing employees, p. 265 [323]
— mining, p. 292 [346]
— mining employees, p. 265 [323]
— paid civilian employment in federal government, p. 267 [324]
— pensions, p. 599 [680]
— public utilities, p. 299 [351]
— public utilities employees, p. 265 [323]
— real estate, p. 286 [342]
— real estate employees, p. 265 [323]
— retail trade, p. 295 [348]
— retail trade employees, p. 265 [323]
— services, p. 296 [349]
— services sector employees, p. 265 [323]
— Social Security benefits, beneficiaries, and payments, p. 551 [625]
— state and local government employment, p. 270 [327]
— state government, p. 298 [350]
— transportation, p. 299 [351]
— transportation employees, p. 265 [323]
— unemployed, p. 489 [549]
— unemployed men with work disabilities, p. 508 [569]
— unemployed women with work disabilities, p. 512 [572]
— unemployment, p. 434 [487]
— wholesale trade, p. 301 [352]
— wholesale trade employees, p. 265 [323]
— work disability rates, p. 513 [573]
— workers' compensation payments, p. 795 [819]
Conner Peripherals Inc.
— employment growth, p. 426 [478]
Conrail
— pension income, p. 601 [682]
Conservation and renewable natural resources
— academic awards and degrees, p. 626 [715]
Consolidated Omnibus Budget Reconcilliation Act
— health plan coverage, p. 585 [662]
Construction
— academic awards and degrees, p. 626 [715]
— all occupations, p. 303 [353]
— annual wages, p. 282 [340]
— blue-collar worker supervisors, p. 315 [365]
— bookkeeping, accounting, and auditing clerks, p. 316 [366]
— bus and truck mechanics and diesel engine specialists, p. 318 [367]

Construction continued:
— carpenters, p. 320 [369]
— collective bargaining agreements, p. 279 [336]
— compensation, p. 233 [279]
— construction and maintenance painters and paperhangers, p. 328 [378]
— construction trade helpers, p. 330 [379]
— drafting occupations, p. 335 [384]
— earnings, p. 236 [282]
— earnings of union members, p. 279 [337]
— electricians, p. 339 [388]
— employees, p. 265 [323]
— employees and earnings, p. 244 [291]
— employees, hours, and earnings, p. 293 [347]
— employment, pp. 261, 282, 303 [319, 340, 354]
— employment projections, p. 303 [354]
— establishments, p. 282 [340]
— financial managers, p. 345 [395]
— general managers and top executives, p. 352 [402]
— general office clerks, p. 353 [403]
— general utility maintenance repairers, p. 354 [404]
— groundskeepers and gardeners, p. 350 [400]
— health insurance, p. 239 [286]
— injury and illness incidence rates, p. 274 [332]
— liability claims against directors and officers, p. 812 [843]
— mechanics, installers, and repairers, p. 379 [429]
— minimum wage, p. 237 [283]
— multiple job holders, p. 422 [474]
— plumbers, pipefitters, and steamfitters, p. 385 [435]
— productivity, p. 420 [471]
— purchasing agents, p. 392 [443]
— secretaries, p. 403 [454]
— self-employed, p. 423 [475]
— truck drivers, p. 413 [465]
— unemployment rates, p. 271 [328]
— union membership, p. 280 [338]
— wages and salaries, p. 233 [279]
— weekly wages, p. 282 [340]
— welders and cutters, p. 417 [469]
— work fatalities, p. 277 [334]
Construction and related machinery
— employees and earnings, p. 248 [299]
— machinists, p. 372 [422]
— output per hour, p. 418 [470]
— welders and cutters, p. 417 [469]
Construction, heavy See: Heavy construction
Construction, highway and street See: Highway and street construction
Consumer Price Index
— earnings, p. 530 [593]
Containers and boxes, paperboard See: Paperboard containers and boxes
Containers, metal shipping See: Metal cans and shipping containers
Containers, wood See: Wood containers
Controlling devices See: Measuring and controlling devices
Conversion Industries
— earnings of John McGrain, p. 10 [13]

Numbers following p. or pp. are page references. Numbers in [ ] are table references.

952

Numbers following p. or pp. are page references. Numbers in [ ] are table references.

Keyword Index

Numbers following p. or pp. are page references. Numbers in [ ] are table references.

Keyword Index

Numbers following p. or pp. are page references. Numbers in [ ] are table references.

955

Numbers following p. or pp. are page references. Numbers in [ ] are table references.

Keyword Index

Numbers following p. or pp. are page references. Numbers in [ ] are table references.

Numbers following p. or pp. are page references. Numbers in [ ] are table references.

Keyword Index

Numbers following p. or pp. are page references. Numbers in [ ] are table references.

Numbers following p. or pp. are page references. Numbers in [ ] are table references.

Keyword Index

Numbers following p. or pp. are page references. Numbers in [ ] are table references.

Keyword Index

Numbers following p. or pp. are page references. Numbers in [ ] are table references.

Numbers following p. or pp. are page references. Numbers in [ ] are table references.

964

Keyword Index

Numbers following p. or pp. are page references. Numbers in [ ] are table references.

Numbers following p. or pp. are page references. Numbers in [ ] are table references.

Numbers following p. or pp. are page references. Numbers in [ ] are table references.

967

Keyword Index

Numbers following p. or pp. are page references. Numbers in [ ] are table references.

Numbers following p. or pp. are page references. Numbers in [ ] are table references.

Numbers following p. or pp. are page references. Numbers in [ ] are table references.

Numbers following p. or pp. are page references. Numbers in [ ] are table references.

971

Keyword Index

Numbers following p. or pp. are page references. Numbers in [ ] are table references.

Keyword Index

Numbers following p. or pp. are page references. Numbers in [ ] are table references.

973

Numbers following p. or pp. are page references. Numbers in [ ] are table references.

Numbers following p. or pp. are page references. Numbers in [ ] are table references.

Numbers following p. or pp. are page references. Numbers in [ ] are table references.

Keyword Index

Numbers following p. or pp. are page references. Numbers in [ ] are table references.

Numbers following p. or pp. are page references. Numbers in [ ] are table references.

978

Numbers following p. or pp. are page references. Numbers in [ ] are table references.

979

Numbers following p. or pp. are page references. Numbers in [ ] are table references.

Numbers following p. or pp. are page references. Numbers in [ ] are table references.

981

Numbers following p. or pp. are page references. Numbers in [ ] are table references.

Numbers following p. or pp. are page references. Numbers in [ ] are table references.

983

Numbers following p. or pp. are page references. Numbers in [ ] are table references.

Keyword Index

Numbers following p. or pp. are page references. Numbers in [ ] are table references.

Keyword Index

Numbers following p. or pp. are page references. Numbers in [ ] are table references.

987

Numbers following p. or pp. are page references. Numbers in [ ] are table references.

Keyword Index

Numbers following p. or pp. are page references. Numbers in [ ] are table references.

Numbers following p. or pp. are page references. Numbers in [ ] are table references.

Keyword Index

Numbers following p. or pp. are page references. Numbers in [ ] are table references.

991

Hospitals continued:
— secretaries, p. 403 [454]
— short order and fast food cooks, p. 404 [455]
— social workers, p. 404 [456]
— switchboard operators, p. 408 [460]
— telephone operators, p. 411 [463]
— typists and word processors, p. 414 [466]
— vocational education and training teachers and
    instructors, p. 415 [467]
— waiters and waitresses, p. 416 [468]
— workers' compensation medical costs, p. 794 [817]
**Hotel Employees and Restaurant Employees
International Union**
— union membership, p. 855 [899]
Hotels and lodging places
— academic awards and degrees, p. 630 [719]
— bartenders, p. 312 [362]
— business travel expenses, p. 539 [606]
— butchers and meat cutters, p. 319 [368]
— cashiers, p. 321 [370]
— child care workers, p. 322 [371]
— dining room and cafeteria attendants and bar helpers,
    p. 334 [383]
— employees and earnings, p. 254 [309]
— employment, pp. 262, 304 [319, 354]
— employment projections, p. 304 [354]
— food counter, fountain, and related workers, p. 347 [397]
— food service and lodging managers, p. 349 [399]
— general utility maintenance repairers, p. 354 [404]
— groundskeepers and gardeners, p. 350 [400]
— guards and police, p. 355 [405]
— injury and illness incidence rates, p. 275 [332]
— institution or cafeteria cooks, p. 364 [414]
— janitors, cleaners, maids, and housekeeping cleaners,
    p. 366 [416]
— output per hour, p. 419 [470]
— productivity, p. 420 [471]
— restaurant cooks, p. 396 [447]
— restaurant, lounge, or coffee shop hosts and
    hostesses, p. 397 [448]
— switchboard operators, p. 408 [460]
— telephone operators, p. 411 [463]
— waiters and waitresses, p. 416 [468]
— workplace violence, p. 800 [825]
Hours
— construction, p. 293 [347]
— financial services, p. 293 [347]
— government employees, p. 293 [347]
— high school seniors, p. 500 [560]
— hours at work, pp. 496-497, 829 [556-557, 864]
— insurance, p. 293 [347]
— manufacturing, p. 293 [347]
— manufacturing productivity percent changes, p. 826 [860]
— mining, p. 293 [347]
— public utilities, p. 293 [347]
— real estate, p. 293 [347]
— retail trade, p. 293 [347]
— services, p. 293 [347]

Hours continued:
— telecommuters, p. 840 [883]
— transportation, p. 293 [347]
— weekly, p. 499 [559]
— wholesale trade, p. 293 [347]
House of Representatives, U.S. *See:* U.S. House of
    Representatives
Household appliances
— assemblers and fabricators, p. 310 [359]
— employees and earnings, p. 244 [292]
— injury and illness incidence rates, p. 273 [330]
— output per hour, p. 418 [470]
Household audio and video equipment
— employees and earnings, p. 244 [292]
Household furniture
— assemblers and fabricators, p. 310 [359]
— employees and earnings, p. 261 [318]
— output per hour, p. 418 [470]
Household International
— pension income, p. 602 [682]
Household laundry equipment
— injury and illness incidence rates, p. 273 [330]
Households, private *See:* Private households
Housing and community development
— city government employment and payroll, p. 240 [289]
— city government payroll, p. 240 [289]
— persons with work disabilities, p. 509 [570]
— public housing, p. 509 [570]
— subsidized housing, p. 509 [570]
Housing and Urban Development, U.S. Department of *See:*
    U.S. Department of Housing and Urban Development
Houston, Texas
— accountants and auditors, p. 63 [91]
— administrative support occupations, p. 64 [92]
— annual pay, p. 565 [640]
— apparel sales workers, p. 65 [93]
— assemblers, p. 66 [94]
— automobile mechanics, p. 67 [95]
— bank tellers, p. 68 [96]
— bartenders, p. 69 [97]
— bookkeeping, accounting, and auditing clerks, p. 70 [98]
— bus drivers, p. 71 [99]
— business service sales occupations, p. 72 [100]
— butchers and meat cutters, p. 73 [101]
— carpenters, p. 74 [102]
— cashiers, p. 75 [103]
— city government employment and payroll, p. 242 [290]
— civilian labor force, p. 480 [542]
— clergy, p. 76 [104]
— clinical laboratory technologists and technicians, p. 77 [105]
— commodity sales workers, p. 78 [106]
— computer operators, p. 79 [107]
— computer programmers, p. 80 [108]
— computer systems analysts and scientists, p. 81 [109]
— construction and maintenance painters, p. 82 [110]
— construction laborers, p. 83 [111]
— construction supervisors, p. 84 [112]
— cooks, p. 85 [113]

Numbers following p. or pp. are page references. Numbers in [ ] are table references.

992

Keyword Index

Numbers following p. or pp. are page references. Numbers in [ ] are table references.

993

Hunterdon, New Jersey continued:
— civilian labor force, p. 481 [542]
— unemployment rate, p. 481 [542]
Huntsman Design
— OSHA Star certification, p. 784 [802]
Huntsville, Alabama
— annual pay, p. 566 [640]
Husbands
See also: Widows and widowers
— unemployment, p. 518 [579]
— weekly earnings, pp. 502, 558 [562, 632]
IBM
— health care benefits to retirees, p. 547 [619]
— OSHA Star certification, p. 784 [802]
Idaho
— agriculture, p. 281 [339]
— average annual pay, p. 569 [643]
— civilian labor force, p. 439 [493]
— civilian labor force characteristics, p. 476 [539]
— civilian noninstitutionalized population, p. 439 [493]
— construction, p. 283 [340]
— construction employees, p. 266 [323]
— earnings in state and local government, p. 255 [310]
— educational attainment, p. 664 [735]
— employed men with work disabilities, p. 507 [568]
— employed women with work disabilities, p. 510 [571]
— employment, p. 439 [493]
— employment in state and local government, p. 255 [310]
— employment status of Hispanics, p. 439 [493]
— employment status of married persons, p. 439 [493]
— employment status of men, p. 439 [493]
— employment status of single persons, p. 439 [493]
— employment status of teens, p. 439 [493]
— employment status of whites, p. 439 [493]
— employment status of women, p. 439 [493]
— enrollment in higher education, p. 765 [779]
— federal government, p. 284 [341]
— financial services, p. 286 [342]
— financial services employees, p. 266 [323]
— fishing, p. 281 [339]
— forestry, p. 281 [339]
— government employees, p. 266 [323]
— insurance, p. 286 [342]
— insurance industry employees, p. 266 [323]
— jury duty pay, p. 614 [698]
— local government, p. 289 [344]
— manufacturing, p. 291 [345]
— manufacturing employees, p. 266 [323]
— mining, p. 292 [346]
— mining employees, p. 266 [323]
— paid civilian employment in federal government, p. 268 [324]
— pensions, p. 599 [680]
— public utilities, p. 299 [351]
— public utilities employees, p. 266 [323]
— real estate, p. 286 [342]
— real estate employees, p. 266 [323]
— retail trade, p. 295 [348]

Idaho continued:
— retail trade employees, p. 266 [323]
— services, p. 296 [349]
— services sector employees, p. 266 [323]
— Social Security benefits, beneficiaries, and payments, p. 551 [625]
— state and local government employment, p. 270 [327]
— state government, p. 298 [350]
— transportation, p. 299 [351]
— transportation employees, p. 266 [323]
— unemployed, p. 489 [549]
— unemployed men with work disabilities, p. 508 [569]
— unemployed women with work disabilities, p. 512 [572]
— unemployment, p. 439 [493]
— wholesale trade, p. 301 [352]
— wholesale trade employees, p. 266 [323]
— workers' compensation payments, p. 796 [819]
Illinois
— agriculture, p. 281 [339]
— average annual pay, p. 569 [643]
— civilian labor force, p. 440 [494]
— civilian labor force characteristics, p. 476 [539]
— civilian noninstitutionalized population, p. 440 [494]
— construction, p. 283 [340]
— construction employees, p. 266 [323]
— earnings in state and local government, p. 255 [310]
— educational attainment, p. 666 [736]
— employed men with work disabilities, p. 507 [568]
— employed women with work disabilities, p. 510 [571]
— employment, p. 440 [494]
— employment in state and local government, p. 255 [310]
— employment status of blacks, p. 440 [494]
— employment status of Hispanics, p. 440 [494]
— employment status of married persons, p. 440 [494]
— employment status of men, p. 440 [494]
— employment status of single persons, p. 440 [494]
— employment status of teens, p. 440 [494]
— employment status of whites, p. 440 [494]
— employment status of women, p. 440 [494]
— enrollment in higher education, p. 765 [779]
— federal government, p. 284 [341]
— financial services, p. 286 [342]
— financial services employees, p. 266 [323]
— fishing, p. 281 [339]
— forestry, p. 281 [339]
— government employees, p. 266 [323]
— insurance, p. 286 [342]
— insurance industry employees, p. 266 [323]
— jury duty pay, p. 614 [698]
— local government, p. 289 [344]
— manufacturing, p. 291 [345]
— manufacturing employees, p. 266 [323]
— mining, p. 292 [346]
— mining employees, p. 266 [323]
— paid civilian employment in federal government, p. 267 [324]
— pensions, p. 599 [680]
— public utilities, p. 299 [351]
— public utilities employees, p. 266 [323]

Numbers following p. or pp. are page references. Numbers in [ ] are table references.

Numbers following p. or pp. are page references. Numbers in [ ] are table references.

Keyword Index

Numbers following p. or pp. are page references. Numbers in [ ] are table references.

Numbers following p. or pp. are page references. Numbers in [ ] are table references.

Keyword Index

Numbers following p. or pp. are page references. Numbers in [ ] are table references.

1000

Keyword Index

Numbers following p. or pp. are page references. Numbers in [ ] are table references.

Numbers following p. or pp. are page references. Numbers in [ ] are table references.

Numbers following p. or pp. are page references. Numbers in [ ] are table references.

1003

Numbers following p. or pp. are page references. Numbers in [ ] are table references.

Keyword Index

Numbers following p. or pp. are page references. Numbers in [ ] are table references.

Numbers following p. or pp. are page references. Numbers in [ ] are table references.

Numbers following p. or pp. are page references. Numbers in [ ] are table references.

1007

Numbers following p. or pp. are page references. Numbers in [ ] are table references.

Numbers following p. or pp. are page references. Numbers in [ ] are table references.

Keyword Index

1009

Numbers following p. or pp. are page references. Numbers in [ ] are table references.

Keyword Index

Numbers following p. or pp. are page references. Numbers in [ ] are table references.

Numbers following p. or pp. are page references. Numbers in [ ] are table references.

Keyword Index

Numbers following p. or pp. are page references. Numbers in [ ] are table references.

Numbers following p. or pp. are page references. Numbers in [ ] are table references.

Keyword Index

Numbers following p. or pp. are page references. Numbers in [ ] are table references.

1016

Keyword Index

Numbers following p. or pp. are page references. Numbers in [ ] are table references.

Numbers following p. or pp. are page references. Numbers in [ ] are table references.

Keyword Index

Numbers following p. or pp. are page references. Numbers in [ ] are table references.

Numbers following p. or pp. are page references. Numbers in [ ] are table references.

Keyword Index

Numbers following p. or pp. are page references. Numbers in [ ] are table references.

Numbers following p. or pp. are page references. Numbers in [ ] are table references.

Numbers following p. or pp. are page references. Numbers in [ ] are table references.

Numbers following p. or pp. are page references. Numbers in [ ] are table references.

Keyword Index

Numbers following p. or pp. are page references. Numbers in [ ] are table references.

National Employee Database
— online resumes, p. 838 [879]
National Maritime Union
    See also: Marine Engineers Beneficial Association
— union membership, p. 855 [899]
Natural gas *See:* Crude petroleum, natural gas, and gas liquids
Natural gas liquids *See:* Crude petroleum, natural gas, and gas liquids
Natural resources
    See also: Conservation and renewable natural resources
— government employment, p. 248 [298]
— government payroll, p. 248 [298]
Natural resources, renewable *See:* Conservation and renewable natural resources
Navigation equipment *See:* Search and navigation equipment
Nebraska
— agriculture, p. 281 [339]
— average annual pay, p. 569 [643]
— civilian labor force, p. 451 [508]
— civilian labor force characteristics, p. 476 [539]
— civilian noninstitutionalized population, p. 451 [508]
— construction, p. 283 [340]
— construction employees, p. 266 [323]
— earnings in state and local government, p. 255 [310]
— educational attainment, p. 701 [750]
— employed men with work disabilities, p. 507 [568]
— employed women with work disabilities, p. 511 [571]
— employment, p. 451 [508]
— employment in state and local government, p. 255 [310]
— employment status of blacks, p. 451 [508]
— employment status of married persons, p. 451 [508]
— employment status of men, p. 451 [508]
— employment status of single persons, p. 451 [508]
— employment status of teens, p. 451 [508]
— employment status of whites, p. 451 [508]
— employment status of women, p. 451 [508]
— enrollment in higher education, p. 766 [779]
— federal government, p. 285 [341]
— financial services, p. 286 [342]
— financial services employees, p. 266 [323]
— fishing, p. 281 [339]
— forestry, p. 281 [339]
— government employees, p. 266 [323]
— insurance, p. 286 [342]
— insurance industry employees, p. 266 [323]
— jury duty pay, p. 614 [698]
— local government, p. 289 [344]
— manufacturing, p. 291 [345]
— manufacturing employees, p. 266 [323]
— mining, p. 292 [346]
— mining employees, p. 266 [323]
— paid civilian employment in federal government, p. 267 [324]
— pensions, p. 600 [680]
— public utilities, p. 300 [351]
— public utilities employees, p. 266 [323]

Nebraska continued:
— real estate, p. 286 [342]
— real estate employees, p. 266 [323]
— retail trade, p. 295 [348]
— retail trade employees, p. 266 [323]
— services, p. 297 [349]
— services sector employees, p. 266 [323]
— Social Security benefits, beneficiaries, and payments, p. 551 [625]
— state and local government employment, p. 271 [327]
— state government, p. 298 [350]
— transportation, p. 300 [351]
— transportation employees, p. 266 [323]
— unemployed, p. 489 [549]
— unemployed men with work disabilities, p. 508 [569]
— unemployed women with work disabilities, p. 512 [572]
— unemployment, p. 451 [508]
— wholesale trade, p. 301 [352]
— wholesale trade employees, p. 266 [323]
— work disability rates, p. 513 [573]
— workers' compensation payments, p. 796 [819]
Necks
— work injuries, p. 782 [800]
Neenah, Wisconsin
— farmers, p. 99 [127]
— machine operators, p. 126 [153]
Netherlands
— employment of foreign affiliates, p. 425 [477]
— manufacturing productivity indexes, p. 825 [859]
— strikes, p. 852 [896]
Networking
— recruiting, p. 483 [544]
Neurological impairments
— Americans With Disabilities Act complaints, p. 779 [794]
— return-to-work success rate, p. 781 [798]
Nevada
— agriculture, p. 281 [339]
— average annual pay, p. 569 [643]
— civilian labor force, p. 452 [509]
— civilian labor force characteristics, p. 476 [539]
— civilian noninstitutionalized population, p. 452 [509]
— construction, p. 283 [340]
— construction employees, p. 266 [323]
— earnings in state and local government, p. 255 [310]
— educational attainment, p. 704 [751]
— employed men with work disabilities, p. 507 [568]
— employed women with work disabilities, p. 511 [571]
— employment, p. 452 [509]
— employment in state and local government, p. 255 [310]
— employment status of blacks, p. 452 [509]
— employment status of Hispanics, p. 452 [509]
— employment status of married persons, p. 452 [509]
— employment status of men, p. 452 [509]
— employment status of single persons, p. 452 [509]
— employment status of teens, p. 452 [509]
— employment status of whites, p. 452 [509]
— employment status of women, p. 452 [509]
— enrollment in higher education, p. 766 [779]

Numbers following p. or pp. are page references. Numbers in [ ] are table references.

1028

Numbers following p. or pp. are page references. Numbers in [ ] are table references.

Numbers following p. or pp. are page references. Numbers in [ ] are table references.

Numbers following p. or pp. are page references. Numbers in [ ] are table references.

1031

Keyword Index

Numbers following p. or pp. are page references. Numbers in [ ] are table references.

Numbers following p. or pp. are page references. Numbers in [ ] are table references.

Numbers following p. or pp. are page references. Numbers in [ ] are table references.

Keyword Index

Numbers following p. or pp. are page references. Numbers in [ ] are table references.

Oakland, California continued:
— janitors, cleaners, maids, and housekeeping cleaners, p. 121 [148]
— laborers, p. 122 [149]
— lawyers, p. 123 [150]
— licensed practical nurses, p. 124 [151]
— machine operators, pp. 125-127 [152-154]
— machinists, p. 129 [155]
— maids and housemen, p. 130 [156]
— management analysts, p. 131 [157]
— management-related occupations, p. 132 [158]
— managers and administrators, pp. 133-134 [159-160]
— marketing, advertising, and public relations managers, p. 135 [161]
— mechanic and repairer supervisors, p. 136 [162]
— mining, manufacturing, and wholesale sales representatives, p. 137 [163]
— motor vehicle and boat sales workers, p. 138 [164]
— nursing aides, orderlies, and attendants, p. 139 [165]
— packaging and filling machine operators, p. 140 [166]
— personnel and labor relations managers, p. 141 [167]
— personnel, training, and labor relations specialists, p. 142 [168]
— physicians, p. 143 [169]
— plumbers, pipefitters, and steamfitters, p. 145 [170]
— postal clerks, p. 146 [171]
— postal service mail carriers, p. 147 [172]
— postsecondary teachers, p. 148 [173]
— printing press operators, p. 149 [174]
— private household cleaners and servants, p. 150 [175]
— production inspectors, checkers, and examiners, p. 151 [176]
— production occupation supervisors, p. 152 [177]
— property and real estate managers, p. 153 [178]
— public administration administrators and officials, p. 154 [179]
— public service police and detectives, p. 155 [180]
— real estate sales occupations, p. 156 [181]
— receptionists and information clerks, p. 157 [182]
— registered nurses, p. 158 [183]
— salaried sales occupation supervisors and proprietors, p. 159 [184]
— secondary school teachers, p. 161 [186]
— secretaries, p. 162 [187]
— securities and financial services sales occupations, p. 163 [188]
— self-employed sales occupation supervisors and proprietors, p. 160 [185]
— service organization managers, p. 164 [189]
— social workers, p. 165 [190]
— stock and inventory clerks, p. 166 [191]
— stock handlers and baggers, p. 167 [192]
— teacher aides and educational assistants, p. 169 [194]
— teachers, p. 168 [193]
— technicians, p. 170 [195]
— textile sewing machine operators, p. 171 [196]
— traffic, shipping, and receiving clerks, p. 172 [197]
— truck drivers, p. 173 [198]

Oakland, California continued:
— typists and word processors, p. 174 [199]
— unemployment rate, p. 480 [542]
— waiters and waitresses, p. 176 [201]
— waiters' and waitresses' assistants, p. 177 [202]
— welders and cutters, p. 178 [203]
Occidental Petroleum
— earnings of Ray Irani, p. 10 [13]
Occupational diseases
See also: specific diseases and illnesses
— deaths, p. 774 [788]
— new cases, p. 780 [796]
— return-to-work success rate, p. 782 [799]
Occupational safety
See also: Accidents; Fatalities; Injuries
— employee injuries, p. 272 [329]
— fatalities, p. 783 [801]
— work fatalities, pp. 277, 773, 775-777, 797 [334, 787, 789-790, 792, 820]
— work injuries, pp. 782-783 [800-801]
Occupational Safety and Health Administration
— Star certification, p. 784 [802]
— violations, p. 785 [803]
Occupational tenure
— employer tenures, p. 60 [88]
— longest, p. 60 [88]
— older Americans, p. 520 [581]
Occupations
See also: Occupation Index
— employment projections, pp. 302, 305-318, 320-328, 330-331, 333-390, 392-417 [353, 355-469]
— fastest declining, p. 179 [204]
— fastest growing, p. 180 [205]
— largest job growth, p. 181 [206]
— longest tenures, p. 60 [88]
— of the employed, p. 61 [90]
Ocean, New Jersey
— annual pay, p. 566 [640]
Office and Professional Employees International Union
— union membership, p. 855 [899]
Office Depot Inc.
— employment growth, p. 426 [478]
Office equipment See: Computer and office equipment
Office furniture
— employees and earnings, p. 261 [318]
— lost workdays, p. 274 [331]
— output per hour, p. 418 [470]
Office of Administration
— civilian employment, p. 264 [321]
Office of Management and Budget
— civilian employment, p. 264 [321]
Office of Personnel Management
— accessions to and separations from employment, p. 263 [320]
— civilian employment, p. 264 [321]
Office of the Vice-President
— civilian employment, p. 264 [321]
Office supplies See: Pens, pencils, office and art supplies

Numbers following p. or pp. are page references. Numbers in [ ] are table references.

1037

Numbers following p. or pp. are page references. Numbers in [ ] are table references.

Keyword Index

Numbers following p. or pp. are page references. Numbers in [ ] are table references.

1039

Oregon continued:
— unemployed women with work disabilities, p. 512 [572]
— unemployment, p. 459 [518]
— wholesale trade, p. 301 [352]
— wholesale trade employees, p. 266 [323]
— work disability rates, p. 513 [573]
— workers' compensation payments, p. 796 [819]
Organ transplants
— health care benefits, p. 588 [666]
Orlando, Florida
— civilian labor force, p. 481 [542]
— construction supervisors, p. 84 [112]
— food preparation and service occupation supervisors, p. 102 [130]
— food service and lodging managers, p. 104 [132]
— groundskeepers and gardeners, p. 110 [138]
— maids and housemen, p. 130 [156]
— real estate sales occupations, p. 156 [181]
— unemployment rate, p. 481 [542]
— waiters and waitresses, p. 176 [201]
— waiters' and waitresses' assistants, p. 177 [202]
Ortho Diagnostic Systems
— OSHA Star certification, p. 784 [802]
Orthoptics
— health care benefits, p. 588 [666]
Oshkosh, Wisconsin
— farmers, p. 99 [127]
— machine operators, p. 126 [153]
Osteopaths' offices
See also: Physicians' offices
— bill and account collectors, p. 314 [363]
— billing, cost, and rate clerks, p. 314 [364]
— clerical supervisors and managers, p. 324 [373]
— clinical laboratory technologists and technicians, p. 325 [374]
— file clerks, p. 344 [394]
— health professionals and paraprofessionals (nonspecific), p. 360 [410]
— licensed practical nurses, p. 369 [419]
— medical secretaries, p. 380 [430]
— nursing aides, orderlies, and attendants, p. 381 [431]
— physicians, p. 384 [434]
— receptionists and information clerks, p. 394 [445]
— registered nurses, p. 395 [446]
— social workers, p. 405 [456]
— switchboard operators, p. 408 [460]
— telephone operators, p. 411 [463]
— typists and word processors, p. 414 [466]
Outerwear, girls' and children's See: Girls' and children's outerwear
Outerwear, women's and misses' See: Women's and misses' outerwear
Outpatient care
— full-time workers, p. 591 [669]
— insurance plan coverage, p. 593 [671]
— insurance plans in state and local government, p. 594 [672]
Outplacement
See also: Displaced workers
— employee assistance programs, p. 623 [710]

Outplacement continued:
— time limits, p. 863 [907]
Output
See also: Productivity
— output per hour, pp. 825-829 [859-860, 862-864]
Overtime
See also: Hours
— hours per week, p. 827 [861]
— payroll cost reduction, p. 536 [602]
Oxnard, California
— annual pay, p. 566 [640]
OxyChem Petrochemicals
— OSHA Star certification, p. 784 [802]
Oxygen deficiency
— fatal work injuries, p. 775 [789]
Pacific Bell
— downsizing, p. 861 [905]
Pacific Islanders
See also: Asians
— accountants and auditors, p. 62 [91]
— administrative support occupations, p. 64 [92]
— apparel sales workers, p. 65 [93]
— assemblers and fabricators, p. 66 [94]
— automobile mechanics, p. 67 [95]
— bank tellers, p. 68 [96]
— bartenders, p. 69 [97]
— bookkeeping, accounting, and auditing clerks, p. 70 [98]
— bus drivers, p. 71 [99]
— business service sales occupations, p. 72 [100]
— butchers and meat cutters, p. 73 [101]
— carpenters, p. 74 [102]
— cashiers, p. 75 [103]
— clergy, p. 76 [104]
— clinical laboratory technologists and technicians, p. 77 [105]
— commodity sales workers, p. 78 [106]
— computer operators, p. 79 [107]
— computer programmers, p. 80 [108]
— computer systems analysts and scientists, p. 81 [109]
— construction and maintenance painters, p. 82 [110]
— construction laborers, p. 83 [111]
— construction supervisors, p. 84 [112]
— cooks, p. 85 [113]
— data entry keyers, p. 86 [114]
— designers, p. 87 [115]
— drafting occupations, p. 88 [116]
— early childhood teachers' assistants, p. 89 [117]
— education administrators, p. 90 [118]
— educational attainment| 634, 636, 639, 641, 644, 646, 649,
— electrical and electronic engineers, p. 91 [119]
— electrical and electronic equipment assemblers, p. 92 [120]
— electrical and electronic technicians, p. 93 [121]
— electricians, p. 94 [122]
— elementary school teachers, p. 95 [123]
— engineers, p. 96 [124]
— experienced unemployed, p. 175 [200]
— family child care providers, p. 97 [125]
— farm workers, p. 98 [126]
— farmers, p. 99 [127]

Numbers following p. or pp. are page references. Numbers in [ ] are table references.

Numbers following p. or pp. are page references. Numbers in [ ] are table references.

Numbers following p. or pp. are page references. Numbers in [ ] are table references.

Numbers following p. or pp. are page references. Numbers in [ ] are table references.

Keyword Index

1043

Numbers following p. or pp. are page references. Numbers in [ ] are table references.

Numbers following p. or pp. are page references. Numbers in [ ] are table references.

Keyword Index

Numbers following p. or pp. are page references. Numbers in [ ] are table references.

Keyword Index

Numbers following p. or pp. are page references. Numbers in [ ] are table references.

Numbers following p. or pp. are page references. Numbers in [ ] are table references.

Numbers following p. or pp. are page references. Numbers in [ ] are table references.

Keyword Index

Numbers following p. or pp. are page references. Numbers in [ ] are table references.

Numbers following p. or pp. are page references. Numbers in [ ] are table references.

Keyword Index

Numbers following p. or pp. are page references. Numbers in [ ] are table references.

Numbers following p. or pp. are page references. Numbers in [ ] are table references.

Keyword Index

Numbers following p. or pp. are page references. Numbers in [ ] are table references.

Numbers following p. or pp. are page references. Numbers in [ ] are table references.

Keyword Index

1055

Retirees
See also: Older Americans
— employee benefits, p. 611 [694]
— health care plans, p. 610 [692]
— health insurance, pp. 543, 547, 608-611 [611, 619, 690-691, 693-694]
— medical plans of large employers, p. 577 [654]
— Social Security benefits, beneficiaries, and payments, pp. 551-552 [625-626]

Retirement
— benefits at women-owned small businesses, p. 583 [660]
— cost, p. 529 [592]
— cost to self-employed, p. 531 [594]
— defined contribution plans, p. 597 [677]
— early withdrawal of funds, p. 598 [679]
— employee assistance programs, p. 623 [710]
— employee benefits, p. 582 [658]
— employer costs, p. 531 [595]
— federal civil service, p. 598 [678]
— full-time workers, p. 604 [685]
— job loss relief, p. 862 [906]
— large employers, p. 577 [654]
— part-time workers, p. 605 [686]
— small establishments, p. 606 [687]
— state and local government systems, p. 608 [689]

Rhode Island
— agriculture, p. 282 [339]
— average annual pay, p. 569 [643]
— civilian labor force, p. 461 [520]
— civilian labor force characteristics, p. 477 [539]
— civilian noninstitutionalized population, p. 461 [520]
— construction, p. 283 [340]
— construction employees, p. 266 [323]
— earnings in state and local government, p. 256 [310]
— educational attainment, p. 731 [762]
— employed men with work disabilities, p. 507 [568]
— employed women with work disabilities, p. 511 [571]
— employment, p. 461 [520]
— employment in state and local government, p. 256 [310]
— employment status of blacks, p. 461 [520]
— employment status of Hispanics, p. 461 [520]
— employment status of married persons, p. 461 [520]
— employment status of men, p. 461 [520]
— employment status of single persons, p. 461 [520]
— employment status of teens, p. 461 [520]
— employment status of whites, p. 461 [520]
— employment status of women, p. 461 [520]
— enrollment in higher education, p. 766 [779]
— federal government, p. 285 [341]
— financial services, p. 287 [342]
— financial services employees, p. 266 [323]
— fishing, p. 282 [339]
— forestry, p. 282 [339]
— government employees, p. 266 [323]
— insurance, p. 287 [342]
— insurance industry employees, p. 266 [323]
— jury duty pay, p. 615 [698]
— local government, p. 289 [344]

Rhode Island continued:
— manufacturing, p. 291 [345]
— manufacturing employees, p. 266 [323]
— mining, p. 292 [346]
— mining employees, p. 266 [323]
— paid civilian employment in federal government, p. 267 [324]
— pensions, p. 600 [680]
— public utilities, p. 300 [351]
— public utilities employees, p. 266 [323]
— real estate, p. 287 [342]
— real estate employees, p. 266 [323]
— retail trade, p. 295 [348]
— retail trade employees, p. 266 [323]
— services, p. 297 [349]
— services sector employees, p. 266 [323]
— sexual harassment, p. 814 [845]
— Social Security benefits, beneficiaries, and payments, p. 551 [625]
— state and local government employment, p. 271 [327]
— state government, p. 298 [350]
— transportation, p. 300 [351]
— transportation employees, p. 266 [323]
— unemployed, p. 489 [549]
— unemployed men with work disabilities, p. 508 [569]
— unemployed women with work disabilities, p. 512 [572]
— unemployment, p. 461 [520]
— wholesale trade, p. 302 [352]
— wholesale trade employees, p. 266 [323]
— workers' compensation payments, p. 796 [819]

Richland, Washington
— farm workers, p. 98 [126]

Richmond, Virginia
— machine operators, p. 126 [153]

Ripken, Cal, Jr.
— strike-related pay losses, p. 850 [894]

Riverside, California
— accountants and auditors, p. 62 [91]
— administrative support occupations, p. 64 [92]
— apparel sales workers, p. 65 [93]
— assemblers and fabricators, p. 66 [94]
— automobile mechanics, p. 67 [95]
— bank tellers, p. 68 [96]
— bartenders, p. 69 [97]
— bookkeeping, accounting, and auditing clerks, p. 70 [98]
— bus drivers, p. 71 [99]
— business service sales occupations, p. 72 [100]
— butchers and meat cutters, p. 73 [101]
— carpenters, p. 74 [102]
— cashiers, p. 75 [103]
— civilian labor force, p. 480 [542]
— clergy, p. 76 [104]
— clinical laboratory technologists and technicians, p. 77 [105]
— commodity sales workers, p. 78 [106]
— computer operators, p. 79 [107]
— computer programmers, p. 80 [108]
— computer systems analysts and scientists, p. 81 [109]
— construction and maintenance painters, p. 82 [110]
— construction laborers, p. 83 [111]

Numbers following p. or pp. are page references. Numbers in [ ] are table references.

1056

Numbers following p. or pp. are page references. Numbers in [ ] are table references.

Keyword Index

1057

Numbers following p. or pp. are page references. Numbers in [ ] are table references.

1058

Numbers following p. or pp. are page references. Numbers in [ ] are table references.

Keyword Index

Numbers following p. or pp. are page references. Numbers in [ ] are table references.

Numbers following p. or pp. are page references. Numbers in [ ] are table references.

Keyword Index

Numbers following p. or pp. are page references. Numbers in [ ] are table references.

Numbers following p. or pp. are page references. Numbers in [ ] are table references.

Keyword Index

Numbers following p. or pp. are page references. Numbers in [ ] are table references.

Numbers following p. or pp. are page references. Numbers in [ ] are table references.

Numbers following p. or pp. are page references. Numbers in [ ] are table references.

Numbers following p. or pp. are page references. Numbers in [ ] are table references.

Keyword Index

Numbers following p. or pp. are page references. Numbers in [ ] are table references.

Keyword Index

Numbers following p. or pp. are page references. Numbers in [ ] are table references.

Numbers following p. or pp. are page references. Numbers in [ ] are table references.

Keyword Index

Numbers following p. or pp. are page references. Numbers in [ ] are table references.

Numbers following p. or pp. are page references. Numbers in [ ] are table references.

Keyword Index

Numbers following p. or pp. are page references. Numbers in [ ] are table references.

Numbers following p. or pp. are page references. Numbers in [ ] are table references.

Keyword Index

Numbers following p. or pp. are page references. Numbers in [ ] are table references.

Keyword Index

Numbers following p. or pp. are page references. Numbers in [ ] are table references.

Keyword Index

Numbers following p. or pp. are page references. Numbers in [ ] are table references.

Numbers following p. or pp. are page references. Numbers in [ ] are table references.

Trenton, New Jersey continued:
— marketing, advertising, and public relations managers, p. 135 [161]
— mechanic and repairer supervisors, p. 136 [162]
— mining, manufacturing, and wholesale sales representatives, p. 137 [163]
— motor vehicle and boat sales workers, p. 138 [164]
— nursing aides, orderlies, and attendants, p. 139 [165]
— packaging and filling machine operators, p. 140 [166]
— personnel and labor relations managers, p. 141 [167]
— personnel, training, and labor relations specialists, p. 142 [168]
— physicians, p. 143 [169]
— plumbers, pipefitters, and steamfitters, p. 145 [170]
— postal clerks, p. 146 [171]
— postal service mail carriers, p. 147 [172]
— postsecondary teachers, p. 148 [173]
— printing press operators, p. 149 [174]
— private household cleaners and servants, p. 150 [175]
— production inspectors, checkers, and examiners, p. 151 [176]
— production occupation supervisors, p. 152 [177]
— property and real estate managers, p. 153 [178]
— public administration administrators and officials, p. 154 [179]
— public service police and detectives, p. 155 [180]
— real estate sales occupations, p. 156 [181]
— receptionists and information clerks, p. 157 [182]
— registered nurses, p. 158 [183]
— salaried sales occupation supervisors and proprietors, p. 159 [184]
— secondary school teachers, p. 161 [186]
— secretaries, p. 162 [187]
— securities and financial services sales occupations, p. 163 [188]
— self-employed sales occupation supervisors and proprietors, p. 160 [185]
— service organization managers, p. 164 [189]
— social workers, p. 165 [190]
— stock and inventory clerks, p. 166 [191]
— stock handlers and baggers, p. 167 [192]
— teacher aides and educational assistants, p. 169 [194]
— teachers, p. 168 [193]
— technicians, p. 170 [195]
— textile sewing machine operators, p. 171 [196]
— traffic, shipping, and receiving clerks, p. 172 [197]
— truck drivers, p. 173 [198]
— typists and word processors, p. 174 [199]
— waiters and waitresses, p. 176 [201]
— waiters' and waitresses' assistants, p. 177 [202]
— welders and cutters, p. 178 [203]
Trim, metal See: Metal doors, sash, and trim
Troy, New York
— annual pay, p. 567 [640]
— public administration administrators and officials, p. 154 [179]
— secondary school teachers, p. 161 [186]
— teacher aides and educational assistants, p. 169 [194]

Truck and bus bodies
— injury and illness incidence rates, p. 273 [330]
Truck trailers
— injury and illness incidence rates, p. 273 [330]
Trucking
See also: Courier services
— automobile mechanics, p. 311 [360]
— billing, cost, and rate clerks, p. 315 [364]
— blue-collar worker supervisors, p. 316 [365]
— bus and truck mechanics and diesel engine specialists, p. 317 [367]
— employee injuries, p. 272 [329]
— employees and earnings, p. 259 [315]
— hand packers and packagers, p. 358 [408]
— industrial truck and tractor operators, p. 363 [413]
— injury and illness incidence rates, p. 275 [332]
— truck drivers, p. 413 [465]
Trunks (body)
— work injuries, p. 782 [800]
Tucson, Arizona
— city government employment and payroll, p. 242 [290]
Tuition reimbursement
— benefits at women-owned small businesses, p. 583 [660]
Tulare, California
— farm workers, p. 98 [126]
— farmers, p. 99 [127]
Tulsa, Oklahoma
— city government employment and payroll, p. 243 [290]
— welders and cutters, p. 178 [203]
Typing
— repetitive motion injuries, p. 780 [797]
Undergarments, women's and children's See: Women's and children's undergarments
Unemployed
— blacks, pp. 505-506 [566-567]
— civilian labor force, p. 493 [553]
— displaced workers, p. 860 [904]
— duration of unemployment, pp. 483, 485 [545-546]
— educational attainment, p. 492 [552]
— Hispanics, pp. 514-516 [574-576]
— insured, p. 489 [549]
— men, pp. 490, 516, 518 [550, 577, 579]
— men looking for full-time work, p. 501 [561]
— men looking for part-time work, p. 501 [561]
— number, pp. 427-428, 489 [479-480, 549]
— older Americans, p. 491 [551]
— percent of labor force, pp. 427-428 [479-480]
— school enrollment, p. 767 [780]
— social insurance coverage, p. 550 [624]
— teens, p. 491 [551]
— unemployment rate of men, p. 476 [539]
— unemployment rate of women, p. 476 [539]
— whites, pp. 520-521 [582-583]
— women, pp. 476, 490, 521, 523 [539, 550, 584, 586]
— women looking for full-time work, p. 501 [561]
— women looking for part-time work, p. 501 [561]
Unemployment
— ages, p. 491 [551]

Numbers following p. or pp. are page references. Numbers in [ ] are table references.

Keyword Index

1081

Numbers following p. or pp. are page references. Numbers in [ ] are table references.

Numbers following p. or pp. are page references. Numbers in [ ] are table references.

Keyword Index

Numbers following p. or pp. are page references. Numbers in [ ] are table references.

Keyword Index

Numbers following p. or pp. are page references. Numbers in [ ] are table references.

Numbers following p. or pp. are page references. Numbers in [ ] are table references.

Numbers following p. or pp. are page references. Numbers in [ ] are table references.

Keyword Index

Numbers following p. or pp. are page references. Numbers in [ ] are table references.

Numbers following p. or pp. are page references. Numbers in [ ] are table references.

Keyword Index

Numbers following p. or pp. are page references. Numbers in [ ] are table references.

Numbers following p. or pp. are page references. Numbers in [ ] are table references.

Keyword Index

Numbers following p. or pp. are page references. Numbers in [ ] are table references.

Keyword Index

Numbers following p. or pp. are page references. Numbers in [ ] are table references.

Numbers following p. or pp. are page references. Numbers in [ ] are table references.

Numbers following p. or pp. are page references. Numbers in [ ] are table references.

Keyword Index

Numbers following p. or pp. are page references. Numbers in [ ] are table references.

Numbers following p. or pp. are page references. Numbers in [ ] are table references.

Wyoming continued:
— sexual harassment, p. 814 [845]
— Social Security benefits, beneficiaries, and payments,
　　p. 551 [625]
— state and local government employment, p. 271 [327]
— state government, p. 299 [350]
— transportation, p. 300 [351]
— transportation employees, p. 266 [323]
— unemployed, p. 490 [549]
— unemployed men with work disabilities, p. 509 [569]
— unemployed women with work disabilities, p. 513 [572]
— unemployment, p. 469 [531]
— wholesale trade, p. 302 [352]
— wholesale trade employees, p. 266 [323]
— workers' compensation payments, p. 796 [819]
X-rays *See:* Radiology
Yakima, Washington
— farm workers, p. 258 [313]
Yarn mills *See:* Weaving, finishing, yarn, and thread mills
Yarn spinning mills
— output per hour, p. 418 [470]
York, Pennsylvania
— machine operators, p. 128 [154]
Zoological gardens *See:* Museums, botanical, zoological
　gardens

Keyword Index